1999

HISTORIC DOCUMENTS
OF
1999

Cumulative Index, 1995–1999

CQ PRESS

A Division of Congressional Quarterly Inc.

Historic Documents of 1999

Editors: Martha Gottron, John Felton, Bruce Maxwell
Production and Associate Editor: Kerry V. Kern
Indexer: Victoria Agee

"To Err Is Human," copyright © 1999 by the National Academy of Sciences.
Reprinted courtesy of the National Academy Press, Washington, D.C.

Copyright © 2000 Congressional Quarterly Inc.
1414 22nd Street, N.W.
Washington, D.C. 20037

Printed in the United States of America

**The Library of Congress cataloged the first issue of this
title as follows:**

Historic documents. 1972—
      Washington. Congressional Quarterly Inc.

      1. United States—Politics and government—1945– —Yearbooks.
2. World politics—1945– —Yearbooks. I. Congressional Quarterly Inc.

E839.5H57   917.3'03'9205   72-97888

      ISBN 1-56802-489-4
      ISSN 0892-080X

PREFACE

More than a half-century after world leaders solemnly signed treaties and established institutions intended to prevent a recurrence of the horrors of World War II, a new generation of leaders was forced in 1999 to confront the fact that new evils were arising in place of the old. The NATO alliance went to war in March to halt the latest episode of "ethnic cleansing" in the former Yugoslavia, only to discover that Serbian authorities in the beleaguered province of Kosovo used the NATO bombings as an excuse to accelerate their attacks on the ethnic Albanian majority there. More than a million Albanians fled from their homes and an estimated ten thousand were killed during three months of Serbian brutality. With its massive air strikes, NATO drove Serbian forces out of Kosovo and established a peacekeeping force that enabled nearly all the Albanians to return, in many cases to homes and villages that had been destroyed. But NATO, and the UN administration that sought to rebuild Kosovo's civil society, quickly found that rebuilding Kosovo would be an expensive and difficult process. It was far from clear that European nations would follow through on the promises they made during the war to provide the money and resources for postwar reconstruction. President Bill Clinton was among the Western leaders who appealed to the Kosovar Albanians to forgive the Serbs who remained, but such appeals appeared to be falling on deaf ears.

The United Nations found it necessary to make two apologies for its failures earlier in the decade to protect civilians in war zones. In Rwanda in 1994 the UN and its member states failed to take effective action to stop an ethnic slaughter that, in less than one hundred days, led to the deaths of an estimated 800,000 people. Later declared to be a "genocide" as defined by the UN's 1948 Genocide Convention, it was the greatest single killing of people since more than 1 million Cambodians lost their lives during the brutal Khmer Rouge regime in the middle 1970s. A high-level board of inquiry reported in December that the UN Security Council and its member nations—most notably the United States—had refused to provide adequate resources to a UN peacekeeping unit in Rwanda, leaving it helpless to confront the mounting terror as the government and an extremist Hutu militia systematically slaughtered political opponents and civilians belonging to the rival Tutsi ethnic group.

How to Use This Book

The documents are arranged in chronological order. If you know the approximate date of the report, speech, statement, court decision, or other document you are looking for, glance through the titles for that month in the table of contents.

If the table of contents does not lead you directly to the document you want, turn to the index at the end of the book. There you may find references not only to the particular document you seek but also to other entries on the same or a related subject. The index in this volume is a five-year cumulative index of *Historic Documents* covering the years 1995–1999. There is a separate volume, *Historic Documents Index, 1972–1995*, which is comprehensive and is scheduled for periodic updating by the publisher.

The introduction to each document is printed in italic type. The document itself, printed in roman type, follows the spelling, capitalization, and punctuation of the original or official copy. Where the full text is not given, omissions of material are indicated by the customary ellipsis points. Additions, explanatory information, and corrections that have been made to the documents are enclosed in brackets.

Similarly, UN secretary general Kofi Annan issued a report in November apologizing for the world body's failure in 1995 to protect Muslim civilians living in an area of Bosnia that the UN had declared a "safe haven." During the closing months of the three-year ethnic war in Bosnia, Serbian forces attacked the town of Srebrenica, overwhelmed a small UN detachment of peacekeepers from the Netherlands, and proceeded to kill more than 7,000 Muslim men and boys. It was the worst single ethnic slaughter in Europe since World War II. In his report, Annan acknowledged that the UN did not keep its promise of safety to the Muslims.

Even as the UN was preparing its reports on recent tragedies, another one was unfolding on the tiny Pacific island of Timor. Indonesia had occupied East Timor for a quarter century and in 1999 agreed to allow a vote on independence there. The UN-arranged referendum at the end of August went smoothly, and more than three-quarters of East Timorese voters opted for independence. In response, anti-independence militias that had been armed and trained by the Indonesian military went on a rampage and killed thousands of civilians before world leaders intervened and forced the military to withdraw. An Australian-led peacekeeping force moved in, and East Timor became a UN protectorate. Once again, there was criticism that the United Nations failed to protect innocent civilians who had assumed that its presence meant they were safe.

All four cases—Kosovo, Rwanda, Bosnia, and East Timor—led to a reconsideration by world leaders of such long-treasured concepts as national sovereignty and the neutrality of the UN. NATO intervened in Kosovo without any authorization from the UN and despite the fact that Kosovo was an undisputed province of Serbia. Serbia's allies in Russia objected, and China raised concerns, but there was remarkably little debate around the world about NATO's unprecedented intervention in the internal affairs of a UN member state. Reflecting on the tragedies, Annan said the UN had for too long hidden behind its neutrality when confronted with massive human rights violations. In his report on Srebrenica he declared that deliberate attacks on an entire people, wherever they occurred, "must be met decisively with all necessary means, and with the political will to carry the policy through to its logical conclusion."

Despite such expressions of determination, world leaders had limited success in halting the biggest conflict under way anywhere in 1999: a regional war in the Democratic Republic of the Congo (formerly Zaire) that involved a half-dozen nations. In many ways that war was a direct outgrowth of the conflicts earlier in the decade in Rwanda and its neighbor, Burundi, that had sent more than 1 million refugees into Zaire. The UN and African leaders helped negotiate a peace agreement in Congo, but the fighting continued. At year's end Annan was attempting to arrange a UN peacekeeping mission that would avoid the failure of previous missions that were sent into conflict zones before peace was truly established.

An even more insidious killer was on the loose in Africa: AIDS. Two-thirds of the 33 million people infected with HIV, the virus that causes the incurable disease, lived in sub-Saharan Africa. In some African countries as much as one-fourth of the population was infected with the AIDS virus; in addition to destroying families and communities, the disease was expected to slow economic growth significantly. Nor was Africa the only continent affected. International health officials worried that Asia could soon be enveloped in an equally devastating epidemic of AIDS, one that could have even greater repercussions for the world economy.

Yet another conflict raging at the end of the year put Western leaders in a difficult position, morally and politically. Russia in September launched an attack on Islamic separatists in the republic of Chechnya, in effect repeating a 1994–1996 invasion that led to a humiliating defeat of the Russian army. President Clinton and his counterparts in other Western capitals gradually escalated their criticism of the army's reportedly indiscriminate bombing of civilian areas in the Chechen capital, Grozny. But the West hesitated to push Moscow too hard on the matter, fearing that outside pressure might destabilize Russia's still-developing democracy.

As the war in Chechnya raged, Russian president Boris Yeltsin, a man of many surprises, had one last shock for his nation and the world. On December 31 he suddenly announced that he was resigning—six months before the end of his five-year term—and handing the presidency to his designated successor, Prime Minister Vladimir Putin. Yeltsin's resignation helped make Putin, who was riding on a wave of popularity from his management of the war in Chechnya, the favored candidate in the next presidential elections. The fact that Russia was about to have its third contested presidential election was undoubtedly Yeltsin's greatest accomplishment during his nine years in office. Yeltsin appeared on the world stage just in time to help push the crumbling Soviet Union out of existence, and he had the vision to plan a future for Russia as a democracy. Despite his many failings—most important his inability to manage the difficult transition from communism to capitalism—he stuck with that vision and gave Russia a democracy. Messy and turbulent it might be, but it was the only true freedom Russia had ever known.

One element of the Russian democracy was the parliament's power to try to impeach the president, and Yeltsin's opponents used that impeachment power to try to force Yeltsin from office because of the failed 1994–1996 war in Chechnya. Yeltsin easily beat back that impeachment move in May, becoming the second major world figure during the year to survive an impeachment grounded largely in partisanship.

The first was Clinton, who was acquitted by the Senate in February on two charges stemming from his sexual relationship with a former White House intern, Monica Lewinsky. The Republican-led House of Representatives in December 1998 had voted, mostly along party lines, to impeach Clinton, a Democrat, on charges that he had lied to a grand jury about his relationship with Lewinsky and had used his official powers to block an investigation of his wrongdoing. There was never much chance that the Senate would muster the needed two-thirds vote to convict the president and force him from office, but the Senate gathered all its dignity, minimized its partisan squabbling, and conducted a trial in January and February. A clear majority of fifty-five senators rejected the charge that Clinton had lied under oath, and the Senate split fifty-fifty on the obstruction of justice count. A humbled Clinton apologized for the trauma he had caused the nation.

The impeachment, coupled with the fact that Clinton was entering the end of his two terms in office, weakened the president's political standing and muted the power of his moral authority. But Clinton was still able to best his Republican opponents in Congress on some issues of substance, including the one that was most important to the functioning of the government: the budget. For the fifth year in a row, Clinton used his veto power and superior negotiating skills to win most of his battles with Congress on spending priorities. For the second year in a row, those spending battles were fought in the context of a budget surplus. The government had showed its first overall budget surplus in the fiscal year ending in 1998, and the fiscal 1999 budget (counting all items, including Social Security) was $123 billion in the black. Clinton and Congress hotly disputed what to do with the surplus, and the president appeared to have won broad public support for his priority of setting money aside to ensure the future of Social Security and Medicare and to begin paying off the enormous national debt. Republicans had put their emphasis on a multiyear tax cut, a proposal that appealed to the party's well-to-do core constituency, but that failed to generate much broad-based enthusiasm.

Clinton's fading but still evident political magic failed him in at least one major battle during the year on Capitol Hill. The president had set as his chief foreign policy priority Senate approval of an international treaty banning all nuclear weapons tests. The Comprehensive Test Ban Treaty, first proposed by President Dwight Eisenhower in the 1950s, had been completed in 1996 and had been on the Senate's agenda since 1997. Clinton failed to lay the political groundwork for the treaty, however, and when treaty supporters began pushing for Senate action on it during the late summer they discovered that Republican opponents had quietly lined up enough votes to kill the treaty. Clinton found himself pleading with the Republican leaders to delay the vote he had long requested, but they refused. The Senate rejected the treaty on a 48–51 vote; among the no voters were several moderate Republican leaders who normally backed such measures. The defeat was one of the most important foreign policy setbacks Clinton had ever suffered, and it alarmed many world leaders who saw rejection of the treaty as evidence of resurgent isolationism in the United States.

Violence also dominated headlines at home. In April two teenage boys, armed with guns and homemade bombs, rampaged through Columbine High School in Littleton, Colorado, killing twelve students and a teacher before turning the weapons on themselves. Self-styled outcasts filled with hatred of Jews, blacks, and their more popular classmates, the two left behind tapes and diaries indicating that they had hoped to kill as many as five hundred students. They also left behind a grief-stricken community and a nation wondering how to stop school violence. The shootings helped gun control forces win passage in the Senate of legislation regulating some sales of guns, but the House blocked similar legislation. Clinton convened a White House conference on the issue of school violence but was criticized for not taking a stronger stand for gun control and against violence in the media, which many Americans believed fomented violence among teenagers and young adults.

Despite the focus on the Columbine shootings, crime rates, including homicides and crimes in which guns were used, continued to decline in 1999. Use of illegal drugs among teenagers also dropped, although it remained fairly stable in the population overall. In two major reports by the surgeon general, substance abuse was found to be a significant contributor to mental illness and the incidence of suicide. According to the "nation's doctor," David Satcher, one of five Americans was afflicted with mental disorders during any given year, but two-thirds of those never received treatment, largely for fear of being stigmatized by society. Stressing that mental illness was not a moral failing but rather a physical illness that could be treated, Satcher urged anyone with a mental health problem or symptoms of mental disorder, such as depression or anxiety, to seek help. The surgeon general said he hoped the report would be even more influential than the first surgeon general's report in 1964, which warned the public about the dangers of smoking.

Another report, this one by a prestigious body of doctors and scientists, found that as many as 98,000 Americans died every year from medical mistakes, half of which were preventable. The report laid out several recommendations to "design" safety into the nation's health care system; Congress and Clinton took these recommendations under immediate consideration. The White House and Congress were unable to agree, however, on legislation protecting patients' rights, including giving patients the right to sue their managed care health plans for malpractice. On this issue, as well as on gun control and several other perennial controversies, Democrats and Republicans alike were calculating their legislative votes with an eye to the 2000 presidential elections.

Experts noted that 1999 technically was just the next-to-last year of the twentieth century and of the second millennium. Officially, they said, the year 2000 had the honor of ending both historic periods, and 2001 would mark the beginning of a new era. But popular perception ran a year ahead of the experts, and so the stroke of midnight on December 31, 1999, was widely celebrated as the end of the twentieth century and 2000 as the opening of a new millennium. For years there had been worries that computer systems, designed in the days when only two digits were used to record the year, would fail once 1999 gave way to 2000. The government and private businesses in the United States spent more than $300 billion updating their computer systems, and many Western countries followed suit. Despite the worries—and possibly because of all that work—the dawning of the new year saw remarkably few computer failures.

The millions of people who worried about their computers might have saved a considerable amount of money had they instead paid just 5 cents, the standard fee for reassuring advice from Lucy, one of the regular characters in the enormously popular comic strip, "Peanuts." Charles Schulz, who created Lucy, Charlie Brown, Snoopy, Linus, and the other characters who represented the wisdom and foibles of the human race, announced his retirement on December 14. It was clear that "good ol' Charlie Brown" and the rest of Schulz's lovable characters would live on, through the magic of reruns and the memories of millions of fans.

These are only some of the topics of national and international interest chosen by the editors for *Historic Documents of 1999*. This edition marks the twenty-eighth volume of a Congressional Quarterly project that began with *Historic Documents of 1972*. The purpose of the series is to give students, librarians, journalists, scholars, and others convenient access to documents on a wide range of topics that set forth some of the most important issues of the year. In our judgment, the official statements, news conferences, speeches, special studies, and court decisions presented here will be of lasting interest.

Each document is preceded by an introduction that provides context and background material and, when relevant, an account of continuing developments during the year. We believe these introductions will become increasingly useful as memories of current events fade.

John Felton and Martha Gottron

CONTENTS

January

Supreme Court on State Ballot Initiatives   3

Excerpts from the majority opinion, written by Ruth Bader Ginsburg, and a dissenting opinion written by Chief Justice William H. Rehnquist, in the case of *Buckley v. American Constitutional Law Foundation,* in which the Supreme Court ruled on January 12, 1999, that the Colorado law requiring circulators of initiative petitions to be registered voters, to wear badges identifying them by name, and to disclose how much they had been paid to circulate the petitions imposed an unconstitutional infringement on their right of free speech.

Statements from Clinton's Impeachment Trial   15

Excerpts from a presentation to the Senate on January 16, 1998, by Rep. Henry J. Hyde, R-Ill., chairman of the House Judiciary Committee and chairman of the House managers in the impeachment trial of President Bill Clinton, and from a presentation to the Senate on January 21, 1998, by former Democratic senator Dale Bumpers of Arkansas, acting as a defense counsel for President Clinton.

State of the Union Address and Republican Response   41

Texts of President Bill Clinton's State of the Union address, delivered to a joint session of Congress on January 19, 1999, and the Republican response by Representatives Jennifer Dunn of Washington and Steve Largent of Oklahoma.

Federal Report on Quality of Public School Teachers   64

Text of the executive summary from a report released January 28, 1999, by the National Center for Education Statistics, entitled "Teacher Quality: A Report on the Preparation and Qualifications of Public School Teachers."

February

European Central Bank President on the Euro   75

Excerpts from a speech by Willem F. Duisenberg, president of the European Central Bank, delivered February 1, 1999, to the Council on Foreign Relations in Chicago, in which he explained the introduction of the euro and Europe's new common monetary policies.

President's Economic Report, Economic Advisers' Report   **85**
Text of the Economic Report of the President and excerpts from chapters
1 and 3 of the Annual Report of the Council of Economic Advisers, both
released February 4, 1999.

March

U.S. Investigating Committee on Olympic Bribery Scandal   **105**
Executive summary of the report submitted to the U.S. Olympic Committee on March 1, 1999, by the Special Bid Oversight Commission,
chaired by former senator George Mitchell and with Kenneth Duberstein,
Donald Fehr, Roberta Cooper Ramo, and Jeffrey G. Benz as members.

Transportation Safety Board Chairman on Aviation Safety   **113**
An excerpt from testimony delivered March 10, 1999, to the House
Appropriations Subcommittee on Transportation and Related Agencies by
Jim Hall, chairman of the National Transportation Safety Board.

Statements Marking Addition of Three Nations to NATO   **119**
Excerpts from statements made at a ceremony in Independence, Missouri,
on March 12, 1999, by Jan Kavan, foreign minister of the Czech Republic;
Janos Martonyi, minister of foreign affairs of the Republic of Hungary;
Bronislav Geremek, minister of foreign affairs of the Republic of Poland;
and Madeleine K. Albright, secretary of state of the United States, marking the accession of the Czech Republic, Hungary, and Poland to full membership on the North Atlantic Treaty Organization.

Clinton on Air War Against Serbian Forces in Kosovo   **134**
Text of a televised address by President Bill Clinton on March 24, 1999,
announcing a NATO bombing campaign against the Federal Republic of
Yugoslavia.

United Nations Observer on Human Rights Situation in Iraq   **144**
Excerpts from a statement given March 31, 1999, to the United Nations
Commission on Human Rights by Max van der Stoel, the commission's special rapporteur on Iraq, in which he analyzed the human rights situation in
that country.

April

New European Commission President on Reforms   **155**
Excerpts from an address to the European Parliament on April 13 by
Romano Prodi, who had been named the new president of the European
Commission following publication of an investigating report into fraud and
mismanagement at the commission.

Starr on the Future of the Independent Counsel Law   165

Excerpts from testimony delivered April 14, 1999, by Kenneth W. Starr, the independent counsel investigating President Bill Clinton, to a hearing of the Senate Committee on Governmental Affairs in which Starr called on Congress not to renew the statute authorizing the appointment of independent counsels.

Astronomers on Discovery of a Multiplanet Solar System   173

Excerpts from a statement released March 15, 1999, by San Francisco State University; the Harvard-Smithsonian Center for Astrophysics in Cambridge, Massachusetts; and the University Corporation for Atmospheric Research in Boulder, Colorado, announcing the discovery of three large gaseous planets around the star Upsilon Andromedae.

Vice President on Shootings at Columbine High School   179

Text of a speech delivered April 25, 1999, by Vice President Al Gore in Littleton, Colorado, commemorating those who died or were wounded in the mass shooting at Columbine High School on April 20.

GAO on Health Threat from Drug-Resistant Bacteria   185

Excerpts from the report, "Antimicrobial Resistance: Data to Assess Public Health Threat from Resistant Bacteria Are Limited," prepared by the Health, Education, and Human Services Division of the U.S. General Accounting Office and presented April 28, 1999, to the Senate committees on health and agriculture.

May

SEC Chairman Levitt on Online Investing   203

Excerpts from an address, "Plain Talk About On-line Investing," delivered by Securities and Exchange Commission Chairman Arthur Levitt to the National Press Club in Washington, D.C., on May 4, 1999.

Supreme Court on Student Sexual Harassment   215

Excerpts from the majority and dissenting opinions in the case of *Davis v. Monroe County Board of Education,* in which the Supreme Court ruled, 5–4, on May 24, 1999, that a school district could be liable for student sexual harassment of another student if it knew about the harassment but did nothing about it and if the harassment was so severe and pervasive that the victim was denied access to educational benefits guaranteed under Title IX of the Education Amendments of 1972.

House Committee on Theft of U.S. Nuclear Secrets by China   235

Excerpts from the "Overview" of the declassified version of a report released May 25, 1999, by the House of Representatives Select Committee on U.S. National Security and Military/Commercial Concerns with the People's Republic of China; two statements released April 21, 1999, by

George Tenet, the director of central intelligence, follow: "Key Findings" from "The Intelligence Community Damage Assessment on the Implications of China's Acquisition of U.S. Nuclear Weapons Information on the Development of Future Chinese Weapons" and the "Introductory Note" from a review panel, chaired by retired admiral David Jeremiah, which examined the intelligence community damage assessment.

GAO Report on the Effects of Welfare Reform   257
Excerpts of testimony titled "Welfare Reform: States' Implementation Progress and Information on Former Recipients," given May 27, 1999, by Cynthia M. Fagnoni, director of education, workforce, and income security issues for the General Accounting Office, before the House Ways and Means Subcommittee on Human Resources on the experiences of former welfare recipients.

Obasanjo on His Inauguration as President of Nigeria   272
Text of the inaugural address of Olusegun Obasanjo, president of Nigeria, given May 29, 1999.

June

United Nations Security Council Resolution on Kosovo   285
Excerpts from United Nations Security Council Resolution 1244, adopted June 10, 1999, which established the basis for international peacekeeping and humanitarian aid efforts in Kosovo, a province of the Federal Republic of Yugoslavia.

Mbeki on His Inauguration as President of South Africa   297
Text of the inaugural address of Thabo Mbeki, president of South Africa, given June 16, 1999.

State Department on U.S. Bombing of Chinese Embassy   304
Excerpts from a statement given June 17, 1999, by U.S. Undersecretary of State Thomas R. Pickering to senior Chinese diplomatic officials in Beijing offering an explanation for the mistaken bombing May 7, 1999, of the Chinese embassy in Belgrade, Yugoslavia; the State Department released the text of the statement July 6, 1999.

Supreme Court on the Definition of Disability   317
Excerpts from the majority opinions in two Supreme Court rulings issued June 22, 1999, dealing with the Americans with Disabilities Act. In the first, *Sutton v. United Air Lines,* the Court ruled, 7–2, that individuals with correctable impairments are not automatically defined as being disabled under the act; in the second, *Olmstead v. L.C.,* the Court ruled, 6–3, that the disabilities act and its regulations obliged states to place mentally disabled people in the least restrictive setting possible, consistent with the condition and wishes of the patient and the resources of the state.

Supreme Court on States Rights   333

Excerpts from the majority and dissenting opinions in the case of *Alden v. Maine,* handed down June 23, 1999, in which the Supreme Court by a 5–4 vote ruled that Congress did not have the power under Article I of the Constitution to authorize private suits seeking to enforce federal law in state courts without the consent of the state.

President Clinton's Remarks on the Budget Surplus   350

Statement by President Bill Clinton at the White House on June 28, 1999, during which he announced higher estimates on expected surpluses in the federal budget during fiscal years 2000 to 2009 and beyond.

July

Israeli Prime Minister Barak on the New Government   359

Excerpts from an address July 6, 1999, by Israeli prime minister Ehud Barak, in which he announced his cabinet and his government program to the Knesset.

Report on "Digital Divide" in Access to Computers, Internet   368

Excerpts from the report, "Falling Through the Net: Defining the Digital Divide," issued July 8, 1999, by the National Telecommunications and Information Administration of the U.S. Commerce Department.

Federal Report on the Well-Being of Children   384

Text of the highlights section of "America's Children: Key National Indicators of Well-Being," a report issued July 8, 1999, by the Federal Interagency Forum on Child and Family Statistics.

Census Bureau Report on Measures of Well-Being   390

Excerpts from the report, "Extending Measure of Well-Being: Meeting Basic Needs," issued July 8, 1999, by the U.S. Census Bureau.

Agriculture Secretary on Biotechnology in Agriculture   401

Excerpts from a speech delivered July 13, 1999, by Agriculture Secretary Dan Glickman at the National Press Club in Washington, D.C., on the safety of genetically altered food crops.

Inspector General on Federal Oversight of Hospitals   412

Executive summary from the report, "The External Review of Hospital Quality: A Call for Greater Accountability," released July 20, 1999, by the Office of Inspector General in the Department of Health and Human Services.

Sen. Edward M. Kennedy's Eulogy for John F. Kennedy Jr.   422

Text of the eulogy delivered July 23, 1999, by Sen. Edward M. Kennedy for his nephew John Kennedy Jr., at the Church of St. Thomas in New York City.

UN Refugee Commissioner on Promoting Peace in Africa   **428**
Excerpts from an address to the United Nations Security Council in New
York on July 26, 1999, by Sadako Ogata, the UN high commissioner for
refugees, in which she addressed the needs of refugees in Africa.

Surgeon General on Suicide Prevention   **439**
Text of "The Surgeon General's Call to Action to Prevent Suicide, 1999"
released July 28, 1999, by the U.S. Public Health Service.

August

Federal Survey on Drug Use   **459**
Text of the "highlights" section from the "Summary of Findings" of the
1998 National Household Survey on Drug Abuse, released August 18,
1999, by Donna Shalala, secretary of the U.S. Department of Health and
Human Services.

USAID on Earthquake in Turkey   **465**
Excerpts from "Turkey—Earthquake Fact Sheet #6," issued August 20,
1999, by the U.S. Agency for International Development, describing the
situation in Turkey following a powerful earthquake that struck the country on August 17, 1999.

September

Secretary of State Albright on U.S. Consulate in Vietnam   **475**
Text of remarks by Secretary of State Madeleine K. Albright at a ceremony
September 7, 1999, marking the dedication of a new U.S. consulate build-
ing in Ho Chi Minh City, Vietnam.

Attorney General and Special Counsel on Waco Investigation   **480**
Excerpts from a news conference September 9, 1999, at which Attorney
General Janet Reno announced her appointment of former senator John
Danforth as special counsel to investigate the government's handling of
the April 19, 1993, siege of the Branch Davidian compound in Waco,
Texas.

UNICEF Director on the Spread of AIDS in Africa   **489**
Excerpts from a speech delivered September 15, 1999, by Carol Bellamy,
executive director of the United Nations Children's Fund, at the
International Conference on AIDS and Sexually Transmitted Diseases,
held in Lusaka, Zambia.

National Security Commission on Threats in the Next Century   **499**
Excerpts from the "introduction" and "major themes and implications"
from the report, "New World Coming: American Security in the 21st

Century," issued September 15, 1999, by the congressionally mandated
United States Commission on National Security/21st Century.

**UN Human Rights Commissioner on Independence
in East Timor**   511
"Report of the High Commissioner for Human Rights on the Human Rights
Situation in East Timor," issued September 17, 1999, by Mary Robinson,
the UN High Commissioner for Human Rights, describing the conditions in
East Timor following the August 30, 1999, referendum in which a majority
of East Timorese voted for independence from Indonesia.

**UN Secretary General on the Situation
in Afghanistan**   524
Excerpts from a report, "The Situation in Afghanistan and Its Implications
for International Peace and Security," submitted September 21, 1999, by
United Nations Secretary General Kofi Annan to the UN General Assembly
and Security Council.

Justice Department Allegations of Fraud by Tobacco Industry   536
Excerpts from the civil complaint filed September 22, 1999, by the U.S.
Department of Justice against tobacco manufacturers, seeking to recover
damages from the American tobacco industry, which the department
alleged had conspired to mislead and defraud the American public about
the health risks associated with smoking.

Army Secretary on Investigation of Korean War Massacre   552
Excerpts from a news conference September 30, 1999, in which U.S. Army
Secretary Louis Caldera announced an investigation into charges that the
army had killed several hundred South Korean refugees at the village of
No Gun Ri during the first weeks of the Korean War in July 1950.

October

Census Bureau on Health Insurance Coverage   561
Excerpts from a report on health insurance coverage, issued October 4,
1999, by the U.S. Census Bureau.

Former Defense Secretary on U.S. Policy Toward North Korea   568
Excerpts from the unclassified version of a report released October 12,
1999, by the State Department, entitled "Review of United States Policy
Toward North Korea: Findings and Recommendations," by William J.
Perry, a special adviser to President Bill Clinton who conducted a review
of U.S. policy toward North Korea.

UN on World Population Reaching Six Billion People   584
Text of a statement made October 12, 1999, in Sarajevo, Bosnia, by United
Nations Secretary General Kofi Annan, honoring the symbolic designation

of a baby born in that city as the world's six billionth person; excerpts
follow from the introduction and highlights sections of *The World at Six
Billion,* issued October 12, 1999, by the United Nations Population
Division.

Clinton on "Roadless Initiative" for Protecting Federal Forests   **592**
Excerpts from a speech delivered October 13, 1999, by President Bill
Clinton in which he announced a "roadless initiative" for protecting approximately 40 million acres of National Forest land from development by banning construction of roads for logging and other commercial purposes.

Clinton and Lott on Defeat of the Nuclear Test Ban Treaty   **600**
Excerpts from statements October 14, 1999, by President Bill Clinton and
Senate Majority Leader Trent Lott, R-Miss., commenting on the Senate's
rejection the previous day of the Comprehensive Test Ban Treaty.

NSF Director on Emergency Rescue of South Pole Doctor   **611**
Text of a statement released October 15, 1999, by Rita Colwell, director of
the National Science Foundation, announcing the successful emergency
rescue from the South Pole of Jerri Nielsen, a doctor who had been
stranded at a polar research station after finding a lump in her breast.

FBI Report on Crime   **614**
Press release issued October 17, 1999, by the Federal Bureau of
Investigation summarizing the findings of its annual report, *Crime in the
United States, 1998.*

Pakistani General Musharraf on Military Coup   **623**
Excerpts from a televised speech delivered October 17, 1999, by General
Pervez Musharraf, who had taken control of Pakistan five days earlier after
ousting the prime minister, Nawaz Sharif.

AFL-CIO President on Advances for the Labor Movement   **630**
Excerpts from a speech, "Building a Labor Movement for the Next
Century," delivered October 20, 1999, by John J. Sweeney, president of the
AFL-CIO, at Georgetown University Law Center in Washington, D.C.

Armenian President on Shootings in Parliament   **639**
Text of a speech delivered October 31, 1999, by Armenian president
Robert Kocharian at the funeral for Prime Minister Vazgen Sarkisian,
Speaker of Parliament Karen Demirchian, and other officials killed during
the October 27 attack on Parliament.

November

UN Secretary General Annan on the War in Congo   **645**
Excerpts from a report sent November 1, 1999, to the United Nations
Security Council by Secretary General Kofi Annan, in which he described

the conflict in the Democratic Republic of Congo and international attempts to end the fighting.

U.S. District Court on Microsoft's Monopoly Power   **654**
Excerpts from the "findings of fact," issued November 5, 1999, by U.S. District Court Judge Thomas Penfield Jackson, in the case of *United States of America v. Microsoft Corporation,* in which the judge determined that Microsoft had monopoly power in the market for personal computer operating systems and had used that power to harm competitors and consumers.

State Department Evaluation of U.S. Diplomatic Posts   **690**
Executive summary of the report, "America's Overseas Presence in the 21st Century," issued November 5, 1999, by the U.S. State Department's Overseas Presence Advisory Panel.

Clinton on the Fall of "The Wall" and an "Activist" Foreign Policy   **699**
Excerpt from a speech delivered November 8, 1999, by President Bill Clinton at Georgetown University in Washington, D.C., marking the tenth anniversary of the fall of the Berlin Wall.

NASA Investigation into the Loss of the *Mars Climate Orbiter*   **711**
Text of the executive summary from the "Phase I" report by the Mars Climate Orbiter Mishap Investigation Board, released November 10, 1999, in which an investigative panel of senior NASA engineers and scientists assessed the causes of the failure on September 23, 1999, of the *Mars Climate Observer* mission.

Clinton and Wahid on Renewal of Democracy in Indonesia   **718**
Excerpts from a news conference held November 12, 1999, in Washington, D.C., by President Bill Clinton and the newly elected Indonesian president, Abdurrahman Wahid.

Announcement on U.S.-China Bilateral Trade Agreement   **724**
Text of a communiqué issued November 15, 1999, in Beijing by the governments of the United States and China following the signing of a bilateral trade agreement between the two countries; the communiqué is followed by excerpts from a news conference in Beijing held by Charlene Barshefsky, the United States trade representative, and Gene Sperling, President Bill Clinton's economic advisor.

United Nations Report on the Fall of Srebrenica   **735**
Excerpts from the "assessment" section of the report, "The Fall of Srebrenica," submitted November 15, 1999, to the United Nations General Assembly by UN Secretary General Kofi Annan, in which he reviewed the events leading to the 1995 massacre of thousands of Muslim men and boys in a Bosnian town the UN had promised to protect.

CONTENTS

Northern Ireland Leaders on Status of the Peace Process   753
Three statements on the status of the peace process in Northern Ireland:
first, a statement November 16, 1999, by David Trimble, leader of the
Ulster Unionist Party; then a statement the same day by Gerry Adams,
leader of Sinn Fein (the political arm of the Irish Republican Army); and
finally a statement issued November 17, 1999, by the Irish Republican
Army.

Commerce Department on Y2K Preparations   760
Executive summary of the report, "The Economics of Y2K and the Impact
on the United States," released November 17, 1999, by the Economics and
Statistics Administration of the U.S. Department of Commerce.

OSHA on Proposed Ergonomics Standards   769
Texts of two background documents that accompanied the proposed
ergonomics regulations issued November 22, 1999, by the Occupational
Safety and Health Administration, describing the agency's proposed
ergonomics regulations and explaining why they were necessary.

Institute of Medicine on Medical Mistakes   779
Executive summary of a report on medical mistakes, "To Err Is Human:
Building a Safer Health System," issued November 29, 1999, by the
Institute of Medicine.

December

U.S. Trade Representative on World Trade Organization Talks   797
Text of a statement by Charlene Barshefsky, the U.S. trade representative
and the chair of the ministerial meeting of the World Trade Organization
held in Seattle from November 30, 1999, to December 3, 1999, in which
she announced that the meeting had failed to reach agreement on a new
round of multilateral trade negotiations.

Reports on Human Rights Violations in Kosovo   802
Excerpts from two reports, "Ethnic Cleansing in Kosovo: An Accounting,"
issued December 9, 1999, by the U.S. State Department, describing
human rights violations in Kosovo during 1999; and from the executive
summary of the "Report on Human Rights Findings of the OSCE Mission
in Kosovo: As Seen, As Told, Part II," issued December 6, 1999, by the
Organization for Security and Cooperation in Europe describing human
rights violations in Kosovo from mid-June to late October 1999.

European Council on a New European Defense Force   817
Excerpts from two reports, "Ethnic Cleansing in Kosovo: An Accounting,"
issued December 9, 1999, by the U.S. State Department, describing
human rights violations in Kosovo during 1999; and from the executive
summary of the "Report on Human Rights Findings of the OSCE Mission

in Kosovo: As Seen, As Told, Part II," issued December 6, 1999, by the Organization for Security and Cooperation in Europe describing human rights violations in Kosovo from mid-June to late October 1999.

Department of Justice Report on Capital Punishment   828
Excerpts from the report, "Capital Punishment 1998," released December 12, 1999, by the Department of Justice's Bureau of Justice Statistics.

Surgeon General's Report on Mental Health   836
Excerpts from the preface and chapter 1 of "Mental Health: A Report of the Surgeon General," released December 13, 1999, by Surgeon General David Satcher at a White House news conference.

Former President Carter on the Panama Canal Transfer   850
Text of a speech delivered December 14, 1999, by former president Jimmy Carter during a ceremony in Panama marking the transfer of control of the Panama Canal from the United States to Panama.

Cartoonist Charles M. Schulz on His Retirement   856
Statement released December 14, 1999, by the cartoonist Charles M. Schulz, announcing that he was retiring and ending his comic strip, "Peanuts"; and a comment by President Bill Clinton December 15 on Schulz's retirement.

United Nations Report on the 1994 Genocide in Rwanda   860
Excerpts from the "Report of the Independent Inquiry into the Actions of the United Nations During the 1994 Genocide in Rwanda," released December 16, 1999.

Remarks at Peace Talks Between Israel and Syria   890
Remarks by President Bill Clinton, Israeli prime minister Ehud Barak, and Syrian foreign minister Farouk al-Shara at a ceremony December15, 1999, at the White House marking the first high-level peace negotiations between Israel and Syria.

Vermont Supreme Court on the Rights of Homosexuals   898
Excerpts from the majority opinion in the case of *Baker v. State of Vermont*, in which the Vermont Supreme Court ruled December 20, 1999, that the state had to give homosexual couples all the rights and protections that it extended to heterosexual couples.

UN Human Rights Official on the War in Chechnya   909
Text of a statement issued December 20, 1999, by Francis M. Deng, the representative of the United Nations secretary general on internally displaced persons, in which he called on the Russian government to protect civilians in Chechnya from attacks by the Russian military.

CONTENTS

Boris Yeltsin on His Resignation as Russian President   **917**
   Text of a speech delivered December 31, 1999, by Russian president Boris
   Yeltsin, in which he announced that he was resigning and turning the gov-
   ernment over to Vladimir Putin as acting president.

Index   **925**

January

Supreme Court on
State Ballot Initiatives 3

Statements from Clinton's
Impeachment Trial 15

State of the Union Address
and Republican Response 41

Federal Report on Quality
of Public School Teachers 64

SUPREME COURT ON
STATE BALLOT INITIATIVES
January 12, 1999

The Supreme Court dealt a setback to state efforts to regulate the ballot initiative process when it ruled on January 12 that parts of a Colorado law unduly hindered "political conversation and the exchange of ideas." Ballot initiatives, a process that allowed voters to circumvent a state legislature and vote directly on an issue, had become increasingly popular during the 1990s. In 1998 more than two hundred initiatives were on the ballots of the twenty-five jurisdictions that permitted them, seeking to write state laws on a broad range of topics, such as banning billboards, legalizing marijuana, and barring assisted suicide.

Supporters of the process argued that ballot initiatives were a necessary means of ensuring that voters have access to the ballot. But detractors, which included several states, contended that their popularity and commercialization were undermining the American system of representative government in general and jeopardizing the integrity of the petition process in particular. Colorado sought to blunt the use of ballot initiatives there by passing a state law that required petition collectors to be registered to vote in Colorado and to wear badges displaying their names when they circulated petitions. The law also required petition organizers to file periodic statements saying how much each signature collector had been paid. In striking down these provisions, the Court majority held that the state had not shown sufficient reason why such forms of political speech should be limited.

Ballot Initiatives: Populist Expression
or a Tool of Special Interests?

The ballot initiative is a form of direct legislation permitted by twenty-four states, mostly in the West and Midwest, and the District of Columbia. The process had its beginnings in the populist movement at the turn of the century, when South Dakota in 1902 became the first state to permit its use. The ballot initiative was intended to give local citizens a way to counter the

3

special interests that had captured many state legislatures. In essence, if a sufficient number of registered voters in a state signed a petition in support of a specific ballot initiative, then that initiative would go on the state election ballot. The initiative would become state law if a simple majority, or in some cases a two-thirds majority, voted for it.

For much of the century the ballot initiative was used sparingly. In 1978 the process itself captured national attention when a group in California used it to pass Proposition 13, which placed limits on state taxes and spending. Similar laws quickly swept across the country. Voter referendums were used more often in the 1990s than at any other time in history to place a broad assortment of issues on state ballots. Many of these, such as bond issues for schools and road projects, were mundane questions of local or regional interest. But others, including legalizing marijuana and assisted suicide, banning partial birth abortions and same-sex marriages, and providing state aid for private schools and public funds for political candidates, were highly controversial nationally. California was particularly known for its controversial voter referendums, having voted in recent years to end state affirmative action programs, ban bilingual education, and trim benefits to illegal aliens.

Supporters of particular issues turned to the state ballot initiative for any number of reasons. Often initiatives resulted from the refusal or failure of the U.S. Congress or the state legislature to act on an issue. Supporters of a ban on partial birth abortions hoped to accomplish what Congress was unable to do and override President Bill Clinton's veto of a national ban on the procedure. In other cases, initiatives were used to overturn other laws. Supporters of state initiatives to legalize the use of marijuana for medical purposes, for example, sought to circumvent federal laws prohibiting the medical use of the drug. Alternatively, supporters might use the initiative process to test the political waters in a few key states before mounting a national campaign. "It's a way of gauging public opinion before you finalize your legislative policy," a spokesperson for the Center for Responsive Politics said.

The increasing popularity of ballot initiatives quickly turned them into big business. Backers of a particular initiative often hired political consulting companies, sometimes from outside the state, to mount publicity campaigns in favor of the initiative. Other firms specialized in organizing drives to collect petition signatures; these firms often used paid collectors who moved from state to state in signature-gathering campaigns. One firm filed a brief in the Colorado case saying that it had collected more than 18 million signatures in the course of more than 150 signature drives conducted in thirty-six states. Such campaigns cost hundreds of thousands of dollars or more, not to mention the sums that might be spent by opponents of the initiative. The Human Rights Campaign, for example, estimated that it spent more than $1.1 million in what turned out to be an unsuccessful effort to defeat a ballot initiative in Hawaii in 1998 that would bar the state from recognizing gay marriages.

Those who supported the initiative process argued that it was a valuable tool for guaranteeing voters access to the ballot. The initiative is "a safety valve," said one proponent in Oregon. "Powerful groups have great influence in our legislature. 'Good old boy' clubs develop and the average citizen feels left out. With the initiative, if you've got a gripe, you can get access. You don't have to take up arms." But the "professionalization" of the ballot initiative process led many critics to observe that a tool created to fight the special interests had been coopted by those very interests. "The initiative process has become dominated by wealthy special interests," the Council of States Governments said in a brief filed in behalf of Colorado. Others worried that the overuse or misuse of voter referendums could undermine democratic government. "The more you substitute a plebiscite for the checks and balances of the legislative process, the more you run afoul of the fundamental idea of our constitution," David Frohnmayer, the president of the University of Oregon, told the Washington Post.

Colorado was in the vanguard of states that attempted to control the process through regulation. In 1988, in the case of Meyer v. Grant, *the Supreme Court struck down the state's prohibition on paid signature collectors as a violation of the First Amendment's guarantee of free speech. The majority in that case held that petition circulation was "core political speech" because it involved "interactive communication concerning political change."*

An Excessive Restriction on Free Speech

A 1999 case, Buckley v. American Constitutional Law Foundation, *centered on Colorado's subsequent attempts to restrict ballot initiatives. Writing the majority opinion for the Court, Justice Ruth Bader Ginsburg discussed each restriction separately but said that all three inhibited communication with voters and that the state interests used to justify the regulations—administrative efficiency, fraud detection, and informing voters—were not sufficiently compelling to override free speech protections. The state's argument that petition circulators be registered to vote in Colorado to reduce the potential for fraud was already served, Ginsburg said, by the valid requirement that circulators submit affidavits listing their address. Requiring circulators to be registered voters, Ginsburg said, "cuts down the number of message carriers in the ballot-access arena without impelling cause." (Ginsburg noted that the majority had not addressed the question whether a state residency requirement would be permissible.)*

The requirement that signature collectors wear a badge identifying them by name so that the state could apprehend those who engaged in misconduct was also overly restrictive. The state had other ways to identify such collectors, Ginsburg said, while the badge requirement exposed circulators "to the risk of 'heat of the moment' harassment" and discouraged participation in the petition process. Finally, the majority said the state had shown no apparent reason why it should be permitted to require that the amounts paid to each petition circulator be disclosed. The law already required the organizers of a petition campaign to disclose their names and the total amount paid to circulators information that the majority thought was sufficient to serve as a check on domination of the process by special interest groups. Moreover, Ginsburg said, paying petition circulators did not involve the same "risk of 'quid pro quo' corruption present when money is paid to, or for, candidates."

Ginsburg's opinion was joined by Justices John Paul Stevens, Antonin Scalia, Anthony M. Kennedy, and David H. Souter. Justice Clarence Thomas concurred with the judgment of the majority but not the reasoning. He argued that all the restrictions should have been examined under the most strict forms of scrutiny; in his opinion all would have been found wanting under such an examination.

In dissent, Chief Justice William H. Rehnquist said he found it ironic that, in the name of the First Amendment, the majority "strikes down the attempt of a State to allow its own voters (rather than out-of-state persons and political drop-outs) to decide what issues should go on the ballot to be decided by the State's registered voters." He also raised broader concerns about the majority ruling, suggesting that it called into question laws in at least nineteen states that required those who circulated petitions to put candidates on the ballot to be registered voters.

Although he dissented from the majority opinion, Rehnquist agreed that requiring petition circulators to wear badges identifying them by name was unconstitutional. In a separate opinion Justices Sandra Day O'Connor and Stephen G. Breyer concurred that the name badges were unconstitutional but disagreed with the majority on the registration and disclosure rulings.

> *Following are excerpts from the majority opinion, written by Ruth Bader Ginsburg, and a dissenting opinion written by Chief Justice William H. Rehnquist, in the case of* Buckley v. American Constitutional Law Foundation, *in which the Supreme Court ruled on January 12, 1999, that the Colorado law requiring circulators of initiative petitions to be registered voters, to wear badges identifying them by name, and to disclose how much they had been paid to circulate the petitions imposed an unconstitutional infringement on their right of free speech:*

No. 97-930

Victoria Buckley, Secretary of
State of Colorado, Petitioner

v.

American Constitutional Law
Foundation, Inc., et al.

On writ of certiorari to the United
States Court of Appeals for the
Tenth Circuit

[January 12, 1999]

JUSTICE GINSBURG delivered the opinion of the Court.

Colorado allows its citizens to make laws directly through initiatives placed on election ballots. We review in this case three conditions Colorado places on the ballot-initiative process: (1) the requirement that initiative-petition circulators be registered voters, (2) the requirement that they wear an identification badge bearing the circulator's name; and (3) the requirement that proponents of an initiative report the names and addresses of all paid circulators and the amount paid to each circulator.

Precedent guides our review. In *Meyer* v. *Grant* (1988), we struck down Colorado's prohibition of payment for the circulation of ballot-initiative petitions. Petition circulation, we held, is "core political speech," because it involves "interactive communication concerning political change." First Amendment protection for such interaction, we agreed, is "at its zenith." We have also recognized, however, that "there must be a substantial regulation of elections if they are to be fair and honest and if some sort of order, rather than chaos, is to accompany the democratic processes." *Storer* v. *Brown* (1974). Taking careful account of these guides, the Court of Appeals for the Tenth Circuit upheld some of the State's regulations, but found the three controls at issue excessively restrictive of political speech, and therefore declared them invalid. We granted certiorari, and now affirm that judgment.

I

The complaint in this action was filed in 1993 in the United States District Court for the District of Colorado. . . ; it challenged six of Colorado's many controls on the initiative-petition process. Plaintiffs, now respondents, included American Constitutional Law Foundation, Inc., a nonprofit, public interest organization that supports direct democracy, and several individual participants in Colorado's initiative process. In this opinion we refer to plaintiffs-respondents, collectively, as ACLF. ACLF charged that the following prescriptions of Colorado's law governing initiative petitions violate the First Amendment's freedom of speech guarantee: (1) the requirement that petition circulators be at least 18 years old; (2) the further requirement that they be registered voters; (3) the limitation of the petition circulation period to six months; (4) the requirement that petition circulators wear identification badges stating their names, their status as "VOLUNTEER" or "PAID," and if the latter, the name and telephone number of their employer; (5) the requirement that circulators attach to each petition section an affidavit containing, *inter alia*, the circulator's name and address and a statement that "he or she has read and understands the laws governing the circulation of petitions"; and (6) the requirements that initiative proponents disclose (a) at the time they file their petition, the name, address, and county of voter registration of all paid circulators, the amount of money proponents paid per petition signature, and the total amount paid to each circulator, and (b) on a monthly basis, the names of the proponents, the name and address of each paid circulator, the name of the proposed ballot measure, and the amount of money paid and owed to each circulator during the month.

The District Court, after a bench trial, struck down the badge requirement and portions of the disclosure requirements, but upheld the age and affidavit requirements and the six-month limit on petition circulation. The District Court also found that the registration requirement "limits the number of persons available to circulate . . . and, accordingly, restricts core political speech." Nevertheless, that court upheld the registration requirement. In 1980, the District Court noted, the registration requirement had been adopted by Colorado's voters as a constitutional amendment. For that reason, the District Court believed, the restriction was "not subject to any level of scrutiny."

The Court of Appeals affirmed in part and reversed in part. . . . Initiative-petition circulators, the Tenth Circuit recognized, resemble handbill distributors, in that both seek to promote public support for a particular issue or position. Initiative-petition circulators also resemble candidate-petition signature gatherers, however, for both seek ballot access. In common with the District Court, the Tenth Circuit upheld, as reasonable regulations of the ballot-initiative process, the age restriction, the six-month limit on petition circulation, and the affidavit requirement. The Court of Appeals struck down the requirement that petition circulators be registered voters, and also held portions of the badge and disclosure requirements invalid as trenching unnecessarily and improperly on political expression.

[II omitted]
III

By constitutional amendment in 1980, and corresponding statutory change the next year, Colorado added to the requirement that petition circulators be residents, the further requirement that they be registered voters. Registration, Colorado's Attorney General explained at oral argument, demonstrates "commit[ment] to the Colorado law-making process," and facilitates verification of the circulator's residence. Beyond question, Colorado's registration requirement drastically reduces the number of persons, both volunteer and paid, available to circulate petitions. We must therefore inquire whether the State's concerns warrant the reduction.

When this case was before the District Court, registered voters in Colorado numbered approximately 1.9 million. At least 400,000 persons eligible to vote were not registered.

Trial testimony complemented the statistical picture. Typical of the submissions, initiative proponent Paul Grant testified: "Trying to circulate an initiative petition, you're drawing on people who are not involved in normal partisan politics for the most part. . . . [L]arge numbers of these people, our natural support, are not registered voters."

As earlier noted, the District Court found from the statistical and testimonial evidence: "The record does show that the requirement of registration limits the number of persons available to circulate and sign [initiative] petitions and, accordingly, restricts core political speech." Because the requirement's source was a referendum approved by the people of Colorado, however, the District Court deemed the prescription "not subject to any level of [judicial] scrutiny." That misjudgment was corrected by the Tenth Circuit: "The voters may no more violate the United States Constitution by enacting a ballot issue than the general assembly may by enacting legislation."

The Tenth Circuit reasoned that the registration requirement placed on Colorado's voter-eligible population produces a speech diminution of the very kind produced by the ban on paid circulators at issue in *Meyer*. We agree. The requirement that circulators be not merely voter eligible, but registered voters . . . decreases the pool of potential circulators as certainly as that pool is decreased by the prohibition of payment to circulators. Both provisions "limi[t] the number of voices who will convey [the initiative proponents'] message" and, consequently, cut down "the size of the audience [proponents] can reach." In this case, as in *Meyer*, the requirement "imposes a burden on political expression that the State has failed to justify."

Colorado acknowledges that the registration requirement limits speech, but not severely, the State asserts, because "it is exceptionally easy to register to vote." The ease with which qualified voters may register to vote, however, does not lift the burden on speech at petition circulation time. Of course there are individuals who fail to register out of ignorance or apathy. But there are also individuals for whom, as the trial record shows, the choice not to register implicates political thought and expression. A lead plaintiff in this case, long active in ballot-initiative support-a party no doubt " 'able and willing' to convey a political message"-testified that his refusal to register is a "form of . . . private and public protest." Another initiative proponent similarly stated that some circulators refuse to register because "they don't believe that the political process is responsive to their needs." For these voter-eligible circulators, the ease of registration misses the point.

The State's dominant justification appears to be its strong interest in policing lawbreakers among petition circulators. Colorado seeks to ensure that circulators will be amenable to the Secretary of State's subpoena power, which in these matters does not extend beyond the State's borders. The interest in reaching law violators, however, is served by the requirement, upheld below, that each circulator submit an affidavit setting out, among several particulars, the "address at which he or she resides, including the street name and number, the city or town, [and] the county." This address attestation, we note, has an immediacy, and corresponding reliability, that a voter's registration may lack. The attestation is made at the time a petition section is submitted; a voter's registration may lack that currency.

ACLF did not challenge Colorado's right to require that all circulators be residents, a requirement that, the Tenth Circuit said, "more precisely achieved" the State's subpoena service objective. Nor was any eligible-to-vote qualification in contest in this lawsuit. Colorado maintains that it is more difficult to determine who is a state resident than it is to determine who is a registered voter. The force of that argument is diminished, however, by the affidavit attesting to residence that each circulator must submit with each petition section.

In sum, assuming that a residence requirement would be upheld as a needful integrity-policing measure-a question we, like the Tenth Circuit, have no occasion to decide because the parties have not placed the matter of residence at issue-the added registration requirement is not warranted. That requirement cuts down the number of message carriers in the ballot-access arena without impelling cause.

IV

Colorado enacted the provision requiring initiative-petition circulators to wear identification badges in 1993, five years after our decision in *Meyer*. The Tenth Circuit held the badge requirement invalid insofar as it requires circulators to display their names. The Court of Appeals did not rule on the constitutionality of other elements of the badge provision, namely the "requirements that the badge disclose whether the circulator is paid or a volunteer, and if paid, by whom." Nor do we.

Evidence presented to the District Court, that court found, "demonstrated that compelling circulators to wear identification badges inhibits participation in the petitioning process." The badge requirement, a veteran ballot-initiative-petition organizer stated, "very definitely limited the number of people willing to work for us and the degree to which those who were willing to work would go out in public." Another witness told of harassment he personally experienced as circulator of a hemp initiative petition. He also testified to the reluctance of potential circulators to face the recrimination and retaliation that bearers of petitions on "volatile" issues sometimes encounter: "[W]ith their name on a badge, it makes them afraid." Other petition advocates similarly reported that "potential circulators were not willing to wear personal identification badges."

Colorado urges that the badge enables the public to identify, and the State to apprehend, petition circulators who engage in misconduct. Here again, the affidavit requirement, unsuccessfully challenged below, is responsive to the State's concern; as earlier noted, each petition section must contain, along with the collected signatures of voters, the circulator's name, address, and signature. This notarized submission, available to law enforcers, renders less needful the State's provision for personal names on identification badges.

While the affidavit reveals the name of the petition circulator and is a public record, it is tuned to the speaker's interest as well as the State's. Unlike a name badge worn at the time a circulator is soliciting signatures, the affidavit is separated from the moment the circulator speaks. As the Tenth Circuit explained, the name badge requirement "forces circulators to reveal their identities at the same time they deliver their political message"; it operates when reaction to the circulator's message is immediate and "may be the most intense, emotional, and unreasoned." The affidavit, in contrast, does not expose the circulator to the risk of "heat of the moment" harassment. . . .

The injury to speech is heightened for the petition circulator because the badge requirement compels personal name identification at the precise moment when the circulator's interest in anonymity is greatest. . . .

V

. . . In ruling on Colorado's disclosure requirements for paid circulations, the Court of Appeals looked primarily to our decision in *Buckley* v. *Valeo* (1976). In that decision, we stated that "exacting scrutiny" is necessary when compelled disclosure of campaign-related payments is at issue. We nevertheless upheld, as substantially related to important governmental interests, the recordkeeping, reporting, and disclosure provisions of the Federal Election Campaign Act of 1971. We explained in *Buckley* that disclosure provides the electorate with information "as to where political campaign money comes from and how it is spent," thereby aiding electors in evaluating those who seek their vote. We further observed that disclosure requirements "deter actual corruption and avoid the appearance of corruption by exposing large contributions and expenditures to the light of publicity."

Mindful of *Buckley*, the Tenth Circuit did not upset Colorado's disclosure requirements "as a whole." Notably, the Court of Appeals upheld the State's requirements for disclosure of *payors*, in particular, proponents' names and the total amount they have spent to collect signatures for their petitions. In this regard, the State and supporting *amici* stress the importance of disclosure as a control or check on domination of the initiative process by affluent special interest groups. . . .

Through the disclosure requirements that remain in place, voters are informed of the source and amount of money spent by proponents to get a measure on the ballot; in other words, voters will be told "who has proposed [a measure]," and "who has provided funds for its circulation." The added benefit of revealing the names of paid circulators and amounts paid to each circulator, the lower courts fairly determined from the record as a whole, is hardly apparent and has not been demonstrated.

We note, furthermore, that ballot initiatives do not involve the risk of *"quid pro quo"* corruption present when money is paid to, or for, candidates. . . .

VI

Through less problematic measures, Colorado can and does meet the State's substantial interests in regulating the ballot-initiative process. Colorado aims to protect the integrity of the initiative process, specifically, to deter fraud and diminish corruption. To serve that important interest . . . Colorado retains an arsenal of safeguards. To inform the public "where [the] money comes from," we reiterate, the State legitimately requires sponsors of ballot initiatives to disclose who pays petition circulators, and how much.

To ensure grass roots support, Colorado conditions placement of an initiative proposal on the ballot on the proponent's submission of valid signatures representing five percent of the total votes cast for all candidates for Secretary of State at the previous general election. Furthermore, in aid of efficiency, veracity, or clarity, Colorado has provided for an array of process measures not contested here by ACLF. These measures prescribe, *inter alia*, a single subject per initiative limitation, a signature verification method, a large, plain-English notice alerting potential signers of petitions to the law's requirements, and the text of the affidavit to which all circulators must subscribe.

* * *

For the reasons stated, we conclude that the Tenth Circuit correctly separated necessary or proper ballot access controls from restrictions that unjustifiably inhibit the circulation of ballot-initiative petitions. Therefore, the judgment of the Court of Appeals is

Affirmed.

CHIEF JUSTICE REHNQUIST, dissenting.

The Court today invalidates a number of state laws designed to prevent fraud in the circulation of candidate petitions and to ensure that local issues of state law are decided by local voters, rather than by out-of-state interests. Because I believe that Colorado can constitutionally require that those who circulate initiative petitions *to* registered voters actually *be* registered voters themselves, and because I believe that the Court's contrary holding has wide-reaching implication for state regulation of elections generally, I dissent.

I

Ballot initiatives of the sort involved in this case were a central part of the Progressive movement's agenda for reform at the turn of the 20th century, and were advanced as a means of limiting the control of wealthy special interests and restoring electoral power to the voters. However, in recent years, the initiative and referendum process has come to be more and more influenced by out-of-state interests which employ professional firms doing a nationwide business. The state laws that the Court strikes down today would restore some of this initial purpose by limiting the influence that such out-of-state interests may have on the in-state initiative process. The ironic effect of today's opinion is that, in the name of the First Amendment, it strikes down the attempt of a State to allow its own voters (rather than out-of-state persons and political dropouts) to decide what issues should go on the ballot to be decided by the State's registered voters.

The basis of the Court's holding is that because the state laws in question both (1) decrease the pool of potential circulators and (2) reduce the chances that a measure would gather signatures sufficient to qualify for the ballot, the measure is unconstitutional under our decision in *Meyer* v. *Grant* (1988). *Meyer*, which also dealt with Colorado's initiative regulations, struck down a criminal ban on *all* paid petition circulators. But *Meyer* did not decide that a State cannot impose reasonable regulations on such circulation. Indeed, before today's decision, it appeared that under our case law a State could have imposed reasonable regulations on the circulation of initiative petitions, so that some order could be established over the inherently chaotic nature of democratic processes. Today's opinion, however, calls into question the validity of *any* regulation of petition circulation which runs afoul of the highly abstract and mechanical test of diminishing the pool of petition circulators or making a proposal less likely to appear on the ballot. It squarely holds that a State may not limit circulators to registered voters, and maintains a sphinx-like silence as to whether it may even limit circulators to state residents.

II

. . . State ballot initiatives are a matter of state concern, and a State should be able to limit the ability to circulate initiative petitions to those people who can ultimately vote on those initiatives at the polls. If eligible voters make the conscious decision not to register to vote on the grounds that they reject the democratic process, they should have no right to complain that they cannot circulate initiative petitions to people who *are* registered voters. . . .

But the implications of today's holding are even more stark than its immediate effect. Under the Court's interpretation of *Meyer*, any ballot initiative regulation is unconstitutional if it either diminishes the pool of people who can circulate petitions or makes it more difficult for a given issue to ultimately appear on the ballot. Thus, while today's judgment is ostensibly circumscribed in scope, it threatens to invalidate a whole host of historically established state regulations of the electoral process in general. Indeed, while the Court is silent with respect to whether a State can limit initiative petition circulation to state residents, the implication of its reading of *Meyer*-that being unable to hire out-of-state circulators would "limi[t] the number of voices who will convey [the initiative proponents'] message"-is that under today's decision, a State cannot limit the ability to circulate issues of local concern to its own residents.

May a State prohibit children or foreigners from circulating petitions, where such restrictions would also limit the number of voices who could carry the proponents' message and thus cut down on the size of the audience the initiative proponents could reach? And if initiative petition circulation cannot be limited to electors, it would seem that a State can no longer impose an elector or residency requirement on those who circulate petitions to place candidates on ballots, either. At least 19 States plus the District of Columbia explicitly require that candidate petition circulators be electors, and at least one other State requires that its petition circulators be state residents. Today's decision appears to place each of these laws in serious constitutional jeopardy.

III

As to the other two laws struck down by the Court, I agree that the badge requirement for petition circulators is unconstitutional. . . .

I disagree, however, that the First Amendment renders the disclosure requirements unconstitutional. The Court affirms the Court of Appeals' invalidation of only the portion of the law that requires final reports to disclose information specific to each paid circulator-the name, address, and amount paid to each. Important to the Court's decision is the idea that there is no risk of *"quid pro quo"* corruption when money is paid to ballot initiative circulators, and that paid circulators should not have to surrender the anonymity enjoyed by their volunteer counterparts. I disagree with this analysis because, under Colorado law, *all* petition circulators must surrender their anonymity under the affidavit requirement. Colorado law requires that each circulator must submit an affidavit which must include the circulator's "name, the address at which he or she resides, including the street name and number, the city or town, [and] the county." This affidavit requirement was upheld by the Tenth Circuit as not significantly burdening political expression, and is relied upon by the Court in holding that the registered voter requirement is unconstitutional. The only additional piece of information for which the disclosure requirement asks is thus the amount paid to each circulator. Since even after today's decision the identity of the circulators as well as the total amount of money paid to circulators will be a matter of public record, I do not believe that this additional requirement is sufficient to invalidate the disclosure requirements as a whole. They serve substantial interests and are sufficiently narrowly tailored to satisfy the First Amendment.

IV

Because the Court's holding invalidates what I believe to be legitimate restrictions placed by Colorado on the petition circulation process, and because its reasoning calls into question a host of other regulations of both the candidate nomination and petition circulation process, I dissent.

STATEMENTS FROM CLINTON'S IMPEACHMENT TRIAL
January 16 and 21, 1999

President Bill Clinton in 1998 became the second president of the United States to be impeached by the House of Representatives for "high crimes and misdemeanors." In 1999, after a trial of thirty-seven days in the Senate, Clinton became the second president acquitted of impeachment charges; the first was Andrew Johnson in 1868. After the Republican-led House voted in a highly partisan atmosphere to impeach Clinton, a Democrat, there never was a serious prospect that he would be convicted by a two-thirds majority of the Senate and removed from office. Even so, the trauma of the impeachment crisis strained the public's faith in government and ensured that Clinton's presidency would forever be tarred by scandal. At the end of 1999 the residue of impeachment was still hampering the ability of Clinton and Congress to work together and causing political difficulty for Vice President Al Gore, who was hoping to succeed Clinton.

Throughout the ordeal, politicians in Washington and citizens throughout the country disagreed about the gravity of Clinton's wrongdoing. After months of denial, the president in August 1998 acknowledged that he had engaged in improper "intimate contact" with a White House intern, Monica Lewinsky. Most Republican leaders in Congress argued that Clinton had committed perjury in his denials of a relationship with Lewinsky and had obstructed justice during his numerous efforts to head off an inquiry into the matter by independent counsel Kenneth W. Starr. Clinton and those who defended him-however reluctantly-argued that he was the victim of a partisan witch hunt into what was essentially a sex scandal, not an abuse of power.

Midterm elections in 1998 and the consistent findings of opinion polls showed that most of the public wanted the Lewinsky matter concluded as rapidly as possible. Throughout the year-long scandal, Clinton enjoyed extraordinarily high popularity ratings in the polls, despite public disgust with his personal behavior. Clinton's Republican accusers suffered a comparable level of public disapproval. In that political atmosphere, the trial became an exercise in damage control for the Republican-led Senate, with members of both parties anxious to be seen as handling the case expeditiously but with dignity. Except for diehard Clinton opponents, most Americans appeared satisfied with the outcome, if unhappy that Clinton and his Republican accusers had forced the country to go through the turmoil. Starr, a former federal judge who since 1994 had tenaciously pursued Clinton, left Washington in October 1999-nearly four months after Congress allowed the independent counsel statute under which he had operated to expire.

The Lewinsky scandal had its origins in a sexual harassment lawsuit filed against Clinton in 1994 by Paula Corbin Jones. Jones accused Clinton of requesting oral sex from her in a Little Rock hotel room in 1991, when he was governor of Arkansas and she was a state employee. Attempting to demonstrate a pattern of behavior, Jones's attorneys compiled a list of women whose names had been linked with Clinton, publicly or privately. Lewinsky's name appeared on that list because she had told several friends that she had a relationship with the president, beginning in November 1995. However, Lewinsky filed a sworn affidavit on January 7, 1998, denying ever having sexual relations with Clinton. Within weeks of that testimony, news of the alleged relationship between the president and Lewinsky became public, setting in motion a political and constitutional crisis resulting in Clinton's impeachment by the House on December 19, 1998. (Jones case, Historic Documents of 1997, p. 290; Lewinsky scandal, Clinton impeachment, Historic Documents of 1998, pp. 564, 632, 695, 958; independent counsel law, p. 165)

Establishing Trial Procedures

As the Senate convened in January 1999 for the second session of the 106th Congress, its first order of business was to deal with the two articles of impeachment that had been voted by the full House three weeks earlier. Article one accused the president of committing perjury in his August 17, 1998, grand jury testimony in which he attempted to skirt questions about his relationship with Lewinsky. Article two charged that the president had obstructed justice through a series of actions related to the Jones case and Starr's inquiry. The House had rejected two other impeachment articles that had been endorsed by its Judiciary Committee.

The Senate formally opened the Clinton trial on January 7, with Supreme Court Chief Justice William H. Rehnquist presiding, as mandated by the Constitution. The next day, all 100 senators met privately in the Old Senate Chamber in the Capitol for an extraordinary "bipartisan caucus" that produced a general agreement on the conduct of the trial. The overwhelming majority of senators appeared to want the trial to be as short as possible but long enough to assure the public that the Senate had taken its constitutional responsibilities seriously.

The House, in the meantime, had appointed thirteen "managers" to present the impeachment case to the Senate. All were Republican members of the Judiciary Committee, headed by committee chairman Henry J. Hyde of Illinois. Democrats had refused to serve as impeachment managers, in large part to highlight the essentially partisan nature of the House case against Clinton.

Despite occasional efforts by both sides to portray the trial as a bipartisan, or even nonpartisan affair, partisan politics also played a major role in the Senate deliberations. Three key votes in late January demonstrated the deep divide between the parties. Two of those votes came on January 27. First, the Senate rejected, 44–56, a motion by senior Democrat Robert C. Byrd of West Virginia to dismiss the charges against Clinton; then the Senate voted to summon Lewinsky and two other witnesses for closed-door depositions. Both votes were along party lines, except for Democrat Russell D. Feingold of Wisconsin, who voted with the majority Republicans. The next day, in a vote strictly along party lines, the Senate adopted a Republican plan for the closing stages of the trial. Even though the Democrats were on the losing side in all three votes, the tallies clearly demonstrated there would not be 68 votes in the Senate to convict Clinton on either impeachment charge.

As the trial continued, the major procedural issues involved the number of witnesses the House managers could call and the format of their testimony. The managers wanted the right to call several dozen witnesses to bolster their case, many of whom had not testified during the House Judiciary Committee hearings in the fall of 1998. Senate Democrats, and even many Republicans, objected to the House maneuver, saying it would delay the trial unnecessarily and arguing that the place for detailed testimony and cross-examination of witnesses was during the Judiciary committee hearings, not the Senate trial.

The key step in the witness issue came on February 4, when senators voted 70–30 not to require Lewinsky to testify in person before the full Senate. Instead, the Senate approved a procedure under which videotaped testimony Lewinsky had given House managers on February 1 would be available for either side during the presentation of arguments in the Senate. Senators agreed to a similar procedure for the videotaped testimony by two other witnesses: Vernon Jordan, a Washington lawyer and one of Clinton's closest friends, who Republicans suspected had tried to silence Lewinsky by finding a job for her in New York City; and Sidney Blumenthal, a Clinton aide deeply involved in the White House public relations offensive against the Republicans.

The House Case Against Clinton

Led by Judiciary Committee Chairman Hyde, the thirteen House managers began presenting their case against Clinton on January 14. Each of the managers made one or more presentations highlighting specific parts of the impeachment articles. From the outset, the House managers faced an uphill struggle because of the difficulty—if not impossibility—of swaying enough senators to secure a conviction. Perhaps because the outcome was *a foregone conclusion, the House managers devoted much of their effort to a public relations campaign countering Clinton's defense and attacking the Senate trial procedures. Hyde and other managers staged numerous press conferences just outside the Senate chamber, to the annoyance of many senators. Hyde on January 22 acknowledged the uneasy relationship between the House managers and the senators, telling them: "I know, oh do I know, what an annoyance we are in the bosom of this great body. But we're a constitutional annoyance, and I remind you of that fact."*

In their presentations to the senators, some of the House managers engaged in florid denunciations of the president's actions during the Lewinsky affair. Hyde, in particular, used numerous quotations from Shakespeare, along with allusions to historical events, such as the signing of the Magna Carta, the American Revolution, and the Civil War. "This case is a test of whether what the Founding Fathers described as 'sacred trust' still has meaning in our time, 222 years after those two words, 'sacred honor,' were inscribed in our country's birth certificate, our national charter of freedom, our Declaration of Independence," Hyde told the senators in a January 16 summary of the manager's initial presentation.

Other House managers gave detailed analyses of how the charges contained in the two impeachment articles constituted impeachable offenses. Several senators later said the most compelling presentations were made by Representative Asa Hutchinson, an Arkansas Republican whose brother, Tim, was a senator. Representative Hutchinson used detailed charts attempting to demonstrate that Clinton had obstructed justice through such actions as orchestrating efforts to find a job for Lewinsky in New York City.

For many senators and other observers, the strongest argument made by the House managers was that Clinton should face the consequences of his actions, even if he was president. Several House managers noted that the Senate had repeatedly removed federal judges from office for offenses bearing some similarity to the president's, and that military officers had suffered serious penalties for lying about adulterous relationships. F. James Sensenbrenner Jr. (R-Wis.) summarized that argument in his closing remarks to the Senate: "To keep a president in office, whose gross misconduct and criminal actions are a well-established fact, will weaken the authority of the presidency, undermine the rule of law, and cheapen those words which have made America different from most other nations in the earth: 'equal justice under law.' "

One of the highlights of the House case came February 6, when prosecutors showed senators a videotape of Lewinsky's testimony, contrasting the former White House intern with videotape of Clinton's denials of a sexual relationship between the two of them. It was the first time the public had a chance to hear Lewinsky speak directly about her relationship with the president. Lewinsky said Clinton had never asked her to lie about their relationship-contradicting numerous media reports shortly after the scandal emerged early in 1998. However, she said she had known during the relationship that she would deny involvement with the president because "it was part of the pattern of the relationship."

Clinton's Defense

The president's defenders opened their case January 19, accusing the Republican House managers of constructing a flimsy case against the president. Led by White House Counsel Charles F. C. Ruff, the president's lawyers gave a point-by-point response to the charges contained in the two impeachment articles-at several stages ridiculing the allegations as lacking any basis in fact. In one particularly memorable and damaging line, Ruff summarized a key part of the House Republican case as consisting of "sealing wax and strings and spider's webs."

From the outset, Clinton's lawyers opted for a strategy of acknowledging that the president's behavior with Lewinsky had been inexcusable and wrong. The lawyers also admitted that Clinton had misled the public about his relationship with Lewinsky and had been "evasive" and "misleading" in his grand jury testimony. But, the lawyers insisted, the president had not committed perjury and had not obstructed justice-as the impeachment articles alleged-and therefore should not be removed from office. The House charges against Clinton were "frivolous" and not worthy of the impeachment standards envisioned in the Constitution, said White House lawyer Gregory B. Craig. "If you convict and remove President Clinton on the basis of these allegations, no president of the United States will ever be safe from impeachment again."

One of the key elements of the obstruction-of-justice charge was that Clinton had conspired with Lewinsky to hide numerous gifts that the two had exchanged during their relationship. The House managers repeatedly drew attention to a meeting between the two on December 28, 1997, during which Lewinsky asked Clinton if she should hide or return the gifts he had given her. In a January 19 presentation to the Senate, Cheryl D. Mills, an assistant White House counsel, derided the House manager's focus on the gift issue, and in particular the December 28 meeting between Clinton and Lewinsky. Noting that Clinton gave Lewinsky more gifts at that meeting, Mills said: "Why would the president give Ms. Lewinsky gifts if he wanted her to give them right back?" Mills said this was one of several examples of how the House case against Clinton could not withstand the presence of "stubborn facts."

The president's lawyers also sought to focus attention on the actions of those who had investigated Clinton, primarily Starr and the House Republicans. In the midst of the trial, Starr's office handed the White House a political bonus by leaking word to the New York Times that Starr was considering seeking an indictment against Clinton after he left office. The newspaper's report, on January 31, set off a flurry of charges and countercharges about Starr's handling of his investigation, in particular his apparent use of news leaks to shape public opinion. All this played into the hands of the president's defenders.

To cap the defense of the president, the White House turned January 21 to one of the most eloquent speakers from the ranks of the Senate itself: Dale Bumpers, an Arkansas Democrat who had retired from the Senate just a few weeks earlier. A longtime friend of the president, Bumpers nevertheless described his friend's conduct as "indefensible, outrageous, unforgivable, shameless." Even so, Bumpers said, the Senate would be committing folly if it removed Clinton from office. "If you vote to convict, in my opinion, you're going to be creating more havoc than he could ever possibly create," he told his former colleagues. "After all, he's only got two years left."

The Votes to Acquit

Senators voted February 9 to conduct their final deliberations in private. After three days of closed-door speeches to each other-speeches that many senators later delivered in public news conferences-senators opened the doors to their chamber for a public reckoning on February 12. "Senators, how say you? Is the respondent, William Jefferson Clinton, guilty or not guilty?" Chief Justice Rehnquist asked. One by one, senators stood at their desks as their names were called and responded, "guilty" or "not guilty" to the two articles of impeachment.

On article one, accusing Clinton of perjury, the Senate voted 45 in favor of conviction and 55 against, far short of the two-thirds vote necessary for conviction. Ten Republicans joined all 45 Democrats in voting "not guilty." All ten were moderate or liberal Republicans who said they strongly disapproved of Clinton's behavior but did not believe his denials in the Lewinsky case amounted to a perjury offense for which he should be removed from office.

On article two, accusing Clinton of obstruction of justice, the Senate was evenly divided, 50–50. Five Republicans joined the 45 Democrats in voting "not guilty." Five of the Republicans who had voted to acquit Clinton on the perjury count switched sides on article two.

In statements explaining their votes, even those senators voting to acquit Clinton expressed strong disapproval of his behavior. John H. Chafee, a moderate Republican from Rhode Island, summarized the views of many senators when he said: "Overshadowing all this has been the president's reckless, tawdry behavior, coupled with misleading statements, that have undermined the dignity of the presidency and brought about a divisive and unpleasant chapter in our history."

Rehnquist praised the Senate for its deliberations, even while confessing his bewilderment at the procedural differences between the Supreme Court and the Senate-institutions separated by one street and some 200 years of established practice. The Senate, in turn, passed a resolution thanking Rehnquist for his work as its temporary president.

Senators gave various views of the performance of their institution during the impeachment proceedings. Some, such as Byrd, a Senate historian and senior statesman, insisted the chamber "under all these circumstances did pretty well." Others were not so certain that the Senate had properly fulfilled its constitutional mandate. Arlen Specter of Penn-

sylvania was one of the ten Republicans who voted to acquit Clinton on both impeachment charges. But to protest what he at one point called a "sham" trial, Specter twice cast his vote as "not proven, therefore, not guilty." Specter said he was using a standard of Scottish law to demonstrate his belief that the prosecutors had not proven their case, rather than that the president was innocent.

After the Senate votes, Clinton made his most direct apology for his actions. "I want to say again to the American people how profoundly sorry I am for what I said and did to trigger these events and the great burden they have imposed on the Congress and on the American people," he said in a televised address from the Rose Garden at the White House. "Now, I ask all Americans, and I hope all Americans here in Washington and throughout our land, will rededicate ourselves to the work of serving our nation and building our future together."

A Failed Attempt at Censure

In both the House, during its 1998 impeachment deliberations, and in the Senate, during its 1999 trial, some Democrats and Republicans sought a compromise demonstrating congressional disapproval of Clinton's behavior but stopping short of removing him from office. For the most part, these members hoped Congress could adopt a resolution of "censure," similar to resolutions that the two chambers occasionally adopted when members had violated established rules or customs.

The censure option was blocked in both chambers by Republican leaders on two principal grounds. First, they argued that the Constitution did not provide for a congressional censure of the president. Unpleasant and tortuous as it might be, impeachment was the only route constitutionally open for Congress in cases of extreme presidential misbehavior, they said. Second, and perhaps more important in political terms, Republican leaders viewed censure as providing political "cover" for members who did not want to vote to remove the president in the face of public opposition.

In the final days of the Senate trial, Democrats Joseph I. Lieberman of Connecticut and Dianne Feinstein of California, along with Republican Robert F. Bennett of Utah, developed a draft bipartisan resolution denouncing Clinton's "shameless, reckless and indefensible" behavior in the Lewinsky affair. Moments after Chief Justice Rehnquist graveled the impeachment trial to a close, Feinstein rose in the Senate to ask permission to offer that censure resolution. The Senate blocked her move by a vote of 43–56, effectively killing any prospect for censure.

Postimpeachment Developments

The not guilty verdict in the Senate trial did not end Clinton's legal troubles. Two months later, on April 12, Susan Webber Wright, a U.S. District Court judge in Arkansas, issued a ruling holding Clinton in contempt of court for providing false evidence in a January 17, 1998, deposition in the Paula Corbin Jones case. Clinton had testified that he did not have sexual relations with Lewinsky.

21

Judge Wright, who had studied law with Clinton, said in her finding: "The record demonstrates by clear and convincing evidence that the president responded to plaintiff's [Jones's lawyers'] questions by giving false, misleading, and evasive answers that were designed to obstruct the judicial process." Judge Wright ordered Clinton to pay "any reasonable expenses" incurred by Jones as a result of his testimony. Jones's lawyers sought a total of $496,000 from the president, but Judge Wright on July 29 reduced the payments to $89,483, which Clinton later paid. Clinton in November 1998 had agreed to pay Jones $850,000 as part of an out-of-court settlement of her claim against him. Clinton made that payment to Jones in January 1999, just as his Senate trial was getting underway.

Kenneth Starr's long-running inquiry into numerous aspects of Clinton's past also continued in the months after the Senate verdict. Starr had originally been appointed as an independent counsel in 1994 to investigate the involvement of Clinton and his wife, Hillary Rodham Clinton, in a failed real estate deal in Arkansas, known as "Whitewater." Starr won the conviction of three Clinton associates, including former Arkansas governor Jim Guy Tucker, but he never brought charges against either of the Clintons. Starr stepped down as independent counsel on October 18 to return to private law practice in Washington. He was replaced by Robert W. Ray, who had been a lawyer in Starr's office. In a meeting with reporters December 3, Starr defended his inquiry, which had cost the taxpayers more than $47 million, and called on Clinton to admit that he had lied under oath in his depositions. The president, Starr said, should "get himself right with the law."

In December Lewinsky testified in a pretrial hearing in a case brought by Maryland prosecutors against Linda R. Tripp, a former friend who had secretly taped her telephone conversations with Lewinsky. Taping telephone conversations without the knowledge of the other party was illegal under Maryland law.

Following are excerpts from a presentation to the Senate on January 16, 1999, by Rep. Henry J. Hyde, R-Ill., chairman of the House Judiciary Committee and chairman of the House managers in the impeachment trial of President Bill Clinton, and from a presentation to the Senate on January 21, 1999, by former Democratic senator Dale Bumpers of Arkansas, acting as a defense counsel for President Clinton:

HYDE'S SUMMATION

Mr. Chief Justice, counsel for the president, distinguished members of the Senate: 139 years ago—136 years ago—at a small military cemetery in Pennsylvania, one of Illinois' most illustrious sons asked a haunting question: Whether a nation conceived in liberty and dedicated to the proposition that all men are created equal can long endure.

America is an experiment never finished; it's a work in progress. And so, that question has to be answered by each generation for itself, just as we will have to answer whether this nation can long endure.

This controversy began with the fact that the president of the United States took an oath to tell the truth in his testimony before the grand jury, just as he had on two prior occasions, sworn a solemn oath to preserve, protect and defend the Constitution and to faithfully execute the laws of the United States.

One of the most memorable aspects of this entire proceeding was the solemn occasion wherein every senator in this chamber took an oath to do impartial justice under the Constitution. But I must say, despite massive and relentless efforts to change the subject, the case before you, Senators, is not about sexual misconduct, infidelity, adultery. Those are private acts and are none of our business.

It's not even a question of lying about sex. The matter before this body is a question of lying under oath. This is a public act. The matter before you is a question of the willful, premeditated, deliberate corruption of the nation's system of justice through perjury and obstruction of justice.

These are public acts. And when committed by the chief law enforcement officer of the land, the one who appoints every United States district attorney, every federal judge, every member for the Supreme Court, the attorney general, they do become the concern of Congress. And that's why your judgment, respectfully, should rise above politics, above partisanship, above polling data.

This case is a test of whether what the Founding Fathers described as "sacred honor" still has meaning in our time 222 years after those two words, "sacred honor," were inscribed in our country's birth certificate, our national charter of freedom, our Declaration of Independence.

Every school child in the United States has an intuitive sense of the sacred honor that is one of the foundation stones of the American house of freedom, for every day in every classroom in America, our children and grandchildren pledge allegiance to a nation under God.

That statement is not a prideful or arrogant claim. It's a statement of humility. All of us as individuals stand under the judgment of God or the transcendent truths by which we hope finally to be judged. So does our country.

The presidency is an office of trust. Every public office is a public trust, but the office of the president is a very special public trust. The president is the trustee of the national conscience. No one owns the office of the president—the people do. The president is elected by the people and their representatives in the Electoral College. And accepting the burdens of that great office, the president in his inaugural oath enters into a covenant, a binding agreement of mutual trust and obligation with the American people.

Shortly after his election and during his first few months in office, President Clinton spoke with some frequency about a new covenant in America. In this instance, let's take the president at his word that his office is a covenant, a solemn pact of mutual trust and obligation with the American people. Let's take the president seriously when he speaks of covenants, because a covenant is about promise-making and promise-keeping.

For it's because the president has defaulted on the promises he made, it's because he has violated the oaths he has sworn, that he has been impeached. The debate about impeachment during the constitutional convention of 1787 makes it clear that the framers regarded impeachment and removal from office on conviction as a remedy for a fundamental betrayal of trust by the president.

The framers had invested the presidential office with great powers. They knew that those powers could be and would be abused if any president were to violate in a fundamental way the oath he had sworn to faithfully execute the nation's laws.

["The Covenant of Trust"]

For if the president did so violate his oath of office, the covenant of trust between himself and the American people would be broken. Today, we see something else, that the fundamental trust between America and the world can be broken if a presidential perjurer represents our country in world affairs.

If the president calculatedly and repeatedly violates his oath, if the president breaks the covenant of trust he's made with the American people, he can no longer be trusted. And because the executive plays so large a role in representing our country to the world, America can no longer be trusted.

It's often said we live in an age of increasing interdependence. If that's true—and the evidence for it is all around us—then the future will require an even stronger bond of trust between the president and the nation, because with increasing interdependence comes an increased necessity of trust.

This is one of the basic lessons of life. Parents and children know it; husbands and wives know it; teachers and students know it; as do doctors, patients, suppliers, customers, lawyers, clients, clergy and parishioners.

The greater the interdependence, the greater the necessity of trust. The greater the interdependence, the greater the imperative of promise-keeping.

Trust, not what James Madison called the parchment barriers of laws, is the fundamental bond between the people and their elected representatives; between those who govern and those who are governed.

Trust is the mortar that secures the foundations of the American house of freedom. And the Senate of the United States, sitting in judgment on this impeachment trial, should not ignore or minimize or dismiss the fact that that bond of trust has been broken, because the president has violated both his oaths of office and the oath he took before his grand jury testimony.

In recent months, it's often been asked: So what? What is the harm done by this lying under oath, by this perjury?

Well, what is an oath? An oath is an asking almighty God to witness to the truth of what you're saying. Truth telling, truth telling, is the heart and soul of our justice system. I think the answer would have been clear to those who once pledged their sacred honor to the cause of liberty. The answer would have been clear to those who crafted the world's most enduring written constitution.

No greater harm can come—can come than breaking the covenant of trust between the president and the people, between the three branches of our government, and between our country and the world, for to break that covenant of trust is to dissolve the mortar that binds the foundation stones of our freedom into a secure and solid edifice. And to break the covenant of trust by violating one's oath is to do grave damage to the rule of law among us.

That none of us is above the law is a bedrock principle of democracy. To erode that bedrock is to risk even further injustice. To erode that bedrock is to subscribe to a divine right of kings theory of governance in which those who govern are absolved from adhering to the basic moral standards to which the governed are accountable.

We must never tolerate one law for the ruler and another for the ruled. If we do, we break faith with our ancestors from Bunker Hill, Lexington and Concord to Flanders Fields, Normandy, Hiroshima, Panmunjom, Saigon and Desert Storm.

Let's be clear: The vote you are asked to cast is in the final analysis a vote about the rule of law. The rule of law is one of the great achievements of our civilization, for the alternative to the rule of law is the rule is the rule of raw power.

["We're the Heirs"]

We here today are the heirs of 3000 years of history in which humanity, slowly and painfully, and at great cost, evolved a form of politics in which law, not brute force, is the arbiter of our public destinies.

We're the heirs of the Ten Commandments and the Mosaic law, moral code for a free people, who having been liberated from bondage, saw in law a means to avoid falling back into the habits of slaves. We're the heirs of Roman law, the first legal system which peoples of different cultures, languages, races and religions came to live together to form a political community.

We're the heirs of the Magna Carta, by which the free men of England began to break the arbitrary and unchecked power of royal absolutism. We're the heirs of a long tradition of parliamentary development in which the rule of law gradually came to replace royal prerogative as the means for governing a society of free men and free women.

Yes, we're the heirs of 1776 and of an epic moment in human affairs— when the founders of this republic pledged their lives, their fortunes and yes, their sacred honor to the defense of the rule of law.

Now we're the heirs of a tragic civil war which vindicated the rule of law over the appetites of some for owning others. We're the heirs of the 20th century's great struggles against totalitarianism in which the rule of law was defended at immense cost against the worst tyrannies in human history.

The rule of law is no pious aspiration from a civics textbook. The rule of law is what stands between us and the arbitrary exercise of power by the state. The rule of law is the safeguard of our liberties. The rule of law is what allows us to live our freedom in ways that honor the freedom of others while strengthening the common good.

Lying under oath is an abuse of freedom. Obstruction of justice is a degradation of law. There are people in prison for such offenses. What in the world do we say to them about equal justice if we overlook this conduct by the president?

Some may say, as many have in recent months, that this is to pitch the matter too high. The president's lie, it is said, was about a trivial matter; it was a lie to spare embarrassment about misconduct on a private occasion.

The confusing of what is essentially a private matter and none of our business with lying under oath to a court and a grand jury has been only one of the distractions we've had to deal with.

Senators, as men and women with a serious experience of public affairs, we can all imagine a situation in which a president might shade the truth when a great issue of national interest or national security is at stake. We've been all over that terrain.

We know the thin ice on which any of us skates when blurring the edges of the truth for what we consider a compelling, demanding public purpose.

Morally serious men and women can imagine the circumstances at the far edge of the morally permissible when, with the gravest matters of national interest at stake, a president could shade the truth in order to serve the common good. But under oath for a private pleasure?

In doing this, the office of the president of the United States has been debased and the justice system jeopardized. In doing this, he's broken his covenant of trust with the American people.

The framers also knew that the office of the president could be gravely damaged if it continued to be unworthily occupied. That's why they devised the process of impeachment by the House and trial by the Senate.

It is in truth a direct process. If on impeachment the president is convicted, he's removed from office and the office itself suffers no permanent damage. If on impeachment the president is acquitted, the issue is resolved once and for all and the office is similarly protected from permanent damage.

But, if on impeachment the president is not convicted and removed from office despite the fact that numerous senators are convinced that he has, in the words of one proposed resolution of censure, "egregiously failed the test of his oath of office, violated the trust of the American people, and dishonored the office by which they entrusted to him," then the office of the presidency has been deeply and perhaps permanently damaged.

And that is a further reason why President Clinton must be convicted of the charges brought before you by the House and removed from office. To fail to do so, while conceding that the president has engaged in egregious and dishonorable behavior, that has broken the covenant of trust between himself and the American people, is to diminish the office of president of the United States in an unprecedented and unacceptable way.

Now, Senators, permit me a word on my own behalf and on behalf of my colleagues in the House. I want to clarify an important point. None of us comes to this chamber today without a profound sense of our own responsibilities in life and of the many ways in which we have failed to meet those responsibilities to one degree or another. None of us comes to you claiming to be a perfect man or a perfect citizen.

Just as none of you imagines yourself perfect, all of us, members of the House and Senate, know we come to this difficult task as flawed human beings under judgment. That is the way of this world—flawed human beings must, according to the rule of law, judge other flawed human beings.

But the issue before the Senate of the United States is not the question of its own members' personal moral condition, nor is the issue before the Senate the question of the personal moral condition of the members of the House of Representatives.

The issue here is whether the president has violated the rule of law and thereby broken the covenant of trust with the American people. This is a public issue involving the gravest matter of public interest. And it's not affected one way or another by the personal moral condition of any member of either House of Congress or by whatever expressions of personal chagrin the president has managed to express.

Senators, we of the House don't come before you today lightly. And if you will permit me, it is a disservice to the House to suggest that it has brought these articles of impeachment before you in a mean-spirited or irresponsible way. That is not true.

We have brought these articles of impeachment because we're convinced in conscience that the President of the United States lied under oath, that the president committed perjury on several occasions before a federal grand jury. We have brought these articles of impeachment because we are convinced in conscience that the president willfully obstructed justice and thereby threatened the legal system he swore a solemn oath to protect and defend.

["These Are Not Trivial Matters"]

These are not trivial matters. These are not partisan matters. These are matters of justice, the justice that each of you has taken a solemn oath to serve in this trial.

Some of us have been called Clinton-haters. I must tell you distinguished senators, that this impeachment trial is not, for those of us from the House, a question of hating anyone. This is not a question of who we hate, it's a question of what we love.

And among the things we love are the rule of law, equal justice before the law and honor in our public life. All of us are trying as hard as we can to do our duty as we see it; no more and no less.

Senators, the trial is being watched around the world. Some of those watching thinking themselves superior in their cynicism wonder what it's all about.

But others know, political prisoners know, that this is about the rule of law, the great alternative to arbitrary and unchecked state powers. The families of executed dissidents know that this is about the rule of law, the great alternative to the lethal abuse of power by the state. Those yearning for freedom know this about the rule of law—the hard, one structure by which men and women can live by their God-given dignity and secure their God-given rights in ways that serve the common good.

If they know this, can we not know it?

If across the river in Arlington Cemetery there are American heroes who died in defense of the rule of law, can we give less than the full measure of our devotion to that great cause?

I wish to read you a letter I recently received that expresses my feelings far better than my poor words:

> *Dear Chairman Hyde: My name is William Preston Summers. How are you doing? I am a third-grader in room 504 at Chase elementary school in Chicago.*
>
> *I am writing this letter because I have something to tell you. I have thought of a punishment for the president of the United States of America. The punishment should be that he should write a 100 word essay by hand. I have to write an essay when I lie. It is bad to lie because it just gets you in more trouble. I hate getting in trouble.*
>
> *It's just like the boy who cried wolf, and the wolf ate the boy. It is important to tell the truth. I like to tell the truth because it gets you in less trouble. If you do not tell the truth people do not believe you.*
>
> *It is important to believe the president because he is a important person. If you cannot believe the president, who can you believe. If you have no one to believe in, then how do you run your life. I do not believe the president tells the truth anymore right now. After he writes the essay and tells the truth, I will believe him again.*
>
> *William Summers*

Then there's a P.S. from his dad:

> *Dear Representative Hyde: I made my son William either write you a letter or an essay as a punishment for lying. Part of his defense for his lying was that the President lied. He's still having difficulty understanding why the President can lie and not be punished.*
>
> *Bobby Summers*

Mr. Chief Justice and Senators, on June 6, 1994, it was the 50th anniversary of the American landing at Normandy, and I went ashore at Normandy and walked up to the cemetery area where, as far as the eye could see, there were white crosses, Stars of David. And the British had a bagpipe band scattered among the crucifixes, the crosses, playing Amazing Grace with that pierceful, mournful sound that only the bagpipe can make.

And if you could keep your eyes dry you were better than I. But I walked up to one of these crosses marking a grave because I wanted to personalize the experience. I was looking for a name. But there was no name. It said, "Here lies in honored glory a comrade in arms known but to God."

How do we keep faith with that comrade in arms? Well, go to the Vietnam memorial and the national mall and press your hands against the 58,000, a few of the 58,000 names carved into that wall and ask yourself how we can redeem the debt we owe all those who purchased our freedom with their lives. How do we keep faith with them?

I think I know. We work to make this country the kind of America they were willing to die for. That's an America where the idea of sacred honor still has the power to stir men's souls.

My solitary, solitary hope is that 100 years from today people will look back at what we've done and say, "they kept the faith."

I'm done.

BUMPERS'S DEFENSE SUMMATION

Mr. Chief Justice, distinguished House managers from the House of Representatives, colleagues, I have seen the look of disappointment on many faces because I know a lot of people thought you were rid of me once and for all.

And I've taken a lot of ribbing this afternoon, but I have seriously negotiated with some people, particularly on this side by an offer to walk out and not deliver this speech in exchange for a few votes. I understand three have it under active consideration.

It is a great joy to see you, and it is especially pleasant to see an audience which represents about the size of the cumulative audience I had over a period of 24 years.

I came here today for a lot of reasons. One was that I was promised a 40-foot cord—and I've been shorted 28 feet. [Sen.] Chris[topher J.] Dodd [D-Conn.] said that he didn't want me in his lap, and I assume that he arranged for the cord to be shortened.

I want to especially thank some of you for your kind comments in the press when it received some publicity that I would be here to close the debate on behalf of the White House counsel and the president. I was a little dismayed by Sen. [Robert F.] Bennett's [R-Utah] remark. He said, "Yes, Sen. Bumpers is a great speaker, but I never—he was never persuasive with me because I never agreed with him." I thought he could have done better than that.

You can take some comfort, colleagues, in the fact that I'm not being paid. And when I'm finished you will probably think the White House got their money's worth.

I have told audiences that over 24 years that I went home almost every weekend and returned usually about dusk on Sunday evening. And you know the plane ride into National Airport, when you can see the magnificent Washington Monument and this building from the window of the airplane. And I've told these students at the university, in a small, liberal arts school at home, Hendricks, after 24 years of that, literally hundreds of times, I never failed to get goosebumps. Same thing is true about this chamber.

I can still remember as though it were yesterday the awe I felt when I first stepped into this magnificent chamber so full of history, so beautiful.

And last Tuesday as I returned after only a short three-week absence, I still felt that same sense of awe that I did the first time I walked in this chamber.

Colleagues, I come here with some sense of reluctance. The president and I have been close friends for 25 years. We've fought so many battles back home together in our beloved Arkansas. We tried mightily all of my years as governor and his, and all of my years in the Senate when he was governor, to raise the living standards in the Delta area of Mississippi, Arkansas and Louisiana, where poverty is unspeakable, with some measure of success— not nearly enough. We tried to provide health care for the lesser among us, for those who are well-off enough they can't get on welfare, but not making enough to buy health insurance.

We have fought, above everything else, to improve the educational standards for a state that, for so many years, was at the bottom of the list or near the bottom of the list of income, and we have stood side-by-side to save beautiful, pristine areas in our state from environmental degradation.

We even crashed a twin-engine Beech Bonanza trying to get to the Gillette coon supper, a political event that one misses at his own risk. And we crashed this plane on a snowy evening on a rural airport, off the runway, sailing out across the snow, jumped out, jumped out and ran away unscathed, to the dismay of every budding politician in Arkansas.

The president and I have been together hundreds of times—at parades, dedications, political events, social events. And in all of those years, and all those hundreds of times we've been together, both in public and in private, I have never one time seen the president conduct himself in a way that did not reflect the highest credit on him, his family, his state, and his beloved nation.

The reason I came here today with some reluctance—please don't misconstrue that. It has nothing to do with my feelings about the president, as I've already said. But it's because we are from the same state and we are long friends, and I know that that necessarily diminishes to some extent the effectiveness of my words.

[Constitutional Punishment]

So if Bill Clinton the man, Bill Clinton the friend, were the issue here, I'm quite sure I would not be doing this. But it is the weight of history on all of us, and it is my reverence for that great document you heard me rail about for 24 years that we call our Constitution, the most sacred document to me next to the holy Bible.

These proceedings go right to the heart of our Constitution where it deals with impeachment, the part that provides the gravest punishment for just about anybody, the president, even though the framers said we're putting this in to protect the public, not to punish the president.

Ah, colleagues, you have such an awesome responsibility. My good friend, the senior senator from New York, has said it well. He says this: A decision to convict holds the potential for destabilizing the office of the presidency.

And those 400 historians—and I know some have made light of that; about those historians, are they just friends of Bill? And last evening, I went over that list of historians, many of whom I know, among them C. Van Woodward. In the South we love him. He is the preeminent Southern historian in the nation. I promise you, he may be a Democrat, he may be even a friend of the president. [But] when you talk about integrity, he is the walking personification, exemplification of integrity.

[Historic Proceedings?]

Well, colleagues, I have heard so many adjectives to describe this gathering and these proceedings. Historic, memorable, unprecedented, awesome—all of those words, all of those descriptions are apt. And to those I would add the word "dangerous"—dangerous not only for the reasons I just stated, but because it's dangerous to the political process, and it's dangerous to the unique mix of pure democracy and republican government Madison and his colleagues so brilliantly crafted and which has sustained us for 210 years.

Mr. Chief Justice, this is what we lawyers call "dicta." This costs you nothing. It's extra. But the more I study that document and those four months in Philadelphia in 1787, the more awed I am. And you know what Madison did? The brilliance was in its simplicity. He simply said: Man's nature is to get other people to dance to their tune. Man's nature is to abuse his fellow man sometimes.

And he said, the way to make sure that the majorities don't abuse the minorities, and the way to make sure that the bullies don't run over the weaklings, is to provide the same rights for everybody.

And I had to think about that a long time before I delivered my first lecture at the University of Arkansas last week. And it made so much sense to me. But the danger, as I say, is to the political process. And dangerous for reasons feared by the framers about legislative control of the executive.

That single issue and how to deal with impeachment was debated off and on for the entire four months of the constitutional convention. But the word dangerous is not mine. It's Alexander Hamilton's—a brilliant, good-looking guy [White House Counsel] Mr. [Charles F.C.] Ruff quoted extensively on Tuesday afternoon in his brilliant statement here. He quoted Alexander Hamilton precisely, and it's a little arcane, it isn't easy to understand. So if I may, at the expense of being slightly repetitious, let me paraphrase what Hamilton said.

He said the Senate had a unique role in participating with the executive branch in appointment. And too, it had a role in participating with the executive in the character of a court for the trial of impeachments.

But he said—and I must say this, and you all know it—he said it would be difficult to get what he called a well-constituted court from wholly elected members. He said passions would agitate the whole community and divide it between those who were friendly and those who had inimical interest to the accused, namely the president.

And then he said, and this is his words, the greatest danger was that the decision would be based on the comparative strength of the parties rather than the innocence or guilt of the president.

[Why Are You Here?]

You have a solemn oath. You have taken a solemn oath to be fair and impartial. I know you all, I know you as friends, and I know you as honorable men, and I'm perfectly satisfied to put that in your hands under your oath.

This is the only caustic thing I will say in these remarks this afternoon, but the question is, "How did we come to be here?" We are here because of a five-year, relentless, unending investigation of the president. Fifty million dollars, hundreds of FBI agents fanning across the nation examining in detail the microscopic lives of people—maybe the most intense investigation not only of a president but of anybody ever.

I feel strongly just because of my state, and what we have endured. So you'll have to excuse me, but that investigation has also shown that the judicial system in this country can and does get out of kilter unless it's controlled. Because there are innocent people who have been financially and mentally bankrupted. One woman told me two years ago that her legal fees were $95,000. She said, "I don't have $95,000, and the only asset I have is the equity in my home, which just happens to correspond to my legal fees of $95,000." And she says, "The only thing I can think of to do is to deed my home." This woman was innocent—never charged, testified before the grand jury a number of times. And since that time, she has accumulated an additional $200,000 in attorney fees.

Javert's pursuit of Jean Valjean in *Les Miserables* pales by comparison.

I doubt that there are few people, maybe nobody in this body, who could withstand such scrutiny. And in this case, those summoned were terrified not because of their guilt, but because they felt guilt or innocence was not really relevant. But after all of those years and $50 million of Whitewater, Travelgate, Filegate, you name it, nothing, nothing, the president was found guilty of nothing, official or personal.

You're here today because the president suffered a terrible moral lapse, a marital infidelity. Not a breach of the public trust, not a crime against society, the two things Hamilton talked about in *Federalist Paper* number 65—I recommend it to you before you vote—but it was a breach of his marriage vows. It was a breach of his family trust.

The Human Element

It is a sex scandal. H. L. Mencken said one time, "When you hear somebody say, 'This is not about money,' it's about money." And when you hear somebody say, "This is not about sex," it's about sex.

You pick your own adjective to describe the president's conduct. Here are some that I would use: *indefensible, outrageous, unforgivable, shameless.* I promise you the president would not contest any of those or any others.

But there's a human element in this case that has not even been mentioned, and that is the president and Hillary and Chelsea are human beings. This is intended only as a mild criticism of our distinguished friends in the House, but as I listened to the presenters—to the managers—make their opening statements, they were remarkably well-prepared, and they spoke eloquently, more eloquent than I really had hoped. But when I talk about the human element, I talk about what I thought was, on occasion, unnecessarily harsh and pejorative descriptions of the president. I thought that language should have been tempered somewhat, to acknowledge that he is the president. To say constantly that the president lied about this and lied about that, as I say, I thought that was too much for a family that has already been about as decimated as a family can get.

The relationship between husband and wife, father and child has been incredibly strained, if not destroyed. There's been nothing but sleepless nights, mental agony for this family for almost five years. Day after day, from accusations of having assassinated, or [having] had Vince Foster assassinated, on down. It has been bizarre. But I didn't sense any compassion, and perhaps none is deserved.

The president has said for all to hear that he misled, he deceived, he did not want to be helpful to the prosecution. And he did all of those things to his family, to his friends, to his staff, to his Cabinet and to the American people.

Why would he do that? Well, he knew this whole affair was about to bring unspeakable embarrassment and humiliation on himself, his wife whom he adored, and a child that he worshiped with every fiber in his body, and for whom he would happily have died to spare her this or to ameliorate her shame and her grief.

The House managers have said shame and embarrassment is no excuse for lying. Well, the question about lying, that's your decision. But I can tell you, you put yourself in his position, and you've already had this big moral lapse, as to what you would do.

We are none of us perfect. Sure, you say, he should have thought of all that beforehand. And indeed he should. Just as Adam and Eve should have. Just as you and you and you and you, and millions of other people who have been caught in similar circumstances, should have thought of it before.

And I say none of us are perfect.

I remember, Chaplain, the—the chaplain's not here, is he? That's too bad. He ought to hear this story: This evangelist was holding this great revival meeting, and at the close of one of his meetings he said, "Is there anybody in this audience who has ever known anybody who even comes close to the perfection of our Lord and Savior, Jesus Christ?" Nothing.

He repeated the challenge, and finally an itty bitty guy in back of the audience kind of held up his hand, and he said, "You—are you saying you've known such a person? Stand up." He stood up, and he said, "Tell us, share it with us. Who was it?" He said, "My wife's first husband."

Make no mistake about it, removal from office is punishment, it is unbelievable punishment, even though the framers didn't quite see it that way.

Again they said, and it bears repeating over and over again, they said they wanted to protect the people. But I can tell you this: The punishment of removing Bill Clinton from office would pale compared to the punishment he has already inflicted on himself.

There's a feeling in this country that somehow or other Bill Clinton's gotten away with something. Mr. Leader, I can tell you, he hasn't gotten away with anything. And the people are saying, "Please don't protect us from this man, 76 percent of us think he's doing a fine job. Sixty-five to seventy percent of us don't want [him] removed from office."

And some have said, "We're not respected on the world scene." The truth of the matter is, this nation has never enjoyed greater prestige in the world than we do right now. You saw Carlos Menem, the president of Argentina, just here recently, say to the president, "Mr. President, the world needs you."

The war in Bosnia is under control. The president has been as tenacious as anybody could be about Middle East peace. And in Ireland, actual peace, and maybe the Middle East will make it. And he has the Indians and the Pakistanis talking to each other as they've never talked to each other in recent times.

[Czech President] Vaclav Havel said, "Mr. President, for the enlargement of the North Atlantic Treaty Organization there's no doubt in my mind that it was personal leadership that made this historic development possible." [Jordan's] King Hussein: "Mr. President, I've had the privilege of being a friend of the United States and presidents since the late President Eisenhower. And throughout all the years that have passed, I've kept in touch. But on the subject of peace, the peace we're seeking, I have never—with all due respect and all the affection I held for your predecessors—have known someone with your dedication, clearheadedness, focus and determination to help resolve this issue in the best way possible."

Well, I'm not—I've got Nelson Mandela and other world leaders who have said similar things in the last six months. Our prestige, I promise you, in the world is as high as it's ever been.

[Perjury?]

When it comes to the question of perjury, you know, there's perjury and then there's perjury. Let me ask you if you think this is perjury: On Nov. 23, 1997, President Clinton went to Vancouver, British Columbia. And when he returned, Monica Lewinsky was at the White House at some point, and he gave her a carved marble bear. I don't know how big it was.

Question before the grand jury Aug. 6, 1998: "What was the Christmas present or presents that he got for you?"

Answer: "Everything was packaged in a big Black Dog, or big canvas bag from the Black Dog store in Martha's Vineyard. He got me a marble bear's head carving, sort of, you know—a little sculpture, I guess you'd call it, maybe."

"Was that the item from Vancouver?"

"Yes."

Question on the same day of the same grand jury: "OK, good. When the president gave you the Vancouver Bear on the 28th, did he say anything about what it means?"

"Mmm-hmmm."

"Well, what did he say?"

Answer: "I think he—I believe he said that the bear is the, maybe, Indian symbol for strength, you know, and to be strong like a bear."

"And did you interpret that to be strong in your decision to continue to conceal the relationship?"

"No."

House Judiciary Committee report to the full House: "On the other hand, knowing the subpoena requested gifts, his giving Ms. Lewinsky more gifts on Dec. 28 seems odd, but Ms. Lewinsky's testimony reveals why he did so. She said that she 'never questioned that we would ever do anything but keep this private, and that meant to take whatever appropriate steps needed to be taken to keep it quiet.'

"The only logical inference is that the gifts, including the bear symbolizing strength, were a tacit reminder to Ms. Lewinsky that they would deny the relationship even in the face of a federal subpoena."

She just got through saying "No," and yet this report says that's the only logical inference.

And then the brief that came over here accompanying the articles of impeachment said, "On the other hand, more gifts on Dec. 28. . . . Ms. Lewinsky's testimony reveals the answer. She said that she 'never questioned that we were ever going to do anything but keep this private, and that meant to take whatever appropriate steps needed to be taken to keep it quiet.' "

Again, they say in their brief, "the only logical inference is that the gifts, including the bear symbolizing strength, were a tacit reminder to Ms. Lewinsky that they would deny the relationship even in the face of a federal subpoena."

Is it perjury to say the only logical inference is something when the only shred of testimony in the record is, "No, that was not my interpretation. I didn't infer that"? And yet here you have it in the committee report and you have it in the brief.

Now, of course that's not perjury. First of all, it isn't under oath, but as a trial lawyer, I'll tell you what it is: It's wanting to win too badly. I tried 300, 400, maybe 500 divorce cases—incidentally, you're being addressed by the entire South Franklin County, Ark., Bar Association. I can't believe there were that many cases in that little town, but I had a practice in surrounding communities, too. And in all those divorce cases, I would guess that in 80 percent of the contested cases, perjury was committed. And you know what it was about? Sex. Extramarital affairs.

But there's a very big difference in perjury about a marital infidelity in a divorce case, and perjury about whether I bought the murder weapon or whether I concealed the murder weapon or not. And to charge somebody with the first and punish them as though it were the second stands justice, our sense of justice on its head.

There's a total lack of proportionality, a total lack of balance, in this thing. The charge and the punishment are totally out of sync.

All of you have heard or read the testimony of the five prosecutors who testified before the House Judiciary Committee. Five seasoned prosecutors. And each one of them, veterans, said under the identical circumstances, the identical circumstances of this case, we would never charge anybody because we'd know we couldn't get a conviction. And in this case, the charges brought and the punishment sought are totally out of sync. There is no balance, there is no proportionality.

[Historically Speaking]

But even stranger, you think about it, even if this case had originated in the courthouse rather than the Capitol, you would never have heard of it. How do you reconcile what the prosecutors said with what we're doing here?

Impeachment was debated off and on in Philadelphia for the entire four months, as I said. The key players were Gouverneur Morris—Sen. Specter, a brilliant Pennsylvanian—[and] George Mason, the only man reputedly to have been so brilliant that Thomas Jefferson actually deferred to him. And he refused to sign the Constitution, incidentally, even though he was a delegate, because they didn't deal with slavery, and he was a strict abolitionist. And then there was Charles Pinkney—Sen. Hollings, from South Carolina—just a youngster, 29 years old, I believe. Edmund Randolph from Virginia, who had a big role in the Constitution in the beginning; the Virginia Plan. And then there was, of course, James Madison, the craftsman.

They were all key players in drafting this impeachment provision. And uppermost in the mind during the entire time they were composing was, they did not want any kings. They had lived under despots, they had lived under kings, they had lived under autocrats, and they didn't want any more of that. And they succeeded very admirably. We've had 46 presidents, and no kings.

But they kept talking about corruption—maybe that ought to be the reason for impeachment, because they feared some president would corrupt the political process. That's what the debate was about. Corrupt the political process and ensconce himself through a phony election, maybe as something close to a king. They followed the British rule on impeachment, because the British said, the House of Commons may impeach, and the House of Lords must convict. And every one of the colonies had the same procedure: House, Senate.

Though in all fairness, House members, Alexander Hamilton was not very keen on the House participating.

But here was the sequence of events at Philadelphia that brought us here today. They started out with "maladministration," and Madison said that's too vague. What does that mean? So they dropped that. They went from that to "corruption," and they dropped that. Then they went to "malpractice." And they decided that was not definitive enough.

And they went to "treason, bribery and corruption." And they decided that still didn't suit them. But bear in mind one thing: During this entire process, they are narrowing—they are narrowing the things you can impeach the president for. They were making it tougher. Madison said, if we aren't careful, the president will serve at the pleasure of the legislature—the Senate, he said.

And then they went to "treason and bribery," and somebody said that's still not quite enough. And so they went to "treason, bribery," and George Mason added, "or other high crimes and misdemeanors against the United States." And they voted on it, and on Sept. 10 they sent the entire Constitution to a committee.

They called a committee on style and arrangement, which was the committee that would draft the language in a way that everybody would understand; it would be well-crafted from a grammatical standpoint. But that committee, which was dominated by Madison and Hamilton, dropped "against the United States." And historians will tell you that the reason they did that was because of redundance, because that committee had no right to change the substance of anything. They would not have dropped it if they hadn't felt that it was redundant.

And then, they put in for good measure—we can always be grateful—the two-thirds majority.

Now, this is one of the most important points of this entire presentation: The term—first of all—"treason and bribery," nobody quarrels with that, and we're not debating treason and bribery here in this chamber. We're talking about "other high crimes and misdemeanors."

And where did "high crimes and misdemeanors" come from? It came from the English law, and they found it in an English law under a category which said, "distinctly political offenses against the state." Let me repeat that, they said, "high crimes and misdemeanors was to be," because they took it from English law, where they found it in the category that said, "offenses distinctly political against the state."

So colleagues, please, for just one moment, forget the complexities of the facts and the tortured legalisms. And we've heard them all brilliantly presented on both sides, and I'm not getting into that. But ponder this: If "high crimes and misdemeanors" was taken from English law by George Mason, which listed high crimes and misdemeanors as political offenses against the state, what are we doing here?

If, as Hamilton said, it had to be a crime against society or a breach of the public trust, what are we doing here? Even perjury. Concealing or deceiving. An unfaithful relationship does not even come close to being an impeachable offense.

Nobody has suggested that Bill Clinton committed a political crime against the state. So, colleagues, if you honor the Constitution, you must look at the history of the Constitution and how we got to the impeachment clause. And if you do that and you do that honestly according to the oath you took, you cannot—you can censure Bill Clinton, you can hand him over to the prosecutor for him to be prosecuted, but you cannot convict him. And you cannot indulge yourselves the luxury or the right to ignore this history.

[A Look Back]

There's been a suggestion that a vote to acquit would be something of a breach of faith with those who lie in Flanders Field, Anzio and Bunker Hill and Gettysburg and wherever. I didn't hear that; I read about it. But I want to say—and, incidentally, I think it was Chairman Hyde who alluded to this and said, those men fought and died for the rule of law.

I can remember a cold Nov. 3 morning in my little hometown of Charleston, Ark., I was 18 years old. I had just gotten one semester in at the university when I went into the Marine Corps. And so, I reported to Little Rock to be inducted.

My, it was cold. The drugstore was the bus stop. I had to be there by 8 o'clock to be sworn in, and I had to catch the bus down at the drugstore at 3 o'clock in the morning, so my mother and father and I got up at 2 o'clock, got dressed, and went down there.

I'm not sure I can tell you this story.

And the bus came over the hill—I was rather frightened anyway about going in. I was quite sure I was going to be killed, only slightly less frightened that Betty would find somebody else while I was gone.

When the bus came over Schoolhouse Hill, my parents started crying. I had never seen my father cry. I knew I was in some difficulty.

Now, as a parent at my age, I know he thought he was giving not his only begotten son, but one of his begotten sons. Can you imagine? You know that scene. It was repeated across this nation millions of times.

And then happily, I survived that war; saw no combat; was on my way to Japan when it all ended. I'd never had a terrible problem with dropping the bomb, though that's been a terrible moral dilemma for me, because the estimates were that we would lose as many as a million men in that invasion.

But I came home to a generous government who provided me, under the GI Bill, an education in a fairly prestigious law school which my father could never have afforded. And I practiced law in this little town for 18 years; loved every minute of it. But I didn't practice constitutional law, and I knew very little about the Constitution. But when I went into law school, I did study constitutional law, though Mr. Chief Justice, it was fairly arcane to me.

And trying to read *The Federalist Papers* and Tocqueville—all of those things law students are expected to do, that was tough for me, I confess. So after 18 years in law practice, I jumped up and ran for governor, and I served as governor for four years. And I still—I guess I knew what the rule of law was, but I still didn't really have much reverence for the Constitution. I just did not understand any of the things I just got through telling you.

No. My love for that document came day after day and debate after debate right here in this chamber.

Some of you perhaps read an op-ed piece I did a couple of weeks ago, when I said I was perfectly happy for my legacy of a 24-year senator to be I never voted for a constitutional amendment. And it isn't that I wouldn't. I think they made a mistake not giving you fellows four years. You're about to cause me to rethink that one.

And the reason I developed this love of it is because I saw Madison's magic working time and time again, keeping bullies from running over weak people, keeping majorities from running over minorities. And I thought about all the unfettered freedoms we had. The oldest organic law in existence made us the envy of the world.

Mr. Chairman, we've also learned that the rule of law includes presidential elections. That's a part of the rule of law in this country. We have an event, a quadrennial event in this country which we call presidential elections. And that's the day when we reach across this aisle and hold hands, Democrats and Republicans. And we say, "Win or lose, we will abide by the decision."

It is a solemn event, presidential elections, and it should not—they should not be undone lightly. Or just because one side has the clout and the other one doesn't. And if you want to know what men fought for in World War II, for example, or in Vietnam, ask Sen. [Daniel K.] Inouye [D-Hawaii]. He left an arm in Italy.

He and I were in the presence at Normandy on the 50th anniversary. But we started off on Anzio. Sen. [Pete V.] Domenici [R-N.M.], were you with us? It was one of the most awesome experiences I've ever had in my life—certified war hero. I think his relatives were in an internment camp, so ask him what he was fighting for.

Or ask [Sen.] Bob Kerrey [D-Neb.], certified Medal of Honor winner, what was he fighting for. You'll probably get a quite different answer.

Or Sen. [John H.] Chafee [R-R.I.], one of the finest men ever to grace this body and certified Marine hero of Guadalcanal—ask him. And Sen. [John] McCain [R-Ariz.], a genuine hero—ask him.

You don't have to guess. They're with us, and they're living. And they can tell you. And one who is not with us here in the Senate any more, Robert Dole [R-Kan.]. Ask Sen. Dole what he was fighting for. Sen. Dole had what I thought was a very reasonable solution to this whole thing that would handle it fairly and expeditiously.

[Voting the Polls?]

The American people are now and for some time have been asking to be allowed a good night's sleep. They're asking for an end to this nightmare. It is a legitimate request. I'm not suggesting that you vote for or against the polls. I understand that. Nobody should vote against the polls just to show their mettle and their courage. I have cast plenty of votes against the polls, and it's cost me politically a lot of times.

This has been going on for a year, though. And in that same op-ed piece I talked about meeting [former president] Harry Truman my first year as governor of Arkansas. Spent an hour with him; an indelible experience. People at home kid me about this, because I very seldom make a speech that I don't mention this meeting. But I will never forget what he said: "Put your faith in the people. Trust the people. They can handle it." They have shown conclusively time and time again that they can handle it.

Colleagues, this is easily the most important vote you will ever cast. If you have difficulty because of an intense dislike of the president—and that's understandable—rise above it. He is not the issue.

He will be gone. You won't. So don't leave a precedent from which we may never recover and almost surely will regret.

If you vote to acquit, Mr. Leader, you know exactly what's going to happen. You're going to go back to your committees; you're going to get on this legislative agenda; you're going to start dealing with Medicare and Social Security and tax cuts and all those things which the people of the country have a non-negotiable demand that you do.

If you vote to acquit, you go immediately to the people's agenda. If you vote to acquit, you go immediately to the people's agenda. But if you vote to convict, you can't be sure what's going to happen.

James G. Blaine was a member of the Senate when Andrew Johnson was tried in 1868, and 20 years later he recanted. And he said: "I made a bad mistake." And he says, "As I reflect back on it, all I can think about is having convicted Andrew Johnson would have caused much more chaos and confusion in this country than Andrew Johnson could ever conceivably have tried."

And so it is with William Jefferson Clinton. If you vote to convict, in my opinion you're going to be creating more havoc than he could ever possibly create. After all, he's only got two years left. So don't, for God's sake, heighten people's alienation that is at an all-time high toward their government.

The people have a right, and they are calling on you to rise above politics, rise above partisanship. They're calling on you to do your solemn duty. And I pray you will.

Thank you, Mr. Chief Justice.

STATE OF THE UNION ADDRESS AND REPUBLICAN RESPONSE
January 19, 1999

For the second year in a row, President Bill Clinton turned in a bravura performance as he delivered the annual State of the Union Address. His 1998 speech was delivered only a week after reports were made public that Clinton had had an affair with a White House intern. The 1999 speech came just one month after the House had impeached the president on two counts of perjury and obstruction of justice stemming from those allegations and just hours after his attorneys had begun his defense in the Senate on those charges. In both speeches the president appeared poised and confident as he proclaimed the nation to be strong and moving forward.

In some respects Clinton's 1999 speech was almost anticlimactic. Almost no one thought that the Senate would convict him of the impeachment charges; even a handful of Republican senators had let it be known that they did not believe the president's conduct was an abuse of power that should force him from office. Public opinion polls had repeatedly shown that the vast majority of the American public, although dismayed and disgusted with Clinton's personal conduct, wanted its politicians to turn their attention away from impeachment and toward issues of governing. (Lewinsky scandal, Clinton impeachment, Historic Documents of 1998, pp. 564, 632, 695, 958; Senate trial, p. 15)

The speech was thus an opportunity for the president to set the agenda for his final two years in office and the run-up to the November 2000 elections. During his seventy-seven-minute speech, Clinton never referred directly to his impeachment or trial. He instead focused on the issues that had led the American people to elect him twice and that Democrats hoped would keep a Democrat in the White House and give the party control of Congress in the elections of 2000. Clinton's major initiative was a plan to "save Social Security now," but his list also included new and old proposals on health care, education, crime, trade, the environment, and campaign finance reform.

Clinton also had good news to report. The nation was enjoying the longest peacetime economic expansion in its history, inflation and unemployment were both low, welfare rolls had dropped, and the violent crime rate had fallen dramatically. In addition, the federal budget was in balance for the first time in three decades. The government had moved from a $290 billion deficit in 1992 to a projected surplus of $70 billion in 1998 and budget surpluses were expected for the next several years. It was against this background that Clinton walked onto the House floor projecting an image of a confident leader proud of his administration's past accomplishments and eager to tackle a long list of unfinished legislative items before leaving office in January 2001—at the end of his second full term in the White House.

Immediately after the speech Clinton's approval rating rose to a record 76 percent in an NBC News poll, confirming that the president had lost none of his charisma with the public. Although many Republican legislators gave Clinton only tepid applause or refused to applaud at all, others ruefully acknowledged the brilliance of Clinton's performance. "Whether you agree with him philosophically or not," Republican senator Richard C. Shelby of Alabama said, "he's gifted." Even conservative television evangelist Pat Robertson said the following day that in the wake of Clinton's speech Republicans "might as well dismiss the impeachment hearing and get on with something else, because it's over as far as I'm concerned."

Competing Legislative Agendas

"With our budget surplus growing, our economy expanding, our confidence rising, now is the moment for this generation to meet its historic responsibility to the twenty-first century," Clinton said, outlining an ambitious legislative agenda. The centerpiece of the president's proposals called for setting aside 62 percent of the projected budget surplus for the next fifteen years to shore up Social Security's cash reserves. Clinton said his plan would maintain the public retirement system's solvency to 2055; without some action, Social Security was expected to run out of funds after 2032. Clinton also proposed that another 16 percent of the budget surpluses be used to ensure the solvency of Medicare until 2020. Without a further infusion of cash, the federal health insurance program for the elderly and disabled was expected to run out of funds by about 2010. Clinton also asked Congress to take steps to make schools more accountable for the educational achievement of their students, to pass campaign finance reform, to boost the minimum wage by $1 an hour, to restore the five-day waiting period for handgun purchases, and to approve a patients' bill of rights. (Budget surplus, p. 350)

Predictably, the Republican-led Congress found little to praise and much to criticize in the president's legislative program. "Ninety-some percent of his proposal was all more government," said Majority Whip Don Nickles of Oklahoma. "I don't think you'll see this Congress pass it. Most of it I'll be working very aggressively to see it doesn't pass." Republicans *offered their own alternative to Clinton's legislative agenda, calling for a 10 percent across-the-board cut in income taxes. "Next year there will be a $63 billion budget surplus," Rep. Jennifer Dunn of Washington said in the official Republican response to the State of the Union. "Mr. President, give it back."*

A Predictable Stalemate

As the legislative year played out, neither Clinton nor the Republicans saw their major proposals enacted into law. Republicans managed to pass a broad tax cut plan, but it won little public support and Republicans leaders did not even attempt to override Clinton's veto. While both parties agreed in principle with Clinton's proposal to set aside much of the surplus for Social Security and Medicare, they were unable to agree on a means to do that. Moreover, Congress and the president dipped into the Social Security surplus to help finance the fiscal year 2000 appropriations. Republicans also flatly rejected Clinton's call to invest part of the surplus earmarked for Social Security in the stock market. "No, no, a thousand times no," said House Ways and Means Committee Chairman Bill Archer of Texas, said after the speech. Republican leaders preferred to modify the retirement program to allow individuals to invest a portion of their Social Security taxes in personal retirement accounts. The two sides were unable to come to any agreement during the year on an overhaul of Social Security.

Republicans also gave short shrift to Clinton's calls for a hike in the minimum wage and for tougher handgun controls. Clinton's request for renewal of the president's fast-track trade negotiating authority was given the cold shoulder by legislators from both parties. Republicans and Democrats were unable to reach agreement on campaign finance reform, the House and Senate were far apart in their approaches to protecting patients' rights, and Congress dealt the president a major blow when it rejected ratification of the Comprehensive Nuclear Test Ban Treaty. (Health care, p. 561; test ban treaty, p. 600)

Yet Clinton did not go away empty-handed. Congress appropriated new money to hire more teachers and police, it voted to release funding to pay the United Nations some of the back dues that the United States owed, and it funded the purchase of environmentally and culturally significant lands to protect them from development. Overall, Clinton once again got most of his budget priorities through the Republican-controlled Congress.

Following are texts of President Bill Clinton's State of the Union address, delivered to a joint session of Congress on January 19, 1999, and the Republican response by Representatives Jennifer Dunn of Washington and Steve Largent of Oklahoma:

STATE OF THE UNION ADDRESS

Mr. Speaker [Dennis Hastert], Mr. Vice President [Al Gore], members of Congress, honored guests, my fellow Americans. Tonight I have the honor of reporting to you on the State of the Union.

Let me begin by saluting the new Speaker of the House and thanking him especially tonight for extending an invitation to two guests sitting in the gallery with Mrs. Hastert. Lynn Gibson and Wei Ling Chestnut are the widows of the two brave Capitol Hill police officers who gave their lives to defend freedom's house.

Mr. Speaker, at your swearing in, you asked us all to work together in a spirit of civility and bipartisanship. Mr. Speaker, let's do exactly that.

Tonight I stand before you to report that America has created the longest peacetime economic expansion in our history, with nearly 18 million new jobs, wages rising at nearly twice the rate of inflation, the highest homeownership in history, the smallest welfare rolls in 30 years and the lowest peacetime unemployment since 1957. For the first time in three decades, the budget is balanced. From a deficit of $290 billion in 1992, we had a surplus of $70 billion last year, and now we are on course for budget surpluses for the next 25 years.

Thanks to the pioneering leadership of all of you, we have the lowest violent crime rate in a quarter-century and the cleanest environment in a quarter-century. America is a strong force for peace, from Northern Ireland to Bosnia to the Middle East.

Thanks to the pioneering leadership of Vice President Gore, we have a government for the Information Age; once again, a government that is a progressive instrument of the common good, rooted in our oldest values of opportunity, responsibility and community, devoted to fiscal responsibility, determined to give our people the tools they need to make the most of their own lives in the 21st century, a 21st century government for 21st century America.

My fellow Americans, I stand before you tonight to report that the state of our union is strong.

America is working again. The promise of our future is limitless. But we cannot realize that promise if we allow the hum of our prosperity to lull us into complacency. How we fare as a nation far into the 21st century depends upon what we do as a nation today.

So with our budget surplus growing, our economy expanding, our confidence rising, now is the moment for this generation to meet our historic responsibility to the 21st century.

Our fiscal discipline gives us an unsurpassed opportunity to address a remarkable new challenge: the aging of America.

[The Coming "Senior Boom"]

With the number of elderly Americans set to double by 2030, the Baby Boom will become a "senior boom." So first and above all, we must save

Social Security for the 21st century. Early in this century, being old meant being poor. When President [Franklin D.] Roosevelt created Social Security, thousands wrote to thank him for eliminating what one woman called the "stark terror of penniless, helpless old age." Even today, without Social Security, half our nation's elderly would be forced into poverty.

Today Social Security is strong. But by 2013, payroll taxes will no longer be sufficient to cover monthly payments. By 2032, the trust fund will be exhausted and Social Security will be unable to pay the full benefits older Americans have been promised.

The best way to keep Social Security a rock-solid guarantee is not to make drastic cuts in benefits, not to raise payroll tax rates, not to drain resources from Social Security in the name of saving it. Instead, I propose that we make the historic decision to invest the surplus to save Social Security.

Specifically, I propose that we commit 60 percent of the budget surplus for the next 15 years to Social Security, investing a small portion in the private sector just as any private or state government pension would do. This will earn a higher return and keep Social Security sound for 55 years.

But we must aim higher. We should put Social Security on a sound footing for the next 75 years. We should reduce poverty among elderly women, who are nearly twice as likely to be poor as our other seniors, and we should eliminate the limits on what seniors on Social Security can earn.

Now, these changes will require difficult but fully achievable choices over and above the dedication of the surplus. They must be made on a bipartisan basis. They should be made this year. So let me say to you tonight, I reach out my hand to all of you in both houses and both parties and ask that we join together in saying to the American people: We will save Social Security now.

Now, last year, we wisely reserved all of the surplus until we knew what it would take to save Social Security. Again, I say we shouldn't spend any of it, not any of it, until after Social Security is truly saved. First things first.

Second, once we have saved Social Security, we must fulfill our obligation to save and improve Medicare. Already, we have extended the life of the Medicare Trust Fund by 10 years, but we should extend it for at least another decade. Tonight I propose that we use one out of every six dollars in the surplus for the next 15 years to guarantee the soundness of Medicare until the year 2020.

But again, we should aim higher. We must be willing to work in a bipartisan way and look at new ideas, including the upcoming report of the bipartisan Medicare commission. If we work together, we can secure Medicare for the next two decades and cover the greatest growing need of seniors: affordable prescription drugs.

Third, we must help all Americans from their first day on the job to save, to invest, to create wealth. From its beginning, Americans have supplemented Social Security with private pensions and savings. Yet today, millions of people retire with little to live on other than Social Security. Americans living longer than ever simply must save more than ever.

[New Pension Initiative]

Therefore, in addition to saving Social Security and Medicare, I propose a new pension initiative for retirement security in the 21st century. I propose that we use a little over 11 percent of the surplus to establish Universal Savings Accounts—USA Accounts—to give all Americans the means to save. With these new accounts, Americans can invest as they choose, and receive funds to match a portion of their savings, with extra help for those least able to save. USA Accounts will help all Americans to share in our nation's wealth and to enjoy a more secure retirement. I ask you to support them.

Fourth, we must invest in long-term care. I propose a tax credit of $1,000 for the aged, ailing or disabled and the families who care for them. Long-term care will become a bigger and bigger challenge with the aging of America, and we must do more to help our families deal with it.

I was born in 1946, the first year of the Baby Boom. I can tell you that one of the greatest concerns of our generation is our absolute determination not to let our growing old place an intolerable burden on our children and their ability to raise our grandchildren. Our economic success and our fiscal discipline now give us an opportunity to lift that burden from their shoulders and we should take it.

Saving Social Security, Medicare, creating USA Accounts—this is the right way to use the surplus. If we do so—if we do so—we will still have resources to meet critical needs in education and defense.

And I want to point out that this proposal is fiscally sound. Listen to this: If we set aside 60 percent of the surplus for Social Security and 16 percent for Medicare, over the next 15 years that saving will achieve the lowest level of publicly held debt since right before World War I, in 1917.

So, with these four measures—saving Social Security, strengthening Medicare, establishing the USA Accounts, supporting long-term care—we can begin to meet our generation's historic responsibility to establish true security for 21st century seniors.

Now, there are more children from more diverse backgrounds in our public schools than at any time in our history. Their education must provide the knowledge and nurture the creativity that will allow our entire nation to thrive in the new economy. Today we can say something we could not say six years ago: With tax credits and more affordable student loans, with more work-study grants and more Pell grants, with education IRAs and the new HOPE Scholarship tax cut that more than 5 million Americans will receive this year, we have finally opened the doors of college to all Americans.

With our support, nearly every state has set higher academic standards for public schools, and a voluntary national test is being developed to measure the progress of our students. With over $1 billion in discounts available this year, we are well on our way to our goal of connecting every classroom and library to the Internet.

Last fall you passed our proposal to start hiring 100,000 new teachers to reduce class size in the early grades. Now I ask you to finish the job.

You know, our children are doing better. SAT scores are up. Math scores have risen in nearly all grades. But there is a problem: While our fourth-graders outperform their peers in other countries in math and science, our eighth-graders are around average, and our 12th-graders rank near the bottom. We must do better.

Now each year, the national government invests more than $15 billion in our public schools. I believe we must change the way we invest that money, to support what works and to stop supporting what does not work.

[Accountability in Education]

First, later this year, I will send to Congress a plan that for the first time holds states and school districts accountable for progress and rewards them for results. My Education Accountability Act will require every school district receiving federal help to take the following five steps:

First, all schools must end social promotion.

Now, no child should graduate from high school with a diploma he or she can't read. We do our children no favors when we allow them to pass from grade to grade without mastering the material.

But we can't just hold students back because the system fails them. So my balanced budget triples the funding for summer school and after-school programs to keep a million children learning. If you doubt this will work, just look at Chicago, which ended social promotion and made summer school mandatory for those who don't master the basics. Math and reading scores are up three years running, with some of the biggest gains in some of the poorest neighborhoods. It will work, and we should do it.

Second, all states and school districts must turn around their worst-performing schools, or shut them down. That's the policy established in North Carolina by Gov. [James B.] Hunt [Jr.]. North Carolina made the biggest gains in test scores in the nation last year. Our budget includes $200 million to help states turn around their own failing schools.

Third, all states and school districts must be held responsible for the quality of their teachers. The great majority of our teachers do a fine job. But in too many schools, teachers don't have college majors—or even minors—in the subjects they teach.

New teachers should be required to pass performance exams, and all teachers should know the subjects they are teaching.

This year's balanced budget contains resources to help them reach higher standards. And to attract talented young teachers to the toughest assignments, I recommend a sixfold increase in our program for college scholarships for students who commit to teach in the inner cities and isolated rural areas and in Indian communities. Let us bring excellence to every part of America.

Fourth, we must empower parents with more information and more choices. In too many communities, it's easier to get information on the quality of the local restaurants than on the quality of the local schools. Every school district should issue report cards on every school.

47

And parents should be given more choice in selecting their public schools. When I became president, there was one independent, public charter school in all America. With our support, on a bipartisan basis, today there are 1,100. My budget assures that early in the next century, there will be 3,000.

Fifth, to assure that our classrooms are truly places of learning, and to respond to what teachers have been asking us to do for years, we should say that all states and school districts must both adopt and implement sensible discipline policies.

Now, let's do one more thing for our children. Today too many schools are so old they're falling apart, are so overcrowded students are learning in trailers. Last fall Congress missed the opportunity to change that. This year, with 53 million children in our schools, Congress must not miss that opportunity again. I ask you to help our communities build or modernize 5,000 schools.

Now if we do these things—end social promotion; turn around failing schools; build modern ones; support qualified teachers; promote innovation, competition and discipline—then we will begin to meet our generation's historic responsibility to create 21st century schools.

Now we also have to do more to support the millions of parents who give their all every day at home and at work. The most basic tool of all is a decent income. So let's raise the minimum wage by $1 an hour over the next two years. And let's make sure that women and men get equal pay for equal work by strengthening enforcement of equal pay laws. . . .

Working parents also need quality child care. So again this year, I ask Congress to support our plan for tax credits and subsidies for working families, for improved safety and quality, for expanded after-school programs. And our plan also includes a new tax credit for stay-at-home parents too. They need support as well.

Parents should never have to worry about choosing between their children and their work. Now, the Family [and] Medical Leave Act—the very first bill I signed into law—has since 1993 helped millions and millions of Americans to care for a newborn baby or an ailing relative without risking their jobs. I think it's time, with all the evidence that it has been so little burdensome to employers, to extend family leave to 10 million more Americans working for smaller companies. And I hope you will support it.

Finally, on the matter of work, parents should never have to face discrimination in the workplace. So I want to ask Congress to prohibit companies from refusing to hire or promote workers simply because they have children. That is not right.

["Patients' Bill of Rights"]

America's families deserve the world's best medical care. Thanks to bipartisan federal support for medical research, we are now on the verge of new treatments to prevent or delay diseases from Parkinson's to Alzheimer's to arthritis to cancer, but as we continue our advances in medical science, we can't let our health care system lag behind.

Managed care has transformed medicine in America, driving down costs, but threatening to drive down quality as well. I think we ought to say to every American: You should have the right to know all your medical options, not just the cheapest. If you need a specialist, you should have a right to see one. You have a right to the nearest emergency care if you are in an accident. These are things that we ought to say, and I think we ought to say you should have a right to keep your doctor during a period of treatment, whether it's a pregnancy or chemotherapy treatment or anything else. I believe this.

Now, I have ordered these rights to be extended to the 85 million Americans served by Medicare, Medicaid and other federal health programs.

But only Congress can pass a Patients' Bill of Rights for all Americans. Now, last year Congress missed that opportunity, and we must not miss that opportunity again. For the sake of our families, I ask us to join together across party lines and pass a strong, enforceable Patients' Bill of Rights.

As more of our medical records are stored electronically, the threats to all our privacy increase. Because Congress has given me the authority to act if it does not do so by August, one way or another, we can all say to the American people we will protect the privacy of medical records and we will do it this year.

Now, two years ago, the Congress extended health coverage to up to 5 million children. Now, we should go beyond that. We should make it easier for small businesses to offer health insurance. We should give people between the ages of 55 and 65 who lose their health insurance the chance to buy into Medicare, and we should continue to ensure access to family planning. No one should have to choose between keeping health care and taking a job. And therefore, I especially ask you tonight to join hands to pass the landmark bipartisan legislation proposed by Sens. [Edward M.] Kennedy [D-Mass.] and [James M.] Jeffords [R-Vt.], [William V.] Roth [Jr., R-Del.] and [Daniel Patrick] Moynihan [D-N.Y.], to allow people with disabilities to keep their health insurance when they go to work.

We need to enable our public hospitals, our community, our university health centers to provide basic, affordable care for all the millions of working families who don't have any insurance. They do a lot of that today, but much more can be done. And my balanced budget makes a good down payment toward that goal. I hope you will think about them and support that provision.

Let me say we must step up our efforts to treat and prevent mental illness. No American should ever be afraid, ever, to address this disease. This year we will host a White House Conference on Mental Health. With sensitivity, commitment and passion, Tipper Gore is leading our efforts here, and I thank her for what she's done on it.

As everyone knows, our children are targets of a massive media campaign to hook them on cigarettes. Now I ask this Congress to resist the tobacco lobby, to reaffirm the FDA's [Food and Drug Administration] authority to protect children from tobacco, and to hold the tobacco companies accountable while protecting tobacco farmers.

[Federal Litigation on Tobacco]

Smoking has cost taxpayers hundreds of billions of dollars under Medicare and other programs. You know, the states have been right about this: Taxpayers shouldn't pay for the costs of lung cancer, emphysema and other smoking-related illnesses, the tobacco companies should. So tonight I announce that the Justice Department is preparing a litigation plan to take the tobacco companies to court, and with the funds we recover, to strengthen Medicare.

Now, if we act in these areas—minimum wage, family leave, child care, health care, the safety of our children—then we will begin to meet our generation's historic responsibility to strengthen our families for the 21st century.

Today, America is the most dynamic, competitive, job-creating economy in history. But we can do even better in building a 21st century economy that embraces all Americans.

Today's income gap is largely a skills gap. Last year, the Congress passed a law enabling workers to get a skills grant to choose the training they need, and I applaud all of you here who were part of that. This year, I recommend a five-year commitment to the new system so that we can provide over the next five years appropriate training opportunities for all Americans who lose their jobs and expand rapid response teams to help all towns which have been really hurt when businesses close. I hope you will support this.

Also, I ask for a dramatic increase in federal support for adult literacy, to mount a national campaign aimed at helping the millions and millions of working people who still read at less than a fifth-grade level. We need to do this.

Here's some good news: In the past six years, we have cut the welfare rolls nearly in half. Two years ago from this podium, I asked five companies to lead a national effort to hire people off welfare. Tonight, our Welfare to Work Partnership includes 10,000 companies who have hired hundreds of thousands of people. And our balanced budget will help another 200,000 people move to the dignity and pride of work. I hope you will support it.

We must do more to bring the spark of private enterprise to every corner of America, to build a bridge from Wall Street to Appalachia to the Mississippi Delta to our Native American communities, with more support for community development banks, for empowerment zones, for 100,000 more vouchers for affordable housing. And I ask Congress to support our bold new plan to help businesses raise up to $15 billion in private sector capital to bring jobs and opportunities to our inner cities and rural areas—with tax credits and loan guarantees, including the new American Private Investment Companies modeled on the Overseas Private Investment Company [OPIC].

Now, for years and years and years we've had this OPIC, this Overseas Private Investment Corporation, because we knew we had untapped markets overseas. But our greatest untapped markets are not overseas; they are right here at home, and we should go after them.

We must work hard to help bring prosperity back to the family farm. As this Congress knows very well, dropping prices and the loss of foreign markets have devastated too many family farms. Last year the Congress provided substantial assistance to help stave off a disaster in American agriculture, and I am ready to work with lawmakers of both parties to create a farm safety net that will include crop insurance reform and farm income assistance.

I ask you to join with me and do this. This should not be a political issue. Everyone knows what an economic problem is going on out there in rural America today, and we need an appropriate means to address it.

We must strengthen our lead in technology. It was government investment that led to the creation of the Internet. I propose a 28 percent increase in long-term computing research.

[Y2K Computer Problem]

We also must be ready for the 21st century, from its very first moment, by solving the Y2K computer problem. Remember, this is a big, big problem. And we've been working hard on it. Already we've made sure that the Social Security checks will come on time. But I want all the folks at home listening to this to know that we need every state and local government, every business, large and small, to work with us to make sure that this Y2K computer bug will be remembered as the last headache of the 20th century, not the first crisis of the 21st.

Now, for our own prosperity, we must support economic growth abroad. You know, until recently, a third of our economic growth came from exports. But over the past year and a half, financial turmoil overseas has put that growth at risk. Today much of the world is in recession, with Asia hit especially hard.

This is the most serious financial crisis in half a century. To meet it, the United States and other nations have reduced interest rates and strengthened the International Monetary Fund. And while the turmoil is not over, we have worked very hard with other nations to contain it.

At the same time, we have to continue to work on the long-term project, building a global financial system for the 21st century that promotes prosperity and tames the cycles of boom and bust that have engulfed so much of Asia. This June I will meet with other world leaders to advance this historic purpose. And I ask all of you to support our endeavors.

I also ask you to support creating a freer and fairer trading system for 21st century America.

I'd like to say something really serious to everyone in this chamber and both parties. I think trade has divided us and divided Americans outside this chamber for too long. Somehow we have to find a common ground on which business and workers, and environmentalists, and farmers and government can stand together. I believe these are the things we ought to all agree on. So let me try.

First, we ought to tear down barriers, open markets and expand trade. But at the same time, we must ensure that ordinary citizens in all countries actually benefit from trade—a trade that promotes the dignity of work and the rights of workers—and protects the environment. We must insist that international trade organizations be open to public scrutiny instead of mysterious, secret things subject to wild criticism.

When you come right down to it, now that the world economy is becoming more and more integrated, we have to do in the world what we spent the better part of this century doing here at home—we have got to put a human face on the global economy.

Now, we must enforce our trade laws when imports unlawfully flood our nation. I have already informed the government of Japan that if that nation's sudden surge of steel imports into our country is not reversed, America will respond.

We must help all manufacturers hit hard by the present crisis with loan guarantees and other incentives to increase American exports by nearly $2 billion.

I'd like to believe we can achieve a new consensus on trade based on these principles, and I ask the Congress again to join me in this common approach and to give the president the trade authority long used, and now overdue and necessary, to advance our prosperity in the 21st century.

Tonight, I also issue a call to the nations of the world to join the United States in a new round of global trade negotiation to expand exports of services, manufacturers and farm products.

Tonight I say we will work with the International Labor Organization on a new initiative to raise labor standards around the world. And this year, we will lead the international community to conclude a treaty to ban abusive child labor everywhere in the world.

If we do these things—invest in our people, our communities, our technology, and lead in the global economy—then we will begin to meet our historic responsibility to build a 21st century prosperity for America.

You know, no nation in history has had the opportunity and the responsibility we now have to shape a world that is more peaceful, more secure, more free.

[Peacekeeping and Arms Control]

All Americans can be proud that our leadership helped to bring peace in Northern Ireland. All Americans can be proud that our leadership has put Bosnia on the path to peace. And with our NATO allies, we are pressing the Serbian government to stop its brutal repression in Kosovo, to bring those responsible to justice and to give the people of Kosovo the self-government they deserve.

All Americans can be proud that our leadership renewed hope for lasting peace in the Middle East. Some of you were with me last December as we watched the Palestinian National Council completely renounce its call for the destruction of Israel. Now I ask Congress to provide resources so that all parties can implement the Wye Agreement, to protect Israel's security, to stimulate the Palestinian economy, to support our friends in Jordan. We must not, we dare not, let them down. I hope you will help.

As we work for peace, we must also meet threats to our nation's security, including increased dangers from outlaw nations and terrorism. We will defend our security wherever we are threatened, as we did this summer when we struck at Osama bin Laden's network of terror. The bombing of our embassies in Kenya and Tanzania reminds us again of the risks faced every day by those who represent America to the world. So let's give them the support they need, the safest possible workplaces, and the resources they must have so America can continue to lead.

We must work to keep terrorists from disrupting computer networks. We must work to prepare local communities for biological and chemical emergencies, to support research into vaccines and treatments.

We must increase our efforts to restrain the spread of nuclear weapons and missiles, from Korea to India and Pakistan. We must expand our work with Russia, Ukraine and the other former Soviet nations to safeguard nuclear materials and technology so they never fall into the wrong hands.

Our balanced budget will increase funding for these critical efforts by almost two-thirds over the next five years.

With Russia, we must continue to reduce our nuclear arsenals. The START II Treaty and the framework we have already agreed to for START III could cut them by 80 percent from their Cold War height.

It's been two years since I signed the Comprehensive Test Ban Treaty. If we don't do the right thing, other nations won't either. I ask the Senate to take this vital step: Approve the Treaty now, to make it harder for other nations to develop nuclear arms and to make sure we can end nuclear testing forever.

For nearly a decade, Iraq has defied its obligations to destroy its weapons of terror and the missiles to deliver them. America will continue to contain [Iraqi President] Saddam [Hussein], and we will work for the day when Iraq has a government worthy of its people.

Now, last month, in our action over Iraq, our troops were superb. Their mission was so flawlessly executed that we risk taking for granted the bravery and the skill it required. Capt. Jeff Taliaferro, a 10-year veteran of the Air Force, flew a B-1B bomber over Iraq as we attacked Saddam's war machine. He is here with us tonight. I'd like to ask you to honor him and all the 33,000 men and women of Operation Desert Fox.

[Building Up the Defense Budget]

It is time to reverse the decline in defense spending that began in 1985. Since April, together we have added nearly $6 billion to maintain our military readiness. My balanced budget calls for a sustained increase over the next six years for readiness, for modernization, and for pay and benefits for our troops and their families.

You know, we are the heirs of a legacy of bravery represented in every community of America by millions of our veterans. America's defenders today still stand ready at a moment's notice to go where comforts are few and dangers are many, to do what needs to be done as no one else can. They always come through for America. We must come through for them.

The new century demands new partnerships for peace and security. The United Nations plays a crucial role, with allies sharing burdens America might otherwise bear alone. America needs a strong and effective U.N. I want to work with this new Congress to pay our dues and our debts.

We must continue to support security and stability in Europe and Asia, expanding NATO and defining its new missions, maintaining our alliance with Japan, with Korea, with our other Asian allies, and engaging China.

In China last year, I said to the leaders and the people what I'd like to say again tonight: Stability can no longer be bought at the expense of liberty. But I'd also like to say again to the American people: It's important not to isolate China. The more we bring China into the world, the more the world will bring change and freedom to China.

Last spring, with some of you, I traveled to Africa, where I saw democracy and reform rising, but still held back by violence and disease. We must fortify African democracy and peace by launching Radio Democracy for Africa, supporting the transition to democracy now beginning to take place in Nigeria, and passing the African Trade and Development Act.

We must continue to deepen our ties to the Americas and the Caribbean, our common work to educate children, fight drugs, strengthen democracy and increase trade. In this hemisphere, every government but one is freely chosen by its people. We are determined that Cuba, too, will know the blessings of liberty.

The American people have opened their hearts and their arms to our Central American and Caribbean neighbors who have been so devastated by the recent hurricanes. Working with Congress, I am committed to help them rebuild. When the first lady and Tipper Gore visited the region, they saw thousands of our troops and thousands of American volunteers. In the Dominican Republic, first lady Hillary [Clinton] helped to rededicate a hospital that had been rebuilt by Dominicans and Americans working side by side. With her was someone else who has been very important to the relief efforts.

You know, sports records are made, and sooner or later, they are broken. But making other people's lives better—and showing our children the true meaning of brotherhood—that lasts forever. So for far more than baseball, Sammy Sosa, you are a hero in two countries tonight. Thank you.

So I say to all of you, if we do these things—if we pursue peace, fight terrorism, increase our strength, renew our alliances—we will begin to meet our generation's historic responsibility to build a stronger 21st century America in a freer, more peaceful world.

As the world has changed, so have our own communities. We must make them safer, more livable and more united. This year, we will reach our goal of 100,000 community police officers ahead of schedule and under budget. The Brady bill has stopped a quarter- million felons, fugitives and stalkers from buying handguns. And now, the murder rate is the lowest in 30 years, and the crime rate has dropped for six straight years. Tonight I propose a 21st century crime bill, to deploy the latest technologies and tactics to make our communities even safer.

Our balanced budget will help put up to 50,000 more police on the street in the areas hardest hit by crime and then to equip them with new tools, from crime-mapping computers to digital mug shots. We must break the deadly cycle of drugs and crime. Our budget expands support for drug testing and treatment, saying to prisoners, "If you stay on drugs, you have to stay behind bars," and to those on parole, "If you want to keep your freedom, you must stay free of drugs."

[Gun Control]

I ask Congress to restore the five-day waiting period for buying a handgun and extend the Brady bill to prevent juveniles who commit violent crimes from buying a gun.

We must do more to keep our schools the safest places in our communities. Last year every American was horrified and heartbroken by the tragic killings in Jonesboro, Paducah, Pearl, Edinboro, Springfield. We were deeply moved by the courageous parents, now working to keep guns out of the hands of children, and to make other efforts so that other parents don't have to live through their loss.

After she lost her daughter, Suzann Wilson of Jonesboro, Ark., came here to the White House with a powerful plea. She said, "Please, please, for the sake of your children, lock up your guns. Don't let what happened in Jonesboro happen in your town." It is a message she is passionately advocating every day. Suzann is here with us tonight with the first lady. I'd like to thank her for her courage and her commitment.

In memory of all the children who lost their lives to school violence, I ask you to strengthen the Safe and Drug-Free School Act, to pass legislation to require child trigger locks, to do everything possible to keep our children safe.

A century ago, President Theodore Roosevelt defined our "great, central task" as "leaving this land even a better land for our descendants than it is for us." Today, we are restoring the Florida Everglades, saving Yellowstone, preserving the red-rock canyons of Utah, protecting California's redwoods and our precious coasts. But our most fateful new challenge is the threat of global warming. 1998 was the warmest year ever recorded. Last year's heat waves, floods and storms are but a hint of what future generations may endure if we do not act now.

Tonight, I propose a new clean air fund to help communities reduce greenhouse and other pollution, and tax incentives and investment to spur clean energy technologies. And I want to work with members of Congress in both parties to reward companies that take early, voluntary action to reduce greenhouse gases.

Now, all our communities face a preservation challenge as they grow and green space shrinks. Seven thousand acres of farmland and open space are lost every day. In response, I propose two major initiatives. First, a $1 billion Livability Agenda to help communities save open space, ease traffic congestion and grow in ways that enhance every citizen's quality of life. And second, a $1 billion Lands Legacy Initiative to preserve places of natural beauty all across America, from the most remote wilderness to the nearest city park.

These are truly landmark initiatives which could not have been developed without the visionary leadership of the vice president, and I want to thank him very much for his commitment here.

Now, to get the most out of your community, you have to give something back. That's why we created AmeriCorps—our national service program that gives today's generation a chance to serve their communities and earn money for college. So far, in just four years, 100,000 young Americans have built low-income homes with Habitat for Humanity, helped to tutor children with churches, worked with FEMA [the Federal Emergency Management Agency] to ease the burden of natural disasters, and performed countless other acts of service that have made America better. I ask Congress to give more young Americans the chance to follow their lead and serve America in AmeriCorps.

We must work to renew our national community as well for the 21st century. Last year, the House passed the bipartisan campaign finance reform legislation sponsored by Reps. [Christopher] Shays [R-Conn.] and [Martin T.] Meehan [D-Mass.] and Sens. [John] McCain [R-Ariz.] and [Russell D.] Feingold [D-Wis.]. But a partisan minority in the Senate blocked reform. So I'd like to say to the House: Pass it again, quickly.

And I'd like to say to the Senate, I hope you will say yes to a stronger American democracy in the year 2000.

[Initiative on Race]

Since 1997, our Initiative on Race has sought to bridge the divides between and among our people. In its report last fall, the initiative's advisory board found that Americans really do want to bring our people together across racial lines. We know it's been a long journey. For some it goes back to before the beginning of our republic, for others back since the Civil War, for others throughout the 20th century. But for most of us alive today, in a very real sense this journey began 43 years ago when a woman named Rosa Parks sat down on a bus in Alabama and wouldn't get up. She's sitting down with the first lady tonight, and she may get up or not, as she chooses.

We know that our continuing racial problems are aggravated, as the presidential initiative said, by opportunity gaps. The initiative I have outlined tonight will help to close them. But we know that the discrimination gap has not been fully closed, either.

Discrimination or violence because of race or religion, ancestry or gender, disability or sexual orientation is wrong and it ought to be illegal. Therefore, I ask Congress to make the Employment Non-Discrimination Act and the Hate Crimes Prevention Act the law of the land.

Now, since every person in America counts, every American ought to be counted. We need a census that uses [the] most modern scientific methods to do that.

Our new immigrants must be part of our one America. After all, they're revitalizing our cities, they're energizing our culture, they're building up our new economy. We have a responsibility to make them welcome here, and they have a responsibility to enter the mainstream of American life. That means learning English and learning about our democratic system of government. There are now long waiting lines of immigrants that are trying to do just that. Therefore, our budget significantly expands our efforts to help them meet their responsibility. I hope you will support it.

Whether our ancestors came here on the Mayflower, on slave ships, whether they came to Ellis Island or LAX in Los Angeles, whether they came yesterday or walked this land a thousand years ago, our great challenge for the 21st century is to find a way to be one America. We can meet all the other challenges if we can go forward as one America.

You know, barely more than 300 days from now, we will cross that bridge into the new millennium. This is a moment, as the first lady has said, to honor the past and imagine the future. I'd like to take just a minute to honor her for leading our Millennium Project, for all she's done for our children, for all she has done in her historic role to serve our nation and our best ideals at home and abroad. I honor her.

Last year I called on Congress and every citizen to mark the millennium by saving America's treasures. Hillary has traveled all across the country to inspire recognition and support for saving places like Thomas Edison's invention factory or Harriet Tubman's home. Now we have to preserve our treasures in every community. And tonight, before I close, I want to invite every town, every city, every community to become a nationally recognized "millennium community" by launching projects that save our history, promote our arts and humanities, prepare our children for the 21st century.

Already, the response has been remarkable, and I want to say a special word of thanks to our private sector partners and to members in Congress, of both parties, for their support. Just one example: Because of you, the Star Spangled Banner will be preserved for the ages.

In ways large and small, as we look to the millennium, we are keeping alive what George Washington called "the sacred fire of liberty."

Six years ago, I came to office in a time of doubt for America, with our economy troubled, our deficit high, our people divided. Some even wondered whether our best days were behind us. But across this country, in a thousand neighborhoods, I have seen, even amidst the pain and uncertainty of recession, the real heart and character of America. I knew then that we Americans could renew this country.

Tonight, as I deliver the last State of the Union address of the 20th century, no one anywhere in the world can doubt the enduring resolve and boundless capacity of the American people to work toward that "more perfect union" of our founders' dreams. We're now at the end of a century when generation after generation of Americans answered the call to greatness, overcoming Depression, lifting up the dispossessed, bringing down barriers to racial prejudice, building the largest middle class in history, winning two world wars and the "long twilight struggle" of the Cold War.

We must all be profoundly grateful for the magnificent achievements of our forebears in this century. Yet perhaps in the daily press of events, in the clash of controversy, we do not see our own time for what it truly is: a new dawn for America.

A hundred years from tonight, an American president will stand in this place to report on the State of the Union. He—or she—will look back on a 21st century shaped in so many ways by the decisions we make here and now. So let it be said of us then that we were thinking not only of our time, but of their time; that we reached as high as our ideals; that we put aside our divisions and found a new hour of healing and hopefulness; that we joined together to serve and strengthen the land we love.

My fellow Americans, this is our moment. Let us lift our eyes as one nation, and from the mountain top of this American century, look ahead to the next one, asking God's blessing on our endeavors and on our beloved country.

Thank you, and good evening.

REPUBLICAN RESPONSE

Dunn: Good evening. I'm Jennifer Dunn. I represent the people of the Eighth District of Washington state.

Largent: And I'm Steve Largent, from the First District of Oklahoma.

Dunn: As you might imagine, if you had been sitting with us in the House chamber tonight as the president was giving his speech, you could have felt the swirl of history. These are disturbing and controversial times in our nation's capital. A couple of weeks ago, I even heard a network anchor say the capital is in chaos. Another proclaimed we are in the midst of a constitutional crisis.

Ladies and gentlemen, our country is not in crisis. There are no tanks in the streets. Our system of government is as solid as the Capitol dome you see behind me. Our democracy is sound. Our economy is prosperous. The state of our union is strong. And no matter what the outcome of the president's situation, life in America will go on. Our lives will continue to be filled with practical matters, not constitutional ones.

I've been a single mother since my boys were little, 6 and 8. My life in those days was taken up with meeting—trying to make ends meet, trying to get to two soccer games at the same time on two different fields, worrying about dropping the boys off early at school in order for me to get to work on time. I know how that knot in the pit of your stomach feels. I've been there.

I'm still a practical person. You heard the president make a lot of promises to a lot of people tonight. But I'd like to talk to you about two very practical Republican priorities: tax relief and Social Security reform.

Our current tax system is a burden on the economy and on the American people. Let me tell you a story about a fellow I represent from North Bend, Wash., whose name is Robert Allen. A few years ago the IRS denied his right to file a joint return with his wife because they said his wife Shirley was deceased. Well, I've seen Shirley. She looks pretty good for a dead person. Robert took Shirley to the IRS office in Seattle. The IRS was not convinced. So the Allens brought in their family doctor, and in his medical opinion he pronounced Shirley alive. The IRS was still not convinced. It took intervention by a member of Congress—me—to resolve this comedy, which in truth is a tragedy, because it's symbolic of how removed our entire tax system has become from reality and from common sense.

Last year we passed legislation reining in the IRS so that taxpayers are now considered innocent until proven guilty. But so much more needs to be done. Next year there will be a $63 billion budget surplus. Mr. President, give it back.

Last year a typical mother and father who both worked paid nearly 40 percent of their income in taxes. That means 40 cents out of every dollar they earned went to the government in federal, state or local taxes. That's the highest percentage of income ever paid in taxes by American families.

I don't know about you, but that really bothers me. No wonder so many American families are struggling. Get married and your taxes go up. Save for your children's education and your taxes go up. And when you die—that's right—your taxes go up. The government gets a bigger piece of your life's work than all your children put together.

So what can you expect from Republicans? Expect action.

First, tonight, we're proposing a 10 percent, across-the-board cut in tax rates for every working American. That's the down payment on a simpler, fairer, flatter tax system.

Second, we must end the marriage penalty. We should honor commitment, not tax it.

And third, we must cut death taxes so that families don't have to sell their businesses and farms when Mom and Dad die.

In all of our tax policies, we start from this premise: The people's money belongs to the people, not to the government.

The second thing I want to talk about is Social Security. A year ago, in his State of the Union speech, the president said he was committed to saving Social Security.

I'm glad to hear him discuss it again this evening. Unfortunately, spending the surplus as he proposes will not save Social Security; it just temporarily props it up with some extra cash. Mr. President, we're still waiting for real legislation. We've reserved HR 1, the very first bill of this Congress, for the president's Social Security plan.

There's one thing we can all agree on, one non-negotiable principle: We must keep our contract with our senior citizens who depend on Social Security for part or all of their retirement income. This nation made that promise long ago and we will keep that promise.

But Social Security needs not just to be patched up, it needs to be updated for the 21st century. People today want and expect to have more control over their lives and over their money. But President Clinton's approach, as you just heard, gives the government more control of your retirement income. The Social Security dollars deducted from your paycheck currently earn less than 3 percent a year. That's not enough of a return. That's not going to keep Social Security solvent. And it's especially not fair to young people and to women.

For example, the current system works against mothers who choose to step out of their job for a while, away from their career, to raise children or to care for parents. It works against wives, who more often than not survive their husbands and they end up living for more years on fewer dollars.

And it works against young people, who believe they'll never see a Social Security check.

Here's a better way: Give working Americans the choice to invest some of their Social Security dollars in personal retirement accounts. We can do this without touching a dime in Social Security funds, without raising one nickel in taxes, and without touching one penny of current benefits.

A new century requires a new beginning in approaches, in ideas, and yes, in civility and cooperation between political parties.

I'd like to close on a personal note. I'm a mother, a gardener, a Republican and a member of Congress. Believe me, all four take patience. My boys, thankfully, turned out to be wonderful young men. My plants at home, unfortunately, need a lot of work. And as for my efforts in the Congress, I am constantly planting and watering.

As one citizen to another, in spite of all the troubling things you hear about our nation's capital, I believe that good ideas can take root here. Good things can grow here, and good things can blossom here.

And now, my friend, Steve Largent.

Largent: Thanks, Jennifer. First, let me say what a special privilege it is to speak to you and give my response and the Republicans' response to the president's remarks.

Let me tell you a bit about myself. I grew up in Oklahoma and was born in the very district I'm now proud to represent. I was raised in a broken home, and thanks to my mom, I stayed in school, stayed out of most trouble and went to college.

I married my high school sweetheart, Terry, a cheerleader. And for the next 14 years I got to live every boy's dream: playing in the National Football League, for the Seattle Seahawks. After I concluded my career in the NFL, I started my own marketing and advertising business back in Tulsa.

But in 1994, I campaigned for the first elective office in my life—and won. I came to Washington with a group of Republicans committed to balancing the budget, slowing the growth of government, cutting taxes, reforming welfare and saving Medicare. And that's exactly what we did.

But as Babe Ruth once said, yesterday's home runs don't win today's games. It's time to step up to the plate once again.

Prior to 1994, my wife and I, we weren't political. We were like most families—raising four kids, hustling from one school or sports event to another, our car littered by fast-food wrappers and french fries. In fact, it wasn't until after I was elected that I attended a Republican function where a banner hung that read, "GOP." I had to ask someone what those letters stood for. They said, "Grand Old Party, of course."

I believe tonight is an appropriate time to ask once again, what does the GOP stand for? What does the party of Lincoln and Reagan stand for today? What are the lasting bedrock principles that personify and distinguish the Republican Party? It's these questions I want to answer tonight, because the answer is why I ran for office in the first place.

Here's the 15-second sound bite answer: The Republican Party's mission is to promote, preserve and protect individual liberty, free enterprise and limited government. But what does that mean to my family and your family?

Let's start with individual liberty. We must preserve the notion that true liberty and freedom come from God and are his blessing on this land, and that freedom reigns only as we act responsibly—toward God, each other and his creation. Our freedom was bought at a great price, and our most important responsibility is to defend this sacred gift and to keep our country secure.

Tonight we support our troops that are stationed in Bosnia, the Middle East and around the world. And the good news is that after six years of cutting spending for our armed forces, the president has signaled that he's ready to join us in strengthening our national defense. We must never be complacent in what is still a dangerous world. Terrorists and rogue nations are rapidly acquiring technology to deliver weapons of mass destruction to our very doorstep. Most Americans are shocked to discover that our country is unshielded from the accidental or ruthless launch of even a single missile over our skies. Mr. President, we urge you, join Congress in establishing a viable missile defense system to protect the United States.

Protecting individual liberty also means protecting the unborn. Again, this year, overwhelming majorities in both houses will urge the president to end the dreadful and unwarranted practice of "partial-birth" abortion. We must uphold the sanctity of life amidst the tragedies of abortion, euthanasia and assisted suicide.

Republicans also promote free enterprise. We believe market principles like competition really work.

At the heart of free enterprise is good education. For far too long we've allowed Washington to dictate how our children are taught. One of our priorities is to give control of our schools to local communities. We want the most important election affecting your children's education to be the one that decides who sits on the school board, not who you send to Washington. Parents deserve the opportunity to choose the best school with the best curriculum, the best teachers and the safest environment for their children.

I recently met with a room full of teachers in Jenks, Oklahoma. I came out of that meeting convinced, more than ever, that teachers like these know best how federal education dollars should be spent. That's why Republicans are leading the effort that will ensure 90 cents of every federal education dollar goes directly to the classroom, empowering parents and teachers, not bureaucrats.

And if we really want to "free" enterprise and the economy, let's scrap the Internal Revenue tax code. The 8,000-plus pages of confusion, contradiction and confiscation are choking small business and driving the average tax-payer mad.

Republicans want to establish a date by which the tax code will be abolished and replaced by something that's simple, fair and takes a smaller bite from the family's pocketbook.

Finally, Republicans stand for limited government. Ronald Reagan reminded us that a government that is big enough to give you everything you want is also big enough to take everything you have. And tonight, the federal government is still too big and taking more than it should. We will continue our efforts to control Washington's wasteful spending and its insatiable appetite for your money.

Well, this is what the Grand Old Party stands for, and if this represents your hopes and dreams, we ask not that you pull for us, but that you push with us. Back in my district, Oklahomans are steeped in America's deep tradition of faith, family, hard work and strong neighborhoods. They represent the values that hold communities together, and they believe in the power of a better tomorrow.

There's still a lot to be done, but I too am more optimistic than ever. These last four years have given me the unique opportunity to witness the grit and determination of the American people—our greatest resource.

Yesterday marked the 70th year since the birth of a great American leader and hero, Dr. Martin Luther King. In one of his last sermons, in 1968, Dr. King warned that while the world is a closer neighborhood, we are experiencing less brotherhood. That's equally true today. It is no longer the aggression from without that is America's greatest threat, but alienation from within; alienation at every level—husband from wife, mother from father, parent from child, black from white, Republican from Democrat, liberal from conservative. And there's only one solution: reconciliation. Ironically, the word Congress itself is made of two Latin words that mean "to walk together." Reconciliation requires the humility and courage to say, "I'm sorry. I was wrong. Will you forgive me?" Therein lies the healing salve for the wounded soul of our nation. You see, the body of our country is strong. It's the heart that needs attention.

On Christmas Eve, my family and I packed up our kids and gifts and headed to grandma's house. In the car, we sang along with Vince Gill's Christmas tape. As we sang one particular song, I was struck by the words and by their poignancy for our country tonight. The chorus went, "Let there be peace on Earth and let it begin with me."

So, let there be peace on Earth and let it begin with me. And let it begin with Republicans and Democrats and blacks and whites and moms and, yes, especially dads. Let there be peace on Earth and let it begin with all of us who comprise one nation, under God, indivisible.

And if we work together and walk together and if we have a Congress motivated not by the maintenance of power, but by principle, then I believe historians will tell our children's children, "There walked a great people—a nation that preserved the wonderful promise that we call America."

May God bless you and your family, and may God continue to bless this great nation.

Dunn: Thank you for listening. Good night.

FEDERAL REPORT ON QUALITY OF PUBLIC SCHOOL TEACHERS
January 28, 1999

The quality of the nation's public school teachers was the subject of renewed scrutiny in 1999 as government and school officials, academic experts, and parents all sought ways to improve the academic achievement of the nation's elementary and secondary school students. The National Center for Education Statistics (NCES) released a major survey of full-time public school teachers that found that fewer than half felt well prepared to implement new methods of teaching or new curriculum and performance standards. A bluntly worded report from the American Council on Education laid much of the blame for unqualified teachers at the feet of mediocre teacher education programs. And after wrangling over priorities, Congress and President Bill Clinton agreed not only to appropriate more money to hire teachers and reduce classroom size, but also to allow a greater proportion of that money to be used for professional development and training. Both Republicans and Democrats were eager to appeal to voters, who were telling pollsters that improved teacher quality was one of the best ways to improve student achievement.

The poor quality of many elementary and secondary school teachers was often cited as a chief contributor to low student achievement in the nation's public schools. Relatively low pay and status, poorly equipped classrooms, underfunded education programs, unruly students, and a host of duties and responsibilities not directly related to teaching were all said to drive many of the most qualified teachers into other more rewarding and less frustrating careers and to discourage potential teachers from entering the field. Many of the teachers remaining or coming into the classroom were said to be ill-prepared to deal with many of the demands made on them, from teaching children with limited English proficiency or physical and mental disabilities, to implementing new curriculum requirements, to using computers and other technology in their teaching.

A severe teacher shortage was exacerbating the problem. Many schools were asking teachers to teach subject areas in which they had little or no academic background and were hiring teachers who had not completed all their state certification requirements. Teachers' aides had also been pressed into duties that they had not been trained or certified for, according to some reports. The teacher shortage was expected to get worse in the first ten years of the new century. According to Secretary of Education Richard W. Riley, 2.2 million teachers would be needed to replace teachers who had been hired during the baby boom and were now reaching retirement age and to cover increasing enrollments resulting from the "baby boom echo"—the sons and daughters of the baby boom generation. The number of public and private school students was projected to increase from 53.2 million in 1999—the highest level yet recorded—to 54.2 million in 2009.

National Survey on Teacher Preparedness

On January 28, 1999, the National Center for Education Statistics released the first of what it projected to be a biennial series of surveys. According to Pascal D. Forgione Jr., commissioner of education statistics, the national profile of teacher quality was a "necessary tool for tracking our progress toward improving the quality of classroom teachers." Teacher quality was "a complex phenomenon" surrounded by controversy over how to define and measure it, he said. Teacher preparation (consisting of postsecondary training and certification and continued learning) was one of two broad components of teacher quality, he said. The other was the "actual behavior and practices" that teachers display in the classroom. The report released on January 28 surveyed only the first component—preparation and qualifications.

The survey found that only 41 percent of all full-time public school teachers felt "very well prepared" to introduce new methods of training into their classrooms and that only 36 percent felt very well prepared to implement new curriculum and performance standards imposed by the state or school district. Only 20 percent of all teachers felt very well prepared to integrate educational technology into their teaching or to address the needs of students with disabilities or students from diverse cultural backgrounds—a finding that the report found "particularly unsettling" given the great diversity of the student population and the great resources that had been spent on putting computers and the Internet into classrooms.

The survey looked at academic background and found that although virtually all full-time public school teachers had at least a bachelor's degree, only 38 percent had majored in an academic field in college. The rest had majored in subject area education, such as mathematics education (18 percent); general education (37 percent); or some other form of education, including special education and educational administration (7 percent). Teaching was more specialized in high school, and the survey found that 95 percent of all high school teachers had majored either in an academic field (66 percent) or in subject area education (29 percent). Not surprisingly, 58 percent of all elementary school teachers majored in general education.

The survey found that a significant number of teachers were teaching "out of their field," that is, they were teaching a subject area for which they had not themselves received academic training. Eighteen percent of mathematics teachers, 14 percent of English and language arts teachers, 12 percent of science teachers, and 11 percent of social studies teachers in grades 7 through 12 were teaching out of their field. The problem was most prevalent in grades 7 and 8.

Virtually all teachers also participated in some sort of professional development in the year before the survey was conducted, but most spent eight hours or less in any specific development activity, such as learning how to help students with disabilities or how to use the Internet in the classroom. Only a small proportion of these teachers reported that they thought the activity had improved their teaching "a lot." Roughly three times as many of the teachers who spent more than eight hours on any one activity said that it had improved their teaching "a lot." Forgione said these findings confirmed criticisms that professional development activities were often too superficial. The survey showed "that teachers find more time in these activities to be highly beneficial."

A Focus on Teacher Training

The American Council on Education, the country's largest association of colleges and universities, took its own members to task in a report released October 25. Taking note of the findings of the NCES survey, as well as data showing that elementary school teachers generally took less challenging courses in college and performed less well on standardized tests than their peers, the report declared that the nation's students deserved better. "That many students in America—often those most in need of excellent teachers—are taught by unqualified teachers is a reprehensible form of publicly sanctioned malpractice," the report said. "Just as no person should receive medical care from a person who is not qualified or reliably certified as a health care professional, no student should face an unqualified or uncertified teacher."

The report, entitled "To Touch the Future," proposed that the nation's 1,300 teacher education programs be audited and accredited by an outside agency, much as medical and law schools were. It also called for more funding for research on how to train effective teachers.

Federal Funding to Hire More Teachers

An end-of-session compromise between President Clinton and congressional Republicans appropriated $1.325 billion for fiscal 2000 to help many of the nation's schools hire teachers and thereby reduce class size. The program to hire 100,000 new teachers so that classrooms in grades 1 through 3 would have eighteen or fewer students was the centerpiece of Clinton's education program; in 1998 Congress appropriated $1.2 billion for it. But this year Republicans wanted to fold the program into a block grant that would give states greater authority over how to spend federal education grants. In return for dropping the block grant approach, the

*White House agreed to increase, from 15 to 25 percent, the portion of the
hiring grants that school districts could use for professional training.*

*The Council of the Great City Schools reported in early November that
about 3,500 teachers had been hired under the program in its first year in
forty of the nation's largest cities and that another 22,000 teachers received
professional training. Most of the new teachers taught math, reading, bilingual classes, and special education.*

> *Following is the text of the executive summary from a report
> released January 28, 1999, by the National Center for Education
> Statistics, entitled "Teacher Quality: A Report on the Prepara-
> tion and Qualifications of Public School Teachers":*

Background

In his 1997 State of the Union Address, President Clinton issued a "Call to
Action" that included as a priority improving the quality of teachers in every
American classroom. President Clinton's speech reflects growing concern
over the condition of education and the nation's need for excellent teachers.
The nation's educational system must provide our children with the knowledge, information, and skills needed to compete in a complex international
marketplace. Good teachers are the hallmark of such an educational system;
they are integral to children's intellectual and social development.

In response to these concerns and expectations, this study, undertaken by
the National Center for Education Statistics (NCES), using its Fast Response
Survey System (FRSS), provides a profile of the quality of the nation's teachers. Providing such a profile is not an easy task. Teacher quality is a complex
phenomenon, and there is little consensus on what it is or how to measure it.
For example, definitions range from those that focus on what should be
taught and how knowledge should be imparted to the kinds of knowledge and
training teachers should possess. There are, however, two broad elements
that most observers agree characterize teacher quality: (1) teacher preparation and qualifications, and (2) teaching practices. The first refers to preservice learning (e.g., postsecondary education, certification) and continued
learning (e.g., professional development, mentoring). The second refers to
the actual behaviors and practices that teachers exhibit in their classrooms.
Of course, these elements of teacher quality are not independent; excellent
teacher preparation and qualifications should lead to exemplary teaching
behaviors and practices.

This FRSS report is based on current NCES efforts to collect data on the
first of these elements (i.e., teacher preparation and qualifications), using a
nationally representative survey of full-time public school teachers whose
main teaching assignment is in English/language arts, social studies/social
sciences, foreign language, mathematics, or science, or who teach a self-con-
tained classroom. Specifically, it includes indicators of preservice and con-

tinued learning (e.g., degrees held, certification, teaching assignment, professional development opportunities, and collaboration with other teachers). In addition, because schools and communities play an important role in shaping and maintaining high-quality teachers, this study examines the work environments in which educators teach (e.g., formal induction procedures for new teachers, parental support).

This report is timely in light of recent concerns over the quality of our educational system and our teachers. Teachers' professional preparation (as well as their working conditions) has been identified as fundamental to improving elementary and secondary education. At the core of educational reforms to raise standards, reshape curricula, and restructure the way schools operate is the call to reconceptualize the practice of teaching. Teachers are being asked to learn new methods of teaching, while at the same time they are facing the greater challenges of rapidly increasing technological changes and greater diversity in the classroom.

The FRSS survey indicates that currently less than half of American teachers report feeling "very well prepared" to meet many of these challenges:

- Although many educators and policy analysts consider educational technology a vehicle for transforming education, relatively few teachers reported feeling very well prepared to integrate educational technology into classroom instruction (20 percent).
- While 54 percent of the teachers taught limited English proficient or culturally diverse students, and 71 percent taught students with disabilities, relatively few teachers who taught these students (about 20 percent) felt very well prepared to meet the needs of these students. Their feelings of preparedness did not differ by teaching experience.
- Only 28 percent of teachers felt very well prepared to use student performance assessment techniques; 41 percent reported feeling very well prepared to implement new teaching methods, and 36 percent reported feeling very well prepared to implement state or district curriculum and performance standards.

This national profile of teacher preparation, qualifications, and work environments provides a context for understanding why many teachers do not report feeling very well prepared to meet many of the challenges they currently face in their classrooms. Key findings are provided in three major areas: (1) preservice learning and teaching assignment; (2) continued learning; and (3) supportive work environment.

Key Findings

Preservice Learning and Teaching Assignment

Growing concern that a number of the nation's teachers are underqualified to teach our children has focused attention on their preservice learning. For example, concern regarding preservice learning has been directed toward teachers' postsecondary degrees—that is, the idea that teachers, particularly secondary teachers, should have an academic major rather than a general education degree. In addition, certification policies have drawn criticism—specifically, that a growing number of the nation's teachers are entering classrooms with emergency or temporary certification. Finally, attention is increasingly directed toward teaching assignments—that is, teachers being assigned to teach subjects that do not match their training or education. Results of the 1998 FRSS survey indicate that:

- Virtually all teachers had a bachelor's degree, and nearly half (45 percent) had a master's degree. More high school teachers had an undergraduate or graduate major in an academic field (66 percent), compared with elementary school teachers (22 percent) and middle school teachers (44 percent).

- Most of the teachers (92 percent and 93 percent, for departmentalized and general elementary, respectively) were fully certified in the field of their main teaching assignment. However, emergency and temporary certification was higher among teachers with 3 or fewer years of experience compared to teachers with more teaching experience. For example, 12 percent of general elementary classroom teachers with 3 or fewer years of experience had emergency or temporary certification, whereas less than 1 percent of general elementary classroom teachers with 10 or more years of experience had emergency or temporary certification. The results are similar for departmentalized teachers.

- Despite the fact that the measure of out-of-field teaching used in this report is conservative—it only includes teachers' main teaching assignments in core fields—the results indicate that a number of educators were teaching out of field. For example, the percent of teachers in grades 9 through 12 who reported having an undergraduate or graduate major or minor in their main teaching assignment field was 90 percent for mathematics teachers, 94 percent for science teachers, and 96 percent for teachers in English/language arts, social studies/social science, and foreign language. This means that 10 percent of mathematics teachers, 6 percent of science teachers, and 4 percent of English/language arts, foreign language, and social studies/social science teachers in grades 9 through 12 were teaching out of field. The percent of teachers who reported having an undergraduate or graduate major or minor in their main teaching assignment field was significantly lower for teachers of grades 7 through 12 than for teachers of grades 9 through 12 for mathematics (82 percent), science (88 percent), English/language arts (86 percent), and social studies/social sciences (89 percent), indicating that teachers in grades 7 and 8 are less likely to be teaching in field than are teachers in grades 9 through 12.

Continued Learning: Professional Development and Teacher Collaboration

In order to meet the changing demands of their jobs, high-quality teachers must be capable and willing to continuously learn and relearn their trade. Professional development and collaboration with other teachers are strategies for building educators' capacity for effective teaching, particularly in a profession where demands are changing and expanding. However, traditional approaches to professional development (e.g., workshops, conferences) have been criticized for being relatively ineffective because they typically lack connection to the challenges teachers face in their classrooms, and they are usually short term. Research suggests that unless professional development programs are carefully designed and implemented to provide continuity between what teachers learn and what goes on in their classrooms and schools, these activities are not likely to produce any long-lasting effects on either teacher competence or student outcomes. In addition to quality professional development, peer collaboration has also been recognized as important for teachers' continuous learning. The 1998 survey indicates that:

- Virtually all teachers participated in professional development activities (99 percent) and at least one collaborative activity (95 percent) in the last 12 months. Participation in professional development activities typically lasted from 1 to 8 hours, or the equivalent of 1 day or less of training. Teachers were most likely to participate in professional development activities focused toward areas that reformers emphasize (e.g., implementing state or district curriculum and performance standards, integrating technology into the grade or subject taught, using student performance assessment techniques).
- Nineteen percent of teachers had been mentored by another teacher in a formal relationship; 70 percent of teachers who were mentored at least once a week reported that it improved their teaching "a lot."
- Increased time spent in professional development and collaborative activities was associated with the perception of significant improvements in teaching. For every content area of professional development, a larger proportion of teachers who participated for more than 8 hours believed it improved their teaching "a lot" compared with teachers who participated for 8 hours or less. For example, teachers who spent more than 8 hours in professional development on in-depth study in the subject area of their main teaching assignment were more likely than those who spent 1 to 8 hours to report that participation in the program improved their teaching a lot (41 percent versus 12 percent). Moreover, teachers who participated in common planning periods for team teachers at least once a week were more likely than those who participated a few times a year to report that participation improved their teaching a lot (52 percent versus 13 percent).

Supportive Work Environment

Teachers' work environment is the final aspect of teacher quality addressed in this report. In addition to teacher learning, one key factor to understanding teacher quality is to focus on what happens to teachers once they enter the work force, including if they receive support from the schools and communities in which they work and from the parents of the children they teach. The 1998 FRSS survey indicates that:

- One-third of teachers had participated in an induction program when they first began teaching. However, newer teachers were more likely to have participated in some kind of induction program at the beginning of their teaching careers than were more experienced teachers (65 percent of teachers with 3 or fewer years of experience versus 14 percent of teachers with 20 or more years of experience). This FRSS survey did not elicit information regarding the intensity or usefulness of the induction programs.
- Teachers perceived relatively strong collegial support for their work; 63 percent strongly agreed that other teachers shared ideas with them that were helpful in their teaching. In addition, many teachers also felt supported by the school administration, with 55 percent agreeing strongly that the school administration supported them in their work and 47 percent agreeing strongly that goals and priorities for the school were clear.
- Teachers perceived somewhat less support from parents than from other teachers and the school administration. Only one-third of teachers agreed strongly that parents supported them in their efforts to educate their children.
- Collegial, school, and parental support varied by the instructional level of the school, with elementary school teachers perceiving stronger support than high school teachers.

The results of this survey provide a national profile of teacher quality, specifically focused on teachers' learning (both preservice and continued) and the environments in which they work. Included is important information regarding teachers' education, certification, teaching assignments, professional development, collaboration, and supportive work environment. In addition, comparisons by instructional level and poverty level of the school provide information about the distribution of teacher quality. This information provides a context for understanding why few teachers report feeling very well prepared to meet the challenges they face in their classrooms. This report is the first in a series of biennial reports that will be undertaken by NCES. Thus, the information provided here should provide a benchmark for these important dimensions of teacher quality and preparation.

February

European Central Bank
    President on the Euro. 75
President's Economic Report,
    Economic Advisers' Report 85

EUROPEAN CENTRAL BANK
PRESIDENT ON THE EURO
February 1, 1999

A consolidated currency for eleven European countries—the euro—made its debut on January 1, 1999, adding a vital element to decades-old plans to convert Europe into a single economic market. The euro promptly began a year-long slide against the dollar and yen, generating concerns about the real strength of European economic expansion. But the euro's weakness in the currency markets partly disguised its rapid success in transforming business practices on the continent. Experts noted that almost overnight the euro created a corporate bond market in Europe, making it easier for companies around the world to finance startups, expansions, and mergers and acquisitions there.

European political and economic leaders repeatedly expressed confidence in the underlying strength of their economies and brushed aside concerns about the euro's year-long sag. On December 2 European Central Bank President Willem F. Duisenberg predicted at least two years of strong economic growth, with low inflation, for Europe as a whole. Asked whether he was concerned about stability of the euro, he said: "I would become concerned if—what our strong belief is, the upward appreciation possibility of the euro, the future strength of the euro—if that were not over time to materialize. But these things always take time." Center-right parties, including some that had opposed the euro or expressed skepticism about it, prevailed in European Parliament elections in mid-June, raising questions, at least for the moment, about the underlying strength of public support in Europe for the unified currency. (Euro background, Historic Documents of 1998, p. 271)

Euro Value and European Economic Strength

The euro became a reality on January 1, 1999, when computerized systems around the world officially began recognizing the unified currency for financial trading. The first business day of the new year was January 4, and the euro opened trading at a value of about $1.17 against the U.S. dollar.

The euro effectively locked together the currencies of eleven of the fifteen member nations of the European Union: Austria, Belgium, Finland, France, Germany, Ireland, Italy, Luxembourg, the Netherlands, Portugal, and Spain. For convenience, journalists labeled the eleven countries as "Euroland" or the "Eurozone."

Britain, Denmark, and Sweden opted not to participate in the euro; Greece wanted to participate but it failed to meet minimum requirements the European Union had established to ensure that weak economies did not drag down the others. British prime minister Tony Blair on February 23 outlined a timetable for his country to adopt the euro following the next general elections, scheduled for 2002. But the euro's weakness against the pound sterling later in the year heightened opposition within Britain to joining the common currency.

During its first three years, the euro was to exist solely as an electronic currency, used for trading in stocks, bonds, and other financial transactions. Consumers could make credit card purchases and borrow money in euros, but actual bills and coins were not to enter circulation until the first six months of 2002.

The introduction of the euro generated much excitement, both in financial markets and on the streets of European cities. Companies eager to take advantage of a unified European economy quickly adjusted their bookkeeping to reflect the new currency; shopkeepers, restaurateurs, and service providers enthusiastically posted prices in euros as well as local currencies, such as the franc, lira, and deutschemark.

But within days currency traders began sending a different kind of message as they abandoned the euro for U.S. dollars, Japanese yen, and British pounds. The euro's slide against the dollar continued with only brief interruptions until the middle of July, when it picked up again for a few weeks, then headed back down until early December. On December 2 the euro briefly fell below the dollar in trading for the first time. The euro staged a modest recovery during the rest of December and ended the year at just about parity to the dollar-a drop of about 15 percent. The euro fell even more dramatically against the yen, ending the year at about 30 percent below its opening level.

Economists and financial experts offered numerous explanations for the euro's slide in the markets. There was consensus on the most important reason: the strength of the U.S. economy, which continued to grow at a faster pace than most of Europe through 1999, made the United States a more attractive place for investments. At the end of 1999 the U.S. economy was approaching a record for duration of an economic expansion, which began in 1992 and showed no signs of immediate reversal.

When the Federal Reserve Board began raising interest rates during the second half of 1999 to keep the expansion on course without risking inflation, U.S. financial investments became even more of a lure on the world markets. The bad news for the United States was that rising interest rates and the strength of the dollar versus the euro made American products more expensive in Europe, and therefore less attractive to European consumers-helping to put the U.S. trade deficit at record highs.

Throughout the year, investors watched for signs that European leaders would stick to their pledges to reduce budget deficits and resist the temptation to intervene in their economies to protect them against international competition. All eleven Eurozone countries had imposed austerity measures during the mid-1990s to reach economic and budget targets that had been agreed on for the introduction of the euro. In several cases the pain of austerity had translated into political disaster for the governments in office at the time, most notably the 1997 electoral defeat of the center-right part in France and the 1998 unseating of German Chancellor Helmut Kohl, one of the chief architects of the euro. (German election, Historic Documents of 1998, p. 815)

Despite the political agony and social upheaval caused by the austerity measures, the end result was a boom for most European economies during 1999. Economic growth for the eleven Eurozone countries was estimated at about 3 percent for the year, a welcome contrast to the lengthy recessions that many European countries had experienced earlier in the decade.

Even so, political leaders were under enormous pressure to protect workers against inevitable job losses as companies faced the realities of a globalized economy. In perhaps the most highly publicized backtracking on the earlier austerity promises, Gerhard Schroeder, who defeated Kohl, on November 24 ordered a $2.2 billion bail-out of a bankrupt construction company, Philipp Holzmann A. G. The action taken by Schroeder raised alarms among investors, who wanted decisions on the life and death of companies to be based on economic realities rather than political concerns.

At year's end financial analysts were divided in their predictions for the future course of the euro. Some experts said the continued strength of the U.S. economy would make it difficult for the euro to recover its original value. But others said the euro's setbacks in 1999 were only temporary, and they predicted that within a few years the euro would supplant the U.S. dollar as the world's dominant currency.

Impact on European Financing

If currency traders shied away from the euro during its first year, business leaders had the opposite reaction, flocking to the euro as the currency of choice to finance their operations. Hundreds of European firms—as well as some based in the United States and other countries—issued euro-based corporate bonds. The British Broadcasting Corporation reported December 30 that corporate bonds denominated in euros totaled about $590 billion in 1999—three times the value of European corporate bonds in 1998.

The emergence of a European bond market represented a significant change in business practices. In the past, most European companies borrowed from banks to finance new projects or to purchase assets of other companies. But the availability of a unified currency reduced the risks of international exchange rates, encouraging corporate borrowers to turn to bonds that could be bought easily by investors worldwide. "We have created one large capital market out of eleven small ones, and it has created a real shift," Thomas Mayer of the Goldman Sachs Group Inc. in Frankfurt told the Washington Post. *"Companies can finance themselves in more efficient ways. They don't need banks as much anymore."*

The euro also helped spur a new wave of corporate mergers and takeovers in Europe, parallel to the consolidation boom that had been underway in the United States for several years. The year saw 12,000 mergers and acquisitions in Europe, with a total value of $1.2 trillion, according to a report by Thomson Financial Securities Data. Those figures represented a 20 percent increase in the number of transactions and a doubling of the value, compared to 1998. Just as the euro made it safer and easier for business leaders and investors to issue and buy corporate bonds, analysts said, the unified currency eased the complex process of merging companies across national boundaries.

Following are excerpts from a speech by Willem F. Duisenberg, president of the European Central Bank, delivered February 1, 1999, to the Council on Foreign Relations in Chicago, in which he explained the introduction of the euro and Europe's new common monetary policies:

The euro—the new European currency—has made its debut this year. Its successful launch constitutes a milestone in the process of European integration and, in consequence, is bound to have a profound impact upon the euro area as well as the world economy in the years to come. In fact, the process of European integration started immediately after the Second World War. Its objectives were not and are not only economic, nor even primarily economic, but also political. European integration aims at the creation of a stable, prosperous and peaceful Europe. For a large part, economic integration has been the engine of this process. Economic integration has its own merits, but it is also likely to contribute to better relations among the countries concerned. And, on balance, although this process has had its ups and downs, it has been successful. However, there is no room for complacency. The introduction of the euro is an important step in this process, but it is not the end of it. New challenges lie ahead. The euro has been launched successfully but, as you know, the launch is only the start of a mission.

Following almost a decade of meticulous preparation and economic convergence, a single monetary policy for the entire euro area, encompassing almost 300 million people in eleven countries, is now determined by the Governing Council of the European Central Bank (ECB). This Council consists of the eleven governors of the national central banks (NCBs) of the participating Member States and the six members of the Executive Board of the ECB. Each member of this 17-member Governing Council has one vote. Monetary policy is conducted by the Eurosystem, which is comprised of the ECB and the eleven national central banks of the participating Member States. Like the FED [U.S. Federal Reserve], the Eurosystem is a federal system. Our "Washington" is "Frankfurt" in Germany, where the ECB is located. The Executive Board of the ECB which, as I have mentioned, consists of six members, is a separate decision-making body. It has to ensure that the tasks conferred upon the European System of Central Banks (ESCB) are implemented, either by its own activities or through the national central banks. The ECB has currently a staff of some 600. This number will grow to around 750 in the course of this year and is likely to increase further in the years to come.

The ECB's Monetary Policy

Let me elaborate on Europe's single monetary policy framework. In accordance with the Treaty on European Union, the primary objective of the single monetary policy is to maintain price stability. Price stability is a necessary condition for promoting sustainable economic growth and better employment prospects for the citizens of the euro area. The stability-oriented monetary policy strategy announced by the Governing Council last year, and currently shaping monetary policy decisions, was conceived with the intention of making the best possible contribution to the achievement of this objective.

At the centre of the stability-oriented monetary policy strategy lies the quantification of the primary objective of price stability. By announcing a quantitative definition of price stability, the Governing Council has provided a clear guide for the formulation of expectations of future price movements. At the same time such a quantitative definition has the distinct advantage of complying with the principles of transparency and accountability. This is so because, on the one hand, it clarifies how the Treaty's mandate is interpreted by the Governing Council while, on the other, it gives the public a yardstick against which the success of the single monetary policy can be evaluated.

Price stability has been defined and publicly announced as a year-on-year increase in the Harmonised Index of Consumer Prices (HICP) for the euro area of below 2%. This definition mirrors our aversion to both inflation and deflation. Hence neither price increases in excess of 2% nor deflation—that is, a persistent fall in the price level—would be deemed to be consistent with price stability. Based on the latest data available, the current annual rate of inflation, measured on a harmonised basis at around 1%, is consistent with the definition of price stability.

Price stability is to be maintained over the medium term. This emanates from the need for monetary policy to be forward-looking. It also recognises the reality that monetary policy cannot compensate for factors such as changes in indirect taxes or commodity prices that could distort price level movements in the short run.

The Governing Council of the ECB has founded its stability-oriented strategy upon two pillars. The first pillar relates to the prominent role assigned to money, given that the origins of inflation over the longer term are monetary in nature. Thus a quantitative reference value for the growth of a broad monetary aggregate, namely M3 [a catch-all term for all elements of the money supply, including currency, checks, money market accounts, and other financial deposits], has been announced. An annual rate of 4 1/2% has been set as the first reference value. The reference value for M3 is consistent with maintaining price stability over the medium term, while allowing for sustainable output growth and taking account of the trend decline in the velocity of circulation of M3. I wish to emphasise, however, that interest rates will not be changed in a "mechanistic" way in order to react to deviations of monetary growth from the reference value in the short term. Rather, such deviations will be regularly and thoroughly analysed for the signals that they convey about future price developments. If a deviation is considered to be posing a threat to price stability, monetary policy will then react accordingly to counter this threat.

In parallel with the evaluation of monetary growth, it is imperative to monitor a broad range of other economic and financial indicators, including economic forecasts. Thus our monetary policy strategy rests also upon a second pillar. This pillar comprises a broadly-based assessment of the outlook for price developments and the risks to price stability in the euro area as a whole. This systematic analysis of all other relevant information about economic and financial conditions will ensure that the Governing Council is as well informed as possible when formulating its monetary policy decisions. . . .

What the Monetary Policy of the ESCB Can Do

The Treaty [on the European Union] states that the ESCB, while having price stability as a primary objective, shall support the general economic policies in the European Community; moreover, it will operate in such a way as to be consistent with the establishment of free and competitive markets. The Treaty therefore provides an explicit order of priority for the objectives: price stability is the first reference point for the monetary policy of the Eurosystem, and only within the limits of price stability can there be scope to contribute to the achievement of the other objectives of the European Community. As a consequence, the role of other Community objectives in the monetary policy of the Eurosystem is conditional upon the achievement of the overriding target of price stability.

The high unemployment rate in Europe represents the main concern of economic policy-makers. I should like to stress that the Eurosystem shares these concerns and will do its utmost to help find a solution to this problem. That said, however, we should realise that what monetary policy is able to contribute to economic policy and the reduction of unemployment, is the achievement of price stability. By creating optimal conditions for a sustainable and strong pace of economic activity, price stability will ultimately spur employment growth and foster higher living standards. The high unemployment rate in Europe is far more the consequence of structural rigidities within the European labour and product markets than a result of adverse cyclical developments. The solution is thus to be found, above all, in structural reforms. The European unemployment rate has, indeed, been high and stable over the business cycles in the past decade. However, over the same period, unemployment was significantly reduced in those EU [European Union] countries which succeeded in creating better-functioning labour and product markets, which allowed wages and prices to adjust when economic conditions changed. A clear example can be found in the Netherlands, where a substantial reduction in unemployment has been effected in recent years by reforming the labour market, while following the same monetary policy as Germany, where the unemployment rate is still close to 10%.

The medium-term orientation of the monetary policy of the Eurosystem should help to avoid excessive fluctuations in real economic activity. Given the fact that the Eurosystem does not aim to stabilise every short-term deviation of price developments from the predetermined path of price stability, it contributes to the stabilisation of economic activity around its long-run potential growth path. I should like to add, however, that the room for manoeuvre of monetary policy and the degree of success in terms of maintaining price stability crucially depend on the support of sound fiscal policies and responsible wage settlements in the euro area.

The Links with Other Economic Policies

I should now like to address the way in which the economic environment and the economic policies of both the Community and the governments of Member States will affect the functioning of monetary policy. A monetary policy reaction to inflationary or deflationary pressures may cause short-run fluctuations in real output. Flexible and competitive goods and labour markets, however, would soften this trade-off, thereby allowing central banks to attain the goal of price stability with less serious adverse consequences for real output. The establishment of free and competitive markets for labour, goods and services would facilitate to a large extent the functioning of monetary policy in the euro area.

Market flexibility may also help to reduce regional asymmetries in the effects of the single monetary policy. The monetary policy of the ESCB will be geared towards the euro area as a whole and will not be able to take into account purely national or regional developments. Moreover, the cyclical positions of participating countries will not completely converge at the start of Stage Three, although, with the single currency in place, some national differences may disappear over time. In the past, asymmetric shocks across European countries were sometimes dealt with via movements in the exchange rates. In the EMU [European Monetary Union] environment, which is characterised by a single and uniform monetary policy aimed at maintaining price stability in the euro area as a whole, the required adjustments will have to stem from fiscal policies and national prices and wages, in addition to mobility of labour and capital.

Budgetary policies also play a major role in conditioning monetary policy. Sound budgetary policies enhance the credibility of monetary policy by preventing inflationary pressures. Furthermore, fiscal discipline exerts a downward influence on the risk premia embedded in nominal long-term interest rates. Moreover, given the requirements of the so-called Stability and Growth

Pact, a budgetary position which is close to balance or in surplus in normal conditions may allow scope for reaction to unforeseen regional or local shocks that could bring about heavy real output losses. This would also contribute to alleviating the possible asymmetric impact of monetary policy actions on single countries.

Where Do We Stand at Present?

Let me now turn to the operational aspects of the changeover to the new currency and the first experiences in financial markets. The start of Stage Three of EMU proved to be a formidable operation, yet it was clearly a success. In spite of the extraordinary operational risks involved, the changeover passed without any serious incident affecting the orderly conditions of the monetary system. The monitoring of the Eurosystem's activities to convert the former national currencies into the euro progressed smoothly. There was no need to invoke any contingency measure, whether "ordinary" or "extraordinary". This smooth introduction of the euro was the result of years of thorough preparatory work involving the ECB, the NCBs and a large number of public and private institutions which represent the core of the financial infrastructure in the euro area. This has been reflected clearly in the way in which financial markets have received the euro. . . .

As regards the broadly based assessment of the outlook for price developments, the second pillar—financial indicators—suggests that markets expect the current environment of price stability to be maintained over the medium to longer term. This outlook is supported by the significant fall observed in nominal short and long-term interest rates following the co-ordinated interest rate cut at the beginning of December. With regard to the real-side indicators for the euro area, the signals are mixed. On the one hand, euro area real GDP growth is generally expected to slow down somewhat in 1999 and business confidence, orders and capacity utilisation have been less favourable in recent months. On the other hand, the latest increase in employment figures, the acceleration in retail sales and the recent boost in consumer confidence point towards a more favourable outlook. Finally, subdued wage growth, moderate food price increases and declining energy prices have contributed to a lower rate of inflation for the euro area of just below 1%. On balance, therefore, the evidence suggests that there are no significant upward or downward pressures on the price level, at least at this juncture. Therefore, we have announced our decision to set and maintain the interest rate on our main refinancing operations at 3% for the foreseeable future.

Of course, I recognise that potential risks to price stability do exist. First, the floating and subsequent depreciation of Brazil's currency has given rise to renewed fears of a disruption in world financial markets and, potentially, of a further decline in world output growth in 1999. Second, wage demands in excess of labour productivity growth and a relaxation of the fiscal stance by national governments in the euro area constitute upward risks. The Governing Council will continue to monitor all these developments very closely, and will act, should the need arise, in order to prevent either inflationary or deflationary pressures becoming entrenched.

The International Role of the Euro

The introduction of the euro has created a single currency area which approximately matches the United States in terms of economic size, is larger with respect to its share in total world exports and ranks only second in terms of the size of its capital market. Such an event will have important implications for the economies outside the euro area and the international capital markets. In this context, a few words seem to be in order to clarify our view on the international role of the euro and, particularly, the policy stance of the Eurosystem with regard to such a role.

With reference to the use of the euro as an international currency, I should like to remind you that the primary objective of the Eurosystem is the maintenance of price stability. Having an international currency will be advantageous for both businesses and consumers. At the same time, though, the conduct of monetary policy could become complicated should the fraction of the money stock circulating outside the euro area increase significantly. The Eurosystem does not intend either to foster or to hinder the development of the euro as an international currency. It will take a neutral stance and leave it to market forces to determine that role. There is no conscious policy of challenging the dollar. Naturally, to the extent that the Eurosystem is successful in maintaining price stability, this will in itself foster the use of the euro as an international currency. It is hard to make a prediction with regard to the pace at which the euro will emerge as an international currency. An educated guess is that the process will be a gradual one. Nevertheless, the possibility of the euro assuming a prominent role more rapidly than is perhaps suggested by past experience cannot be ruled out.

A second aspect of the international role of the euro relates to the exchange rate of the euro against the US dollar or the Japanese yen. The Eurosystem in its monetary strategy deliberately does not specify a target for the exchange rate of the euro. The euro area is a large, relatively closed economy, similar in this respect to the United States. The maintenance of price stability could easily be undermined if a target for the euro exchange rate were to be vigorously pursued. Rather, in accordance with the Eurosystem's monetary policy strategy, the euro exchange rate will depend upon current and expected economic policies and developments and upon the interpretation markets attach to these policies and developments. The absence of an exchange rate objective against major currencies does not mean that the Eurosystem will be indifferent toward the euro exchange rate. The exchange rate is one of the indicators of monetary policy that are monitored under the second pillar of our strategy, that is the broadly based assessment of the outlook for price developments. If its development poses a threat to price stability in the euro area, this threat will be assessed and a response will be given, if considered necessary.

Moreover, the lack of a target for the euro exchange rate against the major international currencies does not necessarily mean that these rates should become more volatile. I am in favour of reasonably stable exchange rates. Who is not? However, just as a fever cannot be prevented by restricting the movement of the thermometer, we cannot ensure the absence of exchange rate pressures simply by announcing targets for exchange rates. The pursuit of stability-oriented monetary and fiscal policies at home constitutes a fundamental prerequisite for fostering a stable exchange rate environment. The Eurosystem's stability-oriented monetary policy strategy provides a significant contribution in this regard. Nonetheless, absolute stability of the exchange rate is impossible to guarantee. Such an outcome may not even be desirable if, for example, the United States and the euro area were to go through business cycles that were not fully synchronised. Such a prospect cannot be ruled out, as even recent history has shown.

Finally, I should like briefly to touch upon the issue of the role of the ECB in international co-operation. It is clear that a central bank that acts on behalf of a monetary union comparable in economic size to the United States and which is responsible for managing a major currency is bound to play an important international role. The ECB will meet this challenge by assuming the responsibility that comes with this role. Its role will develop gradually, since it is a young institution. We will also build on the experience of those central banks which have played an important international role in the past. You may guess which central bank outside the euro area I have in mind in particular. . . .

The euro—the new European currency—is a reality. The single monetary policy is in place and the Governing Council of the ECB has assumed responsibility for steering it. There is no doubt in my mind that the real challenges for the Eurosystem still lie ahead. I am confident that the Eurosystem, through its stability-oriented monetary policy strategy, will stand up to these challenges and be successful in maintaining price stability in the euro area. In doing so, it will not only provide for a better future for all the citizens of the euro area but will also contribute to a stable international financial system.

PRESIDENT'S ECONOMIC REPORT, ECONOMIC ADVISERS' REPORT
February 4, 1999

The American economy is "at the pinnacle of power and success," President Bill Clinton proudly proclaimed in his sixth annual economic report to Congress. In 1998, the president said, wages rose at twice the rate of inflation; home ownership was at its highest level ever; inflation, unemployment, and the welfare rolls were at their lowest levels in three decades; and the federal government was showing a surplus for the second year in a row after running a deficit for a generation. Already experiencing the longest peacetime expansion in the nation's history, the U.S. economy was poised to keep growing in 1999, the administration predicted, although at a slower pace than it had in 1998. If the economy continued to expand through February 2000, it would become the longest expansion on record, surpassing the 106-month expansion of 1961–1969, which encompassed the first years of the Vietnam War.

Moreover, the president said, the current expansion was "both broad and deep," with incomes and employment rising for all income groups, including African Americans and Hispanics who had been left behind in the supply-side expansion of 1982–1990, when Republicans Ronald Reagan and George Bush were in the White House, and in the early years of the current expansion. Jobless rates among blacks and Hispanics fell to their lowest levels since the federal government began tracking them, while hourly wages for blacks rose even faster in 1998 than those for whites. In addition to beginning to narrow the inequality between rich and poor, white and black, the tight labor market also helped keep welfare rolls and crime rates down, the Council of Economic Advisers said.

These economic successes were not accidental, the president said, but the result of the administration's strategy to maintain fiscal discipline, invest in education and technology, and expand exports. "Continuing with this proven strategy is the best way to maintain our prosperity and meet the challenges of the twenty-first century," Clinton maintained. While welcoming the good economic news, Republicans said the report did *not give enough credit to the monetary policies of the Federal Reserve and its chairman, Alan Greenspan, or to the Republican welfare reform bill signed into law in 1996 and Republican contributions to the balanced budget.*

The president's Council of Economic Advisers said that it saw no signs that the expansion was nearing its end. Inflation, the usual event triggering the end of the nation's post–World War II expansions, was mild and likely to remain so, they said. The Consumer Price Index, the chief measure of inflation, rose by only 1.6 percent in 1998, its second smallest increase since 1964. Average unemployment fell to 4.5 percent, its lowest level since 1969. Although such a tight labor market has traditionally been considered inflationary, other factors in the economy put downward pressure on inflation, keeping it well in check. These favorable conditions included a continuing drop in computer and oil prices. Moreover, industrial capacity continued to increase at a faster pace than wage rates, which meant that even though they were paying their workers more, companies still had to price their goods and services at competitive rates.

The Economic Year in Review

Consumer spending and business investment were the keys to the expanding economy in 1998, the Council of Economic Advisers said in its annual report, released February 4 in conjunction with the president's report. Household spending grew at an annual rate of about 6 percent in the first six months of 1998 before moderating somewhat later in the year. Several reasons accounted for the boost in personal consumption. First, real disposable income continued to rise, at a rate of about 3.25 percent in the first three quarters of 1998. Second, spreading ownership of stocks and a sharp run-up in stock prices sent household wealth soaring to nearly six times income. Some two-fifths of all American families owned stock directly or indirectly, compared with just one-third ten years earlier. Continuing low interest rates and easy availability of credit—made possible because the federal government was no longer competing for funding to finance its deficit—also spurred household spending, especially on housing. Single-family housing starts were the highest since 1978, and single-family home sales reached record levels, as did the percentage of Americans who owned their own home. By the end of the year, nearly two-thirds of all Americans owned their own homes.

Business investment also rose sharply in 1998, increasing at an annual rate of 15 percent in the first half of the year before slowing in the last half. Business spending on computers and peripheral equipment rose 75 percent in the first three quarters, while spending on communications equipment jumped about 20 percent. At the same time, the federal government's consumption spending (not including transfer payments, interests, or grants to state and local governments) continued to decline. Defense spending fell by about 2 percent, more than offsetting a 1 percent increase in nondefense spending.

Throughout the year, economists, investors, and others worried that the financial and currency crisis that had struck East Asia in the summer of 1997 and then spread to Russia and Brazil in 1998 would undermine the U.S. economy. Russia's devaluation of the ruble and its default on some of its debt did cause sharp drops in the U.S. stock markets in August and September. Banks and many businesses were forced to write off millions in loans to faltering emerging markets, and farmers and many manufacturers were hurt by falling prices for their exports. Those tensions were eased late in the year when the Federal Reserve reduced interest rates. The stock market recovered most of its earlier losses, and business investment picked up again. While lower prices for commodities such as oil and steel were bad for their producers, they helped keep overall inflation down. (East Asian crisis, Historic Documents of 1998, p. 532; Russian economic crisis, Historic Documents of 1998, p. 601)

Benefits of a Strong Labor Market

One of the more troubling facets of the economic expansion of 1982–1990 and the early years of the current one was that although the expanding economies benefited the well-off and well-educated population, the poor and less educated were experiencing increasing unemployment rates and declining wages. It was thus with great pride that the president and his advisers reported that the employment and income gaps appeared to be narrowing. Overall, 133 million Americans had jobs at the end of 1998 and only 4.3 percent of the workforce was unemployed.

The jobless rate for whites was 3.8 percent, about what it had been throughout the year, while the jobless rate for blacks fell to 7.9 percent, down more than two percentage points from its 10.1 percent standing in December 1997 and the first time it had fallen below 8 percent since the federal government began tracking joblessness for African Americans in 1972. Nonetheless, the administration said the unemployment rate for minorities was "still unacceptably high."

The tight labor market was also benefiting those people at the lower end of the educational attainment scales. Employment levels for high school dropouts rose more than 9 percent between 1993 and 1996, while employment among those with only a high school diploma or a few years of college rose about 3 percent. Employment among college graduates, which had always been high, remained about the same.

People at the low end of the pay scale also began to make up for ground they lost in the previous two decades. Real hourly wages for men in the bottom fifth of the wage distribution increased by about 6 percent between 1993 and 1998, or about half of what they had lost between 1979 and 1993. Real hourly wages for black men rose nearly 6 percent in 1997 and 1998. In 1998 black men earned $10.57 an hour, compared with $14.41 for white men. Black women and Hispanics also recorded significant gains. The median wage for high school dropouts and high school graduates also turned around since 1993. High school graduates with no college experi-

ence saw their median wage rise 2.8 percent since 1993, reversing a nearly 22 percent decline between 1979 and 1993. The median real wage for high school dropouts increased in 1998 for the first time since at least 1979, rising by 7 percent. One factor contributing to these higher wage rates, the advisers said, was the increase in the minimum wage that Congress approved in 1996 over the objections of the Republican leadership. (Raising the minimum wage, Historic Documents of 1996, p. 563)

Predictions for 1999

The Council of Economic Advisers said it expected growth in 1999 to slow to about 2 percent, inflation to rise to a still comfortable 2.3 percent, and unemployment to rise to 4.8 percent. The advisers said that unemployment could not decline much further "without inflationary consequences" and that consumption spending was unlikely to continue its fast growth "unless the stock market continues to surge."

Speaking at the Economic Strategy Institute in Washington on February 11, a week after the economic report was released, Jeffrey Frankel, a member of the Council of Economic Advisers, said that the administration's growth estimate for 1999 "already looks like it may be too conservative." Although Frankel maintained that some slowdown in growth was inevitable, "chances are pretty good that this time next year, we'll be marking the longest expansion ever." Although final figures for 1999 would not be available until well into 2000, Frankel's assessment appeared to be accurate. The economy grew at an annual rate of 5.8 percent in the last three months of 1999, according to preliminary data, while the inflation rate rose to 2.3 percent. The rapid pace of growth fueled fears that the Federal Researve would soon increase interest rates to keep inflation in check.

Following are the text of the Economic Report of the President and excerpts from chapters 1 and 3 of the Annual Report of the Council of Economic Advisers, both released February 4, 1999:

ECONOMIC REPORT OF THE PRESIDENT

To the Congress of the United States:

I am pleased to report that the American economy today is healthy and strong. Our Nation is enjoying the longest peacetime economic expansion in its history, with almost 18 million new jobs since 1993, wages rising at twice the rate of inflation, the highest home ownership ever, the smallest welfare rolls in 30 years, and unemployment and inflation at their lowest levels in three decades.

This expansion, unlike recent previous ones, is both wide and deep. All income groups, from the richest to the poorest, have seen their incomes rise since 1993. The typical family income is up more than $3,500, adjusted for inflation. African-American and Hispanic households, who were left behind during the last expansion, have also seen substantial increases in income.

Our Nation's budget is balanced, for the first time in a generation, and we are entering the second year of an era of surpluses: our projections show that we will close out the 1999 fiscal year with a surplus of $79 billion, the largest in the history of the United States. We are on course for budget surpluses for many years to come.

These economic successes are not accidental. They are the result of an economic strategy that we have pursued since 1993. It is a strategy that rests on three pillars: fiscal discipline, investments in education and technology, and expanding exports to the growing world market. Continuing with this proven strategy is the best way to maintain our prosperity and meet the challenges of the 21st century.

The Administration's Economic Agenda

Our new economic strategy was rooted first and foremost in fiscal discipline. We made hard fiscal choices in 1993, sending signals to the market that we were serious about dealing with the budget deficits we had inherited. The market responded by lowering long-term interest rates. Lower interest rates in turn helped more people buy homes and borrow for college, helped more entrepreneurs to start businesses, and helped more existing businesses to invest in new technology and equipment. America's economic success has been fueled by the biggest boom in private sector investment in decades—more than $1 trillion in capital was freed for private sector investment. In past expansions, government bought more and spent more to drive the economy. During this expansion, government spending as a share of the economy has fallen.

The second part of our strategy has been to invest in our people. A global economy driven by information and fast-paced technological change creates ever greater demand for skilled workers. That is why, even as we balanced the budget, we substantially increased our annual investment in education and training. We have opened the doors of college to all Americans, with tax credits and more affordable student loans, with more work-study grants and more Pell grants, with education IRAs and the new HOPE Scholarship tax credit that more than 5 million Americans will receive this year. Even as we closed the budget gap, we have expanded the earned income tax credit for almost 20 million low-income working families, giving them hope and helping lift them out of poverty. Even as we cut government spending, we have raised investments in a welfare-to-work jobs initiative and invested $24 billion in our children's health initiative.

Third, to build the American economy, we have focused on opening foreign markets and expanding exports to our trading partners around the world. Until recently, fully one-third of the strong economic growth America has enjoyed in the 1990s has come from exports. That trade has been aided by 270 trade agreements we have signed in the past 6 years.

Addressing Our Nation's Economic Challenges

We have created a strong, healthy, and truly global economy—an economy that is a leader for growth in the world. But common sense, experience, and the example of our competitors abroad show us that we cannot afford to be complacent. Now, at this moment of great plenty, is precisely the time to face the challenges of the next century.

We must maintain our fiscal discipline by saving Social Security for the 21st century—thereby laying the foundations for future economic growth.

By 2030, the number of elderly Americans will double. This is a seismic demographic shift with great consequences for our Nation. We must keep Social Security a rock-solid guarantee. That is why I proposed in my State of the Union address that we invest the surplus to save Social Security. I proposed that we commit 62 percent of the budget surplus for the next 15 years to Social Security. I also proposed investing a small portion in the private sector. This will allow the trust fund to earn a higher return and keep Social Security sound until 2055.

But we must aim higher. We should put Social Security on a sound footing for the next 75 years. We should reduce poverty among elderly women, who are nearly twice as likely to be poor as other seniors. And we should eliminate the limits on what seniors on Social Security can earn. These changes will require difficult but fully achievable choices over and above the dedication of the surplus.

Once we have saved Social Security, we must fulfill our obligation to save and improve Medicare and invest in long-term health care. That is why I have called for broader, bipartisan reforms that keep Medicare secure until 2020 through additional savings and modernizing the program with market-oriented purchasing tools, while also providing a long-overdue prescription drug benefit.

By saving the money we will need to save Social Security and Medicare, over the next 15 years we will achieve the lowest ratio of publicly held debt to gross domestic product since 1917. This debt reduction will help keep future interest rates low or drive them even lower, fueling economic growth well into the 21st century.

To spur future growth, we must also encourage private retirement saving. In my State of the Union address I proposed that we use about 12 percent of the surplus to establish new Universal Savings Accounts—USA accounts. These will ensure that all Americans have the means to save. Americans could receive a flat tax credit to contribute to their USA accounts and additional tax credits to match a portion of their savings—with more help for lower income Americans. This is the right way to provide tax relief to the American people.

Education is also key to our Nation's future prosperity. That is why I proposed in my State of the Union address a plan to create 21st-century schools through greater investment and more accountability. Under my plan, States and school districts that accept Federal resources will be required to end social promotion, turn around or close failing schools, support high-quality teachers, and promote innovation, competition, and discipline. My plan also proposes increasing Federal investments to help States and school districts take responsibility for failing schools, to recruit and train new teachers, to expand after school and summer school programs, and to build or fix 5,000 schools.

At this time of continued turmoil in the international economy, we must do more to help create stability and open markets around the world. We must press forward with open trade. It would be a terrible mistake, at this time of economic fragility in so many regions, for the United States to build new walls of protectionism that could set off a chain reaction around the world, imperiling the growth upon which we depend. At the same time, we must do more to make sure that working people are lifted up by trade. We must do more to ensure that spirited economic competition among nations never becomes a race to the bottom in the area of environmental protections or labor standards.

Strengthening the foundations of trade means strengthening the architecture of international finance. The United States must continue to lead in stabilizing the world financial system. When nations around the world descend into economic disruption, consigning populations to poverty, it hurts them and it hurts us. These nations are our trading partners; they buy our products and can ship low-cost products to American consumers.

The U.S. proposal for containing financial contagion has been taken up around the world: interest rates are being cut here and abroad, America is meeting its obligations to the International Monetary Fund, and a new facility has been created at the World Bank to strengthen the social safety net in Asia. And agreement has been reached to establish a new precautionary line of credit, so nations with strong economic policies can quickly get the help they need before financial problems mushroom from concerns to crises.

We must do more to renew our cities and distressed rural areas. My Administration has pursued a new strategy, based on empowerment and investment, and we have seen its success. With the critical assistance of Empowerment Zones, unemployment rates in cities across the country have dropped dramatically. But we have more work to do to bring the spark of private enterprise to neighborhoods that have too long been without hope. That is why my budget includes an innovative "New Markets" initiative to spur $15 billion in new private sector capital investment in businesses in underserved areas through a package of tax credits and guarantees.

Going Forward Together in the 21st Century

Now, on the verge of another American Century, our economy is at the pinnacle of power and success, but challenges remain. Technology and trade and the spread of information have transformed our economy, offering great opportunities but also posing great challenges. All Americans must be equipped with the skills to succeed and prosper in the new economy. America must have the courage to move forward and renew its ideas and institutions to meet new challenges. There are no limits to the world we can create, together, in the century to come.

William J. Clinton
The White House
February 4, 1999

THE ANNUAL REPORT OF THE
COUNCIL OF ECONOMIC ADVISERS

Chapter 1: Meeting Challenges and Building for the Future

The economic policies of the past 6 years have nurtured and sustained what is now the longest peacetime expansion on record. By December 1998, the 93rd month since the bottom of the last recession, 18.8 million jobs had been created (17.7 million of them since January 1993). More Americans are working than ever before, the unemployment rate is the lowest in a generation, and inflation remains tame. This record of achievement is especially noteworthy in light of the troubles experienced in the international economy in 1998. The United States has not entirely escaped the effects of this turmoil—and calm has not been restored completely abroad. But the fundamental soundness of the U.S. economy prevented it from foundering in 1998's storms.

This Administration laid a strong policy foundation for growth in 1993 when the President put in place an economic strategy grounded in deficit reduction, targeted investments, and opening markets abroad. Since then the Federal budget deficit has come down steadily, and in 1998 the budget was in the black for the first time since 1969. This policy of fiscal discipline, together with an appropriately accommodative monetary policy by the Federal Reserve, produced a favorable climate for business investment and a strong, investment-driven recovery from the recession and slow growth of the early 1990s. Even while reducing Federal spending as a share of gross domestic product (GDP), the Administration has pushed for more spending in critical areas such as education and training, helping families and children, the environment, health care, and research and development. And although international economic conditions have led to a dramatic widening of the trade deficit, the United States has succeeded in expanding exports in real (inflation-adjusted) terms by almost 8 percent per year since 1993. . . .

Policy Lessons from Three Long Expansions

The current economic expansion is only the third that has lasted at least 7 years, according to business-cycle dating procedures that have been applied back to 1854. . . . It is useful to review and compare the histories of each of these long expansions in order to understand the role of macroeconomic policy in promoting balanced and noninflationary growth.

The Employment Act of 1946 (which created the Council of Economic Advisers) established a policy framework in which the Federal Government is responsible for trying to stabilize short-run economic fluctuations, promote balanced and noninflationary economic growth, and foster low unemployment. Although the U.S. economy has continued to experience fluctuations in output and employment in the more than half a century since then, it has avoided anything like the prolonged contraction of 1873–79, or the 30 percent contraction in output and 25 percent unemployment rate of the Great Depression. Moreover, the three longest expansions of the past century—including the current one—have all occurred since the Employment Act was passed.

Each of these three long expansions can be interpreted as an experiment in macroeconomic policy. The longest—the expansion of 1961–69, which lasted 106 months—was associated with the first self-consciously Keynesian approach to economic policy. It was also associated with Vietnam War spending. The longest peacetime expansion before the current one was the expansion of 1982–90, which lasted 92 months. Although the economic philosophy underlying the policies of that period is often characterized as anti-Keynesian, this expansion, too, featured a stimulative fiscal policy. The current expansion is the only one of the three in which fiscal policy was contractionary rather than expansionary, reflecting the budget situation at the time and the view that fiscal discipline would lower interest rates and spur long-term economic growth.

Keynesian Activism in the 1961–69 Expansion

In the early 1960s the Council of Economic Advisers advocated activist macroeconomic policies based on the ideas of the British economist John Maynard Keynes. The Council diagnosed the economy at that time as suffering from "fiscal drag" arising from a large structural budget surplus. (The structural budget balance is the deficit or surplus that would arise from the prevailing fiscal stance if the economy were operating at full capacity.) The marginal tax rates then in effect, which were far higher than today's, were seen as causing tax revenues to rise rapidly as the economy approached full employment, draining purchasing power and slowing demand before full employment could be achieved. The problem was not the fact that Federal Government receipts and expenditures were sensitive to changes in economic activity—this sensitivity plays an important automatic stabilizing role, particularly when economic activity falters, as reduced tax payments and increased unemployment compensation help preserve consumers' purchasing power. The problem was that the automatic stabilizers kicked in too strongly on the upside, not only preventing the economy from reaching full employment but also, ironically, preventing the actual budget from balancing. Thus, President John F. Kennedy proposed a tax cut in 1962, which was enacted in 1964, after his death.

This tax cut provided further stimulus to the economic recovery that had begun in 1961. The unemployment rate continued to fall, until early in 1966 it dropped below the 4 percent rate that was considered full employment at the time. Inflation had been edging up as the unemployment rate came down, but it then began to rise sharply. . . . Although the changed conditions appeared to call for fiscal restraint, President Lyndon B. Johnson was reluctant to raise taxes or scale back his Great Society spending initiatives. Meanwhile Vietnam War spending continued to provide further stimulus.

At the time, policymakers believed that the rise in inflation could be unwound simply by moving the economy back to 4 percent unemployment, but when restraint was finally applied it produced a rise in unemployment with little reduction in inflation. This so-called stagflation, together with a slowdown in productivity and a series of oil price shocks in the 1970s, dealt a serious setback to the prevailing view among economists that economic policy could be easily adjusted to achieve the goals of the Employment Act.

The Supply-Side Revolution and the 1982–90 Expansion

At the beginning of the Administration of President Ronald Reagan in 1981, the economy was bouncing back from the short 1980 recession, but it was also experiencing very high inflation. President Reagan's program for economic recovery called for large tax cuts, increased defense spending, and reduced domestic spending. Although advocates of these policies invoked the 1964 tax cut as precedent, the justification offered for this policy was not Keynesian demand stimulus. Rather it was the "supply-side" expectation that substantial cuts in marginal tax rates would call forth so much new work effort and investment that the economy's potential output would grow rapidly, easing inflationary pressure and bringing in sufficient new revenue to keep the budget deficit from increasing. In the short run, however, this expansionary fiscal policy collided with an aggressive anti-inflationary monetary policy on the part of the Federal Reserve. The budget deficit ballooned in the deep recession of 1981–82, and it stayed large even after the Federal Reserve eased and the economy began to recover.

Compared with the 1961–69 expansion, the 1982–90 expansion was marked by higher levels of both inflation and unemployment. But the main distinguishing feature of this expansion was the large Federal budget deficits and their macroeconomic consequences. In the early 1980s the combination of an expansionary fiscal policy and a tight monetary policy produced high real interest rates, an appreciating dollar, and a large current account deficit. (The current account, which includes investment income and unilateral transfers, is a broader measure of a country's international economic activity than the more familiar trade balance.) Although borrowing from abroad offset some of the drain on national saving that the budget deficit represented, and prevented the sharp squeeze on domestic investment that would have taken place in an economy closed to trade and foreign capital flows, the effect of this policy choice was a decline in net national saving and investment after 1984. As in the 1961–69 expansion, inflation began to rise as the economy moved toward high employment. By this time, however, the prevailing view was that inflation could not be reversed simply by returning to the full-employment unemployment rate.... Instead the economy would have to go through a period of subnormal growth in order to squeeze out inflation.

Deficit Reduction and the Current Expansion

The economy was out of the 1990–91 recession when President Bill Clinton took office, but the recovery was weak and job growth appeared slow. Budget deficits were very large, partly because of the recession but also because the structural deficit remained large. The President's economic program sought to get the economy moving again while bringing the budget deficit under control. It was based on the idea that reducing the Federal budget deficit would bring down interest rates and stimulate private investment. With a responsible fiscal policy in place, and with favorable developments in inflation and productivity, the decline in the unemployment rate to less than 5 percent did not lead to interest rate hikes that could have choked off the expansion prematurely. In fact, the economy witnessed a combination of low consumer price inflation and low unemployment that compared favorably with the low "misery index" achieved in the late 1960s. (The misery index is the sum of the inflation and unemployment rates.) This time, however, inflation is tame rather than rising.

Judged by the objectives of stabilization policy (inflation and unemployment), the current economic expansion has been very successful.... Three-quarters of the way through the eighth year of expansion, inflation remains low even though the unemployment rate has been below most estimates of the NAIRU. This situation stands in marked contrast to the sharply rising inflation experienced at the end of the 1960s expansion and the milder price acceleration seen at the end of the 1980s expansion. To be sure, this good inflation performance has been aided by favorable conditions such as a continuing sharp decline in computer prices, a drop in oil prices, rapid growth of industrial capacity, and downward pressure on prices of traded goods due to weakness in the world economy. And ... the Administration (as well as the consensus of private forecasts) projects a moderating of growth over the next 2 years. What is significant, however, is that the actions taken over the past 6 years to reduce the budget deficit created conditions in which the Federal Reserve could accommodate steady noninflationary growth. And, of course, the strong economic performance helped improve the budget balance even further.

Growth in GDP has also been solid. With slower growth in the working-age population and slower trend productivity growth since the early 1970s, it is understandable that GDP has grown more slowly than it did in the 1960s.... Moreover, growth over the 1980s expansion partly reflects how far below potential output the economy was at the start of that expansion, which followed a deep recession, rather than a particularly strong underlying growth trend. Finally, growth in aggregate income matters for some purposes, but productivity growth is what matters for real wages and a rising standard of living over the longer term. And productivity growth has continued relatively strong well into this expansion—it has not exhibited the decline that often occurs late in expansions. Nevertheless, the rate of productivity growth over this expansion remains well below that achieved in the 1960s, before the productivity slowdown.

Relatively slow productivity growth continues to prevent the kind of wage and income growth that produced a doubling in living standards between 1948 and 1973. . . . [H]owever, the sustained tight labor market that this expansion has created in the past few years has brought benefits to the vast majority of American workers, including groups that had fallen behind over the past two decades or so, such as low-wage workers and minorities. A labor market like that of today has numerous benefits. It increases the confidence of job losers that they will be able to return to work; it lures discouraged workers back into the labor force; it enhances the prospects of those already at work to get ahead; it enables those who want or need to switch jobs to do so without a long period of joblessness; and it lowers the duration of the typical unemployment spell. It can reduce long-term structural unemployment by providing jobs and experience to younger and less skilled workers, thus increasing their longer run attachment to the labor force. In short, a sustained tight labor market helps the rising tide of economic growth lift all boats.

This expansion has illustrated how the mix of monetary and fiscal policy can affect the composition of output. Unlike the expansion of the 1980s, which saw an expansionary fiscal policy restrained by tight monetary policy, the current expansion has taken place under conditions of fiscal restraint and an accommodative monetary policy. The 1980s policy mix brought with it relatively high real interest rates, declining net national saving and investment, and a large current account deficit, which changed the United States from the world's largest creditor Nation to its largest debtor. Strong performance by the U.S. economy in the 1990s is again associated with a strong dollar and, most recently, a widening trade deficit, as the United States has continued to absorb foreign goods while weakness abroad has reduced demand for U.S. goods. On balance, however, the current account deficits of the 1990s have been the result of generally rising net national investment remaining greater than generally rising net national saving.

The current account balance depends on the gap between saving and investment. But future growth depends on the levels of saving and investment. Since 1993, net national saving has increased by about 3 percentage points as a share of GDP, to better than 6 1/2 percent in the first three quarters of 1998. The current expansion has been distinguished by the large contribution of private fixed investment to GDP growth and the negligible contribution of government spending. . . . Strong investment has already been associated with strong growth in capacity, which has helped keep inflation in check, and may have contributed to maintaining growth in productivity as the expansion has matured. . . .

Conclusion

Through a combination of sound policy, other favorable conditions, and of course the energetic efforts of millions of American workers and businesses, the current economic expansion has achieved both high employment and low inflation. Longer run trends in productivity and population growth will ultimately determine how fast the economy grows. But the investment that has driven the current expansion should pay off in stronger growth and productivity and higher future standards of living than otherwise would have been the case. With the Federal budget once more under control, large deficits will not constrain future policy choices. . . .

Chapter 3: Benefits of a Strong Labor Market

The Nation's labor market is performing at record levels: the number of workers employed is at an all-time high, the unemployment rate is at a 30-year low, and real (inflation-adjusted) wages are increasing after years of stagnation. Groups whose economic status has not improved in the past decades are now experiencing progress. The real wages of blacks and Hispanics have risen rapidly in the past 2 to 3 years, and their unemployment rates are at long-time lows; employment among male high school dropouts, single women with children, and immigrants, as well as among blacks and Hispanics, has increased; and the gap in earnings between immigrant and native workers is narrowing.

The most recent data also show that the employment relationship is strong. Job displacement—job losses due to layoffs, plant closures, and the like—has declined substantially since the 1993–95 period, and among those who have been displaced, the share that have found new work has increased. These reemployed workers still typically earn less on the new job than at the job they lost, but these wage losses are at record lows. Moreover, the popular assertion that secure lifetime jobs are disappearing appears to be overstated. This is not to suggest that the picture is entirely benign: some groups have experienced declines in job tenure since the 1980s, and the rate of job displacement remains relatively high given the current strength of the labor market. To address these and other problems, this Administration has undertaken a number of measures to strengthen education and job training and to promote lifelong learning.

Besides spreading the benefits of economic growth more widely, the robust labor market has generated other, less obvious benefits. It has contributed to a decrease in welfare case loads, allowing States and localities to focus increased resources on designing and implementing welfare reform. In addition, low unemployment and, especially, the rise in average wages may have contributed to a reduction in crime. Several studies have demonstrated an inverse relationship between labor market opportunities and criminal behavior: the better the options in legal employment, the less likely are potential criminals to commit crimes. . . .

Economy-wide Developments in the Labor Market

Employment

The usual indicators of labor market progress—employment, unemployment, and wages—show that working men and women continue to benefit from the ongoing economic expansion. Employment is at an all-time high, with 133 million Americans at work in December 1998, and only 4.3 percent of the labor force unemployed. Having fallen from 7.3 percent in January 1993, the unemployment rate is at its lowest level since February 1970. . . .

Data on discouraged workers provide further evidence of a strong labor market. The number of discouraged workers—workers who are not employed and who have not looked for work in the past 4 weeks because they did not think they could find a job—has shrunk by one-third since 1994, the earliest year for which comparable data are available. Discouraged workers are not counted in the labor force and therefore are not captured in the official unemployment rate. However, because there are so few discouraged workers, redefining the unemployment rate to include them as unemployed increases the unemployment rate by no more than 0.4 percentage point.

Much of the growth in employment reflects an increase in the share of women looking for and finding jobs. More women than ever before have joined the labor force: among women aged 25–64, 72.4 percent were working or seeking work in 1998, up from 70.2 percent in 1993 and 33.1 percent in 1948. The labor force participation rate among men aged 25–64 gradually declined during the 1960s and early 1970s, but it has remained steady at about 88 percent ever since.

A tight labor market in a high-employment economy means that more men and women who are looking for jobs are finding them, and finding them faster. Those unemployed in 1998 had been searching for work an average of 14.5 weeks, down from 18.8 weeks in 1994, the earliest year with comparable data. The average length of a spell of unemployment is sensitive to the number of those undergoing long spells. In 1998, 14.1 percent of the unemployed had been searching for a job for over 27 weeks, far below the 1994 figure of 20.3 percent. By contrast, the share of those unemployed for less than 15 weeks rose from 64.2 percent to 73.6 percent during the same period.

Wages

One of the best documented labor market trends of the past few decades has been the decline in real wages among men. According to the Current Population Survey (CPS) . . . between 1979 and 1993 the median real wage for men fell by 11.1 percent. . . . However, progress has been made since 1996: the median real wage for men rose 1.7 percent in 1997 and 2.3 percent in

1998. Women experienced slightly stronger real wage growth in 1997 of 1.9 percent, but their wages were flat in 1998. Other measures of compensation show similar increases. Data reported by establishments (businesses and government agencies; the CPS data cited above are from surveys of households) show that, after stabilizing in the early 1990s, real hourly earnings of production and nonsupervisory workers have risen by 5.4 percent since 1993. The employment cost index . . . shows that total compensation (wages and salaries plus benefits) per worker increased by 2.2 percent in real terms from the third quarter of 1997 to the third quarter of 1998. Employers' wage and salary costs in that period rose by 2.7 percent and benefit costs (health insurance, paid leave, supplemental pay, retirement benefits, and the like) by 1.2 percent. Establishment data also show that the average workweek for production and nonsupervisory workers continued to hover between 34.4 and 34.8 hours, as it has since the mid-1980s.

Disadvantaged Groups

A strong labor market is particularly important to less advantaged groups in the labor market, such as workers with less education, younger workers, racial and ethnic minorities, and immigrants. The unemployment rates of these groups typically swing up and down more than the average during expansions and recessions. When employers find it hard to fill vacancies, they are more willing to hire and train workers whom they might pass over when they have fewer openings and an abundance of applicants.

For the same reason, a tight labor market can also pull up wages for disadvantaged workers. When labor is scarce, these workers can command better pay than at other times. The current expansion is especially important for disadvantaged workers given their experience from the late 1970s to the early 1990s, when wage inequality grew and less skilled groups faced persistently declining wages, on average.

The reasons for these wage declines and the rise in inequality that accompanied them were discussed in the 1997 *Economic Report of the President* and are still being debated, but it seems clear that demand for highly skilled workers has been expanding faster than supply, whereas demand for less skilled workers has declined even faster than supply. Even though the fraction of the population without a high school diploma has shrunk, as older, less educated cohorts have retired and been replaced by younger, more educated ones, the number of jobs available to high school dropouts shrank even faster from the late 1970s to the early 1990s. An important explanation is technological change in manufacturing, as a result of which the manufacturing sector requires fewer workers to produce more output than in the past. Competition from lower wage, low-skilled labor in other countries may also have been a factor, although most studies find that technological change is more important than increased international trade in explaining the declining demand in the United States for workers with no more than a high school diploma. Meanwhile, employment has expanded dramatically in the financial, professional, and business services industries, where most jobs require a college education or beyond.

Unions have historically helped less educated workers obtain higher wages than they could get otherwise. As employment in the highly unionized goods-producing, transport, and utilities industries has declined as a share of the work force since the 1950s, however, so has union membership. Like the American economy in general, the labor market has become more competitive in recent decades, with compensation and job security more often determined by market forces than before. This has benefited many American workers who were in a position to take advantage of the new job opportunities, but it has been hard on less skilled workers at the lower end of the wage distribution.

The Administration's efforts to keep the economy expanding and to make work pay have been particularly important to these workers. Not only is the overall labor market performing at record levels, but several groups of workers who had been experiencing low employment rates, declining wages, and high rates of unemployment have begun to show marked improvements. . . .

Low-Wage Workers

It is well established that workers at the lower end of the wage distribution have not fared well in recent decades: from the late 1970s through the early 1990s, the purchasing power of their wages declined. Between 1979 and 1993 the real hourly wages of male and female workers (including part-timers) at the 10th percentile of the wage distribution fell by 14.8 percent and 15.8 percent, respectively. . . . More recently, however, these lowest paid workers have seen significant gains. Real hourly wages for men 16 and older at the 10th and 20th percentiles have increased by about 6 percent since 1993, with especially large gains in the past 2 years. One might expect the earnings of low-wage women to have declined in recent years as supply expanded when a large number of them left welfare and entered the labor force. But on the contrary, wage increases for women were significant, with wages for those at the 20th percentile increasing by 4.7 percent since 1993.

These gains have not been confined to the lower end of the wage distribution. Real hourly earnings of the median male worker have increased by 3.6 percent since 1993, while those of the highest earning men and women (measured at the 90th percentile . . .) have increased by 6.4 percent and 6.2 percent, respectively.

Less Educated Workers

Education is a key determinant of labor market success, and much of the decrease in real wages for low-wage workers over the past two decades may be due to changes in the economy that have placed increasing value on skilled labor. The shift from goods-producing industries to services and to a more technology-intensive workplace has increased the premium on education, and particularly on workers who have at least a bachelor's degree. In this new economic environment it is important to monitor the progress of those with less education, who risk missing out on gains in the economy as a whole. During the current economic expansion, however, those with less education appear to be sharing in the benefits of the tight labor market in a number of ways.

Since 1993 the strong labor market has sharply reduced unemployment rates for workers at all levels of educational attainment. Particularly interesting, however, are changes in the employment-to-population ratio for people with different levels of attainment. . . . [H]igh school dropouts have experienced a much larger relative increase in their employment rate than have workers with more education. This increase is the joint result of increased labor force participation among dropouts and decreased unemployment among those dropouts who are in the labor force. The economy created enough low-skilled jobs to employ a larger share of the dropout population, which is shrinking as more-educated younger cohorts replace older ones. . . .

Workers with less education are not only experiencing employment gains; they are also beginning to share in wage gains. From 1993 to 1998, male high school graduates aged 20 and over without any college attendance experienced a real increase in their median wage of 2.8 percent. Although small, this was an improvement over their experience from 1979 to 1993, when their median wage fell by 21.8 percent. In 1998 the median real wage of male high school dropouts aged 20 and over finally increased, for the first time since at least 1979, by 7.0 percent. . . .

Blacks and Hispanics

After years of decline, the real wages of black men began to increase in 1993; they have risen by 5.8 percent since 1996 alone. Black women and Hispanic men and women have also experienced recent gains. . . . Because blacks and Hispanics are disproportionately represented in the lower end of the wage distribution, the long-run trends in their wages are similar to those for low-wage workers generally. Both of these minority groups have less education on average than the rest of the work force, and Hispanics are younger on average. When the real wages of workers without a college education started declining in the 1970s, the median real wages of black and Hispanic men started declining as well. In the last few years, however, their wages have been rising.

Employment opportunities are also expanding for minorities. The unemployment rates for blacks and Hispanics in 1998 were the lowest ever recorded, and were 4.1 and 3.6 percentage points lower, respectively, than in 1993. But minority unemployment is still unacceptably high, at 8.9 percent for blacks and 7.2 percent for Hispanics in 1998, compared with 3.9 percent for whites.

The tight labor market of the 1990s appears to be helping even young minority workers, who suffered greater wage declines than others in the

1980s and who typically have extraordinarily high unemployment rates. By 1998 the unemployment rate among black youth aged 16-24 was 20.7 percent, lower than in any year since the data series began in 1973. And the unemployment rate among young Hispanics aged 16-24 dropped 3.7 percentage points between 1993 and 1998. . . . Moreover, the median real wages of young black males aged 16-24 rose by 6.2 percent in 1998 alone. . . .

March

**U.S. Investigating Committee
on Olympic Bribery Scandal** **105**

**Transportation Safety Board
Chairman on Aviation Safety** **113**

**Statements Marking Addition
of Three Nations to NATO** **119**

**Clinton on Air War Against
Serbian Forces in Kosovo** **134**

**United Nations Observer on
Human Rights Situation in Iraq** **144**

U.S. INVESTIGATING COMMITTEE ON OLYMPIC BRIBERY SCANDAL
March 1, 1999

The Olympics—for millions of people around the world a hopeful symbol of individual excellence, teamwork, and international cooperation—came under unprecedented criticism during 1999 because of a scandal involving greed. The scandal led to revelations of cozy relationships and bribery among top Olympics officials, tarnishing the once sterling reputation of the Olympics and forcing the adoption of reforms.

The scandal became public in December 1998 with reports that backers of a bid by Salt Lake City, Utah, to host the winter Olympics in 2002 had provided expensive vacations and other gifts to members and relatives of the International Olympics Committee (IOC), which choose sites for the quadrennial competitions. Investigations quickly confirmed that more than a dozen IOC members had accepted gifts, for themselves and family members, which were intended to influence their 1995 decision on where to hold the 2002 Olympics. Reports surfaced that Olympics officials had accepted similar gifts over the years on behalf of the Olympics bids by other cities, including Sydney's for the 2000 summer Olympics and Atlanta's for the 1996 summer Olympics.

Six IOC members were expelled and four resigned during the year. An IOC-appointed commission recommended reforms in basic management of the Olympics system, which the IOC adopted in December. The Justice Department launched a criminal investigation into the matter, which was still underway at year's end. Congress threatened to intervene by placing restrictions on U.S.-based sponsors who provided the bulk of financial support for the Olympics but backed off once the reforms were put in place.

The Salt Lake City Bribes

Salt Lake City news organizations in November and December 1998 provided the first public details about the frantic efforts of the Salt Lake City Olympics Organizing Committee to win IOC approval for the winter games in 2002. Initial reports said the Salt Lake committee had paid for, or arranged for, expensive vacations, college tuition, medical treatment, and even jobs for IOC members and their relatives.

An IOC investigating committee, headed by Montreal lawyer Richard W. Pound (an IOC vice president), quickly confirmed details of the news reports and found other incidents of wrongdoing in the Salt Lake City bid. Pound's panel submitted a report to the IOC on January 24. That report said fourteen IOC members or their relatives had received gifts with an estimated value of nearly $800,000 from the Salt Lake Olympic organizers.

Meeting at Olympics headquarters in Lausanne, Switzerland, after receiving the report, the IOC executive committee voted to recommend the expulsion of six members, accepted the resignation of a seventh member, issued a warning to one other member, and continued investigating the actions of three additional members. Two other members had resigned previously in response to reports about gifts to their family members, and another member implicated in the scandal had died by the time of the January action. The punishments were by far the most severe ever imposed upon top Olympics officials in the movement's history. Several of those punished said they would appeal the disciplinary action to the full Olympics committee.

On February 9, three weeks after the IOC executive committee action, the Salt Lake committee issued its own investigating report providing new details on payments made on behalf of IOC members and their families. The Salt Lake committee had paid for such things as shopping trips, violin and ski lessons, medical treatments, college tuition, and trips to the Super Bowl for IOC members and their relatives. Two Salt Lake representatives even flew to Washington, D.C., to help the daughter of one IOC member move into a new apartment. In all, the report said twenty-four IOC members had received gifts of one type or another, ten more than the fourteen members implicated in the earlier IOC investigation.

Among those named in the February 9 report was Kim Un Yong, a member of the IOC executive committee who had been considered a possible successor to the committee's long-time chairman, Juan Antonio Samaranch. The report said the Salt Lake Olympics organizers had arranged and paid for a job for Kim's son and had arranged for his daughter to perform with the Utah Symphony. Kim was not among the members who had been punished by the IOC on January 24.

The report laid most of the blame for the bribes on the two men who had headed the Salt Lake Olympics committee when it was appealing to the IOC for the 2002 games: former president Tom Welch and vice president David R. Johnson. Lawyers for the two men said their clients had done nothing illegal but had simply followed precedents by other cities in their bids to host the Olympics. Welch had resigned as committee president in 1997.

Utah governor Mike Leavitt praised the February 9 report and said it was a major step in correcting mistakes of the past. "Olympic corruption didn't start here, but it must end here," he said.

Later that day, Olympics officials received the first solid indication that the bribery scandal might have serious financial consequences. David D'Alessandro, president and chief operations officer of the John Hancock Mutual Life Insurance Company, said he was suspending negotiations with NBC, which had broadcast rights for the Olympics. D'Alessandro said his company had paid $50 million to be designated the "official" life insurance and annuities company of the Olympics but would not "buy a nickel" of advertising for the Olympics until the IOC "is going in the right direction." Other corporations that had been major sponsors of the Olympics later voiced similar sentiments, adding to the pressure on Olympics officials.

Report of U.S. Committee

A third investigation of the Olympic bribery scandal was led by a five-member panel appointed by the U.S. Olympic Committee and chaired by former senator George Mitchell, the Maine Democrat who also played a key role in peace talks for Northern Ireland. Mitchell's panel, the Special Bid Oversight Committee, on March 1 released a damning report that urged wide-range reforms at all levels of the Olympics system, from the IOC down to local organizing committees. "The credibility of the Olympic movement has been gravely damaged and reform must occur," Mitchell said at a New York news conference in releasing the report.

Mitchell's commission said the Salt Lake committee had reported spending $3 million on gifts and other benefits for IOC members during its 1989–1995 campaign to win the 2002 winter Olympics. But that figure "understates" the actual total, the commission said, because it did not include "value in-kind" gifts—such as medical benefits, jobs, clothing, travel, and other items—provided by other organizations under arrangements with the Salt Lake committee. Adding the value of those gifts would put the total benefits paid to IOC members at between $4 million and $7 million, the Mitchell commission said.

The commission rejected the contention of the Salt Lake ethics panel that former Salt Lake committee officials Welch and Johnson were primarily to blame. "It strains credulity to believe that so many responsible citizens could participate in such a long and highly public campaign to influence IOC members and spend so much money in the process, but that only Messrs. Welch or Johnson were aware of the improprieties surrounding these activities," the Mitchell panel said. "Rather, it appears that an 'everybody does it' attitude took hold and many good people in Salt Lake City got swept up in what was seen as a good civic effort."

The commission said the bribery scandal stemmed from the fact that the Olympics had become "big business" and there was "intense competition" among communities to host the events. Furthermore, weak regulations within the Olympic organization and a tradition of secrecy in decision-making had permitted the growth of a "broader culture of improper gift giving" by cities wooing the IOC, the commission said. The Olympic organiz-

ers in Salt Lake City "did not invent this culture," the commission said. "They joined one that was flourishing."

In calling for reforms throughout the Olympics system, the Mitchell commission said the basis should be the concept of "fair play"—that the selection of Olympics sites "should not be weighed in favor of a city that spends the most on IOC members" but rather on the basis of "which city can best stage the Olympics games."

The commission also recommended that bid cities be prohibited from making gifts of more than "nominal value" to Olympics officials, including IOC members; that the U.S. Olympics Committee strengthen its oversight of the site selection process involving U.S. cities; that the IOC make "fundamental reforms" such as setting term limits for members, establishing and enforcing rules on the acceptance of gifts, and making public the audits of its financial records; and that the U.S. government consider designating the IOC a "public international organization," thereby making its operations subject to U.S. antibribery laws.

IOC Expels Six Members

On March 17–18, the full IOC held its first meeting since the beginning of the bribery scandal and took initial steps toward reforms. With 90 of the 108 current members in attendance, the committee voted to expel 6 members who had refused to resign after being named in the earlier IOC report. The committee also voted to continue the investigation of charges against Kim, the member whose son and daughter had received benefits from the Salt Lake committee.

In addition, the committee, by a vote of 86–2, with 2 abstentions, voiced its confidence in Samaranch, who had been the IOC president since 1980. Samaranch had not been linked personally to the Salt Lake City bribes, but critics outside the IOC said he had long tolerated the payment of benefits to IOC members by local organizing committees. The IOC named a committee to recommend institutional reform, and Samaranch took the chairmanship.

Despite the unprecedented expulsion of some members, the IOC's actions did little to convince some critics that it was taking the bribery scandal seriously. "This is not cleaning house," said Kenneth Duberstein, a member of the Mitchell commission. "This is the beginning of the cleaning of one room." And John McCain, an Arizona Republican who chaired the Senate Commerce, Science, and Transportation Committee and had sponsored legislation to review the IOC's tax-exempt status, denounced Samaranch for failing to name an independent committee on reforms. "I am afraid the IOC leadership is less concerned about reform than in preserving the power of an elite few," McCain said.

IOC Adopts Reforms

The IOC reform committee met throughout the summer and fall, and on October 30 approved a list of fifty recommendations, which were made pub-

lic November 24. The eighty-two member committee included numerous Olympics officials, athletes, and public figures, such as former secretary of state Henry Kissinger and former United Nations secretary general Boutros Boutros-Ghali.

A major recommendation would revamp the IOC membership to include (for the first time) fifteen active Olympic athletes elected by their peers, as well as public figures and representatives of national Olympic committees and international sports federations. Members would serve eight-year, renewable terms and would be subject to mandatory retirement at age seventy (current members could serve until age eighty). Other recommendations would require that cities bidding to host the Olympics sign contracts including a code of conduct with sanctions for violations, would prohibit or strictly control visits to bidding cities by IOC members, and would require that the IOC publish financial reports for the first time.

Meeting at its Lausanne headquarters on December 12, the IOC adopted the measures urged by Samaranch and his reform panel. Most of the proposals were adopted by unanimous votes, and only one became a serious point of contention. Strengthening the proposal of his own reform committee, Samaranch proposed that IOC members be prohibited from visiting cities that were bidding to host Olympics. Thirty-six members took the floor to discuss that proposal during the IOC debate, most of them speaking against it. But on the vote, the ban was adopted 89–10, with 1 abstention.

Samaranch declared the IOC meeting a success. "The problem we faced at the beginning of the year, today we will say this problem is solved," he said. Three days later, Samaranch became the first IOC president ever to appear before Congress. Testifying before the House Commerce Subcommittee on Oversight and Investigations, Samaranch defended his handling of the bribery scandal and said that "we've cleaned house" by expelling members and adopting what he called a "fundamental package of reforms."

In a city where political connections mean everything, Samaranch also received a boost from a well-connected critic—Kenneth Duberstein, a member of the Mitchell commission and a former White House chief of staff under President George Bush. Testifying after Samaranch, Duberstein said the IOC needed "close monitoring" by outsiders but told the subcommittee that the reform package "represents real progress."

> *Following is the executive summary of the report submitted to the U.S. Olympics Committee on March 1, 1999, by the Special Bid Oversight Commission, chaired by former senator George Mitchell and with Kenneth Duberstein, Donald Fehr, Roberta Cooper Ramo, and Jeffrey G. Benz as members:*

This Commission was created by Bill Hybl, the President of the United States Olympic Committee (USOC). He promised us full support and total independence and he kept his promises. For that we thank him.

Throughout this process, the USOC has demonstrated a deep concern for the problems facing the Olympic Movement and a willingness to learn from the mistakes of the past including, its own. For that we commend them.

The findings and recommendations in our report are exclusively those of the members of this Commission and its counsel. We are unanimous in our conclusions; there is no disagreement among us. Each member of the Commission volunteered many hours of time and effort. Counsel worked exceptionally hard to complete this report in a tight time frame.

The troubling events in Salt Lake City and other host cities are attributable to the fact that ethical governance has not kept pace with the rapid expansion of the Olympic Movement. The Olympic Games have become big business for sponsors host cities athletes and the organizations that make up the Olympic Movement.

The intense competition to host the Olympic Games, coupled with the multi-billion dollar enterprise that results from winning that competition, have exposed the weaknesses in the Movement's governing structure and operational controls. Despite the fact that everyone recognizes the Olympics to be a huge commercial enterprise, the IOC and its constituent organizations lack the accountability and openness in keeping with the role the Olympic Games play in the world today. The commercial success of the Olympic Games creates both the opportunity to better the Games and the potential for abuse. To preserve the integrity of the Olympic Games, especially with the public, there must be reform at every level of the Olympic Movement.

It was wrong for Salt Lake City officials to give money to IOC members and their families to win their votes. But what happened in Salt Lake City was not unique. In 1991, Toronto officials reported to the IOC an experience in the Olympic site selection process. In strikingly prophetic language, they warned of the consequences of such improper behavior. The Toronto prophecy has come true. As a result, credibility of the Olympic Movement has been gravely damaged.

As the organization with exclusive responsibility over the conduct of the Olympic Games when held in the United States, the USOC shares responsibility for the improper conduct of the bid and organizing committees in Salt Lake City. This responsibility stems from its failure to assure that United States candidate cities not seek to influence IOC members in the selection process by improperly providing them with things of value. This responsibility also extends to the USOC by virtue of the admitted recognition by certain USOC personnel that the bid and organizing committees were using the USOC's International Assistance Fund to influence or pay back IOC members for their site selection votes.

We were asked to review "the circumstances surrounding Salt Lake City's bid to host the Olympic Winter Games" and to make recommendations "to improve the policies and procedures related to bid processes." We have done that. In the process, we have concluded that it will be impossible to improve such policies and procedures unless there is significant change by and within the IOC. That is because the activity in which the Salt Lake committees engaged was part of a broader culture of improper gift giving in which candidate cities provided things of value to IOC members in an effort to buy their votes. This culture was made possible by the closed nature of the IOC and by the absence of ethical and transparent financial controls in its operations.

In each improper transaction, there was a giver and a taker; often the transaction was triggered by a demand from the taker. We do not excuse or condone those from Salt Lake City who did the giving. What they did was wrong. But, as we have noted, they did not invent this culture; they joined one that was already flourishing.

The rationale behind the governance changes proposed by the Commission is that the integrity of the Olympic Movement must be restored and protected. Reform and restoration will be effective only if they reach the entire Olympic Movement. The IOC must be reformed. For too long, it has tolerated the culture of improper gift giving, which affected every city bidding for the Olympic Games. The Commission's call for reform is rooted in the concept of fair play. Competition should not be weighted in favor of a city that spends the most on IOC members. The selection process should be free of improper influence on IOC members and should be made, instead, on the basis of which city can best stage the Olympic Games.

We believe those concerned about the future of the Olympic Games must recognize that true accountability for this mess does not end with the mere pointing of the finger of accusation at those who engaged in the improper conduct. Those responsible for the Olympic trust should have exercised good management practices, should have inquired into the purpose and propriety of programs, should have followed expenditures, and should have set a proper framework for those competing to host the Games.

In our Report we make a series of recommendations Principal among them are:

1. Bid cities should be prohibited from giving to members of the USOC or the IOC anything of more than nominal value, and from directly paying the expenses of members of the USOC or IOC. Travel to bid cities and other expenses should be paid out of a central fund administered by the USOC in the selection of a United States candidate city, and out of a central fund administered by the IOC in the selection of a host city.

2. The USOC must strengthen its oversight of the site selection process by:

(a) establishing an independent Office of Bid Compliance;

(b) prohibiting bid and candidate cities from having or participating in any international assistance program;

(c) strictly applying the criteria for the award and administration of its International Assistance Fund; and

(d) strengthening its Bid Procedures Manual and its Candidate City Agreement.

3. The IOC must make fundamental structural changes to increase its accountability to the Olympic Movement and to the public:

(a) a substantial majority of its members should be elected by the National Olympic Committees for the country of which they are citizens, by the International Federations, and by other constituent organizations. The athlete members should be chosen by athletes. There should be members from the public sector who best represent the interests of the public;

(b) Its members and leaders should be subject to periodic re-election with appropriate term limits;

(c) Its financial records should be audited by an independent firm, and the results of the audit disclosed publicly, at least yearly; and

(d) appropriate gift giving rules and strict travel and expense rules should be adopted and vigorously enforced.

4. The USOC should request the President of the United States to consider, in consultation with other governments, naming the IOC "a public international organization" within the meaning of Foreign Corrupt Practices Act, as amended.

The IOC should not award the Olympic Games to any city whose country has not taken steps to enact a law that applies the principles of the Anti-Bribery Convention of the Organization for Economic Cooperation and Development, signed by 34 governments, including the United States. Of the twenty-one nations that have hosted or are scheduled to host the Olympic Games, nineteen are signatories to the OECD Convention. Only the cities of Moscow and Sarajevo are located in countries that are not signatories to the Convention. The Convention entered into force on February 15, 1999.

Timely aggressive reform goes hand-in-hand with acceptance of responsibility. It is the true measure of commitment. Each Olympic entity has pledged to reform. The seriousness of that commitment and the credibility of the Olympic Movement turn on the extent to which that reform is undertaken. The Olympic flame must burn clean once again.

TRANSPORTATION SAFETY BOARD CHAIRMAN ON AVIATION SAFETY
March 10, 1999

Embattled federal agencies continued to struggle during 1999 with the task of helping promote safety and security at the nation's airlines and airports. The Federal Aviation Administration (FAA) was working to implement recommendations for improved safety inspections but was continuing to experience management problems, according to a report by the congressional watchdog agency, the General Accounting Office (GAO). And the National Transportation Safety Board (NTSB)—the agency that investigated crashes of airliners and trains and had been highly critical of the FAA—came in for criticism itself; a report found that agency was underfunded, overworked, and badly managed.

Testifying before a House subcommittee on March 10, NTSB Chairman Jim Hall sought to focus attention on air safety standards in other countries and at foreign-owned airlines. There was a "growing likelihood" that Americans traveling overseas would use foreign airlines, many of which did not have safety records comparable to U.S. air carriers, he said.

The only U.S.-related commercial air disaster of 1999 involved a foreign airliner. On October 31, a half-hour after taking off from New York's Kennedy Airport, Egyptair Flight 990 crashed into the Atlantic Ocean south of Nantucket Island. All 217 people on board were killed. Investigators quickly developed evidence appearing to show that one of pilots may have put the plane into a deliberate dive, but no formal findings had been issued by year's end.

FAA's New Inspection Program

The FAA was responsible for monitoring the safety of the nation's airline industry, as well as staffing the air traffic control network. For years the FAA had been criticized by government watchdog agencies and aviation experts on numerous grounds, including mismanagement, misplaced priorities, and excessive reliance on bureaucratic red tape.

A high-level commission headed by Vice President Al Gore in 1996 and 1997 issued reports containing dozens of recommendations for improving aviation safety and security—including a massive revamping of the FAA's air traffic control network. The process of implementing many of the Gore commission recommendations began in 1997 and continued through 1999, but the expensive work on the air traffic control system was expected to take many years. (Gore commission, Historic Documents of 1997, p. 116; Reports on airline safety, Historic Documents of 1998, p. 169)

Implementing suggestions by the Gore commission and the GAO, the FAA in October 1998 began a new system of airline safety inspections. The new Air Transportation Oversight System was intended to make inspections more thorough and useful, in large part by replacing spot-checks by individual inspectors with a more systematic approach using teams that examined a broad range of problems with airlines and their equipment. The FAA said it was stepping up its training of inspectors, an area that had been widely criticized.

In a review for Congress, the GAO on June 28 praised the general approach of the new FAA inspection program but said it had so far shown only limited success in reaching the stated goals. The GAO cited numerous management problems, including that FAA was still failing to make sure that inspectors were qualified, that it had not provided enough guidance to enable inspectors to do their jobs, and that it was having problems with high turnover of inspectors and assigning inspectors to the proper locations. The FAA did not dispute the substance of the GAO report but complained that its negative tone might imply that the new safety program should be abandoned.

Airport Security Failings

Another perennial issue for the FAA and the nation's aviation industry involved airport security—or the lack of it. Over the years the GAO and other agencies had produced numerous reports saying that airports needed to tighten security procedures, especially to prevent unauthorized individuals from entering sensitive areas.

Investigators for the Transportation Department—the parent agency of the FAA—in December offered the latest evidence that airport security remained inadequate. Undercover agents from the department's inspector general's office easily penetrated supposedly "secure" areas at major airports, including those in New York City, Washington, D.C., Atlanta, Chicago, and Miami. Agents walked unnoticed into cargo areas, through boarding gates, and even managed to board planes without showing tickets or boarding passes. The agents made 173 attempts to enter areas where they were not allowed; they succeeded in 117 of those tries.

In a statement, Inspector General Kenneth Mead said the FAA—which had supervisory authority over airport security—"has been slow to take actions necessary to strengthen access control requirements and adequately oversee the implementation of existing controls." The FAA responded to the report by saying it was taking steps to increase airport security by working with airlines to improve training of employees and to punish employees who violate security rules.

Safety Board Overload

The NTSB, which in years past had been critical of safety efforts at its sister agency, the FAA, came in for some criticism itself. The safety board was an independent federal agency responsible for monitoring the safety of both air and ground transportation. It was headed by five board members appointed by the president and confirmed by the Senate. In 1999 the board had about 400 staff members, one-third of whom were assigned to investigate aviation accidents.

A report by the Rand Institute of Santa Monica, California, released on December 9, said the board was underfunded, its staff was overworked, and many of its management and investigative procedures were "archaic." The NTSB had commissioned the study in 1998 at a cost of $400,000, in part to convince the administration and Congress of its need for a bigger budget. The board said the Rand study was the most complete analysis of its operations in its thirty-year history.

"The NTSB is an agency coping with serious overload and is in urgent need of additional resources and management reform," the report said. Cynthia Lebow, lead researcher on the study, told reporters that the board lacked adequate equipment, facilities, and staff to conduct the investigations for which it was responsible. The board's work was of a high quality, she said, but "that is only through the heroic efforts of its staff."

The study identified numerous management problems, some stemming from an inadequate budget but others the result of outdated and sloppy procedures. As one example, the Rand researchers found that the board lacked the organized budgeting system needed to determine how much its investigations cost.

The report also criticized the safety board's reliance on those involved in airline crashes—including the airlines, plane manufacturers, and others—to provide technical expertise for investigations. This so-called party system enabled the board to keep down its costs but also compromised the board's independence in conducting investigations. Rand researchers acknowledged that the board in many cases had no choice but to rely on the parties involved in a crash for help, but suggested that the board also could get independent assistance from the Pentagon, NASA, and other agencies with technical expertise.

Hall accepted the general thrust of the Rand report and said it bolstered his contention that the board needed an additional forty to fifty staff members. Hall blamed the White House Office of Management and Budget for repeatedly "zeroing out" his annual requests for additional funding.

Boeing 737 Issues

The NTSB issued two reports during 1999 on mechanical problems with the Boeing 737, the world's most popular airliner. The board for nearly eight years had been investigating numerous incidents involving the plane, including a 1991 United Airlines crash in Colorado that killed 25 people and a 1994 USAir crash near Pittsburgh that killed 132 people. The board praised the general safety record of the plane, but said specific shortcomings probably caused those two crashes and led to other serious problems.

In March the safety board said it had concluded that malfunctioning controls for the rudder—the movable portion of the horizontal tail fin—could force a plane into an uncontrollable dive. A key valve had been redesigned and was being installed on the 3,000 Boeing 737s around the world, but the board said that step was not sufficient. Instead, the board called for installation of multiple valves, similar to those used on most other commercial airliners.

"Consumer-Friendly" Rules at Airlines

Responding to growing passenger dissatisfaction with service, major U.S. airlines in June and September announced joint rules to improve customer service. In many cases the rules were little more than reformulations of existing regulations that airlines had never enforced; other cases involved new rules intended to respond to the most common passenger complaints. The airlines acted to head off proposals pending in both chambers of Congress for a passenger "bill of rights" legally requiring service improvements by the airlines.

Several of the new rules dealt with improved procedures for notifying passengers when their flights were delayed, canceled, or overbooked. For years airliner passengers had complained that most airlines were unable or unwilling to provide timely information about such situations. Under the new rules, the airlines promised that their personnel would have better access to flight information and would be instructed to pass that information on to passengers. The airlines also promised to guarantee quoted fares for twenty-four hours, to tell passengers about the lowest available fares, and improve procedures for finding and delivering lost baggage.

> *Following is an excerpt from testimony delivered March 10, 1999, to the House Appropriations Subcommittee on Transportation and Related Agencies by Jim Hall, chairman of the National Transportation Safety Board:*

As you are all probably aware, 1998 was the first year that no passenger died on a scheduled Part 121 or Part 135 carrier in the United States. This is a remarkable achievement considering the statistics: in 1998, the airlines carried about 611 million passengers on almost 11 million flights. The more than 500,000 people employed by scheduled air carriers in the United States and the 40+ thousand employees of the FAA should be commended for this outstanding record.

My prepared testimony discusses five safety issues, but in the interest of time, I will briefly discuss only 2—flight recorders and collision avoidance systems. I will, of course, be happy to answer your questions on these and the other three issues—aircraft icing, runway incursions, and child safety.

The upgrading of accident recorders is a top priority at the Safety Board, and an issue on the Board's Most Wanted list of safety improvements since 1990. The purpose of flight recorders—whether it be a cockpit voice recorder [CVR] or a flight data recorder—is to collect data that can help us learn. What these important devices tell us can prevent accidents. The Safety Board and this Subcommittee have for many years prodded the FAA to require upgraded recorders on transport category aircraft, but sadly most of the U.S. fleet is still equipped with outmoded models. Just two weeks ago, a control incident involving a Metrojet Boeing 737 occurred. That aircraft had an 11-parameter recorder on board. Once again, because of FAA and industry inaction, the Safety Board does not have important information needed to find out what happened on that 737.

As you are aware, the Safety Board has urgently recommended that the FAA require all transport category aircraft to have upgraded flight recorder capability and asked that the FAA expedite this action with regard to the Boeing 737. Although the FAA has published a final rule mandating the inclusion of almost all of the data parameters we originally recommended, we are concerned that the completion of the upgrade is 3 years away. In addition, the FAA chose not to single out the 737 as urgently requested by the Board. The Board's safety recommendation asked for an effective date of December 30, 1995—the FAA's rule has an effective date of 2002.

In addition, the Metrojet's in-flight event was not preserved on the aircraft's cockpit voice recorder because the 30-minute continuous loop had recorded over the event. Important safety information is often lost on CVRs that record for only 30 minutes, and two years ago the Safety Board recommended that the FAA move expeditiously to equip aircraft with 2-hour cockpit voice recorders so that valuable investigative data could be retrieved during accident and incident investigations. To date, the FAA has yet to require the 2-hour recorder.

Another problem is the loss of recorder data due to interruption of aircraft electrical power. The Canadian's investigation of Swissair flight 111 has been hampered because the cockpit voice recorder and the digital flight data recorder both stopped nearly 6 minutes before the airplane hit the water. The NTSB and the Canadian Transportation Safety Board yesterday recommended that CVRs be retrofitted, on all airplanes required to carry both a CVR and an FDR, with a CVR that is capable of recording the last 2 hours of audio, and that it be fitted with an independent power source that will provide 10 minutes of operation whenever aircraft power to the recorder ceases.

The second issue I want to discuss is traffic alert collision avoidance systems [TCAS]. We believe the regulation regarding the phased installation program of TCAS II should include cargo aircraft. A week ago yesterday two large cargo planes nearly collided at 33,000 feet over Kansas after both planes apparently lost radio contact with an air traffic control center. Domestic air cargo nearly tripled between 1980 and 1996. The growth in cargo operations, including 8-million pounds of hazardous materials freight shipped by air daily, has brought about an increase in daytime flying for cargo operators, which means they are increasingly using the same airspace at the same time as passenger carriers. This traffic mix and density increases the challenge of maintaining safe separation among aircraft. While it is encouraging that since the incident last week the FAA has issued press statements that it now favors installation of TCAS on cargo carriers, no official documentation has been released.

Mr. Chairman, before closing I would like to briefly mention the Board's increased activity in foreign aviation accident investigations. In 1998, 110 United States citizens were killed in foreign aviation accidents, and a United States citizen can be found on most air carrier flights anywhere in the world. This is, in part, as a result of ever-increasing code-sharing arrangements with foreign airlines. You will recall that several years ago the FAA acted on Safety Board recommendations regarding one level of safety between smaller commuter airlines and large air carriers. As code sharing agreements continue to increase, we plan to monitor this situation closely to determine whether safety recommendations are appropriate.

It is apparent to me, Mr. Chairman, that issues of aviation safety are no longer parochial, but are international in nature. The NTSB expects to be more and more involved in foreign accident and incident investigations, as U.S. airlines become more entwined with foreign counterparts, and U.S. aircraft and engine manufacturers find themselves competing more and more with foreign companies. . . .

STATEMENTS MARKING ADDITION OF THREE NATIONS TO NATO
March 12, 1999

The Czech Republic, Hungary, and Poland on March 12, 1999, officially joined the North Atlantic Treaty Organization (NATO), expanding the alliance membership to nineteen nations and formally ending the sharp military and political divisions between western and central Europe.

On April 23–24, the leaders of those three countries joined other NATO leaders at a gala summit meeting in Washington, D.C., to celebrate the alliance's fiftieth anniversary. The glow of that summit was somewhat dimmed by the fact that NATO was then engaged in its largest military operation ever: an aerial bombardment of the former Yugoslavia to force Belgrade to end its ruthless grip on the territory of Kosovo. (Kosovo bombing, p. 134)

The Kosovo war illustrated the tensions facing NATO as it entered a new era as the most successful alliance in modern history. Although there was little disagreement within NATO that something had to be done about Kosovo, alliance members were not entirely united on the wisdom of the U.S.-led bombing campaign. The Kosovo operation served as a painful reminder to some European leaders of their own inability to deal with conflicts on the continent without turning to Washington for leadership. The European Union on December 10 approved a plan for its own military force for crisis intervention should the United States not want to get involved. European leaders acknowledged that simply putting such a plan in place was potentially difficult and contentious. (European defense force, p. 817)

NATO Expansion

Largely at the initiative of the Truman administration, NATO was founded in 1949 to provide a military counterbalance to the Soviet Union, which had consolidated its hold on nearly all of Eastern Europe in the aftermath of World War II. The original alliance had twelve members, all on continental Europe except for the United States, Canada, the United Kingdom, and Iceland. Greece and Turkey joined in 1952, and Germany in 1956.

With the admission of Spain in 1982, the alliance stretched across much of Europe. Countering NATO was the Warsaw Pact, the alliance of nations dominated by the Soviet Union.

NATO's founders gave the alliance two principal tasks: preventing Europe's persistent conflicts from erupting into another worldwide conflagration and thwarting Soviet expansion into the rest of Europe. Both assignments were fraught with peril and difficulty, but the remarkable unity among alliance members enabled NATO to achieve both purposes. There were conflicts in Europe in the five decades after World War II, but until the Kosovo crisis none seriously threatened to spread regionwide. The cold war between NATO and the Soviet alliance ended as peacefully as possible, starting with the dismantling of the Berlin Wall in 1989 and culminating with the collapse of the Soviet Union itself in 1991. No other alliance in modern history had been so successful in achieving its goals. (Soviet Union collapse, Historic Documents of 1991, p. 785)

With success came questions about NATO's future. Should NATO simply declare victory and disband? Or should an alliance committed to peace and democracy continue pursuing those goals in a world where both were under constant challenge? By the mid-1990s the Clinton administration was pursuing an activist approach to NATO's future, calling for admission of some of the former Soviet allies and proposing a "charter" between NATO and Russia (the successor to most of the Soviet Union) to calm Moscow's fears about the eastward expansion of NATO. Some U.S. allies in Europe took a different view of security issues in the post-cold war era and cut their military spending. (NATO expansion, Historic Documents of 1997, p. 514; Historic Documents of 1998, p. 912)

Eastern European countries responded eagerly to the prospect of joining NATO—even though doing so required them to modernize their military operations to meet NATO standards. From a list of a half-dozen serious prospects, NATO in 1997 selected the Czech Republic, Hungary, and Poland for early membership. Russia was adamantly opposed to the expansion of NATO into the former Warsaw Pact region, but the government of President Boris Yeltsin gradually became resigned to the fact that former Soviet allies were in fact about to become part of the Western alliance. NATO and Russia in 1997 signed a document called the "Founding Act" in which the alliance promised not to station nuclear weapons or large numbers of troops on the territory of its new members that had once been part of the Soviet empire.

Questions about NATO's expansion also arose in the West, including in the U.S. Senate, which was required to vote on an amendment to the Atlantic Alliance treaty that created NATO. Among the arguments raised by opponents were that antagonizing Russia was too risky, that expanding NATO could create new divisions in Europe similar to the "Iron Curtain" that separated West and East during the cold war, and that Washington inevitably would have to subsidize the costs of NATO expansion. Despite such arguments, the Senate overwhelmingly approved NATO expansion in 1998.

Even before the three new members were inducted into the alliance, all had participated in NATO operations, most importantly in Bosnia, where the alliance was enforcing the 1995 Dayton peace agreement. Hungarian engineers, for examples, had rebuilt dozens of bridges that were destroyed during the devastating civil war in Bosnia. (Bosnia peace, Historic Documents of 1995, p. 717; Historic Documents of 1997, p. 342)

For symbolic reasons, the Harry S Truman Presidential Library in Independence, Missouri, was chosen as the site for the ceremony at which the three new members would formally join NATO. Truman was president in the years immediately following World War II, and historians had generally given him and his secretary of state, Dean Acheson, chief credit for establishing NATO. Also for symbolic reasons—as well as to comply with diplomatic protocol—Secretary of State Madeline K. Albright presided over the March 12 ceremony at the Truman library. Albright was born in Prague, the daughter of a Czech diplomat, and as a child fled with her family to the West in 1948 after the communist takeover. Since becoming secretary of state in 1997, Albright had been one of the most outspoken proponents of NATO expansion.

Joining Albright at the ceremony were the foreign ministers of the three new NATO nations: Jan Kavan of the Czech Republic, Janos Martonyi of Hungary, and Bronislav Geremek of Poland. All three had been opponents of the communist regimes that ruled their countries for more than forty years. Geremek, who had been a leader of the anticommunist Solidarity labor movement, declared: "Poland forever returns where she has always belonged; the free world." Recalling popular uprisings against the communist regimes in each of the three nations, Geremek said Czechs, Hungarians, and Poles "have proved the democratic credentials which give them the right to be here today."

Kavan acknowledged that NATO membership brought with it serious responsibilities for each of three nations, including the ability to share in the collective defense of all alliance members. The armed forces of all three countries lagged well behind those of existing NATO members, and each was barely able to meet NATO's minimum standards for admission. "We are determined not to become a burden to the alliance," Kavan said. "We are prepared to fulfill our part of the responsibilities and the commitments of member states, and to meet all the obligation and duties which stem from this membership."

In her speech celebrating the status of NATO's three new allies, Albright emphasized the importance of maintaining the strength and unity of the alliance. "[I]f NATO does not respond to the twenty-first-century security challenges facing our region, who will? If NATO cannot prevent aggressors from engulfing whole chunks of Europe in conflict, who can? And if NATO is not prepare to respond to the threat posed to our citizens by weapons of mass destruction, who will have that capability?" she asked.

Washington Summit

Five weeks after the ceremony in Independence, NATO heads of state and other officials gathered in Washington, D.C., for a glittering celebration of the alliance's fiftieth anniversary. In planning for years, that celebration

121

was at least somewhat overshadowed by NATO's air war against Yugoslav forces in Kosovo. Rather than discussing long-term issues—such as the future of the alliance in the post-cold war world—NATO officials spent much of the summit trying to figure out how best to bring the Kosovo conflict to a successful conclusion.

Ostensibly, the primary business of the summit was to approve a document called a "Strategic Concept" that had been in preparation for more than a year. That document outlined both general and specific steps for how the alliance was carry to out its responsibilities in the twenty-first century. None of the points represented a dramatic departure from how NATO had been functioning in the nearly ten years since the collapse of Soviet communism. Rather, they were incremental steps for dealing with other challenges, such as the proliferation of nuclear and chemical weapons and the outbreak of regional and ethnic conflicts following the disintegration of Yugoslavia and the Soviet Union. NATO leaders also approved a forty-five-point "Washington Communiqué" that covered many of the same items as those in the "Strategic Concept" but in broader political terms.

One issue left unresolved at the summit was the pace of future NATO expansion. Some NATO members had been pressing for rapid addition of nations such as Slovakia and Romania, while others had been urging a pause in further expansion, in part to calm Russian jitters. NATO leaders gave priority to Romania and Slovenia, two countries that had been considered for membership as of 1999 but had been delayed because they had not yet made all the military and political reforms required for membership in the alliance. The other nations put on the list for potential membership were, in order: the three Baltic states of Estonia, Latvia and Lithuania; Bulgaria; Slovakia; Macedonia; and Albania.

Following are excerpts from statements made at a ceremony in Independence, Missouri, on March 12, 1999, by Jan Kavan, foreign minister of the Czech Republic; Janos Martonyi, minister of foreign affairs of the Republic of Hungary; Bronislav Geremek, minister of foreign affairs of the Republic of Poland; and Madeleine K. Albright, secretary of state of the United States, marking the accession of the Czech Republic, Hungary, and Poland to full membership on the North Atlantic Treaty Organization:

Foreign Minister Kavan of the Czech Republic: Madame Secretary [Albright], Mr. [Bronislav] Geremek, Mr. [Janos] Martonyi, ladies and gentleman, my country's accession to the North Atlantic Treaty fills me with satisfaction and pride. The deposit of ratification instruments seals off the entry of the Czech Republic into this successful and very important alliance.

It is a very special and a unique feeling of a Czech politician to deposit these certification papers in a country where the basic ideas and principles of the new Czechoslovak state were first formulated and announced in 1918 in Philadelphia. It is therefore symbolic to mark today our historic accession to NATO in the country which stood at the birth of independent Czechoslovakia. And we will always remember the invaluable role of President Woodrow Wilson as the new Czechoslovakia was founded on treaties for which he was primarily responsible.

I am satisfied that we proved to be able to meet the minimal military requirements in time for today's accession to this efficient and strong political and military alliance. We appreciate that we are now an integral part of NATO's collective defense system. And we are determined not to become a burden to the Alliance—just a country. We are prepared to fulfill our part of the responsibilities and the commitments of member states, and to meet all the obligations and duties which stem from this membership.

We highly appreciate that our accession to NATO was fully supported by all member states of the Alliance. We also interpret it as recognition of the fact that we all share common values and common interests.

Today, at the moment of joining the Alliance, allow me to express my conviction that the Czech traumas of this century has now been relegated forever only to history. I have in mind, for example, the dismemberment of the independent, democratic, pre-War Czechoslovakia which was betrayed by its allies; the fascist protectorate; the horrors of World War II; the 40 years of communist dictatorship and the death of the Prague Spring, which was crushed by the Soviet-led Warsaw Pact invasion.

At the same time, the entry of the three new member nations into NATO is also a great vindication for the renewed Czech democracy, helped to get on its feet also by the United States of America, and for the transformation reforms for which the "Velvet Revolution" opened the way almost ten years ago. More generally, the admission of the first three new NATO members is a recognition of the strategic changes in Central and Eastern Europe after the fall of the Berlin Wall. It's also a manifestation of NATO's adaptation to the challenges of the post-Cold War period.

The process of European integration of today would not be possible without active and strong involvement of the United States since the Second World War. We, the Central Europeans, will remember what the United States has done for the Old Continent. NATO is the strongest link between Europe and North America. The Czech Republic shares the interest to keep this transatlantic link strong, in order to be able to deal with the risks and threats of the 21st Century security environment.

The Czech Republic also appreciates the value the United States and NATO attach to the concept of European defense identity. We fully support it, as we strongly believe that Europe should significantly contribute to its own defense and to the solutions of crises on its own continent. The NATO's new strategic concept will provide an updated political and conceptual basis for the foreseeable future. It will have to be far more clearly the basis for the new Article V missions, which are the most likely way of employing NATO's military power in the current situation.

We look forward to the successful Washington Summit, which will outline the future development of NATO, including the stages of its future enlargement. NATO is not only the bedrock of our common defense, but also an instrument for projecting cooperation, peace and stability beyond the treaty territory.

The Partnership for Peace has become the most successful cooperative security project in the post-Cold War world. We very much appreciate that the Alliance reached agreements on cooperation with both Russia and Ukraine. This, we believe, is very important for the European security of the 21st Century.

Allow me a brief personal note. I was in this area only once in my life. It was a few miles away from here, in Kansas City. The date was August 21, 1968, the day when Russian tanks swept into Prague and the occupation of Czechoslovakia began. The power of anger which then swept me is indescribable. And while working for the Czech opposition for the subsequent 20 years and cooperating closely with Polish and Hungarian opposition during that time, I was dreaming about the day when Central and Eastern Europe would become independent, democratic and secure. It is for me very symbolic that it is precisely here that we today accept a guarantee that my country will never again become a powerless victim of a foreign invasion.

Madame Secretary, ladies and gentlemen, the Czechs will remember the support of the American people and of its representatives for the country's entry into the Alliance. Today is a good occasion to thank the US Congress, President Clinton, you personally, Madame Secretary, and many others here in the United States for what you have done for us. Thank you all very much.

Foreign Minister Martonyi of the Republic of Hungary: Madame Secretary, Ministers, senators, congressmen, ladies and gentlemen, dear friends. Next year, Hungary will celebrate a very special anniversary, a thanksgiving for the millennium of her statehood. Ours has been a rich but stormy history.

Through all the struggles for freedom and independence, Hungarians have developed a deep sense of belonging to a larger entity, to the community of Western democracies. For a long time, it has been our aspiration to become part of this family. The best of Hungarians were dreaming of this when fighting foreign occupation and sinister ideologies forced upon them.

This is the part Hungarians (played) when they drove the first nail into the coffin of communism in 1956. It is my duty and a privilege for me to pay tribute here to the heroes of that desperate struggle—and now, ultimately, victorious struggle. How symbolic it is that the revolution which shook the empire of oppression flamed up from demonstrations of Solidarity with Poland.

In 1956, alien boots stamped out that flame in Budapest. But sparks from it reappeared on the streets of Prague in 1968. They reappeared again in the shipyard from Gdansk in 1981. They reappeared ten years ago when lawful revolutions swept through Central Europe to restore democracy there. It's not by chance that I share this rostrum with friends from Poland and the Czech Republic.

As Thomas Paine wrote, "Tyranny is not easily conquered, yet we have this consolation within us that the harder the conflict, the more glorious the triumph. What we attempt too cheap, we esteem too lightly."

For Hungarians, Czechs and Poles liberty was obtained very dear. We know that, having our freedom. Sovereign again, Hungary is now a genuine and stable democracy. A flourishing market economy has been established, and a historic choice has been made.

We Hungarians made this decision on our own, free from any outside interference. We applied for joining NATO, the largest network of security that history has ever known. Yet, the decision was not only about security. NATO accession is also about returning Hungary to her natural habitat. It has been our manifest destiny to rejoin those with whom we share the same values, interests and goals.

Let me thank the governments and the legislatures and all of the persons in the member states—all those who supported the cost of our membership. They understood that we wanted to join NATO for the same reasons for which no member wants to leave it. They know by joining the Alliance we want not to win but to prevent wars. They realize that NATO enlargement is not a zero-sum game but part of a prudent strategy benefiting all nations of Europe and all members of the Atlantic community.

George Bernard Shaw once said, "Liberty means responsibility. That's why most people dread it." We do not.

Hungarians know that membership in NATO is a combination of advantages to enjoy and obligations to meet. Hungary will continue to focus her attention on Central and Southeastern Europe. We want all its nations to be stable, democratic, prosperous and secure. In terms of development, it is the most dynamic region of the world. We want it to keep this distinction.

We want human rights to be fully respected; national identities to be fully preserved and expressed. For us, it is a matter of vital importance that our states of our region remain connected to Germany and NATO. Hungary will support their aspirations in two ways. First, we shall prove that new members can indeed add to the weight of the Alliance. Second, we will continue to engage prospective members and to have a meaningful partnership with them.

Ladies and gentlemen, in the past, Hungarians often complained of being abandoned or of standing up alone. At long last, that is over. Hungary has come home. We are back in the family. Together with all of you, we have just started a new chapter in history. From this day on, we are the closest of allies in our great endeavor: the quest for peace and prosperity.

As said by President Truman 54 years ago, "We all look forward to the day when the law, rather than force, will be the arbiter of international relations. We shall strive to make that day come soon. Until it does come, let us make sure that no possible aggressor is going to be tempted by any weakness on our part."

Dear friends, we shall show the world the strength of this commitment and the spirit of our alliance. Thank you.

Foreign Minister Geremek of the Republic of Poland: Madame Secretary of State, my dear friends the Czech and Hungarian Ministers, excellencies, ladies and gentlemen. Fifty-three years ago in nearby Fulton, Missouri, Winston Churchill delivered his famous speech, in which he said, "From Stettin in the Baltics to Trieste in the Adriatic, an Iron Curtain has descended and closed the continent."

Today with joy and pride, we celebrate the end of the bipolar blight symbolized by the Iron Curtain. This brings satisfaction especially to those who sacrificed so much in the struggle for freedom over the last 50 years.

For the people of Poland, the Cold War, which forcibly excluded our country from the West, ends with our entry to NATO. Poland is a member of the most powerful Alliance, bringing together democratic nations of Western Europe and North America, joining the vital process of bridging old divisions and contributes to the security and stability in Europe.

This remarkable achievement would not have taken place without the leadership, vision and courage of individuals who have played a pivotal role in this process. We owe our deep gratitude to President Bill Clinton and Secretary of State Madeleine Albright. We are grateful to the US Senate. We are grateful to the American people, who have continuously expressed their support for our aspirations.

Today's ceremony confirms that the Alliance is a community of values. The success of NATO over the last 50 years has been built on the principles of democracy, civil rights and liberties, shared by all of its members. The nations who join this community today were denied these values until 1989. On the streets of Budapest in 1956; Prague in 1968; and Gdansk in 1970 and 1981, they paid a heavy price. They have proved the democratic credentials which give them the right to be here today.

Poland in the Alliance will be a good and credible ally for good and bad weather. We are prepared to both take advantage of the rights of membership and build the obligations the membership carries. We shall contribute substantially to bolster this organization and to developing its political and military strengths. I want to assure our allies that we will not lack the determination, courage and imagination needed to bring forth our own capability as a member of the Alliance.

We are convinced that NATO must remain a defensive alliance based on the principle of solidarity. To quote President Harry Truman, "The security and the welfare of each member of this community depends upon the security and the welfare of all. None of us alone can achieve economic prosperity or military security. None of us alone can assure the continuance of freedom."

We consider the Alliance, to use Senator [Arthur] Vandenberg's words, "a fraternity of peace." We share the view that NATO has a wider role to play to further the cause of democracy, human rights and solidarity.

Let me say a word about the relations between America and Europe. Poland is a wholly dedicated advocate both of the processes of European integration and the strong transatlantic link. The United States has given the Atlantic community leadership, stability and strength. Europe continuously needs some American anchor for its security and growth. Conversely, American security and prosperity depends on a reliable and flourishing Europe. We should keep the door of the Alliance open for those who have fought for freedom of those nations in Central Europe. . . .

An Iron Curtain must never again descend on Europe. Also it would lack the rigidity of the old iron one; it would almost certainly become as cruel. It would keep us divided economically if not politically.

Based on common values, principles, NATO must promote a value-oriented approach to democracy, stability and peace. The challenge facing us in the coming century, the challenge of creating a new international order, must be an indispensable and inseparable part of our agenda. To meet this challenge, we must seek out democratic values incorporated in the Washington Treaty, the ability to defend ourselves and the strong transatlantic ties. These are the sources of our strength. We cannot let them fade away in the future.

Let me say in this room, just a few words in my language, in Polish.

(In Polish:) "This is a great day for Poland, as well as for millions of Poles scattered all over the world. Poland forever returns where she has always belonged: to the free world. Poland is no longer alone in the defense of her freedom. We are in NATO, as you used to say, for your freedom and ours."

For the Harry Truman Presidential Library, I bring from Poland some records of history of our road to freedom and to make them a poster of 1989 elections, with a picture of Gary Cooper from the film, *High Noon*.

It helped us in Poland to win. For the people of Poland, *High Noon* comes today. Dear friends, in an hour and some seconds, it's a great day for Poland and for the world. Thank you.

[The instruments are signed and deposited.]

Secretary of State Albright of the United States: . . . Minister [Jan] Kavan, Minister Martonyi, and Minister Geremek, excellencies from the diplomatic corps, Admiral Gough, General Anderson and other leaders of our armed forces, officials of the Truman Library—thank you for remembering my daughter—honored guests, colleagues, and friends, today is a day of celebration and re-dedication and remembrance and renewal.

Today we recognize in fact what has always been true in spirit. Today we confirm through our actions that the lands of King Stephen and Cardinal Mindszenty, Charles the Fourth and Vaclav Havel, Copernicus and Pope John Paul II reside fully and irrevocably within the Atlantic community for freedom. And to that I say, to quote an old Central European expression, "Hallelujah."

History will record March 12, 1999, as the day the people of Hungary, the Czech Republic and Poland strode through NATO's open door and assumed their rightful place in NATO's councils.

To them I say that President Clinton's pledge is now fulfilled. Never again will your fates be tossed around like poker chips on a bargaining table. Whether you are helping to revise the Alliance's strategic concept or engaging in NATO's partnership with Russia, the promise of "nothing about you without you," is now formalized. You are truly allies; you are truly home.

This is a cause for celebration not only in Prague, Budapest and Warsaw, but throughout the Alliance. For the tightening of transatlantic ties that we mark today inspired the vision of transatlantic leaders half a century ago. That generation, which in Dean Acheson's famous phrase was "present at the creation," emerged from the horror of World War II determined to make another such war impossible. They had seen—and paid in blood—the price of division; so their policies were inclusive. They wanted to help build a transatlantic community of prosperity and peace that would include all of Europe.

But between the 1947 offering of the Marshall Plan and the forging of NATO two years later, it became evident that the reality of their times did not match the boldness of their vision. The Iron Curtain descended; and across the body of Europe, a brutal and unnatural division was imposed. Now, due to bravery on both sides, that curtain has lifted, and links that should have been secured long ago are being soldered together.

Today is evidence of that. For this morning, NATO is joined by three proud democracies—countries that have proven their ability to meet Alliance responsibilities, uphold Alliance values and defend Alliance interests.

Since the decision to invite new members was first made, President Clinton has argued that a larger NATO would make America safer, our Alliance stronger and Europe more peaceful and united. Today, we see that this is already the case. For NATO's new members bring with them many strengths. Their citizens have a tradition of putting their lives on the line for liberty: Witness Hungary's courageous freedom fighters in 1956; the students who faced down tanks in the streets of Prague 12 years later; and the workers of Gdansk whose movement for Solidarity ushered in Europe's new dawn.

As young democracies, these countries have been steadfast in supporting the vision of an integrated Europe. Their troops are serving alongside NATO forces in Bosnia. And each is contributing to stability in its own neighborhood.

As a daughter of the region, and a former professor of Central and East European affairs, I know many Americans have not always had the understanding of this region that they now do. Earlier this century, when Jan Masaryk, son of the Czech President, came to the United States, an American Senator asked him, how is your father; and does he still play the violin?

Jan replied, sir, I fear that you are making a small mistake. You are perhaps thinking of Paderewski and not Masaryk. Paderewski plays the piano, not the violin, and was President not of Czechoslovakia, but of Poland.

Of our Presidents, Benes was the only one who played; but he played neither the violin nor the piano, but football. In all other respects, your information is correct.

Later, after his father had died and World War II had been fought, Jan Masaryk became Czechoslovak Foreign Minister—my father's boss. It soon became clear that the revival of Czechoslovak democracy and Czechoslovak aspirations to be part of the West would be short-lived.

Czechoslovakia was also invited to join the Marshall Plan. However, Foreign Minister Masaryk was summoned to Moscow and told that Czechoslovakia had to refuse the invitation. He returned to Prague to tell his colleagues, "I now know I am not the Foreign Minister of a sovereign country."

Masaryk's statement reminds us of another great gift the Czech Republic, Poland and Hungary bring to our Alliance for freedom: the living memory of living without freedom.

NATO's success has enabled generations protected by the Alliance to grow up and grow old under democratic rule. For that, we are enormously grateful.

But we must also guard against a danger. For there is a risk that to people who have never known tyranny, an Alliance forged before they were born to counter an enemy that no longer exists, to defend freedoms some believe are no longer endangered, may appear no more relevant than the fate of Central Europe did to some of our predecessors 60 years ago.

The Truman Library is a fit place for plain speaking. So let me speak plainly now. It is the job of each and every one of us, on both sides of the Atlantic, to bring home to the generations of today and tomorrow the compelling lessons of this century.

We must never fall back into complacency or presume that totalitarianism is forever dead or retreat in the face of aggression. We must learn from history, not repeat it. And we must never forget that the destinies of Europe and North America are inseparable; and that this is as true now as it was when NATO was founded 50 years ago.

Of course, there will always be differences between Europe and America. We have been aptly called cousins, but we will never be mistaken for clones. Today, there are splits on trade and other issues—some of which are quite controversial. But do not exaggerate, these are differences within the family.

However, I think I can speak for each of my Alliance colleagues when I say that on the central questions that affect the security and safety of our people, our Alliance is and will remain united, as it must. For the hopes of future generations are in our hands. We cannot allow any issue to undermine our fundamental unity. We must adapt our alliance and strengthen our partnerships. We must anticipate and respond to new dangers. And we must not count on second chances; we must get it right—now.

This requires understanding that the more certain we are in preparing our defense, the more certain we may be of defending our freedom without war. NATO is the great proof of that. For its success over five decades is measured not in battles won, but rather in lives saved, freedoms preserved and wars prevented. That is why President Truman said that the creation of NATO was the achievement in which he took the greatest pride.

Today we, too, have grounds for pride. For NATO enlargement is a sign that we have not grown complacent about protecting the security of our citizens. The nations entering our alliance today are the first new members since the Cold War's end, but they will not be the last. For NATO enlargement is not an event; it is a process.

It is our common purpose, over time, to do for Europe's east what NATO has already helped to do for Europe's west. Steadily and systematically, we will continue erasing without replacing the line drawn in Europe by Stalin's bloody boot.

When President Clinton welcomes his counterparts to Washington next month to mark NATO's 50th anniversary, they will affirm that the door of the Alliance does remain open; and they will announce a plan to help prepare aspiring members to meet NATO's high standards.

But enlargement is only one element in our effort to prepare NATO for its second 50 years. The Washington Summit will be the largest gathering of international leaders in the history of Washington, D.C. It will include representatives from NATO and its partner countries—44 in all—and it will produce a blueprint for NATO in the 21st Century.

Our leaders will, I am confident, agree on the design of an Alliance that is not only bigger, but also more flexible; an Alliance committed to collective defense, and capable of meeting a wide range of threats to its common interests; an Alliance working in partnership with other nations and organizations to advance security, prosperity and democracy in and for the entire Euro-Atlantic region.

The centerpiece of the Summit will be the unveiling of a revised strategic concept that will take into account the variety of future dangers the Alliance may face.

Since 1949, under Article V of the North Atlantic Treaty, the core mission of our alliance has been collective defense. That must not change, and will not change. NATO is a defensive alliance, not a global policeman.

But NATO's founders understood that what our alliance commits us to do under Article V is not all we may be called upon to do, or should reserve the right to do. Consider, for example, that when French Foreign Minister Robert Schuman signed the North Atlantic Treaty, he characterized it as "insurance against all risks—a system of common defense against any attack, whatever its nature."

During the Cold War, we had no trouble identifying the risks to our security and territory. But the threats we face today and may face tomorrow are less predictable. They could come from an aggressive regime, a rampaging faction, or a terrorist group. And we know that, if past is prologue, we face a future in which weapons will be more destructive at longer distances than ever before.

Our alliance is and must remain a Euro-Atlantic institution that acts by consensus. We must prevent and, if necessary, respond to the full spectrum of threats to Alliance interests and values. And when we respond, it only makes sense to use the unified military structure and cooperative habits we have developed over the past 50 years. This approach shouldn't be controversial. We've been practicing it successfully in Bosnia since 1995.

We are also taking steps, as we plan for the summit, to ensure that NATO's military forces are designed, equipped and prepared for 21st Century missions. And we expect the summit to produce an initiative that responds to the grave threat posed by weapons of mass destruction and their means of delivery.

Clearly, NATO's job is different now than when we faced a single mono-lithic adversary across a single, heavily-armed frontier. But NATO's purpose is enduring. It has not changed. It remains to prevent war and safeguard free-dom. NATO does this only by deterring, but also by unifying. And let no one underestimate its value here, as well. For if NATO can assure peace in Europe, it will contribute much to stability around the globe.

The history of this century and many before it has been marked by shift-ing patterns within Europe as empires rose and fell, borders were drawn and redrawn, and ethnic divisions were exploited by aggressors and demagogues. Twice this century, conflicts arose which required American troops to cross the Atlantic and plunge into the cauldron of war.

NATO and NATO's partners have closed that book and are authoring a new one. In collaboration with regional institutions, we are encouraging the reso-lution of old antagonisms, promoting tolerance, ensuring the protection of minority rights and helping to realize, for the first time in history, the dream of a Europe whole and free.

So let us not hesitate to rebut those who would diminish the role of our alliance, dispute its value, or downplay the importance of its unity and pre-paredness. For if NATO does not respond to the 21st Century security chal-lenges facing our region, who will? If NATO cannot prevent aggressors from engulfing whole chunks of Europe in conflict, who can? And if NATO is not prepared to respond to the threat posed to our citizens by weapons of mass destruction, who will have that capability?

The 20th Century has been the bloodiest and most destructive in human history; and despite the Cold War's end, many threats remain. But we have learned some hard lessons from this history of conflict, and those lessons underlie all our planning for the Washington Summit.

We know that when the democracies of Europe and America are divided, crevices are created through which forces of evil and aggression may emerge; and that when we stand together, no force on Earth is more power-ful than our solidarity on behalf of freedom.

That is why NATO is focused not only on welcoming new members, but also on strengthening its valuable partnerships with Russia, Ukraine and Europe's other democracies. Their inclusion and full participation in the transatlantic community is essential to the future we seek. For NATO's pur-pose is not to build new walls, but rather to tear old walls down.

Five years ago, while serving as US Permanent Representative to the UN, I traveled with General Shalikashvili to Central and Eastern Europe, to out-line President Clinton's plan for a Partnership for Peace. That concept con-tinues to deepen and pay dividends for countries whether or not they aspire to NATO membership. Today, former adversaries are talking to each other, training with each other, carrying out missions together, and planning together for the future. By fostering that process, we prevent potentially dangerous misunderstandings, address present problems and lay a solid foundation for future cooperation.

We also remind ourselves, that although NATO stands tall, it does not stand alone. The EU, OSCE and NATO and its partners form the core of a broader system for protecting vital interests and promoting shared values.

We learned in Bosnia earlier this decade how vital such a system is. We face a test of that system now in Kosovo, and we welcome Russian Foreign Minister Ivanov's efforts in Belgrade today to help achieve our common goal.

There, together, we have backed diplomacy with tools ranging from humanitarian relief to OSCE verifiers to the threatened use of NATO force. Together, we have hammered out an interim political settlement which meets the needs and respects the rights of all concerned.

When talks resume next week, we must be firm in securing this agreement. We must be clear in explaining that a settlement without NATO-led enforcement is not acceptable because only NATO has the credibility and capability to make it work. And we must be resolute in spelling out the consequences of intransigence.

To those abroad and in my own country who have raised doubts, I reply that the plan we and our partners have developed is not risk-free. But we prefer that risk to the certainty that inaction would lead to a renewed cycle of repression and retaliation, bloodletting and ethnic cleansing. The path we have chosen for our alliance in Kosovo is not easy; but it is right. It serves NATO interests, and it upholds the values of our alliance for which it was created and which we will defend.

Today, as NATO embarks upon a new era, our energy and vision are directed to the future. But we are mindful, as well, of the past. For as we welcome three new members, we have a debt we cannot fail to acknowledge.

In this room today are ambassadors and foreign ministers and generals and members of Congress. In this room, there is great pride and good reason for it. But let us never forget upon whose shoulders we stand. We pay homage to our predecessors and to the millions of soldiers and sailors and aviators and diplomats who, throughout the past half-century, have kept NATO vigilant and strong.

We pay homage, as well, to those who fought for freedom on the far side of freedom's curtain. For the Berlin Wall would be standing today; the Fulda Gap would divide Europe today; the Warsaw Pact would remain our adversary today, if those who were denied liberty for so long, had not struggled so bravely for their rights.

Let us never forget that freedom has its price. And let us never fail to remember how our alliance came together, what it stands for, and why it has prevailed.

Upon the signing of the North Atlantic Treaty, President Harry Truman referred to the creation of NATO as a "neighborly act." "We are like a group of householders," he said, "who express their community of interests by entering into an association for their mutual protection."

At the same time, Canadian Secretary of State Lester Pearson said, "The North Atlantic community is part of the world community, and as we grow stronger to preserve the peace, all free men and women grow stronger with us."

Prime Minister Spaak of Belgium added, "The new NATO pact is purely defensive; it threatens no one. It should therefore disturb no one, except those who might foster the criminal idea of having recourse to war."

Though all the world has changed since these statements were made, the verities they express have not. Our alliance still is bound together by a community of interests. Our strength still is a source of strength to those everywhere who labor for freedom and peace. Our power still shields those who love the law and still threatens none, except those who would threaten others with aggression and harm. Our alliance endures because the principles it defends are timeless and because they reflect the deepest aspirations of the human spirit.

It is our mission now, working across the Atlantic, to carry on the traditions of our alliance and prepare NATO for the 21st Century. To that end, we take a giant step today. And we look forward with confidence and determination to the historic summit in Washington and further progress tomorrow.

Thank you all very much.

CLINTON ON AIR WAR AGAINST
SERBIAN FORCES IN KOSOVO
March 24, 1999

*It took the biggest war in Europe since World War II to end—at least tem-
porarily—an ethnic conflict in Kosovo, a tiny province of Serbia in the former Yugoslavia. For seventy-eight days, beginning on March 24, NATO airplanes and missiles attacked Serbian military and economic targets to halt
Serbia's campaign of terror against the ethnic Albanian majority in
Kosovo. Serbian leader Slobodan Milosevic relented and withdrew his
forces from Kosovo after NATO had caused extensive damage both in
Kosovo and in greater Serbia. A NATO-led peacekeeping force, acting under
a United Nations mandate, took up positions in Kosovo in mid-June to
supervise the return of refugees and the beginning of reconstruction in the
embattled province.* (Peacekeeping and postwar developments, p. 285)

*Between January 1998, when fighting broke out between Serbian secu-
rity forces and the Kosovo Albanian independence movement, and the end
of NATO bombing in June 1999, an estimated 1.4 million Kosovo Albanians were forced from their homes. A U.S. State Department report issued in
December estimated that approximately 10,000 Kosovar Albanians had
been killed by Serbian forces and that tens of thousands of homes, farms,
and businesses were destroyed or damaged. Several news reports late in the
year suggested that the State Department figures were too high; even so,
there was no doubt that the war's toll in human lives and property damage
was enormous.* (1998 Kosovo events, Historic Documents of 1998, p. 827; ethnic cleansing reports, p. 802)

An Escalating Crisis

*Kosovo's Albanian majority had enjoyed a substantial degree of auton-
omy until 1989, when Milosevic imposed direct rule on Kosovo from Belgrade. The Serbian crackdown inspired a Kosovo independence movement,
which conducted nonviolent resistance through the early 1990s, following
the breakup of Yugoslavia. When Serbian repression intensified in 1996,
the Kosovo Liberation Army launched periodic bombings and other attacks,*

culminating in a military offensive early in 1998. Counter-attacks by the Serbian police in February and March 1998 included raids in which villages were burned and dozens of Albanians were murdered.

The escalation of violence in Kosovo in 1998 captured international attention. Western leaders worried that a civil war in Kosovo could spill over into neighboring Albania and Macedonia and possibly even into Greece and Turkey, two NATO allies that historically were antagonists. The UN Security Council passed resolutions demanding that Serbian security forces halt their attacks on civilians, and NATO leaders authorized air strikes against Belgrade if the attacks did not stop. But those resolutions and threats had little effect, and by September 1998 the government had wiped out much of the Kosovar resistance. Having achieved most of his goals, Milosevic in October 1998 signed a U.S.-brokered cease-fire agreement, to be monitored by an international force of up to 2,000 unarmed observers. By the time of the cease-fire, an estimated 1.45 million Kosovar Albanians (about 90 percent of the population) had been forced from their homes; about 860,000 of them had taken refuge in neighboring countries and elsewhere in Europe.

The cease-fire did not completely stop the fighting, but it did help contain the level of violence. The international monitors said that for a few months they had been able to prevent an explosion of ethnic violence while political leaders considered their next steps.

The escalation of violence that led to the bombing war started on January 15, 1999, when Serbian security forces massacred forty ethnic Albanians in the village of Racak. It was one of the largest, and most blatant, assaults in the year-long series of attacks between the two sides. The next day, William Walker, an American diplomat who headed the international observer mission in Kosovo, visited Racak and denounced the killings as a "crime against humanity" that had been committed by the Yugoslav military. In response, the Yugoslav government labeled Walker an "undesirable person" and ordered him to leave the country—a demand that was retracted under international pressure.

The Racak massacre was the first of a new series of Serbian attacks on Albanian villages. Alarmed by the renewed violence, Western leaders decided to attempt to negotiate peace in Kosovo before turning to a military solution. The six nations of a "contact group," established in 1992 to deal with the unraveling of Yugoslavia, met on January 29 and agreed to convene peace talks between Serbian authorities and Kosovar Albanian leaders under international monitoring.

Negotiations began February 6 at a chateau in Rambouillet, France. U.S. diplomats presented a draft peace agreement calling for a new constitution establishing a multiethnic legislature in Kosovo, with the province gradually gaining autonomy—but not full independence—during a three-year period. Compliance with the agreement was to be monitored by a NATO peacekeeping force. U.S. negotiators, including Secretary of State Madeleine K. Albright, gave each side no alternative but to sign the agree-

ment. Despite that pressure, neither side was prepared to take the first step, and the Rambouillet talks ended February 23 without an agreement. After a second round of negotiations in Paris March 1518, the Albanian delegation reluctantly signed the U.S.-drafted accord. But the Yugoslav delegation, acting under orders from Milosevic, refused to sign, setting in motion NATO's previously prepared plans for air strikes against Yugoslavia.

There were two last steps before NATO launched its air war against Yugoslavia. First, on March 19 the 1,400 international monitors were evacuated from Kosovo. The monitors left behind some 1,500 Kosovar staff members, including translators, bodyguards, and drivers—some of whom reportedly were killed because of their association with the international mission. On March 21 U.S. special envoy Richard Holbrooke, who had negotiated a 1995 peace agreement ending the civil war in Bosnia and the October 1998 Kosovo cease-fire, flew to Belgrade to deliver what the Clinton administration called a "final warning" to Milosevic. Unable to secure any concessions from the Yugoslav leader, Holbrooke left Belgrade on March 23.

NATO Secretary-General Javier Solano, who had been given authority by alliance foreign ministers to launch air attacks, issued the go-ahead orders later on March 23, and the first strikes came March 24. That night, President Clinton delivered a televised address from the White House announcing the air strikes. The NATO allies were acting to force Milosevic to end the terror campaign against Albanians in Kosovo, Clinton said. The president also stated a broader objective of preventing the war in Kosovo from spreading throughout the Balkans. "Let a fire burn here in this area and the flames will spread," he said. "Eventually, key U.S. allies could be drawn into a wider conflict, a war we would be forced to confront later only at far greater risk and greater cost. . . ."

Congress and the majority of the American public, according to opinion polls, supported U.S. involvement in the war. But some Republican leaders expressed opposition, saying Clinton had not adequately justified U.S. intervention in Kosovo's civil war. Don Nickles of Oklahoma, the Senate majority whip, was among Republican opponents; he warned that getting involved in Kosovo was "breaking new ground" and might establish a precedent for intervention in ethnic and political conflicts such as those in Indonesia, Turkey, the Sudan, Burundi, and Rwanda.

Air War Against Yugoslavia

NATO officials had hoped that a limited round of air strikes against Serbian military targets would be enough to persuade Milosevic to ease his grip on Kosovo. This hope was based on previous incidents in which Milosevic had staked out a hard line and then retreated under international pressure. But as the Kosovo air war entered its initial phases, it became clear that Milosevic was determined to hold out as long a possible, perhaps in the hope that NATO allies would tire of the war before he did. President Clinton at first ruled out a ground invasion of Yugoslavia, despite wide-

spread skepticism that aerial attacks alone would be enough to force Milosevic to yield. The air campaign worked as Clinton promised, but it took much longer than NATO military planners had hoped.

When NATO intensified its bombing, Serbian security forces stepped up terror attacks against the Albanian community in Kosovo, forcing tens of thousands of people from their homes. On March 27 Kosovar Albanians began pouring into neighboring countries, including Albania, Bosnia, Macedonia, and Montenegro. By March 29 observers estimated that refugees were fleeing Kosovo at a rate of 4,000 an hour, the vast majority of them traveling on foot over mountain passes. The refugee flow reached a daily peak of 20,000 on April 16.

The massive influx of refugees severely strained the resources of countries in the region, which were struggling just to meet the needs of their own populations. International organizations rushed food and temporary shelter to the thousands of refugees camped in muddy fields. By mid-April, refugee totals exceeded 359,000 in Albania, 132,000 in Macedonia, 50,000 in Montenegro, and 30,000 in Bosnia. Thousands more Kosovar Albanians who had fled their homes were unable or unwilling to travel to other countries.

Secretary of Defense William S. Cohen said the tactical aim of the NATO campaign was to "degrade" Yugoslav military capabilities to the point that Milosevic would have no choice but to sue for peace. With that goal in mind, NATO planned an air campaign of gradually increasing pressure. Initial targets included Yugoslav military positions in Kosovo and in neighboring regions of Serbia. After the bombing of those targets had no discernible impact on Milosevic, NATO bombed the Yugoslav interior and defense ministries in Belgrade and then attacked "infrastructure" targets such as bridges over the Danube River and electrical installations. NATO on May 23 began systematic attacks on the Yugoslav electrical grid, disrupting power and water supplies throughout the country. By late May the formidable Yugoslav military had been severely damaged and the country's economy—still reeling from international sanctions imposed during the three-year war in Bosnia—had all but collapsed.

All nineteen NATO member nations contributed to the campaign, but the bulk of the actual bombing was carried out by U.S. forces, along with planes and missiles from Britain and France. Greece, which stood to suffer the most immediate consequences if the Kosovo war spread throughout the Balkans, was the only NATO nation that sought to distance itself from the bombing. The Greek government repeatedly called for a negotiated end to the conflict and on May 17 said NATO should declare a cease-fire "to give diplomacy a chance." But Athens took no direct steps to hinder NATO operations or to challenge the political unity of the alliance.

Late in May NATO military commander General Wesley K. Clark pressed for serious consideration of a ground attack. Although top U.S. officials, including Clinton, were reluctant to entertain the notion of sending ground troops into Kosovo, they did allow planning for such a move to begin. Clark and some military analysts later said it was the possibility of a massive invasion that ultimately convinced Milosevic he had to give in.

As could be expected from such a massive campaign, NATO committed several mistakes, some of them significant. On May 7 NATO planes bombed the Chinese embassy in Belgrade, killing three people and wounding twenty. The Clinton administration said the bombing was a mistake that resulted from the use of outdated maps. The Chinese government refused to accept the U.S. apology, however, and the incident severely strained relations between the two countries for several months. (Embassy bombing, p. 304)

NATO planes and missiles also killed numerous Kosovar Albanians. In one highly publicized incident on May 14, an estimated eighty-seven Albanians were killed by NATO bombs in the village of Korisa. The Yugoslav government accused NATO of deliberately targeting civilians, but NATO suggested that the Yugoslav military was using the Albanians as "human shields" by putting them in areas known to be military targets.

As the NATO bombing campaign neared its conclusion, a UN tribunal investigating war crimes in the former Yugoslavia stepped up political pressure on Milosevic by indicting him. Milosevic and four other Serbian leaders were charged with committing "crimes against humanity" by ordering the killings of Kosovar Albanians. The main practical effect of the indictment was to lock Milosevic inside his own country, since he would be subject to arrest if he traveled outside Yugoslavia. The indictment also weakened Milosevic internationally and domestically by affirming the seriousness of atrocities committed under his supervision.

On June 1 the Milosevic government announced that it was ready to accept a set of peace principles laid down by the "Group of Eight" major industrialized countries. Milosevic then met with Finnish president Martti Ahtisaari (acting in his capacity as president of the European Union) and Russian envoy Viktor Chernomyrdin and on June 3 accepted terms for an end to the war. The key terms were the withdrawal of all but a few hundred Serbian security forces from Kosovo, the open-ended deployment of a NATO-led peacekeeping force, and "substantial autonomy" for Kosovo. NATO suspended its bombing while NATO and Yugoslav military representatives haggled over an agreement establishing technical details of a Yugoslav pullout from Kosovo. Yugoslav began withdrawing from Kosovo on June 10, and later in the day Secretary General Solano ordered a suspension of the air attacks. Also on June 10, the UN Security Council adopted resolution 1244 establishing procedure for a NATO-led peacekeeping force in Kosovo. (UN resolution, p. 285)

Hours before the peacekeeping forces were to enter Kosovo on June 12, Russian troops entered the capital city, Pristina, and occupied the airport. That action angered Western leaders, who saw it as an effort by Moscow to establish a Russian-protected Serbian enclave in Kosovo, and led to a tense standoff between NATO and Russian forces lasting more than a week. The standoff was resolved when Russia agreed not to establish a protectorate in

Kosovo and said its forces would serve inside U.S., French, and German zones.

Yugoslavia completed withdrawal of its military and security forces from Kosovo on June 20, and Solano formally ordered an end to the air war. The NATO assault on Yugoslavia was massive. During the ten weeks of active warfare, NATO planes flew about 35,000 missions (of which nearly 10,000 were bombing runs) and dropped about 23,000 bombs and missiles in Serbia (including Kosovo) and Montenegro, the junior partner in the Federal Republic of Yugoslavia. NATO commander Clark on September 16 released a report saying that the bombing had destroyed or seriously damaged about one-third of the Yugoslav army's weapons and vehicles in Kosovo. The totals included 933 tanks, 153 armored personnel carriers, 389 artillery pieces, and 339 jeeps and trucks, he said.

The Yugoslav government said NATO bombing had killed between 1,200 and 2,000 civilians. The Pentagon insisted those figures were too high and said the number of civilians killed during the bombing was in the "low hundreds."

In a televised address on June 11, President Clinton hailed the outcome of the war and promised that the NATO allies would provide "security and dignity for the people of Kosovo." Speaking directly to the people of Serbia, Clinton said they had endured NATO bombing "not to keep Kosovo a province of Serbia, but simply because Mr. Milosevic was determined to eliminate Kosovar Albanians from Kosovo, dead or alive. As long as he remains in power, as long as your nation is ruled by an indicted war criminal, we will provide no support for the reconstruction of Serbia. But we are ready to provide humanitarian aid now, and to help build a better future or Serbia, too, when its government represents tolerance and freedom, not repression and terror."

Clinton acknowledged during a news conference June 25 that he had underestimated Milosevic's determination to withstand a NATO attack. Clinton said he had expected that Milosevic would relent on Kosovo "after a couple of days" of NATO bombing. Clinton said he was proud that there were no American combat deaths in the nearly three months of fighting (although two Army pilots had died in a training mission in Albania on May 5).

Following is the text of a televised address by President Bill Clinton on March 24, 1999, announcing a NATO bombing campaign against the Federal Republic of Yugoslavia:

My fellow Americans, today our Armed Forces joined our NATO allies in air strikes against Serbian forces responsible for the brutality in Kosovo. We have acted with resolve for several reasons.

We act to protect thousands of innocent people in Kosovo from a mounting military offensive. We act to prevent a wider war; to diffuse a powder keg at the heart of Europe that has exploded twice before in this century with catastrophic results. And we act to stand united with our allies for peace. By acting now we are upholding our values, protecting our interests and advancing the cause of peace.

Tonight I want to speak to you about the tragedy in Kosovo and why it matters to America that we work with our allies to end it. First, let me explain what it is we are responding to. Kosovo is a province of Serbia, in the middle of southeastern Europe, about 160 miles east of Italy. That's less than the distance between Washington and New York, and only about 70 miles north of Greece. Its people are mostly ethnic Albanian and mostly Muslim.

In 1989, Serbia's leader, Slobodan Milosevic, the same leader who started the wars in Bosnia and Croatia, and moved against Slovenia in the last decade, stripped Kosovo of the constitutional autonomy its people enjoyed; thus denying them their right to speak their language, run their schools, shape their daily lives. For years, Kosovars struggled peacefully to get their rights back. When President Milosevic sent his troops and police to crush them, the struggle grew violent.

Last fall our diplomacy, backed by the threat of force from our NATO Alliance, stopped the fighting for a while, and rescued tens of thousands of people from freezing and starvation in the hills where they had fled to save their lives. And last month, with our allies and Russia, we proposed a peace agreement to end the fighting for good. The Kosovar leaders signed that agreement last week. Even though it does not give them all they want, even though their people were still being savaged, they saw that a just peace is better than a long and unwinnable war.

The Serbian leaders, on the other hand, refused even to discuss key elements of the peace agreement. As the Kosovars were saying "yes" to peace, Serbia stationed 40,000 troops in and around Kosovo in preparation for a major offensive—and in clear violation of the commitments they had made.

Now, they've started moving from village to village, shelling civilians and torching their houses. We've seen innocent people taken from their homes, forced to kneel in the dirt and sprayed with bullets; Kosovar men dragged from their families, fathers and sons together, lined up and shot in cold blood. This is not war in the traditional sense. It is an attack by tanks and artillery on a largely defenseless people, whose leaders already have agreed to peace.

Ending this tragedy is a moral imperative. It is also important to America's national interest. Take a look at this map. Kosovo is a small place, but it sits on a major fault line between Europe, Asia and the Middle East, at the meeting place of Islam and both the Western and Orthodox branches of Christianity. To the south are our allies, Greece and Turkey; to the north, our new democratic allies in Central Europe. And all around Kosovo there are other small countries, struggling with their own economic and political challenges—countries that could be overwhelmed by a large, new wave of refugees from Kosovo. All the ingredients for a major war are there: ancient grievances, struggling democracies, and in the center of it all a dictator in

Serbia who has done nothing since the Cold War ended but start new wars and pour gasoline on the flames of ethnic and religious division.

Sarajevo, the capital of neighboring Bosnia, is where World War I began. World War II and the Holocaust engulfed this region. In both wars Europe was slow to recognize the dangers, and the United States waited even longer to enter the conflicts. Just imagine if leaders back then had acted wisely and early enough, how many lives could have been saved, how many Americans would not have had to die.

We learned some of the same lessons in Bosnia just a few years ago. The world did not act early enough to stop that war, either. And let's not forget what happened—innocent people herded into concentration camps, children gunned down by snipers on their way to school, soccer fields and parks turned into cemeteries; a quarter of a million people killed, not because of anything they have done, but because of who they were. Two million Bosnians became refugees. This was genocide in the heart of Europe—not in 1945, but in 1995. Not in some grainy newsreel from our parents' and grandparents' time, but in our own time, testing our humanity and our resolve.

At the time, many people believed nothing could be done to end the bloodshed in Bosnia. They said, well, that's just the way those people in the Balkans are. But when we and our allies joined with courageous Bosnians to stand up to the aggressors, we helped to end the war. We learned that in the Balkans, inaction in the face of brutality simply invites more brutality. But firmness can stop armies and save lives. We must apply that lesson in Kosovo before what happened in Bosnia happens there, too.

Over the last few months we have done everything we possibly could to solve this problem peacefully. Secretary Albright has worked tirelessly for a negotiated agreement. Mr. Milosevic has refused.

On Sunday I sent Ambassador Dick Holbrooke to Serbia to make clear to him again, on behalf of the United States and our NATO allies, that he must honor his own commitments and stop his repression, or face military action. Again, he refused.

Today, we and our 18 NATO allies agreed to do what we said we would do, what we must do to restore the peace. Our mission is clear: to demonstrate the seriousness of NATO's purpose so that the Serbian leaders understand the imperative of reversing course. To deter an even bloodier offensive against innocent civilians in Kosovo and, if necessary, to seriously damage the Serbian military's capacity to harm the people of Kosovo. In short, if President Milosevic will not make peace, we will limit his ability to make war.

Now, I want to be clear with you, there are risks in this military action— risks to our pilots and the people on the ground. Serbia's air defenses are strong. It could decide to intensify its assault on Kosovo, or to seek to harm us or our allies elsewhere. If it does, we will deliver a forceful response.

Hopefully, Mr. Milosevic will realize his present course is self-destructive and unsustainable. If he decides to accept the peace agreement and demilitarize Kosovo, NATO has agreed to help to implement it with a peace-keeping force. If NATO is invited to do so, our troops should take part in that mission to keep the peace. But I do not intend to put our troops in Kosovo to fight a war.

Do our interests in Kosovo justify the dangers to our Armed Forces? I've thought long and hard about that question. I am convinced that the dangers of acting are far outweighed by the dangers of not acting—dangers to defenseless people and to our national interests. If we and our allies were to allow this war to continue with no response, President Milosevic would read our hesitation as a license to kill. There would be many more massacres, tens of thousands more refugees, more victims crying out for revenge.

Right now our firmness is the only hope the people of Kosovo have to be able to live in their own country without having to fear for their own lives. Remember: We asked them to accept peace, and they did. We asked them to promise to lay down their arms, and they agreed. We pledged that we, the United States and the other 18 nations of NATO, would stick by them if they did the right thing. We cannot let them down now.

Imagine what would happen if we and our allies instead decided just to look the other way, as these people were massacred on NATO's doorstep. That would discredit NATO, the cornerstone on which our security has rested for 50 years now.

We must also remember that this is a conflict with no natural national boundaries. Let me ask you to look again at a map. The red dots are towns the Serbs have attacked. The arrows show the movement of refugees—north, east and south. Already, this movement is threatening the young democracy in Macedonia, which has its own Albanian minority and a Turkish minority. Already, Serbian forces have made forays into Albania from which Kosovars have drawn support. Albania is a Greek minority. Let a fire burn here in this area and the flames will spread. Eventually, key U.S. allies could be drawn into a wider conflict, a war we would be forced to confront later—only at far greater risk and greater cost.

I have a responsibility as President to deal with problems such as this before they do permanent harm to our national interests. America has a responsibility to stand with our allies when they are trying to save innocent lives and preserve peace, freedom and stability in Europe. That is what we are doing in Kosovo.

If we've learned anything from the century drawing to a close, it is that if America is going to be prosperous and secure, we need a Europe that is prosperous, secure undivided and free. We need a Europe that is coming together, not falling apart; a Europe that shares our values and shares the burdens of leadership. That is the foundation on which the security of our children will depend.

That is why I have supported the political and economic unification of Europe. That is why we brought Poland, Hungary and the Czech Republic into NATO, and redefined its missions, and reached out to Russia and Ukraine for new partnerships.

Now, what are the challenges to that vision of a peaceful, secure, united, stable Europe? The challenge of strengthening a partnership with a democratic Russia, that, despite our disagreements, is a constructive partner in the work of building peace. The challenge of resolving the tension between Greece and Turkey and building bridges with the Islamic world. And, finally, the challenge of ending instability in the Balkans so that these bitter ethnic problems in Europe are resolved the force of argument, not the force of arms; so that future generations of Americans do not have to cross the Atlantic to fight another terrible war.

It is this challenge that we and our allies are facing in Kosovo. That is why we have acted now—because we care about saving innocent lives; because we have an interest in avoiding an even crueler and costlier war; and because our children need and deserve a peaceful, stable, free Europe.

Our thoughts and prayers tonight must be with the men and women of our Armed Forces who are undertaking this mission for the sake of our values and our children's future. May God bless them and may God bless America.

UNITED NATIONS OBSERVER ON HUMAN RIGHTS SITUATION IN IRAQ
March 31, 1999

Eight years after the Persian Gulf war, the United Nations and Iraq remained locked in a standoff concerning central issues such as weapons inspections, economic sanctions, and human rights. Under UN prodding, the Iraqi government made limited progress during 1999 in using oil revenue to improve the living conditions of its people—but the United States and other critics said the Baghdad regime was more interested in rebuilding its army and palaces for its leaders than in providing food and medicine for the population.

Diplomatically and economically, Iraq was one of the most isolated countries on earth. Economic sanctions imposed in 1990 by the UN Security Council to protest Iraq's invasion of Kuwait remained in effect because of Baghdad's failure to cooperate fully with a UN program to dismantle its nuclear, chemical, and biological weapons. The government also refused to cooperate with UN efforts to monitor the human rights situation in Iraq.

At year's end the UN Security Council approved a new system for monitoring the destruction of Iraq's weapons of mass destruction. But the Baghdad government rejected the plan, raising questions about whether it would ever be put in place. (Sanctions against Iraq, Historic Documents of 1991, p. 165)

Human Rights Report

The frequent and high-profile confrontations between the UN and Iraq over weapons inspections pushed to the background another source of conflict: Baghdad's near-total disregard for human rights and political freedoms. The regime headed by President Saddam Hussein was one of the most authoritarian in the world, and it resisted all calls from the outside, including from the United Nations, for reform.

The United Nations Commission on Human Rights in 1991 appointed Max van der Stoel, a former foreign minister of the Netherlands, as a "spe-

cial rapporteur" to investigate the human rights situation in Iraq. Van der Stoel issued his first report in 1992, calling the Iraqi government one of the most repressive anywhere since the end of World War II. His report enraged Baghdad, which refused to allow him into the country afterward. Van der Stoel continued his investigations from afar, interviewing Iraqi exiles, visitors to the country, human rights experts, and others.

On March 31, 1999, he presented the Human Rights Commission in Geneva with what turned out to be his final formal report on the human rights situation in Iraq. Recalling his 1992 statement that the Iraqi human rights situation "had few comparisons in the world" since World War II, van der Stoel told the commission he regretted that he had no cause to change his view. "The prevailing regime in Iraq has effectively eliminated the civil rights to life, liberty, physical integrity, and the freedoms of thought, expression, association and assembly; the rights of political participation have been flouted, while all available resources have not been used to ensure the enjoyment of economic, social and cultural rights," he said.

Van der Stoel said Saddam Hussein's regime was concerned primarily with remaining in power. Saddam had consolidated power to such an extent, he said, that "the mere suggestion that someone is not a supporter of the president carries the prospect of the death penalty."

An example of the regime's ruthlessness, van der Stoel said, was the assassination on February 19 of one of the country's leading Shiite Muslim clerics, Grand Ayatollah Mohammed Sadeq al-Sadr, and his two sons. Saddam's regime had long suppressed members of the Shiite branch of Islam, who constituted a majority of Iraq's population; Saddam and leading figures in his regime belonged to the Sunni branch of Islam. The killing of Ayatollah al-Sadr set off public protests in Iraq and several neighboring countries. The government blamed the assassination on disaffected Shiites, but van der Stoel dismissed that claim and suggested it was part of Baghdad's "systematic suppression" of Shiite leaders.

Van der Stoel said Saddam's repression of his people went beyond curbing political dissent and included a fundamental disregard for the wellbeing of the populace. Baghdad for five years had refused to cooperate with a UN program allowing it to sell oil to raise money for food and medicine, he noted, and since accepting that program in 1996 had failed to make full use of it and had stockpiled medicines rather than distributing them to the public. The government's failure to cooperate with the UN program "is not only a serious violation" of UN human rights covenants, signed by the Iraqi government, van der Stoel said, "but I believe it reveals a great deal about the overall attitude of the government of Iraq."

Iraqi officials objected to van der Stoel's report, saying it was part of a campaign against the country launched by "hostile states"—a reference to the United States. Addressing the Human Rights Commission shortly after van der Stoel presented his report, Iraqi representative Mohammed al Humaimeedi said van der Stoel had the "poisonous aim" of "provoking sec-

*tarianism" and division among the Iraqi people. The government had com-
plied with its international obligations on human rights, Humaimeedi
said.*

*Van der Stoel resigned his post in November, after issuing another
report saying that the humanitarian situation in Iraq was worsening. Van
der Stoel called on Iraq to accept the stationing of UN human rights monitors throughout the country. Amnesty International, the London-based
human rights monitoring organization, issued a report November 23
detailing Baghdad's use of torture, secret arrests and detention, and executions to curb political dissent. "Those suspected of any involvement in
opposition activities can be expected to be arrested without a warrant, held
in secret detention, be brutally tortured . . . and finally could face execution," the report said.*

Oil-for-Food Program

*UN agencies and the Iraqi government also sparred during the year over
implementation of the so-called oil-for-food program, which allowed Baghdad to sell limited quantities of oil on the world market, with the proceeds
used to buy food, medicine, and other humanitarian supplies for the Iraqi
people.*

*The Security Council first offered an oil-for-food program in 1991, in
response to reports of widespread hunger following the Gulf War in February. The government refused that offer and later ones until 1996, when it
accepted a complex program allowing it to sell predetermined amounts of
oil for set periods and authorizing UN agencies to monitor how the proceeds were spent on humanitarian supplies. The Iraqi government was
responsible for providing supplies to the southern two-thirds of the country; the UN administered the provision of supplies to three northern districts, inhabited primarily by Iraqi Kurds.*

*Iraq exported its first oil under the UN program in late 1996, and the
first shipments of humanitarian supplies arrived early in 1997. Almost
immediately, UN officials complained about Iraq's procedures for distributing the supplies. Among other things, observers said the government was
failing to order adequate food supplies for young children and their mothers and was sending millions of dollars worth of medicine to warehouses
rather than making it available to the public.*

*In response to reports that Iraq's oil industry was so damaged by the
Gulf War that it was incapable of meeting production quotas, the Security
Council in 1998 and 1999 authorized up to $900 million from oil revenue
to buy spare parts and equipment. The worldwide drop in oil prices in
1998 reduced Iraq's income from oil sales, creating shortfalls in the oil-for-
food program.*

*In the initial phases the Security Council authorized the oil-for-food
program for six-month periods, but disputes between the UN and Iraq led
the Security Council on November 19 to approve an extension of just two
weeks. Three days later Baghdad said it was halting its oil shipments to*

protest the UN action. Negotiations between UN officials and Iraq led to Security Council approval on December 10 of a new resolution authorizing another six-month extension of the oil-for-food program. Under that resolution Iraq could sell $5.26 billion worth of oil through the first half of 2000 to buy food, medicine, other humanitarian supplies, and spare parts of the oil industry. Iraq accepted that extension and resumed its oil exports in late December.

The Security Council on December 17 liberalized the oil-for-food program by eliminating the limit on how much oil Iraq could export to buy humanitarian supplies. The council also dropped a provision requiring that Iraq obtain advance approval from the UN for all purchases made under the program. However, all money earned by Iraq had to go into a UN-supervised escrow account.

Standoff on Weapons Inspections

Ever since the end of the Persian Gulf War the most contentious issue between the United Nations and Iraq involved the nuclear, chemical, and biological weapons that Baghdad had developed before the war. The Security Council in 1991 established procedures under which the International Atomic Energy Agency would locate and destroy Iraq's nuclear arsenal, and a new body, called the United Nations Special Commission, would catalogue and destroy chemical and biological weapons. Most of the nuclear weapons had been found and dismantled by the mid-1990s, but Iraq cooperated only fitfully with the UN commission, provoking a series of confrontations. The United States government, which saw itself as the ultimate enforcer of UN Security Council resolutions because of its military might in the Middle East, was the most adamant in insisting that Baghdad cooperate fully with the UN commission.

Iraq posed numerous hurdles to the commission during 1998, resulting in a December 15 report to the Security Council by Richard Butler, an Australian diplomat who chaired the UN commission, saying that Iraq was not cooperating. Butler ordered his weapons inspectors to leave Iraq, and on December 16 President Bill Clinton ordered a series of air strikes against Iraqi military facilities. Baghdad said it would never again permit UN weapons inspectors on its territory.

Butler presented his final report to the Security Council in January 1999. Russia, which tended to side with Iraq, prevented the Security Council from publishing Butler's report as an official UN document, but other diplomats made it available to reporters. The report detailed an eight-year effort by the Baghdad government to conceal its weapons of mass destruction from the UN inspectors. When confronted with evidence about the weapons, Butler's report said, the Iraqis resorted to lies, delaying tactics, and other means to prevent the commission from uncovering the truth and the weapons themselves. Iraq destroyed some weapons on its own, preventing the commission from discovering the full extent of the country's arsenal.

The commission report provided the most details to date on Iraq's bio-logical weapons program. Baghdad for several years denied it had tried to develop biological weapons; confronted in 1995 with evidence developed by the commission, the government gradually acknowledged various aspects of that weapons program. Butler's report compared Iraq's assertions to evidence developed by the commission on weapons systems that had been equipped with biological agents. For example, the report said Iraq had claimed to have installed biological weapons on twenty-five medium-range ballistic missiles. But, according to the report, "confusion reigns, even among Iraqi officials, over how many warheads were filled with [biological weapons] agents" and exactly what type of weapons were used. Iraq also claimed to have made 200 bombs for its biological weapons program, but the report cited evidence that "more than 200 were available" for the program.

Attempts by UN Security Council members to negotiate a new system of weapons inspections for Iraq made no headway during most of 1999. The issue was complicated in part by news reports early in the year that U.S. intelligence services had placed agents in the UN weapons commission who had installed sophisticated monitoring devices to spy on the Iraqi military. The U.S. government and Butler denied the reports.

The five permanent members of the Security Council—each with a veto—were divided on the issue. The United States and Britain advocated continuing hard-nosed inspections to locate Iraq's banned weapons, while China, France, and Russia pushed for a weaker system and for a gradual lifting of economic sanctions against Iraq.

After numerous false starts, the Security Council on December 17 approved resolution 1284 authorizing creation of a new agency, the UN Monitoring, Verification, and Inspection Commission (called UNMOVIC) to finish the task of dismantling Iraq's weapons of mass destruction. The resolution required that Iraq give the new agency "immediate, unconditional, and unrestricted access" to all facilities and records that it wanted to inspect. The resolution also held out the prospect that economic sanctions could be suspended for renewable 120-day periods if the commission reported that Iraq was cooperating "in all respects." The resolution directed UN Secretary General Kofi Annan to name a chairman for the commission, subject to approval by the Security Council.

China, France, and Russia abstained on the resolution, providing the latest indication that the Security Council remained divided on how vigorously to confront Iraq on the weapons issue. Tariq Aziz, the Iraqi deputy prime minister who represented Baghdad in negotiations with the UN, said on December 18 that Iraq would refuse to accept the new weapons monitors. Aziz called the resolution a U.S.-inspired "trick" that "failed to meet Iraq's legitimate demand for the lifting of sanctions."

Following are excerpts from a statement given March 31, 1999, to the United Nations Commission on Human Rights by Max

van der Stoel, the commission's special rapporteur on Iraq, in
which he analyzed the human rights situation in that country:

The Commission on Human Rights decided at its session early in 1991 to appoint two independent experts to investigate and assess, respectively, the actions of the Iraqi authorities during their occupation of Kuwait and the actions of the Iraqi authorities within Iraq. Professor Walter Kälin of Switzerland reported on the situation of human rights in Kuwait under Iraqi occupation. Following discontinuation of his mandate, I was assigned responsibility to report on the continuing violation of the missing Kuwaiti and third country nationals. This issue thus became part of my mandate in addition to reporting on violations committed by the Government of Iraq. It is important to note that I have never been mandated to report on the wider context of disputes involving Iraq.

Upon my appointment, I was overwhelmed by the mass of material which was put before me. United Nations files were already full of thousands of documented cases of disappeared persons, of cases of alleged torture, arbitrary execution and other serious violations of human rights. The cases, having occurred over several years but with increasing frequency since the early 1980s, bore considerable similarities. But there had never been a country-specific mandate to study the situation as a whole. I was now confronted by not only this compiled material, but also the new mass of allegations which flowed from the recent events in Iraq. Having examined the submissions, I immediately undertook to meet with alleged victims. Their personal testimonies were wholly consistent with the documentary material. Accordingly, I submitted a summary of the allegations to the Government of Iraq in order to learn their views. I received back only their denials and excuses. I then embarked upon a mission to visit not only Iraq, but also the neighbouring countries where I met with large numbers of persons who had recently fled from all parts of Iraq. I received their testimonies, ranging from individuals who showed me their scars and wounds from torture to the hundreds of Kurdish women who held up their fingers indicating the numbers of family members who had been taken by the Iraqi authorities and subsequently disappeared. I also met representatives of the hundreds of thousands of Iraqi citizens who had been arbitrarily expelled from Iraq merely because of their supposed "Persian" ancestry. The testimonies I received, supplemented by documentation and sometimes physical evidence, were again wholly consistent. And so was my own experience of the police-State in which I found myself upon visiting Iraq. In sum, the evidence revealed a pattern of systematic gross violations of human rights.

I reported this to the Commission on Human Rights in 1992. The Government of Iraq denied everything, refused me a return visit to the country, and eventually cut off contacts with me. Nevertheless, I have continued to seek and receive information, and I have continued to report my findings. The Government has continued simply to deny everything or to offer limpid excuses even for its own laws which blatantly sanction arbitrary killing for anyone who insults the President or institutions of the regime, and laws which prescribe tortures for criminal acts like petty theft or evasion from military service. Increasingly, the Government of Iraq seems to find comfort in attacking my personal integrity—attacking the messenger since they are unable to refute the message. And all the while, there have continued widespread and systematic violations of human rights in Iraq.

These past eight years I have submitted almost a thousand pages of reporting on the situation of human rights in Iraq. I have analysed and reported upon the situation of civil, cultural, economic, political, and social rights. I have studied the politico-legal regime which affects the whole population, and especially tolerates no political dissent. I have also studied the special situations of persons in particular regions of Iraq—the north and the south—and of particular communities: the Kurds, the Turkomans, the Assyrians, the Marsh Arabs and the Shi'ite religious community. I have also reported upon the effects of Government policy on particularly vulnerable groups: women, children, the elderly, and refugees. All the while, the violations have continued without the slightest indication of any change in Government policy—of any effort or intention to improve the situation of human rights in Iraq. And all the while the Government has simply denied everything.

In my current report to the Commission on Human Rights, I have the sad duty yet again to report: allegations of numerous and systematic arbitrary executions; interferences with the independent religious practice of the Shi'ite community; continuing internal deportations of ethnic Kurds; violations of the rights to food and health; violations of the rights of the child; and the Government's continuing failure even to cooperate in efforts to resolve the hundreds of cases of missing Kuwaitis and others who disappeared under the Iraqi occupation of Kuwait.

In the past year, I have received allegations of arbitrary executions from various sources. It is my duty to evaluate and report upon these allegations, especially as they fall within the same pattern of previously established violations. They allege executions of large numbers of persons within Iraqi prisons for various crimes including for political reasons. Reports indicate that army officers have been among those executed, including some top officers in the last few weeks allegedly for planning a military coup and also others in relation to unrest in southern Iraq following the assassination of Ayatollah Mohammed Sadek al-Sadr and his two sons.

The assassination of Ayatollah al-Sadr on 19 February 1999 merits further attention. In itself, the killing of one of the leading Shi'ite clerics is important because it shows the risks which such persons suffer in Iraq. Ayatollah al-Sadr had been gaining in popularity in Iraq, especially since he has called for the release of Shi'ite prisoners—an action which apparently angered the Iraqi authorities. As a leader of the Shi'ite religious establishment, the Ayatollah enjoys considerable prestige among the Shi'ite community of Iraq which constitutes a majority of the population. In a country well-known not to tolerate the least spectre of opposition, the Ayatollah's modest actions placed him at serious risk. But, his risk and eventual assassination must be seen in the wider context of the string of assassinations of Shi'ite clerics, including two other leading Ayatollahs in April and June of last year. Moreover, ever since the attacks against the Shi'ite religious establishment in April 1991, when Ayatollah al-Khoie was forcibly abducted and imprisoned by the Iraqi authorities together with numerous other clerics, there has continued systematic suppression of religious activity among the Shi'ite community. Well over 100 clerics and religious scholars remain missing from their April 1991 abduction, and the once large religious establishment in the holy cities of Najaf and Karbala has steadily declined. The Government denies any responsibility. But, how is it possible in a country like Iraq where security is so well organized and maintained—where internal movement and external frontiers are strictly controlled—that high Shi'ite clerics and their family members are murdered at regular intervals? And why only this group of persons in particular? The Government has the audacity to lay the blame at the feet of Shi'ite faithful themselves, and agents from hostile countries. But what kind of perverse logic would motivate Shi'ite faithful to kill their own religious leaders apparently only to embarrass the Government of Iraq?

The situation in Iraq, the reports of executions and the assassination of Ayatollah al-Sadr must be seen in the wider context also of other violations by the Government of Iraq. Among these is the systematic and forcible internal deportation of Kurds and Turkomans from the city and region of Kirkuk. This policy of ethnic transformation—of "Arabization"—has been going on for many years. Not trusting ethnic Kurds and Turkomans, the Government has been rewarding loyal Arabs with houses and jobs in Kirkuk in place of Kurds and Turkomans. This is not a fanciful invention of anyone's imagination. Many of the displaced persons flee to the northern Governorates of Dahuk, Arbil and Suleiymaniyah where they are assisted by independent bodies such as the UNHCR and the WFP. Officers of these organizations can attest to the numbers of internally displaced to whom they distribute humanitarian supplies donated in measure by other governments. This is the reality of life in Iraq today.

Regarding the broader humanitarian situation in Iraq, it is important to note that the Government is not only the cause of great suffering, but it has even on a number of occasions interfered with efforts to improve the situation. For example, in the period 1992/1997, landmines placed by the Government of Iraq have caused more than 15,000 casualties of which 30% of the victims were children. Yet, the Government has so far failed meaningfully to cooperate in facilitating the work of the United Nations demining programme. As for the rights to food and health, affecting especially the most vulnerable in Iraq, the Government has for years on end failed to cooperate fully with the United Nations to end the sanctions or to take full advantage of the "food-for-oil" formula which was made available years ago. For almost five years, the Government simply refused to cooperate at all. And since finally accepting to cooperate, the Secretary-General's own reports specify that the Government has failed to facilitate fully the programme either by failing to make orders for necessary foodstuffs and medicines or failing to distribute goods received. Specifically, as of 31 January 1999, the Secretary-General reports that some USD 275 million worth of medicines and medical supplies had accumulated in warehouses in Iraq. Failure to cooperate in this humanitarian programme is not only a serious violation of the Covenant on Economic, Social and Cultural Rights, but I believe it reveals a great deal about the overall attitude of the Government of Iraq.

In my current report to the Commission, I have also reported again on the still missing 604 Kuwaitis and some others who were taken by Iraqi forces during the illegal occupation of 1990-1991. Unfortunately, there has been very little progress in the last several years and now the Government of Iraq has simply discontinued its cooperation with the International Committee of the Red Cross and the other members of the Tripartite Commission on Missing Persons. Apparently, the Government of Iraq wants the world just to forget about these people and the pain caused to their families.

I submit that it is not a difficult task to clarify unequivocally the situation of human rights in Iraq. In the first place, Iraq is a State Party without reservation to almost all human rights treaties. In addition, the Government of Iraq has never deemed it necessary to derogate from any of its obligations. At the same time, the mass of evidence—testimonial, documentary, and physical—is so abundant and so consistent, including straightforward provisions of law, that one cannot escape reaching conclusions of serious violations of human rights in Iraq simply as a matter of logic. However, to reveal absolutely the emptiness of Iraqi denials and excuses, I have consistently recommended the sending to Iraq of United Nations human rights monitors who could move freely throughout the country and report daily on the situation as they see it. If the Government of Iraq have nothing to hide, then they should have no problem accepting this proposal. Indeed, any open society generally respecting human rights should have no problem accepting such independent and impartial observers. But, tellingly, Iraq has steadfastly refused this simple proposal.

Regrettably, the situation of human rights has not improved in Iraq, nor does it show any sign of improving. In my view, so long as there remains the same politico-legal order in Iraq, serious violations of human rights will continue. I believe it is up to the Government of Iraq to take steps to change the situation. It can begin by accepting, at long last, United Nations human rights monitors throughout the country.

April

New European Commission
   President on Reforms 155

Starr on the Future of the
   Independent Counsel Law 165

Astronomers on Discovery of
   a Multiplanet Solar System 173

Vice President on Shootings
   at Columbine High School 179

GAO on Health Threat
   from Drug-Resistant Bacteria 185

NEW EUROPEAN COMMISSION PRESIDENT ON REFORMS
April 13, 1999

A scandal involving fraud and mismanagement led in March to the mass resignation of the twenty members of the European Commission—the powerful body responsible for establishing and administering the policies of the European Union. The scandal followed years of allegations about favoritism and bloated bureaucracy in Brussels, where the commission was headquartered. European leaders quickly appointed a new commission, including some of the members who had just resigned, and pledged reforms.

The commission administered a budget approaching $100 billion and had overall authority for policies on trade, transport, communications, and other matters involving the fifteen nations belonging to the European Union. The scandal-forced resignations came just ten weeks after the successful introduction of a common currency for most of Europe—the euro. Some observers said the two events heightened the contrast between a progressive Europe working for common solutions to problems and a tradition-bound Europe accustomed to tolerating fraud and favoritism as part of daily life. (Euro introduction, p. 75)

One immediate outcome of the scandal appeared to be increased influence for the European Parliament, long considered a toothless debating society composed of politicians with little support or power back in the countries they represented. The parliament initiated an investigation of irregularities that led to the commission's resignation, and it won increased powers, including the right to approve all nominations to the commission.

Background to the Scandal

The twenty European Commission members were appointed by the fifteen-member nations of the European Union: two each from Britain, France, Germany, Italy, and Spain, and one each from the ten smaller nations. Each commissioner had responsibility for a specific area of pol-

icy, such as trade or agriculture. Most commissioners had been prominent leaders in their home countries; commission president Jacques Santer, for example, had been prime minister of Luxembourg, and commissioner Neil Kinnock had been leader of Britain's Labour Party.

Commissioners drew salaries of about $200,000 each, plus expenses, and managed a staff of more than 17,000. The commission had sole authority to propose Europe-wide legislation, which it submitted to the parliament for approval.

Reports of corruption at commission headquarters began emerging in the early 1990s. Little action was taken until December 1998 when a Dutch employee of the commission, Paul van Buitenen, sent the parliament a scathing critique detailing what he called the "incompetence and unwillingness of the administration to deal efficiently with fraud and irregularities."

In response, the parliament refused what normally would have been routine approval of the commission's account books for fiscal year 1996 and initiated a no-confidence motion against the commission. A resulting confrontation between the commission and the parliament produced two actions: the commission adopted a code of conduct, and the parliament appointed a five-member committee to investigate the allegations raised by van Buitenen and others.

A Report and Resignations

The investigating panel presented its report to the parliament and Santer on March 15. Within a few hours, the commission made the stunning announcement that all twenty members had resigned. Describing the decision, Santer said: "The commission thus assumes its responsibilities consistent with the commitment it made to follow up on the report" of the investigators. Within twenty-four hours, however, Santer and several other commissioners made it clear they hoped to be reappointed to their posts.

The investigators' report painted a general picture of a European Commission that tolerated cozy business relationships, inattention to detail, and sloppy management. Five commission members were criticized by name, including Santer, who was cleared of personal wrongdoing but was cited for failure to stop fraudulent activities in a security office he supervised.

Commissioner Edith Cresson, a former prime minister of France, came under the most serious criticism from the investigators. Cresson had responsibility for the research, education, and training programs of the commission. The investigators concentrated on allegations, raised in numerous press reports, that Cresson had issued lucrative consulting contracts to a friend with no obvious qualifications for the jobs involved. The friend, Rene Berthelot, was a retired dentist from Cresson's hometown of Chatellerault, France; the contracts paid him nearly $200,000 over a three-year period, and investigators could find no evidence that he performed any work.

The investigators uncovered fraudulent billings for work never performed in connection with job training programs under Cresson's supervision and for European aid programs in the former Yugoslavia and Africa. None of the cases of fraud involved enormous amounts of money in the context of the commission's multibillion dollar budget, and the investigators found no evidence that individual commissioners benefited financially from fraudulent activities. Nevertheless, the investigators faulted the commission collectively and individually for failing to take responsibility to deal with illegal and improper behavior. "The studies carried out by the [investigating] committee have too often revealed a growing reluctance among the members of the hierarchy to acknowledge their responsibility," the panel said. "It is becoming difficult to find anyone who has even the slightest sense of responsibility."

Santer accepted the investigating report on behalf of the commission, then convened a commission meeting, which lasted for three hours. Afterward, Santer announced that all twenty members had submitted their resignations but would stay in office until their successors had been appointed.

Leaders of the European Parliament expressed relief at the outcome and said they would move to tighten regulations governing the conduct of commissioners and other European Union officials, including members of parliament. "We are making a transition towards more control of the executive, towards accepting individual responsibility, and toward establishing proper standards in European life," said Patrick Cox, leader of the Liberal Party in the parliament.

Within twenty-four hours, however, Santer and several other commissioners appeared to renege on their new-found willingness to accept responsibility for wrongdoing documented by the investigators. Santer denounced the report as "unbalanced" and "shameful" and said his own reputation was "whiter than white." Cresson vigorously denied that she had done anything wrong and used faulty judgment. "I think I can be satisfied," she said of her service as a commissioner.

If Santer believed he could win reappointment to office, he was quickly disappointed by the statements of British prime minister Tony Blair, who called for "root and branch reform" of the commission, and German chancellor Gerhard Schroeder, who held the rotating presidency of the European Union and who said he would push for a replacement for Santer.

Meeting in Berlin on March 24, European leaders agreed to name Romano Prodi, a former prime minister of Italy, to replace Santer when his term of office expired at the end of 1999. Prodi was a centrist politician who had been prime minister in 1997–1998. In a speech to the European Parliament on April 13, Prodi said European institutions "and I mean all of them, must renew and reform themselves."

The European Parliament approved the appointment of Prodi on May 5, and on September 15 confirmed the other nineteen commission members. Among the members of the "new" commission were several holdovers, none *of whom had been named in the investigators' report. All were to take office at the beginning of 2000.*

Commission member Kinnock, who headed efforts to develop reform proposals, made a twenty-one point "reform strategy" public on December 14. He said it called for "radical overhaul and modernization" of the commission bureaucracy, including hiring civil servants on the basis of merit rather than personal relationships. The new commission was to adopt a detailed reform plan early in 2000.

Despite its new influence, the European Parliament failed to generate much public enthusiasm. Elections for the 626 seats in mid-June produced the lowest turnout in the twenty years of the parliament's existence: an average of 43 percent. Center-right parties scored victories in most countries; analysts said the outcomes tended to reflect sentiment on domestic concerns in most cases and that voters were sending messages of dissatisfaction to the center-left governments that were in power in much of Europe.

Expanding the European Union

Two years after temporarily suspending moves to expand membership, the European Union in December agreed on a list of thirteen potential new members. If all thirteen were admitted, the union's membership would balloon to twenty-eight, representing the bulk of nations on the European continent, with Russia as the most prominent outsider. No new members were expected to be admitted prior to late in 2002.

Six nations named by the union as potential members in 1997 were Cyprus, the Czech Republic, Estonia, Hungary, and Poland. At a December 14 meeting in Helsinki, European leaders agreed to add seven nations to that list: Bulgaria, Latvia, Lithuania, Malta, Slovakia, Slovenia, and Turkey. But, as they had in 1997, European leaders expressed doubts about Turkey, saying that country needed to improve its human rights record and accept the jurisdiction of the International Court of Justice at the Hague as the arbiter of a territorial dispute with Greece over the divided island of Cyprus. Turkey invaded Cyprus in 1974 and backed a Turkish-Cypriot regime on the northern half of the island.

> *Following are excerpts from an address to the European Parliament on April 13, 1999, by Romano Prodi, who had been named the new president of the European Commission following publication of an investigating report into fraud and mismanagement at the commission:*

When, in September 1996, I decided to step up Italy's efforts to prepare for joining the European Monetary Union at its inception, I felt the historical responsibility of the contribution made by my country to the European project over the last forty or so years.

But I felt even more strongly that only a solid bond with Europe could guarantee each individual country and each individual citizen a future of peace and progress in a world increasingly characterised by globalisation. For this reason I staked all the political capital I had accumulated on this objective.

Today, I am delighted to be standing before you, not only to assure you that I intend to bring the same determination to this new phase of the European project, but also to assure you that I and the next Commission will make all possible efforts to lead Europe into a time of major reforms and change. A time of major reforms and change.

The European institutions—and I mean all of them—must renew and reform themselves, both in terms of their policies towards the outside world and to the forms and methods of organisation within. As I say, it is time for reform for all the European institutions. The Commission, of course, but also the Council and Parliament itself.

We are not here to preserve what we have. We are here to reform.

The challenge facing us today is to prevent recent economic and political adversities from putting a stop to our process of integration. At stake is the hard-won credibility of the European undertaking. We do not simply fear delays in accomplishing our project. We fear, above all, that we will waste an opportunity to make our own indispensable contribution to resolving conflicts between countries on our doorstep.

My Vision of the European Project

This is why it is right to ask me about my vision of the European project, even at this early stage of my relationship with the European Union and my first encounter with a plenary session of Parliament. In the eighties, the single market for goods and factors of production was the major issue; in the nineties it was monetary union. Today we must tackle the difficult task of moving towards a single economy and a single politics.

While our countries have developed different models of social organisation, each has taken care to create a fair and united basis for its society. This tradition must be defended and, at the same time, reformed to make it compatible with the world outside.

This means we must reform the welfare model that the countries of Western Europe have developed and which has provided us with a high degree of social cohesion.

In the course of these reforms the individual Member States will be the leading actors, but Parliament and the Commission will need to provide momentum and coordination to enable national reforms to achieve a more efficient organisation of the labour market, which will stimulate social mobility and movement between the regions of Europe.

While competitiveness is not the sole objective for the new Europe, I am aware that a high degree of competition is a necessary instrument to reduce our unnecessary pockets of inefficiency.

The reason for us to move in this direction derives from the fact that Europe will be the largest area in the world and will be the first to have to deal with the problems of an ageing population.

The consequences of an ageing population go beyond social policies. They require a response in terms of the productivity of the economic system as a whole in order to maintain solidarity between the generations with less conflict.

The creation of a vast and efficient market for European risk capital is a prerequisite for raising productivity.

This market can also encourage our production facilities to concentrate on high-growth sectors and innovation.

There should be more direct action by governments and the Commission to stimulate investment in research and development, especially in the new electronic computer and communications technologies, but also in the chemical industry, in pharmaceuticals, biotechnology and, more generally, in the life sciences.

The key to the future of our Continent is in the hands of hi-tech, knowledge-based industries, at the cutting edge of research. These industries are not just the future of European industry or finance; they are the future of European society as a whole.

Just think of the Internet. It can change the whole organisation of production, reducing stocks and creating virtual products. Direct access to information must be increased for all. It is a long, hard road we have to travel to bridge the gap between us and the United States. Much of our work will concentrate on reducing this gap.

I have a vision, which I would like to become a commitment for the Commission, for Parliament and for the Governments of Europe. A vision that, in five years, young Europeans completing their secondary education will find themselves as well equipped as their best contemporaries anywhere in the world when it comes to using the technologies of the information society.

Europe has a great cultural tradition and a vast heritage of scientific knowledge locked away in its universities and research centres. Where Europe falls down, it is in its capacity to transform this tradition and this knowledge into opportunities for growth; it needs above all to improve the links between the world of science and the world of production.

From a macroeconomic point of view, the surrendering of monetary sovereignty has increased the importance of fiscal policies. There needs to be greater coordination to permit fiscal policies to act as a stabilising influence in the face of events or situations occurring in the various countries (known as asymmetric shocks) and, to take a more long-term view, to arrive at the genuine harmonisation of national economic systems.

The coordination of economic policies is also necessary to counteract divergences in regional economies which could develop.

The international shock waves which swept out of Asia, Russia and Brazil have prevented EMU from freeing up the same sort of growth potential that was unleashed by the prospect of the single market in the second half of the eighties and that the creation of the single currency prepared for the end of this century. Companies and families seem uncertain about the future and the events of the war in Yugoslavia only serve to further undermine their confidence.

This assessment, which is now shared by all bodies, has prompted the European Central Bank to shoulder the great responsibilities of the tasks involved in managing European monetary policy. It is now the turn of national budget authorities to work together to ensure, within the framework set out by the Maastricht Treaty and the Stability and Growth Pact, that everything possible is done to sustain growth in Europe. The Commission, in turn, will have to do its best to implement the agreements reached in Berlin on Agenda 2000 as quickly as possible and to launch, within the budgetary constraints, European projects which not only sustain demand within Europe, but also make the activities of the Union clear to see for all its citizens. This means that the Commission will also have to do its utmost to resolve the causes of tension in international trade between Europe and the United States and restore confidence to our producers. Growth is the necessary condition for European policy to play a part in reducing unemployment, but there is no guarantee that it will be enough. Therefore, now is the time for the Commission to push for a more rapid review of the rules governing labour markets and professional markets to lower the barriers preventing access and increase the personal involvement in work. The aim of all this is to make the employment situation more responsive to economic growth.

The emerging situation can only be faced successfully by the new monetary and financial stability created by the development of the single currency. We must redouble our efforts in this direction, because the high level of unemployment is the principal cause of the anxiety which seems to be spreading among the people of Europe. The declining population, mass migrations, doubts about the possibility of maintaining intact the European model of social welfare: these are the dark fears casting their shadows over the future of the Continent. If the links between the various generations and groups of citizens are not sufficiently nurtured, at European level as at all others, they will gradually crack.

To achieve these objectives we must embark on a new phase of intense economic growth. But this will happen only if we can make public administrations lighter of touch and introduce the sort of microeconomic reforms I have mentioned.

Political Aspects

At the political level, the prospects for the European Union in the international field have never looked so promising. From the enlargement of the Union to the universal assertion of the principles of liberty and democracy, the desire for Europe and its presence is a sentiment which we are morally and politically obliged to satisfy. . . .

The Union has grown enormously and is still growing. The tasks it has set itself need stronger, more cohesive institutions, closer dialogue and a stronger democratic process. In the history of the Union and in its institutional philosophy, the three principal institutions must establish stronger links: Parliament and the Council should steadily increase their role of management and guidance, whilst the Commission should increasingly be able to improve its ability to guide the growth of the Union. The different national governments and the institutions and bodies at local level will have a decisive role to play.

A united Europe is only as strong as its autonomous components.

This means that the Commission has to pursue two strategic objectives. The first is to help map out the future.

The second is to ensure that the Union as a whole enjoys effective administrative structures. I have already said that the Commission has to be the "guardian of the Treaties"; but it is only if there is a productive, honest and open relationship between Commission, Parliament and Council that we will be able to evolve a Europe that grows closer and closer to its citizens.

The ambitious tasks I have set out for the Europe of the future cannot be pursued for any length of time with the Community institutions as they stand, which the Amsterdam Treaty has only just begun to reform. Enlargement itself makes action necessary, since institutions designed for six members, and which are already inadequate now, will certainly not be in a position to govern a Union made up of 20 or 25 countries.

There will have to be thoroughgoing reform of the Commission, and the portfolios will have to be reorganised to reflect the great new political priorities and the shifting nature of its tasks. But if European institutions which are growing daily in importance are to enjoy democratic legitimacy, and if the policies pursued by the Union are to be effective, there will have to be a more ambitious programme, based on a strengthening of Parliament's powers of codecision, more frequent resort to majority voting in the Council, and full implementation of the Amsterdam Treaty's provisions on the role of the President of the Commission in the selection of Commissioners and the distribution of their powers.

I am fully aware of the fact that this House, the Governments of the Member States and more generally public opinion throughout Europe have very high expectations of the reform of the Commission's internal workings which will we have to carry out.

This reform will be one of the foundations of the programme of the new Commission, and will require the application of at least three principles: greater efficiency, absolute transparency, and full accountability. But I can assure the House right away that we will show no toleration towards corruption; that there will be ever greater openness in our work, and that we will be prepared to account readily for our actions; and that we will take full responsibility for what we do, both as a body and as individual Commissioners. . . .

Conclusions

I have frequently had occasion to observe that, in a sense, the search for a European "soul" is increasingly proving to be the major problem facing our continent as it looks to the future. It is certainly a mistake to be thinking of a possible way ahead for the European institutions (a strengthening of Parliament, use of the right of veto in exceptional cases and a reorganising of the Commission and its powers) without tackling the problem of how to gradually build up a shared feeling of belonging to Europe.

There is no dominant culture in Europe, which I think is a genuine stroke of luck. Europe would not have been what it has been in history, or be what it is now, if its various individual national cultures had not survived through the centuries and were not now flourishing.

But—and this seems to me something less positive—there are no philosophers, thinkers or "lifestyle gurus" that we can look up to nowadays right across the continent.

There is, however, a risk that what is happening on the financial markets may start happening in the area of culture and values. The euro is forming a single market out of so many different forces, but it is able to perform this unifying function, in these early months, largely thanks to American commercial banks and investment funds.

The power of American culture in the broad sense and as expressed in symbolic form by the media is actually believed by some to be capable of acting as a single point of reference for a Europe in quest of its soul.

There is nothing discreditable about such a supposition, especially since the world in store for us will depend for its balance on ever closer cooperation between Europe and the United States in the fields of politics, the economy and defence.

This assumes a degree of affinity, as far as the broad lines go, in the understanding of society on either side. I would point out, however, that Europe in the course of its history has had a great heritage to live up to, a heritage which still forms the richest store of culture and knowledge amassed by mankind. Unfortunately, there are no ready-made experiments or recipes for achieving this objective.

The only thing that remains is to take the confusion of the present day as our starting point for moving against the dispersal of knowledge and culture, for beating back the Babel of languages till we find a shared form of speech, a way of talking to one another which every day becomes more of a necessity. We cannot lock ourselves in the past. The ready-made nostrums of the past century are no longer enough.

Europe offers a great opportunity for talking our past over again, for comparing it with the experiences of others, for freeing ourselves once for all from inheritances which were originally supposed to bring us together but have instead kept us apart.

No leader and no nation can on its own abandon the past and build the future. But it can be done by the peoples and governments of Europe all working together.

That is why we have to have Europe: we cannot find the new way forward on our own. On our own, we cannot tackle the most basic problems of the present day either, beginning with the greatest one of all, in other words our relationship with the peoples who live around us and who look to us to help build their political and economic future.

No single country by itself can give them an answer: only Europe can give the answer. Just as the economic objectives are being hit by the effects of international developments, so, too, may this political project for Europe be put at risk by the serious events going on in the war in Yugoslavia. If the project is to survive now, it needs to be speeded up. The tragedy of Kosovo makes it dramatically clear that the European Union has to play an increasingly important part in guaranteeing security and democracy in areas which are of vital importance for our future.

This future is something we must build ourselves, with the strength of our institutions, by bringing into being the shared defence structures and the common foreign policy promised to Europe's peoples by the Treaties of Maastricht and Amsterdam.

The Commission will shoulder its full responsibility for showing the citizens of the Union the reforms which will have to be carried out to bring that future into being.

This is a move which will only succeed if the European Parliament supports it.

STARR ON THE FUTURE OF THE INDEPENDENT COUNSEL LAW
April 14, 1999

Congress in 1999 allowed to lapse the law authorizing appointment of independent counsels in cases of alleged wrongdoing by high government officials. The lack of congressional support for the long-controversial law stemmed, in large part, from heated partisan disputes over the actions of Kenneth W. Starr, the independent counsel whose investigations led to the impeachment of President Bill Clinton in 1998. Starr himself testified to Congress on April 14 that the law authorizing his work was unconstitutional and troublesome.

Congress wrote the independent counsel law in 1978 in reaction to the Watergate scandal that forced President Richard Nixon to resign. The law never lacked detractors, and Congress ensured repeated controversy by requiring that the law be subject to renewal every five years. Even so, the law survived these controversies until 1992, an election year, when it was allowed to lapse because of Republican discontent with the prolonged investigation by independent counsel Lawrence Walsh into the Iran-contra dealings of the Reagan administration. Congress summoned enough support to revive the law in 1994, but by 1999 few in Congress appeared to have the appetite to take on the issue anytime soon. (Independent counsel law, Historic Documents of 1998, p. 905; Iran-contra affair, Historic Documents of 1994, p. 8)

Attorney General Janet Reno stepped into the void created by the death of the independent counsel statute. On July 1 she published regulations for the appointment of a special counsel by the attorney general. However, Reno's regulations gave special counsels much less independence than independent counsels enjoyed under the expired law. Reno on September 9 made her first appointment under the new regulations, naming former senator John C. Danforth, a Missouri Republican, to examine the government's review of its own actions in the deaths of seventy-six people at a compound of the Branch Davidian cult in Waco, Texas, in 1993. (Waco investigation, p. 480)

Starr Testimony

Twenty-one independent counsels had been appointed since the law authorizing the position was enacted in 1978, and several had conducted controversial investigations into sensitive matters, such as the Iran-contra affair and a scandal involving senior officials of the Department of Housing and Urban Development during the administration of Ronald Reagan. But none of the investigations or independent counsels had caused nearly as much controversy or upheaval as the five-year probe by Kenneth Starr into various actions by President Clinton.

A three-judge panel in 1994 named Starr, a former federal judge active in Republican circles, to investigate the actions of Clinton and his wife Hilary Rodham Clinton in connection with a failed real estate deal in Arkansas called "Whitewater." Starr gradually expanded his probe to include other controversies involving Clinton and his aides, including alleged improprieties at the White House travel office, the suicide of White House counsel Vincent W. Foster, the alleged misuse by the White House of FBI investigative files, and charges of unethical actions by former deputy attorney general Webster L. Hubbell.

Early in 1998 Starr asked for and received permission from Reno to examine allegations that Clinton had lied under oath while testifying about a suit brought against him by Paula Corbin Jones. A former Arkansas state employee, Jones alleged that Clinton—when governor of Arkansas—solicited sex from her in a hotel room. Starr in September 1998 submitted to Congress a report alleging that Clinton had committed eleven impeachable offenses in connection with his testimony about the Jones case and his affair with White House intern Monica Lewinsky. The House of Representatives in December 1998 voted two articles of impeachment against Clinton, citing evidence compiled by Starr. Clinton was acquitted by the Senate in February 1999. (Starr report and impeachment, Historic Documents of 1998, pp. 632, 958; Senate acquittal of Clinton, p. 15)

Many Democrats attacked Starr and his prosecutorial methods, accusing him of conducting a partisan vendetta against the president. Among other things, Democrats said Starr began investigating Clinton's sex life only because he was unable to develop any damaging evidence against the president in the Whitewater case—the original reason for his appointment. Democrats also denounced repeated news reports that appeared to originate from Starr's office. A chief complaint against Starr was his decision to send Congress thousands of pages of material about Clinton's affair with Lewinsky, including secret grand jury testimony. The House Judiciary Committee later voted, along partisan lines and without objection from Starr, to release the material to the public—a step that Democrats and many legal experts said damaged the grand jury process. Most Republicans defended Starr and his methods, saying he had to take an aggressive approach in investigating wrongdoing by a president who had a history of lying about his actions.

It was in this context, just two months after the Senate acquitted Clinton, that Starr appeared before the Senate Committee on Governmental Affairs on April 14 and urged that Congress allow the independent counsel statute to lapse when its authorization expired June 30. Starr argued against the statute on constitutional, procedural, and political grounds. While acknowledging that the Supreme Court had upheld the constitutionality of the statute, Starr argued that it violated the Constitution because it attempted to "cram a fourth branch of government into our three-branch system." Under the statute, he said, an independent counsel was separated from, and generally unaccountable to, the legislative, executive, and judicial branches—in effect a fourth branch of government. Starr said the statute also established vague criteria regulating the cases in which an attorney general was to initiate steps leading to appointment of an independent counsel. And while the law was supposed to remove sensitive inquiries from partisan politics, he said, in actual practice independent counsels "are especially vulnerable to partisan attack" because they had no institutional support within the government. "In this fashion, the legislative effort to take politics out of law enforcement sometimes has the ironic effect of politicizing it," Starr said.

After listening to Starr's testimony, Democrats on the committee professed astonishment. "If you live long enough, you'll experience everything," Sen. Robert G. Torricelli of New Jersey said. Sen. Richard J. Durbin of Illinois said Starr had appeared before Congress asking its members to "stop me before I prosecute again."

Under harsh questioning by Democrats, Starr defended his inquiry and said he had followed standard Justice Department prosecutorial regulations. He noted that federal judges who exercised supervision over his work had never rebuked him.

Starr resigned as independent counsel on October 18, having spent more than $40 million on his inquiry into the Clintons. He was succeeded by a staff attorney, Robert W. Ray, who was one of several independent counsels allowed to continue working under a "grandfather clause" of the expired law.

Views of Other Experts

In other hearings on the issue during the early months of 1999, congressional panels heard conflicting views from legal experts, former independent counsels, and former members of Congress and administration officials. The Clinton administration, reversing its previous position of supporting the law, on March 2 announced its opposition to renewing it.

One experienced voice urging Congress to take its time to decide the issue was that of Howard H. Baker, a former Republican senator from Tennessee who sat on the Senate Watergate Committee and had briefly served as chief of staff to President Reagan. While saying the law should be allowed to lapse, Baker said Congress should take no irrevocable action on the issue. "I recommend . . . that we cool it. We think about it for a while.

*We let the temper of these times soften. There's no absolute urgency in pass-
ing anything," Baker told the Senate Committee on Governmental Affairs
on February 24.*

*The American Bar Association, which had been among the initial advo-
cates of an independent counsel law in the wake of the Watergate scandal,
switched position in 1999. Meeting in Los Angeles on February 8, the bar
association's House of Delegates voted 384–49 to oppose renewal of the
statute "in any form." The organization adopted a report of a special task
force that found that the law was proving unworkable and counterproductive.*

*Several attorneys who had served as independent counsels under the
statute, or as special counsels investigating government scandals, argued
for preserving most aspects of the law. Among them were Walsh, the Iran-
contra prosecutor; Samuel Dash, chief counsel of the Senate Watergate
Committee; and Henry Ruth, a senior attorney in the Watergate special
prosecutor's office. But even these men said the law should be changed.
Walsh said independent counsels should be appointed only to investigate
alleged wrongdoing by presidents and attorneys general; Dash called for
specific changes in the law, such as making it extremely difficult for independent counsels to expand the scope of their inquiries.*

*Yet another view on the issue came in May with a report commissioned
by two of Washington's most influential think tanks, the Brookings Institution and the American Enterprise Institute. The two organizations asked
former Senate majority leaders Robert J. Dole, a Republican, and George J.
Mitchell, a Democrat, to chair a committee of legal experts to examine possible changes in the independent counsel law. In their report, Dole and
Mitchell acknowledged that Congress appeared likely not to renew the law.
As an alternative, they suggested new legislation authorizing the attorney
general to appoint special counsels to investigate high-level wrongdoing.
The counsels should have a high degree of independence, the committee
said, with full authority to conduct grand jury proceedings, initiate
indictments, conduct trials, and appeal decisions—so long as they adhered
to standard Justice Department guidelines for federal prosecutors.*

New Justice Department Regulations

*With the expiration of the independent counsel law on June 30, Attorney
General Reno put into effect a new set of regulations for special counsels.
Under Reno's regulations, the attorney general could determine that it
would be "in the public interest" to appoint a special counsel from outside
the Justice Department to conduct an investigation. That broad language
replaced the often-criticized portion of the independent counsel law requiring the attorney general to go through complex procedural maneuvers to
determine whether grounds existed for a special investigation.*

*The core of Reno's new regulation involved the degree of independence to
be accorded special counsels. In an introductory section, Reno acknowledged
that "there is no perfect solution" to the issue. She said she attempted to strike*

a balance between the sometimes conflicting principles of independence and accountability—a balance giving the special counsel "day-to-day independence" but retaining ultimate responsibility with the attorney general.

Under Reno's regulations, a special counsel would have "the full power and independent authority" to conduct investigations and prosecute cases, including taking such steps as presenting evidence to grand juries, preparing indictments, and taking cases to trial. However, the regulations gave the attorney general the right to review any action by the special counsel and determine that "the action is so inappropriate or unwarranted under established departmental practices" that it should not be taken. The attorney general could also remove a special counsel for "good cause," such as willful violation of Justice Department policies and regulations.

> *Following are excerpts from testimony delivered April 14, 1999, by Kenneth W. Starr, the independent counsel investigating President Bill Clinton, to a hearing of the Senate Committee on Governmental Affairs in which Starr called on Congress not to renew the statute authorizing the appointment of independent counsels:*

After carefully considering the statute and its consequences, both intended and unintended, I concur with the Attorney General. The statute should not be reauthorized.

The reason is not that criminality in government no longer exists. Nor is the reason that the public has grown serenely indifferent to our tradition of holding government officials to a high standard. Rather, the reason is this: By its very existence, the Act promises us that corruption in high places will be reliably monitored, investigated, exposed, and prosecuted, through a process fully insulated from political winds. But that is more than the Act delivers, and more than it *can* deliver under our constitutional system. Briefly:

- The statutory trigger is unenforceable. If we're going to rely on the Attorney General's good faith, then we should do so forthrightly. We should acknowledge that the Attorney General is the indispensable actor in federal law enforcement, and hold her accountable for the exercise of that authority. Significantly, this is the view of Attorney General [Janet] Reno and all of her predecessors who have testified here or in the House this year.
- The mechanical simplicity of the language in the statute camouflages the inescapable exercise of professional judgment and discretion. The focus should be on whether the Department is capable of conducting an impartial investigation. The statute, by trying to create a litmus test for partiality, distracts us from that central concern.
- Because the Independent Counsel is vulnerable to partisan attack, the investigation is likely to be seen as political. If politicization and the loss

of public confidence are inevitable, then we should leave the full responsibility where our laws and traditions place it, on the Attorney General (or, where she deems it appropriate, her appointee as special counsel) and on the Congress.

- The statute leaves the Independent Counsel substantially dependent on the Department of Justice, which may have incentives to impede, or at least not assist, his work.
- The law may have the unfortunate effect of eroding respect for the judiciary, through attacks—unanswered and institutionally unanswerable—on the Special Division. It is one thing to turn the political attack machine on a prosecutor; it is quite another to turn it on the judiciary.
- The law also may have the effect of discouraging vigorous oversight by the Congress, in a departure from our traditions.
- In a variety of ways, the statute tries to cram a fourth branch of government into our three-branch system. But, invariably, this new entity lacks (in Madison's phrase) the "constitutional means ... to resist encroachments." The result is structurally unsound, constitutionally dubious, and—in overstating the degree of institutional independence—disingenuous.

To be sure, returning to the pre-Act regime entails undisputed disadvantages. There was no golden age of special prosecutors.

If the past is any guide, more investigations are likely to stay in the Justice Department, with no outsider appointed. That means—again, if the past is any guide—more politically tinged cases in which the investigation will be seen, fairly or unfairly, as something less than thoroughgoing.

Then there is the possibility that politics will play a role. On occasion, as Timothy Flanigan [a former assistant attorney general] pointed out last month, "men and women who are deeply involved in the political passions of their times" will be overseeing a law enforcement investigation "that may have far-reaching political implications."

Professor Cass Sunstein, though he opposes the statute, acknowledges that the law probably has deterred crime by (in his words) "letting high-level officials know of the serious consequences of any illegal conduct." As investigations into public corruption are seen as becoming less vigorous, the deterrent effect will diminish.

When a case is closed with no indictments, the public may be more skeptical. As Nathan Lewin pointed out, a statutory Independent Counsel provides additional reassurance of fairness and thoroughness in such instances.

More gravely, restoring the regime of regulatory special counsels may invite another Saturday Night Massacre [President Nixon's firing of special Watergate counsel Archibald Cox in 1973], this time with a different outcome. The "thin thread," as Mr. [Henry] Ruth [former Watergate special counsel lawyer] put it, may give way the next time; the final cover-up may succeed—as, in the view of some historians, occurred in the 1870s when President Grant fired a special prosecutor at a crucial moment of the investigation.

We should not overlook these risks. But we have to make trade-offs. In light of all the factors, I respectfully recommend that the statute not be reenacted.

If, however, the Congress does decide to modify and reenact the statute, I urge you to beware of gimmicks. Attorney General Reno said of the current system, "It can't get any worse. . . ." With all due respect, I disagree. The system could indeed be made worse, and one of the proposals before you would have just that effect.

I speak of the proposal to impose a time limit on investigations. As Senator [Carl] Levin [D-Mich.] said in 1993, "Complex Federal criminal cases often take years to investigate." And, as Senator Levin also wisely noted, many of the people who complain the loudest about the slow pace of an investigation tend to be the ones who themselves have delayed it.

Remember, too, the tactics of defense attorneys. According to his biographer, the legendary trial lawyer Edward Bennett Williams invariably employed the same strategy in each major criminal case that he handled. The strategy: delay. As Mr. Ruth said before this Committee last month, "[t]he second you set a time limit, 23 people get a one-way trip to China," for "delay is the first principle of defense."

A time limit, even if it allowed extensions in unusual circumstances, would confer few benefits while imposing significant costs. Any attorney worth his or her salt knows how to delay proceedings in subtle and not-so-subtle ways, such as the sixteen months we lost while litigating jurisdiction in the *Tucker* case [Starr's prosecution of Arkansas governor Jim Guy Tucker]. A Procrustean time limit would invite lawyers to run out the clock.

If you do reauthorize the statute, I urge you to broaden the Attorney General's discretion. Greater emphasis should be placed on Section 591(c), which gives the Attorney General the authority to seek appointment of an Independent Counsel whenever an investigation raises a conflict of interest. The list of categorical triggers in Section 591(b) should be shortened. As for the preliminary investigation under Section 592, the time limit should be extended or abandoned. The Attorney General should be given authority to use traditional law enforcement tools to gather information, and the authority to take into account the full panoply of traditional prosecutorial considerations.

Some witnesses have suggested that the Independent Counsel's jurisdictional limits be tightened, perhaps by eliminating the provision for expansions. In the view of these witnesses, an Independent Counsel with an expanding mandate, as the law now permits, may appear to be pursuing a personal vendetta, or at least a prosecutorial fiefdom.

In our investigation, the Department and the Special Division expanded our jurisdiction four times, to cover matters related to the firing of White House Travel Office employees, the accumulating of FBI files in the White House, the Congressional testimony of a former White House Counsel, and, finally, Monica Lewinsky. In some of those instances, the expansion came at the Department's initiative; we agreed to accept the added jurisdiction, which we had not sought. The number of expansions is unique, and it may have fed the misconception that we were investigating individuals rather than crimes. Let me make clear: that was not the case. Indeed, I am as proud of our decisions *not* to bring several indictments as I am of anything else we have done.

Keep in mind that in each of the jurisdictional expansions, the Attorney General concluded that she faced a conflict of interest. If she had not acted to expand our jurisdiction, she would have been obliged to seek the appointment in each instance of a *new* Independent Counsel. Eliminating jurisdictional expansions thus will substantially increase start-up costs and delays. It also may produce even more litigation over jurisdiction, leading to still greater costs and delays.

There is one proposal that I endorse wholeheartedly: Senator Baker's suggestion that the Congress postpone any decision on the statute for a cooling-off period, or, perhaps more aptly, a ceasefire. Let the statute lapse. Monitor the Justice Department's record in selecting regulatory special counsels. And then reassess after the current intensities have passed, and when—in the words of *Federalist 2*—no one will be "influenced by any passions except love for their country."

In conclusion, I think it is fair to say that the Act has been a worthwhile experiment. Like most experiments that are professionally conducted, it has yielded significant results. The results, I believe, support this conclusion: Jurisdiction and authority over these cases ought to be returned to the Justice Department. And who will oversee them? The Congress, the press, and the public.

This is not, as I said, a perfect solution. It will no doubt give rise to imperfect outcomes. But it puts me in mind of Winston Churchill's famous remark about democracy—the worst system, he called it, except for all the others. Returning the authority over these prosecutions to Attorneys General, and relying on them to appoint outside counsel when necessary, is the worst system—except for all the others.

In this difficult realm, solutions are bound to be transitory. Twenty-five years after the Saturday Night Massacre, we are still searching for a reasonable, effective, and constitutional approach. No matter what the Congress decides, no matter what microsurgical precision is applied to fine-tune the statute, these problems will endure.

ASTRONOMERS ON DISCOVERY OF A MULTIPLANET SOLAR SYSTEM
April 15, 1999

Scientists in 1999 came closer than ever to finding evidence that the Earth's solar system is not unique in the universe. For the first time, astronomers located another system with multiple planets circling a living star, similar to the Sun. The giant planets were composed of hot gas and were thought incapable of supporting life. But their existence gave new support to theories that the universe had other solar systems where life might exist.

Technology available in 1999 was incapable of determining many details about the newly discovered planetary system. The system centered around the star Upsilon Andromedae in the Andromeda constellation, a member of the Milky Way galaxy. The star was forty-four light years (about 260 trillion miles) from Earth. Space explorations planned by the National Aeronautics and Space Administration (NASA) for the second and third decades of the twenty-first century were expected to provide more information, including whether the Upsilon Andromedae system contained planets with Earth-like characteristics.

Discovering Planets

For hundreds of years, scientists and philosophers had imagined that some of the billions of stars in the universe were host to planetary systems similar to the solar system. The Milky Way—the galaxy in which the solar system is located—contains an estimated 200 billion stars, and scientists believed it was likely that planets had formed around many of them. Nine planets orbit the Sun; the Earth is the only one known to be able to sustain life.

It was not until the 1990s that astronomers developed hard evidence that other planets existed outside the solar system. In 1992 astronomers detected planets around an exploded dead star (called a pulsar) in the constellation Virgo. In 1995 Michael Mayor of the Geneva Observatory in Switzerland found the first evidence of a planet around a living star simi-

lar to the Sun. Other planets around stars were found throughout the late 1990s, bringing the total to about twenty. Most of the solitary planets were larger than Jupiter and scientists believed all were composed of gas, not solid material like the Earth.

In 1996 Geoffrey Marcy of San Francisco State University (SFSU) and R. Paul Butler of the Anglo-Australian Observatory detected a gaseous planet, about two-thirds the size of Jupiter, orbiting near Upsilon Andromedae. In February and March 1999, Marcy and colleagues at SFSU detected two more plants orbiting that star—meaning that Upsilon Andromedae was the first living star known to have a "system" composed of more than one planet.

The findings of the SFSU scientists, based on observations at the Lick Observatory near San Jose, California, were independently confirmed by another team of astronomers using data from the Whipple Observatory near Tucson, Arizona. The latter team included scientists from the Harvard-Smithsonian Center for Astrophysics in Cambridge, Massachusetts, and the High Altitude Observatory in Boulder, Colorado.

The teams jointly announced their findings on March 15. Marcy, generally considered one of the world's leading planetary researchers, said the findings meant that "here, for the first time, we can see a kinship between these planets and our own solar system." Debra Fischer, a colleague at SFSU, said the findings also implied that "planets can form more easily than we ever imagined, and that our Milky Way is teeming with planetary systems."

As of early 1999, all the astronomers' "observations" of distant planets were made indirectly. The planets could not be seen directly by telescopes that collected rays of lights or radio emissions. Instead, astronomers inferred the existence of the planets from the gravitational effects they had on the stars they orbited. As a planet orbited a star, it created what scientists called "wobbles" or "reflex motions" on the star itself. Careful observation of the motion of the star enabled scientists to determine the existence of the planet and some information about it, such as its orbit and its mass.

Although scientists were excited by the findings of planets around Upsilon Andromedae, they also were mystified by one of the central elements: all three planets were huge, gaseous masses similar to Jupiter, and two of them orbited near the star. The inner-most planet, in fact, was so close that it completed its orbit every 4.6 days. Existing scientific theory held that large, gaseous, Jupiter-like planets could not form so close to a living star because the region was too hot. Scientists said they would have to develop new theories to account for the system they found around Upsilon Andromedae. Perhaps, one scientist said, the planets might have formed further away from the star and then moved inward, for unknown reasons.

The presence of the giant Jupiter-like planets made it unlikely that Earth-like planets orbited Upsilon Andromedae in what scientists called the "habitable zone" around the star—close enough to absorb some of the star's heat but not so close as to be scorched. If any Earth-like planets developed in that zone, they probably would have been quickly pushed out of the way by the much larger gaseous planets.

More Planetary Findings

Astronomers had plenty of additional planetary news in 1999. In November astronomer Greg Henry of Tennessee State University reported the first direct observation of a planet around a star: HD 209458 in the constellation Pegasus. Using data from telescopes in Arizona, Henry watched the shadow of a planet as it crossed the star at exactly the time predicted by indirect observations of a wobble in the star's motion. Marcy, the SFSU scientist who had provided the clues for Henry's findings, said the planetary shadow proved that the planets he had detected by indirect observation "really are planets."

Marcy and other astronomers on November 29 announced they had found six additional planets, each orbiting a star. Five of the six planets were in the "habitable zone" of their stars, but all appeared to be giant balls of gas and therefore unlikely to support any form of life similar to that known on Earth. The November announcement brought to twenty-eight the number of planets discovered outside the solar system, as of late 1999.

Findings on Mars and Jupiter's Moons

Interplanetary missions by NASA spacecraft provided new details in 1999 about space bodies much closer to home: the planet Mars and two of the moons orbiting Jupiter. NASA had mixed luck with its missions to Mars. Two satellites that were to explore the red planet disappeared in separate incidents in August and December. (Mars mission failures, p. 711)

But in March another mission, the Mars Global Surveyor, *began its scheduled two-year task of mapping the Martian surface. The* Global Surveyor *reached its orbit in September 1997, but it took NASA technicians more than a year to correct a malfunction in the craft's solar power panels and get it into place for its mapping mission. In the meantime,* Global Surveyor *sent photographs and other data that provided spectacular details about Mars, especially its volcanic past. Scientists said the photographs proved that Mars once had water, lots of it, which flooded parts of the planet's surface and created scars still visible today.*

NASA also continued to collect vast amounts of data about the moons orbiting Jupiter. The data was sent back to Earth by the Galileo *spacecraft, which had been orbiting Jupiter since 1995. In September NASA reported that* Galileo *had detected large quantities of sulfuric acid—the harsh acid used in car batteries—on the surface of Jupiter's moon Europa. The spacecraft also produced data leading scientists to believe that an ocean of liquid, possibly including water, might lie beneath the icy crust of Europa. In December NASA reported that* Galileo *had observed lava spewing from a volcano on another Jovian moon, Io. One fountain of lava shot more than a mile above the moon's surface, a massive eruption compared to the gen-*

erally more sedate volcanic lava flows on Earth. (Galileo findings, Historic Documents of 1997, p. 202)

> *Following are excerpts from a statement released March 15, 1999, by San Francisco State University; the Harvard-Smithsonian Center for Astrophysics in Cambridge, Massachusetts; and the University Corporation for Atmospheric Research in Boulder, Colorado, announcing the discovery of three large gaseous planets around the star Upsilon Andromedae:*

Astronomers from four research institutions have discovered strong evidence for a trio of extrasolar planets that orbit the star Upsilon Andromedae. This is the first multiple planet system ever found around a normal star, other than the nine planets in our Solar System. The closest planet in the Upsilon Andromedae system was detected in 1996 by San Francisco State University (SFSU) astronomers Geoffrey Marcy and R. Paul Butler. Now, after 11 years of telescope observations at the Lick Observatory near San Jose, CA, the signals of two additional planets have emerged from the data. Therefore, Upsilon Andromedae harbors the first planetary system that is reminiscent of our own Solar System.

In parallel, a team of astronomers from the Harvard-Smithsonian Center for Astrophysics (CFA) in Cambridge, MA and the High Altitude Observatory (HAO) in Boulder, CO have independently found the two outer planets around Upsilon Andromedae. This team has been studying the star for more than 4 years at the Whipple Observatory near Tucson, AZ.

This first planetary system, found from a survey of 107 stars, suggests that planetary systems like our own are abundant in our Milky Way Galaxy, which contains 200 billion stars. SFSU researcher Dr. Debra Fischer said, "It implies that planets can form more easily than we ever imagined, and that our Milky Way is teeming with planetary systems."

The innermost (and previously known) of the three planets contains at least three-quarters of the mass of Jupiter and orbits only 0.06 AU from the star. (One "AU" equals the distance from the Earth to the Sun). It traverses a circular orbit every 4.6 days. The middle planet contains at least twice the mass of Jupiter and it takes 242 days to orbit the star once. It resides approximately 0.83 AU from the star, similar to the orbital distance of Venus. The outermost planet has a mass of at least four Jupiters and completes one orbit every 3.5 to 4 years, placing it 2.5 AU from the star. The two outer planets are both new discoveries and have elliptical (oval) orbits which is characteristic of the nine other extrasolar planets in distant orbits around their stars.

No current theory predicted that so many giant worlds would form around a star. "I am mystified at how such a system of Jupiter-like planets might have been created," said Marcy, SFSU's Distinguished Professor of Science. "This will shake up the theory of planet formation." Robert Noyes, a professor of astronomy at Harvard-Smithsonian CFA and a member of the CFA-HAO team, said, "A nagging question was whether the massive bodies orbiting in apparent isolation around stars really are planets, but now that we see three around the same star, it is hard to imagine anything else."

Currently a staff astronomer at the Anglo-Australian Observatory, Butler is the lead author of the paper, submitted to the *Astrophysical Journal,* announcing the triple planet system. Along with Marcy, Fischer, and Noyes, the authors include Sylvain Korzennik, Peter Nisenson, and Adam Contos of the Harvard-Smithsonian CFA, and Timothy Brown of the HAO. "Both of our groups found essentially the same size and shape for the orbits of the companions", said Korzennik. "The chances of this happening by accident are infinitesimal." Fischer added, "This is an extraordinary finding and it demands extraordinary evidence. Having two completely independent sets of observations gives us confidence in this detection."

Marcy and Butler had suspected that there was something strange about Upsilon Andromedae. The velocity variations that revealed the closest planet to the star in 1996 had an unusual amount of scatter. Not until early this year had enough observations been made of the star to confirm the presence of an additional planet, which explained some of the confusing pattern in the data. But another object still seemed to be tugging on the star. "We looked at the two planet solution that we had been expecting and there was still too much extra noise," said Fischer. "We arrived at the conclusion that the extra observed wobble could only be explained by the presence of a third planet." Both teams of astronomers considered astrophysical effects that could mimic the velocity signature from these planets, but no such effects are viable. A computer simulation by Greg Laughlin of U.C. Berkeley suggests that these three giant planets could co-exist in stable orbits.

One big question left to answer is how such a solar system arose. "The usual picture is that gas giant planets form at least four AU away from a star, where temperatures are low enough for ice to condense and start the process of planet formation," said Brown. "But all three giant planets around Upsilon Andromedae now reside inside this theoretical ice boundary." The planets may have formed close to the host star, or, like balls on a billiard table, the planets may have scattered off of each other, migrating into their current orbits from a more distant place of origin.

The discovery of this multiple planet system suggests a new paradigm for planet formation where many small seed planets known as planetesimals might develop in the disk of matter surrounding a star. Those planets that grow fastest would engage in a gravitational tug of war that weeds out some of the smaller worlds and determines which planets ultimately remain in orbit. "The Upsilon Andromedae system suggests that gravitational interactions between Jupiter-mass planets can play a powerful role in sculpting solar systems," said Butler.

If these Jupiter-mass planets are like our own Jupiter, they would not be expected to have solid Earth-like surfaces. But, Nisenson noted, "our observations can't rule out Earth-sized planets as well in this planetary system, because their gravity would be too weak for them to be detectable with present instruments."

A bright star visible to the naked eye starting this June, Upsilon Andromedae is 44 light-years away from Earth and it is roughly 3 billion years old, two-thirds the age of the Sun. This star should make an ideal target for NASA's upcoming Space Interferometry Mission (SIM). Expected to launch in 2005, SIM will spend five years probing nearby stars for Earth-sized planets and will test technology slated for future planet-searching telescopes. The ongoing ground-based planet search will enable SIM to home in on those stars most likely to harbor small planets.

VICE PRESIDENT ON SHOOTINGS AT COLUMBINE HIGH SCHOOL
April 25, 1999

Late on a Tuesday morning in April two high school seniors rampaged through Columbine High School in Littleton, Colorado, throwing pipe bombs and shooting semiautomatic guns at anyone they could find. When the assault was over some five hours later, thirteen people had been gunned down, the two shooters had committed suicide, twenty-three people were wounded, a community had been plunged into shock and grief, and a nation was anxiously searching for causes and answers.

Self-styled loners and outcasts, the two shooters, Eric Harris, eighteen, and Dylan Klebold, seventeen, left behind tapes and diaries showing their rage at being taunted by classmates and others for refusing to dress and act like other teenagers. They also expressed open hatred of blacks, Jews, and other minorities. The two had planned the massacre for at least a year, apparently in an effort to draw attention to themselves. The diaries indicated that Harris and Klebold wanted to kill as many as five hundred of their classmates and teachers.

For the next several days, as the families of the twelve murdered students and one teacher buried their loved ones and the police began their investigations, much of the nation publicly agonized over the causes of the Columbine massacre and other school shootings. Although more people were killed and injured in the Columbine incident than in any other single mass shooting in a school, additional school shootings had occurred between October 1997 and May 1998, with thirteen students and teachers killed and forty-six wounded. The shootings left students, their parents, school authorities, and government officials searching for ways to prevent similar rampages elsewhere. Predictably, there were loud calls for tighter gun controls, less violence on television and in the movies, and better school security. (School safety, Historic Documents of 1998, p. 735)

Day of Rage

The shootings at Columbine High began about 11:30 A.M. on April 20 when Harris and Klebold began to walk through the school firing semiau-

tomatic weapons. Some students and their teachers fled the school; others were trapped in classrooms and closets. Some students used their cell phones to call police, parents, and the media. The next hours were filled with confusion as police moved methodically through the school looking for the gunmen. The two were found dead in the school library, along with ten of the victims. Survivors told gruesome stories of how Harris and Klebold had taunted their victims before coldly killing them. The last of the bodies was not removed from the school until the following day because police were concerned about time bombs.

It was later reported that in addition to a semiautomatic rifle and pistol and two shotguns, the police had found fifty-one bombs in the school and in Harris's home. Most were pipe bombs, filled with shrapnel to inflict more damage. The police also reported that the two teenagers had put a multi-gallon propane tank, set to explode with a timer mechanism, in the school cafeteria. The timer failed, as did their efforts to detonate it with gunshots. How the two had accumulated such an arsenal and smuggled it into the school without their families or anyone at the school discovering it remained unclear. A friend was reported to have bought at least one of the guns at a local gun show. In a videotape, Klebold filmed Harris in his bedroom showing the guns, bombs, and ammunition he had hidden in his room. The tape was one of several the two had made as they planned their shooting spree.

The tapes, which were released in December, confirmed what had been widely speculated at the time of the shootings. They showed two teenagers, alienated from their peers and filled with rage and anger, who wanted to "get paybacks" against classmates and relatives they believed had slighted them. Many people, however, especially in the days immediately after the shootings, were still trying to understand how such emotions could escalate into the carnage that Harris and Klebold inflicted. "All of us are struggling to understand what happened and why," President Bill Clinton said April 21. Four days later, Vice President Al Gore told 60,000 people gathered in a shopping mall parking lot near Columbine High School that he "would be misleading you if I said I understand this; I don't." Gore then praised the Columbine students for their courage and called for an end to the violence. "Parents, we can stop the violence and hate," Gore said April 25. "In a culture ripe with violence where too many young people place too little value on human life, we can rise up and we can say, no more."

Sporadic threats of violent actions directed at students and schools forced the temporary closing of various schools across the nation during 1999 and resulted in the suspension and arrest of numerous youngsters alleged to be responsible for the threats. One of the schools closed, for two days in December, was Columbine itself. Two other school shooting incidents also occurred in 1999; neither resulted in loss of life. On May 20, a fifteen-year-old sophomore in Conyers, Georgia, opened fire on groups of students standing outside the high school waiting for classes to begin. The student, T. J. Solomon, who was reported to be despondent over breaking up with his girlfriend, wounded six classmates before other students disarmed him. On December 6 a seventh grader from Fort Gibson, Oklahoma, shouted "I'm crazy, I'm crazy" and fired a semiautomatic handgun into groups of middle-school students waiting outside the school for class to start. He wounded five before being subdued.

Tightening School Security

The deliberate nature of the Columbine shootings, combined with the large number of killed and wounded, tended to overshadow the fact that school violence was decreasing, mirroring an overall decrease in crime generally. The second annual report on school safety, released by the Departments of Justice and Education on October 19, showed that the overall crime rate in schools had fallen about one-third between 1993 and 1997, from 155 crimes for every 1,000 students in 1993 to 102 crimes in 1997. Students ages twelve through eighteen were three times more likely to be victims of serious violent crimes away from school than in school, and the percentage of high school students who carried a gun or other weapon to school had also declined significantly. (Overall crime trends, p. 614)

Such reports, while welcome, did little to calm the fears of students and their parents, who felt increasingly vulnerable with each new incident of mass school shootings. Schools around the country moved to install new security measures, including requiring students to use mesh bookbags that made it harder to conceal weapons; some schools were also removing student lockers. Surveillance cameras, metal detectors, computerized identification cards, and on-site police or security guards became commonplace in urban and many suburban schools. Schools adopted a combination of strategies to keep their students and teachers safe, including dress codes or uniforms to help cut down on peer pressure, deter gang activity, and identify students; stiffer penalties imposed on students for making violent threats and violating disciplinary rules; readily available counseling services; and training for both students and teachers in recognizing and dealing with troubled students.

The Federal Response

At the national level, Surgeon General David Satcher announced that the government would conduct a new study on the causes of violence among adolescents, looking particularly at popular culture, peer pressure, mental illness, and the availability of guns. But little else of real substance transpired. President Clinton convened a White House "summit" meeting on ways to prevent school violence, but he was criticized for not taking a stronger stance against the gun lobby and the entertainment industry.

The summit meeting, held May 10, brought together gun control lobbyists, representatives of gun manufacturers and hunting groups, entertainment executives, law enforcement officials, education officials, clergy, and children's advocates. Clinton did not ask the media to stop making violent movies and video games but to stop marketing them to children. He also said that parents should not buy products that glorified violence, and they should monitor what their children watched on television and supervise their activities on the Internet. After the meeting, which was closed to the press, Clinton said it "was exactly the kind of session I had hoped for, where everyone was talking about the problems and the opportunities. No one was pointing the finger of blame." Others were more critical, saying that the president had failed to take a firm stand either on gun control or violence in popular culture for fear of political retaliation from two of the most powerful lobbying organizations in Washington.

Gun control advocates won a momentary victory on May 20, when the Senate approved a juvenile justice measure only hours after the school shooting in Conyers, Georgia. Among other things, the bill would have required safety locks on all handguns and background checks on people who bought guns at gun shows. The gun show provision was adopted only after Vice President Gore cast a tie-breaking vote. In the House, however, opponents of gun control split those provisions from the rest of the its juvenile justice bill and then voted down the gun control provisions. At year's end, the two versions of the legislation were languishing in a House-Senate conference.

Following is the text of a speech delivered April 25, 1999, by Vice President Al Gore in Littleton, Colorado, commemorating those who died or were wounded in the mass shooting at Columbine High School on April 20:

Nothing that I can say today to you can bring comfort. Nothing that anyone else can say can bring comfort. But there is a voice that speaks without words, and addresses us in the depths of our being. And that voice says to our troubled souls, peace be still.

The scripture promises that there is a peace that passes understanding.

I would be misleading you if I said I understand this; I don't. Why human being[s] do evil I do not understand. Why bad things happen to good people, I do not understand. Like everyone of you at such a time as this I go on my knees and ask why, oh Lord, why.

I do know this, at a such a time we need each other. To the families of all those who died here, I say you are not alone. The heart of America aches with yours. We hold your agony in the center of our prayers. The entire nation is a community of shock, of love, and of grief.

May you feel the embrace of the literally hundreds of millions who weep with you.

"Blessed are those who mourn, for they shall be comforted."

And our thoughts are with the many who bore injury. We hope and pray along with their families that they will be whole again.

One of the hidden truths of the human condition is that suffering binds us together. Suffering lays bare our common human need for love, kindness and grace. In our suffering, all of us stand naked before God.

And for all of us, the scripture says "though it may be darkness now, joy cometh in the morning."

Here in Jefferson county, the spring has yielded to a cold winter of the heart, but I am reminded of the words of a sage writer who said "in the depths of winter, I finally learned that within me there lay an invincible summer."

To the world that is watching us, let us remind them that the young killers of Columbine High School do not stand for the spirit of America. [America] is a good and decent place, and our a goodness is a light to all the nations of the world.

We have seen in this community so much of that goodness, so much healing, so much of what is best in our country. You have shown us that even in this ashen moment there is a spark that lights our way forward.

At Columbine High School last week, this great goodness was expressed in the bravery of the teachers who risked [their] own lives to protect the lives of their students.

These teachers knew their pupils and loved them as if they were their own children. No one can doubt that. Their love was made not of words. Their love was made of acts. We remember among them coach and teacher Dave Sanders who bravely lead so many to safety, but never made it out of the building himself.

The young too were brave. The student with first aid training who swallowed his fear and went back into that awful smoke filled, terror filled corridor to lead others in a three-hour crusade to try to save his teacher's life.

There were countless other acts of heroism that saved many lives. And there was profound heroism among those who died.

Among them we remember Cassie Bernall, whose final words as she stared death in the face, were "Yes, I do believe in God."

"Those who suffer for righteousness sake, theirs is the kingdom of God."

Now as we are brought to our knees in the shock of this moment, what say we? What say we into the open muzzle of this tragedy, cocked and aimed at our hearts?

If our spiritual courage can match the eternal moment, we can make manifest in our lives, the truth of the prophesy that the sufferings of this present time are not worthy to be compared with the glory that shall be revealed in us.

All of us must change our lives to honor these children.

More than ever I realize that every one of us is responsible for all the children. There are children today hungering for their parents to become more involved in their schools, and to fill the spiritual void in their lives. If you are a parent, your children need attention. If you are a grandparent, they need your time. If you not have children, there are kids who need your example and your presence. Somewhere, somewhere in the reach of every adult in this country, is a child to hold and teach, a child to save.

We must have the courage not to look away in life or in death from those who feel despised and rejected, those for whom we are taught "sin lieth crouching at the door."

All adults in this nation must take on the challenge of creating in all of God's children, a clean heart and a right spirit within. Children look to us; they learn from us. They don't always know when to look away.

We must teach them right from wrong. We must protect them from the violence and cruelty in our popular culture.

We must teach them why embracing the right values transcends a moment's cheap sensation.

I believe the best antidote to vulgarity and brutality is the power of a better example, of love over indifference . . . "the power of a higher affection."

The human heart responds to goodness. I believe this. I wouldn't think life worth living if it were not so.

After the death of a loved one, a poetess wrote, "gently they go, the beautiful, the tender, the kind, quickly they go, the intelligent, the witty, the brave. I know, but I do not approve and I am not resigned."

Parents, we can stop the violence and the hate. In a culture ripe with violence where too many young people place too little value on a human life, we can rise up and we can say, no more.

We have seen enough of violence in our schools. We must replace a culture of violence and mayhem with one of values and meaning. It is too easy for a young child to get a gun, and everywhere we look there are too many lessons in how to use one. We can do something about that.

We need more discipline and character in our schools and more alternatives to drugs and crime. We can do something about that.

We need to recognize the earliest signs of trouble and teach our children to resolve their difference with reason and conscience. We can do something about that.

No society will ever be perfect, but we know the way things should be, and America can be what we are meant to be, a community of goodness, of reason, of moral strength.

As the Psalmist prayed I also prayed, so "teach us to number our days that we may apply our hearts unto wisdom."

If we can work our way as a people to that place, where caring and compassion open us to the lives of all our children, then those children who died here will not have died in vain. And then in the words of the prophet, "no more shall be heard the sound of weeping and the cry of distress. They shall not labor in vain or bear children for calamity, for they shall be the offspring of the blessed of the Lord, and their children with them, and never again shall they hurt or destroy in all God's holy mountain."

For now I know only that my heart weeps with you, and with you I yearn that we may come through this dark passage a stronger, and more caring people for I believe with all my heart that earth hath no sorrows that heaven cannot heal.

GAO ON HEALTH THREAT
FROM DRUG-RESISTANT BACTERIA
April 28, 1999

Indications that bacteria and other microbes were growing increasingly resistant to drugs continued to mount in 1999, as public health officials and others called for action to avert a potentially serious public health problem. Although data on the problem were limited, the General Accounting Office (GAO), the investigative arm of Congress, reported that "resistant bacteria are emerging around the world, that more kinds of bacteria are becoming resistant, and that bacteria are becoming resistant to multiple drugs." Strains of bacteria have developed a tolerance to penicillin and erythromycin, two of the most valuable drugs in use. Resistance to these and other drugs increased the risk of serious and life-threatening illness, especially for vulnerable populations, such as the elderly and people with weakened immune systems.

The success of the drugs in treating stubborn but common illnesses was the root cause of the problem. The GAO and the federal Centers for Disease Control (CDC), among other national and international health agencies, said the resistance was caused by the overuse and misuse of antibiotics and other drugs. The CDC was mounting a public health campaign to inform doctors and the public of the dangers caused from overprescribing antibiotics, while the Food and Drug Administration (FDA) was writing proposed regulations to bar the use of certain antibacterials in animal feed. Those regulations were bound to be opposed by meat and poultry producers and the pharmaceutical industry.

Although drug resistance was showing up in viruses, fungi, and parasites, all of which could cause serious disease, most concern was focused on bacteria, partly because the use of antibacterials was so widespread. Antibiotics were used to treat serious infectious diseases not only in humans, but also in plants and animals. Antibiotics were also widely used to stimulate growth in food-producing animals. Moreover, antibacterials were prevalent in the antiseptics and disinfectants used in hospitals, restaurants, and industrial settings, and in a wide range of consumer products from soap to kitty litter to children's toys. Although most cases of documented bacterial resistance had been in connection with drugs, scientists had found some instances where the bacterial resistance seemed to have derived from exposure to disinfectants and antiseptics.

Bacteria developed resistance to antibiotics either by acquiring resistance genes from other bacteria or by spontaneously mutating their own genetic material. Some bacteria were naturally resistant. Resistance spreads by a process of selection: bacteria susceptible to an antibiotic die, leaving behind resistant strains that then pass on their resistance to other bacteria. Settings such as hospitals, where patients and health care workers were exposed to infections, were potential breeding grounds for resistant bacteria and other microbes. The great increase in international travel and trade also contributed to the spread of bacterial resistance throughout the world.

GAO Report on Scope of the Problem

In a report released April 28, 1999, the GAO said that without routine testing and systematic data collection throughout the world, the prevalence of drug-resistant bacteria could not be determined. The report cited several diseases, including tuberculosis, gonorrhea, and some forms of pneumonia, where bacteria were showing resistance to the preferred treatment drugs. Resistance had also been found to treatments for several common diseases, such as otitis media (the ear infection frequently seen in children), cystitis, strep throat, and gastric ulcers.

The GAO report said lack of data made it impossible to determine how many people died from drug-resistant infections, but one recent study found that patients with staphylococcus infections that were resistant to the drug methicillin were two-and-a-half times more likely to die than patients whose staph infections were not resistant to the drug. The report also said that infections caused by drug-resistant microbes were likely to be more costly to treat because patients were sicker longer and the only effective drugs available were usually more expensive or had to be used in combination with other drugs, which also pushed up the cost.

Overuse of Antibiotics in Humans

Scientists and public health officials said overuse and misuse of antibiotics in humans was a major contributor to the increase in bacterial resistance. Vancomycin, for example, was the one antibiotic that doctors used as their last resort when bacteria proved resistant to other treatments. But the CDC said that its overusestudies estimated that it is misused in humans 30 to 80 percent of the timewas a leading cause for an increase in vancomycin-resistant enterococci (VRE). This organism, generally contracted in hospitals, caused serious, sometimes untreatable, infections in humans.

The number of prescriptions for drugs to treat more common illnesses had also grown. According to one study, 4.2 million prescriptions were written for amoxicillin in 1980; by 1992 the number of prescriptions had risen to 12.4 million—nearly three times as many. Prescriptions for the class of antibiotics known as cephalosporins shot up, from 876,000 prescriptions in 1980 to nearly 7 million in 1992. According to the CDC, many patients took these antibiotics to treat conditions that were not caused by bacteria and therefore could not be cured by antibiotics. Among these were the common cold (which was caused by a virus), most forms of bronchitis, and many kinds of sinus infection. The CDC estimated that up to one-third of the 150 million antibiotics prescribed each year were unnecessary and they caused harm in the sense that they gave bacteria more opportunities to develop resistance. Patients who did not complete their course of treatment also could contribute to the spread of resistance; if the bacteria causing the infection were not all killed, the ones most likely to survive were those most resistant to the drug.

Surveys and focus groups showed that doctors, perhaps under pressure from the patient to "do something," prescribed antibiotics even when they know the drugs would not be effective. This was a particular problem for children, who contracted many common infections and were prescribed antibiotics at three times the rate prescribed for adults. In a survey of 610 pediatricians around the country, researchers at Boston University found that parental pressure, more than medical efficiency or fears of malpractice, was the major reason that these doctors prescribed antibiotics for children. Of those polled, 96 percent said that in the previous months parents had asked them to prescribe antibiotics; 80 percent said they rarely or never prescribed antibiotics over the phone, but more than 30 percent acknowledged that they often or occasionally prescribed antibiotics that they considered unnecessary to appease parents. The results of the survey were published in the February 1999 issue of the journal Pediatrics. *In conjunction with the American Academy of Pediatrics, the CDC has mounted a public awareness campaign targeted at both physicians and parents. Its main thrust was explaining why antibiotics were not effective against most ordinary colds, coughs, and runny noses, and it gave alternative solutions for care and treatment.*

Antibiotic Use in Animals

*An estimated 40 to 50 percent of all antibiotics used in the United States were used to treat or prevent disease in food animals and plants, to prevent the spread of disease among groups of animals, and to promote growth in animals used for human food. Experts at the FDA and the CDC believed that drug-resistant strains of three food-borne organisms that cause disease in humans—*Salmonella, Campylobacter, *and* E. coli—*were linked directly to the use of antibiotics in animals. Most of the time these diseases were relatively harmless, but occasionally they caused severe illness, especially among the young, the aged, and people whose immune systems were weakened by other disease. Scientists believed that the organisms acquired resistance to antibiotics in the animal and that these resistant bacteria* *were then passed on to humans either through food or through contact with the animal itself or animal waste. Some scientists also believed that the use of antibiotics as a feed supplement could reduce the effectiveness of related antibiotics in humans; they postulated that resistance developed to one antibiotic in a particular class of antibiotics would increase resistance to all antibiotics in that class.*

In 1999 the FDA began to revise its guidelines for the use of antibiotics in animals. Under the proposed revisions, drug manufacturers would be required to test certain new drugs intended for use in livestock to determine whether they created a drug resistance that could prove harmful to humans. Drugs that were shown to have such potential could then be banned from use as growth stimulants in animals. The agricultural and pharmaceutical industries challenged the proposed revisions, saying that the link between antibiotic use in animals and drug resistance in humans had not been proved, and that, even if it had, it would be only one of several important contributors to drug resistance. Furthermore, they argued, antibiotic use was critical to the continued production of safe and affordable food.

Public health officials and consumer advocates argued that overuse of antibiotics as a growth stimulant was already putting human health at risk. FDA officials said they had decided to act when they found that bacteria were developing resistance to fluoroquinolones, the last new class of antibiotics to be approved for use in humans, and that a new class of antibiotics was not likely to be ready in the near future. Approved in 1986, fluoroquinolones were particularly effective in treating gastrointestinal infections caused by salmonella. A coalition led by the Center for Science in the Public Interest petitioned the FDA to prohibit any drug used to treat disease in humans from also being used as a growth promoter in animals.

The agricultural use of antibiotics had been debated since at least the mid-1970s, but lack of data to prove or disprove that agricultural use was threatening human health left the matter unresolved. Several countries in Europe were not so reticent. The United Kingdom banned the use of penicillin and tetracycline as a growth stimulant in the early 1970s. Sweden banned that use for all antibiotics in 1986. And on July 1, 1999, the European Union banned four antibiotics widely used to promote growth in their fifteen member countries.

> *Following are excerpts from the report, "Antimicrobial Resistance: Data to Assess Public Health Threat from Resistant Bacteria Are Limited," prepared by the Health, Education, and Human Services Division of the U.S. General Accounting Office and presented April 28, 1999, to the Senate committees on health and agriculture:*

The *Staphylococcus aureus* bacterium (*S. aureus*)—one of the most common causes of infections worldwide—has long been considered treatable with antimicrobial drugs. Recently, however, a number of *S. aureus* infections were found that resisted most available antimicrobials including vancomycin, the last line of treatment for these and some other infections. For example, several years ago in Japan, a 4-month-old infant who had developed an *S. aureus* infection following surgery died after a month of treatments with various antimicrobials, including vancomycin. About a year later, three elderly patients in the United States with multiple chronic conditions were infected with this type of *S. aureus*—now known as vancomycin intermediate-resistant *Staphylococcus aureus* (VISA). They were treated with numerous antimicrobials for an extended period of time and eventually died, but it is unclear what role VISA played in their deaths. More recently, a middle-aged cancer patient in Hong Kong was admitted to a hospital with a fever and died despite 2 weeks of treatment for VISA.

Cases like these have heightened concern about antimicrobial resistance. To better understand the potential threat to the public's health, you asked us to (1) summarize what is known about the current public health burden—in terms of illnesses, deaths, and treatment costs due to antimicrobial resistance; (2) assess the potential future burden, given what is known about the development of resistance in microbes and usage of antimicrobials; and (3) describe federal efforts to gather and provide information about resistance. Although resistance has been observed in many kinds of microbes including bacteria, viruses, parasites, and fungi the scope of this report, the first in a series you have requested, is limited to bacteria. To conduct our work, we reviewed scientific and medical literature and spoke with experts in government agencies as well as in academia and private industry. We conducted our work between June 1998 and April 1999 in accordance with generally accepted government auditing standards. . . .

Results in Brief

Although many studies have documented cases of infections that are difficult to treat because they are caused by resistant bacteria, the full extent of the problem remains unknown. More specifically, we found many sources of information about the public health burden in the United States attributable to resistant bacteria, but each source has limitations and provides data on only part of the burden. For example, the public health burden attributable to resistant tuberculosis (TB) and gonorrhea is relatively well characterized because nationwide surveillance systems monitor these diseases. However, little is known about the extent of most other diseases that can be caused by resistant bacteria, such as otitis media (middle ear infection), gastric ulcers, and cystitis (inflammation of the bladder) because they are not similarly monitored.

The development and spread of resistant bacteria worldwide and the widespread use of various antibacterials create the potential for the U.S. public health burden to increase. Data indicate that resistant bacteria are emerging around the world, that more kinds of bacteria are becoming resistant, and that bacteria are becoming resistant to multiple drugs. While little information is publicly available about the actual quantities of antibacterials produced, used, and present in the environment, it is known that antibacterials are used extensively around the world in human and veterinary medicine, in agricultural production, and in industrial and household products and that they have been found in food, soil, and water.

A number of federal agencies and international organizations that receive U.S. funds collect information about different aspects of antibacterial resistance, and some ongoing efforts involve collaboration among agencies. For example, the Centers for Disease Control and Prevention (CDC) is the primary source of information about the number of infections caused by resistant bacteria. CDC also collects information on resistance found in bacterial samples and the use of antibacterial drugs in human medicine. The U.S. Department of Agriculture (USDA) collects information about resistant bacteria in animals and antibacterial drug residues in food. The Food and Drug Administration (FDA) also has a program to monitor antibacterial residues in food. CDC, USDA, and FDA are collaborating on efforts to monitor resistant bacteria that can contaminate the food supply. The Department of Defense conducts surveillance for antibacterial resistance at 13 military sites in the United States and at its 6 tropical overseas laboratories. Internationally, the World Health Organization serves as a clearinghouse for data on resistance in bacteria isolated from people and animals from many different countries. Over the next several years, ongoing efforts to improve existing data sources and to create new ones may allow better characterization of the public health burden. Moreover, several agencies have data or access to data that, although not originally intended for these purposes, could be used to learn more about the number of resistant infections, treatment costs, and antibacterial usage.

Background

Bacteria exist almost everywhere—in water, soil, plants, animals, and humans. Bacteria can transfer from person to person, among animals and people, from animals to animals, and through water and the food chain. Most bacteria do little or no harm, and some are even useful to humans. However, others are capable of causing disease. Moreover, the same bacteria can have different effects on different parts of the host body. For example, *S. aureus* on the skin can be harmless, but when they enter the bloodstream through a wound they can cause disease.

An antibacterial is anything that can kill or inhibit the growth of bacteria, such as high heat or radiation or a chemical. Antibacterial chemicals can be grouped into three broad categories: antibacterial drugs, antiseptics, and disinfectants. Antibacterial drugs are used in relatively low concentrations in or upon the bodies of organisms to prevent or treat specific bacterial diseases without harming the organism. They are also used in agriculture to enhance the growth of food animals. Unlike antibacterial drugs, antiseptics and disinfectants are usually nonspecific with respect to their targets they kill or inhibit a variety of microbes. Antiseptics are used topically in or on living tissue, and disinfectants are used on objects or in water. . . .

Antibacterial resistance describes a feature of some bacteria that enables them to avoid the effects of antibacterial agents. Bacteria may possess characteristics that allow them to survive a sudden change in climate, the effects of ultraviolet light from the sun, or the presence of an antibacterial chemical in their environment. Some bacteria are naturally resistant. Other bacteria acquire resistance to antibacterials to which they once were susceptible.

The development of resistance to an antibacterial is complex. Susceptible bacteria can become resistant by acquiring resistance genes from other bacteria or through mutations in their own genetic material (DNA). Once acquired, the resistance characteristic is passed on to future generations and sometimes to other bacterial species.

Antibacterials have been shown to promote antibacterial resistance in at least three ways: through (1) encouraging the exchange of resistant genes between bacteria, (2) favoring the survival of the resistant bacteria in a mixed population of resistant and susceptible bacteria, and (3) making people and animals more vulnerable to resistant infection. Although the contribution of antibacterials in promoting resistance has most often been documented for antibacterial drugs, there are also reports of disinfectant use contributing to resistance and concerns about the potential for antiseptics to promote resistance. For example, in the case of disinfectants, researchers have found that chlorinated river water contains more bacteria that are resistant to streptomycin than does nonchlorinated river water. Also, it has been shown that some kinds of *Escherichia coli* (*E. coli*) resist triclosan—an antiseptic used in a variety of products, including soaps and toothpaste. This raises the possibility that antiseptic use could contribute to the emergence of resistant bacteria.

While antibacterials are a major factor in the development of resistance, many other factors are also involved—including the nature of the specific bacteria and antibacterial involved, the way the antibacterial is used, characteristics of the host, and environmental factors. Therefore, the use of antibacterials does not always lead to resistance.

Data Insufficient to Determine Full Extent of Public Health Burden Associated with Antibacterial Resistance

Although we found many sources of information about the public health burden in the United States attributable to resistant bacteria, each source provides data on only part of the burden. Specifically, we found information about resistant diseases that result in hospitalization or are acquired in the hospital and information about two specific diseases—TB and gonorrhea. Moreover, no systematic information is available about deaths from diseases caused by resistant bacteria or about the costs of treating resistant disease. Consequently, the overall extent of disease, death, and treatment costs resulting from resistant bacteria is unknown.

Estimates from Hospital Data

The primary source of information on cases of disease caused by resistant bacteria is the National Hospital Discharge Survey (NHDS)—conducted annually by CDC's National Center for Health Statistics (NCHS). It estimates drug-resistant infections among hospitalized patients, including both patients with a resistant infection that caused them to be hospitalized and patients who acquired a resistant infection while in the hospital for another reason. According to this survey, in 1997, hospitals discharged 43,000 patients who had been diagnosed with and treated for infections from drug-resistant bacteria. . . .

These numbers, however, should be interpreted cautiously. The survey's diagnostic codes for designating infections with drug-resistant bacteria are, in most cases, not required for reimbursement, and they went into effect only in October 1993—though the survey has been conducted since 1965. Therefore, estimating the number of cases of infections with drug-resistant bacteria based on these codes likely results in an underestimate. In addition, increases in the number of discharged patients who had been treated for infections from drug-resistant bacteria may reflect an increase in the use of the new codes and not an actual increase in the incidence of resistant infections.

Data on five predominant bacterial infections acquired in hospitals from CDC's Hospital Infections Program further suggest that the estimates derived from NHDS may be too low. Since the discharge survey is not limited to specific infections and includes diseases acquired outside the hospital, it would be expected that estimates derived from the survey would be greater. However, estimates from the Hospital Infections Program indicate that the number of resistant infections acquired in hospitals is many times greater [279,000 cases in 1995]. . . .

These estimates should also be interpreted cautiously. CDC estimated the number of cases for each type of resistant bacteria by extrapolating from data on the 276 hospitals participating in CDC's National Nosocomial Infections Surveillance (NNIS) system to all hospitals in the United States. NNIS hospitals, however, are not representative of all hospitals; they are disproportionately large, urban, and affiliated with medical schools, and therefore likely to have more severely ill patients. Moreover, unlike NHDS, which surveys discharge codes that denote actual infections, the NNIS hospitals test bacterial samples in laboratories and thus may be detecting resistant bacteria that did not necessarily result in a patient treated for infection. Consequently, these CDC extrapolations probably overestimate the number of cases of these types of resistant bacterial disease.

Data from Surveillance of Disease

Another source of information on cases of disease caused by resistant bacteria is data developed through surveillance of infectious diseases. However, nationwide data on such diseases are currently limited to TB and gonorrhea.

Tuberculosis

CDC's Division of Tuberculosis Elimination collects reports of all verified TB cases from states. TB is an infectious disease, most commonly of the lungs, caused by *Mycobacterium tuberculosis*. In response to increased incidence of TB in the late 1980s and early 1990s, CDC, in conjunction with state and local health departments, expanded national surveillance to include tests for resistance for all confirmed cases reported in 1993 and later. In 1997, the most recent year for which data have been published, tests were performed on 88.5 percent of confirmed TB cases reported in the United States. Of these, 12.6 percent were resistant to at least one antituberculosis drug. Although the number of cases of TB has declined, the proportion of cases that are resistant has remained relatively stable. . . .

Gonorrhea

Through its Division of Sexually Transmitted Disease Prevention, CDC also conducts nationwide surveillance of gonorrhea, which is caused by the bacterium *Neisseria gonorrhoea*. CDC supplements nationwide surveillance of gonorrhea infections with a Gonococcal Isolate Surveillance Project (GISP), a network consisting of clinics in 27 cities. In 1997, 33.4 percent of the gonococcal samples collected by GISP were resistant to penicillin, or tetracycline, or both. . . . [T]he proportion of gonorrhea resistant to these drugs has remained relatively stable since 1991.

Other Diseases

Nationwide data on other diseases that can be caused by resistant bacteria are not yet available, but efforts are under way to monitor invasive diseases caused by *Streptococcus pneumoniae* (*S. pneumoniae*), including meningitis and bacteremia. This bacterium was once routinely treatable with penicillin; however, since the mid-1980s, penicillin resistance has emerged, and some infections are susceptible only to vancomycin. In 1995, resistant *S. pneumoniae* was designated as a nationally reportable disease, and by 1998, 37 states were conducting public health surveillance on this bacterium.

We found no efforts yet under way to collect systematic information on bacterial resistance in other diseases that have exhibited resistance to the antibacterial drugs usually used to treat them. Many common diseases caused by bacteria that have exhibited resistance—such as otitis media, gastric ulcers, cystitis, and strep throat—are typically acquired outside the hospital. In addition, they typically do not result in hospitalization, are often treated without laboratory identification of the underlying cause, and are not notifiable. Thus, they are not reflected in existing data sources.

Deaths and Treatment Costs

The number of deaths caused by resistant bacteria cannot be determined because the standard source of data on deaths—vital statistics compiled from death certificates—does not distinguish resistant infections from susceptible ones. A number of studies provide some information about deaths, but they are generally small studies of outbreaks in a single hospital or community. These studies suggest that infections from resistant bacteria are more likely to be fatal than those from nonresistant bacteria. One recent study on deaths in a larger population over a relatively longer period of time—all hospitalized patients in 13 New York City metropolitan area counties in 1995—found that patients with infections from methicillin-resistant *Staphylococcus aureus* (MRSA) were more than 2.5 times more likely to die than patients with infections from methicillin-sensitive *Staphylococcus aureus* (MSSA). . . .

Because the number of cases of resistant disease is not known and the average treatment cost of cases is not available, we are unable to estimate the overall cost of treating drug-resistant bacterial disease. Although information about the cost of treating infections caused by resistant bacteria is limited, it suggests that resistant infections are generally more costly to treat than those caused by susceptible bacteria. For example, in the study of the impact of *S. aureus* infections in metropolitan New York City hospitals, direct medical costs—consisting of hospital charges, professional fees during hospitalization, and medical services after discharge—were 8 percent higher for a patient with MRSA than for a patient with MSSA. The higher cost of treating MRSA infections reflects the higher cost of vancomycin use, longer hospital stay, and patient isolation procedures. Similarly, a study of the cost of treating TB, based on a survey of five programs in Alabama; Illinois; New Jersey; Texas; and Los Angeles, California showed that outpatient therapy costs for multidrug-resistant TB were more than 3 times as great as for susceptible TB. . . .

Increasing Resistance and Widespread Antibacterial Use Could Increase Public Health Burden

Existing data on resistant bacteria, which can cause infections, and antibacterial use, which can promote the development of resistance, provide clues for understanding how the future U.S. public health burden could develop. Because resistant bacteria from anywhere in the world could result in an infection in the United States, the development of resistance globally must also be considered. The data available suggest that antibacterial resistance is increasing worldwide and that antibacterial agents are used extensively. Consequently, the U.S. public health burden could increase.

Available Data Indicate that Antibacterial Resistance Is Increasing

Without routine testing and systematic data collection globally, the prevalence of resistant bacteria worldwide cannot be determined. Data from laboratories that monitor for resistant bacteria, however, show that resistance in human and animal bacteria is increasing in four ways.

- *Bacteria known to be susceptible are becoming resistant.* Some bacteria that were once susceptible to certain antibacterials are now resistant to them. For example, *Yersinia pestis*, which causes plague, was universally susceptible to streptomycin, chloramphenicol, and tetracycline. Extensive testing of samples of specific kinds of *Yersinia pestis* collected between 1926 and 1995 in Madagascar had not detected any multidrug resistance. In 1995, however, a multidrug-resistant sample was isolated from a 16-year old boy in Madagascar.

- *The proportion of resistant bacteria is increasing in some populations of bacteria.* Although existing surveillance systems predominantly monitor the development of resistance in bacteria from sick people in specific countries, and while different geographical areas may exhibit different antibacterial resistance patterns, data overall indicate that a greater proportion of samples being tested are positive for resistance. For example, according to data from CDC, *S. pneumoniae* is becoming increasingly resistant in the United States that is, an increasing percentage of S. pneumoniae samples that are tested in CDC laboratories are resistant to penicillin. . . .

    Studies also show that resistance is increasing in other countries. For example, a DOD-funded study on diarrhea-causing bacteria isolated from indigenous persons in Thailand over 15 years shows that ciprofloxacin resistance among *Campylobacter* samples increased from 0 percent before 1991 to 84 percent in 1995. In Iceland, the frequency of penicillin-resistant samples of *S. pneumoniae* rose from 2.3 percent in 1989 to 17 percent in 1992, after detecting penicillin-resistant *S. pneumoniae* for the first time in 1988. In the Netherlands, metronidazole-resistant *Helicobacter pylori* in several Dutch hospitals increased from 7 percent in 1993 to 32 percent in 1996.

    In addition to increases in resistance in bacteria that affect people, resistance among bacteria in animals has also been increasing. In Finland, two surveys—carried out in 1988 and 1995—studied the prevalence of inflamed udders in cows and the antibacterial susceptibility of the bacteria that caused them. The investigators found that the proportion of certain types of *S. aureus* resistant to at least one antibacterial drug increased from 37 percent in 1988 to almost 64 percent in 1995. In the Netherlands, a study of *Campylobacter* isolated from poultry products between 1982 and 1989 showed that resistance to quinolones increased from 0 percent to 14 percent.

- *Bacteria are becoming resistant to additional antibacterials.* Some bacteria that were considered resistant to a particular antibacterial drug have developed resistance to additional antibacterials. For example, in 1989, a multiresistant clone of MRSA was detected in Spain and a multiresistant clone of penicillin-resistant *S. pneumoniae* was detected in Iceland. Similarly, a few cases of MRSA have exhibited an intermediate level of resistance to vancomycin, in addition to their resistance to many other antibacterials.

- *Resistant bacteria are spreading.* Over the past decade, a number of resistant bacteria are also believed to have spread around the world. Bacteria can be traced by their DNA patterns. Evidence that the DNA patterns of resistant bacteria from geographically diverse places are the same or very similar combined with evidence that resistance in these bacteria have been prevalent in one place and not in the other allows researchers to conclude that a bacterial clone has spread. With international travel and trade and the continuous exchange of bacteria among people, animals, and agricultural hosts and environments, resistant bacteria can spread from one country to another. For example, in 1989, a multidrug-resistant MRSA, known as the Iberian clone, was identified during an outbreak in Spain. This clone has spread to hospitals in Portugal, Italy, Scotland, Germany, and Belgium. In 1998, resistant *Shigella* on parsley entered the United States from Mexico, causing two outbreaks of shigellosis in Minnesota.

Antibacterials Are Used Widely, but Data Quantifying Use and Residues Are Limited

Antibacterials are used around the world for a number of purposes in various settings, and their use can vary from country to country. Antibacterial drugs are used in both people and animals. Antiseptics and disinfectants are used in hospitals, homes, schools, restaurants, farms, food processing plants, water treatment facilities, and other places. While measures of total antibacterial use in most countries are not available, some data have been published on the total amount of antibacterials produced or sold in the United States. . . .

According to the Environmental Protection Agency (EPA), a total of 3.3 billion pounds of active ingredients were produced for disinfectants in 1995. We found no estimates of production, sales, or usage of antiseptics. Overall accumulations of antibacterial residue in soil, water, and food are unknown. However, studies have shown that while some antibacterial drugs are rapidly degraded in soil, others remain in their active form indefinitely and that 70 to 80 percent of the drugs administered on fish farms end up in the environment.

- *Antibacterial drugs are used to prevent and treat disease in humans.* NCHS estimates that from 1980 until 1997, the U.S. antibacterial drug prescription rate remained approximately constant at about 150 prescriptions per 1,000 physician office visits. . . . Since 1992, NCHS has collected data on drugs prescribed in hospital emergency and outpatient departments. These data indicate that in 1996, the last year for which all data are available, antibacterial drugs were prescribed 19 million times a year in emergency departments and 8 million times a year in outpatient departments, for a total of 133 million prescriptions for physician office, hospital emergency, and outpatient settings combined.

  In general, use of antibacterial drugs differs among the countries that have been studied. (Most countries studied are developed countries, but India, South Africa, several Latin American nations, and other less developed countries have also been studied.) For example, Japan and Spain have higher rates of cephalosporin sales than do the other countries studied. The Danish Antimicrobial Resistance Monitoring and Research Programme has reported that antibiotic consumption in Denmark's primary care sector declined from 12.8 defined daily doses per 1,000 population in 1994 to 11.3 in 1997. Available reports indicate that the amount of antibacterial drug use per person in some other developed countries, such as Canada, is greater than in the United States. In less developed countries—including Kenya, Bangladesh, and Nigeria—use of some antibacterial drugs tends to be relatively great for the segment of the population who can afford them.

- *Antibacterial drugs are used to prevent and treat disease in food animals, pets, and plants.* Antibacterial drugs, often the same ones used to prevent and treat disease in humans, are also used in veterinary medicine, fish farming, beekeeping, and agriculture. Veterinarians prescribe antibacterial drugs to treat disease in food animals, such as cattle and swine, and in companion animals, such as dogs and cats. A variety of antibacterial drugs are available without prescription in feed stores and pet stores. Fish farmers who raise fish, such as salmon, catfish, and trout, put antibacterial drugs in water to treat bacterial infection; and beekeepers use antibacterial drugs to prevent and treat bacterial infection in honeybees. Antibacterial drugs are also sprayed on some fruits and vegetables, such as pears and potatoes, as well as on other crops, such as rice and orchids. Chemical industry sources estimated that in 1985, the total weight of antibacterial drugs used to treat and prevent disease in cattle, swine, and poultry in the United States was 13.8 million pounds, but they have not published more recent estimates.

- *Antibacterial drugs are used to enhance the growth of food animals and other commercially important animals.* Antibacterial drugs are also often administered in the United States as feed additives to enhance growth and increase feed efficiency. As feed additives, they are primarily used for food animals, such as livestock and poultry, but they are also given to other commercially important animals, such as mink. Many antibacterial drugs used to promote growth can be purchased without a prescription.

  Chemical industry sources estimated that in 1985, 4.5 million pounds of antibacterial drugs were used for growth enhancement in cattle, swine, and poultry.

  Some other developed countries, such as Canada, also use antibacterial drugs for growth enhancement. However, because of concerns about antibacterial resistance, several countries have banned certain uses of some drugs or particular drugs altogether. For example, Sweden banned all antibacterials for use in animal feed without prescription, and the European Union banned several specific antibacterial feed additives. FDA has efforts under way to determine if similar actions are warranted in this country.

- *Antibacterials are applied to various surfaces and environments to inhibit bacterial growth.* Antibacterials are also used to disinfect various surfaces and environments in institutional settings, such as hospitals and laboratories; in industrial settings, such as food processing and manufacturing plants; and in environmental health settings, such as water treatment facilities. They are also used as antiseptics to disinfect skin and wounds. The presence of antibacterials in hundreds of consumer products, including soaps, cat litter, cutting boards, and even ballpoint pens, contributes to the public's exposure to them. According to industry sources, almost 700 new antibacterial products were introduced between 1992 and the middle of 1998. Many of these, such as cribs and toys, are for use by children. The American Academy of Pediatrics' Committee on Infectious Diseases is conducting a study of the use and safety of antibacterials in these products and other consumer products, such as hand soaps, that children may come into contact with.

- *Antibacterial residues in some foods are monitored, but little is known about other residues.* USDA inspects meat and poultry for antibacterial residues and reports on all samples with detectable levels. However, the levels of antibacterials in food that might promote resistance are not known and, therefore, cannot be factored into the current limits. USDA also regularly tests samples of fruits and vegetables for contamination by certain pesticides, such as insecticides, but not for antibacterials. EPA assesses risks of toxicity, but not antibacterial resistance, from residues on fruits and vegetables using data collected by USDA.

  Residues can also end up in water and soil. Studies in Europe have shown that antibacterials can be found in bodies of water that supply drinking water. However, we know neither the extent to which antibacterials in the environment promote the development of resistance nor how much antibacterial residue ends up in the environment or in food (with the exception of meat) or drinking water. . . .

Conclusions

Although many studies have documented cases of infections that are difficult to treat because they are caused by resistant bacteria, the full extent of the problem remains unknown. The development and spread of resistant bacteria worldwide and the widespread use of various antibacterials create the potential for the U.S. public health burden to increase. A number of federal and federally funded agencies are collecting information about different aspects of antibacterial resistance, and some ongoing efforts involve collaboration among agencies. However, there is little information about the extent of the following:

- common diseases that can be caused by resistant bacteria, are acquired in the community, and do not typically result in hospitalization, such as otitis media;
- the development of resistant properties in bacteria that do not normally cause disease but that can pass these properties on to bacteria that do;
- antibacterial use, particularly in animals, and antibacterial residues in places other than food; and
- the development of resistant disease and resistant bacteria and the use of antibacterials globally.

Without improvements in existing data sources and more information in these areas, it is not possible to accurately assess the threat to the U.S. public health posed by resistant bacteria. As you have requested, we will be conducting further studies to (1) explore options for improving existing data sources and developing new ones; (2) identify the factors that contribute to the development and spread of antimicrobial resistance; and (3) consider alternatives for addressing the problem. . . .

May

SEC Chairman Levitt
  on Online Investing 203

Supreme Court on Student
  Sexual Harassment 215

House Committee on Theft of
  U.S. Nuclear Secrets by China. 235

GAO Report on the Effects
  of Welfare Reform 257

Obasanjo on His Inauguration
  as President of Nigeria 272

SEC CHAIRMAN LEVITT
ON ONLINE INVESTING
May 4, 1999

Rapid technological advances and the explosive growth of the Internet during the 1990s made it much easier for people to manage their own investments in the stock market. But those advances also heightened the prospect that many of them would take inappropriate risks and would be misled by fraudulent services and false advertising. During 1999 federal and state regulators and the securities industry began investigating how to protect investors against online wrongdoing. Even as they considered changes in laws and regulations, authorities said investors themselves were primarily responsible for weighing the risks of their investments.

By 1999 technological changes had helped spawn new ways for people to invest in stocks. One was online investing, which involved buying and selling stocks through sites on the Internet or via direct computer hookups to the stock markets. A study by the U.S. Bancorp estimated that some 5.8 million people engaged in online stock trading in 1999, and a study by Jupiter Communications put the value of assets traded online at $415 billion in 1998. Both figures represented a small but fast-growing segment of the investment community.

Another small but spreading trend was called "day-trading." According to various estimates, between 6,000 and 15,000 people were using computer systems owned by specialty firms to make very rapid purchases and sales of stocks—often within a matter of seconds—to take advantage of small price fluctuations. Most day-traders had little or no experience and training in stock market investing; often they had been lured to day-trading by advertisements promising huge profits. A few day-traders had managed to make money with these investments, but studies showed that the vast majority lost money.

Arthur Levitt, the chairman of the Securities and Exchange Commission (SEC), gave a series of speeches during the year warning the public to beware of the lure of quick profits through online investing or day-trading, referring to the latter as "gambling" rather than investing or even speculat-

ing. Investors needed to pay more attention to what they bought, Levitt said, adding: "I'm often surprised by investors who spend more time deciding what movie they'll rent than on which stock to buy."

Largely in response to the rising popularity of online investing, the major stock exchanges laid plans to extend trading hours, possibly by 2000. The New York Stock Exchange and American Stock Exchange for decades had kept their trading floors open only from 9 A.M. to 4 P.M. Monday through Friday. But the stock markets were under pressure from millions of investors who wanted to make trades on their home computers at night and on weekends.

In a related development, the New York and American exchanges made plans to convert to for-profit organizations in 2000, scrapping their long-time status as membership organizations. Levitt said that development raised questions about whether the exchanges should continue to police themselves. In the past, the stock markets, the National Association of Securities Dealers, and similar groups were considered "self-regulating organizations" that developed and enforced their own rules within broad parameters set by law and SEC rules. But once the stock markets became profit-making organizations, Levitt said, their self-regulatory functions should be taken over by independent organizations.

Online Investing

By the mid-1980s brokerage firms had developed systems enabling investors to buy and sell stocks using their computers, usually over direct modem-to-modem hookups. The growth of the Internet starting in the mid-1990s made direct online investing more accessible to a broader public. Having established an account, investors could log onto a brokerage firm's Web site and buy and sell stocks more quickly than ever before. Studies showed most online investors tended to be well-educated, with higher-than-average incomes and substantial stock portfolios.

In a report published November 23, 1999, the SEC predicted continued rapid growth of online investing. The SEC cited studies by private consultants who estimated that 9.7 million to 20.3 million households would engage in online trading by 2003. One survey of investors found that more than one-fourth said they were likely to use the Internet for stock trading in the next twelve months. Perhaps the most telling indicator of the importance of online trading was that several major full-service brokerage firms that had resisted the trend jumped on the bandwagon during 1999.

Securities regulators and other experts praised online trading as offering the potential to "democratize" the stock market by making it more accessible to people of all backgrounds and income levels. But online trading also posed numerous issues for government and private regulators who had the job of preventing fraud and ensuring the fundamental soundness of the financial markets.

Laws and regulations intended for traditional transactions—in which investors typically had a long-term relationship with a broker who bought and sold stocks on their behalf—did not always apply to the world of online trading. Investors who used their computers to access the stock markets often had little direct contact with a broker and relied instead on written material posted on a Web site. Moreover, millions of investors who turned to online services had little knowledge about or experience with the stock market and were vulnerable to misleading sales pitches and short-term trends. Levitt said he was worried that most of these investors, attracted by the bull market of the 1990s, had never experienced a "down" market and would not be able to withstand even modest financial losses.

One major issue concerning regulators involved a standard they called "suitability"—the National Association of Security Dealers requirement that stock brokers and dealers recommend only stocks that they believe to be "suitable" for their customers. Brokers and dealers were required to make that determination based on what their customers told them about their financial status, securities holdings, investing needs, and other factors. The New York Stock Exchange and other "self-regulating organizations" had imposed similar requirements on their members.

In its November 23 report, the SEC said online trading raised numerous questions about application of the suitability rule, most importantly: at what point is an online broker considered to have made a specific recommendation to an individual customer, thereby invoking the suitability rule? Some online firms insisted that their stock recommendations were aimed at a general audience, not at specific customers, and so were not covered by the suitability rule. Other experts said the suitability rule should apply to many types of online trading because brokers were able to use financial profiles stored in their computer systems to make recommendations to individual customers. Such a recommendation would be customer-specific, although less personal than a telephone call from a broker to a client.

In its report, the SEC said securities regulators should investigate the issue further before reshaping suitability rules to apply specifically to online trading. In any event, the report said the field of online trading was changing so rapidly that new developments would help determine what types of actions should be taken.

Regulators also expressed concern about the use of false or misleading advertising and other forms of information on the Internet. Some online firms failed to disclose all fees customers would pay or made exaggerated claims about potential profits from investing. Many Internet sites also featured "chat rooms" where investors traded advice and stock tips; in some cases the advice came from people with undisclosed financial interests in promoting specific stocks.

Other issues confronted by regulators dealt with the technical capacity of online services to handle the volume of business generated by Internet trading. Some firms had experienced computer and electrical outages that affected their services. In other cases, online customers discovered that orders they thought had been placed or canceled were never acted on, even when they had received an electronic receipt. Some online firms also failed to update customers' accounts on a regular basis, with the result that a customer might make investment decisions based on out-of-date information. Levitt advised customers to keep careful records of their own and to never assume that an order placed over the Internet was carried out.

Despite their concerns about these and other issues, key officials said they did not want to move so quickly in passing new regulations that the budding online industry would be damaged. "I don't want to stamp out the on-line brokers, and I think if we came down too hard on them right now that's what we'd do," Laura Unger, the SEC commissioner responsible for the November 23 report, told the Washington Post.

The Day-Trading Phenomenon

The rapid growth in the number of day-traders was posing a similar set of issues for securities regulators. SEC chairman Levitt told a Senate subcommittee on September 16 that more than 100 firms were offering day-trading services, with an estimated 5,800 to 6,800 people using those services full-time. Other estimates pegged the number of full-time and part-time day-traders at upwards of 15,000.

In most cases, day-traders used computers and software provided by firms that specialized in that service. On any given day a day-trader might make dozens or even hundreds of transactions, usually buying a stock in small quantities then selling it a few seconds or minutes later. Only rarely would a day-trader hold a stock overnight. In theory, a day-trader would make a small profit on each transaction, with the profits adding up to a sizable amount by the end of each day.

Levitt and others said day-traders faced numerous hazards, the most important of which was that few of them actually made any money. The vast majority of day-traders lost money during the first few months, and only those who had substantial amounts of capital before entering day-trading could absorb the continuing losses. Most day-traders had little experience in or knowledge about the stock market, Levitt said. For training, many day-traders relied on crash courses offered by the firms whose services they had contracted to use. Some firms used what Levitt called "exaggerated claims of profitability" to attract people. In one highly publicized commercial, a firm featured a tow truck driver who was said to have made enough money day-trading to buy a tropical island; the firm withdrew its commercial following complaints.

Levitt told the Senate panel that the SEC was investigating the practices of more than forty day-trading firms to determine whether they were complying with securities laws and regulations. As of mid-September, he said, the investigations had not found "marked and widespread fraud" by the firms but had raised numerous concerns about the extent to which some of them were complying with bookkeeping requirements and rules governing prudent and ethical behavior by securities dealers. The commission "will vigorously pursue any firms that violate" those rules, he said.

Levitt also noted that some day-trading firms were taking advantages of loopholes in securities laws and regulations to engage in dangerous or unethical practices. For example, he said, some day-trading firms used lending among the accounts of their customers to cover "margin deficiencies," or the difference between the amount a trader put down for a stock and the total price of the stock. This lending among customers—a practice known as "journaling"—was rarely used by traditional stockbrokers but was becoming common practice among some day-trading firms, Levitt said. That development raised "significant concerns" for regulators, he said, because the firms might not fully disclose the potential risks to their customers, some of whom might not understand that they were "trading beyond their own means."

Following are excerpts from an address, "Plain Talk About On-line Investing," delivered by Securities and Exchange Commission Chairman Arthur Levitt to the National Press Club in Washington, D.C., on May 4, 1999:

Today, you can hardly pick up a newspaper, turn on a television, overhear a conversation, or talk to a friend without mention of the Internet. It has done nothing short of change the way our world works and the way our nation invests. And overall, it has changed us for the better.

I'm here today not to extol the Internet's virtues—as they are self-evident—or to raise a red flag of danger. Instead, I want to talk plainly and sensibly about the challenges it presents in the most practical ways.

Last week, I visited Martin Luther King High School in New York City to talk about the importance of financial literacy. The first question I got was from a young student who asked what "Internet stock should I buy." We are living in a time when the stock market is more a part of the American consciousness than ever before. After years of nothing but "up" markets and empowering technology, the investor psyche has gone through a lot of changes. Memories have shortened and important points may have gotten lost in the excitement.

We—as a nation, as investors, as businesses and as regulators—should not get manic about the mania. One day, a little-known company stock soars 38,000 percent after on-line investors invest using the wrong ticker symbol. Another day, someone fabricates a news story by copying a web page of a news organization and the stock in question rises 32 percent. Or, sadly, it's an investor who didn't take the time to appreciate what he was getting into and ended up losing his life savings in one fell swoop. It seems that with every passing day, we come across one story more amazing than the other.

As cliché as it may be, fundamentals still apply. I want to review them here—whether they take the form of advice to investors, guidance to brokers, or reasoned action for regulators.

I want to discuss a number of important issues that should give all of us sufficient pause. First, to investors, I want to talk about your responsibilities when investing over the Internet; second, to on-line brokerages, in the enthusiasm over on-line trading, you can never lose sight of the fundamental obligations to customers; and third, I want to discuss how the SEC [Securities and Exchange Commission] is responding to these rapid changes to protect investors and help maintain market integrity.

By one account, more than seven million Americans trade on-line—comprising 25 percent of all trades made by individual investors. In 1994, not one person traded over the Internet. In the next few years, the number of on-line brokerage accounts will roughly equal the metropolitan populations of Seattle, San Francisco, Boston, Dallas, Denver, Miami, Atlanta and Chicago, combined.

The breadth and pace of change prompted by the Internet are phenomenal. But, while it changes the way millions of Americans invest, on-line investing does not alter the basic framework that has governed our markets for the past 65 years.

The laws regulating our markets are a product of the New Deal era. To me, their concepts are as indelible as the Constitution. They have weathered challenge after challenge, decade after decade, and are every bit as relevant and effective today as they were the day they were written. Companies offering their shares—whether off a website or through a paper prospectus—still have to disclose what they are selling and why. Brokers—whether traditional or on-line—still have the same obligations to their customers. And fraud—whether perpetrated over the Internet, on the phone, or in-person—is still fraud.

Consequently, I am not convinced it's necessary for the SEC to pronounce a totally new and radical scheme of regulation specifically tailored to on-line investing. Yet, I don't rule out the possibility that there may come a time when the SEC sees a need for new approaches to better meet the imperatives of the Internet.

What must occur now is a greater recognition by investors of their individual responsibility. I'm talking specifically about an individual investor's duty to understand and control the level of risk he or she is assuming. That level can vary with the type of activity an investor undertakes. On one end of the spectrum lie investors who trade occasionally on-line and hold their investments for the longer term. They are basically retail investors who manage their portfolios through on-line accounts.

On the other end of that spectrum are so-called "day traders" whose time horizon for moving in and out of stock positions is measured by minutes, if not seconds. Some argue day trading is really nothing more than speculation. And, speculation is not new to our markets. Personally, I don't think day traders are speculating because traditional speculation requires some market knowledge. They are instead gambling, which doesn't. Historically, short-term trading has been an activity filled by a relatively small number of professional traders.

I am concerned that more and more people may be undertaking day trading strategies without a full appreciation of the risk and difficulty involved. No one should have any illusions of what he is getting involved in. I know of one state that recently found that 67 out of 68 day traders at a firm had in fact lost money.

Somewhere in the middle of this spectrum—with long-term investors on one side and day traders on the other—is an increasing number of Americans who use their on-line accounts both to invest longer term and to trade short term on momentum or small changes in the price of a stock. Call this mixed strategy day trading "light."

I'm concerned about the great influx of new and relatively inexperienced investors who may be so seduced by the ease and speed of Internet trading that they may be trading in a way that does not match their specific goals and risk tolerance. I also wonder about many of these investors who have never experienced a down market. On the other hand, a greater number of Americans investing for their futures and helping to raise capital is, in the long-term, good for our markets and good for our country.

Individual Responsibility

As far as I'm concerned, for most individuals, the stock market is best used for investing, not trading. And, it's important to make that distinction. On-line trading may be quick and easy; on-line investing—and I emphasize investing—requires the same old-fashioned elbow grease like researching a company or making the time to appreciate the level of risk. I'm often surprised by investors who spend more time deciding what movie they'll rent than on which stock to buy.

Regardless of how frequently a person trades or invests, the opportunity to make these decisions comes with the responsibility to take the time to understand the implications of those decisions. We have noticed four common misconceptions that investors have about on-line trading.

The first is that although the Internet makes it seem as if you have a direct connection to the securities markets, you don't. When you push that enter key, your order is sent to your broker, who then sends it to a market to be executed. This process is usually seamless and electronic; it is not, however, guaranteed. Lines may clog; systems may break; orders may back-up.

Even when automated systems can handle a lot of investors who want to buy or sell the same stock at the same time, a line often forms. Price quotes are only for a limited number of shares; some investors may not receive the currently quoted price. And, as you would expect, the price of that stock will then go up if there are more buyers and down if there are more sellers. By the time you get to the front of the line, the price of the stock could be very different.

So, how do investors protect themselves from a rapid change in the price of a stock? One way is to use a limit order. That's the second thing every on-line investor needs to know. A limit order buys or sells a security at a specific price. In other words, the order can be executed only if the market price has not moved past a certain level. On the other hand, a market order buys or sells the stock at whatever price the security is at the time the order reaches the market. So, if you place a market order to buy an IPO [initial public offering] stock at $9, you could end up paying $90 by the time your order is executed.

This isn't theoretical. More than a few investors have lost most of their savings—thousands and thousands of dollars—because they failed to limit their price. Now, sometimes limit orders may not get executed in a fast moving market and some firms may charge more for them. But, at the very least, I'd rather not own a stock or pay a little more upfront than be totally unprepared or incapable of paying a whole lot more later. My goals as an investor may be different from yours, but considering the costs and benefits of a limit order is part of responsible investing in today's market.

The third misconception is that an order is canceled when you hit "cancel" on your computer. But, the fact is it's canceled only when the market receives the cancellation. You may get an electronic confirmation, but that may only mean your request to cancel was received—not that your order was actually canceled. Recently, one major brokerage wasn't able to process 20 percent of the cancellation orders on a fast moving IPO. One investor placed an on-line order for 2,000 shares of the stock—thought she canceled it—and then placed another order for 1,000 shares.

After realizing that she had two orders outstanding, she tried to cancel both. Instead, she owed her broker over a quarter-million dollars for 3,000 shares after wanting to invest roughly $18,000. Most cases may not be this exceptional, but I urge investors to contact their firms to see how they can ensure a cancellation order actually worked.

Fourth, if you plan to borrow money to buy a stock, you also need to know the terms of the loan your broker gave you. This is called margin. When you buy on margin, the stock you purchase is collateral for that loan. In volatile markets, investors who put up an initial margin payment for a stock may find themselves required to provide additional cash if the price of the stock falls.

But, some investors have been shocked to find out that if they don't meet the margin call the brokerage firm has the right to sell their securities—without any notification and potentially at a substantial loss to the investor. Others investors have been surprised to learn that they are lending to or borrowing from other customers in their firm through excess balances in their margin accounts. It's clear that if an investor fails to understand the use and consequences of a margin account, he does so at his own peril.

You also may have heard about plans by the major markets to extend their trading hours into the evening. That's another way the markets are being responsive to ever-changing investment patterns brought about by individual investors. But with this new flexibility comes a catch—the price you pay or receive might be affected by the fewer number of people in the market at that hour. That's simply a product of the law of supply and demand.

The Cardinal Rule of Acting in the Customer's Interest

Let me turn to some of the concerns I have about the role of on-line firms. Firms should remember that while on-line trading may place significantly more responsibility in the hands of investors, it doesn't absolve the firms of their obligations to customers. Most firms are doing a pretty good job—especially in light of the dramatic growth they are experiencing. But as the Internet rapidly becomes more and more an integral part of investing for more and more Americans, I ask brokerage firms to help protect the integrity of it for the long-run.

First, firms need to ensure that their ability to provide effective customer service keeps pace with their growth. If you're marketing your firm to new customers, you'd better be able to provide them service when they do business with you. Firms are opening roughly 15,000 new accounts a day. That means 15,000 new potential complaints a day—especially if a system goes down. Are investors having a hard time getting their e-mails answered? Are customer service 800 numbers always busy? Are complaints about failures or delays in order execution, account accessibility, and other issues overwhelming the firm's compliance department?

If the answer to any of these questions is "yes," then what are firms doing about it? It doesn't take a regulator to tell you what unhappy customers mean to a company's future, or more broadly, to the future of on-line investing.

Second, all firms—whether on-line, discount or full service—have an obligation to ensure the best execution of their customers' orders. That's not just good business practice; it's a legal obligation. Firms have this same duty to their customers to find the best prices—whether they charge $10 per trade or $100 per trade.

The Commission has long stressed to firms the importance of obtaining the best possible price when they route their customers' orders. They simply can't let payment for order flow or other relationships or inducements determine where they do business. That's why I have directed our examiners to focus in on firms' order routing practices in an examination sweep. I urge all firms now to review their practices to ensure they're doing right by their customers.

Third, firms need to communicate more clearly to investors. We have reviewed the disclosure in account agreements both on paper and on web pages. Overall, we found that most firms address the different types of orders available, fewer firms discuss how market volatility and the use of margin can affect on-line investors, and almost none talk about the risks or what to do in the event of system capacity and outage problems. I know that customers' orders can be slowed down for reasons outside of a firm's control. But explaining clearly to customers rather than merely disclaiming liability through complex and legalistic language would go a long way toward reducing the complaints pouring into the SEC, Congress and firms.

So, to every on-line firm I challenge you to meaningfully communicate with your customers. Talk in realistic terms; let them know their options; and focus on the quality of your disclosure in your agreements, instead of just the acceptability of them.

Lastly, I worry about how some on-line firms advertise. Quite frankly, some advertisements more closely resemble commercials for the lottery than anything else. When firms, again and again, tell investors that on-line investing can make them rich, it creates unrealistic expectations. And, when firms sow

211

those grandiose and unrealistic expectations, they stand a good chance of reaping the adverse results when many of them go unmet.

Now, in today's Bull Market, there may be an increasing population of tow truck drivers who now own their own islands as a result of on-line investing. Assuming there's not, I don't rule out the fact that some of these commercials are tongue-in-cheek. But, in a market environment where many investors are susceptible to quixotic euphoria, I'm worried these commercials step over the line and border on irresponsibility.

I recently saw one commercial that showed two women rushing in from their jog to trade before the stock market closed. After a few clicks of the mouse, one woman proclaims, "I just made $1700." The other woman sheepishly replies by admitting she invests in mutual funds. What's the implication of the message here? Has it become passé to invest for the longer-term and to diversify your risk?

Now, some may argue that we shouldn't tell firms how to sell their products as long as its lawful. I agree. But selling securities is not like selling soap. Brokers have always had duties to their customers that go beyond simply "buyer beware."

I've asked the NASD [National Association of Securities Dealers] regulatory unit to hold a roundtable on advertising to add to the work they're already doing to improve fairness in advertising. I call on all of the firms to join in this effort. I've also asked Jay Chiat, former head of the advertising firm, Chiat Day, to work with the NASD and industry leaders to consider the public interest issues this type of advertising implicates.

What the SEC Is Doing

Today, I've talked about what investors need to be aware of if they invest over the Internet and I've also discussed some of the issues firms should be addressing. As technology recasts our markets and helps attract more and more investors than ever before, the SEC's mission to protect investors and maintain market integrity remains absolute.

Securities fraud perpetrated over the Internet represents a signal challenge for the SEC. While the scams we have seen on the Internet are the same basic frauds that have always accompanied the flow of money, the Internet's speed, low cost and relative anonymity give con artists access to an unprecedented number of innocent investors.

Policing this marketplace will require more resources, more manpower, and more money. Nevertheless, we are prepared to do whatever is necessary to help protect investors. While we contend with the Internet's growing presence, it offers us important tools to track down and catch criminals. Law enforcement will tell you that it's a lot easier to catch someone who uses the Internet than the telephone. For example, although the individual who perpetrated last month's news hoax about a corporate takeover tried to cover up his footprints, we tracked him down within a week.

Last year, we created the SEC's Cyberforce—a specially trained nationwide corps of 125 attorneys, accountants and analysts tasked with searching for

Internet fraud. This year, we will increase that number by 100 percent. For next year, the Commission has asked for an $11 million increase to expand our efforts to combat fraud. And, with the support and insight of Congressional and Administration leaders, we will continue to step up our efforts in the future.

In the mean time, we are vigilantly pursuing those who seek to take advantage of innocent investors. In the next two weeks, the SEC's Enforcement Division will present a number of cases charging fraudulent offerings over the Internet. These cases would charge issuers and promoters with making false claims about companies or offering investments in entirely fictitious companies. We have also been working with the FBI on a project called "Operation InvestNet"—a nationwide initiative to address fraudulent securities activities taking place over the Internet.

Second, the SEC's Office of Compliance and Inspections will continue to inspect firms offering on-line trading. We've already conducted inspections of firms that represent 80 percent of the market share. Based on our initial findings, I sent a letter this morning to all of the on-line brokerage firms asking them to improve the quality of their disclosure to investors. When firms achieve the highest quality of service and continually act in the interests of their customers, they create a customer for life—instead of just another short-term trading opportunity.

The SEC and the self-regulatory agencies are also inspecting all of the brokerage firms that specialize in day trading. Clearly providing day trading opportunities is not itself against the law, but these firms should be on notice that they are still broker-dealers and must operate within the existing rules. That means complying with disclosure, capital, margin, and best execution requirements as well as maintaining updated and comprehensive books and records. And any firm, whether day trading or on-line, that recommends a type of investment strategy or customizes research should ensure that it is suitable for its customers.

Third, I'm announcing today the formation of a formal SEC private sector Advisory Committee on Technology. The Advisory Committee's mandate will be a broad one. It will encompass not only how the Commission might better leverage its resources to protect investors and safeguard market integrity, but also examine issues specifically relating to on-line trading. I've asked General Ken Minihan, former head of the National Security Agency and Bran Ferren, a true innovator in technology, to lead this effort in lending cutting edge expertise to the SEC.

As its first priority, I will ask the Committee to convene a group of industry executives to hear their thoughts and concerns about how technology will affect our markets and its participants.

Fourth, the Commission is unveiling its new Investor Education Web Page. The Web site is *www.sec.gov/invkhome.htm*. It includes detailed information and tips on on-line investing, how to detect fraud both on and off the Internet and other important information on saving and investing.

In addition, in the letter that I sent to on-line firms, I have asked them to create links from their web sites to the SEC's investor education site. This is an idea that came up during a Senate hearing on this subject. I hope we can all agree that an informed and knowledgeable investor is good for the industry and good for individual businesses.

Lastly, I want to raise some points about chat rooms, which increasingly have become a source of information and mis-information for many investors. They have been compared to a high-tech version of morning gossip or advice at the company water cooler. But, at least you knew your co-workers at the water cooler. That just isn't true on the Internet. And, I hope investors recognize that.

I wonder how many chat room participants realize that if someone is waxing poetic about a certain stock, that person could well be paid to do it. For the future sake of this medium, I encourage investors to take what they see over chat rooms—not with a grain of salt—but with a rock of salt. By doing so, you protect yourself and you protect the Internet.

I've asked the major Internet providers who host these chat rooms to place a link to the SEC's website where investors can learn more about on-line investing and file a complaint with us if necessary. I want everyone in a chat room to know that if someone is taking advantage of the technology, you have the opportunity to shine the light on it. Think of it as neighborhood watch on the Internet. With the help of investors, we can get those people who have only one motivation—to ruthlessly make money at the expense of others—out of our communities.

The SEC will do everything it can to protect and inform investors during this time of great innovation and change. But, I've said many times before that investor protection—at its most basic and effective level—starts with the investor. In this day and age, there simply is no substitute for a person's awareness and wariness.

Conclusion

Many of the issues I have raised today were not even a blip on the screen a few years ago. Who can confidently say what on-line issues will demand our time and attention in the future? But we won't stop examining and thinking about how the Internet will affect investors and our markets. Through the efforts of Commissioner Unger who is spearheading the Commission's work on technology issues and the rest of the SEC staff, we are going to do our best to ensure investors remain protected and our markets remain the strongest in the world.

All of us are participants in an extraordinary social phenomena. The democratization of our markets is a desirable development which regulators should not frustrate. Our mission is not to prevent losers or to modulate the sometimes mercurial movement of our markets. The standard by which we will determine our methods of surveillance, education, market structure, disclosure and , if need be, enforcement will be an unyielding commitment to the well being of investors. I call on all market participants, the media, fellow regulators and lawmakers to help us fulfill this commitment by working together to make the 21st Century defined as much by trust as technology.

SUPREME COURT ON
STUDENT SEXUAL HARASSMENT
May 24, 1999

In one of its more controversial decisions of the year, the Supreme Court ruled, 5–4, that public schools could be sued in federal court for failing to prevent students from sexually harassing their classmates. Under the ruling, handed down May 24, 1999, schools that received federal funding were liable for money damages if school officials knew of the harassment but were "deliberately indifferent" to it. Moreover, Justice Sandra Day O'Connor wrote for the majority, the harassment had to be "so severe, pervasive, and objectively offensive that it effectively bars the victim's access to an educational opportunity or benefit."

Although O'Connor made a point of saying that conduct such as teasing or name calling would not by itself constitute sexual harassment under the ruling, Justice Anthony M. Kennedy, writing for the minority, said the ruling was an unwarranted federal intrusion into the classroom, a judicial overreaction to "routine problems of adolescence" that would make "the federal courts the final arbiters of school policy and of almost every disagreement between students." Joining O'Connor in the majority were Justices John Paul Stevens, David H. Souter, Ruth Bader Ginsburg, and Stephen G. Breyer. In the minority with Kennedy were Chief Justice William H. Rehnquist and Justices Antonin Scalia and Clarence Thomas.

Some observers suggested that the minority's dire portrait of the consequences of the ruling was overdrawn, in part because many schools already had policies in place to help teachers and students understand and deal with sexual harassment and in part because the threshold for liability was so high. Julie Underwood, general counsel for the National School Boards Association, which had filed a brief in behalf of the school district involved in the case, was one who said that school administrators should be able to live with the decision. "The Court stated that school districts would be held liable if they were deliberately indifferent to known and pervasive harassment. These are rare occasions," Underwood told the Washington Post.

Still others, including the Washington Post *in an editorial, said that the minority's concerns might be well-founded. "It would be naive to think that this decision will not encourage myriad suits against school districts, and . . . that the threat of such actions will not affect the tone and substance of educational instruction," the editorial said. "Experience will show whether this decision proves to be the narrow exception the majority intends or the opening of the floodgates that the minority fears."*

The Court's ruling in the case of Davis v. Monroe County Board of Education *extended its interpretation of the protections provided by the Title IX of the Education Amendments of 1972, which barred gender discrimination by any school system that accepted federal funding. In 1998 the Court ruled that school districts were liable to suit under Title IX for sexual harassment of students by teachers if school administrators knew of the harassment but were deliberately indifferent to it.* (Sexual harassment by teachers, Historic Documents of 1998, p. 442)

The facts in the Davis *case seemed almost tailor-made to fit the standard the Court set out in the 1998 case. In this case, however, the harasser was not a teacher, but a classmate. For months, beginning in late 1992, fifth grader LaShonda Davis came home from her elementary school in Monroe County, Georgia, with complaints that one of her classmates, a boy who sat next to her, was harassing her. According to LaShonda, the boy would grab at her breasts, rub up against her, and tell her he wanted to "get in bed" with her. As the months passed, the girl grew depressed, her grades fell, and she even wrote a note talking about committing suicide. LaShonda and her mother, Aurelia Davis, repeatedly asked teachers and school officials to do something about the situation. Other girls had also complained about the boy's conduct, but the school did not respond to the complaints. One day, when LaShonda came home crying, Aurelia Davis decided she had had enough. She went to the local sheriff (and the boy ultimately pleaded guilty to sexual battery). A year later she sued the Monroe County school board for failing to do enough to protect her daughter from sexual harassment.*

The federal district court ruled in favor of the board of education, which argued that Davis had no standing to sue because nothing in Title IX put schools on notice that they could be held financially liable for student-on-student harassment. Although a three-judge panel of the Court of Appeals for the Eleventh Circuit reversed that ruling, the panel's decision was overruled by the full Appeals Court. Davis appealed to the Supreme Court.

A New Standard: Narrowly Drawn or Overly Broad?

In reversing the lower courts, the majority stated a new standard for judging liability for student harassment. Schools that receive federal funding, O'Connor wrote, "are properly held liable in damages only where they are deliberately indifferent to sexual harassment, of which they have actual knowledge, that is so severe, pervasive, and objectively offensive that it can be said to deprive the victims of access to the educational opportunities or benefits provided by the school." O'Connor emphasized that the majority had carefully drawn the standard to exclude all but the most egregious conduct. "At least early on," she wrote, "students are still learning how to interact appropriately with their peers. It is thus understandable that, in the school setting, students often engage in insults, banter, teasing, shoving, pushing, and gender-specific conduct that is upsetting to the students subjected to it. Damages are not available for simple acts of teasing and name-calling among school children, however. . . ."

A single incident of harassment was unlikely to trigger liability, she said, noting that the standard was limited to cases where the harassment had "a systemic effect on educational programs or activities." O'Connor also took issue with the minority for suggesting that schools would be held liable under the standard if they did not actually remedy the harassment. To the contrary, she said, the standard requires only that the school "respond to known peer harassment in a manner that is not clearly unreasonable."

Throughout her opinion, O'Connor noted instances where she said the minority had misinterpreted or misrepresented what the ruling would and would not permit. Remanding the case to the lower courts for review under the new standard, O'Connor cautioned them not to be misled by the minority into imposing "more sweeping liability than we read Title IX to require."

Kennedy, in an unusual judicial diatribe, said the majority had overstepped its authority by reading more into Title IX than Congress had intended. In doing so, the majority had set forth an overly broad standard in an attempt to control conduct that could not "be identified by either schools or courts with any precision." For example, he said, "teenage romantic relationships are a part of everyday life. . . . A teenager's romantic overtures to a classmate (even when persistent and unwelcome) are an inescapable part of adolescence."

The broad standard endorsed by the majority would open a potential floodgate of litigation, Kennedy said, and "breed a climate of fear that encourages school administrators to label even the most innocuous of childish conduct sexual harassment." He cited a North Carolina school's suspension of a six-year-old boy who kissed a female classmate on the cheek. The costs of defending against this torrent of liable suits "could overwhelm many school districts," he said.

Perhaps Kennedy's most scathing comments castigated the majority for thrusting a federal presence in the nation's public schools. "Enforcement of the federal right recognized by the majority means that the federal influence will permeate everything from curriculum decisions to day-to-day classroom logistics and interactions," he wrote. "After today, Johnny will find that the routine problems of adolescence are to be resolved by invoking a federal right to demand assignment to a desk two rows away."

Reactions: Nonsense or a Workable Standard?

Some commentators clearly sided with the minority in their view of the case. Writing in Newsweek, *columnist George F. Will said the case "illus-*

217

*trates how law metastasizes from words by Congress, to rules from bureau-
crats, to fiats from judges, to a torrent of litigation that will divert school
districts' financial resources from educational functions and force schools
into defensive silliness."*

*Others took a more tempered approach. Warren Plowden, who argued the
case for the Monroe County school board said he thought the standard the
majority set was high enough that the Davises might not prevail when
their case was reviewed in the lower court. "It's going to be tough for any
plaintiff to win any of these cases unless she can show that the school did
nothing," he said.*

*Stephen R. Yurek, of the National Association of Secondary School Prin-
cipals, said the decision reaffirmed what his association had long been
telling its members. "The days of boys will be boys and girls will be girls
are long gone," he said. "The school needs to address all elements of the
school environment and teach core values, including respect. There won't
be liability if you are proactive and out there teaching kids about appropriate behavior."*

> *Following are excerpts from the majority and dissenting opin-
> ions in the case of* Davis v. Monroe County Board of Education,
> *in which the Supreme Court ruled, 5–4, on May 24, 1999, that a
> school district could be liable for student sexual harassment of
> another student if it knew about the harassment but did nothing
> about it and if the harassment was so severe and pervasive that
> the victim was denied access to educational benefits guaranteed
> under Title IX of the Education Amendments of 1972:*

No. 97–843

Aurelia Davis, as next friend of LaShonda D., Petitioner *v.* Monroe County Board of Education et al.	On writ of certiorari to the United States Court of Appeals for the Eleventh Circuit

[May 24, 1999]

JUSTICE O'CONNOR delivered the opinion of the Court.

Petitioner brought suit against the Monroe County Board of Education
and other defendants, alleging that her fifth-grade daughter had been the victim of sexual harassment by another student in her class. Among petitioner's
claims was a claim for monetary and injunctive relief under Title IX of the
Education Amendments of 1972 (Title IX), as amended. The District Court
dismissed petitioner's Title IX claim on the ground that "student-on-student,"

or peer, harassment provides no ground for a private cause of action under the statute. The Court of Appeals for the Eleventh Circuit, sitting en banc, affirmed. We consider here whether a private damages action may lie against the school board in cases of student-on-student harassment. We conclude that it may, but only where the funding recipient acts with deliberate indifference to known acts of harassment in its programs or activities. Moreover, we conclude that such an action will lie only for harassment that is so severe, pervasive, and objectively offensive that it effectively bars the victim's access to an educational opportunity or benefit.

I

. . .

A

Petitioner's minor daughter, LaShonda, was allegedly the victim of a prolonged pattern of sexual harassment by one of her fifth-grade classmates at Hubbard Elementary School, a public school in Monroe County, Georgia. According to petitioner's complaint, the harassment began in December 1992, when the classmate, G.F., attempted to touch LaShonda's breasts and genital area and made vulgar statements such as " 'I want to get in bed with you' " and " 'I want to feel your boobs.' " Similar conduct allegedly occurred on or about January 4 and January 20, 1993. *Ibid.* LaShonda reported each of these incidents to her mother and to her classroom teacher, Diane Fort. Petitioner, in turn, also contacted Fort, who allegedly assured petitioner that the school principal, Bill Querry, had been informed of the incidents. Petitioner contends that, notwithstanding these reports, no disciplinary action was taken against G.F.

G.F.'s conduct allegedly continued for many months. In early February, G.F. purportedly placed a door stop in his pants and proceeded to act in a sexually suggestive manner toward LaShonda during physical education class. LaShonda reported G.F.'s behavior to her physical education teacher, Whit Maples. Approximately one week later, G.F. again allegedly engaged in harassing behavior, this time while under the supervision of another classroom teacher, Joyce Pippin. Again, LaShonda allegedly reported the incident to the teacher, and again petitioner contacted the teacher to follow up.

Petitioner alleges that G.F. once more directed sexually harassing conduct toward LaShonda in physical education class in early March, and that LaShonda reported the incident to both Maples and Pippen. In mid-April 1993, G.F. allegedly rubbed his body against LaShonda in the school hallway in what LaShonda considered a sexually suggestive manner, and LaShonda again reported the matter to Fort.

The string of incidents finally ended in mid-May, when G.F. was charged with, and pleaded guilty to, sexual battery for his misconduct. The complaint alleges that LaShonda had suffered during the months of harassment, however; specifically, her previously high grades allegedly dropped as she became unable to concentrate on her studies, and, in April 1993, her father discovered that she had written a suicide note. The complaint further alleges that, at one point, LaShonda told petitioner that she " 'didn't know how much longer she could keep [G.F.] off her.' "

Nor was LaShonda G.F.'s only victim; it is alleged that other girls in the class fell prey to G.F.'s conduct. At one point, in fact, a group composed of LaShonda and other female students tried to speak with Principal Querry about G.F.'s behavior. According to the complaint, however, a teacher denied the students' request with the statement, " 'If [Querry] wants you, he'll call you.' "

Petitioner alleges that no disciplinary action was taken in response to G.F.'s behavior toward LaShonda. In addition to her conversations with Fort and Pippen, petitioner alleges that she spoke with Principal Querry in mid-May 1993. When petitioner inquired as to what action the school intended to take against G.F., Querry simply stated, " 'I guess I'll have to threaten him a little bit harder.' " Yet, petitioner alleges, at no point during the many months of his reported misconduct was G.F. disciplined for harassment. Indeed, Querry allegedly asked petitioner why LaShonda " 'was the only one complaining.' "

Nor, according to the complaint, was any effort made to separate G.F. and LaShonda. On the contrary, notwithstanding LaShonda's frequent complaints, only after more than three months of reported harassment was she even permitted to change her classroom seat so that she was no longer seated next to G.F. Moreover, petitioner alleges that, at the time of the events in question, the Monroe County Board of Education (Board) had not instructed its personnel on how to respond to peer sexual harassment and had not established a policy on the issue.

B

On May 4, 1994, petitioner filed suit in the United States District Court for the Middle District of Georgia against the Board, Charles Dumas, the school district's superintendent, and Principal Querry. The complaint alleged that the Board is a recipient of federal funding for purposes of Title IX, that "[t]he persistent sexual advances and harassment by the student G.F. upon [LaShonda] interfered with her ability to attend school and perform her studies and activities," and that "[t]he deliberate indifference by Defendants to the unwelcome sexual advances of a student upon LaShonda created an intimidating, hostile, offensive and abus[ive] school environment in violation of Title IX." The complaint sought compensatory and punitive damages, attorney's fees, and injunctive relief.

The defendants (all respondents here) moved to dismiss petitioner's complaint under Federal Rule of Civil Procedure 12(b)(6) for failure to state a claim upon which relief could be granted, and the District Court granted respondents' motion. With regard to petitioner's claims under Title IX, the court dismissed the claims against individual defendants on the ground that only federally funded educational institutions are subject to liability in private causes of action under Title IX. As for the Board, the court concluded that Title IX provided no basis for liability absent an allegation "that the Board or an employee of the Board had any role in the harassment."

Petitioner appealed the District Court's decision dismissing her Title IX claim against the Board, and a panel of the Court of Appeals for the Eleventh Circuit reversed. Borrowing from Title VII law, a majority of the panel determined that student-on-student harassment stated a cause of action against the Board under Title IX: "[W]e conclude that as Title VII encompasses a claim for damages due to a sexually hostile working environment created by co-workers and tolerated by the employer, Title IX encompasses a claim for damages due to a sexually hostile educational environment created by a fellow student or students when the supervising authorities knowingly fail to act to eliminate the harassment." The Eleventh Circuit panel recognized that petitioner sought to state a claim based on school "officials' failure to take action to stop the offensive acts of those over whom the officials exercised control," and the court concluded that petitioner had alleged facts sufficient to support a claim for hostile environment sexual harassment on this theory.

The Eleventh Circuit granted the Board's motion for rehearing en banc, and affirmed the District Court's decision to dismiss petitioner's Title IX claim against the Board. The en banc court relied, primarily, on the theory that Title IX was passed pursuant to Congress' legislative authority under the Constitution's Spending Clause, and that the statute therefore must provide potential recipients of federal education funding with "unambiguous notice of the conditions they are assuming when they accept" it. Title IX, the court reasoned, provides recipients with notice that they must stop their employees from engaging in discriminatory conduct, but the statute fails to provide a recipient with sufficient notice of a duty to prevent student-on-student harassment. . . .

We granted certiorari in order to resolve a conflict in the Circuits over whether, and under what circumstances, a recipient of federal educational funds can be liable in a private damages action arising from student-on-student sexual harassment. . . . We now reverse.

II

Title IX provides, with certain exceptions not at issue here, that

"[n]o person in the United States shall, on the basis of sex, be excluded from participation in, be denied the benefits of, or be subjected to discrimination under any education program or activity receiving Federal financial assistance.

Congress authorized an administrative enforcement scheme for Title IX. Federal departments or agencies with the authority to provide financial assistance are entrusted to promulgate rules, regulations, and orders to enforce the objectives of [Title IX] and these departments or agencies may rely on "any . . . means authorized by law," including the termination of funding, to give effect to the statute's restrictions.

There is no dispute here that the Board is a recipient of federal education funding for Title IX purposes. Nor do respondents support an argument that student-on-student harassment cannot rise to the level of "discrimination" for purposes of Title IX. Rather, at issue here is the question whether a recipient of federal education funding may be liable for damages under Title IX under any circumstances for discrimination in the form of student-on-student sexual harassment.

A

Petitioner urges that Title IX's plain language compels the conclusion that the statute is intended to bar recipients of federal funding from permitting this form of discrimination in their programs or activities. She emphasizes that the statute prohibits a student from being "*subjected to discrimination* under any education program or activity receiving Federal financial assistance." (emphasis supplied). It is Title IX's "unmistakable focus on the benefited class," rather than the perpetrator, that, in petitioner's view, compels the conclusion that the statute works to protect students from the discriminatory misconduct of their peers.

Here, however, we are asked to do more than define the scope of the behavior that Title IX proscribes. We must determine whether a district's failure to respond to student-on-student harassment in its schools can support a private suit for money damages. See *Gebser* v. *Lago Vista Independent School Dist.* (1998). . . . This Court has indeed recognized an implied private right of action under Title IX, and we have held that money damages are available in such suits. Because we have repeatedly treated Title IX as legislation enacted pursuant to Congress' authority under the Spending Clause, however, private damages actions are available only where recipients of federal funding had adequate notice that they could be liable for the conduct at issue. . . .

. . . [R]espondents urge that Title IX provides no notice that recipients of federal educational funds could be liable in damages for harm arising from student-on-student harassment. Respondents contend, specifically, that the statute only proscribes misconduct by grant recipients, not third parties. Respondents argue, moreover, that it would be contrary to the very purpose of Spending Clause legislation to impose liability on a funding recipient for the misconduct of third parties, over whom recipients exercise little control.

We agree with respondents that a recipient of federal funds may be liable in damages under Title IX only for its own misconduct. . . .

We disagree with respondents' assertion, however, that petitioner seeks to hold the Board liable for G.F.'s actions instead of its own. Here, petitioner attempts to hold the Board liable for its *own* decision to remain idle in the face of known student-on-student harassment in its schools. In *Gebser*, we concluded that a recipient of federal education funds may be liable in damages under Title IX where it is deliberately indifferent to known acts of sexual harassment by a teacher. . . .

We consider here whether the misconduct identified in *Gebser*—deliberate indifference to known acts of harassment—amounts to an intentional violation of Title IX, capable of supporting a private damages action, when the harasser is a student rather than a teacher. We conclude that, in certain limited circumstances, it does. . . . [T]the regulatory scheme surrounding Title IX has long provided funding recipients with notice that they may be liable for their failure to respond to the discriminatory acts of certain non-agents. The Department of Education requires recipients to monitor third parties for discrimination in specified circumstances and to refrain from particular forms of interaction with outside entities that are known to discriminate.

The common law, too, has put schools on notice that they may be held responsible under state law for their failure to protect students from the tortious acts of third parties. In fact, state courts routinely uphold claims alleging that schools have been negligent in failing to protect their students from the torts of their peers.

This is not to say that the identity of the harasser is irrelevant. On the contrary, both the "deliberate indifference" standard and the language of Title IX narrowly circumscribe the set of parties whose known acts of sexual harassment can trigger some duty to respond on the part of funding recipients. Deliberate indifference makes sense as a theory of direct liability under Title IX only where the funding recipient has some control over the alleged harassment. A recipient cannot be directly liable for its indifference where it lacks the authority to take remedial action. . . .

These factors combine to limit a recipient's damages liability to circumstances wherein the recipient exercises substantial control over both the harasser and the context in which the known harassment occurs. Only then can the recipient be said to "expose" its students to harassment or "cause" them to undergo it "under" the recipient's programs. . . .

Where, as here, the misconduct occurs during school hours and on school grounds—the bulk of G.F.'s misconduct, in fact, took place in the classroom—the misconduct is taking place "under" an "operation" of the funding recipient. . . . In these circumstances, the recipient retains substantial control over the context in which the harassment occurs. More importantly, however, in this setting the Board exercises significant control over the harasser. We have observed, for example, "that the nature of [the State's] power [over public schoolchildren] is custodial and tutelary, permitting a degree of supervision and control that could not be exercised over free adults." *Vernonia School Dist. 47J* v. *Acton* (1995). On more than one occasion, this Court has recognized the importance of school officials' "comprehensive authority . . ., consistent with fundamental constitutional safeguards, to prescribe and control conduct in the schools." *Tinker* v. *Des Moines Independent Community School Dist.* (1969). . . .

At the time of the events in question here, in fact, school attorneys and administrators were being told that student-on-student harassment could trigger liability under Title IX. In March 1993, even as the events alleged in petitioner's complaint were unfolding, the National School Boards Association issued a publication, for use by "school attorneys and administrators in understanding the law regarding sexual harassment of employees and students," which observed that districts could be liable under Title IX for their failure to respond to student-on-student harassment. . . .

Likewise, although they were promulgated too late to contribute to the Board's notice of proscribed misconduct, the Department of Education's Office for Civil Rights (OCR) has recently adopted policy guidelines providing that student-on-student harassment falls within the scope of Title IX's proscriptions. . . .

We stress that our conclusion here—that recipients may be liable for their deliberate indifference to known acts of peer sexual harassment—does not mean that recipients can avoid liability only by purging their schools of actionable peer harassment or that administrators must engage in particular disciplinary action. We thus disagree with respondents' contention that, if Title IX provides a cause of action for student-on-student harassment, "nothing short of expulsion of every student accused of misconduct involving sexual overtones would protect school systems from liability or damages." . . . Likewise, the dissent erroneously imagines that victims of peer harassment now have a Title IX right to make particular remedial demands. . . . In fact, as we have previously noted, courts should refrain from second guessing the disciplinary decisions made by school administrators. School administrators will continue to enjoy the flexibility they require so long as funding recipients are deemed "deliberately indifferent" to acts of student-on-student harassment only where the recipient's response to the harassment or lack thereof is clearly unreasonable in light of the known circumstances. The dissent consistently mischaracterizes this standard to require funding recipients to "remedy" peer harassment, . . . and to "ensur[e] that . . . students conform their conduct to" certain rules. Title IX imposes no such requirements. On the contrary, the recipient must merely respond to known peer harassment in a manner that is not clearly unreasonable. This is not a mere "reasonableness" standard, as the dissent assumes. In an appropriate case, there is no reason why courts, on a motion to dismiss, for summary judgment, or for a directed verdict, could not identify a response as not "clearly unreasonable" as a matter of law.

Like the dissent, we acknowledge that school administrators shoulder substantial burdens as a result of legal constraints on their disciplinary authority. To the extent that these restrictions arise from federal statutes, Congress can review these burdens with attention to the difficult position in which such legislation may place our Nation's schools. We believe, however, that the standard set out here is sufficiently flexible to account both for the level of disciplinary authority available to the school and for the potential liability arising from certain forms of disciplinary action. A university might not, for example, be expected to exercise the same degree of control over its students that a grade school would enjoy, and it would be entirely reasonable for a school to refrain from a form of disciplinary action that would expose it to constitutional or statutory claims.

While it remains to be seen whether petitioner can show that the Board's response to reports of G.F.'s misconduct was clearly unreasonable in light of the known circumstances, petitioner may be able to show that the Board "subject[ed]" LaShonda to discrimination by failing to respond in any way over a period of five months to complaints of G.F.'s in-school misconduct from LaShonda and other female students.

B

The requirement that recipients receive adequate notice of Title IX's proscriptions also bears on the proper definition of "discrimination" in the context of a private damages action. . . . Having previously determined that "sexual harassment" is "discrimination" in the school context under Title IX, we are constrained to conclude that student-on-student sexual harassment, if sufficiently severe, can likewise rise to the level of discrimination actionable under the statute. . . . The statute's other prohibitions, moreover, help give content to the term "discrimination" in this context. Students are not only protected from discrimination, but also specifically shielded from being "excluded from participation in" or "denied the benefits of" any "education program or activity receiving Federal financial assistance." The statute makes clear that, whatever else it prohibits, students must not be denied access to educational benefits and opportunities on the basis of gender. We thus conclude that funding recipients are properly held liable in damages only where they are deliberately indifferent to sexual harassment, of which they have actual knowledge, that is so severe, pervasive, and objectively offensive that it can be said to deprive the victims of access to the educational opportunities or benefits provided by the school.

The most obvious example of student-on-student sexual harassment capable of triggering a damages claim would thus involve the overt, physical deprivation of access to school resources. Consider, for example, a case in which male students physically threaten their female peers every day, successfully preventing the female students from using a particular school resource—an athletic field or a computer lab, for instance. District administrators are well aware of the daily ritual, yet they deliberately ignore requests for aid from the female students wishing to use the resource. The district's knowing refusal to take any action in response to such behavior would fly in the face of Title IX's core principles, and such deliberate indifference may appropriately be subject to claims for monetary damages. It is not necessary, however, to show physical exclusion to demonstrate that students have been deprived by the actions of another student or students of an educational opportunity on the basis of sex. Rather, a plaintiff must establish sexual harassment of students that is so severe, pervasive, and objectively offensive, and that so undermines and detracts from the victims' educational experience, that the victim-students are effectively denied equal access to an institution's resources and opportunities.

Whether gender-oriented conduct rises to the level of actionable "harassment" thus "depends on a constellation of surrounding circumstances, expectations, and relationships," including, but not limited to, the ages of the harasser and the victim and the number of individuals involved. Courts, moreover, must bear in mind that schools are unlike the adult workplace and that children may regularly interact in a manner that would be unacceptable among adults. . . . Indeed, at least early on, students are still learning how to interact appropriately with their peers. It is thus understandable that, in the school setting, students often engage in insults, banter, teasing, shoving, pushing, and gender-specific conduct that is upsetting to the students subjected to it. Damages are not available for simple acts of teasing and name-calling among school children, however, even where these comments target differences in gender. Rather, in the context of student-on-student harassment, damages are available only where the behavior is so severe, pervasive, and objectively offensive that it denies its victims the equal access to education that Title IX is designed to protect.

The dissent fails to appreciate these very real limitations on a funding recipient's liability under Title IX. It is not enough to show, as the dissent would read this opinion to provide, that a student has been "teased," or "called . . . offensive names." Comparisons to an "overweight child who skips gym class because the other children tease her about her size," the student "who refuses to wear glasses to avoid the taunts of 'four-eyes,'" and "the child who refuses to go to school because the school bully calls him a 'scardy-cat' at recess," are inapposite and misleading. Nor do we contemplate, much less hold, that a mere "decline in grades is enough to survive" a motion to dismiss. The drop-off in LaShonda's grades provides necessary evidence of a potential link between her education and G.F.'s misconduct, but petitioner's ability to state a cognizable claim here depends equally on the alleged persistence and severity of G.F.'s actions, not to mention the Board's alleged knowledge and deliberate indifference. We trust that the dissent's characterization of our opinion will not mislead courts to impose more sweeping liability than we read Title IX to require.

Moreover, the provision that the discrimination occur "under any education program or activity" suggests that the behavior be serious enough to have the systemic effect of denying the victim equal access to an educational program or activity. Although, in theory, a single instance of sufficiently severe one-on-one peer harassment could be said to have such an effect, we think it unlikely that Congress would have thought such behavior sufficient to rise to this level in light of the inevitability of student misconduct and the amount of litigation that would be invited by entertaining claims of official indifference to a single instance of one-on-one peer harassment. By limiting private damages actions to cases having a systemic effect on educational programs or activities, we reconcile the general principle that Title IX prohibits official indifference to known peer sexual harassment with the practical realities of responding to student behavior, realities that Congress could not have meant to be ignored. Even the dissent suggests that Title IX liability may arise when a funding recipient remains indifferent to severe, gender-based mistreatment played out on a "widespread level" among students. . . .

C

Applying this standard to the facts at issue here, we conclude that the Eleventh Circuit erred in dismissing petitioner's complaint. Petitioner alleges that her daughter was the victim of repeated acts of sexual harassment by G.F. over a 5-month period, and there are allegations in support of the conclusion that G.F.'s misconduct was severe, pervasive, and objectively offensive. The harassment was not only verbal; it included numerous acts of objectively offensive touching, and, indeed, G.F. ultimately pleaded guilty to criminal sexual misconduct. Moreover, the complaint alleges that there were multiple victims who were sufficiently disturbed by G.F.'s misconduct to seek an audience with the school principal. Further, petitioner contends that the harassment had a concrete, negative effect on her daughter's ability to receive an education. The complaint also suggests that petitioner may be able to show both actual knowledge and deliberate indifference on the part of the Board, which made no effort whatsoever either to investigate or to put an end to the harassment. . . . Accordingly, the judgment of the United States Court of Appeals for the Eleventh Circuit is reversed, and the case is remanded for further proceedings consistent with this opinion.

It is so ordered.

JUSTICE KENNEDY, with whom THE CHIEF JUSTICE, JUSTICE SCALIA, and JUSTICE THOMAS join, dissenting.

The Court has held that Congress' power " 'to authorize expenditure of public moneys for public purposes is not limited by the direct grants of legislative power found in the Constitution.' " As a consequence, Congress can use its Spending Clause power to pursue objectives outside of "Article I's 'enumerated legislative fields' " by attaching conditions to the grant of federal funds. So understood, the Spending Clause power, if wielded without concern for the federal balance, has the potential to obliterate distinctions between national and local spheres of interest and power by permitting the federal government to set policy in the most sensitive areas of traditional state concern, areas which otherwise would lie outside its reach.

A vital safeguard for the federal balance is the requirement that, when Congress imposes a condition on the States' receipt of federal funds, it "must do so unambiguously." As the majority acknowledges, "legislation enacted . . . pursuant to the spending power is much in the nature of a contract," and the legitimacy of Congress' exercise of its power to condition funding on state compliance with congressional conditions "rests on whether the State voluntarily and knowingly accepts the terms of the 'contract.' ". . .

Our insistence that "Congress speak with a clear voice" to "enable the States to exercise their choice knowingly, cognizant of the consequences of their participation," is not based upon some abstract notion of contractual fairness. Rather, it is a concrete safeguard in the federal system. Only if States receive clear notice of the conditions attached to federal funds can they guard against excessive federal intrusion into state affairs and be vigilant in policing the boundaries of federal power. . . . While the majority purports to give effect to these principles, it eviscerates the clear-notice safeguard of our Spending Clause jurisprudence.

Title IX provides:

> "No person in the United States shall, on the basis of sex be [1] excluded from participation in, [2] be denied the benefits of, or [3] be subjected to discrimination under any education program or activity receiving Federal financial assistance."

To read the provision in full is to understand what is most striking about its application in this case: Title IX does not by its terms create any private cause of action whatsoever, much less define the circumstances in which money damages are available. The only private cause of action under Title IX is judicially implied.

The Court has encountered great difficulty in establishing standards for deciding when to imply a private cause of action under a federal statute which is silent on the subject. We try to conform the judicial judgment to the bounds of likely congressional purpose but, as we observed in *Gebser* v. *Lago Vista Independent School District* (1998), defining the scope of the private cause of action in general, and the damages remedy in particular, "inherently entails a degree of speculation, since it addresses an issue on which Congress has not specifically spoken."

When the statute at issue is a Spending Clause statute, this element of speculation is particularly troubling because it is in significant tension with the requirement that Spending Clause legislation give States clear notice of the consequences of their acceptance of federal funds. Without doubt, the scope of potential damages liability is one of the most significant factors a school would consider in deciding whether to receive federal funds. Accordingly, the Court must not imply a private cause of action for damages unless it can demonstrate that the congressional purpose to create the implied cause of action is so manifest that the State, when accepting federal funds, had clear notice of the terms and conditions of its monetary liability.

Today the Court fails to heed, or even to acknowledge, these limitations on its authority. The remedial scheme the majority creates today is neither sensible nor faithful to Spending Clause principles. In order to make its case for school liability for peer sexual harassment, the majority must establish that Congress gave grant recipients clear and unambiguous notice that they would be liable in money damages for failure to remedy discriminatory acts of their students. The majority must also demonstrate that the statute gives schools clear notice that one child's harassment of another constitutes "discrimination" on the basis of sex within the meaning of Title IX, and that—as applied to individual cases—the standard for liability will enable the grant recipient to distinguish inappropriate childish behavior from actionable gender discrimination. The majority does not carry these burdens.

Instead, the majority finds statutory clarity where there is none and discovers indicia of congressional notice to the States in the most unusual of places. It treats the issue as one of routine statutory construction alone, and it errs even in this regard. In the end, the majority not only imposes on States liability that was unexpected and unknown, but the contours of which are, as yet, unknowable. The majority's opinion purports to be narrow, but the limiting principles it proposes are illusory. The fence the Court has built is made of little sticks, and it cannot contain the avalanche of liability now set in motion. The potential costs to our schools of today's decision are difficult to estimate, but they are so great that it is most unlikely Congress intended to inflict them.

The only certainty flowing from the majority's decision is that scarce resources will be diverted from educating our children and that many school districts, desperate to avoid Title IX peer harassment suits, will adopt whatever federal code of student conduct and discipline the Department of Education sees fit to impose upon them. The Nation's schoolchildren will learn their first lessons about federalism in classrooms where the federal government is the ever-present regulator. The federal government will have insinuated itself not only into one of the most traditional areas of state concern but also into one of the most sensitive areas of human affairs. This federal control of the discipline of our Nation's schoolchildren is contrary to our traditions and inconsistent with the sensible administration of our schools. Because Title IX did not give States unambiguous notice that accepting federal funds meant ceding to the federal government power over the day-to-day disciplinary decisions of schools, I dissent.

[I omitted]

II

Our decision in *Gebser* makes clear that the Spending Clause clear-notice rule requires both that the recipients be on general notice of the kind of conduct the statute prohibits, and—at least when money damages are sought—that they be on notice that illegal conduct is occurring in a given situation. . . . Title IX, however, gives schools neither notice that the conduct the majority labels peer "sexual harassment" is gender discrimination within the meaning of the Act nor any guidance in distinguishing in individual cases between actionable discrimination and the immature behavior of children and adolescents. The majority thus imposes on schools potentially crushing financial liability for student conduct that is not prohibited in clear terms by Title IX and that cannot, even after today's opinion, be identified by either schools or courts with any precision.

The law recognizes that children—particularly young children—are not fully accountable for their actions because they lack the capacity to exercise mature judgment. . . . It should surprise no one, then, that the schools that are the primary locus of most children's social development are rife with inappropriate behavior by children who are just learning to interact with their peers. The *amici* on the front lines of our schools describe the situation best:

> "Unlike adults in the workplace, juveniles have limited life experiences or familial influences upon which to establish an understanding of appropriate behavior. The real world of school discipline is a rough-and-tumble place where students

practice newly learned vulgarities, erupt with anger, tease and embarrass each other, share offensive notes, flirt, push and shove in the halls, grab and offend." Brief for National School Boards Association et al. as *Amici Curiae* 10–11 (hereinafter school *amici*).

No one contests that much of this "dizzying array of immature or uncontrollable behaviors by students," is inappropriate, even "objectively offensive" at times, and that parents and schools have a moral and ethical responsibility to help students learn to interact with their peers in an appropriate manner. It is doubtless the case, moreover, that much of this inappropriate behavior is directed toward members of the opposite sex, as children in the throes of adolescence struggle to express their emerging sexual identities.

It is a far different question, however, whether it is either proper or useful to label this immature, childish behavior gender discrimination. Nothing in Title IX suggests that Congress even contemplated this question, much less answered it in the affirmative in unambiguous terms.

The majority, nevertheless, has no problem labeling the conduct of fifth graders "sexual harassment" and "gender discrimination." . . . To treat that proposition as establishing that the student conduct at issue here is gender discrimination is to erase, in one stroke, all differences between children and adults, peers and teachers, schools and workplaces.

In reality, there is no established body of federal or state law on which courts may draw in defining the student conduct that qualifies as Title IX gender discrimination. Analogies to Title VII hostile environment harassment are inapposite, because schools are not workplaces and children are not adults. The norms of the adult workplace that have defined hostile environment sexual harassment are not easily translated to peer relationships in schools, where teenage romantic relationships and dating are a part of everyday life. Analogies to Title IX teacher sexual harassment of students are similarly flawed. A teacher's sexual overtures toward a student are always inappropriate; a teenager's romantic overtures to a classmate (even when persistent and unwelcome) are an inescapable part of adolescence. . . .

The difficulties schools will encounter in identifying peer sexual harassment are already evident in teachers' manuals designed to give guidance on the subject. For example, one teachers' manual on peer sexual harassment suggests that sexual harassment in kindergarten through third grade includes a boy being "put down" on the playground "because he wants to play house with the girls" or a girl being "put down because she shoots baskets better than the boys." Yet another manual suggests that one student saying to another, "You look nice" could be sexual harassment, depending on the "tone of voice," how the student looks at the other, and "who else is around." Blowing a kiss is also suspect. This confusion will likely be compounded once the sexual-harassment label is invested with the force of federal law, backed up by private damages suits.

The only guidance the majority gives schools in distinguishing between the "simple acts of teasing and name-calling among school children," said not to be a basis for suit even when they "target differences in gender," and actionable peer sexual harassment is, in reality, no guidance at all. The majority proclaims that "in the context of student-on-student harassment, damages are available only in the situation where the behavior is so serious, pervasive, and objectively offensive that it denies its victims the equal access to education that Title IX is designed to protect." The majority does not even purport to explain, however, what constitutes an actionable denial of "equal access to education." Is equal access denied when a girl who tires of being chased by the boys at recess refuses to go outside? When she cannot concentrate during class because she is worried about the recess activities? When she pretends to be sick one day so she can stay home from school? It appears the majority is content to let juries decide.

The majority's reference to a "systemic effect" does nothing to clarify the content of its standard. The majority appears to intend that requirement to do no more than exclude the possibility that a single act of harassment perpetrated by one student on one other student can form the basis for an actionable claim. That is a small concession indeed.

The only real clue the majority gives schools about the dividing line between actionable harassment that denies a victim equal access to education and mere inappropriate teasing is a profoundly unsettling one: On the facts of this case, petitioner has stated a claim because she alleged, in the majority's words, "that the harassment had a concrete, negative effect on her daughter's ability to receive an education." In petitioner's words, the effects that might have been visible to the school were that her daughter's grades "dropped" and her "ability to concentrate on her school work [was] affected." Almost all adolescents experience these problems at one time or another as they mature.

III

The majority's inability to provide any workable definition of actionable peer harassment simply underscores the myriad ways in which an opinion that purports to be narrow is, in fact, so broad that it will support untold numbers of lawyers who will prove adept at presenting cases that will withstand the defendant school districts' pretrial motions. Each of the barriers to run-away litigation the majority offers us crumbles under the weight of even casual scrutiny.

For example, the majority establishes what sounds like a relatively high threshold for lliability—"denial of equal access" to education—and, almost in the same breath, makes clear that alleging a decline in grades is enough to [meet that threshold] and, it follows, to state a winning claim. The majority seems oblivious to the fact that almost every child, at some point, has trouble in school because he or she is being teased by his or her peers. The girl who wants to skip recess because she is teased by the boys is no different from the overweight child who skips gym class because the other children tease her about her size in the locker room; or the child who risks flunking out because he refuses to wear glasses to avoid the taunts of "four-eyes"; or the child who refuses to go to school because the school bully calls him a "scaredy-cat" at recess. Most children respond to teasing in ways that detract from their ability to learn. The majority's test for actionable harassment will, as a result, sweep in almost all of the more innocuous conduct it acknowledges as a ubiquitous part of school life. . . .

The majority's limitations on peer sexual harassment suits cannot hope to contain the flood of liability the Court today begins. The elements of the Title IX claim created by the majority will be easy not only to allege but also to prove. A female plaintiff who pleads only that a boy called her offensive names, that she told a teacher, that the teacher's response was unreasonable, and that her school performance suffered as a result, appears to state a successful claim.

There will be no shortage of plaintiffs to bring such complaints. Our schools are charged each day with educating millions of children. Of those millions of students, a large percentage will, at some point during their school careers, experience something they consider sexual harassment. A 1993 Study by the American Association of University Women Educational Foundation, for instance, found that "fully 4 out of 5 students (81%) report that they have been the target of some form of sexual harassment during their school lives." The number of potential lawsuits against our schools is staggering.

The cost of defending against peer sexual harassment suits alone could overwhelm many school districts, particularly since the majority's liability standards will allow almost any plaintiff to get to summary judgment, if not to a jury. In addition, there are no damages caps on the judicially implied private cause of action under Title IX. As a result, school liability in one peer sexual harassment suit could approach, or even exceed, the total federal funding of many school districts. Petitioner, for example, seeks damages of $500,000 in this case. Respondent school district received approximately $679,000 in federal aid in 1992–1993. . . .

The prospect of unlimited Title IX liability will, in all likelihood, breed a climate of fear that encourages school administrators to label even the most innocuous of childish conduct sexual harassment. It would appear to be no coincidence that, not long after the DOE issued its proposed policy guidance warning that schools could be liable for peer sexual harassment in the fall of 1996, a North Carolina school suspended a 6-year-old boy who kissed a female classmate on the cheek for sexual harassment. A week later, a New York school suspended a second-grader who kissed a classmate and ripped a button off her skirt. The second grader said that he got the idea from his favorite book "Corduroy," about a bear with a missing button. School administrators said only, "We were given guidelines as to why we suspend children. We follow the guidelines." . . .

A school faced with a peer sexual harassment complaint in the wake of the majority's decision may well be beset with litigation from every side. One student's demand for a quick response to her harassment complaint will conflict with the alleged harasser's demand for due process. Another student's demand for a harassment-free classroom will conflict with the alleged harasser's claim to a mainstream placement under the Individuals with Disabilities Education Act or with his state constitutional right to a continuing, free public education. On college campuses, and even in secondary schools, a student's claim that the school should remedy a sexually hostile environment will conflict with the alleged harasser's claim that his speech, even if offensive, is protected by the First Amendment. In each of these situations, the school faces the risk of suit, and maybe even multiple suits, regardless of its response. . . .

Disregarding these state-law remedies for student misbehavior and the incentives that our schools already have to provide the best possible education to all of their students, the majority seeks, in effect, to put an end to student misbehavior by transforming Title IX into a Federal Student Civility Code. . . . I fail to see how federal courts will administer school discipline better than the principals and teachers to whom the public has entrusted that task or how the majority's holding will help the vast majority of students, whose educational opportunities will be diminished by the diversion of school funds to litigation. The private cause of action the Court creates will justify a corps of federal administrators in writing regulations on student harassment. It will also embroil schools and courts in endless litigation over what qualifies as peer sexual harassment and what constitutes a reasonable response.

In the final analysis, this case is about federalism. Yet the majority's decision today says not one word about the federal balance. Preserving our federal system is a legitimate end in itself. It is, too, the means to other ends. It ensures that essential choices can be made by a government more proximate to the people than the vast apparatus of federal power. Defining the appropriate role of schools in teaching and supervising children who are beginning to explore their own sexuality and learning how to express it to others is one of the most complex and sensitive issues our schools face. Such decisions are best made by parents and by the teachers and school administrators who can counsel with them. The delicacy and immense significance of teaching children about sexuality should cause the Court to act with great restraint before it displaces state and local governments.

Heedless of these considerations, the Court rushes onward, finding that the cause of action it creates is necessary to effect the congressional design. It is not. Nothing in Title IX suggests that Congress intended or contemplated the result the Court reaches today, much less dictated it in unambiguous terms. Today's decision cannot be laid at the feet of Congress; it is the responsibility of the Court.

The Court must always use great care when it shapes private causes of action without clear guidance from Congress, but never more so than when the federal balance is at stake. . . . Whether the Court ever should have embarked on this endeavor under a Spending Clause statute is open to question. What should be clear beyond any doubt, however, is that the Court is duty-bound to exercise that discretion with due regard for federalism and the unique role of the States in our system. The Court today disregards that obligation. I can conceive of few interventions more intrusive upon the delicate and vital relations between teacher and student, between student and student, and between the State and its citizens than the one the Court creates today by its own hand. Trusted principles of federalism are superseded by a more contemporary imperative.

Perhaps the most grave, and surely the most lasting, disservice of today's decision is that it ensures the Court's own disregard for the federal balance soon will be imparted to our youngest citizens. The Court clears the way for the federal government to claim center stage in America's classrooms. Today's decision mandates to teachers instructing and supervising their students the dubious assistance of federal court plaintiffs and their lawyers and makes the federal courts the final arbiters of school policy and of almost every disagreement between students. Enforcement of the federal right recognized by the majority means that federal influence will permeate everything from curriculum decisions to day-to-day classroom logistics and interactions. After today, Johnny will find that the routine problems of adolescence are to be resolved by invoking a federal right to demand assignment to a desk two rows away.

As its holding makes painfully clear, the majority's watered-down version of the Spending Clause clear-statement rule is no substitute for the real protections of state and local autonomy that our constitutional system requires. If there be any doubt of the futility of the Court's attempt to hedge its holding about with words of limitation for future cases, the result in this case provides the answer. The complaint of this fifth grader survives and the school will be compelled to answer in federal court. We can be assured that like suits will follow—suits, which in cost and number, will impose serious financial burdens on local school districts, the taxpayers who support them, and the children they serve. Federalism and our struggling school systems deserve better from this Court. I dissent.

HOUSE COMMITTEE ON THEFT OF U.S. NUCLEAR SECRETS BY CHINA
May 25, 1999

A special committee of the House of Representatives created a political sensation during 1999 with the release of a report charging that China had "stolen" many nuclear weapons secrets from the United States and would soon pose a direct threat to U.S. interests. The committee report set off a round of finger pointing about who was responsible for lax security at U.S. nuclear weapons laboratories. The Clinton administration noted that the actions cited by the committee had occurred during both Republican and Democratic administrations, and the administration claimed it was the first to take concrete steps to counter the Chinese espionage. President Bill Clinton said he had ordered tighter security at the weapons laboratories.

A Chinese-American scientist at Los Alamos National Laboratory in New Mexico was one of the first targets of investigations into the matter. Wen Ho Lee was arrested in December and charged with illegally copying an enormous quantity of computerized information about U.S. weapons systems. Lee was not charged with espionage because investigators were unable to develop evidence that he had passed the secret information onto China or any other country. Lee vigorously denied wrongdoing and said he was singled out for arrest because of racism.

In addition to creating a furor about Chinese espionage, the House committee report focused new attention on the status of U.S. research capabilities. National security specialists had been warning for years that research into advanced weapons systems was lagging in the United States. The House committee and two groups of experts empanelled by the Clinton administration agreed with this assessment and called for more spending on weapons research. The administration experts also agreed with the House committee assessment that the United States needed to bolster its commercial satellite-launching capabilities. Some of the incidents cited by the House committee stemmed from U.S. dependence on China for lower-cost launching of commercial satellites.

The Chinese government repeatedly denied that it had stolen U.S. nuclear weapons technology. Responding to the House committee report, Chinese foreign ministry spokesman Zhu Bangzao said: "Some people in the United States stubbornly cling to a cold war mentality, are full of bias and hostility toward China and have tried in all possible ways to create rumors about China. Their goal is to spread the theory of a 'China threat' and divert attention away from the embassy bombing." This was a reference to a dispute over the U.S. bombing of China's embassy in Belgrade, during the NATO air campaign against the former Yugoslavia. (Embassy bombing, p. 304)

Cox Committee Report

Chaired by Christopher Cox, R-Calif., the committee had five Republican and four Democratic members. Its formal title was the Select Committee on U.S. National Security and Military/Commercial Concerns with the People's Republic of China. The committee was originally formed to investigate charges that two U.S. satellite manufacturers had illegally given China information about ballistic missiles. During the course of its probe in 1998 the committee expanded its inquiry into a broad range of questions about how China obtained secret information about U.S. strategic weapons programs.

The committee announced December 1998 that it had concluded its work. President Clinton received a copy of the report January 4, 1999, and the White House released the committee's thirty-eight recommendations in February. After an intensive review process by intelligence agencies, the committee was allowed to release an unclassified version of its full report on May 25. (Committee background, Historic Documents of 1998, p. 976)

The committee adopted its report by a unanimous vote, although one Democrat—John M. Spratt Jr. of South Carolina—challenged the validity of some key conclusions. Norm Dicks, of Washington, the panel's ranking Democrat, also sought to soften the impact of the committee findings by saying they were based on "worst-case" assumptions and should not be read as definitive.

The report said the Chinese government began systematic espionage against U.S. nuclear installations in the late 1970s—about the time diplomatic relations between the two countries were normalized—and that espionage was continuing as of 1999. At the time of the report, the committee said, China's acquisition of nuclear knowledge had not yet altered the military balance between the two countries because the United States had thousands of nuclear weapons and China had only a few dozen. But China's nuclear program already threatened U.S. allies in the Asia-Pacific region and ultimately could pose a threat to U.S. military forces and the mainland, the committee said.

The headline-catching portion of the Cox panel report was its assertion that China had stolen "design information" on seven advanced nuclear weapons. Among the weapons were the W-88 warhead, used on missiles carried by the Trident D-5 submarine; that warhead contained several miniaturized nuclear bombs and was the most advanced weapon in the U.S. arsenal. The Cox panel also said China had stolen design information about the "neutron bomb," a nuclear warhead designed to destroy tanks and infantry while leaving buildings undamaged. Although the United States had developed the technology for the neutron bomb, it had not deployed the weapon in its arsenal.

"These thefts of nuclear secrets from our national weapons laboratories enabled the PRC [the People's Republic of China] to design, develop, and successfully test modern strategic nuclear weapons sooner than would otherwise have been possible," the Cox committee said in a summary of its findings. "The stolen U.S. nuclear secrets give the PRC the design information on thermonuclear weapons on a par with our own."

The latter statement was the most hotly contested item in the entire report. "Now, that's alarming, but is it accurate?" Spratt asked rhetorically in questioning the statement. "I do know that we have had 1,100 nuclear tests, as opposed to 50 on their part," Spratt said. "We've built over 30,000 nuclear warheads, as opposed to a few hundred, at most, on their part. So that would suggest to you that we have a somewhat greater capability for nuclear design than they do." Cox and other committee Republicans defended the assertion, saying that China had acquired enough information to be able to replicate the most advanced U.S. weapons.

The Cox panel devoted an extensive section of its report to the original point of its inquiry: allegations that two U.S. satellite manufacturers—Hughes Space and Communications Co. and Loral Space and Communications Systems Ltd.—had improperly divulged to China secret information about U.S. ballistic missile guidance technology. Representatives of the companies had worked with Chinese technicians following the failure of three Chinese rocket launches between 1993 and 1998. The committee alleged that information provided by the companies could be useful in China's military ballistic missile program. Both companies denied wrongdoing. The Justice Department in 1998 opened an investigation into the matter, but no findings were made public by the end of 1999.

Some Republican leaders, especially in the House, sought to use the China-nuclear issue for political attacks against the Clinton administration. House Majority Whip Tom DeLay, of Texas, strongly implied that Clinton's acceptance of 1996 campaign contributions from sources linked to the Chinese government may have affected his judgment on national security. "We are forced to question whether the president and vice president deliberately ignored the reality of Chinese spying and theft because they had ulterior economic and political motives," DeLay said when the Cox report was released.

House Majority Whip Richard Armey, of Texas, sought to focus attention on the actions of Samuel R. ("Sandy") Berger, Clinton's national security adviser. Armey noted that Berger originally told the Cox committee that he had briefed Clinton about the Chinese nuclear-espionage matter in 1998, and the committee cited that date in its report. But after the report was completed, Berger told the panel he had in fact briefed the president in July 1997. Insisting that the Clinton administration in general, and Berger in particular, had not taken the issue seriously enough, Armey called for Berger to resign. Berger refused the suggestion.

Administration Response and Actions

Attempting to defuse a politically sensitive issue, the Clinton administration took the position of agreeing with most of the policy recommendations of the Cox committee, even while disputing the accuracy of some of the factual findings and analyses. Administration officials also pointedly noted that many of the lapses cited by the committee had occurred during Republican administrations.

The White House issued a detailed response to the committee report on May 25, generally praising the panel for focusing on an important issue but also stressing the administration's long-standing commitment to fixing the problems highlighted by the panel. Among other things, the White House noted that the president in February 1998 issued an executive order ("Presidential Decision Directive 61") setting rules of tightened security at the national laboratories. That order, the White House said, was "the most comprehensive and vigorous attempt ever taken to strengthen security and counterintelligence" at the national laboratories. The administration also said it was working to correct deficiencies noted by the Cox committee in controlling exports to China and other nations of items such as high-performance computers and satellite-launching technology.

After receiving a classified version of the Cox panel report on January 4, 1999, Clinton ordered the director of central intelligence, George Tenet, to conduct an assessment of the issues raised by the report. That assessment was conducted by a committee of high-level intelligence officials, chaired by Robert Walpole, the Central Intelligence Agency's national intelligence officer for strategic and nuclear programs. Walpole's panel completed its work in March. Its work was reviewed, in turn, by another committee of former senior government officials, headed by retired admiral David Jeremiah. Jeremiah's panel concurred with the findings of the Walpole committee.

Tenet on April 21 released a declassified version of the Walpole committee's "key findings," along with an "introductory note" from the Jeremiah review panel. In those documents, both panels agreed with the underlying findings of the Cox committee that China for more than two decades had been working aggressively to obtain information about U.S. nuclear weapons programs. However, both the Walpole and Jeremiah panels took a more low-key approach than did the Cox committee to describing the consequences of Chinese espionage. The Walpole committee, while noting that China had obtained information on a "variety of U.S. weapon design concepts and weaponization features" (including the neutron bomb and the W-88 warhead), said it could not determine "the full extent of weapon infor-

mation obtained" by China. "For example, we don't know whether any weapon design document or blueprints were acquired," the committee said. In addition, the Walpole committee said it was more likely that the Chinese used information obtained from the United States "to inform their own program than to replicate U.S. weapons designs"—as the Cox committee had appeared to assume.

Overall, the Walpole committee said, the Chinese intelligence effort "has not resulted in any apparent modernization of their deployed strategic force or any new nuclear weapons deployment." The Jeremiah committee also noted that China was just one of several countries that had succeeded in obtaining secret information about U.S. weapons programs. The United States had remained "technologically ahead" of those countries, the committee said, but recent cutbacks in research efforts "have diminished the protective edge we could have over those using our information, making such losses more significant in today's world."

Yet another study was conducted at Clinton's request by the President's Foreign Intelligence Advisory Board, chaired by former senator Warren B. Rudman, Republican of New Hampshire. That panel focused on security procedures at the weapons laboratories of the Department of Energy (DOE). Its report, issued in June, said the department's "organizational disarray, managerial neglect and a culture of arrogance" left it incapable of reforming itself. Rudman's committee also agreed with the bulk of the findings by the two other administration panels of experts.

Criticisms of Cox Report

Numerous intelligence experts in government and academic circles criticized the sharp-edged tone of the Cox committee report and many of its conclusions. In general, the critics said the committee was correct in noting deficiencies in U.S. defenses against espionage by China and other countries. But, the critics said, the committee overstepped the available evidence in claiming that China posed an imminent threat primarily because of secret information it may have stolen from the United States.

One of the broadest attacks on the Cox committee report came in a study released December 15 by the Center for International Security and Cooperation at Stanford University in California. That study was written by five foreign policy and weapons experts, two of whom had close ties with the Lawrence Livermore National Laboratory. The Stanford scholars strongly questioned the underlying assumption of the Cox committee—that China had been able to develop advanced nuclear weapons in large part through "theft" of secret information from the United States. The Cox panel provided "no evidence" for many of its central conclusions, the Stanford experts said.

As an example, the Stanford authors challenged the Cox committee's attack on an exchange program that enabled nuclear experts from the United States, China, and Russia to visit installations in each others' countries. That program had been "carefully controlled" by U.S. security officials, the Stanford authors said, and the Cox committee failed to document charges against it.

The Stanford authors also played down the prospect that specific Chinese weapons programs directly resulted from information stolen from the United States, noting that China had its own experts who were capable, over time, of developing the same weapons system as U.S. scientists. In addition, the authors noted that the Cox committee made no distinction between information that China might have obtained legally from public sources and that might have been acquired through theft or espionage. The Cox panel treated all information acquired by the Chinese as "stolen," the authors said.

Security at Nuclear Weapons Laboratories

The Cox committee report and other disclosures during 1999 opened to public view long-standing concerns within the government and among security experts about protecting classified information at three national weapons laboratories owned by the DOE. Several officials were quoted during the year as saying that experts had questioned information-security procedures at some of the laboratories for decades, but successive administrations had done little to address those concerns.

Secretary of Energy Bill Richardson, who took office in 1998 just before the national outcry began over nuclear weapons security, said he was determined to "clean up a mess" that he had inherited. "We have undertaken a total overhaul of the Department of Energy counterintelligence program."

One of Richardson's most dramatic moves came April 6, when he ordered all scientific work on classified computer systems at the national laboratories halted while security improvements were made. The "stand-down" lasted two weeks. During that period, scientists at the laboratories were required to attend training sessions on computer security.

Richardson in June named retired air force general Eugene E. Habiger, a former chief of the Strategic Air Command, to head a new Office of Security and Emergency Operations, which would be in charge of the security improvements. Habiger began an intensive review of DOE procedures, but told reporters in December that his work was hampered by congressional budget cuts. He said he had requested $65 million for fiscal 2000 but Congress had approved only $10 million.

In a review released September 20, the DOE said it had found that security procedures had improved at the Los Alamos laboratory but remained below standard at Lawrence-Livermore Laboratory in California and Sandia Laboratory in New Mexico.

Congress in September cleared legislation, as part of the fiscal year 2000 defense authorization bill (PL 106–65) to restructure nuclear weapons programs by putting them under the National Nuclear Security Administration, a new agency that was to be semiautonomous within the DOE. Richardson at first opposed creation of the new agency but relented when Congress approved it by overwhelming votes in both chambers. Neverthe-

less, Richardson persuaded Clinton to name him as head of the agency—in addition to his duties as energy secretary—until he was able to negotiate changes in the new law during 2000.

Charges Against Wen Ho Lee

Federal investigations into possible Chinese espionage at U.S. weapons laboratories turned up one immediate suspect: Wen Ho Lee, a physicist at the Los Alamos National Laboratory in New Mexico. Lee was born on Taiwan and came to the United States in 1964, eventually becoming an American citizen and taking a research job at Los Alamos in 1978. After an investigation found that Lee had copied vast quantities of computerized information about weapons design and other matters, Lee was fired by the DOE on March 8. A federal grand jury on December 10 indicted Lee on fifty-nine counts of illegally removing computer data at the laboratory and violating the Atomic Energy Act and the Foreign Espionage Act. Lee pleaded not guilty. The indictment alleged that Lee had copied thousands of pages of sensitive information onto ten computer tapes in 1993, 1994, and 1997. The documents allegedly copied by Lee contained design information and other details on nearly every major nuclear weapon system in the U.S. arsenal, the indictment said. The FBI said it had been able to recover only seven of the ten computer tapes and that the other three were missing. Lee was not charged with espionage or turning secrets over to a foreign government, however.

In December Lee's children filed a lawsuit in federal district court in Washington, D.C., accusing the FBI and the energy and justice departments of selectively leaking information to the news media, including information about the family's history and personal finances. Other critics complained about the government's investigation of Lee, but for a different reason: they noted that Lee had come under suspicion of security violations in 1982 and again in 1995, but no definitive steps had been taken to curtail his access to classified information. Critics also said the FBI and other agencies had bungled the investigation into Lee's use of computerized information.

The case against Lee sparked controversy over whether he was a victim of racial bias. Robert S. Vrooman, who headed counterintelligence operations at Los Alamos until March 1998 and had investigated Lee's activities for nearly three years, said in August 1999 that Lee's ethnic background was "a major factor" in his being targeted. Vrooman said he had uncovered "not one shred of evidence" that Lee had spied for China. Other DOE officials denied Vrooman's charge.

Following are excerpts from the "Overview" of the declassified version of a report released May 25, 1999, by the House of Representatives Select Committee on U.S. National Security and Military/Commercial Concerns with the People's Republic of China; two statements released April 21, 1999, by George Tenet, the director of central intelligence, follow: "Key Findings" from "The Intelligence Community Damage Assessment on the Implications of China's Acquisition of U.S. Nuclear Weapons Information on the Development of Future Chinese Weapons" and the "Introductory Note" from a review panel, chaired by retired admiral David Jeremiah, which examined the intelligence community damage assessment:

OVERVIEW

1.

A. The People's Republic of China (PRC) has stolen design information on the United States' most advanced thermonuclear weapons.

The People's Republic of China (PRC) has stolen classified design information on the United States' most advanced thermonuclear weapons. These thefts of nuclear secrets from our national weapons laboratories enabled the PRC to design, develop, and successfully test modern strategic nuclear weapons sooner than would otherwise have been possible. The stolen U.S. nuclear secrets give the PRC design information on thermonuclear weapons on a par with our own.

The PRC thefts from our National Laboratories began at least as early as the late 1970s. Significant secrets are known to have been stolen, from the laboratories or elsewhere, as recently as the mid-1990s. Such thefts almost certainly continue to the present. . . .

In addition, in the mid-1990s the PRC stole from a U.S. national weapons laboratory classified thermonuclear weapons information that cannot be identified in this unclassified Report. Because this recent espionage case is currently under investigation and involves sensitive intelligence sources and methods, the Clinton administration has determined that further information cannot be made public without affecting national security or ongoing criminal investigations.

The W-88, a miniaturized, tapered warhead, is the most sophisticated nuclear weapon the United States has ever built. In the U.S. arsenal, it is mated to the D-5 submarine-launched ballistic missile carried aboard the Trident nuclear submarine. The United States learned about the theft of the W-88 Trident D-5 warhead information, as well as about the theft of information regarding several other nuclear weapons, in 1995.

The PRC has stolen U.S. design information and other classified information for neutron bomb warheads. The PRC stole classified U.S. information about the neutron bomb from a U.S. national weapons laboratory. The U.S. learned of the theft of this classified information on the neutron bomb in 1996.

In the late 1970s, the PRC stole design information on the U.S. W-70 warhead from the Lawrence Livermore Laboratory. The U.S. government first learned of this theft several months after it took place. The W-70 warhead contains elements that may be used either as a strategic thermonuclear weapon, or as an enhanced radiation weapon ("neutron bomb"). The PRC tested the neutron bomb in 1988.

The Select Committee is aware of other PRC thefts of U.S. thermonuclear weapons-related secrets. The Clinton administration has determined that further information about PRC thefts of U.S. thermonuclear weapons-related secrets cannot be publicly disclosed without affecting national security.

The PRC acquired this and other classified U.S. nuclear weapons information as the result of a 20-year intelligence collection program to develop modern thermonuclear weapons, continuing to this very day, that includes espionage, review of unclassified publications, and extensive interactions with scientists from the Department of Energy's national weapons laboratories.

The Select Committee has found that the primary focus of this long-term, ongoing PRC intelligence collection effort has been on the following national weapons laboratories: Los Alamos, Lawrence Livermore, Oak Ridge, Sandia.

The Select Committee judges that the PRC will exploit elements of the stolen design information on the PRC's next generation of thermonuclear weapons. The PRC plans to supplement its silo-based CSS-4 ICBMs [intercontinental ballistic missiles] targeted on U.S. cities with mobile ICBMs, which are more survivable because they are more difficult to find than silo-based missiles.

The PRC has three mobile ICBM programs currently underway—two road-mobile and one submarine-launched program—all of which will be able to strike the United States.

The first of these new People's Liberation Army (PLA) mobile ICBMs, the DF-31, may be tested in 1999, and could be deployed as soon as 2002. These mobile missiles require small warhead designs, of which the stolen U.S. design information is the most advanced in the world.

In addition, the PRC could choose to use elements of the stolen nuclear weapons design information—including the neutron bomb—on intermediate- and short-range ballistic missiles, such as its CSS-6 missiles. . . .

The PRC has the infrastructure and technical ability to use elements of the stolen U.S. warhead design information in the PLA's next generation of thermonuclear weapons. The Select Committee concludes that the production tools and processes required by the PRC to produce small thermonuclear warheads based on the stolen U.S. design information, including the stolen W-88 information, would be similar to those developed or available in a modern aerospace or precision-guided munitions industry. The Select Committee judges that the PRC has such infrastructure and is capable of such production.

The Select Committee judges that the PRC is likely to continue its work on advanced thermonuclear weapons based on the stolen U.S. design information. The PRC could begin serial production of such weapons during the next decade in connection with the development of its next generation of intercontinental ballistic missiles.

A series of PRC nuclear weapons test explosions from 1992 to 1996 began a debate in the U.S. Government about whether the PRC's designs for its new generation of nuclear warheads were in fact based on stolen U.S. classified information. The apparent purpose of these PRC tests was to develop smaller, lighter thermonuclear warheads, with an increased yield-to-weight ratio.

The United States did not become fully aware of the magnitude of the counterintelligence problem at the Department of Energy national weapons laboratories until 1995. . . .

The stolen U.S. nuclear secrets give the PRC design information on thermonuclear weapons on a par with our own. Currently deployed PRC ICBMs targeted on U.S. cities are based on 1950s-era nuclear weapons designs. With the stolen U.S. technology, the PRC has leaped, in a handful of years, from 1950s-era strategic nuclear capabilities to the more modern thermonuclear weapons designs. These modern thermonuclear weapons took the United States decades of effort, hundreds of millions of dollars, and numerous nuclear tests to achieve.

Such small, modern warheads are necessary for all of the elements of a modern intercontinental nuclear force, including:

- road-mobile ICBMs
- submarine-launched ICBMs
- ICBMs with multiple warheads (MRVs or MIRVs)

The PRC has an ongoing program to use these modern thermonuclear warheads on its next generation of ICBMs, currently in development. Without the nuclear secrets stolen from the United States, it would have been virtually impossible for the PRC to fabricate and test successfully small nuclear warheads prior to its 1996 pledge to adhere to the Comprehensive Test Ban Treaty.

B. The Select Committee judges that elements of the stolen information on U.S. thermonuclear warhead designs will assist the PRC in building its next generation of mobile ICBMs, which may be tested this year.

The stolen U.S. design information will assist the PRC in building smaller nuclear warheads—vital to the success of the PRC's ongoing efforts to develop survivable, mobile missiles. Current PRC ICBMs, which are silo-based, are more vulnerable to attack than mobile missiles.

The PRC has currently underway three intercontinental mobile missile programs—two road-mobile, and one submarine-launched. All of these missiles are capable of targeting the United States.

The first of these, the road-mobile solid-propellant DF-31, may be tested in 1999. Given a successful flight-test program, the DF-31 could be ready for deployment in 2002.

The Select Committee judges that the PRC will in fact use a small nuclear warhead on its new generation ICBMs. The small, mobile missiles that the PRC is developing require smaller warheads than the large, heavy, 1950s-era warheads developed for the PRC's silo-based missiles. The main purpose of a series of nuclear tests conducted by the PRC between 1992 and 1996 was evidently to develop new smaller, lighter warheads with an increased yield-to-weight ratio for use with the PRC's new, mobile nuclear forces.

The Select Committee judges that the PRC will exploit elements of the stolen U.S. thermonuclear weapons designs on its new ICBMs currently under development. The advanced U.S. thermonuclear warheads for which the PRC has stolen U.S. design information are significantly smaller than those for which the PRC's silo-based missiles were designed. The U.S. designs, unlike those in the PRC's currently-deployed arsenal, can be used on smaller mobile missiles. . . .

These small warhead designs will make it possible for the PRC to develop and deploy missiles with multiple reentry vehicles (MRVs or independently targetable MIRVs).

Multiple reentry vehicles increase the effectiveness of a ballistic missile force by multiplying the number of warheads a single missile can carry as many as ten-fold. Multiple reentry vehicles also can help to counter missile defenses. For example, multiple reentry vehicles make it easier for the PRC to deploy penetration aids with its ICBM warheads in order to defeat anti-missile defenses.

The Select Committee is aware of reports that the PRC has in the past undertaken efforts related to technology with MIRV applications. Experts agree that the PRC now has the capability to develop and deploy silo-based intercontinental ballistic missiles with multiple reentry vehicles (MIRVs or MRVs).

Experts also agree that the PRC could have this capability for its new mobile intercontinental ballistic missiles within a reasonable period of years that is consistent with its plans to deploy these new mobile missiles. The PRC could pursue one or more penetration aids in connection with its new nuclear missiles.

If the PRC violates the Comprehensive Test Ban Treaty by testing surreptitiously, it could further accelerate its nuclear development.

The Select Committee judges that, if the PRC were successful in stealing nuclear test codes, computer models, and data from the United States, it could further accelerate its nuclear development. By using such stolen codes and data in conjunction with High Performance Computers (HPCs) already acquired by the PRC, the PRC could diminish its need for further nuclear testing to evaluate weapons and propose design changes.

The possession of the stolen U.S. test data could greatly reduce the level of HPC performance required for such tasks. For these reasons, the Select Committee judges that the PRC has and will continue to aggressively target for theft our nuclear test codes, computer models, and data.

Although the United States has been the victim of systematic espionage successfully targeted against our most advanced nuclear weapons designs—and although the Select Committee judges that the PRC will exploit elements of those designs for its new generation of ICBMs—the United States retains an overwhelming qualitative and quantitative advantage in deployed strategic nuclear forces. Nonetheless, in a crisis in which the United States confronts the PRC's conventional and nuclear forces at the regional level, a modernized PRC strategic nuclear ballistic missile force would pose a credible direct threat against the United States.

Neither the United States nor the PRC has a national ballistic missile defense system.

In the near term, a PRC deployment of mobile thermonuclear weapons, or neutron bombs, based on stolen U.S. design information, could have a significant effect on the regional balance of power, particularly with respect to Taiwan. PRC deployments of advanced nuclear weapons based on stolen U.S. design information would pose greater risks to U.S. troops and interests in Asia and the Pacific.

In addition, the PRC's theft of information on our most modern nuclear weapons designs enables the PRC to deploy modern forces much sooner than would otherwise be possible.

At the beginning of the 1990s, the PRC had only one or two silo-based ICBMs capable of attacking the United States. Since then, the PRC has deployed up to two dozen additional silo-based ICBMs capable of attacking the United States; has upgraded its silo-based missiles; and has continued development of three mobile ICBM systems and associated modern thermonuclear warheads.

If the PRC is successful in developing modern nuclear forces, as seems likely, and chooses to deploy them in sufficient numbers, then the long-term balance of nuclear forces with the United States could be adversely affected.

C. Despite repeated PRC thefts of the most sophisticated U.S. nuclear weapons technology, security at our national nuclear weapons laboratories does not meet even minimal standards.

The PRC stole design information on the United States' most advanced thermonuclear weapons as a result of a sustained espionage effort targeted at the United States' nuclear weapons facilities, including our national weapons laboratories. The successful penetration by the PRC of our nuclear weapons laboratories has taken place over the last several decades, and almost certainly continues to the present.

More specifically, the Select Committee has concluded that the successful penetration of our National Laboratories by the PRC began as early as the late 1970s; the PRC had penetrated the Laboratories throughout the 1980s and 1990s; and our Laboratories almost certainly remain penetrated by the PRC today.

Our national weapons laboratories are responsible for, among other things, the design of thermonuclear warheads for our ballistic missiles. The information at our national weapons laboratories about our thermonuclear warheads is supposed to be among our nation's most closely guarded secrets.

Counterintelligence programs at the national weapons laboratories today fail to meet even minimal standards. Repeated efforts since the early 1980s have failed to solve the counterintelligence deficiencies at the National Laboratories. While one of the Laboratories has adopted better counterintelligence practices than the others, all remain inadequate.

Even though the United States discovered in 1995 that the PRC had stolen design information on the W-88 Trident D-5 warhead and technical information on a number of other U.S. thermonuclear warheads, the White House has informed the Select Committee, in response to specific interrogatories propounded by the Committee, that the President was not briefed about the counterintelligence failures until early 1998.

Moreover, given the great significance of the PRC thefts, the Select Committee is concerned that the appropriate committees of the Congress were not adequately briefed on the extent of the PRC's espionage efforts.

A counterintelligence and security plan adopted by the Department of Energy in late 1998 in response to Presidential Decision Directive 61 is a step toward establishing sound counterintelligence practices. However, according to the head of these efforts, significant time will be required to implement improved security procedures pursuant to the directive. Security at the national weapons laboratories will not be satisfactory until at least sometime in the year 2000. . . .

2.

A. The PRC has stolen U.S. missile technology and exploited it for the PRC's own ballistic missile applications.

The PRC has proliferated such military technology to a number of other countries, including regimes hostile to the United States.

The Select Committee has found that the PRC has stolen a specific U.S. guidance technology used on current and past generations of U.S. weapons systems. The stolen guidance technology is currently used on a variety of U.S. missiles and military aircraft, including:

- The U.S. Army Tactical Missile System (ATACMS)
- The U.S. Navy Stand-off Land Attack Missile-Extended Range (SLAM-ER)
- The U.S. Navy F-14
- The U.S. Air Force F-15, F-16, and F-117 fighter jets

The stolen guidance technology has direct applicability to the PRC's intercontinental, medium- and short-range ballistic missiles, and its spacelift rockets.

The theft of U.S. ballistic missile-related technology is of great value to the PRC. In addition to ICBMs and military spacelift rockets, such technology is directly applicable to the medium- and short-range PLA missiles, such as the

CSS-6 (also known as the M-9), the CSS-X-7 (also known as the M-11), and the CSS-8 that have been developed for, among other purposes, striking Taiwan.

CSS-6 missiles were, for example, fired in the Taiwan Strait and over Taiwan's main ports in the 1996 crisis and confrontation with the United States.

The Select Committee has uncovered instances of the PRC's use of this specific stolen U.S. technology that:

- Enhance the PRC's military capabilities
- Jeopardize U.S. national security interests
- Pose a direct threat to the United States, our friends and allies, or our forces

The Clinton administration has determined that particular uses by the PRC of this stolen U.S. technology cannot be disclosed publicly without affecting national security.

The PRC has proliferated weapons systems and components to other countries including Iran, Pakistan, Libya, Syria, and North Korea.

B. In the late 1990s, the PRC stole or illegally obtained U.S. developmental and research technology that, if taken to successful conclusion, could be used to attack U.S. satellites and submarines.

During the late 1990s, U.S. research and development work on electromagnetic weapons technology has been illegally obtained by the PRC as a result of successful espionage directed against the United States. Such technology, once developed, can be used for space-based weapons to attack satellites and missiles.

In 1997, the PRC stole classified U.S. developmental research concerning very sensitive detection techniques that, if successfully concluded, could be used to threaten U.S. submarines.

C. Currently-deployed PRC ICBMs targeted on the United States are based in significant part on U.S. technologies illegally obtained by the PRC in the 1950s.

This illustrates the potential long-term effects of technology loss.

Even in today's rapidly changing technological environment, technology losses can have long-term adverse effects. Currently-deployed PRC ICBMs targeted on the United States are based on U.S. and Russian technologies from the 1950s and 1960s.

In the 1950s, a U.S. military officer and associated members of the design team for a U.S. ICBM program (the "Titan" missile program) emigrated to the PRC and illegally gave U.S. missile and missile-related technology to the PRC.

This information formed the basis for the up to two dozen PRC CSS-4 ICBMs that are currently targeted on the United States.

All but two of these missiles have been deployed by the PRC for the first time in this decade.

D. In the aftermath of three failed satellite launches since 1992, U.S. satellite manufacturers transferred missile design information and know-how to the PRC without obtaining the legally required licenses.

This information has improved the reliability of PRC rockets useful for civilian and military purposes.

The illegally transmitted information is useful for the design and improved reliability of future PRC ballistic missiles, as well.

U.S. satellite manufacturers analyzed the causes of three PRC launch failures and recommended improvements to the reliability of the PRC rockets. These launch failure reviews were conducted without required Department of State export licenses, and communicated technical information to the PRC in violation of the International Traffic in Arms Regulations.

The Select Committee has concluded that the PRC implemented a number of the recommended improvements to rocket guidance and to the fairing (or nose cone), which protects a satellite during launch. These improvements increased the reliability of the PRC Long March rockets. It is almost certain that the U.S. satellite manufacturers' recommendations led to improvements in the PRC's rockets and that the improvements would not have been considered or implemented so soon without the U.S. assistance.

It is possible or even likely that, absent the U.S. satellite manufacturers' interventions on the problems associated with the defective fairing on the PRC's Long March 2E rocket and the defective guidance system on the PRC's Long March 3B rocket, one or more other PRC launches would have failed.

The PRC Long March rockets improved by the U.S. technology assistance are useful for both commercial and military purposes. The military uses include launching:

- Military communications and reconnaissance satellites
- Space-based sensors
- Space-based weapons, if successfully developed
- Satellites for modern command and control and sophisticated intelligence collection

The Select Committee judges that the PRC military has important needs in these areas, including notably space-based communications and reconnaissance capabilities.

In addition, design and testing know-how and procedures communicated during the launch failure reviews could be applied to the reliability of missiles or rockets generally. U.S. participants' comments during the failure investigations related to such matters as:

- Missile design
- Design analysis
- Testing procedures
- The application of technical know-how to particular failure analyses

To the extent any valuable information was transferred to the PRC's space program, such information would likely find its way into the PRC's ballistic missile program. The ballistic missile and space launch programs have long been intertwined and subordinate to the same ministry and state-owned corporation in the PRC.

For example, the PRC's Long March 2 rockets and their derivatives (including the Long March 2E, on which Hughes advised the PRC) were derived directly from the PRC's silo-based CSS-4 intercontinental ballistic missiles that are currently targeted on the United States.

The various institutes and academies in the PRC involved in ballistic missile and rocket design also share design and production responsibilities. Many of the PRC personnel in these organizations have responsibilities for both commercial rocket and military missile programs. Attendees at important failure review meetings included PRC personnel from such organizations.

In fact, information passed during each of the failure analyses has the potential to benefit the PRC's ballistic missile program. The independent experts retained by the Select Committee judge that information valuable to the PRC's ballistic missile and space programs was transferred to the PRC in the failure investigations.

The rocket guidance system on which Loral and Hughes provided advice in 1996 is judged by the Select Committee to be among the systems capable of being adapted for use as the guidance system for future PRC road-mobile intercontinental ballistic missiles, although if a better system is available, it is more likely to be chosen for that mission.

The Select Committee judges that information on rocket fairings (that is, nose cones) provided to the PRC by Hughes may assist the design and improved reliability of future PRC MIRVed missiles, if the PRC decides to develop them, and of future submarine-launched ballistic missiles.

When Loral and Hughes assisted the PRC, they could not know whether the PRC would in fact use such information in their military programs.

i. In 1993 and 1995, Hughes showed the PRC how to improve the design and reliability of PRC rockets.

Hughes' advice may also be useful for design and improved reliability of future PRC ballistic missiles.

Hughes deliberately acted without seeking to obtain the legally required licenses. . . .

ii. In 1996, Loral and Hughes showed the PRC how to improve the design and reliability of the guidance system used in the PRC's newest Long March rocket.

Loral's and Hughes' advice may also be useful for design and improved reliability of elements of future PRC ballistic missiles.

Loral and Hughes acted without the legally required license, although both corporations knew that a license was required. . . .

E. In light of the PRC's aggressive espionage campaign against U.S. technology, it would be surprising if the PRC has not exploited security lapses that have occurred in connection with launches of U.S. satellites in the PRC.

The original policy permitting U.S. manufactured satellites to be launched in the PRC envisioned strict compliance with requirements to prevent unauthorized technology transfers.

These requirements are encompassed in U.S. regulations and licenses. Pursuant to a bilateral agreement between the United States and the PRC, the requirements include U.S. control over access to the satellite while it is in the PRC. Many of these requirements imposed on exporters are to be closely monitored by U.S. Government officials provided by the Defense Department.

The Select Committee has found numerous lapses in the intended pre-launch technology safeguards. Defense Department monitors have reported numerous security infractions by exporters. Exporters often hire private security guards to assist in the performance of their duties to prevent technology transfers, and these private guards have also reported security lapses. . . .

F. Foreign brokers and underwriters of satellite and space launch insurance have obtained controlled U.S. space and missile-related technology outside of the system of export controls that applies to U.S. satellite manufacturers.

While existing laws address such exports, U.S. export control authorities may not be adequately enforcing these laws in the space insurance industry context, nor paying sufficient attention to these practices. . . .

G. The Strom Thurmond National Defense Authorization Act took important steps to correct deficiencies in the administration of U.S. export controls on commercial space launches in the PRC.

But the aggressive implementation of this law is vital, and other problems with launches in the PRC that the Act does not address require immediate attention. . . .

H. It is in the national security interest of the United States to increase U.S. domestic launch capacity.

While U.S. policy since 1988 has permitted launching satellites in the PRC, U.S. national security interests would be advanced by avoiding the need for foreign launches through increased domestic launch capability.

The Reagan administration's decision to permit launches in the PRC was affected by two factors: insufficient domestic launch options in the aftermath of the *Challenger* disaster, and the perception of the PRC as a strategic balance against the Soviet Union in the context of the Cold War. These factors are no longer applicable today.

Launching Western satellites has provided the PRC with additional experience that has improved its space launch capabilities. Even in the absence of any loss of U.S. technology, such experience benefits a potential long-run competitor of the United States. . . .

3.

A. Recent changes in international and domestic export control regimes have reduced the ability to control transfers of militarily useful technology.

i. The dissolution of COCOM [the Coordinating Committee for Multilateral Export Controls] in 1994 left the United States without an effective, multilateral means to control exports of militarily useful goods and technology. . . .

ii. The expiration of the Export Administration Act in 1994 has left export controls under different legislative authority that, among other things, carries lesser penalties for export violations than those that can be imposed under the Act. . . .

iii. U.S. policy changes announced in 1995 that reduced the time available for national security agencies to consider export licenses need to be reexamined in light of the volume and complexity of licensing activities. . . .

B. Dividing the licensing responsibilities for satellites between the Departments of Commerce and State permitted the loss of U.S. technology to the PRC.

The 1996 decision to give Commerce the lead role in satellite exporting was properly reversed by the Congress. . . .

C. U.S. policies relying on corporate self-policing to prevent technology loss have not worked.

Corporate self-policing does not sufficiently account for the risks posed by inherent conflicts of interest, and the lack of priority placed on security in comparison to other corporate objectives. . . .

D. The PRC requires high performance computers (HPCs) for the design, modeling, testing, and maintenance of advanced nuclear weapons based on the nuclear weapons design information stolen from the United States.

The United States relaxed restrictions on HPC sales in 1996; and the United States has no effective way to verify that HPC purchases reportedly made for commercial purposes are not diverted to military uses.

The Select Committee judges that the PRC has in fact used HPCs to perform nuclear weapons applications. . . .

E. The PRC has attempted to obtain U.S. machine tools and jet engine technologies through fraud and diversions from commercial end uses.

In one 1991 case studied by the Select Committee, the Department of Commerce decontrolled jet engines without consulting either the Defense Department or the State Department. . . .

4.

A. The PRC has mounted a widespread effort to obtain U.S. military technologies by any means—legal or illegal.

These pervasive efforts pose a particularly significant threat to U.S. export control and counterintelligence efforts. . . .

B. Efforts to deny the PRC access to U.S. military technology are complicated by the broad range of items in which the PRC is interested, and by transfers to the PRC of Russian military and dual-use technologies, which may make the consequences of the PRC's thefts of U.S. technology more severe. . . .

C. The PRC uses commercial and political contacts to advance its efforts to obtain U.S. military, as well as commercial, technology. . . .

D. The PRC has proliferated nuclear, missile, and space-related technologies to a number of countries.

The PRC is one of the leading proliferators of complete ballistic missile systems and missile components in the world.

The PRC has sold complete ballistic missile systems, for example, to Saudi Arabia and Pakistan, and missile components to a number of countries including Iran and Pakistan. The PRC has proliferated military technology to Iran, Pakistan, and North Korea.

In 1991, the PRC agreed to adhere to the April 1987 Missile Technology Control Regime (MTCR) guidelines, but the PRC has not accepted the revisions to those guidelines issued in 1993. The 1993 MTCR guidelines increase the kinds of missile systems subject to controls and call for a "strong presumption to deny" both sales of complete missile systems and components that could be used in ballistic missiles.

The PRC has provided, or is providing, assistance to the missile and space programs of a number of countries according to the Congressional Research Service. These countries include, but are not limited to:

- **Iran.** The PRC has provided Iran with ballistic missile technology, including guidance components and the recent transfer of telemetry equipment. The PRC reportedly is providing Iran with solid-propellant missile technology. Additionally, the PRC provided Iran with the 95-mile

range CSS-8 ballistic missile. Since the mid-1980s, the PRC has transferred C-802 anti-ship cruise missiles to Iran. The PRC has also provided
assistance to Iran's nuclear programs.

- **Pakistan.** The PRC has provided Pakistan with a wide range of assistance. The PRC reportedly supplied Pakistan with CSS-X-7/M-11 mobile
  missile launchers and reportedly has provided Pakistan with the facilities necessary to produce M-11 missiles. The PRC provides Pakistan
  with assistance on uranium enrichment, ring magnets, and other technologies that could be used in Pakistan's nuclear weapons program.
- **Saudi Arabia.** The PRC provided a complete CSS-2 missile system to
  Saudi Arabia in 1987. The conventionally-armed missile has a range of
  1,200 to 1,900 miles.
- **North Korea.** The Select Committee judges that the PRC has assisted
  weapons and military-related programs in North Korea.

The Select Committee is aware of information of further PRC proliferation
of missile and space technology that the Clinton administration has determined cannot be publicly disclosed without affecting national security.

KEY FINDINGS

The Intelligence Community Damage Assessment on the Impli-
cations of China's Acquisition of US Nuclear Weapons Informa-
tion on the Development of Future Chinese Weapons

Chinese strategic nuclear efforts have focused on developing and deploying a survivable long-range missile force that can hold a significant portion of
the US and Russian populations at risk in a retaliatory strike. By at least the
late 1970s the Chinese launched an ambitious collection program focused on
the US, including its national laboratories, to acquire nuclear weapons technologies. By the 1980s China recognized that its second strike capability
might be in jeopardy unless its force became more survivable. This probably
prompted the Chinese to heighten their interest in smaller and lighter nuclear
weapon systems to permit a mobile force.

- China obtained by espionage classified US nuclear weapons information that probably accelerated its program to develop future nuclear
  weapons. This collection program allowed China to focus successfully
  down critical paths and avoid less promising approaches to nuclear
  weapon designs.
- China obtained at least basic design information on several modern US
  nuclear reentry vehicles, including the Trident II (W88).
- China also obtained information on a variety of US weapon design concepts and weaponization features, including those of the neutron
  bomb.

- We cannot determine the full extent of weapon information obtained. For example, we do not know whether any weapon design documentation or blueprints were acquired.
- We believe it is more likely that the Chinese used US design information to inform their own program than to replicate US weapon designs.

China's technical advances have been made on the basis of classified and unclassified information derived from espionage, contact with US and other countries' scientists, conferences and publications, unauthorized media disclosures, declassified US weapons information, and Chinese indigenous development. The relative contribution of each cannot be determined.

Regardless of the source of the weapons information, it has made an important contribution to the Chinese objective to maintain a second strike capability and provided useful information for future designs.

Significant deficiencies remain in the Chinese weapons program. The Chinese almost certainly are using aggressive collection efforts to address deficiencies as well as to obtain manufacturing and production capabilities from both nuclear and nonnuclear sources.

To date, the aggressive Chinese collection effort has not resulted in any apparent modernization of their deployed strategic force or any new nuclear weapons deployment.

China has had the technical capability to develop a multiple independently targetable reentry vehicle (MIRV) system for its large, currently deployed ICBM for many years, but has not done so. US information acquired by the Chinese could help them develop a MIRV for a future mobile missile.

We do not know if US classified nuclear information acquired by the Chinese has been passed to other countries. Having obtained more modern US nuclear technology, the Chinese might be less concerned about sharing their older technology.

INTRODUCTORY NOTE

This damage assessment was reviewed by a panel of independent, national security and weapons experts—Admiral David Jeremiah, General Brent Scowcroft, Dr. John Foster, Mr. Richard Kerr, Dr. Roland Herbst, and Mr. Howard Schue—prior to its publication. The panel members reviewed the report, held a question-and-answer session with the team, discussed the report amongst themselves, and concluded that they concurred with the report. The panel then worked with the team to develop a set of unclassified findings, which are completely consistent with the classified Key Findings in the damage assessment.

The panel would add the following observations:

- It is important to understand Chinese strategic objectives in assessing their efforts to acquire technical information on US nuclear weapons. The need to preserve their second strike capability, their regional concerns, and their perceptions of future national and regional ballistic defenses have driven collection efforts.

- The Chinese continue to have major gaps in their weapons program. We should seek to identify Chinese efforts to fill these gaps as indicators of future program direction and to provide insight into counterintelligence issues.

- The panel feels strongly that there is too little depth across the Intelligence Community's analytic elements and they are too frequently occupied with whatever current crisis takes front stage. The necessity to pull Intelligence Community analysts and linguists off other activities to assess the compromises to US nuclear weapons programs and their value to the Chinese further reinforces the panel's view that the depth of Intelligence Community technical and language expertise has eroded.

- A separate net assessment should be made of formal and informal US contacts with the Chinese (and Russian) nuclear weapons specialists. The value of these contacts to the US, including to address issues of concern—safety, command and control, and proliferation—should not be lost in our concern about protecting secrets.

- The panel recognizes that countries have gained access to classified US information on a variety of subjects for decades, through espionage, leaks, or other venues. While such losses were and continue to be unacceptable, our research and development efforts generally kept us technologically ahead of those who sought to emulate weapons systems using our information. However, decreases in research efforts have diminished the protective edge we could have over those using our information, making such losses much more significant in today's world.

GAO REPORT ON THE EFFECTS
OF WELFARE REFORM
May 27, 1999

State and federal welfare reforms combined with a strong economy to cut the national welfare caseload nearly in half in five years. But while millions of Americans had moved from welfare to work, many of them were working at low-wage, low-skill jobs, and it was unclear how economically stable these families were or how well they would fare if the economy were to slow down. Such were the conclusions of two major reports on welfare reform issued in 1999, one by the General Accounting Office (GAO), the investigative arm of Congress, and the other by the Urban Institute, an independent, nonpartisan research organization.

According to federal reports, the number of families receiving welfare assistance dropped 45 percent, from a peak of approximately 5 million families in 1994 to approximately 2.7 million families at the end of 1998—far more than even the most ardent supporters of welfare reform had predicted. Much of that decline occurred after the federal welfare laws were reformed in 1996; the national caseload fell 32 percent in 1997 and 1998 alone. But the decline had begun even before the 1996 law was enacted, when several states reformed their own welfare programs to experiment with new ways to move people from welfare to work. Overall, the decline was aided by an increase in the minimum wage and a surging economy that saw unemployment levels drop to their lowest levels in thirty years. (Increase in minimum wage, Historic Documents of 1996, p. 563; 1999 economic report, p. 85)

The drop in the welfare rolls was hailed by the Clinton administration and by congressional Republicans; both sides claimed political credit for passing the 1996 reform law. "The president's strategy of requiring work and rewarding people who go to work is working," declared Bruce Reed, director of the White House Domestic Policy Council. House Republican leaders issued a fact sheet claiming that the welfare reform law was "one of the most successful pieces of social legislation in American history." That law (PL 104–193) eliminated the decades-old concept that needy Ameri-

cans with children were entitled to government aid and set up new block grants to the states, called Temporary Assistance to Needy Families. To underline the "temporary" aspect of the aid, states were required to impose work requirements on adults receiving welfare. With few exceptions, adults could receive assistance for no more than two years, and families could receive aid for no more than five years. In addition, the law provided several incentives to help states reduce their welfare rolls, including increased flexibility to use federal funding to provide child care, transportation, and other services that would ease the transition from welfare to work. (Welfare reform enacted, Historic Documents of 1996, p. 450)

In 1998 the GAO reported that the new law appeared to be having its desired effect of encouraging welfare recipients to find work and become more self-sufficient. But the report also said it was too early to answer numerous questions about the effect of welfare reform on the families who had been receiving aid. Were these families actually attaining self-sufficiency? How many families were returning to welfare? What was happening to welfare recipients who left welfare but still had no job? And how were these families likely to fare in an economic slowdown? Although no one could yet answer these questions definitely, the GAO and Urban Institute studies began to fill in some of the blanks. (1998 GAO report, Historic Documents of 1998, p. 354)

The GAO Report

The GAO report, released May 27, 1999, reviewed state-sponsored studies in seven states—Indiana, Maryland, Oklahoma, South Carolina, Tennessee, Washington, and Wisconsin—that reported on the status of families that left welfare in 1995 or later. (Several other studies had also been conducted, but GAO determined that they were not representative of all families who had left the welfare rolls in a particular state.) Testifying before the House Ways and Means Subcommittee on Human Resources the same day, Cynthia M. Fagnoni, director of education, workforce, and income security issues of the GAO's Health, Education, and Human Services Division, said that the studies differed in several key aspects, but they nonetheless suggested "a pattern of what is happening to such families." Among the findings were the following:

- *Between 61 and 87 percent of those who left and remained off welfare were employed at some time after leaving welfare. Estimated annual average earnings for these workers ranged from $9,536 to $15,144, more than a three-person family with no other income could have received in cash assistance and food stamps in those states, but in most cases still under the federal poverty level ($13,650 for a family of three in 1998).*
- *Although the studies provided some information on earned incomes, little was known about total family household income, including earned income from other family members, child support payments,*

or financial assistance from friends and relatives. Oklahoma reported that 57 percent of its former welfare families had total household incomes at or below the federal poverty level. A Wisconsin study found that total income from earnings varied by the size of the family. Substantially more families with only one or two children earned above the poverty level than families with three or more children.

- *Between 44 and 83 percent of the former welfare families still received Medicaid benefits; between 31 and 60 percent still received food stamps. (Only five of the seven states tracked these benefits.)*
- *Little was known about the families who had left welfare but were not working. The most frequent reason former welfare recipients in South Carolina and Wisconsin gave for not working was their own physical or mental illness, followed by inability to find a job, lack of transportation, and lack of child care.*
- *The studies also revealed that the percentage of families who returned to welfare was "significant," according to the GAO, from 19 percent after three months in Maryland to 30 percent after fifteen months in Wisconsin. As increasing numbers of families reach their lifetime limitation on welfare aid, the GAO report said, "the issue of families needing to return to welfare will become more important."*
- *The studies provided little if any information about housing, health, education, or nutrition for the former welfare families, but, Fagnoni said, preliminary evidence did not show an increase in homelessness for the families or an increased need for foster care for the children.*

Fagnoni stressed that the studies did not answer several critical questions, including whether former welfare recipients earned enough to stay off welfare and upgrade their job skills or were still dependent on income supports, such as Medicaid, food stamps, subsidized child care, and the earned income credit. Nor was it clear what would happen to those welfare recipients who were unable to find jobs because of health problems or substance abuse. Some states had already noticed that the rate of decline in their welfare rolls was slowing, indicating that most of the remaining recipients probably faced significant barriers to finding and holding a job.

The Urban Institute Report

The Urban Institute report, written by Pamela Loprest and released in late July, was based on data from the National Survey of America's Families, which was conducted by the institute. The study looked specifically at people who had left welfare between 1995 and 1997. Because of the eligibility rules for receiving welfare, most of the former recipients were young women (under age thirty-five) with children. Loprest thus compared them with other low-income women to gauge how well the former welfare recipients were doing.

The Urban Institute report confirmed the GAO findings that most people were leaving welfare because they had found a job. Loprest reported that

69 percent of those surveyed said they left welfare because of increased earnings on an existing job or a new job. The remaining 31 percent left because they no longer wanted the benefits, did not want to comply with the program requirements, or were no longer eligible. The median hourly wage for employed former recipients was $6.61, with 25 percent of the former recipients earning $8 or more an hour and 25 percent earning less than $5.29. Nearly 40 percent of former welfare recipients worked in service jobs, which typically offered little room for advancement, and more than 25 percent worked at night. At least 65 percent did not have health insurance through their employer.

For many of these former welfare recipients, economic survival was tenuous. More than 30 percent of the families said they had skipped meals or cut down on the size of meals because they did not have enough money for food. Thirty-nine percent said they had been unable to pay their rent, mortgage, or utility bills at least once in the past year; 7 percent said they had moved in with family or friends because they could no longer afford housing.

These people, the report stressed, were the former welfare recipients who had jobs. About 20 percent of those who had left welfare were not working, did not have a spouse who was working, and were not relying on government disability benefits. Twenty-nine percent of those who left welfare between 1995 and 1997 returned to welfare. And if the first to leave welfare were the most "amenable" to work, as many poverty experts believed, then those who remained on the rolls were likely to have a much harder transition. All these groups, the report said, "could face greater obstacles" to becoming self-sufficient in the future.

Supreme Court on Two-Tier Benefits

In a related development, the Supreme Court on May 17 struck down a California law that would have allowed the state to pay new residents, for their first year in the state, the same level of welfare benefits that they had received in their home state. The vote was 7–2. California, which had one of the highest welfare payments in the country, had hoped to save an estimated $10.9 million a year through the double-tier system. The majority said, however, that states were required to treat all their citizens equally. "Citizens of the United States, whether rich or poor, have the right to choose to be citizens 'of the state wherein they reside,' " Justice John Paul Stevens wrote for the majority. "The states, however, do not have any right to select their citizens."

In holding that such double-tier benefits were unconstitutional, the court, by implication, struck down a provision of the 1996 welfare reform law that allowed states to set up such systems. Fifteen states, including New York and New Jersey, had adopted such laws, but most had been blocked by state or federal court action.

In 1969 the Supreme Court had established a fundamental "right to travel" when it held that states could not bar new residents from receiving welfare benefits altogether. In the 1999 case, Saenz v. Roe, *the Court said it based its decision on language in the Fourteenth Amendment stating that "no state shall make or enforce any law which shall abridge the privileges or immunities of citizens of the United States." This revival of the long-unused "privileges or immunities" clause was hailed by legal experts across the ideological spectrum; it was seen as a potentially powerful new source of protection for individual rights.*

> *Following are excerpts of testimony titled "Welfare Reform: States' Implementation Progress and Information on Former Recipients," given May 27, 1999, by Cynthia M. Fagnoni, director of education, workforce, and income security issues for the General Accounting Office, before the House Ways and Means Subcommittee on Human Resources on the experiences of former welfare recipients:*

Madam Chair and Members of the Subcommittee:

Thank you for inviting me here today to discuss our work on state implementation of welfare reform and information on families who have left welfare. The Personal Responsibility and Work Opportunity Reconciliation Act of 1996 (PRWORA) (PL 104–193) significantly changed federal welfare policy for low-income families with children, building upon and expanding state-level reforms. The act ended the federal entitlement to assistance for eligible needy families with children under Aid to Families With Dependent Children (AFDC) and created the Temporary Assistance for Needy Families (TANF) block grant, designed to help low-income families reduce their dependence on welfare and move toward economic independence. Under TANF, states have much greater flexibility than before to design and implement programs that meet state and local needs. At the same time, states must impose federal work and other program requirements on most adults receiving aid and enforce a lifetime limit of 5 years, or less at state option, on the length of time federal assistance is received.

These recent federal and state reforms represent significant departures from previous policies for helping needy families with children. To better understand states' program changes and the status of families who have left welfare, your Subcommittee, in concert with the Senate Finance Committee, asked us to review and report on state implementation of welfare reform and information on families who have left welfare. To respond to your requests, in June 1998 we issued a report on implementation of welfare reform in seven states, and today the Subcommittee has released a second report that reviews and summarizes state-sponsored studies of families who left the welfare rolls during or after 1995. Today I will summarize these reports' findings, discussing (1) states' implementation of welfare reform, (2) what state-sponsored studies tell us about the status of children and families leaving welfare, and (3) key issues involved in assessing the success of welfare reform.

In summary, our work shows that states are transforming the nation's welfare system into a work-focused, temporary assistance program for needy families. Many states are refocusing their programs on moving people into employment rather than signing them up for monthly cash assistance. To better support this new work focus, many states are changing how their offices and workers do business, expanding the roles of welfare workers to include helping clients address and solve problems that interfere with employment. These changes, made in times of strong economic growth, have been accompanied by a 45-percent decline in the number of families receiving welfare—from a peak of about 5 million families in 1994 to fewer than 3 million families as of December 1998.

Caseload reductions serve as only one indication of progress in meeting the goals of welfare reform, however. An essential question is: What do these program changes and caseload reductions mean for needy families with children? Early indications from our review of state-sponsored studies in seven states conducted at various periods from 1995 to 1998 are that most of the adults who left welfare were employed at some time after leaving the rolls, often at low-paying jobs. There was little evidence of increased incidence of homelessness or of children entering foster care after families left welfare, in the few cases in which these studies addressed these issues. However, much remains unknown about the economic status and well-being of most former welfare families nationwide.

Many efforts are under way to provide more information on the families who have left welfare and the effects of welfare reform. As this information becomes available, it will permit a more comprehensive assessment of welfare reform, which will need to address the following key issues:

- How do low-wage earners and their families fare after leaving welfare for work?
- What is happening to eligible families seeking welfare who are provided other forms of aid, such as job search assistance, instead of welfare or other aid?
- How effectively are states working with hard-to-serve welfare recipients who remain on the TANF rolls?
- How would an economic downturn affect states' welfare reform programs?

Background

PRWORA specified that the goals of TANF include providing assistance to needy families so that children may be cared for in their own homes or in the homes of relatives; ending the dependence of needy parents on government benefits by promoting job preparation, work, and marriage; preventing and reducing the incidence of out-of-wedlock pregnancies; and encouraging the formation and maintenance of two-parent families. In fiscal year 1998, states expended or obligated $12.2 billion of the $14.8 billion in federal funds available for TANF. In addition, states spent $11 billion of their own funds on needy families with children, meeting the requirement to maintain a specified minimum level of their own spending to receive federal TANF funds. The Department of Health and Human Services (HHS) oversees TANF at the federal level.

Before PRWORA, many states received waivers from federal rules under the AFDC program to allow them to strengthen work requirements for adults, impose time limits on the receipt of aid, and change other aspects of their programs. As a result, at the time PRWORA was enacted, states were at different stages of implementing their reform efforts. State programs continue to evolve at different paces. The great extent of state experimentation and sweeping changes at the federal level have generated interest among program administrators, state and local policymakers, welfare advocates, and the public in general about state and local welfare programs and the status of families no longer receiving cash assistance under AFDC or TANF.

States Are Changing Their Welfare Programs to Emphasize Work

States' have made progress in restructuring their programs to emphasize work and to reduce families' dependence on welfare. State efforts include requiring more welfare recipients to look for work or participate in work activities; providing other forms of aid, such as child care and transportation, to keep families from needing monthly cash assistance; and focusing more on helping families solve problems that interfere with employment. Although caseloads have declined, it is not yet clear to what extent states' program changes, rather than the strong economy, have contributed to the decline.

Our work and other studies show that many states and localities are transforming their welfare offices into job placement centers. The seven states we reviewed in depth generally had increased the percentage of their clients required to participate in work-related activities from an average of 44 percent in 1994 to 65 percent in the early months of TANF implementation in 1997. In some instances, applicants are now expected to engage in job search activities as soon as they apply for assistance. To emphasize the importance of work, five of the seven states have more strongly enforced work requirements by adopting provisions for terminating assistance to the entire family for noncompliance with program requirements. In addition, we recently reported that 17 states are drawing upon their existing workforce development systems to help welfare clients get jobs, often through the use of the Department of Labor's one-stop career center system.

Many States Are Using New Strategies to Divert Families from Welfare

Requiring applicants to search for work as soon as or before they apply for aid is part of a major new strategy many states are using to divert some applicants from monthly cash assistance. With the end of the entitlement to cash aid and the increased flexibility now granted states under TANF, states are sometimes providing other forms of assistance—such as one-time, lump-sum payments; support services, such as child care and transportation; and assistance with job searches—in an attempt to keep families from needing monthly cash assistance. One-time cash payments can help families to catch up on rent, repair their car, or get through a medical emergency, allowing adults within the families to be more able to obtain or retain a job. Support services such as child care and transportation may also enable families to maintain their self-sufficiency without going on the welfare rolls. A study sponsored by HHS showed that, as of August 1998, 31 states had reported using at least one diversion strategy in at least part of the state. A 1999 Rockefeller Institute review of 20 states' welfare programs found that states and localities have developed a range of diversion programs. For example, a diversion program in Texas allows caseworkers to provide families with employment counseling or refer them to public or private agencies for a variety of services, while Arizona's diversion program offers families emergency shelter, rent or mortgage assistance, or assistance with utility payments.

Along with this new emphasis on diverting families from receiving monthly cash assistance comes concern among some policymakers, program administrators, and others that families in need of and eligible for Medicaid and food stamps may not be receiving these benefits. To ensure continued Medicaid coverage for low-income families, PRWORA generally preserves the Medicaid entitlement, setting eligibility standards at the AFDC levels in effect on July 16, 1996. Moreover, many families who do not meet state-defined eligibility criteria for TANF can still be eligible for food stamps. We have ongoing work for Representatives Levin and Coyne addressing Medicaid and food stamp issues that we will be reporting on later this year.

States Are Providing Supportive Services to Families to Decrease Welfare Dependence

As many welfare offices have increased their emphasis on work activities, welfare offices and workers are also focusing more on helping clients address and solve problems that interfere with employment. The seven states we visited used some of the additional budgetary resources available under TANF to provide services to help families address barriers to employment, including lack of child care, lack of transportation, and more complex mental and physical health problems. States are also continuing to provide services to families that have left the welfare rolls as a result of employment, including, in some cases, providing case management services to help ensure that families can deal with problems that might put parents' jobs at risk. In addition, some states are providing services to low-income working families not receiving cash.

States Are Anticipating Difficulty in Serving Families Still on the Welfare Rolls

As states require larger percentages of their welfare caseloads to participate in work-related activities—including some recipients who were previously exempted because of a determination of physical or mental disability—

and as the most readily employable recipients leave welfare for employment, states are concerned that they will be left with a more difficult-to-serve population. Finding ways to involve these recipients in work activities was one of the most challenging and widespread implementation issues cited in the seven states we visited.

Studies of these hard-to-serve recipients have found that, in addition to being less likely to have prior work experience and more likely to have lower literacy levels, they tend to have multiple problems that make participation in work-related activities more difficult. These problems include physical and mental health issues such as depression, anxiety, personality disorders, substance abuse, and domestic violence. To move these recipients toward economic self-sufficiency, states have sought to enhance their capacity to provide mental and physical health services. For example, in our June 1998 report, we noted that Oregon officials had estimated that about 50 percent of the state's welfare caseload requires drug or alcohol treatment services. Oregon introduced mental health and drug and alcohol services by integrating them into some of their training classes for welfare recipients and by placing counselors on-site at welfare offices.

Welfare Caseloads Have Declined, but
No Consensus Exists on the Cause of the Decline

States' implementation of more work-focused programs, undertaken under conditions of strong economic growth, has been accompanied by a 45-percent decline in the number of families receiving welfare—from a high of about 5 million families in 1994 to 2.7 million families as of December 1998. A large part of the reduction occurred after enactment of federal reform in August 1996: the national caseload declined 32 percent between January 1997 and December 1998 alone. Thirty-five states had caseload reductions of 25 percent or more during that same time period. While economic growth and state welfare reforms have been cited as key factors to explain nationwide caseload declines, there is no consensus about the extent to which each factor has contributed to these declines. In any case, it is important to view caseload reductions as only one measure of progress in meeting the goals of welfare reform. As stated, the goals of PRWORA include ending the dependence of needy parents on government benefits by promoting job preparation, work, and marriage; encouraging two-parent families; and helping families care for their children in their own or relatives' homes. As a result, outcomes for families in the areas of economic status, family composition, and family and child well-being need to be assessed.

Several Studies Show Most Adults in Former
Welfare Families Were Employed at Some Time After
Leaving Welfare; Little Is Known About Family Well-Being

There are no federal requirements for states to report on the status of former welfare recipients. As a result, the only systematic data currently available on families who have left welfare come from research efforts initiated by states. We identified a total of 18 state-conducted or -sponsored studies in 17 states—2 studies in Wisconsin and 1 in each of the other 16 states—that reported on the status of families who left welfare in 1995 or later. . . . These state studies differed in important ways, such as when they were conducted, the categories of families tracked, the length of time families were tracked, and the extent to which the families for whom data were available were representative of all families in the population from which the sample was drawn.

Taking these factors into account, we determined that only 8 of the 18 tracking studies, covering seven states, had sufficient data on a sample of families to conclude that the sample represented the population from which it was taken. These states are Indiana, Maryland, Oklahoma, South Carolina, Tennessee, Washington, and Wisconsin. The eight studies from these states had data on at least 70 percent of the sample of families from the population of interest in the state or included a nonresponse analysis that showed no important differences between the respondents and the nonrespondents. We estimated that these seven states accounted for about 8 percent of the families who left welfare nationwide between October 1993 and June 1997. . . .

Because the seven states' studies differ in key ways, including time periods covered and categories of families studied, the results are not completely comparable. However, the studies provide information on the status of families who had left welfare in these states at the time of the studies and, because certain results are consistent across the studies, suggest a pattern of what is happening to such families.

Adults Had Employment Rates of 61 Percent to 87 Percent, but Little Is Known About Household Income

Seven of the state studies reported that most of the adults in families remaining off the welfare rolls were employed at some time after leaving welfare. . . . . [E]mployment rates ranged from 61 percent to 87 percent for adults in these families. However, these employment rates were measured in different ways. Studies measuring employment at the time of follow-up reported employment rates from 61 percent to 71 percent. Studies measuring whether an adult in a family had ever been employed since leaving welfare reported employment rates from 63 percent to 87 percent. These employment rates generally exclude families who returned to welfare, which can be a substantial portion of the families who leave welfare. The percentages of families who initially left welfare and then returned to the rolls were significant, ranging from 19 percent after 3 months in Maryland to 30 percent after 15 months in Wisconsin. The issue of families' needing to return to welfare will become more important as increasing numbers of recipients reach their time limit on aid, since returning to the rolls will no longer be an option for them.

Turning to the incomes of those who left welfare, average quarterly earnings ranged from $2,378 to $3,786 in the studies that either reported quarterly earnings or for which we estimated quarterly earnings. . . . Extrapolating these quarterly earnings to a year results in estimated average annual earnings for former welfare recipients in the seven states that range from $9,512 to $15,144. . . . These amounts of annual earned income are greater than the maximum annual amount of cash assistance and food stamps that a three-person family with no other income could have received in these states. However, if these earnings were the only source of income for families after they left welfare, many of them would remain below the federal poverty level.

While the tracking studies provide information on individuals' earned incomes, much remains unknown about families' total household incomes. For example, the studies generally do not provide complete information on other forms of household income, such as earnings by other household members, child support payments, and financial assistance from relatives and friends. Three of the eight state studies provided some information on total household income. In the Oklahoma study, 57 percent of the former welfare families reported household incomes at or below the federal poverty level. In the Indiana study, 57 percent of the families off welfare at follow-up reported monthly household income below $1,000. In contrast, the Washington study reported average total family income, including child support payments, equal to 130 percent of the federal poverty level for a family of three. In addition, the 1995–96 Wisconsin study, which focused on earnings rather than income, found that the proportion of families who had left and remained off welfare for at least 1 year who had earnings above the federal poverty level varied by family size. While 35 percent of the families with one child and 24 percent of the families with two children had earnings above the poverty level, only 11 percent of the families with three or more children did.

In addition to information on total household income, information on the receipt of government supports is key to understanding the condition of former welfare recipients and the extent to which they continue to rely on government aid and have not become economically self-sufficient. Five of the seven states' studies had some information on the receipt of benefits. For example, between 44 and 83 percent of the families who left welfare received Medicaid benefits, and between 31 and 60 percent received food stamps. As we discussed earlier, some policymakers and administrators are concerned that families seeking assistance and being diverted from welfare may be inappropriately diverted from receiving Medicaid and food stamps and that those who leave welfare may not receive Medicaid and food stamps even though they continue to be eligible for those programs. For example, families that leave TANF for employment generally may continue to receive Medicaid for 12 months. In addition, Medicaid coverage is also available for many low-income children even if their parents are not eligible.

In addition to interest in welfare recipients who have left welfare and are employed, there is great interest in how those families who have left welfare and are not employed are faring. The South Carolina and Wisconsin surveys asked nonworking former recipients what stopped them from working for pay. In both states, the most frequently mentioned reason was their own physical or mental illness, followed by the inability to find a job, lack of transportation, and lack of child care. The Wisconsin study attempted to determine how these families were supporting themselves. Of the 142 former recipients not currently working, 18 percent were living with employed spouses or partners. Sixty-five percent of the families of the remaining nonworking former recipients were receiving Social Security, state unemployment insurance, child support, or foster care payments; 23 percent were not receiving cash assistance but were receiving noncash assistance, such as free housing, rent subsidies, Medicaid, or food stamps.

Studies in Seven States Provided Limited Information on the Well-Being of Children and Families

The seven states' studies generally provided no information on changes in family composition, such as changes in marital status or formation of two-parent families, and provided little information on how former welfare children and families were doing relative to housing, health, education, and nutrition. However, preliminary evidence from a few of these studies shows no increased incidence in homelessness or entry of children into foster care at the time of follow-up.

Three studies—from Maryland, Oklahoma, and Washington—reported on the number of children in former recipient families that had ever been involved with child protective services and found few cases in which children had been involved with child protective services since leaving welfare. For example, the Maryland study reviewed state data from its foster care program to determine the number of children placed in foster care after their families left welfare. This study reported that less than one-half of 1 percent of the children studied entered foster care after their families left cash assistance. In addition, South Carolina, in separate analyses, compared the number of incidents of maltreatment reported to the Child Protective Services' Central Registry for a sample of families who had left welfare with the number of incidents for families still on welfare; it also compared the number of incidents of maltreatment in a sample of former welfare families before and after leaving welfare. The differences were not statistically significant for either comparison.

Two studies, South Carolina's as well as Wisconsin's recent survey of families leaving welfare during the first quarter of 1998, asked former recipients to compare several aspects of their general well-being after leaving welfare with their situation when they were on welfare. Because Wisconsin used a modified version of the interview schedule developed in South Carolina, the data are comparable, even though the programs that the recipients participated in are not. . . . Former welfare recipients in both states more often experienced deprivations after leaving welfare than while on welfare. At the same time, 76 percent and 68 percent of respondents in South Carolina and Wisconsin, respectively, disagreed or strongly disagreed with the statement that life was better when you were getting welfare. Regarding housing status, an important aspect of well-being, the limited information from the studies did not suggest increased incidence of homelessness at the time of follow-up.

Efforts Are Under Way to Further Assess the Success of Welfare Reform

While we were able to learn some things about the status of former welfare recipients in several states, we could not draw conclusions about the status of most families that have left welfare nationwide. In our attempt to describe the condition of former welfare families, we were constrained by the data available from these early state tracking studies. However, efforts are under way at both the federal and state levels to improve the usefulness of the data being collected to assess the status of former welfare families. A total of 39 states and the District of Columbia already are tracking or plan to track families leaving welfare. In addition, HHS has recently funded 14 projects to track and monitor families who have left welfare as part of its overall strategy to evaluate welfare reform and to respond to the Congress' earmarking of $5 million for HHS to study the outcomes of welfare reform. The HHS projects will cover families who leave welfare in 10 states, five counties in 2 other states, and the District of Columbia and, in some cases, will study eligible families diverted from welfare. The limited nature of the information currently available emphasizes the importance of additional state efforts such as those funded by HHS. HHS is funding other efforts also, including 23 studies in 20 states of welfare reforms that began under waivers of the AFDC program. Most of these efforts are looking at issues such as duration and amount of welfare receipt and measures of employment, earnings, and income. Five of these states' studies also will include information on outcomes for children.

Other efforts are also under way to provide information to better understand the effects of welfare reform on families. For example, to assess the post-reform status of all low-income families, not just former welfare families, the U.S. Census Bureau at the direction of the Congress is conducting a longitudinal survey of a nationally representative sample of families called the Survey of Program Dynamics. The survey particularly asks about eligibility for and participation in welfare programs, employment, earnings, out-of-wedlock births, and adult and child well-being. In addition, the Urban Institute is conducting a multiyear project monitoring program changes and fiscal developments along with changes in the well-being of children and families. As part of this project, the Urban Institute has surveyed nearly 50,000 people to obtain comprehensive information on the well-being of adults and children as welfare reform is being implemented in the various states. A second survey is planned for 1999. Full results from the Census Bureau and Urban Institute surveys may not be available until the year 2000. In addition, a multitude of other studies—some by us, HHS, and other federal agencies; states and localities; and other researchers—that will be providing information in the future on various aspects of welfare reform are under way or planned. In the near and long term, these efforts promise to provide more data to help us understand the effects of welfare reform on families.

In the meantime, our work shows that states have clearly made progress in restructuring their programs to emphasize the importance of employment to both clients and welfare workers. In addition, the information currently available from several states consistently shows that most families who have left welfare have at least some attachment to the workforce. In the longer term, the information that becomes available from ongoing and future studies will permit a more comprehensive assessment of welfare reform. Such an assessment will need to take into account some key questions.

How Do Families Fare After Leaving Welfare for Work?

Our work and other studies consistently show that many of the individuals in families who have left welfare are employed in low-wage jobs. While they are now employed, these families' prospects for achieving some measure of economic stability remain an important issue in light of prior research showing that AFDC mothers, who often found jobs with low wages, generally experienced little rise in wages over time after they began working. To the extent that these families' earnings do not increase over time and their employment-based fringe benefits are limited, the families' ability to maintain employment and support themselves may depend to a great extent on the availability of income supports, such as Medicaid, food stamps, subsidized child care, and the earned income credit. The recently expanded earned income credit, for example, can increase the incomes of qualified low-income families by as much as $2,271 for families with one child and $3,756 for families with two or more children. In some instances, states and localities have undertaken efforts to help these low-wage workers upgrade their skills to improve their job prospects. Federal and state policies and programs for assisting low-income working families are likely to play a critical role in the future success of welfare reform.

What Is Happening to Families Who Sought but Were Diverted from Cash or Other Assistance?

In recent years, welfare caseloads have dropped dramatically. While we have focused in this testimony on families who have left welfare, states' diverting eligible families from receiving cash assistance may have contributed to the large decline. Any comprehensive assessment of welfare reform and outcomes for families will need to explore state and local practices of diverting families from aid and the impact of these practices on families.

How Effective Are States in Working with Welfare Recipients Who Are Difficult to Employ?

Another issue that has emerged as states have experienced large caseload reductions is that many of the remaining recipients have multiple barriers to participation in work activities, such as mental health and substance abuse problems and domestic violence. As a result, even if economic conditions remain favorable, states' initial successes with moving applicants and recipients into employment will probably slow over time. In response, states will need to adjust their approaches to better enable families with a range of problems to take steps toward becoming more self-supporting. More research will be needed to identify promising approaches for working with these welfare families.

How Would an Economic Downturn Affect States' Welfare Reform Programs?

In many states, favorable economic conditions appear to have facilitated implementation of more work-focused approaches. It is not yet known, however, how states' welfare reform programs will perform under weaker economic conditions. For example, some adults who had previously left welfare for work could become unemployed. While they could be eligible for unemployment insurance, some could once again apply for cash assistance after their unemployment insurance ran out. Furthermore, if caseloads did increase significantly in a worsening economy, it is unclear what budgetary responses states would take in an environment of fixed federal TANF funding.

While welfare agencies' increased emphasis on employment, the large number of welfare recipients transitioning into jobs, and caseload reductions indicate progress in meeting the goals of welfare reform, additional information from ongoing and future studies will help us better understand the evolving story of welfare reform and its impact on families and children. . . .

OBASANJO ON HIS INAUGURATION AS PRESIDENT OF NIGERIA
May 29, 1999

Nigeria, Africa's most populous and one of its most troubled nations, may have entered a new era in 1999 with the election of a popular new president. Olusegun Obasanjo, one of several generals who had dominated Nigerian political life since independence from Great Britain in 1960, became the first elected president in twenty years—and only the third elected president in the nation's history. Obasanjo promised to root out corruption, eliminate military domination of Nigerian society, and lead his country toward democracy and economic prosperity. Fully achieving just one of those goals would be a major accomplishment for a country that had seen little but despotism, corruption, and ethnic strife in the previous four decades.

With more than 110 million citizens, Nigeria was home to about one-sixth of all Africans. The country had vast reserves of oil, but its governments had squandered billions of dollars worth of oil wealth though corruption and mismanagement, plunging the economy into near bankruptcy by the late 1990s. A succession of military regimes deprived Nigerians of civil and human liberties.

Supporters, including Western governments that were relieved to see responsible leadership in Nigeria, said Obasanjo had the necessary determination and political support to bring his nation back from the brink of ruin. Critics within Nigeria said Obasanjo, sixty-one at the time of his inauguration on May 29, 1999, was so dependent on the military that he would be unable to implement the broad range of reforms he had promised.

Many Nigerian leaders and international observers said the elections represented more of a beginning of a transition to stable democracy than the culmination of that process. They noted that Obasanjo and many of the leading figures in the new government were former generals from previous military regimes or recycled officials from the last civilian government, which was widely considered to be one of the country's most corrupt. Many Nigerians said they assumed the experiment with democracy would be temporary and that the military was merely biding its time until the next opportunity arose to take power.

But when critics attacked Obasanjo as a "tool" of the military, he turned that argument to his advantage. As a former general, he said, he would be a "bridge" between the military rulers of the past and a full-scale democracy of the future. His background would help thwart another military takeover, he said. "Election is not the end of democracy," he said on March 1, when he was declared the winner. "Democracy is a process. Election is just one important event in the process, and democracy under my own leadership will continue."

Despite Nigeria's many problems, the election of Obasanjo may have come at a fortuitous moment in terms of the economy. The world's sixth largest oil producer, Nigeria depended heavily on oil exports, which had declined sharply during the mid-1990s because of a worldwide oil glut and because of social turmoil in the southern oil-producing region. But the world's oil-producing nations curtailed their production in 1999 to force a rise in prices—offering the prospect of at least a short-term economic upturn in Nigeria.

Four Decades of Turmoil and Violence

Nigeria became a British colony in 1861 and gained its independence in 1960 during the rush of decolonization in Africa. For five years the country was a "republic" with civilian leadership. But a legacy of the colonial era led to chronic in-fighting; the British had divided Nigeria into three administrative districts, each dominated by one major ethnic group: in the north, the Hausa-speakers, most of whom were Muslim; in the southwest, the Yoruba, most of whom also were Muslim; and in the southeast, the Ibo, most of whom were Christian.

The first of a series of military coups took place in January 1966. Little more than a year later, in May 1967, the Ibo-dominated "Eastern region" seceded and declared the independent state of Biafra. A brutal three-year war killed hundreds of thousands, most of them Ibos, and resulted in the failure of the independence movement.

After another succession of coups and military governments, Obasanjo, a British-trained military officer, rose to power in 1976. His government was little better than those preceding it, but he earned international praise with one act: in 1979 he held elections and handed the government over to an elected civilian leadership, becoming the first Nigerian general to do so. Obasanjo then retired to a farm where he raised chickens and pigs.

The civilian government proved that democracy does not guarantee quality leadership; by nearly all accounts it was one of Nigeria's most corrupt and inept. A military coup overthrew the civilian regime in 1983. Ten years later, the military rulers at the time called elections under rigged procedures, but when it became clear that a popular Yoruba leader, Moshood K.O. Abiola, had won despite the rigging, the military invalidated the results. When Abiola protested, he was thrown in prison.

273

Yet another coup brought to power General Sani Abacha, who quickly distinguished himself by heading what was generally considered the most brutal and corrupt regime in the nation's history. Under Abacha, Nigeria became an international pariah state. Western and other African governments regularly denounced Abacha's excesses and sought to distance themselves from him. (Human rights conditions in Nigeria, Historic Documents of 1995, p. 696; religious persecution in Nigeria, Historic Documents of 1997, p. 575; political conditions in Nigeria, Historic Documents of 1998, p. 220)

Abacha died of a heart attack on June 8, 1998. He was succeeded by General Abdulsalami Abubakar who came under intense international and domestic pressure to undertake political reforms. As Abubakar was taking hesitant steps toward reform, Nigeria was shaken in July 1998 by the sudden death in prison of opposition leader Abiola. Despite widespread protests among Abiola's Yoruba supporters—and suspicion that he had been killed by the military—an autopsy performed by Western doctors found that Abiola had died of heart disease.

Abiola's death served to stiffen pressure on Abubakar. In July he announced plans for local, state, and national elections beginning at the end of 1998 and running through early 1999. Abubakar also pledged to hand over power to an elected president on May 29, 1999. Immediately, political attention turned to Obasanjo, who had been imprisoned by Abacha in 1995 and was released by Abubakar during his 1998 reform movement. Under pressure from Abubakar and other military leaders, Obasanjo agreed to run for president, heading the People's Democratic Party.

The Electoral Process

Nigeria's sudden leap into democracy, after fifteen years of military dictatorship, began with local elections in December 1998 that were plagued by technical problems and violence in many years. Follow-up elections in thirty-five of the nation's thirty-six states on January 9, 1999, went more smoothly and were generally endorsed by international observers. The People's Democratic Party, headed by Obasanjo, won the majority of those elections.

The People's Democratic Party was by far the best financed and organized of Nigeria's three main political parties. The other two parties, the Alliance for Democracy (dominated by Yorubas) and the All People's Party (which included many former allies of Abacha), agreed on a joint candidate to oppose Obasanjo. He was Olu Falae, a former finance minister who headed the Alliance for Democracy. Falae's campaign was badly managed and strapped for funding, and observers said he was unable to spread his message nationwide. His principal argument was that Obasanjo would represent a continuation of military rule under a civilian guise.

Obasanjo scored an overwhelming victory in the February 27 presidential election, with 63 percent of the vote. His opponent, Falae, bitterly denounced the voting procedures as unfair, pointing to numerous cases of fraud. Most international observers agreed that there had been widespread fraud but said those problems were not serious enough to have made a significant difference in the outcome. Among the observers was former U.S. president Jimmy Carter, who had been in office during Obasanjo's first stint as president; the two men had been friends ever since. Obasanjo was officially declared the winner on March 1.

Obasanjo: Democrat or Military Front-Man?

For two decades, Obasanjo had been one of the best known African figures around the world. Inside Nigeria, Obasanjo was remembered as one of a series of military dictators; outside Nigeria, especially in Western capitals, he was remembered as the only Nigerian military leader who had voluntarily given up power to an elected civilian government.

During the election campaign, Obasanjo said he was committed to democracy and to ending corruption and mismanagement in Nigerian society. Critics insisted Obasanjo was merely a tool of the military establishment and that General Abubakar had chosen Obasanjo as his successor and had arranged for the financing of his campaign.

Once in office, Obasanjo moved to prove his critics wrong. He replaced nearly one hundred top military officers with men who had not been involved in previous military regimes. Obasanjo canceled dozens of contracts that had been issued by the Abubakar regime during its final months in office. Among those contracts were eleven licenses for oil exploration awarded, without competitive bids, to firms associated with ruling military officers or their families. The new government also established a commission to investigate past human rights abuses, similar to the Truth and Reconciliation Commission in South Africa. (South African commission, Historic Documents of 1998, p. 755)

Obasanjo drew widespread criticism, both domestically and internationally, for his failure to address one key issue: the imbalance of political and economic power between the national government, which received all revenues from oil production, and the state governments, including those in the oil-producing Niger Delta region. The desperate poverty in that region led to severe rioting in 1999, including sabotage against oil facilities.

U.S. Policy

During the years of military rule in Nigeria, successive administrations in the United States followed carefully balanced policies toward that country. Washington expressed disapproval of the brutal dictatorships and warned against the consequences of the corruption that was draining Nigeria's oil wealth. But officials in Washington also were cautious not to upset U.S. economic interests in Nigeria, which supplied about 8 percent of U.S. oil imports. The Mobil and Chevron oil companies had major production facilities in Nigeria.

Secretary of State Madeleine K. Albright visited Nigeria on October 20 during a week-long visit to Africa. She praised progress made by

Obasanjo's government and promised that the Clinton administration would ask Congress for more aid money for Nigeria.

Obasanjo met with President Bill Clinton in Washington on October 28 and pleaded for faster action on international debt forgiveness. Nigeria owed international financial institutions, other governments, and private lenders more than $30 billion. Clinton had proposed a broad debt forgiveness plan for developing countries, but Nigeria—with its vast oil reserves—was not to be one of the prime beneficiaries.

Obasanjo assured audiences in Washington that he was serious about rooting out corruption and making Nigeria a more attractive place for international investment. "To invite investment into Nigeria, we have to create conducive environment for business to thrive," he said at a joint news conference with Clinton.

Following is the text of the inaugural address of Olusegun Obasanjo, president of Nigeria, given May 29, 1999:

Fellow Nigerians, we give praise and honour to God Almighty for this day specially appointed by God Himself. Everything created by God has its destiny and it is the destiny of all of us to see this day.

Twelve months ago, no one could have predicted the series of stunning events that made it possible for democratic elections to be held at the Local Government level, the State level, and culminating in the National Assembly Elections. Thereafter, you the good people of Nigeria elected me, a man who had walked through the valley of the shadow of death, as your President, to head a democratic civilian administration. I believe that this is what God Almighty has ordained for me and for my beloved country Nigeria and its people. I accept this destiny in all humility and with the full belief that with the backing of our people we shall not fail.

I wish, at this point, to thank all you good Nigerians for the confidence reposed in me. I wish to pay tribute to the great and gallant Nigerians who lost their lives in the cause of the struggle for liberty, democracy and good governance. They held the beacon of freedom and liberty high in the face of state terrorism and tyranny. We thank God that their sacrifice has not been in vain. We will always remember them.

Our thanks go also to the friends of Nigeria in many lands for the commitment and unrelenting support they gave throughout the dark, ominous days of the struggle.

Nigerians living in foreign lands deserve special tribute for not forgetting their fatherland and for making their voices heard persistently in defence of freedom. And I must commend you my home-based fellow Nigerians for the way you bore unprecedented hardship, deprivation of every conceivable rights and privileges that were once taken for granted.

I commend General Abdulsalami Abubakar and members of the Provisional Ruling Council (PRC) for the leadership they gave the country in the last eleven months and for keeping meticulously to their announced timetable of handing over to a democratically elected government today. As officers and gentlemen, they have kept their word.

The Independent National Electoral Commission (INEC) also deserves the thanks of all of us. In the face of doubt and skepticism and great time constraints, the Chairman and his commissioners conducted elections right from Local Government level to the Presidential level. They acquitted themselves creditably and they deserve our gratitude.

Nigeria is wonderfully endowed by the Almighty with human and other resources. It does no credit either to us or the entire black race if we fail in managing our resources for quick improvement in the quality of life of our people. Instead of progress and development, which we are entitled to expect from those who governed us, we experienced in the last decade and a half, and particularly in the last regime but one, persistent deterioration in the quality of our governance, leading to instability and the weakening of all public institutions. Good men were shunned and kept away from government while those who should be kept away were drawn near. Relations between men and women who had been friends for many decades, and between communities that had lived together in peace for many generations became very bitter because of the actions or inaction of government. The citizens developed distrust in government, and because promises made for the improvement of the conditions of the people were not kept all statements by government met with cynicism.

Government officials became progressively indifferent to propriety of conduct and showed little commitment to promoting the general welfare of the people and the public good. Government and all its agencies became thoroughly corrupt and reckless. Members of the public had to bribe their way through in ministries and parastatals to get attention and one government agency had to bribe another government agency to obtain the release of their statutory allocation of funds.

The impact of official corruption is so rampant and has earned Nigeria a very bad image at home and abroad. Besides, it has distorted and retrogressed development.

Our infrastructures—NEPA [National Electric Power Authority], NITEL [Nigerian Telecommunications], roads, railways, education, housing and other social services—were allowed to decay and collapse. Our country has thus been through one of its darkest periods.

All these have brought the nation to a situation of chaos and near despair. This is the challenge before us. Fellow Nigerians, let us rise as one, to face the tasks ahead and turn this daunting scene into opportunities in a New Dawn. Let us make this the beginning of a genuine Renaissance.

Fellow Nigerians, the entire Nigerian scene is very bleak indeed. So bleak people ask me where do we begin? I know what great things you expect of me at this New Dawn. As I have said many times in my extensive travels in the country, I am not a miracle worker. It will be foolish to underrate the task ahead. Alone, I can do little.

You have been asked many times in the past to make sacrifices and to be patient. I am also going to ask you to make sacrifices, and to exercise patience. The difference will be that in the past sacrifices were made and patience exercised with little or no results. This time, however, the results of your sacrifice and patience will be clear and manifest for all to see. With God as our guide, and with 120 million Nigerians working with me, with commitment, sustained effort, and determination, we shall not fail. On my part, I will give the forthright, purposeful, committed, honest and transparent leadership that the situation demands.

I am determined with your full cooperation, to make significant changes within a year of my administration.

Together we shall take steps to halt the decline in the human development indices as they apply to Nigeria. All the impacts of bad governance on our people that are immediately removable will be removed, while working for medium and long term solutions.

Corruption

Corruption, the greatest single bane of our society today, will be tackled head-on at all levels. Corruption is incipient in all human societies and in most human activities.

But it must not be condoned. This is why laws are made and enforced to check corruption, so that society would survive and develop in an orderly, reasonable and predictable way. No society can achieve anything near its full potential if it allows corruption to become the full-blown cancer it has become in Nigeria. One of the greatest tragedies of military rule in recent times, is that corruption was allowed to grow unchallenged, and unchecked, even when it was glaring for everybody to see. The rules and regulations for doing official business were deliberately ignored, set aside or by-passed to facilitate corrupt practices. The beneficiaries of corruption in all forms will fight back with all the foul means at their disposal. We shall be firm with them. There will be no sacred cows. Nobody, no matter who and where, will be allowed to get away with the breach of the law or the perpetration of corruption and evil.

Under the administration, therefore, all the rules and regulations designed to help honesty and transparency in dealings with government will be restored and enforced. Specifically, I shall immediately reintroduce "Civil Service Rules", and "Financial Instructions" and enforce compliance. Other regulations will be introduced to ensure transparency. The rampant corruption in the public service and the cynical contempt for integrity that pervades every level of the bureaucracy will be stamped out. The public officer must be encouraged to believe once again that integrity pays. His self-respect must be restored and his work must be fairly rewarded through better pay and benefits, both while in service and in retirement.

Restoration of Confidence in Government

I am very aware of the widespread cynicism and total lack of confidence in government arising from the bad faith, deceit and evil actions of recent administrations. Where official pronouncements are repeatedly made and not matched by action, government forfeits the confidence of the people and their trust. One of the immediate acts of this administration will be to implement quickly and decisively, measures that would restore confidence in governance. These measures will help to create the auspicious atmosphere necessary for the reforms and the difficult decisions and the hard work required to put the country back on the path of development and growth.

The issue of crime requires as much attention and seriousness as the issue of corruption. Although the Police are in the forefront of fighting crimes and ensuring our security, it is our responsibility to help the police to be able to help us. The police will be made to do their job. All Nigerian citizens and residents in our midst are entitled to the protection of life and property. A determined effort will be made to cut down significantly the incidence of violent crime.

Priority Issues

I believe that this administration must deal with the following issues even in these difficult times of near economic collapse:

(i)   The crisis in the Oil Producing Areas,
(ii)   Food Supply, food security and Agriculture,
(iii) Law and order with particular reference to armed robbery and to cultism in our educational institutions,
(iv)   Exploration and production of petroleum,
(v)   Education,
(vi)   Macro-economic policies—particularly, exchange rate management etc.,
(vii) Supply and distribution of petroleum products,
(viii) The debt issue,
(ix)   Corruption, drugs, organised fraud called 419 activities and crimes leading to loss of lives, properties and investment,
(x)   Infrastructure—Water supply, Energy, Telecommunication, Ports, airways, National Shipping, Nigerian Railways, etc.,
(xi)   Resuscitation of the Manufacturing Industries,
(xii) Job creation and creation of conducive environment for investment,
(xiii) Poverty alleviation,
(xiv) Housing—both
       • Civilian Housing Programmes; and
       • Barrack refurbishment and new construction for the Armed Forces and the Police,
(xv)   ECOMOG [Economic Community of West African States Monitoring Group],
(xvi) Health Services,
(xvii) Political and Constitutional Dialogue, and
(xviii) Women and Youth Empowerment.

In pursuit of these priorities, I have worked out, measures which must be implemented within the first six months.

279

Details of the focus and measures of this administration on these and other matters, will be announced from time to time. I shall quickly ascertain the true state of our finances and the economy and shall let the nation know. In the light of resources available, I shall concentrate on those issues that can bring urgent beneficial relief to our people.

Cabinet

I will need good men and women of proven integrity and record of good performance to help me in my cabinet. I appreciate that the quality and calibre of the members of my cabinet and top appointments will send a positive or negative signal to Nigerians and the international community as to the seriousness of the administration to make salutary changes. In our difficult and abnormal situation, great care and circumspection are called for in appointments to the cabinet and high public positions. To be appointed a minister or to any other public office is not a licence to loot public funds. It is a call to national service. It is one of the best ways of rendering dedicated services to humanity. In this administration, being a minister or holding any other public office will not deprive you of what you have before you come into office but you will not be allowed to have conflict of interest, abuse of office or illicit acquisition. Service to be satisfying must entail sacrifice.

Regular weekly meetings of Cabinet will be reinforced to enrich the quality of decisions of government through open discussions of memoranda in Council. Before any issues are introduced to the cabinet, the time-tested procedure of inter-ministerial consultations would have been made. The conclusions of Council, circulated to all ministers and permanent secretaries will, as used to be the practice in the past, be the authority for executive action and for incurring expenditure of public funds. This will help the cohesion of the government, ensure discipline, and hinder corrupt intentions, since all major contracts must go to Council for open consideration.

A code of conduct for Ministers and other public offices will be introduced. Other measures for individual and collective self-control and self-discipline of ministers and other public officers will be introduced.

Political Reconciliation

I am determined to stretch my hand of fellowship to all Nigerians regardless of their political affiliations. I intend to reconcile all those who feel alienated by past political events and I will endeavour to heal divisions, and to restore the harmony we used to know in this country.

Crisis in the Niger Delta

A bill will be forwarded within weeks of the inception of the administration to the National Assembly, for a law providing for 13% derivation in Revenue Allocation to be used for ecological, rehabilitation, infrastructural and other developments.

A competent group will be set up immediately to prepare a comprehensive Development Plan for the Niger-Delta Area. Dialogue will be held at all levels with the real representatives of all sections of the oil producing communities to improve communication and better mutual understanding. The responsibility and initiative for resolving the crisis rests with the Government.

ECOMOG

Nigeria has over the years played a very active role in ECOMOG for the restoration of peace in Liberia and Sierra Leone. Our national interest requires the establishment and maintenance of peace and stability in the West African Sub-region. Specifically in the case of Sierra Leone, we shall endeavour to ensure a quick resolution of the crisis by dialogue and diplomatic means by increasing activity on the second track of peace and reconciliation. This will enable us reduce our commitments in both theatres but particularly in Sierra Leone.

External Relations

Nigeria, once a well-respected country and a key role player in international bodies, became a pariah nation. We shall pursue a dynamic foreign policy to promote friendly relations with all nations and will continue to play a constructive role in the United Nations and the Organisation of African Unity, and other international bodies. We shall continue to honour existing agreements between Nigeria and other countries.

Let me, once again, thank our international friends who fought for democracy alongside with us. Today, we are taking a decisive step on the path of democracy. We will leave no stone unturned to ensure sustenance of democracy because it is good for us; it is good for Africa; and it is good for the world. We call on the world, particularly the Western World to help us sustain democracy by sharing with us the burden of debt which may be crushing and destructive to democracy in our land.

The Nigeria Armed Forces

The incursion of the military into government has been a disaster for our country and for the military over the last thirty years. The esprit-de-corps amongst military personnel has been destroyed; professionalism has been lost. Youths go into the military not to pursue a noble career but with the sole intention of taking part in coups and to be appointed as military administrators of states and chairmen of task forces.

As a retired officer, my heart bleeds to see the degradation in the proficiency of the military. A great deal of reorientation has to be under taken and a re-definition of roles, re-training and re-education will have to be done to ensure that the military submits to civil authority and regains its pride, professionalism and traditions. We shall restore military cooperation and exchanges with our traditional friends. And we will help the military to help itself.

Harmony Within the Three Arms of Government

It is my resolve to work harmoniously with the legislature and the judiciary to ensure that Nigerians enjoy good and civilized governance. I am also determined to build a broad consensus amongst all parties to enhance national harmony and stability and thus ensure success in the long struggle ahead.

Politicians have a duty, in whatever capacity they may find themselves, whether as legislators or ministers, to be committed, and be seen to be committed to the public good. Politicians must carefully examine the budget to ensure that public funds are judiciously spent. They must avoid damage to their own credibility and not vote for themselves special privileges. They must join in the campaign against corruption and help re-establish integrity in the conduct of public affairs. I assure you all that it is the policy of this government to ensure fair remuneration in service and in retirement to public servants, which includes legislators, civil servants, the police and members of the armed forces, parastatals and public-owned educational institutions.

I call on all Nigerians but particularly on our religious leaders to pray for moral and spiritual revival and regeneration in our nation.

Conclusion

I shall end this address by stressing again that we must change our ways of governance and of doing business on this eve of the coming millennium. This we must do to ensure progress, justice, harmony and unity and above all, to rekindle confidence amongst our people. Confidence that their conditions will rapidly improve and that Nigeria will be great and will become a major world player in the near future.

May the Almighty help us.

June

United Nations Security Council
  Resolution on Kosovo 285

Mbeki on His Inauguration
  as President of South Africa 297

State Department on U.S
  Bombing of Chinese Embassy 304

Supreme Court on the
  Definition of Disability 317

Supreme Court on
  States Rights 333

President Clinton's Remarks
  on the Budget Surplus 350

UNITED NATIONS SECURITY COUNCIL RESOLUTION ON KOSOVO
June 10, 1999

The June 10, 1999, end of NATO's eleven-week air war forced Serbia to ease its grip on Kosovo and marked the beginning of a massive international effort to bring peace and stability to the troubled province. Acting under a United Nations Security Council mandate, NATO nations, Russia, and a dozen other countries sent nearly 50,000 peacekeepers to Kosovo. International relief organizations shipped tons of food, clothing, housing supplies, and other items essential for helping Kosovo's nearly 2 million citizens return to some semblance of a normal life. (Kosovo air war, p. 134)

Despite these efforts, Kosovo at the end of 1999 resembled the American Wild West of the late 1800s, ruled as much by vigilante groups and organized crime as by UN-appointed representatives who were supposed to lead the way toward democracy. Most of the million-plus Kosovar Albanians who had fled to neighboring countries in response to Serbia's terror campaign had returned by late 1999. Many found their homes and villages burned and destroyed, and they faced an almost total lack of public services, such as electricity and clean water. Seeking revenge, Albanian nationalists attacked and killed hundreds of Serbs and gypsies, who they accused of cooperating with the Yugoslav regime headed by Slobodan Milosevic. The Kosovo Liberation Army (KLA), which had battled for independence before the NATO bombing campaign, gave up most of its weapons, as required by the UN decree. But the KLA became the dominant political force in the province, pushing aside moderate leaders who represented Kosovo's intellectual elite. KLA fighters were accused of confiscating property from fellow ethnic Albanians and organizing revenge attacks against Serbs.

The international community in July pledged more than $2 billion in aid for Kosovo, but at year's end UN operations were desperately short of money for supplies and salaries. NATO secretary general Lord Robertson said a "small investment" by the international community "will save a colossal amount of money later if it all goes wrong."

The U.S.-led bombing campaign that forced the Serbian government out of Kosovo had little immediate impact on Yugoslav leader Milosevic, who was accused by the West of masterminding the ethnic terror in Kosovo. Internal opposition to Milosevic grew after the war, as illustrated by several anti-Milosevic demonstrations and petitions. The largest demonstration occurred August 19, when a crowd of more than 50,000 people gathered in front of the Yugoslav parliament building in Belgrade to demand that Milo- sevic resign. But there was no conclusive evidence that Milosevic had lost his grip on the Yugoslav military, which was the basis of his hold on power.

UN Resolution

Terms for the security and political settlement of the Kosovo war were based on Resolution 1244, adopted June 10 by the UN Security Council. The vote was 14-0, with China abstaining. The resolution was largely derived from a set of principles adopted May 6 by the foreign ministers of the Group of Eight—the major industrialized nations, plus Russia. The Secu- rity Council resolution incorporated the Group of Eight principles as annexes to Resolution 1244, effectively making them UN policy. The key principles dealt with demilitarization of the province. All Serbian-Yugoslav security forces were required to leave Kosovo, thereby eliminating Bel- grade's means of controlling the province, and the KLA was required to dis- band and turn over the bulk of its weapons.

In essence, the resolution endorsed NATO plans for a massive peace- keeping operation to make Kosovo a safe place and to protect the Albanian and Serbian communities there from each other. The UN was to have over- all responsibility for establishing political institutions, providing human- itarian assistance, and reviving the economy of Kosovo. In other words, the UN was taking on Kosovo as a virtual protectorate.

This complex Kosovo operation bore numerous similarities to the one established in the former Yugoslav republic of Bosnia after the end of a bru- tal three-year war. In both countries, NATO was keeping the peace while UN diplomats and relief agencies were supervising key aspects of domestic pol- icy. One important difference was that Kosovo was still a province of a country—the former Yugoslavia—which accepted the international pres- ence only because it was defeated in war, whereas Bosnia had become an independent state totally dependent on international help. The UN resolu- tion said Kosovo was to have "substantial autonomy" from Yugoslavia, but the resolution did not declare Kosovo to be independent. That deliberately ambiguous language skirted the underlying dispute between Albanians who wanted independence and Serbs who wanted Kosovo to remain part of Serbian-dominated Yugoslavia. Over the long term, however, it appeared likely that Kosovo gradually would become independent of Yugoslavia. (Bosnia peacekeeping, Historic Documents of 1995, p. 717)

In previous years, a resolution giving NATO and the UN such vast pow- ers to intervene in the internal affairs of a UN-member country, such as Yugoslavia, would have caused deep controversy. But Yugoslavia's terror campaign against thousands of its own citizens had caused so much revul- sion around the world that there was little hesitation on the matter. The

Chinese, Cuban, and Russian ambassadors condemned the NATO bombing of Yugoslavia, but most countries represented on the Security Council portrayed the world's response to events in Kosovo as a seminal victory for human rights. "Today, no sovereign state has the right to terrorize its own citizens," the ambassador of the Netherlands, Peter Van Walsum, told the Security Council.

One of the key elements of the Security Council resolution dealt with timing. Although the resolution established an initial one-year mandate for the NATO peacekeeping force, in effect it provided for an indefinite mandate by stating that NATO would remain in Kosovo "unless the Security Council decides otherwise." Because key NATO members, including the United States, had a veto power over Security Council resolutions, that language meant that a decision to end NATO's presence in Kosovo would have to be made by consensus.

Peacekeeping Gets Under Way

NATO's peacekeeping plans, implicitly endorsed by the UN Security Council resolution, called for dividing Kosovo into sectors controlled by U.S., British, French, and German contingents. The peacekeeping force was called KFOR, for Kosovo Force.

The first challenge for KFOR came June 12, even before it entered Kosovo, when Russian troops raced ahead of NATO troops and occupied the airport at Pristina, the Kosovar capital. Russian diplomats in Moscow called the action a mistake, but military officers on the scene refused to budge, and the incident developed into a tense standoff between Western governments and Moscow, which wanted a larger and more independent role in Kosovo peacekeeping than NATO had planned. The dispute was resolved June 17, when Russia agreed to have its troops in Kosovo serve alongside NATO forces.

Western European nations contributed the bulk of troops to KFOR, which reached full strength of 47,000 by late November. Most of the troops were stationed in Kosovo, but several thousand were on duty in Albania and Macedonia, helping guard borders and aid shipments into Kosovo. The U.S. contingent totaled 7,500; of those, some 6,000 soldiers were stationed at Camp Bondsteel, a large U.S. army base in southeastern Kosovo.

NATO officials said that nearly one-half of the KFOR troops were dedicated to protecting Serbs, gypsies, and other minorities against attacks by the majority Albanians in Kosovo. Most of the remaining peacekeepers were acting as security officers in towns and villages, which lacked any organized police presence; were manning checkpoints and border patrols; and were helping provide humanitarian supplies and services, such as building refugee camps and sanitation facilities and restoring railways.

One of the slowest elements of the international effort in Kosovo was the development of a police force. NATO members and other nations promised to send several thousand policemen to Kosovo, but by year's end only a few hundred were on the scene. UN Special Representative Bernard Kouchner, of France, said in late November that he needed about 6,000 police officers to stem the province's crime wave. Kosovo also lacked anything approaching a criminal justice system, with the result that criminals could act with impunity.

Disarming the KLA

Of all the tasks confronting KFOR, probably the most difficult was dealing with the KLA, the Albanian guerrilla group that had been fighting for independence from Yugoslavia for more than three years. At the end of the NATO bombardment, the KLA had several thousand fighters, many of them heavily armed with weapons provided by Albania. UN Security Council Resolution 1244 specifically called for the KLA to stop "all offensive actions" and to be "demilitarized" under procedures to be established by KFOR.

KFOR's first commander, British General Michael Jackson, set a September 1 deadline for all KLA fighters to hand over their weapons. When that goal was not met, Jackson extended the deadline. By September 21 KFOR officials determined that the KLA had been substantially demilitarized, even though many guerrillas kept handguns and rifles. KLA fighters were to be incorporated into an unarmed, nonmilitary public service organization, the Kosovo Protection Corps, described by international officials as a way of keeping the fighters busy and out of trouble.

An equally serious challenge for the international agencies in Kosovo was the largely successful effort by the KLA commanders to set themselves up as the province's de facto political leaders. A senior KLA commander, Hashim Thaci, in June appointed himself "prime minister" of a provisional government and named numerous relatives and rebel associates to head ministries. Ibrahim Rugova, a moderate Albanian who headed the Democratic League for Kosovo, established a competing interim government.

In December the United Nations negotiated a power-sharing arrangement for running the province until elections could be held, possibly in the second half of 2000. Under that deal, UN Special Representative Kouchner was to serve as governor, heading an interim council. Appointed by UN Secretary General Kofi Annan, Kouchner was well-known internationally as the founder of the aid agency Medicins sans Frontieres (Doctors Without Borders). The leaders of three factions of ethnic Albanians, including Thaci, were to serve as council members, along with one ethnic Serb representative. However, Serb leaders rejected the agreement and boycotted a December 15 signing ceremony. The agreement required Thaci and Rugova to disband their competing governments and instead work within the UN administration. At year's end it was unclear how effective that agreement would be.

Meeting Humanitarian Needs

Nearly a year and a half of war left Kosovo in shambles. For much of 1998 and into the early months of 1999 Serbian security forces burned and bulldozed hundreds of villages inhabited by ethnic Albanians, driving nearly 400,000 people from their homes. And during the eleven weeks of NATO bombing as many as 1 million more ethnic Albanians were forced from their homes—again, most of them by Serbian security forces who destroyed their homes and villages after they left. NATO's bombing also destroyed much of the province's infrastructure, including electrical production, water service, and roads.

On July 26 the United Nations High Commissioner for Refugees released a review of 456 villages affected by the war. The survey estimated that 54 percent of the houses in those villages suffered severe damage or complete destruction. Altogether, officials estimated that about 125,000 homes were damaged in Kosovo. Nearly half of Kosovo's villages were reported to have inadequate water supplies, and the main electrical generating plant for all Kosovo was so antiquated and damaged by the war that power outages were common.

At a donors conference in Brussels on July 28, industrialized nations pledged nearly $2.1 billion in aid for Kosovo. The United States pledged an additional $556 million, an amount provided in a supplemental appropriation approved by Congress in May. Another donors conference in November generated an additional $1 billion in pledges, but many countries were slow to provide the money they promised.

UN agencies were also slow to begin their operations in Kosovo, with the result that thousands of people were left without the help they had been promised by the international community. The most serious problem was shortage of shelter. International agencies promised heated housing units for more than 300,000 Kosovars, but by the onset of winter in November fewer than half those units were in place. Many of the delays were unavoidable, given the cost and logistical difficulties of meeting the massive needs of the war-damaged province. Actions by countries in the region also posed hurdles. On November 4, for example, the government of Macedonia— reportedly angered by Western nations' failures to follow through on promises of aid for that country—began forcing humanitarian aid convoys bound for Kosovo to undergo searches at the border, tying up shipments for days at a time. Bureaucratic infighting among aid agencies also contributed to delays in delivering aid to those most in need.

Some critics warned that the massive infusion of foreign aid had the potential of permanently distorting the Kosovo economy, which historically had been based on subsistence agriculture. Among other things, critics noted that aid agencies were paying Kosovo civilians exceptionally high salaries—by local standards—to serve in support functions, including as translators, drivers, and cooks. Many of those people, the critics said, would be of greater long-term help to their country by returning to their former jobs as teachers, doctors, lawyers, farmers, and other civilian occupations.

Continuing Serbian-Albanian Conflict

One of the chief concerns of international officials in the wake of the war was stemming the desire of Kosovar Albanians for revenge against their

Serbian neighbors. Fearing retribution, thousands of Serbs fled Kosovo at war's end—mirroring, in smaller numbers, the earlier flood of Albanians seeking to escape Serbian security forces. Officials of the United Nations and other agencies pleaded with Kosovar Serbs to return home, and their pleas were echoed by the Serbian government in Belgrade. During a visit to Kosovo in late July, U.S. Secretary of State Madeleine K. Albright said Serbs needed to contribute to a multiethnic society, and she said KFOR "is set up to protect them."

By late November UN officials estimated that 60,000 to 70,000 Serbs remained in Kosovo, compared to a population of more than 200,000 before the outbreak of serious ethnic conflict early in 1998. Nearly all Serbs had left or been forced out of Kosovo's three principal cities (Pristina, Pec, and Prizren) and were concentrated in the north of the province, near the border with Serbia. In effect, Kosovo was becoming partitioned, with its two main ethnic groups separated by the armed guards of KFOR.

Throughout the last half of 1999 there were numerous incidents of attacks on Serbs, the single most brutal of which was the shooting of fourteen Serb farmers in the village of Gracko on July 23. Louise Arbour, the chief prosecutor of the UN war crimes tribunal promised an investigation of that incident, and KFOR on July 29 detained three ethnic Albanians as part of an investigation. In its December report on atrocities in Kosovo the State Department estimated that between 200 and 400 Serbians were killed in the wake of the war.

Human Rights Watch on August 3 published a report detailing atrocities in Kosovo against Serbs and gypsies. Human Rights Watch did not directly accuse the KLA of ordering or approving atrocities, but the organization said the KLA should "take swift and decisive action" to prevent attacks on Serbs by its members.

President Bill Clinton visited Kosovo for the first time on November 23 and pleaded with ethnic Albanians to forgive the Serbs. "You cannot forget the injustice that was done to you," he told several hundred Kosovars in the village of Urosevac. "No one can force you to forgive what was done to you. But you must try." Clinton's plea was met with silence.

Following are excerpts from United Nations Security Council Resolution 1244, adopted June 10, 1999, which established the basis for international peacekeeping and humanitarian aid efforts in Kosovo, a province of the Federal Republic of Yugoslavia:

The Security Council,

Bearing in mind the purposes and principles of the Charter of the United Nations, and the primary responsibility of the Security Council for the maintenance of international peace and security,

Recalling its resolutions 1160 (1998) of 31 March 1998, 1199 (1998) of 23 September 1998, 1203 (1998) of 24 October 1998 and 1239 (1999) of 14 May 1999,

Regretting that there has not been full compliance with the requirements of these resolutions,

Determined to resolve the grave humanitarian situation in Kosovo, Federal Republic of Yugoslavia, and to provide for the safe and free return of all refugees and displaced persons to their homes,

Condemning all acts of violence against the Kosovo population as well as all terrorist acts by any party,

Recalling the statement made by the Secretary-General on 9 April 1999, expressing concern at the humanitarian tragedy taking place in Kosovo,

Reaffirming the right of all refugees and displaced persons to return to their homes in safety,

Recalling the jurisdiction and the mandate of the International Tribunal for the Former Yugoslavia,

Welcoming the general principles on a political solution to the Kosovo crisis adopted on 6 May 1999 (annex 1 to this resolution) and welcoming also the acceptance by the Federal Republic of Yugoslavia of the principles set forth in points 1 to 9 of the paper presented in Belgrade on 2 June 1999 (annex 2 to this resolution), and the Federal Republic of Yugoslavia's agreement to that paper,

Reaffirming the commitment of all Member States to the sovereignty and territorial integrity of the Federal Republic of Yugoslavia and the other States of the region, as set out in the Helsinki Final Act and annex 2,

Reaffirming the call in previous resolutions for substantial autonomy and meaningful self-administration for Kosovo,

Determining that the situation in the region continues to constitute a threat to international peace and security,

Determined to ensure the safety and security of international personnel and the implementation by all concerned of their responsibilities under the present resolution, and acting for these purposes under Chapter VII of the Charter of the United Nations,

1. Decides that a political solution to the Kosovo crisis shall be based on the general principles in annex 1 and as further elaborated in the principles and other required elements in annex 2;

2. Welcomes the acceptance by the Federal Republic of Yugoslavia of the principles and other required elements referred to in paragraph 1 above, and demands the full cooperation of the Federal Republic of Yugoslavia in their rapid implementation;

3. Demands in particular that the Federal Republic of Yugoslavia put an immediate and verifiable end to violence and repression in Kosovo, and begin and complete verifiable phased withdrawal from Kosovo of all military, police and paramilitary forces according to a rapid timetable, with which the deployment of the international security presence in Kosovo will be synchronized;

4. Confirms that after the withdrawal an agreed number of Yugoslav and Serb military and police personnel will be permitted to return to Kosovo to perform the functions in accordance with annex 2;

5. Decides on the deployment in Kosovo, under United Nations auspices, of international civil and security presences, with appropriate equipment and personnel as required, and welcomes the agreement of the Federal Republic of Yugoslavia to such presences;

6. Requests the Secretary-General to appoint, in consultation with the Security Council, a Special Representative to control the implementation of the international civil presence, and further requests the Secretary-General to instruct his Special Representative to coordinate closely with the international security presence to ensure that both presences operate towards the same goals and in a mutually supportive manner;

7. Authorizes Member States and relevant international organizations to establish the international security presence in Kosovo as set out in point 4 of annex 2 with all necessary means to fulfil its responsibilities under paragraph 9 below;

8. Affirms the need for the rapid early deployment of effective international civil and security presences to Kosovo, and demands that the parties cooperate fully in their deployment;

9. Decides that the responsibilities of the international security presence to be deployed and acting in Kosovo will include:

(a) Deterring renewed hostilities, maintaining and where necessary enforcing a ceasefire, and ensuring the withdrawal and preventing the return into Kosovo of Federal and Republic military, police and paramilitary forces, except as provided in point 6 of annex 2;

(b) Demilitarizing the Kosovo Liberation Army (KLA) and other armed Kosovo Albanian groups as required in paragraph 15 below;

(c) Establishing a secure environment in which refugees and displaced persons can return home in safety, the international civil presence can operate, a transitional administration can be established, and humanitarian aid can be delivered;

(d) Ensuring public safety and order until the international civil presence can take responsibility for this task;

(e) Supervising demining until the international civil presence can, as appropriate, take over responsibility for this task;

(f) Supporting, as appropriate, and coordinating closely with the work of the international civil presence;

(g) Conducting border monitoring duties as required;

(h) Ensuring the protection and freedom of movement of itself, the international civil presence, and other international organizations;

10. Authorizes the Secretary-General, with the assistance of relevant international organizations, to establish an international civil presence in Kosovo in order to provide an interim administration for Kosovo under which the people of Kosovo can enjoy substantial autonomy within the Federal Republic of Yugoslavia, and which will provide transitional administration while

establishing and overseeing the development of provisional democratic self-governing institutions to ensure conditions for a peaceful and normal life for all inhabitants of Kosovo;

11. Decides that the main responsibilities of the international civil presence will include:

(a) Promoting the establishment, pending a final settlement, of substantial autonomy and self-government in Kosovo, taking full account of annex 2 and of the Rambouillet accords [a peace agreement signed in March 1999 by Kosovar Albanians but not by the Federal Republic of Yugoslavia];

(b) Performing basic civilian administrative functions where and as long as required;

(c) Organizing and overseeing the development of provisional institutions for democratic and autonomous self-government pending a political settlement, including the holding of elections;

(d) Transferring, as these institutions are established, its administrative responsibilities while overseeing and supporting the consolidation of Kosovo's local provisional institutions and other peace-building activities;

(e) Facilitating a political process designed to determine Kosovo's future status, taking into account the Rambouillet accords;

(f) In a final stage, overseeing the transfer of authority from Kosovo's provisional institutions to institutions established under a political settlement;

(g) Supporting the reconstruction of key infrastructure and other economic reconstruction;

(h) Supporting, in coordination with international humanitarian organizations, humanitarian and disaster relief aid;

(i) Maintaining civil law and order, including establishing local police forces and meanwhile through the deployment of international police personnel to serve in Kosovo;

(j) Protecting and promoting human rights;

(k) Assuring the safe and unimpeded return of all refugees and displaced persons to their homes in Kosovo;

12. Emphasizes the need for coordinated humanitarian relief operations, and for the Federal Republic of Yugoslavia to allow unimpeded access to Kosovo by humanitarian aid organizations and to cooperate with such organizations so as to ensure the fast and effective delivery of international aid;

13. Encourages all Member States and international organizations to contribute to economic and social reconstruction as well as to the safe return of refugees and displaced persons, and emphasizes in this context the importance of convening an international donors' conference, particularly for the purposes set out in paragraph 11 (g) above, at the earliest possible date;

14. Demands full cooperation by all concerned, including the international security presence, with the International Tribunal for the Former Yugoslavia;

15. Demands that the KLA and other armed Kosovo Albanian groups end immediately all offensive actions and comply with the requirements for demil-

itarization as laid down by the head of the international security presence in consultation with the Special Representative of the Secretary-General;

16. Decides that the prohibitions imposed by paragraph 8 of resolution 1160 (1998) shall not apply to arms and related materiel for the use of the international civil and security presences;

17. Welcomes the work in hand in the European Union and other international organizations to develop a comprehensive approach to the economic development and stabilization of the region affected by the Kosovo crisis, including the implementation of a Stability Pact for South Eastern Europe with broad international participation in order to further the promotion of democracy, economic prosperity, stability and regional cooperation;

18. Demands that all States in the region cooperate fully in the implementation of all aspects of this resolution;

19. Decides that the international civil and security presences are established for an initial period of 12 months, to continue thereafter unless the Security Council decides otherwise;

20. Requests the Secretary-General to report to the Council at regular intervals on the implementation of this resolution, including reports from the leaderships of the international civil and security presences, the first reports to be submitted within 30 days of the adoption of this resolution;

21. Decides to remain actively seized of the matter.

Annex 1

Statement by the Chairman on the conclusion of the meeting of the G-8 Foreign Ministers held at the Petersberg Centre on 6 May 1999.

The G-8 Foreign Ministers adopted the following general principles on the political solution to the Kosovo crisis:

- Immediate and verifiable end of violence and repression in Kosovo;
- Withdrawal from Kosovo of military, police and paramilitary forces;
- Deployment in Kosovo of effective international civil and security presences, endorsed and adopted by the United Nations, capable of guaranteeing the achievement of the common objectives;
- Establishment of an interim administration for Kosovo to be decided by the Security Council of the United Nations to ensure conditions for a peaceful and normal life for all inhabitants in Kosovo;
- The safe and free return of all refugees and displaced persons and unimpeded access to Kosovo by humanitarian aid organizations;
- A political process towards the establishment of an interim political framework agreement providing for a substantial self-government for Kosovo, taking full account of the Rambouillet accords and the principles of sovereignty and territorial integrity of the Federal Republic of Yugoslavia and the other countries of the region, and the demilitarization of the KLA;
- Comprehensive approach to the economic development and stabilization of the crisis region.

Annex 2

Agreement should be reached on the following principles to move towards a resolution of the Kosovo crisis:

1. An immediate and verifiable end of violence and repression in Kosovo.

2. Verifiable withdrawal from Kosovo of all military, police and paramilitary forces according to a rapid timetable.

3. Deployment in Kosovo under United Nations auspices of effective international civil and security presences, acting as may be decided under Chapter VII of the Charter, capable of guaranteeing the achievement of common objectives.

4. The international security presence with substantial North Atlantic Treaty Organization participation must be deployed under unified command and control and authorized to establish a safe environment for all people in Kosovo and to facilitate the safe return to their homes of all displaced persons and refugees.

5. Establishment of an interim administration for Kosovo as a part of the international civil presence under which the people of Kosovo can enjoy substantial autonomy within the Federal Republic of Yugoslavia, to be decided by the Security Council of the United Nations. The interim administration to provide transitional administration while establishing and overseeing the development of provisional democratic self-governing institutions to ensure conditions for a peaceful and normal life for all inhabitants in Kosovo.

6. After withdrawal, an agreed number of Yugoslav and Serbian personnel will be permitted to return to perform the following functions:

- Liaison with the international civil mission and the international security presence;
- Marking/clearing minefields;
- Maintaining a presence at Serb patrimonial sites;
- Maintaining a presence at key border crossings.

7. Safe and free return of all refugees and displaced persons under the supervision of the Office of the United Nations High Commissioner for Refugees and unimpeded access to Kosovo by humanitarian aid organizations.

8. A political process towards the establishment of an interim political framework agreement providing for substantial self-government for Kosovo, taking full account of the Rambouillet accords and the principles of sovereignty and territorial integrity of the Federal Republic of Yugoslavia and the other countries of the region, and the demilitarization of UCK. Negotiations between the parties for a settlement should not delay or disrupt the establishment of democratic self-governing institutions.

9. A comprehensive approach to the economic development and stabilization of the crisis region. This will include the implementation of a stability pact for South-Eastern Europe with broad international participation in order to further promotion of democracy, economic prosperity, stability and regional cooperation.

10. Suspension of military activity will require acceptance of the principles set forth above in addition to agreement to other, previously identified, required elements. . . . A military-technical agreement will then be rapidly concluded that would, among other things, specify additional modalities, including the roles and functions of Yugoslav/Serb personnel in Kosovo:

Withdrawal

- Procedures for withdrawals, including the phased, detailed schedule and delineation of a buffer area in Serbia beyond which forces will be withdrawn;

Returning personnel

- Equipment associated with returning personnel;
- Terms of reference for their functional responsibilities;
- Timetable for their return;
- Delineation of their geographical areas of operation;
- Rules governing their relationship to the international security presence and the international civil mission.

MBEKI ON HIS INAUGURATION AS PRESIDENT OF SOUTH AFRICA
June 16, 1999

Nelson Mandela, one of the towering figures of the last half of the twenti-eth century, stepped down as president of South Africa on June 16, 1999. He was succeeded by his deputy, Thabo Mbeki, who had exercised day-to-day supervision of the South African government for most of the previous five years. The smooth transition followed parliamentary elections in which the ruling African National Congress scored an overwhelming victory.

Mandela oversaw the transition of South Africa from a dictatorship of the white minority to a multiracial democracy dominated by the black majority. During his tenure, Mandela had emphasized what he called the "reconciliation" of the races in one of the most racially polarized nations in the world. Mbeki said he would stress the "transformation" of South African society to fulfill the promise of democracy for the millions of impoverished blacks who had suffered under a half-century of white-imposed segregation called "apartheid."

The challenges facing Mbeki were enormous. Although its economy remained the biggest and most prosperous in Africa, South Africa was struggling with the consequences of more than a decade of economic decline. Whites still controlled most of the nation's wealth, but many were increasingly alienated from the new black-led government. Blacks were still waiting for the improvements in education, jobs, infrastructure, and social services they believed were due following the end of apartheid.

Mandela's Legacy

As a leader of the African National Congress, Nelson Mandela spent twenty-seven years in prison for his opposition to apartheid. In 1990, under intense international pressure to end apartheid, the white regime headed by F. W. de Klerk released Mandela from prison, setting in motion a series of dramatic events that led to the nation's first multiracial elections in 1994. The African National Congress easily won the elections, with more than 60 percent of the vote. The first multiracial parliament chose Mandela as South Africa's first black president. De Klerk briefly served as one of Mandela's two deputy presidents; the other deputy was Mbeki. (Mandela release, Historic Documents of 1990, p. 68; elections, Historic Documents of 1994, p. 247)

Mandela proved to be the ideal leader for South Africa in its initial phase of transition from white rule to black leadership. At nearly every crucial point, he stressed the need for reconciliation among all the country's racial groups. Mandela had an uncanny knack for making exactly the right gesture or choice of words to reassure whites that they had a place in the new South Africa and offer renewed hope to blacks. He vigorously opposed moves within the African National Congress to punish all white society for the sins of the white leadership during apartheid. In numerous trips to the world's capitals, Mandela was treated as a heroic symbol of opposition to tyranny. His presence sparked renewed, if modest, international investment in South Africa after years of economic sanctions.

Mandela's government took important first steps to improve the lives of the nation's 31 million black citizens who had been denied all political and economic rights under apartheid. The government built 600,000 new homes and provided telephone lines, electric power, and clean water to several million people.

The pace of change satisfied few in South Africa. Many blacks argued that Mandela's government was not doing enough to improve their lives; they said they had expected a black-led government to move more quickly to lift millions of people out of poverty. Many whites were upset by their sudden loss of political power and feared that Mandela would socialize the economy, stripping whites of their economic prosperity and forcibly transferring the wealth to blacks. Whites also were distressed by the numerous shortcomings of the nation's new black leaders, who were unaccustomed to managing a large country with a complex economy. Public opinion polls during the 1999 election campaign showed that racial attitudes were hardening again, following a brief moment of reconciliation early in Mandela's tenure as president.

Although he may have disappointed the extremes on both sides, Mandela created bargaining room for the compromises necessary for the survival of democracy in a country as diverse as South Africa. Although it was clear that blacks held the final say, at least politically, Mandela recognized that continuing white control of the economy imposed limits on how far and fast changes could be made.

Despite the Mandela government's efforts to improve the lives of blacks, aspects of the country's underlying social ills worsened during the first five years of the postapartheid era. The soaring crime rate was perhaps the most worrisome problem, a manifestation of high unemployment (estimated at upward of 40 percent) and inadequate housing and education for most blacks. Thousands of whites—and a growing number of middle-class blacks—were sealing off their neighborhoods with security fences and armed guards. The crime epidemic was matched by an AIDS (acquired immunodeficiency syndrome) epidemic. By 1999 South Africa had one of the world's fastest-growing rates of infection by HIV (human immunodeficiency virus), the virus that causes AIDS; an estimated one-fourth of its 40 million people were infected. Crime and AIDS were among the leading contributors to a spreading fear among many South Africans of all races was that the country might be slowly disintegrating.

Mandela made no effort to play down the nation's problems and often lectured his fellow citizens on their civic responsibilities. In his last state of the nation address, on February 5, Mandela said: "Quite clearly there is something wrong with a society where freedom is interpreted to mean that teachers or students get to school drunk; warders chase away management and appoint their own friends to lead institutions; striking workers resort to violence and destruction of property; business people lavish money in court cases simply to delay implementation of legislation they do not like; and tax evasion turns individuals into heroes of dinner-table talk." What South Africa needed, he said, was to "infuse itself with a measure of discipline, a work ethic and responsibility for the actions we undertake."

Mbeki's Rise to Power

If Mandela was widely perceived as a noble father-figure striving to keep his unruly South African family in line through persuasion, Mbeki was generally considered a pragmatist who would take a more assertive approach to dealing with the country's problems. Born in 1942, Mbeki was the son of communists who insisted that he receive an education in mission schools. The African National Congress, which was then waging a guerrilla war against the white government, helped to arrange for Mbeki to go into exile in Great Britain, where he attended Sussex University and received a master's degree in economics. In 1963 his father, Govan, was arrested in the same government crackdown on ANC officials that led to Mandela's imprisonment. After he finished his schooling, Thabo Mbeki became an ANC organizer in London and traveled to the Soviet Union for training in guerrilla tactics before joining the ANC headquarters in Lusaka, Zambia. Oliver Tambo, the ANC leader in exile, appointed Mbeki as his chief spokesman and diplomat. Mbeki served as the ANC's contact with the de Klerk government during secret talks in 1989 and 1990 that led to Mandela's release from prison and the initial steps toward the transfer of power from whites to blacks.

When he became president in 1994, Mandela asked Mbeki to be one of his two vice presidents, along with de Klerk. Mbeki quickly took on the role of unofficial prime minister, supervising day-to-day operations of the government while Mandela campaigned for interracial harmony and traveled overseas to promote business investment in South Africa. Throughout Mandela's five-year term, it was clear that Mbeki was his chosen successor. Supporters said Mbeki was an intelligent and efficient administrator with the vision to lead South Africa into a new era of transformation. But some critics said he was too hungry for power and overly sensitive to criticism; they noted that he had been very aggressive in elbowing aside other ANC officials who might have become candidates for the role of Mandela's successor.

Under Mbeki's leadership, the ANC scored an overwhelming victory in the June 3 parliamentary elections, winning 266 of the 400 seats, just one seat short of a two-thirds majority. Some whites had warned of ANC "tyranny" if it gained the two-thirds majority necessary to change the 1994 constitution, but Mbeki said the party had no desire to amend the constitution.

The former National Party, which had imposed apartheid on South Africa during nearly a half-century in power and then renamed itself the New National Party, was the big loser in the 1999 elections. The party won just twenty-eight seats, compared with eighty-two seats in the previous parliament. Its place as the official opposition party was taken by the Democratic Party, a white-led liberal alliance.

The parliament formally chose Mbeki as president on June 14; there were no other candidates. At the inaugural ceremony June 16, Mbeki promised to speed up the pace of change and to improve the lives of millions of South Africans caught in poverty. "As the sun continues to rise to banish the darkness of the long years of colonialism and apartheid, what the new light over our land must show is a nation diligently at work to create a better life for itself," he said. "What it must show is a palpable process of the comprehensive renewal of our country—its rebirth—driven by the enormous talents of all our people, both black and white, and made possible by the knowledge and realization that we share a common destiny, regardless of the shapes of our noses."

Mbeki laid out a detailed plan for his presidency in a speech to the parliament June 25. He said fighting crime would be a top priority, and he announced plans to improve education and training of police officers and to establish an elite unit to combat "national priority crimes," such as corruption and organized crime. Mbeki endorsed the free-market economic policies he inherited from Mandela—policies that were largely Mbeki's handiwork.

Following is the text of the inaugural address of Thabo Mbeki, president of South Africa, given June 16, 1999:

Your Majesties, Your Royal Highnesses, Your Excellencies, President of the Constitutional Court, Chief Justice, Isithwalandwe Nelson Mandela, Distinguished guests, Fellow South Africans,

I am honoured to welcome you all to our seat of government as we carry out the solemn act of the inauguration of the President of our Republic.

I feel greatly privileged that so many of you could travel from all corners of the globe, from everywhere in Africa and from all parts of our country to lend importance and dignity to this occasion.

That sense of privilege, which will stay with us for all time, is intensified by our recognition of the fact that never before have we, as a people, hosted this large a number of high level delegations representing the peoples of the world.

We thank you most sincerely for your presence which itself constitutes a tribute to the millions of our people and a profound statement of hope that all of us will, together, continue to expand the frontiers of human dignity.

For us, as South Africans, this day is as much a Day for the Inauguration of the new government as it is a Day of Salute for a generation that pulled our country out of the abyss and placed it on the pedestal of hope, on which it rests today.

I speak of the generation represented pre-eminently by our outgoing President, Nelson Mandela—the generation of Oliver Tambo, Walter Sisulu, Govan Mbeki, Albertina Sisulu, Ray Alexander and others.

Fortunately, some of these titans are present here today, as they should be. None of us can peer into their hearts to learn what they feel as this infant democracy they brought into the world begins its sixth year of existence.

But this I can say, that we who are their offspring know that we owe to them much of what is humane, noble and beautiful in the thoughts and actions of our people, as they strive to build a better world for themselves.

For throughout their lives, they struggled against everything that was ugly, mean, brutish and degrading of the dignity of all human beings.

And because they did, being prepared to pay the supreme price to uphold good over evil, they planted a legacy among our people which drives all of us constantly to return to the starting point and say—I am my brother's keeper! I am my sister's keeper!

And because we are one another's keepers, we surely must be haunted by the humiliating suffering which continues to afflict millions of our people.

Our nights cannot but be nights of nightmares while millions of our people live in conditions of degrading poverty.

Sleep cannot come easily when children get permanently disabled, both physically and mentally, because of lack of food.

No night can be restful when millions have no jobs, and some are forced to beg, rob and murder to ensure that they and their own do not perish from hunger.

Our minds will continue the restless inquiry to find out how it is possible to have a surfeit of productive wealth in one part of our common globe and intolerable poverty levels elsewhere on that common globe.

There can be no moment of relaxation while the number of those affected by HIV-AIDS continue to expand at an alarming pace.

Our days will remain forever haunted when frightening numbers of the women and children of our country fall victim to rape and other crimes of violence.

Nor can there be peace of mind when the citizens of our country feel they have neither safety nor security because of the terrible deeds of criminals and their gangs.

Our days and our nights will remain forever blemished as long as our people are torn apart and fractured into contending factions by reason of the racial and gender inequalities, which continue to characterise our society.

Neither can peace attend our souls as long as corruption continues to rob the poor of what is theirs and to corrode the value system, which sets humanity apart from the rest of the animal world.

The full meaning of liberation will not be realised until our people are freed both from oppression and from the dehumanising legacy of deprivation we inherited from our past.

What we did in 1994 was to begin the long journey towards the realisation of this goal. When the millions of our people went to the polls 12 days ago, they mandated us to pursue this outcome.

Our country is in that period of time which the seTswana-speaking people of Southern Africa graphically describe as *"mahube a naka tsa kgomo"*—the dawning of the dawn, when only the tips of the horn of the cattle can be seen etched against the morning sky.

As the sun continues to rise to banish the darkness of the long years of colonialism and apartheid, what the new light over our land must show is a nation diligently at work to create a better life for itself.

What it must show is a palpable process of the comprehensive renewal of our country—its rebirth—driven by the enormous talents of all our people, both black and white, and made possible by the knowledge and realisation that we share a common destiny, regardless of the shapes of our noses.

What we will have to see in the rising light is a government that is fully conscious of the fact that it has entered into a contract with the people, to work in partnership with them to build a winning nation.

In practical and measurable ways, we have to keep pace with the rising sun, progressing from despair to hope, away from a brutal past that forever seeks to drag us backwards towards a new tomorrow that speaks of change in a forward direction.

History and circumstance have given us the rare possibility to achieve these objective.

To ensure that we transform the possibility to reality, we will have to nurture the spirit among our people which made it possible for many to describe the transition of 1994 as a miracle—the same spirit which, in many respects, turned this year's election campaign into a festival in celebration of democracy.

As Africans, we are the children of the abyss, who have sustained a backward march for half-a-millennium.

We have been a source for human slaves. Our countries were turned into the patrimony of colonial powers. We have been victim to our own African predators.

If this is not merely the wish being father to the thought, something in the air seems to suggest that we are emerging out of the dreadful centuries which in the practice, and in the ideology and consciousness of some, defined us as sub-human.

As South Africans, whatever the difficulties, we are moving forward in the effort to combine ourselves into one nation of many colours, many cultures and diverse origins.

No longer capable of being falsely defined as a European outpost in Africa, we are an African nation in the complex process simultaneously of formation and renewal.

And in that process, we will seek to educate both the young and ourselves about everything all our forebears did to uphold the torch of freedom.

It is in this spirit that we are, this year, observing the Centenary of the Commencement of the Anglo-Boer War and the 120th Anniversary of the Battle of Isandhlwana.

We will also work to rediscover and claim the African heritage, for the benefit especially of our young generations.

From South Africa to Ethiopia lie strewn ancient fossils which, in their stillness, speak still of the African origins of all humanity.

Recorded history and the material things that time left behind also speak of Africa's historic contribution to the universe of philosophy, the natural sciences, human settlement and organisation and the creative arts.

Being certain that not always were we the children of the abyss, we will do what we have to do to achieve our own Renaissance.

We trust that what we will do will not only better our own condition as a people, but will also make a contribution, however small, to the success of Africa's Renaissance, towards the identification of the century ahead of us as the African Century.

Twenty-three years ago this day, children died in Soweto, Johannesburg in a youth uprising which democratic South Africa honours as our National Youth Day.

As we speak, both our own, as well as international athletes, are competing in our annual Comrades Marathon which, this year, is dedicated to Nelson Mandela.

Our best wishes go to all these, the long distance runners of the Marathon.

Those who complete the course will do so only because they do not, as fatigue sets in, convince themselves that the road ahead is still too long, the inclines too steep, the loneliness impossible to bear and the prize itself of doubtful value.

We too, as the peoples of South Africa and Africa, must together run our own Comrades Marathon, as comrades who are ready to take to the road together, refusing to be discouraged by the recognition that the road is very long, the inclines very steep and that, at times, what we see as the end is but a mirage.

When the race is run, all humanity and ourselves will acknowledge the fact that we only succeeded because we succeeded to believe in our own dreams!

Every year the rains will fall to bless our efforts!

That too is a dream!

But because it is our dream, we are able still to demand of our ancestors—
pula! nala!

STATE DEPARTMENT ON U.S
BOMBING OF CHINESE EMBASSY
June 17, 1999

Relations between the United States and the People's Republic of China—often on a razor's edge because of longstanding conflicts over foreign policy, human rights, and trade issues—suffered a stunning setback in May when U.S. bombers accidentally destroyed the Chinese embassy in Belgrade, Yugoslavia. The embassy was hit May 7, 1999, during the eleven-week air war by NATO allies that forced Yugoslavia to abandon control of the province of Kosovo. Three Chinese journalists were killed and twenty-seven others, most of them embassy staff members, were wounded in the attack.

President Bill Clinton apologized to China for the bombing, which his aides said resulted from a series of mistakes by U.S. intelligence services and military planners. The Chinese government, which opposed the NATO campaign against Yugoslavia, did not fully accept the U.S. explanation. Nevertheless, the two countries reached agreements under which the United States would pay $4.5 million in compensation for the victims of the bombing and $28 million in compensation for the embassy in Belgrade, and China would pay the United States $2.87 million to compensate for damage to U.S. diplomatic posts in China during anti-American rioting following the Belgrade bombing. (Kosovo war, p. 134)

The embassy bombing occurred within weeks of the release of a congressional committee report denouncing China's "theft" of important information about U.S. nuclear weapons. The two events combined for a particularly sour period in relations between Washington and Beijing. But leaders in both capitals worked through the year to repair the damage, and on November 15 U.S. and Chinese trade representatives signed a landmark agreement intended to resolve significant trade disputes. Over the long term, the trade accord was likely to have substantially more impact on U.S.-China relations than either the embassy bombing incident or the furor over nuclear espionage. (Nuclear weapons report, p. 235; U.S.-China trade agreement, p. 724)

The Embassy Bombing and Aftermath

Early in the morning of May 7, B-2 "Stealth" bombers based at Whiteman Air Force Base in Missouri dropped satellite-guided bombs on several targets in downtown Belgrade, during the seventh week of the NATO air war against Yugoslavia. One of the targets was intended to be the headquarters of the Federal Directorate for Supply and Procurement, later described by U.S. officials as the Yugoslav military procurement agency. Unbeknownst to the B-2 crew that dropped five bombs on that target, the building they bombed had been used as the Chinese embassy for nearly two years. The agency that was supposed to be the bombing target actually was located about 300 yards away on the same street.

Three Chinese journalists living in the embassy building were killed and twenty-seven people in the building at the time were injured. The building was so heavily damaged that it was considered destroyed.

U.S. officials in Washington and NATO officials in Brussels immediately said the bombing had been a mistake, and they identified the intended target. "NATO did not intentionally target the Chinese embassy in Belgrade last night," NATO spokesman Jamie Shea said. "The wrong building was attacked. This was a terrible accident." Allied officials promised a full investigation into the matter. President Clinton on May 8 called the bombing a "tragic mistake" and said he was offering "my sincere regret and my condolences to both the leaders and the people of China."

Such expressions of regret did little to satisfy Chinese leaders, who organized protest demonstrations at the U.S. embassy in Beijing, beginning May 8. The largest demonstration was on May 9, when thousands of people massed outside the embassy compound and shouted slogans and carried anti-American signs. Many of the demonstrators threw stones, eggs, and paint-filled balloons at the embassy. By day's end many of the building's windows had been broken, and the facade was splattered with red and blue paint. Protesters also attacked the British embassy but caused less damage there. Anti-American protests occurred in other Chinese cities, including Chengdu, where the home of the U.S. consul general was set on fire.

Speaking on television that night, Chinese vice president Hu Jintao supported the demonstrations but urged moderation. The Chinese government announced on May 9 that it was suspending some of its discussions with the United States, including meetings between senior military officials, to protest the embassy bombing.

Mass protests at the American embassy in Beijing continued through May 11, by which time police had developed a system of escorting groups of protesters to the embassy and allowing them set periods of time to shout slogans and throw stones and pieces of concrete at the building. On May 11 Chinese foreign minister Tang Jiaxuan telephoned U.S. ambassador James Sasser—who was trapped inside the embassy—with four demands of the United States: an official apology for the embassy bombing, a complete investigation, prompt disclosure of the results of the investigation, and severe punishment of "those responsible for the attack." The anti-American demonstrations tapered off on May 12, but the war of words emanating from Beijing continued for several weeks.

The U.S. Explanation

Six weeks after the bombing, Undersecretary of State Thomas R. Pickering traveled to Beijing, with an entourage of senior diplomatic and security officials, to explain the results of the official U.S. investigation into the embassy bombing. In a private meeting with Foreign Minister Tang and other high-level Chinese officials, Pickering read from a prepared statement that detailed how "a series of errors and omissions" led to the inclusion of the Chinese embassy building on the list of bombing targets in Belgrade.

Pickering said the Central Intelligence Agency chose the Yugoslav arms agency as a potential target and determined its location by its street address. Unfortunately, Pickering said, none of the maps or any other information sources consulted by U.S. officials indicated that the building presumed to house the arms agency actually was the Chinese embassy. The selection of targets in Belgrade underwent several reviews, both in Washington and at NATO military headquarters in Europe—but none of the reviews challenged the underlying, inaccurate information about the location of the arms agency. During the review process, Pickering said, inaccurate information "took on the mantle of fact."

Many U.S. and NATO diplomats almost certainly knew the location of the Chinese embassy, but they were not consulted in the process of selecting and validating targets, Pickering stated. One unnamed intelligence officer had expressed doubts about whether the arms agency was located in the targeted building, but Pickering said the officer was unable to communicate his concerns to high-level officials in time to avert the mistaken bombing.

Pickering told his Chinese counterparts that the incident had pointed out flaws in the process of selecting military targets and in verifying the accuracy of those selections. As a result, he said, the U.S. government was taking "corrective actions to prevent mistakes like this from happening in the future." As an example, he said that intelligence and military agencies were updating their databases, especially in reference to the location of "nostrike" facilities such as embassies, hospitals, and schools.

In perhaps the most diplomatically sensitive portion of his presentation, Pickering sought to counter speculation within China that the United States had deliberately targeted the embassy because of Beijing's opposition to the NATO air campaign against Yugoslavia. President Clinton, who had a "strong personal commitment" to improving U.S.-Chinese relations, would never have approved an attack on the embassy, Pickering said. Moreover, it "would have made absolutely no sense" to deliberately undertake such a provocative action at a time when Washington was trying to win Chinese support for a diplomatic solution to the crisis in Kosovo. Because China was one of five permanent United Nations Security Council mem-

bers holding a veto over any proposed settlement that came before the UN, Pickering said, "we knew we would need China's support in this matter. Bombing your embassy was hardly the way to persuade you to help."

Pickering's statement was an extraordinary confession by the U.S. government of flawed work by its intelligence and military agencies. Even so, the Chinese government rejected the explanation as "unconvincing" and demanded even more information from the United States. The Communist Party newspaper, the People's Daily, *said Pickering's "inadequate explanation only shows that the United States lacks any sincerity."*

Subsequent Negotiations

Despite Chinese dissatisfaction with the official U.S. explanation, negotiations between the two countries continued. On July 25, Secretary of State Madeleine K. Albright and Chinese foreign minister Tang met over lunch in Singapore. Albright said the result was "an easing of tensions."

Five days later, on July 30, David Andrews, a State Department legal adviser, reached an agreement with his Chinese counterparts under which the United States would pay $4.5 million in compensation for the victims of the mistaken bombing. Andrews said the Chinese government would determine how the money was to be distributed among the families of the three journalists who were killed and the twenty-seven people who were wounded.

On December 16 Andrews reached a follow-up agreement in Beijing providing for the two nations to reimburse each other for damage to their respective embassies. The United States would pay China $28 million to compensate for damage to the embassy in Belgrade. That amount was to be included in the fiscal 2001 State Department budget, requiring congressional approval. In turn, China would pay the United States $2.87 million for damage caused the embassy in Beijing and other diplomatic missions during the anti-American protests in mid-May. "I hope this day marks the beginning of a more positive trend in U.S.-China relations," Andrews told reporters in announcing the agreement.

> *Following are excerpts from a statement given June 17, 1999, by U.S. Undersecretary of State Thomas R. Pickering to senior Chinese diplomatic officials in Beijing offering an explanation for the mistaken bombing May 7, 1999, of the Chinese embassy in Belgrade, Yugoslavia; the State Department released the text of the statement July 6, 1999:*

I am here at the instruction of President Clinton as his personal envoy. He has asked me to deliver a letter from him to President Jiang [Zemin]; to present the official report of our investigation into the accidental bombing of your embassy in Belgrade; and to answer any questions you may have about the report. My remarks and comments will constitute a full report to you.

The attack was a mistake. Our examination explains how a series of errors and omissions led to that mistake. Let me emphasize: no one targeted the Chinese Embassy. No one, at any stage in the process, realized that our bombs were aimed at the Chinese Embassy.

It is entirely appropriate that we provide you with an explanation of how this awful tragedy occurred. The U.S. government recognizes our responsibility to provide a full explanation. We have undertaken our own internal investigation into this matter and want to share our results with you.

I have brought with me a high-level delegation of representatives from the White House, Department of State, Department of Defense, and the Intelligence Community.

The delegation includes officials who have been directly involved in the investigation and the preparation of the report. Let me introduce them. . . .

My intention is to provide information and explanation as we proceed. We will also show you some charts and photos to help illustrate some of the basic results of our investigation. After that, we will turn to providing answers to your questions.

Introduction

First let me express the heartfelt condolences of the American people and government to the families of the three Chinese journalists who died in the bombing of your Embassy in Belgrade on May 7th. Let me convey also our sympathy for the 20 Embassy staff members who were injured. We realize that no amount of explanation will make up for the personal tragedy suffered by these individuals and their loved ones.

I am here, as you know, to provide the explanation and the investigation report in fulfillment of President Clinton's comments in his telephone conversation and letters to President Jiang.

I want to underline that this report has been prepared by senior U.S. Government officials from our intelligence and military organizations.

The report shows that multiple factors and errors in several parts of the U.S. Government were responsible for the mistaken bombing. Beginning as early as 1997, mistakes in different parts of our government contributed to this tragic set of errors; and our operational procedures failed to catch these errors.

The CIA and Defense Department are continuing to interview individuals in the field who were involved in various aspects of the decisions that led to the bombing. Because the NATO air campaign has only just concluded, it has not been possible to debrief fully every person involved and to reach conclusions regarding responsibility for mistakes that led to the bombing. The Director of Central Intelligence, who is also Chief of the Intelligence Community, has directed the conduct of an accountability review which will go into the issue of responsibility, the appropriate results of which will be made available.

The bombing resulted from three basic failures. First, the technique used to locate the intended target—the headquarters of the Yugoslav Federal

Directorate for Supply and Procurement (FDSP)—was severely flawed. Second, none of the military or intelligence databases used to verify target information contained the correct location of the Chinese Embassy. Third, nowhere in the target review process was either of the first two mistakes detected. No one who might have known that the targeted building was not the FDSP headquarters—but was in fact the Chinese Embassy—was ever consulted.

To help better understand the circumstances which led to the mistaken bombing, let me offer a chronology of events.

Mistargeting

The first major error stemmed from mislocating the intended target.

In March of this year, officers at the Central Intelligence Agency began considering the Federal Directorate for Supply and Procurement (FDSP) as a potential target for NATO Allied Force strike operations. The FDSP, because of its role in military procurement, was a legitimate target.

We had a street address of the FDSP headquarters: "Bulevar Umetnosti 2" in New Belgrade. But military forces require precise geographic coordinates to conduct an attack with precision munitions. During a mid-April selection and designation of the target, three maps were used in an attempt to locate physically the address of the FDSP headquarters: two local commercial maps from 1996 and 1989, and the then most recent U.S. government map produced in 1997.

None of these maps had any reference to the FDSP building. And none accurately identified the current location of the Chinese Embassy.

As you can see, the 1997 U.S. Government city map shows the Embassy in Old Belgrade and depicts an unidentified building at the actual Embassy site in New Belgrade. The 1996 commercial map made no reference to the Embassy at either location. The 1989 map predated the Embassy's move.

Please keep in mind that the location of the Chinese Embassy was not a question that anyone would have asked when assembling this particular target package since it was not connected in any way to our intent to strike the FDSP headquarters.

In an effort to locate the FDSP building at Bulevar Umetnosti 2, an intelligence officer in Washington used land navigation techniques taught by the U.S. military to locate distant or inaccessible points and objects. These techniques—which involve the comparison of addresses from one street to another—can be used for general geographic location, but are totally inappropriate for precision targeting, and were used uniquely in this case. Using this process, the individual mistakenly determined that the building which we now know to be the Chinese Embassy was the FDSP headquarters. To use these techniques for targeting purposes was a serious mistake. The true location of the FDSP headquarters was some 300 meters away from the Chinese Embassy. This flaw in the address location process went undetected by all the others who evaluated the FDSP as a military target.

Because this first error was so fundamental, let me walk you through it.

The method for determining the location of the intended target—the FDSP—was seriously flawed. It was not based on certain knowledge of the numbering sequence for addresses on the Bulevar Umetnosti. Rather, our attempts to determine the location of the building employed a method that is used in the field by the Army, but is not normally used for aerial targeting purposes. The system will provide an approximation of location, but cannot guarantee an accurate geographic fix.

A 1997 National Imaging and Mapping Agency (NIMA) map was first used to display the grid pattern of the streets in New Belgrade. Next, in order to identify locations to use as reference points, they identified and drew on the NIMA map to locate the Hyatt Hotel, the Intercontinental Hotel, and the Serbian Socialist Party Headquarters. Each of these buildings—which were clearly labeled on the maps being used—were approximately one mile east of Bulevar Umetnosti. Using these locations and their street addresses as reference points, parallel lines were drawn that intersected both the known addresses and Bulevar Umetnosti. In what proved to be a fundamental error, those same numbers were then applied to locations on Bulevar Umetnosti, assuming that streets were numbered in the same fashion along parallel streets. The effectiveness of this method depends on the numbering system being the same on parallel streets, that the numbers are odd and even on the same sides of the street and that the street numbers are used in the same parallel sequence even if the street names change. Unfortunately, a number of these assumptions were wrong.

Using this approximation method, your embassy building was designated as the target when in fact the Embassy was located on a small side street at some distance on Bulevar Umetnosti from where the intended target was actually located at number 2 Bulevar Umetnosti. Let me show you a satellite photograph and some maps to illustrate the method and the error it produced.

The identification of the building that actually was the Chinese Embassy as the FDSP building subsequently and in error took on the mantle of fact. It was not questioned nor reviewed up the chain of command. This was in part because everyone involved had, as a result of so many previously correct locations, assumed generally high confidence in our procedures to locate, check and verify such analytical facts. In this particular, and singular, case, our system clearly failed. In part it failed also because every established procedure in the review of this target was not followed.

Maps and satellite imagery were also analyzed to look for any possible collateral damage issues near the target. There was no indication that the targeted building was an embassy—no flags, no seals, no clear markings showed up. There were no collateral damage issues in the vicinity.

Flawed Databases

The second major error stemmed from flawed databases.

The incorrect location of the FDSP building was then fed into several U.S. databases to determine whether any diplomatic or other facilities off-limits to targeting were nearby. We do our best to avoid damage to sensitive facilities such as embassies, hospitals, schools and places of worship. Viewed from space, there was no indication that the office building being targeted was an embassy. On the satellite imagery available to U.S., there were no flags, seals, or other markings to indicate that the building was an embassy. And unfortunately, in this instance none of the database sources that were checked correctly identified the targeted building as the Chinese Embassy.

Multiple databases within the Intelligence Community and the Department of Defense all reflected the Embassy in its pre-1996 location in Old Belgrade. Despite the fact that U.S. officials had visited the Embassy on a number of occasions in recent years the new location was never entered into intelligence or military targeting databases. If the databases had accurately reflected the current location of the Embassy, the mistaken identification of the FDSP building would have been recognized and corrected.

Why was the Chinese Embassy not correctly located? It is important to understand that our ability to verify the location of fixed targets depends heavily on the accuracy of the databases, and the databases in this case were wrong. Further, it is difficult to keep current databases for cities around the globe. In general, diplomatic facilities have been given relatively little attention in our efforts to update our databases because such facilities are not targets. Military targets are the top priority in these databases because of the danger they pose to our own forces. Unfortunately, locations where strikes should be avoided had lower priority and our databases contained errors, notably in the failure to include the new location of the Embassy of China.

Now, this is an important point, so let me expand upon it.

The databases which contained information about the physical location of organizations in Belgrade—including the so-called "no hit list" of buildings that should not be targeted—were faulty.

Although database maintenance is one the basic elements of our intelligence efforts, it has been routinely accorded low priority.

The target and "no-hit" databases were not independently constructed. Outdated information that placed the Chinese Embassy in its former location in Old Belgrade was not updated when the Embassy moved. Because various databases were not independently constructed, this wrong information was duplicated. So when target information was checked against the no-hit list, the error was not detected.

Many U.S. and other NATO diplomats must have visited the new building. The address was in the phone book, the diplomatic list and perhaps other sources, including Yugoslav maps. Certainly, many citizens and officials of the United States were aware of the correct location of the Chinese Embassy in Belgrade. However, in error, their knowledge was not recorded in any of the military or intelligence databases used in the targeting process.

In addition, the correct location of the Chinese Embassy was not known to targeteers or NATO commanders because we were not, in fact, looking for it. Since your Embassy was not a target, and because we were unaware of any diplomatic or civilian facilities in the immediate vicinity of the presumed

311

FDSP building, no effort was made to verify or precisely locate the where-abouts of your Embassy.

We have subsequently found some maps which show the correct current location of the Chinese Embassy, although there are others, including some produced in recent years by the Yugoslav government, which do not.

Since the incident, the United States has updated its databases to show the best known location of diplomatic facilities. The databases will be updated as new information becomes available. Maps are out of date almost as soon as they are printed. Databases can and should be maintained to be effective.

Faulty Checks

The third problem was faulty checks.

Once the target was proposed, the focus of the review was on the military value of the target, how best to attack it, and the issue of collateral damage. No one in any of the succeeding reviews questioned the accuracy of the loca-tion. The formal recommendation of the FDSP target was forwarded in late April to military staffs both in the U.S. and Europe, who were responsible for reviewing and identifying targets for Operation Allied Force. Maps and satel-lite imagery were analyzed to look for any possible collateral damage con-cerns near the target. We conducted a target review in Europe, and again, no significant risks to civilian or diplomatic facilities were uncovered.

Following submission by the European Command for approval, the target package mistakenly received no additional examination outside of the Defense Department. It did go through additional review at the Pentagon, but this review found nothing different from the review that took place in Europe. There were no known collateral damage concerns. From that point on the building incorrectly identified as an FDSP facility was included on a list of potential Allied Force strike targets.

Some of our employees knew the location of the new Chinese Embassy. But keep in mind that we were not looking for it, since the database with the old location was assumed to be correct. None of these individuals was con-sulted as the target was reviewed and, as a result, we lost any opportunity to learn that the building targeted was the new Chinese Embassy. We have also found one report from 1997 which gave the correct address of the Chinese Embassy, but unfortunately the correct address was not entered into the data-base.

To further explain: Once the wrong target was selected, the system of checks that NATO and U.S. command forces had in place to catch target errors did not reveal the mistake. The database reviews conducted by the European Command (EUCOM) were limited to validating the target data sheet coordinates with the information put into the database by NIMA ana-lysts. Such a circular process could not uncover the original error and exposes our susceptibility to a single point of database failure.

There has been much press coverage of the fact that the U.S. and NATO relied on out-of-date maps to check targets. In fact, since any physical map can quickly become out of date, the key question is one of accurate databases. These were not properly maintained and did not catch the error. Furthermore, persons familiar with the layout of the city of Belgrade were not consulted in the construction of the target and no-hit databases. They were also not involved in a review of this target. This points up a flaw in our procedures.

The only question about the target information was raised by an intelligence officer who had doubts as to whether the building targeted was in fact the FDSP headquarters or might be some other unidentified building. At no time was there any suspicion that the building might be an embassy. This question was not raised to senior levels and the strike went ahead.

Let me explain further this attempt by an intelligence officer to question the reliability of the target information related to the FDSP. There was information that suggested a discrepancy between the selected target and the actual location of the FDSP. There was no information that the target location was the Chinese Embassy, only that it was perhaps the wrong building. However, there was a series of frustrating miscommunications—missed phone calls and lack of follow-up—which led to these doubts not being aired at a command level in time to stop the attack. (The officer had doubts early on in the process because of his own knowledge about the location of the FDSP building; attempted to check with working-level contacts; was continuing to check when the bombing happened; and was not able to communicate his suspicions to senior officers.)

The Bombing

The air strike then proceeded as planned on May 7 without any of the mistakes having been detected or doubts about the reliability of the target information having been addressed.

At 2146 Zulu (about midnight local time in Belgrade) on 7 May 1999 one of the fleet of B-2 bombers from Whiteman Air Force Base (AFB) in Missouri dropped 5 Joint Direct Attack Munitions (JDAM) 2000 lb. GPS-guided bombs on the target designated as the FDSP building but which was, in fact, the Chinese Embassy in Belgrade. All B-2 strikes on Yugoslavia were flown from Whiteman AFB. The bombs were Global Positioning System (GPS) guided weapons and operate in all weather and at night using a satellite-based navigation system of a high order of accuracy.

The air crews carried out their mission as planned. They had no idea they were in fact bombing the Chinese Embassy. As a result, it is obvious that they bear no responsibility for this failure; the problem, as I have outlined, occurred earlier.

They had no way of seeing any identifying markers that would show the building was an embassy. A flag in front of the building or any such features would not be discernible at night and at the speeds and altitudes at which our planes fly.

No other buildings in the immediate vicinity were hit. Our weapons hit the target they were aimed at. Unfortunately, we did not realize the true nature of the target.

To Review

In summary, there were several crucial errors which led to the Chinese Embassy being struck.

There was an error in locating the target. The approach used to attempt to locate the FDSP building was severely flawed.

All sources of information used to prevent precisely this type of accident were either inaccurate or incomplete.

The review process did not catch the locational error and did not consult any material or any person which could have provided correct information.

The United States is, as I speak, continuing to conduct an in-depth review of this tragic accident. Based on our initial findings, it is clear that this terrible mistake occurred not because of just one organization, or because of any one individual.

There was in the immediate aftermath of the bombing some confusion as to what had happened and some of our early public statements were confused and contradictory. To summarize clearly and precisely: the attack on the PRC [People's Republic of China] Embassy was the result of a series of errors that led to the destruction of the PRC Embassy instead of the Serb military target that was intended. The use of a map containing an error—the inaccurate location of the Chinese Embassy—contributed to the tragic mistake—but this was not due solely to a "map error."

What went wrong was, first and foremost, that the approach used to locate the Bulevar Umetnosti 2, the address of the FDSP, was severely flawed.

Second, the databases used to check and prevent this type of targeting error were also inaccurate, incomplete, and not fully independent.

And third, the target review process did not detect the first two mistakes, nor did it involve people and information that could have provided additional data to correct or detect these errors.

As the President has already expressed, we are deeply sorry that we made these tragic errors.

Following the accident, the President of the United States and the Secretary General of NATO separately expressed to China's leaders their sincere apologies for the mistaken attack on the embassy and their sympathy to the families of those who died and to the injured.

Our government has also undertaken corrective actions to prevent mistakes like this from happening in the future.

New updated city maps have been published detailing locations of diplomatic sites and other "no-strike" facilities in and around Belgrade. Additionally, databases are being updated as changes occur. We rely on these databases for our most current information, because maps themselves are inevitably out of date the day or the week they are published.

Intelligence and Defense organizations have strengthened their internal mechanisms and procedures for selecting and verifying targets, and have placed new priority on keeping our databases current.

All U.S. Government sources will be required to report whenever foreign embassies move or are established. This information will then be forwarded and incorporated into our intelligence and military databases.

The U.S. Government will seek direct contact with other governments and interested organizations and persons to obtain their assistance in identifying and locating facilities and places of interest or concern.

And as I noted earlier, we are continuing our internal reviews of the causes of the accident, and when these reviews are completed, we will determine whether any disciplinary action is called for.

U.S. Intentions

I would like now to address various speculative theories that appear to be held by some people in China.

We have heard that many people believe that our attack on your Embassy was intentional.

Clearly the United States had absolutely no reason to want to attack your protected embassy facility. Any such decision to bomb an Embassy would have been contrary to U.S. doctrine and practice and against international standards of behavior and established international accords. No such decision was ever proposed or indeed made.

Bombing the Chinese Embassy also would have been completely antithetical to President Clinton's strong personal commitment to strengthening the relationship between the United States and China; he has defended this relationship and our engagement policy in the face of vociferous domestic criticism. It is not imaginable that President Clinton would make such a decision.

Moreover, bombing the Chinese Embassy in Belgrade would have made absolutely no sense in terms of our policy objectives in Kosovo. The objective of the NATO bombing campaign was to diminish and degrade the capacity of the Yugoslav government and military for repression in Kosovo. The Embassy of China played no role in that set of activities. It had always been the intention of the U.S. and NATO to bring the Kosovo effort to conclusion through diplomatic efforts, including of the G-8 and in the UN Security Council.

The accidental bombing of your Embassy not only intensified international criticism of the NATO bombing campaign, it also had negative effects on our diplomatic efforts, and affected in a deeply negative fashion China's attitude and policies toward our effort in Yugoslavia.

In particular, as Secretary Albright told Premier Zhu in April, we always expected that China, as a permanent member of the UN Security Council, would need to be a part of the resolution of the Kosovo crisis. We knew we would need China's support in this matter. Bombing your Embassy was hardly the way to persuade you to help.

Thus, the bombing was contrary to two critically important U.S. foreign policy goals: the further development of U.S.-China relations and the resolution of the Kosovo situation.

I also have heard that some people in China subscribe to the theory that the bombing was caused by one or several individuals working in our government who conspired to subvert U.S.-China relations or who may have concluded that China was too friendly to Belgrade or that the Embassy was playing some role in assisting Belgrade.

We have found no evidence of an unauthorized conspiracy to attack the Chinese Embassy, for any reason whatsoever, or of any "rogue element" within the U.S. Government. The errors we have identified as producing the accident took place in three separate and independent areas. There was a series of three separate sets of events, some of which affecting the databases occurred as far back as 1997, when no one could have predicted this present set of circumstances. It is just not conceivable, given the circumstances and errors committed, that the attack could have been brought about by a conspiracy or by "rogue elements."

Science has taught us that a direct explanation, backed up by full knowledge of facts obtained through a careful investigation, is always preferable to speculation and far fetched, convoluted or contrived theories with little or no factual backing.

In this tragic case, the facts show a series of errors: that the target was mislocated; the databases designed to catch mistakes were inaccurate and incomplete; and none of the reviews uncovered either of the first two errors.

Compensation

The bombing of the embassy in Belgrade was a tragic accident occurring during a time of ongoing hostilities in Yugoslavia. While the action was completely unintended, the United States and NATO nevertheless recognize that it was the result of a set of errors which led to the embassy being mistakenly targeted.

In view of these circumstances, and recognizing the special status of the diplomatic personnel who were affected, the United States wishes to offer immediate *ex gratia* payments to those individuals who were injured in the bombing and to the families of those killed, based on current experience internationally for the scale of such payments.

I have asked Ambassador Sasser to discuss the particulars of this offer on our part with you in the next few days.

As for the damage to the embassy property in Belgrade, this is clearly a more complicated question. There is also the question of damage suffered by U.S. diplomatic and consular facilities in China in early May due to attacks by demonstrators.

Because of their complexity, these latter issues will need to be examined with some care. We believe they too can be discussed through diplomatic channels and are ready to do so at a mutually suitable time.

SUPREME COURT ON THE
DEFINITION OF DISABILITY
June 22, 1999

In a series of rulings in 1999 the Supreme Court sharply restricted the number of Americans defined as disabled under the Americans with Disabilities Act (ADA) of 1990 and then reinforced the federal protections barring discrimination against those who fell within the definition of disabled. In a related development, Congress passed and President Bill Clinton signed legislation that would allow certain low-income people to retain their Medicare or Medicaid benefits when they found employment.

The ADA barred discrimination in employment, public services, and public accommodations against people with disabilities that "substantially impaired" their ability to perform "major life activities." Since the ADA's enactment in 1990, more than 100,000 complaints had been filed with the Equal Employment Opportunity Commission under the act, about half of which were dismissed as groundless. Employers said the law was unclear about exactly who the ADA was intended to cover, while advocates for the disabled sought the broadest possible coverage. The first case testing the scope of the ADA did not reach the Supreme Court until 1998. Then, in what many interpreted as an expansive ruling, a divided Court held that people with HIV (human immunodeficiency virus), the virus that causes AIDS (acquired immunodeficiency syndrome), may be protected from discrimination under the ADA even though they showed no outward symptoms of the disease. (HIV infection as a disability, Historic Documents of 1998, p. 378)

The rulings in 1999 further delineated both the definition of disability under the law and the scope of the protections afforded to those who fell within that definition. In three cases decided June 22, the Court ruled that people with physical disabilities who could function normally with medicine or corrective devices, such as glasses or hearing aids, could not typically be considered "disabled" under the federal disability law and were therefore not entitled to its protections against discrimination. The decisions were likely to affect millions of Americans with a wide range of rela-

tively common impairments, from diabetes and high blood pressure, to vision and hearing problems, to some forms of depression or anxiety. In a separate decision handed down the same day, the Court ruled that the ADA's protection against discrimination by public agencies required states to move mentally disturbed people from state psychiatric hospitals to community homes under certain conditions. Earlier in the year, the Court ruled that a second federal law, the Individuals with Disabilities Education Act, required school districts to pay for the special needs of disabled students so long as those needs could be provided by someone other than a doctor.

Defining Disability

The three cases seeking a definition of disability all involved people with common physical impairments that were correctable for most normal activities but not enough to meet the minimum standards set for the jobs they were seeking. The leading case, Sutton v. United Air Lines, *involved twin sisters with severe myopia that was correctable to 20/20. The sisters, both licensed pilots, sued under the ADA after United Air Lines turned them down for jobs as pilots because their uncorrected vision did not meet United's minimum requirements.*

In agreeing with the lower courts that correctable disabilities did not automatically entitle a person to the ADA's protections, the seven-justice majority in Sutton *said it was "apparent" from "looking at the act as a whole" that the effects of correcting or mitigating measures must be taken into account when determining whether a person was "substantially limited" in a major life activity and therefore disabled under the meaning of the ADA. Writing for the majority, Justice Sandra Day O'Connor said the law was "properly read as requiring that a person be presently—not potentially or hypothetically—substantially limited in order to demonstrate a disability." A disability, she added, existed under the ADA "only where an impairment 'substantially limits' a major life activity, not where it 'might,' 'could,' or 'would' be substantially limiting if mitigating measures were not taken."*

O'Connor also noted that the text of the ADA stated that "some 43 million Americans have one or more physical or mental disabilities." Although the source of that number was uncertain, O'Connor said that Congress could not have meant to include all the people who wore glasses or had some other correctable problem because the number then would have been closer to 160 million. "The 43 million figure reflects an understanding that those whose impairments are largely corrected by medication or other devices are not 'disabled' within the meaning" of the ADA, she said.

O'Connor observed that even with corrective medication or devices, a person might still be considered disabled under the act. The sisters, however, also failed to show that they met either of the other two tests required, namely, that they had been substantially limited in a major life activity or that the airline had regarded them as being disabled. O'Connor was joined by Chief Justice William H. Rehnquist and Justices Antonin Scalia,

Anthony M. Kennedy, David H. Souter, Clarence Thomas, and Ruth Bader Ginsburg.

In dissent Justices John Paul Stevens and Stephen Breyer said that "to be faithful to the remedial purpose of the act, we should give it a generous, rather than a miserly, construction." Stevens noted that since the purpose of the act was to bar job discrimination against people with disabilities, "it is especially ironic to deny protection for persons with substantially limiting impairments that, when corrected, render them fully able and employable."

*The two other cases involved a man with high blood pressure, who was able to work as a mechanic but even with medication was unable to meet minimum federal standards for driving a truck (*Murphy v. United Parcel Service*); and a truck driver, blind in one eye, who saw adequately for most purposes but who was fired from his job after he failed a vision test because he could not meet federal standards for a commercial driver even with corrective lenses (*Kirkingburg v. Albertson's*).*

Employers and employer organizations were relieved by the majority's interpretation of disability. "The great fear was a dramatic expansion in lawsuits, with a lot of people without clearly defined disabilities clearly empowered to seek legal relief," said Stephen Bokat, the general counsel for the United States Chamber of Commerce. "That was very, very scary for employers." But advocates for the disabled were appalled by the rulings. Chai Feldblum, a professor at Georgetown University Law School and one of the drafters of the ADA legislation, said the decisions "create the absurd result of a person being disabled enough to be fired from a job, but not disabled enough to challenge the firing." Senator Tom Harkin, D-Iowa, who was a chief sponsor of the ADA legislation, lamented that he did not "know how many people with disabilities are going to be denied jobs before people recognize the wrongness of this decision."

Protecting the Disabled

Advocates for the disabled found a great deal more to celebrate in the Court's ruling in a fourth case handed down June 22. At issue was a regulation promulgated under the ADA that required public services to be offered "in the most integrated setting appropriate to the needs" of people with disabilities. The case, Olmstead v. L.C., *was brought on behalf of two women who suffered from mental retardation and other mental disorders and who sought to be moved from a large state psychiatric hospital in Georgia into a smaller, community-based home. Their doctors had said the more homelike setting would be appropriate both medically and socially. The available homes had long waiting lists, however, and the state of Georgia argued that the regulation exceeded the scope of the ADA, and that the failure to move the women into smaller homes was due to fiscal constraints, not discrimination.*

In ruling against the state, the Court, in an opinion written by Justice Ginsburg, said that keeping the mentally ill in a hospital did in fact

*amount to illegal discrimination "when the state's treatment professionals
have determined that community placement is appropriate, the transfer
from institutional care to a less restrictive setting is not opposed by the
affected individual, and the placement can be reasonably accommodated,
taking into account the resources available to the state." Five justices—
Stevens, O'Connor, Kennedy, Souter, and Breyer—joined Ginsburg in the
judgment and various parts of her opinion. Chief Justice Rehnquist and
Justices Scalia and Thomas dissented, arguing that the majority's definition of discrimination was overly broad and that the Court was wrongly
imposing federal standards on the states.*

*"Olmstead is huge," said one disability rights advocate after the decision
was announced. "The Court has said that unjustified isolation equals prohibited discrimination under the ADA, and we couldn't be happier about
that."*

Continuing Insurance Coverage

*Disability rights activists were also pleased with federal legislation
passed in 1999 that would allow individuals receiving Social Security
Disability Insurance and Supplemental Security Income (SSI) to retain
their Medicare or Medicaid health benefits if they returned to work. Many
of the 8 million people on the federal disability rolls were too impaired to
work, but many others were hesitant to take advantage of the opportunities for work offered by computers and other technologies for fear of losing
their health benefits. The legislation (PL 106–170) also authorized the
states to extend their Medicaid programs to people with disabilities who
earned too much to qualify for the program. Under the new law, states
could allow individuals to buy into Medicaid on a sliding scale depending
on their income. Those making more than $75,000 would pay the full pre-
mium.*

*Following are excerpts from the majority opinions in two
Supreme Court rulings issued June 22, 1999, dealing with the
Americans with Disabilities Act. In the first,* Sutton v. United Air
Lines, *the Court ruled, 7–2, that individuals with correctable
impairments are not automatically defined as being disabled
under the act; in the second,* Olmstead v. L.C., *the Court ruled,
6–3, that the disabilities act and its regulations obliged states to
place mentally disabled people in the least restrictive setting possible, consistent with the condition and wishes of the patient
and the resources of the state:*

No. 97–1943

Karen Sutton and Kimberly Hinton,
Petitioners
v.
United Air Lines, Inc.

On writ of certiorari to the United
States Court of Appeals for the
Tenth Circuit

[June 22, 1999]

JUSTICE O'CONNOR delivered the opinion of the Court.

The Americans with Disabilities Act of 1990 (ADA or Act) prohibits certain employers from discriminating against individuals on the basis of their disabilities. Petitioners challenge the dismissal of their ADA action for failure to state a claim upon which relief can be granted. We conclude that the complaint was properly dismissed. In reaching that result, we hold that the determination of whether an individual is disabled should be made with reference to measures that mitigate the individual's impairment, including, in this instance, eyeglasses and contact lenses. In addition, we hold that petitioners failed to allege properly that respondent "regarded" them as having a disability within the meaning of the ADA.

I

. . . Petitioners are twin sisters, both of whom have severe myopia. Each petitioner's uncorrected visual acuity is 20/200 or worse in her right eye and 20/400 or worse in her left eye, but "[w]ith the use of corrective lenses, each . . . has vision that is 20/20 or better." Consequently, without corrective lenses, each "effectively cannot see to conduct numerous activities such as driving a vehicle, watching television or shopping in public stores," but with corrective measures, such as glasses or contact lenses, both "function identically to individuals without a similar impairment."

In 1992, petitioners applied to respondent for employment as commercial airline pilots. They met respondent's basic age, education, experience, and FAA certification qualifications. After submitting their applications for employment, both petitioners were invited by respondent to an interview and to flight simulator tests. Both were told during their interviews, however, that a mistake had been made in inviting them to interview because petitioners did not meet respondent's minimum vision requirement, which was uncorrected visual acuity of 20/100 or better. Due to their failure to meet this requirement, petitioners' interviews were terminated, and neither was offered a pilot position.

In light of respondent's proffered reason for rejecting them, petitioners filed a charge of disability discrimination under the ADA with the Equal Employment Opportunity Commission (EEOC). After receiving a right to sue letter, petitioners filed suit in the United States District Court for the District of Colorado, alleging that respondent had discriminated against them "on the basis of their disability, or because [respondent] regarded [petitioners] as having a disability" in violation of the ADA. Specifically, petitioners alleged that due to their severe myopia they actually have a substantially limiting impairment or are regarded as having such an impairment, and are thus disabled under the Act.

The District Court dismissed petitioners' complaint for failure to state a claim upon which relief could be granted. Because petitioners could fully correct their visual impairments, the court held that they were not actually substantially limited in any major life activity and thus had not stated a claim that they were disabled within the meaning of the ADA. The court also determined that petitioners had not made allegations sufficient to support their claim that they were "regarded" . . . as having an impairment that substantially limits a major life activity. The court observed that "[t]he statutory reference to a substantial limitation indicates . . . that an employer regards an employee as handicapped in his or her ability to work by finding the employee's impairment to foreclose generally the type of employment involved." But petitioners had alleged only that respondent regarded them as unable to satisfy the requirements of a particular job, global airline pilot. Consequently, the court held that petitioners had not stated a claim that they were regarded as substantially limited in the major life activity of working. Employing similar logic, the Court of Appeals for the Tenth Circuit affirmed the District Court's judgment.

The Tenth Circuit's decision is in tension with the decisions of other Courts of Appeals. We granted certiorari and now affirm.

II

The ADA prohibits discrimination by covered entities, including private employers, against qualified individuals with a disability. Specifically, it provides that no covered employer "shall discriminate against a qualified individual with a disability because of the disability of such individual in regard to job application procedures, the hiring, advancement, or discharge of employees, employee compensation, job training, and other terms, conditions, and privileges of employment." . . . A "qualified individual with a disability" is identified as "an individual with a disability who, with or without reasonable accommodation, can perform the essential functions of the employment position that such individual holds or desires." In turn, a "disability" is defined as:

> "(A) a physical or mental impairment that substantially limits one or more of the major life activities of such individual;
>
> "(B) a record of such an impairment; or
>
> "(C) being regarded as having such an impairment."

Accordingly, to fall within this definition one must have an actual disability . . . , have a record of a disability . . . , or be regarded as having one. . . .

III

With this statutory and regulatory framework in mind, we turn first to the question whether petitioners have stated a claim under subsection (A) of the disability definition, that is, whether they have alleged that they possess a physical impairment that substantially limits them in one or more major life activities. Because petitioners allege that with corrective measures their vision "is 20/20 or better," they are not actually disabled within the meaning of the Act if the "disability" determination is made with reference to these measures. Consequently, with respect to subsection (A) of the disability definition, our decision turns on whether disability is to be determined with or without reference to corrective measures.

Petitioners maintain that whether an impairment is substantially limiting should be determined without regard to corrective measures. They argue that, because the ADA does not directly address the question at hand, the Court should defer to the agency interpretations of the statute, which are embodied in the agency guidelines issued by the EEOC and the Department of Justice. These guidelines specifically direct that the determination of whether an individual is substantially limited in a major life activity be made without regard to mitigating measures.

Respondent, in turn, maintains that an impairment does not substantially limit a major life activity if it is corrected. It argues that the Court should not defer to the agency guidelines cited by petitioners because the guidelines conflict with the plain meaning of the ADA. The phrase "substantially limits one or more major life activities," it explains, requires that the substantial limitations actually and presently exist. Moreover, respondent argues, disregarding mitigating measures taken by an individual defies the statutory command to examine the effect of the impairment on the major life activities "of such individual." And even if the statute is ambiguous, respondent claims, the guidelines' directive to ignore mitigating measures is not reasonable, and thus this Court should not defer to it.

We conclude that respondent is correct that the approach adopted by the agency guidelines—that persons are to be evaluated in their hypothetical uncorrected state—is an impermissible interpretation of the ADA. Looking at the Act as a whole, it is apparent that if a person is taking measures to correct for, or mitigate, a physical or mental impairment, the effects of those measures—both positive and negative—must be taken into account when judging whether that person is "substantially limited" in a major life activity and thus "disabled" under the Act. . . .

Three separate provisions of the ADA, read in concert, lead us to this conclusion. The Act defines a "disability" as "a physical or mental impairment that substantially limits one or more of the major life activities" of an individual . . . . Because the phrase "substantially limits" appears in the Act in the present indicative verb form, we think the language is properly read as requiring that a person be presently—not potentially or hypothetically—substantially limited in order to demonstrate a disability. A "disability" exists only where an impairment "substantially limits" a major life activity, not where it "might," "could," or "would" be substantially limiting if mitigating measures were not taken. A person whose physical or mental impairment is corrected by medication or other measures does not have an impairment that presently "substantially limits" a major life activity. To be sure, a person whose physical or mental impairment is corrected by mitigating measures still has an impairment, but if the impairment is corrected it does not "substantially limi[t]" a major life activity.

The definition of disability also requires that disabilities be evaluated "with respect to an individual" and be determined based on whether an impairment substantially limits the "major life activities of such individual." Thus, whether a person has a disability under the ADA is an individualized inquiry. . . .

The agency guidelines' directive that persons be judged in their uncorrected or unmitigated state runs directly counter to the individualized inquiry mandated by the ADA. The agency approach would often require courts and employers to speculate about a person's condition and would, in many cases, force them to make a disability determination based on general information about how an uncorrected impairment usually affects individuals, rather than on the individual's actual condition. For instance, under this view, courts would almost certainly find all diabetics to be disabled, because if they failed to monitor their blood sugar levels and administer insulin, they would almost certainly be substantially limited in one or more major life activities. A diabetic whose illness does not impair his or her daily activities would therefore be considered disabled simply because he or she has diabetes. Thus, the guidelines approach would create a system in which persons often must be treated as members of a group of people with similar impairments, rather than as individuals. This is contrary to both the letter and the spirit of the ADA.

The guidelines approach could also lead to the anomalous result that in determining whether an individual is disabled, courts and employers could not consider any negative side effects suffered by an individual resulting from the use of mitigating measures, even when those side effects are very severe. . . . This result is also inconsistent with the individualized approach of the ADA.

Finally, and critically, findings enacted as part of the ADA require the conclusion that Congress did not intend to bring under the statute's protection all those whose uncorrected conditions amount to disabilities. Congress found that "some 43,000,000 Americans have one or more physical or mental disabilities, and this number is increasing as the population as a whole is growing older." This figure is inconsistent with the definition of disability pressed by petitioners. [Discussion of origin of 43 million figure omitted.]

Regardless of its exact source, however, the 43 million figure reflects an understanding that those whose impairments are largely corrected by medication or other devices are not "disabled" within the meaning of the ADA. . . .

Because it is included in the ADA's text, the finding that 43 million individuals are disabled gives content to the ADA's terms, specifically the term "disability." Had Congress intended to include all persons with corrected physical limitations among those covered by the Act, it undoubtedly would have cited a much higher number of disabled persons in the findings. That it did not is evidence that the ADA's coverage is restricted to only those whose impairments are not mitigated by corrective measures.

The dissents suggest that viewing individuals in their corrected state will exclude from the definition of "disab[led]" those who use prosthetic limbs or take medicine for epilepsy or high blood pressure. This suggestion is incorrect. The use of a corrective device does not, by itself, relieve one's disability. Rather, one has a disability under subsection A if, notwithstanding the use of a corrective device, that individual is substantially limited in a major life activity. For example, individuals who use prosthetic limbs or wheelchairs may be mobile and capable of functioning in society but still be disabled because of a substantial limitation on their ability to walk or run. The same may be true of individuals who take medicine to lessen the symptoms of an impairment so that they can function but nevertheless remain substantially limited. Alternatively, one whose high blood pressure is "cured" by medication may be regarded as disabled by a covered entity, and thus disabled under subsection C of the definition. The use or nonuse of a corrective device does not determine whether an individual is disabled; that determination depends on whether the limitations an individual with an impairment actually faces are in fact substantially limiting.

Applying this reading of the Act to the case at hand, we conclude that the Court of Appeals correctly resolved the issue of disability in respondent's favor. As noted above, petitioners allege that with corrective measures, their visual acuity is 20/20, and that they "function identically to individuals without a similar impairment." In addition, petitioners concede that they "do not argue that the use of corrective lenses in itself demonstrates a substantially limiting impairment." Accordingly, because we decide that disability under the Act is to be determined with reference to corrective measures, we agree with the courts below that petitioners have not stated a claim that they are substantially limited in any major life activity. . . .

No. 98–536

Tommy Olmstead, Commissioner, Georgia Department of Human Resources, et al., Petitioners v. L.C., by Jonathan Zimring, guardian ad litem and next friend, et al.	On writ of certiorari to the United States Court of Appeals for the Eleventh Circuit

[June 22, 1999]

JUSTICE GINSBURG announced the judgment of the Court and delivered the opinion of the Court with respect to Parts I, II, and III-A, and an opinion with respect to Part III-B, in which O'CONNOR, SOUTER, and BREYER, JJ., joined.

This case concerns the proper construction of the anti-discrimination provision contained in the public services portion (Title II) of the Americans with Disabilities Act of 1990. Specifically, we confront the question whether the proscription of discrimination may require placement of persons with mental disabilities in community settings rather than in institutions. The answer, we hold, is a qualified yes. Such action is in order when the State's treatment professionals have determined that community placement is appropriate, the transfer from institutional care to a less restrictive setting is not opposed by the affected individual, and the placement can be reasonably accommodated, taking into account the resources available to the State and the needs of others with mental disabilities. In so ruling, we affirm the decision of the Eleventh Circuit in substantial part. We remand the case, however, for further consideration of the appropriate relief, given the range of facilities the State maintains for the care and treatment of persons with diverse mental disabilities, and its obligation to administer services with an even hand.

I

. . . In the opening provisions of the ADA, Congress stated findings applicable to the statute in all its parts. Most relevant to this case, Congress determined that

> (2) historically, society has tended to isolate and segregate individuals with disabilities, and, despite some improvements, such forms of discrimination against individuals with disabilities continue to be a serious and pervasive social problem;
>
> (3) discrimination against individuals with disabilities persists in such critical areas as . . . institutionalization. . . .
>
> (5) individuals with disabilities continually encounter various forms of discrimination, including outright intentional exclusion, . . . failure to make modifications to existing facilities and practices, . . . [and] segregation . . . .

Congress then set forth prohibitions against discrimination in employment (Title I), public services furnished by governmental entities (Title II), and public accommodations provided by private entities (Title III). The statute as a whole is intended "to provide a clear and comprehensive national mandate for the elimination of discrimination against individuals with disabilities."

This case concerns Title II, the public services portion of the ADA. The provision of Title II centrally at issue reads:

> "Subject to the provisions of this subchapter, no qualified individual with a disability shall, by reason of such disability, be excluded from participation in or be denied the benefits of the services, programs, or activities of a public entity, or be subjected to discrimination by any such entity."

. . . As Congress instructed, the Attorney General issued Title II regulations, including one modeled on the §504 regulation just quoted; called the "integration regulation," it reads:

"A public entity shall administer services, programs, and activities in the most integrated setting appropriate to the needs of qualified individuals with disabilities."

The preamble to the Attorney General's Title II regulations defines "the most integrated setting appropriate to the needs of qualified individuals with disabilities" to mean "a setting that enables individuals with disabilities to interact with non-disabled persons to the fullest extent possible." Another regulation requires public entities to "make reasonable modifications" to avoid "discrimination on the basis of disability," unless those modifications would entail a "fundamenta[l] alter[ation]"; called here the "reasonable-modifications regulation," it provides:

"A public entity shall make reasonable modifications in policies, practices, or procedures when the modifications are necessary to avoid discrimination on the basis of disability, unless the public entity can demonstrate that making the modifications would fundamentally alter the nature of the service, program, or activity."

We recite these regulations with the caveat that we do not here determine their validity. While the parties differ on the proper construction and enforcement of the regulations, we do not understand petitioners to challenge the regulatory formulations themselves as outside the congressional authorization.

II

With the key legislative provisions in full view, we summarize the facts underlying this dispute. Respondents L.C. and E.W. are mentally retarded women; L.C. has also been diagnosed with schizophrenia, and E.W., with a personality disorder. Both women have a history of treatment in institutional settings. In May 1992, L.C. was voluntarily admitted to Georgia Regional Hospital at Atlanta (GRH), where she was confined for treatment in a psychiatric unit. By May 1993, her psychiatric condition had stabilized, and L.C.'s treatment team at GRH agreed that her needs could be met appropriately in one of the community-based programs the State supported. Despite this evaluation, L.C. remained institutionalized until February 1996, when the State placed her in a community-based treatment program.

E.W. was voluntarily admitted to GRH in February 1995; like L.C., E.W. was confined for treatment in a psychiatric unit. In March 1995, GRH sought to discharge E.W. to a homeless shelter, but abandoned that plan after her attorney filed an administrative complaint. By 1996, E.W.'s treating psychiatrist concluded that she could be treated appropriately in a community-based setting. She nonetheless remained institutionalized until a few months after the District Court issued its judgment in this case in 1997.

A

In May 1995, when she was still institutionalized at GRH, L.C. filed suit in the United States District Court for the Northern District of Georgia, challenging her continued confinement in a segregated environment.... L.C. alleged that the State's failure to place her in a community-based program, once her treating professionals determined that such placement was appropriate, violated, inter alia, Title II of the ADA. L.C.'s pleading requested, among other things, that the State place her in a community care residential program, and that she receive treatment with the ultimate goal of integrating her into the mainstream of society. E.W. intervened in the action, stating an identical claim.

The District Court granted partial summary judgment in favor of L.C. and E.W. The court held that the State's failure to place L.C. and E.W. in an appropriate community-based treatment program violated Title II of the ADA. In so ruling, the court rejected the State's argument that inadequate funding, not discrimination against L.C. and E.W. "by reason of" their disabilities, accounted for their retention at GRH. Under Title II, the court concluded, "unnecessary institutional segregation of the disabled constitutes discrimination per se, which cannot be justified by a lack of funding."

In addition to contending that L.C. and E.W. had not shown discrimination "by reason of [their] disabilit[ies]," the State resisted court intervention on the ground that requiring immediate transfers in cases of this order would "fundamentally alter" the State's activity. The State reasserted that it was already using all available funds to provide services to other persons with disabilities. Rejecting the State's "fundamental alteration" defense, the court observed that existing state programs provided community-based treatment of the kind for which L.C. and E.W. qualified, and that the State could "provide services to plaintiffs in the community at considerably less cost than is required to maintain them in an institution."

The Court of Appeals for the Eleventh Circuit affirmed the judgment of the District Court, but remanded for reassessment of the State's cost-based defense. As the appeals court read the statute and regulations: When "a disabled individual's treating professionals find that a community-based placement is appropriate for that individual, the ADA imposes a duty to provide treatment in a community setting—the most integrated setting appropriate to that patient's needs"; "[w]here there is no such finding [by the treating professionals], nothing in the ADA requires the deinstitutionalization of th[e] patient."

The Court of Appeals recognized that the State's duty to provide integrated services "is not absolute"; under the Attorney General's Title II regulation, "reasonable modifications" were required of the State, but fundamental alterations were not demanded. The appeals court thought it clear, however, that "Congress wanted to permit a cost defense only in the most limited of circumstances." In conclusion, the court stated that a cost justification would fail "[u]nless the State can prove that requiring it to [expend additional funds in order to provide L.C. and E.W. with integrated services] would be so unreasonable given the demands of the State's mental health budget that it would fundamentally alter the service [the State] provides." Because it appeared that the District Court had entirely ruled out a "lack of funding" justification, the appeals court remanded, repeating that the District Court should consider, among other things, "whether the additional expenditures necessary to treat L.C. and E.W. in community-based care would be unreasonable given the demands of the State's mental health budget."

We granted certiorari in view of the importance of the question presented to the States and affected individuals.

III

Endeavoring to carry out Congress' instruction to issue regulations implementing Title II, the Attorney General, in the integration and reasonable-modifications regulations, made two key determinations. The first concerned the scope of the ADA's discrimination proscription; the second concerned the obligation of the States to counter discrimination. As to the first, the Attorney General concluded that unjustified placement or retention of persons in institutions, severely limiting their exposure to the outside community, constitutes a form of discrimination based on disability prohibited by Title II. . . . Regarding the States' obligation to avoid unjustified isolation of individuals with disabilities, the Attorney General provided that States could resist modifications that "would fundamentally alter the nature of the service, program, or activity."

The Court of Appeals essentially upheld the Attorney General's construction of the ADA. . . .

We affirm the Court of Appeals' decision in substantial part. Unjustified isolation, we hold, is properly regarded as discrimination based on disability. But we recognize, as well, the States' need to maintain a range of facilities for the care and treatment of persons with diverse mental disabilities, and the States' obligation to administer services with an even hand. Accordingly, we further hold that the Court of Appeals' remand instruction was unduly restrictive. In evaluating a State's fundamental-alteration defense, the District Court must consider, in view of the resources available to the State, not only the cost of providing community-based care to the litigants, but also the range of services the State provides others with mental disabilities, and the State's obligation to mete out those services equitably.

A

We examine first whether, as the Eleventh Circuit held, undue institutionalization qualifies as discrimination "by reason of . . . disability." The Department of Justice has consistently advocated that it does. Because the Department is the agency directed by Congress to issue regulations implementing Title II, its views warrant respect . . . .

The State argues that L.C. and E.W. encountered no discrimination "by reason of" their disabilities because they were not denied community placement on account of those disabilities. Nor were they subjected to "discrimination," the State contends, because " 'discrimination' necessarily requires uneven treatment of similarly situated individuals," and L.C. and E.W. had identified no comparison class, i.e., no similarly situated individuals given preferential treatment. We are satisfied that Congress had a more comprehensive view of the concept of discrimination advanced in the ADA.

The ADA stepped up earlier measures to secure opportunities for people with developmental disabilities to enjoy the benefits of community living. [Citing the Developmentally Disabled Assistance and Bill of Rights Act of 1975 and the Rehabilitation Act of 1973.] Ultimately, in the ADA, enacted in 1990, Congress not only required all public entities to refrain from discrimination; additionally, in findings applicable to the entire statute, Congress explicitly identified unjustified "segregation" of persons with disabilities as a "for[m] of discrimination." See 42 U.S.C. §12101(a)(2) ("historically, society has tended to isolate and segregate individuals with disabilities, and, despite some improvements, such forms of discrimination against individuals with disabilities continue to be a serious and pervasive social problem"); §12101(a)(5) ("individuals with disabilities continually encounter various forms of discrimination, including . . . segregation").

Recognition that unjustified institutional isolation of persons with disabilities is a form of discrimination reflects two evident judgments. First, institutional placement of persons who can handle and benefit from community settings perpetuates unwarranted assumptions that persons so isolated are incapable or unworthy of participating in community life. . . . Second, confinement in an institution severely diminishes the everyday life activities of individuals, including family relations, social contacts, work options, economic independence, educational advancement, and cultural enrichment. Dissimilar treatment correspondingly exists in this key respect: In order to receive needed medical services, persons with mental disabilities must, because of those disabilities, relinquish participation in community life they could enjoy given reasonable accommodations, while persons without mental disabilities can receive the medical services they need without similar sacrifice. . . .

We emphasize that nothing in the ADA or its implementing regulations condones termination of institutional settings for persons unable to handle or benefit from community settings. Title II provides only that "qualified individual[s] with a disability" may not "be subjected to discrimination." "Qualified individuals," the ADA further explains, are persons with disabilities who, "with or without reasonable modifications to rules, policies, or practices, . . . mee[t] the essential eligibility requirements for the receipt of services or the participation in programs or activities provided by a public entity."

Consistent with these provisions, the State generally may rely on the reasonable assessments of its own professionals in determining whether an individual "meets the essential eligibility requirements" for habilitation in a community-based program. Absent such qualification, it would be inappropriate to remove a patient from the more restrictive setting. . . . In this case, however, there is no genuine dispute concerning the status of L.C. and E.W. as individuals "qualified" for noninstitutional care: The State's own professionals determined that community-based treatment would be appropriate for L.C. and E.W., and neither woman opposed such treatment.

B

The State's responsibility, once it provides community-based treatment to qualified persons with disabilities, is not boundless. The reasonable-modifications regulation speaks of "reasonable modifications" to avoid discrimination, and allows States to resist modifications that entail a "fundamenta[l] alter[ation]" of the States' services and programs. The Court of Appeals construed this regulation to permit a cost-based defense "only in the most limited of circumstances," and remanded to the District Court to consider, among other things, "whether the additional expenditures necessary to treat L.C. and E.W. in community-based care would be unreasonable given the demands of the State's mental health budget."

The Court of Appeals' construction of the reasonable-modifications regulation is unacceptable for it would leave the State virtually defenseless once it is shown that the plaintiff is qualified for the service or program she seeks. If the expense entailed in placing one or two people in a community-based treatment program is properly measured for reasonableness against the State's entire mental health budget, it is unlikely that a State, relying on the fundamental-alteration defense, could ever prevail. . . . Sensibly construed, the fundamental-alteration component of the reasonable-modifications regulation would allow the State to show that, in the allocation of available resources, immediate relief for the plaintiffs would be inequitable, given the responsibility the State has undertaken for the care and treatment of a large and diverse population of persons with mental disabilities.

When it granted summary judgment for plaintiffs in this case, the District Court compared the cost of caring for the plaintiffs in a community-based setting with the cost of caring for them in an institution. That simple comparison showed that community placements cost less than institutional confinements. As the United States recognizes, however, a comparison so simple overlooks costs the State cannot avoid; most notably, a "State . . . may experience increased overall expenses by funding community placements without being able to take advantage of the savings associated with the closure of institutions."

As already observed, the ADA is not reasonably read to impel States to phase out institutions, placing patients in need of close care at risk. Nor is it the ADA's mission to drive States to move institutionalized patients into an inappropriate setting, such as a homeless shelter, a placement the State proposed, then retracted, for E.W. Some individuals, like L.C. and E.W. in prior years, may need institutional care from time to time "to stabilize acute psychiatric symptoms." . . . For other individuals, no placement outside the institution may ever be appropriate. . . .

To maintain a range of facilities and to administer services with an even hand, the State must have more leeway than the courts below understood the fundamental-alteration defense to allow. If, for example, the State were to demonstrate that it had a comprehensive, effectively working plan for placing qualified persons with mental disabilities in less restrictive settings, and a waiting list that moved at a reasonable pace not controlled by the State's endeavors to keep its institutions fully populated, the reasonable-modifications standard would be met. . . . In such circumstances, a court would have no warrant effectively to order displacement of persons at the top of the community-based treatment waiting list by individuals lower down who commenced civil actions.

* * *

For the reasons stated, we conclude that, under Title II of the ADA, States are required to provide community-based treatment for persons with mental disabilities when the State's treatment professionals determine that such placement is appropriate, the affected persons do not oppose such treatment, and the placement can be reasonably accommodated, taking into account the resources available to the State and the needs of others with mental disabilities. The judgment of the Eleventh Circuit is therefore affirmed in part and vacated in part, and the case is remanded for further proceedings consistent with this opinion.

It is so ordered.

SUPREME COURT ON
STATES RIGHTS
June 23, 1999

By a trio of 5–4 votes the Supreme Court sharply tilted the balance of power toward the states and away from the federal government, ruling that individuals did not have the right to sue states for alleged breaches of federal law. The effect of the rulings not only altered a long-standing relationship between the federal and state governments, but also limited the ability of any individual or business to sue a state in order to obtain federally guaranteed benefits or rights from that state. In curbing Congress's authority to force the states to defend themselves against such suits, the majority held that Congress "must accord states the esteem due to them as joint participants in a federal system."

The decisions—and the majority and dissenting opinions that accompanied them—forcefully demonstrated that finding the proper balance between national and state powers may be the single issue that most deeply divided the current court. Lining up behind a strong role for the states within the federal government were Chief Justice William H. Rehnquist and Justices Antonin Scalia, Sandra Day O'Connor, Anthony M. Kennedy, and Clarence Thomas. In dissent were Justices John Paul Stevens, David H. Souter, Stephen G. Breyer, and Ruth Bader Ginsburg.

The divide was palpable in the courtroom June 23, 1999, when the justices convened to hand down the decisions. After the author of each of three majority opinions summarized that decision, one of the four dissenters responded. On occasion the comments on both sides sounded less than judicial. Justice Antonin Scalia, for example, accused the minority of defending their argument "in a degree of repetitive detail that has despoiled our Northern woods," while Justice John Paul Stevens derided the majority for fashioning a doctrine of sovereign immunity "much like a mindless dragon that indiscriminately chews gaping holes in federal statutes." The exchanges from the bench underscored an observation made by a veteran court reporter for the New York Times. *Clearly, she said, the "fault line" running through the current court does not involve race, religion, abortion, or due process, but federalism. "[F]or these Justices, the question of the proper allocation of authority within the American system is not abstract of theoretical but urgent and fundamental. . . ."*

The rulings, which were handed down on the final day of the 1998–1999 term, involved three separate cases. The lead case, Alden v. Maine, *was brought by state probation officers who had sought to sue the state of Maine for overtime wages they said were due under the federal Fair Labor Standards Act. The other two cases involved a company seeking to sue Florida in one case for patent infringement* (Florida v. College Savings Bank) *and in a second case for false advertising in violation of a federal law* (College Savings Bank v. Florida).

Likely Effect of the Rulings

The rulings appeared to complete a turnaround begun in 1996 when, in the case of Seminole Tribe v. Florida, *the same 5–4 majority overturned an earlier precedent. In the* Seminole *case the Court held that Congress did not have the authority to force states to defend themselves in federal courts against private suits brought under federal laws. Read together, the 1996 case and the three 1999 cases meant that states that denied certain federally guaranteed benefits or protections to private individuals could not be sued by those individuals in either federal or state court. The federal government could still sue in state court in behalf of individuals alleging that the state had denied them federally guaranteed benefits; for example, the U.S. Labor Department could sue the state of Maine for denying the state probation officers overtime pay. But it was highly unlikely that the federal agencies had either the time or the resources to pursue such cases. The rulings did not affect individual rights guaranteed under the Fourteenth Amendment, but only those federal laws Congress enacted under its powers enumerated in Article I of the Constitution, including its powers to tax and regulate interstate commerce.*

The decisions had a potentially significant effect on state employees who were brought under federal minimum wage and hour rules in 1974. In 1976 the Supreme Court declared that extension unconstitutional, but nine years later, in the case of Garcia v. San Antonio Metropolitan Transit Authority, *the Court reversed itself. The vote in that decision was 5–4, and at the time Rehnquist, who was then an associate justice, said he would work to have the Court reverse itself once again. Although the Court did not explicitly overturn the Garcia ruling in* Alden v. Maine, *it effectively did so by stripping state employees of the means to enforce federal time and wage standards.*

The decisions also were expected to have a potentially significant effect on publishing houses and other companies that relied on federal law for protections against copyright and trademark infringement and other intellectual property issues. The private companies complained that immunity from suit was likely to give the states, including state universities, a competitive edge in fields such as biotechnology and publishing.

*The Court was scheduled to hear arguments in at least two other feder-
alism cases in the 1999–2000 term, one of which centered on whether state
employees could sue a state for violation of the federal age discrimination
law. In 1995 the Court, by the same 5–4 vote, ruled that Congress had
exceeded its power to regulate interstate commerce when in 1990 it made
possession of firearms within 1,000 feet of a school a federal crime. In 1997
the Court struck down a federal law Congress had passed in 1993 to make
it easier for religious organizations to win exemptions from laws that incidentally infringed on their religious practices. By a 6–3 vote, the Court
said that Congress had intruded both on judicial powers and on traditional
state powers.* (Gun-free school zones, Historic Documents of 1995, p. 183;
Religious Freedom Restoration Act, Historic Documents of 1997, p. 406)

Immunity a "Fundamental Aspect" of State Sovereignty

*The Eleventh Amendment to the Constitution explicitly protected states
from suit by citizens of other states, and the Court had long construed that
amendment to also bar citizens from suing their own state in federal court
unless Congress explicitly granted that right. In his majority opinion in*
Alden v. Maine, *Justice Kennedy argued that the Eleventh Amendment did
not establish state sovereign immunity as a constitutional principle but
simply confirmed it. State immunity from suit, he argued, "is a fundamental aspect of the sovereignty" that the states enjoyed before the Constitution was ratified and that they retained afterward. Moreover, Kennedy
wrote, implicit in this "constitutional design" was a bar against Congress
subjecting the states to private suits in their own courts without their consent. "A power to press a State's own courts into federal service to coerce the
other branches of the State . . . is the power first to turn the State against
itself and ultimately to commandeer, the entire political machinery of the
State against its will and at the behest of individuals. Such plenary federal
control of state governmental processes denigrates the separate sovereignty
of the States."*

*If Congress could authorize private suits against states without their
consent, Kennedy said, it could impose "staggering burdens" on the states.
Private suits could threaten financial integrity of the states and make
"unwarranted strain" on the states' ability to govern. "If the principle of
representative government is to be preserved to the States, the balance
between competing interests must be reached after deliberation by the political process established by the citizens of the State, not by judicial decree
mandated by the Federal Government and invoked by the private citizen."*

*The dissenters said the majority had given the states far more immunity
than the Framers of the Constitution had ever contemplated. Maintaining
that the majority was "mistaken" on each point it had raised in defense of
its position, Justice Souter said the rulings were reminiscent of decisions
in the early years of the century, when the court majority sought to protect
business against government regulation of economic activity. That era*

came to an end in the late 1930s when, under pressure from the public and President Franklin D. Roosevelt's "court-packing" plan, the justices began to reverse earlier rulings and hand down decisions upholding a broad federal power to regulate the economy. Souter said the rulings in the current cases would "prove the equal of [the court's] earlier experiment in laissez-faire, the one being as unrealistic as the other, as indefensible, and probably as fleeting."

> *Following are excerpts from the majority and dissenting opinions in the case of* Alden v. Maine, *handed down June 23, 1999, in which the Supreme Court by a 5–4 vote ruled that Congress did not have the power under Article I of the Constitution to authorize private suits seeking to enforce federal law in state courts without the consent of the state:*

No. 98–436

John H. Alden, et al., Petitioners v. Maine	}	On writ of certiorari to the Supreme Judicial Court of Maine

[June 23, 1999]

JUSTICE KENNEDY delivered the opinion of the Court.

In 1992, petitioners, a group of probation officers, filed suit against their employer, the State of Maine, in the United States District Court for the District of Maine. The officers alleged the State had violated the overtime provisions of the Fair Labor Standards Act of 1938 (FLSA), and sought compensation and liquidated damages. While the suit was pending, this Court decided *Seminole Tribe of Fla. v. Florida* (1996), which made it clear that Congress lacks power under Article I to abrogate the States' sovereign immunity from suits commenced or prosecuted in the federal courts. Upon consideration of Seminole Tribe, the District Court dismissed petitioners' action, and the Court of Appeals affirmed. Petitioners then filed the same action in state court. The state trial court dismissed the suit on the basis of sovereign immunity, and the Maine Supreme Judicial Court affirmed.

The Maine Supreme Judicial Court's decision conflicts with the decision of the Supreme Court of Arkansas, *Jacoby v. Arkansas Dept. of Ed.* (1998), and calls into question the constitutionality of the provisions of the FLSA purporting to authorize private actions against States in their own courts without regard for consent. In light of the importance of the question presented and the conflict between the courts, we granted certiorari. The United States intervened as a petitioner to defend the statute.

We hold that the powers delegated to Congress under Article I of the United States Constitution do not include the power to subject nonconsenting States to private suits for damages in state courts. We decide as well that the State of Maine has not consented to suits for overtime pay and liquidated damages under the FLSA. On these premises we affirm the judgment sustaining dismissal of the suit.

I

The Eleventh Amendment makes explicit reference to the States' immunity from suits "commenced or prosecuted against one of the United States by Citizens of another State, or by Citizens or Subjects of any Foreign State." We have, as a result, sometimes referred to the States' immunity from suit as "Eleventh Amendment immunity." The phrase is convenient shorthand but something of a misnomer, for the sovereign immunity of the States neither derives from nor is limited by the terms of the Eleventh Amendment. Rather, as the Constitution's structure, and its history, and the authoritative interpretations by this Court make clear, the States' immunity from suit is a fundamental aspect of the sovereignty which the States enjoyed before the ratification of the Constitution, and which they retain today (either literally or by virtue of their admission into the Union upon an equal footing with the other States) except as altered by the plan of the Convention or certain constitutional Amendments.

A

Although the Constitution establishes a National Government with broad, often plenary authority over matters within its recognized competence, the founding document "specifically recognizes the States as sovereign entities." . . . Various textual provisions of the Constitution assume the States' continued existence and active participation in the fundamental processes of governance. . . . The limited and enumerated powers granted to the Legislative, Executive, and Judicial Branches of the National Government, moreover, underscore the vital role reserved to the States by the constitutional design, . . . Any doubt regarding the constitutional role of the States as sovereign entities is removed by the Tenth Amendment, which, like the other provisions of the Bill of Rights, was enacted to allay lingering concerns about the extent of the national power. The Amendment confirms the promise implicit in the original document: "The powers not delegated to the United States by the Constitution, nor prohibited by it to the States, are reserved to the States respectively, or to the people."

The States thus retain "a residuary and inviolable sovereignty." . . . They are not relegated to the role of mere provinces or political corporations, but retain the dignity, though not the full authority, of sovereignty.

B

The generation that designed and adopted our federal system considered immunity from private suits central to sovereign dignity. When the Constitution was ratified, it was well established in English law that the Crown could not be sued without consent in its own courts. . . .

Although the American people had rejected other aspects of English political theory, the doctrine that a sovereign could not be sued without its consent was universal in the States when the Constitution was drafted and ratified. . . .

The ratification debates, furthermore, underscored the importance of the States' sovereign immunity to the American people. Grave concerns were raised by the provisions of Article III which extended the federal judicial power to controversies between States and citizens of other States or foreign nations. . . . The leading advocates of the Constitution assured the people in no uncertain terms that the Constitution would not strip the States of sovereign immunity. . . . Although the state conventions which addressed the issue of sovereign immunity in their formal ratification documents sought to clarify the point by constitutional amendment, they made clear that they, like Hamilton, Madison, and Marshall, understood the Constitution as drafted to preserve the States' immunity from private suits. . . .

Despite the persuasive assurances of the Constitution's leading advocates and the expressed understanding of the only state conventions to address the issue in explicit terms, this Court held, just five years after the Constitution was adopted, that Article III authorized a private citizen of another State to sue the State of Georgia without its consent. *Chisholm v. Georgia* (1793). . . .

An initial proposal to amend the Constitution was introduced in the House of Representatives the day after Chisholm was announced; the proposal adopted as the Eleventh Amendment was introduced in the Senate promptly following an intervening recess. Congress turned to the latter proposal with great dispatch; little more than two months after its introduction it had been endorsed by both Houses and forwarded to the States.

Each House spent but a single day discussing the Amendment, and the vote in each House was close to unanimous. . . . All attempts to weaken the Amendment were defeated. . . .

[T]he swiftness and near unanimity with which the Eleventh Amendment was adopted suggest "either that the Court had not captured the original understanding, or that the country had changed its collective mind most rapidly." . . . The more reasonable interpretation, of course, is that regardless of the views of four Justices in Chisholm, the country as a whole—which had adopted the Constitution just five years earlier—had not understood the document to strip the States of their immunity from private suits. . . .

C

The Court has been consistent in interpreting the adoption of the Eleventh Amendment as conclusive evidence "that the decision in Chisholm was contrary to the well-understood meaning of the Constitution," and that the views expressed by Hamilton, Madison, and Marshall during the ratification debates, and by Justice Iredell in his dissenting opinion in Chisholm reflect the original understanding of the Constitution. . . . In accordance with this understanding, we have recognized a "presumption that no anomalous and unheard-of proceedings or suits were intended to be raised up by the Constitution—anomalous and unheard of when the constitution was adopted."... As a consequence, we have looked to "history and experience, and the established order of things," rather than "[a]dhering to the mere letter" of the Eleventh Amendment in determining the scope of the States' constitutional immunity from suit.

Following this approach, the Court has upheld States' assertions of sovereign immunity in various contexts falling outside the literal text of the Eleventh Amendment. In *Hans v. Louisiana* [1890], the Court held that sovereign immunity barred a citizen from suing his own State under the federal-question head of jurisdiction. The Court was unmoved by the petitioner's argument that the Eleventh Amendment, by its terms, applied only to suits brought by citizens of other States.... Later decisions rejected similar requests to conform the principle of sovereign immunity to the strict language of the Eleventh Amendment in holding that nonconsenting States are immune from suits brought by federal corporations, *Smith v. Reeves* (1900), foreign nations, *Principality of Monaco* [1934], or Indian tribes, *Blatchford v. Native Village of Noatak* (1991), and in concluding that sovereign immunity is a defense to suits in admiralty, though the text of the Eleventh Amendment addresses only suits "in law or equity," *Ex parte New York* (1921).

These holdings reflect a settled doctrinal understanding, consistent with the views of the leading advocates of the Constitution's ratification, that sovereign immunity derives not from the Eleventh Amendment but from the structure of the original Constitution itself.... The Eleventh Amendment confirmed rather than established sovereign immunity as a constitutional principle; it follows that the scope of the States' immunity from suit is demarcated not by the text of the Amendment alone but by fundamental postulates implicit in the constitutional design....

II

... While the constitutional principle of sovereign immunity does pose a bar to federal jurisdiction over suits against nonconsenting States, this is not the only structural basis of sovereign immunity implicit in the constitutional design. Rather, "[t]here is also the postulate that States of the Union, still possessing attributes of sovereignty, shall be immune from suits, without their consent, save where there has been 'a surrender of this immunity in the plan of the convention.' "... This separate and distinct structural principle is not directly related to the scope of the judicial power established by Article III, but inheres in the system of federalism established by the Constitution. In exercising its Article I powers Congress may subject the States to private suits in their own courts only if there is "compelling evidence" that the States were required to surrender this power to Congress pursuant to the constitutional design. Blatchford.

A

Petitioners contend the text of the Constitution and our recent sovereign immunity decisions establish that the States were required to relinquish this portion of their sovereignty. We turn first to these sources.

1

Article I, §8 grants Congress broad power to enact legislation in several enumerated areas of national concern. The Supremacy Clause, furthermore, provides:

> "This Constitution, and the Laws of the United States which shall be made in Pursuance thereof . . . shall be the supreme Law of the Land; and the Judges in every State shall be bound thereby, any Thing in the Constitution or Laws of any state to the Contrary notwithstanding." U.S. Const., Art. VI.

It is contended that, by virtue of these provisions, where Congress enacts legislation subjecting the States to suit, the legislation by necessity overrides the sovereign immunity of the States.

As is evident from its text, however, the Supremacy Clause enshrines as "the supreme Law of the Land" only those federal Acts that accord with the constitutional design. Appeal to the Supremacy Clause alone merely raises the question whether a law is a valid exercise of the national power. . . .

The Constitution, by delegating to Congress the power to establish the supreme law of the land when acting within its enumerated powers, does not foreclose a State from asserting immunity to claims arising under federal law merely because that law derives not from the State itself but from the national power. . . . When a State asserts its immunity to suit, the question is not the primacy of federal law but the implementation of the law in a manner consistent with the constitutional sovereignty of the States.

Nor can we conclude that the specific Article I powers delegated to Congress necessarily include, by virtue of the Necessary and Proper Clause or otherwise, the incidental authority to subject the States to private suits as a means of achieving objectives otherwise within the scope of the enumerated powers.

Although some of our decisions had endorsed this contention, see *Parden v. Terminal R. Co. of Ala. Docks Dept.* (1964); *Pennsylvania v. Union Gas Co.* (1989) (plurality opinion), they have since been overruled, see *Seminole Tribe; College Savings Bank v. Florida Prepaid Postsecondary Ed. Expense Bd.* [1999]. . . .

The cases we have cited, of course, came at last to the conclusion that neither the Supremacy Clause nor the enumerated powers of Congress confer authority to abrogate the States' immunity from suit in federal court. The logic of the decisions, however, does not turn on the forum in which the suits were prosecuted but extends to state-court suits as well.

The dissenting opinion seeks to reopen these precedents, contending that state sovereign immunity must derive either from the common law (in which case the dissent contends it is defeasible by statute) or from natural law (in which case the dissent believes it cannot bar a federal claim). As should be obvious to all, this is a false dichotomy. The text and the structure of the Constitution protect various rights and principles. Many of these, such as the right to trial by jury and the prohibition on unreasonable searches and seizures, derive from the common law. The common-law lineage of these rights does not mean they are defeasible by statute or remain mere common-law rights, however. They are, rather, constitutional rights, and form the fundamental law of the land.

Although the sovereign immunity of the States derives at least in part from the common-law tradition, the structure and history of the Constitution make clear that the immunity exists today by constitutional design. The dissent has provided no persuasive evidence that the founding generation regarded the States' sovereign immunity as defeasible by federal statute. . . .

2 [omitted]

B

Whether Congress has authority under Article I to abrogate a State's immunity from suit in its own courts is, then, a question of first impression. In determining whether there is "compelling evidence" that this derogation of the States' sovereignty is "inherent in the constitutional compact," . . . we continue our discussion of history, practice, precedent, and the structure of the Constitution.

1

We look first to evidence of the original understanding of the Constitution. Petitioners contend that because the ratification debates and the events surrounding the adoption of the Eleventh Amendment focused on the States' immunity from suit in federal courts, the historical record gives no instruction as to the founding generation's intent to preserve the States' immunity from suit in their own courts.

We believe, however, that the founders' silence is best explained by the simple fact that no one, not even the Constitution's most ardent opponents, suggested the document might strip the States of the immunity. . . .

2

. . . The provisions of the FLSA at issue here . . . are among the first statutory enactments purporting in express terms to subject nonconsenting States to private suits. Although similar statutes have multiplied in the last generation, "they are of such recent vintage that they are no more probative than the [FLSA] of a constitutional tradition that lends meaning to the text. Their persuasive force is far outweighed by almost two centuries of apparent congressional avoidance of the practice."

Even the recent statutes, moreover, do not provide evidence of an understanding that Congress has a greater power to subject States to suit in their own courts than in federal courts. On the contrary, the statutes purport to create causes of actions against the States which are enforceable in federal, as well as state, court. To the extent recent practice thus departs from longstanding tradition, it reflects not so much an understanding that the States have surrendered their immunity from suit in their own courts as the erroneous view, perhaps inspired by Parden and Union Gas, that Congress may subject nonconsenting States to private suits in any forum.

3 [omitted]

4

Our final consideration is whether a congressional power to subject nonconsenting States to private suits in their own courts is consistent with the structure of the Constitution. We look both to the essential principles of federalism and to the special role of the state courts in the constitutional design.

Although the Constitution grants broad powers to Congress, our federalism requires that Congress treat the States in a manner consistent with their status as residuary sovereigns and joint participants in the governance of the Nation. . . .

Petitioners contend that immunity from suit in federal court suffices to preserve the dignity of the States. Private suits against nonconsenting States, however, present "the indignity of subjecting a State to the coercive process of judicial tribunals at the instance of private parties" . . . regardless of the forum. Not only must a State defend or default but also it must face the prospect of being thrust, by federal fiat and against its will, into the disfavored status of a debtor, subject to the power of private citizens to levy on its treasury or perhaps even government buildings or property which the State administers on the public's behalf.

In some ways, of course, a congressional power to authorize private suits against nonconsenting States in their own courts would be even more offensive to state sovereignty than a power to authorize the suits in a federal forum. Although the immunity of one sovereign in the courts of another has often depended in part on comity or agreement, the immunity of a sovereign in its own courts has always been understood to be within the sole control of the sovereign itself. A power to press a State's own courts into federal service to coerce the other branches of the State, furthermore, is the power first to turn the State against itself and ultimately to commandeer the entire political machinery of the State against its will and at the behest of individuals. Such plenary federal control of state governmental processes denigrates the separate sovereignty of the States.

It is unquestioned that the Federal Government retains its own immunity from suit not only in state tribunals but also in its own courts. In light of our constitutional system recognizing the essential sovereignty of the States, we are reluctant to conclude that the States are not entitled to a reciprocal privilege.

Underlying constitutional form are considerations of great substance. Private suits against nonconsenting States—especially suits for money damages—may threaten the financial integrity of the States. It is indisputable that, at the time of the founding, many of the States could have been forced into insolvency but for their immunity from private suits for money damages. Even today, an unlimited congressional power to authorize suits in state court to levy upon the treasuries of the States for compensatory damages, attorney's fees, and even punitive damages could create staggering burdens, giving Congress a power and a leverage over the States that is not contemplated by our constitutional design. The potential national power would pose a severe and notorious danger to the States and their resources.

A congressional power to strip the States of their immunity from private suits in their own courts would pose more subtle risks as well. . . . When the States' immunity from private suits is disregarded, "the course of their public policy and the administration of their public affairs" may become "subject to and controlled by the mandates of judicial tribunals without their consent, and in favor of individual interests." In re Ayers. While the States have relinquished their immunity from suit in some special contexts . . . , this surrender carries with it substantial costs to the autonomy, the decisionmaking ability, and the sovereign capacity of the States.

A general federal power to authorize private suits for money damages would place unwarranted strain on the States' ability to govern in accordance with the will of their citizens. Today, as at the time of the founding, the allocation of scarce resources among competing needs and interests lies at the heart of the political process. While the judgment creditor of the State may have a legitimate claim for compensation, other important needs and worthwhile ends compete for access to the public fisc. Since all cannot be satisfied in full, it is inevitable that difficult decisions involving the most sensitive and political of judgments must be made. If the principle of representative government is to be preserved to the States, the balance between competing interests must be reached after deliberation by the political process established by the citizens of the State, not by judicial decree mandated by the Federal Government and invoked by the private citizen. . . .

In light of history, practice, precedent, and the structure of the Constitution, we hold that the States retain immunity from private suit in their own courts, an immunity beyond the congressional power to abrogate by Article I legislation.

[III omitted]

IV

The sole remaining question is whether Maine has waived its immunity. The State of Maine "regards the immunity from suit as 'one of the highest attributes inherent in the nature of sovereignty,' " and adheres to the general rule that "a specific authority conferred by an enactment of the legislature is requisite if the sovereign is to be taken as having shed the protective mantle of immunity" [quoting Maine court decisions]. Petitioners have not attempted to establish a waiver of immunity under this standard. . . . The State, we conclude, has not consented to suit.

V

This case at one level concerns the formal structure of federalism, but in a Constitution as resilient as ours form mirrors substance. Congress has vast power but not all power. When Congress legislates in matters affecting the

States, it may not treat these sovereign entities as mere prefectures or corporations. Congress must accord States the esteem due to them as joint participants in a federal system, one beginning with the premise of sovereignty in both the central Government and the separate States. Congress has ample means to ensure compliance with valid federal laws, but it must respect the sovereignty of the States.

In apparent attempt to disparage a conclusion with which it disagrees, the dissent attributes our reasoning to natural law. We seek to discover, however, only what the Framers and those who ratified the Constitution sought to accomplish when they created a federal system. We appeal to no higher authority than the Charter which they wrote and adopted. Theirs was the unique insight that freedom is enhanced by the creation of two governments, not one. We need not attach a label to our dissenting colleagues' insistence that the constitutional structure adopted by the founders must yield to the politics of the moment. Although the Constitution begins with the principle that sovereignty rests with the people, it does not follow that the National Government becomes the ultimate, preferred mechanism for expressing the people's will. The States exist as a refutation of that concept. In choosing to ordain and establish the Constitution, the people insisted upon a federal structure for the very purpose of rejecting the idea that the will of the people in all instances is expressed by the central power, the one most remote from their control. The Framers of the Constitution did not share our dissenting colleagues' belief that the Congress may circumvent the federal design by regulating the States directly when it pleases to do so, including by a proxy in which individual citizens are authorized to levy upon the state treasuries absent the States' consent to jurisdiction.

The case before us depends upon these principles. The State of Maine has not questioned Congress' power to prescribe substantive rules of federal law to which it must comply. Despite an initial good-faith disagreement about the requirements of the FLSA, it is conceded by all that the State has altered its conduct so that its compliance with federal law cannot now be questioned. The Solicitor General of the United States has appeared before this Court, however, and asserted that the federal interest in compensating the States' employees for alleged past violations of federal law is so compelling that the sovereign State of Maine must be stripped of its immunity and subjected to suit in its own courts by its own employees. Yet, despite specific statutory authorization, see 29 U.S.C. §216(c), the United States apparently found the same interests insufficient to justify sending even a single attorney to Maine to prosecute this litigation. The difference between a suit by the United States on behalf of the employees and a suit by the employees implicates a rule that the National Government must itself deem the case of sufficient importance to take action against the State; and history, precedent, and the structure of the Constitution make clear that, under the plan of the Convention, the States have consented to suits of the first kind but not of the second. The judgment of the Supreme Judicial Court of Maine is

Affirmed.

JUSTICE SOUTER, with whom JUSTICE STEVENS, JUSTICE GINSBURG, and JUSTICE BREYER join, dissenting.

In *Seminole Tribe of Fla. v. Florida* (1996), a majority of this Court invoked the Eleventh Amendment to declare that the federal judicial power under Article III of the Constitution does not reach a private action against a State, even on a federal question. In the Court's conception, however, the Eleventh Amendment was understood as having been enhanced by a "background principle" of state sovereign immunity (understood as immunity to suit) that operated beyond its limited codification in the Amendment, dealing solely with federal citizen-state diversity jurisdiction. To the Seminole Tribe dissenters, of whom I was one, the Court's enhancement of the Amendment was at odds with constitutional history and at war with the conception of divided sovereignty that is the essence of American federalism.

Today's issue arises naturally in the aftermath of the decision in Seminole Tribe. The Court holds that the Constitution bars an individual suit against a State to enforce a federal statutory right under the Fair Labor Standards Act of 1938 (FLSA), when brought in the State's courts over its objection. In thus complementing its earlier decision, the Court of course confronts the fact that the state forum renders the Eleventh Amendment beside the point, and it has responded by discerning a simpler and more straightforward theory of state sovereign immunity than it found in Seminole Tribe: a State's sovereign immunity from all individual suits is a "fundamental aspect" of state sovereignty "confirm[ed]" by the Tenth Amendment. As a consequence, Seminole Tribe's contorted reliance on the Eleventh Amendment and its background was presumably unnecessary; the Tenth would have done the work with an economy that the majority in Seminole Tribe would have welcomed. Indeed, if the Court's current reasoning is correct, the Eleventh Amendment itself was unnecessary. Whatever Article III may originally have said about the federal judicial power, the embarrassment to the State of Georgia occasioned by attempts in federal court to enforce the State's war debt could easily have been avoided if only the Court that decided *Chisholm v. Georgia* (1793) had understood a State's inherent, Tenth Amendment right to be free of any judicial power, whether the court be state or federal, and whether the cause of action arise under state or federal law.

The sequence of the Court's positions prompts a suspicion of error, and skepticism is confirmed by scrutiny of the Court's efforts to justify its holding. There is no evidence that the Tenth Amendment constitutionalized a concept of sovereign immunity as inherent in the notion of statehood, and no evidence that any concept of inherent sovereign immunity was understood historically to apply when the sovereign sued was not the font of the law. Nor does the Court fare any better with its subsidiary lines of reasoning, that the state-court action is barred by the scheme of American federalism, a result supposedly confirmed by a history largely devoid of precursors to the action considered here. The Court's federalism ignores the accepted authority of Congress to bind States under the FLSA and to provide for enforcement of federal rights in state court. The Court's history simply disparages the capacity of the Constitution to order relationships in a Republic that has changed since the founding.

On each point the Court has raised it is mistaken, and I respectfully dissent from its judgment.

I

The Court rests its decision principally on the claim that immunity from suit was "a fundamental aspect of the sovereignty which the States enjoyed before the ratification of the Constitution," an aspect which the Court understands to have survived the ratification of the Constitution in 1788 and to have been "confirm[ed]" and given constitutional status by the adoption of the Tenth Amendment in 1791. If the Court truly means by "sovereign immunity," what that term meant at common law, its argument would be insupportable. While sovereign immunity entered many new state legal systems as a part of the common law selectively received from England, it was not understood to be indefeasible or to have been given any such status by the new National Constitution, which did not mention it. Had the question been posed, state sovereign immunity could not have been thought to shield a State from suit under federal law on a subject committed to national jurisdiction by Article I of the Constitution. Congress exercising its conceded Article I power may unquestionably abrogate such immunity. I set out this position at length in my dissent in Seminole Tribe and will not repeat it here.

The Court does not, however, offer today's holding as a mere corollary to its reasoning in Seminole Tribe, substituting the Tenth Amendment for the Eleventh as the occasion demands, and it is fair to read its references to a "fundamental aspect" of state sovereignty as referring not to a prerogative inherited from the Crown, but to a conception necessarily implied by statehood itself. The conception is thus not one of common law so much as of natural law, a universally applicable proposition discoverable by reason. This, I take it, is the sense in which the Court so emphatically relies on Alexander Hamilton's reference in *The Federalist* No. 81 to the States' sovereign immunity from suit as an "inherent" right, a characterization that does not require, but is at least open to, a natural law reading.

I understand the Court to rely on the Hamiltonian formulation with the object of suggesting that its conception of sovereign immunity as a "fundamental aspect" of sovereignty was a substantially popular, if not the dominant, view in the periods of Revolution and Confederation. There is, after all, nothing else in the Court's opinion that would suggest a basis for saying that the ratification of the Tenth Amendment gave this "fundamental aspect" its constitutional status and protection against any legislative tampering by Congress. The Court's principal rationale for today's result, then, turns on history: was the natural law conception of sovereign immunity as inherent in any notion of an independent State widely held in the United States in the period preceding the ratification of 1788 (or the adoption of the Tenth Amendment in 1791)?

The answer is certainly no. There is almost no evidence that the generation of the Framers thought sovereign immunity was fundamental in the sense of being unalterable. Whether one looks at the period before the framing, to the ratification controversies, or to the early republican era, the evidence is the same. Some Framers thought sovereign immunity was an obsolete royal prerogative inapplicable in a republic; some thought sovereign immunity was a common-law power defeasible, like other common-law rights, by statute; and perhaps a few thought, in keeping with a natural law view distinct from the common-law conception, that immunity was inherent in a sovereign because the body that made a law could not logically be bound by it. Natural law thinking on the part of a doubtful few will not, however, support the Court's position.

[Subsections A–F omitted]

II

The Court's rationale for today's holding based on a conception of sovereign immunity as somehow fundamental to sovereignty or inherent in statehood fails for the lack of any substantial support for such a conception in the thinking of the founding era. The Court ... has a second line of argument looking not to a clause-based reception of the natural law conception or even to its recognition as a "background principle," but to a structural basis in the Constitution's creation of a federal system. Immunity, the Court says, "inheres in the system of federalism established by the Constitution[.]" ... That is, the Court believes that the federal constitutional structure itself necessitates recognition of some degree of state autonomy broad enough to include sovereign immunity from suit in a State's own courts, regardless of the federal source of the claim asserted against the State. ... [T]he Court's argument that state court sovereign immunity on federal questions is inherent in the very concept of federal structure is demonstrably mistaken.

A

... [T]he general scheme of delegated sovereignty as between the two component governments of the federal system was clear, and was succinctly stated by Chief Justice Marshall: "In America, the powers of sovereignty are divided between the government of the Union, and those of the States. They are each sovereign, with respect to the objects committed to it, and neither sovereign with respect to the objects committed to the other." *McCulloch v. Maryland* (1819).

Hence the flaw in the Court's appeal to federalism. The State of Maine is not sovereign with respect to the national objective of the FLSA. It is not the authority that promulgated the FLSA, on which the right of action in this case depends. That authority is the United States acting through the Congress, whose legislative power under Article I of the Constitution to extend FLSA coverage to state employees has already been decided, see *Garcia v. San Antonio Metropolitan Transit Authority* (1985), and is not contested here.

Nor can it be argued that because the State of Maine creates its own court system, it has authority to decide what sorts of claims may be entertained there, and thus in effect to control the right of action in this case. Maine has created state courts of general jurisdiction; once it has done so, the Supremacy Clause of the Constitution, Art. VI, cl. 2, which requires state courts to enforce federal law and state-court judges to be bound by it, requires the Maine courts to entertain this federal cause of action. . . . The Court's insistence that the federal structure bars Congress from making States susceptible to suit in their own courts is, then, [a] plain mistake.

B

It is symptomatic of the weakness of the structural notion proffered by the Court that it seeks to buttress the argument by relying on "the dignity and respect afforded a State, which the immunity is designed to protect" (quoting *Idaho v. Coeur d'Alene Tribe of Idaho* (1997)), and by invoking the many demands on a State's fisc. Apparently beguiled by Gilded Era language describing private suits against States as "neither becoming nor convenient" (quoting *In re Ayers* (1887)), the Court calls "immunity from private suits central to sovereign dignity," and assumes that this "dignity" is a quality easily translated from the person of the King to the participatory abstraction of a republican State. . . . It would be hard to imagine anything more inimical to the republican conception, which rests on the understanding of its citizens precisely that the government is not above them, but of them, its actions being governed by law just like their own. Whatever justification there may be for an American government's immunity from private suit, it is not dignity.

It is equally puzzling to hear the Court say that "federal power to authorize private suits for money damages would place unwarranted strain on the States' ability to govern in accordance with the will of their citizens." So long as the citizens' will, expressed through state legislation, does not violate valid federal law, the strain will not be felt; and to the extent that state action does violate federal law, the will of the citizens of the United States already trumps that of the citizens of the State: the strain then is not only expected, but necessarily intended.

Least of all does the Court persuade by observing that "other important needs" than that of the "judgment creditor" compete for public money. The "judgment creditor" in question is not a dunning bill-collector, but a citizen whose federal rights have been violated, and a constitutional structure that stints on enforcing federal rights out of an abundance of delicacy toward the States has substituted politesse in place of respect for the rule of law.

III

. . . Least of all is it to the point for the Court to suggest that because the Framers would be surprised to find States subjected to a federal-law suit in their own courts under the commerce power, the suit must be prohibited by the Constitution. . . . The Framers' intentions and expectations count so far as they point to the meaning of the Constitution's text or the fair implications of its structure, but they do not hover over the instrument to veto any application of its principles to a world that the Framers could not have anticipated.

If the Framers would be surprised to see States subjected to suit in their own courts under the commerce power, they would be astonished by the reach of Congress under the Commerce Clause generally. The proliferation of Government, State and Federal, would amaze the Framers, and the administrative state with its reams of regulations would leave them rubbing their eyes. But the Framers' surprise at, say, the FLSA, or the Federal Communications Commission, or the Federal Reserve Board is no threat to the constitutionality of any one of them. . . .

[IV omitted]

V

The Court has swung back and forth with regrettable disruption on the enforceability of the FLSA against the States, but if the present majority had a defensible position one could at least accept its decision with an expectation of stability ahead. As it is, any such expectation would be naive. The resemblance of today's state sovereign immunity to the Lochner era's industrial due process is striking. The Court began this century by imputing immutable constitutional status to a conception of economic self-reliance that was never true to industrial life and grew insistently fictional with the years, and the Court has chosen to close the century by conferring like status on a conception of state sovereign immunity that is true neither to history nor to the structure of the Constitution. I expect the Court's late essay into immunity doctrine will prove the equal of its earlier experiment in laissez-faire, the one being as unrealistic as the other, as indefensible, and probably as fleeting.

PRESIDENT CLINTON'S REMARKS ON THE BUDGET SURPLUS
June 28, 1999

President Bill Clinton, a Democrat, and the Republican-led Congress learned a lesson during 1999 they had already expected: the politics of a budget surplus could be just as rough-and-tumble as the politics of a deficit. After years of arguing over how to reduce a mammoth federal deficit, Congress and the president spent much of the year disputing how to "spend" a growing surplus. Republican leaders wanted to put much of the money into tax cuts, but Clinton, congressional Democrats, and even many Republicans advocated using the surplus to ensure continued solvency of the Social Security and Medicare systems and to begin paying off the national debt.

Budget disputes between the president and Congress had led to chaotic end-of-session scenes in most of the years since Republicans took control of Congress in 1995. That year saw several short-term closings of much of the federal government as Republicans sought, unsuccessfully, to use their new majority to force concessions from Clinton. In 1998 Congress failed for the first time ever to pass an overall budget blueprint, as required by law. A massive catch-all appropriations bill enacted at the end of the 1998 session was a bloated, complex monument to political failure. Despite his weakened position, Clinton skillfully used his political leverage to win most of what he wanted from Congress in each of those four years. (Budget battles, Historic Documents of 1995, p. 737; Historic Documents of 1996, p. 147; Historic Documents of 1997, p. 602; Historic Documents of 1998, p. 500)

The federal government had ended fiscal year 1998 in surplus for the first time in a generation. But that surplus was made possible only by borrowing from profits in the Social Security and U.S. Postal Service accounts. The following year the administration announced October 27 that fiscal year 1999 ended with a surplus of $123 billion. In nominal terms it was the largest surplus in history, and it represented the first back-to-back surplus since 1956-1957, during the presidency of Dwight Eisenhower. But as with the case a year earlier, the books for 1999 were balanced only by borrowing from a current surplus in Social Security revenue. Without the

350

Social Security surplus, the government's regular operations would have showed a deficit of about $1 billion.

Negotiating a Surplus

Despite the surplus, few in Washington had expectations that budget battles during 1999 would be any different from the previous four years. The Republican failure to oust Clinton from office in the Lewinsky sex scandal had little apparent effect on the budget process. On the face of it, Clinton's political standing on Capitol Hill was weaker than ever in the months after the Senate rejected impeachment charges against him, but as a practical matter the president benefited from divisions among Republicans and his demonstrated ability to use the veto power and other bargaining tools to his own advantage. (Clinton's impeachment trial, p. 15)

The year's budget skirmishing began with predictions in January that the budget surplus for fiscal 1999 would reach about $79 billion, including the borrowing from Social Security. The Congressional Budget Office estimated on January 29 that surpluses over the next ten years would total nearly $800 billion.

Clinton on February 1, 1999, set the year's budget skirmishes in motion with a fiscal 2000 budget request totaling nearly $1.8 trillion, leaving a surplus of $117 billion for the year. Clinton proposed setting aside 62 percent of that surplus for a yet-to-be-negotiated program to shore up the Social Security and Medicare systems. Most of the remaining surplus would be used to begin paying off the nation's $3.7 trillion pubic debt. But Clinton said enough money remained to pay for increased spending on his domestic priorities, including education and environmental programs.

Republicans rejected Clinton's approach but for months failed to agree on a unified alternative. Most congressional leaders put their emphasis on a large tax cut, but some wanted more money reserved for Social Security reform and paying off the national debt.

A major restraint facing both the president and Congress was a series of "budget caps" they had agreed to in 1997. In theory, the caps imposed tight limits on so-called discretionary spending, the parts of the budget over which Congress and the president had control. Both sides had violated the caps in 1998, and from the start it appeared likely they would do so again in 1999.

At the insistence of the new Speaker of the House, Dennis Hastert, Congress worked diligently on a budget resolution (H Con Res 68) setting overall spending targets for fiscal 2000 and managed to pass one by April 15, tax day. That resolution provided for a tax cut totaling $142 billion during the five fiscal years of 2000 to 2004; over a ten-year period the tax cut could total a estimated $788 billion.

Clinton sought once again to seize the high political ground with a June 28 announcement that new estimates showed the surplus growing at a faster pace than had been anticipated. The fiscal 1999 budget would show a surplus of $99 billion, Clinton said, a $20 billion increase over estimates made just *five months earlier. Over a ten-year period (fiscal 2000 through 2009), the surplus would total $2.93 trillion, Clinton said. That represented an increase of more than $500 billion over the February estimate. Clinton attributed all the increases in budget surplus to the nation's booming economy.*

Politics of Tax Cuts

Clinton undoubtedly knew that the new forecasts for budget surpluses would only fuel the appetite among Republicans for a major tax cut. Less than a month later, on July 22, the House passed a bill calling for a tax cut of nearly $800 billion over ten years, and the Senate followed suit on July 30. The two bills took markedly different approaches, however; the House measure was weighted heavily toward business tax reductions, while the Senate bill focused tax reductions on individual taxpayers, especially those in the lowest (15 percent) tax bracket. Conferees agreed on a compromise relatively quickly, however, and both chambers approved it (HR 2488) on August 5. The final product promised to cut taxes by $792 billion over ten years, with broad cuts in individual income taxes—including a $117 billion cut in the so-called marriage penalty, the controversial tax provision that forced most couples to pay higher taxes once they married than they did as two individuals.

As promised, Clinton vetoed the tax cut bill on September 23. Clinton said the bill gave too much relief to high-income taxpayers and soaked up money that should have been left for debt reduction and improving high-priority federal programs. "The bill is too big, too bloated, [and] places too great a burden on America's economy," Clinton said.

White House officials said Clinton might accept a much smaller tax cut—in the neighborhood of $300 billion—but only if it was targeted to middle- and low-income taxpayers. Republicans were unable to capitalize politically on Clinton's veto, largely because the president had successfully popularized the idea of using most of the budget surplus to protect Social Security and to pay down the national debt. Opinion surveys showed that most Americans sided with him on those priorities and played down the need for a big tax cut.

Back to the Budget Negotiations

With the tax cut issue out of the way, White House and congressional negotiators focused their attention on resolving dozens of issues in the budget for fiscal 2000, which began on September 30. The biggest hurdles were the budget caps from 1997, which Congress had reinforced with its fiscal 2000 budget resolution, and a desire by both sides to avoid dipping into Social Security surpluses to pay for ongoing programs. In the end, Congress and the administration gave way on both counts, exceeding the budget caps by more than $30 billion and spending about $15 billion from the expected Social Security surpluses for the year.

Congress also was unable to avoid rolling several of the thirteen annual spending bills into one big catchall measure, called an "omnibus" appro-

priations bill. That happened because Republican leaders sent Clinton four spending measures he had threatened to veto, and when he followed through on his promise, time and political circumstances dictated that an omnibus bill was necessary.

In the end, Congress rolled five of the spending bills into an omnibus measure (HR 3194–PL 106-113), those covering the Commerce, State, and Justice departments; the District of Columbia; foreign aid; the Interior Department; and the Labor, Health and Human Services, and Education departments. As in the past, Clinton's veto-then-negotiate strategy served him well, enabling him to win more funding than Republicans had wanted for his priority programs, including subsidies for local hiring of police officers and teachers, payment of nearly $1 billion in overdue U.S. payments to the United Nations, and the purchase by the federal government of environmentally sensitive and historically important lands.

Congress approved the omnibus bill on November 19, and Clinton signed it into law on November 29. In addition to busting budget caps and dipping into Social Security funds, the bill used what observers said was an unprecedented number of accounting tricks to foster the appearance of holding down spending. One maneuver required federal agencies to cut thirty-eight cents from every $100 they spent—in effect an across-the-board cut intended to save about $1.3 billion. The bill also pushed the last federal pay day for fiscal 2000 into the following fiscal year, cutting $3.6 billion from the 2000 budget, but adding to the total for the following year, when the budget surplus was expected to be higher.

Republicans pledged to tackle Clinton once again on the tax cut and other issues during 2000, an election year. "We'll be back next year," said Pete Domenici, the New Mexico Republican who chaired the Senate Budget Committee.

Following is a statement by President Bill Clinton at the White House on June 28, 1999, during which he announced higher estimates on expected surpluses in the federal budget during fiscal years 2000 to 2009 and beyond:

Good morning. Six years ago, we put in place a new economic strategy for the Information Age. We put our fiscal house in order, we invested in our people, we expanded trade in American goods and services. By making tough decisions, America has reaped rich rewards. We built the longest peacetime expansion in our history.

Last week we learned that in the first three months of 1999, the economy grew at a 4.3 percent rate, with very low inflation. With record numbers of new homes being built, paychecks increasing, hundreds of thousands of young people getting new help to go to college, new businesses opening their doors, a surging market on Wall Street, we are truly widening the circle of opportunity in America.

I'm here to report to the American people on more good news about our budget. As required by law, my administration is releasing the mid-session review of the budget. Here is what we have found. When I took office, the national government had a record deficit of $290 billion, projected to increase indefinitely. Last year, for the first time in 29 years, we balanced the budget.

In January this year, we projected a surplus for this year of $79 billion. Today, I am pleased to report that, in fact, the budget surplus for 1999 will be $99 billion, the largest as a share of our economy since 1951. For next year, we now project a budget surplus of $142 billion, a surplus of $5 billion not counting the receipts from Social Security. In fact, improvements in the outlook since February have added $179 billion to the projected budget surplus over five years, half a trillion dollars over ten years, and $1 trillion over 15 years.

Fiscal discipline does bring real results. I want to thank my economic team for all the work that they have done. Lower interest rates have led to a boom in business investment, to lower mortgage rates, to lower credit card rates, to lower student loan rates. Fiscal discipline has widened opportunity and created hope for all working people in our country. Now we have a chance to do even more—to use the fruits of our prosperity today to strengthen our prospects for tomorrow; indeed, for tomorrows well into the 21st century.

In my State of the Union address, I set out a plan for how to use the budget surplus. Today, in light of the unexpectedly large surplus, I am proposing to build on that budget framework, with a new approach that honors our values, meets our commitments, and makes it possible to reach bipartisan agreement on a budget for America.

First, we can strengthen our commitment to use the bulk of the surplus to save Social Security and Medicare, and to pay down the national debt. The new budget numbers mean that we will run a surplus in the non-Social Security part of the budget, starting next year, much earlier than previously expected. I am pleased that Republicans and Democrats in Congress have agreed to use the Social Security surpluses to reduce the national debt. But we must go forward and achieve an even stronger lock box than one proposed by Congress. Social Security taxes should be saved for Social Security, period. Let's finish the job and work to extend the solvency of Social Security. I'm encouraged that Republicans and Democrats on the House Ways and Means Committee are meeting together to try to accomplish this goal.

Second, our new large surplus will help us to strengthen and modernize Medicare while providing a prescription drug benefit. Tomorrow I will reveal the details of my plan to modernize Medicare. The steps I will propose to use the surplus will increase Medicare's solvency for at least 25 years. By taking additional measures to increase competition, combat fraud, and reduce costs, we can provide a new prescription drug benefit and still pay down our national debt.

Third, our new budget framework will use part of the surplus to provide substantial tax relief. It will maintain USA accounts, the largest and most progressive tax incentive ever offered to encourage savings. USA accounts will allow every American to begin saving from the first day in the work force, providing more help for those who need it, giving every American a stake in our shared prosperity.

In addition to the USA accounts, I have proposed tax cuts, targeted and paid for, for child care, for stay-at-home mothers, for long-term care, to encourage businesses to invest in poor communities, and to modernize 6,000 schools. But first things first.

Fourth, we can use this surplus to meet other vital national needs, such as maintaining military readiness, honoring our veterans, protecting the environment, promoting health research, farm security and other core functions of our government.

Beyond this, we have a chance to use the surplus not only to care for our parents through Social Security and Medicare, but to give a greater chance in life to our young children. So today I am proposing a new $156 billion children's and education trust fund. This commitment can enable us to offer Head Start pre-school to a million children, to hire those 100,000 teachers, to provide extra help for a million children in our poorest communities, to pay for dramatic improvements in children's health.

And finally, by investing to save Social Security and strengthen Medicare, my plan now will entirely pay off our national debt. In the 12 years before I took office, reckless fiscal policies quadrupled our debt, bringing us higher interest rates, higher unemployment, higher inflation. By balancing the budget we have begun to reduce the debt. But today our national debt still totals $13,400 for every man, woman and child. If we maintain our fiscal discipline, using the surplus to pay down the debt and using the savings to strengthen Social Security, America will entirely pay off the national debt by 2015.

If you look at this chart, you will see that we have now cut up Washington's credit card. Now we can pay off the debt; by 2015, this country can be entirely out of debt. This is a remarkable milestone, but it is clearly within reach, if we do not squander the surplus by choosing short-term gain over long-term national goals.

The surplus is the hard-earned product of our fiscal discipline. We should use it to prepare for the great challenges facing our country—caring for our parents, caring for our children, freeing our nation from the shackles of debt so that we can have long-term, sustained economic prosperity.

Keep in mind what this means to ordinary people. If you pay this debt off, it means interest rates will be lower. It means there will be more business investment. It means there will be more new jobs. It means there will be more money left over for higher wages. It means the cost to families of homes and cars and college educations will be lower. That's what being out of debt means.

It means the next time there is an international financial crisis, we will be relatively less vulnerable because we won't have to borrow so much money, and the poorer countries will be able to borrow more money at lower interest rates, bringing greater global prosperity and stability. This is a very significant achievement for our country, and for a more stable and peaceful and prosperous world.

So I hope very much to work with Congress in the weeks ahead—to pay off the debt, to finish the work of strengthening Social Security and Medicare, and to make a real commitment to our children and our future.

Again, let me thank the national economic team, and all others who have supported these initiatives over the last six years. Thank you very much.

July

Israeli Prime Minister Barak
on the New Government 359

Report on "Digital Divide" in
Access to Computers, Internet 368

Federal Report on the
Well-Being of Children 384

Census Bureau Report on
Measures of Well-Being 390

Agriculture Secretary on
Biotechnology in Agriculture 401

Inspector General on Federal
Oversight of Hospitals 412

Sen. Edward M. Kennedy's
Eulogy for John F. Kennedy Jr. 422

UN Refugee Commissioner on
Promoting Peace in Africa 428

Surgeon General on
Suicide Prevention 439

ISRAELI PRIME MINISTER BARAK ON THE NEW GOVERNMENT
July 6, 1999

After three years of confrontation, both domestically and in foreign affairs, Israeli voters in 1999 turned to a new leader who promised to work for internal harmony and to complete the unfinished process of making peace with the country's Arab neighbors. Ehud Barak, a decorated war hero and former army chief of staff with little political experience, overwhelmingly won election as prime minister on May 17, 1999. He defeated Benjamin Netanyahu, who had thrived on confrontation during three years in office but ultimately found it to be his undoing.

Barak, the leader of the left-of-center Labor Party, portrayed himself as the successor to Yitzhak Rabin, the Labor prime minister who in 1993 reached a peace agreement with the Palestine Liberation Organization and was assassinated by an Israeli extremist in 1995. "I know that if Yitzhak today is looking at us from the sky, he is proud of us, just as we are proud of him, and that he knows that together we will fulfill his legacy," Barak told cheering supporters in claiming victory. (Israel-Palestinian peace accord, Historic Documents of 1993, p. 747; Rabin assassination, Historic Documents of 1995, p. 689; Netanyahu election, Historic Documents of 1996, p. 337)

Barak's first challenge was to craft a coalition government, and it took him nearly seven weeks to cobble together enough support from a wide range of parties to form a working majority in Israel's parliament, the Knesset. Within a matter of months Barak turned his attention to his biggest long-term challenges, completing a peace agreement with the Palestinians and negotiating a settlement to Israel's three-decade standoff with Syria. With diplomatic guidance from the United States, negotiations on both fronts were under way at year's end—but with no guarantees of success. (Middle East peace talks, p. 890)

Defeat for Netanyahu, Victory for Barak

Many analysts said the election was primarily a referendum on Netanyahu and his aggressive style, and only secondarily an affirmation of

*confidence in Barak. During his three years in office, Netanyahu—the leader
of the Likud Party coalition—had managed to alienate supporters and opponents alike with his hard-edged approach to nearly every issue. Netanyahu
raised self-confidence and self-righteousness to a new level, even for a country whose leaders frequently invoked a holy mandate for their decisions. Perhaps the most telling aspect of Netanyahu's final year in power was that key
leaders of the political opposition had once been among his most senior
advisers, including his former defense and foreign ministers.*

*Netanyahu came to office in 1996 promising to take a tough line with
Israel's longtime Arab neighbors. In particular, Netanyahu pledged to
refuse any concessions to the Palestinians, who were demanding that Israel
cede control of the West Bank of the Jordan River, which had been seized by
Israel from Jordan during the Six-Day War of 1967. Netanyahu effectively
froze U.S.-sponsored peace talks between Israel and the Palestinians,
encouraged the construction of settlements by religious nationalists in the
occupied territories, and gave at least tacit support to openly anti-Arab elements of his constituency. While popular among Netanyahu's supporters,
these actions did nothing to broaden his political base; opinion polls consistently showed that a majority of Israelis wanted more emphasis on
peace and less on confrontation.*

*Netanyahu also was plagued by a series of scandals involving key sup-
porters. One of the most damaging involved the ultraorthodox Shas Party,
a key element of Netanyahu's coalition, which represented Israelis of
Sephardic descent, whose origins are from the non-Western and Mediter-
ranean regions (including Spain, Turkey, Greece, Iraq, and Morocco) and
make up 60 percent of the Jewish population. Aryeh Deri, the charismatic
Shas leader, was convicted on bribery charges shortly before the election.
Deri's conviction did little to damage his personal support—Shas managed
to increase its Knesset representation in the May 17 election—but it reinforced an image among moderate Israelis of corruption within the
Netanyahu coalition.*

*Barak, by contrast, managed to portray himself as representing the best
of Israel and its ideals. As a former general known for his personal tough-
ness, Barak said he could be trusted to guard Israel's security in the unruly
neighborhood of the Middle East. But Barak said he also knew when to be
conciliatory for the sake of long-term peace and security. To Israelis tired
of Netanyahu's in-your-face assertiveness, Barak offered a reassuring alternative of blandness. He deliberately adopted a low-key posture, avoiding
controversy as much as possible and relying on advice from American
campaign experts who used polling data to gauge voter sentiment.*

*Barak's approach appeared to be exactly what the voters wanted. In a
country accustomed to close elections, Barak won 56 percent of the direct
vote for prime minister, with Netanyahu far behind at 44 percent. It was
only the second election in which the prime minister was elected directly
by the voters. Prior to Netanyahu's election in 1996, the prime minister
was selected by the Knesset.*

A Divided Knesset, Again

Barak's solid victory was not mirrored in parliamentary elections held the same day. While backing a candidate for prime minister who represented moderation, Israeli voters elected dozens of legislators representing the extremes of the country's political life. Among the parties, the biggest victor was the ultraorthodox Shas Party, which won 17 seats, an increase of 10 over its representation in the previous Knesset. At the other end of the spectrum, the leftist Meretz Party, which had been shut out of the Knesset in the previous election, managed to win 7 seats; that party's platform included granting full equality to all inhabitants of Israel, agreeing to establishment of a Palestinian state, and withdrawing from all territories occupied in the 1967 war. In total, fifteen parties managed to secure at least 1 seat in the 120-seat parliament; six of those parties were new.

The two mainstream parties—Barak's Labor Party and Netanyahu's Likud coalition—both lost seats in the election. Labor and a coalition partner won 27 seats, a drop of 7 from the previous election, and Likud lost 13 seats, falling to just 19 representatives.

In the weeks following the election, Barak did something practically unknown in Israeli politics: he stayed out of the limelight, conducting negotiations with potential coalition partners in private and avoiding saying anything that might stir controversy. His strategy appeared to be that of a skilled card player, refusing to show his hand and waiting for others to make the first move. The strategy took a long time to succeed but produced results. One of the most important was the resignation of the convicted Deri as head of the Shas Party. Barak had said he was willing to take Shas (which favored peace talks) as a coalition partner, but only if Deri stepped down. Deri's resignation as party leader in mid-June cleared the way for Shas to join the government and boosted Barak's reputation as a shrewd negotiator.

By law, Barak had forty-five days to form a coalition government, and he took most of that time. What emerged from seven weeks of backroom maneuvering was a broad coalition representing nearly two-thirds of the 120 votes in the Knesset—but also a range of factions with little in common. Many analysts said the coalition of seven parties had the potential to unravel easily if Barak failed to tend to its health on a regular basis. Explaining his moves, Barak said he was "forced by the lessons of Jewish history and the deep divide within our people to form a government that will be able to function during the most difficult times with the wide acceptance of the majority."

Among those excluded from the coalition were some parties that might have appeared to be Barak's natural allies, including one secular moderate party and two parties representing Israel's Arab minority. But leaders of those parties were expected to support Barak on crucial votes in the Knesset concerning peace issues.

Barak unveiled his government on July 6 and immediately came under criticism for the composition of the seventeen-member cabinet. Barak took the most important post—that of defense minister—for himself and put several other key ministries in the hands of men considered to be politically weak or unassertive. Critics said Barak appeared to want a cabinet composed of men (only one member was a woman) who would pose no challenge to him. As an example, the critics pointed to Barak's choice for foreign minister, David Levy, who had held the same post under Netanyahu before breaking with the latter's inflexible approach on peace talks. Barak lost one early internal struggle when his coalition chose Avraham Burg, a rival figure within the Labor Party, as speaker of parliament, rejecting Barak's hand-picked candidate.

In his opening speech to parliament later on July 7, Barak took a conciliatory approach, expressing empathy with North African-born Jews and others who had felt excluded from Israeli society and reaching out to the Palestinians and Syrians whom he expected to face across the peace table. Addressing himself directly to Syrian president Hafez al-Assad, Barak said: "We have been harsh and bitter enemies on the battlefield. Now it is time to form an open and brave peace that will insure the future and security of our peoples, our children, and our grandchildren." Peace negotiations would be "difficult," Barak said, but he added: "If we find the same determination on the other side, no power in the world will stop us."

Barak moved quickly to restart peace negotiations with the Palestinians. Those talks bore fruit with an agreement on September 4 that reformulated a U.S.-brokered compromise from 1998 on the transfer of West Bank land to the Palestinians.

Following are excerpts from an address July 6, 1999, by Israeli prime minister Ehud Barak, in which he announced his cabinet and his government program to the Knesset:

Let me begin with a personal comment. I have been a soldier for practically all my adult life. I have known the pride of victory, but also the pain of failure. And as one whose only clothes, for decades, wore olive-drab uniforms, I tell you today that, in the words of the poet Hillel, "We—the gray soldiers, whose hands are blackened with war, whose nostrils reek with death, whose throats are hoarse—we cry love to inside your souls."

I am not alone here today on this podium. Together with me are generations of IDF [Israel Defense Force] soldiers who withstood the most severe trials of fire in order to secure our liberty. Together with me are those who returned at dawn from the nighttime inferno, carrying on their shoulders the silent stretchers bearing their lifeless comrades.

I am not alone here today on this podium. Together with me are the white-coated hi-tech people in Herzliya and the struggling unemployed, without a livelihood from Dimona, Ofakim and Hazor, rabbis and secular Jews, field-workers, gardeners and construction workers. I am not alone.

I am not alone today. Together with me are the mothers who do not sleep at night and the fathers tormented by anguish. Together with me are all the dreamers and the fighters.

And speaking for myself and the entire Israeli government which is setting forth today, I assure you that we have not closed our eyes in the last month, and we will not close our eyes as long as is needed in the future so that mothers in Israel sleep peacefully in the coming years.

Mr. Speaker, Members of the Knesset:

In the annals of the Knesset there are turning points, ends of eras and beginnings of new ones. Today a new government in Israel starts out, resting on the broad-based confidence of the House and most of the people.

I believe that this day will be chronicled as a milestone and turning point— a time of reconciliation, unity and peace. . . .

I am proud to submit to the people and the House a new, broad-based, good, representative government, supported by the large majority of Knesset members and the citizens of the state. It was not in vain that I took advantage of the full time allotted by law to form the government. I did not take the easy way. The lessons of Jewish history and the depth of the social and political chasm in Israel today required me to choose the long and patient way in order to achieve the goal which I had set for myself: to form a government which will act during a time of difficult national decisions, through consent and balance between most sections of the people. I did not accept any disqualification of any side.

During the negotiations I seriously examined the possibility of expanding the basis of the coalition even further. This was not possible and in retrospect, this may have been best. In a democratic system, there is great importance to the role of a parliamentary opposition, and it is my intention to express my recognition of this by maintaining ongoing contacts with, providing information to and holding consultations with the heads of those factions which are not members of the coalition. I expect substantive and constructive criticism from the opposition which will also enable consideration of its opinion in managing affairs of state.

Mr. Speaker, Members of the Knesset,

The basic guidelines of the Government and the coalition agreements are before you. Everything is open and fully disclosed. Nothing is concealed, there are no secret agreements, no "under-the-table" understandings, and as you have seen, there are neither financial commitments nor favors to specific sectors or groups.

I will not go into the details of all the Government guidelines. The guidelines constitute the identity card of the government, the principles of its policy and its declaration of intent. All previous governments had good intentions. Not all were equally successful in putting them into practice. I know that the Government will be judged by its actions, not its intentions. I will try will all my might to ensure that the gap between its good intentions and its actions is as narrow as possible. . . .

... We know that the victory of Zionism will not be complete until the achievement of genuine peace, full security, and relations of friendship, trust and cooperation with all our neighbors. And therefore, the Government's supreme goal will be to bring peace and security to Israel, while safeguarding the vital interests of the State of Israel. The great historic breakthrough to peace took place 20 years ago, through the vision and courage of two outstanding leaders: the late Menahem Begin [former Israeli prime minister] and the late Anwar Sadat [former president of Egypt] may they rest in peace.

A further milestone was the Madrid Conference during the tenure of Prime Minister Yitzhak Shamir.

Renewed and far-reaching impetus was imparted by Yitzhak Rabin, the courageous and unswerving leader, from whom I learned so much, and who was assassinated during the struggle for his path, the path of peace, and with him, by our friend Shimon Peres.

The government of Benjamin Netanyahu indeed opened with the Hebron Agreement, but it was unable to implement the Wye accords which it had signed.

Now it is our duty to complete the mission, and establish a comprehensive peace in the Middle East which has known so much war. It is our duty to ourselves and our children to take decisive measures to strengthen Israel by ending the Arab-Israeli conflict. This government is determined to make every effort, pursue every path and do everything necessary for Israel's security, the achievement of peace and the prevention of war.

We have an historic obligation to take advantage of the "window of opportunity" which has opened before us in order to bring long-term security and peace to Israel. We know that comprehensive and stable peace can be established only if it rests, simultaneously, on four pillars: Egypt, Jordan, and Syria and Lebanon, in some sense as a single bloc, and of course the Palestinians. As long as peace is not grounded on all these four pillars, it will remain incomplete and unstable. The Arab countries must know that only a strong and self-confident Israel can bring peace.

Here, today, I call upon all the leaders of the region to extend their hands to meet our outstretched hand, and toward a "peace of the brave," in a region which has known so much war, blood and suffering. To our neighbors the Palestinians, I wish to say: the bitter conflict between us has brought great suffering to both our peoples. Now, there is no reason to settle accounts over historical mistakes. Perhaps things could have been otherwise, but we cannot change the past; we can only make the future better. I am not only cognizant of the sufferings of my people, but I also recognize the sufferings of the Palestinian people. My ambition and desire is to bring an end to violence and suffering, and to work with the elected Palestinian leadership, under Chairman Yasser Arafat, in partnership and respect, in order to jointly arrive at a fair and agreed settlement for co-existence in freedom, prosperity and good neighborliness in this beloved land where the two peoples will always live.

To Syrian President Hafez Assad, I say that the new Israeli government is determined, as soon as possible, to advance the negotiations for the achievement of full, bilateral treaty of peace and security, on the basis of Security Council Resolutions 242 and 338.

We have been tough and bitter adversaries on the battlefield. The time has come to establish a secure and courageous peace which will ensure the futures of our peoples, our children and our grandchildren.

It is my intention to bring an end to the IDF presence in Lebanon within one year, to deploy the IDF, through agreement, along the border, and to bring our boys home—while also taking the necessary measures to guarantee the welfare and security of residents along the northern border, as well as the future of the Lebanese security and civilian assistance personnel who have worked alongside us, over all these years, for the sake of the residents of the region.

I wish to take advantage of this opportunity to praise the residents of Kiryat Shmona and communities along the confrontation line for their firm stand in the face of the Katyushas [rockets launched from Palestinian bases in southern Lebanon]. From here, on behalf of us all, I offer my support to them. Their determination and the strength of the IDF are what will enable us to create the new situation.

Mr. Speaker, distinguished Knesset,

These two missions—arriving at a permanent settlement with the Palestinians, and achieving peace with Syria and Lebanon—are, in my eyes, equally vital and urgent. One neither outranks the other, nor has priority over it.

The Government's objective will be to act, at the same time, to bring peace closer on all fronts, but without compromising on Israel's security needs and most vital interests—first and foremost among them, a united Jerusalem, the eternal capital of Israel, under our sovereignty. We will not be deterred by the difficulties.

I know very well that difficult negotiations, replete with crises and ups-and-downs, await us before we reach our desired goal.

I can only promise that, if the other side displays the same degree of determination and good will to reach an agreement as on our side, no force in the world will prevent us from achieving peace here.

In this context, I attach the greatest importance to the support of our partners to peace treaties: Egypt and Jordan. I believe that President Hosni Mubarak and King Abdullah can play a vital role in creating the dynamics and an atmosphere of trust so needed for progress toward peace. They can also advance education for peace among the children of Egypt and Jordan, the Palestinians and, in the future, also of Syria and Lebanon—education for peace, which is a condition for any long-term, stable peace. I am convinced that King Hassan of Morocco can also contribute to this, as can other countries who already, in the past, opened channels of communication with Israel, cooperating with the peace process in various spheres. My aspiration will be to firmly resume these contacts in order to create a favorable regional atmosphere that can assist the negotiations.

It goes without saying that the assistance of the United States is a fundamental condition for any progress toward resolving the conflict in the region. The friendship of America, under the leadership of President Clinton, its generosity and the intensity of its support for the peace process in the Middle East constitute a vital component in the chance to achieve our goal. I will soon leave for the United States, at the invitation of President Clinton, a loyal friend of Israel, in order to discuss the gamut of issues facing us, first and foremost, the renewal of the peace process on all tracks, and the fortification of the strength and security of Israel.

Mr. Speaker, Members of the Knesset,

The guarantee of the peace agreements and their implementation lies in the strength of the Israel Defense Forces. As such, we will attend to bolstering the IDF, the quality of its commanders and soldiers, its equipment—with the best educational and technological systems—training and fitness, its ability to always be prepared to deter and provide a response to distant and near dangers, and to all kinds of threats, whether conventional or otherwise. But security is not only provided with tanks, planes or missile boats. Security is, first and foremost, provided by individuals. It is they who shape the integrity of the society and of the national strength of Israel. Therefore, together with the promotion of security and peace, and foreign policy, and with no less urgency and importance, the Government is obliged to contend with the challenges of society, the economy and the needs of the citizen.

Israeli society is a unique society: a fascinating mosaic of hues and opinions, cultures and creeds—veteran residents and new immigrants, people from different Diasporas, religious and ultra-Orthodox and traditional and secular, Jews and Arabs and Druze and Circassians. Together, equally, they are Israel. A society where none are better or less good, but where, as in every human society, there are fringes of poverty and backwardness. There are weak sectors of hundreds of thousands of agonizing citizens who are unable, without growth or stimulus, to maintain the rapid pace of progress. We must not rush forward and leave them behind by the roadside.

The Government, under my leadership, is committed to waging war on the unemployment and poverty threatening to undermine and unravel our social fabric, and to struggling toward the strengthening of the health system and the improvement of the welfare services in the State of Israel. We will introduce a new national order of priorities.

The most important mission which the Government will take upon itself in the social sphere is the positioning of education as its top priority. I always viewed education as the most correct and worthwhile long-term investment. Therefore, we will aspire to provide the best possible education to every single child and adolescent in Israel, from kindergarten through university. . . .

I wish to say something to those citizens who are members of minority communities in the State of Israel: I wholeheartedly believe in the equal value of all humankind, in equality between people and between citizens, without distinction. The State of Israel has not always been sufficiently wise to grant all its citizens a sense of equality and partnership. The disparities are great, and the sentiment of bitterness is not unjustified. I know that you have heard innumerable slogans and promises, and I pledge today that the Government, under my leadership, will make every effort to gradually bridge the gaps, dissipate the alienation and provide equality for all sectors of the population in

Israel. The Rabin and Peres governments began a focused effort to bring about this change. We will continue along this path with renewed vigor.

Mr. Speaker, Members of the Knesset,

Emphasizing the social aspect of Government policy is not in contradiction with a policy of free and productive economics, free unnecessary government interference. An economy which will act as a magnet for foreign investment, and be increasingly based on hi-tech industries and domestic research and development which will put Israel at the forefront of scientific and technological progress—because there can be no healthy society without a healthy economy, and vice versa. The creation of 300,000 new jobs in the next four years—as I pledged in my election campaign—is a concrete and possible objective for reducing the shame of unemployment and strengthening the entire economy. At the same time, this goal is contingent upon imparting a new impetus to the economy, as a result of restored confidence in a future of peace for the region and the country. . . .

The primary consideration which guided me in composing this government was the need to find the broadest possible common denominator in order responsibly bring together representatives of parties and sectors from various, even opposing, sides of Israeli society. This is not simple, and it comes at a cost. We will first have to make the painful compromises among ourselves, via a policy which is the fruit of a broad-based, sober and realistic consensus—an honest policy, confident in our strength, which is not conceived of wishful thinking and vacuous arrogance, of indecent haste, hesitation and missed opportunity, of vacillation and the intoxication of power, but which is marked by great love for all parts of our homeland and the painful acknowledgment of the ties of others as well.

This government will not turn its back on any group, portion, sector or ideological stream in Israeli society. This will be a government of constant dialogue, openness and attentiveness, a government that will aspire a "new national consensus," but not shirk from decisions or resign itself to paralysis and be stalemated. I know and understand exactly where the government must head and the destination it must reach, and I intend to lead this march to the finish line.

Ultimately, as I have pledged, if and when cardinal historic decisions are required, the entire public will be called to take a decision, in accordance with its sovereign will, in a referendum. . . .

Today, millions of eyes in Israel, millions of eyes of Jews around the world, and millions of eyes around the whole world are focused on us, praying that we will know to lead the country, with determination and a sure hand toward a new path, momentum and a new page in the chronicles of the State of Israel. A new page of peace in an arena which, in recent generations, has almost except pain, bereavement and suffering.

Accompanied by the blessings and concern of everyone, we embark today on the long and arduous path. I would be most appreciative if you would express your confidence in the Government today and wish it well and God speed.

REPORT ON "DIGITAL DIVIDE" IN ACCESS TO COMPUTERS, INTERNET
July 8, 1999

For the third time in five years, the U.S. Commerce Department reported significant disparities among Americans in access to computer technology and the Internet. Whites, the wealthy, and the well-educated were significantly more likely to have entered the computer age than were blacks and Hispanics and those with less money and education, according to a study by the department's National Telecommunications and Information Administration.

The study, "Falling Through the Net: Defining the Digital Divide," was issued July 8, 1999, and offered no policy suggestions for narrowing the gap between those who had access to computer technology and those who did not. Even so, the Clinton administration used the study to support policies such as a controversial national tax on telephone service that subsidized Internet access at schools and public libraries. President Bill Clinton on December 9 signed an executive memorandum declaring a "national goal of making computers and Internet access available for every American."

Some critics said the Commerce Department study was overblown. They noted that throughout history all technological advances reached the wealthy and powerful first and then spread through the rest of society. In fact, these critics said, computers were becoming widely accessible to American society at a faster rate than such previous inventions as the automobile, telephone, and television.

By 1999 there was little dispute that computers and the Internet were nearly essential tools for education and the workplace and were becoming increasingly important at home. The personal computer was popularized in the early 1980s and within fifteen years became nearly universal in offices and schools. The rate of computer ownership increased during the late 1990s as prices for home computers dropped markedly. In the early 1990s the general public began widespread use of the Internet—in its form as the World Wide Web—and within less than five years it too had developed into a powerful medium for dispensing information and marketing any-thing from books to luxury automobiles.

Detailing the Digital Divide

The 1999 Commerce Department report was intended to update findings of similar studies published in 1995 and 1998. Each of the studies was based on Census Bureau interviews conducted the previous year; the 1999 report came from a national sample of 48,000 households.

In general, the report found that the higher the levels of education and income, the more likely it was that households would have computers and access to the Internet. In addition, whites and people of Asian descent were more likely to use computer technology, both at home and at work, than blacks and Hispanics. Similar trends emerged in the 1995 and 1998 reports, although the percentages of computer access were higher among all groups by 1999.

Nationally, the study found that 42.1 percent of households owned at least one computer (compared with 24.1 percent in 1994 and 36.6 percent in 1994), and 26.2 percent had home access to the Internet (compared with 18.6 percent in 1997).

As could be expected, high-income households were much more likely to own computers and have home access to the Internet than low-income households. For example, the study noted that households with annual incomes higher than $75,000 were more than five times as likely to own computers and seven times more likely to be connected to the Internet than households with incomes lower than $10,000. Among households with at least one member holding a college degree, 68.7 percent owned a computer and 44.6 percent had Internet access at home; among households with the highest educational achievement being a high school diploma, the figures were 31.2 percent and 13.8 percent, respectively.

Among racial groups, households whose members were of Asian/Pacific Island descent were by far the most likely to own a computer (55 percent), followed by whites (46.6 percent), Hispanics (25.5 percent), and blacks (23.2 percent). The trend was the same for Internet access, although at lower percentage levels for each race group. Millions of Americans who did not have computers or Internet access at home were using facilities at schools, local libraries, or at "community access centers" that were funded by public or private sources. Not surprisingly, the study found that members of disadvantaged groups were more likely to depend upon such public facilities than were the more well-to-do and highly educated Americans.

The report also showed disparities by geographical region, but it was difficult to draw general conclusions about the reasons for those dispari-ties. Residents of the nine southeastern and Appalachian states (except for Florida) were at the bottom of the list, with an average of less than 33 per-cent of households owning computers, compared with the national average of 42.1 percent. Mississippi ranked last among the states: 25.7 percent of its households reported owning a computer. At the top of the list were

Alaska (62.4 percent) and Utah (60.1 percent). Other states with more than half of households reporting computer ownership were, in descending order, Washington, Colorado, New Hampshire, Oregon, and Idaho.

The authors of the report drew special attention to one set of statistics they said demonstrated that the "digital divide" between whites and Asians, on the one hand, and blacks and Hispanics, on the other, was becoming a "racial ravine." The report noted, for example, that in 1994 there was a 16.8 percentage point difference in computer ownership between white and black households; by 1998 that difference had grown to 23.4 percentage. Similarly, the report said the gap between whites and Hispanics had grown over the same period from 14.8 percentage points to 21.1 points.

In releasing the report, Clinton said "there is a growing digital divide between those who have access to the digital economy and the Internet and those who don't, and the divide exists along the lines of education, income, region and race." To "unlock the potential of our workers," he said, "we have to close that gap."

A Critique of the Study

A detailed criticism of the Commerce Department study came from David Boaz, executive vice president of the Cato Institute, a Washington, D.C.-based libertarian think tank. In a commentary entitled "A Snapshot View of a Complex World," Boaz argued that the study represented merely a limited "snapshot" of a "dynamic world." Noting the rapid rate at which Americans at all levels had acquired computers and access to the Internet, Boaz said: "When you look at the progress, not the snapshot, the progress is amazing. It is sheer scaremongering to write reports about 'information haves and have-nots.' The reality is a little less exciting: have nows and have-laters. Families that do not have a computer now are going to have them in a few years."

Boaz also criticized the Commerce Department study for its use of statistics to support its claim of a widening "racial ravine" in computer ownership. Using data from the study—but looking at them differently than did the Commerce Department authors—he noted that in 1994 whites were 2.6 times as likely as blacks to own a computer; by 1998 that figure had been reduced to 2.0. Looked at another way, Boaz said, between 1994 and 1998 computer ownership rose by 72 percent in white households and by 125 percent in black households. "That is good news all around," Boaz said, adding that the Commerce Department report "picked the reading that would justify claiming the existence of a 'racial ravine.'"

Programs to Boost Internet Access

Beginning in the early 1990s, government agencies, foundations, and private companies developed numerous programs to make computers and the Internet more accessible to disadvantaged populations. Some of these programs were national in scope; others were developed at the state and local level.

The best known and most controversial national program was known as E-rate. Authorized by Congress as part of the 1996 Telecommunications Act (PL 104-104), this program gave discounts of 20 to 90 percent on telecommunications services to schools and libraries in low-income, rural, or otherwise disadvantaged areas. Money for the program came from a national tax on telephone service, averaging about $8 annually per telephone line. The Federal Communications Commission (FCC) administered the program, for which Congress established an annual spending limit of $2.25 billion.

Another federal program, also funded through FCC fees, subsidized telecommunications services for hospitals and other health care providers in rural areas. The Clinton administration praised these programs as important means of ensuring equal access to computer technology. Critics, including key Republicans in Congress, objected to forcing the general public, through taxation, to subsidize Internet access for limited populations.

On a state level, public utilities commissions in California and Ohio were among those using corporate mergers to help subsidize Internet access for disadvantaged communities. As part of their review of mergers between telephone companies, the California and Ohio commissions required the merging companies to establish funds and other programs to benefit consumers, especially those in low-income areas. In California, for example, Pacific Bell established a fund to provide $5 million annually in grants to broaden technology access in disadvantaged communities.

The Benton Foundation, a Washington, D.C.-based organization that promoted public access to the communications media, also was working with communications and technology companies and organizations such as the National Urban League to develop programs for making computers and Internet access available to "underserved communities." One of the most ambitious aspects of the foundation's programs was the creation of a "Digital Divide Network." The network was described as a national clearinghouse of information on public and private programs to broaden access to computer technology.

As a follow-up to the Commerce Department report, the Clinton administration on December 9 hosted a conference in Washington of civil rights groups, community organizations, technology companies, and others interested in the "digital divide" issue. As the conference was getting started, Clinton announced that he had signed an executive memorandum committing the federal government to a "national goal" of making computer technology and Internet access available to all Americans. Clinton directed Commerce Secretary William Daley to develop a strategy for reaching that goal. At the conference, many participants stressed an additional goal: encouraging the development of content on the Internet that would serve the needs of minorities and other disadvantaged groups.

Following are excerpts from the report, "Falling Through the Net: Defining the Digital Divide," issued July 8, 1999, by the National Telecommunications and Information Administration of the U.S. Commerce Department:

Part I

Household access

A. Introduction

Over the last five years, NTIA [National Telecommunication and Information Administration] has measured household connectivity as a means of determining which Americans are connected to the nation's telecommunications and information infrastructure. Part I updates the earlier household penetration surveys released in NTIA's *Falling Through the Net: A Survey of the "Have Nots" in Rural and Urban America* (July 1995) and *Falling Through the Net II: New Data on the Digital Divide* (July 1998). As in our earlier surveys, we have measured household telephone, computer, and Internet penetration rates across America to determine which Americans own telephones and personal computers (PCs) and access the Internet at home.

The 1998 data reveal that, overall, U.S. households are significantly more connected by telephone, computer, and the Internet since NTIA issued the first *Falling Through the Net* report, which was based on 1994 Current Population Survey (CPS) results. Penetration rates have risen across all demographic groups and geographic areas. Nevertheless, penetration levels currently differ—often substantially—according to income, education level, race, household type, and geography, among other demographic characteristics. The differences in connectivity are most pronounced with respect to computers and Internet access.

The following examples highlight the breadth of the digital divide today:

- Those with a college degree are more than *eight times* as likely to have a computer at home, and nearly *sixteen times* as likely to have home Internet access, as those with an elementary school education.
- A high-income household in an urban area is more than *twenty times* as likely as a rural, low-income household to have Internet access.
- A child in a low-income White family is *three times* as likely to have Internet access as a child in a comparable Black family, and *four times* as likely to have access as children in a comparable Hispanic household.
- A wealthy household of Asian/Pacific Islander descent is nearly *thirteen times* as likely to own a computer as a poor Black household, and nearly *thirty-four times* as likely to have Internet access.
- Finally, a child in a dual-parent White household is nearly twice as likely to have Internet access as a child in a White single-parent household,

while a child in a dual-parent Black family is almost *four times* as likely to have access as a child in a single-parent Black household.

The data reveal that the digital divide—the disparities in access to telephones, personal computers (PCs), and the Internet across certain demographic groups—still exists and, in many cases, has *widened significantly*. The gap for computers and Internet access has generally grown larger by categories of education, income, and race. . . .

B. Telephone Penetration

As a mature technology, telephones are now a likely feature in most American homes. Unlike computer and Internet use, telephone penetration rates have generally stabilized (at about 94%). That stabilization, however, masks disparities that still exist among different demographic groups. Certain groups, such as low-income, young, and certain minority households, are still far less likely to own telephones than higher income, older, or White or Asian/Pacific Islander households. These disparities are particularly noticeable in rural areas.

The good news is that the differential between traditional "haves" and "have nots" has decreased in recent years. For example, no group is more likely to own a telephone today than Black households earning $75,000 or more (traditionally less connected than White households at the same income level).

1. Stable Telephone Penetration

As noted, the 1998 data reveal that telephone penetration rates among households have changed little overall in the last few years. From 1994 to 1998, at-home telephone ownership in America has increased slightly from 93.8% to 94.1%. All geographic locations—whether rural, urban, or central city—have experienced a similar marginal growth, although central cities have continued to lag behind rural and urban areas.

2. Disparities in Telephone Penetration

The likelihood of owning a phone still varies significantly, however, by the household's income, education level, race, age, or household makeup. Additionally, where a person lives can also greatly influence the likelihood of telephone ownership. While rural areas are generally as connected as urban areas, those groups that are less likely to own phones have especially low penetration rates in rural areas. . . .

3. Closing Penetration Gaps

While there are still acute disparities among different demographic groups, the encouraging news is that certain disparities appear to be shrinking over time. The racial divide, for example, between Whites and Blacks, and Whites and Hispanics, has shrunk significantly between 1994 and 1998. In 1994, there was a 10.6 percentage point difference between telephone penetration rates in White and Black households. By 1998, that gap decreased (by 25.5%) to a

7.9 percentage point difference. Similarly, the White/Hispanic differential of 10.2 points in 1994 has decreased by 37.3% to a 6.4 percentage point gap in 1998. . . .

C. Access to Electronic Services

While telephone penetration has remained stable across the nation, significant changes have occurred for personal computer ownership and Internet access. For the latter two categories, household rates have soared since 1994 for all demographic groups in all locations. These increases indicate that Americans across the board are increasingly embracing electronic services by employing them in their homes.

Despite increasing connectivity for all groups, in some areas the digital divide still exists and, in a number of cases, is *growing*. Some groups (such as certain minority or low-income households in rural America) still have PC and Internet penetration rates in the single digits. By contrast, other groups (such as higher-income, highly educated, or dual-parent households) have rising connectivity rates. One promising sign of change is that the gap between races for PC ownership has narrowed significantly at the highest income level (above $75,000).

1. Expanding Access to Electronic Services

Americans of every demographic group and geographic area have experienced a significant increase in computer ownership and Internet access. Nationwide, PC ownership is now at 42.1%, up from 24.1% in 1994 and 36.6% in 1997 (an increase of 74.7% and 15.0%, respectively). Households across rural, central city, and urban areas now own home computers in greater numbers; each area experienced at least a sixteen percentage point increase since 1994, and at least a five percentage point increase since 1997. Similarly, households of all ethnic groups, income levels, education levels, and ages have experienced a significant increase. Black and Hispanic households, for example, are now twice as likely to own PCs as they were in 1994.

Internet access has also grown significantly in the last year: 26.2% of U.S. households now have Internet access, up from 18.6% in 1997 (an increase of 40.9%). As with computer ownership, Internet access has increased for all demographic groups in all locations. In the last year alone, for example, Internet access increased 52.8% for White households, 52.0% for Black households, and 48.3% for Hispanic households.

2. Disparities in Access to Electronic Services

Despite these gains across American households, distinct disparities in access remain. Americans living in rural areas are less likely to be connected by PCs or the Internet—even when holding income constant. Indeed, at most income brackets below $35,000, those living in urban areas are at least 25% more likely to have Internet access than those in rural areas. Additionally, groups that already have low penetration rates (such as low-income, young, or certain minority households) are the least connected in rural areas and central cities.

Most of this closure has occurred just in the last year. In the period between 1997 and 1998, the White/Black household gap decreased by 20.2% (from a difference of 9.9 percentage points in 1997 to a gap of 7.9 percentage points in 1998), and the White/Hispanic household gap decreased by 31.9% (from a difference of 9.4 percentage points in 1997 to a gap of 6.4 percentage points in 1998). . . .

The following demographic and geographic breakdowns are significant determinants of a household's likelihood of owning a computer or accessing the Internet from home:

Income. PC and Internet penetration rates both increase with higher income levels. Households at higher income levels are far more likely to own computers and access the Internet than those at the lowest income levels. Those with an income over $75,000 are more than *five times* as likely to have a computer at home and are more than *seven times* as likely to have home Internet access as those with an income under $10,000.

Low income households in rural areas are the least connected, experiencing connectivity rates in the single digits for both PCs and Internet access. The contrast between low income households (earning between $5,000 and $9,999) in rural America and high income households (earning more than $75,000) in urban areas is particularly acute: 8.1% versus 76.5% for computer ownership, and 2.9% versus 62.0% for Internet access.

The impact of income on Internet access is event even among families with the same race and family structure. Among similarly-situated families (two parents, same race), a family earning more than $35,000 is two to almost six times as likely to have Internet access as a family earning less than $35,000. The most significant disparity is among Hispanic families: two-parent households earning more than $35,000 are nearly *six times* as likely to have Internet access as those earning less than $35,000.

Race/Origin. As with telephone penetration, race also influences connectivity. Unlike telephone penetration, however, households of Asian/Pacific Island descent have the clear lead in computer penetration (55.0%) and Internet access rates (36.0%), followed by White households (46.6% and 29.8%, respectively). Black and Hispanic households have far lower PC penetration levels (at 23.2% and 25.5%), and Internet access levels (11.2% and 12.6%).

Again, geography and income influence these trends. Urban Asians/Pacific Islanders have the highest computer penetration rates (55.6%) and Internet access rates (36.5%). By contrast, rural Black households are the least connected group in terms of PC ownership (17.9%) or Internet access (7.1%). Black households earning less than $15,000 are also at the opposite end of the spectrum from high income Asians/Pacific Islanders for PC ownership (6.6% versus 85.0%).

The role of race or ethnic origin is highlighted when looking at similarly-situated families. A White, two-parent household earning less than $35,000 is nearly *three times* as likely to have Internet access as a comparable Black household and nearly *four times* as likely to have Internet access as Hispanic households in the same income category.

Education. Access to information resources is closely tied to one's level of education. Households at higher education levels are far more likely to own computers and access the Internet than those at the lowest education levels. Those with a college degree or higher are more than *eight times* as likely to have a computer at home (68.7% versus 7.9%) and are nearly *sixteen times* as likely to have home Internet access (48.9% versus 3.1%) as those with an elementary school education. In rural areas, the disparity is even greater. Those with a college degree or higher are more than *eleven times* as likely to have a computer at home (6.3% versus 69.7%) and are more than *twenty-six times* as likely to have home Internet access (1.8% versus 47.0%) as those with an elementary school education.

Household Type. As with telephones, the makeup of the household influences the likelihood of the household's access to electronic services. Computer ownership lags among single-parent households, especially female-headed households (31.7%), compared to married couples with children (61.8%). The same is true for Internet access (15.0% for female-headed households, 39.3% for dual-parent households).

When holding race constant, it is clear that family composition can still have a significant impact on Internet access. Overall, dual-parent White families are nearly twice as likely to have Internet access as single-parent White households (44.9% versus 23.4%). Black families with two parents are nearly *four times* as likely to have Internet access as single-parent Black households (20.4% versus 5.6%). And, children of two-parent Hispanic homes are nearly *two and a half times* as likely to have Internet access as their single-parent counterparts (14.0% versus 6.0%).

These differences are modified somewhat when income is taken into account. Nevertheless, even when comparing households of similar incomes, disparities in Internet access persist. At all income levels, Black, Asian, and Native American households with two parents, are twice as likely to have Internet access as those with one parent. For Hispanics and White households with two parents, on the other hand, clear-cut differences emerge only for incomes above $35,000. For these households, Whites are one and a half times more likely and Hispanics are *twice* as likely to have Internet access.

Age. Age also plays a role in access to information resources. While seniors have the highest penetration rates for telephones, they trail all other age groups with respect to computer ownership (25.8%) and Internet access (14.6%). Young households (under age 25) exhibit the second lowest penetration rates (32.3% for PCs, 20.5% for Internet access). Households in the middle-age brackets (35–55 years) lead all others in PC penetration (nearly 55.0%) and Internet access (over 34.0%). The contrasts among age groups are particularly striking between rural seniors (23.3% for PCs, 12.4% for Internet) and young, rural households (27.7% for PCs, 13.3% for Internet) on the one hand, and urban 45–54 year-olds on the other (55.3% for PCs, 36.5% for Internet).

Region. The region where a household is located also impacts its access to electronic services. The West is the clear-cut leader for both computer penetration (48.9%) and Internet access (31.3%). At the other end of the spectrum is the South at 38.0% for PC penetration and 23.5% for Internet access. Looking at the degree of urbanization, the lowest rates are in Northeast central cities (30.4% for PCs, 18.7% for Internet access); the highest are in the urban West (49.2% for PCs, 32.0% for Internet access).

State. As with telephones, computer penetration among states is grouped according to tiers due to the ranges of certainty created by the use of 90% confidence intervals. The top tier ranges from Alaska's 62.4% to Wyoming's 46.1%. The middle grouping is bounded by Arizona (44.3%) and Pennsylvania (39.3%). The low tier includes principally southern states, ranging from Oklahoma (37.8%) to Mississippi (25.7%). Regarding Internet access, the ordering of the states—ranging from Alaska (44.1%) to Mississippi (13.6%)—tracks relatively closely the PC rankings, but often with confidence intervals at the 90% level.

In sum, disparities with respect to electronic access clearly exist across various demographic and geographic categories. Similar to telephone penetration, electronic access comes hardest for Americans who are low-income, Black or Hispanic or Native American, less educated, single-parent families (but especially single-female householders), young heads-of-households, and who live in the South, rural areas or central cities. Dissimilar to the phone profile, however, senior "have nots" are less connected in terms of electronic access. And Asians/Pacific Islanders have reached a leading status with respect to computers and Internet access that they have not enjoyed in telephone comparisons.

3. Expanding Digital Divide

The chief concern with respect to household computer and Internet access is the growing digital divide. Groups that were already connected (*e.g.*, higher-income, more educated, White and Asian/Pacific Islander households) are now far more connected, while those with lower rates have increased less quickly. As a result, the gap between the information "haves" and "have nots" is growing over time. The increasing divides are particularly troublesome with regard to Internet access.

a. Divide by Race/Origin. The digital divide has turned into a "racial ravine" when one looks at access among households of different races and ethnic origins. With regard to computers, the gap between White and Black households *grew 39.2%* (from a 16.8 percentage point difference to a 23.4 percentage point difference) between 1994 and 1998. For White versus Hispanic households, the gap similarly *rose by 42.6%* (from a 14.8 point gap to 21.1 point gap).

Minorities are losing ground even faster with regard to Internet access. Between 1997 and 1998, the gap between White and Black households *increased by 53.3%* (from a 13.5 percentage point difference to a 20.7 percentage point difference), and *by 56.0%* (from a 12.5 percentage point difference to a 19.5 percentage point difference) between White and Hispanic households.

Even when holding income constant, there is still a yawning divide among different races and origins. At the lowest income levels, the gap has waned considerably for computer ownership. For households earning less than $15,000, the gaps rose substantially: by 73.0% or an additional 4.6 points between White and Black households, and by 44.6% or an additional 2.5 points between White and Hispanic households. For the households earning between $15,000 and $34,999, the disparities between White and Black households has increased by 61.7% (or 5.0 percentage points), and 46.0% or (4.0 percentage points) between White and Hispanic households.

For the same period, the increases for the $35,000–$74,999 bracket are much smaller for both the White/Black gap (a growth of 6.4%, or 1.0 percentage points) and the White/Hispanic divide (a growth of 15.2%, or 1.5 percentage points). The most striking finding, however, concerns the highest income level of $75,000 or more. For that income range, the gap between White and Black households has *declined* substantially (by 76.2%, or 6.4 percentage points), while the gap between White and Hispanic households has grown by 4.9 percentage points.

b. Divide Based on Education Level. Households at higher education levels are now also much more likely to own computers and access the Internet than those at the lowest education levels. In the last year alone, the gap in computer use has grown 7.8% (from a 56.4 to a 60.8 percentage point difference). The divide with respect to Internet access has waned 25.0% (from a 36.6 to a 45.8 percentage point difference). Not all groups, however, are lagging further behind the front-runners. Those with some college education, and those with a high school diploma, are now closing in on those with a college education.

c. Divide Based on Income. The digital divide has waned substantially when comparing households of different incomes. In the last year, the divide between the highest and lowest income groups grew 29.0% (from a 42.0 to a 52.2 percentage point difference) for Internet access. The same trends are recurring with respect to all income levels lower than $50,000. Interestingly, however, the gap appears to be narrowing for the mid-range and upper income groups. Households earning between $50,000–$74,999 are now actually closer (by 0.4 percentage points) to those at the highest income level than they were in 1997.

Middle-income households are faring far better with regard to computers. A significant drop of 11.1% (from a 15.3 to a 13.6 percentage point difference) occurred between the highest ($75,000+) and second highest ($50,000–$74,999) income brackets. And the gaps are also narrowing—though less significantly—for those earning more than $25,000.

D. Conclusion

The Census data reveal a number of trends. On the positive side, it is apparent that *all* Americans are becoming increasingly connected—whether by telephone, computer, or the Internet—over time. On the other hand, it is also apparent that certain groups are growing far more rapidly, particularly with respect to Internet connectivity. This pattern means that the "haves" have only become more information-rich in 1998, while the "have nots" are lagging even further behind.

As the Internet becomes a more mature and pervasive technology, the digital divide among households of different races, incomes, and education levels may narrow. This pattern is already occurring with regard to home computers. Race matters less at the highest income level, and the gap is narrowing among households of higher income and education levels.

Even so, it is reasonable to expect that many people are going to lag behind in absolute numbers for a long time. Education and income appear to be among the leading elements driving the digital divide today. Because these factors vary along racial and ethnic lines, minorities will continue to face a greater digital divide as we move into the next century. This reality merits a thoughtful response by policymakers consistent with the needs of Americans in the Information Age. . . .

Part III

Challenges Ahead

Traditionally, our notion of being connected to the nation's communications networks has meant having a telephone. Today, Americans' increased use of computers and the Internet has changed that notion. To be connected today increasingly means to have access to telephones, computers, and the Internet. While these items may not be necessary for survival, arguably in today's emerging digital economy they are necessary for success. As the Department of Commerce has found in its *Emerging Digital Economy* reports, the dramatic growth of electronic commerce and the development of information technology (IT) industries are changing the way Americans work, communicate, purchase goods, and obtain information. Jobs in the new economy now increasingly require technical skills and familiarity with new technologies. Additionally, obtaining services and information increasingly requires access to the Internet.

Policymakers have achieved high levels of telephone connectivity through the implementation of two key initiatives. Pro-competition policies at the state and national levels have resulted in lower prices for consumers of telephone services. Universal service policies have helped assure that most Americans can enjoy affordable access today. Assistance for low-income households (e.g., the Federal Communications Commission's Lifeline Assistance and Link-Up America and state programs) and support for high-cost regions of the country (e.g., the FCC's Universal Service Fund; other State and Federal rate-averaging) are prime examples of such programs. And the U.S. Department of Agriculture's Rural Utilities Service (RUS) provides targeted lending and technical advice to help ensure that advanced telecommunications infrastructure is in place for rural communities.

With the data in this report, we are in a better position to identify where and how to reach everyone. Policymakers should explore ways to continue to boost telephone penetration, particularly among the underserved, and to expand computer and Internet connectivity. For some individuals, it is an economic solution. Lower prices, leasing arrangements, and even free computer deals will bridge the digital gap for them. For high cost communities and low-income individuals, universal service policies will remain of critical importance. For other individuals, there are language and cultural barriers that need to be addressed. Products will need to be adapted to meet special needs, such as those of the disabled community. Finally, we need to redouble our outreach efforts, especially directed at the information disadvantaged.

Promoting Competition and Universal Service

To some extent, the surging use of computers and the Internet among American households reflects the success of our nation's pro-competition policies. A significantly higher percentage of households owned PCs in 1998 (42.1%) than in 1997 (36.6%), and experienced greater Internet access during the same period (26.2% versus 18.6%). The increased competition among PC-providers and lower costs of manufacturing have resulted in PCs selling for well below $1000. The increasing use of other Internet-accessing devices, such as televisions, palm computers, and Internet phones, should further invigorate competition among manufacturers and reduce prices for consumers.

While competition has made computers and the Internet increasingly affordable, these technologies still remain beyond the budget of many American households. When asked why they lacked Internet access, a significant portion of households (16.8%) responded that it was too expensive. Respondents particularly cited the cost of monthly bills, followed by toll calling for ISP access. A significantly higher percentage of minority and low-income households reported that Internet access was cost prohibitive. In addition, cost ranked highest among reasons given by those who discontinued Internet use. And, the proportion of non-use would surely be higher still for those who do not yet own PCs or other Internet-access devices. Policymakers, such as the Federal-State Universal Service Joint Board, State Public Service Commissions, and the Federal Communications Commission should carefully consider these facts in their attempts to evaluate the new universal service and access needs.

These findings suggest that further competition and price reductions will be vital to making information tools affordable for most Americans. Going forward, it will be important to promote policies that directly enhance competition among companies manufacturing computers and other Internet devices, as well as among Internet service providers. Expanding competition in rural areas and central cities is particularly significant, as these areas lag behind the national averages for PC-ownership and household Internet access.

At the same time, the data demonstrate the need for continued universal service support for telephony, particularly in rural and other high-cost areas. And we need to encourage the buildout of broadband networks to rural and other underserved areas of our nation, so that all Americans can take full advantage of new information technologies and services.

Expanding Community Access Centers

Competition is a significant answer to providing affordable access to computers and the Internet, but it is not the total solution. It is highly unlikely that, in the foreseeable future, prices will fall to the point where most homes will have computers and Internet access. As a result, a digital divide may continue to exist at home between the information rich and the information poor. Given the great advantages accruing to those who have access, it is not economically or socially prudent to idly await the day when most, if not all, homes can claim connectivity. Part of the short-term answer lies in providing Internet access at community access centers (CACs), such as schools, libraries, and other public access facilities.

The 1998 data demonstrate why providing public access to the Internet at these external sources is critical. To begin with, these sources tend to be used by groups that lack Internet access at home or at work; chiefly, minorities, people earning lower incomes, those with lower education levels, and the unemployed. Households with incomes of less than $20,000 and Black households, for example, are twice as likely to get Internet access through a public library or community center than are households earning more than $20,000 or White households. Similarly, low-income households and households with lower education levels are obtaining access at schools at far higher rates.

Moreover, the same households that are using community access centers at higher rates are also using the Internet more often than other groups to find jobs or for educational purposes. CACs are, therefore, providing the very tools these groups need to advance economically and professionally.

The data support the continued funding of CACs by both industry and government. Industry has already come forward with significant assistance. Companies are supporting the creation of community technology centers, helping connect schools through "NetDays," and donating computers and software to schools and neighborhood centers. NTIA's Telecommunications and Information Infrastructure Assistance Program (TIIAP) has funded a number of pioneering CAC efforts. The U.S. Department of Education's new Community Technology Centers (CTC) program will enable the funding of CACs in economically distressed communities on a broader scale.

The 1998 data also underscore the importance of the Administration's efforts to ensure that all schools and libraries have affordable access to the Internet. Under the E-rate program, telecommunications carriers are providing eligible schools and libraries with a discounted rate for telecommunications services, internal connections among classrooms, and Internet access. As a result, the E-rate program is helping to connect more than 80,000 schools and libraries and is enabling children and adults to both learn new technologies and have new points of access. The data demonstrate that these community access centers are, indeed, used by people who lack access at home and merit further funding.

In addition, we should look to other community-based organizations that can help us achieve these goals—traditional community centers, churches, credit unions, housing projects, senior centers, museums, fire and police stations, and more. Each community knows best how to reach and connect its residents.

Building Awareness

While many Americans are embracing computers and the Internet, there are many others who do not realize that this technology is relevant to their lives. We need to reach out to these communities and let them know why they should care—how new technologies can open new opportunities for them and their children.

We also need to find out *why* people are or are not connected. While such outreach works best at the local level, this type of information should be shared with policymakers at all levels of government—local, state, tribal, and federal. Only when we have a good understanding about why different communities do or do not have access to digital tools can we fashion appropriate policies.

Addressing Content Concerns

The data show that Americans are concerned about invasions of their privacy caused by accessing the Internet. Almost two-thirds of American are either "very concerned" or "somewhat concerned" about confidentiality on the Internet. There are legitimate concerns regarding the collection and transmission of personal information via the Internet, especially information gathered from children. The Administration has set forth an Electronic Bill of Rights, proposing that every consumer have: the right to choose whether her personal information is disclosed; the right to know how, when and how much of that information is being used; the right to see that information; and the right to know if information is accurate and to be able to correct it if it is not.

The Administration believes that the private sector should take the lead in implementing meaningful, consumer-friendly privacy regimes. We would like for companies to take steps to notify customers of their privacy policies, process consumer privacy preferences, protect customer data, and handle inquiries and complaints. Several promising private sector initiatives are underway, such as BBBOnline and TRUSTe, which require merchants to adhere to fair trade practices. These programs provide a seal to businesses that post privacy policies that meet certain criteria.

Parents are also concerned about their children's safety while using the Internet. The data show that one of the reasons that households with a computer have never used the Internet is "concerns with children." The Administration is committed to empowering parents, teachers, and other guardians with tools to keep children safe while online. The Administration has encouraged private sector initiatives, such as "One Click Away," which are designed to give parents technology and educational resources to protect their children from material that they deem to be inappropriate and to know who to contact when their children encounter dangerous situations online. The Administration has also promoted the concept of "greenspaces"—educational, age-appropriate, noncommercial content that is easily identifiable for families online.

Continued Monitoring

Good public policy requires a good factual foundation. Continued studies—public and private—are vital to permitting policymakers to make prudent decisions. Policymakers should explore ways to improve the availability of reliable penetration data for historically small but vitally important groups, such as Native Americans and Asians/Pacific Islanders. Potential solutions include "over-sampling" as part of a broader-based survey or conducting special studies that target these groups. A new analytical tool to gauge the status of Internet connectivity could be a Household Access Index [HAI], designed to highlight progress or deficiencies in this regard. A composite index could be developed that represents the country's combined penetration for telephones, computers, other Internet access devices, and the Internet. In 1998, the HAI for U.S. households would have equaled 162.4%, increasing from 149.0% in 1997.

In the final analysis, no one should be left behind as our nation advances into the 21st Century, where having access to computers and the Internet may be key to becoming a successful member of society.

FEDERAL REPORT ON THE WELL-BEING OF CHILDREN
July 8, 1999

A spate of reports in 1999 on the well-being of children both in the United States and throughout the world led to a stark conclusion. The longest period of sustained economic growth in U.S. history was helping to improve the overall well-being of America's children. At the same time, war and disease in many of the world's poorest areas were putting children in those places at increasing jeopardy.

Improvement in the Welfare of American Children

The broadest survey of child welfare in the United States was entitled "America's Children: Key National Indicators of Well-Being," issued July 8, 1999. The report was the third in a series of annual reports issued by the Federal Interagency Forum on Child and Family Statistics, a group of eighteen federal agencies with responsibility for some aspect of child welfare. The sixty-four-page report compiled indicators for economic security, health, education, and behavior, such as smoking.

On average, the report said, children were doing better in several categories than they had in recent years. Death rates were down at all age levels, and preschool enrollment rates were up, especially among African Americans. Daily smoking among teenagers, which had increased gradually since 1992, dropped in 1998, although it still remained high. The percentage of high school seniors who smoked every day dropped from 25 percent in 1997 to 22 percent in 1998. Birth rates among teenage girls also declined, from 38.7 live births to girls ages fifteen to seventeen in 1991 to 32.1 live births in 1997. Crimes committed by and against children were also down, mirroring a downward trend in crime generally. (Crime report, p. 614)

Although the proportion of children living in poverty was relatively unchanged at about 19 percent (roughly the same rate it was in 1980), the strong economy and federal and state welfare reforms seemed to have benefited poor children to some degree—more of them had vaccines than ever

*before, and more children were living with at least one parent who worked.
But children in poverty were still more likely than better-off children to live
in substandard housing, to have a disability, and to receive inadequate
nutrition. Moreover, the proportion of children living in extreme poverty
had increased (from 7 percent in 1980 to 8 percent since 1997), as had the
proportion living in high-income families (from 17 percent to 25 percent),
while the proportion of children in families with medium incomes had
declined.* (Economic report, p. 85; welfare reform, p. 257)

*A new indicator in the 1999 report measured the quality of children's
diets. It found that between 1994 and 1996 most children and adolescents
had diets that were "poor" or "needed improvement," and older children had
poorer diets than younger ones. Nearly 25 percent of children ages two to
five had good diets, for example, while 8 percent had poor diets, and the
remainder had diets that needed improvement. Only 6 percent of teenagers
had a good diet, while 20 percent had poor diets, largely because of declines
in their milk and fruit consumption.*

*A report released November 29 took a bleaker view of the data. The report,
sponsored by the National School Boards Association, the National League
of Cities, the Joe DiMaggio Children's Hospital, and the Youth Crime Watch
of America, was called "Ten Critical Threats to America's Children: Warning Signs for the Next Millennium." The report listed ten dangers to children: teenage pregnancy, abuse and neglect at home, inadequate child care,
poor schools, lack of health care, substance abuse, poverty, absent parents,
crime, and environmental dangers. Each danger was then coupled with a
potential solution, such as increases in the minimum wage and universal
health care.*

*A spokesman for the coalition said the report was intended to raise
awareness about the dangers to children in American society rather than to
advance any specific legislative agenda. "What these groups have done is to
say there needs to be a national agenda on children's issues," the spokesman
said. "These problems are not new. They are chronic; they are pervasive."*

*A separate report on teen pregnancy, released October 26 by the National
Center for Health Statistics, said that the birth rate among fifteen- to sev-
enteen-year-old girls continued to fall in 1997, reaching its lowest level in
forty years, and that the birth rate for younger girls had fallen to its lowest
level since 1969. The teenage birth rate had reached a peak in 1991. Birth
rates among African American girls dropped to their lowest level since
1960, when such data were first collected, and the rate among Hispanic
women also declined dramatically. "There has definitely been a decline in
sexual activity among teenagers, both boys and girls," Stephanie Ventura,
the author of the report, told the* New York Times. *"There is also more consistent use of birth control, especially condoms. Finally, you have to look at
the widespread attention this subject has gotten."* (1998 report on teenage
pregnancy, Historic Documents of 1998, p. 260)

*While welcoming the news, health care officials cautioned that teenage
pregnancy was still a significant problem. "This new data is terrific news,"*

said Sarah Brown, director of the National Campaign to Prevent Teen Pregnancy, "but we still remain the industrialized country with the highest degree of teen pregnancy and abortion. And even if we don't compare ourselves to other countries, we still have too many girls giving birth."

American attitudes about children and teenagers did not change much over the last two years, according to a report issued May 3 by Public Agenda. A majority of Americans still described children as "lazy," "spoiled," and "rude" and said that teenagers were "irresponsible" and "wild." The report, "Kids These Days 99: What Americans Really Think About the Next Generation," was cosponsored by Ronald McDonald House Charities and the Advertising Council; it was the second in a biennial survey. (1997 report, Historic Documents of 1997, p. 422)

About the same percentage of those surveyed in 1999 as in 1997 expressed concern that children seemed to lack values such as honesty, civility, and responsibility, but a higher proportion placed the primary blame on "irresponsible parents" (49 percent in 1999, compared with 44 percent in 1997). In both years, most of those surveyed said parents were not commonly good role models for their children and did not teach them right from wrong. Slightly more than half of those surveyed said that it was "very common" for people to have children before they were ready, to divorce too easily, and to think that buying things for their children was equivalent to caring for them.

As in 1997, survey respondents said the most effective ways to help kids would be to improve the quality of public schools and provide more after-school programs. Interestingly, the number of people who said employers should offer parents flexible work schedules so they could spend more time with their children rose from 55 percent in 1997 to 59 percent in 1999. At a time when Congress and state legislators were pursuing tougher sentences for children who commit crimes, the number of those surveyed who thought that was an effective way to help children fell, from 48 percent in 1997 to 44 percent in 1999.

UNICEF Report on Children Around the World

In its annual report, "The State of the World's Children 2000," released on December 13, the United Nations International Children's Emergency Fund (UNICEF) found that a century of medical and technological advances had improved children's lives worldwide but cautioned that war and the spread of AIDS threatened to reverse gains for children in many of the poorest nations. In the last hundred years, the report said, small pox had been eradicated, and polio nearly so. Iodine supplements available throughout the world had eliminated a leading cause of mental disease. Most children were receiving at least a basic education, and millions of children had been freed from labor. Infant mortality rates were declining in developing and industrialized nations alike.

Yet 540 million children—one child in four—had been displaced by violent conflict or lived on the edge of war. Eleven million children and young *adults had acquired immunodeficiency syndrome (AIDS), and every minute five more were infected with human immunodeficiency virus (HIV), the virus that caused AIDS. Despite a $30 trillion global economy, 600 million children, more than 25 percent, lived on less than $1 a day. About 130 million children, two-thirds of them girls, were denied a quality education. "These problems are not new," the report said, "but they are more widespread and profoundly entrenched than they were even a decade ago."*

Children in some countries, such as Angola, Sierra Leone, and Somalia, often went unvaccinated not only because civil strife prevented aid workers from reaching them, but also because the primary caregiver who would have brought them to be vaccinated had died of AIDS. In some countries such as Afghanistan, the Sudan, and the Democratic Republic of Congo, UNICEF and other aid workers had negotiated "days of tranquillity" with the ruling factions so that the health care workers could inoculate children in strife-torn areas. "It turns out the major obstacles now to eradicating polio are not 'Do we have a vaccine or do we have enough money.' . . . The biggest single process is access," said Carol Bellamy, executive director of UNICEF.

> *Following is the text of the highlights section of "America's Children: Key National Indicators of Well-Being," a report issued July 8, 1999, by the Federal Interagency Forum on Child and Family Statistics:*

America's Children: Key National Indicators of Well-Being, 1999 is the third annual report to the Nation on the condition of our most precious resource, our children. Included are six contextual measures that describe the changing population and family context in which children are living, and 23 indicators of well-being in the areas of economic security, health, behavior and social environment, and education. This year, a special feature is presented on Children Who Have Difficulty Performing Everyday Activities.

Part I: Population and Family Characteristics

- America's children continue to grow in racial and ethnic diversity. In 1998, 65 percent were white, non-Hispanic; 15 percent were black, non-Hispanic; 15 percent were Hispanic; 4 percent were Asian/Pacific Islander; and 1 percent were American Indian/Alaska Native. Hispanic children slightly outnumber black, non-Hispanic children.
- The percentage of children living with two parents declined from 77 percent in 1980 to 68 percent in 1996, and has remained stable since then. There are large differences across racial and ethnic groups, however. In 1998, 76 percent of white, non-Hispanic children lived with two parents, compared to 36 percent of black children and 64 percent of Hispanic children.

- The percentage of births that are to unmarried women stabilized since 1994 at about 32 percent, after rising sharply from 18 percent in 1980.

Part II: Indicators of Children's Well-Being

Economic Security Indicators

- The poverty rate of children was at 19 percent in 1997, about the same as it has been since 1980. The proportion of children living in families with high income increased from 17 percent in 1980 to 25 percent in 1997, while the proportion of children living in extreme poverty grew slightly from 7 to 8 percent over the same period. These shifts reflect a growing income disparity among children.
- The percentage of children living with their parents who had at least one parent working full time all year increased 5 percentage points to 76 percent from 1993 to 1997. A large share of this increase was due to the increase in the percentage of children living with employed single mothers, which increased from 33 percent in 1993 to 41 percent in 1997.
- Most American children and adolescents had a diet that was poor or needed improvement in 1996. As children get older, the quality of their diet declines: 24 percent of 2- to 5-year-olds had a good diet, compared with only 6 percent of teenagers ages 13 to 18.
- Teenagers are also less likely than younger children to have a usual source of medical care. In 1996, 8 percent of all adolescents ages 12 to 17 lacked a usual source of care. Over 27 percent of uninsured adolescents in this age group lacked a usual source of care.

Health Indicators

- The percentage of infants born with low birthweight (weighing less than about 5 1/2 pounds) continues to rise. In 1997, this percentage was the highest in over 20 years, at 7.5 percent. The increase in low birthweight is partly due to the rising number of twin and other multiple births.
- The percentage of children in families living in poverty who have received the combined series of vaccines has increased between 1996 and 1997, from 69 to 71 percent.
- While the mortality rate for almost all groups of children continues to fall, it has fallen most dramatically among black children ages 1 to 4, from 67.6 per 100,000 in 1996 to 59.2 in 1997, according to preliminary data. This rate, however, remains almost twice the rate for whites, at 31.5 per 100,000 according to 1997 preliminary data.
- Death rates among adolescents, particularly among black males, have dropped dramatically after rising rapidly during the early 1990s. In 1996, the adolescent firearm mortality rate was at the lowest point since 1989 for both blacks and whites. The rate among black males dropped from 120.3 per 100,000 in 1995 to 108.7 in 1996, and the rate among white males dropped from 27.9 per 100,000 in 1995 to 23.1 in 1996.

- The birth rate for teenagers ages 15 to 17 dropped from 1991 to 1997, after rising during the late 1980s. In 1997, the rate was 32.1 live births per 1,000 females ages 15 to 17, down from 38.7 in 1991.

Behavior and Social Environment Indicators

- The percentage of 10th- and 12th-grade students who reported smoking daily dropped in 1998 after generally increasing since 1992. Among 10th-graders, the percentage dropped from 18 percent in 1997 to 16 percent in 1998, and among 12th-graders it dropped from its recent high of 25 percent in 1997 to 22 percent in 1998. This rate is still high compared to previous years, however.
- Youth ages 12 to 17 were victims of serious violent crime at the rate of 27 crimes per 1,000 in 1997, down from 44 per 1,000 in 1993. Juveniles were identified as perpetrators of serious violent crimes at the rate of 31 crimes per 1,000 in 1997, down from 52 per 1,000 in 1993.

Education Indicators

- A higher percentage of children were enrolled in preschool in 1997 than in 1996—48 percent compared to 45 percent. Preschool enrollment particularly increased among black, non-Hispanic children, from 45 to 55 percent, and among children living in poverty, from 34 to 40 percent.
- In 1998, about 8 percent of the Nation's 16- to 19-year-olds were neither enrolled in school nor working, a significant decrease from 9 percent in 1997.

Special Feature

- About 12 percent of children ages 5 to 17 have difficulty performing one or more everyday activities, including learning, communication, mobility, and self-care. Difficulty with learning is the most common of these four types of limitations. Children in families with lower socioeconomic status are at greater risk than other children of having difficulty performing everyday activities.

CENSUS BUREAU REPORT ON MEASURES OF WELL-BEING
July 9, 1999

The longest economic expansion in the nation's history was helping to pull some American families out of poverty, as 1.1 million Americans rose above the federal poverty level in 1998. But income inequality between the rich and poor continued unabated, and various federal reports showed that a rising number of households were going hungry and were unable to afford some of the other basic necessities of life, such as adequate housing. Worldwide, the poverty indicators were even bleaker. A World Bank report released at the end of the year said that the global financial crisis of 1997-1998 had brought a halt to a slow decline in poverty in developing countries. Although countries were beginning to recover, that recovery was "uneven and fragile," the report said, and the number of people living in poverty in developing countries was on the rise.

The United States:
Rising Incomes, Greater Inequality

According to Census Bureau data released September 30, 1999, the overall income and poverty picture for the United States showed strong improvement. Incomes rose enough in 1998 to push the median household income up 3.5 percent, to $38,885, past its previous high of $37,997, registered in 1989. At the same time, the number of people with incomes below the poverty line fell 0.6 percent from 1997, to 12.7 percent, or 34.5 million people. The poverty rate among Hispanics showed the most improvement, falling 1.5 percentage points from its 1997 level to 25.6 percent. For the first time since 1993, the rate for African Americans did not change significantly from the previous year. The poverty rate for African Americans was 26.1 percent. That was the lowest level on record, but it was still 2.5 times higher than the poverty rate for whites.

The same data showed that income inequality—the gap between the richest and poorest—remained virtually unchanged in 1998, with the richest households earning about eight times as much as the poorest ones. A con-

troversial study issued by the Center on Budget and Policy Priorities, which advocates tax and spending programs for the poor, said that the after-tax income for the richest fifth, or quintile, of all Americans had increased 43 percent since 1977, while after-tax incomes for the poorest quintile had fallen 9 percent. That report, which was released in early September, was based on income figures that included income from capital gains; the Census Bureau data looked only at earned income.

In a separate report issued July 9, the Census Bureau revealed that about 49 million people—nearly one in five Americans—lived in a household that had trouble meeting one or more basic need in 1995. Basic needs were defined as not paying utility bills, not paying the rent or mortgage, needing to see a doctor or dentist but not going, having a utility disconnected, or being evicted for failure to pay. About 10 percent of all Americans did not pay their full utility bills, while 1.9 percent had a utility disconnected and 0.4 percent were evicted. Not surprisingly, the Census Bureau found that poorer people had the most difficulty meeting basic needs. More than one-third of the households in the lowest quintile had trouble meeting one of the basic needs, and more than one-fifth of the lowest income group had trouble meeting two or more. The study also found that African Americans were more than twice as likely as whites to have trouble. More than one-third of all people living in households that could not meet basic needs were children under eighteen. (Indicators of children's well-being, p. 384)

The Census Bureau also found that nearly one in five Americans reported that they either did not get enough to eat or could not buy the kinds of food they wanted to eat. Those figures were confirmed by the Agriculture Department, which released state-by-state data on October 14 showing that hunger was widespread in the United States despite the booming economy and low unemployment rate. According to the data, 9.7 percent of households nationally either experienced hunger or were in danger of being without enough to eat. At 15.1 percent, New Mexico had the highest rate of households considered "food insecure," while North Dakota had the lowest, at 4.6 percent. Altogether eighteen states had food insecurity rates above 10 percent.

Nationwide, food stamp use had fallen 27 percent since 1995, and the Clinton administration had begun a public awareness campaign to let people know that they might be eligible for the benefits. The program was aimed primarily at the working poor, but researchers had observed that many of the families that had left welfare for work were not using food stamps even though many of them were still eligible for the benefits. (Welfare reform, p. 257)

More low-income families were also having trouble finding affordable housing, partly because rents were rising twice as fast as inflation and partly because the number of affordable rental units was declining. The Department of Housing and Urban Development (HUD) said that waiting lists to live in public housing and to receive rent assistance had shown increases of 10 to 25 percent in the last two years. According to one depart-

ment study, 5.3 million families were either paying more than they could afford for housing or living in substandard housing. "The sad truth is that more and more people working at low-wage jobs, as well as older Americans living on fixed incomes, are being priced out of the housing market as rents rise," said HUD secretary Andrew M. Cuomo.

A national survey of the homeless, the first such study since 1987, found that almost half were experiencing their first bout with homelessness and that 44 percent had worked at least part time in the past month. It also found that two-thirds were suffering from chronic or infectious diseases other than AIDS and that 55 percent did not have health insurance. Thirty-nine percent showed signs of mental illness, and 27 percent reported that they spent some of their childhood in foster care or an institution. Contrary to common perceptions, 42 percent said what they most wanted was help finding a job, and more than half of the homeless left shelters for permanent housing when they received needed services, such as housing subsidies, health care, job training, and treatment for substance abuse.

The study did not estimate the size of the homeless population, but one of its many figures estimated that the 470,000 homeless people in shelters on an average night in February 1996 represented about one-fourth of all people who were homeless at any given time. The 600-page survey was based on census data from 1995 and 1996 and surveys of about 40,000 programs that served the homeless nationwide. The report took three years to complete and involved twelve federal agencies and numerous experts on homelessness both in and outside the government. It was released by HUD on December 8.

The International Picture

Many developing countries experienced rapid economic growth in the early 1990s, which helped to improve living conditions in some places. But the global economic crisis that affected several East Asian economies and then spread to Russia and elsewhere in 1997 and 1998 severely weakened the economies in developing countries, and they had not yet fully recovered. As a consequence, the number of poor people, which had been declining in the mid-1990s, was once again rising, wiping out many of the gains that had been made. According to a World Bank report, "Global Economic Prospects and the Developing Countries," about 1.2 billion people—more than one-sixth of the world's population—lived on less than $1 a day in 1998, the same number as in 1987. The World Bank said it expected average per capita incomes to fall in developing countries outside Asia in 1999, and that economic growth in these countries between 2002 and 2008 would be less than it was in the early 1990s before the crisis. It also predicted that an international goal to cut worldwide poverty in half by 2015 was unlikely to be met. (UN report on poverty, Historic Documents of 1995, p. 134)

The gap between rich and poor nations also appeared to be growing, leading to warnings of potential political unrest. "Global inequalities in *income and living standards have reached grotesque proportions," the United Nations Development Programme (UNDP) said in its annual report, released July 12. In 1960, the report said, the richest fifth of the world's population had thirty times as much income as the world's poorest fifth. In 1997 that ratio had more than doubled to seventy-four to one. Just three men—Bill Gates, Paul Allen, and Steve Ballmer, the top officers of Microsoft—had more assets (nearly $140 billion combined) than the combined gross national products of the forty-three least-developed nations and their 600 million people.*

The report blamed much of the growth in inequality on economic globalization, which was increasingly dominated by a relatively few corporations in the wealthiest countries. Moreover, the high technology industries that were driving the globalization were also overwhelmingly concentrated in the United States and a few other industrialized nations, the report said. "The privatization and concentration of technology are going too far," the report warned.

"Competitive markets may be the best guarantee of efficiency but not necessarily of equity," the report said. "Many activities and goods that are critical to human development are provided outside the market, but these are being squeezed by the pressures of global competition." The report suggested that if the gap in the distribution of the nations' wealth grew too wide, public sentiment could develop in the poorer countries that might destabilize the global economy. Voicing similar warnings earlier in the year, United Nations Secretary General Kofi Annan said the global economy was "vulnerable to all the 'isms' of our post-cold war world: protectionism, populism, nationalism, ethnic chauvinism, fanaticism, and terrorism."

The UNDP said that challenge was "not to stop the expansion of global markets" but to "find the rules and institutions for stronger governance" that would ensure that "globalization works for people, not just for profits." The UN agency recommended several steps that it said could help to even out the disparities between rich and poor countries, including giving the World Trade Organization antimonopoly powers to prevent a few global corporations from dominating an industry, monetary rules that would allow developing countries to impose capital controls to protect their economies, a global investment trust to moderate flows of capital into and out of developing countries, and a global central bank that would help regulate financial markets and act as a lender of last resort to financially strapped countries.

One step toward greater cooperation came December 16, when financial ministers and central bankers from the Group of Seven industrialized countries met in Berlin with their counterparts from the other leading economies to discuss ways to avoid future global financial crises and promote greater economic growth and stability among developing countries. The so-called Group of 20 included Canada, France, Germany, Italy, Japan, the United Kingdom, and the United States—the Group of Seven—

plus Argentina, Australia, Brazil, China, India, Indonesia, Mexico, Russia, Saudi Arabia, South Africa, South Korea, and Turkey, as well as representatives from the European Union, itself a collection of fifteen member countries and the world's leading commercial power.

Following are excerpts from the report, "Extending Measures of Well-Being: Meeting Basic Needs," issued July 8, 1999, by the U.S. Census Bureau:

It should not be surprising that many Americans have trouble paying bills and making ends meet. There is evidence all around—from rising consumer debt levels to increases in personal bankruptcy. Doubtless, most people have had times when paying the bills has been difficult. But how extensive is the problem? What types of people find their budget exceeding their resources? How often do people end up with serious problems like not getting enough to eat or foregoing needed medical care? Where do people get help when the going gets rough?

Personal or household income is generally regarded as the single best measure of the degree to which people are "well off." However, other factors also contribute to people's well-being. To assess some of these other dimensions, the Census Bureau administered questions on basic needs, food sufficiency, and income adequacy as a supplement to the Survey of Income and Program Participation [SIPP] in October 1995 through January 1996. This report presents the findings for these extended measures of well-being.

Difficulty Meeting Basic Needs:
How Extensive Is the Problem?

In 1995, approximately 49 million people—about 1 person in 5—lived in a household that had at least one difficulty meeting basic needs. These included households that didn't pay utility bills, didn't pay mortgage or rent, needed to see the doctor or dentist but didn't go, had telephone or utility service shut off, were evicted, didn't get enough to eat, or otherwise didn't meet essential expenses. Eleven percent lived in households where more than one of these difficulties took place. . . .

Many also had problems paying specific types of bills. Of the total population, 9.9 percent were in households that didn't pay gas, oil, or electricity bills. It was less common to reside in a household that didn't pay the full amount of rent or mortgage or in a household that didn't get needed medical care or dental care. . . . (There was no significant difference between the proportion who didn't pay rent or mortgage and the proportion who didn't visit the dentist.) Least common were situations where the household got so far behind in paying bills that they had their utilities or phone service cut off or were evicted from their apartment or home.

When people did have difficulty meeting basic needs, they often faced more than one problem at a time. Of those with difficulty meeting basic needs, 54 percent experienced more than one problem. . . . For each of the specific types of difficulties meeting basic needs, at least 60 percent of people lived in households with two or more difficulties. Researchers who have examined the "survival strategies" of families with limited budgets have noted that they often play one type of need off against another. They might scrimp on food to buy Christmas presents or forestall paying one bill in order to pay another. This implies that, over the course of a year, those who have limited resources would experience more than one type of difficulty meeting basic needs. This relationship is definitely borne out by the data collected in this survey. For most of those who were exposed to at least one difficulty meeting basic needs in 1995, it was not an isolated incident.

Income and Basic Needs

Having low household income greatly raised a person's chance of having difficulty meeting basic needs. Levels of income can be described by quintiles, i.e., dividing households into five equal groups ranging from those with the highest incomes to those with the lowest. In the lowest income quintile, 37.8 percent of people lived in households with at least one difficulty meeting basic needs, and more than one-fifth lived in households with more than one type of difficulty meeting basic needs. . . . A majority of those in households with at least one difficulty were in the two lowest income quintiles (31.7 million people). People in the lowest income quintile were more likely than those in the next income quintile to live in households with difficulties meeting basic needs of every type. . . . Overall, income was very strongly associated with the ability to meet basic needs.

Age and Basic Needs

Nearly every type of difficulty was more common among children than among adults aged 60 and over. . . . Children were more likely than adults to live in households that didn't pay gas and electric bills, didn't pay rent or mortgage, didn't visit the dentist or doctor, or had services disconnected. Among children, 8.8 percent lived in a household where someone needed to see the dentist but didn't go, and 7.0 percent lived in a house where someone needed to see the doctor but didn't go. By contrast, around 3.0 percent of people 60 and over lived in households where each of these conditions was reported.

In 1995, more than a quarter of children (28.5 percent of those under age 10, 27.8 percent of those ages 10 to 17) lived in a household in which someone reported at least one difficulty meeting basic needs. Less than 10 percent of those in the oldest age category (70 and older) were in this situation. . . . Overall, there were 18.1 million children who were in households with at least one difficulty meeting basic needs. More than one-third of all people living in households with at least one difficulty meeting basic needs were children.

The strong association between age and difficulty meeting basic needs indicates that the lack of resources may not be the only explanation for households not meeting their needs. The oldest age groups reported they were able to meet their basic needs even though, on average, they had low incomes. In fact, even with control for income and other factors associated with ability to meet basic needs, the effect of age remained essentially unchanged. There are several possible explanations of this pattern. Older respondents may have experienced lower living standards when they were younger (for example, during the Great Depression), they may have lower expenses, or they may be more reluctant to admit to problems. It also might be that basic needs can be met in households with stable and predictable circumstances—those without disruptions to income or living situation. As people age, they tend to have fewer life changing events such as marriage, childbirth, job change, and migration that might lead to a temporary strain on the budget and difficulties meeting basic needs.

Other Characteristics and Basic Needs

Besides income and age, a number of other characteristics were associated with at least one difficulty meeting basic needs in 1995. . . . Race and ethnicity were associated fairly strongly. Blacks were more likely than Whites to experience difficulty meeting basic needs. Hispanics, who can be of any race, were also more likely than (non-Hispanic) Whites to experience a difficulty meeting basic needs. These differences may be partially explained by differences in income, education, and other characteristics between these groups. Difficulty meeting basic needs was also associated with barriers to productive labor force participation. Greater difficulty was observed among those who were unemployed, those who had a work disability, and those who had low levels of education. Difficulty meeting basic needs was also more common among those who lacked health insurance and those who were unmarried. In all these groups, there is a large share who lack the resources necessary to meet basic needs in their households.

Those who rented rather than owned their homes were more likely to experience at least one difficulty meeting basic needs. Renters tend to have lower incomes, fewer assets and other resources to draw on, and less stability in their circumstances. Those who moved within the last year were also more likely to have experienced at least one difficulty. It could be that the instability of moving contributed to unmet needs, or it could be that the inability to meet basic needs contributed to the necessity of moving.

There was a 1.4 percent gender difference in the experience of difficulty meeting basic needs. The difference is as small as it is because most households contain both males and females. When a household has difficulty meeting basic needs, it affects both genders at the same time. By contrast, people living in households with a female householder were significantly more likely to experience difficulty meeting basic needs than people in households with a male householder.

Lack of Health Insurance and Difficulties Meeting Basic Needs

People who were without health insurance for at least 1 of the 4 months prior to interview were more than twice as likely to live in a household with

any difficulty meeting basic needs as those who had continuous coverage. . . .
Likewise, the percentage with multiple difficulties was much higher for those
without health insurance than for those who were insured.

A growing number of people in the United States lack health insurance.
There is some question about the extent to which those who lack insurance
do so out of choice or by necessity. The finding in this report of greater difficulty meeting basic needs among those without insurance suggests that
people who lack health insurance may do so because of other pressing
needs. A greater concern, perhaps, is the degree to which those without
health insurance are forced to go without needed medical care. Lack of
health insurance strongly affected the probability that there would be a person in the household who needed to see the doctor but did not go. While only
3.1 percent of the insured population lived in a household where needed
medical care was not obtained, 14.9 percent of those without health insurance faced this situation.

Not Getting Enough to Eat

Another measure of well-being is food sufficiency—which can be measured by looking at both the quantity and quality of food. The SIPP asks about
the kind and amount of food in a household, the length of time food was in
short supply, and the amount of money it would have taken to balance the
food budget. Approximately 1 person in 20 (4.8 percent) lived in a household
reporting that members sometimes did not get enough to eat. . . . A larger portion, nearly one in five (18.8 percent), lived in households that either did not
get enough or did not get the kind of foods they wanted to eat. Thus, even
though the great majority of people lived in households where adequate
amounts of nutritious food were available, there was a small segment of the
population in 1995 that lacked adequate amounts of food.

When they occurred, food shortfalls were fairly large. Among those in
households that did not get enough food in the last 30 days, the average time
they reported being short of food was over a week, and on average, it would
have taken about $100 for these households to bring their food budget into
balance.

Getting enough food was strongly associated with income, age, race and
Hispanic origin, gender of householder, and health insurance coverage. The
difference between males and females was not significant. Among children,
7.3 percent lived in households which didn't have enough to eat. . . , compared to 1.9 percent of those age 60 and above. About one person in ten (9.3
percent) among Blacks lived in households with insufficient food. Among
Hispanics, 11.7 percent lived in households where there wasn't enough to eat.
It was rare for people in the top income quintile to live in households that did
not have enough food, with only 0.8 percent falling in this category, but 11.2
percent of those in the lowest income quintile were in households that did not
get enough food. The percentage of low-income households with not enough
food was not significantly different from the percentage of Hispanics with not
enough food.

Where to Go When the Going Gets Rough: Getting Help

Another measure of well being is the availability of help to households that had difficulty meeting basic needs. The SIPP asked households with difficulty meeting basic needs whether they received any help, and if so, where it came from—family, friends, community organizations, or government.

Only 17.2 percent of people who experienced difficulties in their household said they received help from others.... Help was most likely to come from family, friends and community organizations—altogether, 13.1 percent. Government agencies provided help to 4.9 percent. Those whose household incomes fell in the lowest quintile were more likely to get help than those with higher incomes.

One in four (26.0 percent) of the lowest income group received help, while lower portions of most other income groups did. In the lowest income quintile, people who experienced difficulties meeting basic needs more often received assistance from government programs than those with higher incomes who experienced difficulties. Assistance from non-governmental sources was also more common among those in the lowest income quintile than those in higher income quintiles.

There was little variation in the rate of receiving help between those of different age groups, although there were significant contrasts between people in the 40-60 age range and those under 30. There was no significant difference in help received by race. In a few other cases there were significant differences between groups. Those with college educations were less likely than others to receive help. Compared to those living with male householders, people living with female householders were more likely to have received help when they experienced difficulty meeting basic needs. Renters were more likely to get help when in need than were homeowners. There was a higher probability of help for those who recently moved compared with those who didn't, and for unmarried people compared with married people. Renters, movers, and the unmarried might have occasional problems paying bills because of instability in their life situations, and not always because of lack of income. This may be why they have less trouble getting help when they have difficulty meeting basic needs.

Who Would Be There if Help Were Needed?

Even if they didn't have difficulty meeting basic needs, all respondents were asked about sources of help that would be available if it were needed. More than two-thirds were in a household where all or most of the help they need would be available from family.... Just over half lived where help was available from friends. Finally, less than one-third lived in households where they could get help from community agencies. Since the majority of people did not experience difficulties meeting basic needs in 1995, this information provides a broader picture of available help than information from people who actually experienced difficulties meeting basic needs.

A majority of those in all groups (age groups, race groups, etc.) lived in households reporting that help would be available if it were needed. Moreover, the proportions fell in a relatively narrow band. Children under the age of 10 were quite likely to live where help would be available, with 81.4 percent in such a household. Help would be available to around 80 percent of people in various other groups—people between the ages of 18 and 39, people in the highest two income quintiles, the college educated, Midwesterners, and those who had not moved recently. At the other extreme, help would be available for approximately 70 percent of those with less than a high school education, those who were unemployed and those with work disabilities. In all other groups, the proportion living where help would be available was between 70 and 80 percent.

Help Expected and Help Received

The contrast between help people received when they had actual need and the help they expected if need arose presents a seeming paradox. People with lower incomes were more likely than people with high incomes to be in households that received help from others when they experienced difficulties meeting basic needs. But when asked about help available in a hypothetical situation, low-income people were less likely than high-income people to be in households where help was available. A possible explanation is that poor people were caught in a bind. Asking for help from others usually generates feelings of obligation or actual obligations. Those with low incomes might have been reluctant to ask for help or might have used up the generosity of those willing to help, especially if those available to help had similarly low incomes.

There are other contrasts between help anticipated and help received. When asked about help they would receive if needed, 77.3 percent said help would be available from some source. By contrast, when people experienced financial troubles, only 17.2 percent did receive help. . . . Part of the reason for this seeming contradiction may be the difference between the hypothetical situation posed (sickness or moving), and the actual situation where help might have been needed (bill-paying problems). In addition, the hypothetical situation clearly specified that it would be one where the respondent needed help. However, part of the reason could well be that people are overly optimistic about the help that would be available to them, or that they are reluctant to ask for help when they need it.

. . . [T]here are also contrasts involving the source of help received. Among those in households that expected to get help, 88.4 percent lived where help would be forthcoming from family. Of those in households that had difficulties meeting basic needs and received help, a much smaller percentage actually got help from family, only 43.3 percent. A similar situation existed when it came to help from friends. Around 69.8 percent of people in households that expected to get help said help would be forthcoming from friends, but friends accounted for only 17.2 percent of help received when need arose. By contrast, other agencies in the community were a larger part of actual help received than they were of help expected. Community agencies were credited with being able to offer needed help by only 36.9 percent, but when actual need arose, the percentage who got help from this source was 44.3 percent.

Extended Measures of Well-Being

There are many aspects of well-being, including some that have been examined in previous Census Bureau reports. This report has focused on several key aspects—difficulty meeting basic needs, food sufficiency, and getting help when it is needed. Those least likely to experience difficulties were those who were older, had greater resources, and were more established in their living patterns (married, employed, homeowners, etc.). Those who experienced the most serious difficulties—inadequate food or medical care were members of groups that lack needed resources, especially income and health insurance. Many people were able to get help from others when they ran into difficulties, but most tried to deal with the problems on their own.

Traditional measures of income, wealth, and poverty provide basic information about the well-being of the population. On the other hand, extended measures such as those examined in this report can provide insight into aspects of well-being not fully captured by traditional measures. Collection and examination of data on extended measures of well-being will allow us to develop a more complete picture of the quality of life. . . .

AGRICULTURE SECRETARY ON BIOTECHNOLOGY IN AGRICULTURE
July 13, 1999

Longstanding opposition in Europe and many developing countries to genetically engineered foods began to have an impact in the United States in 1999 as Americans increasingly questioned the safety of the products. American agribusiness and pharmaceutical companies were at the forefront of developing and growing genetically modified crop seed, arguing that the higher yields of pest-resistant, vitamin-enriched crops were the best means to ensure an abundant global food supply. But highly publicized protests in Europe by consumers and environmentalists, who claimed the altered crops were untested and possibly unsafe, began to catch the attention of U.S. consumers. At the same time, trade restrictions in Europe began to dampen farmers' enthusiasm for the crops. By year's end a few major food producers had pledged not to use altered crops in their products, and many American farmers were saying they would go back to using unaltered seeds to ensure markets for their crops.

A retreat by American farmers would have a major effect on the genetic seed market. Modified primarily to improve the plants' resistance to pests and plant disease, genetically altered varieties of corn, soybeans, wheat, and cotton had proved popular among American farmers since they were first approved for use by the Agriculture Department in 1996. The farmers found that improved pest resistance not only led to higher yields, but also lessened the need for expensive and environmentally damaging pesticides. In 1998, 25 percent of the U.S. corn crop, 38 percent of the soybean crop, and 45 percent of the cotton acreage was planted with altered seed. The genetically engineered crops ended up in a wide range of everyday consumer products, from clothing using altered cotton seeds to soft drinks and baked goods that contained bioengineered corn syrup and corn starch.

The federal government had sided with farmers and pharmaceutical manufacturers in their efforts to expand trade in the bioengineered products. Early in the year U.S.-led opposition stalled international negotia-

tions on a treaty that would have sharply restricted exports of goods containing genetically modified material. But as pressure from domestic consumer advocates and environmentalists mounted, the administration signaled a willingness to be more responsive to safety concerns. In a major policy address on July 12, Agriculture Secretary Dan Glickman announced that the government would undertake long-term studies of the safety of genetically altered foods. Late in the year the Food and Drug Administration (FDA) held a series of public hearings on safety issues surrounding genetically modified food.

Pros and Cons of Genetically Altered Crops

Genetic modification of plants involved selecting certain genes from one kind of organism and inserting them into another organism to produce a seed with enhanced characteristics, such as higher nutrient levels or a greater ability to withstand drought or disease. Most altered seeds currently available were designed to be more resistant to pests or weeds, but biotechnology companies were exploring a wide range of possibilities, including edible vaccines built into potatoes, reduced saturated fats in vegetable oils, and vegetables and fruits that stayed fresh longer. They also said bioengineered crops would do less damage to the environment than traditional farming by using less land, less water, and fewer pesticides and other harmful chemicals.

Although their developers and the government said that the genetically altered seeds already in the marketplace were safe, consumer and environmental groups argued that the seeds had not been thoroughly tested and that the long-term effects on humans and the environment were therefore unknown. A potential problem was allergic reaction. One company that used a gene from the Brazil nut to enhance the protein in soybeans abandoned the project when it discovered that the altered soybeans caused the same allergic reaction as the Brazil nut. That incident not only intensified safety concerns but bolstered the arguments of those who demanded that bioengineered food products be labeled appropriately.

Environmentalists were concerned that genetically altered seed might crowd out conventional crops, reduce biodiversity, and transfer their heightened pest resistance to other plants and bugs, creating superweeds and superbugs. Instead of helping developing countries, these critics said, the crops might in fact harm them. Many small farmers in developing countries could not afford the altered seed and thus were unlikely to reap many of its benefits. These countries also worried that altered products might someday replace their specialty crops, undermining their already fragile economies.

Critics also expressed concern about the potential for the major biotechnology companies to manipulate the global food supply for their own profit. As an example, they cited efforts by Monsanto and other manufacturers to engineer a so-called terminator gene that would make the plant sterile and force farmers to buy new seed every year. That effort particularly angered governments of developing countries where, by some estimates, as many as 80 percent of all farmers saved seed from one year's crop to plant the next year.

Spreading Opposition

Developing countries pushed their concerns at meetings in Cartagena, Colombia, in February 1999, where negotiators from more than 170 nations had gathered to draw up a "biosafety protocol." The proposed treaty was an outgrowth of the Convention on Biological Diversity, which came out of the June 1992 Earth Summit in Rio de Janeiro. The protocol was intended to protect biodiversity by establishing procedures for the safe handling and transfer in international trade of biotech products that could affect the environment. These products included food, vaccines, and other drugs that were bioengineered. Several developing countries demanded strict trade restrictions on all food and clothing products made with genetically altered ingredients. The United States, joined by other major agricultural exporters such as Argentina, Australia, and Canada, wanted the trade restrictions to apply only to genetically engineered living seeds and organisms that had the potential to multiply and spread in the environment. The talks were suspended when it became clear that the issue was not going to be resolved during the meetings. (Rio summit, Historic Documents of 1992, p. 499)

Meanwhile, protests against genetically engineered crops were mounting. Various groups demonstrated outside grocery and fast-food stores in France and destroyed altered crops growing in test fields in England. England's Prince Charles and the singer Paul McCartney spoke out against altered crops. Several factors contributed to the European distaste for what some were calling "Frankenstein" foods. Among them were heightened awareness of food safety in general, brought on by incidents such as the discovery of cancer-causing dioxins in several Belgian food products in 1999 and an outbreak in the United Kingdom in the early 1990s of "mad cow disease," a brain disease in beef cattle that was linked to human brain disease. In response to the furor, several European governments banned the use or import of genetically altered products, and in June the European Union's environmental ministers agreed to what was effectively a moratorium on genetically altered seeds.

Pressure from environmental and consumer groups in the United States also began to be felt. Food manufacturers H.J. Heinz and Gerber and pet food manufacturer Iams announced they would no longer buy genetically altered crops. Legislation was introduced in Congress to force food companies to label food products containing genetically engineered ingredients. In May the public's attention was piqued by widespread media reports of laboratory tests showing that the caterpillars of monarch butterflies were killed by pollen from corn that had been modified to resist the corn borer. Although no field tests had yet confirmed those findings, the Environmental Defense Fund petitioned the Environmental Protection Agency for a reg-

*ulation requiring farmers to plant a buffer zone of conventional corn
around their genetically altered corn to protect the butterflies.*

Administration Response

*Faced with mounting demands for labeling and more thorough testing
from American consumers and deepening trade tensions with Europe and
elsewhere, the Clinton administration sought to defuse the situation. On
July 13, in a "major policy" address at the National Press Club in Washington, D.C., Agriculture Secretary Glickman took the first conciliatory
steps. The "promise and potential" of biotechnology were enormous, the secretary said, "but so too are the questions many of which are completely
legitimate. Today . . . we have to grapple with and satisfy those questions
so we can in fact fulfill biotechnology's awesome potential."*

*Saying that "we cannot take consumers for granted," Glickman
announced that the department would undertake long-term studies of the
safety of genetically altered food products, something consumer and environmental groups had long demanded. He stressed that the genetically
altered foods posed no known health risks to humans, but conceded that the
no long-term studies had been conducted. He also said he thought "some
type of informational labeling is likely to happen," but added that it was
"imperative" that the labeling "not undermine trade" in "this promising
new technology." Glickman also said that the developers of the altered products had to take responsibility for notifying the government of any unexpected or potentially adverse effects of their products as soon as they are
discovered.*

*Glickman laid out five principles to guide government approach to bio-
engineered food products: an arm's length regulatory process in which regulators kept a "dispassionate distance" from manufacturers and based regulations on protecting public health, safety, and the environment;
consumer acceptance, which Glickman said was dependent on sound regulation; fairness to farmers, which meant that "biotechnology has to result
in greater, not fewer, options for farmers"; corporate citizenship, meaning
that biotech companies must understand and respect the roles of regulators,
farmers, and consumers; and free and open trade, meaning the government
would not permit unfounded and unwarranted scientific claims to block
commerce in bioengineered agricultural products.*

*Consumer and environmental groups generally applauded Glickman's
speech. "The U.S. has realized it can't bully its way out of this problem,"
said Rebecca Goldberg, a leading scientist with the Environmental Defense
Fund. "Just a year ago, I don't think there was anyone in the Agriculture
Department that would have acknowledged the legitimate issues of risk."*

*Following are excerpts from a speech delivered July 13, 1999, by
Agriculture Secretary Dan Glickman at the National Press Club
in Washington, D.C., on the safety of genetically altered food
crops:*

... [F]irst of all, and if you come away with a dominant point from my remarks, it is that I want you to know that biotechnology has enormous potential.

Biotechnology is already transforming medicine as we know it. Pharmaceuticals such as human insulin for diabetes, interferon and other cancer medications, antibiotics and vaccines are all products of genetic engineering. Just yesterday I read that scientists at Virginia Polytechnic Institute will process drugs from milk from genetically altered cows. One new drug has the potential to save hemophiliacs from bleeding to death. Scientists are also looking at bananas that may one day deliver vaccines to children in developing countries.

Agricultural biotechnology has enormous potential to help combat hunger. Genetically modified plants have the potential to resist killer weeds that are, literally, starving people in Africa and other parts of the developing world.

Biotechnology can help us solve some of the most vexing environmental problems: It could reduce pesticide use, increase yields, improve nutritional content, and use less water. We're employing bioengineered fungi to remove ink from pulp in a more environmentally sensitive manner.

But, as with any new technology, the road is not always smooth. Right now, in some parts of the world there is great consumer resistance and great cynicism toward biotechnology. In Europe protesters have torn up test plots of biotechnology-derived crops and some of the major food companies in Europe have stopped using GMOs—genetically-modified organisms—in their products.

Yesterday's news was that the WTO [World Trade Organization] affirmed our view that the EU [European Union] is unjustifiably blocking US ranchers from selling beef produced with completely tested and safe growth hormones. Today we're seeing that the G-8 [Group of Eight industrialized countries] agreed to a new review of food safety issues and, having myself just come back from France a couple of weeks ago, I can assure you that trade in GMOs is looming larger over US-EU trade relations in all areas.

Now, more than ever, with these technologies in their relative infancy, I think it's important that, as we encourage the development of these new food production systems, we cannot blindly embrace their benefits. We have to ensure public confidence in general, consumer confidence in particular, and assure farmers the knowledge that they will benefit.

The important question is not, do we accept the changes the biotechnology revolution can bring, but are we willing to heed the lessons of the past in helping us to harness this burgeoning technology. The promise and potential are enormous, but so too are the questions many of which are completely legitimate. Today, on the threshold of this revolution, we have to grapple with and satisfy those questions so we can in fact fulfill biotechnology's awesome potential.

To that end, today I am laying out 5 principles I believe should guide us in our approach to biotechnology in the 21st century. They are:

1. *An Arm's Length Regulatory Process.* Government regulators must continue to stay an arm's length, dispassionate distance from the companies developing and promoting these products; and continue to protect public health, safety and the environment.

2. *Consumer Acceptance.* Consumer acceptance is fundamentally based on an arm's length regulatory process. There may be a role for information labeling, but fundamental questions to acceptance will depend on sound regulation.

3. *Fairness to Farmers.* Biotechnology has to result in greater, not fewer options for farmers. The industry has to develop products that show real, meaningful results for farmers, particularly small and medium size family farmers.

4. *Corporate Citizenship.* In addition to their desire for profit, biotechnology companies must also understand and respect the role of the arm's length regulator, the farmer, and the consumer.

5. *Free and Open Trade.* We cannot let others hide behind unfounded, unwarranted scientific claims to block commerce in agriculture.

Arm's Length Regulatory Process

When I was a school board member in Wichita, Kansas, one of my tasks was to study the level of student participation in the school lunch program. I quickly learned if the food didn't taste or look good, no matter how nutritious it was, the kids wouldn't eat it.

With all that biotechnology has to offer, it is nothing if it's not accepted. This boils down to a matter of trust—trust in the science behind the process, but particularly trust in the regulatory process that ensures thorough review—including complete and open public involvement. The process must stay at arm's length from any entity that has a vested interest in the outcome.

By and large the American people have trust and confidence in the food safety efforts of USDA [U.S. Department of Agriculture], the FDA [Food and Drug Administration], EPA [Environmental Protection Agency], CDC [Centers for Disease Control] and others because these agencies are competent and independent from the industries they regulate, and are viewed as such, That kind of independence and confidence will be required as we deal with biotechnology.

The US regulatory path for testing and commercializing biotechnology products as they move from lab to field to marketplace is over a decade old. We base decisions on rigorous analysis and sound scientific principles. Three federal agencies USDA, FDA, and EPA each play a role in determining the use of biotechnology products in the United States: USDA evaluates products for potential risk to other plants and animals. FDA reviews biotechnology's effect on food safety. And the EPA examines any products that can be classified as pesticides.

Right now, there are about 50 genetically altered plant varieties approved by USDA. And so far, thanks to the hard work and dedication of our scientists, the system is keeping pace. But, as I said, the system is tried and tested, but not perfect and not inviolate and should be improved where and when possible.

To meet the future demand of the thousands of products in the pipeline will require even greater resources, and a more unified approach and broader coordination.

When I chaired the US delegation to the World Food Conference in Rome in 1996, I got pelted with genetically modified soybeans by naked protesters. I began to realize the level of opposition and distrust in parts of Europe to biotechnology for products currently on the market or in the pipeline.

I believe that distrust is scientifically unfounded. It comes in part from the lack of faith in the EU to assure the safety of their food. They have no independent regulatory agencies like the FDA, USDA or EPA. They've had many food scares in recent years—mad-cow disease, and in just the last several weeks, dioxin-tainted chicken—that have contributed to a wariness of any food that is not produced in a traditional manner notwithstanding what the science says. Ironically they do not share that fear as it relates to genetically modified pharmaceuticals.

But, GMO foods evoke in many circles a very volatile reaction. And that has created a serious problem for the U.S. and other countries as we try to sell our commodities in international markets.

We need to make sure our regulatory system has the foresight to begin addressing issues even before they arise. So to keep pace with the accelerating growth of agricultural biotechnology, I am taking several additional steps to ensure we are fully prepared to meet the regulatory challenges of this new technology.

Today I'm announcing that I will be asking for an independent scientific review of USDA's biotech approval process. The purpose of this review will be to ensure that, as we are faced with increasingly complex issues surrounding biotechnology, our scientists have the best information and tools to ensure our regulatory capabilities continue to evolve along with advances in the new technology. And to address complex issues like pharmaceutical producing plants or genetically modified livestock we will need to consult the experts, many of whom are outside USDA.

Two of the more significant challenges we face are grower and consumer awareness, and improving monitoring on a long term basis. . . .

So, USDA will propose the establishment of regional centers around the country to evaluate biotech products over a long period of time and to provide information on an ongoing basis to growers, consumers, researchers and regulators.

To strengthen biotechnology guidelines to ensure we can stay on top of any unforeseen adverse effects after initial market approval, I am requesting all developers of biotech products to report any unexpected or potentially adverse effects to the Department of Agriculture immediately upon discovery.

Finally, we need to ensure that our regulators just regulate and only regulate. A few years ago, we created a food safety agency separate and distinct from any and all marketing functions to ensure that no commercial interests have even the appearance of influence on our decisions regarding food safety. It needs to be the same with biotechnology. The scientists who evaluate and approve biotech products for the market must be free of any hint of influence from trade support and other non-regulatory areas within USDA.

We at USDA will undertake a review to reinforce the clear line between our regulatory functions and those that promote and support trade. This reaffirms our basic principle that we will remain scrupulously rigid in maintaining an arm's length regulatory process.

Consumer Acceptance

However strong our regulatory process is, it is of no use if consumer confidence is low and if consumers cannot identify a direct benefit to them.

I have felt for some time that when biotechnology products from agriculture hit the market with attributes that, let's say, reduce cholesterol, increase disease resistance, grow hair, lower pesticide and herbicide use, and are truly recognized as products that create more specific public benefits, consumer acceptance will rise dramatically.

There's been a lot of discussion as to whether we should label GMO products. There are clearly trade and domestic implications to labeling to be considered in this regard. I know many of us in this room are sorting out these issues. At the end of the day many observers, including me, believe some type of informational labeling is likely to happen. But, I do believe that it is imperative that such labeling does not undermine trade and this promising new technology.

The concept of labeling particular products for marketing purposes is not a radical one. For example, USDA has already decided that for a product to be certified as organic under our pending organic agriculture rules, a GMO product would not qualify. And that does not mean that USDA believes organic is safer or better than non-organic all approved foods are safe it just means that consumers are given this informed choice.

There clearly needs to be a strong public education effort to show consumers the benefits of these products and why they are safe. Not only will this be the responsibility of private industry and government, but I think the media will play a vital role. It's important that the media treat this subject responsibly and not sensationalize or fan consumer fears. That's what we're seeing happen in the EU and the outcome is fear, doubt and outright opposition.

What we cannot do is take consumers for granted. I cannot stress that enough. A sort of if-you-grow-it-they-will-come mentality. I believe farmers and consumers will eventually come to see the economic, environmental, and health benefits of biotechnology products, particularly if the industry reaches out and becomes more consumer accessible.

But, to build consumer confidence, it is just like it is with the way we regulate our airlines, our banks and the safety of our food supply consumers must have trust in the regulatory process. That trust is built on openness. Federal agencies have nothing to hide. We work on behalf of the public interest.

Understanding that will go a long way to solving the budding controversy over labeling and ensuring that consumers will have the ability to make informed choices.

Fairness to Farmers

Like consumers, farmers need to have adequate choices made available to them. But today, American agriculture is at a crossroads. Farmers are currently facing extremely low commodity prices and are rightfully asking what will agriculture look like in the years to come and what will their roles be.

That also means they have more responsibility and more pressure. And much of the pressure they face originates from sources beyond their control. We are seeing social and economic trends that have a powerful effect on how farmers do business. We are seeing increased market concentration, a rise in contracting, rapidly evolving technologies such as information power and precision agriculture in addition to biotechnology. We are seeing different marketing techniques such as organics, direct marketing, coops and niche markets, and an expansion of non-agricultural industrial uses for plants.

One of my biggest concerns is what biotechnology has in store for family farmers. Consolidation, industrialization and proprietary research can create pitfalls for farmers. It threatens to make them servants to bigger masters, rather than masters of their own domains. In biotechnology, we're already seeing a heated argument over who owns what. Companies are suing companies over patent rights even as they merge. Farmers have been pitted against their neighbors in efforts to protect corporate intellectual property rights.

We need to ensure that biotechnology becomes a tool that results in greater—not fewer—options for farmers. For example, we're already hearing concerns from some farmers that to get some of the more highly desirable non-GMO traits developed over the years, they might have to buy biotechnology seeds. For some, that's like buying the car of your dreams but only if you get it in yellow. On the other hand, stress-tolerant plants are in the pipeline which could expand agricultural possibilities on marginal lands which could be a powerful benefit to poor farmers.

The ability of farmers to compete on a level playing field with adequate choices available to them and without undue influence or impediments to fair competition must be preserved. As this technology develops, we must achieve a balance between fairness to farmers and corporate returns.

We need to examine all of our laws and policies to ensure that, in the rush to bring biotech products to market, small and medium family farmers are not simply plowed under. We will need to integrate issues like privatization of genetic resources, patent holders rights and public research to see if our approach is helping or harming the public good and family farmers.

It is not the government who harnesses the power of the airwaves, but it is the government who regulates it. That same principle might come to apply to discoveries in nature as well. And that debate is just getting started.

Corporate Citizenship

If the promises hold true, biotechnology will bring revolutionary benefits to society. But that very promise means that industry needs to be guided by a broader map and not just a compass pointing toward the bottom line.

Product development to date has enabled those who oppose this technology to claim that all the talk about feeding the world is simply cover for corporate profit-making. To succeed in the long term, industry needs to act with greater sensitivity and foresight.

In addition, private sector research should also include the public interest, with partnerships and cooperation with non-governmental organizations here and in the developing world ensuring that the fruits of this technology address the most compelling needs like hunger and food security.

Biotechnology developers must keep farmers informed of the latest trends, not just in research but in the marketplace as well. Contracts with farmers need to be fair and not result in a system that reduces farmers to mere serfs on the land or create an atmosphere of mistrust among farmers or between farmers and companies.

Companies need to continue to monitor products, after they've gone to market, for potential danger to the environment and maintain open and comprehensive disclosure of their findings.

We don't know what biotechnology has in store for us in the future, good and bad, but if we stay on top of developments, we're going to make sure that biotechnology serves society, not the other way around.

These basic principles of good corporate citizenship really just amount to good long-term business practices. As in every other sector of the economy, we expect responsible corporate citizenship and a fair return. For the American people, that is the bottom line.

Free and Open Trade

The issues I have raised have profound consequences in world trade. Right now, we are fighting the battles on ensuring access to our products on many fronts. We are not alone in these battles; Canada, Australia, Mexico, many Latin American, African and Asian nations agree with us that sound science ought to establish whether biotech products are safe and can move in international commerce.

These are not academic problems. . . . While only a few varieties of GMO products have been approved for sale and use in Europe, many more have been put on hold by a de facto European moratorium on new GMO products.

Two weeks ago I went to France and met with the French Agriculture Minister at the request of the US ambassador there, Felix Rohatyn, to see if we can break this logjam which directly threatens US-EU relations at a delicate time when we are commencing the next WTO round in Seattle.

Quite frankly the food safety and regulatory regimes in Europe are so split and divided among the different countries that I am extremely concerned that failure to work out these biotech issues in a sensible way could do deep damage to our next trade round and effect both agricultural and non- agricultural issues. For that reason, the French Minister's agreement to have a short-term working group with USDA on biotech approval issues, and his willingness to come to the US in the fall to further discuss the situation, is encouraging.

To forestall a major US-EU trade conflict, both sides of the Atlantic must tone down the rhetoric, roll up our sleeves and work toward conflict resolution based on open trade, sound science and consumer involvement. I think this can be done if the will is there.

However, I should warn our friends across the Atlantic that, if these issues cannot be resolved in this manner, we will vigorously fight for our legitimate rights.

Conclusion

Finally, I've established a Secretary's Advisory Committee on Agricultural Biotechnology—a cross-section of 25 individuals from government, academia, production agriculture, agribusiness, ethicists, environmental and consumer groups. The committee, which will hold its first meeting in the fall, will provide me with advice on a broad range of issues relating to agricultural biotechnology and on maintaining a flexible policy that evolves as biotechnology evolves.

Public policy must lead in this area and not merely react. Industry and government cannot engage in hedging or double talking as problems develop, which no doubt they will.

At the same time, science will march forward, and especially in agriculture, that science can help to create a world where no one needs to go hungry, where developing nations can become more food self-sufficient and thereby become freer and more democratic, where the environmental challenges and clean water, clean air, global warming and climate change, must be met with sound and modern science and that will involve biotechnological solutions.

Notwithstanding my concerns raised here today, I would caution those who would be too cautious in pursuing the future. As President Kennedy said, "We should not let our fears hold us back from pursuing our hopes."

So let us continue to move forward thoughtfully with biotechnology in agriculture but with a measured sense of what it is and what it can be. We will then avoid relegating this promising new technology to the pile of what-might-have-beens, and instead realize its potential as one of the tools that will help us feed the growing world population in a sustainable manner.

Thank you.

INSPECTOR GENERAL ON FEDERAL OVERSIGHT OF HOSPITALS
July 20, 1999

A two-year study of the independent agencies that inspect the nation's 6,200 hospitals found "major deficiencies" in the system for ensuring the safety and quality of hospital care. The report said that the system relied too much on trust and cooperation and not enough on the sort of in-depth probing required to protect patients from "questionable providers and sub- standard practices." One of the authors of the report said that "if there were something seriously wrong" at a hospital, the agencies would not be able to find it under the current system. The report, "The External Review of Hos- pital Quality: A Call for Greater Accountability," was issued July 20, 1999, by the Office of Inspector General in the Department of Health and Human Services (HHS).

Studies had found evidence of serious problems resulting from negligent or inappropriate hospital care. For example, a study in 1997 of about one thousand patients at a large teaching hospital found that approximately 18 percent of those patients received inappropriate care that resulted in a seri- ous problem. A much earlier study of hospitals in New York estimated that, in 1984, 1 percent of all patients suffered from negligent care, resulting in nearly 27,000 injuries, including 7,000 deaths and 1,000 cases of perma- nent and total disability.

These studies, together with vivid media reports about poor hospital care, were just one element undermining the public's confidence in the nation's health care system. Charges that managed care insurers were denying patients necessary medical treatment to keep costs down and prof- its up were behind several lawsuits and a push in Congress to adopt a "patient's bill of rights." Late in the year, President Bill Clinton called on health care providers to work with the government to cut back on medical errors that each year cost as many as 98,000 patients their lives. (Patients' bill of rights, p. 561; medical mistakes, p. 779)

Shortcomings in Hospital Oversight

The HHS report found that the system for overseeing hospitals was not doing enough to ensure accountability either on the part of the hospitals or the agencies that were meant to ensure their quality. The federal oversight system, designed to ensure that hospitals met minimum requirements for participating in Medicare, was based on a combination of private accreditation and state certification. A private entity called the Joint Commission on the Accreditation of Healthcare Organizations accredited about 80 percent of all hospitals, while state agencies were responsible for certifying the other 20 percent. The joint commission and the state agencies reported to the HHS Health Care Financing Administration (HCFA), which was responsible for administering the Medicare program.

The joint commission, which was funded by hospitals, had adopted a collegial approach to hospital oversight. This approach sought to improve overall hospital performance through education and therefore relied on professional accountability and cooperative relationships to achieve its objectives. The commission encouraged cooperation by telling hospitals that they would not be penalized for reporting problems to the commission. While the collegial approach had its value, the inspector general's report said, it was unlikely to uncover hospital conditions or practices that could result in harm to patients. Hospitals had advance warning that commission agents were about to visit; the agents rarely had any background knowledge about any problems facing the hospitals; and instead of reviewing medical records chosen at random, they generally reviewed medical records chosen by the hospital staff.

The state agencies took a more regulatory approach to oversight, seeking to ensure that hospitals met required minimum standards for participating in Medicare. Although this investigatory approach was more likely to protect patients than the collegial approach, the state certification system was flawed because the state agencies were so far behind in their review. About half of all nonaccredited hospitals in 1997 had not been surveyed within the three-year industry standard, and some rural hospitals had not been surveyed for as many as eight years.

Moreover, the HCFA was prodding state agencies to follow the joint commission's lead and adopt the collegial approach. Yet, by paying "insufficient attention" to in-depth investigations, the report said, the "emerging dominance of the collegial approach may undermine the existing system of patient protection." The report noted that recent concerns about the quality of care in nursing homes had led the HCFA to toughen enforcement, including more immediate penalties for violations of care regulations, surprise surveys, and posting survey results on the Internet. "Such a heavy regulatory emphasis may well not be required for hospitals," the report said, "but it does reinforce the point that when patients are found to be at risk, regulatory approaches have an important part to play." The report added that *recent studies and media reports "make it clear" that inappropriate care in hospitals "can and frequently does" put patients at risk.*

Finally, the report took the HCFA to task for failing to demand more accountability from either the joint commission or the state agencies, for providing only limited feedback to these bodies on their overall performance, and for making little information available to the public on the performance either of hospitals or their overseers.

Recommendations and Reactions

The report offered one "guiding principle" and two recommendations that it urged the HCFA to adopt. As a guiding principle, the report said, the HCFA should steer the joint commission and state agencies to strike a balance between the collegial and regulatory approaches to oversight. Such a balance would provide for both announced and unannounced on-site hospital surveys and the capacity to respond quickly to complaints of poor quality care. The report listed several specific recommendations for each of the three entities.

In a letter on an earlier draft of the report, the administrator of the HCFA assured the inspector general that the agency agreed that the approaches to oversight should be balanced, issued a preliminary plan for incorporating more accountability into the oversight process, and said such accountability would be "consumer and purchaser-driven." In his response to an earlier draft, Dennis S. O'Leary, president of the joint commission, said the inspector general's criticisms of his agency were "unfounded." But in an interview with the New York Times *after the release, O'Leary said he agreed with much of the report.*

The nation's largest health care union said the report did not go far enough. "Without fundamental reforms, the current system of letting the hospital industry monitor itself is a joke," said Andrew L. Stern, president of the Service Employees International Union. Stern contended that oversight of hospitals would not be improved until doctors, nurses, and other health care workers were involved in the process. "Nobody knows what needs to be improved better than the people on the front lines providing patient care," he said. The union represented more than 600,000 health care workers, including 100,000 nurses and 20,000 physicians.

Following is the executive summary from the report, "The External Review of Hospital Quality: A Call for Greater Accountability," released July 20, 1999, by the Office of Inspector General in the Department of Health and Human Services:

Purpose

To provide a summary and recommendations based on our assessment of the external review of hospitals that participate in Medicare.

Background

External Quality Review of Hospitals in the Medicare Program

Hospitals are a vital part of our healthcare system, routinely providing valuable services. But they are also places where poor care can lead to unnecessary patient harm. This reality was clearly underscored in 1991, when a Harvard medical practice study revealed the results of its review of about 30,000 randomly selected records of patients hospitalized in New York State during 1984. The study found that 1 percent of the hospitalizations involved adverse events caused by negligence. On the basis of these findings, it estimated negligent care in New York hospitals in that year was responsible for about 27,000 injuries, including almost 7,000 deaths and close to 1,000 instances of "permanent and total disability." More recently, a 1997 study of about 1,000 hospitalized patients in a large teaching hospital found that almost 18 percent of these patients received inappropriate care resulting in a serious adverse event. In the public eye, such scholarly inquiries have been overshadowed by media reports that describe, often in graphic detail, the harm done to patients because of poor hospital care.

Hospitals rely upon many internal mechanisms to avoid such incidents and to improve the quality of care. External review serves as an additional safeguard. The Federal government relies primarily on two types of external review to ensure hospitals meet the minimum requirements for participating in Medicare: accreditation, usually by the Joint Commission on Accreditation of Healthcare Organizations, and Medicare certification, by State Agencies. About 80 percent of the 6,200 hospitals that participate in Medicare are accredited by the Joint Commission.

This Summary Report

This report synthesizes the findings we present in three parallel reports. It is based on our broad inquiry of the external quality oversight of hospitals, for which we drew on aggregate data, file reviews, surveys, and survey observations from a rich variety of sources, including the Health Care Financing Administration (HCFA), the Joint Commission, State agencies, and other stakeholders.

The report, as our study as a whole, focuses on the roles played by the Joint Commission and the State agencies in reviewing hospitals and by HCFA in overseeing these bodies. Other bodies, most especially the Medicare Peer Review Organizations and State Professional Licensure Boards, play important related roles. We have reviewed their performance in numerous prior studies and will continue our examination of them in future studies. They are not discussed in this report.

Findings

The current system of hospital oversight has significant strengths that help protect patients.

Joint Commission surveys provide an important vehicle for reducing risk and fostering improvement. Hospital leadership takes these accreditation surveys seriously. Hospitals spend months preparing for them, seeking to ensure that their hospitals meet and, where possible, exceed the Joint Commission's standards.

State agency investigations offer a timely, publicly accountable means for responding to complaints and adverse events. The HCFA funds these investigations as a high priority. For both accredited and nonaccredited hospitals, they serve as a significant front-line response to major incidents involving patient harm.

But it also has major deficiencies.

Joint Commission surveys are unlikely to detect substandard patterns of care or individual practitioners with questionable skills. Quick-paced, tightly structured, educationally oriented surveys afford little opportunity for in-depth probing of hospital conditions or practices. Rather than selecting a random sample, the surveyors tend to rely on hospital staff to choose the medical records for review. Further, the surveyors typically begin the process with little background information on any special problems or challenges facing a hospital.

The State agencies rarely conduct routine, not-for-cause surveys of nonaccredited hospitals. The percent of nonaccredited hospitals that have not been surveyed within the 3-year industry standard has grown from 28 percent in 1995 to 50 percent in 1997. In some cases, nonaccredited hospitals, usually in rural areas, have gone as long as 8 years without a survey.

Overall, the hospital review system is moving toward a collegial mode of oversight and away from a regulatory mode.

A collegial mode of oversight is one that focuses on education and improved performance. It emphasizes a trusting approach to oversight, rooted in professional accountability and cooperative relationships. A regulatory mode focuses on investigation and enforcement of minimum requirements. It involves a more challenging approach to oversight, grounded in public accountability. It is helpful to consider external hospital oversight in terms of a continuum, characterized by the collegial approach on one side and the regulatory approach on the other.

The Joint Commission, the dominant force in external hospital review, is leading this movement. It is grounded in a collegial approach to review that stresses education and improvement. It focuses on systems in its quest to improve hospital processes and patient outcomes.

The State agencies are rooted in a more regulatory approach to oversight. But HCFA, through the proposed Medicare conditions of participation, is looking for them to follow the Joint Commission's lead. Traditionally, the State agencies have emphasized investigatory approaches that aim to protect patients from harm more than to improve the overall standard of care. The proposed conditions call for them to move in a direction parallel to that of the Joint Commission.

The emerging dominance of the collegial mode may undermine the existing system of patient protection afforded by accreditation and certification practices. It contrasts significantly with the current regulatory emphasis in nursing home oversight. Both the collegial and regulatory approaches to oversight have value. As the system increasingly tilts toward the collegial mode, however, it could result in insufficient attention to investigatory efforts intended to protect patients from questionable providers and substandard practices.

For nursing homes, recent concerns about the quality of care provided have led to a HCFA crack-down involving more immediate penalties, surprise surveys, and posting of survey results on the Internet, with scant attention to collegial approaches. Such a heavy regulatory emphasis may well not be required for hospitals, but it does reinforce the point that when patients are found to be at risk, regulatory approaches have an important part to play. As we have noted, many recent studies and media reports make it clear that hospitals, too, are places where inappropriate care can and frequently does put patients at risk.

The HCFA does little to hold either the Joint Commission or the State agencies accountable for their performance overseeing hospitals.

The HCFA obtains limited information on the performance of the Joint Commission or the States. In both cases, HCFA asks for little in the way of routine performance reports. To assess the Joint Commission's performance, HCFA relies mainly on validation surveys conducted, at HCFA's expense, by the State agencies. But for a number of reasons the value of these surveys has been limited. The methodology for selecting the hospitals to survey fails to consider hospital size, type, or past performance. More fundamentally, the surveys have been based on different standards (the Medicare Conditions of Participation as opposed to the Joint Commission standards) and have been conducted subsequent to the Commission's surveys (when hospital conditions could have changed). During 1996 and 97, HCFA piloted 20 observation surveys—during which State and HCFA officials accompanied Joint Commission surveyors. This approach appears to have much promise, but HCFA has not yet issued any evaluation of the pilots.

The HCFA observes few hospital surveys conducted by State agencies and conducts no validation surveys of them.

The HCFA provides limited feedback to the Joint Commission and the State agencies on their overall performance. Its feedback to the Joint Commission is more deferential than directive. Its major vehicle for feedback to the Joint Commission is its annual Report to Congress, which is based on the validation surveys and has typically been submitted years late. The HCFA is more directive to the State agencies, which carry out their survey work in accord with HCFA protocols, but gives them little feedback on how well they perform their hospital oversight work.

Public disclosure plays only a minimal role in holding Joint Commission and State agencies accountable. The HCFA makes little information available to the public on the performance of either hospitals or of the external reviewers. By contrast, HCFA posts nursing home survey findings on the Internet and requires nursing homes to post them as well. The Joint Commission has been more proactive than HCFA in making hospital survey results widely available on the Internet and through other means.

Recommendations

We offer one guiding principle and two recommendations that set forth ways in which HCFA can, over time, provide leadership to address the shortcomings we have identified in our inquiry, holding the Joint Commission and State agencies more accountable for their performance.

Guiding Principle

The HCFA, as a guiding principle, should steer external reviews of hospital quality so that they ensure a balance between collegial and regulatory modes of oversight.

The HCFA must recognize that both approaches have value and that a credible system of oversight must reflect a reasonable balance between them. In our assessment, a balanced system would involve the continued presence of on-site hospital surveys, both announced and unannounced; an ongoing capacity to respond quickly and effectively to complaints and adverse events; further development and application of standardized performance measures; and, even though it is not much in evidence at this time, a mechanism for conducting retrospective reviews of the appropriateness of hospital care. A balanced system would also be one in which performance measures are used to protect patients from harm as well as to improve the standard of care.

In its steering role, HCFA must recognize the inherent strengths and limitations of accrediting bodies and the State agencies. Each contributes to the external review of hospitals, but they do so differently. Thus, in steering, HCFA should look to the Joint Commission to tilt (but not too far) toward the collegial end and the State agencies to tilt (but not too far) toward the regulatory end.

Recommendation 1:

The HCFA should hold the Joint Commission and State agencies more fully accountable for their performance in reviewing hospitals.

- Revamp Federal approaches for obtaining information on Joint Commission and State agency performance by de-emphasizing validation surveys, giving serious consideration to the potential of observation surveys, and calling for more timely and useful reporting of performance data.
- Strengthen Federal mechanisms for providing performance feedback and policy guidance to the Joint Commission and State agencies. Given the major role played by the Joint Commission, the public purposes associated with its special deemed status authority, and the importance of achieving a more balanced system of external review, HCFA should negotiate with the Joint Commission to achieve the following changes:
  — Conduct more unannounced surveys.
  — Make the "accreditation with commendation" category more meaningful, or do away with it altogether.
  — Introduce more random selection of records as part of the survey process.

- — Provide surveyors with more contextual information about the hospitals they are about to survey.
- — Jointly determine some year-to-year survey priorities, with an initial priority on examining credentials and privileges.
- — Conduct more rigorous assessments of hospitals' internal continuous quality improvement efforts.
- — Enhance the capacity of surveyors to respond to complaints within the survey process.
- • Assess periodically the justification for the Joint Commission's deemed status authority.
- • Increase public disclosure on the performance of hospitals, the Joint Commission, and State agencies, by, at a minimum, posting more detailed information on the Internet.

Recommendation 2:

The HCFA should determine the appropriate minimum cycle for conducting certification surveys of nonaccredited hospitals.

Nonaccredited hospitals are subject to limited external review other than those reviews triggered by complaints and adverse events. Unlike nursing homes and home health agencies, hospitals lack a mandated minimum cycle for surveys. While complaints and adverse events may well warrant priority over routine surveys, such surveys play an important role in external review, and by determining a minimum cycle HCFA can increase the level of attention to hospital oversight.

Comments

Within the Department of Health and Human Services, we received comments on our draft reports from HCFA—the Departmental agency to which all of our recommendations are directed. We also solicited and received comments from the following external organizations: the Joint Commission on Accreditation of Healthcare Organizations, the Association of Health Facility Survey Agencies, the American Osteopathic Association, the American Hospital Association, the American Association for Retired Persons, the Service Employees International Union, the National Health Law Program, and Public Citizen's Health Research Group. . . . Below, we summarize the thrust of the comments and, in italics, offer our responses.

HCFA Comments

The HCFA reacted positively to our findings and recommendations. It offered a detailed hospital oversight plan that incorporates our many recommendations. The plan reflects HCFA's commitment to more frequent surveys of nonaccredited hospitals, to strengthened oversight of both the State agencies and the Joint Commission, and to a balance between collegial and regulatory approaches to oversight. In addition, HCFA presented a hospital performance measurement strategy based on developing standardized performance measures that are consumer- and purchaser-driven and that are in the public domain.

The HCFA's action plan is highly responsive to the recommendations we set forth. As it is carried out, it can be of considerable value in improving patient safety and the quality of patient care.

Joint Commission and Association of Health Facility Survey Agencies Comments

The Joint Commission and the State survey agencies, which the Association of Health Facility Survey Agencies represents, are the two key parties that HCFA relies upon to conduct external reviews of hospital quality. The Joint Commission agreed with the principle of balance between collegial and regulatory approaches, but regarded our concerns about an emerging dominance of the collegial approach to be unfounded. It also objected to the limitations we cited about its survey approach and to our conclusion that the Joint Commission devotes minimal attention to complaints. It did express support for stronger, more performance-oriented HCFA oversight of the Joint Commission. The Association, while agreeing with the thrust of our assessment, noted some reservations about phasing out the validation surveys in favor of an observation survey approach that is largely untested.

We stress here, as we did in the text, the importance of a balance in oversight that avoids tilting too far toward either the collegial or the regulatory ends. We believe that we established credible bases for such a balanced approach. Similarly, we believe that our assessments of Joint Commission practices are balanced and well-supported. We identified various strengths that the Joint Commission brings to the field of quality oversight. We regard the limitations that we cited as an important part of the overall picture. With respect to the Association's reservations about the observation surveys as a tool of oversight, we suggest that the problems we pointed out about the validation process are significant ones and that the potential of the observation surveys is compelling enough to warrant further exploration.

Comments of Other External Organizations

Overall, the other stakeholder organizations offered considerable support for our findings and recommendations. But they also expressed concerns. The American Hospital Association took issue with how we applied the collegial and regulatory concepts and stressed that hospital liability concerns preclude the kind of public disclosure we urge. The American Osteopathic Association noted reservations about more unannounced surveys and suggested that a closer review of medical care during on-site surveys would be more productive. The American Association of Retired Persons agreed with the thrust of our recommendations.

The Service Employees International Union, the National Health Law Program, and Public Citizen's Health Research Group called for even stronger Federal actions than we recommended. These included a stronger emphasis on regulatory approaches, greater reliance on unannounced surveys, more extensive public disclosure, and firmer HCFA action in overseeing the Joint Commission and in reassessing its deeming authority.

These stakeholders raise concerns and urge directions that we often heard expressed during our study. As HCFA carries out its hospital quality oversight plan, we suggest that it take these perspectives into account. We believe that our recommendations (and HCFA's announced action plan) sets forth a balanced course of action that draws to some degree on the insights of each of these stakeholders. This course is one that can substantially improve the external review of hospital quality in the years ahead.

SEN. EDWARD M. KENNEDY'S
EULOGY FOR JOHN F. KENNEDY JR.
July 23, 1999

The American public lost a favorite son and the Kennedy family suffered another heartbreaking misfortune when a small plane piloted by John F. Kennedy Jr. crashed into the Atlantic Ocean just off the coast of Martha's Vineyard on the evening of July 16, 1999. Also killed were Kennedy's wife of three years, Carolyn Bessette Kennedy, and her sister Lauren Bessette.

The accident was under investigation by federal authorities, who were not expected to make a final determination of its causes until sometime in 2000. But wreckage recovered from the crash site showed no signs of malfunctioning equipment or defect in the aircraft, and speculation quickly centered on the theory that Kennedy, a novice pilot, may have become disoriented in the dark and hazy night and lost control of the plane. "It appears to be an all-too-ordinary type of accident involving extraordinary people," one federal investigator told the Chicago Tribune.

Although he had never held public office and had not deliberately sought the limelight, Kennedy was a celebrity throughout his life. An adoring public that had watched Kennedy play in the White House Oval Office as a toddler was shocked and dismayed by the news that his plane had disappeared. For a week the nation's attention was focused on the search for the wreckage, the recovery of the bodies, and the memorial services that followed. Coverage of the crash and its aftermath saturated the media for days. Kennedy's life and death inevitably drew comparisons with Diana, Princess of Wales, who died in a car crash in Paris in August 1997. (Historic Documents of 1997, p. 647)

The death of the son of the late president was the latest in a string of untimely deaths that had plagued what many Americans had come to think of as the nation's "first family." President John F. Kennedy was assassinated in November 1963; his older brother, Joseph Kennedy Jr., was killed in 1944 on a World War II bombing mission; and his younger brother Robert F. Kennedy was assassinated in 1968 after winning the California presidential primary. In July 1969 a car driven by Sen. Edward M.

Kennedy went off a bridge on Chappaquiddick Island, killing Kennedy's passenger, Mary Jo Kopechne. A son of Robert Kennedy, David Kennedy, died of a drug overdose in 1984, and another son, Michael, died in a skiing accident in 1997.

A Celebrity Life

Born November 25, 1960, just weeks after his father was elected president, the young Kennedy was a celebrity throughout his life. "The whole world knew his name before he did," Sen. Kennedy, said in a moving eulogy for his nephew, delivered July 23 at a memorial service in Manhattan. Perhaps the most heart-rending memory many Americans carried from the assassination of President Kennedy was an image of the toddler saluting his father's coffin outside St. Matthew's Cathedral in Washington, D.C.; it was the young Kennedy's third birthday.

Kennedy went to private schools and then to Brown University, where he majored in American history. He went to law school at New York University and failed the New York bar exam twice before finally passing. "Hunk Flunks" screamed the tabloid headlines. After working as an assistant district attorney in Manhattan for four years, Kennedy left and eventually started George, *a glossy political magazine. Although he showed little interest in running for office, Kennedy helped the Democratic Party raise money and devoted a great deal of his own time and money to underprivileged children and the disabled.*

Until his marriage to Caroline Bessette in 1996, Kennedy was one of the most sought-after bachelors in the world. His name was frequently linked with glamorous women, and in 1988 People *magazine deemed him "the sexiest man alive." Yet by most accounts, Kennedy was a self-effacing man who frequently used public transportation and had time for strangers who spoke to him on the street. "I have a pretty normal life, surprisingly," he once said.*

Also by most accounts, Kennedy was a good but relatively inexperienced pilot. He had gotten his pilot's license in 1998, had logged about 200 hours of flying time, and was learning how to fly his high-performance Piper Saratoga by instruments alone. On July 16 Kennedy and his wife planned to fly her sister to the Martha's Vineyard Island airport before flying on to Hyannis Port on Cape Cod to attend a family wedding. The three took off from the Essex County Airport in Fairfield, New Jersey, at 8:38 P.M., a few minutes after sunset. Radar readings later showed that Kennedy's plane began a normal descent beginning about thirty miles from the Martha's Vineyard airport, then inexplicably turned away from the island and climbed a few hundred feet. It then turned back toward the island and began a second descent. It abruptly turned right a second time and went into a steep descent. When the radar lost contact with the plane, it was in a dive only about a thousand feet above the water.

A massive search coordinated by the Coast Guard began early on July 17, and the wreckage and three bodies were found July 21, more than one hun-

dred feet under the surface of the water. On July 22 family members boarded the naval destroyer Briscoe *and the cremated remains of Kennedy and the two women were buried at sea off the coast of Martha's Vineyard in a private ceremony. Kennedy was not automatically entitled to the naval burial at sea, but Defense Secretary William S. Cohen authorized the service at Senator Kennedy's request. A larger but still private memorial mass was held for Kennedy on July 23 at the Church of St. Thomas in Manhattan.*

Likely Explanations: Disorientation and Inexperience

Although the investigation had not been completed by the end of the year, most aviation experts speculated that Kennedy had become disoriented in the hazy night, turned the wrong way, and then gone into a dive as he tried to correct his descent. "We call this getting yourself in a square corner, when you run out of ideas and experience at the same time," said Michael L. Barr shortly after the accident. Barr was the director of the Aviation Safety Program at the University of Southern California, one of the leading training centers for aviation accident investigators. Kennedy "would have been looking straight out at the dark ocean on a nearly moonless night," Barr said. "He probably looked over his right shoulder for lights, then when he started to sink, he would have been trying to get the nose back to the horizon, get the wings level and find where he was, all at the same time. Even for a good pilot, that could produce a death spiral."

The number of crashes in general (noncommercial) aviation had been steadily declining, from 721 in 1978 to 361 in 1998. According to the Aircraft Owners and Pilots Association, pilots with low levels of training who found themselves in conditions requiring instrument-only skills caused more accidents than most weather hazards combined.

Another celebrity, professional golfer Payne Stewart, was killed in 1999 when the chartered Learjet in which he was a passenger crashed after flying off course by about 1,500 miles. The bizarre incident began at about 9:15 A.M. on October 25, when the small jet, carrying two pilots and three other passengers, left Orlando, Florida, for Dallas, Texas. Air traffic controllers lost radio contact with the plane about half an hour into the flight while the plane was still climbing to its cruising altitude of 39,000 feet. Air force planes caught up with the plane as it climbed to 45,000 feet and then tailed it helplessly as it flew, apparently unpiloted, for nearly four hours, before running out of fuel and crashing near Aberdeen, South Dakota, at about 1:30 in the afternoon.

The causes of the crash had not been confirmed by the end of the year. The Air force pilots said the windows of the Lear jet were frosted over, a sign that the plane may have sustained a rapid loss of cabin pressure, which could have caused all on board to pass out or even die from lack of oxygen. A low pressure alarm, but no voices, were captured on the cockpit voice recorder, which bolstered that hypothesis. One of the most popular players on the pro golf circuit, Stewart had won his second U.S. Open in June and was the third highest money winner on the 1999 tour.

Following is the text of the eulogy delivered July 23, 1999, by Sen. Edward M. Kennedy for his nephew John Kennedy Jr., at the Church of St. Thomas in New York City:

Thank you, President and Mrs. Clinton and Chelsea, for being here today. You've shown extraordinary kindness throughout the course of this week.

Once, when they asked John what he would do if he went into politics and was elected president, he said: "I guess the first thing is call up Uncle Teddy and gloat." I loved that. It was so like his father.

From the first day of his life, John seemed to belong not only to our family, but to the American family.

The whole world knew his name before he did.

A famous photograph showed John racing across the lawn as his father landed in the White House helicopter and swept up John in his arms. When my brother saw that photo, he exclaimed, "Every mother in the United States is saying, 'Isn't it wonderful to see that love between a son and his father, the way that John races to be with his father.' Little do they know—that son would have raced right by his father to get to that helicopter."

But John was so much more than those long ago images emblazoned in our minds. He was a boy who grew into a man with a zest for life and a love of adventure. He was a pied piper who brought us all along. He was blessed with a father and mother who never thought anything mattered more than their children.

When they left the White House, Jackie's soft and gentle voice and unbreakable strength of spirit guided him surely and securely to the future. He had a legacy, and he learned to treasure it. He was part of a legend, and he learned to live with it. Above all, Jackie gave him a place to be himself, to grow up, to laugh and cry, to dream and strive on his own.

John learned that lesson well. He had amazing grace. He accepted who he was, but he cared more about what he could and should become. He saw things that could be lost in the glare of the spotlight. And he could laugh at the absurdity of too much pomp and circumstance.

He loved to travel across this city by subway, bicycle and roller blade. He lived as if he were unrecognizable—although he was known by everyone he encountered. He always introduced himself, rather than take anything for granted. He drove his own car and flew his own plane, which is how he wanted it. He was the king of his domain.

He thought politics should be an integral part of our popular culture, and that popular culture should be an integral part of politics. He transformed that belief into the creation of *George*. John shaped and honed a fresh, often irreverent journal. His new political magazine attracted a new generation, many of whom had never read about politics before.

John also brought to *George* a wit that was quick and sure. The premier issue of *George* caused a stir with a cover photograph of Cindy Crawford dressed as George Washington with a bare belly button. The "Reliable

Source" in the *Washington Post* printed a mock cover of *George* showing not Cindy Crawford, but me dressed as George Washington, with my belly button exposed. I suggested to John that perhaps I should have been the model for the first cover of his magazine. Without missing a beat, John told me that he stood by his original editorial decision.

John brought this same playful wit to other aspects of his life. He campaigned for me during my 1994 election and always caused a stir when he arrived in Massachusetts. Before one of his trips to Boston, John told the campaign he was bringing along a companion, but would need only one hotel room.

Interested, but discreet, a senior campaign worker picked John up at the airport and prepared to handle any media barrage that might accompany John's arrival with his mystery companion. John landed with the companion all right—an enormous German Shepherd dog named Sam he had just rescued from the pound.

He loved to talk about the expression on the campaign worker's face and the reaction of the clerk at the Charles Hotel when John and Sam checked in.

I think now not only of these wonderful adventures, but of the kind of person John was. He was the son who quietly gave extraordinary time and ideas to the Institute of Politics at Harvard that bears his father's name. He brought to the Institute his distinctive insight that politics could have a broader appeal, that it was not just about elections, but about the larger forces that shape our whole society.

John was also the son who was once protected by his mother. He went on to become her pride—and then her protector in her final days. He was the Kennedy who loved us all, but who especially cherished his sister Caroline, celebrated her brilliance, and took strength and joy from their lifelong mutual admiration society.

And for a thousand days, he was a husband who adored the wife who became his perfect soul-mate. John's father taught us all to reach for the moon and the stars. John did that in all he did—and he found his shining star when he married Carolyn Bessette.

How often our family will think of the two of them, cuddling affectionately on a boat—surrounded by family, aunts, uncles, Caroline and Ed and their children, Rose, Tatiana, and Jack, Kennedy cousins, Radziwill cousins, Shriver cousins, Smith cousins, Lawford cousins as we sailed Nantucket Sound.

Then we would come home, and before dinner, on the lawn where his father had played, John would lead a spirited game of touch football. And his beautiful young wife, the new pride of the Kennedys, would cheer for John's team and delight her nieces and nephews with her somersaults.

We loved Carolyn. She and her sister Lauren were young extraordinary women of high accomplishment and their own limitless possibilities. We mourn their loss and honor their lives. The Bessette and Freeman families will always be part of ours.

John was a serious man who brightened our lives with his smile and his grace. He was a son of privilege who founded a program called "Reaching

Up," to train better caregivers for the mentally disabled. He joined Wall Street executives on the Robin Hood Foundation to help the city's impoverished children. And he did it all so quietly, without ever calling attention to himself.

John was one of Jackie's two miracles. He was still becoming the person he would be, and doing it by the beat of his own drummer. He had only just begun. There was in him a great promise of things to come.

The Irish Ambassador recited a poem to John's father and mother soon after John was born. I can hear it again now, at this different and difficult moment:

> *We wish to the new child*
> *A heart that can be beguiled*
> *By a flower*
> *That the wind lifts*
> *As it passes.*
> *If the storms break for him*
> *May the trees shake for him*
> *Their blossoms down.*
> *In the night that he is troubled,*
> *May a friend wake for him,*
> *So that his time be doubled,*
> *And at the end of all loving*
> *and love,*
> *May the Man above*
> *Give him a crown.*

We thank the millions who have rained blossoms down on John's memory. He and his bride have gone to be with his mother and father, where there will never be an end to love. He was lost on that troubled night—but we will always wake for him, so that his time, which was not doubled, but cut in half, will live forever in our memory, and in our beguiled and broken hearts.

We dared to think, in that other Irish phrase, that this John Kennedy would live to comb grey hair, with his beloved Carolyn by his side. But like his father, he had every gift but length of years.

We who have loved him from the day he was born, and watched the remarkable man he became, now bid him farewell. God bless you, John and Carolyn. We love you, and we always will.

UN REFUGEE COMMISSIONER ON PROMOTING PEACE IN AFRICA
July 26, 1999

Bringing and maintaining peace in long-troubled regions of Africa became a high priority for the international community, particularly the United Nations, during 1999. Peace agreements were negotiated to end two of the continent's most brutal wars—in Sierra Leone and the Democratic Republic of Congo—but considerable doubt remained about the durability of those accords. Short of money and international confidence in its abilities, the UN was struggling with the responsibility of mounting difficult and expensive missions to keep the peace.

Perhaps at no other time since the end of colonialism in the 1960s had there been such a sharp contrast between progress in some parts of Africa and a reversion to bloody conflict elsewhere. Nigeria and South Africa held successful democratic elections during 1999, and several other African nations were continuing to develop democratic institutions and revive their economies through free-market practices and international trade. But ethnic, tribal, and regional conflict raged in nearly a dozen countries, in some cases with consequences that damaged entire regions. By 1999, according to UN figures, more than 7 million Africans had been forced from their homes by fighting. Many African nations were losing an even more insidious and murderous war as their populations were being ravaged by AIDS (acquired immunodeficiency syndrome). (Nigerian election, p. 272; South African election, p. 297; AIDS in Africa, p. 489)

The focus on peacekeeping during 1999 came just one year after President Bill Clinton's historic trip to Africa gave extraordinary international attention to a series of positive developments on the continent. Clinton and others had declared in 1998 that Africa was turning to a new chapter in its history. The overthrow of dictators, such as Zaire's Mobutu Sese Seko in 1997, and the coming to power of a new generation of progressive leaders seemingly interested more in the welfare of their countries than in lining their own pockets, were among the factors that had led some optimists to declare a "renaissance" in Africa. By 1999 much of the optimism had faded. (Clinton trip, Historic Documents of 1998, p. 159; Mobutu ouster, Historic Documents of 1997, p. 877)

A Matter of Priorities

During the first half of 1999, much of the world was preoccupied with the conflict in Kosovo, where NATO used massive military intervention on behalf of ethnic Albanians who had been terrorized by Serbian security forces. The continued killing in Africa during the same period was met with comparatively little international response. Addressing the United Nations Security Council on July 26, 1999, Sadako Ogata, the UN High Commissioner for Refugees, noted a "perception of disparity in the assistance given, for example, to displaced persons from Kosovo, as opposed to that given to African refugees." Factors such as strategic interest and intense media coverage were partly responsible for the extraordinary outpouring of Western support for Kosovar refugees, she said. "Undeniably, this [level of support] has not been true-and continues not to be true—in other situations," including those in Africa, she added. (Kosovo conflict, pp. 134, 285, 802)

Ogata appealed for UN support for enforcing the security provisions of political agreements that attempted to end Africa's wars. "Throughout my recent travels in Africa, I sensed that there is now a strong expectation for the United Nations to provide more support and be more actively involved in keeping and building peace," she told the Security Council. In essence, she said, that meant active UN participation in peacekeeping or monitoring forces.

Ogata also lectured the council on the obligations of the international community to support long-term development efforts in countries where civil wars have ended. In Rwanda, for example, she noted that humanitarian aid programs were "relatively well supported" by international donors immediately following the gruesome civil war in 1994, but development efforts since then received "much more timid inputs" from development agencies and donor nations.

United Nations Secretary General Kofi Annan, a Ghanaian, echoed these sentiments in several speeches and reports during the year. Addressing the Security Council on September 29, Annan noted that the international community had to respond to every world crisis "on its own merits." But for the UN and the Security Council "to retain their credibility and the support of the world's peoples, the commitment to peacekeeping, humanitarian assistance and other such action must be applied fairly and consistently, irrespective of region or nation," he said. Annan also pursued a theme he had developed in a controversial 1998 report on Africa: that Africans for too long had blamed all their troubles on the legacy of colonialism, and that only by accepting responsibility for their own failures would they be able to learn how to achieve political and economic stability. (Annan report, Historic Documents of 1998, p. 220)

Annan and Ogata acknowledged that the UN faced two key problems in responding to the peacekeeping and humanitarian challenge posed by Africa's wars. The first was financial; paying for humanitarian aid and the thousands of troops needed to monitor peace agreements was expensive, and key donors, especially the United States, were balking at the cost. The second hurdle was the logistical difficulty of aiding refugees and reconstructing countries devastated by years of war. By 1999 Africa's wars had become so complex, each involving numerous countries and competing guerrilla groups, that negotiating peace agreements was just the first of many difficult phases of actually ending fighting and restoring peace. In her address to the Security Council, Ogata noted that Africa was plagued with "multiple, inter-related conflicts and smaller human displacement crises," rather than the massive conflicts and refugee displacements common in earlier wars in Rwanda, Zaire, and other countries.

The Clinton administration, which had begun paying increased attention to Africa during the late 1990s, insisted that the United States was willing to meet its responsibilities to the region. But during a trip to several African nations in October, Secretary of State Madeleine K. Albright blamed Congress for failing to approve adequate foreign aid. Africans, she said in Kenya, find it "very hard to understand that we have the world's greatest economy and we have a huge budget surplus and they are digging themselves out of garbage."

Conflicts in Congo and Sierra Leone

By far the biggest conflict in Africa was taking place in the Democratic Republic of Congo, a mammoth country involved with six other countries and numerous guerrilla factions battling either to support or to overthrow the self-declared president, Laurent Kabila. The major parties signed a peace agreement during the summer, but the fighting did not stop. (Congo war, p. 645)

Another fragile peace accord was reached during 1999 offering the prospect of ending one of the most brutal civil wars in modern African history. In the tiny nation of Sierra Leone on the West African coast, a guerrilla group, the Revolutionary United Front, had battled the government since March 1991. The conflict killed an estimated 50,000 people and drove 500,000 people (10 percent of the total population) from their homes, according to UN figures. Another 100,000 people—and possibly many more, by some estimates—were mutilated by government and rebel fighters who intimidated opponents by hacking off victims' hands, arms, and legs. Briefing the Security Council, Ogata said of the conflict: "I have rarely seen consequences of physical and psychological violence as horrifying as those affecting civilians who survived killings and were left traumatized by beatings, amputations, and rape."

African nations, with help from the United States, negotiated a ceasefire agreement, signed May 24, and a full peace afford, signed July 7 by President Ahmad Kabbah and rebel leader Foday Sankoh. Fighting continued even after the peace agreement was signed, however, and international human rights groups said guerrillas were continuing to terrorize civilians with killings and maimings.

The UN Security Council on October 22 authorized a peacekeeping force of 6,000 armed troops and 260 observers, most of them from Nigeria and other members of the West African economic community, ECOWAS. The cost for the first year was projected at $200 million. The first peacekeepers arrived in late November. Rebel Sankoh announced creation of a political party to contest elections scheduled for 2000, but at year's end the guerrilla group had split into two factions that were battling each other.

Other African Conflicts

Significant regional conflicts were under way in other parts of Africa during 1999.

Angola. A peace agreement between the government and UNITA [National Union for the Total Independence of Angola] rebels, signed in 1994, collapsed in December 1998, resulting in intense fighting early in 1999. UNITA captured several key towns, and in February UN Secretary General Annan took the unprecedented step of withdrawing UN peacekeeping forces from Angola.

The Republic of Congo. This small nation just to the west of the massive Democratic Republic of Congo was engulfed in what Ogata referred to as an "almost forgotten civil war." Tens of thousands of civilians were forced from the capital, Brazzaville, and neighboring towns, and there was little prospect of a settlement between the government and rebel factions.

Ethiopia and Eritrea. A border dispute between Ethiopia and the breakaway province of Eritrea erupted into fighting in May 1998, then lapsed for about eight months before becoming a full-scale war in February 1999 that featured massive trench warfare and "wave attacks" reminiscent of World War I. The Organization of African Unity negotiated a peace plan, which Eritrea accepted in August. The plan received an ambiguous response from Ethiopia, and fighting continued throughout the year.

Sudan. The longest-running conflict in Africa, other than Angola's twenty-five-year conflict, was in the Sudan, where for sixteen years the Islamic government in Khartoum had battled rebel groups in the southern part of the country. The government during 1999 announced its willingness to let the south secede, and in August proposed a nationwide cease-fire. But the rebels rejected the proposal, insisting that the government was violating its promise to stop bombing and other attacks. At year's end, it appeared that internal divisions within the Khartoum government might weaken the influence of Islamic extremists who had controlled the country for most of the 1990s.

Following are excerpts from an address to the United Nations Security Council in New York on July 26, 1999, by Sadako Ogata, the UN high commissioner for refugees, in which she addressed the needs of refugees in Africa:

Refugee Problems in Africa—
Opportunities for Solutions?

As the head of an Office which spends over 40% of its resources in Africa, and having personally visited West Africa in February, and Central Africa last month, I shall provide you with a first hand perspective on problems of human displacement on the continent. My impressions of the last Summit of the Organization of African Unity [OAU], which I attended in Algiers two weeks ago, are a good starting point.

I found this year's summit—the seventh such gathering to which I have been invited as observer—particularly encouraging. Like Secretary-General Kofi Annan, I sensed a real spirit of openness and noted positive signs that existing problems could be solved. In attendance were the newly, democratically elected Presidents of South Africa and Nigeria. It was a powerful symbol that these two key African countries are ready to provide an essential contribution to peace, democratization and economic development throughout the continent. This year's host country for the Summit, Algeria, may also be auspiciously emerging from nine years of internal instability under the direction of a new President. Another remarkable feature of the Summit was that it took place at the same time as a cease-fire agreement on the conflict in the Democratic Republic of the Congo and a peace agreement between the government and rebel forces in Sierra Leone were being signed. We should be realistic: there will be delays and setbacks in the advancement towards peace and prosperity, but for the first time in years I felt that the election of some remarkable leaders, their presence at the Summit, and developments on the ground, marked a hope for progress. And from the perspective of UNHCR [United Nations High Commissioner for Refugees], these positive steps towards peace raise hopes that many refugees will eventually return home.

. . . [T]he challenge before us is to act rapidly to support the implementation of political agreements. Since the signature of the initial cease-fire agreement on 24 May, for example, hostilities have not resumed in Sierra Leone. From UNHCR's perspective, both agreements may be rare coincidences of opportunities which—if properly and quickly seized by the international community—may lead to the resolution of some of the worst refugee problems in Africa. There are about six million people "of concern" to my Office on the continent. If you analyze a "map of human displacement" you will clearly see that people in flight are invariably an indicator of situations of poverty, or conflict, or a combination of both.

The main refugee groups caused by recent crises continue to be the over half a million Sierra Leoneans in West Africa; the 260,000 Burundians in Tanzania; the 150,000 people who have fled conflict in the Democratic Republic of the Congo in various countries. As we speak, people are fleeing the Republic of Congo (Brazzaville) to the Democratic Republic of the Congo and Gabon. There are older, unresolved conflict situations which have produced refugees many years ago—more than 370,000 Sudanese continue to be refugees in Uganda and Ethiopia; 120,000 Saharan refugees are still in camps in Algeria and other countries; there are 150,000 Angolan refugees, mostly in the Democratic Republic of the Congo—tens of thousands of these are actually newly arrived people fleeing fresh fighting in their country. In both Sudan and Angola, as well as in war-torn areas at the border between Ethiopia and Eritrea, there are also tens of thousands of internally displaced people. In Liberia, where 280,000 refugees have returned home and where we hope to finish the repatriation of the remaining quarter of a million by mid-2000, recent episodes of insecurity betray internal tensions and the fragility of peace.

Supporting Peace Processes and Addressing Refugee Problems in West and Central Africa

In February, when I visited Guinea, Sierra Leone, Liberia and Côte d'Ivoire, hopes for a settlement in Sierra Leone were still fragile. I therefore welcome the recent Lomé agreement [a peace agreement to end the civil war in Sierra Leone, signed at Lome, Togo], although the road to peace is undoubtedly going to be long and difficult. The end of the civil war in Sierra Leone may bring about a positive solution to the worst current refugee problem in Africa—the plight of over half a million people, about 10% of the entire Sierra Leonean population, who have fled violence and fighting in various waves in the last few years. Most of them have taken refuge in Guinea and Liberia, which, in spite of their very limited resources, have generously provided asylum to this large refugee population—a true example to the international community. Sierra Leonean refugees, as has been frequently reported to the Council, have suffered unspeakable violence during the conflict. I have rarely seen consequences of physical and psychological violence as horrifying as those affecting civilians who survived killings and were left traumatized by beatings, amputations, and rape.

My first key message here today is therefore a plea for all necessary resources to be provided to Sierra Leone and governments in the sub-region so that the Lomé agreement can be implemented—and implemented very rapidly. Peace is at hand, but - especially seen from the vantage point of hundreds of villages still exposed to violence, pillaging and retaliation—it is very fragile. From the humanitarian perspective, resources will soon be needed to support the return and reintegration of refugees and internally displaced people in their communities of origin. This is of paramount importance because the violence of the Sierra Leonean conflict has created deep divisions and mistrust. As we see in other situations, the longer people stay away from their communities, the more difficult and complex reconciliation becomes. Repatriation will take time, but we must of course get prepared for it as quickly as possible, while continuing to assist refugees and local communities hosting them in countries of asylum. I would also like to take this opportunity to make a special appeal to help those—thousands, unfortunately—who have suffered physical amputations. My visit to a center for the rehabilitation of amputees from Sierra Leone, last February in Guinea, was one of the most shocking experiences of my eight years as High Commissioner. Their courageous efforts to learn again to walk, eat, and write, deserve special attention and sustained support.

In the Democratic Republic of the Congo, the Lusaka agreement [a peace agreement to end the Congo's civil war, signed in Lusaka, Zambia], although not yet signed by all parties, is a welcome development for which governments in the region should be commended. It is not only immediately important as a positive step towards resolving conflict in Central Africa—it is also an encouraging indication that peace in Africa can be attained when African leaders are committed to work together towards this goal, in spite of all differences and difficulties. As with the Lomé agreement, however, it is now imperative that the Lusaka agreement receives strong, clear international support, so that all parties to the conflict adhere to it and its rapid implementation can become a reality. In spite of the progress made, war has not ended - witness the recent influx into the Central African Republic of thousands of Congolese fleeing fresh fighting in the Equateur province, a very destabilizing situation in this fragile area.

The Democratic Republic of the Congo desperately needs peace. Visiting the country last month, I was shocked by the deteriorating living conditions of the Congolese population at large. The informal economy, once the backbone of this resilient country, has all but collapsed—poverty is rampant, almost 150,000 refugees have fled and there are countless internally displaced people. In Algiers, I met President Kabila and asked him to take the initiative in granting humanitarian agencies access to all those in need. I was encouraged by his positive reply. Humanitarian assistance is needed to bring relief to hundreds of thousands of suffering people, but it can also contribute to the peace process and be a first step towards a much needed stabilization of the country and of the sub-region. I therefore wish to renew my appeal to all parties to the conflict to allow the delivery of aid to refugees, displaced people and all civilians in need.

The situation in the entire Central African sub-region has shifted from one of massive refugee movements to one of multiple, inter-related conflicts and smaller human displacement crises. However, the potential for larger, and more dramatic displacement, exists. Refugees are often manipulated by states and rebel groups alike. At the present juncture, it is very difficult to pursue a comprehensive effort to enforce refugee protection principles with due consideration for the security concerns of states, as we had promoted at the Kampala regional meeting on refugee issues in May 1998. While the Lusaka peace process continues, UNHCR will therefore concentrate on trying to address, if not resolve, individual situations of displacement.

The most pressing issue is to tackle the problem of Rwandans who have not yet returned after fleeing the country in the aftermath of genocide, and particularly of the largest groups, which are in the two Congos. A solution to this problem has been made easier by improvements in the security and internal stability of Rwanda. On the other hand, the presence of armed elements among bona fide refugees continues to be a serious problem in several countries, with security implications affecting and slowing down the peace process. In this respect I am pleased to report that during my recent trip to the sub-region I have taken two key decisions. First, from offices in Bukavu and Goma, UNHCR will resume support to the repatriation of Rwandans still in the eastern part of the Democratic Republic of the Congo. We have received assurances from rebel authorities controlling these areas that we shall be granted access to those requesting repatriation, and that the voluntary character of return will be respected; I informed President Bizimungu of Rwanda, who encourages and supports our role in this operation; I also informed President Kabila, who did not object to UNHCR's involvement. Second, we shall offer Rwandans in the Republic of Congo (Brazzaville) to either repatriate, or to settle in areas in the north of their host country, where they can receive a one-time assistance package to facilitate local integration. This scheme is presently under discussion with the authorities in Brazzaville.

Prospects for a solution to the plight of Burundian refugees in Tanzania, on the other hand, appear less promising. Peace talks in Arusha between the government of Burundi and its opponents continue. Meanwhile, however, refugee repatriation movements are now limited to a few individuals per day. I am very concerned by this situation, which exposes refugees (and the local population) to a situation of serious tension and insecurity at the border between Burundi and Tanzania—a situation that can only be resolved when refugees return home voluntarily. In asking the Council to encourage an early and positive conclusion of the Arusha peace process, I would also like to request that refugee issues be addressed from a humanitarian viewpoint, in respect of international norms. On our side, we shall continue to support Tanzania in ensuring that refugee camps maintain their civilian character; and we stand ready to resume the voluntary repatriation, and support the reintegration of Burundian refugees in their country.

Before concluding on Central Africa, I would like to draw the Council's attention to several other situations of conflict and displacement, which currently offer little or no hope for early solutions and where UNHCR must therefore continue to provide care and maintenance support, and emergency assistance in the case of new refugee outflows. I am thinking of the situation in Western Sahara, where UNHCR continues to make preparations for repatriation in March next year, but where the likelihood of the return of refugees depends entirely on the progress of political negotiations. I am referring as well to the Angolan conflict, which is pushing thousands of people to flee their homes—I visited an Angolan refugee camp in the Bas-Congo province of the Democratic Republic of the Congo, and observed that no return can be possible under the present circumstances. I am referring also to the war in southern Sudan, one of the oldest and most violent conflicts in the world, the effects of which—both in terms of refugee movements and of general insecurity—are widely felt in the region.

And finally I would particularly like to draw the attention of the Security Council to the violent, and almost forgotten civil war in the Republic of Congo (Brazzaville). Thousands of inhabitants of Brazzaville and of neighbouring areas, caught in the fighting between government and rebel forces, have been compelled to flee in the past few months, and have been able to return home only by transiting through the Democratic Republic of the Congo: among them, there are thousands of victims of frightening acts of violence, including torture and rape. In the last few days, 30,000 new refugees have arrived in Gabon—this is a new, worrying development, that indicates how destabilizing this war may become for the entire region—especially given its proximity to other conflicts. UNHCR has already dispatched an emergency team to Libreville and stands ready to provide support to the authorities to protect and assist refugees. I fully realize the burden that these refugees place on the country's resources, but wish to appeal here to the government of Gabon to provide asylum to those fleeing the war. It is very urgent, however, that the international community takes a much stronger stance with respect to the Congolese conflict, and does all that is in its power to put an end to the senseless violence of which thousands of civilians are the victims.

One striking feature of all these conflicts is that they are closely inter-linked. The Lusaka peace process addresses only one of them, but the central position of the Democratic Republic of the Congo makes the process crucial to peace in the entire sub-region. Furthermore, the presence of armed elements—some of them closely related to refugee groups—and the uncontrolled flow of heavy and light weapons, are both causes and effects of the intertwined wars affecting Central Africa. Once more, I would like to urge the Security Council to examine these issues and take concrete action to address them.

Both in Central and West Africa, UNHCR continues its work. Let me however repeat once more my key message of today. If refugee problems in these two sub-regions are to be resolved in a durable fashion, it is essential that support be provided to the political agreements. I would like to draw the Council's attention in particular to the importance of the actual implementation of the security provisions of these agreements, as rapidly as possible and in the most appropriate form—be it through the direct deployment of peace-keepers or observers, or through the provision of logistical support to forces deployed by other countries. African leaders have taken political initiatives to address conflicts. Throughout my recent travels in Africa, I sensed that there is now a strong expectation for the United Nations to provide more support and be more actively involved in keeping and building peace. Lusaka and Lomé are windows of opportunity. They may not remain open for long. Let us seize these opportunities now.

Peace Building After Conflicts

We, at UNHCR, deal every day, in the field, with millions of women, men and children who flee from war. We understand very well the importance of stopping conflicts—which is what the Lomé and Lusaka peace negotiations aim to do. But we also help refugees return home after conflicts have ended, often to situations of very fragile peace—often to communities that war has left divided and torn. We therefore constantly insist on the importance of consolidating peace, after peace has been "signed", and of avoiding a dangerous gap between the provision of humanitarian assistance and of longer-term development cooperation.

I have repeated this point so many times that I risk sounding like a broken record. However—and again, I wish to refer to my recent trips to Africa—such situations of gap continue to exist. Take the example of Rwanda. Most refugees have returned—returnees make about 25% of the entire population. The phase of humanitarian assistance—relatively well supported by donors—has been followed by much more timid inputs by development agencies and bilateral actors. Resources are simply not forthcoming substantially enough for peace to be consolidated. This is dangerous, and—in my opinion—potentially very destabilizing. In the Great Lakes region, like in most parts of Africa, there is a close link between poverty, conflict and the forced displacement of people.

I was proud to visit areas in which UNHCR has done substantial work to support the reintegration of two million returnees—including the construction or rehabilitation of 100,000 houses and of communal facilities. This is a remarkable result, I believe, but a humanitarian agency cannot go beyond this type of work, on such a scale. Who will sustain these accomplishments? Who will provide support to the people and the government?

I agree with those who say that much remains to be done in terms of democratization, power sharing and reconciliation in Rwanda. Efforts, however, are being made. I was encouraged by a much greater emphasis on reconciliation, for example, in addition to the focus on justice—attempts to bring people together are now systematic, widespread and very professional. Such efforts must be supported. I am concerned that in these and other situations—for example Liberia, which I have mentioned earlier—the fragility of governments and their weak implementation capacity discourage the provision of development resources. While I fully understand that humanitarian assistance is much freer from political constraints than development cooperation—and it should be—I would nevertheless urge governments not to forget people when planning and implementing longer term aid programmes. Often, by giving people a chance—whatever the political and economic context—we can start processes leading to the democratization of institutions and ultimately to the peace and stability of countries and regions. . . .

Disparities in Humanitarian Assistance?

I would like to conclude by referring to a problem that has received much attention in the last few months. I am aware that there is a perception of disparity in the assistance given, for example, to displaced persons from Kosovo, as opposed to that given to African refugees. I know that many of you have also been concerned by this complex and difficult problem.

Emergencies, of course, attract more attention than other programmes—and the Kosovo crisis has been a very serious and very large refugee emergency. Crises in Africa at certain times have also received heightened attention and financial support - think of the Horn in the 80s, or the Great Lakes region a few years ago. It is true, however, that Kosovo has been the focus of unprecedented political attention and material support by the international community, by Western countries in particular. Undeniably, proximity, strategic interest and extraordinary media focus have played a key role in determining the quality and level of response. Undeniably, this has not been true—and continues not to be true—in other situations, including some of those that I have spoken of today.

But let me go back to the point I made at the beginning. The positive indications of the OAU Summit in Algiers may signal—*will* signal, I hope—a renewed commitment by African governments to take their future, and the future of their people, more resolutely in their own hands—and to address and resolve their problems, including refugee problems, through negotiations rather than force. This is a fundamental pre-condition for international support. On the other hand, we—who shoulder global, and not just regional responsibilities—should make all that is in our power to back efforts to resolve conflicts, in Africa and in other parts of the world. And while I can only appeal to you, and to governments, to be as balanced as possible in your support to peace endeavours, I can certainly assure you that my Office will continue to fulfil its own responsibilities towards all those compelled to flee heir homes—and especially those who do so away from the limelight of international attention.

SURGEON GENERAL ON
SUICIDE PREVENTION
July 28, 1999

In an unprecedented action, Surgeon General David Satcher issued a "call to action" July 28, 1999, identifying suicide as a "serious public health problem." He laid out a strategy for raising public awareness of the problem, identifying people at risk, and improving intervention and treatment programs. It was the first time that a U.S. surgeon general had made a mental health problem a public health priority. "The nation must address suicide as a significant public health problem and put into place national strategies to prevent the loss of life and suffering suicide causes," Satcher said. "We must act now."

Although it was often overshadowed by the high murder rates of the late 1980s and early 1990s, suicide was one of the leading causes of death in America. In the late 1990s about 30,000 people a year killed themselves, roughly half again as many as the number of people who were murdered annually. Each year approximately 500,000 people required emergency room treatment as a result of attempted suicide. Suicide was typically associated with mental disorders and substance abuse. Like those diseases, it was shrouded in fear and stigma and seldom discussed. The surgeon general's call to action, like a much more comprehensive report on mental health issued in December, was intended in part to lift the silence that prevented a fuller understanding of suicide and ways to prevent it. (Mental health report, p. 836)

Even as the health care community worked on ways to prevent suicide, a debate continued to rage over whether physicians should be permitted to help terminally ill patients end their own lives. Late in the year, the U.S. House of Representatives voted to make it a federal crime for physicians to prescribe drugs to help terminally ill patients kill themselves. The national legislators were reacting to a state law in Oregon that permitted such physician-assisted suicides under carefully controlled circumstances. In 1998, the first full year the Oregon law was in effect, fifteen people ended their lives using lethal doses of drugs prescribed by their physicians.

The "Call to Action"

The rate of suicide had remained fairly stable for several decades, actually declining a percentage point between 1976 and 1996, the last year for which statistics were available when the surgeon general issued his call to action. But the rates among various age, gender, and ethnic groups had changed substantially. The highest suicide rate was among white males over age 65, accounting for 20 percent of all suicides. But the suicide rate nearly tripled between 1952 and 1996 among adolescents and young adults and was the third leading cause of death for people aged fifteen to twenty-four. The suicide rate for children aged ten to fourteen had doubled since 1980, to nearly 300 a year. The rate among African American males aged fifteen to nineteen also doubled during that time period, and most of the increase was attributable to the use of guns. According to data released later in the year, guns were used in 17,566 suicides committed in 1997, compared with 13,522 homicides.

Those data, combined with a call from the World Health Organization to all nations to give suicide prevention higher priority, led the surgeon general to convene a national conference in Reno, Nevada, in October 1998 to determine what was known and unknown about suicide and to develop a national prevention strategy. Participants included researchers, experts in mental health and substance abuse, community leaders, suicide survivors, and policymakers. Although a comprehensive national strategy was not expected to be offered until early in 2000, convention attendees agreed on fifteen recommendations that Satcher decided should be the basis of a public awareness campaign. "Our feeling was, this is too important to wait for the full-blown, comprehensive strategy," said Damon Thompson, the surgeon general's spokesman. "It's simple, it's understandable, and there's near universal agreement that these fifteen steps can prevent suicide."

The surgeon general's call to action had two main purposes: to inform the public that many suicides were preventable, and to diminish the stigma that is attached to suicide and the mental disorders that generally underlie it. The report listed several suicide risk and protective factors that were critical to prevention strategies. These factors included genetic, neurobiological, psychological, social, and cultural characteristics of individuals and groups, as well environmental factors, such as the availability of guns. Understanding risk factors, the report said, should "help dispel the myths that suicide is a random act or results from stress alone." Among the risk factors were a previous suicide attempt or a family history of suicide; mental disorders, particularly depression and bipolar disorder; mental disorders combined with alcohol or other substance abuse; feelings of hopelessness and isolation; impulsive or aggressive tendencies; barriers to getting mental health treatment; relational, social, work, or financial loss; physical illness; easy access to a means of death, such as a gun; unwillingness to seek help because of the stigma attached to mental and substance abuse disorders; and outside influences, such as a cultural or religious belief that *embraces suicide, a family member, celebrity, or peer that has committed suicide, or a local epidemic of suicide.*

Protective factors included effective and appropriate clinical care for mental and substance abuse disorders; early access to a variety of clinical interventions; restricted access to highly lethal methods of suicide, especially guns; continued support from medical and mental health care providers, learned skills in problem solving, conflict resolution, and nonviolent handling of disputes; and cultural and religious beliefs that discourage suicide and support self-preservation instincts.

The report warned that "indiscriminate suicide awareness efforts" and overly inclusive lists of potential risk factors could "promote suicide as a possible solution to ordinary distress or suggest that suicidal thoughts and behaviors are normal responses to stress." To avoid increasing the risk of suicide particularly among young people, the report said, "efforts must be made to avoid normalizing, glorifying, or dramatizing suicidal behavior, reporting how-to methods, or describing suicide as an understandable solution to a traumatic or stressful life event."

The recommendations dealt with educating the public to learn how to recognize valid warning signs and get prevention help. The campaign was directed not only at health care workers, but at anyone in the community in a position to hear other people's problems. "We want coaches, we want school teachers, we want hairdressers, we want people who interact with the community," Thompson said. Many of the recommendations for intervention emphasized earlier and improved clinical treatment as well as better access to treatment for mental and substance abuse disorders. Other elements of the public awareness campaign included a PBS video called "Depression: On the Edge" that the government planned to distribute to school counselors and a media campaign to reduce the stigma attached to mental illness.

House Bar on Physician-Assisted Suicide

The House on October 27 passed, 271-156, a bill making it a federal crime for physicians to prescribe drugs "for the purpose of causing death." Penalties included up to twenty years in prison. Introduced by Rep. Henry J. Hyde, R-Ill., chairman of the House Judiciary Committee, the legislation was a reaction to an Oregon state law.

In 1994, 51 percent of Oregon's voters passed a state referendum permitting doctors to help terminally ill patients commit suicide under carefully controlled circumstances designed to ensure that the patient was not acting out of clinical depression or being coerced. In 1997, 60 percent of the state's voters voted down an attempt to repeal the law. After that vote, the federal Drug Enforcement Administration (DEA) wrote a letter, at Rep. Hyde's request, saying that any physician who prescribed a lethal dose of narcotics with the intent of helping a patient commit suicide would be in violation of the Controlled Substances Act. The DEA letter was nullified by Attorney General Janet Reno in June 1998, who issued a ruling stating that penalties under the Controlled Substances Act did not reach physicians in Oregon who prescribed controlled drugs for terminally ill patients under the state's laws. (Oregon law, Historic Documents of 1994, p. 501; Historic Documents of 1997, p. 459)

Hyde and others immediately introduced legislation to overturn Reno's ruling, but it was not passed in 1998, in part because the American Medical Association (AMA) raised concerns about governmental interference in a private decision between doctor and patient. The AMA was also concerned that the legislation might make doctors wary of prescribing narcotics for pain management and "palliative"—end-of-life—care. In 1999 Hyde refined the legislation to make clear that using narcotics for palliative care was a "legitimate medical purpose" under the Controlled Substances Act even if the use of the narcotic "may increase the risk of death." Although many individual doctors continued to oppose the legislation, the AMA endorsed the Hyde legislation. (End-of-life care, Historic Documents of 1997, p. 325)

Hyde and other supporters of the legislation said they were trying to preserve the sanctity of life. A physician who assists suicide "no longer has an ethical right to care for that patient," said Rep. Tom Coburn, R-Okla., who was a medical doctor. But opponents said it was hypocritical for Republicans, who usually supported states' rights, to overturn a law that had been approved twice by the voters of Oregon. They also argued that the law was likely to have a chilling effect on the use of narcotics in palliative care. "This bill authorizes the Drug Enforcement Administration to second-guess physicians all across America, and its effects on pain management will be devastating," said Rep. David Wu, D-Ore. Similar legislation had been introduced in the Senate, but no action was taken on it by the end of the year.

In a related event, Jack Kevorkian, the Michigan pathologist sometimes referred to as "Dr. Death," was sentenced to ten to twenty-five years in prison for murder. Kevorkian, who was no longer licensed to practice medicine, had administered a lethal injection of barbiturates to a terminally ill man, videotaped the injection and the man's death, and sent it to CBS's Sixty Minutes, which aired the tape in November 1998. Kevorkian, who claimed to have helped more than 130 people kill themselves, had been tried four times earlier on charges of illegally assisting suicide; he was acquitted in three of those cases, and the jury was unable to reach a verdict in the fourth. In sentencing Kevorkian, the judge said that the trial was not about assisted suicide but about lawlessness. Kevorkian, she said, had broken the law and then dared the legal system to stop him. "Well, sir, consider yourself stopped," she concluded.

Following is the text of "The Surgeon General's Call to Action to Prevent Suicide, 1999" released July 28, 1999, by the U.S. Public Health Service:

Suicide is a serious public health problem. In 1996, the year for which the most recent statistics are available, suicide was the ninth leading cause of mortality in the United States, responsible for nearly 31,000 deaths. This number is more than 50% higher than the number of homicides in the United States in the same year (around 20,000 homicides in 1996). Many fail to realize that far more Americans die from suicide than from homicide. Each year in the United States, approximately 500,000 people require emergency room treatment as a result of attempted suicide. Suicidal behavior typically occurs in the presence of mental or substance abuse disorders—illnesses that impose their own direct suffering. Suicide is an enormous trauma for millions of Americans who experience the loss of someone close to them. The nation must address suicide as a significant public health problem and put into place national strategies to prevent the loss of life and the suffering suicide causes.

In 1996, the World Health Organization (WHO), recognizing the growing problem of suicide worldwide, urged member nations to address suicide. Its document, *Prevention of Suicide: Guidelines for the Formulation and Implementation of National Strategies*, motivated the creation of an innovative public/private partnership to seek a national strategy for the United States. This public/private partnership included agencies in the U.S. Department of Health and Human Services, encompassing the Centers for Disease Control and Prevention (CDC), the Health Resources and Services Administration (HRSA), the Indian Health Service (IHS), the National Institute of Mental Health (NIMH), the Office of the Surgeon General, and the Substance Abuse and Mental Health Services Administration (SAMHSA) and the Suicide Prevention Advocacy Network (SPAN), a public grassroots advocacy organization made up of suicide survivors (persons close to someone who completed suicide), attempters of suicide, community activists, and health and mental health clinicians.

An outgrowth of this collaborative effort was a jointly sponsored national conference on suicide prevention convened in Reno, Nevada, in October 1998. Conference participants included researchers, health and mental health clinicians, policy makers, suicide survivors, and community activists and leaders. They engaged in careful analysis of what is known and unknown about suicide and its potential responsiveness to a public health model emphasizing suicide prevention.

This *Surgeon General's Call To Action* introduces a blueprint for addressing suicide—Awareness, Intervention, and Methodology, or *AIM*—an approach derived from the collaborative deliberations of the conference participants. As a framework for suicide prevention, *AIM* includes 15 key recommendations that were refined from consensus and evidence-based findings presented at the Reno conference. Recognizing that mental and substance abuse disorders confer the greatest risk for suicidal behavior, these recommendations suggest an important approach to preventing suicide and injuries from suicidal behavior by addressing the problems of undetected and undertreated mental and substance abuse disorders in conjunction with other public health approaches.

These recommendations and their supporting conceptual framework are essential steps toward a comprehensive *National Strategy for Suicide Prevention*. Other necessary elements will include constructive public health policy, measurable overall objectives, ways to monitor and evaluate progress toward these objectives, and provision of resources for groups and agencies identified to carry out the recommendations. The nation needs to move forward with these crucial recommendations and support continued efforts to improve the scientific bases of suicide prevention.

Many people, from public health leaders and mental and substance abuse disorder health experts to community advocates and suicide survivors, worked together in developing and proposing *AIM* for the American public. *AIM* and its recommendations chart a course for suicide prevention action now as well as serve as the foundation for a more comprehensive *National Strategy for Suicide Prevention* in the future. Together, they represent a critical component of a broader initiative to improve the mental health of the nation. I endorse the ongoing work necessary to complete a *National Strategy* because I believe that such a coordinated and evidence-based approach is the best way to use our resources to prevent suicide in America.

But even the most well-considered plan accomplishes nothing if it is not implemented. To translate AIM into action, each of us, whether we play a role at the federal, state, or local level, must turn these recommendations into programs best suited for our own communities. We must act now. We cannot change the past, but together we can shape a different future.

David Satcher, M.D., Ph.D.
Assistant Secretary for Health
and Surgeon General

Suicide as a Public Health Problem

On average, 85 Americans die from suicide each day. Although more females attempt suicide than males, males are at least four times more likely to die from suicide. Firearms are the most common means of suicide among men and women, accounting for 59% of all suicide deaths.

Over time, suicide rates for the general population have been fairly stable in the United States. Over the last two decades, the suicide rate has declined from 12.1 per 100,000 in 1976 to 10.8 per 100,000 in 1996. However, the rates for various age, gender and ethnic groups have changed substantially. Between 1952 and 1996, the reported rates of suicide among adolescents and young adults nearly tripled. From 1980 to 1996, the rate of suicide among persons aged 15–19 years increased by 14% and among persons aged 10–14 years by 100%. Among persons aged 15–19 years, firearms-related suicides accounted for 96% of the increase in the rate of suicide since 1980. For young people 15–24 years old, suicide is currently the third leading cause of death, exceeded only by unintentional injury and homicide. More teenagers and young adults die from suicide than from cancer, heart disease, AIDS, birth defects, stroke, pneumonia and influenza, and chronic lung disease *combined*. During the past decade, there have also been dramatic and disturbing increases in reports of suicide among children. Suicide is currently the fourth leading cause of death among children between the ages of 10 and 14 years.

Suicide remains a serious public health problem at the other end of the age spectrum, too. Suicide rates increase with age and are highest among white American males aged 65 years and older. Older adult suicide victims, when compared to younger suicide victims, are more likely to have lived alone, have been widowed, and to have had a physical illness. They are also more likely to have visited a health care professional shortly before their suicide and thus represent a missed opportunity for intervention.

Other population groups in this country have specific suicide prevention needs as well. Many communities of Native Americans and Alaskan Natives long have had elevated suicide rates. Between 1980 and 1996, the rate of suicide among African American males aged 15-19 years increased 105% and almost 100% of the increase in this group is attributable to the use of firearms.

It is generally agreed that not all deaths that are suicides are reported as such. For example, deaths classified as homicide or accidents, where individuals may have intentionally put themselves in harm's way are not included in suicide rates.

Compounding the tragedy of loss of life, suicide evokes complicated and uncomfortable reactions in most of us. Too often, we blame the victim and stigmatize the surviving family members and friends. These reactions add to the survivors' burden of hurt, intensify their isolation, and shroud suicide in secrecy. Unfortunately, secrecy and silence diminish the accuracy and amount of information available about persons who have completed suicide— information that might help prevent other suicides.

Methodology

Developing Recommendations for a National Strategy for Suicide Prevention

Developing and implementing a *National Strategy for Suicide Prevention* should achieve a significant, measurable, and sustained reduction in suicidal behaviors. The action steps presented in this document were prioritized from among a variety of recommendations developed through a public-private collaboration of nongovernmental organizations, federal and state governmental agencies, corporations and foundations, and public health, health, mental health experts.

Before the Reno Conference, experts evaluated research studies, programs, policies, and best interventions to prevent suicide among five U.S. population groups known to be at high risk of suicide. Those identified as being at increased risk were youth, the medically ill, specific population groups, persons with mental and substance abuse disorders, and the elderly. Following review of the evidence by a second expert, the lead expert extracted recommendations for suicide prevention. In extracting recommendations, experts were instructed to consider the robustness of the available data; an intervention's likelihood of reducing suicide; its perceived suitability for implementation in the real world; and estimates of the lead-time to put the recommendation into practice and produce its intended effect. They were also asked to consider the ethical implications and cultural appropriateness of each recommendation.

Those experts' draft recommendations were brought to the Reno conference. A broad cross section of conference participants and a highly varied expert panel were identified to work with the recommendations and evaluate each one. The panel and the invited conference participants represented diverse areas of expertise and included researchers, suicide survivors, persons who had attempted suicide, public health leaders, community volunteers, clinicians, educators, consumers of mental health services, and corporate/nonprofit advocates. Financial support was made available so that socioeconomic status would not exclude panelists and participants who wanted to contribute from attending the conference. The Regional Health Administrators of the U.S. Public Health Service served as facilitators in working with over 400 participants to refine recommendations during the conference. The expert panel received over 700 written comments from participants during the course of their deliberations.

The expert panel's recommendations were derived from a rigorous review of suicide and suicide prevention research. Existing suicide research is strongest in the identification of risk factors, particularly mental and substance abuse disorders, less developed in categorizing protective factors, and only beginning to analyze the mutual interactions among risk and protective factors. Some treatments for mental and substance abuse disorders have been associated with a reduction in suicidal behaviors. Further research is needed to determine whether these benefits will occur if treatments are offered to groups outside the small populations that were studied.

The recommendations the panel developed include past and current initiatives, programs, and interventions. Other recommendations pragmatically extend findings from existing suicide and suicide prevention research into proposed applications. Suicide prevention experts from multiple disciplines endorsed these proposed recommendations as having the greatest potential for effectiveness.

By the end of the conference, the expert panel had advanced 81 recommendations for consideration for inclusion in a *National Strategy for Suicide Prevention*. These recommendations were posted on the SPAN Web site to allow a period of further reflection and public comment. The CDC developed a tool for priority ranking the 81 recommendations. Respondents from all interested sectors prioritized the recommendations using criteria of feasibility, necessity, clarity, and likelihood of being funded. Recommendations with the highest priority scores and broadest support were combined and edited to serve as the essential first steps of an action agenda for suicide prevention.

Results

AIM to Prevent Suicide

This *Surgeon General's Call to Action* introduces an initial blueprint for reducing suicide and the associated toll that mental and substance abuse disorders take in the United States. As both evidence-based and highly prioritized by leading experts, these 15 key recommendations listed below should serve as a framework for immediate action. These recommended first steps are categorized as *Awareness, Intervention, and Methodology*, or *AIM.*

Awareness: Appropriately broaden the public's awareness of suicide and its risk factors

Intervention: Enhance services and programs, both population-based and clinical care

Methodology: Advance the science of suicide prevention

Awareness: Appropriately Broaden the Public's Awareness of Suicide and Its Risk Factors

- Promote public awareness that suicide is a public health problem and, as such, many suicides are preventable. Use information technology appropriately to make facts about suicide and its risk factors and prevention approaches available to the public and to health care providers.
- Expand awareness of and enhance resources in communities for suicide prevention programs and mental and substance abuse disorder assessment and treatment.
- Develop and implement strategies to reduce the stigma associated with mental illness, substance abuse, and suicidal behavior and with seeking help for such problems.

Intervention: Enhance Services and Programs, Both Population-Based and Clinical Care

- Extend collaboration with and among public and private sectors to complete a *National Strategy for Suicide Prevention.*
- Improve the ability of primary care providers to recognize and treat depression, substance abuse, and other major mental illnesses associated with suicide risk. Increase the referral to specialty care when appropriate.
- Eliminate barriers in public and private insurance programs for provision of quality mental and substance abuse disorder treatments and create incentives to treat patients with coexisting mental and substance abuse disorders.
- Institute training for all health, mental health, substance abuse and human service professionals (including clergy, teachers, correctional workers, and social workers) concerning suicide risk assessment and recognition, treatment, management, and aftercare interventions.
- Develop and implement effective training programs for family members of those at risk and for natural community helpers on how to recognize,

respond to, and refer people showing signs of suicide risk and associated mental and substance abuse disorders. Natural community helpers are people such as educators, coaches, hairdressers, and faith leaders, among others.

- Develop and implement safe and effective programs in educational settings for youth that address adolescent distress, provide crisis intervention and incorporate peer support for seeking help.
- Enhance community care resources by increasing the use of schools and workplaces as access and referral points for mental and physical health services and substance abuse treatment programs and provide support for persons who survive the suicide of someone close to them.
- Promote a public/private collaboration with the media to assure that entertainment and news coverage represent balanced and informed portrayals of suicide and its associated risk factors including mental illness and substance abuse disorders and approaches to prevention and treatment.

Methodology: Advance the Science of Suicide Prevention

- Enhance research to understand risk and protective factors related to suicide, their interaction, and their effects on suicide and suicidal behaviors. Additionally, increase research on effective suicide prevention programs, clinical treatments for suicidal individuals, and culture-specific interventions.
- Develop additional scientific strategies for evaluating suicide prevention interventions and ensure that evaluation components are included in all suicide prevention programs.
- Establish mechanisms for federal, regional, and state interagency public health collaboration toward improving monitoring systems for suicide and suicidal behaviors and develop and promote standard terminology in these systems.
- Encourage the development and evaluation of new prevention technologies, including firearm safety measures, to reduce easy access to lethal means of suicide.

Discussion

Risk and Protective Factors

Suicide risk and protective factors and their interactions form the empirical base for suicide prevention. Risk factors are associated with a greater potential for suicide and suicidal behavior while protective factors are associated with reduced potential for suicide.

Substantial age, gender, ethnic, and cultural variations in suicide rates provide opportunities to understand the different roles of risk and protective factors among these groups. Risk and protective factors encompass genetic, neurobiological, psychological, social, and cultural characteristics of individuals and groups and environmental factors such as easy access to firearms.

This expanding base of empirical evidence generates promising ideas about what can be changed or modified to prevent suicide.

Clear progress has been made in the scientific understanding of suicide, mental and substance abuse disorders, and in developing interventions to treat these disorders. For example, increased understanding of brain systems regulated by chemicals called neurotransmitters holds promise for understanding the biological underpinnings of depression, anxiety disorders, impulsiveness, aggression, and violent behaviors. Much remains to be learned, however, about the common risk factors for mental disorders and substance abuse, suicide and other forms of intentional violence including homicide, domestic violence, and child abuse. Expanding the base of scientific evidence will help in the development of more effective interventions for these harmful behaviors.

Advances in neurobiology and the behavioral sciences and their application in developing effective treatments for mental and substance abuse disorders have generated much hope. Wider public understanding of the science of the brain and behavior can reduce the stigma associated with seeking help for mental and substance abuse disorders and consequently may contribute to reducing the risk for suicidal behavior.

Risk Factors

Understanding risk factors can help dispel the myths that suicide is a random act or results from stress alone. Some persons are particularly vulnerable to suicide and suicidal self-injury because they have more than one mental disorder present, such as depression with alcohol abuse. They may also be very impulsive and/or aggressive, and use highly lethal methods to attempt suicide. As noted above, the importance of certain risk factors and their combination vary by age, gender, and ethnicity.

The impact of some risk factors can be reduced by interventions (such as providing effective treatments for depressive illness). Those risk factors that cannot be changed (such as a previous suicide attempt) can alert others to the heightened risk of suicide during periods of the recurrence of a mental or substance abuse disorder, or following a significant stressful life event.

Risk factors include:

- Previous suicide attempt
- Mental disorders—particularly mood disorders such as depression and bipolar disorder
- Co-occurring mental and alcohol and substance abuse disorders
- Family history of suicide
- Hopelessness
- Impulsive and/or aggressive tendencies
- Barriers to accessing mental health treatment
- Relational, social, work, or financial loss
- Physical illness
- Easy access to lethal methods, especially guns

- Unwillingness to seek help because of stigma attached to mental and substance abuse disorders and/or suicidal thoughts
- Influence of significant people—family members, celebrities, peers who have died by suicide—both through direct personal contact or inappropriate media representations
- Cultural and religious beliefs—for instance, the belief that suicide is a noble resolution of a personal dilemma
- Local epidemics of suicide that have a contagious influence
- Isolation, a feeling of being cut off from other people

Some lists of warning signs for suicide have been created in an effort to identify and increase the referral of persons at risk. However, the warning signs given are not necessarily risk factors for suicide and may include common behaviors among distressed persons, behaviors that are not specific for suicide. If such lists are applied broadly, for instance in the general classroom setting, they may be counterproductive. In effect, indiscriminate suicide awareness efforts and overly inclusive screening lists may promote suicide as a possible solution to ordinary distress or suggest that suicidal thoughts and behaviors are normal responses to stress. Efforts must be made to avoid normalizing, glorifying, or dramatizing suicidal behavior, reporting how-to methods, or describing suicide as an understandable solution to a traumatic or stressful life event. Inappropriate approaches could potentially increase the risk for suicidal behavior in vulnerable individuals, particularly youth.

Protective Factors

Protective factors can include an individual's genetic or neurobiological makeup, attitudinal and behavioral characteristics, and environmental attributes. Measures that enhance resilience or protective factors are as essential as risk reduction in preventing suicide. Positive resistance to suicide is not permanent, so programs that support and maintain protection against suicide should be ongoing.

Protective factors include:

- Effective and appropriate clinical care for mental, physical, and substance abuse disorders
- Easy access to a variety of clinical interventions and support for help seeking
- Restricted access to highly lethal methods of suicide
- Family and community support
- Support from ongoing medical and mental health care relationships
- Learned skills in problem solving, conflict resolution, and nonviolent handling of disputes
- Cultural and religious beliefs that discourage suicide and support self-preservation instincts

The risk factors that lead to suicide (especially mental and substance abuse disorders) and the protective factors that safeguard against it form the conceptual framework for the prevention recommendations developed and presented in this document and in the evolving *National Strategy for Suicide Prevention.*

Identifying and Addressing Risk

Unfortunately, it is difficult to identify particular individuals at greatest risk for suicidal behaviors or completed suicide. Measures to screen the general population for suicide risk lack the precision needed to identify in advance only those people who eventually would die by suicide. Because suicide screening in the general population currently is not feasible, it is especially important for suicide prevention programs to include broader approaches that benefit the whole population as well as efforts focused on smaller, high-risk subgroups that can be identified. Within those subgroups, a different approach to screening—screening programs for specific disorders, like depression, that are associated with suicide—can be used to identify and direct people to highly effective treatments that may lower their risk of suicide.

Often, the suicide prevention efforts in place are directed primarily at improving clinical care for the individual already struggling with suicidal ideas or the individual requiring medical attention for a suicide attempt. Suicide prevention also demands approaches that reduce the likelihood of suicide before vulnerable individuals reach the point of danger. Applying the public health approach to the problem of suicide in the United States will maximize the benefits of efforts and resources for suicide prevention.

The Public Health Approach

Suicide is a public health problem that requires an evidence-based approach to prevention. In concert with the clinical medical approach, which explores the history and health conditions that could lead to suicide in a single individual, the public health approach focuses on identifying and understanding patterns of suicide and suicidal behavior throughout a group or population. The public health approach defines the problem, identifies risk factors and causes of the problem, develops interventions evaluated for effectiveness, and implements such interventions widely in a variety of communities.

Although this description suggests a linear progression from the first step to the last, in reality the steps occur simultaneously and depend on each other. For example, systems for gathering information to define the exact nature of the suicide problem may also be useful in evaluating programs. Similarly, information gained from program evaluation and implementation may lead to new and promising interventions. Public health has traditionally used this model to respond to epidemics of infectious disease. During the past few decades, the model has also been used to address other problems that are likewise complicated and challenging to prevent, such as chronic disease and injury.

The Public Health Approach Applied to Suicide Prevention

Defining the Problem

The first step includes collecting information about incidents of suicide and suicidal behavior. It goes beyond simple counting. Information is gathered on characteristics of the persons involved, the circumstances of the incidents, events that may have precipitated the act, the adequacy of support and health services received, and the severity and cost of the injuries. This step covers the who, what, when, where, how, and how many of the identified problem.

Identifying Causes and Protective Factors

The second step focuses on why. It addresses risk factors such as depression, alcohol and other drug use, bereavement, or job loss. This step may be used to define groups of people at higher risk for suicide. Many questions remain, however, about the interactive matrix of risk and protective factors in suicide and suicidal behavior and, more importantly, how this interaction can be modified.

Developing and Testing Interventions

The next step involves developing approaches to address the causes and risk factors that have been identified. Testing the effectiveness of each approach is a critical part of this step to ensure that strategies are safe, ethical, and feasible. Pilot testing, which may reveal differences among particular age, gender, ethnic and cultural groups, can help determine for whom a suicide prevention strategy is best fitted.

Implementing Interventions

The final step is to implement interventions that have demonstrated effectiveness in preventing suicide and suicidal behavior. Implementation requires data collection as a means to continue evaluating effectiveness of an intervention. This is essential because an intervention that has been found effective in a clinical trial or academic study may have different outcomes in other settings. Ongoing evaluation builds the evidence base for refining and extending effective suicide prevention programs. Determination of an intervention's cost-effectiveness is another important component of this step. This ensures that limited resources can be used to achieve the greatest benefit.

As interventions for preventing suicide are developed and implemented, communities must consider several key factors. Interventions have a much greater likelihood of success if they involve a variety of services and providers. This requires community leaders to build effective coalitions across traditionally separate sectors, such as the health care delivery system, the mental health system, faith communities, schools, social services, civic groups, and the public health system. Interventions must be adapted to support and reflect the experience of survivors and specific community values, cultures, and standards. They must also be designed to benefit from multi-ethnic and culturally diverse participation from all segments of the community.

As it evolves, America's *National Strategy for Suicide Prevention* must recognize and affirm the value, dignity, and importance of each person. Everyone concerned with suicide prevention shares the responsibility to help change and eliminate the societal conditions and attitudes that often contribute to suicide. Individuals, communities, organizations, and leaders at all levels should collaborate in promoting suicide prevention. Final development of a *National Strategy for Suicide Prevention* and the success of these essential action steps ultimately rest with individuals and communities and institutions and policy makers across the United States.

Implementing AIM as an Action Agenda in Communities

As states and local communities apply the public health approach to AIM recommendations, they must consider both population-based and clinical care initiatives. Their first step is to define and to describe the problem of suicide and its associated risk factors locally and measure their magnitude. Next, causes of the conditions found must be identified. Then, community interventions must be designed to address the identified needs through attention to the causes revealed. Evaluating project effectiveness provides guidance for refining the intervention and expanding benefits to other settings. The following hypothetical descriptions of community suicide prevention activities have been created to illustrate applied public health and clinical management prevention models.

Youth

Recognizing the state's increasing rates of substance abuse and suicide among youth, the state public health director in consultation with the Regional Health Administrator brought together concerned representatives to form a state youth suicide, substance abuse and depression prevention coalition. The coalition members reflected many sectors in the community including suicide survivors, educators, social service agencies, the faith community, businesses, the state cooperative extension programs (4-H), school psychologists, child psychiatrists, the PTA, substance abuse treatment counselors, public officials, and the juvenile justice system. The coalition also established a youth advisory board.

After collecting detailed information on the dimensions of youth substance abuse, depression and suicide in the state and identifying how few school systems had screening, referral, and crisis plans, the coalition formed a multidisciplinary study committee to develop a model suicide prevention plan. A broad array of public and professional organizations in the state studied and endorsed the model plan. A corporate partner from the business community provided a grant to distribute the model plan along with a curriculum guide for natural helpers to identify high-risk youth. As school districts adapted the plan and implemented it locally, followup surveys were conducted to determine patterns of use, satisfaction with the model plan and guide, and impact on substance abuse, depression and suicidal behaviors in communities statewide. Based on evidence collected from the evaluations, the model plan was revised to include more guidance on working with the media to de-sensationalize coverage of suicide, and promote abstinence from substance use as well as encourage youth to seek treatment for both substance abuse and depression.

The Elderly

The public health approach has revealed that suicide rates are highest among the elderly and that most elderly suicide victims are seen by their primary care provider within a few weeks of their suicide and are experiencing a first episode of mild to moderate depression. Recognizing that clinical depression is a highly treatable illness, but treatment has not yet been adequately provided in primary care settings, a state with a large elderly population brought together a group of health professionals and community advocates. Together they devised and supported a pilot program to follow depression screening in the primary care setting with the addition of an on-site nurse or social worker specializing in depression services. These on-site specialists ensured that those elderly patients who screened positive for depression received depression treatment and follow up from the physician and assessed patient progress so that ongoing treatments could be adjusted to increase their effectiveness. Outcomes for patients in the pilot project were compared to those patients receiving usual treatment in comparable primary care settings. This evaluation provided information to fine tune the program and extend its benefits to other primary care settings in the state.

Advancing a National Suicide Prevention Strategy

The 15 recommendations (AIM) presented in this *Surgeon General's Call to Action* propose a nationwide, collaborative effort to reduce suicidal behaviors, and to prevent premature death due to suicide across the life span. The conceptual framework for AIM incorporates analysis of suicide risk and protective factors and emphasizes the benefits of effectively treating mental and substance abuse disorders. A comprehensive *National Strategy for Suicide Prevention* should include these elements along with supportive government policy, measurable objectives for the *Strategy*, means of monitoring and evaluating progress, and provision of authority and resources to carry out the *Strategy's* recommendations.

To realize success in preventing suicide and suicidal behaviors, collaboration must be fostered on this public health priority across a broad spectrum of agencies, institutions, groups, and representative individuals throughout the country. As additional elements of a comprehensive *Strategy* evolve, the public and prospective implementation partners must also sustain awareness that improved detection and treatment of mental and substance abuse disorders represent a primary approach to suicide prevention. These partners must ensure the availability of evidence-based guidance for communities to develop and refine effective suicide prevention approaches. Likewise, as communities implement approaches to recognize and reduce risk factors to prevent suicide, they must be aware of the dangers of inadvertently glamorizing suicide, and remain vigilant to avoid doing so. Ongoing review of research, policy, and program advances in suicide prevention may expand the number of effective initiatives and interventions for incorporation into the *Strategy*. Work should continue that outlines measurable objectives for an overall *Strategy*, provides mechanisms for tracking these objectives, and develops means of communicating significant progress in preventing suicide and suicidal self-injury.

Conclusion

Americans in communities nationwide can make a significant difference in preventing suicide and suicidal behaviors. The recommendations presented in AIM provide a blueprint and call for action now. Programs and activities that are carried out and evaluated today will generate additional recommendations for effective suicide prevention initiatives in the future. Working together locally, in states, and at the federal level to complete and implement a *National Strategy for Suicide Prevention* is an important step in responding to the major public health problem of suicide in the United States.

1999 HISTORIC DOCUMENTS

August

Federal Survey on Drug Use. 459

USAID on Earthquake in Turkey 465

FEDERAL SURVEY
ON DRUG USE
August 18, 1999

An annual federal survey on drug use found that overall levels of drug abuse remained stable in 1998 but that drug use among teenagers had dropped. That decline indicated that the country had "turned the corner" on the use of illicit drugs, Donna Shalala, secretary of the Department of Health and Human Services (HHS), said as she and Barry McCaffrey, director of the White House Office of National Drug Control Policy, released the report August 18, 1999. But any euphoria the announcement might have raised was dashed later in the year by another major report showing that drug use among teens was holding steady in 1999 and that use of some drugs appeared to be increasing. Both surveys found that teenage alcohol use and smoking remained essentially unchanged.

The two surveys were not strictly comparable but, read together, they provided a reasonably good indication of trends in illegal drug use. The survey released in August was the 1998 National Household Survey on Drug Abuse, which was based on interviews with 25,500 people who responded to questions about their illegal drug usage during the previous thirty days. It was thus a "snapshot" of drug abuse. The survey had been conducted annually since 1971; since 1992 it has been under the auspices of the Substance Abuse and Mental Health Services Administration in HHS.

The second survey, released December 17, was directed only at teenagers in the eighth, tenth, and twelfth grades. About 45,000 students from 433 schools across the country were asked questions about their illicit drug usage in their lifetime, in the last year, and in the last month. This survey thus provided a more complete picture of drug usage among a narrow but important population group. Called Monitoring the Future, this survey was conducted by the University of Michigan Institute for Social Research and funded by the National Institute on Drug Abuse.

The National Household Survey

Overall, according to the 1998 National Household Survey on Drug Abuse, 13.6 million Americans, or 6.2 percent of those aged twelve and over, were current users of illegal drugs in 1998. That level had remained about the same for the past five years, but it was nearly half the 1979 peak of about 25 million users. Marijuana continued to be the most frequently used illegal drug; approximately 60 percent of those who used illegal drugs used marijuana only. An estimated 1.8 million people used cocaine, while about 437,000 used crack cocaine.

Among twelve- to seventeen-year-olds, 9.9 percent reported using illicit drugs in the previous month. This percentage was down from the 11.4 percent recorded in 1997. But teenage drug use had fluctuated by one or two percentage points a year since 1995. Like their adult counterparts, most teenage drug users used marijuana. The number of teenagers using inhalants dropped by nearly half, from 2.0 percent to 1.1 percent.

Levels of alcohol use among all Americans had not changed significantly since 1988. According to the 1998 survey, 113 million Americans reported using alcohol in the past month. More than 25 percent of these (about 33 million) were binge drinkers, meaning that they had five or more drinks on a single occasion during the month, and about 12 million were heavy drinkers (five or more drinks on one occasion on five or more days during the month). About 10.5 million drinkers were ages twelve through twenty in 1998; about 50 percent of those (5.1 million) engaged in binge drinking. No changes in the levels of underage drinking had been recorded since 1994.

The one area in which there was a significant drop was in overall smoking, which fell to 27.7 percent in 1998 from 29.6 percent in 1997. The rate of smoking among twelve- to seventeen-year-olds remained relatively stable, at 18.2 percent, as did the rate of new underage smokers. Despite massive national campaigns to reduce smoking among children, roughly 3,000 teenagers began smoking every day. Smoking among young adults (ages eighteen through twenty-five) continued to increase, from 34.6 percent in 1994, to 40.6 percent in 1997, to 41.6 percent in 1998. (Tobacco settlement, Historic Documents of 1998, p. 842; tobacco company fraud, p. 536)

Monitoring the Future Survey

Like the National Household Survey, the Monitoring the Future Survey showed that use of illegal drugs, alcohol, and tobacco among teenagers in 1999 remained about the same as it had been for the past two years. But because the monitoring survey looked at use over different time periods, it picked up possible trends that the household survey did not. So, although the rate of cigarette smoking did not change much among teenagers overall, smoking among eighth graders in the past month was down from 19.1 percent in 1998 to 17.5 percent in 1999. This same age group indicated that cigarettes were not as available to them as they had been in previous years, reflecting new restrictions on selling tobacco products to minors.

Among the few statistically significant changes that the survey found were an increase among tenth and twelfth graders in the use of "ecstasy," an inhibition-relaxing synthetic drug known as a "club drug" because of its popularity among teenagers attending all-night dances, known as "raves."

Ecstasy and other similar drugs were thought to cause potentially lasting damage to the brain. Steroid use among eighth and tenth graders also increased in 1999. Some researchers attributed some of that increase to the revelation that baseball star Mark McGwire had used a muscle-building steroid, androstenedione, when he set a new home run record in 1998. (Breaking the home run record, Historic Documents of 1998, p. 626)

At a news conference releasing the results of the survey, Shalala and McCaffrey continued to paint a cautiously optimistic picture of the Clinton administration's war against drug use. "Today's report confirms that we have halted the dangerous trend of increased drug use among our young people," Shalala said. "Our job now is to continue the momentum we have built up with local communities, parents and teachers, and to work even harder to let teenagers know the real danger of alcohol, tobacco, and drugs."

Following is the text of the "highlights" section from the "Summary of Findings" of the 1998 National Household Survey on Drug Abuse, released August 18, 1999, by Donna Shalala, secretary of the U.S. Department of Health and Human Services:

This report presents the first results from the 1998 National Household Survey on Drug Abuse, an annual survey conducted by the Substance Abuse and Mental Health Services Administration (SAMHSA). This survey has been the primary source of estimates of the prevalence and incidence of illicit drug, alcohol, and tobacco use in the population since 1971. The survey is based on a nationally representative sample of the civilian, noninstitutionalized population of the United States age 12 years and older. A sample of 25,500 persons was interviewed for the 1998 survey; this sample included augmented samples in California and Arizona (4,903 and 3,869 respectively). Selected findings are presented below:

Illicit Drug Use

- An estimated 13.6 million Americans were current users of illicit drugs in 1998, meaning they used an illicit drug at least once during the 30 days prior to the interview. Although this number is slightly less than the 13.9 million estimate for 1997, the difference is not statistically significant. By comparison, the number of current illicit drug users was at its highest level in 1979 when the estimate was 25.0 million.
- 9.9 percent of youths age 12–17 reported current use of illicit drugs in 1998. This estimate represents a statistically significant decrease from the estimate of 11.4 percent in 1997. The rate was highest in 1979 (16.3 percent), declined to 5.3 percent in 1992, then increased to 10.9 percent in 1995. The percent of youth reporting current use of illicit drugs has fluctuated since 1995 (9.0 percent in 1996 and 11.4 percent in 1997).

461

- 8.3 percent of youths age 12–17 were current users of marijuana in 1998. The prevalence of marijuana use among youth did not change significantly between 1997 when it was 9.4 percent and 1998 when it was 8.3 percent. Youth marijuana use reached a peak of 14.2 percent in 1979, declined to 3.4 percent in 1992, more than doubled from 1992 to 1995 (8.2 percent), and has fluctuated since then (7.1 in 1996 and 9.4 percent in 1997).
- An estimated 1.8 million (0.8 percent) Americans age 12 and older were current users of cocaine in 1998. The estimate was 1.5 million (0.7 percent) in 1997; but the difference is not statistically significant. Cocaine use reached a peak of 5.7 million or 3.0 percent of the population in 1985.
- The percent of youths reporting current use of inhalants decreased significantly from 2.0 percent in 1997 to 1.1 percent in 1998.
- An estimated 4.1 million people met diagnostic criteria for dependence on illicit drugs in 1997 and 1998, including 1.1 million youths age 12–17.

Alcohol Use

- In 1998, 113 million Americans age 12 and older reported current use of alcohol, meaning they used alcohol at least once during the 30 days prior to the interview. About 33 million of this group engaged in binge drinking, meaning they drank 5 or more drinks on one occasion during that 30 day period. 12 million were heavy drinkers, meaning they had 5 or more drinks on one occasion 5 or more days during the past 30 days. The percentages of the population falling into these different groups have not changed since 1988.
- Although consumption of alcoholic beverages is illegal for those under 21 years of age, 10.5 million current drinkers were age 12–20 in 1998. Of this group, 5.1 million engaged in binge drinking, including 2.3 million who would also be classified as heavy drinkers. There have been no statistically significant changes in the rates of underage drinking since 1994.

Tobacco Use

- An estimated 60 million Americans age 12 and older reported current cigarette use, meaning smoking cigarettes at least once during the 30 days prior to the interview. This estimate represents a rate of 27.7 percent, which is a statistically significant decline from the 1997 rate of 29.6 percent.
- The current rate of smoking among young adults age 18–25 has increased from 34.6 percent in 1994 to 40.6 percent in 1997 and 41.6 percent in 1998.
- An estimated 18.2 percent of youths age 12–17, or 4.1 million, were current cigarette smokers in 1998. There was no significant change in this rate between 1997 (19.9 percent) and 1998; the rate for this group has remained relatively stable since 1988.

- Youths age 12–17 who currently smoked cigarettes were 11.4 times more likely to use illicit drugs and 16 times more likely to drink heavily than nonsmoking youths.
- The rate of current cigar use among those 12 and older increased from 5.9 percent in 1997 to 6.9 percent in 1998, a statistically significant increase. An estimated 5.6 percent of youths age 12–17 were current cigar smokers in 1998. This compares to 5.0 percent in 1997, not a statistically significant difference.

Perceived Risk and Availability of Drugs

- Between 1997 and 1998, there was no change in the percentages of youths age 12–17 reporting great risk from using cigarettes, marijuana, cocaine, or alcohol.
- 56 percent of youths age 12–17 reported marijuana was easy to obtain in 1998. 21 percent said it was easy to obtain heroin. 14 percent of youths reported being approached by someone selling drugs during the 30 days prior to the interview. None of these measures changed significantly between 1997 and 1998.

Trends in New Use of Substances (Incidence)

Because information on when people first used a substance is collected on a retrospective basis, information on first time use or incidence is always one year behind information on current use.

- An estimated 2.1 million persons first used marijuana in 1997. This translates to about 5,800 new marijuana users per day. The rate of first use of marijuana among youths age 12–17 declined significantly from 79 per thousand potential new users in 1996 to 64 per thousand potential new users in 1997. This rate had increased from 38 to 73 between 1991 and 1994; that is, use of marijuana by youths who had never previously used the substance doubled during that time period. The youth incidence rate was stable from 1994 to 1996.
- An estimated 81,000 persons used heroin for the first time in 1997. The rate of initiation for youths from 1994 to 1997 was at the highest level since the early 1970s.
- There were an estimated 730,000 new cocaine users in 1997. The rate of new use among youths did not change between 1996 (11.1) and 1997 (10.8). However, there was a statistically significant increase in the rate from 1991 (4.1) to 1997. The 1997 rate for youths is similar to the high initiation rates of the early 1980s.
- There were an estimated 1.1 million new hallucinogen users in 1997. The rate of initiation among youths age 12–17 increased between 1991 and 1995, from 11.1 to 25.0 per thousand potential new users, and was constant from 1995 to 1997 (23.9).

- An estimated 2.1 million people began smoking cigarettes daily in 1997. More than half of these new smokers were younger than age 18, which translates to more than 3,000 new youth smokers per day.

Drug Use in California and Arizona

- In 1998, the prevalence of illicit drug use among persons 12 years and older was 7.2 percent in California, 7.4 percent in Arizona, and 6.1 percent in the rest of the United States. These differences are not statistically significant.
- 14.4 percent of the youths age 12–17 in Arizona were current drug users in 1998. The rate in Arizona was significantly greater than the rates in California (9.9 percent) and in the rest of the United States (9.9 percent).
- There was no significant change in illicit drug use in California between 1997 and 1998, either for youths or for adults. By contrast there were significant decreases in Arizona during the same period in the rates of illicit drug use among youths age 12–17 and young adults 18–25 years of age.
- In 1997 Californians and Arizonians were less likely than other Americans to perceive great risk in using marijuana.

USAID ON EARTHQUAKE
IN TURKEY
August 20, 1999

Powerful earthquakes struck Turkey and Taiwan late in 1999, killing thousands of people and causing tens of billions of dollars in property damage. Both countries were ill-prepared to respond to the quakes, and both countries discovered that faulty building standards were responsible for much of the damage and loss of life.

International agencies rushed millions of dollars worth of aid to Turkey and Taiwan, and by the end of the year most of those made homeless by the quakes had been given temporary shelter. Even so, officials said it would take years for both countries to recover fully; the earthquakes hit the industrial centers of both countries. Turkey's misfortune turned out to have two positive side effects: it helped stimulate efforts already underway toward closer relations with Greece, an historic enemy; and public anger at the government's slow response gave impetus for political reform in Turkey.

Two Earthquakes Hit Turkey

Turkey was hit by two major earthquakes, each of which had a serious aftershock. The first, and most powerful, temblor came at 3:02 A.M., local time, on August 17, 1999, and was centered at the industrial city of Izmit, about 55 miles southeast of Istanbul. The quake lasted about forty-five seconds and was recorded at 7.4 on the Richter scale. The U.S. National Earthquake Information Center said it was one of the most powerful earthquakes of the twentieth century, nearly as powerful as the 7.9 magnitude quake that destroyed much of San Francisco in 1906.

The earthquake caused serious damage in Istanbul, Turkey's largest city, but did not affect the religious and historic monuments for which the city was famous. Other cities affected by the earthquake included Bursa, Bolu, Eskisehir, and Sakrya. The earthquake was felt 200 miles away in Ankara, the capital city.

An estimated 17,000 people were killed as a result of the earthquake, some 24,000 were reported injured, and more than 250,000 were forced *permanently out of their homes. As of mid-September, the government re-ported that more than 60,000 homes were totally destroyed, and twice as many suffered moderate or light damage. The government estimated the total damage to houses, workplaces, and public facilities at more than $25 billion.*

An aftershock, measured at 5.8 on the Richter scale, struck the same region on September 13, killing six people and injuring about 500.

Turkey was still digging out from the August earthquake when a second major temblor hit at 6:58 P.M., local time, on November 12. Measured at 7.2 on the Richter scale, that earthquake was centered in the city of Duzce in northwestern Turkey, about 115 miles east of Istanbul. Parts of the area hit by that earthquake also had been damaged by the August 17 quake. In the city of Kaynasli, for example, officials reported that nearly 90 percent of all buildings collapsed after the November 12 earthquake, many of them having been damaged by the earlier one.

The government announced two weeks later that 730 people were confirmed dead and more than 5,000 were reported injured by the November 12 earthquake. An aftershock measuring 5.0 on the Richter scale hit the same area on November 18 but caused limited damage.

The earthquakes represented an immense human tragedy for Turkey, a country that had been struggling to modernize its economy. Rescue efforts after the August earthquake were hampered first by the searing late-summer heat (with temperatures over 100 degrees Fahrenheit common), then by heavy rains. It quickly became clear that the Turkish government was not prepared to respond to a disaster of that magnitude. Critics, including some senior government officials, said Ankara's bureaucracy was slow and disorganized in sending emergency aid to the disaster scenes. Food, medicine, water, and emergency housing all were in short supply. Bodies piled up in city streets.

A week after the August 17 earthquake, the country's tourism minister, Erkan Mumcu, said the government's inability to help its own people represented "a declaration of bankruptcy for the Turkish political and economic system." The Turkish news media, which generally voiced only mild discontent with the government, gave vent to angry outbursts from citizens about Ankara's inability to organize timely rescue and relief efforts. Many Turks were especially angered by the comments of the health minister, Osman Durmus, who said the country should reject assistance from other countries that "do not suit our culture."

Despite the health minister's misgivings, Turkey received rapid aid from overseas, including from the United States and the United Nations relief agencies. High-profile rescue missions by teams from Israel and Greece were warmly embraced by the Turkish public. Turkey was able to repay Greece in September when a milder earthquake hit Athens. Work by a Turkish rescue team was featured on Greek television, helping stimulate a thaw in the always frosty relations between the two countries. In December Greece modified its long-standing objections to Turkish membership in the European Union. Israel's dispatch of rescue teams helped cement rela-tions between the Jewish state and Turkey, which had a secular Islamic society. (European Union expansion, p. 119)

Public anger in Turkey quickly found another target: contractors who in the previous twenty years had built offices and apartment complexes in the country's industrial heartland. In theory, those structures were supposed to meet modern standards of earthquake resistance. But many citizens and experts said the government had not seriously enforced building standards and unscrupulous contractors took advantage of the lax oversight by tak-ing shortcuts that ultimately cost hundreds or thousands of people their lives. "The inevitable happened, despite years and years of repeated warn-ings," Ahmet Ercan, a professor of geophysics at Istanbul Technical Uni-versity told the New York Times. *Officials "never insisted that contractors survey the risk and build earthquake-resistant structures."*

On November 16, four days after the second major earthquake in Turkey, President Bill Clinton visited the country to survey the damage and offer words of hope to its battered people. Speaking in Izmit to sur-vivors of the August 17 quake, many still living in tents, Clinton said: "Keep your spirits up, keep the smiles on your children's faces, keep help-ing the people who lost their loved ones in the earthquake, and know that together we will get through this to better days."

Clinton brought with him news that the United States was continuing to provide aid to the survivors, including 500 winterized military tents that would house up to 10,000 people. Overall, the U.S. Agency for International Development (USAID) said U.S. aid totaled about $14.5 million in response to the August earthquake and $3.8 million in response to the November quake. The World Bank in November advanced $758 million in loans for Turkey, about one-third of which was for aid to those still home-less and the rest for programs to improve the country's building standards and emergency response systems.

A Similar Story in Taiwan

At 1:47 A.M. local time on September 21, a massive earthquake struck the island of Taiwan in the China Sea. The epicenter of the quake was in a rural areas in the mountainous interior of the island, but several cities suffered damage, including Nantou, Taichung City, and Tungshih. Dam-age was moderate in Taipei, the capital, about ninety miles north of the epicenter. Scores of modern high-rise office buildings and apartment com-plexes in cities collapsed or toppled over like dominoes. Roads and bridges leading to the mountainous interior also were damaged, complicating relief efforts.

The Taiwan government said the earthquake killed 2,300 and damaged 82,000 housing units. Total property damage was estimated at $9.2 bil-lion.

Offers of aid came in from around the world, including from the com-munist government on mainland China, which regarded Taiwan as a *"renegade" province. President Jiang Zemin reminded the people of Taiwan that they were linked to the mainland by "flesh and blood." The United States provided $2.5 million in emergency aid.*

Taiwan had adopted stringent requirements for modern buildings to meet earthquake resistant standards, and experts said many of the island's offices and apartments were in compliance. But in its rush to provide housing and offices, Taiwan had allowed developers to build in reclaimed marshland and other areas unsuitable for large buildings. As a result, even buildings that met international standards could tumble when a major earthquake struck. As in Turkey, officials and observers said some developers had managed to sidestep legal requirements, using shoddy materials and cutting corners, rendering their buildings vulnerable to even a modest earthquake.

The Taiwan government quickly identified eighteen contractors suspected of failing to meet building standards. Investigators found that some contractors had diluted concrete with such material as plastic foam and wads of newspaper. The Associated Press quoted one American rescue worker as saying that some buildings in Taiwan were more shoddily constructed than those he had seen after the earthquake in Turkey. On December 4 one contractor was charged with negligence, endangering public safety, and other crimes in the construction of a high-rise apartment building in the central city of Dali.

Other Natural Disasters

Colombia, India, and Venezuela were among other countries that experienced significant natural disasters during 1999. An earthquake registering 6.0 on the Richter scale struck central Colombia in the early morning hours of January 25. The Colombian Red Cross reported 1,171 confirmed deaths and nearly 4,800 injured. Officials said about 45,000 houses were destroyed or damaged, leaving about 150,000 people homeless. The hardest hit cities were Armenia, Calarca, and Pereira. In Armenia, scores of looters went on a rampage after the earthquake, adding to the damage and turmoil

As in Turkey, the government's disorganized response angered victims and the public generally. Observers said the government's inability to provide rapid relief for victims and to control looting had undermined public support and damaged President Andres Pastrana's fledgling effort to negotiate peace with leftist guerrillas.

Two massive cyclones in the Bay of Bengal struck the eastern coast of India in October, one on October 1819, and the other on October 29. The government estimated in mid-November than nearly 9,500 people had been killed and 2,300 injured by floods and high winds resulting from the storms. But the storms had other impacts that were almost beyond belief, judged by Western standards. An estimated 7.5 million people were left homeless; in some areas officials said more than 70 percent of the housing was completely destroyed. More than 11,000 schools were destroyed or

468

severely damaged, and millions of acres of crops were ruined. The govern-
ment said it needed emergency food aid for nearly 2.3 million people, for
at least a month. International aid agencies rushed food, medicine, and
other supplies. The United States contributed about $7.5 million through
mid-November.

Venezuela suffered its greatest natural disaster of modern times in
December when torrential rains caused widespread floods and mud slides
along the northern coast. Flood waters engulfed entire towns and cities,
burying people and buildings in mud and washing others into the
Caribbean Sea. At year's end no accurate casualty estimates were avail-
able, but some government officials said 30,000 or more people might have
died and well over 100,000 were homeless. Many of those swept away by
the floods lived in shanty towns built on mountainsides. One Venezuelan
Red Cross official said that "no one really knows" how many people lived
in the affected areas.

Following are excerpts from "Turkey—Earthquake Fact Sheet
#6," issued August 20, 1999, by the U.S. Agency for Interna-
tional Development, describing the situation in Turkey follow-
ing a powerful earthquake that struck the country on August 17,
1999:

Background: On August 17 at 3:02 A.M. local time, an earthquake lasting 45 seconds and reported to be between 7.4 and 7.8 on the Richter scale, hit Izmit, Turkey, approximately 55 miles east-southeast of Istanbul. Major affected areas include various districts of Istanbul and provinces of Izmit (Kocaeli), Adapazari (Sakarya), Yalova, Bursa, Eskishir, and Bolu to east and southeast of Istanbul. The Government of Turkey (GOT) also reports that Turkey's main naval base at Golcuk was hard-hit. Geophysicists at the U.S. National Earthquake Information Center described the quake as one of the most powerful recorded in the 20th century, nearly rivaling the 7.9-magnitude temblor that devastated San Francisco in 1906. It was felt as far east as Ankara, 200 miles away, and across parts of the Balkans.

Numbers Affected: Latest CNN reports confirm nearly 10,000 deaths and 34,000 injured persons. Approximately one million people are now camped outdoors for fear of more destruction. Smashed sewage lines and the number of homeless living on garbage-strewn streets without portable toilets or fresh water is compounding the risk of cholera or other infectious diseases spreading.

Current Situation: USAID [U.S. Agency for International Develop-ment]/OFDA [Office of U.S. Foreign Disaster Assistance] Search and Rescue Team 1 (Fairfax County) has rescued a total of four people alive from col-lapsed buildings in Izmit. The team reports that 11 rescues have been made in the sector in which the team is working, including recent rescues by the

Swiss and Hungarian teams. However, even with the assistance of a thousand professional rescue workers from around the world, many earthquake victims will not be reached and will die of injuries, or thirst and exposure. The Turkish military seconded a liaison officer and a military contingent to USAID/OFDA Team 1 to assist with search and rescue operations. U.S. Ambassador [Mark Robert] Parris and Turkish President [Suleyman] Demirel visited the team on 19 August.

At local time this morning, firefighters brought the blaze at the Tupras oil refinery under control.

Storage, identification and burial of the victims are fast becoming a major problem, as makeshift morgues in skating rinks, fishermen's warehouses and refrigerated trucks are filled to capacity.

The situation is further aggravated by a lack of water and sanitation in many places and by daytime high temperatures of 95 degress Fahrenheit. Turkish health officials are working to establish a hygienic environment to prevent contagious diseases. Five teams have been sent to different parts of the quake-hit zone to collect garbage, put chlorine into water reservoirs, and pick up dead bodies. Vomiting and diarrhea began showing up last night in Adapazari, especially among children and the elderly.

The USAID/DART [Disaster Assistance Response Team] reports that local and international medical staff appear to be meeting medical needs in Izmit.

The USAID/DART visited the Izmit crisis center to try to determine relief effort coordination. The DART found that the crisis center staff had been overwhelmed by requests for assistance from local residents and had abandoned efforts to track the requests.

The electricity distribution systems in Izmit (Kocaeli) and Adapazari (Sakarya) are reported to be working in a fragmentary fashion. However, distribution is limited to hospitals, bakeries, main arteries, and the water pumps at the Tupras refinery; there is no distribution to homes.

U.S. Government Response: The U.S. Government has responded with the immediate deployment of a Disaster Assistance Response Team (DART) composed of four persons and a USAID-supported 70-person search and rescue team from Fairfax County Fire Department. The DART/Fairfax County Search and Rescue team deployed to Izmit on the night of 18 August and established a base of operations in the Yavuz Sultan Maii neighborhood in the southeast quadrant of Izmit. Search and rescue operations began on the morning of 19 August, local time.

At 11:00 EDT on 19 August, USAID/OFDA ordered the deployment of a second 70-person search and rescue team. Miami Metro Dade has fielded a team, which is due in country at 09:30 local time on 21 August.

USAID also seconded an eight-person team to assist the On-Site Operations Coordination Center (OSOCC) established by the United Nations Office for the Coordination of Humanitarian Assistance (UNOCHA). USAID/OFDA's assistance to the OSOCC includes search and rescue management personnel, an information officer, and a mapping expert.

The USAID plane carrying emergency medical supplies and USAID/BHR

[Humanitarian Response Bureau] Assistant Administrator Hugh Parmer arrived at 05:45 local time on 21 August.

In addition to staff already deployed, two epidemiologists from the U.S. Centers for Disease Control and a water/sanitation specialist were deployed on 19 August and will arrive shortly to assess emergency health and water/sanitation needs.

A second USAID/OFDA-funded airlift carrying reverse osmosis water purification units, capable of assisting 28,000 persons, also is scheduled to arrive in Istanbul in the coming days.

Three U.S. warships carrying 2,100 Marines from the 26th Marine Expeditionary Unit departed Spain on 19 August. The USS *Kearsarge* and USS *Gunston Hall* are expected to arrive on 22 August; the USS *Ponce* is due on 23 August. The Kearsarge Amphibious Ready Group has 60 hospital beds, six operating rooms and five x-ray rooms. Its personnel comprise eight doctors, three dentists and 88 medical corpsmen.

The U.S. Department of Defense deployed a 22-member crisis response medical team and a three-member team of medical disaster assessment experts, both of which arrived in county on 19 August.

On 19 August, the U.S. Department of Defense announced that it will be sending aerial firefighting equipment and 30,000 tents to help victims of Tuesday's massive earthquake. In addition, a humanitarian assistance survey team is being deployed by the U.S. European Command in Stuttgart, Germany. More than 100,000 humanitarian daily rations, stored in Europe because of the Kosovo crisis, will also be made available to Turkey if needed. . . .

Relief Efforts: The Turkish Coordination Council for Relief, operating under the leadership of the Prime Minister, is overseeing all relief operations in the affected region being carried out by national forces, Turkish Red Crescent, and volunteers.

Turkish authorities have requested the following relief supplies: 5,000 body bags, heavy gloves and masks for clearing rubble, parabolic microphones, blankets, medicine and first-aid material, soup kitchens and food, range water, and water purification systems.

UNOCHA has activated its Disaster Response System, which includes establishing the United Nations Disaster Assessment and Coordination (UNDAC) team and an On-Site Operations Coordination Center (OSOCC). In collaboration with Turkish authorities, UNDAC has established a reception center at the Istanbul airport to facilitate the movement of arriving relief items.

As of 1000 EDT 19 August, search and rescue teams from 21 countries are assisting the relief effort.

The International Federation of Red Cross and Red Crescent Societies (IFRC) has launched a preliminary appeal for 10.52 million Swiss francs (approximately US$7.1 million) to assist 100,000 victims of the earthquake. Funds will be used to support the Turkish Red Crescent relief operation and to purchase locally relief items such as food, water, blankets, and tents.

According to CNN, the Red Cross will bring in 600 tons of food during the next few days. . . .

September

Secretary of State Albright on
U.S. Consulate in Vietnam 475

Attorney General and Special
Counsel on Waco Investigation 480

UNICEF Director on the
Spread of AIDS in Africa 489

National Security Commission
on Threats in the Next Century 499

UN Human Rights Commissioner
on Independence in East Timor 511

UN Secretary General on
the Situation in Afghanistan 524

Justice Department Allegations
of Fraud by Tobacco Industry 536

Army Secretary on Investigation
of Korean War Massacre 552

SECRETARY OF STATE ALBRIGHT
ON U.S. CONSULATE IN VIETNAM
September 7, 1999

The United States and Vietnam on September 7, 1999, reached another important milestone in their drive to move past the bitter experience of the Vietnam War. Secretary of State Madeleine K. Albright dedicated a new U.S. consulate in Ho Chi Minh City (formerly Saigon), adjacent to the site of the old embassy, from which the U.S. ambassador and staff fled in the closing days of the Vietnam War in 1975.

"The United States and Vietnam will forever be linked by history," Albright said at a dedication ceremony. "But by continuing to work together to transcend that tragic legacy, we can add to our shared history bright new chapters of hope and mutual prosperity."

Halting progress was made during 1999 on one of the most substantive elements of a new relationship between the United States and Vietnam: a bilateral trade agreement. Negotiators for the two countries on July 25 reached an agreement in principle to normalize trade relations, including sharply reducing tariffs. But despite personal coaxing from Albright, senior Vietnamese officials later balked at signing the accord. The issue remained unresolved at year's end.

Human rights and political freedoms continued to be contentious issues between Vietnam and the United States. The Hanoi government released several prominent dissidents during 1998 and 1999, but human rights organizations and U.S. officials said Vietnam continued to intimidate and harass anyone who sought to open the political system. Albright said that "by not permitting more open and inclusive politics and media, Vietnam is denying itself the benefits of greater international standing, as well as those of more productive public participation in civic and economic affairs."

A New Consulate

The United States and Vietnam began the process of normalizing relations in 1992, when Vietnam allowed representatives from the U.S. Defense

Department to begin looking for the bodies of American soldiers and air-men missing in action since the war. Bolstered by cooperation on that symbolically important issue, the two countries made steady progress in settling other disagreements, including the lifting of U.S. economic sanctions against Vietnam in 1994. In 1995 they agreed to restore full diplomatic relations. The United States established an embassy in Hanoi in 1996, and a year later Douglas "Pete" Peterson, a former prisoner of war and representative from Florida, arrived as the first U.S. ambassador there. (Sanctions lifted, Historic Documents of 1994, p. 95; Establishment of diplomatic relations, Historic Documents of 1995, p. 472)

Another key step came in 1997 when Albright visited Ho Chi Minh City for a ceremony initiating construction of the new consulate. At that time, Albright symbolically laid a brick that came from the prison in Hanoi (known in the United States as the "Hanoi Hilton") where Peterson and several hundred other American servicemen had been held during the war. (Consulate construction, Historic Documents of 1997, p. 489)

The consulate was completed just years later, ahead of schedule and under budget. U.S. diplomats and staff moved into the building in June and a month later began issuing visas—the main task projected for the facility. At full staffing the building was to house 20 U.S. and more than 150 Vietnamese employees. Charles Ray, who served two tours of duty in the Vietnam War as an army captain, was the first consul general.

The State Department estimated that the consulate would process about 25,000 immigrant visas annually, making it one of the busiest such facilities in the world. Most of the visas were expected to be for Vietnamese citizens wanting to visit relatives in the United States, where more than 1.5 million people of Vietnamese background lived. Before the consulate was opened, Vietnamese were required to travel to the U.S. consulate in Bangkok, Thailand, to obtain the most common types of visas.

In her remarks at the ceremony dedicating the consulate, Albright noted that the building—located in the former courtyard of the old U.S. embassy, since demolished—was "surrounded by reminders of the past." Even so, she said, the United States and Vietnam "will be moving resolutely toward a better future."

Earlier that same day, Albright was in Hanoi for a grimmer type of ceremony: the loading into caskets of boxes containing the remains of four bodies presumed to be American servicemen missing since the Vietnam War. While praising Vietnam for cooperation on the matter, Albright said that locating remains of the missing servicemen "remains paramount to the United States." As of late 1999 the Pentagon had identified the remains of more than 500 servicemen and returned them to their families, with another 1,500 still missing. The Hanoi government said that some 200,000 Vietnamese soldiers remained unaccounted for. The Pentagon in 1999 agreed to open its archives to Vietnamese researchers looking for information about those missing soldiers.

Moving Toward a Trade Agreement

U.S.-Vietnamese progress on political issues was not fully matched on the economic front. In the mid-1980s the communist rulers of Vietnam began restructuring their economy by opening it to outside private investment. A decade later several hundred firms from the United States, Europe, Japan, and other nations had established modest operations in Hanoi and Ho Chi Minh City. But bureaucratic hurdles and the chronic inefficiencies of the Vietnamese state-run economy made operating there difficult, and many firms were paring back their commitments or even leaving. The World Bank estimated new foreign investment in Vietnam during 1999 at $600 million, the lowest figure since 1992. Vietnam's fragile economy also was shaken severely by the Asian financial crisis of 1997 and 1998. (Asian crisis, Historic Documents of 1998, p. 722)

Following the normalization of their diplomatic relations, the United States and Vietnam in 1996 began negotiating a bilateral trade agreement that would reduce tariffs from levels as high as 200 percent. The agreement would open the Vietnamese economy to imports of U.S. goods and services, and for the first time enable low-cost Vietnamese goods to enter the United States in marketable quantities. The accord also dealt with intellectual property rights and investment issues.

Partly because of lingering suspicions on both sides and partly because of the enormous disparities between the two economies, the negotiations at times were contentious and took many years. After a marathon session July 24, the two sides the next day announced that they had reached an agreement "in principle" that covered the main issues, including numerous steps Vietnam needed to take to relax government control of the economy. U.S. Trade Representative Charlene Barshefsky called the tentative agreement "a major step forward," one that would mark the full return of U.S. "economic reengagement with Indochina." Washington already had normalized trade relations with Cambodia and Laos. From Vietnam's perspective, completion of the agreement was expected to pave the way for membership in the World Trade Organization, the international body that set worldwide regulations on trade.

But in the weeks following the tentative agreement, senior Vietnamese officials reportedly had serious second thoughts about their willingness to open the country's economy to the brisk winds of international trade. According to media reports, many officials in Hanoi expressed concerns about the consequences of the inevitable "westernization" of Vietnam once multinational corporations began large-scale operations there.

During her visit to Hanoi September 6-7, Albright met with senior government officials to encourage them to proceed with the agreement. At a news conference September 6, Albright pointedly said that "we must reach closure on a landmark trade agreement which, if approved by Congress, would open the door to normal trade relations between our countries. After nearly four years of effort, and in light of the congressional calendar, prompt action is needed if this major opportunity is not to be come a missed opportunity." Albright's reference to Congress was an indication that the Clinton administration hoped for congressional action on a trade agreement during 1999 so that the sensitive question of improving ties with Vietnam would not become a political issue during the 2000 elections.

Albright's appeals appeared to have little or no impact on officials in Hanoi, who continued to balk at completing the final details needed before the trade agreement could be signed and submitted to each country's legislature. At year's end the agreement remained unsigned.

Following is the text of remarks by Secretary of State Madeleine K. Albright at a ceremony September 7, 1999, marking the dedication of a new U.S. consulate building in Ho Chi Minh City, Vietnam:

I want to welcome our extraordinary Ambassador to Vietnam, Pete Peterson; Consul General Ray; our distinguished Vietnamese friends and members of the diplomatic community; consulate staff, family and friends.

In the spring of 1997, I had the high diplomatic honor of throwing out the ceremonial first pitch of the season for the Baltimore Orioles. So at the ground-breaking here two years ago—with that very different Opening Day fresh on my mind—I said that was the first time I had ever been asked to throw out the first brick.

That's why it's especially gratifying to come back today and see what became of that brick—and what a magnificent new Consulate has been built upon this site. It even takes the sting off the fact that Senator [Chuck] Hagel [R-Neb.] beat me to the punch here three weeks ago.

I want to express special thanks to Chairman Thanh and the other authorities here in Ho Chi Minh City. Their cooperation allowed us to complete construction here not only on time, but ahead of time. And I want to congratulate our foreign buildings staff for its major role in that achievement.

This Consulate General marks another important step forward in the relationship between the United States and Vietnam. For in this place—surrounded by reminders of the past—our two countries will be moving resolutely toward a better future.

Soon we will be able to provide full visa services here for the first time in almost a quarter century. And within a year, we expect this consulate to be one of our busiest visa-issuing posts in the world.

This new facility will allow us to accelerate refugee processing and foster family reunification—two important humanitarian goals.

It will enhance our people-to-people ties with Vietnam, as tourism and travel become easier in both directions.

It will deepen our commercial ties, as bilateral trade grows and Vietnam moves ahead with reforms that encourage entrepreneurs and attract investors.

It will help us better serve the American business community which is concentrated here in the South.

It will enhance our capacity to follow up concerns on human rights, labor rights and religious freedoms.

And it will help us pursue what remains our paramount goal in Vietnam, which is to obtain the fullest possible accounting of Americans still missing or otherwise unaccounted for in Southeast Asia. Vietnam's cooperation with this effort in recent years has paved the way to the normal consular ties our two countries celebrate today.

The United States and Vietnam will forever be linked by history. But by continuing to work together to transcend that tragic legacy, we can add to our shared history bright new chapters of hope and mutual prosperity.

It is in this spirit that I commission this Consulate as a symbol of America's commitment to continued progress towards full reconciliation and normalization between the people of America and the people of Vietnam.

And it is in this same spirit that I will now present a very special Fiancée Visa to be issued by this new Consulate. Congratulations, Miss Lien—on both your engagement and your visa. You have our best wishes.

And thank you all very much.

ATTORNEY GENERAL AND SPECIAL COUNSEL ON WACO INVESTIGATION
September 9, 1999

One of the first crises of Bill Clinton's presidency—the 1993 assault on the Branch Davidian compound in Waco, Texas—continued to plague his administration as he neared the end of his two terms in office. New disclosures in 1999 cast serious doubt on key claims by the Justice Department and the Federal Bureau of Investigation (FBI) about the handling of the Waco incident, which resulted in the deaths of some eighty members of the Branch Davidian cult. Angered by the FBI's possible withholding of important information, Attorney General Janet Reno on September 9, 1999, appointed former senator John Danforth, R-Mo., as a special counsel with broad powers to investigate the government's handling of the incident.

The Waco case had become a cause célèbre among both mainstream conservatives, who portrayed it as an example of Clinton administration incompetence, and far-right antigovernment groups, who said Waco represented authoritarian tactics. In 1995, on the second anniversary of the Waco assault, Timothy McVeigh, a former army soldier apparently embittered by the deaths in Waco, bombed the federal building in Oklahoma City, killing 168 people and wounding hundreds of others. (Waco assault, Historic Documents of 1993, pp. 293, 819; Oklahoma City bombing, Historic Documents of 1995, p. 176)

New Evidence Emerges

Led by the charismatic David Koresh, more than one hundred members of the Branch Davidian cult lived in a complex of buildings near Waco, Texas. The federal Bureau of Alcohol, Tobacco, and Firearms (ATF) surrounded the compound early in 1993, saying that cult members possessed an enormous quantity of illegal weapons. ATF agents stormed the compound February 28, 1993, setting off a gun battle in which four agents and two cult members died. The FBI then took control of the situation, mounting a siege of the compound that lasted fifty-one days. During that period thirty adults and children left the compound; some of the departures resulted from intense negotiations between cult leaders and representatives of the FBI's "hostage rescue" team at the site.

Insisting that further negotiations would be useless, the FBI on April 19 mounted an assault on the Branch Davidian compound, using military-style tanks to punch holes in the main building and firing tear gas canisters. About six hours after the assault began, fires broke out within the compound. The fires burned out of control for several hours; when the flames finally were subdued, agents found the bodies of more than eighty men, women, and children. Most had died as a result of the fires, but autopsies showed that some died of self-inflicted gunshot wounds.

Arson investigators determined that the fires resulted when cult members sprinkled gasoline around the compound and set it ablaze. The Justice Department conducted an investigation of the entire incident, finding no serious cases of wrongdoing by FBI agents or other officials involved. The investigations did not head off criticism, however, and numerous critics called the probe superficial. In 1996 the House Governmental Reform Committee held hearings that offered an opportunity for critics to denounce nearly every aspect of the Clinton administration's handling of the case.

Throughout various examinations of the Waco incident, the administration insisted that on April 19, 1993, FBI agents did not fire weapons at the Branch Davidian members and did not do anything to cause the fires that killed most of them. Specifically, Reno and her aides said the tear gas canisters fired by FBI agents during the morning of April 19 could not have ignited the fires because they were a nonincendiary type.

On August 24, 1999, the Dallas Morning News *reported that a former senior FBI official, Danny O. Coulson, said in an interview that he had recently learned that FBI agents had fired two military-type tear gas canisters, which contained incendiary agents, at the Branch Davidian compound during the early phase of the April 19 assault. Reversing its long-standing denials, the FBI acknowledged on August 25 that its agents had used a "pyrotechnic" type of tear gas canister, but the agency staunchly denied that those canisters were responsible for the fires. Later that day, Reno and FBI director Louis J. Freeh jointly announced a new investigation of the agency's role in the Waco assault. On August 26 Reno acknowledged that the new revelations had damaged her credibility and said she would "pursue it until I get to the truth."*

The new FBI probe quickly turned up one piece of hard evidence that was made public September 2: an infrared videotape from the day of the assault that captured a conversation in which Richard M. Rogers, the assistant special agent in charge of the FBI hostage rescue team at Waco, authorized the use of "military rounds" of tear gas. The tape was one of many items that had been stored at an FBI warehouse in Virginia and possibly never made available during prior investigations. In an extraordinary move, Reno ordered U.S. marshals to seize material about the Waco assault from the FBI headquarters, located just across Pennsylvania

481

Avenue from the Justice Department in Washington. Reno's action was widely seen as indicating her lack of faith in the bureau's handling of information about the case.

A second infrared videotape, released September 3, showed more detail about the use of the military-style tear gas canister, known as an M651 cartridge. That type of cartridge relied on a burning fuse to turn solid material into CS gas, which was emitted through a vent. Experts said the fuse could, under certain circumstances, start a fire. According to FBI videotape, at about 8 A.M. on April 19 an FBI agent fired one M651 cartridge at an underground concrete storm shelter located near the main portion of the Branch Davidian compound, but the cartridge failed to penetrate the building and bounced into a field. According to various reports, one or two additional canisters were fired at the storm shelter, but it was unclear whether any penetrated the building.

While acknowledging that the videotape cast doubt on the administration's contentions about the Waco assault, Reno insisted that none of the new information indicated that the FBI was responsible for the fires. Reno and other officials noted that the military canisters were fired at the storm shelter—where there was no fire—several hours before fires broke out in the main part of the Branch Davidian complex.

News organizations reported later in September and October that the FBI had turned over to investigators additional documents that raised questions about other FBI assertions, including that no agents had directed sniper fire at the Branch Davidian compound during the assault. Rep. Dan Burton, R-Ind., who chaired the House Government Reform Committee and had been a staunch critic of Reno, said he would conduct new hearings on the Waco incident. Burton was especially angered by reports that the Justice Department had cut a page mentioning the military tear gas canisters from an FBI report given to Congress in 1995. On September 13 Rep. Henry A. Waxman, a senior Democrat on Burton's committee, released documents showing that the FBI in 1995 had turned other information over to both Congress and the Justice Department indicating that "military rounds" of tear gas had been used in the Waco assault. It appeared that congressional staff members, members of Congress, and senior Justice officials may not have understood the significance of that information at the time.

Danforth Appointment

Under fire from Burton and other Republicans on Capitol Hill, Reno moved quickly to distance herself and the Justice Department from the Waco case, saying she was looking for a respected individual to lead an independent investigation. On September 9 she announced the appointment of Danforth as special counsel. She described him as "someone who is independent and someone who has the wisdom and determination to do the job the right way." A moderate Republican widely respected in Washington, Danforth represented Missouri in the Senate for three terms. Following his retirement from the Senate, Danforth joined a prominent St.

Louis legal firm. Danforth told reporters he would continue with that position while serving as independent counsel. He named Edward Dowd, the U.S. attorney in St. Louis and a Democrat, as his deputy.

Danforth said he would focus his investigation on whether there was any wrongdoing by federal authorities during the siege and final assault on the Branch Davidian compound, but would not second-guess the policy judgments of top officials. "What we're going to be looking at is whether there were bad acts, not whether there was bad judgment," he told reporters. "Our country can survive bad judgment. But the thing that really undermines the integrity of government is whether there were bad acts, whether there was a cover-up and whether the government killed people."

Danforth was the first special counsel named under provisions of regulations issued by Reno on July 1, following the expiration of a twenty-year-old law that authorized the appointment of independent counsels to investigate high-level wrongdoing. Congress allowed that law to expire in large part because of the controversy generated by the wide ranging investigation of President Clinton conducted by independent counsel Kenneth W. Starr. (Independent counsel issue, p. 165)

Along with attorneys representing the Branch Davidian survivors and relatives, Danforth's office pressed for a filmed reenactment of a portion of the Waco assault to determine whether federal agents fired on the compound. The test was to be filmed with an infrared camera similar to one used by the FBI on the day of the siege. Some government critics had contended that flashes shown on a film of the siege must have been caused by gunfire from FBI agents. The Justice Department insisted that there was no gunfire from government positions and for several weeks in late 1999 opposed a filmed reenactment. But U.S. District Court Judge Walter Smith on November 17 ordered the test to determine whether gunfire would produce flashes such as those shown on the film of the assault. The Justice Department relented on the matter in late December and signed an agreement setting details of the test. At year's end Danforth's office was attempting to borrow a camera similar to the one used at Waco from an unnamed foreign country because one could not be located in the United States, according to the Dallas Morning News.

Following are excerpts from a news conference September 9, 1999, at which Attorney General Janet Reno announced her appointment of former senator John Danforth as special counsel to investigate the government's handling of the April 19, 1993, siege of the Branch Davidian compound in Waco, Texas:

Attorney General Janet Reno: Good morning. I have been working to identify an individual outside the Department of Justice who could head up the investigation into the events at Waco, Texas on April 19, 1993.

During that time, I have tried to find someone with impeccable credentials, someone with bipartisan support in Washington, who is widely regarded throughout the country; someone who is independent and someone who has the wisdom and determination to do the job the right way.

I have found that person in Senator John Danforth. Senator Danforth will have the authority to investigate whether any government employee or agent, one, suppressed information relating to the events on April 19th; made false statements or misleading statements concerning those events; used any pyrotechnic or incendiary devices or engaged in gunfire on that day; and took any action that started or contributed to the spread of the fire. In addition, he is authorized to investigate whether there is any—was any illegal use of the armed forces.

More than two weeks ago, I said I wanted to set up an investigation to find answers and present those answers to the American public. I believe the system we have agreed upon today will enable Senator Danforth to do just that. Under the order I have signed today, Senator Danforth will have the same authority as that which any special counsel would have under our new special counsel regulations.

As for any limited role that I would otherwise have in supervising such an outside inquiry, I've asked Deputy Attorney General Eric Holder to handle those duties, since he was not involved in any way with Waco. I have spoken with Director Freeh and he agrees with the choice of Senator Danforth and says he feels it is an excellent choice.

The recent revelations have caused the American people to raise new questions—questions that deserve to be answered. Senator Danforth, I think, is a person who can find those answers.

Senator?

Former senator John Danforth: I think you'll understand that once an investigation gets going, it's really not appropriate to have a running commentary on a day-to-day or week-to-week basis as to what's going on in the investigation.

But before it gets started—and it's going to take, you know, a few days to gear it up—I think it's important for me to be accessible to the media and to the American people to try to make it clear what's going to happen and what this investigation is about and what it is not about.

I, when I was first approached by the attorney general, made it clear that it is very important for this investigation to have definition, to have some mission statement of what it is and what it isn't. And the attorney general's order spells out what it is. And I want to just summarize it for you so that there is a total understanding of this.

Basically, when you boil down the half-dozen points that are in the order, they amount to two big questions that have to be resolved.

The first question is, was there a cover-up?

And the second question is, did federal officials kill people? That's the question of the cause of the fire, whether there was shooting, and so forth.

And those are the two big questions. And those are the questions that we will be examining in this investigation.

In other words, what we're going to be looking at is whether there were bad acts, not whether there was bad judgment. I want that understood.

Our country can survive bad judgment. I take it that every day for the history of America there's been bad judgment, but the thing that really undermines the integrity of government is whether there were bad acts, whether was a cover-up and whether there was government—and whether the government killed people.

So what we are not going to be looking is whether it was advisable in the first place for ATF [Bureau of Alcohol, Tobacco, and Firearms] to be concerned about the Branch Davidians, whether it was a good idea or not to stage the raid in February of 1993 or in April of 1993 for that matter or the psychological efforts that took place in between.

Those, I don't minimize the importance of those questions at all, but I don't think that those should be the questions for a special counsel. I think that they are questions that Congress can address, that the media can address or the American people can address or the political process can address. But they are really not subject of this—of this investigation.

Now, another point that should be made about the attorney general's order is at the very end of the order, where it says, "In addition to the confidential report, the special counsel to the maximum extent possible and consistent with his duties and the law shall submit to the attorney general a final report and such interim reports in the form that will permit public dissemination."

The first priority is to get to the facts. And the attorney general has armed me with all the authority under the law necessary to get to the facts, including, if necessary, the power to empanel a grand jury. That's the first priority, to get to the facts.

However, it is my hope and my intention that the facts that are discovered will be made available to the American people, for that is very, very important.

And as we proceed with the investigation, we have to bear in mind that, you know, if we ever get to the grand jury point, obviously secrecy is in place. And I'm just telling you the balancing act that we are going to have to go through along the way. Getting the facts, that's order number one, but hopefully in a form that can be made public.

It is clear to me that the quality of the product of what we hope to produce is going to be dependent on the quality of the people who produce it.

And it was clear to me that I needed, as a deputy, somebody who was very, very experienced in prosecutions, in investigations, and somebody in whom I could have confidence. And I asked for the help of Ed Dowd, a person I have known—he's from St. Louis, and he is a person who is very highly regarded in our community, and a very, very experienced prosecutor to be the deputy special counsel. And I'm happy to say that he has accepted that.

Obviously this means that he will be leaving the U.S. attorney's office. He will be, in fact, joining the law firm that I'm in—Bryan Cave—and he will be working on this project with me. And I am very grateful for that.

Question: Senator, who's going to do the leg work? It's been speculated that you will not use FBI agents, even though, as I understand it, some FBI agents who have no connection to Waco are available for that leg work.

Danforth: I don't believe that the FBI should be investigating the FBI. And I think that that's the reason for a special counsel. I would hope, to the maximum extent that I can, to use people who are in the private sector. I think that it is possible and even likely that we will need some help from government investigators. In that case, I would hope to go outside the Justice Department to the maximum extent that I can.

I can't say that under no circumstances would I call on any help at all from the FBI because I don't know how the course of this will proceed. But my basic thought is that the FBI should not be investigating the FBI.

Question: How long [off-mike] this investigation [off-mike]

Danforth: No, I don't know how long. I think that it would be a mistake to set a fixed time limit. I can tell you that my goals are first of all to be absolutely objective, and I go into this with no preconceived ideas whatever. So I'm going to be totally, totally objective. I'm going to call them as I see them.

Secondly, to be thorough, to do all the work that should be done to try to bring these questions to an answer. And finally, to try to be expeditious. The first two priorities are the priorities, but consistent with that, I don't myself want this to go on and on. I don't think that serves anybody's purpose. . . .

Question: Is there any hesitation, Senator, into stepping into the middle of a situation that has become so politically sensitive? Any hesitation, any reluctance on your part to take this job?

Danforth: Well, as a friend of mine said, this is not what you call a good career move. And I have—I got out of government for the reason that I wanted to go home, and I wanted to really be in the private sector. So, this goes against that.

On the other hand, this is really a big thing. And I think that it is very important to try to get answers to questions that are important for the whole integrity of our government, so that's how I feel about it. . . .

Question: Senator, is there any authority that you asked for that you did not receive from the attorney general?

Danforth: No, no. No, I made it clear to the attorney general first of all that we needed a deputy who was first rate, in whom I had confidence and who had extensive experience in prosecution; secondly, that we needed a mission statement that had definition to it, which I think is what we have. And third, that I have the powers, if necessary to use those powers, to find out all the facts.

And I'm satisfied that I have all of those. . . .

Question: Senator, you characterize this as a big deal. What exactly do you see at stake here?

Danforth: Well, I see at stake the beginning of the Declaration of Independence; that the point of government—the purpose of government—is to protect the life and liberty and the pursuit of happiness of the American people. And if government doesn't do that, if government covers things up, if government kills people, if that's what happened, and I don't prejudge that, then that undermines what Jefferson talked about as being the very foundation of government.

And I further believe that, as the Declaration of Independence says, that the just powers of government are derived from the consent of the people. And it's very important to have the consent of the American people. And that consent is based on knowledge of what happened.

So I think that my role is to give the American people knowledge of what happened and to hope that the American people will do as I do, and that is keep their minds open about what happened until a full factual presentation is made. . . .

Question: Senator, Congressman [Henry] Hyde [chairman of the House Judiciary Committee] and others have talked about their concerns that the Justice Department somehow obstruct your investigation. What do you make of those concerns, and what assurances have you gotten over the last couple of days that you will be given independence to. . . ?

Danforth: I know I will be given the independence because I wouldn't have done this without it.

Question: Have you been assured of that?

Danforth: Well, I have been assured of it and I have asked that question and I have accepted the job on that basis. And I know that we have sufficient legal powers to pursue this. And I have no doubt that we will pursue it diligently.

Question: Senator, what's your biggest concern, going into this, as you look at all of the dynamics surrounding the mission that you've have, all the way back to the Declaration of Independence? What's your single biggest concern as you take on this assignment?

Danforth: Well, I mean, what the goal is is to produce something that the American people can see. So, I guess my biggest concern is the balancing act, because we have to get the facts, even if it entails a grand jury to get the facts.

But we also want to present something that, you know, is the basis of the consent of the people. And so, doing that balancing, I think, is going to be a challenge.

Question: Do you feel like you can satisfy all the conspiracy theorists who are out there? Whatever you do will be attacked by some sector?

Danforth: I have never been in a pursuit where you can satisfy 100 percent of the people, but I would hope people would know that I am trying and that our group is going to try to do a careful job and that we go into this with no preconceived ideas and that we will call them as we see them. And that's what I'm going to do.

Question: Also, some people say that the Davidians did commit suicide, but they did so because of the government tactics. Given that criticism, can you look at—can you fulfill your mission without looking at the entire episode?

Danforth: I think that it is important, and the reason for having this defined mission, is to keep parameters on what we're doing. And I think that what you've asked is really an important question and it's important to understand it.

I take it that if, for example, ATF had never thought about the Branch Davidians, there wouldn't have been this loss of life. So in a way, you could say that any decision that was made, you know, was a decision that led up to what eventually happened.

But I am not going to get into that. I'm not going to get into judgment calls, even if those judgments led to the eventual result, because I think that bad judgments—and I'm not saying they were bad judgments, I'm not presupposing that at all, I have no opinion of it—but whether they were good judgments or bad judgments is a different question than the dark question.

And I think my job is to answer the dark question or the dark questions: Was there a cover up? That's a dark question. Did the government kill people? That's—how did the fire start? And was there shooting?

I mean those are questions that have been raised. Those are—those are questions that go to the basic integrity of government, not judgment calls. And I do want to make it clear in the next few days, while I can still speak about this, what that distinction is.

I don't think that you get a special counsel with subpoena powers to deal with the judgment calls. I just don't think so. I think we try to deal with factual questions, and did the government—really, ultimately, did the government kill people and did the government cover things up, not, you know, what was the chain of events going back to, you know, some earlier time that led eventually to a set of circumstances that led to this. . . .

UNICEF DIRECTOR ON THE SPREAD OF AIDS IN AFRICA
September 15, 1999

New drugs, massive information campaigns, and greater community health efforts were not enough to prevent the spread of AIDS (acquired immunodeficiency syndrome) and infection by HIV (human immunodeficiency virus), the virus that causes the incurable disease, from continuing "nearly unabated" in many parts of the world in 1999. An estimated 2.6 million people were expected to die of AIDS in 1999, the highest yearly total since the epidemic began in the late 1970s. Another 5.6 million would become infected with HIV, bringing the worldwide total for HIV infection to an estimated 33.6 million in 1999. Altogether more than 16 million people had died of the disease. "With an epidemic of this scale, every new infection adds to the ripple effect, impacting families, communities, households and increasingly, businesses and economies," said Dr. Peter Piot, executive director of the United Nations Programme on HIV/AIDS (UNAIDS). Piot released the 1999 data at a news conference in November.

Nowhere was the devastation from the disease greater than in sub-Saharan Africa, where 22 million people were living with HIV. Two million people in Africa died of AIDS—ten times as many as were killed in the region's many wars and civil conflicts. Life expectancy rates—a chief indicator of a country's development status—were declining significantly in several of the countries hardest his by the AIDS epidemic. "By any measure . . . the HIV/AIDS pandemic is the most terrible undeclared war in the world, with the whole of sub-Saharan Africa a killing field," Carol Bellamy, the executive director of the United Nations Children's Fund (UNICEF), told an international conference on AIDS in Africa. (1998 report on AIDS epidemic, Historic Documents of 1998, p. 878)

In the United States, deaths from AIDS continued to decline, in large part because of the availability of antiretroviral drugs that slowed the progress of the disease. But there was no significant change in the HIV infection rate of about 40,000 new cases a year, and the decline in the death rate appeared to be leveling off. AIDS deaths fell by 20 percent between 1997 and 1998, to 17,047 people, but they fell 42 percent between 1996 and 1997. Officials were also concerned about reports that an increasing number of gay men, apparently lulled by the availability of the new drugs, were failing to practice safe sex. If those numbers increased sufficiently, these officials warned, the rate of infection might begin to climb again.

Modern Incarnation of Dante's Inferno

Ninety-five percent of people infected with HIV lived in the Third World, where poverty, limited resources, and inadequate health services allowed the disease to spread nearly unchecked. Roughly 70 percent of all cases occurred in sub-Saharan Africa, where more women than men were infected, reversing the trend in the rest of the world. In the United States and elsewhere, AIDS was spread primarily through homosexual intercourse and by intravenous drug users. The proportion of women infected with HIV through heterosexual intercourse was relatively low; in 1999 women accounted for 20 percent of HIV-infected people in the United States. In Africa, however, HIV spread primarily through heterosexual intercourse. According to the UNAIDS report, about six women were infected for every five men. Girls ages fifteen to nineteen were five times more likely than boys in the same age group to become infected, in part because male-to-female transmission was easier than female to male, and in part because teenage girls often had sexual contact with older men, who were more likely to be infected than teenage boys. Older men often coerced younger girls into sex or bought their favors with gifts, according to the report.

Increasing HIV infection among women also had serious consequences for their children, many of whom had been infected by their mothers either during birth or through nursing. Millions of others were orphaned when their parents died. Worldwide an estimated 8 million children, most of them in Africa, had lost their mothers or both parents to AIDS. In Uganda, 11 percent of the children under age fifteen had lost one or both parents to AIDS.

With both men and women in the prime of life falling victim to the disease, communities across sub-Saharan Africa were finding it hard to absorb the social and economic consequences. In Zimbabwe, where nearly 25 percent of the country's residents were infected, so many farmers had died from AIDS that agricultural production was down 20 percent in 1998. Not only were farmers and laborers dying, but so were teachers, managers, military officers, and others with skills that could not be replaced quickly or easily. "Fundamentally, AIDS is . . . stifling the economic and social infrastructure of the entire continent. It is killing the most productive age group," Stephen Lewis, deputy executive director of UNICEF, said in July. "It is the modern incarnation of . . . Dante's Inferno. Never has Africa faced such a plague."

The consequences of AIDS—a shrinking labor pool, increased health and welfare costs, reduced spending power, and lost investment—were expected to reduce economic growth in sub-Saharan Africa by 1.4 percentage points for each the next twenty years. "HIV is now the single greatest threat to future economic development in Africa," Callisto Madavo, the World Bank's vice president for Africa, told the Washington Post. *Moreover, HIV infection appeared to be growing rapidly in parts of Asia, and some feared that Asia might soon replace Africa as the region with the most people infected.*

A Question of Political Will

Speaking at an international conference on aids in Lusaka, Zambia, on September 15, UNICEF executive director Bellamy challenged political leaders in both Africa and the industrialized world to deal with the AIDS epidemic in Africa with the same intensity that they had devoted to trying to end the region's many armed conflicts. Bellamy outlined five priorities UNICEF had set for combating AIDS, including focusing prevention efforts on adolescents, strengthening community capacities to deal with the crisis, and improving and providing access to health services. But, she said, "we can achieve these goals only with the sustained support of officials at the highest levels of government." She urged political leaders to set goals that could be achieved in the short term, such as ensuring that within two years 70 percent of all women attending prenatal clinics would have access to testing so that they would know their HIV status and be able to take precautions against passing the infection to their babies.

Bellamy also called on governments to devote greater resources to stemming the epidemic. For example, she said, the United States spent $880 million a year to fight 40,000 new cases of HIV infection a year. In Africa, only $160 million was spent to cope with 4 million new cases a year. "This is simply unacceptable," Bellamy declared.

The politics of AIDS struck close to home in 1999, when noisy protests by an AIDS activist group forced a change in U.S. trade policy. Drugs were widely available in the United States through various health insurance and other programs, but most HIV/AIDS patients in developing countries could not afford them. Although some countries had the capability to develop and manufacture less expensive generic drugs, the Clinton administration sought to protect the patents of its pharmaceutical companies by threatening to bring trade sanctions against foreign companies that manufactured generic drugs before the patents on those drugs had expired. A loophole in the international trade agreement permitted countries facing health emergencies to make their own generics if they paid a licensing fee to the patent holder, but the United States decided to interpret this provision strictly and threatened trade sanctions against countries that did not go along with its interpretation. In 1998 a threatened sanction induced Thailand to drop its plans to produce a generic AIDS drug. In 1999 the Clinton administration also threatened South Africa with sanctions, but after activists with the domestic group ACT-UP (AIDS Coalition to Unleash Power) began disrupting Vice President Al Gore's campaign appearances, Gore met with South African president Thabo Mbeki, and the trade threats were lifted September 17.

The U.S. policy had also been criticized by Doctors Without Borders, the group that won the Nobel Peace Prize in 1999 for its work in war-ravaged countries around the world, and by World Bank officials. One official said that drug price structure in the United States "shows an increasing disconnect with the needs of the majority of the people in the world." The drugs at issue were not the antivirals that slowed the progress of HIV for many American patients; these were not only too expensive but also required a more sophisticated health delivery system than most developing countries could afford. The real focus was on drugs to treat the opportunistic diseases associated with AIDS, such as tuberculosis, meningitis, and diarrhea, which caused 80 percent of all deaths in AIDS patients. At the World Trade Organization meeting in Seattle in November, Clinton promised that the United States would show "flexibility" in granting countries the right to develop cheaper drugs to treat HIV- and AIDS-related illnesses. (WTO meeting, p. 797)

Following are excerpts from a speech delivered September 15, 1999, by Carol Bellamy, executive director of the United Nations Children's Fund, at the International Conference on AIDS and Sexually Transmitted Diseases, held in Lusaka, Zambia:

Mr. Chairman, Professor Luo, Excellencies, Distinguished Delegates, Ladies and Gentlemen:

On behalf of the United Nations Children's Fund, I am very pleased to join you for this vitally important Conference. The high level of representation here is a sign of the gravity with which Africa and the international community are treating the crisis of HIV/AIDS—and of the urgent need to set priorities for prevention and treatment.

Mr. Chairman, I will not dwell for long on the statistics. The litany of devastation is familiar to all of you:

- Some 200,000 people, most of them children and women, died in 1998 as a result of armed conflict on the African continent—and yet as you have heard, 2 million Africans were killed by AIDS in that same year.
- In sub-Saharan Africa, there are 22 million people living with HIV—two-thirds of the world's total.
- Mother-to-child transmission continues to be the leading cause of infection among young children.
- More than 8 million children have lost their mother or both parents to AIDS, with the total expected to reach 13 million by the year 2000, with the vast majority of them in sub-Saharan Africa.
- The number of child-headed households is rising sharply;
- Millions of children are suffering the effects of being stigmatised;
- And decades of gains for child survival and development are being wiped out, threatening prospects for social progress and better standards of life for all.

By any measure, Mr. Chairman, the HIV/AIDS pandemic is the most terrible undeclared war in the world, with the whole of sub-Saharan Africa a killing field.

The international community, the United Nations, the Organisation of African Unity (OAU) and African leaders at many levels have worked tirelessly to bring peace to places like Liberia and Sierra Leone, using the same combination of tenacity and skill that President Chiluba recently brought to bear in talks to end the conflict in the Democratic Republic of the Congo—talks that were concluded in this very hall just a few weeks ago, before throngs of world media representatives.

Mr. Chairman, we must ratchet up the fight against HIV/AIDS to that same level of intensity and public visibility—and we must do it now.

As Peter Piot put it, AIDS in Africa, far from being "a larger-than-usual medical problem," is in fact a massive development catastrophe requiring an emergency response. The question is how to organise a response that is both urgent and commensurate with the scale of the pandemic.

UNICEF has identified five priority areas as part of our contribution to the International Partnership Against AIDS in Africa.

First, we must mobilize commitment and capacity to act. This includes breaking, once and for all, the "conspiracy of silence" that continues to hide the dimensions of the HIV/AIDS crisis from the very people most affected by it. It means supporting the development of policies and strategies; building partnerships; and mobilizing resources.

Second, we must focus prevention efforts among young people, through such efforts as promoting youth-friendly health services, life-skills training and social mobilization.

Third, we must reduce the risk of mother-to-child transmission of HIV by encouraging all women to learn their HIV status, and by supporting preventative measures, including advice on infant-feeding options.

Fourth, we must provide greatly expanded care for orphans and children affected by HIV/AIDS. This means strengthening families and community capacities to protect and care for children and providing access to basic services.

Fifth, UNICEF intends to take the lead to provide care and support for our own staff who are living with HIV, and to help ensure that we provide a model that other organisations and industries can emulate.

Mr. Chairman, we can achieve these goals only with the sustained support of officials at the highest levels of government.

At the same time, the international community and multilateral agencies and non-governmental groups have a major role to play.

Prevention can succeed only if we help vulnerable countries to strengthen their health systems to cope with the huge new demands that are being placed on them by the pandemic.

Poor countries need more than encouragement. They need income support, debt relief and strong social safety nets.

Most of all, they need resources. Mr. Chairman, if the international community is to come to grips with HIV/AIDS, it must eliminate the staggering inequities and inequalities that are contributing to the spread of the pandemic—along with many other consequences of global poverty.

The United States, for example, spends $880 million a year fighting HIV/AIDS, in the face of 40,000 new cases annually. But Africa, which must deal with 4 million new cases a year, spends only between $149 million and $160 million. This is simply unacceptable.

UNICEF, for its part, is moving to significantly strengthen our support of governments and non-governmental partners to combat HIV/AIDS in Africa, bolstering our staff in regional and country offices while stepping up our country-level support for practical action. At the same time, UNICEF, with the help of its partners in UNAIDS, is working to coordinate closely with other UN agencies.

All these things are more essential than ever, for the explosive spread of the virus is straining resources and capabilities at all levels.

Care-givers throughout sub-Saharan Africa—ordinary people, mostly women—are rendering heroic services in tending to so many terminally ill people through home-based care, and helping orphans and other vulnerable children through informal networks. They are to be congratulated for their efforts, for they are working against tremendous odds.

For example, we are seeing that the traditional African way of relying on the extended family to care for children orphaned by AIDS is becoming increasingly untenable. Many households can barely afford to keep the children, let alone afford to send them to school—and as a result, orphans are often among the first to be denied the right to an education.

Given these worsening conditions, it is clear that alternative models of orphan care are needed.

Important groundwork has already been laid. Since the early part of the decade, the Government of Uganda has actively promoted new approaches for orphan care, drawing on the collaborative energy of non-governmental organisations and community-based groups.

One outcome has been the establishment of the Ugandan Community-Based Association for Children, a national association set up with assistance from UNICEF that provides training to local groups in such areas as child care, organisational management, and information exchange.

In Malawi, the Government began formulating a national policy for orphans in 1991, a policy that it has kept up and developed. It includes actively promoting community-based programmes for orphans with the cooperation of NGOs and churches and the support of UNICEF.

A National Coordinating Board—a collaborative body not controlled by a Government ministry and without paid staff—trains communities and organisations in all aspects of child care. Malawi also offers free primary education for all children.

In another area, the prevention of mother-to-child transmission of HIV, UNICEF—working closely with WHO [World Health Organization] and UNFPA [UN Family Planning Agency] and the UNAIDS Secretariat—is taking the lead in supporting government efforts in many of the most severely affected countries of sub-Saharan Africa.

Last year, we began launching pilot interventions in 11 countries—interventions designed to reduce the paediatric HIV infection rate while simultaneously strengthening health facilities for women and their partners.

The principal aim of these efforts is to provide voluntary HIV testing and counseling for pregnant women. An estimated 30,000 women who are found to be HIV-positive will then be provided with one of the recently developed short anti-retroviral drug regimens; advice on infant feeding; and support for the feeding method of their choice.

These interventions can reduce transmission rates by half. In this connection, Mr. Chairman, we are greatly encouraged by the very recent news of a promising and dramatically more affordable drug regimen to prevent mother-to-child transmission of HIV.

UNICEF is working on an urgent basis with WHO and other UNAIDS partners assess the implications of this drug, Nevirapine, whose effectiveness has undergone initial study in Uganda by the US National Institutes of Health—the results of which are described in the latest issue of the medical journal *The Lancet*. The indications are that Nevirapine can reduce HIV transmission by 50 per cent with a single dose of the drug to the mother and infant—at a per-treatment cost of about $4.

Mr. Chairman, it is true that even a $4 drug treatment will challenge the health budgets of many African countries—but the cost of failing to introduce this preventative regimen will be incalculably higher.

If immediate steps are not taken to dramatically reduce the risk of mother-to-child transmission, already overburdened health services will simply be unable to cope with the needs of the huge numbers of very sick and dying young children.

The problems that communities face in coping with orphans is enormous, but they will be far much worse if a substantial proportion of those orphans are also sick with AIDS—a problem that we hope can be substantially prevented.

Mr. Chairman, the figures on HIV/AIDS in Africa that you have heard in recent days are framed by one terrible, inescapable fact—that it is young people, people up to the age of 24, who are bearing the brunt of the casualties. This is especially true of young girls, who have significantly higher infection rates.

Young people are disproportionately at risk because, in a time of sexual awakening, they are deprived of the right to health services and nutrition, and to a safe and supportive environment free of exploitation and abuse—including protection from coerced sex. And more often than not, they are denied the right to participate and to make their views heard in matters that affect them.

Mr. Chairman, the future course of the HIV/AIDS pandemic lies in the hands of young people. It is absolutely vital that we do everything necessary to arm them with the knowledge they need to protect themselves and their communities.

That is why UNICEF has moved to redouble our efforts to mobilize and support programmes to address the rights of young people to development and to participation.

These include:

- Supporting the right of adolescents to information and life skills, which UNICEF and its partners are doing through a range of activities in schools and through NGOs and the media in countries like Uganda, Zimbabwe, Zambia and Namibia;
- Promoting youth-friendly services, such as health care in countries like Zambia and Kenya
- Building safe and supportive environments with programmes that draw on the help of peers, parents, teachers and health workers in countries like Cote D'Ivoire and Mali
- And providing opportunities for adolescents to participate in decisions, not only in matters that affect them directly, but in the larger decisions that are taken in civil society.

As you heard during Monday's presentation on "young people's perspectives on HIV programmes," many young people have some knowledge about HIV/AIDS—but consultations with them and existing data show that they do not have all the information they need. Indeed, in sub-Saharan Africa, it has been estimated that 90 per cent of HIV-positive people are unaware that they are infected.

We urgently need to address this knowledge gap, using language and formats that young people can appreciate.

At the same time, we also know that the acquisition of knowledge about how to prevent and treat HIV does not necessarily bring about broad behavioural change among youth. However, there is increasing evidence that awareness of one's HIV status can be a powerful motivating force for behavioural change.

To counter the rising HIV infection rate among young people, the UNAIDS World AIDS Campaign has focused on young people for the last two years. This year's theme, Listen, Learn, Live, is aimed at promoting the participation of young people in prevention efforts, raising public awareness of the crisis, harnessing public and private resources—and strengthening support for young people affected by the pandemic.

The UNAIDS Secretariat together with its co-sponsors has been particularly active in widening the network of public and private-sector partnerships.

You may have seen Bill Roedy, the President of MTV, discussing HIV/AIDS issues with young people at the Youth Village this week. MTV deserves immense credit for its ongoing efforts to broadcast the importance of HIV-prevention messages on their music television throughout the world, which are reaching and influencing millions of young people.

What is needed now are increased efforts to promote youth participation and commitment; more services aimed at youth; more parental involvement; more education and information, using schools and other sites; more protection for girls, orphaned children, and young women; and more partnerships with people with HIV and AIDS.

Those measures are already being applied in such places as Zambia, where increasing numbers of young people are working as educators and peer counselors, helping to de-stigmatise HIV/AIDS for other youths, and easing the burden on health workers.

These are important beginnings. But more effective approaches are needed—and they must be put in place quickly if Africa is to make significant headway in stemming the pandemic.

Mr. Chairman, Excellencies, Distinguished Delegates: let us speak frankly.

It is already obvious that at the rate the disease is spreading, governments cannot keep up with increasing demands to help support children orphaned by AIDS; provide adequate levels voluntary and confidential testing; or mount effective and widespread prevention and treatment programmes for young people.

The seriousness of the situation can be seen in the number of seemingly simple things that have not been done.

For example, in many sub-Saharan African countries, it has been found that more than 25 per cent of women aged 15 to 19 are unaware of even one effective way of avoiding HIV infection. And in recent representative surveys, over 30 per cent of young women in virtually all countries expressed the view that a healthy looking person could not possibly be infected with the AIDS virus.

What I am suggesting, Mr. Chairman, is that we have reached a point at which governments may need to consider new ways in which to do business.

It is a process that national leaders can begin by recognising the capabilities of communities and the poor to help themselves.

This means empowering communities—especially poor people—to mobilize themselves to act, and to do so in ways that they are able to see and understand the results of their actions.

Mr. Chairman, the very complexity of the HIV/AIDS problem is why no standard solution exists. But there is every reason to believe that those most directly affected by the problem are in the best position to find solutions that work for them. The key is to recognise the poor as key actors in their own development, rather than as passive recipients of services and commodities dispensed by health care workers, teachers, religious leaders and others.

Distinguished Delegates, I am convinced there is a need to identify some practical things that all countries in sub-Saharan Africa can do to bring about real results in a short period of time.

I am talking about a very limited number of goals—goals that we know can be achieved in a short time if we pull together—that would be relevant to all of the countries in this part of the world—and that could be easily monitored.

You yourselves need to identify what these goals are. But let me suggest some possibilities:

1. Begin an effort to ensure that by a target date—say the end of the year 2002—that most adolescent women will have sufficient knowledge of the

risks of contracting HIV/AIDS—and of the ways in which they can protect themselves.

2. Take steps to ensure that within two years, at least 70 per cent of all women attending ante-natal clinics will have access to voluntary and confidential testing so that they will know their HIV status.

3. Institute steps to make sure that by the end of 2002, at least half of all local authorities will have found a way to make sure that families caring for orphans are able to supply them with adequate food, access to education and to basic health care.

Mr. Chairman, Excellencies, Distinguished Delegates: time is running out.

The monstrous proportions of the HIV/AIDS pandemic in sub-Saharan Africa show that, far from simply another new problem among other development problems, the disease is rapidly becoming a significant and growing threat to peace and stability in the world.

Let us ensure that all our actions are commensurate with the danger.

Thank you.

NATIONAL SECURITY COMMISSION ON THREATS IN THE NEXT CENTURY
September 15, 1999

The federal government received a barrage of warnings during 1999 that the greatest threat to the United States and its citizens during the twenty-first century was likely to come from terrorism, both at home and abroad. Experts on foreign policy and national security issued a series of reports suggesting that ethnic conflicts around the world, the collapse of nation-states following the end of the cold war, global economic interdependence, and the ready availability of chemical and biological weapons were factors that would make terrorism increasingly prevalent in the future. The United States, because of its position—at least for the foreseeable future—as the world's most powerful nation and biggest economy would be an attractive target for disaffected groups and individuals, the experts said.

As if to prove the point, federal officials in December intercepted what appeared to be a plot to smuggle bomb-making equipment into the United States. Authorities on December 14 captured, and then lodged charges against, an Algerian man, Ahmed Ressem, who crossed into Washington state from Canada carrying a large quantity of material suitable for making bombs. Five days later a Canadian woman, Lucia Garofalo, was arrested at a Vermont border crossing with another Algerian man. Federal officials said on December 31 that Ressem and Garofalo—along with a third man arrested in New York City on December 30—had ties to an Algerian terrorist organization, the Armed Islamic Group. The arrests, shortly before the New Year, heightened public fears that terrorists would try to capitalize on worldwide celebrations commemorating the last year of the second millennium. U.S. officials heightened security at many border crossings. No significant terrorism incidents occurred, and the prospect of Middle Easterners lobbing bombs into crowded shopping malls quickly faded from the headlines.

Commission on National Security Report

At least four major reports detailing national security concerns for the twenty-first century landed on the desks of policymakers and opinion lead-

*ers during 1999, each the result of careful study by experts who had been
assembled to peer into their collective crystal balls. The common theme
among all the reports was that the United States probably had more to fear
from what the experts called "nontraditional" threats, such as terrorism
and the accidental or purposeful disruption of economically vital computer
systems, than from the large-scale wars that characterized the previous
three centuries.*

*The one report that appeared to have the greatest potential to influence
national policy came from a panel appointed by the Defense Department
and consisting of influential Washington insiders and national security
experts from both major political parties. Called the United States Commission on National Security/21st Century, the panel was chaired by former senators Gary Hart, a Democrat, and Warren B. Rudman, a Republican. Among its members were former defense secretary James Schlesinger,
former House Speaker Newt Gingrich, and former House Foreign Affairs
Committee chairman Lee Hamilton.*

*The commission made the first phase of its report public on September
15. That report described the likely national security challenges and threats
of the twenty-first century. Second and third phases, planned for release
during 2000 and 2001, were to describe U.S. national security interests
and objectives and lay out prescriptions for changes in policy and legislation. Members said they hoped their findings would influence decisions
made by the president and members of Congress elected in 2000.*

*Perhaps the fundamental message of the commission report was that
recognizing threats in the twenty-first century might not be as easy as in
the past. The major threats faced by the United States in the twentieth century—including fascism, communism, and the economic chaos of the
Great Depression—were readily acknowledged by most Americans, and
when the time came for action there was a general consensus about how to
counter those threats.*

*In the future, the commission said, threats to U.S. national and eco-
nomic security likely would be more diffuse, coming in a variety of forms
and from sources that might not always be apparent, even to the country's
leadership. Such threats, the panel said, might consist of "unannounced
attacks by subnational groups using genetically engineered pathogens
against American cities. They may consist of attacks against an increasingly integrated and vulnerable international economic infrastructure over
which no single body exercises control. They may consist, too, of an unraveling of the fabric of national identity itself, leading several important
countries to fail or disintegrate, generating catalytic regional crises in
their wake."*

*While steering away from a frightening prediction of global chaos dur-
ing the twenty-first century, the panel did suggest that numerous trends
underway at the close of the twentieth century had the potential for serious
risks to world peace and, therefore, American security. The United States
would remain the single greatest global power, both militarily and eco-*

nomically, through at least the first quarter of the century, the commission said. But U.S. power would come under escalating challenges, both from other countries and groups that transcend national boundaries. Those challenges would limit the U.S. ability "to impose our will" and would make Americans increasingly vulnerable to attacks, both at home and abroad.

"States, terrorists, and other disaffected groups will acquire weapons of mass destruction, and some will use them," the commission said. "Americans will likely die on American soil, possibly in large numbers."

The most significant technological developments of the late twentieth century—growing access to high-speed computers, the birth of the Internet, and biotechnology—will pose national security challenges in the next century, the commissioners said. Governments and groups hostile to the United States will have access to those technologies and will use them to launch "nontraditional attacks," offsetting American military and economic might. As it becomes more dependent on technology, and as its economy becomes more intertwined with the rest of the world, the United States will be increasingly vulnerable to attacks such as disruptions of computer services, the commission noted. Disruptions of economically vital energy supplies also could occur, the commission said, theorizing for example about the prospect of an anti-American regime coming to power in Saudi Arabia or other oil-producing states and cutting the flow of oil to the United States and its allies.

Some of the sources of future threats already were obvious at the end of the twentieth century, the commission said. For example, the collapse of the Soviet Union had led to the revival of ethnic conflicts in the Balkans and the Caucasus that had been suppressed for nearly a half-century by communist regimes. The United States and its NATO allies went to war for eleven weeks in 1999 to try to stop ethnic bloodshed in Kosovo. Similar challenges will arise in the twenty-first century, the commission said, forcing the major powers to "struggle to devise an accountable and effective institutional response. . . ."

Dealing with the new threats to security and global peace could be more difficult than in the past, the commission added. Deterring threats by maintaining massive military forces capable of defeating any combination of enemies—the underlying concept of U.S. security for more than two generations—"will not work as it once did," the commission said. "In many cases it may not work at all." The big challenge for the United States will be to find a balance "between activism and restraint" in a world where even the most important global power will have to understand the limits to its power

Rudman said the commission would face its own challenge in coming up with recommendations for restructuring U.S. military and national security forces to meet the threats of the twenty-first century. He noted that the U.S. national security establishment—the military services and the foreign policy and intelligence agencies—was built on legislation enacted in 1947, in response to the lessons of World War II. "But we are not in 1947, we are looking from 2000 to 2025," Rudman told reporters. Some of the necessary changes might be "highly controversial" in the short term, he said.

Countering Terrorism

Several other reports published during 1999 contained specific warnings about the dangers posed by terrorism and the lack of preparation in the United States to meet those dangers. Experts said American officials and citizens had become complacent about terrorism, often viewing it as something more common overseas. But several major terrorism incidents during the 1980s and 1990s—the bombings of the World Trade Center in New York City and of the federal building in Oklahoma City, for example— should alert Americans that terrorists and deranged individuals could strike within U.S. boundaries, the reports said.

One of the reports was submitted to the president and Congress on December 15 by the Advisory Panel to Assess Domestic Response Capabilities for Terrorism Involving Weapons of Mass Destruction. That panel was chaired by Virginia governor James S. Gilmore III, and included retired military officers and intelligence officials, emergency planners, medical experts, and state and local officials. Congress had mandated the panel in the fiscal 1999 defense authorization bill (PL 105–261), enacted in 1998.

The advisory panel used as a focal piece the 1995 attack on the Tokyo subway system by an apocalyptic religious cult, the Aum Shinrikyo, using nerve gas. Twelve people were killed by the attack, but police uncovered enough nerve gas in the cult's possession to kill more than 4 million people. The panel called that attack a "turning point" in terrorism because it was the first time a "nonstate group" had used chemical weapons against civilians, and it might serve as an example for other groups. Perhaps the most frightening aspect of the attack, the panel said, was that it undermined the conventional wisdom that terrorists almost always had rational motives and were primarily interested in gaining publicity for their cause—not in killing people—and that careful investigative work might be able to uncover such plots beforehand. The Tokyo case showed that terrorists could act for reasons totally incomprehensible to governments and could be interested in killing as many people as possible.

With the Tokyo case in mind, the advisory panel devoted much of its report to what it said was a lack of communication and coordination among federal, state, and local agencies responsible for dealing with emergency incidents such as a terrorism attack. Local and state governments had difficulty in getting information and assistance from the federal agencies that tracked terrorism threats, the panel said, and often there was no clear strategy for determining which agencies had what responsibilities in the event of a terrorist attack. Despite efforts in recent years to improve coordination, the panel said that "too much ambiguity remains about the issue of 'who's in charge' if an incident occurs."

Another commission authorized by Congress submitted a report with many of the same findings on July 8. Headed by John Deutch, the former director of the Central Intelligence Agency, and Senator Arlen Specter, R-Pa., that panel called on the president to appoint a national director responsible for combating weapons proliferation and coordinating the response of dozens of federal, state, and local agencies to terrorist incidents.

The General Accounting Office (GAO), the congressional watchdog agency, also released a series of reports about terrorism issues during 1999, some of which focused on countering the threat of chemical and biological terrorism. In a report sent to Congress September 14, the GAO said federal agencies, including the FBI, needed to provide better assessments than in the past on the potential threat of chemical and biological terrorism. Noting that President Bill Clinton had requested $10 billion for counterterrorism programs in fiscal 2000—more than a 30 percent increase over the fiscal 1999 level—the GAO said Congress needed more information on how best to combat domestic terrorism.

While not playing down the prospect that terrorist organizations would use chemical or biological weapons, the GAO said a terrorist organization had to be extremely well organized and financed, with highly trained personnel, if it was to succeed in launching a successful attack. The agency noted that Aum Shinrikyo possessed those characteristics but was unable to carry out the widespread, crippling attack it planned.

In a report issued in June, the GAO focused on exercises held by federal agencies to train personnel and test response capabilities for terrorism incidents. The GAO said agencies had been holding an increasing number of such exercises in recent years, but it suggested that more of them should be of the "no notice" variety, in which tests were run without warning to determine how well individuals and agencies responded in a real emergency.

Following are excerpts from the "introduction" and "major themes and implications" from the report, "New World Coming: American Security in the 21st Century," issued September 15, 1999, by the congressionally mandated United States Commission on National Security/21st Century:

Introduction

The future, in essence, is this: The American "moment" in world politics, which combines bloodless victory in the final stage of the Cold War with the apparent global triumph of fundamental American ideals, will not last forever. Nothing wrought by man does. In the next 25 years, the United States will engage in an increasingly complex world to assure the benefits that we—and most of the world with us—derive from American leadership.

As powerful as the United States may well be over the next 25 years, the world will not be tidily managed, whether from Washington or from anywhere else. History has not ended, mankind's cultural diversity endures, and both the will to power and the pull of passionate ideas remain as relevant as ever in political life both within and among nations.

A diffusion of power thus stands before us, but not necessarily one of the classical sort. A new balance of power may arise that would be intelligible even to the statesmen of the 18th and 19th centuries, but something more, and some-thing different, will overlap and perhaps overwhelm it. The ever tighter harnessing of science to technological innovation, and of that innovation to global economic integration, is changing the rules of international engagement. It is even affecting the identity of its engaging parties. The sway of state power has always fluctuated within society, and states have often competed with other institutions for influence beyond their borders. But the challenges now being mounted to national authority and control—if not to the national idea itself—are both novel and mighty.

It is not a foregone conclusion that the role of the state will be permanently diminished, or the system of sovereign states reformed or replaced on account of these challenges. But both the system and its member units are certain to change as a consequence, as they have always changed from having been tested. In the years ahead, borders of every sort—geo-graphical, communal, and psychological—will be stressed, strained, and compelled to reconfiguration. As the elements and vulnerabilities of national power shift, they will often leave current institutional arrangements at logger-heads with reality. Already the traditional functions of law, police work, and military power have begun to blur before our eyes as new threats arise.

Notable among these new threats is the prospect of an attack on U.S. cities by independent or state-supported terrorists using weapons of mass destruction. Traditional distinctions between national defense and domestic security will be challenged further as the new century unfolds, and both conventional policies and bureaucratic arrangements will be stretched to and beyond the breaking point unless those policies and arrangements are reformed.

The future is also one of rising stakes, for good and for ill. Humanity may find ways to compose its disagreements, succor its poor, heal its sick, and find new purpose in common global goals. But if it fails at these tasks, it stands to fail more spectacularly than ever. That is because greater global connectedness leads one way to benefit and another way to misfortune. Economic downturns that have usually been episodic and local may become, thanks to the integration of global financial markets, more systemic in their origins and hence more global in their effects. The greater wealth that may be expected to flow from global economic integration will nevertheless produce growing inequality within and among nations. The march of science and technology, too, will provide ever more powerful tools—tools that can be used for benefit in the right hands, but that may pose even genocidal dangers should they fall into the wrong ones. The next 25 years may well force mankind back to first principles over the ethical dilemmas inherent in biotechnology. Our concept of national security will expand. Our political values will be tested as our society changes. In every sphere, our moral imaginations will be exercised anew.

Some things, however, will not change. We will no doubt revisit many times the three oldest questions of political life: How is legitimate authority constituted? What is fair in social and economic life? How do we reconcile disagreements? Historical principles will still apply as we ponder these and other questions. There will still be great powers, and their mutual engagement will still matter. As ever, much will depend on the sagacity and good character of leadership. Misunderstandings, misjudgments, and mistakes will still occur, but so will acts of brave leadership borne on the insight of exceptional men and women.

The upshot of the changes ahead is that Americans are now, and increasingly will become, less secure than they believe them-selves to be. The reason is that we may not easily recognize many of the threats in our future. They will differ significantly from the dangers to which history has accustomed us: ranting dictators spouting hatred, vast armies on the march, huge missiles at the ready. They may consist instead of unannounced attacks by sub-national groups using genetically engineered pathogens against American cities. They may consist of attacks against an increasingly integrated and vulnerable international economic infrastructure over which no single body exercises control. They may consist, too, of an unraveling of the fabric of national identity itself, leading several important countries to fail or disintegrate, generating catalytic regional crises in their wake. . . .

Major Themes and Implications

The foregoing analysis leads us to the following general conclusions about the world that is now emerging, and the American role in it for the next 25 years.

1. America will become increasingly vulnerable to hostile attack on our homeland, and our military superiority will not entirely protect us.

The United States will be both absolutely and relatively stronger than any other state or combination of states. Although a global competitor to the United States is unlikely to arise over the next 25 years, emerging powers—either singly or in coalition—will increasingly constrain U.S. options regionally and limit its strategic influence. As a result, we will remain limited in our ability to impose our will, and we will be vulnerable to an increasing range of threats against American forces and citizens overseas as well as at home. American influence will increasingly be both embraced and resented abroad, as U.S. cultural, economic, and political power persists and perhaps spreads. States, terrorists, and other disaffected groups will acquire weapons of mass destruction and mass disruption, and some will use them. Americans will likely die on American soil, possibly in large numbers.

2. Rapid advances in information and biotechnologies will create new vulnerabilities for U.S. security.

Governments or groups hostile to the United States and its interests will gain access to advanced technologies. They will seek to counter U.S. military advantages through the possession of these technologies and their actual use in non-traditional attacks. Moreover, as our society becomes increasingly dependent on knowledge-based technology for producing goods and providing services, new vulnerabilities to such attacks will arise.

3. New technologies will divide the world as well as draw it together.

In the next century people around the world in both developed and developing countries will be able to communicate with each other almost instantaneously. New technologies will increase productivity and create a transnational cyberclass of people. We will see much greater mobility and emigration among educated elites from less to more developed societies. We will be increasingly deluged by information, and have less time to process and interpret it. We will learn to cure illnesses, prolong and enrich life, and routinely clone it, but at the same time, advances in biotechnology will create moral dilemmas. An anti-technology backlash is possible, and even likely, as the adoption of emerging technologies creates new moral, cultural, and economic divisions.

4. The national security of all advanced states will be increasingly affected by the vulnerabilities of the evolving global economic infrastructure.

The economic future will be more difficult to predict and to manage. The emergence or strengthening of significant global economic actors will cause realignments of economic power. Global changes in the next quarter-century will produce opportunities and vulnerabilities. Overall global economic growth will continue, albeit unevenly. At the same time, economic integration and fragmentation will co-exist. Serious and unexpected economic downturns, major disparities of wealth, volatile capital flows, increasing vulnerabilities in global electronic infrastructures, labor and social disruptions, and pressures for increased protectionism will also occur. Many countries will be simultaneously more wealthy and more insecure. Some societies will find it difficult to develop the human capital and social cohesion necessary to employ new technologies productively. Their frustrations will be endemic and sometimes dangerous. For most advanced states, major threats to national security will broaden beyond the purely military.

5. Energy will continue to have major strategic significance.

Although energy distribution and consumption patterns will shift, we are unlikely to see dramatic changes in energy technology on a world scale in the next quarter century. Demand for fossil fuel will increase as major developing economies grow, increasing most rapidly in Asia. American dependence on foreign sources of energy will also grow over the next two decades. In the absence of events that alter significantly the price of oil, the stability of the world oil market will continue to depend on an uninterrupted supply of oil from the Persian Gulf, and the location of all key fossil fuel deposits will retain geopolitical significance.

6. All borders will be more porous; some will bend and some will break.

New technologies will continue to stretch and strain all existing borders—physical and social. Citizens will communicate with and form allegiances to individuals or movements anywhere in the world. Traditional bonds between states and their citizens can no longer be taken for granted, even in the United States. Many countries will have difficulties keeping dangers out of their territories, but their governments will still be committed to upholding the integrity of their borders. Global connectivity will allow "big ideas" to spread quickly around the globe. Some ideas may be religious in nature, some populist, some devoted to democracy and human rights. Whatever their content, the stage will be set for mass action to have social impact beyond the borders and control of existing political structures.

7. The sovereignty of states will come under pressure, but will endure.

The international system will wrestle constantly over the next quarter century to establish the proper balance between fealty to the state on the one hand, and the impetus to build effective transnational institutions on the other. This struggle will be played out in the debate over international institutions to regulate financial markets, international policing and peace-making agencies, as well as several other shared global problems. Nevertheless, global forces, especially economic ones, will continue to batter the concept of national sovereignty. The state, as we know it, will also face challenges to its sovereignty under the mandate of evolving international law and by disaffected groups, including terrorists and criminals. Nonetheless, the principle of national sovereignty will endure, albeit in changed forms.

8. Fragmentation or failure of states will occur, with destabilizing effects on neighboring states.

Global and regional dynamics will normally bind states together, but events in major countries will still drive whether the world is peaceful or violent. States will differ in their ability to seize technological and economic opportunities, establish the social and political infrastructure necessary for economic growth, build political institutions responsive to the aspirations of their citizens, and find the leadership necessary to guide them through an era of uncertainty and risk. Some important states may not be able to manage these challenges and could fragment or fail. The result will be an increase in the rise of suppressed nationalisms, ethnic or religious violence, humanitarian disasters, major catalytic regional crises, and the spread of dangerous weapons.

9. Foreign crises will be replete with atrocities and the deliberate terrorizing of civilian populations.

Interstate wars will occur over the next 25 years, but most violence will erupt from conflicts internal to current territorial states. As the desire for self-determination spreads, and many governments fail to adapt to new economic and social realities, minorities will be less likely to tolerate bad or prejudicial government. In consequence, the number of new states, international protectorates, and zones of autonomy will increase, and many will be born in violence. The major powers will struggle to devise an accountable and effective institutional response to such crises.

10. Space will become a critical and competitive military environment.

The U.S. use of space for military purposes will expand, but other countries will also learn to exploit space for both commercial and military purposes. Many other countries will learn to launch satellites to communicate and spy. Weapons will likely be put in space. Space will also become permanently manned.

11. The essence of war will not change.

Despite the proliferation of highly sophisticated and remote means of attack, the essence of war will remain the same. There will be casualties, carnage, and death; it will not be like a video game. What will change will be the kinds of actors and the weapons available to them. While some societies will attempt to limit violence and damage, others will seek to maximize them, particularly against those societies with a lower tolerance for casualties.

12. U.S. intelligence will face more challenging adversaries, and even excellent intelligence will not prevent all surprises.

Micro-sensors and electronic communications will continue to expand intelligence collection capabilities around the world. As a result of the proliferation of other technologies, however, many countries and disaffected groups will develop techniques of denial and deception in an attempt to thwart U.S. intelligence efforts—despite U.S. technological superiority. In any event, the United States will continue to confront strategic shocks, as intelligence analysis and human judgments will fail to detect all dangers in an ever-changing world.

13. The United States will be called upon frequently to intervene militarily in a time of uncertain alliances and with the prospect of fewer forward-deployed forces.

Political changes abroad, economic considerations, and the increased vulnerability of U.S. bases around the world will increase pressures on the United States to reduce substantially its forward military presence in Europe and Asia. In dealing with security crises, the 21st century will be characterized more by episodic "posses of the willing" than the traditional World War II-style alliance systems. The United States will increasingly find itself wishing to form coalitions but increasingly unable to find partners willing and able to carry out combined military operations.

14. The emerging security environment in the next quarter century will require different military and other national capabilities.

The United States must act together with its allies to shape the future of the international environment, using all the instruments of American diplomatic, economic, and military power. The type of conflict in which this country will generally engage in the first quarter of the 21st century will require sustainable military capabilities characterized by stealth, speed, range, unprecedented accuracy, lethality, strategic mobility, superior intelligence, and the overall will and ability to prevail. It is essential to maintain U.S. technological superiority, despite the unavoidable tension between acquisition of advanced capabilities and the maintenance of current capabilities. The mix and effectiveness of overall American capabilities need to be rethought and adjusted, and substantial changes in non-military national capabilities will also be needed. Discriminating and hard choices will be required.

In many respects, the world ahead seems amenable to basic American interests and values. A world pried open by the information revolution is a world less hospitable to tyranny and more friendly to human liberty. A more prosperous world is, on balance, a world more conducive to democracy and less tolerant of fatalism and the dour dogmas that often attend it. A less socially rigid, freer, and self-regulating world also accords with our deepest political beliefs and our central political metaphors—the checks and balances of our Constitution, the "invisible hand" of the market, our social creed of E Pluribus Unum, and the concept of federalism itself.

Nevertheless, a world amenable to our interests and values will not come into being by itself. Much of the world will resent and oppose us, if not for . . . our preeminence, then for the fact that others often perceive the United States as exercising its power with arrogance and self-absorption. There will also be much apprehension and confusion as the world changes. National leaderships will have their hands full, and some will make mistakes.

As a result, for many years to come Americans will become increasingly less secure, and much less secure than they now believe themselves to be. That is because many of the threats emerging in our future will differ significantly from those of the past, not only in their physical but also in their psychological effects. While conventional conflicts will still be possible, the most serious threat to our security may consist of unannounced attacks on American cities by sub-national groups using genetically engineered pathogens. Another may be a well-planned cyber-attack on the air traffic control system on the East Coast of the United States, as some 200 commercial aircraft are trying to land safely in a morning's rain and fog. Other threats may inhere in assaults against an increasingly integrated and complex, but highly vulnerable, international economic infrastructure whose operation lies beyond the control of any single body. Threats may also loom from an unraveling of the fabric of national identity itself, and the consequent failure or collapse of several major countries.

Taken together, the evidence suggests that threats to American security will be more diffuse, harder to anticipate, and more difficult to neutralize than ever before. Deterrence will not work as it once did; in many cases it may not work at all. There will be a blurring of boundaries: between homeland defense and foreign policy; between sovereign states and a plethora of protectorates and autonomous zones; between the pull of national loyalties on individual citizens and the pull of loyalties both more local and more global in nature.

While the likelihood of major conflicts between powerful states will decrease, conflict itself will likely increase. The world that lies in store for us over the next 25 years will surely challenge our received wisdom about how to protect American interests and advance American values. In such an environment the United States needs a sure understanding of its objectives, and a coherent strategy to deal with both the dangers and the opportunities ahead.

UN HUMAN RIGHTS COMMISSIONER ON INDEPENDENCE IN EAST TIMOR
September 17, 1999

East Timor, an impoverished island province that was occupied by Indonesia in 1975, won the right to independence in 1999—but at a frightful cost. After Timorese voted overwhelmingly in a UN-sponsored referendum for full independence from Indonesia, gangs of militia, supported by the Indonesian military, rampaged through the province, killing thousands of people and setting hundreds of homes and buildings on fire. After nearly two weeks of killings, the Indonesian government acknowledged that it could not control the violence and appealed to the United Nations for a peacekeeping force. More than 7,000 peacekeepers arrived in late September 1999 to calm the situation. At year's end East Timor was under full UN protection, with a UN-appointed special representative managing the province's affairs.

The events in East Timor represented a disaster for the UN, which successfully carried out the referendum under difficult circumstances but failed to provide for the protection of those who supported independence. As machete- and machine gun-wielding militiamen attacked civilians, UN staffers and international observers could do little more than denounce the violence. The Security Council was able to send a peacekeeping force only after the United States and other countries pressured the Indonesian leadership to request the help.

Addressing thousands of Timorese on December 31, Vieira de Mello, the newly appointed UN administrator for East Timor, acknowledged that the world body had failed to predict and prevent the "wave of violence" that engulfed the province. "For that I ask forgiveness from the people of East Timor," de Mello said. "I am not ashamed to ask you to forgive us. I would be ashamed not to acknowledge what happened."

A Troubled History

East Timor comprises about half of a 5,700-square mile island located between the Indonesian island of Java and Australia. Portugal acquired the

province in an 1859 treaty with the Netherlands, the colonial ruler of pre-
sent-day Indonesia. West Timor was a province of Indonesia, both under
colonial rule and after Indonesia gained independence in 1949.

Portugal used East Timor primarily as a penal colony. After Portugal's
right-wing dictatorship was overthrown in 1974, the new Portuguese gov-
ernment suddenly left the colony, and a civil war between pro- and anti-
communist factions broke out.

Fearing a communist victory on East Timor, the Indonesian govern-
ment—with tacit support from the United States and other powers—
invaded the island in 1975 and annexed it a year later. The Indonesian
military launched a brutal crackdown, seeking out communists, their sym-
pathizers, and anyone else who opposed Indonesian rule. Most observers
said the military killed at least 200,000 people in East Timor over the next
quarter century. The UN refused to recognize Indonesian sovereignty over
East Timor.

Indonesian dictator T. N. J. Suharto was driven from office by massive
student protests in May 1998, setting in motion widespread changes in the
country and encouraging a long-suppressed independence movement in
East Timor. In August 1998 Suharto's hand-picked successor, B. J. Habi-
bie, agreed with Portugal to allow a UN-sponsored vote on independence in
the province, and in January he said he would accept the outcome, even if
that meant independence. A formal agreement providing for a referendum
was signed by UN and Indonesian officials on May 5. At the time, many
diplomats expressed private misgivings that the UN had not negotiated
safeguards for the civilian population, such as requiring the Indonesian
government to accept an international peacekeeping presence before and
after the referendum. The agreement provided for the UN forces to admin-
ister the province temporarily after the referendum, if the voting favored
independence. (Suharto resignation, Historic Documents of 1998, p. 284)

The Referendum, Then Violence

The United Nations established a mission in East Timor on June 11,
1999, and began making arrangements for the referendum, the first truly
free vote in the province's history. Even as the UN was getting organized,
the Indonesian military formed and provided weapons for thirteen militia
groups with a total membership of about 10,000, saying they were needed
to provided additional security. But in the months leading up to the refer-
endum the militias kidnapped and killed leaders of the independence move-
ment, burned homes, and forced thousands of people into refugee camps,
some of them in West Timor. The same militia groups later committed
nearly all the postreferendum violence, under the military's protection.

The referendum took place August 30 under generally peaceful condi-
tions, with 98.6 percent of the 450,000 registered voters participating,
according to the UN. As the votes were being counted September 1, militia
groups began attacking groups of foreigners (including news reporters)
and escalated their attacks on pro-independence leaders.

Results of the referendum were announced September 3, with more than 78 percent voting for independence. The militias immediately escalated their attacks on independence supporters, setting up roadblocks in Dili (the capital), burning houses and businesses, and murdering people individually and in groups.

Journalists and UN observers said the Indonesian military and police made no move to stop the violence. In a report issued September 17, Mary Robinson, the UN High Commissioner for Human Rights, said: "United Nations staff in East Timor have on numerous occasions witnessed militia members perpetrating acts of violence in full view of heavily armed police and military personnel who either stood by and watched or actively assisted the militia."

Robinson and other observers reported numerous cases of mass killings, in which groups of several dozen people were rounded up and summarily executed. In one case, approximately one hundred people were killed when militia members set fire to a Catholic church where they had sought shelter. Much of the violence was directed against Catholic priests and nuns— seen by the militias as fomenting the independence movement. Catholic Bishop Carlos Ximenes Belo was awarded the Nobel Peace prize in 1996 for his work to secure rights for the people of East Timor; Belo left the province September 7, 1999, after his home was burned.

Within a few days, more than 200,000 East Timorese, representing about one-fourth of the entire population, fled or were pushed by the militia and military to West Timor. There, they were herded into squalid refugee camps, some of which had been built before the referendum—proving, some observers said, that the military had planned the violence. The refugees were not safe once they reached West Timor; UN officials accused the militiamen of systematically killing men and raping women at the camps. The militias burned hundreds of houses in Dili and destroyed the city's entire business district.

The Indonesian government declared martial law September 7, but the violence continued unabated. World leaders called on the government to rein in the military, even though it was clear that Indonesia's civilian leaders had little control over the situation. To protest the military's involvement in the violence, the United States suspended formal contact with Indonesia's generals and froze commercial arms sales to the country. President Bill Clinton on September 10 called for an international peacekeeping force, and UN Secretary General Kofi Annan warned Indonesian leaders that they might face charges of committing crimes against humanity if they did not allow a peacekeeping force. The World Bank and International Monetary Fund also threatened to suspend billions of dollars worth of financial aid to Indonesia's troubled economy.

Giving in to international pressure, Habibie on September 12 invited the UN to send a peacekeeping force to East Timor. "Too many people have lost their lives since the beginning of the unrest, lost their homes and security," he said. "We cannot wait any longer. We have to stop the suffering and mourning immediately."

It took three days of negotiation among diplomats in New York to reach agreement on details for a peacekeeping force, to be composed of 8,000 armed troops under Australian leadership. On September 15 the UN Security Council approved Resolution 1264 authorizing creation of a multinational force "to restore peace and security" in East Timor and to arrange for the province to come under UN administration. The resolution condemned the violence and demanded that those responsible be brought to justice.

The first units of the Australian-led peacekeeping force arrived in Dili on September 20 and began stabilizing the situation throughout the province. Armed militiamen disappeared or fled into West Timor. In many areas the peacekeepers found that villages had been emptied of residents, with most houses and commercial buildings burnt to the ground.

Some refugees began returning to their villages in late September and early October. But tens of thousands remained in the refugee camps in West Timor, some fearful of encountering militias on the way home, and others terrorized by militia propaganda claiming that the Australian peacekeepers were killing civilians in East Timor.

Moving Toward Recovery and Independence

Meanwhile, political events in Indonesia led to a new government with a new attitude toward East Timor. President Habibie and the ruling party he inherited from Suharto fared poorly in June parliamentary elections, and on October 20 he announced that he was giving up his bid for a full term as president. Parliament immediately chose Abdurrahman Wahid, an Islamic cleric and longtime opposition leader, as the new president. With Wahid's backing, the parliament formally renounced Indonesia's claim to East Timor. (Indonesian election, p. 718)

On October 25 the UN Security Council approved Resolution 1272, effectively putting the UN in charge of East Timor for the foreseeable future. The resolution established a United Nations Transitional Administration in East Timor, with full authority to administer the province for an initial period running until January 31, 2001. Officials said it was likely that time period would need to be extended by at least another year.

The UN administration was to be backed by an international peacekeeping force of 8,950, plus 200 military observers and 1,640 international police officers. The council also authorized an unspecified number of civilian administrators and aid workers. Annan later appointed de Mello, a Brazilian who had been a UN undersecretary general in charge of humanitarian programs, as his special representative in charge of the UN administration. A senior UN official said the East Timor operation would be one of the largest and most expensive in the history of the world body, with the first-year cost estimated at nearly $1 billion.

The last Indonesian army units pulled out of East Timor October 31, leaving the province officially in the hands of UN peacekeepers and administrators. The UN officials closely consulted with leaders of the Timorese independence movement, many of whom had been jailed or exiled for most of the quarter-century of Indonesian occupation. As the last Indonesian army officers left, Jose Alexandre Gusmão (known popularly as Xanana), the guerrilla leader who had fought the Indonesian military and had been imprisoned for seven years, accepted congratulations from UN officials and said, "I feel sensational."

The Indonesian military left behind a province whose infrastructure had been almost totally destroyed during months of violence leading up to and following the referendum. The province had few educated people to serve as teachers, social workers, civil servants, or businessmen. A World Bank spokesman, quoted by the New York Times *on November 2, said aid workers faced a task similar to building a nation from scratch on a desert island. Klaus Rohland, head of a World Bank team assessing the situation, said aid agencies and local leaders needed to take advantage of the international attention—and aid—that East Timor would receive. "East Timor can expect huge international interest maybe for the next three to four years," he said. "After that, it's yet another Pacific island. So whatever money comes in now, if it is not spent properly, it's wasted." The World Bank on December 15 estimated that East Timor would need up to $300 million over a three-year period for humanitarian aid and reconstruction.*

Despite Indonesia's return of East Timor to UN authorities, the Indonesian army and militia groups for months blocked the return of tens of thousands of refugees held in camps in West Timor. Richard C. Holbrooke, the U.S. ambassador to the UN, traveled to the region in late November to press for the return of the refugees. At his urging Bishop Belo appealed to the refugees to ignore militia propaganda about conditions in East Timor, saying "the situation is already good." On December 21 the UN High Commissioner for Refugees issued a statement saying that some 120,000 refugees had returned to East Timor, leaving an estimated 80,000 still in the West Timor camps. Many of those refugees were expected to wait until March 2000—after the rainy season—to return home.

Following is the "Report of the High Commissioner for Human Rights on the Human Rights Situation in East Timor," issued September 17, 1999, by Mary Robinson, the UN High Commissioner for Human Rights, describing the conditions in East Timor following the August 30, 1999, referendum in which a majority of East Timorese voted for independence from Indonesia:

I. Introduction

1. The Commission on Human Rights has been seized with the situation of human rights in East Timor for a number of years. At its fifty-fifth session, the

Commission had before it a report of the Secretary-General on the situation. By a statement of its Chairperson, delivered on 23 April 1999, the Commission on Human Rights expressed its deep concern at the serious human rights situation and at the outbreaks of violence in East Timor.

2. On the basis of a set of agreements of 5 May 1999, signed by the Governments of Indonesia and Portugal and by the United Nations Secretary-General, the population of East Timor participated in a popular consultation on the future of the territory on 30 August 1999. The agreements stressed that the responsibility for ensuring a secure environment devoid of violence or other forms of intimidation would rest with the appropriate Indonesian security authorities. Further, the agreements underscored that the absolute neutrality of the TNI (Indonesian Armed Forces) and the Indonesian Police would be essential. On 11 June 1999, the United Nations Mission in East Timor (UNAMET) was established and proceeded to organize and conduct the popular consultation. In spite of several incidents, in particular violence and threats at the time of registration of voters, the preparations prior to the consultations, as well as the voting itself, proceeded satisfactorily.

3. In announcing the results of the ballot, in which over 78 per cent of voters opted for an independent East Timor, the Secretary-General asked all parties to bring an end to the violence which, for 24 years, had caused untold suffering to East Timor and to begin in earnest a process of dialogue and reconciliation through the East Timor Consultative Commission. Regrettably, this call was not followed and violence by different militia groups, in which elements of the security forces were also involved, targeting those who supported the independence of East Timor, as well as United Nations and other international staff, led to grave human rights violations. Thousands of East Timorese were expelled or fled from the territory. Many were killed. Property was destroyed.

4. It has become a widely accepted principle of contemporary international law and practice that wherever human rights are being grossly violated, the international community has a duty to do its utmost, as a matter of the greatest urgency, to help provide protection to those at risk; that the international community should help bring relief and assistance to those in need; that the facts must be gathered with a view to shedding light on what has taken place and with a view to bringing those responsible to justice; and that the perpetrators of gross violations must be made accountable and justice rendered to the victims. The Vienna Declaration and Programme of Action reconfirmed the promotion and protection of human rights as a legitimate concern of the international community.

5. In a number of recent cases of gross violations of human rights and humanitarian law during internal or international armed conflicts, the various institutions of the United Nations and of regional organizations have sought to comply with these responsibilities and to act in concert to respond to the situation. The cases of Angola, Rwanda, the Democratic Republic of the Congo, Kosovo and Sierra Leone provide examples. During the Rwanda crisis, the then High Commissioner rapidly visited the country, called for a spe-

cial session of the Commission on Human Rights, established an office in Rwanda and reported to the Commission on Human Rights.

6. This year, the High Commissioner has undertaken a number of actions in relation to the situations in Kosovo and Sierra Leone and has reported on them to the Commission on Human Rights. In keeping with this practice, as human rights in East Timor came under grave attack, the High Commissioner, who had sent a personal envoy there in May to assess the human rights situation, issued statements calling upon those concerned to respect fully the human rights of the defenceless civilian population. The High Commissioner consulted the Bureau of the Commission on Human Rights and the Secretary-General of the United Nations and decided to visit the region.

7. The present report presents information available on the human rights situation in East Timor and the results of the High Commissioner's mission.

II. Mission of the High Commissioner to the Area

8. From 10 to 13 September, the High Commissioner visited Darwin, Australia, and Djakarta to assess the situation first hand, to discuss with the authorities involved actions necessary to ensure protection of human rights of civilians, children, women and men, and to gather information that might assist the Commission, the Secretary-General, the Security Council and others in their handling of the situation.

9. In Darwin [Australia], the High Commissioner was briefed on the recent human rights developments in East Timor by UNAMET civilian international police advisers (CIVPOL) officers, military liaison officers, evacuated UNAMET international and local staff and their families, and United Nations Volunteers (UNVs).

10. In Djakarta [Jakarta, Indonesia], the High Commissioner met the President of Indonesia, senior government representatives, as well as the Chairman and some members of the Indonesian Human Rights Commission, civil society leaders, and the leader of the East Timor independence movement.

11. At a meeting on 13 August with President B.J. Habibie, the High Commissioner indicated her deep concern at the human rights situation in East Timor, as well as at the numerous reports of collusion between the TNI and the militia. She stressed the need to address the massive abuse of power committed in East Timor, and proposed the establishment of an international commission of inquiry to gather and analyse evidence of crimes committed. The President asked that the national Human Rights Commission explore with the Office of the United Nations High Commissioner for Human Rights the possibility of establishing a commission of inquiry.

12. The High Commissioner also met Mr. Xanana Gusmão and pledged her Office's support for building upon the new East Timor institutions for an inclusive and democratic society committed to human rights.

13. At a meeting with the High Commissioner, members of Indonesian human rights non-governmental organizations (NGOs), who were concerned about the human rights situation in East Timor and had in some cases been involved in protecting those who fled the violence, briefed her on the human

rights situation in East Timor and provided accounts of extensive violations that had been committed against the East Timorese population.

III. Human Rights Situation in East Timor

Breakdown of law and order

14. The first half of September has seen a dramatic increase in human rights violations in East Timor. Since the results of the popular consultation were announced on 3 September 1999 armed members of pro-integration militia have erected roadblocks throughout Dili and controlled the streets. According to reports received from UNAMET, militia members were terrorizing and murdering unarmed civilians; burning houses; displacing large numbers of people; as well as intimidating, threatening and attacking personnel of international organizations.

15. Martial law, declared on 7 September, did not succeed in stabilizing the situation and was also unable to respond adequately to the humanitarian crisis. Despite assurances by Indonesian authorities that UNAMET's security would be a prime objective of martial law, UNAMET staff reported that on 10 September Aitarak militia were allowed freely past TNI and police checkpoints into the environs of the UNAMET compound. UNAMET personnel then observed TNI soldiers assisting the militia in their attempt to loot UNAMET vehicles. When UNAMET military liaison officers came under direct threat and demanded that TNI act to stop the militiamen, the TNI soldiers informed them that they had no orders to shoot the militia.

16. United Nations staff in East Timor have on numerous occasions witnessed militia members perpetrating acts of violence in full view of heavily armed police and military personnel who either stood by and watched or actively assisted the militia. Whilst prior to the ballot the militia were using machetes and home-made guns, it has been reported that after the ballot the militia were armed with AK-47 and M-16 automatic weapons and hand grenades.

17. It was also reported that there was forced recruitment of young East Timorese men into the militia. Parents were threatened and bribed to coerce the young men and the youths were harassed and intimidated into becoming members of the militia.

18. Reports indicate that Dare, which is situated 9 kilometres from Dili, has been under attack by Kopassus elements of the Indonesian Army. It is believed that the Bishop of Bacua, Rev. Basilio do Nascimento, who was injured on 8 September, and many priests and nuns have been among those hiding in the forest in Dare.

Wanton killings

19. Many pro-independence activists and other community leaders, including the clergy, are reported to have been killed in reprisal for their support of the independence option. There are also reports of mass killings at various locations, including in Dili and a camp for displaced persons in the

church in Sunai. Reports have been received that pro-integration militia murdered approximately 35 young men travelling on the Dobon Solo ferry from Dili to Kupang on 7 September.

20. Some particular groups appear to have been targeted. Many witnesses reported that at the police headquarters, at the docks, on the boats and at the final destinations, screening processes were undertaken. Militia waited at the gangway of the boats, checking papers and looking into the faces of the displaced. Those suspected of being pro-independence activists were taken away. It has been reported that in Atapupu, the port of Atambua in West Timor, those identified by the militia were tied up in the back of trucks to be taken away, or in some instances killed on the spot. In many cases, eyewitnesses reported that these activities were undertaken in the presence of both Indonesian police and military.

21. There are reports that since the beginning of September, at least 20 displaced persons have been killed by militia elements in the town of Maliana, and that another 15 people have been arbitrarily executed in the town of Holo Ruo. Fifteen Catholic priests and the director of the humanitarian organization Caritas, together with many of his staff, have reportedly been summarily executed in Dili. It is further alleged that in early September, at least 100 East Timorese Catholics were killed in Suai when their church, where they were seeking shelter, was set on fire. Priests and nuns have reportedly now gone into hiding fearing for their lives, after having been threatened and attacked by militia forces. Reports also suggest that militia groups have hunted down and summarily executed an unknown number of independence supporters in camps in West Timor.

22. In the attack at the residence of Nobel Peace Prize laureate Bishop Carlos Belo militiamen reportedly hacked to death some 40 persons in the courtyard while TNI soldiers fired into the Bishop's residence from the street.

23. On 30 August, a UNAMET local staff member was killed in Atsabe. On 1 September, at least two persons were killed while seeking refuge in UNAMET headquarters.

24. On 2 September, in Maliana, militia surrounded UNAMET regional headquarters. Two houses belonging to local staff were burned down and two local staff were killed. UNAMET staff sought refuge inside the local police station.

25. Eyewitnesses report that militia members have entered camps for displaced persons throughout West Timor with lists of names of supporters of independence, and that a number of individuals have been executed in the camps or removed from the camps

26. Journalists and international humanitarian workers, as well as displaced persons, have reportedly been assaulted at displaced person camps, possibly by militia members. On 6 September, in Atumbua, a displaced person was reportedly tied up and then repeatedly stabbed until he died, in front of a large number of other displaced persons.

27. On 8 September, the Chairman-Rapporteur of the Working Group on Arbitrary Detention, the Representative of the Secretary-General on inter-

nally displaced persons, the Special Rapporteur on extrajudicial, summary or arbitrary executions and the Special Rapporteur on the question of torture sent an urgent appeal to the Government of Indonesia following information received concerning attacks by regular and irregular armed elements which had resulted in over 100 individuals being killed.

28. On 13 September, the Special Rapporteur on extrajudicial, summary or arbitrary executions and the Special Rapporteur on the question of torture again sent an urgent appeal to the Government of Indonesia in connection with information concerning Mau Hodu, a member of the National Council of Timorese Resistance and the Central Committee of the political party Fretlin. Mau Hodu was allegedly arrested on 8 September in Dili by a joint TNI-militia team. His current whereabouts are unknown.

Forcible expulsions

29. There are reports that 120,000 to 200,000 persons have been forcibly displaced—nearly one fourth of the entire population. The displacement of the population often took the form of forcible expulsions. Instances have been reported of people being rounded up and deported. There are indications that forcible displacement was a deliberate and long-planned action. United Nations personnel reported that the building of the infrastructure in West Timor for the reception of thousands of displaced had begun weeks before the ballot took place. Plans for systematic attacks on villages and the displacement of East Timorese were reportedly leaked as early as July. These reports were denied by the authorities.

30. Reportedly, the entire population of Dili has been forcibly displaced or fled to the hills and forests. Persons fleeing East Timor report having been subjected to extreme intimidation and acts of violence.

31. Churches, houses, schools and other premises in Dili, Aileu, Ermera and Maliana, where displaced persons sought shelter, have allegedly been attacked and those inside massively displaced to camps in West Timor. Reports of massive forced displacement of populations to camps in West Timor have also been received from the western part of East Timor. Sources indicate that the militias are now combing the camps for displaced persons with lists looking for students, intellectuals and activists, then taking them away.

32. On 1 September, an estimated 1,500 persons took shelter in the UNAMET compound after being forced to flee from an adjacent school where they had been sheltering. Automatic weapons with tracer bullets were fired over their heads.

33. On 6 September, UNAMET was forced to evacuate all eight of its regional offices and to evacuate a large number of international staff from UNAMET headquarters in Dili. United Nations vehicles carrying evacuees to the airport were fired upon.

34. On 6 September, armed militiamen carried out attacks against the office of the International Committee of the Red Cross (ICRC) in Dili where some 2,000 displaced people had sought refuge. Despite the ICRC's prior appeals for

police protection, an armed group attacked the compound. The displaced people who were seeking protection on the premises were panic-stricken and feared for their lives as the militiamen opened fire. Following the attack, the 11 ICRC expatriate staff, along with several expatriates from other humanitarian agencies, were separated from the local people and taken at gunpoint to a police station. The ICRC was obliged to evacuate its expatriate staff to Darwin.

Treatment of women

35. According to reports from Kalyanamitra, women were raped and sexually harassed by militia and Indonesian military in Dili between 7 and 10 September. Sexual violence allegedly also occurred during the forced movement of people to West Timor. Reports have been received that many women were raped by militia on a boat taking displaced persons from Dili to West Timor. Furthermore, information has been received that women are being raped in the camps in West Timor.

36. During her meetings with East Timorese whom she met in Darwin and Djakarta, the High Commissioner heard reports that there were three camps between Suai and Atapupu where young women had been held against their will by the militia and raped repeatedly. This information was also corroborated by a member of the Indonesian Commission for Human Rights.

Enforced and involuntary disappearances

37. OHCHR has received reports of thousands of involuntary or enforced disappearances. For example, the whereabouts of some 2,500 persons who had sought shelter at Bishop Belo's residence and who were marched off at gunpoint by militia and TNI on 6 September are unknown.

38. The Office of the United Nations High Commissioner for Refugees (UNHCR) is alarmed by cases of men being separated from their women and children. Reports speak of families being separated while being forcibly taken to West Timor.

Displaced persons

39. United Nations agencies and foreign missions in Djakarta confirmed that thousands of East Timorese had fled to other parts of Indonesia. Many displaced persons have reportedly been transported by Indonesian military ships and aircraft to a number of locations within Indonesia, including Irian Jaya, Ambon, Sulawesi, Surabaya and Bali, some of which are thousands of kilometres from East Timor. Approximately 100,000 displaced East Timorese are in West Timor and on the islands of Flores and Alor. Some 55,000 are at a makeshift camp in Atambua and 22,000 in Kupang. Government sources also report that 20,000 displaced are on the East Timor side of the border, attempting to flee to the western part of the island. Media reports indicate that the militia are preventing men from leaving East Timor.

40. Those displaced by the violence, both in East Timor and West Timor, now face the threat of malnutrition and disease as domestic and international humanitarian efforts are hampered by militia and military activity which

blocks access to camps for displaced persons. They have no access to food, water, urgently needed medicine, shelter, sanitation and human security. Many are barely surviving on roots and leaves. There is no milk for the children. Unless food and water is delivered to these people immediately, the international community will be forced to witness a significant number of unnecessary deaths.

41. Reports continue to be received from East Timorese in the hills and in West Timor of continuing attacks on them by the militia. In West Timor, armed militia are reportedly operating with official support. Many of those displaced into West Timor have reported that their identification documents were confiscated by the militia. In Djakarta alone, United Nations agencies reported that about 700 families were at risk. Many of the family members were pro-independence activists or human rights defenders. At a meeting with the foreign missions and heads of United Nations agencies in Djakarta the High Commissioner urged all those in a position to do so to assist in the protection of these people.

42. The Indonesian military and police have reportedly prevented international aid workers, journalists and observers from visiting camps in West Timor and from interviewing East Timorese.

43. Two UNHCR staff members were injured by an angry crowd of displaced people at an encampment housing thousands of East Timorese near Kupang, West Timor. The UNHCR staff were punched, kicked and had stones thrown at them by opponents of East Timor's independence who had fled to West Timor in the wake of the independence referendum. The UNHCR officials had travelled to West Timor to look at the displacement situation there.

44. On 7 September, four foreign aid workers reportedly sustained injuries after being stoned in the Nolebake camp. On 13 September, two UNHCR staff were also attacked by unidentified assailants at the same location: a man had his throat cut with a machete and his face punched, and a woman was stabbed in the left ribcage. An international aid organization in Kupang is said to have been threatened not to help displaced persons or to give information about the situation in camps to the outside world.

Property

45. In Dili, reliable sources reported that hundreds of houses have been burned, the entire business district completely destroyed and almost all houses emptied of their valuable contents. A similar scenario is believed to have been enacted throughout the western regions although the situation concerning property appears to be less extreme than in the east. On 2 September, the militia rampaged through Maliana all night, burning at least 20 houses. In all cases those involved have acted with impunity and been given protection from the Indonesian police and military.

Media

46. Journalists and observers were reportedly forced at gunpoint by Indonesian police to evacuate their hotels and residences in East Timor and

West Timor on 5 and 6 September and driven to the airport. A small number of journalists refused to leave and took refuge at UNAMET headquarters.

IV. Conclusion

47. There is overwhelming evidence that East Timor has seen a deliberate, vicious and systematic campaign of gross violations of human rights. The High Commissioner condemns those responsible in the strongest possible terms.

48. The High Commissioner has urged the Indonesian authorities to cooperate in the establishment of an international commission of inquiry into the violations so that those responsible are brought to justice. To end the century and the millennium tolerating impunity for those guilty of these shocking violations would be a betrayal of everything the United Nations stands for regarding the universal promotion and protection of human rights.

49. It is the intention of the High Commissioner to remain in contact with the Indonesian authorities with regard to the establishment of an international commission of inquiry. As has been seen recently in a number of situations, the establishment of international commissions of inquiry into massive violations of human rights and humanitarian law is increasingly becoming standard practice - and even imperative. If needed, the High Commissioner is ready to take the initiative in launching such an international commission.

50. The deployment, in accordance with the Security Council resolution 1264 (1999), of a multinational force to assist in restoring peace and security in East Timor is vital for the protection of the human rights of East Timorese. It will help stop systematic killings, displacement, destruction of property and intimidation carried out by militia groups and elements of the security forces.

51. The Indonesian authorities must facilitate the immediate access of aid agencies to those in need. Secure conditions must be created for the safe exercise of the functions of humanitarian aid workers. Airdrops must be deployed to assist the displaced.

52. The cooperation of the Government of Indonesia with the United Nations is vital to ensure effective protection of human rights for all the people in East Timor during the transition process to the full implementation of the agreements of 5 May 1999.

53. The High Commissioner shall continue to keep the Commission informed of developments in the situation of human rights in East Timor and on efforts to bring the perpetrators of gross violations to justice. Meting out justice is the least that can be done on behalf of the innocent victims of this wanton destruction and of gross violations of their human rights.

UN SECRETARY GENERAL ON
THE SITUATION IN AFGHANISTAN
September 21, 1999

*Twenty years after it was invaded and occupied by the Soviet Union in
a last gasp of the cold war, Afghanistan in 1999 remained one of the most
troubled countries on Earth. The Islamic guerrilla army that seized power
in 1996 was locked in a vicious struggle with a rival group—a war that
made some 2.6 million Afghan civilians refugees in their own country. The
United Nations in November imposed economic sanctions against the
Afghan regime because of its refusal to turn over to the United States a
Saudi exile accused of masterminding the 1998 bombing of American
embassies in Kenya and Tanzania. At year's end millions of Afghanis were
facing severe food shortages because of a poor harvest and the country's
war-devastated economy.*

*The Soviet Union invaded Afghanistan in 1979—purportedly to shore up
a teetering communist government—and occupied the country for ten
years, all the time battling fierce guerrilla armies. The last Soviet soldiers
pulled out of Afghanistan in February 1989, leaving the country in the
hands of a pro-Soviet government that also faced guerrilla resistance until
it fell in 1992. After four years of fierce warfare among the rival guerrilla
factions, a Sunni Muslim militia group known as the Taliban, backed by
neighboring Pakistan and representing Afghanistan's majority ethnic
group, the Pashtun, ultimately prevailed by occupying the capital, Kabul.
The Taliban immediately declared a strict Islamic regime and imposed
harsh laws, including amputations and executions for crimes and a prohibition against work and education for women, who were required to
wear garments totally covering their heads and bodies when in public. The
Taliban controlled an estimated 90 percent of Afghanistan; a portion of
northeastern Afghanistan remained in the hands of a guerrilla army, the
United Front.* (Soviet occupation of Afghanistan, Historic Documents of
1979, p. 965; Afghanistan accord, Historic Documents of 1988, p. 257; U.S.
embassy bombings, Historic Documents of 1998, p. 555)

Peace Talks and War

Beginning in 1998, the United Nations attempted peace negotiations under the sponsorship of interested countries known as "six plus two." The six were China, Iran, Pakistan, Tajikistan, Turkmenistan, and Uzbekistan; the "plus" countries were Russia and the United States. Representatives of the Taliban and the United Front attended as "observers." Those talks produced an agreement "in principle" in March 1999 for a coalition government, but the Taliban rejected any compromise.

Another set of peace talks convened July 19, 1999, in Tashkent, Uzbekistan. On July 28 the Taliban launched a major offensive against United Front positions northeast of Kabul. The fighting lasted for a month, with gains and losses on both sides. The UN mission to Afghanistan estimated that 1,200 Taliban and 600 rebel soldiers were killed in the fighting.

In a September 21 report on the Afghanistan situation, UN Secretary General Kofi Annan said it was "profoundly disturbing" that the Taliban launched their offensive just after the UN peace mission convened in Tashkent. That action, he said, "once again raises serious concerns about the intentions of the Taliban leadership, which evidently continues to believe in a military solution to the Afghan conflict." Noting that the rebels had expressed a willingness to negotiate, Annan called on the Taliban "to accept this offer."

Annan expressed special concern about the involvement in the war of "thousands of non-Afghan nationals," a reference to reports that religious students from Pakistan, many of them young teenagers, had joined the Taliban forces. Outside support for the fighting, in both weapons and soldiers, threatened to make it "an even more widespread and destructive regional conflict," Annan said. Without naming names—but in an obvious reference to Pakistan's support for the Taliban and Iran's arms aid for the guerrillas—he noted that some members of the "six plus two" group were taking sides and "appear mostly to be paying lip service" to peacemaking.

Sanctions Imposed

On August 7, 1998, the United States accused Osama bin Laden, a wealthy Saudi businessman, of financing and training the terrorists responsible for bombing U.S. embassies in Kenya and Tanzania. The bombings killed more than 250 people and wounded several thousand others, the vast majority of them Africans. Bin Laden operated out of camps in remote parts of Afghanistan, and the United States retaliated against him by launching missiles against one compound on August 20, 1998. A federal grand jury indicted bin Laden on multiple counts of murder and terrorism, and the State Department offered a reward for information leading to his conviction. The Taliban refused to turn bin Laden over to the United States, saying that Afghan tradition prohibited such treatment of a "guest."

Attempting to pressure the Taliban to expel bin Laden, the Clinton administration on July 5, 1999, imposed unilateral sanctions against

Afghanistan. Those sanctions barred all U.S. investment and trade with Afghanistan, prohibited U.S. citizens from using the Afghan national airline, and froze an estimated $500 million worth of U.S.-based assets held by that airline.

The administration lobbied at the United Nations to broaden the impact of the sanctions, succeeding in winning unanimous approval October 15 by the UN Security Council of Resolution 1267 imposing mandatory international sanctions against Afghanistan. That resolution specifically cited the Taliban's harboring of bin Laden. Although technically not as sweeping as the full trade sanctions imposed by Washington, the UN sanctions had the potential to halt most international trade with Kabul by requiring UN member states to freeze bank accounts belonging to the Taliban. The sanctions also prohibited flights of Taliban-owned aircraft; the main effect was to halt the only scheduled service into Afghanistan, weekly round-trip flights from the United Arab Emirates. The resolution exempted from the sanctions shipments of food and medicine, as well as religious obligations such as travel to the Islamic holy city of Mecca in Saudi Arabia. The UN sanctions took effect November 14 and were to remain in effect until the Taliban turned bin Laden over to the United States or to another country "where he will be arrested and effectively brought to justice."

Taliban officials angrily denounced the sanctions, saying they would hurt Afghanistan's poor. On November 14–15, mobs attacked UN offices in Afghanistan, protesting the sanctions. In a November 16 statement, Security Council president Danilo Turk, of Slovenia, demanded that Afghan authorities provide security for UN offices and personnel and called on the Taliban to comply with the demands for expulsion of bin Laden.

Humanitarian Situation

Annan painted a bleak picture of life in Afghanistan in his September 21 report, saying that "deplorable socio-economic conditions coupled with the direct and indirect impact of the war makes Afghanistan one of the most deadly places on earth, particularly for women, children and others made vulnerable by years of unceasing conflict and growing impoverishment." Both sides had followed a scorched-earth policy, destroying farms and other property, detaining and executing men, abusing women, and forcing children to serve as combatants, he said.

Annan said the upsurge in fighting during 1999 "is having a devastating effect on the lives of civilians" and that the warring parties "have shown little respect for lives and livelihoods." A UN mission to the Panjshir valley, in northern Afghanistan, found in late August that some 100,000 persons had been displaced by the fighting. A spokesman for the UN High Commissioner for Refugees said an estimated 2.6 million Afghanis were refugees in their own country—the largest number of refugees in any country in the world.

Food shortages resulting from the devastation of agricultural areas by twenty years of war were worsened in 1999 by poor harvests resulting from the driest winter in forty years, Annan said. In a statement released December 10 in Pakistan, the World Food Program said several million Afghanis faced severe food shortages during the 1999–2000 winter. That UN organization ran bakeries providing bread to more than 400,000 people in Kabul and Jalalabad.

Despite its confrontation with the Taliban over the presence of bin Laden, the United States was a substantial contributor of humanitarian aid to Afghanistan. In a November 4 statement expressing concern about a pending "serious humanitarian crisis" in Afghanistan, State Department spokesman James Rubin said the United States had pledged $575,000 for immediate aid and was considering additional aid likely to put the total at $1 million. During the previous fiscal year, he said, the United States had provided more than $70 million to Afghans "inside and outside their country," Rubin said.

UN human rights officials visited Afghanistan in September and urged the Taliban to make numerous improvements, including easing discriminatory policies toward women. Annan's special representative on violence against women, Radhika Coomaraswamy, said she had "never seen suffering like in Afghanistan."

Following are excerpts from a report, "The Situation in Afghanistan and Its Implications for International Peace and Security," submitted September 21, 1999, by United Nations Secretary General Kofi Annan to the UN General Assembly and Security Council:

II. Recent Developments in Afghanistan

A. Political Developments

2. At the invitation of the Government of Uzbekistan, the Deputy Ministers for Foreign Affairs of the members of the "six plus two" group met in Tashkent on 19/20 July. My Special Envoy for Afghanistan, Lakhdar Brahimi, participated in the meeting. The two Afghan warring sides were also invited and attended as observers. The Taliban delegation was led by Mullah Muttaqi, the Taliban's acting Minister of Information, and that of the United Front (UF) by Dr. Abdullah, Deputy Foreign Minister of the Rabbani Government. The meeting adopted the Tashkent Declaration on Fundamental Principles for a Peaceful Settlement of the Conflict in Afghanistan. In the Declaration, the members of the group, *inter alia*, reiterated their commitment to a peaceful political settlement of the Afghan conflict and called for the resumption of peace talks between the Taliban and the United Front. Significantly, the group agreed not to provide military support to any Afghan party and to prevent the use of their respective territories for such purposes. I sent a message to the meeting, expressing the hope that the adoption of the Declaration would be

followed by concrete and concerted action by the group to implement their accord. The group, as well as my Special Envoy, made strong appeals to both Afghan sides to refrain from initiating any major new military offensives. However, it is noteworthy that only one week after the Tashkent meeting, the Taliban began a major offensive against the United Front in the Shomali plains, located to the north of Kabul.

3. Since the Tashkent meeting, there has been no direct political contact or meeting between the Taliban and the UF. UNSMA [United Nations Special Mission to Afghanistan] has tried to act as a go-between to keep some contacts alive and has succeeded on occasion in channelling messages between the two leaderships. But the essential stand of both sides remains unaltered. The Taliban insist that the UF must embrace the Emirate system while the UF question the Taliban's popular mandate to make this demand. A large bomb attack, which occurred outside the residence of the Taliban supreme leader Mullah Omar in Kandahar on 25 August and which was apparently designed to kill him, is likely to further reduce the already low level of trust between the two sides. The UF's announcement on 14 September of its intention to form a new 10-member cabinet of ministers will harden the divide between the UF and the Taliban.

4. On 18 August, the Government of Pakistan announced that it was undertaking an initiative to facilitate reconciliation between the two Afghan parties. Accordingly, a Pakistan delegation met a UF delegation in Dushanbe on 18 August and subsequently met with Mullah Omar in Kandahar before returning again to Dushanbe for talks with the UF on 22/23 August. However, the UF has publicly stated that it rejects any mediatory attempt by Pakistan on the grounds that, as the UF asserts, Pakistan's military and political support for the Taliban prevents it from carrying out such a role. As for the Taliban leadership, it does not appear to show interest in the purported Pakistan peace proposals. Nevertheless, the Pakistan delegation is pursuing its initiative and revisited Dushanbe on 14 September and Kandahar on 16 September to meet respectively with UF and Taliban representatives.

5. In another development, the United States of America on 5 July imposed financial and economic sanctions against the Taliban. It is understood that those measures will remain in place until Osama bin Laden, who is accused by the United States in connection with terrorist acts, is expelled or extradited from Afghanistan. United States officials underlined that the imposition of the sanctions was not designed to harm the people of Afghanistan and that the United States would remain one of the largest providers of humanitarian assistance to the Afghan people.

6. As foreshadowed in my last quarterly report, the former King of Afghanistan, Zahir Shah, met in Rome in late June with a group of Afghan intellectuals and political leaders living abroad to consult with them on the next steps to be taken regarding his initiative to convene an emergency Loya Jirgah (Grand Assembly). Ensuing from these consultations was the decision to form a preparatory council to develop the initiative and to launch a campaign within the region to explain the initiative and rally support for it.

B. Military Situation

7. During the period under review, the level of fighting reached an unprecedented scale for 1999 when the Taliban launched their ground and air offensive against the United Front on 28 July. The Taliban offensive was reinforced by 2,000 to 5,000 recruits, mostly emanating from religious schools within Pakistan, many of them non-Afghans and some below the age of 14.

8. North of Kabul, this Taliban offensive led to the capture of most of the Shomali plains up to the entrance to the Panjshir valley. In northern Afghanistan, the Taliban captured the Amu Darya (Oxus) river port of Sher Khan Bandar and the nearby districts of Imam Sahib and Dasht-i-Archi.

9. On 5 August, the UF forces counter-attacked Taliban positions and retook virtually all the territory lost to the Taliban in the previous week. During the fighting the Taliban suffered heavy losses in men and material, particularly in the Shomali plains, where they were attacked from the rear and the flanks by UF fighters who had remained in hiding as the Taliban advanced during their initial offensive.

10. On 11 August, the Taliban regrouped and launched a new attack from the front line north of Kabul, advancing cautiously and securing the terrain through the forced displacement of the civilian population and the destruction of houses and the agricultural infrastructure. The UF reopened new areas of conflict in Kunar and Laghman provinces in the eastern region and in Ghor Province in the central region in an effort to reduce pressure on their forces and draw away some of the Taliban's superior numerical strength. The UF made some minor territorial gains. Additionally, the fighting at Dara-i-Suf in Samangan Province, which had been ongoing since the spring, continued unabated.

11. During the month of fighting between 28 July and 28 August, UNSMA estimates some 1,200 Taliban and 600 UF fighters were killed. In territorial terms, the fighting has not greatly changed the overall balance. The Taliban have established a new front line north of Kabul, running from the "old Kabul road" north of Qarah Bagh, traversing Bagram airbase, which is occupied by the Taliban, and the Kohi Safi mountains, to a point between Tagab and Nijrab. In northern Afghanistan, the Taliban in September continued to exert pressure on UF emplacements to the north of Kunduz city and to the east of Khanabad town in Takhar Province. The UF was keeping up its diversionary attacks in the north-west and the south-east of the country.

12. Prior to the 28 July Taliban offensive, there had been intense fighting to the east of Kunduz city and in the Dara-i-Suf District of Samangan Province, as well as heavy artillery and rocket exchange on the front line north of Kabul. The Taliban airforce kept up its bombing campaign against UF military and civilian targets. The UF continued with rocket attacks against Kabul airport and its environs. On 27 July, 11 rockets struck Kabul airport and the surrounding area, including at a time when a scheduled United Nations flight was making its landing approach within the flight safety time agreed between the United Nations and the two Afghan sides. The United Nations

aborted the aircraft's landing and temporarily suspended further flights to Kabul pending the receipt of a satisfactory explanation and reassurance on safety from both sides. These were subsequently received and the flights resumed a week later.

III. Activities of the Mission

13. UNSMA, through its regular contacts with the two sides to the conflict as well as a wide range of independent Afghan political figures and groups, has continued to work to encourage the Afghans to settle their differences peacefully. While the two sides have not shown much willingness to do so, the Mission has played a useful role in conveying messages and reactions between the leaderships of the two sides as well as keeping Afghans inside and outside Afghanistan informed of each other's thinking.

14. During the reporting period, UNSMA kept a rotational presence in Kabul and visited a number of locations inside the country. It should be recalled in this connection that last April, the Mission's military advisers returned to the Afghan capital for the first time since August 1998. The senior military adviser participated in a number of UNSMA missions, including to Dushanbe, Kandahar and Faizabad.

15. UNSMA has begun the recruitment of a first group of civil affairs officers, including a coordinator for the Civil Affairs Unit. It is expected that, security conditions permitting, the deployment of UNSMA's civil affairs officers will be initiated by the middle of November. As indicated in my last report, in view of the complex and difficult situation on the ground, the objectives of this programme should be regarded as rather modest. During a recent mission to Geneva, UNSMA's acting Head of Mission discussed the establishment of the Civil Affairs Unit with senior United Nations officials, including the United Nations High Commissioner for Human Rights.

IV. My Special Envoy and Activities at United Nations Headquarters

16. As indicated in paragraph 2 above, my Special Envoy, Lakhdar Brahimi, participated on 19/20 July in the Tashkent meeting of the "six plus two" group. . . .

17. In Tashkent, Mr. Brahimi brought together the Taliban and the UF for a face-to-face meeting which lasted some two hours. The UF delegation said in the meeting and publicly afterwards that their side remained ready for an unconditional ceasefire and further direct talks with the Taliban under United Nations auspices without preconditions. Representatives of the Taliban, however, stated that they had no mandate to make similar commitments. They reiterated that they were in no position to contemplate any political solution outside of the "Emirate system". After the end of the "six plus two" meeting, Commander Massoud came to Tashkent and held separate meetings with several delegations as well as with my Special Envoy.

18. In Kabul, Mr. Brahimi met with, among others, Mullah Mohammed Rabbani, the head of the Taliban interim council in Kabul, and Mullah

Mohammed Hassan Akhund, the Taliban's "acting Foreign Minister". In all his meetings, my Special Envoy made an appeal to the Taliban in the strongest terms not to launch their anticipated offensive. His interlocutors in Kabul denied that a large-scale military attack was being planned, while reiterating their strong mistrust of the UF and Commander Massoud [the UF leader]. . . .

V. Humanitarian Activities and Human Rights

A. Humanitarian Situation

21. The upsurge in the conflict is having a devastating effect on the lives of civilians and, as in the past, the warring parties have shown little respect for lives and livelihoods. A United Nations mission to the Panjshir valley at the end of August reported that up to 100,000 persons had been displaced in the area. The World Food Programme (WFP) is preparing a large-scale movement of food commodities to those seriously in need of food. The health situation of the internally displaced persons (IDPs) is reported as being under control, although the availability of shelter materials remains of concern.

22. Lack of access to the Panjshir valley continues to be a serious impediment to providing for those affected by the recent fighting. The Taliban have so far denied access to the Shomali plains, where widespread burning of crops and destruction of homes reportedly have occurred. Emergency task forces in Islamabad, Kabul and Dushanbe are in regular contact to ensure effective coordination and optimize the use of all available information.

23. A further 40,000 persons are in Kabul following forced displacement from the Shomali plains. Since 7 August, WFP has been providing food assistance to the approximately 10,000 people (almost 90 per cent of them women and children) currently housed in the former Soviet embassy compound. The International Committee of the Red Cross (ICRC) is providing food and non-food packages for IDPs in other parts of the city. The United Nations Children's Fund (UNICEF) has participated in the collaborative effort to support IDPs in Kabul through health and supplementary feeding and non-food items such as 10,000 blankets.

24. Ongoing conflict in the central area of Hazarajat has further worsened the plight of civilians in that region. The main focus of humanitarian action has been an inter-agency emergency assistance for food security for 30,000 vulnerable households. Further to this ongoing food security work, the United Nations Coordinator's Office has launched a multi-agency response to conflict-related needs in the Bamyan valley. Some 60,000 people who had been displaced during the conflict earlier in the year have returned. This coordinated response is addressing food, shelter, health and employment needs. The operation is scheduled to continue in additional districts in the coming months.

25. The overall food security situation in Afghanistan is expected to deteriorate because of the 16 per cent reduction in the cereal harvest for 1999 following the driest winter in 40 years. As a result, there will be a greater reliance upon external food assistance, such as that provided through WFP's bakery

projects. WFP currently supports the provision of heavily subsidized bread to over 400,000 of Afghanistan's most vulnerable people in the urban centres of Kabul and Jalalabad. A bakery is also to be opened in Mazar-i-Sharif; it will serve a further 112,000 people identified as particularly vulnerable to food insecurity, such as female-headed households, children and the handicapped.

26. The World Health Organization (WHO) and UNICEF, in collaboration with Afghan health officials and NGOs, completed the second round of National Immunization Days for polio, reaching more than 4 million children. The coverage survey showed that both rounds of the campaign reached about 85 per cent of the children under age 5. WHO and UNICEF also supported a house-to-house "mopping-up" campaign after an acute polio outbreak was identified, with 14 cases of confirmed polio virus in June and July in Kunduz Province. In response to other health needs, UNICEF provided essential life-saving drugs and helped carry out chlorination of water sources in areas affected by cholera and gastroenteritis.

27. Voluntary repatriation of refugees from Pakistan to Afghanistan continues, albeit in smaller numbers than during the second quarter of 1999. The outbreak of heavy fighting at the end of July forced many refugee groups to reconsider and postpone their return. In July and August, with the assistance of the Office of the United Nations High Commissioner for Refugees (UNHCR) 2,564 families (14,024 persons) returned from Baluchistan and the North-West Frontier Province of Pakistan.

28. Following the repatriation of several smaller groups of Afghans from the Islamic Republic of Iran in June, July and August, the planned larger voluntary repatriation programme of Afghans from the Islamic Republic is yet to commence, as negotiations on an agreement between the United Nations and the Iranian authorities remain to be finalized. However, deportations of Afghans from the Islamic Republic are continuing in large numbers, at a rate of more than 1,000 persons per week. Except for a larger-scale joint reintegration project in the eastern region of Afghanistan, UNHCR's efforts in providing initial reintegration assistance to returnees focus on assistance in rebuilding shelter and in providing potable water to returnees and returnee-affected communities.

29. As of the end of July, the United Nations-coordinated Mine Action Programme for Afghanistan had cleared 35.9 square kilometres of mined and battlefield areas and surveyed 54.6 sq km of such areas. The total remaining mined area, including new surveyed areas, is estimated at 704 sq km, of which over 90 per cent is agricultural and grazing land. The Programme has received US$ 16.4 million against its total requirement of $25.6 million for 1999 and has a shortfall of $9.2 million for its activities for the remainder of the year. During the past quarter, as a result of the recent fighting, there have been reports of new mining in the provinces of Baghlan, Kapisa, Badakhshan, Takhar and Kunduz. The Mine Action Programme is investigating the extent of mine contamination in those areas and will implement a mine action plan once the security situation permits. There have been no reports of new mines laid in areas that have been previously cleared.

B. Human Rights

30. The human rights situation of Afghans continues to be of major concern. The combination of widespread poverty and protracted conflict, including the deliberate abuse of civilians and means of livelihood, continues to take an incredible toll. Deplorable socio-economic conditions coupled with the direct and indirect impact of the war makes Afghanistan one of the most deadly places on earth, particularly for women, children and others made vulnerable by years of unceasing conflict and growing impoverishment.

31. Civilians trapped in war zones and areas contested by the Taliban and the UF are seen to be the most vulnerable. Earlier this year, non-combatants in the central highlands of Hazarajat had to flee for their lives as both warring parties attempted to exert control in the area. Many were reported to have been summarily executed, detained or forced to flee their burning homes and property. However, a significant number of those who fled are still at great risk; they continue to suffer disproportionately from the conflict as they struggle to survive in barren and mountainous terrain even though warfare as such has ceased in the central highlands. Many are unable or unwilling to return given the devastation in the area and fear of further violence, including gross violations of human rights.

32. This pattern of warfare—intentional abuse of civilians coupled with the destruction of their property—has characterized the latest bout of fighting in the Shomali plains north of Kabul. Since early August, people have been obliged to abandon their homes as a result of either forced or involuntary displacement. The separation of men from families, their arbitrary detention, violence against women, the use of child soldiers, indiscriminate bombing and the use of landmines continue to add to the dismal human rights record of Afghanistan.

33. The Special Rapporteur on the situation of human rights in Afghanistan, Mr. Kamal Hossain, has been in regular contact with the authorities in Kandahar since his visit last May. However, with regard to the human rights situation in the war-affected central highlands of Hazarajat, the Taliban authorities have neither offered evidence of remedial action as proposed by Mr. Hossain nor given him permission to visit the area. In visits to Kabul from 9 to 12 September, Mr. Hossain and the Special Rapporteur on violence against women, Ms. Radhika Coomaraswamy, met with the authorities and other concerned actors and once again stressed the absolute importance of ending the policy and practice of discrimination against women. Ms. Coomaraswamy remarked that she had "never seen suffering like [she had found] in Afghanistan." While noting some improvements, for example in terms of women's access to health care, she called attention to a systematic pattern of violation of women's rights. She also noted that, notwithstanding the sentiments currently expressed by representatives of the UF on the situation of women, they were responsible for first introducing restrictive practices and their period of rule in Kabul had been one of the worst for Afghan women.

34. An investigation team of the Office of the United Nations High Commissioner for Human Rights has been undertaking research into the alleged massacres of 1997 and 1998. At the request of the Head of the Mission, the High Commissioner has approved an extension of fieldwork which is now scheduled for completion on 23 September 1999. The report of the investigation will be submitted to the High Commissioner by 1 October 1999.

VI. Question of Illegal Drugs

35. The annual opium poppy survey of the United Nations Office for Drug Control and Crime Prevention indicates that Afghanistan is witnessing a major increase in opium poppy cultivation. The Office estimates that this increase will make Afghanistan by far the largest producer of opium, with about 75 per cent of the world's opium production. Its total production of raw opium for 1999 was estimated to be a record of approximately 4,600 metric tonnes. This is more than double the estimated production of 2,100 metric tonnes for 1998. The survey reports that during the 1998/99 growing season an estimated 90,983 hectares of opium poppy were cultivated in Afghanistan. This unprecedented level of opium poppy cultivation represents an increase of approximately 43 per cent over the 1997/98 season. . . .

VII. Observations

37. It is profoundly disturbing that only one week after the meeting of the "six plus two" group in Tashkent on 19/20 July, the Taliban forces started a new military offensive. This flagrant disregard for the Tashkent Declaration (see para. 2) once again raises serious concerns about the intentions of the Taliban leadership, which evidently continues to believe in a military solution to the Afghan conflict. I feel obliged to reiterate my view, which has been endorsed on numerous occasions by the General Assembly and the Security Council, as well as by the "six plus two" group, that there can be no military solution to the conflict in Afghanistan. Peace can only be achieved through negotiations and reconciliation and not by territorial conquest.

38. The UF have repeatedly made clear to my Special Envoy and to UNSMA that they are willing to talk with the Taliban in order to reach a solution to the country's problems. I urge the Taliban leadership to accept this offer. As both sides know full well, UNSMA remains ready and willing to help facilitate talks in a conducive atmosphere.

39. It is my sad duty once more to alert the international community to the worsening human rights situation in Afghanistan. The Taliban's conduct of forced displacement of the civilian population during their recent offensive in the Shomali plains is a particularly alarming signal which reflects the movement's apparent disregard for the concerns expressed by the international community. Since taking office, I have repeatedly raised my own concerns about the human rights situation in Afghanistan. I take this opportunity once again to urge the Afghan parties to take urgent measures to improve the situation and, as an immediate and first step, to ensure the protection of civilians.

40. I am deeply distressed over reports indicating the involvement in the fighting, mainly on the side of the Taliban forces, of thousands of non-Afghan nationals, mostly students from religious schools and some as young as 14 years old. In this connection, I appeal to all parties to respect the Convention on the Rights of the Child. It is indeed very disturbing that, not only are external forces continuing to fuel the fighting inside Afghanistan with deliveries of ammunition and other war-making materials, but an increasing number of other nationals are taking part in the actual combat, as well as the planning of military offensives. If this trend is not halted and reversed, the Afghan conflict will further evolve in the direction of an even more widespread and destructive regional conflict.

41. Furthermore, it is profoundly troubling that Afghanistan seems to be setting new records in drug production, which will have negative consequences for global health. The increased drug-trafficking activities, in particular stemming from Taliban-controlled areas, must also be seen as a vital instrument for fuelling the Afghans' war-making capabilities.

42. The unabated external involvement in the Afghan conflict leads me to raise the question of the role of the "six plus two" group. The group was originally established with the intention of adopting a joint strategy towards reaching a peaceful solution of the Afghan conflict. It appears that, despite the agreements on texts and declarations, the "six plus two" group has not been able to make real progress on a more unified approach vis-à-vis the warring parties in Afghanistan. Words must be put into political practice. In fact, by their continuous support for certain Afghan factions, some members of the "six plus two" appear mostly to be paying lip service to their own stated intentions. I thus share the particular concern of my Special Envoy, Lakhdar Brahimi, about the practical usefulness of the "six plus two" for the United Nations peacemaking efforts in Afghanistan. I therefore support my Special Envoy's recommendation to review the United Nations approach regarding the Afghan conflict, including the mechanism of Member States' support. The outcome of this review will be shared with the General Assembly and the Security Council in my final report of 1999.

43. Before concluding, I should like to pay special thanks and tribute to the Government of Uzbekistan for hosting the Tashkent meeting of the "six plus two" group. I also wish to acknowledge the tireless efforts of Mr. Brahimi, my Special Envoy for Afghanistan, as well as those of the staff of UNSMA, for their continuous endeavours, many times against great political and military odds, to make progress towards a peaceful resolution of the protracted Afghan conflict.

JUSTICE DEPARTMENT ALLEGATIONS OF FRAUD BY TOBACCO INDUSTRY
September 22, 1999

A year after agreeing to the largest settlement in the nation's history, the tobacco industry continued to be the target of lawsuits and other legal challenges. In September 1999 the federal government brought a civil suit against cigarette manufacturers, charging that they had conspired to mislead the American public about the health risks associated with smoking in order to maintain their profits. The suit sought compensation from the companies for federal funds spent on health care for smoking-related illness. In December the Supreme Court heard oral arguments in a case involving the authority of the Food and Drug Administration (FDA) to regulate cigarettes. In Florida a jury in a class-action suit found that the cigarette makers were guilty of conspiring to mislead the public about the dangers of smoking, clearing the way for hundreds of thousands of individual smokers in Florida to sue the companies for compensatory and punitive damages.

The legal actions were the latest in a series of government efforts to reduce smoking in the United States, especially among teenagers, and to force the tobacco industry to pay for smoking-related health care costs borne by public programs such as Medicare and Medicaid. Although the preponderance of medical research showed that smoking was a leading cause of lung cancer, emphysema, and heart disease, the tobacco companies has never acknowledged a direct link between tobacco and illness and had denied that the nicotine in tobacco was addictive. In the early 1990s previously secret documents revealed that the companies had long known about the health hazards of smoking, including the addictive nature of nicotine. The documents also strongly suggested that the companies directed their marketing and advertising to teenagers to ensure a continuing market for their product. That teenagers were attracted to cigarettes was confirmed by the numbers; according to government statistics, every day nearly 3,000 minors started smoking, and 1,000 of those were expected to die prematurely from smoking-related illnesses.

The revelations set off two tracks of attack on the tobacco industry. The FDA, with the strong support of the Clinton White House, issued regulations curbing tobacco sales and advertising aimed at minors. The tobacco industry immediately challenged the FDA's claim that it had the authority to regulate nicotine as an addictive drug and cigarettes as a drug-delivery device. At about the same time states began to file suit against the tobacco companies, seeking to recoup the billions of dollars they had spent under Medicaid to treat thousands of sick smokers. In 1997 the states and the tobacco companies reached agreement on a settlement that had to be approved by Congress before it could take effect. Attacked on several fronts in an intense lobbying campaign, the settlement fell apart in the spring of 1997, and the states then negotiated a scaled-back settlement with the companies that did not have to be approved by Congress. Under that settlement, which was finalized in 1998, the companies did not have to pay as much money as they would have under the first agreements—$246 billion in the 1998 accord, as opposed to at least $368.5 billion in the failed settlement. But they did not get one of the things they wanted most, which was protection from class-action and individual lawsuits. The tobacco companies were still liable to suit from the federal government. (FDA regulations, Historic Documents of 1996, p. 589; initial tobacco settlement, Historic Documents of 1997, p. 331; multistate settlement, Historic documents of 1998, p. 842)

Justice Department Civil Suit

On September 22 the U.S. Department of Justice filed a civil suit in the U.S. District Court for the District of Columbia charging the tobacco industry with conspiracy to commit fraud and seeking the recovery of the Medicare and other funds it had spent and would spend on smoking-related health care costs for the elderly, veterans, and federal employees. The Justice Department said the government spent more than $20 billion a year on such care. At a news conference, Attorney General Janet Reno said that for "the past 45 years the companies that manufacture and sell tobacco have waged an intentional, coordinated campaign of fraud and deceit. As we allege in the complaint, it has been a campaign designed to preserve their enormous profits whatever the costs in human lives, human suffering and medical resources. The consequences have been staggering."

In addition to Philip Morris, the other defendants in the suit were R. J. Reynolds Tobacco Company, the American Tobacco Company, the Brown & Williamson Tobacco Corporation, Lorillard Tobacco Company, and the Liggett Group. Two industry lobbying groups, the Council for Tobacco Research and the Tobacco Institute, also were named, but the industry had disbanded both groups in an effort to clean up its image with the public.

Also on September 22 the Justice Department announced that it was closing its criminal investigation of the tobacco companies. Observers speculated that the government had determined it could not prove allegations of fraud and conspiracy against the companies "beyond a reasonable doubt."

The burden of proof in civil cases was lower, and the government also had the successful state settlement as a guide. The civil suit also represented the first time that the federal government used the Racketeering Influences and Corrupt Organizations Act, known as RICO, to sue an entire industry. Initially passed to fight organized crime, the act often had been used to prosecute businesses alleged to have conspired to cheat the public or the government.

Spokesmen for the tobacco industry said the companies would fight the suit. "We will not succumb to politically correct extortion," said Greg Little, associate general counsel for Philip Morris. "We will not settle this lawsuit. We're right on the law. We're right on the facts. We will prevail in this lawsuit." Some observers noted, however, that the companies had settled, twice, with the states and that the judge appointed to oversee the federal case was known for pushing parties to try to reach agreement outside of court. Others speculated that the companies might stall on settlement until the 2000 presidential elections in the hopes that a Republican victory might be more favorable to their side.

The U.S. Chamber of Commerce also spoke out against the suit, saying that the Clinton administration was bringing it only because it had failed to get a settlement with the tobacco companies through Congress. "No business can feel secure in the United States when the enormous power of the Justice Department can be unleashed against them for the purpose of raising revenue and scoring political points. This is nothing more than taxation through litigation," said Bruce Josten, the chamber executive vice president, in a statement.

Florida Class-Action Case

The July 8 verdict in Miami finding that the tobacco companies had conspired to hide the health risks of smoking was the first class-action suit brought on behalf of individual smokers to reach a verdict. The verdict cleared the way for hundreds of thousands of claims by current and former smokers in Florida who believed they were made ill by smoking, at a potential cost of billions to the tobacco companies. "This could mean a lot of money" for the tobacco companies, one observer said, adding that the claims could also block the Florida courts "for many years to come."

Many observers thought it likely that the tobacco companies would appeal to a higher state court to "decertify," or disband, the class-action. An appeals court could order decertification if it found that the individuals in the class did not have enough factors in common or that resolution of all the claims would unduly encumber the legal system.

FDA Appeal Heard by the Supreme Court

The U.S. Supreme Court heard oral arguments December 1 on whether the FDA had authority to regulate cigarettes as drugs. That claim underlay the regulations the FDA issued in 1996 aimed at reducing smoking among minors by prohibiting or regulating sales and advertising directed at ado-

lescents. The FDA claimed the authority under the Food, Drug, and Cosmetics Act of 1938, as amended, which authorized the agency to regulate any drug "intended to affect the structure or any function of the body." The agency argued that under those terms, it could regulate cigarettes because their manufacturers intended them as a "delivery system" for nicotine, which they knew to be addicting. A federal district court had agreed with the FDA, but the U.S. Court of Appeals for the Fourth Circuit, in Richmond, Virginia, overturned that ruling. The Clinton administration appealed to the Supreme Court, which agreed in April to hear the case.

To win the case, the FDA had to get over at least two hurdles. The first was that until the mid-1990s the agency had steadfastly maintained that it did not have regulatory authority over cigarettes. Solicitor General Seth P. Waxman told the justices that the FDA had changed its mind only when it learned that the companies had known nicotine was addictive and had deliberately engineered their products to convey the precise amounts of nicotine necessary "to obtain its effects." The second hurdle was to explain why the agency had not banned cigarettes if it had the authority it claimed and believed cigarettes were unsafe. The terms of the Food, Drug and Cosmetic Act of 1938 required the FDA to ban any food or drug it found to be unsafe. The administration argued that an outright ban would leave too many adult smokers with painful withdrawal symptoms and would lead to a black market. Although the administration did not mention it, a ban would also lead to substantial economic upheaval not only for the tobacco companies and their investors, but for the thousands of farmers and workers who depended on tobacco for their livelihood. The Supreme Court was expected to hand down its decision in the case in the spring of 2000.

Little Reduction in Smoking Levels

Despite the lawsuits, bans on smoking in public places such as offices and restaurants, and aggressive antismoking campaigns targeted at adolescents, approximately 25 percent of all adults continued to smoke and the rate seemed to have leveled off in the 1990s. According to the Centers for Disease Control and Prevention (CDC), 24.7 percent of American adults smoked in 1997, compared with 25.5 percent in 1990. "During the 1990s we've made virtually no progress whatsoever," said Michael Ericksen, director of the CDC's Office of Smoking and Health. "The fact that we can't get rates below 25 percent really speaks to the addictive power of nicotine." The CDC conceded that it was unlikely to reach its goal of reducing smoking to 15 percent of the population by 2000.

CDC data, based on a nationwide survey conducted in 1997, showed an even more disturbing trend: smoking rates among young adults were going up even as rates for older adults were coming down. Smoking rates for people ages eighteen to twenty-four increased from 24.5 percent in 1990 to 28.7 percent in 1997. Aggressive antismoking campaigns appeared to be having some effect, however. A state-by-state breakdown of the data showed that smoking rates had declined significantly in states such as California,

Massachusetts, and Oregon, which had all implemented tough antismoking programs. Conversely, the CDC said, rates went up in states or stayed about the same in states that imposed few controls and low excise taxes on cigarettes.

> *Following are excerpts from the civil complaint filed September 22, 1999, by the U.S. Department of Justice against tobacco manufacturers, seeking to recover damages from the American tobacco industry, which the department alleged had conspired to mislead and defraud the American public about the health risks associated with smoking:*

Complaint

The United States of America, plaintiff herein, by and through its undersigned attorneys, for its complaint herein, alleges as follows:

Introduction

This is an action to recover health care costs paid for and furnished, and to be paid for and furnished, by the federal government for lung cancer, heart disease, emphysema, and other tobacco-related illnesses caused by the fraudulent and tortious conduct of defendants, and to restrain defendants and their co-conspirators from engaging in fraud and other unlawful conduct in the future, and to compel defendants to disgorge the proceeds of their unlawful conduct.

This action is brought pursuant to the Medical Care Recovery Act ... (Count One), and the Medicare Secondary Payer provisions of Subchapter 18 of the Social Security Act ... (Count Two), and the civil provisions of ... [the] Racketeer Influenced and Corrupt Organizations (" RICO") [Act], that authorize the United States to seek a judicial order preventing and restraining certain unlawful conduct (Counts Three and Four).

Defendants, who manufacture and sell almost all of the cigarettes purchased in this country, and their co-conspirators have for many years sought to deceive the American public about the health effects of smoking. Defendants have repeatedly and consistently denied that smoking cigarettes causes disease, even though they have known since 1953, at the latest, that smoking increases the risk of disease and death. Defendants have repeatedly and consistently denied that cigarettes are addictive even though they have long understood and intentionally exploited the addictive properties of nicotine. Defendants have repeatedly and consistently stated that they do not market cigarettes to children while using advertising and marketing techniques to make their products attractive to children. Even though they have long understood the hazards caused by smoking and could have developed and marketed less hazardous cigarette products, defendants chose and conspired not to do so. Instead, they have knowingly marketed cigarettes—called "low tar/low nicotine" cigarettes—that consumers believed to be less hazardous even though consumers actually receive similar amounts of tar and nicotine as they receive from other cigarettes; and therefore these cigarettes are in fact not less hazardous than other cigarettes.

In all relevant respects, defendants acted in concert with each other in order to further their fraudulent scheme. Beginning not later than 1953, defendants, their various agents and employees, and their co-conspirators, formed an "enterprise" (" the Enterprise"). . . . That Enterprise has functioned as an organized association-in-fact for more than 45 years to achieve, through illegal means, the shared goals of maximizing their profits and avoiding the consequences of their actions. Each defendant has participated in the operation and management of the Enterprise, and has committed numerous acts to maintain and expand the Enterprise.

In order to avoid discovery of their fraudulent conduct and the possibility that they might be called to account for their conduct, defendants engaged in a widespread scheme to frustrate public scrutiny by making false and deceptive statements and by concealing documents and research that they knew would have exposed their public campaign of deceit. This scheme included making false and deceptive statements to the public and in congressional, judicial, and federal agency proceedings.

Defendants' tortious and unlawful course of conduct has caused consumers of defendants' products to suffer dangerous diseases and injuries. As a consequence of defendants' tortious and unlawful conduct, the Federal Government spends more than $20 billion annually for the treatment of injuries and diseases caused by defendants' products. The effect of defendants' fraudulent scheme and wrongful conduct continues to this day; defendants are continuing to prosper and profit from their unlawful and tortious conduct; and, unless restrained by this Court, defendants are likely to continue their unlawful activities into the future. . . .

IV. THE FACTS

A. The Impact of Cigarette Smoking on the American Public

Cigarette smoking is the single largest preventable cause of premature death in the United States. Each year, millions of people suffer from smoking-related diseases, which often require a long-term course of medical and surgical treatment. Each year more than 400,000 Americans die from cigarette smoking. Nearly one in every five deaths in the United States is smoking related.

Each year, as a result of the diseases, illness, or injuries caused by cigarettes, the United States spends more than $20 billion under a variety of programs to pay for or furnish medical care to smokers.

Cigarette smoking causes lung and other types of cancers, emphysema and other chronic lung diseases, heart attacks, strokes, and a variety of other diseases. Cigarette smoking by pregnant women is also a leading cause of low birth weight infants.

Cigarettes contain nicotine, which is an addictive drug. The addictiveness of cigarette smoking significantly increases the adverse health consequences of cigarette smoking.

Although it is illegal to sell cigarettes to children, the vast majority of adults who smoke began smoking before they were 18. Children are particularly susceptible to cigarette advertising, especially advertising that presents smoking as a rite of passage into adulthood. When they first begin to smoke, children do not believe that they will have difficulty in quitting, but because of the addictive nature of nicotine, many are unable to quit once they have started.

More than one million children under age 18 begin smoking each year in America. Of these children, most continue as adult smokers and will suffer from some smoking-related illness and diminished health, which will directly and indirectly have an enormous adverse effect on public welfare and the public fisc; and approximately one in three of these children who become regular smokers will die of a smoking-related disease.

B. The Formation of the Enterprise and the Nature of the Conspiracy

In the 1940's and early 1950's, scientific researchers published findings that indicated a relationship between cigarette smoking and diseases, including lung cancer.

Senior Cigarette Company executives and researchers closely monitored such research and knew that if the public came to understand that cigarette smoking causes cancer and other diseases, the Cigarette Companies' profits would decline and the industry would face the prospect of civil liability and government regulation. In response to the published research linking cigarettes and disease, in December 1953, Paul Hahn, President of American Tobacco Company, sent a telegram to the other Cigarette Company presidents, suggesting a meeting to formulate "an industry response" to the studies.

As a direct result of Mr. Hahn's telegram, on December 15, 1953, the chief executives of American, Brown & Williamson, Lorillard, Philip Morris, and Reynolds met at the Plaza Hotel in New York City. At that meeting, these chief executives agreed that the published studies were "extremely serious" and "worthy of drastic action." At the meeting, the chief executives determined to respond to this serious public health issue with a concerted public relations campaign intended to preserve their profits.

The decisions made by these chief executives at the Plaza Hotel meeting have shaped the actions of the Cigarette Companies, including companies not in attendance at the meeting, to this day. The chief executives at the Plaza Hotel agreed that the strategy they were implementing was a "long-term one" that required defendants to act in concert with each other on the current health controversy, as well as on issues that would face them in the future. This Enterprise and conspiracy still continues today.

The fundamental goal of the Enterprise and conspiracy was to preserve and expand the market for cigarettes and to maximize the Cigarette Companies' profits. To achieve this goal, defendants' strategy was to respond to scientific evidence of the adverse health consequences of cigarette smoking with fraud and deception. Rather than provide full disclosure to the public and in congressional, federal agency, and judicial proceedings about what they knew or learned about the dangers of cigarette smoking, defendants and their agents determined, in furtherance of this Enterprise and conspiracy, to deny that smoking caused disease and to maintain that whether smoking caused disease was an "open question," despite having actual knowledge that smoking did cause disease.

Defendants sought to ensure that no company—in the United States or overseas—broke ranks from defendants' public posture, which was based on falsehood and deception. If any Company admitted that smoking was hazardous, that nicotine was addictive, that the delivery of nicotine was manipulated by the Cigarette Companies, that defendants' research commitment was a sham, or that the Cigarette Companies marketed to children, the conspiracy would be endangered. To further and protect the Enterprise and conspiracy and their profits, defendants:

- made false and misleading statements to the public through press releases, advertising, and public statements, such as before Congress, that were intended to be heard by the consuming public.
- adhered to their common scheme of deception and falsehood in lawsuits, including, among other things, destroying and concealing documents.

Throughout the course of the Enterprise and conspiracy and to the present day, defendants have engaged in these acts knowingly and intentionally and with a common purpose. Their own documents—secreted in internal files and revealed only in recent years despite defendants' involvement in continuous litigation about their products for more than 45 years—demonstrate that defendants:

- sought to create false doubt about the health effects of smoking because they knew that such doubt would influence consumers to begin or to continue smoking;
- falsely denied that nicotine was addictive and controlled the nicotine delivery of cigarettes so that they could addict new users and make it more difficult for addicted cigarette smokers to quit;
- suppressed research, destroyed documents, and took steps to prevent discovery of such documents;
- aggressively targeted children as new smokers because children fail to appreciate the hazards of smoking and the addictiveness of nicotine and are more easily induced to start an addiction that would lead to a lifetime of cigarette purchases; and
- knew that use of their product was unreasonably and unnecessarily dangerous to the lifelong customers that they sought to addict.

C. False Statements About Smoking and Disease

Consistent with the recommendations made in connection with the December 1953 meeting at the Plaza Hotel, defendants formed the TIRC and, on January 4, 1954, caused to be published a full-page statement to the American public called "A Frank Statement to Cigarette Smokers" in 448 newspapers in the United States. . . . [The "frank statement' said that although there was no conclusive link between smoking and lung cancer, and that the companies believed their products were "not injurious to health," they nevertheless pledged to "cooperate closely with those whose task it is to safeguard the public health." To that end, the companies agreed to establish the Tobacco Industry Research Committee (TIRC), to be directed by medical scientists "disinterested in the cigarette industry." The committee would assist "the research effort into all phases of tobacco use and health.]

Before the Frank Statement's claim that "there is no proof that cigarette smoking is one of the causes" of lung cancer, defendants knew of the published literature on smoking and health and researchers employed by the Cigarette Companies had reported the relationship between smoking and disease. Moreover, although the Cigarette Companies refrained from doing much of the basic biological research related to the effects of their products, by January, 1954, the Companies had identified the presence of carcinogenic substances in tobacco smoke. Thus, defendants were well aware of the health hazards posed by smoking.

Despite their knowledge, which only increased in the ensuing years, at no time did defendants disclose to the public that smoking caused disease or make public their own analyses which confirmed the published literature. Instead, over the last forty-five years, defendants have made false and misleading statements to persuade the American public that there was an "open question" as to whether smoking caused disease. In every available regulatory, judicial, and congressional proceeding, as well as in every public forum, including through press releases and advertisements, defendants denied that smoking caused disease or claimed that there was insufficient proof that smoking caused disease.

The Cigarette Companies went so far as to claim that they would cease selling tobacco if they determined that smoking was harmful or would change the product in order to make certain that it was no longer harmful. . . .

In addition to the false statements made by the Cigarette Companies themselves and in furtherance of their scheme to defraud, in 1958 defendants created the Tobacco Institute, a public relations organization whose function was to make certain that defendants' false and misleading positions on issues related to, among other things, the connection between smoking and disease, were kept constantly before the public, doctors, the press, and the government. At all times, defendants controlled the Tobacco Institute, including its public statements made on behalf of defendants. Examples of the Tobacco Institute's false and misleading statements are identified in the attached Appendix.

In contrast to defendants, who long knew and understood the adverse health effects of cigarette smoking, many members of the public did not fully appreciate the risk to their health posed by cigarettes. At all times, defendants made such false and misleading statements with the express purpose of deceiving the public and inducing smokers and non-smokers to minimize the health risks and continue or start smoking. Defendants also had full knowledge that, as their fraud succeeded, more Americans would suffer from tobacco-related disease. Because they failed to warn consumers and lied about the health effects of smoking, many Americans, including millions of children, became addicted to cigarettes, and many people who were already smoking had more difficulty quitting, with resulting damage to their health.

D. The Myth of Independent Research

1. The "Gentleman's Agreement"

As a means to further the aims of the Enterprise and conspiracy and as an adjunct to their claims that there was an open question as to whether smoking causes disease, defendants—in the "Frank Statement" and repeatedly over the 45 years since then—undertook an obligation to protect the public health by conducting and disclosing unbiased and authenticated research on the health risks of cigarette smoking. This promise was false when made, has been repeatedly reaffirmed throughout the years, and has never been fulfilled.

Contrary to their repeated promises, the Cigarette Companies had a "gentleman's agreement"—so called by defendants themselves—not to perform or commission internal research designed to investigate the relationship between smoking and health. They did not routinely employ or support scientists to conduct such research; and, in the rare instances that the companies did conduct such research internally, they did so in secret and suppressed the results, in some cases by destroying documents and in other cases by taking other steps to shield documents and materials from discovery. . . .

2. The Lack of Independence of CTR

Rather than perform relevant research in-house, the Cigarette Companies claimed that they would fulfill their promise to research and publish their findings about smoking and health by funding independent research through the Tobacco Industry Research Committee ("TIRC"), which was later renamed the Council for Tobacco Research ("CTR"). In the "Frank Statement" of January 1954 and repeatedly over the 45 years since then, the Cigarette Companies told the public, Congress, federal agencies, and the courts that CTR's purpose was to fund and to perform independent scientific research on the issue of smoking and health. . . .

In numerous court cases, defendants made similar claims about their search for the "truth" about smoking and disease. Indeed, in the very first personal injury suit litigated in federal court following the 1954 "Frank Statement," the Reynolds Tobacco Company stated in interrogatory answers that the purposes of TIRC was to sponsor research into the health aspects of tobacco and to advance medical knowledge on smoking and disease.

These and similar statements were false and misleading when made. From its inception, TIRC (later CTR) was essentially a public relations organization designed to counter adverse publicity concerning smoking and health, and not as an independent research organization dedicated to getting to the bottom of the smoking and health controversy. TIRC/CTR's true purpose, as acknowledged by Cigarette Company executives, was to provide a cover for defendants' efforts to conceal the truth about smoking and health. While TIRC/CTR served as a front for the Cigarette Companies' claim that they were committed to independent research, TIRC/CTR funds were actually funneled into research controlled by defendants and designed to advance defendants' interests in litigation. . . .

Special Projects were often funded when the SAB would not approve the proposed research or when the Cigarette Companies needed favorable research for litigation and wanted it done quickly. On occasion, the industry would use TIRC/CTR to publicize the results of carefully selected Special Projects-funded work that was favorable to the industry, so that the work would be more credible due to TIRC/CTR's purported independence. Defendants also planned to protect the projects funded through Special Projects by invoking the attorney-client privilege and work product doctrine. Through Special Projects, the Cigarette Companies funded many research projects that were controlled by their lawyers and intended to advance the Companies' interests in lawsuits and legislative proceedings. By design, these projects were secret unless and until defendants decided to make them public.

The Cigarette Companies knew that the "Special Projects" work was neither independent science nor good science. Internal company documents express concern about the "degree to which [Special Projects] make advocacy primary and science becomes secondary," and that, to aid in litigation, the companies, through Special Projects, were funding science that was "not worth a damn."

When researchers funded by TIRC/CTR reached conclusions that threatened to confirm the link between smoking and disease, the companies, at times, terminated the research and concealed the results. For example, when Dr. Freddy Homburger concluded in 1974 that his study of smoke exposure on hamsters indicated that cigarettes were addictive and caused disease, CTR Scientific Director Robert Hockett and CTR lawyer Ed Jacob threatened to cut off Dr. Homburger's funding if his paper were published without deleting the word "cancer."

E. Misrepresentations about Nicotine's Addictiveness and Manipulation of Nicotine Delivery

The primary factor that prevents cigarette smokers from quitting smoking is their addiction to nicotine, and their need for continuing intake of nicotine in order to avoid nicotine withdrawal. The addictive nature of nicotine is directly related to the harm caused by cigarettes, because the risk from smoking increases with prolonged use.

Defendants and their agents have long known that nicotine is an addictive drug and have sought to hide its addictive and pharmacological qualities. They also have long recognized that getting smokers addicted to nicotine is what preserves the market for cigarettes and ensures their profits. In contrast, the average consumer has not been fully aware of the addictive properties of nicotine, and most beginning smokers—particularly children—falsely believe that they will be able to quit after smoking for a few years and thereby avoid the diseases caused by smoking. By hiding their knowledge of nicotine and making false and misleading statements concerning nicotine, defendants have induced existing smokers to continue using their products, and induced others to begin to smoke, particularly children, who believe, usually mistakenly, that they will be able to quit and avoid the diseases caused by smoking.

Defendants have understood nicotine's addictive properties since the early 1960's at the latest. For example, Philip Morris internally discussed methods for increasing the nicotine content of cigarettes as early as 1960. Sir Charles Ellis, scientific advisor to the board of directors of BAT Industries, asserted in a 1962 meeting attended by Brown & Williamson representatives that "smoking is a habit of addiction," and scientists in the Geneva laboratories of the International Division of the Battelle Memorial Institute reported to BAT Industries on the mechanics of nicotine addiction in 1963. BAT sponsored research at the Battelle Memorial Institute at Geneva to investigate the physiological aspects of smoking. B&W general counsel Addison Yeaman stated in 1963 that "nicotine is addictive" and that "we are . . . in the business of selling nicotine, an addictive drug[.]" Reynolds, understanding the importance of retaining sufficient nicotine to maintain dependence on its so-called "low tar/low nicotine" cigarettes, internally proposed in 1971 that the company undertake research into determining more exactly the "habituating level of nicotine."

Defendants concealed their research on the addictiveness of nicotine because they have known that revelation of that research might substantially change the market for cigarettes and result in successful lawsuits against defendants. The Cigarette Companies thus performed much of their research clandestinely, and in at least one case threatened scientists who sought to publish their research on addiction. All of this constituted a comprehensive campaign by the Cigarette Companies to keep secret their knowledge of nicotine's addictive nature. . . .

Defendants' efforts to suppress information on the addictiveness of nicotine continue today. For example, in 1997, Liggett broke ranks and began placing a statement on the packs of cigarettes manufactured by it specifically warning that smoking is addictive. On or about January 12, 1999, Philip Morris entered into an agreement with Liggett to purchase certain brands of cigarettes previously manufactured by Liggett, including Lark, Chesterfield, and L&M, each of which, at the time of their sale to Philip Morris, contained the warning concerning the addictiveness of smoking. After it purchased these brands, Philip Morris altered the packaging of Lark, Chesterfield, and L&M cigarettes to eliminate the warning concerning addictiveness. These brands of cigarettes were no less addictive after their purchase by Philip Morris than when they had been manufactured by Liggett. This alteration continued defendants' efforts to conceal from cigarette purchasers, and from the public in general, the addictive nature of cigarette smoking. . . .

At the same time they were denying the addictiveness of nicotine, the Cigarette Companies were developing and using highly sophisticated technologies designed to deliver nicotine in precisely calculated ways that are more than sufficient to create and sustain addiction in the vast majority of individuals who smoke regularly. The Cigarette Companies control the nicotine content of their products through selective breeding and cultivation of plants for nicotine content and careful tobacco leaf purchasing and blending plans, and control nicotine delivery (i.e., the amount absorbed by the smoker) with various design and manufacturing techniques. . . .

The Cigarette Companies have also investigated a wide variety of other additives, ingredients, and techniques aimed at improving their control of nicotine and thereby their ability to manipulate the addictiveness of cigarettes. Cigarette Companies' use of certain ingredients in their products has been predicated on the belief that they increased the potency, absorption, or effect of nicotine.

The Cigarette Companies have repeatedly (and falsely) denied that they manipulate the nicotine levels and nicotine delivery in their products. . . .

F. Deceptive Marketing to Exploit Smokers' Desire for Less Hazardous Products

The Cigarette Companies have misled consumers by marketing products that consumers believe are less harmful, even though they are not. . . .

In response to concern among smokers about the adverse health effects of cigarette smoking, the Cigarette Companies sought to boost sales during the 1950's by advertising filtered cigarettes with explicit warranties of tar/nicotine content and health claims. These claims were also misleading and made without adequate investigation or testing of the Cigarette Companies' products.

Consumers continued to be concerned about the adverse health effects of smoking, and, in the 1960's, the Cigarette Companies responded by developing and marketing so-called "light" or "low tar/low nicotine" cigarettes. These cigarettes are designed to generate lower tar and nicotine on standard machine smoking tests than do other cigarettes, and they do so. Consequently, the Cigarette Companies have marketed these products with claims such as "light" and "ultra low tar" to suggest to consumers that smokers of these products inhale less tar and nicotine than smokers of other cigarettes. Consumers therefore believe that these products are less hazardous. However, the Cigarette Companies deliberately designed these cigarettes in a way that, as actually smoked by most cigarette smokers, they typically do not actually deliver less tar or nicotine. As a result, there is no basis for believing they are safer than other cigarettes. . . .

G. Targeting the Youth Market

For most of this century, it has been illegal to sell cigarettes to children in most states. Currently, it is illegal to sell cigarettes to children under the age of 18 in all states.

Defendants used the Tobacco Institute to shield the Cigarette Companies' advertising to minors. In 1964, defendants publicized a voluntary "cigarette advertising code" that had been agreed to by all the major cigarette manufacturers. The code prohibited advertising directed at young people or the use of celebrities or sports figures in advertisements for cigarettes. Over the next thirty years, defendants, primarily through publications of the Tobacco Institute and in congressional testimony, reiterated their pledge to avoid advertising directed at young people, while at the same time individual companies were aggressively marketing cigarettes to young people through advertising.

Despite the illegality of sales to children, and despite denying that they do so, the Cigarette Companies have engaged in a campaign to market cigarettes to children. The Cigarette Companies have long known that recruiting new smokers when they are teenagers ensures a stream of profits well into the future because these new smokers will become addicted and continue to smoke for many years, and the young smokers are "replacements" for older smokers who either reduce or cease smoking or die.

Recognizing the profits to be had from this illegal market, the Cigarette Companies researched how to target their marketing at children and actively marketed cigarettes to children. As a result of this research—including research conducted in the 1950's into the smoking habits of 12-year-olds— defendants have long known that young people tend to begin smoking for reasons unrelated to the presence of nicotine in cigarette smoke, but then become confirmed, long-term smokers because they become addicted to nicotine. Defendants are further aware that although beginning smokers realize that there are some health risks associated with long-term smoking, beginning smokers almost universally fail to appreciate the addictive nature of cigarette smoking, and therefore fail to appreciate the risk that, by engaging in smoking while they are adolescents, they will become long-term smokers because of the development of an addiction to nicotine. Moreover, the earlier a person begins to smoke, the more likely it is that he or she will develop a smoking related disease.

The Cigarette Companies have aggressively targeted their advertising campaigns to children. Cigarette Companies' advertising glamorizes smoking and its content is intended to entice young people to smoke, for example, as a rite of passage into adulthood or as a status symbol. Among the techniques used by the Cigarette Companies to attract underage smokers were advertising in stores near high schools, promoting brands heavily during spring and summer breaks, giving cigarettes away at places where young people are likely to be present in large numbers, paying motion picture producers for product placement in motion pictures designed to attract large youth audiences, placing advertisements in magazines commonly read by teenagers, and sponsoring sporting events and other activities likely to appeal to teenagers.

During the 1970's and 1980's, Reynolds' substantial market research indicated that Philip Morris, and particularly its Marlboro brand, was dominating the youth market. Reynolds recognized that, in order to maintain its profits over the long term, it was critically important to attract its own cadre of teenage smokers. Internal Reynolds documents specifically cited the need to recruit youths as "replacement smokers." Thus, Reynolds developed the Joe Camel campaign — based on a cartoon character—to appeal to the youngest potential smokers. In 1988, Reynolds began a massive dissemination of products such as matchbooks, signs, clothing, mugs and drink can holders advertising Camel cigarettes. The advertising was effective in attracting adolescents and, as a result of the campaign, the number of teenage smokers who smoked Camel cigarettes rose dramatically. . . .

[Section H omitted]

I. The Present and Continuing Threat

Defendants' conspiracy to deceive, mislead, and withhold information from the public, and from public legislative, regulatory, and judicial bodies about the adverse health effects of smoking, the addictiveness of nicotine, the manipulation of the delivery of nicotine, marketing to children, and the possibility of less hazardous designs has continued up through the present day.

In 1994, the chief executive officers of the Cigarette Companies testified under oath before the Health Subcommittee and once again repeated defendants' "party line." These executives knowingly provided misleading testimony regarding smoking, health, and addiction.

The Cigarette Company executives made these representations, among others, despite the substantial body of evidence, including information developed by the Cigarette Companies themselves dating back for many years prior to their testimony, indicating that nicotine is addictive and is the central reason why people continue to smoke, that the Cigarette Companies sought to ensure that smokers stayed addicted and that cigarettes are potentially lethal to smokers when used as intended by the Cigarette Companies.

In their public statements, the Cigarette Companies continued to deny that nicotine is addictive and, instead, used various misleading explanations for the role of nicotine, such as "enhances the taste of the smoke" and affects "the way it feels on the smoker's palate," and that it provides "satisfaction," "strength," "rich aroma," "mouth impact," and "pleasure," despite widespread agreement in the medical and scientific communities that the primary, if not sole, function of nicotine is to provide a pharmacological effect on the smoker that leads to addiction. According to the 1988 U.S. Surgeon General report: "The pharmacologic and behavioral processes that determine tobacco addiction are similar to those that determine addiction to drugs such as heroin and cocaine."

In addition to their repetition of the same false and misleading statements discussed above, the Cigarette Companies also continued to suppress and conceal documents and information in their possession concerning, inter alia, smoking and health, addiction, the addictiveness of nicotine, the health effects of low tar and low nicotine products, the potential availability of a less hazardous product, and their efforts to market to children.

In January 1998, as Congress was considering comprehensive legislation that might have limited the industry's liability, the Cigarette Companies finally acknowledged that smoking may cause disease. Philip Morris Companies admitted that "a substantial body of evidence which supports the judgment that cigarette smoking plays a causal role in the development of lung cancer and other diseases in smokers." Similarly, the Chairman and CEO of RJR Nabisco, Reynolds' parent corporation, stated his belief that "smoking plays a role in causing cancer, lung cancer in some people."

The Cigarette Company executives also conceded that cigarettes are addictive under some accepted definitions. In early 1998, Brown & Williamson and RJR Nabisco executives agreed that nicotine is addictive under the "man in the street's definition" and as "people use the term [addiction] today." Moreover, the CEO of Brown & Williamson admitted that his personal position —that smoking is not addictive—was at odds with "the rest of the world," and did not dispute the "rest of the world's" use of the word addiction in relation to cigarette smoking.

The Cigarette Companies' careful, semantic admissions were short-lived. In the spring of 1998, during the state of Minnesota's trial against the Cigarette Companies, defendants' officials returned to the same false and misleading statements that they have always made and denied the addictiveness of nicotine and the health effects of smoking.

The Cigarette Companies eventually settled their suits with the states in the fall of 1998. Despite the injunctive relief obtained by the states, defendants continue to market their products in many of the same ways they had before the settlement, and continue to keep secret research and other documents that would provide the public and regulators with a fuller understanding of the health effects of cigarettes, particularly the addictiveness of nicotine. In particular, the results of defendants' research overseas for the last few decades have not been made public.

Indeed, to this day, defendants are continuing to block disclosure of the very documents that reveal the deception in the Cigarette Companies' half-century false and misleading promotion of TIRC/CTR—in public, in Congress, and in court—as an independent organization designed to find out the truth about smoking and health.

The Cigarette Companies, who hold 99% of the market for cigarettes in the United States, pose a continuing threat to the health and well-being of the American public and there is every reason to believe that they will continue with their fraudulent and unlawful conduct.

The effects of defendants' conspiracy will be felt for many years into the future, and the Cigarette Companies continue to benefit from their fraudulent statements, and suppression of information. Smokers remain addicted and will be far into the foreseeable future, and they, as well as the federal government, will be forced to furnish and pay for medical care and treatment for smoking-related diminished health, diseases, illnesses, and injuries well into the next century—all while the tobacco companies continue to earn enormous profits from addicted smokers. . . .

ARMY SECRETARY ON INVESTIGATION OF KOREAN WAR MASSACRE
September 30, 1999

For three days and nights in the opening phase of the Korean War in July 1950, American soldiers and airmen fired on refugees near the front lines, killing dozens or even hundreds of civilians, most of them women and children. Army commanders feared that many of the refugees were North Korean soldiers disguised as civilians. That was the memory of two-dozen Korean survivors and a handful of former U.S. soldiers who had been present at a railroad bridge near the village of No Gun Ri, in the south-central portion of South Korea. Their recollections, first reported in detail September 29, 1999, by the Associated Press (AP), prompted a hurried inquiry by the Pentagon, announced September 30. The AP and other news organizations later uncovered several other incidents involving U.S. attacks on unarmed refugees during the early weeks of the war.

Army investigators visited No Gun Ri on October 29, interviewed some of the Korean survivors, and promised a full inquiry. The Pentagon announced November 2 that seven retired military officers, historians, and other experts would serve as an advisory panel to the investigating team. Officials said they hoped the investigation would be completed by mid-2000.

The Korean survivors in 1997 had unsuccessfully pressed claims for compensation with the South Korean government, and in response the U.S. Army had denied that any massacre had occurred. If documented, the massacre at No Gun Ri—along with other reporting killings of refugees—would represent one of the most blatant atrocities known to have been committed by the U.S. military in modern times. The best-known such incident was the army's slaughter of an estimated 500 civilians at My Lai, Vietnam, in 1968.

One of the soldiers ordered to shoot at the refuges in No Gun Ri—Edward Daily, at the time a nineteen-year-old corporal—told Newsweek *magazine in October 1999 that he could still hear the voices of women and children screaming as they died. "Some of the guys in my unit have talked about this* over the years," Daily said. "But we never really wanted it to come out. We didn't want people to think we were a bunch of women and baby killers. But war is hell, and in war, it's the innocent people who suffer most."

Daily was one of three veterans who met November 10 with four survivors of the No Gun Ri attack at a memorial service in Cleveland, Ohio, sponsored by the National Council of Churches. The survivors said they wanted an apology from the United States. The veterans said they respected the anguish of the Koreans, but asked for understanding of the circumstances they faced as young soldiers thrown into a chaotic war and facing death themselves.

U.S. and South Korean officials said they were working to ensure that passions stirred by reporting of the long-suppressed incidents would not damage relations between the two countries, which had been allies for half a century. "There is room for anti-American elements to exploit this," South Korean foreign affairs minister Hong Soon Young told the Washington Post in an interview published October 27. "We don't want to lose sight of the fact that the U.S. was here to defend human rights and they were here at the invitation of my government and people."

Early Days of the War

Seeking to unite the country divided after World War II, massive waves of North Korean forces invaded South Korea on June 25, 1950, forcing South Korean troops, small contingents of U.S. forces, and millions of refugees south in panic. The United States rushed units to the scene in an attempt to stabilize the situation. Military officials later acknowledged that most of the soldiers were ill-trained and ill-equipped, and that some of their commanders had no combat experience. The North Koreans were soon joined by millions of Chinese troops. (Korean War background, Historic Documents of 1995, p. 507)

By late July 1950 a portion of the front line was near the village of No Gun Ri, about 100 miles south of the South Korean capital, Seoul. Units of the U.S. Army's First Cavalry Division were in the area, trying to prevent the North Korean invaders from continuing their southward push down the Korean peninsula and at the same time manage the massive waves of refugees. According to the AP report and subsequent reporting by other U.S. news organizations in late 1999, U.S. intelligence services had determined early in the war that many North Korean soldiers were infiltrated among the refugees, having donned typical Korean white peasant clothing over their uniforms. Based on that intelligence, army commanders issued orders that civilians be treated with suspicion. One order from First Cavalry headquarters, located by the AP in army archives, stated: "No refugees to cross the front line. Fire [on] everyone trying to cross lines. Use discretion in case of women and children."

The killing of civilians in the area of No Gun Ri began July 26, 1950, just three days after the Seventh Cavalry Battalion of the First Cavalry Division arrived at the front. Several hundred villagers from the area had *been pushed toward No Gun Ri by other elements of the First Cavalry in advance of the invading North Koreans. Upon arriving at No Gun Ri, the villagers were ordered off the main southbound road and onto a railroad track. As they were resting, warplanes—almost certainly American planes, according to the AP report—swooped in and began strafing the refugees, killing as many as one hundred of them, the AP said. Some American troops were caught in the fire and hid in a culvert, along with many of the refugees. The AP quoted veterans as recalling that the strafing might have been a mistaken response to a call for an air strike on North Korean artillery in the area.*

At some point during the day, several hundred refugees were herded into two large railroad underpasses, each eighty feet long, twenty-three feet wide, and thirty feet high, according to the AP. That night, American commanders ordered soldiers manning machine guns near the entrances to the underpasses to fire on the refugees. Daily was one of those gunners. He told Newsweek that he at first aimed fire over the heads of the refugees, then adjusted his gun to hit them. He said he fired for "what seemed like" thirty minutes. "Even above the noise of the gun, I could hear the frightful screams of women and children, crying out with pain and fear. Their dying voices echoed out of the tunnels."

Some of the refugees managed to escape, but most did not. Survivors quoted by news organizations—most of whom had been children at the time—described a night of terror as they hid behind corpses to escape the gunfire and watched as family members were killed.

The shooting continued sporadically for two more days, then on July 29 the First Cavalry retreated in advance of the oncoming North Korean forces. The AP quoted a North Korean newspaper from the time as reporting that invading troops found about four hundred bodies at the No Gun Ri bridge. There was no independent confirmation of how many people died.

News organizations found conflicting recollections among the American veterans about several aspects of the incident. At least one former soldier claimed that gunfire came from the refugees; others said there was no hostile fire from them, only the ricochet of bullets hitting the concrete bridges. One veteran told the AP that he had found the bodies of North Korean soldiers among the dead refugees; others disputed that claim. Some soldiers said they refused to fire on the refugees by aiming guns over their heads; others said they had no choice because they were ordered to fire and they were told that many of the refugees really were North Korean soldiers disguised as civilians.

On at least one significant point there was no uncertainty: the early days of the Korean War were utterly chaotic as the North Koreans pushed the panicked refugees and the South Korean and American forces southward. Secretary of the Army Louis Caldera, in his September 30 announcement of an investigation into the No Gun Ri incident, noted that chaos and said: "U.S. soldiers, although they fought with great courage under very harsh conditions, were ill trained and ill equipped to fight because of the large reduction in resources available to the military for training and equipment following World War II."

Searching for the Truth

Aside from the one report in a North Korean newspaper, there were no contemporary accounts of the No Gun Ri incident. Some American news reporters covering the war mentioned the army's concern about North Korean soldiers hiding among refugees, but no reports mentioned actual attacks on civilians. U.S. Army records uncovered by the AP also contained no references to the events at the No Gun Ri bridge. However, the AP was able to verify key elements of the accounts of survivors and former soldiers by cross-referencing them with army reports on troop movements that had since been declassified.

After the Korean War ended in a stalemate in 1953—with the North Koreans pushed back north to the 38th Parallel—survivors of the No Gun Ri attack made no recorded attempt to gain publicity or compensation for what they had suffered. South Korea remained an impoverished nation for many years, governed by authoritarian regimes supported by the United States because they were strongly anticommunist. Survivors said they were afraid to complain to the government in Seoul, and so they kept silent for four decades.

Starting in 1994, a group of No Gun Ri survivors began sending petitions to both the South Korean and U.S. governments seeking compensation. The Seoul government rejected their petition on the grounds that the statute of limitations had long since passed. The survivors received encouragement in the United States from the National Council of Churches, which pressed their claim with the Defense Department. The Pentagon wrote the council on March 22, 1999, saying that a review of U.S. Army records had found "no evidence to demonstrate U.S. Army involvement" with the killings at No Gun Ri.

Three reporters from the Associated Press—Sang Hun Choe, Charles J. Hanley, and Martha Mendoza—launched an intense investigation of the incident and developed eyewitness testimony of former U.S. soldiers backing the survivors' claims. Asked by a reporter on September 30 why the army had been unable to locate the same information as the AP, Secretary Caldera said that army historians had simply conducted a "documentary review" but that the news organization "has clearly gone further" by interviewing people who were on the scene. This was new information "that demands that it be looked into," he said.

Other Incidents Reported

On October 13, two weeks after the original report on No Gun Ri, the AP filed a follow-up report describing other incidents on August 3, 1950, when the U.S. army blew up two bridges in South Korea as hundreds of refugees were trying to cross. Those incidents happened at the Naktong River, the largest in Korea, where the U.S. Army was attempting to establish a defense against the North Korean advance.

At the town of Waegwan, where a bridge over the river was the last cross-ing available, Major General Hobart R. Gay of the First Cavalry Division ordered engineers to dynamite the bridge and then blow it up to prevent the North Koreans from crossing the river. At the time, several hundred refugees were on the bridge, fleeing the North Koreans.

"It was a tough decision because up in the air with the bridge went hun-dreds of refugees," Gay later wrote to an army historian, according to the AP report. Gay's recollections were briefly mentioned in an official U.S. history of the Korean War published in 1960. Several days after ordering the bridge destroyed, Gay sent boats across the river to rescue an estimated 6,000 stranded refugees.

A similar incident occurred earlier on that same day, according to the AP, when the army blew up a 650-foot bridge over the Naktong River at the village of Tuksong-dong. The AP quoted former U.S. servicemen as saying they tried to prevent refugees from crossing the bridge, which engineers had wired with explosives, but to no avail. At about 7 A.M. August 3, army offi-cers ordered the bridge blown up, and the explosion sent steel girders, pave-ment, and possibly several hundred refugees tumbling into the river.

The October 13 AP report cited other incidents during early August 1950 in which the army attacked refugee groups, believing many of the white-clad "civilians" actually were North Korean soldiers. In one case recalled by First Cavalry Division veterans, a column of several hundred refugees was attacked by mortar fire to prevent them from passing through the front line. One veteran quoted by the AP said he believed about seventy refugees were killed.

In another report December 29, the AP cited declassified Pentagon reports from the Korean War noting that American pilots frequently were ordered to fire on people in white peasant clothes because they might be North Korean infiltrators. In one incident January 20, 1951, the AP quoted Korean War survivors recalling that American firebombs and strafing killed about three hundred civilians trapped in a cave in Youngchoon, about ninety miles southeast of Seoul. Army spokesmen said these other incidents would be investigated after the No Gun Ri case was resolved.

Following are excerpts from a news conference September 30, 1999, in which U.S. Army Secretary Louis Caldera announced an investigation into charges that the army had killed several hundred South Korean refugees at the village of No Gun Ri dur-ing the first weeks of the Korean War in July 1950:

Secretary [of Defense William S.] Cohen has asked me to lead a review on behalf of the Department of Defense to determine the full scope of the facts surrounding press reports of civilian deaths near No Gun Ri, Korea in 1950 early in the Korean conflict. He's asked me to use whatever resources are available to do as quick and thorough a review of these matters, including all military departments and other governmental agencies that are necessary, to do as quick a review as possible.

Today I am directing my Assistant Secretary of the Army for Manpower and Reserve Affairs, Mr. P. T. Henry, to help me oversee this matter. These reports are, of course, very disturbing.

Earlier this year our Army Center for Military History did a search and found nothing in the official records that substantiates the claims that U.S. Army soldiers perpetrated such massacres. This review, of course, is going to go beyond a search of the documentary records; it will be an all- encompassing review. I am committed to finding out the truth of these matters as best we can after these many years.

Although it would not excuse the alleged acts, history records that the early weeks of the Korean conflict were very chaotic. U.S. soldiers, although they fought with great courage under very harsh conditions, were ill-trained and ill-equipped to fight because of the large reduction in resources available to the military for training and equipment following World War II.

More than 30,000 Americans lost their lives in the Korean War. We owe these dead, and the vast, vast majority of our veterans of the Korean War, our nation's gratitude for their sacrifices on behalf of our country. Regardless, we owe the American people, our veterans and the people—our friends and allies of the Republic of Korea—a full accounting of these matters, and I am confident that the review that I have ordered will provide just that. I would be happy to take a few questions.

Question: Just a year ago, the Army and the Armed Forces Investigative Agency found that these American troops were not located near the bridge at the time in question. The Associated Press account looked up the records for this unit, found them there at the time, and talked to people in the unit. Isn't this a cover-up by the Army?

Caldera: The review that was done by the Center for Military History was a documentary review of the records of the units. The Associated Press has clearly gone further in looking up individuals from those units and seeking out individual testimonials, and so clearly has raised new information that demands that it be looked into. And so because of that, this story, we will clearly be doing a full and comprehensive review to try to get down to the truth of these matters as best as we can.

Question: Absent the interview with the individuals, the eyewitness accounts, the records show the unit was there at the time. The Army said it was not there at the time. On the surface of that, it's either a misreading of the records or a lack of an adequate search of the records.

Caldera: Well, we will also look into the investigations that we've done to date, to ensure that there was no such misreading of those records.

Question: Mr. Secretary, under the Uniform Code of Military Justice, is there a statute of limitations on such crimes, or can there still be prosecutions perhaps if you find people who are culpable?

Caldera: I don't want to speculate on the statute of limitations. I believe the answer is no. But I think we need to get you a correct answer, talking to the lawyers first. But I think the point, though, is that it is important to do this review, to get down to the truth of this matter as best as we can, and that rather than speculating at this point about what the consequences would be, that we need to get down to the truth of these matters and then take the appropriate action for our nation with respect to the victims of any such massacre, if it did occur.

Question: How are you going to conduct this review? How are you going to actually conduct the review? Are you going to go back and talk to the people who were there? What else are you going to do?

Caldera: Well, we'll—it is really too early to outline the full scope of the review, except that I want to tell you that we will commit the resources that are necessary. We'll use all the investigative agencies that we have available to us, that it makes sense to dedicate to this effort. And we certainly will be talking to members of those units.

Question: Mr. Secretary, are you going to be using the results of this review or investigation to consider compensation to the victims—at least the 30 Koreans who were mentioned?

Caldera: I think it is important that we do this review to get down to the truth of the matters as best as we can. And if the review shows that something that was inappropriate did occur, then I think it would be appropriate for our country to take the appropriate actions. I would certainly recommend that to the secretary of defense and to the president.

It's still really too early to speculate on what those actions would be. I think we need to do the review first. These kinds of reviews take time. We anticipate it could take a year—at least a year to do the kind of review that is warranted in this kind of situation.

But we are willing to work to get down to the truth of these matters. I'm personally committed to seeing that we do that. And as best as we can, we will do that, and then we will make that information available to the public. . . .

October

Census Bureau on
   Health Insurance Coverage 561

Former Defense Secretary on
   U.S. Policy Toward North Korea . . . 568

UN on World Population
   Reaching Six Billion People 584

Clinton on "Roadless Initiative"
   for Protecting Federal Forests 592

Clinton and Lott on Defeat of
   the Nuclear Test Ban Treaty 600

NSF Director on Emergency
   Rescue of South Pole Doctor 611

FBI Report on Crime 614

Pakistani General Musharraf
   on Military Coup 623

AFL-CIO President on Advances
   for the Labor Movement 630

Armenian President on
   Shootings in Parliament 639

CENSUS BUREAU ON
HEALTH INSURANCE COVERAGE
October 4, 1999

Public pressure continued to build in 1999 to make health insurance more affordable and to make health insurers more accountable to their clients. The House and Senate responded to that pressure by passing measures setting minimum standards for managed health care plans and granting tax breaks to make health insurance more affordable for some individuals and small groups. But the two chambers and the two political parties were so far apart on the provisions of the bills that it was unclear whether Congress could write compromise legislation that President Bill Clinton would sign. The only certainty was that health care would be a major issue in the presidential and congressional elections of 2000.

Meanwhile, the Census Bureau reported that the number of Americans without health insurance grew by 1 million people in 1998, reaching 44.3 million, or 16.3 percent of the population. Insurance coverage was widely considered to be a leading indicator of overall adequacy of medical care. The increase was troubling to many health care experts because it was continuing in the midst of economic prosperity. New government programs to extend coverage also seemed to have had little effect to date. Although the preponderance of the uninsured continued to be poor, less educated, and immigrants, the number of uninsured people in households with annual incomes of $50,000 or more also climbed, to 12.2 million, more than 25 percent of all people without coverage.

Conflicting Views on Managed Care Protections

As soaring health care costs sent insurance premiums skyrocketing in the late 1980s and early 1990s, consumers turned enthusiastically to health maintenance organizations (HMOs) and other managed care plans that promised to hold premiums down. Enthusiasm quickly turned to dissatisfaction when patients realized that HMOs saved money by reducing the length of hospital stays, restricting access to medical specialists, and requiring preauthorization for many diagnostic procedures and treat-

ments, including emergency room care. By the late 1990s managed care providers were frequently characterized as caring more about profits than the health of their patients.

The states, which traditionally regulated insurance, responded by setting minimum standards for HMOs to meet, but these standards varied from state to state, making it difficult for insurers that operated in more than one state. In addition, few states allowed patients to sue their HMOs or even to appeal their HMO's treatment decisions. Moreover, about 48 million of the 161 million Americans covered by managed care and other private insurance were enrolled in plans that were exempt from state regulation.

Backed by patient advocates, the Clinton administration pressed for a federal "patients' bill of rights" that would require minimum coverage and appeals standards for all private insurers. The Republican leadership, much of the managed care industry, and many employer groups opposed federal standards. They argued that standards would increase the costs of health care, drive up premiums, force more employers to stop offering health care benefits to their employees, and add more people to the rolls of the uninsured. In 1998 House Republicans passed patients' rights legislation, but one that offered far fewer protections than Democrats wanted. Both parties went into the general election campaign in 1998 accusing each other of using the issue for their own political ends. (Clinton call for patients' bill of rights, Historic Documents of 1997, p. 787; 1998 congressional action, Historic Documents of 1998, p. 139)

Those charges were leveled even more intensely in 1999, as the Senate and House both debated patient protection measures. In the Senate Republican leaders were able to hold all but two of their members in check to pass a bill with limited protections and limited coverage. As passed July 15, 1999, on a 53–47 vote, the Senate bill would not allow patients to sue their HMOs over treatment decisions, although it did set up an appeals process for an independent review of those decisions. In the House, however, sixty-eight Republicans deserted the leadership to support a much broader and more inclusive measure sponsored by Democratic veteran John D. Dingell of Michigan and Republican Charlie Norwood, a dentist from Georgia. The House version, passed October 7 on a 275–151 vote, would allow patients who claimed that they had been injured when wrongly denied care by their insurers to sue their health plans in state court for damages. Moreover, most of the provisions in the Senate plan applied only to the 48 million privately insured people who were not in plans regulated by the states, while the House bill applied to all 161 million people insured under private plans. Both the House and Senate measures were packaged with tax provisions intended to make health insurance more affordable for some individuals and groups.

President Clinton generally applauded the broader coverage and greater patient protections of the House bill and threatened to veto any bill coming to his desk that resembled the Senate version. Clinton and many other

Democrats also opposed the tax package, arguing that it was a tax break for the wealthy and would do little to help the poor obtain coverage. They accused the Republicans of pursuing a "poison pill" strategy, which would force the president either to accept the tax breaks he opposed in order to get the patient rights he wanted or to kill the tax breaks and forgo patients rights.

It was unclear, however, whether Clinton would ever have to make the choice. Republican leaders in both the House and Senate were vehemently opposed to giving patients the right to sue their managed care plans, claiming that it would lead to a flood of lawsuits that would push health care costs higher. The only ones likely to benefit, they claimed, would be the trial lawyers. Whether they were willing to seek a compromise in a House-Senate conference was an open question at the end of the year. But Democrats and Republicans were already calculating how best to use the health care issue in the 2000 elections. Democrats were likely to characterize Republicans as protecting the interests of insurers and employers at the expense of patients and their families, while Republicans were expected to hold out the specter of rising health care costs. Most political observers seemed to agree that the Democratic message would hold greater sway with a majority of the voters.

Increasing Numbers of Uninsured

According to the Census Bureau report, which was released October 4, 16.3 percent of the population—about one of every six Americans—was without health insurance coverage in 1998, statistically the same proportion as in 1997. "This is a troubling trend," a White House spokesman said. Nor had proportions changed much among specific demographic groups. Thirty percent of young adults ages eighteen to twenty-four were without coverage, Hispanics were three times as likely as non-Hispanic whites to be uncovered, and the foreign-born were more than twice as likely as the native-born to be without coverage.

Experts offered several reasons for the high number of uninsured in the midst of economic prosperity. Although the booming economy meant that more people were working than ever before, many people in low-skill, low-wage jobs were not offered health insurance coverage through their employer or could not afford the premiums. Of the 5.6 million people who worked full-time but were still poor, about half did not have health insurance in 1998. Overall these workers were less likely than poor nonworkers to have coverage, in part because many of the nonworkers qualified for government health insurance programs unavailable to the working poor.

More than 30 percent of the poor, 11.2 million people, did not have health insurance coverage in 1998, about the same rate as in 1997. But the rate of poor people covered by Medicaid insurance, a federal-state program designed specifically for the poor, was down significantly, from 43.3 percent in 1997 to 40.6 percent. Census Bureau officials said that Medicaid coverage might be higher than the bureau reported because some recipients did not realize they had coverage under the program and therefore did not report it. But the data appeared to confirm other reports that Medicaid enrollments were declining, largely because of welfare reform. Experts speculated that many women were leaving welfare for work and either not replacing Medicaid with private insurance when their Medicaid eligibility expired or not realizing that they and their children might still be eligible for Medicaid. In 1998 the number of women without health insurance increased by nearly 1 million, while the number of men without coverage declined by slightly more than 100,000. (Welfare reform, p. 257)

The percentage of children without health care coverage rose slightly from 1997 to 1998, reaching 11.1 million, or 15.4 percent of all children under age eighteen. That increase was particularly disappointing in light of a law passed in 1997 to create a special health insurance program for children. Although the program was just beginning to be implemented when the Census Bureau data were collected, officials had hoped to see some signs that the program was making a difference. A program enacted in 1996 to make it easier for people to retain their health insurance when they changed jobs had also fallen short of expectations. (Health care portability, Historic Documents of 1998, p. 139)

The number of people without health insurance had grown by more than 4.5 million since 1993, when President Clinton took office promising coverage for all Americans. In 1994 widespread opposition among Republicans and the medical community, combined with ineptitude and political miscalculation on the part of the White House, forced the president to abandon that promise. Recent polls showed that a majority of Americans thought the government should pass a law providing coverage for the uninsured, but they were less united on whether such a law should provide coverage for everyone or only those people who did not have it through other sources. (Universal coverage, Historic Documents of 1994, p. 463)

Following are excerpts from a report on health insurance coverage, issued October 4, 1999, by the U.S. Census Bureau:

An estimated 44.3 million people in the United States, or 16.3 percent of the population, were without health insurance coverage during the entire 1998 calendar year. This number was up about 1 million from the previous year; statistically, the proportion was not different than the 1997 value.

The estimates in this report are based on interviewing a sample of the population. Respondents provide answers to the survey questions to the best of their ability. As with all surveys the estimates differed from the actual values.

Other highlights are. . . .

- The number of uninsured children (under 18 years of age) was 11.1 million in 1998, or 15.4 percent of all children. The status of children's health care coverage did not change significantly from 1997 to 1998.

- The medicaid program insured 14.0 million poor people, but 11.2 million poor people still had no health insurance in 1998, representing about one-third of all poor people (32.3 percent).
- The uninsured rate among Hispanics was higher than that of non-Hispanic Whites—35.3 percent compared with 11.9 percent.
- Among the general population 18-64 years old, workers (both full- and part-time) were more likely to be insured than nonworkers, but among the poor, workers were less likely to be insured than nonworkers. About one-half, or 47.5 percent, of poor, full-time workers were uninsured in 1998.
- The foreign-born population was more likely to be without health insurance than natives—34.1 percent compared with 14.4 percent in 1998. Poor immigrants were even worse off—53.3 percent were without health insurance.
- People 18 to 24 years old were more likely than other age groups to lack coverage—30.0 percent were without coverage in 1998. Because of medicare, the elderly were at the other extreme—only 1.1 percent lacked coverage.

Employment remains the leading source of health insurance coverage.

Most people (70.2 percent) were covered by a private insurance plan for some or all of 1998 (a private plan is one that is offered through employment—either one's own or a relative's—or privately purchased). Most private insurance was obtained through a current or former employer or union.

The government also provided health care coverage (24.3 percent of people had government insurance), including medicare (13.2 percent), medicaid (10.3 percent), and military health care (3.2 percent). Many people carried coverage from more than one plan during the year; for example, 7.6 percent of people were covered by both private insurance and medicare.

The poor and near poor are more likely to lack coverage.

Despite the medicaid program, 32.3 percent of the poor (11.2 million people) had no health insurance of any kind during 1998. This percentage—which was about double the rate for all people—was statistically unchanged from the previous year. The uninsured poor comprised 25.2 percent of all uninsured people.

Medicaid was the most widespread type of coverage among the poor, with 40.6 percent (14.0 million) of all poor people covered by medicaid at some time during the year. This percentage is down significantly from the previous year, however, when 43.3 percent of poor people were covered by medicaid.

Among the near poor (those with a family income greater than the poverty level but less than 125 percent of the poverty level), 29.9 percent (3.5 million people) were without health insurance.

Key factors influencing the chances of not having health insurance coverage are:

Age—People 18 to 24 years old were more likely than other age groups to lack coverage during all of 1998 (30.0 percent). Because of medicare, the elderly were at the other extreme (only 1.1 percent lacked coverage). Among the poor, adults aged 18 to 64 had much higher noncoverage rates than either children or the elderly.

Race and Hispanic origin—Among these groups, Hispanics had the highest chance of not having health insurance coverage in 1998. The uninsured rate for Hispanics was 35.3 percent, compared with 11.9 percent for non-Hispanic Whites. Among the poor, Hispanics also had the highest noncoverage rates, with 44.0 percent of that population uninsured in 1998.

Educational attainment—Among all adults, the likelihood of being uninsured declined as the level of education rose. Among those who were poor in 1998, there were no differences across the education groups.

Work experience—Of those 18–64 years old who were employed, part-time workers had a higher noncoverage rate (23.2 percent) than full-time workers (16.9 percent). Among the general population of 18–64 year olds, workers (both full- and part-time) were more likely to be insured than nonworkers. However, among the poor, workers were less likely to be insured than nonworkers. About one-half of poor, full-time workers were uninsured in 1998 (47.5 percent).

Nativity—In 1998, a higher proportion of the foreign-born population was without health insurance (34.1 percent) compared with natives (14.4 percent). Of the foreign-born, noncitizens were more than twice as likely as naturalized citizens to lack coverage—42.9 percent compared with 19.2 percent. Poor immigrants were even worse off—53.3 percent were without health insurance.

Income and firm size play important roles.

Noncoverage rates fall as household income rises. In 1998, the percent of people without health insurance ranged from 8.3 percent among those in households with incomes of $75,000 or more to 25.2 percent among those in households with incomes less than $25,000.

Of the 146.3 million total workers in the United States (15 years and older), 53.3 percent had employment-based health insurance policies in their own name. The proportion varied widely by size of employing firm, with workers employed by firms with fewer than 25 employees being the least likely to be covered. These estimates do not reflect the fact that some workers are covered by another family member's employment-based policy.

Children's health care coverage status was unchanged in 1998.

The number of uninsured children (people less than 18 years of age) was 11.1 million (15.4 percent) in 1998; neither the number nor the percentage was significantly different from the previous year.

Among poor children, 3.4 million (25.2 percent) were uninsured in 1998, also statistically unchanged from the previous year. Poor children made up 30.6 percent of all uninsured children in 1998.

Other findings concerning children:

- Children 12 to 17 years of age were slightly less likely to have health care coverage than those under age 12—16.0 percent were uninsured compared with 15.1 percent.

- Hispanic children were far more likely to be uninsured (30.0 percent) than children in other racial or ethnic groups. The rates were 19.7 percent for Black children, 16.8 percent for Asian and Pacific Islander children, and 10.6 percent for non-Hispanic White children.
- While most children (48.6 million) were covered by an employment-based or privately purchased plan in 1998, about one-fifth (14.3 million) were covered by medicaid.
- In 1998, Black children were more likely to be covered by medicaid than children of any other race or ethnic group. Medicaid provided health insurance for 38.8 percent of Black children, 29.8 percent of Hispanic children, 12.5 percent of non-Hispanic White children, and 19.2 percent of Asian and Pacific Islander children.

Some states have higher noncoverage rates than others.

Uninsured rates ranged from 8.7 percent in Hawaii to 24.4 percent in Texas, based on 3-year averages for 1996, 1997, and 1998. We advise against using these estimates to rank the states, however. For example, the high noncoverage rate for Texas was not statistically different from that in Arizona (24.3 percent), while the rate for Hawaii was not statistically different from Wisconsin (9.4 percent), or Minnesota (9.6 percent). . . .

Comparisons of 2-year averages (1997–1998 versus 1996–1997) show that noncoverage rates fell in eight states: Arkansas, Florida, Iowa, Massachusetts, Missouri, Nebraska, Ohio, and Tennessee. Meanwhile, noncoverage rates rose in 16 states: Alabama, Alaska, California, Illinois, Indiana, Maryland, Michigan, Montana, Nevada, North Dakota, Pennsylvania, South Dakota, Utah, West Virginia, Wisconsin and Wyoming. . . .

FORMER DEFENSE SECRETARY ON U.S. POLICY TOWARD NORTH KOREA
October 12, 1999

The Clinton administration eased economic sanctions against North Korea in 1999 in hopes of encouraging the communist regime in Pyongyang to abandon its efforts to build nuclear weapons and long-range ballistic missiles. The new approach represented the most significant development in U.S.-North Korean relations since 1994, when the two sides negotiated a groundbreaking agreement curbing Pyongyang's nuclear weapons program.

The administration adopted its new policy following a year-long study of North Korea by former defense secretary William J. Perry, aided by senior administration officials. Perry submitted a report to President Bill Clinton in September recommending that a policy of limited "engagement" had the best chance of encouraging North Korea to refrain from attempting to build a weapons arsenal capable of threatening much of Asia and even parts of the United States. Perry recommended a close policy coordination with U.S. allies South Korea and Japan, both of which took comparable moves during 1999.

The allies' tentative steps toward better relations came as North Korea showed some signs of emerging from a prolonged famine. Four years of poor harvests, provoked by devastating floods in 1995, caused the deaths of hundreds of thousands of people. The communist government in Pyongyang put the number at 220,000 out of a prefamine population of about 22 million, but international aid workers estimated that as many as 2 million people died of starvation over the four-year period. United Nations officials reported that North Korea's harvests improved slightly in 1999, but they said the country would remain heavily dependent on international food and humanitarian aid for years to come.

Perry's Policy Review

Perry, who served as defense secretary from 1994 to 1997, began his review of U.S. policy toward North Korea at Clinton's request in late 1998.

In May 1999 he became the highest ranking American official ever to visit North Korea, a country with which the United States did not have official diplomatic relations. Perry submitted a classified report with his recommendations to Clinton in September, and an unclassified version was made public October 12.

Perry based his recommendations on the argument that the single most important issue between the United States and North Korea was the latter's efforts to build nuclear weapons and long-range missiles capable of carrying them deep into Asia and as far as Hawaii and Alaska. U.S. policy had to be centered on convincing North Korea to drop those weapons programs, he argued, and the best way to do that was to reinforce a 1994 accord known as the "agreed framework." Under that agreement, North Korea promised to halt work at—and ultimately dismantle—a plutonium production facility near the city of Yongbyon. U.S. officials said that facility was capable of producing enough plutonium to make about ten nuclear weapons annually. In return, the United States agreed to provide oil for North Korea's electrical utility industries, and South Korea and Japan agreed to finance construction of an electrical generating nuclear reactor to replace the Yongbyon plant. Despite problems in subsequent years, Perry said that agreement was a success because it prevented North Korea from developing enough plutonium for "literally dozens" of nuclear weapons. North Korea's compliance with the 1994 accord was being monitored by the International Atomic Energy Agency, a component of the United Nations.

Despite the apparent success of the 1994 accord in halting work at Yongbyon, two events in 1998 raised renewed concern in Washington and among U.S. allies in East Asia. First, U.S. intelligence agencies reported that North Korea was building an underground facility at Kumchangni that appeared to be large enough to house a nuclear reactor and plutonium reprocessing plant. The Clinton administration demanded the right to inspect that facility, and after a series of diplomatic incidents, an inspection in May 1999 found that Washington's concerns were unfounded.

The second troublesome event was North Korea's launching on August 31, 1998, of a three-stage missile, the Taepo Dong 1, with an estimated range of more than 1,250 miles. That missile flew over Japan, in what intelligence experts said was a failed attempt to launch a satellite. Japan vigorously protested the missile launch and threatened to cut off the funding it had promised North Korea as part of the 1994 agreement. U.S. intelligence agencies said North Korea also appeared to be working on a longer-range missile, the Taepo Dong 2, which could deliver a large nuclear warhead as far as Hawaii or Alaska—or possibly a small warhead to the continental United States.

It was during the furor over the missile test that members of Congress called for an independent review of U.S. policy toward North Korea, and Clinton asked Perry to conduct it. Aided by an interagency task force of diplomats and security officials, Perry began work in November 1998. Perry consulted with administration officials, outside experts, and met with lead-

ers in China, Japan, South Korea, and other nations. In May 1999 he made a historic trip to North Korea, a country rarely visited by high-level officials from the West. Perry later said he also found that the North Korean leaders seemed willing to continue the freeze on their nuclear weapons programs and that they were "very much interested" in improving relations with the United States. The main remaining question was whether North Korea was willing to halt further tests of its long-range missiles.

After Perry's visit, North Korea allowed international inspectors to visit the controversial facility at Kumchangni and determined that it was not intended to produce plutonium for nuclear weapons. In fact, Perry later said the Kumchangni facility was "unsuitable" for that purpose.

Perry's visit also led to three sets of negotiations between Charles Kartman, a senior U.S. diplomat, and North Korean officials on the missile-testing issue. The third round of talks, held in Berlin, produced an agreement September 13 under which the United States would ease its economic sanctions against North Korea in return for Pyongyang's pledge not to conduct any more missile tests.

Keeping the U.S. part of the agreement, the State Department announced on September 17 that Clinton was lifting a broad range of economic sanctions against North Korea, allowing trade between the two countries in many commercial and consumer goods, as well as commercial and personal financial transactions between the two countries. Among other things, U.S. businesses would be allowed for the first time in a half century to invest in North Korea.

The September 17 announcement represented the latest in a series of U.S. steps to ease the total trade embargo against North Korea that the United States imposed at the beginning of the Korean War in 1950. The Bush administration in 1989 eased travel restrictions to allow academic and cultural exchanges between the two countries and allowed humanitarian aid donations to North Korea. After the signing of the agreed framework in 1994, the Clinton administration made modifications to allow limited transactions in telecommunications and finances. The administration also responded to the North Korean famine, starting in 1995, by providing food aid and easing restrictions on humanitarian supplies to North Korea.

Later in September North Korea announced its part of the bargain, saying it would suspend missile tests for the duration of its talks with the United States on improving relations. Perry said he would be looking for "an even more concrete" statement by Pyongyang in the future.

In mid-November, Clinton administration officials expressed concern publicly about apparent moves by South Korea to develop ballistic missiles without notice to, or permission from, the United States. Officials told the New York Times *in November that South Korea had been working on a ballistic missile program for several years and had recently built a facility for stationary testing of missile engines. The newspaper reported that President Clinton and senior aides had raised the issue with their South Korean counterparts and expressed concern about the implications for stability on the Korean peninsula.*

Perry's Recommendations

In his policy recommendations to Clinton and Congress, Perry said a fundamental goal of U.S. policy should be maintaining stability on the Korean peninsula. Achieving that goal, he said, meant ensuring that neither North Korea nor South Korea developed an independent arsenal of nuclear weapons and ballistic missiles capable of threatening each other or other countries in East Asia. For nearly a half century, since the end of the Korean War, he told reporters on October 12, "the threat of another war on the Korean peninsula has hung over our heads like a dark cloud." Getting North Korea to agree to suspend its missile tests, he said, means "that cloud is beginning to drift away."

The United States should keep in place the key elements of its longstanding policies toward the Koreas, Perry said, including a large U.S. military presence in South Korea (about 37,000 troops as of 1999) and an absolute pledge to defend South Korea against an unprovoked attack from the north. Perry said he was confident that the United States and South Korea could defeat North Korea if it attempted to invade the south.

But while keeping military forces in place, Perry said, it was in the U.S. interest to head down a "new path" of improving relations with North Korea in hopes of easing tensions on the Korean peninsula and permitting a peaceful solution to the root disputes between the two Koreas. Ultimately, North and South Korea might reunite, he said, but such a step was in the distant future. Perry said his recommendation for improved relations had the support of South Korea and Japan "at the highest levels."

The first step down the road to better relations was the negotiated agreement in Berlin on suspending missile tests. Eventually, Perry said, North Korea must be convinced to comply with an international agreement called the Missile Technology Control Regime. Countries adhering to that accord promised not to produce, deploy, or export ballistic missiles with a range greater than 300 kilometers (about 190 miles) or a payload of greater than 500 kilograms (about 200 pounds).

In his public report, Perry outlined few specific steps for improved U.S.-North Korean relations beyond the missile testing issue. He suggested that the Clinton administration appoint a high-level diplomat to carry out further talks with North Korea, and he called for continued close consultations on the issue among the United States, South Korea, and Japan.

Policymakers and politicians in Washington needed to understand that North Korea likely would send "mixed signals" in the future and continue to engage in "reprehensible behavior" even while negotiations toward better relations were underway, Perry said. For that reason, U.S. policy would require "steadiness and persistence" and would have to be carried out with the strong backing of Congress, he said.

Secretary of State Madeleine K. Albright told reporters September 17 that the Clinton administration generally embraced Perry's recommendations as pointing toward "long-term stability and even eventual reconciliation on the Korean peninsula." But she warned North Korea that the road to bet-

*ter relations "is not a one way street," and the United States was prepared
to "defend our interests" if conflicted resumed in the Koreas.*

North Korean Famine

*The move toward better relations between Washington and Pyongyang
came in the context of the continuing collapse of the North Korean communist economy. International observers and aid officials said food production improved marginally in North Korea during 1999 after four successive years of poor harvests and famine. But the communist regime was able
to provide a subsistence-level diet for its 22 million people only because of
enormous quantities of food provided by international agencies and other
countries.*

*Aid officials said schools and hospitals were unheated, electrical power
was available for only a fraction of the population, and chronic malnutrition and a severe shortage of medicines had led to high rates of infant mortality.*

*David Morton, the coordinator of UN humanitarian aid programs in
North Korea, told reporters on December 14 that agricultural production in
the country was "on the way to recovery" but the economy was nearly bankrupt because of inefficiencies and the lack of a world market for North
Korean goods. During the cold war North Korea traded almost exclusively
with other communist nations. The collapse of the Soviet Union and the
modernization of China's economy meant that North Korea literally had no
serious trading partners.*

*Improved relations with South Korea and Japan already were helping
some sectors of the North Korean economy, including textile production.
But over the long term, experts said, international investors would enter
the North Korean economy only if Pyongyang moved away from communism and toward a free-market economy. As of the end of 1999 there were
no indications of that happening any time soon.*

> *Following are excerpts from the unclassified version of a report
> released October 12, 1999, by the State Department, entitled
> "Review of United States Policy Toward North Korea: Findings
> and Recommendations," by William J. Perry, a special adviser
> to President Bill Clinton who conducted a review of U.S. policy
> toward North Korea:*

A North Korea policy review team, led by Dr. William J. Perry and working
with an interagency group headed by the Counselor of the Department of
State Ambassador Wendy R. Sherman, was tasked in November 1998 by President Clinton and his national security advisors to conduct an extensive
review of U.S. policy toward the DPRK [Democratic People's Republic of
Korea]. This review of U.S. policy lasted approximately eight months, and

was supported by a number of senior officials from the U.S. government and by Dr. Ashton B. Carter of Harvard University. The policy review team was also very fortunate to have received regular and extensive guidance from the Secretary of State, the Secretary of Defense, the National Security Advisor and senior policy advisors.

Throughout the review the team consulted with experts, both in and out of the U.S. government. Dr. Perry made a special point to travel to the Capitol to give regular status reports to Members of Congress on the progress of this review, and he benefited from comments received from Members on concepts being developed by the North Korea policy review team. The team also exchanged views with officials from many countries with interests in Northeast Asia and the Korean Peninsula, including our allies, the ROK [Republic of Korea] and Japan. The team also met with prominent members of the humanitarian aid community and received a wealth of written material, solicited and unsolicited. Members of the policy review team met with many other individuals and organizations as well. In addition, the team traveled to North Korea this past May, led by Dr. Perry as President Clinton's Special Envoy, to obtain a first-hand understanding of the views of the DPRK Government.

The findings and recommendations of the North Korea Policy Review set forth below reflect the consensus that emerged from the team's countless hours of work and study.

The Need for a Fundamental Review of U.S. Policy

The policy review team determined that a fundamental review of U.S. policy was indeed needed, since much has changed in the security situation on the Korean Peninsula since the 1994 crisis.

Most important—and the focus of this North Korea policy review—are developments in the DPRK's nuclear and long-range missile activities.

The Agreed Framework of 1994 succeeded in verifiably freezing North Korean plutonium production at Yongbyon—it stopped plutonium production at that facility so that North Korea currently has at most a small amount of fissile material it may have secreted away from operations prior to 1994; without the Agreed Framework, North Korea could have produced enough additional plutonium by now for a significant number of nuclear weapons. Yet, despite the critical achievement of a verified freeze on plutonium production at Yongbyon under the Agreed Framework, the policy review team has serious concerns about possible continuing nuclear weapons-related work in the DPRK. Some of these concerns have been addressed through our access and visit to Kumchang-ni.

The years since 1994 have also witnessed development, testing, deployment, and export by the DPRK of ballistic missiles of increasing range, including those potentially capable of reaching the territory of the United States.

There have been other significant changes as well. Since the negotiations over the Agreed Framework began in the summer of 1994, formal leadership of the DPRK has passed from President Kim Il Sung to his son, General Kim Jong Il, and General Kim has gradually assumed supreme authority in title as well as fact. North Korea is thus governed by a different leadership from that with which we embarked on the Agreed Framework. During this same period, the DPRK economy has deteriorated significantly, with industrial and food production sinking to a fraction of their 1994 levels. The result is a humanitarian tragedy which, while not the focus of the review, both compels the sympathy of the American people and doubtless affects some of the actions of the North Korean regime.

An unrelated change has come to the government of the Republic of Korea (ROK) with the Presidency of Kim Dae Jung. President Kim has embarked upon a policy of engagement with the North. As a leader of great international authority, as our ally, and as the host to 37,000 American troops, the views and insights of President Kim are central to accomplishing U.S. security objectives on the Korean Peninsula. No U.S. policy can succeed unless it is coordinated with the ROK's policy. Today's ROK policy of engagement creates conditions and opportunities for U.S. policy very different from those in 1994.

Another close U.S. ally in the region, Japan, has become more concerned about North Korea in recent years. This concern was heightened by the launch, in August 1998, of a Taepo Dong missile over Japanese territory. Although the Diet has passed funding for the Light Water Reactor project being undertaken by the Korean Peninsula Energy Development Organization (KEDO) pursuant to the Agreed Framework, and the government wants to preserve the Agreed Framework, a second missile launch is likely to have a serious impact on domestic political support for the Agreed Framework and have wider ramifications within Japan about its security policy.

Finally, while the U.S. relationship with China sometimes reflects different perspectives on security policy in the region, the policy review team learned through extensive dialogue between the U.S. and the PRC [People's Republic of China], including President Clinton's meetings with President Jiang Zemin, that China understands many of the U.S. concerns about the deleterious effects that North Korea's nuclear weapons and missile activities could have for regional and global security.

All these factors combine to create a profoundly different landscape than existed in 1994. The review team concurred strongly with President Clinton's judgment that these changed circumstances required a comprehensive review such as the one that the President and his team of national security advisors asked the team to conduct. The policy review team also recognized the concerns of Members of Congress that a clear path be charted for dealing with North Korea, and that there be closer cooperation between the executive and legislative branches on this issue of great importance to our security. The review team shared these concerns and has tried hard to be responsive to them.

Assessment of the Security Situation on the Korean Peninsula

In the course of the review, the policy team conferred with U.S. military leaders and allies, and concluded that, as in 1994, U.S. forces and alliances in the region are strong and ready. Indeed, since 1994, the U.S. has strengthened both its own forces and its plans and procedures for combining forces with allies. We are confident that allied forces could and would successfully defend ROK territory. We believe the DPRK's military leaders know this and thus are deterred from launching an attack.

However, in sharp contrast to the Desert Storm campaign in Kuwait and Iraq, war on the Korean Peninsula would take place in densely populated areas. Considering the million-man DPRK army arrayed near the DMZ, the intensity of combat in another war on the Peninsula would be unparalleled in U.S. experience since the Korean War of 1950-53. It is likely that hundreds of thousands of persons—U.S., ROK, and DPRK—military and civilian—would perish, and millions of refugees would be created. While the U.S. and ROK of course have no intention of provoking war, there are those in the DPRK who believe the opposite is true. But even they must know that the prospect of such a destructive war is a powerful deterrent to precipitous U.S. or allied action.

Under present circumstances, therefore, deterrence of war on the Korean Peninsula is stable on both sides, in military terms. While always subject to miscalculation by the isolated North Korean government, there is no military calculus that would suggest to the North Koreans anything but catastrophe from armed conflict. This relative stability, if it is not disturbed, can provide the time and conditions for all sides to pursue a permanent peace on the Peninsula, ending at last the Korean War and perhaps ultimately leading to the peaceful reunification of the Korean people. This is the lasting goal of U.S. policy.

However, acquisition by the DPRK of nuclear weapons or long-range missiles, and especially the combination of the two (a nuclear weapons device mounted on a long-range missile), could undermine this relative stability. Such weapons in the hands of the DPRK military might weaken deterrence as well as increase the damage if deterrence failed. Their effect would, therefore, be to undermine the conditions for pursuing a relaxation of tensions, improved relations, and lasting peace. Acquisition of such weapons by North Korea could also spark an arms race in the region and would surely do grave damage to the global nonproliferation regimes covering nuclear weapons and ballistic missiles. A continuation of the DPRK's pattern of selling its missiles for hard currency could also spread destabilizing effects to other regions, such as the Middle East.

The review team, therefore, concluded that the urgent focus of U.S. policy toward the DPRK must be to end its nuclear weapons and long-range missile-related activities. This focus does not signal a narrow preoccupation with nonproliferation over other dimensions of the problem of security on the Korean Peninsula, but rather reflects the fact that control of weapons of mass destruction is essential to the pursuit of a wider form of security so badly needed in that region.

As the United States faces the task of ending these weapons activities, any U.S. policy toward North Korea must be formulated within three constraining facts:

First, while logic would suggest that the DPRK's evident problems would ultimately lead its regime to change, there is no evidence that change is imminent. United States policy must, therefore, deal with the North Korean government as it is, not as we might wish it to be.

Second, the risk of a destructive war to the 37,000 American service personnel in Korea and the many more that would reinforce them, to the inhabitants of the Korean Peninsula both South and North, and to U.S. allies and friends in the region dictate that the United States pursue its objectives with prudence and patience.

Third, while the Agreed Framework has critics in the United States, the ROK, and Japan—and indeed in the DPRK—the framework has verifiably frozen plutonium production at Yongbyon. It also served as the basis for successful discussions we had with the North earlier this year on an underground site at Kumchang-ni—one that the U.S. feared might have been designed as a substitute plutonium production facility. Unfreezing Yongbyon remains the North's quickest and surest path to nuclear weapons. U.S. security objectives may therefore require the U.S. to supplement the Agreed Framework, but we must not undermine or supplant it.

Perspectives of Countries in the Region

The policy review team consulted extensively with people outside of the Administration to better understand the perspectives of countries in the region. These perspectives are summarized below.

Republic of Korea

The ROK's interests are not identical to those of the U.S., but they overlap in significant ways. While the ROK is not a global power like the United States and, therefore, is less active in promoting nonproliferation worldwide, the ROK recognizes that nuclear weapons in the DPRK would destabilize deterrence on the Peninsula. And while South Koreans have long lived within range of North Korean SCUD ballistic missiles, they recognize that North Korea's new, longer-range ballistic missiles present a new type of threat to the United States and Japan. The ROK thus shares U.S. goals with respect to DPRK nuclear weapons and ballistic missiles. The South also has concerns, such as the reunion of families separated by the Korean War and implementation of the North-South Basic Agreement (including reactivation of North-South Joint Committees). The U.S. strongly supports these concerns.

President Kim Dae Jung's North Korea policy, known as the "engagement" policy, marked a fundamental shift toward the North. Under the Kim formulation, the ROK has forsworn any intent to undermine or absorb the North and has pursued increased official and unofficial North-South contact. The ROK supports the Agreed Framework and the ROK's role in KEDO, but the ROK National Assembly, like our Congress, is carefully scrutinizing DPRK behavior as it considers funding for KEDO.

Japan

Like the ROK, Japan's interests are not identical to those of the U.S., but they overlap strongly. The DPRK's August 1998 Taepo Dong missile launch over the Japanese islands abruptly increased the already high priority Japan attaches to the North Korea issue. The Japanese regard DPRK missile activities as a direct threat. In bilateral talks with Japan, the DPRK representatives exacerbate historic animosities by repeatedly referring to Japan's occupation of Korea earlier in this century. For these reasons, support for Japan's role in KEDO is at risk in the Diet. The government's ability to sustain the Agreed Framework in the face of further DPRK missile launches is not assured, even though a collapse of the Agreed Framework could lead to nuclear warheads on DPRK missiles, dramatically increasing the threat they pose. Japan also has deep-seated concerns, such as the fate of missing persons suspected of being abducted by the DPRK. The U.S. strongly supports these concerns.

China

China has a strong interest in peace and stability on the Korean Peninsula and is aware of the implications of increased tension on the peninsula. China also realizes that DPRK ballistic missiles are an important impetus to U.S. national missile defense and theater missile defenses, neither of which is desired by China. Finally, China realizes that DPRK nuclear weapons could provoke an arms race in the region and undermine the nonproliferation regime which Beijing, as a nuclear power, has an interest in preserving. For all these reasons the PRC concerns with North Korean nuclear weapons and ballistic missile programs are in many ways comparable to U.S. concerns. While China will not coordinate its policies with the U.S., ROK, and Japan, it is in China's interest to use its own channels of communication to discourage the DPRK from pursuing these programs.

The DPRK

Based on extensive consultation with the intelligence community and experts around the world, a review of recent DPRK conduct, and our discussions with North Korean leaders, the policy review team formed some views of this enigmatic country. But in many ways the unknowns continue to outweigh the knowns. Therefore, we want to emphasize here that no U.S. policy should be based solely on conjectures about the perceptions and future behavior of the DPRK.

Wrapped in an overriding sense of vulnerability, the DPRK regime has promoted an intense devotion to self-sufficiency, sovereignty, and self-defense as the touchstones for all rhetoric and policy. The DPRK views efforts by outsiders to promote democratic and market reforms in its country as an attempt to undermine the regime. It strongly controls foreign influence and contact, even when they offer relief from the regime's severe economic problems. The DPRK appears to value improved relations with US, especially including relief from the extensive economic sanctions the U.S. has long imposed.

Key Findings

The policy review team made the following key findings, which have formed the basis for our recommendations:

1. DPRK acquisition of nuclear weapons and continued development, testing, deployment, and export of long-range missiles would undermine the relative stability of deterrence on the Korean Peninsula, a precondition for ending the Cold War and pursuing a lasting peace in the longer run. These activities by the DPRK also have serious regional and global consequences adverse to vital U.S. interests. The United States must, therefore, have as its objective ending these activities.

2. The United States and its allies would swiftly and surely win a second war on the Korean Peninsula, but the destruction of life and property would far surpass anything in recent American experience. The U.S. must pursue its objectives with respect to nuclear weapons and ballistic missiles in the DPRK without taking actions that would weaken deterrence or increase the probability of DPRK miscalculation.

3. If stability can be preserved through the cooperative ending of DPRK nuclear weapons- and long-range missile-related activities, the U.S. should be prepared to establish more normal diplomatic relations with the DPRK and join in the ROK's policy of engagement and peaceful coexistence.

4. Unfreezing Yongbyon is North Korea's quickest and surest path to acquisition of nuclear weapons. The Agreed Framework, therefore, should be preserved and implemented by the United States and its allies. With the Agreed Framework, the DPRK's ability to produce plutonium at Yongbyon is verifiably frozen. Without the Agreed Framework, however, it is estimated that the North could reprocess enough plutonium to produce a significant number of nuclear weapons per year. The Agreed Framework's limitations, such as the fact that it does not verifiably freeze all nuclear weapons-related activities and does not cover ballistic missiles, are best addressed by supplementing rather than replacing the Agreed Framework.

5. No U.S. policy toward the DPRK will succeed if the ROK and Japan do not actively support it and cooperate in its implementation. Securing such trilateral coordination should be possible, since the interests of the three parties, while not identical, overlap in significant and definable ways.

6. Considering the risks inherent in the situation and the isolation, suspicion, and negotiating style of the DPRK, a successful U.S. policy will require steadiness and persistence even in the face of provocations. The approach adopted now must be sustained into the future, beyond the term of this Administration. It is, therefore, essential that the policy and its ongoing implementation have the broadest possible support and the continuing involvement of the Congress. . . .

A Comprehensive and Integrated Approach: A Two-Path Strategy

[The policy recommended by the review panel] is a two-path strategy focused on our priority concerns over the DPRK's nuclear weapons- and missile-related activities. We have devised this strategy in close consultation with the governments of the ROK and Japan, and it has their full support. Indeed, it is a joint strategy in which all three of our countries play coordinated and mutually reinforcing roles in pursuit of the same objectives. Both paths aim to protect our key security interests; the first path is clearly preferable for the United States and its allies and, we firmly believe, for the DPRK.

The first path involves a new, comprehensive and integrated approach to our negotiations with the DPRK. We would seek complete and verifiable assurances that the DPRK does not have a nuclear weapons program. We would also seek the complete and verifiable cessation of testing, production and deployment of missiles exceeding the parameters of the Missile Technology Control Regime, and the complete cessation of export sales of such missiles and the equipment and technology associated with them. By negotiating the complete cessation of the DPRK's destabilizing nuclear weapons and long-range missile programs, this path would lead to a stable security situation on the Korean Peninsula, creating the conditions for a more durable and lasting peace in the long run and ending the Cold War in East Asia.

On this path the United States and its allies would, in a step-by-step and reciprocal fashion, move to reduce pressures on the DPRK that it perceives as threatening. The reduction of perceived threat would in turn give the DPRK regime the confidence that it could coexist peacefully with us and its neighbors and pursue its own economic and social development. If the DPRK moved to eliminate its nuclear and long-range missile threats, the United States would normalize relations with the DPRK, relax sanctions that have long constrained trade with the DPRK and take other positive steps that would provide opportunities for the DPRK.

If the DPRK were prepared to move down this path, the ROK and Japan have indicated that they would also be prepared, in coordinated but parallel tracks, to improve relations with the DPRK.

It is important that all sides make contributions to creating an environment conducive to success in such far-ranging talks. The most important step by the DPRK is to give assurances that it will refrain from further test firings of long-range missiles as we undertake negotiations on the first path. In the context of the DPRK suspending such tests, the review team recommended that the United States ease, in a reversible manner, Presidentially-mandated trade embargo measures against the DPRK. The ROK and Japan have also indicated a willingness to take positive steps in these circumstances.

When the review team, led by Dr. Perry as a Presidential Envoy, visited Pyongyang in May, the team had discussions with DPRK officials and listened to their views. We also discussed these initial steps that would create a favorable environment for conducting comprehensive and integrated negotiations. Based on talks between with Ambassador Charles Kartman and DPRK Vice Foreign Minister Kim Gye Gwan in early September, the U.S. understood and expected that the DPRK would suspend long-range missile testing—to include both No Dong and Taepo Dong missiles—for as long as U.S.-DPRK discussions to improve relations continued. The DPRK subsequently announced a unilateral suspension of such tests while talks between the two countries continued. Accordingly, the Administration has taken steps to ease sanctions. This fall a senior DPRK official will likely visit Washington to reciprocate the Perry visit and continue discussions on improving relations. Both sides have taken a bold and meaningful step along the first path. While it is only an initial step, and both sides can easily reverse this first step, we are hopeful that it begins to take us down the long but important path to reducing threat on the Korean Peninsula.

While the first path devised by the review holds great promise for U.S. security and for stability in East Asia, and while the initial steps taken in recent weeks give us great hope, the first path depends on the willingness of the DPRK to traverse it with us. The review team is hopeful it will agree to do so, but on the basis of discussions to date we cannot be sure the DPRK will. Prudence therefore dictated that we devise a second path, once again in consultation with our allies and with their full support. On the second path, we would need to act to contain the threat that we have been unable to eliminate through negotiation. By incorporating two paths, the strategy devised in the review avoids any dependence on conjectures regarding DPRK intentions or behavior and neither seeks, nor depends upon for its success, a transformation of the DPRK's internal system.

If North Korea rejects the first path, it will not be possible for the United States to pursue a new relationship with the DPRK. In that case, the United States and its allies would have to take other steps to assure their security and contain the threat. The U.S. and allied steps should seek to keep the Agreed Framework intact and avoid, if possible, direct conflict. But they would also have to take firm but measured steps to persuade the DPRK that it should return to the first path and avoid destabilizing the security situation in the region.

Our recommended strategy does not immediately address a number of issues outside the scope of direct U.S.-DPRK negotiations, such as ROK family reunification, implementation of the North-South Basic Agreement (including reactivation of North-South Joint Committees) and Japanese kidnapping cases, as well as other key issues of concern, including drug trafficking. However, the policy review team believed that all of these issues should be, and would be, seriously addressed as relations between the DPRK and the U.S. improve.

Similarly, the review team believed the issue of chemical and biological weapons is best addressed multilaterally. Many recommendations have also been made with respect to Korean unification; but, ultimately, the question of unification is something for the Korean people to decide. Finally, the policy review team strongly believed that the U.S. must not withdraw any of its forces from Korea—a withdrawal would not contribute to peace and stability, but rather undermine the strong deterrence currently in place.

Advantages of the Proposed Strategy

The proposed strategy has the following advantages:

1. *Has the full support of our allies.* No U.S. policy can be successful if it does not enjoy the support of our allies in the region. The overall approach

builds upon the South's policy of engagement with North Korea, as the ROK leadership suggested to Dr. Perry directly and to the President. It also puts the U.S. effort to end the DPRK missile program on the same footing with U.S. efforts to end its nuclear weapons program, as the Government of Japan recommended.

2. *Draws on U.S. negotiating strengths.* Pursuant to the recommended approach, the United States will be offering the DPRK a comprehensive relaxation of political and economic pressures which the DPRK perceives as threatening to it and which are applied, in its view, principally by the United States. This approach complements the positive steps the ROK and Japan are prepared to take. On the other hand, the United States will not offer the DPRK tangible "rewards" for appropriate security behavior; doing so would both transgress principles that the United States values and open us up to further blackmail.

3. *Leaves stable deterrence of war unchanged.* No changes are recommended in our strong deterrent posture on the Korean Peninsula, and the U.S. should not put its force posture on the negotiating table. Deterrence is strong in both directions on the Korean Peninsula today. It is the North's nuclear weapons- and long-range missile-related activities that threaten stability. Likewise, the approach recommended by the review will not constrain U.S. Theater Missile Defense programs or the opportunities of the ROK and Japan to share in these programs; indeed, we explicitly recommended that no such linkage should be made.

4. *Builds on the Agreed Framework.* The approach recommended seeks more than the Agreed Framework provides. Specifically, under the recommended approach the U.S. will seek a total and verifiable end to all nuclear weapons-related activities in the DPRK, and the U.S. will be addressing the DPRK's long-range missile programs, which are not covered by the Agreed Framework. In addition, the U.S. will seek to traverse the broader path to peaceful relations foreseen by both the U.S. and the DPRK in the Agreed Framework, and incorporated in its text.

5. *Aligns U.S. and allied near-term objectives with respect to the DPRK's nuclear and missile activities with our long-term objectives for lasting peace on the Korean Peninsula.* The recommended approach focuses on the near-term dangers to stability posed by the DPRK's nuclear weapons- and missile-related activities, but it aims to create the conditions for lasting peace on the Korean Peninsula in the longer run, as the U.S. seeks through the Four Party Talks. As noted above, the recommended approach also seeks to realize the long-term objectives of the Agreed Framework, which are to move beyond cooperation in the nuclear field to broader, more normal U.S.-DPRK relations.

6. *Does not depend on specific North Korean behavior or intent.* The proposed strategy is flexible and avoids any dependence on conjectures or assumptions regarding DPRK intentions or behavior—benign or provocative. Again, it neither seeks, nor depends upon, either such intentions or a transformation of the DPRK's internal system for success. Appropriate contingencies are built into the recommended framework.

Key Policy Recommendations

In the context of the recommendations above, the review team offered the following five key policy recommendations:

1. Adopt a comprehensive and integrated approach to the DPRK's nuclear weapons- and ballistic missile-related programs, as recommended by the review team and supported by our allies in the region. Specifically, initiate negotiations with the DPRK based on the concept of mutually reducing threat; if the DPRK is not receptive, we will need to take appropriate measures to protect our security and those of our allies.

2. Create a strengthened mechanism within the U.S. Government for carrying out North Korea policy. Operating under the direction of the Principals Committee and Deputies Committee, a small, senior-level interagency North Korea working group should be maintained, chaired by a senior official of ambassadorial rank, located in the Department of State, to coordinate policy with respect to North Korea.

3. Continue the new mechanism established last March to ensure close coordination with the ROK and Japan. The Trilateral Coordination and Oversight Group (TCOG)—established during this policy review and consisting of senior officials of the three governments—is charged with managing policy toward the DPRK. This group should meet regularly to coordinate negotiating strategy and overall policy toward the DPRK and to prepare frequent consultations on this issue between the President and the ROK President and Japanese Prime Minister. The U.S. delegation should be headed by the senior official coordinating North Korea policy.

4. Take steps to create a sustainable, bipartisan, long-term outlook toward the problem of North Korea. The President should explore with the majority and minority leaders of both houses of Congress ways for the Hill, on a bipartisan basis, to consult on this and future Administrations' policy toward the DPRK. Just as no policy toward the DPRK can succeed unless it is a combined strategy of the United States and its allies, the policy review team believes no strategy can be sustained over time without the input and support of Congress.

5. Approve a plan of action prepared for dealing with the contingency of DPRK provocations in the near term, including the launch of a long-range missile. The policy review team notes that its proposed responses to negative DPRK actions could have profound consequences for the Peninsula, the U.S. and our allies. These responses should make it clear to the DPRK that provocative actions carry a heavy penalty. Unless the DPRK's acts transgress provisions of the Agreed Framework, however, U.S. and allied actions should not themselves undermine the Agreed Framework. To do so would put the U.S. in the position of violating the Agreed Framework, opening the path for the DPRK to unfreeze Yongbyon and return us to the crisis of the summer of 1994.

Concluding Thoughts

The team's recommended approach is based on a realistic view of the DPRK, a hardheaded understanding of military realities and a firm determination to protect U.S. interests and those of our allies.

We should recognize that North Korea may send mixed signals concerning its response to our recommended proposal for a comprehensive framework and that many aspects of its behavior will remain reprehensible to us even if we embark on this negotiating process. We therefore should prepare for provocative contingencies but stay the policy course with measured actions pursuant to the overall framework recommended. The North needs to understand that there are certain forms of provocative behavior that represent a direct threat to the U.S. and its allies and that we will respond appropriately.

In this regard, it is with mixed feelings that we recognize certain provocative behavior of the DPRK may force the U.S. to reevaluate current aid levels.

Finally, and to close this review, we need to point out that a confluence of events this past year has opened what we strongly feel is a unique window of opportunity for the U.S. with respect to North Korea. There is a clear and common understanding among Seoul, Tokyo, and Washington on how to deal with Pyongyang. The PRC's strategic goals—especially on the issue of North Korean nuclear weapons and related missile delivery systems—overlap with those of the U.S. Pyongyang appears committed to the Agreed Framework and for the time being is convinced of the value of improving relations with the U.S. However, there are always pressures on these positive elements. Underlying tensions and suspicions have led to intermittent armed clashes and incidents and affect the political environment. Efforts to establish the diplomatic momentum necessary to withstand decades of hostility become increasingly difficult and eventually stall. Nevertheless, the year 1999 may represent, historically, one of our best opportunities to deal with key U.S. security concerns on the Korean Peninsula for some time to come.

UN ON WORLD POPULATION REACHING SIX BILLION PEOPLE
October 12, 1999

The convergence of two important milestones in 1999—the approach of a new millennium and achievement of the 6 billion mark in global population—focused renewed attention on the challenges posed by rapid population growth in much of the world. The twentieth century opened with 1.65 billion people and closed with more than three times as many, by far the fastest acceleration of population growth in human history. The century's population explosion resulted from many factors, most importantly enormous advances in medical care and environmental conditions that reduced infant death rates and improved life expectancy.

During the last two decades of the century, there was a spreading recognition in most of the world that rapid population growth posed serious dangers in terms of feeding, housing, employing, and caring for people. The United Nations, other international agencies, and leading industrialized countries pumped billions of dollars into family planning programs and economic development efforts that focused on the education and employment of women. Despite many setbacks, these programs helped reverse population growth rates worldwide. By 1999 the average family was giving birth to 2.7 children, compared with 4.9 children a half-century earlier.

Although the goal of curbing population growth was supported by most world leaders by the late 1990s, the idea remained controversial in much of the world and among numerous groups. The Roman Catholic Church, many Islamic groups, and other important religious denominations opposed the general concept of artificial birth control. Leaders of some countries made high birth rates a point of national pride, and the education of women lagged behind that of men in most of the world, and was even forbidden in some places, most notably Afghanistan.

The UN held a special three-day session on population and family planning issues on June 30–July 2. It was a follow-up to a 1994 conference in Cairo that established a twenty-year goal of slowing population growth rates around the world. "Since Cairo the world does understand . . . that we

584

have to stabilize the population of this planet," UN Secretary General Kofi Annan said in an opening address to the conference. (Cairo conference, Historic Documents of 1994, p. 351)

Reaching the Six-Billion Mark

Using computer projections, UN demographers determined that world population would reach the 6 billion mark on October 12, 1999, and so the world body laid plans to mark the occasion. The population conference was one such event. On October 12 the UN Population Division published "The World at Six Billion," a snapshot of population trends with projections well into the twenty-first century.

The UN also marked the occasion with a high-profile trip by Annan to Sarajevo, the capital of Bosnia, where for symbolic reasons UN officials decided to declare the first baby born on October 12 as the world's six-billionth person. That honor went to a boy, Adnan Nevic, born to refugees in the province of the former Yugoslavia that was torn by a brutal civil war from 1992 to 1995. Annan said the boy's birth "in a city returning to life, to a people rebuilding their homes, in a region restoring a culture of co-existence after a decade of war, should light a path of tolerance and understanding for all peoples."

As Annan was in Sarajevo, a population clock at UN headquarters in New York raced from 5,999,999,998 to 6,000,000,001, prompting one UN official to remark: "Somebody had triplets."

UN officials and some other international leaders used the occasion to comment on the need to address poverty suffered by most of the world's people. UNICEF director Carol Bellamy noted that one-third of the children born in the world's poorest counties would not live beyond the age of five. President Bill Clinton said: "We must refuse to accept a future in which one part of humanity lives on the cutting edge of a new economy, while another part lives on the edge of survival."

More People, but at a Slower Rate

It took just twelve years for the world to grow from 5 billion to 6 billion people, the speediest billion-person increase in history. The previous cycle was thirteen years. During the twentieth century, total population started at 1.65 billion, reached 2 billion in 1927, 3 billion in 1960, 4 billion in 1974, 5 billion in 1987, and 6 billion in 1999.

Using a "medium-case" projection based on a complex set of factors, the UN Population Division estimated that the world would reach the 7 billion mark in 2013 and the 8 billion mark in 2028. In terms of growth rate, those projections would represent relative stability because the number of years required to reach each successive billion-person mark would increase—fourteen years to reach the 7 billion figure and fifteen years to reach 8 billion.

By the late 1990s, the annual population growth rate worldwide had declined sharply. In the 1960s, the world was adding population at an annual rate of just over 2 percent, meaning that world population would

*double about every fifty years. But family planning programs, the educa-
tion of women, and other factors helped reduce that rate in every region of
the world by the 1995–1999 period, according to UN figures. During the
late 1990s, the worldwide annual growth rate was about 1.3 percent, meaning that it would take seventy-seven years for the population to double. In
some areas of the world—especially the industrialized countries of Europe
and North America—the growth rate had dropped to near zero. The growth
rate was highest in Africa, at 2.4 percent.*

*Another manifestation of the declining birth rate was a dramatic drop
in the average number of children per family. After reaching a peak of 4.9
children per couple in the 1960s, the average declined to 2.7 children at the
end of the 1990s. The rate was lowest, at 1.3 children, in Europe, North
America, and Japan, and highest in Africa at 5.1*

*UN officials and population experts said these declining rates were not
the result of chance but of shifting societal trends and key decisions made
by world leaders in the last half of the twentieth century. Some experts
pointed to Mexico as an example. In the 1970s demographers predicted that
Mexico's population would triple, from about 50 million to nearly 150 million, by the end of the twentieth century. The Mexican government, which
had promoted large families to foster economic growth rates, abruptly
changed course in 1974 and began family planning and education programs that encouraged parents to have fewer children. By 1999 Mexico's
population stood at just under 99 billion—double the number of a quarter-
century earlier but 50 million less than had been projected.*

*UN officials said education was a key component to reducing population
growth. Educated people—and especially educated women—tended to
marry later and have fewer children than those with little or no education.
Educated families also tended to provide better food and health care for
their children, helping them live longer and more productive lives.*

*Another important factor helping to reduce the number of children per
family in Mexico and many other countries was rapid urbanization. Families in rural areas tended to want many children as helping hands in the
fields. By contrast, urban parents tended to be better educated and more
interested in promoting their careers and other goals than in having large
families. Poor families in urban areas realized that many children meant
having many mouths to feed and bodies to care for and clothe.*

*Another country that took stemming population growth seriously was
China. Beginning in the 1980s, with the country's population approaching
the 1 billion mark, China's communist leaders launched a strict one-child-
per-family policy intended to reduce the rate of growth. One consequence of
that policy was that many Chinese families took drastic steps to avoid having girls, who were viewed as an economic drag compared to boys. Late-
term abortions, sterilizations, and the killing of baby girls soared in China,
especially during the 1980s. In response to international protests, officials
in Beijing denied that infanticide was national policy and took limited
steps to curb the practice. However draconian it was, China's one-child pol-*

icy worked: by 1999 the country's population stood at 1.25 billion, about 300 million less than had been projected.

Despite the overall decline in growth rates, demographers said world population would continue to expand simply because there were so many women of child-bearing age. With an estimated 1.8 billion people under the age of eighteen as of 1999, the world was expected to experience a "population momentum" well into the twenty-first century.

UN population projections for individual countries showed sharp contrasts in growth rates resulting from complex factors. One attention-getting statistic was the projection that India would surpass China as the world's most populous country by the middle of the twenty-first century. India was expected to reach the 1 billion mark in May 2000 and 1.5 billion by 2050, just slightly more than China's population at that time.

At the other end of the scale, the UN report listed thirty-two countries where population was expected to decline between 1999 and 2050. For the most part, that list consisted of two major groupings. One group included some of the most highly developed nations on the planet where economic and social factors had led to sharply declining birth rates. Among them, in descending order of projected population loss, were Japan, Italy, Germany, the United Kingdom, the Netherlands, Belgium, Austria, and Switzerland.

The second group facing population declines included nations that had been part of the Soviet bloc or had communist rulers for much of the cold war period, among them Russia, Ukraine, Belarus, Latvia, Lithuania, Slovakia, Estonia, and Cuba, and most of the constituent republics of the former Yugoslavia (Croatia, Slovenia, Yugoslavia, and Bosnia). Most of these countries faced severe economic and societal upheavals in the years following the collapse of communism; the former Yugoslav republics were engulfed in civil war for parts of the 1990s.

The population of the United States was expected to grow at a moderate rate during the first part of the twentieth century. U.S. population grew from 157.8 million in 1950 to 276.2 million in 1999. By 2050 the U.S. population was expected to reach 349 million, an average annual increase of less than 1.5 percent.

Although African countries were expected to continue experiencing the most rapid population growth rates in the world during the twenty-first century, there was one deadly countertrend: the AIDS (acquired immunodeficiency syndrome) epidemic, which in 1999 was more prevalent in Africa than anywhere else. The UN report showed the expected effect, between 2000 and 2015, of the AIDS epidemic on population growth rates in thirty-two countries with high rates of infection with HIV (human immunodeficiency virus), which caused AIDS. All were in Africa except for Haiti, Cambodia, and Thailand. The UN estimated that AIDS would cut the annual growth rate by about 1 percent or more in five countries in southern Africa: Namibia, Botswana, South Africa, Mozambique, and Zimbabwe. In South Africa, for example, the UN estimated that the hypothetical annual population growth rate, without the interference of the AIDS epidemic, would be 1.53 percent; including the impact of AIDS would bring South Africa's average annual growth rate to 0.48 percent. Another way to look at the impact of AIDS was to examine anticipated life-expectancy. In the same five southern African countries, the AIDS epidemic was expected to reduce average life expectancy by seventeen to twenty-six years, depending on the country.

Life Expectancy and Aging

During the twentieth century advances in medical care and improved environmental conditions had two major consequences for overall population rates: infant mortality was dramatically reduced worldwide, and life spans increased just as dramatically. By 1999 the worldwide infant mortality rate was 57 per 1,000 live births, and worldwide life expectancy had reached sixty-five years, an increase of nine years in just two decades.

Those trends in turn were having another impact: the rapid "aging" of the world population. The portion of the world population over the age of 60 rose from 8 percent in 1950 to 10 percent in 1999 and was expected to reach 22 percent in 2050. Similarly, the median age rose from 23.5 years in 1950 to 26.4 years in 1999 and was expected to reach nearly 38 years by 2050. The graying of the population was most dramatic in the developed countries, where the median age stood at 37 years in 1999 and was expected to rise to 45 years in 2050.

One result of population aging with potentially serious consequences was the decline in what demographers called the "support ratio"—the proportion of people in the fifteen to sixty-four year range to those in the sixty-five and older range. In 1999 the support ratio was nine working age persons per one older person worldwide; by 2050 that ratio was expected to decline to two to one in developed regions and four to one in less developed regions.

The majority of older people continued to be women, according to the UN projections. Worldwide, women constituted 55 percent of persons sixty or older and 65 percent of those age eighty or older. The ratio of aged women to men was highest in the developed nations and lowest in the developing world.

> *Following is the text of a statement made October 12, 1999, in Sarajevo, Bosnia, by United Nations Secretary General Kofi Annan, honoring the symbolic designation of a baby born in that city as the world's six billionth person; excerpts follow from the introduction and highlights sections of* The World at Six Billion, *issued October 12, 1999, by the United Nations Population Division:*

THE "DAY OF SIX BILLION" CEREMONY

It is a very special honour for me to mark the Day of Six Billion in the city of Sarajevo. I can think of few peoples with whom I would rather commemorate this milestone of hope for humanity.

The birth today of the six billionth person on the planet—a beautiful boy—in a city returning to life, to a people rebuilding their homes, in a region restoring a culture of co-existence after a decade of war—should light a path of tolerance and understanding for all peoples.

Neither the awful war, nor the merciless siege of Sarajevo, nor even the inhuman policy of "ethnic cleansing" has succeeded in preventing this and so many other births in Bosnia. It is my hope that you will celebrate today's birth by ensuring the rebirth of the tolerant and multi-religious atmosphere that once characterized Sarajevo and Bosnia. This should be our common gift to Baby 6 Billion.

On behalf of the United Nations, it gives me great pleasure to announce a gift of $50,000 to the maternity ward at Kosovo Hospital to help provide even better care and services to the people of Sarajevo.

The birth of Sarajevo's Baby Six Billion will resonate far beyond this city or country or region. The world at large is being transformed by a population growth that has seen the total population double within four decades. Half the world's population today is under 25. There are over a billion young people between 15 and 24.

The challenge to feed and clothe and house this great mass of humanity over the next decades will be immense. The means are available. The question is whether we have the will. Of the 4.8 billion people in developing countries, nearly three fifths lack basic sanitation. Almost a third have no access to clean water. A quarter do not have adequate housing and a fifth have no access to modern health services.

The challenge on the Day of Six Billion is to live up to the promise of our time to give every man, woman and child an opportunity to make the most of their abilities, in safety and in dignity. For the sake of Baby Mevic and all who will follow him, let us rededicate ourselves to this noble aim.

UN POPULATION REPORT

Introduction

According to the latest United Nations population estimates, world population reaches the six billion mark on 12 October 1999, an historic milestone in the growth of world population. The marking of a world of six billion just at the dawn of the new millennium is a convergence of events that is attracting widespread global attention. The *World at Six Billion* was prepared in response to this attention. It provides . . . salient characteristics of past, current and future world population growth.

The twentieth century has witnessed extraordinary population growth. During this century, world population increased from 1.65 billion to 6 billion, and experienced both the highest rate of population growth (averaging 2.04 per cent per year) during the late 1960s, and the largest annual increment to world population (86 million persons each year) in the late 1980s.

The world population growth rate has fallen from its peak of 2 per cent to around 1.3 per cent today. Nonetheless, world population will continue to increase substantially during the twenty-first century. United Nations projections (medium fertility scenario) indicate that world population will nearly stabilize at just above 10 billion persons after 2200. However, the twenty-first century is expected to be one of comparatively slower population growth than the previous century, and be characterized by declining fertility and the ageing of populations.

At the same time that the world population growth rate has declined from its peak, the average number of children per couple has fallen from 4.9 to 2.7 and life expectancy at birth has risen from 56 years to 65 years. The share of the world's population living in urban areas has increased from 36 per cent to 47 per cent and the number of megacities of 10 million persons or more has grown from 5 to 18. The number of persons who have moved to another country has risen to over 125 million today.

In the less developed regions, couples are currently having about two children less than couples did three decades ago. Even though fertility has declined to relatively moderate levels in many developing countries, and to below replacement level in some, a large and growing number of births are occurring annually, due to the continued growth in the number of women of childbearing age; a legacy of past high fertility levels. In the more developed nations, fertility declined from 2.4 births per woman during the late 1960s to an historic low of 1.6 for the current period. In Europe, Northern America and Japan, the current fertility rate is 1.5 births per woman or below.

In spite of the impressive gains in health and life expectancy that the world has exhibited during the past decades, much remains to be done. Recent years has shown a devastating toll from AIDS in a number of countries, particularly in sub-Saharan Africa. In addition, in some countries of Eastern Europe, the health situation has been deteriorating and adult mortality, especially among males, has increased.

The twentieth century has witnessed the growth of urban centres and the concentration of population in urban areas. Half of the world population is expected to be urban by 2006. Giant urban agglomerations are becoming both more numerous and larger in size.

Another major transformation of the twentieth century has been population ageing. In 1999 there were 593 million persons aged 60 years or over in the world, comprising 10 per cent of the world population. By 2050, this figure will triple to nearly 2 billion older persons, comprising 22 per cent of the world population. This changing age structure will have wide-ranging economic and social consequences, affecting such factors as economic growth, savings and investment, labour supply and employment, pension schemes, and health and long-term care. While once limited to developed countries, concern for the consequences of ageing has spread to developing countries. . . .

Highlights

1. World population is estimated to cross the six billion threshold on October 12, 1999.

2. World population is projected to cross the 7 billion mark in 2013; the 8 billion mark in 2028; the 9 billion mark in 2054. World population nearly stabilizes at just above 10 billion after 2200.

3. It has taken just 12 years for the world to add this most recent billion people. This is the shortest period of time in world history for a billion people to be added.

4. World population did not reach one billion until 1804. It took 123 years to reach 2 billion in 1927, 33 years to reach 3 billion in 1960, 14 years to reach 4 billion in 1974 and 13 years to reach 5 billion in 1987.

5. The highest rate of world population growth (2.04 per cent) occurred in the late 1960s. The current rate (1995–2000) is 1.31 per cent.

6. The largest annual increase to world population (86 million) took place in the late 1980s; the current annual increase is 78 million.

7. Of the 78 million people currently added to the world each year, 95 per cent live in the less developed regions.

8. Eighty per cent of the world currently reside in the less developed regions. At the beginning of the century, 70 per cent did so. By 2050, the share of the world population living in the currently less developed regions will have risen to 90 per cent.

9. The population of the world is ageing. The median age increased from 23.5 years in 1950 to 26.4 years in 1999. By 2050, the median age is projected to reach 37.8 years. The number of people in the world aged 60 or older will also rise from the current one-of-ten persons to be two-of-nine by 2050. Currently around one-of-five persons in the developed countries are aged 60 or older; in 2050 nearly one-of-every three persons will be aged 60 or older.

10. World life expectancy at birth is now at 65 years, having increased by a remarkable 20 years since 1950; by 2050 life expectancy is expected to exceed 76 years. However, in spite of these impressive gains, recent years have shown a devastating toll from AIDS in a number of countries. In addition, in some Eastern European countries, health has been deteriorating and mortality, particularly among adult males, has been rising.

11. Couples in developing countries today have on average 3 children each; thirty years ago they had six. More than half of all couples in developing countries now use contraception.

12. The number of persons who have moved to another country has risen to over 125 million migrants today from 75 million in 1965.

13. The world has become increasingly urban. Currently, around 46 per cent of the world population lives in urban areas; the majority of the world's population will be urban by 2006.

CLINTON ON "ROADLESS INITIATIVE" FOR PROTECTING FEDERAL FORESTS
October 13, 1999

Taking a step that had the potential to become one of the most sweeping land-conservation measures in American history, President Bill Clinton on October 13, 1999, ordered a year-long process of determining whether some 40 million acres of federal forest should be kept free of roads. Protecting the forests from the construction of roads would have the effect of protecting them from development, mining, and logging.

The 40 million acres represented the largest chunk of the 192 million acres of Forest Service land that was not subject to logging or other exploitive uses nor fully protected by law and regulation. The government had never built roads on the vast majority of those 40 million acres, and the Clinton administration had imposed a temporary moratorium on road construction in all the national forests. Clinton was seeking to use administrative measures, without the direct involvement of Congress, to ensure that the 40 million acres would remain "roadless" permanently and therefore free from development.

The president's action set off a fierce power struggle in Washington, with the administration and environmental advocacy groups on one side, and business interests, joined by their Republican allies in Congress, in opposition. The administration planned to conclude a year's worth of public hearings, technical reviews, and other administrative procedures, and then put the plan into effect by the end of 2000—just before Clinton was scheduled to leave office.

In an open letter dated December 29, Forest Service chief Mike Dombeck sought to emphasize the big picture behind the roadless initiative. "What distinguishes a truly wealthy nation from one that merely generates wealth is the foresight and wisdom to leave behind a richer legacy than we inherited, to make short-term sacrifices to advance long-term gains, to proceed humbly and cautiously in managing our national resource endowment," Dombeck wrote. He added that the debate over the issue would be a "messy, frustrating and sometimes awkward process," but that was a necessary consequence of the fact that the forests were "the people's lands."

Background to the Plan

The U.S. Forest Service, a division of the Agriculture Department, had stewardship over 192 million acres of national forest land. The majority of forest land was open to timbering, mining, or other forms of economic development. Starting in the 1970s, Congress set aside 34 million acres as "wilderness," meaning that it was unspoiled land that could never be logged, mined, or subject to economic development. Another 50 million to 60 million acres—the exact amount was disputed—was not protected by statute or regulation but had never been developed because of inaccessibility, unsuitability for development, or some other reason. Clinton's October 13 proposal would affect about 40 million of those acres.

Under the proposal, the Forest Service would be barred permanently from developing roads in so-called roadless tracts of 5,000 acres or more: sections of national forests in thirty-five states that were not designated as wilderness but had never had roads built through them.

Clinton announced his plan during a ceremony at a scenic overlook in the George Washington and Jefferson Forest in Virginia. With the region's hardwood trees turning to fall color, Clinton stood next to Peter Pinchot, the grandson of Gifford Pinchot, the Forest Service director, who was generally given much of the credit for President Teddy Roosevelt's actions in preserving 120 million acres of national forests and creating five national parks.

"Our nation has not always honored President Roosevelt's vision," Clinton said. "Too often, we have favored resource extraction over conservation, degrading our forests and the critical values they sustain. As the consequences of these actions have become more apparent, the American people have expressed growing concern and have called on us to restore balance to their forests."

Despite the sweeping scope of the plan, Clinton insisted it would have minimal impact on the logging industry, which had already expressed fierce opposition. Referring to that opposition, Clinton said dryly that some had feared his plan would "end the world as we know it." Clinton cited statistics showing that only 5 percent of the timber harvested each year in the United States came from the national forests, and less than 5 percent of the timber cut in national forests came from the roadless areas he was seeking to protect. "We can easily adjust our federal timber program to replace 5 percent of 5 percent, but we can never replace what we might destroy if we don't protect these 40 million acres," he said.

Perhaps the major detail left unresolved in Clinton's plan was the status of some 2 million roadless acres in the Tongass National Forest in Alaska, the nation's largest. The administration did not specifically include the Tongass forest, apparently leaving the question to the give-and-take of decisionmaking for the final version during 2000. Representatives of some environmental groups said excluding Tongass would substantially weaken the effect of the roadless plan, simply because of the size and environmental importance of that forest. But congressional Republicans from Alaska, and the state's Republican governor, vowed to fight the inclusion of a single

*acre of Tongass. Some observers said it appeared possible that the admin-
istration would use Tongass as a bargaining chip—eventually agreeing to
compromise on Tongass acreage in exchange for Congress backing down
from a direct challenge to the overall policy.*

*The roadless initiative was one of three proposals launched by the
administration in late 1999 on national forest policy. A companion proposal, put under the same review timetable as the roadless initiative, called
for new standards for determining how to maintain and improve the
308,000 miles of roads already built in the forests. Officials said that plan
was intended to make best use of the Forest Service's limited budget for
roads. The Forest Service said it had a backlog of forest road maintenance
and reconstruction projects totaling more than $8 billion because Congress
routinely cut appropriations for that purpose. A third proposal, announced
September 30, would establish new procedures for how the Forest Service
developed and issued regulations governing the forests. In essence, the proposal would make environmental concerns—especially the ecological health
of forests—the primary consideration for Forest Service policy, taking
precedence over timber harvests and other commercial uses.*

Reaction to the Plan

*Public reaction to Clinton's proposal was swift and predictable. Envi-
ronmental groups praised it—although some said it did not go far enough
and expressed concern about whether the administration would stand by it
in the face of congressional opposition. Groups representing logging, mining, and recreational sporting industries were quick to denounce the plan
as a federal "land grab." The critics were joined by key allies in Congress,
including Republican leaders from western states who chaired key committees responsible for environmental and forest-management policy.*

*Clinton acknowledged to reporters that his plan faced many political
hurdles. "We're going to have a big fight on this for about a year," he said.
But in the end "we're going to protect all this before it's too late."*

*The most enthusiastic positive response came from the Heritage Forests
Campaign, an advocacy group established by the Pew Charitable Trusts to
lobby for the policy Clinton had embraced. "This is truly a monumental
moment in conservation and American history," the campaign's director,
Ken Rait said.*

*But Carl Ross, executive director of Save America's Forests, a coalition
of environmental groups, offered a more muted response to the president's
action. "It's simply premature to say that this is a great thing. All he's doing
is setting in motion a study, which may or may not lead to more protection
in the end. It's preservation, with a big asterisk, and maybe with loopholes."*

*Even before Clinton formally announced the proposal, opponents made
it clear they would try to block it in Congress. On October 12 thirty-eight
Republicans from western states sent Forest Service chief Dombeck a letter
denouncing the proposal in harsh terms. "We cannot stand by idly and*

watch our constituents lose the right to travel on the land they own," the Republicans wrote. "While the Forest Service might like this step backward to feudal European policies, it is completely unacceptable to us and those who use our public lands."

Henson Moore, president of the American Forest and Paper Association, called Clinton's plan "an extremist form of preservation" that would cost jobs and would lead to destruction of the very lands Clinton wanted to protect. Moore, a former member of Congress from Alabama, argued that roads were needed in the forests to keep them "healthy." Without lumber harvesting, he said, dead trees build up in forests, providing the fuel necessary for gigantic fires that destroy millions of acres. Moore also argued that logging was beneficial to elk and other wild animals that prefer open land to dense forests.

In the last ten weeks of the year the administration conducted 190 public hearings on the proposal and received an estimated 200,000 comments on it. To bolster support for the plan, the Forest Service established a site on the World Wide Web with photographs and descriptions of the forest lands that would be protected.

Development of Private Land

In a separate but related issue, the Agriculture Department on December 6 released a study showing a rapid rate of development of the nation's privately owned farmland, forests, and wetlands. The study was the latest in a series of five-year series of reports, called the National Resources Inventory, on the effect of urban "sprawl" on farms and other properties.

The study showed that development was speeding up in many areas. Sixteen million acres of farmland and other "undeveloped" land was turned over to housing, shopping malls, industrial sites, and other commercial uses between 1992 and 1997, the study said. That was larger than the 13.9 million acres that were developed during the previous ten years.

Pennsylvania and Texas led all states in the increased rate of land converted to developed uses. The average annual rate in Pennsylvania went from 43,110 acres between 1982 and 1992 to 224,640 between 1992 and 1997. In Texas the comparable average figures were 139,000 acres developed annually between 1982 and 1992 and 243,900 acres between 1992 and 1997.

Following are excerpts from a speech delivered October 13, 1999, by President Bill Clinton in which he announced a "roadless initiative" for protecting approximately 40 million acres of National Forest land from development by banning construction of roads for logging and other commercial purposes:

. . . Peter [Pinchot] talked about his grandfather [Gifford Pinchot, the first chief of the U.S. Forest Service] and Theodore Roosevelt. One of my proudest possessions—some of you know I collect old books about America. I just finished reading a fascinating account by Frances Perkins, the first woman to serve in the Cabinet, who was President Franklin Roosevelt's Labor Secretary during his entire tenure—about her 35-year relationship with Roosevelt. One of my proudest old American books is a first printing of the proceedings of the very first Governors Conference, held at the invitation of Theodore Roosevelt in 1908. The subject was the conservation of America's natural resources.

In my private dining room at the White House I have a picture of Theodore Roosevelt and all those governors, signed by all the governors with whom I served in 1992, when I was elected President. That first Governor's Conference remains one of the most important ever held in the White House. So much of what we've done as a nation to conserve our natural resources extends from that day. Peter's grandfather was a guiding spirit behind that conference.

Theodore Roosevelt, himself, said of Gifford Pinchot, "If it hadn't been for him, this conference neither would have, nor could have, been called." Gifford Pinchot used to say that "we must prefer results to routine." I like that a lot. And let me say that, in my view, no one illustrates that principle in our public life today better than Mike Dombeck, who has done such a remarkable job of returning the Forest Service to the vision of stewardship on which it was founded, And I thank you, sir. Thank you.

A century ago, when Mr. Pinchot was first dreaming up his plan to protect our forests, this vista looked very different than what we see today. In fact, it was more wasteland than forest. According to one eyewitness—and I quote—"weather-white ghosts of trees stood on the desolate slopes as a pitiful, battle-scared fragment of the glory that was once a virgin forest." Not only were the slopes nearly bare, tanneries and dye plants had poisoned the lakes and the mountain streams. The deer and black bear and turkey nearly were wiped out. The land and water were so thoroughly abused that most people thought the area had no value at all.

I know that they don't agree with that now because we have so many of the fine local officials from this area show up here today. I thank them for their presence and they can be proud of what they represent.

Visionaries like Theodore Roosevelt and Gifford Pinchot, the other men and women of the Forest Service who have cared for this land since 1917, made those dark descriptions a part of history. Nowadays, hundreds of thousands of visitors come here every year to hike, swim, bike, hunt, fish, or just to breathe the fresh air and take in the beautiful sights. The land that once no one wanted is now a thriving forest everyone can enjoy.

This kind of land has been important to me since I was a boy, where I learned by walking the Ozark and Quachita National Forests of my home state that national forests are more than a source of timber, they are places of renewal of the human spirit and our natural environment. At the dawn of the new century we have the opportunity to act on behalf of these forests in a way that honors the vision of our forbears, Roosevelt and Pinchot.

Within our national forests there are large parcels of land that don't contain roads of any kind and, in most cases, never have. From the beautiful stretch of the Alleghenys that we see here to the old-growth canyonlands of Tahoe National Forest, these areas represent some of the last, best, unprotected wildland anywhere in our nation. They offer unparalleled opportunities for hikers, hunters and anglers. They're absolutely critical to the survival of many endangered species, as you have just heard.

And I think it's worth pointing out they are also very often a source of clean and fresh water for countless communities. They are, therefore, our treasured inheritance.

Today, we launch one of the largest land preservation efforts in America's history to protect these priceless, back-country lands. The Forest Service will prepare a detailed analysis of how best to preserve our forests' large roadless areas, and then present a formal proposal to do just that. The Forest Service will also determine whether similar protection is warranted for smaller roadless areas that have not yet been surveyed.

Through this action, we will protect more than 40 million acres, 20 percent of the total forest land in America in the national forests from activities, such as new road construction which would degrade the land. We will ensure that our grandchildren will be able to hike up to this peak, that others like it across the country will also offer the same opportunities. We will assure that when they get to the top they'll be able to look out on valleys like this, just as beautiful then as they are now.

We will live up to the challenge Theodore Roosevelt laid down a century ago to leave this land even a better land for our descendants than it is for us.

It is very important to point out that we are not trying to turn the national forests into museums. Even as we strengthen protections, the majority of our forests will continue to be responsibly managed for sustainable timber production and other activities. We are, once again, determined to prove that environmental protection and economic growth can, and must, go hand in hand.

Let me give you an example, because I've seen a lot of people already saying a lot of terrible things about what I'm doing today, and how it is going to end the world as we know it. This initiative should have almost no effect on timber supply. Only five percent of our country's timber comes from the national forests. Less than five percent of the national forests' timber is now being cut in roadless areas. We can easily adjust our federal timber program to replace five percent of five percent, but we can never replace what we might destroy if we don't protect these 40 million acres.

As the previous speaker said, today's action is the latest step taken under the administration of Vice President Gore and me to expand our children's natural treasures. Over the past six and a half years, we've protected millions of acres, from the Yellowstone to the Everglades, from the ancient redwoods of Headwaters to the red rock canyons of Utah. We're working now to save New Mexico's spectacular Baca Ranch.

As Secretary [Bruce] Babbitt [secretary of the Interior Department] has said many times, our administration has now protected more land than any in the history of the country except those of Franklin and Theodore Roosevelt.

I have also proposed an unprecedented $1-billion Lands Legacy Initiative, with permanent funding over the years to guarantee for the first time ever a continuing fund for protecting and restoring precious lands across America. This initiative represents the largest investment in protecting our green and open spaces since President Theodore Roosevelt set our nation on this path nearly a century ago. It would allow us to save Civil War battlefields, remote stretches of the historic Lewis and Clark Trail, nearly half a million acres in California desert parks and wilderness areas. It will also allow us to meet the stewardship challenges of the new century by helping communities save small but sacred spaces closer to home.

Unfortunately, this Congress seems intent on walking away from this opportunity. They're trying to slash Lands Legacy funding by a full two-thirds this year alone, with no action at all to ensure permanent funding in the years ahead. This is not an isolated case, unfortunately. Once again, the leaders of the Republican majority are polluting our spending bills with special interest riders that would promote overcutting in our forests, allow mining companies to dump more toxic waste on public land, and give a huge windfall to companies producing oil on federal lands.

I have vetoed such bills before because they were loaded up with anti-environmental riders. If necessary, I will do so again.

So, as Congress completes its work on the Interior bill, again I ask the leadership to send me a clean bill that adequately funds the Lands Legacy Initiative and other priorities. But let me be clear, if the Interior bill lands on my desk looking like it does now, I will give it a good environmental response— I will send it straight back to the recycling bin.

Ever since that first Governors Conference back in 1908, conservation has been a cause important enough to Americans to transcend party lines. I hope, somehow, we can make it a bipartisan—even a nonpartisan—issue again. Theodore Roosevelt was a great Republican President. Franklin Roosevelt was a great Democratic President. President Nixon signed a bill creating the Environmental Protection Agency. Over and over again in the last seven years in which I have had the honor to serve as President, I have worked with people who were both Democrats and Republicans on conservation issues.

Again I have the feeling that this is not a partisan issue anywhere but Washington, D.C., and perhaps in a few other places throughout the country. We can't afford that.

When I was a boy growing up in my hometown, it was in a national park, and I could never be in the downtown of my hometown, which was a big city by Arkansas standards—35,000 people—that even if you were anywhere downtown, you weren't more than five minutes walk from the woods.

I know what this can mean to our children and our future. When I was governor, I was proud that, after leaving office after 12 years, we had—a higher percentage of our land in Arkansas was timberland than it was on the day that I took office, for the first time. And we always did this across party lines. No state was more active in using the Nature Conservancy to buy land and set it aside, and we always did it across party lines.

When people walk through these woods and run into one another, they may talk a lot of things, but I'll bet you very few of them say, are you a Republican or a Democrat. I'll bet you've never asked anybody that on a mountain trail.

We want this for our children forever. And it is important that we set a good example. Earlier, Mr. Pinchot talked about the deterioration of the rain forests and the loss of biodiversity around the globe. If we want to help other people meet those challenges, and the even larger challenge of climate change, we have to set a good example. We have the wealth and security to do it. We also have no excuse, because now we have the scientific knowledge and the technical means to grow the economy while we improve the environment.

It is no longer necessary to grow a modern economy by destroying natural resources and putting more greenhouse gases into the atmosphere. In fact, we can create more jobs by following a responsible path to sustainable development.

So I hope this day will be important not only for our forestland, but the preservation of fresh water and biodiversity and recreational opportunities. I hope it will be the first step in America resuming a path of responsible leadership toward the environmental future we will increasingly share with our neighbors all across the globe. And I hope all of you will always be very proud of the role you have played in this special day.

CLINTON AND LOTT ON DEFEAT OF THE NUCLEAR TEST BAN TREATY
October 14, 1999

Partisanship—hardened by political miscalculations and misunder-standings—colored the Senate's rejection October 13, 1999, of a global treaty to ban all nuclear weapons tests. The Comprehensive Nuclear Test Ban Treaty was the most important diplomatic accord rejected by the Senate since the Treaty of Versailles, establishing the League of Nations, was defeated in 1919 and again in 1920.

President Bill Clinton had signed the test ban treaty in 1996 and submitted it to the Senate a year later, but had done little to win Senate approval for it until late in 1999. Advocates of the treaty, angered by the refusal of the Senate Republican leadership to bring the measure to a vote, demanded action in October. When Senate Majority Leader Trent Lott (R-Miss.) called their bluff, supporters were unable to muster a simple majority, far short of the sixty-seven votes needed for ratification of a treaty.

Clinton angrily denounced the Senate's action as "reckless partisanship" and said he would abide by the treaty's terms anyway. Lott insisted the treaty was "fundamentally flawed" and deserved to be voted down.

Twenty-six nations had ratified the treaty prior to the Senate's vote. After the U.S. rejection, it was considered doubtful that enough other nations would ratify the treaty to enable it to enter into effect as planned in May 2000. By its terms, the treaty would become effective only after it had been ratified by all forty-four nations considered capable of producing nuclear weapons. The two other major treaty holdouts—China and Russia—had made it clear that their ratification of the treaty depended on U.S. action.

Clinton, other treaty supporters, and even some Republicans who voted against it, said the defeat of the treaty raised serious questions about American diplomatic leadership. Throughout the 1990s, partisan disputes in Washington, coupled with foreign policy missteps by the Bush and Clinton administrations, had led many world leaders to express doubts about U.S. reliability. In the wake of the rejection of a treaty that was initiated by

*the United States and took more than forty years to produce, the only cer-
tainty was that Washington would be unable to erase those doubts any time
soon.*

Test Ban Treaty Background

*President Dwight Eisenhower called for a comprehensive ban on nuclear
tests in 1957, and talks about such an agreement began the next year. The
United States and the Soviet Union in 1963 agreed on a limited, bilateral
treaty banning nuclear tests in the atmosphere, and in 1992 President
George Bush halted all underground tests by the United States. At that point
the United States had conducted 1,030 tests of nuclear weapons, by far the
most of any nation. Only in 1994 did serious negotiations begin in Geneva,
Switzerland, with the aim of writing the worldwide agreement suggested by
Eisenhower. Those negotiations reached a successful conclusion in September 1996 with the signing by Clinton and other leaders of a treaty banning
all testing of nuclear weapons, even tests intended only to verify whether
aging weapons systems still functioned. Clinton said the treaty represented
the best means of halting the global nuclear weapons race.*

*The test ban treaty was instantly controversial once Clinton submitted it
to the Senate in 1997. Key conservative Republicans—notably Lott and Senate Foreign Relations Committee Chairman Jesse Helms, of North Carolina—said they were opposed to the treaty because compliance by nations
such as Iraq or North Korea would be difficult and possibly impossible to
verify. Over the next several years similar doubts were expressed by many
conservative and moderate specialists in foreign policy and national security affairs, including former secretary of state Henry M. Kissinger, former
defense secretary James Schlesinger, and former national security advisor
Richard Cheney. Helms bottled up the treaty in his committee, refusing for
nearly two years even to hold hearings on it.*

*The Clinton administration, meanwhile, allowed the treaty to languish
in the Senate and made no serious effort to press for its approval. Other
issues and events consistently had higher priority for the administration,
most notably the Lewinsky sex scandal, which lead to Clinton's impeachment and consumed nearly all of 1998 and the first six weeks of 1999, and
the crisis in Kosovo, which preoccupied the administration from February
through June of 1999.* (Lewinsky scandal, Historic Documents of 1998, p.
958, Clinton impeachment, p. 15; Kosovo war, p. 134)

Pressing for a Vote

*Treaty supporters, including key Senate Democrats and organizations
that lobbied on behalf of arms control agreements, began pushing in 1998
for Senate action on the test ban treaty. Supporters staged a rally at the
Capitol on September 14, with participants holding mask-like images of
Helms, the treaty's most vocal foe.*

*Sen. Byron Dorgan, D-N.D., one of the most avid supporters of the treaty,
took the Senate floor on September 8 and announced that he would not*

leave—that he would be like a "potted plant"—until the Senate took action on the treaty. Dorgan's action turned out to be a major miscalculation, because by that point treaty opponents had quietly lined up the thirty-four Republican votes to assure the treaty did not have a two-thirds majority among the one hundred senators.

When Democrats, with the support of the Clinton administration, continued pressing for a vote on the treaty, Lott called their bluff. In late September he told key Democrats he would allow a vote in October after accelerated hearings in Helms's committee. At that point the Democrats discovered that they lacked the votes to get the treaty approved, and they turned to an alternative strategy: deferring Senate action on the treaty, possibly until after Clinton had left the White House. The Democrats and White House officials decided that, given the political circumstances, postponing a vote had become preferable to outright rejection of the treaty.

Attempts to negotiate a face-saving alternative to an up-or-down vote on the treaty continued until late October 12, when Lott and Senate Minority Leader Tom Daschle, D-S.D., informally agreed on a procedure to postpone a vote until Clinton's successor took office. But that agreement fell apart because of a dispute over a clause allowing Clinton to press for a vote on the treaty in the event of "extraordinary circumstances." Hard-line treaty opponents objected to giving Clinton a "loophole," and Lott decided to press ahead with a vote October 13. Clinton appealed directly to Lott to postpone a vote, but was brushed aside.

The Senate Votes

The Senate took two votes on the issue October 13. The first was a procedural motion to set aside other business so the Senate could turn to the test ban treaty. Normally such votes were routine, but in this case the procedural vote became a test of whether the Senate would honor Clinton's appeal for a delay or back Lott's determination to proceed. Under those circumstances the vote became a party-line issue; all fifty-five Republicans voted to take up the treaty and all forty-five Democrats voted not to proceed. John Warner, R-Va., who chaired the Armed Services Committee and who had advocated delaying a vote, was among those saying he had no choice but to support his party's leader.

On the treaty itself, the vote was forty-eight for approval and fifty-one against—nineteen votes short of the required two-thirds majority. All Democrats voted yes except Robert C. Byrd, who cast a rare vote of "present" to voice his desire to delay action. Four moderate Republicans split with their party to vote for approval of the treaty.

Among those voting against the treaty were several moderate Republicans, such as Warner and Richard G. Lugar of Indiana, who customarily supported arms control treaties and similar foreign policy initiatives. But those senators said they could not support the test ban treaty because of lingering doubts about whether the United States could verify compliance by other countries.

The Senate action provoked an angry war of words. In a press conference the next day, Clinton read a statement saying the Republican action represented "partisan politics of the worst kind, because it was so blatant and because of the risks it poses to the safety of the American people and the world." Lott responded by saying the treaty was defeated because it was "flawed," and he rejected as "baloney" the claims of Democrats and the president that Republicans had rushed a vote on it. "If there's any partisanship, it's on the other side," Lott said.

Key U.S. allies around the world sided with Clinton, expressing shock and dismay that the Senate would reject a treaty that had been signed by more than 150 nations. French president Jacques Chirac said the vote would cause "serious damage" to diplomatic efforts to control the spread of nuclear weapons, and German foreign minister Joschka Fischer said the Senate had sent "a wrong signal that we deeply regret."

Officials in China and Russia also expressed alarm, saying the Senate vote called into question U.S. determination to adhere to other international agreements. The defeat of the test ban treaty took place in the context of maneuvering by Washington to amend the 1972 antiballistic missile treaty, a key arms control pact in which the United States and the former Soviet Union both pledged not to develop systems to shoot down intercontinental ballistic missiles. Under pressure from Congress, the Clinton administration was testing devices to create a "shield" against a missile attack—something explicitly banned by the 1972 treaty. China, Russia, and even some U.S. allies viewed the U.S. movement toward an antimissile defense as a provocative act that might trigger another nuclear arms race.

Secretary of State Madeleine K. Albright wrote letters in late October to her counterparts in Beijing, Moscow, and other capitals saying the United States would maintain its moratorium on nuclear weapons tests. Albright said she hoped the Senate would reverse its position at some future point.

One immediate result of the Senate action was to undermine Clinton administration efforts to persuade India and Pakistan to sign the test ban treaty. Both nations had tested nuclear weapons in 1998, causing widespread worry about a nuclear arms race on the Indian subcontinent. The day before the Senate vote, Pakistan's military overthrew the country's civilian government, again raising tensions in the region. (India and Pakistan nuclear testing, Historic Documents of 1998, p. 32; Pakistan coup, p. 623)

The Verification Issue

Aside from partisan disputes, the central issue facing the treaty in Washington was whether the United States could be sure that other nations were adhering to it. The issue of verification had frequently plagued arms control agreements. As recently as 1997 a dispute over verification nearly prevented the Senate from approving a worldwide ban on the manufacture, possession, and use of chemical weapons. (Chemical weapons treaty, Historic Documents of 1997, p. 105)

Republican opponents of the test ban treaty argued that, despite its vast intelligence-gathering apparatus, the United States did not have the technical capability to detect, with absolute assurance, tests conducted on very small nuclear weapons. Russia, Iraq, or any other nation could conduct what experts called "low-level" nuclear tests, without U.S. knowledge, and use the results to refine its weapons capability, the opponents said. Concerns about such tests reportedly were heightened by Central Intelligence Agency (CIA) briefings of senators early in October, during which intelligence officials said they could not give assurances that Russia was adhering to its commitment not to conduct nuclear weapons tests. Senator Warner referred to the CIA testimony in telling his colleagues to be concerned about a secret "body of fact" on the verification issue.

Sen. Joseph R. Biden Jr., of Delaware, the ranking Democrat on the Foreign Relations Committee, dismissed the concerns, saying Republicans were demanding that the test ban treaty be "perfectly verifiable," something that no other arms control treaty had been able to achieve. Biden noted that the Senate had approved a treaty, negotiated by President Ronald Reagan, banning intermediate-range missiles carrying nuclear warheads despite concerns about how well Soviet adherence to it could be verified. "The only verifiable, perfectly verifiable treaty that's acceptable [to the test ban treaty opponents] is one that's impossible to be written," Biden said.

Following are excerpts from statements October 14, 1999, by President Bill Clinton and Senate Majority Leader Trent Lott, R-Miss., commenting on the Senate's rejection the previous day of the Comprehensive Nuclear Test Ban Treaty:

CLINTON PRESS CONFERENCE STATEMENT

In recent days, members of the congressional majority have displayed a reckless partisanship—it threatens America's economic well being and, now, our national security.

Yesterday, hard line Republicans irresponsibly forced a vote against the Comprehensive Nuclear Test Ban Treaty. This was partisan politics of the worst kind, because it was so blatant and because of the risks it poses to the safety of the American people and the world.

What the Senate seeks is to abandon an agreement that requires other countries to do what we have already done; an agreement that constrains Russia and China, India and Pakistan from developing more dangerous nuclear weapons; that helps to keep other countries out of the nuclear weapons business altogether; that improves our ability to monitor dangerous weapons activities in other countries. Even worse, they have offered no alternative, no other means of keeping countries around the world from developing nuclear arsenals and threatening our security.

In so doing, they ignored the advice of our top military leaders, our most distinguished scientists, our closest allies. They brushed aside the views of the American people and betrayed the vision of Presidents Eisenhower and Kennedy, who set us on the road to this treaty so many years ago.

Even more troubling are the signs of a new isolationism among some of the opponents of the treaty. You see it in the refusal to pay our U.N. dues. You see it in the woefully inadequate budget for foreign affairs and includes meeting our obligations to the Middle East peace process and to the continuing efforts to destroy and safeguard Russian nuclear materials. You see it in the refusal to adopt our proposals to do our part to stem the tide of global warming, even though these proposals plainly would create American jobs.

But by this vote, the Senate majority has turned its back on 50 years of American leadership against the spread of weapons of mass destruction. They are saying America does not need to lead, either by effort or by example. They are saying we don't need our friends or allies. They are betting our children's future on the reckless proposition that we can go it alone; that at the height of our power and prosperity, we should bury our heads in the sand, behind a wall.

That is not where I stand. And that is not where the American people stand. They understand that, to be strong, we must not only have a powerful military; we must also lead, as we have done time and again, and as the whole world expects us to do, to build a more responsible, interdependent world.

So we will continue to protect our interests around the world. We will continue to seek from Congress the financial resources to make that possible. We will continue to pursue the fight against the spread of nuclear weapons. And we will not—we will not—abandon the commitments inherent in the treaty, and resume testing ourselves.

I will not let yesterday's partisanship stand as our final word on the test ban treaty. Today I say again, on behalf of the United States, we will continue the policy we have maintained since 1992 of not conducting nuclear tests. I call on Russia, China, Britain, France and all other countries to continue to refrain from testing. I call on nations that have not done so to sign and ratify the Comprehensive Test Ban Treaty. And I will continue to do all I can to make that case to the Senate. When all is said and done I have no doubt that the United States will ratify this treaty.

Partisanship also threatens our economic security. Exactly one week from today the continuing resolution I signed on September the 30th to keep the government running will expire. And, yet, Congress is not even close to finishing its work. At this time of unprecedented prosperity we must ask ourselves why is the congressional majority so unwilling, or unable, to make the tough choices. Why would we not be willing—or why would they not be willing to send me a responsible budget that saves Social Security, that strengthens and modernizes Medicare, that honors the priorities of the American people and that clearly continues to pay down our debt keeping interest rates low and the economy growing?

When I signed the continuing resolution two weeks ago, I urged Congress to roll up its sleeves and finish the job the American people sent them here to do. I said they should stop playing politics, stop playing games, start making the necessary tough choices. Instead, we have the Republicans lurching from one unworkable idea to the next. Instead of sending me bills I can sign, the congressional majority is still using what the *Wall Street Journal,* the *New York Times* and others have called "budget gimmicks," to disguise the fact that they are spending the Social Security surplus. Their own budget office says so.

We've even seen them try to raise taxes for our hardest-pressed working families. Now, they're talking about across-the-board budget cuts that could deny tens of thousands of children Head Start opportunities, drastically reduce medical research, sacrifice military readiness, jeopardize the safety of air traffic control. One day they raise the spending, the next day they talk about cutting it again.

I say to the congressional majority: enough is enough. We've got a job to do for the American people; it is not that difficult. Let's just do it. We can work together. We can fashion a budget that builds on our economic prosperity and continues to pay down the debt until it is eliminated in 2015 for the first time since 1835; that extends the life of the Social Security trust fund to 2050, the life expanse of almost all the baby boomers; and that invests in our people and our future, especially in our children's education.

The American people want a world-class education for their children. They want smaller classes, more qualified teachers, more computers in the classrooms, more after-school programs for the children who need it, more Head Start opportunities to ensure that our children all start school ready to learn.

The majority so far has failed to come forward with a plan that protects these goals. I believe these goals are worth fighting for and that's what this debate is all about.

They want us to keep making their communities safer, that's what the American people want. They want us to stay with the plan that has resulted in the lowest crime rate in 26 years. They want us to continue to put more cops on the beat and get guns out of the wrong hands. The majority wants to take us off that course and derail our progress. I want to keep us on track in education, in crime, in the budget, in Social Security, in Medicare.

The American people want us to stand up for the environment by preserving our treasured landscapes and enhancing our community's quality of life. The majority would roll back our progress there, too. I want to build on it. That's what this debate is all about.

I want to work with Congress to fulfill these important obligations. We have proved we can do it with the Welfare Reform Bill, with the Balanced Budget Act; with the budget last year, in the teeth of a partisan election season, which made a big down payment on our goal of 100,000 teachers. We need it again: a workable, bipartisan budget process. We don't have that today; we've got a week to go. They've got to go to work.

There are legitimate differences of opinion. But we can put an end to reckless partisanship, to gimmicks and gamesmanship. We can put people first, and make a principled, honorable compromise. We can work for a season of progress, not a winter of politics. And I am committed to do just that.

Question: Mr. President, hasn't the treaty rejection really wiped out our moral authority to ask other nations around the world to stop testing? And was there—do you think there was a personal element in the Republican—a personal vendetta against you in the turn-down, Republican—

Clinton: Well, to answer the first question, let me say I had the occasion to run into three ambassadors last night, of nations that strongly support the test ban treaty. And they were concerned, they didn't know what to say to their governments back home.

And what I told them was that we were in a battle with the new isolationists in the Republican Party. They see this treaty against the backdrop of the failure to pay the U.N. dues, and the failure to shoulder some of our other responsibilities, the failure to pass a bill that would meet our obligations to the Middle East peace process, and our obligations to keep working with the Russians to take down their nuclear arsenal.

But what I told them was the American people always get it right, and we are not going to reverse 40 years of commitment on nonproliferation, that the treaty is still on the Senate calendar, that it will be considered, that we have to keep working forward, and that I have no intention of doing anything other than honoring the obligations of the treaty imposed on the United States.

So I urged them not to overreact, to make clear their opposition to what the Senate did, but to stay with us and believe in the United States because the American people want us to lead toward nonproliferation.

Now, as to the second element, there were a number of partisan considerations, including some bad feelings between the Republicans and Democrats in the Senate, because the Republicans didn't want to bring this up at all, and then they didn't give us a legitimate process when they did. If you compare the debates here, one day of hearings here, with 14 days on the Chemical Weapons Convention, over 20 days on the INF [Intermediate-range Nuclear Force] Treaty under President Reagan, this was not a legitimate process.

Now, I know some people made some personal remarks on the floor of the Senate in the debate, but, you know, it's been my experience that very often in politics when a person is taking a position that he simply cannot defend, the only defense is to attack the opponent. And that's what I took it, as a form of flattery. They knew they didn't have a very strong case, and so they were looking for some excuse for otherwise inexcusable conduct, and it didn't bother me a bit. . . .

LOTT'S REMARKS IN RESPONSE

I want to emphasize this afternoon that the vote in the Senate last night to vote against ratification of the Comprehensive Test Ban Treaty was not a vote involving personalities. It was not about politics. Is was about the substance of the treaty, and that's all it was.

You should note that a majority of the Senate—51 senators—voted against ratification. Only 48 voted for ratification, and it requires 67 to ratify the treaty. So there was not even a close question about whether or not this treaty would be ratified or whether it should be ratified.

You know, there's an old saying in law school and when you practice law that if the facts are with you, you argue the—if the facts are not with you, you argue the law; if the law is not with you, you argue the facts, and if neither are with you, you just argue. I fear this time, since the substance, the facts were not with the president or the supporters of this treaty, they are saying, oh, well, it was politics. That absolutely was not the case.

We have some of the most thoughtful senators that have ever served in this body that said that this treaty was not verifiable; that it was fundamentally flawed and it should not be ratified. And the list is very long of people that fit into that category, including, of course, the chairman of the Foreign Relations Committee, Jesse Helms, a very senior member of the Foreign Relations Committee, Richard Lugar, the chairman of the Armed Services Committee, John Warner, senators that really know a lot about the subject of nuclear weapons and testing and verification like John Kyl and Jim Inhofe. So there's plenty of room to disagree about the substance, but there are lot of very respected senators that would not like their integrity being questioned by insinuating that they were voting on the basis of anything other than the fact that this was a flawed treaty.

I personally took the time to meet with respected experts to discuss this issue. I read their statements. I talked personally with people like Dick Cheney and Jeane Kirkpatrick. But James Schlesinger was the one that had the greatest impact on me. Because he had such a breadth of experience in this area. He had been head of the CIA, he had been head of the Atomic Energy Commission and he had been secretary of defense.

So, he knew all the different ramifications of testing. How can you test nuclear weapons? How can you make sure they're safe and reliable. How can you, or is it possible to verify testing in countries like Russia or China. Or, in fact, are they doing low level testing now? And we cannot verify that—that's exactly what the CIA said, just last week. Just a couple of days ago, there was an article in one paper indicating that Russia and China had refused to allow us to have sites for monitoring so that we could detect if in fact there might be testing.

This was a treaty that we were being asked to accept on good faith. That if we passed it, the rest of the world would follow our example. Even though, we then, would be in the position of not being able to verify what they were doing or test the safety and reliability of our weapons.

Do we really think that North Korea, Iraq, Iran, or even China or Russia, can be trusted to do that, not to mention, Pakistan and India? So, we went into this very seriously. And we looked at the substance. No senator, no senator was pressured to vote anyway but his or her conscience based on the substance of the treaty.

Now, on purely procedural votes, I acknowledge that I asked my senators to stick with me as the majority leader. But on substance, senators were encouraged to get into the substance and listen and make a decision.

Now, let me give you a little bit of a correction of the revisionist history that perhaps you have just heard. This treaty didn't just pop up. The president, I think, has referred to it in his last two State of the Union addresses.

There have been hearings on this issue, multiple hearings on this issue. Many of them, I have to admit, in the Intelligence Committee, where you can't come out and say to the press, well, this is what I was just told in the Intelligence Committee. But there had been hearings in the Foreign Relations Committee and Armed Services Committee. I know very few issues since I've been the Senate Majority Leader where more time was spent listening to experts asking questions, going over the problems and the concerns in all directions.

Plus, there were some interesting developments with me as Majority Leader. I was being requested repeatedly to have hearings, bring this up without delay and let's have a vote. I was being threatened. As a matter of fact, according to the *Wall Street Journal*, there was a meeting at the White House September 23rd with so-called Democratic Senate leaders—I say so-called because I don't know who was there among that group—meeting with Sandy Berger, which it was agreed that for the rest of the year while we're trying to do the work the president called on us to do; trying to do the business of the people, trying to get the appropriations bill passed, that they—the Democratic leadership—would try to attach a resolution or amendment to every bill that moved, demanding that we have a hearing or that we have a vote or we take this issue up.

So finally, one day I went onto the floor of the Senate and I found that Senator Biden had a resolution on this treaty—relating to this treaty—that he was going to try to offer to the Labor, Health and Human Services and Education Appropriations Bill. Something that would tie the Senate up, that would delay this bill.

That was evidence to me that they were going forward with their strategy to try to tangle every bill that came up on the floor of the Senate with amendments dealing with this treaty.

So I went to Senator [Joseph R.] Biden and said OK. You want it? We'll schedule it for debate and a vote. And that was on a Wednesday, or a Tuesday or a Wednesday. It was not until Friday that the unanimous consent agreement was entered into that we would go forward and have this debate in about 10 days or two weeks—I don't remember the exact amount of time—and that we would have, not the 10 hours for debate that I originally offered, but up to as many as I think 18 hours, which we wound up using about 15 or 16 hours.

And if you want to check the history on that, only one other treaty in recent history had as much as 18 hours of debate, and it was the Chemical Weapons Treaty, and if you'll remember, I was involved in that, too, and worked with senators on both sides and the administration to help get that legislation passed.

So when it's argued that this was precipitous, they didn't know it was coming, they didn't have enough time, there wasn't enough hearings, that is all baloney. I was demanded and forced into having a debate and a vote. And so when we agreed, then they said, well, wait a minute. There may not be the votes to ratify this treaty. Well, I wonder why? Because we had been doing our work. We'd been checking into it. We'd been looking into the substance. We had realized that zero tolerance area that we have in this treaty, that many of the things they agreed to at the end of the—those treaty negotiations, rendered this treaty ineffectual, unverifiable and unenforceable.

When you have quotes from senators like Senator Lugar to this effect: "The treaty's likely ineffectuability will risk undermining support and confidence in the whole concept of multilateral arms control." I don't take that lightly.

So what happened was they demanded that we have hearings, they demanded we have debate and they demanded we have a vote. We did all of the above, and a majority of the United States Senate said this is wrong.

I talked to Secretary Cheney yesterday at noon. And I have a lot of respect for him and I think most of you and I think most Americans do. This is not a man that would take a treaty vote frivolously or lightly at all. Former secretary of defense, former congressman, former member of the Intelligence Committee, and a leader of one of the major corporations in America today. He said this treaty should be defeated.

And he certainly would never recommend that if he thought it was not in our best national security interests. And he had went on to say this will help us in the future in treaty negotiations because our negotiators will be able to say to other countries, while these negotiations are going on, if you go too far, if you put the United States interest at risk, the Senate will not ratify it.

The message is to our treaty negotiators, to this administration and to the rest of the world, the Senate is a co-equal party in treaties. We should be involved in advice and consent. Our advice was not asked and we didn't give our consent. We did our job. We did the right thing for our country. And I'm very proud of it.

I don't want this to become, you know, a situation where we hear talk about vendettas and blatant politics. You can't accuse me of that. I took the heat. I stood in the well of the Senate and I did what I thought was right on the Chemical Weapons Treaty. I supported it and it passed.

And I did what I thought was right yesterday, too. And I thought this treaty should be defeated. It was not about President Clinton. It was not about Trent Lott. It was about my country and about my children. And about the dangers involved, the risks involved. I knew this was serious. I labored over this all weekend, on my birthday, with my children and my grandchildren at my home in Mississippi. I thought about it the whole weekend. I read on it. I took calls from Sandy Berger on Monday about this. So, I reject any suggestion of reckless partisanship. If there is any partisanship, it's on the other side.

Republicans didn't all vote one way. We didn't demand this vote. It was demanded on the other side. . . .

NSF DIRECTOR ON EMERGENCY RESCUE OF SOUTH POLE DOCTOR
October 15, 1999

The New York Air National Guard executed a daring rescue in mid-October of an American female doctor who had been stranded at a South Pole research station after discovering a lump in her breast. The perils faced by Jerri Nielsen, a divorced mother of three children from Canfield, Ohio, near Youngstown, had captivated the nation for three months as rescuers waited for a break in the Antarctic winter so she could be flown to safety.

Nielsen, forty-seven, treated herself with chemotherapy while waiting for her rescue. After returning home she underwent surgery for breast cancer— and told the Youngstown newspaper she wanted to return to the South Pole because her time there had been "the best year of my life."

Nielsen's dramatic rescue was the second high-profile emergency retrieval of a female American scientist in three years. In September 1996 astronaut Shannon Lucid was plucked from the Soviet space station Mir *after spending seven weeks in space longer than planned because of delays in launching the space shuttle needed to give her a ride home. Lucid's extended stay aboard the cramped* Mir *gave her an American space endurance record.* (Lucid mission, Historic Documents of 1996, p. 691)

Living at the Pole

An emergency room doctor who had worked at several hospitals in her native Ohio, Nielsen in 1998 learned of an opportunity to serve as the sole doctor at a National Science Foundation (NSF) research station in Antarctica. The opportunity arose shortly after her divorce following twenty-three years of marriage. Nielsen took the job, and in November 1998 became one of forty-one scientists and support personnel stationed at the Amundsen-Scott South Pole Station, named after the Norwegian and British explorers who raced each other to the South Pole in 1911–1912 (Amundsen won, and Scott perished in his failed attempt).

Nielsen handled routine medical care for the staffers at the South Pole center, which carried out a wide range of studies on climate, astronomy, geology, and other scientific matters. The center was one of three scientific stations in Antarctica managed by the National Science Foundation, an independent federal agency. The station was built in the 1970s, featuring a large geodesic dome, and in 1999 was under reconstruction.

In mid-June 1999, Nielsen discovered a lump in her breast. She notified the NSF and, with advice through satellite phone calls and e-mail from doctors at the National Cancer Institute and other U.S. medical centers, she began treating herself. The timing could not have been worse. Antarctica was then in the middle of winter, with temperatures averaging about –80° F.—far too cold for a rescue plane to land at the South Pole station and then take off again. The last prewinter flight left the South Pole in mid-February, and flights were not scheduled to resume until late October, about a month after the sun was to make its spring appearance over the South Pole.

Despite the risks, NSF officials decided on the temporary alternative of an air-drop of anticancer drugs and diagnostic equipment to Nielsen. An Air Force Reserve C-141 cargo plane made the dangerous trip July 11, dropping supplies by parachute. Most of the supplies landed safely, except for an ultrasound machine, which was destroyed when its crate was smashed on the polar ice. Nielsen began treating herself with chemotherapy and even inserted a needle into her own breast to extract tissue from the tumor for a biopsy, the results of which were not disclosed.

The NSF announced the emergency supply mission on July 11, and two days later foundation director Rita Colwell provided more details on the situation. But at the time the agency refused to disclose Nielsen's identity, saying she had asked for privacy. News reports later revealed her name.

Waiting for a Rescue

The emergency supplies helped Nielsen deal with her medical situation temporarily, but it was clear that she needed to be rescued from the South Pole as soon as possible so she could undergo surgery to remove the tumor from her breast. The critical factor was the temperature. Air force experts said hydraulic fluids in the transport planes that flew to the South Pole would freeze in temperatures of less than about –60° F. In the Antarctic mid-winter, –60° F would mark an unusual warming trend.

Just as explorers were forced to do in the days of Columbus or Lewis and Clark, Nielsen waited for winter to pass. She continued her regimen of chemotherapy and consultations with U.S. doctors and, according to friends and colleagues, she stayed in remarkably good spirits.

Finally, in mid-October, air force officials determined that South Pole temperatures had warmed to a point (about –58° F.) where a rescue mission could be attempted. After waiting three days at McMurdo Station, at the edge of the Ross Sea, for a break in the weather, a New York Air National Guard LC-130 Hercules transport plane flew toward the South Pole early October 16. Equipped with landing skis, the plane touched down on the icy South Pole runway in a blinding snow storm. Nielsen was quickly bundled aboard, her replacement and supplies were unloaded, and the plane took off again in just twenty-two minutes; any longer on the ground and the plane's hydraulic fluids would have frozen.

The pilot, Major George R. McAllister, later told reporters that the plane was operating "at the limit" of its capabilities because of the weather. "The risk factor was high," he said. "On a risk scale of one to ten, it was an eight or nine." Col. Graham Pritchard, commander of the rescue mission, told NBC news that Nielsen "had a big smile on her face and was obviously glad to be back home."

The cargo plane flew Nielsen to McMurdo station and then to Christchurch, New Zealand, where she was met by her brothers, Eric and Scott Cahill. Nielsen turned down an offer of air force transport back to the United States and instead flew by a commercial airliner. Within a matter of days she underwent surgery at an undisclosed location to remove the lump from her breast.

Her hometown newspaper, the Youngstown Vindicator, *quoted her on October 26 as saying she was recovering from the surgery and hoped to return some day to the Antarctic. "It was such a wonderful place. I still love it," Nielsen told the newspaper. "I would do it again. Even knowing what happened to me, it was the best year of my life."*

Following is the text of a statement released October 15, 1999, by Rita Colwell, director of the National Science Foundation, announcing the successful emergency rescue from the South Pole of Jerri Nielsen, a doctor who had been stranded at a polar research station after finding a lump in her breast:

Dr. Jerri Nielsen, the physician at the National Science Foundation's Amundsen-Scott South Pole Station since last November, has safely arrived at McMurdo Station, where she will prepare for her return to the United States as soon as possible and practical. NSF's McMurdo Station is the hub of U.S. Antarctic air operations on the Ross Sea.

I applaud the 109th Airlift Wing of the New York Air National Guard for its successful completion of the roughly six hour round trip flight from McMurdo to the South Pole, and the smoothly executed pick-up and transport of Dr. Nielsen, under very difficult operational conditions. Since the beginning of this mission, the Air National Guard has displayed the utmost professionalism, efficiency, and concern for Dr. Nielsen.

Since Dr. Nielsen's discovery of a breast lump in June, our priorities have been her health and safety, and her desire for privacy during a very personal process. This remains her desire, and it remains our priority. She has become a public figure through circumstance and not through choice. I am grateful to all who have respected her desire, and appeal once again for restraint and respect as she prepares to return to the U.S. and a difficult adjustment under the most trying circumstances.

FBI REPORT ON CRIME
October 17, 1999

Serious reported crime dropped for the seventh consecutive year in 1998 and decreased even more sharply in the first six months of 1999, according to the Federal Bureau of Investigation. "Lawfulness is becoming the norm, and it's contagious," one crime expert said. Overall, however, levels of violent crime were still well above the levels recorded in 1969.

In its annual report, Crime in the United States, *released October 17, the FBI said that violent crimes had dropped 6 percent between 1997 and 1998. Property crimes were down 5 percent. Attorney General Janet Reno credited the continuing decline to "more police officers on the street, greater partnerships between law enforcement agencies, continued efforts to keep guns away from criminals, and a balanced approach that includes prevention, intervention, punishment and supervision."*

Little more than a month later, the FBI released preliminary statistics for the first six months of 1999, which showed that serious crime had dropped 10 percent compared with the first six months of 1998. Each category of violent and property crime showed a decline, and serious crime fell in all geographic regions in all sizes of cities.

Continuing Decline in Violent and Property Crimes

For 1998, according to the FBI's annual Uniform Crime Report, *all violent crimes—murder, rape, robbery, and aggravated assault—fell from 1997 levels in both number and rate. Murder declined 7.4 percent, rape dropped 4.2 percent to its lowest level in fifteen years, robbery was down 11.3 percent, and aggravated assault declined 5.7 percent to its lowest level in ten years. All categories of serious property crimes also declined in 1998. Auto theft was down 9.3 percent, while burglary declined 6.2 percent, and larceny-theft was down 5.7 percent. (Crime in the United States, 1997, Historic Documents of 1998, p. 869)*

The percentage of crimes involving firearms was also down. Murders involving firearms dropped from 67.8 percent in 1997 to 64.9 percent in

1998, while the percentage of robberies involving guns dropped from 39.7 percent to 38.2 percent. "That's a consequence of all the efforts limiting access to guns by people who shouldn't have them," said Alfred Blumstein, professor at Carnegie-Mellon University who directed the National Consortium on Violence Research.

Despite highly publicized mass killings at a handful of schools, such as Columbine High School in Littleton, Colorado, the overall incidence of deadly violence in the nation's schools was also declining. Criminologists expressed concern about the continuing high overall murder rate among teenagers. The teenage murder rate skyrocketed with the crack cocaine epidemic that began in the late 1980s, peaking in 1993 before beginning to decline as the crack epidemic began to wane. Still, in 1998 the murder rate among teenagers was nearly twice as high as it had been in 1984. "Police have adopted smarter strategies, focusing on guns and high-risk juveniles, taking a preventive approach rather than waiting in squad cars for 911 to ring," said James Alan Fox, professor of criminal justice at Northeastern University. "But if we let our guard down, the problem could resurface with a vengeance, because every year for the next couple decades we're going to have a record number of black and Latino teenagers, and they live in the most at-risk situations." (School shootings, p. 179)

The sharp decline in crime in the first six months of 1999 surprised even the experts. "This is astounding," Fox said. "No one could have predicted the drops would have been this deep." According to the preliminary data reported by the FBI, murder dropped 13 percent from its levels during the same period in 1998, followed by robbery, which decreased 10 percent; forcible rape, 8 percent; and aggravated assault, 7 percent. Burglary fell 14 percent; auto theft, 12 percent; and larceny-theft, 8 percent. The only upward movement in this set of statistics was a 1 percent increase in murders in cities with more than one million residents. Fox and Blumstein both suggested that the increase was not likely a signal that violent crime was on the rise but that violent crime rates might have dropped about as low as they could be expected to go. "In the big cities, we've gotten rid of the murderous violence that is readily preventable through gun controls, drug market changes and the strength of the economy," Blumstein said. "At some point, we end up with a wide variety of personal disputes."

A more sober view of the FBI data was taken by the National Commission on the Causes and Prevention of Violence, which found that violent crime in the nation's major cities was 40 percent higher in 1998 than it was in 1969. The commission study was an update of a study the original commission had prepared thirty years earlier. That commission had been established by President Lyndon B. Johnson in the wake of urban riots in the late 1960s. Thirty years ago, the commission would have called the crime rates of today a "disaster," said Elliott Carrie, an author of both the 1969 and the 1999 report. Carrie said the commission was not trying to say that "nothing good" had happened in the last few years, but that perspective could be gained by looking back.

Other Reports on Crime and Criminals

The Department of Justice released several other reports in 1999 dealing with criminal statistics. Among these were the following.

Carjackings. *According to the Bureau of Justice Statistics, there were an estimated 49,000 carjackings a year between 1992 and 1996, roughly 10 percent of all reported robberies, and substantially more than criminologists had expected. A gun was used in nearly half of the hijackings, and a victim was injured in 16 percent of the cases. Relatively few people were murdered in car hijackings, however; the annual estimated average was 27.*

According to Blumstein, two reasons might account for the increased hijackings. First, he posited, drug dealers began to hijack cars because they did not want to risk being caught in their own cars, which police could seize if they found drugs in them. Second, he said, car manufacturers had made it more difficult to "hot wire" car ignitions. Would-be car thieves thus often had to commandeer an occupied car. Traditional auto theft had declined, from 1.66 million vehicles in 1991 to 1.35 million vehicles in 1997.

Incarceration Rates. *According to a report released March 14 by the Bureau of Justice Statistics, the number of people held in prisons and jails increased again in 1998, to a record 1.8 million, despite an overall downward turn in crime rates. The increase of 4.4 percent over 1997, however, was well under the average annual rate of increase of previous years, indicating that the dramatic growth in prison populations might be slowing. Crime experts believed that incarcerating more criminals for longer periods of time had helped to reduce the rates of violent crime. One new study calculated that most of the increase in the number of prison inmates was attributable to more long prison sentences and to more convictions of people arrested, rather than to more arrests of criminals.*

Hate Crimes. *In a separate report on hate crimes, issued November 18, 1999, the FBI confirmed that a total of 7,755 bias-motivated crimes had been reported to the agency from law enforcement agencies in forty-six states and the District of Columbia during 1998. Of the total, 4,321 were racially motivated, 1,390 were attributed to religious bias, and 1,260 were motivated by bias against sexual preference. Because the number of jurisdictions reporting hate crimes varies each year, direct year-to-year comparisons were not possible, but the 1998 figures showed considerably fewer hate crimes than the figures for 1997.*

Eighty percent of hate crimes were directed at people; 38 percent involved intimidation and another 30 percent involved assault. Thirteen people were killed in 1998. Two of these murders were particularly vicious. On June 7, 1998, James Byrd Jr., a black man from Jasper, Texas, was beaten, chained to the back of a pickup truck, and dragged for two miles until his body literally fell apart. Three white men, known for their racist beliefs and support of the local Ku Klux Klan, were quickly arrested. All three were convicted of murder; two were sentenced to death. On October 7,

1998, a passerby found Matthew Shepard, badly beaten and burned, tied to a fence near Laramie, Wyoming. Shepard, a student at the University of Wyoming who was openly gay, died five days later. Authorities quickly arrested two men, who had pretended to be gay to lure Shepard into their vehicle. Both men were sentenced to life in prison.

***Violent Crimes Against Children.** The Justice Department's Office of Juvenile Justice and Delinquency Prevention reported that only 28 percent of violent crimes against children aged twelve to seventeen were reported to police, compared to 48 percent of violent crimes committed against adults. An additional 16 percent of violent crimes against children are reported to other officials, such as school authorities, the report said. Even when all those figures were added together, the report said, only 44 percent of violent crimes against children were reported, compared with 55 percent for adults.*

The authors of the report, David Finkelhor and Richard Ormrod, said there were several reasons for the underreporting. First, they wrote, "there is a cultural predisposition, shared by parents, youth and police, to view nonsexual assaults against juveniles as something other than crimes." Second, they said, teenagers "concerned with personal autonomy" might avoid involving adults in their affairs, even when they are victims of crime. And, finally, they suggested that parents might fear that involving their children with the police might stigmatize the child or even draw a reprisal from the criminals. The report was based on data from the annual National Crime Victimization Survey.

> Following is a press release issued October 17, 1999, by the Federal Bureau of Investigation summarizing the findings of its annual report, Crime in the United States, 1998:

With the publication of *Crime in the United States, 1998*, the Federal Bureau of Investigation confirmed that reported serious crime decreased nationwide for the seventh consecutive year. The final 1998 statistics released by the Bureau's Uniform Crime Reporting (UCR) Program reveal that reported serious crime, comprising both violent and property crimes, was down 5 percent from the 1997 level and 11 percent from the 1994 figures.

According to the FBI, violent crime totals declined 6 percent and property crime totals dropped 5 percent compared to the previous year's totals.

For violent crimes, the reductions in 1998 from 1997 totals included robbery, 10 percent; murder, 7 percent; aggravated assault, 5 percent; and forcible rape, 3 percent. In 1998, the number of violent crimes was 18 percent below the 1994 level and 7 percent below the 1989 level.

For property crimes, the reductions in 1998 from 1997 levels totaled motor vehicle theft, 8 percent and burglary and larceny-theft, 5 percent each. In 1998, the number of property crimes was 10 percent below the 1994 level and 13 percent below the 1989 level.

The 6-percent decline in reported serious crime in the Nation's cities over-all and suburban counties was only slightly higher than the 5-percent decrease in rural areas.

Based on reports from approximately 17,000 city, county, and state law enforcement agencies, *Crime in the United States, 1998*, contains the most current national crime data available. Estimates are included for nonreporting areas.

Highlights from the 1998 edition include:

Crime Volume

- The 1998 Crime Index total of approximately 12.5 million offenses represents a 5-percent decline from the 1997 figure. Five- and 10-year comparisons show the 1998 national total has dropped 11 percent since 1994 and 12 percent since 1989.
- The South, with 35 percent of the Nation's population, recorded 40 percent of total reported crime in 1998; the West, with 22 percent of the population, accounted for 24 percent; the Midwest, with 23 percent of the population, 22 percent; and the Northeast, comprising 19 percent of the population, accounted for 14 percent. Crime dropped 7 percent in both the Northeast and West, 5 percent in the South, and 4 percent in the Midwest.

Crime Rate

- The 1998 Crime Index rate of 4,616 offenses per 100,000 United States inhabitants was 6 percent lower than the 1997 rate, 14 percent below the 1994 rate, and 20 percent lower than the 1989 figure.
- Regionally, the Crime Index rate in the South was 5,223 offenses per 100,000 inhabitants; in the West, 4,879; in the Midwest, 4,379; and the Northeast, 3,474. All regions reported rate declines from 1997 levels.
- Cities outside the Nation's metropolitan areas recorded a Crime Index rate of 4,987 offenses per 100,000 inhabitants; Metropolitan Statistical Areas recorded 4,975 offenses per 100,000 inhabitants; and rural counties, 1,998 per 100,000 inhabitants.

Violent Crime

- There were an estimated 1.5 million violent crimes during 1998. The rate of 566 violent crimes for every 100,000 inhabitants was the lowest since 1985.
- All individual violent crimes (murder, forcible rape, robbery, and aggravated assault) declined in volume and rate from the 1997 levels.
- Data collected on weapons used in connection with violent crimes showed personal weapons (hands, fists, and feet) were used in 31 percent of all murders, robberies, and aggravated assaults, collectively. Aggravated assault accounted for 64 percent of all violent crimes in 1998; robbery accounted for an additional 29 percent; and murder for the

lowest number, 1 percent. Firearms were used in 25 percent of violent crimes; knives or cutting instruments in another 15 percent, and other dangerous weapons were involved in 28 percent.

Property Crime

- All property crime categories (burglary, larceny-theft, and motor vehicle theft) in 1998 decreased in volume and rate.
- The estimated property crime total, 11 million offenses, was 5 percent lower than the 1997 total.
- The 1998 property crime rate dropped 6 percent from the previous year's rate to 4,049 offenses per 100,000 population.
- Estimates place the financial losses associated with stolen property at more than $15.4 billion in 1998, an average loss per offense of $1,407.

Hate Crime

- In 1998, a total of 7,755 hate crime incidents were reported; 4,321 were motivated by racial bias; 1,390 by religious bias; 1,260 by sexual-orientation bias; 754 by ethnic bias; 25 by disability bias; and 5 were multiple-bias incidents.
- A total of 10,461 agencies covering nearly 214 million of the U.S. population participated in hate crime data collection.
- Crimes against persons comprised 68 percent of the 9,235 offenses reported. Among the crimes against persons, intimidation accounted for 55 percent of the total; simple assault and aggravated assault accounted for 27 percent and 17 percent, respectively; murder and rape each accounted for less than 1 percent.

Crime Clearances

- Law enforcement agencies nationwide recorded a 21-percent Crime Index clearance rate in 1998. The clearance rate for violent crimes was 49 percent; for property crimes, 17 percent.
- Among the Crime Index offenses, the clearance rate was highest for murder, 69 percent; and lowest for burglary and motor vehicle theft, 14 percent each.
- Offenses involving only juvenile offenders (under 18 years of age) accounted for 19 percent of the Crime Index offenses cleared; 12 percent of the violent crime clearances; and 21 percent of the property crime clearances.

Arrests

- Law enforcement agencies made an estimated 14.5 million arrests for all criminal infractions, excluding traffic violations, in 1998, a decrease of 1 percent over the previous year's figure. The highest estimated arrest counts were for drug abuse violations at approximately 1.6 million. Driving under the influence arrests were gauged at over 1.4 million. There were an estimated 1.3 million arrests each for larceny-theft and simple assault. The number of arrests in proportion to the total U.S. population was 5,534 arrests per 100,000 inhabitants.

- From 1997 to 1998, juvenile arrests decreased 4 percent while adult arrests fell 1 percent. Violent crime arrests of juveniles decreased 8 percent and those of adults declined 4 percent.
- Of all persons arrested in 1998, 45 percent were under the age of 25 and 18 percent were under the age of 18. Juveniles were most frequently arrested for larceny-theft; adults were most often arrested for drug abuse violations.
- Of those individuals arrested, 78 percent were male, and 68 percent were white.
- Thirty percent of all arrests were for drug abuse violations and alcohol-related offenses. Females were most often arrested for the offense of larceny-theft. Males were most often arrested for drug abuse violations.

Murder

- The number of murders in 1998 was estimated at nearly 17,000, which is 7 percent lower than the 1997 total and 28 percent lower than in 1994. The murder rate was 6 offenses per 100,000 inhabitants, the lowest figure since 1967.
- Based on supplemental data received for 14,088 of the estimated murders, 88 percent of murder victims in 1998 were persons aged 18 years or older and 76 percent were male. The percentage of white and black murder victims was 50 percent and 48 percent, respectively.
- According to data submitted on 16,019 murder offenders, 89 percent of the assailants were male, 88 percent were 18 years of age or older, 49 percent of the offenders were black, and 49 percent were white. The remaining offenders were persons of other races.
- Fifty-one percent of murder victims knew their assailants. Among all female murder victims, 32 percent were slain by husbands or boyfriends, and 4 percent of the male victims were slain by wives or girlfriends.
- Thirty-two percent of all murders were a result of arguments, and 18 percent resulted from felonious activities such as robbery, arson, and other crimes.
- Data indicate that murder is most often an intraracial offense. In 1998, 94 percent of black murder victims were slain by black offenders. Eighty-seven percent of white victims were slain by white offenders.
- Six out of every ten reported murders were committed with a firearm.

Forcible Rape

- The estimated total of 93,103 forcible rapes reported to law enforcement during 1998 was the lowest total in a decade.
- Approximately 67 of every 100,000 females in the country were reported rape victims in 1998, a rate that is 4 percent lower than in 1997.

Robbery

- Robbery declined 10 percent in 1998 as compared to 1997 levels. Estimated robbery totals were 446,625 or 165 robberies per 100,000 population nationwide.
- Nearly $446 million in monetary loss was attributed to property stolen in connection with this offense. Bank robberies resulted in the highest average loss, $4,516 per offense; gas or service station robberies the lowest, $546.
- Street or highway robberies accounted for slightly less than half of the offenses in this category.
- Strong-arm tactics were used in 40 percent of all robberies committed in 1998, and firearms were used in 38 percent. Knives or cutting instruments were involved in 9 percent of the total robberies, and other weapons in 13 percent.

Aggravated Assault

- An estimated 974,402 aggravated assaults were reported to law enforcement in 1998, down 5 percent from the 1997 total.
- Aggravated assault accounted for 64 percent of the violent crimes in 1998.
- Blunt objects or other dangerous weapons were used in 36 percent of aggravated assaults in 1998. Personal weapons such as hands, fists, and feet were used in 27 percent of reported incidents; firearms in 19 percent; and knives or cutting instruments in 18 percent.

Burglary

- An estimated 2.3 million burglaries were reported to law enforcement in 1998, a decline of 5 percent from the 1997 level. Residences were the target of 2 of every 3 burglaries.
- Overall burglary losses were estimated at $3.1 billion in 1998.
- Sixty-five percent of all burglaries involved forcible entry, and 53 percent occurred during daylight hours. The average loss for residential burglaries was $1,299 and for nonresidential, $1,432.

Larceny-theft

- Of the three property crime offenses reported (burglary, larceny-theft, and motor vehicle theft), larceny-theft, with an estimated total of 7.4 million offenses, comprised 67 percent of the property crime total for the year.
- The total dollar loss to victims nationwide due to larceny-theft was nearly $4.8 billion in 1998. Property loss averaged $650 per offense.
- Thirty-six percent of the reported larcenies involved the theft of motor vehicle parts, accessories, and contents.

Motor Vehicle Theft

- In 1998, an estimated 1.2 million motor vehicles were reported stolen nationwide, representing an 8-percent drop in motor vehicle thefts from the 1997 levels and the lowest number since 1986.
- The estimated total value of vehicles stolen nationwide was nearly $7.5 billion. The estimated average value of stolen motor vehicles at the time of theft was $6,030 per vehicle.
- Seventy-six percent of all vehicle thefts involved automobiles. Trucks and buses accounted for 19 percent, and the remainder included other types of vehicles.

Arson

- A total of 78,094 arson offenses were reported in 1998, a 7-percent decline from the previous year's total.
- Structures were the most frequent targets of arsonists, comprising 47 percent of the reported incidents. Residential property was involved in 61 percent of the structural arsons during the year, and 43 percent of these structural arsons were directed at single-family dwellings.
- The monetary value of property damaged due to reported arsons averaged $12,561 per incident.
- Persons under the age of 18 were involved in 45 percent of arson crimes cleared by law enforcement in 1998. Of the eight Crime Index offenses, arson had the highest percentage of juvenile involvement.

Law Enforcement Employees

- A total of 13,865 city, county, and state police agencies reporting to the UCR Program provided law enforcement services to nearly 260 million inhabitants of the United States in 1998. Collectively, these agencies employed 641,208 officers and 253,327 civilians.
- The average rate of 2.5 full-time officers for every 1,000 inhabitants across the country was unchanged from the 1997 total.
- The Nation's cities collectively employed 2.4 officers per 1,000 inhabitants; rural law enforcement, 2.5 officers per 1,000; and suburban law enforcement, 2.6 per 1,000.
- The highest rate of sworn officers to population was recorded in the Northeastern States, with 2.8 officers per 1,000 inhabitants.
- Civilians made up 28 percent of the total United States law enforcement employee force in 1998.

PAKISTANI GENERAL MUSHARRAF ON MILITARY COUP

October 17, 1999

For a brief moment early in 1999, it appeared that India and Pakistan might finally be able to put behind them a half century of bitter rivalry stemming from the British partition of the Indian subcontinent following World War II. In a dramatic gesture toward peace, India's nationalist prime minister on February 20, 1999, rode a bus across the border and embraced the prime minister of Pakistan. A day later the two men signed pledges of peaceful cooperation.

But within a matter of months, domestic political developments and age-old disputes between the two countries nearly led them into a full-scale war for the fourth time in a half century—a war that could easily have led to the use of nuclear weapons both sides had tested just a year before. International mediation helped avert a conflict, but hopes for a long-term reconciliation were shattered. In October the Pakistani prime minister, Nawaz Sharif, was ousted in a bloodless military coup, ending an eleven-year period of democratically elected governments and creating new uncertainty in one of the most troubled regions of the world.

Peace Talks at Lahore

Separated by the British in 1947 and enemies ever since, India and Pakistan seemed almost always on the verge of war. The two countries fought three wars in the fifty years after the British departure from the Indian subcontinent. A majority of Pakistanis were Muslim; India was dominated by Hindus, with a large Muslim minority. One legacy of British partition was the rivalry between India and Pakistan over the territory of Kashmir, a mountainous region bordering the two countries and China. The British gave control of most of Kashmir to India, despite its majority Muslim population. Two of the three Indian-Pakistan wars (in 1947 and 1965) were over Kashmir, and low-level skirmishes were common.

In May 1998 international concern about the rivalry between India and Pakistan reached new heights when both countries tested nuclear weapons.

India, which had first tested a nuclear explosive device in 1974, took the lead again with a series of five underground tests. Pakistan, which had been developing a nuclear device for years, quickly followed suit with five tests of its own. The prospect of an armed conflict between the two countries escalating into a nuclear war caused alarm worldwide. The United States, which had been one of Pakistan's most important allies, imposed economic sanctions against the country and demanded a halt to further tests by either nation. (Nuclear tests, Historic Documents of 1998, p. 326)

Within months the uproar over the nuclear tests faded, and the leaders of the two countries set about to improve relations with a series of meetings and telephone calls. In February 1999 Pakistani prime minister Sharif invited his Indian counterpart, Atai Bihari Vajpayee, for a visit. On February 20 Vajpayee boarded a bus in the Indian city of Armristar and rode across the Punjab plains to the Pakistani border at Wagha. As he crossed the border, Vajpayee said: "I bring good will and hopes of my fellow Indians, who seek abiding peace and harmony with Pakistan. I am conscious that this is a defining moment in South Asia, and I hope we will be able to rise to the challenge." The words were all the more remarkable considering that they came from the leader of India's Hindu nationalist party, an organization long dedicated to opposing Pakistan at any cost.

Vajpayee was enthusiastically greeted by Sharif, the leader of the Pakistani party called the Muslim League. The leaders met for two days at the ancient city of Lahore. On February 21 they signed two agreements pledging negotiations on such issues as trade and visas. The leaders agreed to take steps to avoid a nuclear war, including notifying each other of pending missile tests and any other "accidental, unauthorized, or unexplained incident" that might lead to conflict. And they issued a joint document, called the Lahore Declaration, promising to "intensify their efforts" to resolve the dispute over Kashmir.

Political Maneuvering, and a Flare-up over Kashmir

Both leaders came under political pressure following their goodwill diplomacy, and within a few weeks India and Pakistan were again on the verge of war. In April Vajpayee lost a key ally in parliament, costing his government a working majority. Forced to call new elections in the fall (which his party ultimately won), Vajpayee continued as head of a caretaker government. At about the same time Sharif's chief political foe—former prime minister Benazir Bhutto—was convicted on corruption charges, imprisoned for five years, and barred from holding political office. Also in April both nations conducted tests of ballistic missiles, raising new fears internationally that they might equip missiles with nuclear warheads.

Early in May the two countries came close to a full-scale war when Muslim guerrillas backed by Pakistan blew up an Indian army ammunition dump in a region of Kashmir called Kargil and took up positions on the Indian side of a cease-fire line (called the "line of control") that had sepa-

rated the two countries since 1949. India mounted a vigorous defense and for two months the two sides skirmished along the line of control.

U.S. officials later said that the conflict could easily have escalated into a major war, possibly with one or the other parties resorting to nuclear weapons—most likely Pakistan, since it had a much smaller army. President Bill Clinton helped mediate the conflict, inviting Sharif to Washington. In a meeting July 4 Clinton pressured Sharif to order the Pakistan-backed guerrillas to leave India. Sharif complied, and the crisis abated.

Sharif Ousted

Sharif's concession to Clinton was a major factor leading to his downfall just three months later. Pakistan's military leaders reportedly were deeply angered that Sharif had given up hard-fought gains in Kashmir. The military high command was further angered later in July when Sharif refused to allow retaliation after India shot down a Pakistani military plane, killing sixteen.

Attempting to gain the upper hand with his military leadership, Sharif on October 12 announced that he was replacing the head of the Pakistani armed forces, General Pervez Musharraf. The general, who was in Sri Lanka at the time, hurried back to Pakistan while military units loyal to him took control of the government and placed Sharif under arrest. In a brief televised address at 3 A.M. on October 13, Musharraf said the military had moved "to prevent further destabilization," and was doing so because of "incessant public clamor" for action. It was the fourth military coup in Pakistan's fifty-two-year history, and it brought to an end an eleven-year run of civilian governments.

The Indian government expressed "grave concern" about the coup and placed its military on alert along the line of control in Kashmir. U.S. State Department spokesman James Rubin called for the "earliest possible restoration of democracy" in Pakistan.

In a televised address to the nation October 17, Musharraf said he had taken the title of "chief executive" of Pakistan but insisted that military rule would be temporary. "The armed forces have no intention to stay in charge any longer than absolutely necessary to pave the way for true democracy," he said, without mentioning any plans for new elections. The military had not imposed martial law, he said, and to emphasize the point the printed text of his remarks put those words in capital letters.

Musharraf said the military ousted Sharif because his government had been "intriguing to destroy the last institution of stability left in Pakistan by creating dissension in the ranks of the armed forces." Specifically, Musharraf accused Sharif of attempting to deny his airplane permission to land in Pakistan upon his return from Sri Lanka, in effect forcing the plane "either to land in India or crash." The plane finally was allowed to land in Pakistan with only seven minutes of fuel left in its tanks, he said.

Musharraf promised to crack down on corruption, which he said had reached a "horrendous proportion, threatening the very basis of our soci-

ety." Without naming names, but in an apparent reference to Sharif and his government, Musharraf said anticorruption efforts would target "those guilty of plundering and looting the national wealth."

Pakistan's new leader also sought to calm international fears—especially in India—that the coup meant a victory for hard-line forces bent on renewed confrontation. India and Pakistan "both must sincerely work towards resolving their problems," especially the dispute over Kashmir, he said. Pakistan was committed to a policy of "restraint and sensitivity" in the handling of its new nuclear arsenal, he added.

In his first press conference, held November 1, Musharraf said he had formed a "National Accountability Bureau" to investigate corruption. The military government later filed charges against Sharif, accusing him of corruption as well as kidnapping and attempted murder when he refused Musharraf's plane permission to land in Pakistan.

The United States and most other countries appealed to Musharraf to set a timetable for calling elections and returning democracy to Pakistan. State Department spokesman Rubin said the United States would not conduct "business as usual" with Pakistan, which for many years had been one of Washington's key allies in South Asia. Rubin noted that the administration had curtailed foreign aid and arms sales to Pakistan, as required by law, after Pakistan tested nuclear weapons in 1998.

> *Following are excerpts from a televised speech delivered October 17, 1999, by General Pervez Musharraf, who had taken control of Pakistan five days earlier after ousting the prime minister, Nawaz Sharif:*

Pakistan today stands at the crossroads of its destiny—a destiny which is in our hands to make or break. Fifty-two years ago, we started with a beacon of hope and today that beacon is no more and we stand in darkness. There is despondency, and hopelessness surrounding us with no light visible anywhere around. The slide down has been gradual but has rapidly accelerated in the last many years.

Today, we have reached a stage where our economy has crumbled, our credibility is lost, state institutions lie demolished; provincial disharmony has caused cracks in the federation, and people who were once brothers are now at each other's throat.

In sum, we have lost our honour, our dignity, our respect in the comity of nations. Is this the democracy our Quaid-e-Azam had envisaged? Is this the way to enter the new millennium?

Let us not be despondent. I am an optimist. I have faith in the destiny of this nation; belief in its people and conviction in its future. We were not a poor nation as generally perceived. In fact we are rich. We have fertile land that can produce three crops a year. We have abundant water to irrigate these lands and generate surplus power. We have gas, coal and vast untapped mineral resources—and above all a dynamic and industrious people. All these await mobilization. We have only to awaken, join hands and grasp our destiny. For Allah helps those who help themselves.

My fellow Pakistanis, as you are aware I took over in extremely unusual circumstances—not of my making. It is unbelievable and indeed unfortunate that, the few at the helm of affairs in the last government were intriguing to destroy the last institution of stability left in Pakistan by creating dissention in the ranks of the armed forces of Pakistan. And who would believe that the Chief of Army Staff, having represented Pakistan in Sri Lanka, upon his return was denied landing in his own country and instead circumstances were created which would have forced our plane either to land in India or crash.

Providence ultimately intervened. Praise be to Allah that the plane landed safely when barely seven minutes of fuel was left. I salute my soldiers and men for acting courageously in the supreme interest of the nation. Most of all I salute our people who stood solidly with their armed forces at that critical hour. Quite clearly, what Pakistan has experienced in the recent years has been hardly a label of democracy not the essence of it. Our people were never emancipated from the yoke of despotism. I shall not allow the people to be taken back to the era of sham democracy but to a true one. . . .

My dear countrymen. The choice before us on 12th October was between saving the body (that is the nation) at the cost of losing a limb (which is the Constitution) or saving the limb and losing the whole body. The Constitution is but a part of the nation, therefore I chose to save the nation and yet took care not to sacrifice the Constitution. The Constitution has only been temporarily held in abeyance. This is NOT MARTIAL LAW, only another path towards democracy. The armed forces have no intention to stay in charge any longer than is absolutely necessary to pave the way for true democracy to flourish in Pakistan.

Ever since 12th October I have deliberated, carried out consultations and crystallized my views about the future course to be adopted. I wish to share these with you today. My dear countrymen, our aims and objectives shall be:

- Rebuild national confidence and morale.
- Strengthen federation, remove inter provincial disharmony and restore national cohesion.
- Revive economy and restore investor confidence.
- Ensure law and order and dispense speedy justice.
- Depoliticise state institutions.
- Devolution of power to the grass roots level.
- Ensure swift and across the board accountability.

Good governance is the pre-requisite to achieve these objectives. In the past, our governments have ruled the people. It is time now for the governments to serve the people. The government I plan to institute shall comprise:

Firstly—The President. On my request, President Rafique Tarar has very kindly agreed to stay.

627

Second—A National Security Council headed by the Chief Executive with six members. These members will be Chief of Naval Staff, Chief of Air Staff, a specialist each in Legal, Finance, Foreign Policy and national affairs. A think-tank of experts shall be formed as an adjunct to the National Security Council, to provide institutionalised advice and input.

Third—A Cabinet of Ministers who will work under the guidance of the National Security Council.

Four—The Provinces to be headed by a Governor, functioning through a small provincial cabinet. All these appointments shall be made purely on the basis of professional competence, merit and repute.

Revival of Economy is critical. Our economy is in deep trouble and revolutionary steps are needed to put it back on track. The Pakistani people were subjected to betrayal of trust. Their hard-earned money was frozen or taxed in violation of State commitment. We need to restore this trust. To revitalize our economy in addition to measures like recovery of the looted national wealth—a task that will be ruthlessly pursued, I am identifying policy guidelines. Some of which are:

Rebuilding of investors' confidence through stability and consistency in economic policies, and economic security. The objective is to encourage the local investors, overseas Pakistanis and foreign investors. Increase domestic savings. Carry out pragmatic tax reforms. Turn around the state enterprises towards profitability. Boost agriculture and revive industry. Strict austerity measures.

Next aspect is accountability. Lack of accountability has resulted in corruption of horrendous proportion, threatening the very basis of our society. The term *Ehtesab* has been abused to an extent that it has lost its meaning. There is thus a need to re-establish faith in the process of accountability.

The process of accountability is being directed especially towards those guilty of plundering and looting the national wealth and tax evaders. It is also directed towards loan defaulters and those who have had their loans rescheduled or condoned. The process of accountability will be transparent for the public to see. My advice to the guilty is to return voluntarily national wealth, bank loans and pay their taxes before the hand of law forces them to do so with penalty. As a last chance I urge all defaulters to come forth and settle their debts within a period of four weeks, after which their names will be published and the law will take its due course. They owe this to Pakistan and I expect their spirit of patriotism to guide them. . . .

I wish to reassure the International community that there is no change in our foreign policy. We will continue to honour international obligations and commitments as in the past. It will remain our constant endeavour to promote peace and stability in our region. We would like to maintain our abiding policy of friendship and co-operation with all countries. The strengthening of brotherly ties with the Islamic countries will be a central pillar of our foreign policy. We shall continue our efforts to achieve a just and peaceful solution in Afghanistan. We wish to see a truly representative government in Kabul. We will maintain and further reinforce our traditional and time tested friendship and co-operation with China. We attach the highest importance to our friendly relations with all major powers, especially the United States.

Here I would like to mention two key areas of our external relations: International security and disarmament and our relations with India. Pakistan has always been alive to international non-proliferation concerns. Last year, we were compelled to respond to India's nuclear tests in order to restore strategic balance in the interest of our national security and regional peace and stability. In the new nuclear environment in South Asia, we believe that both Pakistan and India have to exercise utmost restraint and responsibility. We owe it to our people and also to the world. I wish to assure the world community that while preserving its vital security interests Pakistan will continue to pursue a policy of nuclear and missile restraint and sensitivity to global non-proliferation and disarmament objectives.

As for relations with India, let me at the out-set congratulate Mr. Atal Bihari Vajpayee on assumption of office as the Prime Minister of India. I welcome his offer for friendly relations and positively reciprocate. At the turn of the century, South Asia stands at a crucial juncture of its history, 20th Century saw our transition to independence but the region has unfortunately remained mired in conflicts and economic deprivation.

Together Pakistan and India can change this scenario. For this objective both must sincerely work towards resolving their problems, especially the core issue of Jammu and Kashmir. The people of Kashmir have made great sacrifices for the achievement of their rights promised to them by the United Nations. We shall continue our unflinching moral, political and diplomatic support to our Kashmiri brethren in their struggle to achieve their right of self-determination.

India must honour the UN resolutions and its own commitment to the people of Kashmir. It must also end its repression of the Kashmiri people and respect their fundamental human rights. Pakistan would welcome unconditional, equitable and result-oriented dialogue with India. While, our armed forces are fully equipped and ready to defend our national sovereignty and territorial integrity, it is our desire that the situation on our borders with India and on the Line of Control should remain calm and peaceful. I take this opportunity to announce a unilateral military de-escalation on our international borders with India and initiate the return of all our forces moved to the borders in the recent past. I hope this step would serve as a meaningful confidence building measure.

My dear countrymen, to conclude my address let me say that we have hit rock bottom. We have no choice but to rise, and rise we will Inshallah. Our actions shall speak louder than words. Therefore, my countrymen let us RISE TO THE OCCASION AND SEIZE THE OPPORTUNITY. Before I close I would like to give you a personal commitment. I hereby undertake to declare my tax returns and assets to be documented and open for public scrutiny. . . .

AFL-CIO PRESIDENT ON ADVANCES FOR THE LABOR MOVEMENT
October 20, 1999

After decades of declining union membership and political influence, the American labor movement may have begun a turnaround in 1999. Labor unions picked up a net membership of about 265,000 workers, the largest one-year gain in two decades. Union membership as a percentage of the total work force held steady, halting a downward trend that for many years had appeared unstoppable. And in the biggest single organizing victory for labor since 1937, the Service Employees International Union in February won the right to represent nearly 75,000 home care workers in Los Angeles County.

On the political front, organized labor played a significant role in the high-profile collapse of an attempt by the World Trade Organization to organize a new round of international trade negotiations. Labor leaders argued that trade negotiators were not giving due consideration to poor working conditions and the rights of workers. After the trade talks collapsed in Seattle in December, President Bill Clinton said he would push for more consideration of labor issues in any future negotiations. (Trade talks, p. 797)

In a speech at the Georgetown University Law Center on October 20, 1999, AFL-CIO President John J. Sweeney said the labor federation was emphasizing union membership as a "fundamental civil right" and as a needed countervailing force to "corporate power."

AFL-CIO Organizing Efforts

Organized labor reached a peak of membership and influence in the United States in the years following World War II, when the American economy was booming with industrial production and construction. In 1954 labor unions represented more than 35 percent of all American workers. But changes in society and the economy starting in the 1960s led to a long and steady decline in union membership generally and altered the face of the labor movement. The rise of technology and automation in the workplace reduced the importance of industrial workers—long the backbone of labor unions. Seeking to reduce production costs, American corporations moved jobs from the heavily unionized industrial heartland of the Northeast and Midwest, first to the South and then overseas, where unions were less welcome. As more Americans entered the middle class, workers abandoned the unions they viewed as representing the blue-collar past.

By the late 1990s union membership in the United States stood at under 16 million, representing just 14 percent of the total work force. The AFL-CIO, the federation of seventy-three unions that sought to speak for all working people, could claim a total membership of only about 13 million. During the years of overall decline, the major growth area for labor was in the public sector, where unions were able to sign up millions of school teachers and public employees whose pay and working benefits often failed to match their educational backgrounds and responsibilities on the job.

Elected as AFL-CIO president in 1995, Sweeney launched a major campaign to reverse the trend, partly by acknowledging changes in the American workplace and partly by taking a more aggressive stance against the antiunion attitude in corporate board rooms. Labor unions began paying more attention to workers such as women, minorities, and immigrants, millions of whom held low-pay, high-stress jobs in service industries. The AFL-CIO also adopted an approach of emphasizing what it called "economic density"—trying to increase the proportion of organized workers within an industry so they would have greater clout at the bargaining table. This approach took its cue from the auto industry, where unions historically had great influence because they represented high proportions of the total work force. Another AFL-CIO tactic was to focus increased public attention on the antiunion activities of corporations, portraying American business leaders as denying civil rights to workers just as southern segregationists had denied the civil rights of blacks.

Labor's new approach showed signs of paying off in 1998, when total union membership nationally grew by a net of about 100,000, the first significant rise in nearly two decades. And 1999 turned out to be an even better year for labor, with an estimated 600,000 workers joining unions. After subtracting losses incurred when unionized companies cut back their work forces or moved operations overseas, the net gain for labor in the year was about 265,000, according to statistics from the AFL-CIO and the Labor Department's Bureau of Labor Statistics.

"We're at the corner," Sweeney said in summing up labor's new success in halting the slide in membership. "We haven't turned it yet, but we're at the corner."

Two Big Victories for Labor

Labor unions had several major organizing victories during 1999, two of which had enormous psychological impact on the labor movement generally. The first came February 25, when officials certified that a majority of home care workers voting in a representation election had given the Service Employees International Union the right to represent them in negotiations with Los Angeles County. The nearly 75,000 workers provided ser-

vices such as preparing meals and cleaning homes for elderly and disabled residents of the county under Medicare and other programs. In terms of numbers, it was the single biggest gain for labor since 112,000 General Motors workers joined the United Auto Workers in 1937.

The service union had begun its drive to represent the Los Angeles home care workers in 1987. Most of the workers were women and minorities; nearly all earned $5.75, the minimum hourly wage in California, for work that was often stressful and physically demanding. The union's road to victory passed through many hurdles, including a trip to the state legislature in 1992 to win approval of a law establishing counties as the employing agencies for home care workers.

"This is a home run for labor amidst a lot of strike-outs, in that it is a huge victory in a pivotal sector of the economy, the service sector," Harley Shaiken, a labor specialist at the University of California-Berkeley told the New York Times. "And it represents the new face of labor—women workers, minority workers, low-paid workers—people who have been so hard to organize."

In its organizing drive, the service union dealt directly with one issue that often arose in such circumstances: the fear of some workers, and their employers, that union wage demands would raise costs to an unacceptable level and lead to job cutbacks. The contrary was true, the union said: higher wages ultimately would stabilize costs and employment levels and raise quality by encouraging home care workers to stay in jobs that historically experienced turnover as high as 40 percent annually. At least one member of the Los Angeles County Board of Supervisors agreed, saying that elderly citizens who received care from higher paid, better trained workers would be more inclined to stay at home rather than moving into nursing homes, which were much more expensive.

Another organizing victory for labor involved far fewer employees but had major historical and emotional importance for the union movement. In June more than 5,200 employees of a complex of six Fieldcrest Cannon textile plants in Kannapolis, North Carolina, voted narrowly to be represented by the Union of Needletrades, Industrial and Textile Employees (known as UNITE). Owned by Pillowtex Corp., of Dallas, Texas, the plants had been the subject of various union organizing efforts dating to 1921. Kannapolis had been a company town—its homes, shops, and public services were all owned for decades by the textile mills—and the company had spared no effort to keep its workers out of unions. Setting that history aside, Pillowtex Chairman Charles M. Hansen Jr. announced November 10 that the company would recognize UNITE as representing the workers. "The times have changed," he said. "Life is one of change, and one has to adapt to change."

Organizing the Medical Profession

Change also came to the health care industry, where doctors and other medical professionals were increasingly turning to unions in hopes of countering the cost-cutting measures of corporate managed care agencies. The most dramatic move in that direction came on June 23, when the doctors in the American Medical Association (AMA) voted to form a union to represent salaried doctors and medical residents.

The AMA's action was not typical of union organizing drives. With 700,000 members who considered themselves professionals, the AMA established an organization called Physicians for Responsible Negotiation. That organization, in turn, would organize local unions of doctors in communities to bargain with hospitals, health maintenance organizations, and other agencies that employed the doctors. The AMA sought to disassociate itself from typical unions in another important way: doctors would not go on strike because that would represent a break in "the covenant we have with our patients," AMA president Nancy W. Dickey said.

The move toward a union of doctors was not greeted with universal applause. Representatives of the health insurance industry expressed concern about the potential impact on costs, as did Robert Pitofsky, chairman of the Federal Trade Commission, who warned Congress against passing legislation to exempt self-employed health care professionals from antitrust laws. Allowing independent doctors to unionize ultimately would be "bad medicine for consumers," he said. The doctors who would be unionized under the AMA program already were exempt from antitrust laws because they were employees, not independent practitioners.

In a related development, the National Labor Relations Board ruled on November 26 that interns and medical residents at privately owned hospitals had the right to organize unions, and even go on strike, to seek higher wages and better working conditions. The board's decision, on a 3–2 vote, overturned a 1976 ruling that defined interns and residents as students, rather than as employees with the right to organize.

The case involved the Boston Medical Center, where interns and residents were represented by the Committee of Interns and Residents. The formerly public hospital was sold in 1996 to a private company, which sought to decertify the union. In its ruling, the labor relations board said interns and residents in private hospitals had the same right to organize as their counterparts in public institutions. The committee's executive director, Mark Levy, said it would seek to organize an estimated 90,000 interns and residents nationwide at private hospitals. The committee already represented 10,000 interns and residents at sixty public hospitals. Joseph Keye, general counsel of the Association of American Medical Colleges, said the labor relations board made a "wrong decision" that would be "bad for education and labor relations."

Following are excerpts from a speech, "Building a Labor Movement for the Next Century," delivered October 20, 1999, by John J. Sweeney, president of the AFL-CIO, at Georgetown University Law Center in Washington, D.C.:

Today, I want to tell you about the efforts of today's unions to restore the voice of working Americans in their workplaces, their communities, their government, and the world economy as we cross the threshold of the Twenty-First Century.

Just last week, at our convention in Los Angeles, delegates representing more 13 million union members made decisions that will escalate our efforts at organizing, political action, community outreach, and global solidarity.

But, first, I want to talk about why these efforts are so important, not only for our movement but for every American who shares our vision of a shared prosperity, an inclusive society, and a vibrant democracy. . . .

Business, labor, and government all agreed that working people were entitled to a fair share of the wealth they produced. Our economy benefited because high wages generated strong consumer demand. And our social fabric and our political process were strengthened because upward mobility made Americans more confident and cohesive.

Of course, America wasn't perfect—far from it. But shared prosperity made our people more supportive of the struggles for social justice, from the civil rights movement to the women's movement and other efforts to eradicate discrimination of all kinds.

Strong unions helped make all this possible. When unions represented a third of the entire workforce, as they did at the time of the AFL-CIO merger more than four decades ago, they were able to win higher wages and better benefits not only for their own members but for working people throughout the economy.

And unions used their strength to promote the common good in the political arena as well.

At the AFL-CIO, there is an exhibit of a hundred pens that President Johnson gave the labor federation's first president, the legendary George Meany. Johnson had used the pens to sign historic social legislation that the union movement had helped enact, including civil rights, voting rights, Medicare, Medicaid, student loans, and improvements in Social Security.

None of these laws benefitted union members alone. Every one of them advanced the cause of economic security and social justice for every American. That was what a strong union movement meant for all Americans at the middle of this century.

But, for roughly a quarter century, from the early 1970s until just a few years ago, family incomes stagnated, economic inequality increased, and our social fabric frayed.

Much of the deterioration in working families' living standards can be traced to the decline of the labor movement to scarcely a seventh of the workforce. And much of labor's decline can be traced to the erosion of the idea that employees have the right to a voice at work.

That was the promise of the National Labor Relations Act. But, because of corporate America's hostility and official Washington's indifference, that promise has been broken.

It pains me to say this at one of our nation's great law schools, but no laws do less to protect those they are intended to protect than our nation's labor laws. And nothing sums up the problem as well as a few facts.

The fact is: Nine out of ten employers where workers try to form unions force their employees to attend anti-union propaganda meetings.

The fact is: Half of private employers threaten to shut down their operations if their workers exercise their freedom to choose a union.

And the fact is: One in three private-sector employers facing organizing campaigns illegally fires union supporters.

That is why the report of the blue-ribbon, bipartisan, national Commission on the Future of Worker-Management Relations, concluded in 1994—and I quote: "The United States is the only major democratic country in which the choice of . . . workers . . . to be represented by a union is subject to such a confrontational process."

One year after that report was released, American labor elected new leaders, with a mandate to rebuild our movement, so that we can help working families regain their voices.

From the first, we have understood that we cannot restore the world we once knew.

The workforce is becoming more diverse. A new economy is emerging, based on high technology, international trade, and the ability to process information and master new skills. And, just like today's companies, today's unions must change as well.

If we change with the times, and if we work smarter as well as harder, we can build a new labor movement for the new workforce, the new economy, and the next century.

We're beginning our journey of change by reaching out to the new American workforce.

At the AFL-CIO, we're asking unions at every level to shift resources to help workers organize. And more and more are meeting the challenge.

Today's unions are recruiting and training new organizers whose faces reflect the variety of America at work—including more women, more people of color, and more recent immigrants, many of whom come from our own ranks.

We're setting strategies to build and leverage working people's power in their companies, their communities, and entire industries. And, increasingly, our efforts are bearing fruit.

Last year, more than 475,000 Americans gained a voice at work as new union members.

That's a modern-day record. And we're doing even better this year. Seventy-five thousand home-care workers in Los Angeles, sixty-six thousand public employees in Puerto Rico, ninety-four hundred US Airways reservation agents, and, in a struggle that spanned several decades, more than five thousand sturdy souls at the Pillowtex/Cannon textile mills in North Carolina. All have voted this year to join unions.

But we can't afford to kid ourselves. As fast as today's unions are growing, today's economy is growing even faster. And it's growing fastest in industries and communities where we have to work overtime to establish a foothold.

To begin the job, union activists are re-introducing themselves to the communities where we live and work.

We have a compelling message for our friends and neighbors: If we work together, we can create good jobs, strong communities and a voice for working families.

At our convention last week, the delegates debated and decided on plans that will restructure the union movement to build a stronger capability in our cities, our metropolitan areas, and our states. As so many decisions devolve from Washington—and as regions become the most important economic units—working families need to raise their voices at the state and local levels.

Most of all, we need to reach out to our communities.

We're building and bolstering our relationships with community institutions and their leaders—elected officials, congregations, civil and human rights organizations, students and intellectuals, and other proven or potential allies.

We saw this in Los Angeles. In the days before our convention officially began, we held a national conference with leaders from the major faith communities. And, with Monsignor Higgins' help, we are helping to build the new National Interfaith Committee for Worker Justice.

Meanwhile, we also participated in a teach-in at UCLA, with students, professors, and other academics. As with similar events throughout this country, we are reaching out to a new generation of activists who are joining the movement against sweatshops and in support of the right to a voice at work.

Through Union Summer, more than 2,000 interns have learned first-hand how to bring about social change—and many have become union organizers.

Through our Organizing Institute, thousands of dedicated people—many of whom are union members themselves or come from union families—are learning the skills they need to reach out to the new American workforce.

And, in local campaigns for living wage ordinances and boycotts of products made in sweatshops at home or abroad, today's unions are working alongside Americans of good will from every walk of life.

We can see this new energy and new activism here at Georgetown, where law students and undergraduates are working together in the struggle against sweatshops, and I want to thank each and every one of you who are involved in this effort.

As we work with old friends and new allies, we can begin to create a climate where America will restore workers' rights to organize unions.

According to public opinion research, three out of four Americans support strong laws giving workers the right to join and form unions. A strong majority understands that unions offer employees a voice at work. But they just don't know about the lengths to which employers will go to deny workers that voice.

Our challenge is to turn this openness towards unions into outrage against the denial of the right of working men and women to organize unions. It's time to expose injustices, such as what has happened to the workers at the Avondale Shipyard in Louisiana.

Since 1993, when 5000 workers voted for a union, Avondale has been found guilty of more than 100 federal labor law violations, including 28 firings. But the company—a company that exists off taxpayer-funded defense contracts—has yet to reinstate even one worker—or to pay even one dime of the $3 million in penalties that have been assessed against it. That's a scandal, and it has to be stopped.

Through our "Voice at Work" campaign, our unions are working with our allies in communities across this country to expose instances where employers ride roughshod on workers' rights to organize. This effort began with seven days in June of this year, when we held more than 120 events in 38 states. And this effort will continue until we have restored the right to choose a voice at work.

We're going to keep asserting two common-sense principles: First, forming associations in the workplace is a fundamental civil right. And, second, America needs unions, because they offer a countervailing voice to corporate power.

We're already offering working families a stronger voice in the political arena. We're conducting a new kind of political action that stresses working families' issues, not party labels.

By raising our voice on national issues, we have raised the minimum wage and defended Social Security, Medicare, Medicaid, education and the environment. And, by organizing around these issues in election years, we have increased the political participation of working families.

In 1998, 49% of union household members turned out to vote, compared with only 34% of other eligible Americans. In next year's elections, we will make every effort to put working families' issues at the center of public debate—and to encourage even more members of union households to cast their ballots.

And next year we'll be taking our members' civic participation a step further by launching a new internet community—workingfamilies.com—where union members can make their voices heard around social and economic justice issues through cyberspace.

And we're asking union members to do even more. It's not good enough to have public officials who feel for us. We need more public officials who feel with us—who know what it's like to work hard every day and pay the bills at the end of the month.

That is why we were proud that some 626 union members ran for office in 1998, and 420 were elected or re-elected. And that is why we are working towards the goal of having 2000 union members run for office in the year 2000.

When union members participate in politics, we seek justice not only for ourselves but for everyone. Here at Georgetown Law, I'm proud to report that the AFL-CIO is joining the outcry by leading civil rights and women's organizations against the way in which the Far Right is holding hostage the confirmation of qualified nominees for federal judgeships, particularly women and people of color. . . .

When we raise our voices and raise our issues, we can transform public debate. That is what we are doing in the debate about international trade.

Two years ago, we helped beat Fast Track because most Americans believe that international trade agreements must protect the rights of workers and consumers, as well as investors. People understand that the injustices of sweatshops, child labor, and forced labor persist because our existing trade agreements fail to protect human rights in general and workers' rights in particular.

That is why we are challenging employers and governments around the world to create a new system of rules that guarantees that the global economy works for those who create the wealth.

When the World Trade Organization meets in Seattle next month, we'll be there. And we'll insist that international trade rules must be overhauled to ensure basic human rights and reverse the inequities in the global economy.

As a new century begins, the players in today's global economy can take two roads.

If they take the low road, they'll compete by cutting wages, cutting workforces, and cutting corners on quality. That road is paved with exploitation and abuse. And it leads the world's nations on a race to the bottom.

But, if they take the high road, they will compete by improving quality, not impoverishing their employees. The high road leads to a future of high-wage jobs, stable families, strong communities, a well-educated workforce, a well-maintained natural environment, and a shared and sustainable prosperity.

The labor movement of the Twenty-First Century will do everything we can to make sure that our own nation and every other nation takes the high road to the future.

In the days since Henry Kaiser first fought for working Americans in our nation's courtrooms, our economy has come a long way—from the typewriter and the telephone to the Internet and electronic commerce.

But the principles he promoted are still a guidepost for our journeys. America still works best—and does best by working families—when they enjoy a fair share of the bounty they produce and exert an influence on the decisions that shape their lives.

Strong, vibrant, and forward-looking unions are still the best way for working families to raise their voices, lift their livelihoods, and promote economic progress and social justice for every American. And that is why today's unions are rebuilding and revitalizing themselves to take our movement into the Twenty-First Century. . . .

ARMENIAN PRESIDENT ON SHOOTINGS IN PARLIAMENT
October 31, 1999

Gunmen burst into the Parliament chamber in Armenia on October 27 and opened fire, killing the prime minister, the speaker of Parliament, and other officials. The gunmen, who said they intended to kill only the prime minister, appeared to be protesting the country's deteriorating economic situation.

In addition to Prime Minister Vazgen Sarkisian, the gunmen killed Parliament Speaker Karen Demirchian, two deputy speakers, and three other senior government officials. An elderly journalist in the Parliament chamber at the time died of a heart attack, and nine other people were wounded in the shooting. Sarkisian had been prime minister for just five months, and Demirchian had been Armenia's communist leader for fourteen years when Armenia was a republic of the Soviet Union.

After shooting Sarkisian and the other leaders, the gunmen held about forty people—most of them members of Parliament—hostage in the Parliament building. President Robert Kocharian negotiated with the gunmen overnight for the release of the hostages. Bowing to the gunmen's demands, Kocharian promised a fair trial and agreed to broadcast on state-run television a statement in which they demanded a guarantee of personal safety and the bringing to justice of unnamed officials who had "plundered the nation." The hostages were freed October 28 after about thirty hours of captivity. The gunmen surrendered, and three of them were charged with terrorism.

The apparent leader of the assault, Nairi Unanian, had once been a member of a radical Armenian nationalist party, but that group denied any association with him. Unanian told one reporter that the assault was a "patriotic action" to rescue Armenia from a "catastrophic situation." Prosecutors on November 10 charged a member of Parliament, Musheg Movesian, with helping to organize the attack.

A week after the shootings, Kocharian named Sarkisian's brother, Aram, as the new prime minister. Aram Sarkisian had no political experience but had run a large cement factory. He promised to continue economic reforms initiated by his brother and Kocharian.

The U.S. deputy secretary of state, Strobe Talbott, had been in Yerevan meeting with Kocharian and Sarkisian but had left the capital by the time the shootings began. Talbott had been pressing both Armenia and neighboring Azerbaijan to settle a long dispute over a contested territory, Nagorno-Karabakh.

Conflict over Nagorno-Karabakh

In the immediate aftermath of the shootings, much of the speculation about the gunmen's motives centered on the possibility that they were radical nationalists angered by the government's willingness to negotiate with Azerbaijan about Nagorno-Karabakh. Later, it appeared that the attackers were more concerned about Armenia's struggling economy—in many ways a consequence of the Nagorno-Karabakh dispute.

Nagorno-Karabakh was a territory of western Azerbaijan, close to the border with Armenia, populated mostly by Christian Armenians. The two countries went to war in 1988 when Armenian separatists in the territory declared independence from Muslim-dominated Azerbaijan. With the aid of Armenian troops, the nationalists drove Azeri forces from Nagorno-Karabakh. An estimated 35,000 people died in the conflict. Full-scale fighting ended in 1993, and a truce was signed in 1994—with Armenia controlling Nagorno-Karabakh and about 20 percent of Azerbaijan's territory. But intermittent fighting continued into 1999.

In addition to causing thousands of deaths, driving millions of refugees from their homes, and sapping the treasuries of two impoverished countries, the Nagorno-Karabakh war heightened tensions throughout the Caucasus region. The neighboring countries of Iran, Russia, and Turkey all were concerned about the potential for the conflict to spread. Turkey joined with Azerbaijan in imposing an economic blockade that severely curtailed Armenian imports.

The Nagorno-Karabakh issue also threatened international plans for a pipeline to carry oil from enormous but mostly untapped reserves in the Caspian Sea. Some multinational oil firms had wanted the pipeline to run from Azerbaijan through Armenia into Turkey, where it would reach ports that would carry the oil to international markets. But the continuing conflict over Nagorno-Karabak led to the development of alternate routes bypassing Armenia.

The Clinton administration in 1999 initiated high-level contacts between Armenia and Azerbaijan, with Secretary of State Madeleine K. Albright hosting a meeting in her Washington office between Kocharian and Azerbaijani president Heydar Aliyev. The two leaders met four more times before the October 27 shootings, raising hopes in some quarters—and fears among hard-liners in both countries—that a final resolution of the Nagorno-Karabakh question might be possible.

Armenian Politics

The Nagorno-Karabakh conflict was at the heart of Armenian politics during the late 1980s and throughout the 1990s. Many hard-line nationalists insisted there could never be any compromise with Azerbaijan over the status of the territory, but others said a permanent peace settlement was in the long-term interests of both countries.

Levon Ter-Petrosian in 1996 won the presidency in an election that opponents said was invalid. Shortly after taking office he arrested some opponents and imposed tight limits on political activity. Sarkisian, the defense minister at the time, used the military to quell protests against the election results and Ter-Petrosian's crackdown.

Ter-Petrosian undertook new negotiations with Azerbaijan on the issue of Nagorno-Karabakh, prompting new protests among hard-liners who said he was making too many concessions. Under fire on that issue, he resigned in 1998.

Kocharian, an Armenian nationalist from the disputed region, took over as president and named Sarkisian as his prime minister in June 1999. The two men promised to take a harder line at the bargaining table with Azerbaijan and to institute economic reforms to create a free market. But under U.S. pressure, Kocharian and Sarkisian stepped up the pace of negotiations, even as the economy faltered. The United States had been a major source of foreign aid to Armenia; some observers speculated that Kocharian and Sarkisian feared Washington would reduce that aid if Armenia was seen as the recalcitrant party in the peace talks.

Following is the text of a speech delivered October 31, 1999, by Armenian president Robert Kocharian at the funeral for Prime Minister Vazgen Sarkisian, Speaker of Parliament Karen Demirchian, and other officials killed during the October 27 attack on Parliament:

Today the bodies of the distinguished sons of the Armenian people who were wholeheartedly devoted to their nation will be laid to rest. The cruel fate has taken the lives of the people who have unreservedly dedicated themselves to the sacred task of creating prosperity to their homeland and entrenching the Armenian statehood.

Our grief is inconsolable. Armenia and the entire Armenian nation are suffering an irreparable loss. Words will not express the depth of our sorrow. The committed crime with its consequences will long stay as a severe wound.

The independent Republic of Armenia is enduring one of the most critical days of its history. The reputation of the entire nation has been tarnished. The pillars of Armenia's statehood have been undermined and human values shaken up.

Those savages who carried out this crime will answer not only before the law, but also before history, before future generations.

The names of Vazgen Sarkissian, Karen Demirjian, Juri Bakhshian, Rouben Miroian, Henrik Abrahamian, Armenak Armenakian, Michael Kotanian and Leonard Petrossian will forever stay in our memories. They have enjoyed the admiration and respect of the people, they lived difficult though happy lives, for it was their mission to serve the nation and the people. Wherever they tried themselves, be it at the battlefield or in times of peace, they always achieved success, resolving arduous, sometimes even seemingly insurmountable tasks, and inspiring the people with their will, single-mindedness and vigour.

The history will remember Vazgen Sarkissian as a statesman, who stood at the foundations of Armenia's independent statehood. He played a focal role in the creation of the National Army. With his life and unreserved dedication, Vazgen Sarkissian had unlimited influence on the processes of the strengthening of our country.

We bid farewell to Karen Demirjian, one of our most proficient political leaders, whose life has been exemplary in his high sense of statehood and dedication to the nation. The forty-five years of his work will forever remain in the memories of generations.

We must remember the deeds of our other deceased friends. We must also remember the wise counsel that unites them with those of us alive, and that it is our duty to serve without reserve to achieve the ultimate goal of creating prosperity for our nation and our people. Let us learn lessons from this tragedy, let us unite, join forces and strengthen the Republic of Armenia and the entire Armenian nation.

Once again, I would like to convey my heartfelt condolences to the bereaved families, relatives and friends of the victims, to our people. Let us express our resolve to carry forward the mission of our brothers.

Dear compatriots,

The entire world is mourning with us today. Leaders of nearly all the countries of the world have conveyed their condolences to our people. Numerous foreign delegations have arrived here to share with us our grief. I express my deep gratitude to them.

November

UN Secretary General Annan
on the War in Congo 645

U.S. District Court on
Microsoft's Monopoly Power 654

State Department Evaluation
of U.S. Diplomatic Posts 690

Clinton on the Fall of "The Wall"
and an "Activist" Foreign Policy . . . 699

NASA Investigation into the Loss
of the *Mars Climate Orbiter* 711

Clinton and Wahid on Renewal
of Democracy in Indonesia 718

Announcement on U.S.-China
Bilateral Trade Agreement 724

United Nations Report
on the Fall of Srebrenica 735

Northern Ireland Leaders on
Status of the Peace Process 753

Commerce Department on
Y2K Preparations 760

OSHA on Proposed Ergonomics
Standards 769

Institute of Medicine
on Medical Mistakes 779

UN SECRETARY GENERAL ANNAN ON THE WAR IN CONGO
November 1, 1999

Africa was the scene of more than a half-dozen civil wars and regional conflicts during 1999. None was as worrisome, from an international viewpoint, as the brutal war in the Democratic Republic of Congo, formerly known as Zaire. One of the biggest and potentially richest countries on the continent because of its vast mineral wealth, Congo was the center of a complex series of bloody struggles involving six other nations and a myriad of guerrilla groups.

The United Nations struggled throughout the year to come to terms with the Congo war, first by encouraging the parties to sign a fragile peace agreement, then by debating how to enforce compliance with that accord. At year's end the UN Security Council was considering its options—none of which were easy—while fighting continued. (Promoting peace in Africa, p. 428)

A Tangled Web of War

Fighting broke out in August 1998, a little more than a year after an insurgent army led by Laurent Kabila overthrew the corrupt regime of President Mobutu Sese Seko, who had led Zaire for three decades. Kabila, a longtime anti-Mobutu activist with no firm power base of his own, sought to assert control by declaring himself president. In the process, Kabila alienated many of those who had sponsored his drive against Mobutu. (Ouster of Mobutu, Historic Documents of 1997, p. 877)

Prime backers of a campaign to oust Kabila were Rwanda and Uganda, ironically the two countries that had provided much of the firepower for Kabila's guerrilla war that toppled Mobutu. Leaders of those countries had turned against Kabila for numerous reasons. In the case of Rwanda, the chief motivation was Kabila's failure to control Hutu rebels who had fled Rwanda after slaughtering 500,000 Tutsi there in 1994. The Hutus, operating from refugee camps in eastern Congo, had provided most of the troops for Kabila's guerrilla army. Once Kabila had won, the Hutu guerrillas con-

*ducted cross-border raids into Rwanda, which had come under Tutsi lead-
ership after the 1994 killings. Uganda also moved against Kabila; many
observers said that nation's leader, Yoweri Museveni, feared Kabila was
becoming too hungry for power, both within Congo and in the region as a
whole.* (Background on Rwanda, p. 860)

*During the fighting in 1998, the anti-Kabila forces quickly gained con-
trol of more than a third of eastern Congo and within a few weeks seemed
on the verge of capturing the capital, Kinshasa, and driving Kabila from
power. But Kabila turned to Angola, Chad, Namibia, and Zimbabwe, all of
which sent troops and weapons to help him battle the insurgents. Kabila's
key ally was Zimbabwe, which, according to the U.S. State Department, provided hundreds of troops and millions of dollars worth of weapons to
Kabila in return for access to Congo's mineral wealth.*

*In a report to the Security Council on November 1, Secretary General
Kofi Annan said more than 180,000 Congolese had been forced to flee to
neighboring countries and another 800,000 had been forced from their
homes but remained within Congo. Sadako Ogata, the UN Higher Commissioner for Refugees, told the Security Council in July that, during a
visit to Congo a month earlier, she was "shocked by the deteriorating living
conditions of the Congolese population at large."*

Moving Toward Peace

*After more than eight months of savage warfare throughout Congo, the
anti-Kabila rebel forces split into two factions in May 1999, one backed by
Rwanda and one by Uganda. With the conflict in stalemate, African leaders negotiated a peace agreement, which Kabila and chief guerrilla factions
signed in Lusaka, Zambia, on July 10; other guerrilla leaders accepted it
by the end of August.*

*The Lusaka agreement called for a cease-fire, the establishment of an
international peacekeeping force, and a "national dialogue" to resolve disputes between Kabila and the rebel factions. The agreement did little to
stop the fighting, however. Early in August the competing forces backed by
Rwanda and Uganda battled for three days in Kisangani, the most important city in northeastern Congo. Rebel factions in that region continued
their fighting well into October, with one of the factions insisting it had
established a "transitional government" over the territory it claimed to
control.*

*Despite the continued fighting and jockeying for position within Congo,
the peace accord forced international leaders to attempt to seize an opportunity to end the war. Declaring that the Lusaka accord represented "the
most viable basis for a resolution of the conflict," the UN Security Council
on August 6 authorized a force of 90 military liaison personnel to monitor
a cease-fire. In his November 1 report, Annan asked the Security Council to
authorize a larger force of 500 military observers to help determine further
steps for patrolling the peace accord. Annan said he would send the
observers only after he received "security guarantees" from Kabila's gov-*

ernment and assurances from a UN technical team, then traveling in Congo, that "conditions were suitable" for the observers.

The Security Council approved Annan's request November 30 and called on all parties to the conflict to respect the cease-fire. But even as the Security Council acted, Annan was said to have told the council privately that 20,000 or more peacekeepers ultimately would be needed to try to supervise the peace in areas where fighting had ceased. Among its tasks, the peacekeeping force would monitor the withdrawal of foreign troops from Congo and the disarmament of the various rebel factions.

At year's end Annan was attempting to build international support for such a sizable force. Among the issues he faced was the Clinton administration's insistence that the United States would not provide money for a large UN force in Congo until it was clear that fighting had stopped and the warring parties had agreed on a mediator who could help establish a political settlement. Richard C. Holbrooke, Washington's ambassador to the UN, traveled throughout the region in December to push for compliance in deed, as well as in word, with the Lusaka agreement. "This cannot be a situation where the international community tries to impose its will or pacify a country as large and as complex" as Congo, Holbrooke said during a stop in Kinshasa, Congo's capital. The United States generally provided about 30 percent of the funding for UN peacekeeping forces, but no U.S. troops were expected to be part of the Congo operation.

Following are excerpts from a report sent November 1, 1999, to the United Nations Security Council by Secretary General Kofi Annan, in which he described the conflict in the Democratic Republic of Congo and international attempts to end the fighting:

I. Introduction

1. By paragraph 8 of its resolution 1258 (1999) of 6 August 1999, the Security Council authorized the deployment of up to 90 United Nations military liaison personnel, together with the necessary civilian, political, humanitarian and administrative staff, to the capitals of the States signatories to the Lusaka Ceasefire Agreement. The Council also authorized the deployment of liaison officers to the provisional headquarters of the Joint Military Commission (JMC) established by the Agreement and, as security conditions permit, to the rear military headquarters of the main belligerents in the Democratic Republic of the Congo and, as appropriate, to other areas the Secretary-General may deem necessary, for a period of three months.

2. By paragraph 12 of the resolution, the Council requested the Secretary-General to keep it regularly informed of developments in the Democratic Republic of the Congo and to report at the appropriate time on the future presence of the United Nations in the Democratic Republic of the Congo in

support of the peace process. The present report is submitted pursuant to those provisions.

II. Developments in the Peace Process

3. Despite the signature of the Ceasefire Agreement in Lusaka on 10 July 1999 by the six States parties concerned, the two Congolese rebel movements, the Movement for the Liberation of the Congo (MLC) and the Congolese Rally for Democracy (RCD), declined to sign at that time. Jean-Pierre Bemba, the leader of MLC, signed the Agreement in Lusaka on 1 August.

4. Following intense diplomatic activity, especially by President Chiluba of Zambia and his Government and the Government of South Africa and others, representatives of the remaining rebel movement, RCD, signed the Ceasefire Agreement in Lusaka on 31 August.

5. The signing by the RCD representatives was followed by a meeting, on 3 September, of the Political Committee established by the Agreement at the ministerial level to provide overall political coordination in the implementation of the Agreement. The Political Committee agreed that the United Nations and the Organization of African Unity (OAU) should be full participants in its work and in that of JMC and that Zambia should have permanent observer status in the two bodies. The Committee also decided that JMC should establish its headquarters immediately in Zambia and move to the Democratic Republic of the Congo as soon as possible thereafter. A budget for JMC, amounting to some $5 million, was also adopted. . . .

11. The Lusaka Ceasefire Agreement provides for a national dialogue to be held between the Government of the Democratic Republic of the Congo, the armed opposition, namely RCD and MLC, the unarmed opposition and civil society. It also provides for the Organization of African Unity to assist the Democratic Republic of the Congo in organizing these inter-Congolese political negotiations under the aegis of a neutral facilitator chosen by the parties. While the Government of the Democratic Republic of the Congo has accepted the names of the facilitators proposed by OAU—the International Organization of La Francophonie and the Communità Sant'Egidio—the Goma-based RCD has until now withheld its agreement. The importance of the national dialogue in creating the conditions for national reconciliation and what the Lusaka Agreement terms a new political dispensation cannot be overemphasized. I consider it of the utmost importance that this issue be resolved. . . .

13. There have been several accusations and counter-accusations of ceasefire violations by the parties. Troop movements are said to be continuing. Some reports have also indicated a build-up of foreign troops in the areas of Mbuji-Mayi and Kisangani and a serious confrontation between Rwandan and Ugandan troops took place in Kisangani in August/September. The dispute seems to have been subsequently resolved. Some small locations have reportedly been seized recently by the rebels, and so far unverified reports have been received concerning troop movements by the Government forces.

14. The presence of former Rwandan government forces (ex-FAR) and Interahamwe [Hutu] militia elements in the region and the alleged alliances

they are forging with different groups underscore the intricate and interconnected nature of the peace process in the Great Lakes region.

III. Action Taken by the United Nations

15. Immediately upon the issuance of my first report dated 15 July 1999 on the United Nations preliminary deployment in the Democratic Republic of the Congo (S/1999/790), I dispatched an advance civilian and military team to the subregion to establish contacts with the Government of Zambia and other participants in the ceasefire process and to formulate recommendations for the initial deployment of United Nations personnel. . . .

IV. Humanitarian Situation

22. Despite the ceasefire following the signing of the Lusaka peace accord, insecurity remains a major obstacle to humanitarian operations and hampers access to the internally displaced, now numbering more than 800,000 people. Currently, over 180,000 citizens of the Democratic Republic of the Congo are refugees in neighbouring countries, and over 250,000 are refugees with the Democratic Republic of the Congo itself. Reports indicate that inter-ethnic fighting in the north-eastern part of the country has forced over 100,000 people to flee their homes. Additional pockets of displacement have been identified in Equateur, North Kivu, Katanga and Eastern Kasai. Refugees from Angola and the Republic of the Congo continue to arrive in Katanga, Bas Congo and Bandundu provinces of the Democratic Republic of the Congo and a reduced but continuing flight of refugees from the Democratic Republic of the Congo are entering the United Republic of Tanzania and Zambia.

23. Also as a result of the prevailing insecurity, large numbers of civilians continue to be exposed to indiscriminate violence, looting and the destruction of property, including agriculture, in almost all parts of the country. Widespread reports of human rights abuses continue to circulate.

24. The major constraint for the humanitarian community is that priority life-saving operations are severely underfunded. To date, the 1999 Consolidated Appeal for the Democratic Republic of the Congo, which requested $81 million to address life-saving requirements, is less than 25 per cent funded. Greater access in itself would be ineffective without the additional resources required. The World Food Programme (WFP) faces a commodity shortfall of 60,000 metric tons in the coming six months, but expects to receive only 10,000 tons of food during the last quarter of 1999. The consequences of inadequate funding are simple: lives that could have been saved are lost and suffering that could have been lessened is allowed to follow its course.

25. However, the humanitarian community hopes that the deployment of United Nations military and civilian personnel will allow confidence to be restored sufficiently so that commercial routes (by rail, air and through the Congo River) may be reopened.

26. Despite these constraints, humanitarian coordination arrangements exist in most parts of the country, with good contacts with local authorities and within the communities receiving assistance. It is essential that United

Nations humanitarian staff be deployed as part of the military liaison officer teams to the various locations in order to benefit from these linkages with the communities and the interlocutors.

27. On 23 and 24 October, the third and final round of polio immunization took place throughout the country in an attempt to immunize 10 million children under the age of five. In addition, children between 9 and 59 months old were to be immunized against measles. So far, there is no indication of the level of coverage attained in this campaign.

V. Relations with the Organization of African Unity, the Joint Military Commission and the Parties

28. The proper implementation of the Lusaka Agreement will require very close coordination and cooperation between the United Nations, the parties, JMC and OAU. In order to generate this cooperation, the Department of Peacekeeping Operations has been in very close and regular contact with the permanent missions concerned in New York, in addition to the activities of the liaison teams in the capitals.

29. The United Nations and OAU are currently discussing the coordination of the deployment plans and the roles to be played by the respective military personnel. . . .

VI. Next Steps

34. In my 15 July report, I outlined plans to deploy up to 500 United Nations military observers within the Democratic Republic of the Congo and, as required, to the belligerent and other neighbouring States. Their tasks, which would be in accordance with the peacekeeping functions listed in the Lusaka Ceasefire Agreement, would supplement those already being performed by the military liaison officers and would include the following:

- To establish contacts with the various parties at their headquarters locations, including in the capitals of the belligerent States;
- To strengthen liaison with JMC and collaborate with it in the implementation of the Ceasefire Agreement;
- To assist JMC and the parties in investigating alleged violations of the ceasefire;
- To make a general security assessment of the country;
- To secure from the parties guarantees of cooperation and assurances of security for the further deployment in-country of United Nations personnel;
- To determine the present and likely future locations of the forces of all parties with a view to refining and finalizing the concept for deployment of United Nations military personnel;
- To observe, subject to the provision by the parties of adequate security, the ceasefire and disengagement of the forces and their redeployment and eventual withdrawal;
- To facilitate the provision of humanitarian assistance to and protection of displaced persons, refugees, children, and other affected persons, and

to assist and protect human rights and child protection officers in the performance of their duties.

35. It had been my intention to recommend the deployment of military observers on the basis of the report of the technical survey team on its visits to proposed deployment locations. For the reasons given above, the team has not yet been able to report. Nonetheless, in view of the urgency of the situation in the Democratic Republic of the Congo and in order to lend momentum to the peace process, I think it advisable to proceed further to the extent possible.

36. I would therefore seek from the Security Council prior authorization to deploy up to 500 military observers, with the necessary support and protection. I anticipate receiving in due course from the Government of the Democratic Republic of the Congo acceptable guarantees of security and freedom of movement which would make such a deployment possible. The military observers would be deployed as and when confirmation was received from the technical survey team and the military liaison officers deployed to the field headquarters that conditions were suitable.

37. In order to be effective, the military observers will require protection and considerable logistical support, including vehicles and communications, as well as additional air assets to ensure their deployment, supply, rotation and, if necessary, extraction. A medical unit should also be deployed in support of the mission.

38. The security of the military observers, whose mandate is much broader than that of the liaison officers, is of paramount concern. The deployment of United Nations formed units might be necessary to ensure the protection of the observers and other United Nations personnel.

39. Military deployment alone will not be sufficient, however. The humanitarian and human rights aspects of the conflict in the Democratic Republic of the Congo require the deployment of civilian humanitarian, child protection and human rights officers at the earliest stages of the operation, in order to assess the situation and propose further long-term action the United Nations and the international community can take. It is proposed that at this early stage in the operation a number of professional political, humanitarian, human rights, child protection, civilian police, public information, administrative and other personnel will have to be deployed.

40. The plight of child soldiers, and of children in general, is a particular acute feature of the conflict. The protection of children's rights will require immediate and sustained attention, as well as adequate resources throughout the peace process in the Democratic Republic of the Congo. Among the many pressing needs are the disarmament, demobilization and reintegration of child combatants; the protection and safe return of internally displaced and refugee children; the provision of humanitarian assistance to vulnerable populations composed largely of women and children; and the registration, protection and reunification of unaccompanied or orphaned children and children in foster families. Child protection advisers should be an integral part of the mission in all relevant aspects of deployment to the Democratic Republic of the Congo.

VII. Observations and Recommendations

41. The enormous obstacles facing any United Nations operation in the Democratic Republic of the Congo have always been very apparent. The experience gained so far in deploying a small number of military liaison officers in and around the Democratic Republic of the Congo has only served to deepen our appreciation of the difficulties.

42. Nevertheless, the United Nations must continue to support the peace process to the full extent of its capacities. The suffering in the Democratic Republic of the Congo has persisted for far too long for us to miss the chance offered by the Lusaka Ceasefire Agreement.

43. I therefore recommend to the Security Council the extension of the mandate of the United Nations personnel currently in the Democratic Republic of the Congo until 15 January 2000. By then, on the basis of the conclusions of the technical survey team, it should be possible to provide the Council with further details on the possible establishment of a United Nations peacekeeping operation in the Democratic Republic of the Congo.

44. I also request from the Security Council prior authorization for the setting up of a United Nations Observer Mission in the Democratic Republic of the Congo (MONUC) and the deployment of up to 500 military observers with the necessary logistical and personnel support and with the mandate set out above. The provision of the necessary security guarantees would facilitate their expeditious deployment while taking into account the findings of the technical survey team. The observer operation would absorb the existing initial deployment. It should be adequately equipped and should have sufficient numbers of civilian staff, including political, humanitarian, human rights and child protection officers as well as administrative personnel. It should be led by a Special Representative, whom I shall shortly appoint.

45. As I indicated in my 15 July report, the deployment of military observers, should the Council so decide, would constitute the second phase of United Nations involvement in the Democratic Republic of the Congo, security and other conditions permitting. A third phase would be the eventual deployment of a peacekeeping operation with formed units to assist the parties in the implementation of the Lusaka Ceasefire Agreement and in strengthening the peace process in general, as well as to protect the United Nations personnel deployed in the Democratic Republic of the Congo. In order to make up for the delays encountered so far, my next report will cover both those phases.

46. Subject to further progress in the peace process, I therefore envisage reverting to the Security Council within the next few weeks with a further report containing recommendations and a proposed mandate and concept of operations for the deployment of United Nations peacekeeping troops, accompanied by military observers. I trust it will also be possible to provide the Council within the same time-frame the details of the requirements in terms of logistics, communications, transportation, medical support, civilian staff and the associated cost estimates.

47. In the meantime, I shall keep the Council fully informed of developments in the Democratic Republic of the Congo and the activities of the United Nations there, including its relations with the Government of the Democratic Republic of the Congo, JMC and OAU.

48. In that context, I urgently call upon all parties to cooperate fully and closely with the United Nations mission and with my Special Representative (to be appointed). The provision of an acceptable security guarantee and the acceptance by the Government of the Democratic Republic of the Congo of the need for United Nations personnel to be deployed throughout the country are essential preconditions to the mission's ability to deploy and function effectively. I intend to continue to seek pragmatic and feasible solutions to the problems as they arise.

49. The Joint Military Commission established pursuant to the Lusaka Ceasefire Agreement clearly has a central role to play in the peace process. It needs and deserves support in order to function effectively. The deployment of four United Nations military liaison officers, initially in Lusaka, is a first step in this direction. In addition, I commend those Governments that have already made available resources to JMC or pledged to do so, and invite donors to redeem their pledges as rapidly as possible. In the same spirit, I propose that the United Nations provide JMC with the necessary logistical and other operational support.

50. I look forward to continued close cooperation with OAU. The United Nations intends to follow up the dispatch of two military liaison officers to Addis Ababa to consult with OAU officials on closer coordination between our two organizations with additional measures, including the permanent deployment of United Nations military personnel at OAU headquarters.

51. I also express my appreciation to the United Nations political and military staff already deployed in and around the Democratic Republic of the Congo for the efforts they have been making, often in difficult circumstances, and to those countries that have expressed willingness to contribute military observers.

U.S. DISTRICT COURT ON
MICROSOFT'S MONOPOLY POWER
November 5, 1999

In a ruling with the potential to force widespread changes in the fast-evolving technology industry, a federal judge ruled November 5, 1999, that the Microsoft Corporation used its overwhelming power in the personal computer industry to stifle competition that it viewed as threatening to its market share. Judge Thomas Penfield Jackson, of the U.S. District Court for the District of Columbia, determined that Microsoft had monopoly control of the market for operating systems for personal computers and had aggressively used that monopoly to bludgeon its competitors.

Jackson's sweeping ruling, in an antitrust case brought by the Justice Department and nineteen states, set the stage either for a final judgment imposing sanctions against Microsoft or a negotiated agreement between the company and the plaintiffs. Two weeks after issuing his ruling—called a "findings of fact" summarizing months of testimony in the case—Jackson appointed a mediator to oversee negotiations that he said he hoped would lead to a settlement early in 2000. The mediator was Richard Posner, chief judge of the U.S. Court of Appeals for the Seventh Circuit in Chicago.

If the mediation attempts failed to produce a settlement, Jackson was expected to issue a final decision in 2000 finding Microsoft guilty of antitrust violations and imposing remedies, which could include breaking Microsoft into two or more companies—just as AT&T had been broken into a half-dozen companies following an antitrust cases in 1982. (AT&T case, Historic Documents of 1982, p. 17)

Possibly indicating the government's interest in pursuing a breakup of Microsoft, the Justice Department on December 2 hired a New York mergers and acquisitions firm, Greenhill and Company, as a consultant to help devise the "full range of potential remedies" in the case. Microsoft was considered certain to appeal any final decision by Jackson, possibly in hopes of dragging out the case for years.

Jackson's finding prompted a spate of class-action lawsuits against Microsoft. Citing the judge's finding that Microsoft had harmed consumers by restricting their choice of software products, lawyers filed suits in several states alleging damage to thousands of consumers.

Background to the Case

Microsoft was founded in 1975 by William Gates and Paul Allen, college students with an interest in computer software. The two developed an operating system (Microsoft disk operating system, or MS-DOS), which they licensed to the IBM Corp. for use in its personal computers. After Apple Computer introduced its revolutionary Macintosh computer in 1984, Microsoft in 1985 developed a competing system with many of the same features, called Windows. Intended for use on personal computers manufactured by IBM and other companies, Windows quickly grew in popularity and by 1990 had become the dominant operating system for small computers used at home and in many offices.

The Federal Trade Commission in 1990 launched an investigation of Microsoft, but in 1993 closed its case after commissioners could not agree on whether to file a formal complaint charging that Microsoft unfairly monopolized its market. At that point the Justice Department opened its own investigation, which led to a consent decree signed July 17, 1994, in which Microsoft promised to change various business practices to open the field to more competition. The Justice Department alleged in 1997 that Microsoft had violated that consent decree by forcing computer manufacturers to install its software to "browse" the Internet, called the Internet Explorer. That suit led to an injunction, issued by Judge Jackson, barring Microsoft from requiring installation of Internet Explorer. An appeals court later overturned the injunction.

The Justice Department and attorneys general from nineteen states and the District of Columbia filed antitrust suits against Microsoft on May 18, 1998, charging that the company had an illegal monopoly of the market for operating systems in personal computers. Arguments in the case opened in Judge Jackson's court room on October 19, 1998. Hearing the case without a jury, Jackson moved both sides along at what observers said was an astonishing pace for such a complex case; all testimony was concluded by June 24, 1999. Early phases of the trial featured videotaped testimony by Gates, the Microsoft chairman, who insisted he could not remember key events, including memos he had written and meetings he had attended.

The crux of the government's case was that Microsoft had used its monopoly (it controlled an estimated 90 percent of the market for personal computer operating systems) to pressure computer manufacturers, Internet access providers, and other key players into dropping their use of Navigator, a competing Internet browser developed by the Netscape Corporation. Netscape had introduced Navigator in 1994, and the browser quickly dominated the field. Only in 1995, according to court room testimony, did Gates and other top Microsoft executives awaken to the full potential of the Internet and begin a concerted push for adoption of their browser, Internet Explorer.

The government also alleged that Microsoft had used its monopoly to inhibit the growth of computer applications based on a language, called Java, developed by Sun Microsystems. Sun had distributed many Java applications through Netscape.

Jackson's Findings of Fact

In his 205 pages of closely reasoned findings, Jackson sided almost entirely with the government complaint, accepting its characterizations of events and rejecting Microsoft's contention that the company had played hard ball but had done nothing improper or illegal. Jackson's central findings were that Microsoft possessed a monopoly of personal computer operating systems and was determined to protect that monopoly "at any costs"; that Microsoft feared Netscape's Navigator might lead to the development of competing operating systems; and that Microsoft ruthlessly used its monopoly power to pressure and coerce other companies into abandoning Navigator. Jackson concluded that consumers were harmed because Microsoft's actions curtailed their ability to choose software products, and that the company's competitors were discouraged from developing products that might compete with Microsoft and benefit consumers.

Jackson based his findings on seventy-six days of courtroom testimony and more than two million documents. Among the documents were hundreds of internal e-mail memoranda exchanged by senior Microsoft executives, which were turned over to the court in response to government subpoenas. In numerous cases the views expressed by those executives contradicted or undermined the company's assertions in court. Jackson quoted extensively from the e-mails to reinforce his finding that Microsoft was determined to protect its monopoly. Among the memos was a January 2, 1997, message from Microsoft executive James Allchin stating that the company needed to use its control of Windows to make sure that "Netscape never gets a chance" to be included on personal computers.

Jackson methodically developed evidence demonstrating Microsoft's history of using persuasion and coercion to beat back competition, most importantly from Netscape. Starting in 1995, Microsoft officials became convinced that Netscape's Navigator posed a long-term threat to the dominance of Windows because competitors could use Navigator as a "platform" for software applications—just as Windows was the platform for tens of thousands of applications, such as word processing and business management programs.

Microsoft officials held two meetings with senior Netscape executives in June 1995, offering in the second meeting to create a "special relationship" between the two companies if Netscape would agree not to do anything that would create competition for Windows. Under Jackson's interpretation, Microsoft's offer represented an attempt by a monopoly to divide the market with a potential competitor—an illegal activity under antitrust law. Netscape's chief executive officer at the time, James Barkdale, declined to accept the Microsoft offer. Microsoft immediately launched an intense cam-

paign to ensure that computer manufacturers, Internet access providers, and others stopped using Netscape Navigator.

The most important element of the Microsoft campaign against Netscape was the company's decision later in 1995 to offer Internet Explorer to consumers for free—but only as a part of the Windows operating system. This decision undermined Netscape, a much smaller company that had relied on sales of Navigator licenses as a major source of revenue and had no choice but to follow suit by making Navigator available for free.

Microsoft's decision to give Internet Explorer to customers at no charge also led to a series of disputes between the company and several major computer manufacturers—including Compaq, Gateway, and IBM—over the question of how closely linked Internet Explorer was with Microsoft's new Windows products, first Windows 95 and then Windows 98. In "bundling" Internet Explorer with Windows, Microsoft argued that the Internet browser was an essential and integral component of the operating system. Taking Internet Explorer out of Windows—for example, to replace it with Navigator—would damage the operating system, Microsoft officials said. Jackson cited cases in which Microsoft threatened to withhold Windows from computer manufacturers if they tried to delete Internet Explorer from the machines they provided to consumers, or even if they simply tried to make Navigator available as an alternative. Among the companies pressured by Microsoft was IBM, which until the early 1990s was the most powerful force in the computer business.

Jackson cited evidence, including internal memoranda from Microsoft's files, demonstrating that the decision to bundle Internet Explorer with Windows was made to stifle competition from Netscape, not to improve the functionality of either the browser or the operating system. "Web browsers and operating systems are separate products," Jackson ruled, rejecting what had been a central component of the Microsoft legal defense.

Jackson also reviewed Microsoft's successful anti-Netscape efforts among companies that provided access for consumers to the Internet. Microsoft's biggest success came with America On Line, which during the late 1990s was the single most important source of consumer access to the Internet and its component, the World Wide Web. Under pressure from Microsoft, America On Line agreed to use Internet Explorer as its Internet browser and to make it difficult for customers to replace it with Netscape Navigator.

Such arrangements quickly succeeded in substantially reducing Navigator's share of the market. Before Microsoft took on Netscape in 1995, Navigator was used by more than 80 percent all consumers with Internet browsers. By 1998 Navigator's market share had been cut in half. Microsoft's campaign also succeeded in eliminating Netscape as an independent player in the computer industry. In November 1998, after Netscape experienced serious financial difficulty because of its inability to compete with Microsoft, America On Line purchased Netscape for $10 billion. Even after the purchase, America On Line continued to use Inter-

net Explorer as its browser because of contractual obligations to Microsoft.

Despite the fact that it controlled more than 90 percent of the market for personal computer operating systems, Microsoft steadily denied that it had a monopoly and insisted that it faced competition on numerous fronts. As examples, Microsoft cited the rapid rise of Sun Microsystem's Java language and the growing interest during the late 1990s in a computer operating system called Linux, which was available at no charge.

Jackson summarily rejected Microsoft's assertions, saying that the company "enjoys monopoly power in the relevant market" and could, if it wanted, charge almost any price for its Windows products without fear of stifling short-term demand. Microsoft kept most of its prices down for reasons of long-term strategy, Jackson said, noting that many of its actions made business sense only because "they operated to reinforce monopoly power." Jackson cited numerous cases in which Microsoft gave up short-term opportunities to make money and instead focused on ensuring that its clients had no choice but to use Windows products.

The question of whether Microsoft was a monopoly involved more than just scoring debating points. A monopoly can be found to have violated antitrust law if it engaged in actions—such as underpricing its products and pressuring other companies not to do business with competitors—that would be legal for a company that did not have a monopoly.

Ultimately, Jackson found, Microsoft's actions harmed consumers, who faced fewer choices because of the company's aggressive use of its monopoly power. Perhaps Jackson's most damning assertion came in the closing paragraph of his findings, when he directly refuted Microsoft's underlying argument that all its actions had been intended to encourage "innovation" in the technology industry. "Most harmful of all [to consumers] is the message that Microsoft's actions have conveyed to every enterprise with the potential to innovate in the computer industry," he wrote. "Through its conduct toward Netscape, IBM, Compaq, Intel, and others, Microsoft has demonstrated that it will use its prodigious market power and immense profits to harm any firm that insists on pursuing initiatives that could intensify competition against one of Microsoft's core products. Microsoft's past success in hurting such companies and stifling innovation deters investment in technologies and businesses that exhibit the potential to threaten Microsoft. The ultimate result is that some innovations that would truly benefit consumers never occur for the sole reason that they do not coincide with Microsoft's self-interest."

Reactions to the Ruling

Attorney General Janet Reno declared that Jackson's ruling was "a great day for the American consumer." The case was not a dry analysis of antitrust law, she said, but was "about the protection of innovation, competition, and the consumer's right to choose products they want." Joel Klein, the assistant attorney general in charge of the Justice Department's antitrust division, said the ruling showed that "in America, no person and no company is above the law."

James Barkdale, the former head of Netscape whose complaints about Microsoft had formed the basis of the Justice Department suit, said he had been "vindicated" by Jackson's ruling. "I don't think Microsoft is evil. I think they just got carried away," he said. "Practices that served them well when they were young and growing and aggressive are illegal when you become a monopoly."

Reaction among others in the computer software business was mixed. Officials of Sun Microsystems joined Barkdale in expressing pleasure that a federal judge had agreed with their assessment of Microsoft's behavior. But other business executives expressed concern about possible government intervention in the booming software industry. "Any would-be entrepreneur is getting a message from Washington that says, 'Become successful, but not too successful, or we'll ruin your life,'" said Tim Draper a venture capitalist who financed software firms in California's "Silicon Valley."

Microsoft officials expressed disappointment with Jackson's findings and insisted that the judge had overlooked the true source of the company's success, the popularity of its products with millions of consumers. In an interview with the New York Times, *Microsoft president Steve Ballmer took particular exception to Jackson's contention that Microsoft's bundling of Internet Explorer with Windows was an anticompetitive practice. "[T]o say that the most important software product is somehow unable to respond to the most important trend in technology, I wouldn't get that," he said. "I don't understand how that could be good for consumers or business anyplace." Ballmer sent Microsoft's 30,000 employees an e-mail message saying the antitrust case "will be a long process, and we are in it for the long haul."*

> *Following are excerpts from the "findings of fact," issued November 5, 1999, by U.S. District Court Judge Thomas Penfield Jackson, in the case of* United States of America v. Microsoft Corporation, *in which the judge determined that Microsoft had monopoly power in the market for personal computer operating systems and had used that power to harm competitors and consumers:*

III. Microsoft's Power in the Relevant Market

33. Microsoft enjoys so much power in the market for Intel-compatible PC operating systems that if it wished to exercise this power solely in terms of price, it could charge a price for Windows substantially above that which could be charged in a competitive market. Moreover, it could do so for a significant period of time without losing an unacceptable amount of business to

competitors. In other words, Microsoft enjoys monopoly power in the relevant market.

34. Viewed together, three main facts indicate that Microsoft enjoys monopoly power. First, Microsoft's share of the market for Intel-compatible PC operating systems is extremely large and stable. Second, Microsoft's dominant market share is protected by a high barrier to entry. Third, and largely as a result of that barrier, Microsoft's customers lack a commercially viable alternative to Windows.

A. Market Share

35. Microsoft possesses a dominant, persistent, and increasing share of the world- wide market for Intel-compatible PC operating systems. Every year for the last decade, Microsoft's share of the market for Intel-compatible PC operating systems has stood above ninety percent. For the last couple of years the figure has been at least ninety-five percent, and analysts project that the share will climb even higher over the next few years. Even if Apple's Mac OS were included in the relevant market, Microsoft's share would still stand well above eighty percent. . . .

[Following sections define the "applications barrier to entry" faced by anyone wanting to compete with Microsoft in that market. As described in the findings, the barrier existed because consumers would buy an operating system only if a substantial number of software applications (such as word processing and accounting programs) existed that could be used on that system—but software developers would write programs for an operating system only if that system already had a sizable share of the consumer market. It was this "chicken and egg" problem that helped Microsoft maintain is dominant market share of the operating system market.]

C. Viable Alternatives to Windows

53. That Microsoft's market share and the applications barrier to entry together endow the company with monopoly power in the market for Intel-compatible PC operating systems is directly evidenced by the sustained absence of realistic commercial alternatives to Microsoft's PC operating-system products.

54. OEMs [original equipment manufacturers, such as makers of personal computers] are the most important direct customers for operating systems for Intel- compatible PCs. Because competition among OEMs is intense, they pay particularly close attention to consumer demand. OEMs are thus not only important customers in their own right, they are also surrogates for consumers in identifying reasonably-available commercial alternatives to Windows. Without significant exception, all OEMs pre-install Windows on the vast majority of PCs that they sell, and they uniformly are of a mind that there exists no commercially viable alternative to which they could switch in response to a substantial and sustained price increase or its equivalent by Microsoft. . . .

55. OEMs believe that the likelihood of a viable alternative to Windows emerging any time in the next few years is too low to constrain Microsoft

from raising prices or imposing other burdens on customers and users. The accuracy of this belief is highlighted by the fact that the other vendors of Intel-compatible PC operating systems do not view their own offerings as viable alternatives to Windows. Microsoft knows that OEMs have no choice but to load Windows, both because it has a good understanding of the market in which it operates and because OEMs have told Microsoft as much. Indicative of Microsoft's assessment of the situation is the fact that, in a 1996 presentation to the firm's executive committee, the Microsoft executive in charge of OEM licensing reported that piracy continued to be the main competition to the company's operating system products. Secure in this knowledge, Microsoft did not consider the prices of other Intel-compatible PC operating systems when it set the price of Windows 98. . . .

H. Microsoft's Pricing Behavior

62. Microsoft's actual pricing behavior is consistent with the proposition that the firm enjoys monopoly power in the market for Intel-compatible PC operating systems. The company's decision not to consider the prices of other vendors' Intel-compatible PC operating systems when setting the price of Windows 98, for example, is probative of monopoly power. One would expect a firm in a competitive market to pay much closer attention to the prices charged by other firms in the market. Another indication of monopoly power is the fact that Microsoft raised the price that it charged OEMs for Windows 95, with trivial exceptions, to the same level as the price it charged for Windows 98 just prior to releasing the newer product. In a competitive market, one would expect the price of an older operating system to stay the same or decrease upon the release of a newer, more attractive version. Microsoft, however, was only concerned with inducing OEMs to ship Windows 98 in favor of the older version. It is unlikely that Microsoft would have imposed this price increase if it were genuinely concerned that OEMs might shift their business to another vendor of operating systems or hasten the development of viable alternatives to Windows.

63. Finally, it is indicative of monopoly power that Microsoft felt that it had substantial discretion in setting the price of its Windows 98 upgrade product (the operating system product it sells to existing users of Windows 95). A Microsoft study from November 1997 reveals that the company could have charged $49 for an upgrade to Windows 98—there is no reason to believe that the $49 price would have been unprofitable—but the study identifies $89 as the revenue-maximizing price. Microsoft thus opted for the higher price.

64. An aspect of Microsoft's pricing behavior that, while not tending to prove monopoly power, is consistent with it is the fact that the firm charges different OEMs different prices for Windows, depending on the degree to which the individual OEMs comply with Microsoft's wishes. Among the five largest OEMs, Gateway and IBM, which in various ways have resisted Microsoft's efforts to enlist them in its efforts to preserve the applications barrier to entry, pay higher prices than Compaq, Dell, and Hewlett-Packard, which have pursued less contentious relationships with Microsoft.

65. It is not possible with the available data to determine with any level of confidence whether the price that a profit-maximizing firm with monopoly power would charge for Windows 98 comports with the price that Microsoft actually charges. Even if it could be determined that Microsoft charges less than the profit-maximizing monopoly price, though, that would not be probative of a lack of monopoly power, for Microsoft could be charging what seems like a low short-term price in order to maximize its profits in the future for reasons unrelated to underselling any incipient competitors. For instance, Microsoft could be stimulating the growth of the market for Intel-compatible PC operating systems by keeping the price of Windows low today. Given the size and stability of its market share, Microsoft stands to reap almost all of the future rewards if there are yet more consumers of Intel-compatible PC operating systems. By pricing low relative to the short-run profit-maximizing price, thereby focusing on attracting new users to the Windows platform, Microsoft would also intensify the positive network effects that add to the impenetrability of the applications barrier to entry.

66. Furthermore, Microsoft expends a significant portion of its monopoly power, which could otherwise be spent maximizing price, on imposing burdensome restrictions on its customers—and in inducing them to behave in ways—that augment and prolong that monopoly power. For example, Microsoft attaches to a Windows license conditions that restrict the ability of OEMs to promote software that Microsoft believes could weaken the applications barrier to entry. Microsoft also charges a lower price to OEMs who agree to ensure that all of their Windows machines are powerful enough to run Windows NT for Workstations. . . .

I. Microsoft's Actions Toward Other Firms

67. Microsoft's monopoly power is also evidenced by the fact that, over the course of several years, Microsoft took actions that could only have been advantageous if they operated to reinforce monopoly power. These actions are described below. . . .

IV. The Middleware Threats

. . .72. As soon as Netscape [Communications Corporation] released Navigator [an Internet browser] on December 15, 1994, the product began to enjoy dramatic acceptance by the public; shortly after its release, consumers were already using Navigator far more than any other browser product. This alarmed Microsoft, which feared that Navigator's enthusiastic reception could embolden Netscape to develop Navigator into an alternative platform for applications development. In late May 1995, Bill Gates, the chairman and CEO of Microsoft, sent a memorandum entitled "The Internet Tidal Wave" to Microsoft's executives describing Netscape as a "new competitor 'born' on the Internet." He warned his colleagues within Microsoft that Netscape was "pursuing a multi-platform strategy where they move the key API [application programming interfaces] into the client to commoditize the underlying operating system." By the late spring of 1995, the executives responsible for setting Microsoft's corporate strategy were deeply concerned that Netscape was moving its business in a direction that could diminish the applications barrier to entry. . . .

75. Sun [Microsystems] announced in May 1995 that it had developed the Java programming language. Mid-level executives at Microsoft began to express concern about Sun's Java vision in the fall of that year, and by late spring of 1996, senior Microsoft executives were deeply worried about the potential of Sun's Java technologies to diminish the applications barrier to entry. . . .

V. Microsoft's Response to the Browser Threat

A. Microsoft's Attempt to Dissuade Netscape from Developing Navigator as a Platform

79. Microsoft's first response to the threat posed by Navigator was an effort to persuade Netscape to structure its business such that the company would not distribute platform-level browsing software for Windows. Netscape's assent would have ensured that, for the foreseeable future, Microsoft would produce the only platform-level browsing software distributed to run on Windows. This would have eliminated the prospect that non-Microsoft browsing software could weaken the applications barrier to entry.

80. Executives at Microsoft received confirmation in early May 1995 that Netscape was developing a version of Navigator to run on Windows 95, which was due to be released in a couple of months. Microsoft's senior executives understood that if they could prevent this version of Navigator from presenting alternatives to the Internet-related APIs in Windows 95, the technologies branded as Navigator would cease to present an alternative platform to developers. Even if non-Windows versions of Navigator exposed Internet-related APIs, applications written to those APIs would not run on the platform Microsoft executives expected to enjoy the largest installed base, i.e., Windows 95. So, as long as the version of Navigator written for Windows 95 relied on Microsoft's Internet-related APIs instead of exposing its own, developing for Navigator would not mean developing cross-platform. Developers of network-centric applications thus would not be drawn to Navigator's APIs in substantial numbers. Therefore, with the encouragement and support of Gates, a group of Microsoft executives commenced a campaign in the summer of 1995 to convince Netscape to halt its development of platform-level browsing technologies for Windows 95. . . .

[Following sections detail meetings held on June 2 and June 21, 1995, during which Microsoft executives offered Netscape a "special relationship" under which Netscape would receive access to information it needed to make its Navigator browser compatible with Windows 95 if Netscape agreed to ensure that Navigator could not be used for the development of products competitive with Windows. Netscape officials did not immediately accept the offer, and Microsoft withdrew it in mid-July 1995].

C. The Similar Experiences of Other Firms in Dealing with Microsoft

93. Other firms in the computer industry have had encounters with Microsoft similar to the experiences of Netscape described above. These interactions demonstrate that it is Microsoft's corporate practice to pressure other firms to halt software development that either shows the potential to weaken the applications barrier to entry or competes directly with Microsoft's most cherished software products. . . .

[Following sections describe efforts by Microsoft from 1994 to 1997 to persuade the Intel Corporation, Apple Computer, RealNetworks, and IBM Corporation to abandon projects that might have resulted in increased competition for Microsoft products. Section 132 concluded that Microsoft had a policy of "punishing those companies that resist" its demands.]

D. Developing Competitive Web Browsing Software

133. Once it became clear to senior executives at Microsoft that Netscape would not abandon its efforts to develop Navigator into a platform, Microsoft focused its efforts on ensuring that few developers would write their applications to rely on the APIs that Navigator exposed. Developers would only write to the APIs exposed by Navigator in numbers large enough to threaten the applications barrier if they believed that Navigator would emerge as the standard software employed to browse the Web. If Microsoft could demonstrate that Navigator would not become the standard, because Microsoft's own browser would attract just as much if not more usage, then developers would continue to focus their efforts on a platform that enjoyed enduring ubiquity: the 32-bit Windows API set. Microsoft thus set out to maximize Internet Explorer's share of browser usage at Navigator's expense.

134. Microsoft's management believed that, no matter what the firm did, Internet Explorer would not capture a large share of browser usage as long as it remained markedly inferior to Navigator in the estimation of consumers. The task of technical personnel at Microsoft, then, was to make Internet Explorer's features at least as attractive to consumers as Navigator's. Microsoft did not believe that improved quality alone would depose Navigator, for millions of users appeared to be satisfied with Netscape's product, and Netscape was known as 'the Internet company.' As Gates wrote to Microsoft's executive staff in his May 1995 "Internet Tidal Wave" memorandum, "First we need to offer a decent client," but "this alone won't get people to switch away from Netscape." Still, once Microsoft ensured that the average consumer would be just as comfortable browsing with Internet Explorer as with Navigator, Microsoft could employ other devices to induce consumers to use its browser instead of Netscape's.

135. From 1995 onward, Microsoft spent more than $100 million each year developing Internet Explorer. The firm's management gradually increased the number of developers working on Internet Explorer from five or six in early 1995 to more than one thousand in 1999. Although the first version of

Internet Explorer was demonstrably inferior to Netscape's then-current browser product when the former was released in July 1995, Microsoft's investment eventually started to pay technological dividends. When Microsoft released Internet Explorer 3.0 in late 1996, reviewers praised its vastly improved quality, and some even rated it as favorably as they did Navigator. After the arrival of Internet Explorer 4.0 in late 1997, the number of reviewers who regarded it as the superior product was roughly equal to those who preferred Navigator.

E. Giving Internet Explorer Away and Rewarding Firms that Helped Build Its Usage Share

136. In addition to improving the quality of Internet Explorer, Microsoft sought to increase the product's share of browser usage by giving it away for free. In many cases, Microsoft also gave other firms things of value (at substantial cost to Microsoft) in exchange for their commitment to distribute and promote Internet Explorer, sometimes explicitly at Navigator's expense. While Microsoft might have bundled Internet Explorer with Windows at no additional charge even absent its determination to preserve the applications barrier to entry, that determination was the main force driving its decision to price the product at zero. Furthermore, Microsoft would not have given Internet Explorer away to IAPs [Internet access providers], ISVs [independent software vendors], and Apple, nor would it have taken on the high cost of enlisting firms in its campaign to maximize Internet Explorer's usage share and limit Navigator's, had it not been focused on protecting the applications barrier.

137. In early 1995, personnel developing Internet Explorer at Microsoft contemplated charging OEMs and others for the product when it was released. Internet Explorer would have been included in a bundle of software that would have been sold as an add-on, or "frosting," to Windows 95. Indeed, Microsoft knew by the middle of 1995, if not earlier, that Netscape charged customers to license Navigator, and that Netscape derived a significant portion of its revenue from selling browser licenses. Despite the opportunity to make a substantial amount of revenue from the sale of Internet Explorer, and with the knowledge that the dominant browser product on the market, Navigator, was being licensed at a price, senior executives at Microsoft decided that Microsoft needed to give its browser away in furtherance of the larger strategic goal of accelerating Internet Explorer's acquisition of browser usage share. Consequently, Microsoft decided not to charge an increment in price when it included Internet Explorer in Windows for the first time, and it has continued this policy ever since. In addition, Microsoft has never charged for an Internet Explorer license when it is distributed separately from Windows.

138. Over the months and years that followed the release of Internet Explorer 1.0 in July 1995, senior executives at Microsoft remained engrossed with maximizing Internet Explorer's share of browser usage. Whenever competing priorities threatened to intervene, decision-makers at Microsoft

reminded those reporting to them that browser usage share remained, as Microsoft senior vice president Paul Maritz put it, "job #1." For example, in the summer of 1997, some mid-level employees began to urge that Microsoft charge a price for at least some of the components of Internet Explorer 4.0. This would have shifted some anticipatory demand to Windows 98 (which was due to be released somewhat later than Internet Explorer 4.0), since Windows 98 would include all of the browser at no extra charge. Senior executives at Microsoft rejected the proposal, because while the move might have increased demand for Windows 98 and generated substantial revenue, it would have done so at the unacceptable cost of retarding the dissemination of Internet Explorer 4.0. Maritz reminded those who had advocated the proposal that "getting browser share up to 50% (or more) is still the major goal."

139. The transcendent importance of browser usage share to Microsoft is evident in what the firm expended, as well as in what it relinquished, in order to maximize usage share for Internet Explorer and to diminish it for Navigator. Not only was Microsoft willing to forego an opportunity to attract substantial revenue while enhancing (albeit temporarily) consumer demand for Windows 98, but the company also paid huge sums of money, and sacrificed many millions more in lost revenue every year, in order to induce firms to take actions that would help increase Internet Explorer's share of browser usage at Navigator's expense. First, even though Microsoft could have charged IAPs, ISVs, and Apple for licenses to distribute Internet Explorer separately from Windows, Microsoft priced those licenses, along with related technology and technical support, at zero in order to induce those companies to distribute and promote Internet Explorer over Navigator. Second, although Microsoft could have charged IAPs and ICPs substantial sums of money in exchange for promoting their services and content within Windows, Microsoft instead bartered Windows' valuable desktop "real estate" for a commitment from those firms to promote and distribute Internet Explorer, to inhibit promotion and distribution of Navigator, and to employ technologies that would inspire developers to write Web sites that relied on Microsoft's Internet technologies rather than those provided by Navigator. Microsoft was willing to offer such prominent placement even to AOL [America On Line], which was the principal competitor to Microsoft's MSN service. If an IAP was already under contract to pay Netscape a certain amount for browser licenses, Microsoft offered to compensate the IAP the amount it owed Netscape. Third, Microsoft also reduced the referral fees that IAPs paid when users signed up for their services using the Internet Referral Server in Windows in exchange for the IAPs' efforts to convert their installed bases of subscribers from Navigator to Internet Explorer. For example, Microsoft entered a contract with AOL whereby Microsoft actually paid AOL a bounty for every subscriber that it converted to access software that included Internet Explorer instead of Navigator. Finally, with respect to OEMs, Microsoft extended co-marketing funds and reductions in the Windows royalty price to those agreeing to promote Internet Explorer and, in some cases, to abstain from promoting Navigator.

140. Even absent the strategic imperative to maximize its browser usage share at Netscape's expense, Microsoft might still have set the price of an Internet Explorer consumer license at zero. It might also have spent something approaching the $100 million it has devoted each year to developing Internet Explorer and some part of the $30 million it has spent annually marketing it. After all, consumers in 1995 were already demanding software that enabled them to use the Web with ease, and IBM had announced in September 1994 its plan to include browsing capability in OS/2 Warp at no extra charge. Microsoft had reason to believe that other operating-system vendors would do the same.

141. Still, had Microsoft not viewed browser usage share as the key to preserving the applications barrier to entry, the company would not have taken its efforts beyond developing a competitive browser product, including it with Windows at no additional cost to consumers, and promoting it with advertising. Microsoft would not have absorbed the considerable additional costs associated with enlisting other firms in its campaign to increase Internet Explorer's usage share at Navigator's expense. This investment was only profitable to the extent that it protected the applications barrier to entry. Neither the desire to bolster demand for Windows, nor the prospect of ancillary revenues, explains the lengths to which Microsoft has gone. For one thing, loading Navigator makes Windows just as Internet-ready as including Internet Explorer does. Therefore, Microsoft's costly efforts to limit the use of Navigator on Windows could not have stemmed from a desire to bolster consumer demand for Windows. Furthermore, there is no conceivable way that Microsoft's costly efforts to induce Apple to pre-install Internet Explorer on Apple's own PC systems could have increased consumer demand for Windows.

142. In pursuing its goal of maximizing Internet Explorer's usage share, Microsoft actually has limited rather severely the number of profit centers from which it could otherwise derive income via Internet Explorer. For example, Microsoft allows the developers of browser shells built on Internet Explorer to collect ancillary revenues such as advertising fees; for another, Microsoft permits its browser licensees to change the browser's start page, thus limiting the fees that advertisers are willing to pay for placement on that page by Microsoft. Even if Microsoft maximized its ancillary revenue, the amount of revenue realized would not come close to recouping the cost of its campaign to maximize Internet Explorer's usage share at Navigator's expense. The countless communications that Microsoft's executives dispatched to each other about the company's need to capture browser usage share indicate that the purpose of the effort had little to do with attracting ancillary revenues and everything to do with protecting the applications barrier from the threat posed by Netscape's Navigator and Sun's implementation of Java. For example, Microsoft vice president Brad Chase told the company's assembled sales and marketing executives in April 1996 that they should "worry about your browser share as much as Bill G" even though Internet Explorer was "a no revenue product," because "we will lose [sic] the

Internet platform battle if we do not have a significant user installed base."
He told them that "if you let your customers deploy Netscape Navigator, you
will loose [sic] leadership on the desktop."

F. Excluding Navigator from Important
Distribution Channels

143. Decision-makers at Microsoft worried that simply developing its own
attractive browser product, pricing it at zero, and promoting it vigorously
would not divert enough browser usage from Navigator to neutralize it as a
platform. They believed that a comparable browser product offered at no
charge would still not be compelling enough to consumers to detract substantially from Navigator's existing share of browser usage. This belief was
due, at least in part, to the fact that Navigator already enjoyed a very large
installed base and had become nearly synonymous with the Web in the public's consciousness. If Microsoft was going to raise Internet Explorer's share
of browser usage and lower Navigator's share, executives at Microsoft
believed they needed to constrict Netscape's access to the distribution channels that led most efficiently to browser usage.

1. The Importance of the OEM and IAP Channels

144. Very soon after it recognized the need to gain browser usage share at
Navigator's expense, Microsoft identified pre-installation by OEMs and
bundling with the proprietary client software of IAPs as the two distribution
channels that lead most efficiently to browser usage. Two main reasons
explain why these channels are so efficient. First, users must acquire a computer and connect to the Internet before they can browse the Web. Thus, the
OEM and IAP channels lead directly to virtually every user of browsing software. Second, both OEMs and IAPs are able to place browsing software at the
immediate disposal of a user without any effort on the part of the user. If an
OEM pre-installs a browser onto its PCs and places an icon for that browser
on the default screen, or "desktop," of the operating system, purchasers of
those PCs will be confronted with the icon as soon as the operating system
finishes loading into random access memory ("RAM"). If an IAP bundles a
browser with its own proprietary software, its subscribers will, by default, use
the browser whenever they connect to the Web. In its internal decision-making, Microsoft has placed considerable reliance on studies showing that consumers tend strongly to use whatever browsing software is placed most readily at their disposal, and that once they have acquired, found, and used one
browser product, most are reluctant—and indeed have little reason—to
expend the effort to switch to another. Microsoft has also relied on studies
showing that a very large majority of those who browse the Web obtain their
browsing software with either their PCs or their IAP subscriptions. . . .

148. Knowing that OEMs and IAPs represented the most efficient distribution channels of browsing software, Microsoft sought to ensure that, to as
great an extent as possible, OEMs and IAPs bundled and promoted Internet
Explorer to the exclusion of Navigator.

2. Excluding Navigator from the OEM Channel

a. Binding Internet Explorer to Windows

i. The Status of Web Browsers as Separate Products

149. Consumers determine their software requirements by identifying the functionalities they desire. While consumers routinely evaluate software products on the basis of the functionalities the products deliver, they generally lack sufficient information to make judgements based on the designs and implementations of those products. Accordingly, consumers generally choose which software products to license, install, and use on the basis of the products' functionalities, not their designs and implementations.

150. While the meaning of the term "Web browser" is not precise in all respects, there is a consensus in the software industry as to the functionalities that a Web browser offers a user. Specifically, a Web browser provides the ability for the end user to select, retrieve, and perceive resources on the Web. There is also a consensus in the software industry that these functionalities are distinct from the set of functionalities provided by an operating system.

151. Many consumers desire to separate their choice of a Web browser from their choice of an operating system. Some consumers, particularly corporate consumers, demand browsers and operating systems separately because they prefer to standardize on the same browser across different operating systems. For such consumers, standardizing on the browser of their choice results in increased productivity and lower training and support costs, and permits the establishment of consistent security and privacy policies governing Web access.

152. Moreover, many consumers who need an operating system, including a substantial percentage of corporate consumers, do not want a browser at all. For example, if a consumer has no desire to browse the Web, he may not want a browser taking up memory on his hard disk and slowing his system's performance. Also, for businesses desiring to inhibit employees' access to the Internet while minimizing system support costs, the most efficient solution is often using PC systems without browsers.

153. Because of the separate demand for browsers and operating systems, firms have found it efficient to supply the products separately. A number of operating system vendors offer consumers the choice of licensing their operating systems without a browser. Others bundle a browser with their operating system products but allow OEMs, value-added resellers, and consumers either to not install it or, if the browser has been pre-installed, to uninstall it. While Microsoft no longer affords this flexibility (it is the only operating system vendor that does not), it has always marketed and distributed Internet Explorer separately from Windows in several channels. These include retail sales, service kits for ISVs, free downloads over the Internet, and bundling with other products produced both by Microsoft and by third-party ISVs. In order to compete with Navigator for browser share, as well as to satisfy corporate consumers who want their diverse PC platforms to present a common

browser interface to employees, Microsoft has also created stand-alone versions of Internet Explorer that run on operating systems other than 32-bit Windows, including the Mac OS and Windows 3.x.

154. In conclusion, the preferences of consumers and the responsive behavior of software firms demonstrate that Web browsers and operating systems are separate products.

ii. Microsoft's Actions

155. In contrast to other operating system vendors, Microsoft both refused to license its operating system without a browser and imposed restrictions—at first contractual and later technical—on OEMs' and end users' ability to remove its browser from its operating system. As its internal contemporaneous documents and licensing practices reveal, Microsoft decided to bind Internet Explorer to Windows in order to prevent Navigator from weakening the applications barrier to entry, rather than for any pro-competitive purpose.

156. Before it decided to blunt the threat that Navigator posed to the applications barrier to entry, Microsoft did not plan to make it difficult or impossible for OEMs or consumers to obtain Windows without obtaining Internet Explorer. In fact, the company's internal correspondence and external communications indicate that, as late as the fall of 1994, Microsoft was planning to include low-level Internet "plumbing," such as a TCP/IP stack, but not a browser, with Windows 95.

157. Microsoft subsequently decided to develop a browser to run on Windows 95. As late as June 1995, however, Microsoft had not decided to bundle that browser with the operating system. The plan at that point, rather, was to ship the browser in a separate "frosting" package, for which Microsoft intended to charge. By April or May of that year, however, Microsoft's top executives had identified Netscape's browser as a potential threat to the applications barrier to entry. Throughout the spring, more and more key executives came to the conclusion that Microsoft's best prospect of quashing that threat lay in maximizing the usage share of Microsoft's browser at Navigator's expense. The executives believed that the most effective way of carrying out this strategy was to ensure that every copy of Windows 95 carried with it a copy of Microsoft's browser, then code-named "O'Hare." For example, two days after the June 21, 1995 meeting between Microsoft and Netscape executives, Microsoft's John Ludwig sent an E-mail to Paul Maritz and the other senior executives involved in Microsoft's browser effort. "[O]bviously netscape does see us as a client competitor," Ludwig wrote. "[W]e have to work extra hard to get ohare on the oem disks."

158. Microsoft did manage to bundle Internet Explorer 1.0 with the first version of Windows 95 licensed to OEMs in July 1995. It also included a term in its OEM licenses that prohibited the OEMs from modifying or deleting any part of Windows 95, including Internet Explorer, prior to shipment. The OEMs accepted this restriction despite their interest in meeting consumer demand for PC operating systems without Internet Explorer. After all,

Microsoft made the restriction a non-negotiable term in its Windows 95 license, and the OEMs felt they had no commercially viable alternative to pre-installing Windows 95 on their PCs. Apart from a few months in the fall of 1997, when Microsoft provided OEMs with Internet Explorer 4.0 on a separate disk from Windows 95 and permitted them to ship the latter without the former, Microsoft has never allowed OEMs to ship Windows 95 to consumers without Internet Explorer. This policy has guaranteed the presence of Internet Explorer on every new Windows PC system.

159. Microsoft knew that the inability to remove Internet Explorer made OEMs less disposed to pre-install Navigator onto Windows 95. OEMs bear essentially all of the consumer support costs for the Windows PC systems they sell. These include the cost of handling consumer complaints and questions generated by Microsoft's software. Pre-installing more than one product in a given category, such as word processors or browsers, onto its PC systems can significantly increase an OEM's support costs, for the redundancy can lead to confusion among novice users. In addition, pre-installing a second product in a given software category can increase an OEM's product testing costs. Finally, many OEMs see pre-installing a second application in a given software category as a questionable use of the scarce and valuable space on a PC's hard drive.

160. Microsoft's executives believed that the incentives that its contractual restrictions placed on OEMs would not be sufficient in themselves to reverse the direction of Navigator's usage share. Consequently, in late 1995 or early 1996, Microsoft set out to bind Internet Explorer more tightly to Windows 95 as a technical matter. The intent was to make it more difficult for anyone, including systems administrators and users, to remove Internet Explorer from Windows 95 and to simultaneously complicate the experience of using Navigator with Windows 95. As Brad Chase wrote to his superiors near the end of 1995, "We will bind the shell to the Internet Explorer, so that running any other browser is a jolting experience." . . .

[Following sections describe how Microsoft "bound" Internet Explorer to Windows 95 in such a way as to make it difficult to separate them should a user not want Internet Explorer as part of the operating system.]

166. In late 1996, senior executives within Microsoft, led by James Allchin, began to argue that Microsoft was not binding Internet Explorer tightly enough to Windows and as such was missing an opportunity to maximize the usage of Internet Explorer at Navigator's expense. Allchin first made his case to Paul Maritz in late December 1996. He wrote:

> I don't understand how IE is going to win. The current path is simply to copy everything that Netscape does packaging and product wise. Let's [suppose] IE is as good as Navigator/Communicator. Who wins? The one with 80% market share. Maybe being free helps us, but once people are used to a product it is hard to change them. Consider Office. We are more expensive today and we're still winning. My conclusion is that we must leverage Windows more. Treating IE as just an add-on to Windows which is cross-platform [means] losing our biggest advantage—Windows marketshare. We should dedicate a cross group team to come up

with ways to leverage Windows technically more. . . . We should think about an integrated solution—that is our strength.

Allchin followed up with another message to Maritz on January 2, 1997:

> You see browser share as job 1. . . . I do not feel we are going to win on our current path. We are not leveraging Windows from a marketing perspective and we are trying to copy Netscape and make IE into a platform. We do not use our strength—which is that we have an installed base of Windows and we have a strong OEM shipment channel for Windows. Pitting browser against browser is hard since Netscape has 80% marketshare and we have 20%. . . . I am convinced we have to use Windows—this is the one thing they don't have. . . . We have to be competitive with features, but we need something more—Windows integration.
>
> If you agree that Windows is a huge asset, then it follows quickly that we are not investing sufficiently in finding ways to tie IE and Windows together. This must come from you. . . . Memphis [Microsoft's code-name for Windows 98] must be a simple upgrade, but most importantly it must be killer on OEM shipments so that Netscape never gets a chance on these systems.

167. Maritz responded to Allchin's second message by agreeing "that we have to make Windows integration our basic strategy" and that this justified delaying the release of Windows 98 until Internet Explorer 4.0 was ready to be included with that product. Maritz recognized that the delay would disappoint OEMs for two reasons. First, while OEMs were eager to sell new hardware technologies to Windows users, they could not do this until Microsoft released Windows 98, which included software support for the new technologies. Second, OEMs wanted Windows 98 to be released in time to drive sales of PC systems during the back-to-school and holiday selling seasons. Nevertheless, Maritz agreed with Allchin's point that synchronizing the release of Windows 98 with Internet Explorer was "the only thing that makes sense even if OEMs suffer."

168. Once Maritz had decided that Allchin was right, he needed to instruct the relevant Microsoft employees to delay the release of Windows 98 long enough so that it could be shipped with Internet Explorer 4.0 tightly bound to it. When one executive asked on January 7, 1997 for confirmation that "memphis is going to hold for IE4, even if it puts memphis out of the xmas oem window," Maritz responded affirmatively and explained,

> The major reason for this is . . . to combat Nscp, we have to position the browser as "going away" and do deeper integration on Windows. The stronger way to communicate this is to have a 'new release' of Windows and make a big deal out of it. . . . IE integration will be [the] most compelling feature of Memphis.

Thus, Microsoft delayed the debut of numerous features, including support for new hardware devices, that Microsoft believed consumers would find beneficial, simply in order to protect the applications barrier to entry. . . .

172. Microsoft's refusal to respect the user's choice of default browser fulfilled Brad Chase's 1995 promise to make the use of any browser other than Internet Explorer on Windows "a jolting experience." By increasing the like-

lihood that using Navigator on Windows 98 would have unpleasant consequences for users, Microsoft further diminished the inclination of OEMs to pre-install Navigator onto Windows. The decision to override the user's selection of non-Microsoft software as the default browser also directly disinclined Windows 98 consumers to use Navigator as their default browser, and it harmed those Windows 98 consumers who nevertheless used Navigator. In particular, Microsoft exposed those using Navigator on Windows 98 to security and privacy risks that are specific to Internet Explorer and to ActiveX controls..

173. Microsoft's actions have inflicted collateral harm on consumers who have no interest in using a Web browser at all. If these consumers want the non-browsing features available only in Windows 98, they must content themselves with an operating system that runs more slowly than if Microsoft had not interspersed browsing-specific routines throughout various files containing routines relied upon by the operating system. More generally, Microsoft has forced Windows 98 users uninterested in browsing to carry software that, while providing them with no benefits, brings with it all the costs associated with carrying additional software on a system. These include performance degradation, increased risk of incompatibilities, and the introduction of bugs. Corporate consumers who need the hardware support and other non-browsing features not available in earlier versions of Windows, but who do not want Web browsing at all, are further burdened in that they are denied a simple and effective means of preventing employees from attempting to browse the Web.

174. Microsoft has harmed even those consumers who desire to use Internet Explorer, and no other browser, with Windows 98. To the extent that browsing-specific routines have been commingled with operating system routines to a greater degree than is necessary to provide any consumer benefit, Microsoft has unjustifiably jeopardized the stability and security of the operating system. Specifically, it has increased the likelihood that a browser crash will cause the entire system to crash and made it easier for malicious viruses that penetrate the system via Internet Explorer to infect non-browsing parts of the system.

iii. Lack of Justification

175. No technical reason can explain Microsoft's refusal to license Windows 95 without Internet Explorer 1.0 and 2.0. The version of Internet Explorer (1.0) that Microsoft included with the original OEM version of Windows 95 was a separable, executable program file supplied on a separate disk. Web browsing thus could be installed or removed without affecting the rest of Windows 95's functionality in any way. The same was true of Internet Explorer 2.0. Microsoft, moreover, created an easy way to remove Internet Explorer 1.0 and 2.0 from Windows 95 after they had been installed, via the "Add/Remove" panel. This demonstrates the absence of any technical reason for Microsoft's refusal to supply Windows 95 without Internet Explorer 1.0 and 2.0.

176. Similarly, there is no technical justification for Microsoft's refusal to license Windows 95 to OEMs with Internet Explorer 3.0 or 4.0 uninstalled, or for its refusal to permit OEMs to uninstall Internet Explorer 3.0 or 4.0. Microsoft's decision to provide users with an "uninstall" procedure for Internet Explorer 3.0 and 4.0 and its decision to promote Internet Explorer on the basis of that feature demonstrate that there was no technical or quality-related reason for refusing to permit OEMs to use this same feature. Microsoft would not have permitted users to uninstall Internet Explorer, nor would consumers have demanded such an option, if the process would have fragmented or degraded the other functionality of the operating system.

177. As with Windows 95, there is no technical justification for Microsoft's refusal to meet consumer demand for a browserless version of Windows 98. Microsoft could easily supply a version of Windows 98 that does not provide the ability to browse the Web, and to which users could add the browser of their choice. Indicative of this is the fact that it remains possible to remove Web browsing functionality from Windows 98 without adversely affecting non-Web browsing features of Windows 98 or the functionality of applications running on the operating system. . . .

[Following sections discuss the results of a program developed for the Microsoft trial to show the results of removing Internet Explorer from Windows 98.]

186. As an abstract and general proposition, many—if not most—consumers can be said to benefit from Microsoft's provision of Web browsing functionality with its Windows operating system at no additional charge. No consumer benefit can be ascribed, however, to Microsoft's refusal to offer a version of Windows 95 or Windows 98 without Internet Explorer, or to Microsoft's refusal to provide a method for uninstalling Internet Explorer from Windows 98. In particular, Microsoft's decision to force users to take the browser in order to get the non-Web browsing features of Windows 98, including support for new Internet protocols and data formats is, as Allchin put it, simply a choice about "distribution." . . .

187. . . . [I]t is feasible for Microsoft to supply a version of Windows 98 that does not provide the ability to browse the Web, to which users could add a browser of their choice. Microsoft could then readily offer "integrated" Internet Explorer Web browsing functionality as well, either as an option that could be selected by the end user or the OEM during the Windows 98 setup procedure, or as a "service pack upgrade." . . .

191. Therefore, Microsoft could offer consumers all the benefits of the current Windows 98 package by distributing the products separately and allowing OEMs or consumers themselves to combine the products if they wished. In fact, operating system vendors other than Microsoft currently succeed in offering "integrated" features similar to those that Microsoft advertises in Windows 98 while still permitting the removal of the browser from the operating system. If consumers genuinely prefer a version of Windows bundled with Internet Explorer, they do not have to be forced to take it; they can choose it in the market. . . .

[Following sections discuss Microsoft's claim that Internet Explorer is needed to preserve the "integrity" of Windows and the company's claim that Internet Explorer would prove to be the "best of breed" among Internet browsers.]

b. Preventing OEMs from Removing the Ready Means of Accessing Internet Explorer and from Promoting Navigator in the Boot Sequence

202. Since the release of Internet Explorer 1.0 in July 1995, Microsoft has distributed every version of Windows with Internet Explorer included. Consequently, no OEM has ever (with the exception of a few months in late 1997) been able to license a copy of Windows 95 or Windows 98 that has not come with Internet Explorer. Refusing to offer OEMs a browserless (and appropriately discounted) version of Windows forces OEMs to take (and pay for) Internet Explorer, but it does not prevent a determined OEM from nevertheless offering its consumers a different Web browser. Even Microsoft's additional refusal to allow OEMs to uninstall (without completely removing) Internet Explorer from Windows does not completely foreclose a resourceful OEM from offering consumers another browser. For example, an OEM with sufficient technical expertise (which all the larger OEMs certainly possess) could offer its customers a choice of browsers while still minimizing user confusion if the OEM were left free to configure its systems to present this choice the first time a user turned on a new PC system. If the user chose Navigator, the system would automatically remove the most prominent means of accessing Internet Explorer from Windows (without actually uninstalling, i.e., removing all means of accessing, Internet Explorer) before the desktop screen appeared for the first time.

203. If OEMs removed the most visible means of invoking Internet Explorer, and pre-installed Navigator with facile methods of access, Microsoft's purpose in forcing OEMs to take Internet Explorer—capturing browser usage share from Netscape—would be subverted. The same would be true if OEMs simply configured their machines to promote Navigator before Windows had a chance to promote Internet Explorer, Decision-makers at Microsoft believed that as Internet Explorer caught up with Navigator in quality, OEMs would ultimately conclude that the costs of pre-installing and promoting Navigator, and removing easy access to Internet Explorer, outweighed the benefits. Still, those decision-makers did not believe that Microsoft could afford to wait for the several large OEMs that represented virtually all Windows PCs shipped to come to this desired conclusion on their own. Therefore, in order to bring the behavior of OEMs into line with its strategic goals quickly, Microsoft threatened to terminate the Windows license of any OEM that removed Microsoft's chosen icons and program entries from the Windows desktop or the "Start" menu. It threatened similar punishment for OEMs who added programs that promoted third-party software to the Windows "boot" sequence. These inhibitions soured Microsoft's relations with OEMs and stymied innovation that might have made Windows

PC systems more satisfying to users. Microsoft would not have paid this price had it not been convinced that its actions were necessary to ostracize Navigator from the vital OEM distribution channel. . . .

[Following sections discuss actions Microsoft took to prevent computer manufacturers from removing Internet Explorer from their products, making Internet Explorer difficult to use, or making Netscape Navigator readily available. In several cases Microsoft threatened to withdraw licenses for Windows from manufacturers that refused to comply with its demands]

c. Pressuring OEMs to Promote Internet Explorer and to not Pre-Install or Promote Navigator

230. Microsoft's restrictions on modifications to the boot sequence and the configuration of the Windows desktop ensured that every Windows user would be presented with ready means of accessing Internet Explorer. Although the restrictions also raised the costs attendant to pre-installing and promoting Navigator, senior executives at Microsoft were not confident that those higher costs alone would induce all of the major OEMs to focus their promotional efforts on Internet Explorer to the exclusion of Navigator. Therefore, Microsoft used incentives and threats in an effort to secure the cooperation of individual OEMs.

231. First, Microsoft rewarded with valuable consideration those large-volume OEMs that took steps to promote Internet Explorer. For example, Microsoft gave reductions in the royalty price of Windows to certain OEMs, including Gateway, that set Internet Explorer as the default browser on their PC systems. In 1997, Microsoft gave still further reductions to those OEMs that displayed Internet Explorer's logo and links to Microsoft's Internet Explorer update page on their own home pages. That same year, Microsoft agreed to give OEMs millions of dollars in co-marketing funds, as well as costly in-kind assistance, in exchange for their carrying out other promotional activities for Internet Explorer. . . .

[Following sections discuss efforts by Microsoft to pressure computer manufacturers, including Compaq, Gateway, and IBM, to comply with its strategy to promote Internet Explorer as the sole Internet browser on personal computers.]

d. Effect of Microsoft's Actions in the OEM Channel

239. Microsoft has largely succeeded in exiling Navigator from the crucial OEM distribution channel. Even though a few OEMs continue to offer Navigator on some of their PCs, Microsoft has caused the number of OEMs offering Navigator, and the number of PCs on which they offer it, to decline dramatically. Before 1996, Navigator enjoyed a substantial and growing presence on the desktop of new PCs. Over the next two years, however, Microsoft's actions forced the number of copies of Navigator distributed through the OEM channel down to an exiguous fraction of what it had been. By January 1998, Kempin could report to his superiors at Microsoft that, of the sixty OEM sub-channels (15 major OEMs each offering corporate desktop, con-

sumer/small business, notebook, and workstation PCs), Navigator was being shipped through only four. Furthermore, most of the PCs shipped with Navigator featured the product in a manner much less likely to lead to usage than if its icon appeared on the desktop. For example, Sony only featured Navigator in a folder rather than on the desktop, and Gateway only shipped Navigator on a separate CD-ROM rather than pre-installed on the hard drive. By the beginning of January 1999, Navigator was present on the desktop of only a tiny percentage of the PCs that OEMs were shipping.

240. To the extent Netscape is still able to distribute Navigator through the OEM channel, Microsoft has substantially increased the cost of that distribution. Although in January 1999 (in the midst of this trial), Compaq suddenly decided to resume the pre-installation of Navigator on its Presario PCs, Compaq's reversal came only after Netscape agreed to provide Compaq with approximately $700,000 worth of free advertising.

241. In sum, Microsoft successfully secured for Internet Explorer—and foreclosed to Navigator—one of the two distribution channels that leads most efficiently to the usage of browsing software. Even to the extent that Navigator retains some access to the OEM channel, Microsoft has relegated it to markedly less efficient forms of distribution than the form vouchsafed for Internet Explorer, namely, prominent placement on the Windows desktop. Microsoft achieved this feat by using a complementary set of tactics. First, it forced OEMs to take Internet Explorer with Windows and forbade them to remove or obscure it—restrictions which both ensured the prominent presence of Internet Explorer on users' PC systems and increased the costs attendant to pre-installing and promoting Navigator. Second, Microsoft imposed additional technical restrictions to increase the cost of promoting Navigator even more. Third, Microsoft offered OEMs valuable consideration in exchange for commitments to promote Internet Explorer exclusively. Finally, Microsoft threatened to penalize individual OEMs that insisted on pre-installing and promoting Navigator. Although Microsoft's campaign to capture the OEM channel succeeded, it required a massive and multifarious investment by Microsoft; it also stifled innovation by OEMs that might have made Windows PC systems easier to use and more attractive to consumers. That Microsoft was willing to pay this price demonstrates that its decision-makers believed that maximizing Internet Explorer's usage share at Navigator's expense was worth almost any cost.

3. Excluding Navigator from the IAP Channel

242. By late 1995, Microsoft had identified bundling with the client software of IAPs as the other of the two most efficient channels for distributing browsing software. By that time, however, several of the most popular IAPs were shipping Navigator. Recognizing that it was starting from behind, Microsoft devised an aggressive strategy to capture the IAP channel from Netscape. . . .

In the first step of this strategy, Microsoft enticed ISPs with small subscriber bases to distribute Internet Explorer and to make it their default browsing software by offering for free both a license to distribute Internet Explorer and a software kit that made it easy for ISPs with limited resources to adapt Internet Explorer for bundling with their services.

243. Those who planned and implemented Microsoft's IAP campaign believed that, if IAPs gave new subscribers a choice between Internet Explorer and Navigator, most of them would pick Navigator—both because Netscape's brand had become nearly synonymous with the Web in the public consciousness and because Navigator had developed a much better reputation for quality than Internet Explorer. To compensate for Navigator's advantage, Microsoft reinforced its free distribution of Internet Explorer licenses and the access kits with three tactics designed to induce IAPs with large subscriber bases not only to distribute and promote Internet Explorer, but also to constrain severely their distribution and promotion of Navigator and to convert those of their subscribers already using Navigator to Internet Explorer.

244. Microsoft's first tactic was to develop and include with Windows an Internet sign- up program that made it simple for users to download access software from, and subscribe to, any IAP appearing on a list assembled by Microsoft. In exchange for their inclusion on this list, the leading IAPs agreed, at Microsoft's insistence, to distribute and promote Internet Explorer, to refrain from promoting non-Microsoft Web browsing software, and to ensure that they distributed non-Microsoft browsing software to only a limited percentage of their subscribers. Although the percentages varied by IAP, the most common figure was seventy-five percent.

245. In a similar tactic aimed at a more important IAP sub-channel, Microsoft created an "Online Services Folder" and placed an icon for that folder on the Windows desktop. In exchange for the pre-installation of their access software with Windows and for the inclusion of their icons in the Online Services Folder, the leading OLSs agreed, again at Microsoft's insistence, to distribute and promote Internet Explorer, to refrain from promoting non-Microsoft Web browsing software, and to distribute non-Microsoft browsing software to no more than fifteen percent of their subscribers.

246. Finally, Microsoft gave IAPs incentives to upgrade the millions of subscribers already using Navigator to proprietary access software that included Internet Explorer. To IAPs included in the Windows Internet sign-up list, Microsoft offered the incentive of reductions in the referral fees it charged for inclusion in the list. To OLSs in the Online Services Folder, Microsoft offered cash bounties.

247. In sum, Microsoft made substantial sacrifices, including the forfeiture of significant revenue opportunities, in order to induce IAPs to do four things: to distribute access software that came with Internet Explorer; to promote Internet Explorer; to upgrade existing subscribers to Internet Explorer; and to restrict their distribution and promotion of non-Microsoft browsing software. The restrictions on the freedom of IAPs to distribute and promote Navigator were far broader than they needed to be in order to achieve any economic efficiency. This is especially true given the fact that Microsoft

never expected Internet Explorer to generate any revenue. Ultimately, the inducements that Microsoft offered IAPs at substantial cost to itself, together with the restrictive conditions it imposed on IAPs, did the four things they were designed to accomplish: They caused Internet Explorer's usage share to surge; they caused Navigator's usage share to plummet; they raised Netscape's own costs; and they sealed off a major portion of the IAP channel from the prospect of recapture by Navigator. As an ancillary effect, Microsoft's campaign to seize the IAP channel significantly hampered the ability of consumers to make their choice of Web browser products based on the features of those products.

[Following sections discuss Microsoft's actions in persuading Internet access providers, such as America On Line, to use Internet Explorer, rather than Netscape Navigator, as their preferred Internet browser.]

c. The Online Services Folder Agreements

272. In late 1995 and early 1996, senior executives at Microsoft recognized that AOL accounted for a substantial portion of all existing Internet access subscriptions and that it attracted a very large percentage of new IAP subscribers. Indeed, AOL was and is the largest and most important IAP. The Microsoft executives thus realized that if they could convince AOL to distribute Internet Explorer with its client software instead of Navigator, Microsoft would—in a single coup—capture a large part of the IAP channel for Internet Explorer. In the early spring of 1996, therefore, Microsoft exchanged favorable placement on the Windows desktop, as well as other valuable consideration, for AOL's commitment to distribute and promote Internet Explorer to the near exclusion of Navigator. AOL's acceptance of this arrangement has caused an enormous surge in Internet Explorer's usage share and a concomitant decline in Navigator's share. To supplement the effects of the AOL deal, Microsoft entered similar agreements with other OLSs [on-line services]. The importance of these arrangements to Microsoft is evident in the fact that, in contrast to the restrictive terms in the Windows Referral Server agreements, Microsoft has never waived the terms that require the OLSs to distribute and promote Internet Explorer to the near exclusion of Navigator. . . .

[Following sections discuss Microsoft's negotiations with AOL leading to the signing of an agreement on March 12, 1996, in which AOL agreed to use Internet Explorer as its sole Internet browser in return for certain licensing and technical concessions by Microsoft].

295. On October 28, 1996, Microsoft and AOL entered into an additional agreement called the Promotional Services Agreement, whereby AOL agreed to promote its new proprietary access software that included Internet Explorer to existing AOL subscribers, and Microsoft agreed to pay AOL for such promotion based on results. Specifically, Microsoft agreed to pay AOL $500,000, plus twenty-five cents (up to one million dollars) for each subscriber who upgraded from older versions of AOL's proprietary access software to the version that included Internet Explorer, plus $600,000 if AOL suc-

ceeded in upgrading 5.25 million subscribers by April 1997. In addition, AOL's Referral Server agreement with Microsoft provided that AOL would receive a two-dollar credit on referral fees for each new subscriber who used Internet Explorer. So while the March 12, 1996 agreement ensured that nearly all new AOL subscribers would use Internet Explorer, the Promotional Services and Referral Server agreements enlisted AOL in the effort to convert the OLS's millions of existing subscribers to Internet Explorer. In fulfillment of these agreements, AOL began to prompt its subscribers to download the latest version of its client access software, complete with Internet Explorer, every time they logged off the service.

296. It is not surprising, given the terms of the 1996 agreements between Microsoft and AOL, that the percentage of AOL subscribers using a version of the client software that included Internet Explorer climbed steeply throughout 1997. By January 1998, Cameron Myhrvold was able to report to Gates and the rest of Microsoft's executive committee that ninety-two percent of AOL's subscribers (who by then numbered over ten million) were using client access software that included Internet Explorer. A year earlier, the same type of data had shown that only thirty-four percent of AOL subscribers were using AOL client software that included Internet Explorer. The marked increase resulted in no small part from AOL's efforts to convert its existing subscribers to the newest version of its client software. . . .

299. On November 24, 1998, AOL and Netscape agreed that AOL would acquire Netscape for 4.3 billion dollars' worth of AOL stock. In a related transaction, AOL entered into a three-year strategic alliance with Sun, pursuant to which Sun would develop and market both its and Netscape's server software and would manage the companies' joint efforts in the area of electronic commerce. AOL purchased Netscape not just for its browsing technology, but also for its electronic commerce business, its portal site, its brand recognition, and its talented work force. To the extent AOL was paying for Netscape's browser business, its primary goal was not to compete for user share against Internet Explorer. Rather, AOL was interested in Navigator to the extent that it drove Web traffic to Netscape's popular portal site, Net-Center. AOL was also interested in ensuring that an alternative to Internet Explorer remained viable; it wanted the option of dropping Internet Explorer to retain enough vitality so that it would not be at the mercy of Microsoft for software upon which the success of its online service largely depended. Finally, AOL was interested in keeping Navigator alive in order to ensure that Microsoft did not gain total control over Internet standards.

300. AOL had the right under its agreement with Microsoft to terminate the distribution and promotion provisions relating to Internet Explorer on December 31, 1998. If AOL had decided to terminate those provisions, the March 1996 agreement would otherwise have remained in effect, and AOL could have continued to base its proprietary access software on Internet Explorer, taking advantage of Microsoft's engineering and technical support. Microsoft, however, would have had the option of removing AOL from the OLS folder. What is more, Chase informed AOL that Microsoft might react to

AOL's termination of the restrictive provisions by discontinuing the OLS folder altogether, which would have disadvantaged the AOL's subsidiary OLS, CompuServe, which also enjoyed a place in the OLS folder.

301. Despite its acquisition of Netscape, AOL did not exercise its right to terminate the exclusivity provisions of its agreement with Microsoft at the end of 1998. . . .

[Following sections discuss AOL's reasons for continuing to use Internet Explorer as its default browser.]

304. AOL's subscribers now number sixteen million, and a substantial part of all Web browsing is done through AOL's service. By granting AOL valuable desktop real estate (to MSN's detriment) and other valuable consideration, Microsoft succeeded in capturing for Internet Explorer, and holding for a minimum of four years, one of the single most important channels for the distribution of browsing software. Starting the day Microsoft announced the March 1996 agreement with AOL, and lasting at least until AOL announced its acquisition of Netscape in November 1998, developers had reason to look into the foreseeable future and see that non-Microsoft software would not attain stature as the standard platform for network-centric applications. Microsoft exploited that interval to enhance dependence among developers on Microsoft's proprietary interfaces for network-centric applications— dependence that will continue to inure to Microsoft's benefit even if AOL stops distributing Internet Explorer in the future. The AOL coup, which Microsoft accomplished only at tremendous expense to itself and considerable deprivation of consumers' freedom of choice, thus contributed to extinguishing the threat that Navigator posed to the applications barrier to entry.

ii. Other Online Services

305. In the summer and fall of 1996, Microsoft entered into agreements with three other OLSs, namely, AT&T WorldNet, Prodigy, and AOL's subsidiary, CompuServe. The provisions of these agreements were substantially the same as those contained in the March 1996 agreement between Microsoft and AOL. As with the AOL agreement, Microsoft did not deign to waive the restrictive terms in these OLS agreements when it waived similar terms in the Referral Server agreements in the spring of 1998. The OLSs were discontented with the provisions that limited their ability to distribute and promote non-Microsoft browsing software. Prodigy, for one, found those provisions objectionable and tried, unsuccessfully, to convince Microsoft to make the terms less restrictive. AT&T WorldNet's negotiator also told his Microsoft counterpart, Brad Silverberg, that AT&T wanted to remain neutral as to browsing software. Despite their reservations, the OLSs accepted Microsoft's terms because they saw placement in the OLS folder as crucial, and Microsoft made clear that it would only accord such placement to OLSs that agreed to give Internet Explorer exclusive, or at least extremely preferential, treatment. . . .

306. Although none of these OLSs possessed subscriber bases approaching AOL's, they comprised, along with MSN, the most significant OLSs other

than AOL. By making arrangements with them similar to the one it enjoyed with AOL, Microsoft ensured that, for as long as the agreements remained in effect, the overwhelming majority of OLS subscribers would use Internet Explorer whenever they accessed the Internet. Since AOL owns CompuServe, the acquisition of Netscape may affect CompuServe's arrangement with Microsoft in the future; however, the acquisition does not alter the incentives for the other OLSs to enter new agreements with Microsoft similar to the ones signed in 1996.

[Following sections describe Microsoft's success in increasing the usage of Internet Explorer through the inducements it offered, and the restrictions it placed, on Internet access providers]

4. Inducing ICPs to Enhance Internet Explorer's Usage Share at Navigator's Expense

311. ICPs [Internet content providers] create the content that fills the pages that make up the Web. Because this content can include advertisements and links to download sites, ICPs also provide a channel for the promotion and distribution of Web browsing software. Executives at Microsoft recognized that ICPs were not nearly as important a distribution channel for browsing software as OEMs and IAPs. Nevertheless, protecting the applications barrier to entry was of such high priority at Microsoft that its senior executives were willing to invest significant resources to enlist even ICPs in the effort. Executives at Microsoft determined that ICPs could aid Microsoft's browser campaign in three ways. First, ICPs could help build Internet Explorer's usage share by featuring advertisements and links for Internet Explorer, to the exclusion of non-Microsoft browsing software, on their Web pages. Second, those ICPs that distributed software as well as content could bundle Internet Explorer, instead of Navigator, with those distributions. Finally, ICPs could increase demand for Internet Explorer, and decrease demand for Navigator, by creating their content with Microsoft technologies, such as ActiveX, that would make the content more appealing in appearance when accessed with Internet Explorer.

312. As early as the fall of 1995, Microsoft executives saw that they could help reinforce the applications barrier to entry by inducing the leading ICPs to focus on Microsoft's browsing technologies. In the October 1995 memorandum that Microsoft executives sent to Gates on Microsoft's browser campaign, one of the suggestions was, "Get 80% of Top Web Sites to Target Our Client." Specifically, the executives wrote:

> Content drives browser adoption, and we need to go to the top five sites and ask them, "What can we do to get you to adopt IE?" We should be prepared to write a check, buy sites, or add features—basically do whatever it takes to drive adoption.

313. By the middle of 1996, this proposal had become corporate policy. Senior executives at Microsoft believed that inducing the ICPs responsible for the most popular Web sites to concentrate their distributional, promo-

tional, and technical efforts on Internet Explorer to the exclusion of Navigator would contribute significantly to maximizing Internet Explorer's usage share at Navigator's expense. . . .

[Following sections discuss Microsoft's negotiations and agreements with various Internet content providers, and Microsoft's negotiations with Apple Computer. A major point of all these negotiations was Microsoft's insistence that the other companies give priority to Internet Explorer and reduce or abandon their usage of Netscape Navigator.]

355. Apple increased its distribution and promotion of Internet Explorer not because of a conviction that the quality of Microsoft's product was superior to Navigator's, or that consumer demand for it was greater, but rather because of the in terrorem effect of the prospect of the loss of Mac Office. To be blunt, Microsoft threatened to refuse to sell a profitable product to Apple, a product in whose development Microsoft had invested substantial resources, and which was virtually ready for shipment. Not only would this ploy have wasted sunk costs and sacrificed substantial profit, it also would have damaged Microsoft's goodwill among Apple's customers, whom Microsoft had led to expect a new version of Mac Office [a Windows product licensed to Apple]. The predominant reason Microsoft was prepared to make this sacrifice, and the sole reason that it required Apple to make Internet Explorer its default browser and restricted Apple's freedom to feature and promote non-Microsoft browsing software, was to protect the applications barrier to entry. More specifically, the requirements and restrictions relating to browsing software were intended to raise Internet Explorer's usage share, to lower Navigator's share, and more broadly to demonstrate to important observers (including consumer, developers, industry participants, and investors) that Navigator's success had crested. Had Microsoft's only interest in developing the Mac OS version of Internet Explorer been to enable organizational customers using multiple PC operating-system products to standardize on one user interface for Web browsing, Microsoft would not have extracted from Apple the commitment to make Internet Explorer the default browser or imposed restrictions on its use and promotion of Navigator.

356. Microsoft understands that PC users tend to use the browsing software that comes pre-installed on their machines, particularly when conspicuous means of easy access appear on the PC desktop. By guaranteeing that Internet Explorer is the default browsing software on the Mac OS, by relegating Navigator to less favorable placement, by requiring Navigator's exclusion from the default installation for the Mac OS 8.5 upgrade, and by otherwise limiting Apple's promotion of Navigator, Microsoft has ensured that most users of the Mac OS will use Internet Explorer and not Navigator. Although the number of Mac OS users is very small compared to the Windows installed base, the Mac OS is nevertheless the most important consumer-oriented operating system product next to Windows. Navigator needed high usage share among Mac OS users if it was ever to enable the development of a substantial body of cross-platform software not dependent on Windows. By extracting from Apple terms that significantly diminished

the usage of Navigator on the Mac OS, Microsoft severely sabotaged Navigator's potential to weaken the applications barrier to entry.

G. Microsoft's Success in Excluding Navigator from the Channels that Lead Most Efficiently to Browser Usage

357. The cumulative effect of the stratagems described above was to ensure that the easiest and most intuitive paths that users could take to the Web would lead to Internet Explorer, the gate controlled by Microsoft. Microsoft did not actually prevent users from obtaining and using Navigator (although it tried to do as much in June 1995), but Microsoft did make it significantly less convenient for them to do so. Once Internet Explorer was seen as providing roughly the same browsing experience as Navigator, relatively few PC users showed any inclination to expend the effort required to obtain and install Navigator. Netscape could still carpet bomb the population with CD-ROMs and make Navigator available for downloading. In reality, however, few new users (i.e., ones not merely upgrading from an old version of Navigator to a new one) had any incentive to install—much less download and install—software to replicate a function for which OEMs and IAPs were already placing perfectly adequate browsing software at their disposal. The fact that Netscape was forced to distribute tens of millions of copies of Navigator through high-cost carpet-bombing in order to obtain a relatively small number of new users only discloses the extent of Microsoft's success in excluding Navigator from the channels that lead most effectively to browser usage.

H. The Success of Microsoft's Effort to Maximize Internet Explorer's Usage Share at Navigator's Expense

358. Microsoft's efforts to maximize Internet Explorer's share of browser usage at Navigator's expense have done just that. The period since 1996 has witnessed a large increase in the usage of Microsoft's browsing technologies and a concomitant decline in Navigator's share. This reversal of fortune might not have occurred had Microsoft not improved the quality of Internet Explorer, and some part of the reversal is undoubtedly attributable to Microsoft's decision to distribute Internet Explorer with Windows at no additional charge. The relative shares would not have changed nearly as much as they did, however, had Microsoft not devoted its monopoly power and monopoly profits to precisely that end. . . .

1. The Change in the Usage Shares of Internet Explorer and Navigator

[Following sections detail various statistical analyses of the respective market shares of Internet Explorer and Netscape Navigator.]

372. In summary, the estimates on which Microsoft and AOL relied and the measurements made by AdKnowledge and the University of Illinois provide an adequate basis for two findings: First, from early 1996 to the late summer of 1998, Navigator's share of all browser usage fell from above sev-

enty percent to around fifty percent, while Internet Explorer's share rose from about five percent to around fifty percent; second, by 1998, Navigator's share of incremental browser usage had fallen below forty percent while Internet Explorer's share had risen above sixty percent. All signs point to the fact that Internet Explorer's share has continued to rise—and Navigator's has continued to decline—since the late summer of 1998. It is safe to conclude, then, that Internet Explorer's share of all browser usage now exceeds fifty percent, and that Navigator's share has fallen below that mark. . . .

2. The Cause of the Change in Usage Shares

375. The changes in usage share described above would likely not have occurred had Microsoft not improved its browsing software to the point that, by late 1996, the average user could not discern a significant difference in quality and features between the latest versions of Internet Explorer and Navigator. As Microsoft's top executives predicted, however, Internet Explorer's quality and features have never surpassed Navigator's to such a degree as to compel a significant part of Navigator's installed base to switch to Internet Explorer. An internal Microsoft presentation concluded in February 1998 that "[m]any customers see MS and NS as parity products; no strong reason to switch," and another internal review three months later reported, "IE4 is fundamentally not compelling" and "[n]ot differentiated from Netscape v[ersion]4—seen as a commodity." For a time, even among new users, Navigator was likely to win most choices between comparable browser software, because most people associated the Internet and cutting-edge browsing technology with Netscape rather than with Microsoft. So, if Microsoft had taken no action other than improving the quality and features of its browser, Internet Explorer's share of usage would have risen far less and far more slowly than it actually did. While Internet Explorer's increase in usage share accelerated and began to cut deeply into Navigator's share after Microsoft released the first version of Internet Explorer (3.0) to offer quality and features approaching those of Navigator, the acceleration occurred months before Microsoft released the first version of Internet Explorer (4.0) to win a significant number of head-to-head product reviews against Navigator. This indicates that superior quality was not responsible for the dramatic rise Internet Explorer's usage share.

376. Including Internet Explorer with Windows at no additional charge likely helped the usage share of Microsoft's browsing software. It did not, however, prevent OEMs from meeting demand for Navigator, which remained higher than demand for Internet Explorer well into 1998. More-over, bundling Internet Explorer with Windows had no effect on the distrib-ution and promotion of browsing software by IAPs or through any of the other channels that Microsoft sought to pre-empt by other means. Had Microsoft not offered distribution licenses for Internet Explorer—and other things of great value—to other firms at no charge; had it not prevented OEMs from removing the prominent means of accessing Internet Explorer and lim-ited their ability to feature Navigator; and had Microsoft not taken all the

other measures it used to maximize Internet Explorer's usage share at Navigator's expense, its browsing software would not have weaned such a large amount of usage share from Navigator, much less overtaken Navigator in three years.

I. The Success of Microsoft's Effort to Protect the Applications Barrier to Entry from the Threat Posed by Navigator

377. In late 1995 and early 1996, Navigator seemed well on its way to becoming the standard software for browsing the Web. Within three years, however, Microsoft had successfully denied Navigator that status, and had thereby forestalled a serious potential threat to the applications barrier to entry. . . .

379. Not only did Microsoft prevent Navigator from undermining the applications barrier to entry, it inflicted considerable harm on Netscape's business in the process. By ensuring that the firms comprising the channels that lead most efficiently to browser usage distributed and promoted Internet Explorer to the virtual exclusion of Navigator, Microsoft relegated Netscape to more costly and less effective methods of distributing and promoting its browsing software. After Microsoft started licensing Internet Explorer at no charge, not only to OEMs and consumers, but also to IAPs, ISVs, ICPs, and even Apple, Netscape was forced to follow suit. Despite the fact that it did not charge for Internet Explorer, Microsoft could still defray the massive costs it was undertaking to maximize usage share with the vast profits earned licensing Windows. Because Netscape did not have that luxury, it could ill afford the dramatic drop in revenues from Navigator, much less to pay for the inefficient modes of distribution to which Microsoft had consigned it. The financial constraints also deterred Netscape from undertaking technical innovations that it might otherwise have implemented in Navigator. Microsoft was not altogether surprised, then, when it learned in November 1998 that Netscape had surrendered itself to acquisition by another company.

[Following sections discuss various scenarios regarding AOL usage of Internet Explorer and Netscape Navigator.]

384. Although the suspicion lingers, the evidence is insufficient to find that Microsoft's ambition is a future in which most or all of the content available on the Web would be accessible only through its own browsing software. The evidence does, however, reveal an intent to ensure that if and when full-featured, server-based applications begin appearing in large numbers on the Web, the number of them relying solely on middleware APIs (such as those exposed by Navigator) will be too few to attenuate the applications barrier to entry.

385. At least partly because of Navigator's substantial usage share, most developers continue to insist that their Web content be more-or-less as attractive when accessed with Navigator as it is when accessed with Internet Explorer. Navigator will retain an appreciable usage share through the end of 2000. After that point, AOL may be able and willing to prevent Internet

Explorer's share from achieving such dominance that a critical mass of developers will cease to concern themselves with ensuring that their Web content at least be accessible through non-Microsoft browsing software. So, as matters stand at present, while Microsoft has succeeded in forestalling the development of enough full-featured, cross-platform, network-centric applications to render the applications barrier penetrable, it is not likely to drive non-Microsoft PC Web browsing software from the marketplace altogether.

VI. Microsoft's Response to the Threat Posed by Sun's Implementation of Java

386. For Microsoft, a key to maintaining and reinforcing the applications barrier to entry has been preserving the difficulty of porting applications from Windows to other platforms, and vice versa. In 1996, senior executives at Microsoft became aware that the number of developers writing network-centric applications in the Java programming language had become significant, and that Java was likely to increase in popularity among developers. Microsoft therefore became interested in maximizing the difficulty with which applications written in Java could be ported from Windows to other platforms, and vice versa. . . .

[Following sections discuss various efforts by Microsoft to ensure that the use of Sun Microsystem's Java language would not reduce the market share of the Windows operating system or applications produced by Microsoft.]

VII. The Effect on Consumers of Microsoft's Efforts to Protect the Applications Barrier to Entry

408. The debut of Internet Explorer and its rapid improvement gave Netscape an incentive to improve Navigator's quality at a competitive rate. The inclusion of Internet Explorer with Windows at no separate charge increased general familiarity with the Internet and reduced the cost to the public of gaining access to it, at least in part because it compelled Netscape to stop charging for Navigator. These actions thus contributed to improving the quality of Web browsing software, lowering its cost, and increasing its availability, thereby benefitting consumers.

409. To the detriment of consumers, however, Microsoft has done much more than develop innovative browsing software of commendable quality and offer it bundled with Windows at no additional charge. As has been shown, Microsoft also engaged in a concerted series of actions designed to protect the applications barrier to entry, and hence its monopoly power, from a variety of middleware threats, including Netscape's Web browser and Sun's implementation of Java. Many of these actions have harmed consumers in ways that are immediate and easily discernible. They have also caused less direct, but nevertheless serious and far-reaching, consumer harm by distorting competition.

410. By refusing to offer those OEMs who requested it a version of Windows without Web browsing software, and by preventing OEMs from removing Internet Explorer—or even the most obvious means of invoking it—prior

to shipment, Microsoft forced OEMs to ignore consumer demand for a browserless version of Windows. The same actions forced OEMs either to ignore consumer preferences for Navigator or to give them a Hobson's choice of both browser products at the cost of increased confusion, degraded system performance, and restricted memory. By ensuring that Internet Explorer would launch in certain circumstances in Windows 98 even if Navigator were set as the default, and even if the consumer had removed all conspicuous means of invoking Internet Explorer, Microsoft created confusion and frustration for consumers, and increased technical support costs for business customers. Those Windows purchasers who did not want browsing software—businesses, or parents and teachers, for example, concerned with the potential for irresponsible Web browsing on PC systems—not only had to undertake the effort necessary to remove the visible means of invoking Internet Explorer and then contend with the fact that Internet Explorer would nevertheless launch in certain cases; they also had to (assuming they needed new, non-browsing features not available in earlier versions of Windows) content themselves with a PC system that ran slower and provided less available memory than if the newest version of Windows came without browsing software. By constraining the freedom of OEMs to implement certain software programs in the Windows boot sequence, Microsoft foreclosed an opportunity for OEMs to make Windows PC systems less confusing and more user-friendly, as consumers desired. By taking the actions listed above, and by enticing firms into exclusivity arrangements with valuable inducements that only Microsoft could offer and that the firms reasonably believed they could not do without, Microsoft forced those consumers who otherwise would have elected Navigator as their browser to either pay a substantial price (in the forms of downloading, installation, confusion, degraded system performance, and diminished memory capacity) or content themselves with Internet Explorer. Finally, by pressuring Intel to drop the development of platform-level NSP software, and otherwise to cut back on its software development efforts, Microsoft deprived consumers of software innovation that they very well may have found valuable, had the innovation been allowed to reach the marketplace. None of these actions had pro-competitive justifications.

411. Many of the tactics that Microsoft has employed have also harmed consumers indirectly by unjustifiably distorting competition. The actions that Microsoft took against Navigator hobbled a form of innovation that had shown the potential to depress the applications barrier to entry sufficiently to enable other firms to compete effectively against Microsoft in the market for Intel-compatible PC operating systems. That competition would have conduced to consumer choice and nurtured innovation. The campaign against Navigator also retarded widespread acceptance of Sun's Java implementation. This campaign, together with actions that Microsoft took with the sole purpose of making it difficult for developers to write Java applications with technologies that would allow them to be ported between Windows and other platforms, impeded another form of innovation that bore the potential

to diminish the applications barrier to entry. There is insufficient evidence to find that, absent Microsoft's actions, Navigator and Java already would have ignited genuine competition in the market for Intel-compatible PC operating systems. It is clear, however, that Microsoft has retarded, and perhaps altogether extinguished, the process by which these two middleware technologies could have facilitated the introduction of competition into an important market.

412. Most harmful of all is the message that Microsoft's actions have conveyed to every enterprise with the potential to innovate in the computer industry. Through its conduct toward Netscape, IBM, Compaq, Intel, and others, Microsoft has demonstrated that it will use its prodigious market power and immense profits to harm any firm that insists on pursuing initiatives that could intensify competition against one of Microsoft's core products. Microsoft's past success in hurting such companies and stifling innovation deters investment in technologies and businesses that exhibit the potential to threaten Microsoft. The ultimate result is that some innovations that would truly benefit consumers never occur for the sole reason that they do not coincide with Microsoft's self-interest.

STATE DEPARTMENT EVALUATION
OF U.S. DIPLOMATIC POSTS
November 5, 1999

Thousands of diplomats and other U.S. government employees posted overseas worked in outdated, overcrowded facilities that remained vulnerable to terrorist attacks and other security threats, two high-level advisory panels said during 1999. One panel warned that the government was falling behind its program initiated in the mid-1980s to improve the security of diplomatic posts. The other panel said the U.S. government presence overseas was "perilously close to system failure." The latter group recommended a wide-ranging program of upgrading the nation's 252 diplomatic posts and applying private sector methods to the management of the government's overseas presence.

Many of the recommendations of the two panels would require years of effort and billions of dollars of appropriations—all at a time when Congress was becoming increasingly reluctant to spend tax dollars on overseas projects. Secretary of State Madeleine K. Albright promised to try to begin implementing the recommendations during the waning months of the Clinton administration. (Clinton's on "activist" foreign policy, p. 699)

Albright had convened both panels in the wake of terrorist bombings that destroyed U.S. embassies in Nairobi, Kenya, and Dar es Salaam, Tanzania, in August 1998. One panel, chaired by retired admiral William J. Crowe Jr., a former chairman of the Joint Chiefs of Staff, investigated why the two African embassies were so vulnerable and examined the general issues of embassy security worldwide. That panel made its findings public January 8, 1999. A second committee, the Overseas Presence Advisory Panel, had a broader mandate to review the working conditions of the 14,000 Americans and 30,000 foreign nationals at U.S. embassies, consulates, and other non-military posts overseas. That panel made its findings public November 5. (Embassy bombings in Africa, Historic Documents of 1998, p. 555)

Embassy Security Panel Findings

Admiral Crowe chaired two panels that investigated the bombings of the two embassies in August 1998. The bombings—which the United States said were masterminded by a wealthy Saudi Arabian exile, Ossama bin Laden—killed 224 people and injured more than 5,000, most of them Africans.

The panels, called the Accountability Review Boards, issued a joint report that was highly critical of the U.S. government for failing to take steps to protect its diplomatic posts. The panels noted that many of the problems uncovered in 1985 by a previous committee, chaired by Admiral Bobby Ray Inman, had not yet been fixed. In particular, the panel found that few embassies met standards established by Inman's committee for protection against truck bombs—most important, a minimum setback of 100 feet from streets. Embassies in such major cities as London, Paris, Rome, and Tel Aviv fronted on busy streets and could easily be attacked by the kinds of bombs that destroyed a U.S. Marine Corps barracks in Beirut in 1983 and the embassies in Nairobi and Dar es Salaam.

Noting such lapses, Crowe's panels said they were "especially disturbed by the collective failure of the U.S. government over the past decade to provide adequate resources to reduce the vulnerabilities of U.S. diplomatic missions to terrorist attacks in most countries in the world." The panels criticized a State Department policy of ranking the presumed level of threat faced by each diplomatic facility. The two embassies in Africa had been ranked as "low" threat posts. Rather than trying to differentiate the threat levels based on history or circumstances, the panels said, the government should consider every diplomatic post "as a potential target."

Crowe's panels offered numerous suggestions for improving security and the government's ability to respond to emergencies such as the embassy bombings. Their centerpiece recommendation was for additional spending of $1.4 billion annually for ten years to build new embassies, improve antiterrorism security at existing buildings, and hire additional security personnel.

One of the panels' most controversial recommendations asked the State Department to consider consolidating several embassies into regional embassies "located in less threatened and vulnerable countries." Such a step would reduce the number of buildings that needed to be replaced or upgraded, the panels said. Crowe acknowledged that pulling embassies out of countries was a "tender subject" at the State Department, where diplomats believed in having a U.S. presence in every country.

Six weeks after presenting the report, Crowe told the New York Times *that the State Department had been "intimidated by Congress" and had failed to request enough money to improve diplomatic security. Crowe noted that the administration had requested only $3 billion over a five-year period to rebuild embassies—less than one-fourth of what his panels had recommended. "We're talking money versus lives here," he told the newspaper. "The idea that we cannot outspend the terrorists or defeat them runs counter to our history and spirit." Administration officials responded by saying they had done the best job possible given budget constraints.*

Albright sent a report to Congress in April responding to the findings of the Crowe panels. She said she agreed with the findings and was commit-

ted to "implementing them aggressively with only slight differences of tactics on a few" of them. Albright said it would take "sustained support" over many years from both the Congress and the executive branch to remedy the problems found by Crowe's panels.

Findings of the Overseas Presence Panel

Albright also appointed the Overseas Presence Advisory Panel and asked it to "think creatively" about how the U.S. government conducts its non-military business overseas. The panel was chaired by Lewis B. Kaden, a prominent Washington, D.C., attorney. The twenty-four other members included current and retired diplomats and military officers (including Admiral Crowe), former members of Congress, and prominent labor leaders, business executives, and university professors. Panel members visited diplomatic posts in twenty-three countries in Africa, Asia, Europe, the Middle East, and South America and interviewed hundreds of government employees and outside experts.

In general, the panel said it found that many overseas employees of the State Department and thirty other government agencies worked in substandard buildings and lacked access to modern equipment and technology that was standard for private business. "We encountered shockingly shabby and antiquated building conditions at some of the missions we visited," the panel said. "Throughout the world we found worn, overcrowded, and inefficient facilities." Communications systems at many diplomatic posts were "antiquated, grossly inefficient, and incompatible," the panel said, noting that few government officials posted overseas had access at work to electronic mail facilities. The panel cited several cases of substandard facilities, including the garage-like U.S. embassy in Kiev, Ukraine, which employees called the "folding chair embassy" because they needed to fold up their chairs to get into their work spaces. Such conditions "reduce productivity, impair efforts to retain staff, and often leave visitors with an unflattering impression of the United States," the panel said.

Despite the expenditure of billions of dollars to upgrade security at diplomatic posts since the mid-1980s, the panel echoed Crowe's findings that many posts remained vulnerable to even rudimentary security threats. The panel offered a series of recommendations, starting with an endorsement of the security suggestions of the Crowe panels. This panel put an annual price tag of $1.3 billion, for ten years, on its recommendations—just $100,000 less than the amount recommended by Crowe's committees.

To upgrade the general quality of diplomatic posts, the panel suggested an entirely new approach to the way the government managed and financed its overseas facilities. In the past, a State Department bureau, the Foreign Buildings Operation office, was responsible for managing all aspects of 12,000 buildings, more than 80 percent of which were residential facilities. That office had to compete with other agencies, both within the State Department and governmentwide, for funding and priority. Except in rare cases, the office could not charge rent to other agencies using

State Department buildings. As an alternative, the panel recommended establishment of an independent, federally charted Overseas Facilities Authority that would build and manage overseas posts, in consultation with the secretary of state. The authority would charge rent to the agencies using its buildings and would be able to borrow from the government's Federal Financing Bank. In general, the panel said, the new authority could use "best practices" of the private sector to improve diplomatic facilities and the management of them.

Another recommendation was expected to generate considerable debate and opposition within the government: the "right-sizing" of the U.S. government presence overseas. Without getting into specifics, the panel said the United States had too many employees in some countries and regions and not enough in others. An interagency committee, established by presidential executive order, was needed to establish a new set of priorities so that each overseas mission had the appropriate number of employees, the panel sad.

Government agencies also needed to devote considerably more money and effort to recruiting, training, and motivating employees sent overseas. Diplomats and employees of other agencies—such as the Agriculture and Justice departments and the Agency for International Development—were hard working and dedicated, the panel said. But the pay, working conditions, and promotion opportunities for those employees tended to be substantially inferior to those in the private sector, making it difficult for the government to attract and retain qualified personnel.

In one particularly startling finding, the panel estimated that one-half of State Department employees who took overseas assignments in 1998 did not have the appropriate training. The department needed to develop an overall "human resources strategy," that included better training and more emphasis on improving the quality of life for its overseas employees, the panel said.

In accepting the panel's report, Albright said she generally agreed with its conclusions and recommendations and would work within the administration and with Congress to implement them. She noted, however, that the recommendations involving "substantial additional resources" would take time to put into effect.

Following is the Executive Summary of the report, "America's Overseas Presence in the 21st Century," issued November 5, 1999, by the U.S. State Department's Overseas Presence Advisory Panel:

The United States overseas presence, which has provided the essential underpinnings of U.S. foreign policy for many decades, is near a state of crisis. Insecure and often decrepit facilities, obsolete information technology, outmoded administrative and human resources practices, poor allocation of resources, and competition from the private sector for talented staff threaten to cripple our nation's overseas capability, with far-reaching consequences for national security and prosperity.

These are among the major conclusions of the Overseas Presence Advisory Panel (the Panel) established by the Secretary of State, with the support of the President and the Congress, following the tragic bombings of the embassies in Nairobi and Dar Es Salaam. The Panel was formed to consider the future of our nation's overseas representation (other than personnel under area military commanders), to appraise its condition, and to develop practical recommendations on how best to organize and manage our overseas posts.

The condition of U.S. posts and missions abroad is unacceptable. Since the end of the Cold War, the world's political, economic, and technological landscape has changed dramatically, but our country's overseas presence has not adequately adjusted to this new reality. Thirty Federal agencies now operate internationally, yet they lack a common Internet/e-mail-based communications network. There is no interagency process to "right-size" posts as missions change, nor are agencies required, with a few exceptions, to pay their share of the cost of maintaining and renovating facilities. It is ironic that at the moment when our nation's message resonates through history, its voice has been rendered nearly mute by antiquated technologies. The Panel fears that our overseas presence is perilously close to the point of system failure.

Such failure would have serious consequences: less effective representation and advocacy of U.S. interests abroad; a loss of U.S. exports, investment, and jobs; inadequate political and economic information, leading to unexpected crises; less effectiveness in promoting democracy and the rule of law; and a weakening of the fight against international terrorism and drug trafficking. U.S. citizens traveling abroad would not get the assistance that they need and deserve. Our nation would be less able to forge global alliances to respond to regional conflicts or to solve global environmental and social problems. Only by maintaining a robust global presence can our government protect U.S. interests and promote its values.

A New Design for Our Overseas Presence

To address these deficiencies, the Panel has outlined components of a new design for our nation's overseas presence for the 21st century. It recommends eight major types of changes:

1. Improve security and foster greater accountability for security

Major capital improvements to facilities and more accountability for security, as recommended by the Accountability Review Boards (ARBs) headed by Admiral William Crowe, will better protect our representatives abroad from terrorists and other threats. The ARBs' near-term recommendations should be implemented promptly: upgrades in windows and barriers;

improved warning systems and training in emergency response; more and better-trained regional security officers; and improved cooperation with host nations.

Budget Implications: The Panel recommends approximately $1.3 billion annually for the next 10 years ($ 1.0 billion for capital improvement, including security, and $0.3 billion for maintenance, current and deferred). The estimated cost of mandatory security training is $500,000 per year.

2. Create the right size and sites for our overseas presence

The Panel recommends that the President, by Executive order and with the support of Congress, establish a permanent interagency committee to determine the size and shape of overseas posts. The Executive order should mandate the committee to review and streamline every mission and to reallocate all personnel (not just Department of State personnel) as foreign policy needs and objectives change.

The decision-making process would reconcile differences to reach a consensus. The Secretary of State would be responsible for deciding and promulgating proposed staffing plans developed through the interagency process. A department or agency head who disagrees could appeal to the President. Chiefs of Mission should have input to the committee's process as it relates to decisions affecting their posts.

Right-sizing will match staff with mission priorities and can achieve significant overall budget savings by reducing the size of overstaffed posts. Additional posts may be needed to enhance our presence in some countries where the bilateral relationship has become more important.

Budget Implications: While the magnitude of the savings from right-sizing the U.S. overseas presence cannot be known in advance, we believe that significant savings are achievable. (For example, a 10 percent reduction in all agencies' staffing would generate government wide savings of almost $380 million annually.)

3. Establish a new entity for the financing and management of our overseas presence

The Panel recommends the creation of a federally chartered government corporation—an Overseas Facilities Authority (OFA)—to exercise responsibility for building, renovating, maintaining, and managing the Federal Government's civilian overseas facilities, including office and residential facilities. The OFA would replace the Foreign Buildings Operations office of the Department of State (the Department). To the extent possible, the OFA would have the compensation and personnel practices typical of private-sector property management companies. By statute, the OFA's board chairman would be the designee of the Secretary of State. The relationship of the Secretary to the OFA would be analogous to that of the client to the construction manager. The Secretary would continue as now to have responsibility for decisions concerning the security, size, and location of all facilities and would be required to sign off on every OFA capital project, as well as its long-term capital plan. Congressional approval would be required for the establishment of the OFA. Congress would exercise over-sight of the government's overseas capital plans, as it does now.

The OFA should be designed to receive funds from a variety of sources, including rent (plus a capital charge for new facilities) from all agencies occupying space in overseas facilities; annual appropriations; retained proceeds from asset sales; forward funding commitments from the Federal Budget; loans from the U.S. Treasury Federal Financing Bank; and retained service fee revenues from sources approved by Congress.

4. Increase investment in people; adopt the best private-sector practices in human resources management.

The Secretary of State should develop a comprehensive human resources strategy to improve the quality of life for persons serving overseas; to enhance job satisfaction, improve recruiting, expand training and promotion opportunities; and to increase sensitivity to family issues. All overseas agencies should adopt the best private-sector practices for human resources management, including meaningful evaluation procedures, management and leadership development, and rapid promotion opportunities for the most talented personnel.

Budget Implications: The estimated cost of enhanced career training is $6 million per year.

5. Immediately upgrade information and communications technology

The President should direct all overseas agencies to immediately provide all overseas staff with Internet access, e-mail, a secure unclassified Internet Web site, and shared applications permitting unclassified communications among all agencies and around the globe. Furthermore, agencies should initiate planning for a common platform for secure classified information to be implemented over the next two years.

Budget Implications: The estimated cost of a common network linking all agencies in all overseas missions through the Internet and providing all employees with e-mail and other off-the-shelf capabilities is $200 million. A unified classified system allowing all agencies at post to communicate with each other and with Washington will cost nearly $130 million.

6. Reinforce and further improve consular services

The Bureau of Consular Affairs should accelerate efforts at all posts to apply "best practices" for appointments, same-day processing, and waiver processing. The Department should ensure that staff resources can be shifted to match surges in demand for consular services.

Budget Implications: The Panel supports legislation proposed by the Office of Management and Budget (OMB) to allow the Department to keep an additional $500 million of the consular fees it collects overseas in order to address critical shortfalls in infrastructure, personnel systems, capital needs, technology, training, and other needs.

7. Reform administrative services

Up-to-date information and communications technology should be used to support administrative services. The Panel strongly endorses consolidating many administrative functions in regional centers, devolving others to the local level, and bringing some processing functions back to the United States.

Budget Implications: Significant savings and improvements in productivity should result from new information and communications technology, greater employment of foreign nationals, new regional service centers, and other administrative reforms. (For example, a 10 percent improvement would yield $80 to $90 million in annual savings government wide.)

8. Enhance and refocus the role of the Ambassador

The United States should select its Ambassadors carefully, give them sufficient authority to meet their responsibilities, and provide training commensurate with their difficult and complex jobs. The President should issue an Executive order reinforcing the responsibilities and authorities of Ambassadors and codifying the traditional President's letter to Ambassadors. All agencies at a post should be required to work with the Ambassador to formulate a comprehensive, integrated mission plan and a suggested country budget.

Budget Implications: The minimal costs associated with additional training for Ambassadors and Deputy Chiefs of Mission would be approximately $200,000.

Overall Budget Implications

The Panel believes that significant savings are achievable from right-sizing and the reform of administrative functions; however, it is clear that additional investments are required over the near term for information technology, capital needs, and security. The overall implications are that achieving the important goal of an effective overseas presence will require a net investment in certain overseas activities of the U.S. Government.

Implementing the Report

The Panel believes that this report will help create an opportunity for the Federal Government to focus on the critical importance of its overseas missions and the national interest in making needed institutional reforms. Because our overseas presence involves many agencies, only Presidential initiative, the Secretary of State's leadership, bipartisan Congressional support, and cooperation from other agencies and departments can bring about reform. Indeed, the government wide reforms that we propose in technology, right-sizing, training, security, and capital needs will occur only if the President and the Congress play an ongoing role in the effort to implement them.

- The President, by Executive order, should establish an implementation mechanism and enforce a timetable to achieve the reforms that require interagency procedures or White House initiative, such as right-sizing, improved technology, and security. The President should appoint a "Coordinator for Overseas Presence Reform" to manage those aspects of reform where Presidential leadership is needed. The Secretary of State should submit a list of candidates for appointment as the Coordinator. Each agency responsible for making internal reforms should establish a plan and a timetable for implementation. The President should submit to Congress those reforms requiring its approval.

- The Secretary of State, as the President's principal foreign policy adviser, should take the lead in the implementation process, thus enhancing the Secretary's role in coordinating U.S. foreign affairs. Building on existing statutory responsibilities for the location, security, and staffing of overseas facilities, the Secretary must be in the forefront of the new design for the U.S. overseas presence envisioned in the Report. Since the Department of State is the lead agency in our nation's overseas activities, it bears a special responsibility for leadership in carrying out many of the reforms.

- The Congress should take an active role in the implementation and oversight of the new design proposed in this report, authorizing the changes needed and appropriating the funds required to implement them.

We urge the President, the Secretary of State, and Congressional leaders to form a partnership and together embrace this opportunity to modernize and reshape the our country's overseas presence.

CLINTON ON THE FALL OF "THE WALL"
AND AN "ACTIVIST" FOREIGN POLICY
November 8, 1999

Frustrated by congressional opposition to many foreign policy initiatives, President Bill Clinton and his foreign policy advisors late in 1999 condemned what they called a new round of "isolationism" in America. Administration officials denounced the Republican leadership on Capitol Hill for blocking a key nuclear weapons treaty and cutting foreign aid programs. Clinton ultimately won much of the funding he wanted for foreign aid, but only after he exercised his veto power and agreed to put off some issues until 2000.

Republican leaders denied taking an isolationist approach to foreign affairs and said they simply had different viewpoints and priorities than the administration. Many observers also said the administration brought some problems on itself by failing to make a sustained and articulate case for its policies on Capitol Hill and with the public in general.

Battles on Capitol Hill

Clinton faced congressional opposition to his foreign policy initiatives throughout his presidency, and the disagreement became markedly more intense after Republicans took control of Congress in 1995. Even so, the president managed to win most of the important battles, including approval of the North American Free Trade Agreement with Canada and Mexico in 1993 and the expansion of NATO in 1998. (NAFTA, Historic Documents of 1993, p. 953; NATO expansion, Historic Documents of 1998, p. 912)

Disputes between Clinton and Congress over foreign affairs reached a climax in 1999 with the Senate's high-profile rejection of an international treaty banning all nuclear weapons test. The defeat of the treaty by Senate Republicans was one of the most humiliating foreign policy setbacks suffered by any president in modern times. At the same time, the treaty's rejection was a major victory for conservatives in Congress, most notably Jesse Helms, R-N.C., chairman of the Senate Foreign Relations Committee, who argued that Clinton had weakened American authority and power in the world. (Rejection of the test ban treaty, p. 600)

Rejection of the treaty took place in the context of Clinton's struggle to win congressional approval of a series of funding initiatives he said were essential to maintain U.S. leadership. The central issue involved foreign aid. The United States had been a major source of aid for developing and economically troubled countries ever since the close of World War II. Starting with the formation of the World Bank and International Monetary Fund in 1945, and running through the Marshall Plan and other programs, the United States had provided hundreds of billions of dollars for economic and military aid overseas. But foreign aid was never popular among the public at large or on Capitol Hill. Foreign aid consumed less than 1 percent of the federal budget, but opinion polls consistently showed that Americans believed it to be one of the government's biggest spending items; as a consequence, foreign aid invariably was a contentious issue in Congress.

Throughout his years in office, Clinton had battled, with limited success, to win congressional approval for his foreign aid requests. In January, J. Brian Atwood, head of the Agency for International Development, which administered direct U.S. aid to other countries, resigned with blunt language. He attacked the administration for allowing itself to be "pushed around too much" by Congress, which in turn had taken an "unconscionable" approach to the United Nations and other international agencies.

Largely because of the poisoned relations between Clinton and Congress, the annual battle over foreign aid during 1999 was more difficult than usual. Congress took the first step by sending Clinton a foreign aid bill (HR 2606) in October that slashed nearly $2 billion from Clinton's $14.9 billion initial request. That bill also failed to include another $1.8 billion that Clinton wanted to help Israel, Jordan, and the Palestinian Authority implement the 1998 Wye River peace agreement. Clinton vetoed that measure October 18, saying it backtracked on a half-century of America's "active engagement abroad." Clinton compared the congressional cutbacks in the foreign aid bill to the test ban treaty vote and said it "reflects an inexcusable and potentially dangerous complacency about the opportunities and risks America faces in the world today." (Middle east negotiations, p. 890)

Clinton's veto set off a round of negotiations in the closing days of the 1999 congressional session that ultimately gained him much of what he sought. Congress added $2.6 billion to its original aid bill, including the full $1.8 billion Clinton had requested for increased aid to Israel and its negotiating partners and about $500 million for traditional aid programs. Despite anxieties in Congress about political developments in Russia, Congress also gave Clinton most of the $1 billion he had requested for aid to Russia and other republics of the former Soviet Union. (Developments in Russia, pp. 909, 917)

If there was any foreign affairs issue less popular on Capitol Hill than foreign aid, it was the United Nations—a perennial target of conservatives worried about "world government" and the influence within the world body of countries such as China, India, and Cuba.

Congress for years had refused to appropriate the full extent of U.S. mandatory and voluntary payments to the UN and many of its constituent agencies, such as the UN Development Program and the World Food Program. By 1999 the UN calculated that Washington owed nearly $1.7 billion in back dues; the Clinton administration put the figure at closer to $1.1 billion. Clinton had made annual attempts to win congressional approval of the overdue funding but had been thwarted. Helms was the chief opponent, and he used his power as Foreign Relations Committee chairman to block the funding.

The matter threatened to reach a crisis point at the end of 1999 because, under UN rules, the United States would lose its voting rights in the UN General Assembly unless it began paying off its back debt. U.S. participation in the General Assembly carried no great weight in terms of world affairs, but the ouster of the United States from that body would have been a symbolically important embarrassment.

As with the foreign aid bill, Clinton used his veto power to extract congressional approval of UN funding in 1999. Congress ultimately approved payment of $926 million over a three-year period, as part of the fiscal 2000 spending bill for the Commerce, Justice, and State departments (PL 106–133). That figure included $819 million in direct payments to UN bodies and the forgiving of $107 million in debts that the UN owed to the United States. But Congress demanded important concessions from the UN, including a reduction of the U.S. share of the world body's overall budget to 20 percent, from the long-standing figure of 25 percent. Congress also reiterated 1994 legislation (PL 103–263) placing a 25 percent limit on the U.S. share of UN peacekeeping missions, down from a past figure of 31 percent. Senator Helms said the funding agreement "takes away all the United Nations' excuses" for failing to implement a series of management reforms Congress had demanded.

In approving the UN dues, Congress also forced Clinton to accept restrictions on U.S. funding of international family planning programs that he had long opposed. The restrictions mandated by Congress in 1999 barred any U.S. money going to organizations that performed abortions or that advocated access to abortions overseas.

The contrast between the world views from Capitol Hill and from the White House also was illustrated by the congressional handling of international programs to forgive debts owed by the world's poorest countries. Dozens of developing countries in Africa, Asia, and Latin America were struggling under gigantic debt burdens accumulated during the 1960s through 1980s, when they borrowed money to build roads and power plants and stimulate economic development. By the mid-1990s Clinton and other international leaders concluded that forcing these countries to pay back their debts would be counterproductive. At their annual summit meeting in June, leaders of the so-called G-7 economic powers agreed to forgive up to

701

$27 billion in government-to-government debts owed by twenty-six of the poorest countries. Under the plan, debt forgiveness would be contingent on each country pledging to use the money saved on debt payments to boost development programs, especially in education and health. In addition, "multilateral" financial institutions, including the World Bank and the International Monetary Fund, developed a plan to reduce another $50 billion in debt owed by poor countries resulting from lending by those institutions.

To carry out the U.S. portion of the plan, Clinton in September asked Congress to appropriate $1 billion—$600 million for the multilateral debt relief and $400 million to begin writing off debts owed directly to the U.S. government. Congress approved $123 million for bilateral debt relief but put off until 2000 consideration of Clinton's broader request. Under a last-minute agreement at the end of its session, Congress also agreed to allow the International Monetary Fund to use a complex procedure involving revaluing its gold holdings to forgive $3.1 billion in debt owed by poor countries.

Clinton's Call for Activism

In the midst of the foreign policy battles between the White House and Capitol Hill, Clinton and his chief aides launched a public relations campaign to explain the importance of the U.S. role in the world to the American public—and, not incidentally, to denounce congressional interference. Clinton's national security advisor, Samuel R. (Sandy) Berger opened the administration offensive October 21 with a speech to the Council on Foreign Relations in New York denouncing the "new isolationists" in Congress who had blocked the test ban treaty and who, he said, seemed to want to build "a fortified fence around America."

Two weeks later, on November 8, Clinton went before an audience at Georgetown University in Washington to celebrate the tenth anniversary of the fall of the Berlin Wall, an event he recalled as "one of the happiest and most important days of the twentieth century."

Appearing on the stage with Clinton were the prime ministers of the Czech Republic and the Slovak Republic, representing the millions of eastern Europeans who for two generations had lived behind concrete and steel barriers constructed by the Soviet Union and its allies. "Thank you America," Czech prime minister Milos Zeman told the audience.

Clinton said the determination of those who fought communist tyranny during the cold war needed to be matched with a determination to confront the challenges of the world after the cold war. But some Americans, he said, "believe America can and should go it alone, either withdrawing from the world and relying primarily on our military strength, or by seeking to impose our will when things are happening that don't suit us." Instead, he said, Americans "need to maintain the will to lead, to provide the kind of American leadership that for fifty years has brought friends and allies to our side, while moving mountains around the world."

Following is an excerpt from a speech delivered November 8, 1999, by President Bill Clinton at Georgetown University in Washington, D.C., marking the tenth anniversary of the fall of the Berlin Wall:

Today we celebrate one of history's most remarkable triumphs of human freedom: the anniversary of the fall of the Berlin Wall, surely one of the happiest and most important days of the 20th century.

For the young people, the undergraduates who are here who were, at that time, 9 or 10 years old, it must be hard to sense the depth of oppression of the communist system, the sense of danger that gripped America and the world. I still remember all of our air-raid drills when I was in grade school, preparing for the nuclear war as if, if we got in some basement, it would be all right. It, therefore, may be hard to imagine the true sense of exuberance and pride that the free world felt a decade ago.

So, today, I say to you, it is important to recall the major events of that period; to remember the role America was privileged to play in the victory of freedom in Europe; to review what we have done since; to realize the promise of that victory; and most important of all, to reaffirm our determination to finish the job—to complete a Europe whole, free, democratic, and at peace, for the first time in all of history.

Let's start by looking back a decade ago at Berlin. If the Soviet empire was a prison, then Berlin was the place where everyone could see the bars and look behind them. On one side of the wall lived a free people, shaping their destiny in the image of their dreams. On the other lived a people who desperately wanted to be free, that had found themselves trapped behind a wall of deadly uniformity and daily indignities, in an empire that, indeed, could only exist behind a wall, for, ever if an opening appeared, letting ideas in and people out, the whole structure surely would collapse.

In the end, that is exactly what happened in the fall of 1989. Poland and Hungary already were on the road to democracy. President Gorbachev of the Soviet Union had made clear that Soviet forces would not stand in their way. Then, Hungary opened its borders to the West, allowing East Germans to escape. Then the dam broke. Berliners took to the street, shouting, "We are one people." And on November 9th, a decade ago, the wall was breached. Two weeks later, the Velvet Revolution swept Czechoslovakia, started by university students, just like the undergraduates here, marching through Prague, singing the Czech version of "We Shall Overcome." Then, in Romania, the dictator [Nicolae] Ceausescu, fell in the bloody uprising. A little more than a year later, the Soviet Union itself was no more. A democratic Russia was born.

Those events transformed our world and changed our lives and shaped the future of the young people in this grand room today. Yes, the students of our era will still grow to live in a world full of danger, but probably—and hopefully—they will not have to live in fear of a total war in which millions could be killed in a single deadly exchange. Yes, America will still bear global responsibilities, but we will be able to invest more of our wealth in the welfare of our children and more of our energy in peaceful pursuits.

You will compete in a global marketplace, travel to more places than any generation before you, share ideas and experiences with people from every culture—more and more of whom have embraced, and will continue to embrace, both democracy and free markets.

How did all this happen? Well, mostly it happened because, from the very beginning, oppressed people refused to accept their fate. Not in Poland in 1981, when Lech Walesa jumped over the wall at the Gdansk Shipyard and Solidarity first went on strike; or in Czechoslovakia, during the Prague Spring of 1968. I was there a year and a half later as a young student, and I never will forget the look in the eyes of the university students then and their determination eventually to be free.

They did not accept their fate in Hungary in 1956, or even in St. Petersburg way back in 1920, when the sailors who had led the Soviet revolution first rose against their new oppressors. They did not accept their fate in any Soviet home where the practice of religion was preserved, though it was suppressed by the state; or in countless acts of resistance we have never heard of, committed by heroes whose names we will never know.

The amazing fact is that all those years of repression simply failed to crush people's spirits or their hunger for freedom. Years of lies just made them want the truth that much more. Years of violence just made them want peaceful struggle, and peaceful politics, that much more. Though denied every opportunity to express themselves, when they were finally able to do it they did a remarkable job of saying quite clearly what they believed and what they wanted: democratic citizenship, and the blessings of ordinary life.

Of course, their victory also would not have been possible without the perseverance of the United States and our allies, standing firm against the Iron Curtain and standing firm with the friends of freedom behind it. Fifty years ago, when all this began, it was far from certain that we would do that. It took determination—the determination of President Truman to break the blockade of the Soviet Union of Berlin; to send aid to Greece and Turkey; to meet aggression in Korea. It took the determination of all his successors to ensure that Soviet expansion went no further than it did.

It took vision—the vision of American leaders who launched the Marshall Plan, and brought Germany into NATO, not just to feed Europe or to defend it, but to unify it as never before, around freedom and democracy. It took persistence—the persistence of every President, from Eisenhower to Kennedy to Bush, to pursue policies for four decades until they bore fruit.

It took resources to bolster our friends and build a military that adversaries ultimately knew they could not match. It took faith to believe that we could prevail while avoiding both appeasement and war; that our open society would in time prove stronger than any closed and fearful society.

It took conviction—the conviction of President Reagan, who said so plainly what many people on the other side of the Wall had trouble understanding, that the Soviet empire was evil and the wall should be torn down; the conviction of President Carter, who put us on the side of dissidents and kept them alive to fight another day.

And it took leadership in building alliances, and keeping them united in crisis after crisis—and finally, under President Bush, in managing skillfully the fall of the Soviet empire, and the unification of Germany, and setting the stage for a Europe whole and free.

This was the situation, the remarkable situation that I inherited when I took office in 1993. The Cold War had been won. But in many ways, Europe was still divided—between the haves and have-nots; between the secure and insecure; between members of NATO and the EU, and those who were not members of either body and felt left out in the cold; between those who had reconciled themselves with people of different racial and religious and ethnic groups within their borders, and those who were still torn apart by those differences.

And so we set out to do for the Eastern half of Europe what we helped to do for the Western half after World War II—to provide investment and aid, to tear down trade barriers so new democracies could stand on their feet economically; to help them overcome tensions that had festered under communism; and to stand up to the forces of aggression and hate, as we did in the Balkans; to expand our institutions, beginning with NATO, so that a Europe of shared values could become a Europe of shared responsibilities and benefits.

Since then, there have unquestionably been some setbacks—some small and some great. Under communism, most everyone was equally poor. Now, some people race ahead, while others lag far behind. Former dissidents who once struggled for freedom are now politicians trying to create jobs, to fight corruption and crime, to provide basic security for people who are simply tired of having to struggle.

Most terrible of all have been the wars in the former Yugoslavia, which claimed a quarter-million lives and pushed millions from their homes. But, still, 10 years after the fall of the Berlin Wall, most of Europe is unquestionably better off—as these two leaders so clearly demonstrate.

Democracy has taken root, from Estonia in the north to Bulgaria in the south. Some of the most vibrant economies in the world now lie east of the old Iron Curtain. Russia has withdrawn its troops from Central Europe and the Baltics, accepted the independence of its neighbors—and for all its own problems, has not wavered from the path of democracy.

The armed forces of most every country, from Ukraine to Romania all the way to Central Asia, now actually train with NATO. NATO has three new allies—Poland, Hungary, the Czech Republic—three strong democracies that have stood with us in every crisis, from Iraq to Bosnia to Kosovo. Other new democracies are eager to join us as well, including Slovakia, and they know our alliance is open to all who are ready to meet its obligation. Eleven countries are beginning a process that will lead them to membership in the European Union.

And just as important, because we and our allies stood up to ethnic cleansing in Bosnia and Kosovo, the century is not ending on a note of despair with the knowledge that innocent men, women and children on the doorstep of NATO can be expelled and killed simply because of their ethnic heritage and the way they worship their God. Instead, it ends with a ringing affirmation of the inherent human dignity of every individual.

With our alliance of 19 democracies strong and united, working with partners across the continent, including Russia, to keep the peace in the Balkans. With new hope for a Europe that can be, for the first time in history, undivided, democratic and at peace. I hope all of you will be proud of what your country and its allies have achieved, but I hope you will be even more determined to finish the job, for there is still much to be done.

On Friday, I will leave on a trip to Greece and Turkey, Italy and Bulgaria. This trip is about reinforcing ties with some of our oldest allies, and completing the unfinished business of building that stable, unified, and democratic Europe. I believe there are three principal remaining challenges to that vision that we must meet across the Atlantic, and I might say one great challenge we must meet at home.

The first is the challenge of building the right kind of partnership with Russia—a Russia that is stable, democratic and cooperatively engaged with the West. That is difficult to do because Russia is struggling economically. It has tens of thousands of weapons scientists—listen to this—it has tens of thousands of weapons scientists making an average of $100 a month, struggling to maintain the security of a giant nuclear arsenal. It has mired itself again in the cruel cycle of violence in Chechnya that is claiming many innocent lives.

We should protect our interests in Russia, and speak plainly about actions we believe are wrong. But we should also remember what Russia is struggling to overcome and the legacy with which it must deal. Less than a generation ago, the Russians were living in a society that had no rule of law, no private initiative, no truth-telling—no chance for individuals to shape their own destiny. Now they live in a country with a free press, with almost 1 million small businesses, a country that should experience next year its first democratic transfer of power in a thousand years.

Russia's transformation has just begun. It is incomplete; it is awkward. Sometimes it is not pretty. But we have a profound stake in its success. Years from now, I don't think we will be criticized, any of us, for doing too much to help. But we can certainly be criticized if we do too little.

A second challenge will be to implement, with our allies, a plan for stability in the Balkans, so that region's bitter ethnic problems can no longer be exploited by dictators, and Americans do not have to cross the Atlantic again to fight in another war. We will do that by strengthening democracies in the region, promoting investment and trade, bringing nations steadily into Western institutions, so they feel a unifying magnet that is more powerful than the internal forces that divide them.

I want to say that again—I am convinced that the only way to avoid future Balkan wars is to integrate the countries of Southeastern Europe more with each other, and then more with the rest of Europe. We have to create positive forces that pull the people toward unity, which are stronger than the forces of history pulling them toward division, hatred and death.

We must also push for a democratic transition in Serbia. Mr. [Slobodan] Milosevic is the last living relic of the age of European dictators of the communist era. That era came crashing down with the Wall. He sought to preserve his dictatorship by substituting communist totalitarianism with ethnic hatred and the kind of mindless unity that follows if you are bound together by your hatred of people who are different from you. The consequences have been disastrous—not only for the Bosnians and the Kosovars, but for the Serbs, as well.

If we are going to make democracy and tolerance the order of the day in the Balkans, so that they, too, can tap into their innate intelligence and ingenuity and enjoy prosperity and freedom, there can be no future for him and his policy of manipulating human differences for inhuman ends.

A third challenge is perhaps the oldest of them all, and in some ways, perhaps the hardest—to build a lasting peace in the Aegean Sea region, to achieve a true reconciliation between Greece and Turkey, and bridge the gulf between Europe and the Islamic world.

When I am in Greece, I'm going to speak about the vital role Greece is playing and can play in Europe. The world's oldest democracy is a model to the younger democracies of the Balkans, a gateway to their markets, a force for stability in the region. The one thing standing between Greece and its true potential is the tension in its relationship with Turkey.

Greece and Turkey, ironically, are both our NATO allies, and each other's NATO allies. They have served together with distinction in the Balkans. Their people helped each other with great humanity when the terrible earthquakes struck both lands earlier this year. This is a problem that can be solved. Eventually, it will be solved. And I intend to see that the United States does everything we possibly can to be of help. When I go to Turkey, I will point out that much of the history of the 20th century, for better or worse, was shaped by the way the old Ottoman Empire collapsed before and after World War I, and the decisions that the European powers made in the aftermath.

I believe the coming century will be shaped in good measure by the way in which Turkey, itself, defines its future and its role today and tomorrow. For Turkey is a country at the crossroads of Europe, the Middle East and Central Asia; the future can be shaped for the better if Turkey can become fully a part of Europe, as a stable, democratic, secular, Islamic nation.

This, too, can happen if there is progress in overcoming differences with Greece—especially over Cypress; if Turkey continues to strengthen respect for human rights; and if there is a real vision on the part of our European allies, who must be willing to reach out and to believe that it is at Turkey where Europe and the Muslim world can meet in peace and harmony, to give us a chance to have the future of our dreams in that part of the world in the new millennium.

Now, the last challenge is one we can only meet here at home. We have to decide, quite simply, to maintain the tradition of American leadership and engagement in the world that played such a critical role in winning the Cold War and in helping us to win the peace over this last decade.

Think about it—we spent trillions of dollars in the Cold War to defeat a single threat to our way of life. Now, we are at the height of our power and prosperity. Let me just ask you to focus on this and measure where we are as against what has been happening in the debate about maintaining our leadership. We have the lowest unemployment rate in this country in 30 years, the lowest welfare rolls in 30 years, the lowest crime rates in 30 years, the lowest poverty rates in 20 years, the first back to back budget surpluses in 42 years, and the smallest federal government in 37 years. In my lifetime, we have never had—ever—as a people, the opportunity we now have to build the future of our dreams for our children.

In the early 1960s, we had an economy that closely approximated this, but we had to deal with the challenge of civil rights at home and also from the Vietnam War abroad. Today, we are not burdened by crisis at home or crisis abroad, and the world is out there, looking to see what we are going to do with the blessings God has bestowed upon us at this moment in time.

Everything else I said will either happen or not happen without American involvement unless we make up our minds that we are going to stay with the approach to the world that has brought us to this happy point in human history. That is the most important decision of all.

Now, what are we doing? Well, first, our military budget is growing again to meet new demands. That has to happen. But I want to point out to all of you, it is still, in real terms, $110 billion less than it was when the Berlin Wall fell. Everyone agrees that most of that money should be reinvested here at home. But don't you think just a small part of the peace dividend should be invested in maintaining the peace we secured and meeting the unmet challenges of the 21st century?

Look at all the money we spent at such great cost over the last 50 years. The amazing fact is we are not spending a penny more today to advance our interest in the spread of peace, democracy and free markets than we did during the 1980s. Indeed, we are spending $4 billion less each year.

I think it's worth devoting some small fraction of this nation's great wealth and power to help build a Europe where wars don't happen, where our allies can do their share and we help them to do so; to seize this historic opportunity for peace between Arabs and Israelis in the Middle East; to make sure that nuclear weapons from the former Soviet Union don't fall into the wrong hands; to make sure that the nuclear scientists have enough money to live on and to feed their families by doing constructive, positive things so they're not vulnerable to the entreaties of the remaining forces of destruction in the world; to relieve the debts of the most impoverished countries on Earth, so they can grow their economies, build their democracies and be good, positive partners with us in the new century; and to meet our obligations to and through the United Nations, so that we can share the burden of leadership with others, when it obviously has such good results.

I think most Americans agree with this. But some disagree—and it appears they are disproportionately represented in the deciding body. Some believe America can and should go it alone, either withdrawing from the world and relying primarily on our military strength, or by seeking to impose our will when things are happening that don't suit us.

Well, I have taken the stand for a different sort of approach—for a foreign affairs budget that will permit us to advance our most critical priorities around the world. That's why I vetoed the first bill that reached my desk; why I'm pleased that Democrats and Republicans in Congress worked together last week on a strong compromise that meets many of our goals. But we're not finished yet. We still must work to get funding for our United Nations obligations and authorization to allow the use of IMF resources for debt relief.

This is a big issue. It has captured public attention as never before. I mean, just think about it: This issue for debt relief for the millennium is being head-lined by the Pope and Bono, the lead singer for U2. That is very broad base of support for this initiative. Most of the rest of us can be found somewhere in between our pole-star leaders there.

But it's not just a political issue. It is the smart thing to do. If you go to Africa, you see what competent countries can do to get the AIDS rate down, to build democratic structures, to build successful economies and growth. But we have to give them a chance. And the same is true in Latin America, in the Caribbean, in other places. This is a big issue.

I hope the bipartisan agreement we reached over the weekend on the for-eign affairs budget is a good sign that we are now moving to reestablish and preserve the bipartisan center that believes in America's role in the new post-Cold War world.

In the coming year, we have an ambitious agenda that also deserves bipar-tisan support. We have about 100 days to meet the ambitious timetable the leaders of the Middle East have set for themselves to achieve a framework agreement. We have to secure the peace in the Balkans. We have to ease ten-sions between India and Pakistan. We have to help Russia to stabilize its economy, resolve the conflict in Chechnya, and cheer them on as they have their first democratic transfer of power, ever.

We have to bring China into the World Trade Organization, while continu-ing to speak plainly about human rights and religious freedom. We have to launch a new global trade round in African and Caribbean trade bills, press ahead with debt relief, support the hopeful transitions to democracy in Nige-ria and Indonesia, help Colombia defeat the narco traffickers, contain Iraq and restrain North Korea's missile program. We have to continue to do more to fight terrorism around the world. And we must do what is necessary—and for the young people here, I predict for 20 years this will become a national security issue—we have to do more to reverse the very real phenomenon of global warming and climate change.

To meet those challenges and more, we simply must hold on to the quali-ties that sustained us throughout the long Cold War; the wisdom to see that America benefits when the rest of the world is moving toward freedom and prosperity; to recognize that if we wait until problems come home to Amer-ica before we act, they will come home to America.

We need the determination to stand up to the enemies of peace—whether tyrants like Milosevic or terrorists like those who attacked our embassies in

Africa. We need faith in our own capacity to do what is right, even when it's hard—whether that means building peace in the Middle East or democracy in Russia or a constructive partnership with China. We need the patience to stick with those efforts for as long as it takes, and the resources to see them through.

And, most of all, we need to maintain the will to lead; to provide the kind of American leadership that for 50 years has brought friends and allies to our side, while moving mountains around the world.

Years from now, I want people to say those were the qualities of this generation of Americans. I want them to say that when the Cold War ended, we refused to settle for the easy satisfaction of victory, to walk home and let our European friends go it alone. We did not allow the larger prize of a safer, better world to slip through our fingers.

We stood and supported the Germans as they bravely reunified, and supported the Europeans as they built a true union and expanded it. We stood against ethnic slaughter and ethnic cleansing. We stood for the right kind of partnership with Russia. We acted to try to help Christian and Jewish and Muslim people reconcile themselves in the Middle East, and in the bridge represented by Turkey's outreach to Europe. I want them to say that America followed through, so that we would not have to fight again.

A few months ago, my family and I went to a refugee camp full of children from Kosovo. They were chanting their appreciation to the United States, thanking America for giving them a chance to reclaim their lives. It was an incredibly moving event, with children who have been traumatized far beyond their ability even to understand what has happened to them, but who know they have been given a chance to go home now.

Years from now, I believe the young people in this audience will have a chance to go to Europe time and time again, and you will, doubtless, meet some of those children. Or, maybe some of the young people who actually tore down the Berlin Wall, or marched in the Velvet Revolution. They will be older then. I hope they will say, when I was young I sang America's praises with my voice, but I still carry them in my heart. I think that will be true if America stays true. That is what we ought to resolve to do on the anniversary of this marvelous triumph of freedom.

NASA INVESTIGATION INTO THE LOSS OF THE *MARS CLIMATE ORBITER*
November 10, 1999

Dramatic back-to-back failures of two missions to Mars in September and December forced the National Aeronautics and Space Administration (NASA) to admit embarrassing mistakes in program management and to undertake a fundamental reassessment of its interplanetary missions. Officials said the reassessment might cause delays in missions to Mars planned for 2001 and later in the decade. NASA's approach to interplanetary missions had itself resulted from an earlier reassessment following the failure of the $1 billion Mars Observer *mission in 1993.*

The first failure of 1999 came on September 23, when a $125 million spacecraft, the Mars Climate Orbiter, *disappeared as it was descending into orbit around the red planet. An investigation later determined that the mission had been doomed from the start because of a simple misunderstanding over measurement of the spacecraft's engine power. The investigation also uncovered numerous management shortcomings, some resulting from inadequate funding.*

The second failure occurred early in December when the Mars Polar Lander *disappeared as it was descending to the Martian surface. Numerous attempts to establish radio contact with the spacecraft failed, and NASA officials presumed that it had crashed or become dysfunctional. Two probes that were supposed to accompany the* Polar Lander *also disappeared on that $165 million mission. NASA created two review boards to determine the cause of the* Polar Lander *failure.*

In each case, the mission failure was remarkably similar to the fate of the Mars Observer, *which stopped sending signals as it approached the planet in August 1993. The* Mars Observer *was never heard from again, and scientists never fully explained its disappearance beyond conjecturing that a rupture in a fuel line may have caused the craft to lose control. That mission cost $1 billion, and its loss was a devastating blow to NASA's Martian program. That failure led directly to NASA's strategy of using several lower-cost missions to carry out specific tasks, in effect spreading the risks of failure.*

The "smaller, better, cheaper" approach—as NASA administrator Dan Goldin called it—worked with two other Mars missions launched in the 1990s. The Pathfinder *and* Sojourner, *its roving vehicle on the surface, collected geological samples in 1997. The* Mars Global Surveyor *was taking photographs of the planet's surface from orbit; its mission was to look for evidence of water. (*Pathfinder *and* Sojourner *missions,* Historic Documents of 1997, *p. 509)*

*NASA faced difficulties in other programs during 1999, two of which were of the old-fashioned big-ticket variety. The International Space Station, NASA's showcase project involving cooperation with Russia and key European countries, was over budget and behind schedule, largely because of Russian failure to deliver key components. A space shuttle mission to repair the Hubble space telescope was delayed several times past its scheduled launch in October and ultimately was pushed into 2000. An orbiting telescope called the Wide-Field Infrared Explorer (WIRE) lost a protective cover and was destroyed shortly after it was launched in March because of a design flaw. (*Hubble problems, *Historic Documents of 1995, p. 288; space station launch,* Historic Documents of 1998, p. 929)*

Many space experts outside NASA said the problems that arose in 1999 demonstrated that the space agency—under budget pressure from the Clinton administration and Congress—had cut corners when it reduced the cost of its missions. The concept of building more spacecraft at a lower unit cost was sound, they said, but the execution went too far in the direction of paring expenses. "There's a balance between science return, acceptance of risk, and cost reduction," John M. Logsdon, director of the Space Policy Institute at George Washington University told the New York Times. *"Those have gotten out of balance, with too much emphasis on cost reduction."*

In their public statements, most senior NASA officials denied that their programs had been endangered by the low-cost approach. But in announcing a total reassessment of interplanetary missions, the space agency leadership in effect was acknowledging fundamental flaws in the planning and execution of those missions.

Climate Orbiter

Launched in December 1998, the Climate Orbiter's *mission was to examine weather patterns on Mars. The spacecraft also was supposed to serve as a communications relay station, sending messages from the* Polar Lander *crafts back to Earth.*

Early in the morning of September 23 (eastern standard time), the Climate Orbiter *approached the northern hemisphere of Mars, fired its main rocket engine to slow its descent, and then—as planned—went behind Mars, interrupting radio contact with NASA monitors. The spacecraft should have reappeared within a few minutes, but it never did. As the hours ticked by, NASA flight controllers checked and rechecked their data and finally determined that the* Climate Orbiter *had flown closer than planned to the Martian surface and probably had been destroyed.*

Investigations quickly turned up the embarrassing explanation that a misunderstanding over measurements caused the system failure. Engineers at Lockheed-Martin Aeronautics Corporation in Denver, which built the craft, used the Anglo-American measurement of "pounds" to measure the thrust of the Climate Orbiter's *engines; NASA scientists and flight controllers, on the other hand, assumed the measurements were calculated in the metric unit called "newton"—as NASA's contract with Lockheed-Martin required.*

The resulting miscalculations went undetected for months but had a fatal consequence. Throughout its journey to Mars, the course of Climate Orbiter *repeatedly had to be corrected, and when the craft went into a descent to enter an orbit of Mars, it went dangerously off course. Investigators determined that the* Climate Orbiter *descended to within about twenty-seven miles of the planet's surface, far below the ninety-three miles that had been planned, and about sixteen miles below the minimum altitude the craft was built to be able to survive.* Mars Climate Orbiter *simply burned up as it got too close to the Martian surface.*

A review panel appointed by NASA, called the Mars Climate Orbiter Mishap Investigation Board, conducted an investigation into the entire Climate Orbiter *mission. The first phase of that panel's report, made public November 10, confirmed that the critical mistake in measuring engine thrust, calling that lapse the "root cause" of the mission failure. Even more worrisome, the investigators said, was NASA's failure to catch the mistake during the months of planning and execution of the mission. In their report, the investigators said they had uncovered management lapses and misjudgments "that allowed this error to be born and then let it linger and propagate to the point where it resulted in a major error in our understanding of the spacecraft's path as it approached Mars." The investigating panel found eight "contributing causes" that reinforced the original error, among them lack of communication among various staff departments, inadequate staffing of the flight-control team, and inadequate training at several levels.*

One target of the investigation was the Jet Propulsion Laboratory in Pasadena, California, the agency with direct responsibility for managing interplanetary missions. The world famous laboratory had perhaps become too lax in its approach to managing such missions, the investigators found. After thirty years of sending spacecraft to Mars and other distant targets, the investigators said, employees at the laboratory shared "a widespread perception that 'orbiting Mars is routine.' " This perception resulted in inadequate attention to "navigation risk mitigation." The panel made sixteen recommendations for management improvements to prevent similar problems in the future.

Edward Weiler, the associate administrator of NASA for space science, summarized the investigation findings in one sentence: "We need more people asking what can go wrong."

Polar Lander *Failure*

Just ten weeks after the failure of the Climate Orbiter, *NASA had the sickening experience of hearing that something else had gone wrong. On December 3—eleven months after its launch—the* Polar Lander *began its descent to the Martian surface to begin a mission of examining atmosphere and soil. Aboard the* Polar Lander *were two small robot probes, collectively called Deep Space 2, that were to jump off the spacecraft just before landing, dig into the Martian soil, and send their findings back to Earth.*

In mid-afternoon December 3, eastern standard time, the Polar Lander *was to send a report to Earth signaling that the descent had gone smoothly. But no report came. NASA flight controllers offered various explanations and made numerous attempts over the next several days to establish contact—but to no avail. Immediate attention was focused on potential problems with the* Polar Lander *mission that had been noted by the team investigating the* Climate Orbiter *failure. In particular, the investigators had warned that NASA's plan to have all twelve "thrust" engines fire at the same time during the descent was risky and had never been tried before. NASA officials said most of the problems noted by the investigators had been fixed by the time the* Polar Lander *reached Mars.*

Early in the morning of December 7, NASA issued a statement saying that mission officials "hold out very little hope" of reestablishing communication with the Polar Lander *or the Deep Space 2 probes. Subsequent attempts later in December also failed.*

Attempting to put the best face on a second successive failure, project manager Richard Cook, of the Jet Propulsion Laboratory, noted the difficulty and complexity of the mission but said those involved were determined to press ahead. "We hope people, and children in particular, will see from this experience that the mark of a great person, or group of people, is the ability to persevere in the face of adversity," he said in a statement.

A Reassessment

NASA's senior managers apparently decided that persevering might require a totally new approach to interplanetary exploration. Later on December 7, NASA administrator Goldin told reporters: "Clearly, something is wrong, and we have to understand it. It is conceivable that we will completely change our approach." Goldin also said that NASA would undertake a far-reaching review, even if that meant delays in two Mars missions that had been planned for March and April 2001. "Everything is on the table, and we're not going to just go rushing off, build a spacecraft just to meet an arbitrary deadline," he told the Associated Press.

Goldin made it clear that one option was not under consideration: building enormously expensive spacecraft for interplanetary exploration, such as the failed Mars Observer. *"We ain't going back to multibillion dollar spacecraft that take a decade to build and launch," he said. "If you lose a spacecraft like we lost* Mars Observer, *you lose a whole generation of sci-*

entists." NASA's science chief, Weiler, said the combined failure of the 1999 missions was a "wake up call and we are going to respond to it." The New York Times *quoted John C. Beckman, head of the systems division at the Jet Propulsion Laboratory as saying: "We fell into cutting too many corners."*

Scientists and space experts outside NASA agreed that budget-cutting had fundamentally endangered the Mars programs. "It is not as though the people at JPL [the Jet Propulsion Laboratory] have suddenly developed an attack of the stupids," John Pike, director of space policy for the Federation of American Scientists, told the Los Angeles Times. *"You get what you pay for and we are trying to do it on the cheap. Space is enormously unforgiving, the most unforgiving environment there is. You can't fudge it in space."*

Looming on the horizon for NASA was the annual budget cycle in Congress during 2000, an election year. Congressional committees that oversaw the NASA budget planned special hearings on the failure of the Mars missions, and it appeared likely that Goldin—who had developed broad political support on Capitol Hill—might face an uphill battle in winning enough money to continue his agency's Mars exploration programs.

Following is the text of the executive summary from the "Phase I" report by the Mars Climate Orbiter Mishap Investigation Board, released November 10, 1999, in which an investigative panel of senior NASA engineers and scientists assessed the causes of the failure on September 23, 1999, of the Mars Climate Observer *mission:*

This Phase I report addresses paragraph 4.A. of the letter establishing the Mars Climate Orbiter (MCO) Mishap Investigation Board (MIB) (Appendix). Specifically, paragraph 4.A. of the letter requests that the MIB focus on any aspects of the MCO mishap which must be addressed in order to contribute to the Mars Polar Lander's safe landing on Mars. The Mars Polar Lander (MPL) entry-descent-landing sequence is scheduled for December 3, 1999. . . .

The MCO Mission objective was to orbit Mars as the first interplanetary weather satellite and provide a communications relay for the MPL which is due to reach Mars in December 1999. The MCO was launched on December 11, 1998, and was lost sometime following the spacecraft's entry into Mars occultation during the Mars Orbit Insertion (MOI) maneuver. The spacecraft's carrier signal was last seen at approximately 09:04:52 UTC on Thursday, September 23, 1999.

The MCO MIB has determined that the root cause for the loss of the MCO spacecraft was the failure to use metric units in the coding of a ground software file, "Small Forces," used in trajectory models. Specifically, thruster performance data in English units instead of metric units was used in the software application code titled SM FORCES (small forces). A file called Angular Momentum Desaturation (AMD) contained the output data from the SM FORCES software. The data in the AMD file was required to be in metric units per existing software interface documentation, and the trajectory modelers assumed the data was provided in metric units per the requirements.

During the 9-month journey from Earth to Mars, propulsion maneuvers were periodically performed to remove angular momentum buildup in the on-board reaction wheels (flywheels). These Angular Momentum Desaturation (AMD) events occurred 1014 times more often than was expected by the operations navigation team. This was because the MCO solar array was asymmetrical relative to the spacecraft body as compared to Mars Global Surveyor (MGS) which had symmetrical solar arrays. This asymmetric effect significantly increased the Sun-induced (solar pressure-induced) momentum buildup on the spacecraft. The increased AMD events coupled with the fact that the angular momentum (impulse) data was in English, rather than metric, units, resulted in small errors being introduced in the trajectory estimate over the course of the 9-month journey. At the time of Mars insertion, the spacecraft trajectory was approximately 170 kilometers lower than planned. As a result, MCO either was destroyed in the atmosphere or re-entered heliocentric space after leaving Mars' atmosphere.

The Board recognizes that mistakes occur on spacecraft projects. However, sufficient processes are usually in place on projects to catch these mistakes before they become critical to mission success. Unfortunately for MCO, the root cause was not caught by the processes in-place in the MCO project.

A summary of the findings, contributing causes and MPL recommendations are listed below. . . .

Root Cause

Failure to use metric units in the coding of a ground software file, "Small Forces," used in trajectory models.

Contributing Causes

    1. Undetected mismodeling of spacecraft velocity changes
    2. Navigation Team unfamiliar with spacecraft
    3. Trajectory correction maneuver number 5 not performed
    4. System engineering process did not adequately address transition from development to operations
    5. Inadequate communications between project elements
    6. Inadequate operations Navigation Team staffing
    7. Inadequate training
    8. Verification and validation process did not adequately address ground software

MPL Recommendations

- Verify the consistent use of units throughout the MPL spacecraft design and operations

- Conduct software audit for specification compliance on all data transferred between JPL and Lockheed Martin Astronautics
- Verify Small Forces models used for MPL
- Compare prime MPL navigation projections with projections by alternate navigation methods
- Train Navigation Team in spacecraft design and operations
- Prepare for possibility of executing trajectory correction maneuver number 5
- Establish MPL systems organization to concentrate on trajectory correction maneuver number 5 and entry, descent and landing operations
- Take steps to improve communications
- Augment Operations Team staff with experienced people to support entry, descent and landing
- Train entire MPL Team and encourage use of Incident, Surprise, Anomaly process
- Develop and execute systems verification matrix for all requirements
- Conduct independent reviews on all mission critical events
- Construct a fault tree analysis for remainder of MPL mission
- Assign overall Mission Manager
- Perform thermal analysis of thrusters feedline heaters and consider use of pre-conditioning pulses
- Reexamine propulsion subsystem operations during entry, descent, and landing.

CLINTON AND WAHID ON RENEWAL OF DEMOCRACY IN INDONESIA
November 12, 1999

Indonesia, the world's fourth most populous nation, experienced its first taste of democracy in forty-four years during 1999. The result was a clear break from a string of dictatorships aligned with the military and a victory for moderate political forces. Voters in June elected a new national parliament, which in turn named a moderate Islamic cleric, Abdurrahman Wahid, as president in October. Wahid outmaneuvered a competing figure among the groups that had opposed the government—Megawati Sukarnoputri, daughter of Indonesia's founding leader, Sukarno. Megawati's party had won a plurality in the elections, but she was unable to put together a majority coalition in parliament. She accepted the position of Wahid's vice president, instead.

The transition to democracy in Indonesia took place with remarkable speed. A student-led rebellion in 1998 exposed the hollow core of the long-time dictatorship of President Suharto, forcing him out from power. Suharto's hand-picked successor, B. J. Habibie, proved to be a weak figure, but he did set the stage for the free elections in 1999. (Suharto resignation, Historic Documents of 1998, p. 284)

The election of Wahid had the potential to give Indonesia a new kind of stability. A large country sitting astride key trading lanes between the Pacific and Indian oceans, Indonesia long had been a regional power under Suharto's strong-arm rule. With the renewal of democracy Indonesia could focus sustained attention on reviving its troubled economy and finding peaceful resolutions to ethnic and regional conflicts that had long been suppressed by the Suharto dictatorship.

The most visible of those conflicts came to a conclusion during the year, although far from peacefully. The people of East Timor voted in August in favor of independence from Indonesia, an outcome that led to two weeks of bloody attacks by anti-independence militia groups aligned with the Indonesian military. An international outcry forced Indonesia to retreat from East Timor, and the United Nations moved in with a massive peace-

keeping operation intended to put the region on the road to full indepen-dence. (East Timor, p. 511)

Wahid met with President Bill Clinton in Washington on November 12. Clinton praise Wahid and said the United States would support his effort to "build democracy" in Indonesia.

Putting Democracy in Place

When he took over from Suharto in May 1998, Habibie promised to hold free elections within a year, and he was able to keep his promise June 7, 1999. The voting went very smoothly for a country of 216 million people, spread over 13,700 islands, that had not experienced truly free elections in two generations. Thousands of domestic election monitors and some 500 international observers reported few serious irregularities and little violence.

Forty-eight political parties participated in the election, contesting 462 seats in the National Assembly. Another thirty-eight seats were to be filled by the military. Together with 200 additional representatives of groups such as labor unions and farmers, the assembly was to name a new presi-dent and vice president.

Collecting and tabulating election results from the far-flung Indonesian archipelago took more than a month. The final results, announced July 15, showed that Megawati's party, the Indonesian Democratic Party of Strug-gle, had won a plurality with 34 percent of the vote, and the long-time rul-ing party headed by Habibie, Golkar, had finished second with 22 percent. Wahid's National Awakening Party was a distant third.

Wahid at first supported Megawati for president, but withdrew his back-ing when she hesitated to enter into the coalition building needed to form a working majority in advance of the convening in October of the newly elected parliament. Megawati announced in July that she had a "mandate" to form a government and seemed to expect other politicians to fall in line behind her. When they failed to do so—or when she rejected overtures they made to her—Megawati lost much of the political support she needed to win the presidency. By contrast, Wahid was a skilled coalition builder who had developed a loyal following based on his independence from traditional power centers, such as the military and big business.

In the meantime, a banking scandal led to the temporary suspension of $4.7 billion in international loans to Indonesia. Jakarta, the capital city, also experienced a day of rioting late in September when the outgoing par-liament enacted a security bill that critics feared would lead to the imposi-tion of martial law.

Election of Wahid

When the new parliament convened in October, one of its first orders of business was to hear a state of the nation report from Habibie. The acting president fumbled this one opportunity to build support for his candidacy for a full term in office. For nearly a week afterward opposition leaders took turns deriding Habibie for exhibiting weak leadership.

Habibie then suffered two blows. First, the powerful head of the military, General Wiranto, announced that he had declined an invitation from Habibie to run as vice president, a move widely interpreted as signaling the military's abandonment of Habibie. Then, in a close vote October 19, the parliament rejected Habibie's state of the nation address, effectively voting no confidence in him. Habibie immediately withdrew his candidacy, saying he had concluded that "many sons and daughters of Indonesia can do the job better than I have done."

The next day, October 20, Wahid emerged as the winner of backroom negotiations among the eleven factions in the assembly. Wahid defeated Megawati 373–313, with 5 abstentions. The election provoked angry demonstrations by Megawati's supporters, who had expected her to win the presidency, but she called for "the people of Indonesia to accept the results." Wahid then backed Megawati as his vice president, and she was elected October 21.

In his brief inaugural address, Wahid called for national unity, noting that "the ties that bind us as a nation are unraveling." Wahid also called on Indonesians to deepen their commitment to democracy, which he said "can be sustained and developed only by people who understand its essence. This is the only way to uphold sovereignty, justice, freedom of expression and equal treatment for all, irrespective of blood, language, culture, and faith."

The election of Megawati as vice president had more than symbolic importance. Wahid, fifty-nine at the time of his inauguration, was nearly blind and frail from a stroke; it was widely assumed that he might not be able to serve the full five years of his presidential term, much less the second term allowed by law. If Wahid died or resigned because of illness, Megawati would take his place and presumably would have a solid base of support stemming from her party's first-place finish in the elections.

Wahid announced October 26 what he called a "national unity" cabinet reflecting a broad range of the country's political spectrum. It included four holdovers from the Suharto era, among them the military leader, General Wiranto, who was demoted from the post of defense minister but was given a new position as minister for political and security affairs. Wahid appointed a former education minister, Juwono Sudarsono, as defense minister; he was the first civilian to hold the post in many years. Wahid also named several moderate Islamic leaders to key cabinet posts. Several observers said the cabinet offered Wahid short-term backing for his goal of stability, but the competing range of personalities and viewpoints contained the seeds of possible discord in the future.

During his first two months in office Wahid came under some criticism for allowing too much freedom. Many observers, including some political allies, said Wahid had given his cabinet ministers free rein and was failing to exercise decisive leadership.

Reviving the Economy

Aside from holding his country together, Wahid's major challenge was to spur economic regrowth after nearly two years of stagnation caused by the

Asian financial crisis of 1997–1998. Under Suharto, Indonesia had one of the most corrupt economies on the planet. Suharto's relatives and friends dominated major business sectors, thwarting competition, discouraging foreign investment, and distorting the country's economic development.

The new government moved quickly to reassure the international community about its dedication to cleaning up corruption. On November 2 the government turned over to the International Monetary Fund (IMF) an audit report on the banking scandal that had plagued Habibie during his last months in office. The audit examined the transfer of nearly $80 million from the Bank Bali, a large private bank that was nationalized by the government in June, to other banks associated with Suharto's old ruling party. The $80 million had come from funds that were supposed to be used to reform the Indonesian economy under the terms of a $43 billion bailout arranged in 1998 by the IMF and its sister institution, the World Bank. Those institutions had frozen lending to Indonesia, saying it could be resumed only when the audit was released and those responsible for diversion of the $80 million were prosecuted.

During his visit to Washington in November, Wahid said he had decided to pardon Suharto if the former leader was convicted of corruption. He said he feared that Suharto's followers might move to "topple the cart," an apparent reference to the possibility of a military coup should Suharto be thrown in jail for corruption.

Independence Movements

The first major crisis of Wahid's presidency came quickly, early in November, when rebels in Aceh, a province on the island of Sumatra, escalated their long-standing demands for independence and were joined at a rally November 8 by a half-million people. Wahid himself fanned the separatist flames with a remark indicating support for a referendum on independence in the territory, which had rich reserves of oil and natural gas. Antigovernment violence had been a serious problem in Aceh since the late 1980s and had claimed thousands of lives. A military raid on independence backers in mid-July resulted in the deaths of forty-three people.

Unlike East Timor—which was never recognized by the international community as a legitimate part of Indonesia—Aceh had clearly been under Indonesian jurisdiction, even though it had been promised autonomy at the time of Indonesian independence. Many Indonesian leaders and outside observers said allowing Aceh to secede almost certainly would encourage separatist movements in other regions, possibly leading to the "unraveling" of Indonesia that Wahid warned about in his inaugural address and undermining regional stability.

As the number of violent incidents in Aceh grew during November, Wahid apparently rethought his support for an independence referendum. He told fellow leaders November 28 at a summit meeting of the Association of Southeast Asian Nations that he would not support such a referendum. General Wiranto announced December 6 that the government had agreed to give Aceh greater autonomy, and Wahid said Aceh citizens could vote on whether to impose Islamic law in the province, but not on independence.

Other independence moves were underway in Irian Jaya (on the western half of New Guinea island) and on the island of Sulawesi. Sectarian violence also erupted at year's end in the Moluccas, the eastern Indonesian islands formerly known as the Spice Islands.

Following are excerpts from a news conference held November 12, 1999, in Washington, D.C., by President Bill Clinton and the newly elected Indonesian president, Abdurrahman Wahid:

President Clinton: Let me say, it's a great honor for me and for all of our team to welcome President Wahid here, with the members of his government. He is now the leader of the world's third-largest democracy, and we are very encouraged by that. We have seen this peaceful transition in Indonesia; we've seen a resolution in East Timor, even though there's still the problem of refugees in West Timor. And I'm looking very much forward to this visit.

I think the American people know that a strong and stable and prosperous and democratic Indonesia is very much in our interest. That's the sort of partnership we're interested in pursuing, and I hope I can be helpful in that regard.

So I'm delighted to have you here, Mr. President. And if you'd like to make any public comment to the press while you're here—

President Wahid: Well, thank you for putting a little time for me today to visit you, Mr. President, because you know that I come from Indonesia just to make sure that we are still great friends of the United States, that we are still in good touch with you. And I think that in the future, we meet you more than before. So also that you know that although there is a shift in policy, but not at the expense of the American-Indonesian relationship. This is very important to know, since you understand that this is one world, so we have to create that kind of one world.

And I'm interested in the comment you made about our religious dialogue, which goes toward one world, in that sense. You see, from far away we heard that you made very nice comments on those inter-religious dialogues in Indonesia. And I hope that two months to come, in January, we'll have a discussion initiated by the Americans from Philadelphia, with the Foreign Minister to be a participant there, to be on the organizing committee. We will invite, of course, chief rabbi of Israel as well as the—former chief rabbi. And from here, from the Catholic side and so forth, I don't know who will come. But anyway, around 50 people will come there, of the three Abrahamic traditions.

And since, you know, that kind of thing is special for us in Indonesia, I would like to use this occasion to inform you about this, before anything else—economic things. Those are the troubles there.

So I'm very glad. Today I met people from the World Bank and the IMF and then from the Ex-Im Bank, in which we see the possibility of having more hands extended towards us, to help us to overcome the difficulties in the economic shape, now.

Well, you mentioned about East Timor. I think that, of course, we still have trouble, and we would like the United States to take attention to this kind of problem as well. But I would like to inform you, Mr. President, that—will come to Jakarta, and I'll meet him. So I hope that will ease a little bit the situation in that area, because East Timor is, you know, our brothers.

President Clinton: Thank you very much. That's very good news.

Question: President Wahid, sir, President Wahid, sir, why are you inclined to be willing to pardon your predecessor, President Suharto? And President Clinton, what do you think of the possibility of a pardon for him?

President Wahid: I think if we—we will use law, of course. And we would like to know whether he is guilty or not, according to the law. But after that, we will pardon him because of two reasons. First is that he was our President, so we have to be careful about this for the future generations. Second thing is that, you know, that it's not easy, because Mr. Suharto still has big followers. So we have to be careful not to, let's say, topple the cart.

President Clinton: I think the decision, first of all, is one for the Indonesian people and government to make. And I think every country has to decide how to resolve the tension between the pursuit of a particular case and the desire for the reconciliation of people, and to go forward. And I think that that's a decision that the President has to make, and we ought to support his—anything that he's trying to do to build democracy and to take Indonesia into the future.

Question: Mr. President, after this meeting will you resume military assistance to Indonesia?

President Clinton: Well, we're going to talk about that, and about what kinds of things that we both can do, over a period of time, to strengthen our relationships, including the issue of military-to-military ties. And I look forward to talking to the President about that.

Question: How important is the structural integrity—the territorial integrity of Indonesia? And is it more important than the self-determination of the peoples of Indonesia?

President Clinton: Well, I don't think it has to be an either-or thing. I think the—I said, at the time when Indonesia supported giving the East Timorese a vote, that I would support that, and that having given them the vote, that the vote had to be respected.

On the other hand, we support the territorial integrity of Indonesia. And I think we have to acknowledge that it's quite a challenging task to preserve a democracy so widespread and so diverse. And I hope we can be somewhat helpful to the President dealing with this challenge. . . .

ANNOUNCEMENT ON U.S.-CHINA BILATERAL TRADE AGREEMENT
November 15, 1999

Negotiators for the United States and China on November 15, 1999, signed what appeared to be the most important bilateral trade agreement in decades. Intended to normalize trade between the two countries and pave the way for China's entrance into the World Trade Organization (WTO), the agreement was expected to help boost flagging efforts to modernize the Chinese economy. Over the long haul, leaders of both countries expressed hope that the accord would stabilize the often rocky relations between the world's most powerful country and its most populous one.

Most commentators said the agreement represented more than just a technocratic bargain over arcane trade issues, such as tariffs on corn or regulations for business investment. Rather, they said, the accord was a major step toward cooperation and away from confrontation between Washington and Beijing on key global issues.

"This is a profound and historic moment," U.S. Trade Representative Charlene Barshefsky said after signing the agreement in Beijing.

The accord foreshadowed significant changes for China, still struggling to bring its centrally controlled, inefficient economy into a new world of globalization. In signing the agreement, Chinese leaders pledged to dismantle complex protections that had been carefully assembled around the country's state-run industries, exposing them to the brisk winds of international competition and, not incidentally, improving their prospects for attracting international investment and expertise. The theory in both Beijing and Washington was that China would speed up its modernization, and American business would play a significant and profitable role.

The potential economic impact was substantial. As of 1999 the United States had a trade deficit with China of about $35 billion, largely because of American consumer demand for cheap clothing and electronics from China. Once China opened its huge market to U.S. competition, economists and policymakers expected that trade imbalance would gradually shift.

Washington's policymakers hoped for, but were careful not to promise, an additional outcome: a modernized China would become a more open and democratic China, one less likely than in the past to challenge U.S. interests around the globe. Among its key provisions, the trade deal required China to open its mass media, including Internet access, to foreign investment—and mass media had long been a bulwark of the communist regime's hold on power.

But even under the best of circumstances it would take years for key provisions of the agreement to have an impact on global trade. American business leaders expressed concern that Chinese bureaucrats responsible for day-to-day decisions would undermine provisions of the accord, as they often had with previous agreements on narrow trade issues.

Analysts warned of numerous obstacles to the potentially rosy scenario that underpinned the trade agreement. An open Chinese market could prove incapable of facing global competition, perhaps forcing Beijing's leaders to back off their economic reforms just to keep millions of workers employed and off the streets. Disputes between the United States and China over diplomatic and security issues—most notably the future of Taiwan—could worsen and send the bilateral relationship back to the frosty days of the cold war. There was no immediate evidence to support the Clinton administration's hope that economic reform eventually would lead to a parallel opening in China's political system. The Chinese leaders appeared to have calculated that modernizing the economy would, over the long haul, enhance their prospects of holding onto power.

Finally, President Bill Clinton faced the possibility that Congress would block the trade agreement when it reached Capitol Hill in 2000. Labor leaders were mobilizing against the accord because of China's suppression of labor unions, and some conservatives automatically opposed agreements containing any hint of concessions to Beijing's communist rulers. Clinton's political influence on trade issues had been weakened since 1998, when the House killed a move to extend his so-called fast-track authority to negotiate bilateral trade agreements and then submit them to Congress for approval without amendment. The collapse in December of a WTO meeting in Seattle that was supposed to initiate a new round of global talks on trade rules also threatened to undermine Clinton's case for the China deal. (WTO meeting, p. 797)

Negotiating the Deal

As part of his long-term strategy of modernizing his country's economy, Chinese leader Deng Xiaoping began pressing in the mid-1980s for membership in the General Agreement on Tariffs and Trade, the predecessor to the WTO. Deng was the first of China's communist leaders to open his country to foreign investment. Under his reforms, companies from the United States and other industrialized countries provided capital and expertise for free-market enterprises in limited geographic and market sectors of China.

Talks on China's global trade status began in 1986 but were halted after Beijing's crackdown on democracy protesters in Tiananmen Square in 1989. The negotiations later resumed but sputtered along with little progress until President Jiang Zemin—Deng Xiaoping's successor—visited the United States in 1997 for the first bilateral U.S.-China summit since Tiananmen Square. Throughout the process, a trade deal between the United States and China was seen as the key to China's membership in the WTO. (Tiananmen Square demonstrations, Historic Documents of 1989, p. 275; Jiang visit, Historic Documents of 1997, p. 728)

The negotiations finally made serious progress in April 1999 when Prime Minister Zhu Rongji, generally considered the architect of Chinese economic reforms, visited Washington intending to strike a deal. Zhu offered dramatic concessions on several contentious issues and clearly expected some return movement on the American side. But Clinton hesitated to seize the moment and suggested that the time was not ripe for an agreement. News organizations later reported that Clinton's senior advisors were divided on the wisdom of striking a deal, largely for domestic political reasons. The administration at the time was under fire from Capitol Hill for its handling of investigations into China's alleged theft of nuclear secrets from U.S. weapons laboratories. In addition, Clinton was still smarting from Republican charges that his 1996 reelection campaign had improperly taken donations from business interests with ties to the Chinese government. (Election finance allegations, Historic Documents of 1997, p. 822; China nuclear issue, p. 235)

A frustrated Zhu left Washington without an agreement. The New York Times *later reported that Zhu's failure to get a trade deal undermined his political standing back in Beijing. Clinton administration officials quickly realized that the president's rebuff of Zhu had been a mistake.*

Relations spiraled downward May 7, 1999, when U.S. bombers inadvertently destroyed the Chinese embassy in Belgrade during NATO's eleven-week air war to force the former Yugoslavia to withdraw from Kosovo. Three Chinese journalists died and twenty-seven other embassy residents were wounded in the attack. China angrily denounced the attack and rebuffed all explanations that the bombing had been a mistake. U.S.-Chinese relations went into a deep freeze until the end of July when Washington agreed to pay $4.5 million to compensate the survivors and the families of those killed in the embassy bombing. (Embassy bombing, p. 304)

Later in the summer and into the fall, the two sides took tentative steps toward an agreement, and by November Clinton was pressing hard for a deal. Barshefsky and Gene Sperling, Clinton's economic advisor, flew to Beijing on November 8. After a series of tense meetings—including several threats by Barshefsky to leave if no progress was made—Zhu personally intervened in the talks November 13. The two sides then reached a deal, which they announced and signed November 15.

Key Provisions

The essence of the agreement was that China would open its economy to investment and trade from other countries, including the United States. In return, Washington would reduce tariffs and gradually eliminate quotas that had curtailed Chinese exports of low-cost goods to the United States.

Perhaps the most dramatic elements of the accord dealt with foreign investment in China's financial and telecommunications industries, which had been strictly controlled by the communist regime. Beijing agreed to allow foreign banks to offer services in China within two years, and foreign companies could purchase one-third of the shares in Chinese financial industries, such as insurance (that figure would rise to 49 percent over a period of years). Foreign companies also could purchase up to 49 percent of the shares in Chinese telecommunications companies; that figure would rise to 50 percent within two years. In addition, China agreed to allow foreign investments in companies providing Internet services there. China also agreed to allow increased imports of foreign automobiles and movies.

Under the agreement, China's tariffs on imports of industrial goods would drop from an average of 22 percent to 17 percent, and then lower in later years. China also agreed to reduce tariffs on agricultural imports to 15 percent on average and to eliminate government subsidies of food exports. These provisions were expected to be of special benefit to American wheat, corn, rice, and cotton farmers who had previously been unable to crack the Chinese market. Another potentially significant feature required China to allow foreign companies to distribute and provide service for the goods they sold there, rather than having to go through government-controlled marketing channels.

In addition to permanently reducing tariffs on Chinese imports, the principal U.S. concessions concerned protections against "unfair competition" from China. By 2005 the United States would eliminate quotas on imports of Chinese textile products, but Washington retained safeguards against below-market textile imports for up to nine years. Within fifteen years the United States would eliminate general "antidumping" provisions to block massive waves of low-cost Chinese goods intended to undersell U.S. producers.

Political Outlook

President Clinton said he would present the China agreement to Capitol Hill in 2000 and called on Congress to approve it, as it was in the "best interests" of the United States. Technically, Congress would not vote on the actual agreement but on whether the United States should extend normal trade relations to China—a status China had been prohibited from receiving because of its communist form of government.

Since 1980 Congress had approved an intermediate step called "most favored nation" trade privileges that reduced tariffs on imports of Chinese goods but retained other restrictions on bilateral trade. One restriction was that Congress had a right each year to vote on the president's determination to extend that status. Even though Congress had never rejected a presidential determination, the procedure provided an annual forum for members of Congress to denounce China on human rights and other issues.

The debate for 1999 occurred July 27 in the House, which rejected, 270-160, a move to overturn China's trading benefits. That tally was nearly identical to a similar vote the year before. As in the past, some liberal

727

Democrats and conservative Republicans joined to oppose the trade bene-fits, while moderates in both parties provided the bulk of support.

The debate in Congress on the China trade deal in 2000 was expected to pit big business against big labor, with organizations specializing in human rights, the environment, consumer protection, and other issues tending to side with labor. By and large, major business organizations expressed enthusiasm for the trade agreement, saying it would open the Chinese market to American investment and imports of agricultural and industrial products from the United States.

John J. Sweeney, president of the AFL-CIO, said organized labor would fight to block the agreement because of China's record on labor rights. "It is disgustingly hypocritical for the Clinton White House to invoke the need to 'put a human face on the global economy' while prostrating itself in pur-suit of a trade deal with a rogue nation that decorates with human rights abuses as if they were medals of honor," Sweeney said. The "human face" quote was a reference to the administration's contention that the pay and treatment of workers should be a significant consideration in negotiating global trade arrangements.

> *Following is the text of a communiqué issued November 15, 1999, in Beijing by the governments of the United States and China following the signing of a bilateral trade agreement between the two countries; the communiqué is followed by excerpts from a news conference in Beijing held by Charlene Barshefsky, the United States trade representative, and Gene Sperling, President Bill Clinton's economic advisor:*

COMMUNIQUÉ ON TRADE AGREEMENT

From 10th to 15th November 1999, the Chinese Government Delegation headed by Mr. Shi Guangsheng, Minister of Foreign Trade and Economic Cooperation of the People's Republic of China, and the United States' Government Delegation headed by Ambassador Charlene Barshefsky, U.S. Trade Representative and Mr. Gene Sperling, Director of the National Economic Council of the United States of America, held negotiations in Beijing on the issue of China's accession to the World Trade Organization. The two sides signed on November 15th the Bilateral Agreement Between the Government of the People's Republic of China and the Government of the United States of America on China's Accession to the World Trade Organization.

The two delegations have noted that both the Chinese and U.S. governments and their leaders, Presidents Jiang Zemin and Bill Clinton, have attached great importance to the talks, not only for its commercial importance, but also for its importance to the global economy and long term strategic significance. We believe this agreement benefits both China and the United States.

The signing of the aforementioned agreement by China and the United States will help accelerate the process of China's accession to WTO and the development of China-U.S. economic cooperation and trade relations. The two sides are looking forward to close cooperation in the WTO in the future so as to help ensure the sound development of China-U.S. relations and the prosperity of the world economy.

NEWS CONFERENCE REMARKS

Charlene Barshefsky: Let me just make a couple of general comments: I think this is a profoundly important agreement for a number of reasons. As a trade agreement it obviously protects American Commercial interests and enhances significantly America's commercial interests. The agreement itself is absolutely comprehensive. It covers all goods, all services, all of agriculture. It covers a variety of rules with respect to import surges, technology transfers, state trading enterprises, and high dumping, investing, subsidies and other issues.

Second, however, this is an agreement that is fully consistent with China's own policy of economic reform and economic development. And in that regard it will exert a positive effect on the very reforms China itself is trying to make, and of course on the very economic process at which China has been quite successful. This will open markets here. It will improve the efficiency of Chinese companies. It will make them ever more competitive. I think that is a critical point.

Third, this agreement will strengthen the Rule of Law in China. And I think actually, this is the most import aspect of this agreement. The WTO [World Trade Organization] is a rules-based trading regime. It encompasses almost 140 nations. And the rules, the base rules on transparency, no discrimination, judicial review, administrative independence are absolutely critical to the functioning of the modern economy.

And the notion that China will become a member of this rules based regime is of extraordinary long term importance, not only on the commercial side, but with respect to the development of a more full body and robust legal system within China.

And of course, it goes without saying that this agreement will help to strengthen China's relations with its neighbors, will help to further stabilize the economic situation in the region here, and of course will contribute to global prosperity. The ultimate aim of the global trading system. And last, . . . this agreement is an anchoring agreement, and in that regard in particular it is of both profound and historical importance.

The United States and China have had a rather tumultuous relationship as you know—ups and downs and lots of swings. But an agreement of this sort—with its breadth, with its scope, with it emphasis on Rule of Law, in its consistency with China's own internal reform process—can help to anchor the relationship between the United States and China in a most a fundamental way. And from that anchor, I think other good things will emerge, and greater stability in the overall relationship between the two countries will likewise emerge. . . .

Gene Sperling: As Ambassador Barshefsky said this is bigger than a trade agreement; it's about the U.S.-China relationship. It's about the future of the global economy. It's about an increasing trend of countries that have been outside of the global, rule-based trading system coming within it and becoming part of a truly open, free flowing, international economy that we believe will lead to greater freedom and greater global prosperity. We truly praise the President and leadership in China, President Jiang and Premier Zhu for putting the long-term U.S.-China relationship above short-term political expediency. This will be difficult politically for everyone involved, but it is the right thing for the U.S. economy. It is the right thing for Chinese economic reform, and it's the right thing for the future of the global economy. . . .

Let me just make one more comment before opening up to questions. We know that now we will have to make the case in the United States that this is a strong and good agreement. It resolves many of the unresolved issues from the past in a positive way. We feel that it will be very strong for U.S. export-related jobs and for some of the most important export industries in the United States, as well as being a win for Chinese economic reform and Chinese consumers. However, we will throughout the Administration put out an all out effort to work with the Congressional leadership of both parties to pass permanent normal trading relations status through the Congress. We don't expect it to be easy but we expect that when people see this deal, see the agreement and understand the importance of this for the US-China relationship and the future of the global economy, they will understand that this is in our nation's interest. Thank you.

Question: . . . We are writing the lead stories from here but we haven't received any details and it's very hard to write from the press releases which are extremely vague. I'm wondering if there's some way that you can leave behind or give us tonight more details? My question now is if Ms. Barshefsky could describe what were the main points of negotiation during the last six days and some details about how they were resolved?

Barshefsky: Let me give you just some general detail on the overall agreement and then talk about the resolution of some of the unresolved issues from last Spring. These are just a few quick-hit facts.

With respect to overall tariffs. Overall tariff levels on average will decline to about seventeen percent. This is an extremely good figure. With respect to agriculture, tariffs will decline sharply to roughly fourteen and-a-half or fifteen percent. In that range, there will be very significant liberalization in the agriculture sector including, most importantly, with respect to the bulk commodities: corn, wheat, cotton, soy beans. What we view as the big-ticket items. China will also not provide export subsidies. This is very important in the fields of cotton, rice, and some other areas. There will be what's called a tariff rate quota system set up in agriculture. This is a sort of the WTO mode of doing things. This will significantly enhance market access across the board, not only for bulk commodities but all the specialty agricultural products.

On industrial goods, China will grant essentially full trading rights and distribution rights; the right to import and export directly without Chinese middlemen and to market through distribution, wholesale and retail, after sale service, repair, maintenance, transport—the entire range of distribution related services.

With respect to non-tariff barriers, China will eliminate all quotas and all quantitative restrictions. Everything I'm talking about is generally done well within five years, except in a very few cases, and in many of these areas we complete the phase-outs in two to three years. So this is an extremely strong agreement.

With respect to services. We've covered the full range of services: banking, securities, telecom, as I said, distribution, the professions, tourism, travel, transport and so on and so forth. This is just an extremely comprehensive and a very, very strong agreement.

Let me talk a little bit about the resolution of some of the unresolved issues as well as a couple of changes in the agreement. We have tried to be sensitive to concerns that China had on issues that were very difficult for China last spring in particular, while at the same time maintaining the fundamental interests of the United States. I think we have achieved an overall strengthening of this agreement. I will say in that regard we've always taken the position, very consistently for almost seven years, that the only basis on which we could do an agreement would be a commercially sound one. We've never departed from that. This agreement will pass any such test that could possibly be applied.

Two of the most important unresolved issues from last Spring had to do with special rules on import surges and on the application of a particular anti-dumping methodology called the "non-market economy" methodology. Last spring, China took the view that there must be a very restrictive phase-out of these provisions. We certainly agreed with China at that time, that these provisions should not exist in perpetuity, but we believed that they did need to exist for a reasonable period of time. With respect to what was called the "special safeguard rule" which is an anti-import surge rule into the United States, that provision will exist for 12 years. With respect to the application of the "special anti-dumping" methodology, that provision will exist for 15 years. With respect to the anti-dumping methodology, our laws and regulations do provide for the graduation of sectors or an economy as a whole, from these rules if it can demonstrate that it has become market-oriented. And as we've indicated to the Chinese of course, to the extent that they request review of individual sectors, or the economy as a whole, we will do that under the bounds of our law.

Additional issues outstanding last Spring included, for example, audio-visual issues, most especially motion pictures, and that issue has been resolved by the agreement by China to allow for the importation of motion pictures on a revenue-sharing basis. This is extremely important, not only to our industry but to the industry in Europe, Canada and elsewhere. This is quite unprecedented.

With respect to telecom, we also clarified distribution issues on audio-visual, which were unclarified last spring, and that is the right to form joint ventures for distribution for videos and sound recordings and that has now been secured.

With respect to a critical banking issue, and that was the issue of auto finance. China has now agreed to allow non-bank, and it's the non-bank hat's most critical. Foreign financial institutions can provide auto-financing from the date of accession.

What we've done here—because the auto sector is very important, and we have learned from many mistakes in the way which autos have been handled in Japan, over the course of many decades—is that we have put together a very substantial auto package. To do that we agreed with China to extend to 2006 rather than 2005, the phase-down of auto tariffs in China from 80-100 percent to 25 percent. In exchange for the longer phase-out, which was important to China, we have cut tariffs more rapidly in the earlier years than under our previous understanding, because now that we have auto-finance from the date of accession, we want to insure the maximum market access— which means lower tariffs up front, the auto finance from the date of accession, and of course, we have full distribution rights as well as trade rights in that sector. This is very, very important to the United States with respect to autos.

On the question of securities, our main goal had been to insure that the Treasury Department in particular would have a forum in which to consult with China on the development of its securities market, which, as you know, is very underdeveloped. While China typically turned to Hong Kong regulators for advice, and of course they are excellent regulators, we and particularly the Treasury Department, were very anxious to be able to participate in this kind of formulation of regulations and the development of capital markets generally in China, including with respect to market access in the future. You know from Larry Summers' trip here that a capital markets dialogue has now been established to cover the totality of banking issues as well as securities and regulatory issues.

With respect to telecommunications. There was some ambiguity as to coverage of the Internet from last spring. This has now been fully covered. This is terribly important for the development of the Chinese economy as well as for basic access for foreign telecommunications suppliers. In addition, we have clarified further commitments on satellites and we're pleased that we now have full coverage for satellites in the context of telecommunications.

Last, textiles. China has agreed to the incorporation in full of our bilateral textiles agreement. This is a nine-year, pre-existing agreement. Textile quotas would expire in 2005, consistent with WTO rules, but there would be an additional four years after that of a special anti-surge safeguard mechanism to insure a more orderly transition to open trade in textiles with respect to China.

Last, with respect to telecom. Originally, our conception on telecom had been quite limited. Inward investment in telecom culminating in 51 percent four or five years down the road. The 51 percent issue was a very significant issue for China. What we have done instead is to allow for 49 percent investment by foreign telecom providers in China from date of accession. This is very significant and unprecedented. Moving to 50 percent in the second year after accession. And as you know under Chinese law, contractual management and operational participation is possible in a 50/50 situation. Here again, we tried to balance a particular sensitivity of China with the absolute commercial interests of the United States, leading to an overall strengthening of the commitments particularly in terms of earlier access at a much greater level than previous contemplated.

In all of these instances, we have, I think, affected very much a win/win for the United States and China. For example, on autos where a longer phase-in was important to China because somewhat greater earlier access became important to us, in getting auto finance, we balanced our interests, and China was able to secure longer phase-in and we were able to secure tariff cuts much more consistent with the auto financing package. We've done the same in telecom and in a few other areas. We are extremely pleased with the outcome, not just because it favors the United States, but because of the way we were able to balance the interests between the United States and China in a way that strengthened both of us with respect to the overall package. Basically, the rest of the package is as you know it to be. As I said, the test for us has always and consistently been a very strong commercial agreement consistent with China's export capability and its status as one of the world's largest economies and by any measure we have achieved that goal.

Question: I need two quick clarifications. Internet, did you specifically talk about . . . whether Internet content providers, whether they can invest in China?

Barshefsky: Yes. Yes. Yes. No longer an issue. We have rights of investment. We clearly considered that Internet access issues, considering what will be the dramatic growth not only of the Internet worldwide but as you can imagine in China, to be one of the big economic issues for our country. So securing that and making the Internet issues clear and secure were a top priority for us.

Question: And retail banking, U.S. or foreign participation and the percentages.

Barshefsky: . . . Let me just go through the general commitments. Foreign banks will be able to conduct local currency business with Chinese enterprises two years after accession. Foreign banks will be able to conduct local currency business with Chinese individuals five years from accession. Foreign banks will have the same rights as Chinese banks within the various geographic areas, in other words national treatment. This was absolutely critical. Both geographic and customer restrictions will be completely removed in five years.

Branching of course will be permitted. I think those are the major commitments, along with securing the auto finance. With respect to securities, where China has a very underdeveloped market, this is. The capital market dialogue was absolutely critical because of the under-developed and under-regulated nature of Chinese securities markets. What we have done in securities is to, at the present time, have minority, foreign-owned joint ventures able to engage in fund management on the same terms as Chinese firms. As the scope of business expands for Chinese firms, foreign joint ventures will enjoy the same expansion in the scope of business. Again, this national treatment issue is very, very important. Minority joint ventures will also be able to underwrite domestic securities issues and underwrite trade in foreign currency denominated securities, both debt and equity. That, coupled with the Summers' capital markets dialogue as necessary regulation as developed and expanded will go hand in hand within further expansion and market access both for Chinese securities firms as well as US securities firms.

Question: What's the minority stake?

Barshefsky: For the fund management companies it will be initially 33 percent going up to 49 percent in three years. For the securities companies that engage in underwriting it is 33 percent. . . .

UNITED NATIONS REPORT ON THE FALL OF SREBRENICA
November 15, 1999

Four years after a peace agreement reached in Dayton, Ohio, ended Europe's worst conflict since World War II, the guns were still silent in Bosnia-Herzegovina—but peace remained the only significant accomplishment there. Despite a massive international presence of peacekeepers and aid workers, and the expenditure of billions of dollars, most of the people in Bosnia were little better off in 1999 than they had been at the end of the three-and-a-half year war. Few refugees had been able to return to their homes, the economy was still in ruins, and the three ethnic communities that had killed each other with guns were still fighting in just about every other way.

All during 1998 and 1999, the ethnic conflict in nearby Kosovo had shifted international attention away from Bosnia. But a grim reminder of Bosnia's horrific war—and the international community's failure to deal with it—came in November with the release of an extraordinary United Nations report chronicling the single greatest disaster in that war: the Serbian massacre of thousands of Muslim men and boys in Srebrenica in July 1995. UN Secretary General Kofi Annan acknowledged that the world body failed to protect the people of Srebrenica, as it had promised to do when it declared the town a "safe haven." (Bosnia peace agreement, Historic Documents of 1995, p. 717; war in Kosovo, Historic Documents of 1998, p. 827; bombing of Kosovo, p. 134)

The report on Srebrenica was the first of two damning admissions of failure from the UN in 1999. On December 16 Annan released another report acknowledging that failures by the UN and its member nations— most notably the United States—prevented an effective response against the slaughter of an estimated 800,000 people in Rwanda in 1994. (Rwanda report, p. 861)

The Struggle for Recovery

The structure of the Dayton peace agreement was still in place in 1999: Bosnia was divided into two zones, one controlled by Croats and Muslims *(called the "federation") and the other controlled by Serbs. The three communities were represented in a joint presidency that, in theory, established national policy in coordination with a United Nations High Representative (UNHR), who had the authority to impose and implement laws. A NATO peacekeeping force composed of about 60,000 armed troops kept the once-warring factions apart. Hundreds of aid workers from UN agencies and other international organizations were attempting to reconstruct a civil society. By 1999 the aid effort had cost more than $5 billion.*

Journalistic reports and investigations by outside observers all painted a grim picture of Bosnia in 1999. Croats, Muslims, and Serbs—who before the war had lived together in relative harmony—remained divided by wartime barriers in separate enclaves. Hard-line politicians who had led their communities during the war remained the true source of power, and Serbian leaders who had been indicted by a UN war crimes tribunal remained at large. Politicians and civic officials at the local level constantly obstructed the efforts of UN officials to develop the institutions of a civil society.

A strongly worded report issued October 28, 1999, by the International Crisis Group, chaired by former U.S. senator George Mitchell, said Bosnia was heading away from the Dayton agreement's promise of a unified country. The country "has three de facto mono-ethnic entities, three separate armies, three separate police forces, and a national government that exists mostly on paper and operates at the mercy of the entities," the report said. Only the Muslim community clearly supported the peace process envisioned by the Dayton agreement, the report said. The Croats and Serbs seemed to be "prepared to wait until such a time as the international community withdraws and the agreement can be laid to rest." The report suggested that the best solution to Bosnia's woes might be to make it a UN "protectorate"—in essence taking all decision-making power out of the hands of the local leaders who had created the war.

Journalists reported that the people of Bosnia remained stunned by the war. Unemployment in most areas of the country stood at about 50 percent, and the only steady jobs were with the international aid agencies. Thousands of people wounded in the war, civilians as well as fighters, could not work even if there were jobs for them. Tens of thousands of refugees were still unable to return to their homes, in most cases because their towns and villages had been taken over by members of a different ethnic community. Sarajevo, the capital, once was a vibrant city where Muslims, Croats, and Serbs lived together. By 1999 nearly all the Croats and Serbs were gone, their apartments occupied by Muslims driven out of their homes elsewhere in Bosnia. According to one estimate only 20 percent of the residents of Sarajevo were natives.

Corruption, which had been a way of life under the communist Yugoslav regime that governed Bosnia for two generations after World War II, remained a dominant factor in the economy. The New York Times *on August 17 published an account of "widespread corruption," based on the unpublished findings of the UNHR's office. The newspaper said that "as much as a billion dollars" had disappeared from public funds or had been stolen from aid projects. The report generated an international storm of protest, including from the U.S. State Department, which disputed some details of the report and expressed concern that it would undermine support for aid to Bosnia. But the UNHR's office later said the essence of the newspaper's report was correct and that its publication had focused needed attention on a serious problem.*

Richard C. Holbrooke, the American diplomat who had chaired the negotiations leading to the Dayton agreement, acknowledged the failures of the peace process during a special UN Security Council session November 15. Holbrooke said the root problem was the continuing determination of ethnic leaders in Bosnia—along with the Serb leaders of the Yugoslav government in Belgrade—to "obstruct" UN efforts to rebuild Bosnia as a unified society. Even so, he said, the international community had a responsibility to continue its work in Bosnia.

Holbrooke, who had become the U.S. representative to the United Nations, spent six hours on November 14 closeted in his New York apartment with the three members of the Bosnian presidency and won grudging acceptance for a document he called the "Declaration of New York," made public November 15. That declaration proposed several steps toward a unified Bosnian state, including establishment of a state border service, a national passport, and a joint staff for the three-member presidency. Holbrooke said he hoped the declaration represented a commitment by the leaders "to removing the remaining obstacles to the full implementation" of the Dayton agreement.

Fall of Srebrenica

On the same day that Holbrooke and the three Bosnian leaders issued the New York declaration, Secretary General Annan released one of the most revealing documents in the half-century history of the United Nations: an account of the UN's failure to protect Bosnian Muslims in the enclave of Srebrenica. Srebrenica, and the villages surrounding it, had been among several Bosnian areas that the UN had declared in 1993 to be "safe havens" where civilians could escape the war under the protection of armed UN forces, called UNPROFOR (UN Protection Force). Srebrenica was occupied primarily by Muslims but was located in an area of eastern Bosnia, near the border with Serbia, that was under Serbian control. The local unit of UNPROFOR consisted of 150 Dutch soldiers armed with rifles, machine guns, and several armored personnel carriers.

Annan's report described in detail the events leading to the fall of Srebrenica in July 1995 to the Bosnian Serb army and the immediate massacre there of thousands of Bosnian Muslim men and boys. UN investigators later recovered about 2,500 bodies, and the International Committee of the Red Cross said it had compiled the names of 7,336 who were missing from Srebrenica.

A UN war crimes tribunal indicted the two Bosnian Serb leaders held responsible for the massacre, as well as other atrocities during the war: political leader Radovan Karadzic and General Ratko Mladic, the head of the Bosnian Serb army. The tribunal in 1999 also indicted Yugoslav president Slobodan Milosevic and four key aides for war crimes committed during 1998 and 1999 in Kosovo, a province of Serbia within the federation of Yugoslavia.

In the months before the attack on Srebrenica, UN officials—both in the region and back at headquarters in New York—debated whether to bolster the military capability of UNPROFOR. The ultimate decision was against such a move. The UN Secretary General at the time, Boutros Boutros-Ghali, and his aides feared any step that might provoke additional Serb attacks on UN forces and argued that UN members were unlikely to provide enough troops to make any difference in the security situation. Boutros-Ghali also inveighed against allowing the United Nations to become a part of what he called the "culture of death" in Bosnia.

The UN decision left the small Dutch peacekeeping force and the Muslim population in Srebrenica vulnerable to a concerted Serb attack. An attack came with little warning early in the morning of July 6. Serb infantry and tanks, backed by heavy artillery, attacked the positions of both UNPROFOR and local Muslim military units.

Over the next five days Serbian units moved progressively against UN positions, apparently probing to determine how much resistance they would encounter. The Dutch commander on the scene repeatedly asked his superiors to call on NATO warplanes to attack the advancing Serbs. Most of his requests were denied by UN officials or were lost somewhere along the chain of command. Faced with a heavily armed force of at least 2,000 Serbs, the Dutch offered little resistance to the Serbs, never firing a shot directly at them. Serb forces entered Srebrenica early on the afternoon of July 11, virtually unopposed.

Thousands of Muslim civilians fled the Serb advance and moved into villages surrounding Srebrenica. An estimated 15,000 men and boys—about one-third of them armed—began heading on foot to Tuzla, another UN safe haven about thirty miles away, which required breaking through Serb lines and passing through minefields and over mountains. Of that group, only about 5,000 eventually made it to Muslim-held territory; at least 4,000 and possibly as many as 7,500 of the others were never accounted for.

As the Serbs were consolidating their hold on Srebrenica, NATO planes arrived on the scene and dropped two bombs on Serb positions. The Serbs then threatened to shell the town and kill some thirty Dutch troops they had captured; in response to that threat, UN authorities called off further air attacks on the Serb positions.

The Serbs began evacuating at least 20,000 women, children, and elderly men on July 12. An unknown number of those civilians were later killed or raped. The Serbs insisted that all remaining men between the ages of six-

teen and sixty stay behind. By this time the Dutch soldiers could do little more than observe events, to the extent the Serbs would allow them.

As the evacuations were underway, the Security Council met in emergency session and passed a resolution demanding that the Serbs end their offensive and withdraw immediately from Srebrenica. Several representatives expressed concern that the resolution would have little effect since the UN was not prepared to back up its demands with force. Among them, the representative of the Czech Republic said Security Council resolutions had become "paper tigers."

Beginning on the night of July 12, and continuing through the next day, the Serbs herded the Srebrenica men and boys into buses and trucks and sent them to the nearby town of Bratunac. There they were held in several locations, apparently waiting for mass killings. At some locations the men and boys were beaten, one by one. All together, the report said, an estimated 4,000–5,000 men and boys were held by the Serbs in Bratunac.

Among them were 299 men who had taken refuge in the Dutch compound; 239 of them had given their names to the Dutch soldiers. On Serb orders, the Dutch handed over those men on July 13. All 239 of those on the Dutch list "are still missing," the report said. Several of the Dutch soldiers later testified that they saw Serbs executing Bosnian men in small groups but said they had not directly seen killings on a mass scale.

Serb troops also ambushed the column of 15,000 men who were headed toward Tuzla, capturing and killing hundreds of them. In one particularly horrifying episode, several hundred fleeing men were forced into an agricultural warehouse in the town of Kravica and then attacked with small arms and grenades. Several months later, according to the report, UN personnel "were able to see hair, blood and human tissue caked to the walls of this building." One survivor hid under a pile of bodies and escaped; he later described the incident to the UN war crimes tribunal.

The Serbs began their "systematic extermination" of the Muslims held at Bratunac on July 14, the report said. The Muslims were shipped to several remote locations in the area of Bratunac and were killed by the hundreds over the next four days. In some cases, the men were beaten before they were shot; in other cases they were simply lined up and executed. Most of the bodies were thrown into mass graves or dumped in lakes and streams. Many of the victims were forced to dig their own graves. Most of the bodies were later moved to other locations.

The killings were later described by a handful of survivors and a Bosnian Croat soldier who served with the Serb forces. The soldier testified to the UN tribunal that he had no choice but to participate in the killings.

On July 15, as the killings were underway, senior UN officials—who at the time were unaware of the extent of the horror in the Srebrenica area—negotiated an agreement in Belgrade with Yugoslav president Milosevic, who was presumed to have influence over the Bosnia Serbs and Bosnian Serb general Mladic. Among other things, the agreement called for the safe return of the Muslims who had been forced out of Srebrenica and the pro-

*tection of all UN safe havens in Bosnia. The Serbs proceeded to ignore the
agreement, Annan's report said.*

*Public reports of atrocities in the Srebrenica area began to emerge July
17, based in part on accounts from some of the Dutch soldiers who had
been evacuated. UN officials in Bosnia on July 20 sent a preliminary statement to UN headquarters in New York expressing concern about "severe
human rights violations" after the fall of Srebrenica and speculating that
"as many as 3,000" people may have been killed.*

*As of the time of Annan's report, the UN war crimes tribunal had recov-
ered the remains of approximately 2,500 victims, of whom only about 30
had been identified. The International Committee of the Red Cross listed
7,336 people from Srebrenica as missing as of November 1999.*

After Srebrenica

*The emerging reports of atrocities in Srebrenica, coupled with the Serb
capture on July 25, 1995, of Zepa, another UN safe haven, belatedly moved
the international community to action. On July 25 and August 1 NATO
announced that it would launch air strikes if needed to thwart Serb attacks
on other UN safe havens, including Sarajevo. At about the same time, Croatian forces launched a massive and brutal assault (called "Operation
Storm") against the Bosnian Serbs in the southwest of the province, reliev-
ing Serbian pressure on the Muslim areas and forcing some 200,000 Serbs
in Croatia to flee their homes in terror.*

*NATO finally launched intense air strikes against Bosnian Serb targets
on August 30, in response to Serb shelling of Sarajevo. Those strikes, coupled with the success of the Croatian offensive, eventually encouraged the
Serbian leaders to become serious about peace negotiations that had flick-
ered on and off for years. A cease-fire was reached September 13, and in
November Holbrooke supervised the peace talks in Dayton leading to the
November 21 agreement on a peace plan for the future of Bosnia. Just before
Christmas, 1995, the first elements of a 60,000 member NATO peacekeeping
force entered Bosnia, taking the place of the failed UN mission.*

Assessing Blame for Srebrenica

*In his report on the events at Srebrenica, Annan acknowledged that there
were plenty of candidates for blame—starting, of course, with the Serb
leaders who ordered the attack on the town and the massacre of its male
inhabitants. But Annan said clearly that the UN failed to keep its promise
to protect the people of Srebrenica, and that failure held lessons for future
UN peacekeeping missions. Annan admitted that he was among the senior
UN officials responsible for the failure at Srebrenica; at the time he was the
undersecretary general in charge of peacekeeping. Responsibility also
must be shared by the UN Security Council and the member nations that
prevented a more decisive reaction to the events in Srebrenica, he said.*

*"Through error, misjudgment, and an inability to recognize the scope of
the evil confronting us, we failed to do our part to help save the people of*

Srebrenica from the Serb campaign of mass murder," Annan said. "The tragedy of Srebrenica will haunt our history forever."

The "cardinal lesson" of Srebrenica, Annan said, was that deliberate attacks on an entire people, such as the Serb assaults in Bosnia, "must be met decisively with all necessary means, and with the political will to carry the policy through to its logical conclusion." Throughout the war in Bosnia, and again in Kosovo, he said, the UN operated on the false premise that it could avoid using force and could reach a negotiated settlement "with an unscrupulous and murderous regime." In both cases, he said, only the use of force succeeded in stopping the killing.

Annan called for the international community to ensure that the failures of Bosnia and Kosovo are not repeated. "When the international community makes a solemn promise to safeguard and protect innocent civilians from massacre, then it must be willing to back up is promise with the necessary means," he said. "Otherwise, it is surely better not to raise hopes and expectations in the first place, and not to impede whatever capability they may be able to muster in their own defense."

Falling are excerpts from the "assessment" section of the report, "The Fall of Srebrenica," submitted November 15, 1999, to the United Nations General Assembly by UN Secretary General Kofi Annan, in which he reviewed the events leading to the 1995 massacre of thousands of Muslim men and boys in a Bosnian town the UN had promised to protect:

[The first ten sections of the report, comprising paragraphs 1 through 466, review the events leading to the capture of Srebrenica by Bosnian Serb forces and the subsequent massacre of several thousand Bosnian Muslim men and boys by those forces.]

XI. The Fall of Srebrenica: An Assessment

467. The tragedy that occurred after the fall of Srebrenica is shocking for two reasons. It is shocking, first and foremost, for the magnitude of the crimes committed. Not since the horrors of the Second World War had Europe witnessed massacres on this scale. The mortal remains of close to 2,500 men and boys have been found on the surface, in mass graves and in secondary burial sites. Several thousand more men are still missing, and there is every reason to believe that additional burial sites, many of which have been probed but not exhumed, will reveal the bodies of thousands more men and boys. The great majority of those who were killed were not killed in combat: the exhumed bodies of the victims show that large numbers had their hands bound, or were blindfolded, or were shot in the back or the back of the head. Numerous eyewitness accounts, now well corroborated by forensic evidence, attest to scenes of mass slaughter of unarmed victims.

468. The fall of Srebrenica is also shocking because the enclave's inhabitants believed that the authority of the United Nations Security Council, the presence of UNPROFOR [United Nations Protection Force] peacekeepers, and the might of NATO air power, would ensure their safety. Instead, the Bosnian Serb forces ignored the Security Council, pushed aside the UNPROFOR troops, and assessed correctly that air power would not be used to stop them. They overran the safe area of Srebrenica with ease, and then proceeded to depopulate the territory within 48 hours. Their leaders then engaged in high-level negotiations with representatives of the international community while their forces on the ground executed and buried thousands of men and boys within a matter of days.

469. Questions must be answered, and foremost among them are the following: how can this have been allowed to happen? and how will the United Nations ensure that no future peacekeeping operation witnesses such a calamity on its watch? In this assessment, factors ranging from the proximate to the overarching will be discussed, in order to provide the most comprehensive analysis possible of the preceding narrative.

A. Role of the United Nations Protection Force in Srebrenica

470. In the effort to assign responsibility for the appalling events that took place in Srebrenica, many observers have been quick to point to the soldiers of the UNPROFOR Netherlands battalion as the most immediate culprits. They blame them for not attempting to stop the Serb attack, and they blame them for not protecting the thousands of people who sought refuge in their compound.

471. As concerns the first criticism, the Commander of the Netherlands battalion believed that the Bosniacs [Bosnian Muslim military forces] could not defend Srebrenica by themselves and that his own forces could not be effective without substantial air support. Air support was, in his view, the most effective resource at his disposal to respond to the Serb attack. Accordingly, he requested air support on a number of occasions, even after many of his own troops had been taken hostage and faced potential Serb reprisals. Those requests were not heeded by his superiors at various levels, and some of them may not have been received at all, illustrating the command-and-control problems from which UNPROFOR suffered throughout its history. However, after he had been told that the risk of confrontation with the Serbs was to be avoided, and that the execution of the mandate was secondary to the security of his personnel, the battalion withdrew from observation posts under direct attack.

472. It is true that the UNPROFOR troops in Srebrenica never fired at the attacking Serbs. They fired warning shots over the Serbs' heads and their mortars fired flares, but they never fired directly on any Serb units. Had they engaged the attacking Serbs directly it is possible that events would have unfolded differently. At the same time, it must be recognized that the 150 fighting men of Dutchbat [the Dutch battalion stationed in Srebrenica as part of UNPROFOR] were lightly armed and in indefensible positions, and

were faced with 2,000 Serbs advancing with the support of armour and artillery.

473. As concerns the second criticism, it is easy to say with the benefit of hindsight and the knowledge of what followed that the Netherlands battalion did not do enough to protect those who sought refuge in its compound. Perhaps the soldiers should have allowed everyone into the compound and then offered themselves as human shields to protect them. This might have slowed down the Serbs and bought time for higher-level negotiations to take effect. At the same time, it is also possible that the Serb forces would then have shelled the compound, killing thousands in the process, as they had threatened to do. Ultimately, it is not possible to say with any certainty that stronger actions by Dutchbat would have saved lives, and it is even possible that such efforts could have done more harm than good. Faced with this prospect and unaware that the Serbs would proceed to execute thousands of men and boys, Dutchbat avoided armed confrontation and appealed in the process for support at the highest levels.

474. It is harder to explain why the Dutchbat personnel did not report more fully the scenes that were unfolding around them following the enclave's fall. Although they did not witness mass killing, they were aware of some sinister indications. It is possible that if the members of the battalion had immediately reported in detail those sinister indications to the United Nations chain of command, the international community might have been compelled to respond more robustly and more quickly, and that some lives might have been saved. This failure of intelligence-sharing was also not limited to the fall of Srebrenica, but an endemic weakness throughout the conflict, both within the peacekeeping mission, and between the mission and Member States.

B. Role of Bosniac Forces on the Ground

475. Criticisms have also been leveled at the Bosniacs in Srebrenica, among them that they did not fully demilitarize and that they did not do enough to defend the enclave. To a degree, these criticisms appear to be contradictory. Concerning the first criticism, it is right to note that the Bosnian Government had entered into demilitarization agreements with the Bosnian Serbs. They did this with the encouragement of the United Nations. While it is also true that the Bosniac fighters in Srebrenica did not fully demilitarize, they did demilitarize enough for UNPROFOR to issue a press release, on 21 April 1993, saying that the process had been a success. Specific instructions from United Nations Headquarters in New York stated that UNPROFOR should not be too zealous in searching for Bosniac weapons and, later, that the Serbs should withdraw their heavy weapons before the Bosniacs gave up their weapons. The Serbs never did withdraw their heavy weapons.

476. Concerning the accusation that the Bosniacs did not do enough to defend Srebrenica, military experts consulted in connection with this report were largely in agreement that the Bosniacs could not have defended Srebrenica for long in the face of a concerted attack supported by armour and

artillery. The defenders were an undisciplined, untrained, poorly armed, totally isolated force, lying prone in the crowded valley of Srebrenica. They were ill-equipped even to train themselves in the use of the few heavier weapons that had been smuggled to them by their authorities. After over three years of siege, the population was demoralized, afraid and often hungry. The only leader of stature was absent when the attack occurred. Surrounding them, controlling all the high ground, handsomely equipped with the heavy weapons and logistical train of the Yugoslav army, were the Bosnian Serbs. There was no contest.

477. Despite the odds against them, the Bosniacs requested UNPROFOR to return to them the weapons they had surrendered under the demilitarization agreements of 1993. They requested those weapons at the beginning of the Serb offensive, but the request was rejected by UNPROFOR because, as one commander explained, "it was our responsibility to defend the enclave, not theirs". Given the limited number and poor quality of the Bosniac weapons held by UNPROFOR, it seems unlikely that releasing those weapons to the Bosniacs would have made a significant difference to the outcome of the battle; but the Bosniacs were under attack at that time, they wanted to resist with whatever means they could muster, and UNPROFOR denied them access to some of their own weapons. With the benefit of hindsight, this decision seems to have been particularly ill-advised, given UNPROFOR's own unwillingness consistently to advocate force as a means of deterring attacks on the enclave.

478. Many have accused the Bosniac forces of withdrawing from the enclave as the Serb forces advanced on the day of its fall. However, it must be remembered that on the eve of the final Serb assault the Dutchbat Commander urged the Bosniacs to withdraw from defensive positions south of Srebrenica town—the direction from which the Serbs were advancing. He did so because he believed that NATO aircraft would soon be launching widespread air strikes against the advancing Serbs.

479. A third accusation levelled at the Bosniac defenders of Srebrenica is that they provoked the Serb offensive by attacking out of that safe area. Even though this accusation is often repeated by international sources, there is no credible evidence to support it. Dutchbat personnel on the ground at the time assessed that the few "raids" the Bosniacs mounted out of Srebrenica were of little or no military significance. These raids were often organized in order to gather food, as the Serbs had refused access for humanitarian convoys into the enclave. Even Serb sources approached in the context of this report acknowledged that the Bosniac forces in Srebrenica posed no significant military threat to them. The biggest attack the Bosniacs launched out of Srebrenica during the more than two years during which it was designated a safe area appears to have been the raid on the village of Visnjica, on 26 June 1995, in which several houses were burned, up to four Serbs were killed and approximately 100 sheep were stolen. In contrast, the Serbs overran the enclave two weeks later, driving tens of thousands from their homes, and summarily executing thousands of men and boys. The Serbs repeatedly exag-

gerated the extent of the raids out of Srebrenica as a pretext for the prosecution of a central war aim: to create a geographically contiguous and ethnically pure territory along the Drina, while freeing their troops to fight in other parts of the country. The extent to which this pretext was accepted at face value by international actors and observers reflected the prism of "moral equivalency" through which the conflict in Bosnia was viewed by too many for too long.

C. Role of Air Power

480. The next question that must be asked is this: why was NATO air power not brought to bear upon the Bosnian Serbs before they entered the town of Srebrenica? Even in the most restrictive interpretation of the mandate the use of close air support against attacking Serb targets was clearly warranted. The Serbs were firing directly at Dutchbat observation posts with tank rounds as early as five days before the enclave fell.

481. Some have alleged that NATO air power was not authorized earlier, despite repeated requests from the Dutchbat Commander, because the Force Commander or someone else had renounced its use against the Serbs in return for the release of United Nations personnel taken hostage in May-June 1995. Nothing found in the course of the preparation of this report supports such a view.

482. What is clear is that my predecessor, his senior advisers (among whom I was included as Under-Secretary-General for Peacekeeping Operations), his Special Representative and the Force Commander were all deeply reluctant to use air power against the Serbs for four main reasons. We believed that by using air power against the Serbs we would be perceived as having entered the war against them, something not authorized by the Security Council and potentially fatal for a peacekeeping operation. Second, we risked losing control over the process—once the key was turned we did not know if we would be able to turn it back, with grave consequences for the safety of the troops entrusted to us by Member States. Third, we believed that the use of air power would disrupt the primary mission of UNPROFOR as we then saw it: the creation of an environment in which humanitarian aid could be delivered to the civilian population of the country. Fourth, we feared Serb reprisals against our peacekeepers. Member States had placed thousands of their troops under United Nations command. We, and many of the troop-contributing countries, considered the security of those troops to be of fundamental importance in the implementation of the mandate. That there was merit in our concerns was evidenced by the hostage crisis of May-June 1995.

483. At the same time, we were fully aware that the threat of NATO air power was all we had at our disposal to respond to an attack on the safe areas. The lightly armed forces in the enclaves would be no match for (and were not intended to resist) a Serb attack supported by infantry and armour. It was thus incumbent upon us, our concerns notwithstanding, to make full use of the air power deterrent, as we had done with some effect in response

to Serb attacks upon Sarajevo and Gorazde in February and April 1994, respectively. For the reasons mentioned above, we did not use with full effectiveness this one instrument at our disposal to make the safe areas at least a little bit safer. We were, with hindsight, wrong to declare repeatedly and publicly that we did not want to use air power against the Serbs except as a last resort, and to accept the shelling of the safe areas as a daily occurrence. We believed there was no choice under the Security Council resolutions but to deploy more and more peacekeepers into harm's way. The Serbs knew this, and they timed their attack on Srebrenica well. The UNPROFOR Commander in Sarajevo at the time noted that the reluctance of his superiors and of key troop contributors to "escalate the use of force" in the wake of the hostage crisis would create the conditions in which we would then always be "stared down by the Serbs".

D. Unanswered Questions

484. The above assessment leaves unanswered a number of questions often asked about the fall of Srebrenica and the failure of the safe area regime. Two of these questions, in particular, are matters of public controversy and need to be addressed, even if no definitive answer can be provided.

485. The first question concerns the possibility that the Bosnian Government and the Bosnian Serb party, possibly with the knowledge of one or more Contact Group States, had an understanding that Srebrenica would not be vigorously defended by the Bosniacs in return for an undertaking by the Serbs not to vigorously defend territory around Sarajevo. However, the Bosniacs tried to break out of Sarajevo and were repulsed by the Serbs before the Serbs attacked Srebrenica. This would appear to remove any incentive the Bosniac authorities might have had to let the Serbs take Srebrenica. There is no doubt that the capture of Srebrenica and Zepa by the Serbs made it easier for the Bosniacs and Serbs to agree on the territorial basis of a peace settlement: the Serbs, who believed that they needed to control the border with Serbia for strategic reasons, had the territory they wanted and would not trade it back; the Bosniacs, who believed that they needed to control Sarajevo and its approaches, were able to demand this in exchange for Srebrenica and Zepa. The fact that the result of the tragedy in Srebrenica contributed in some ways to the conclusion of a peace agreement—by galvanizing the will of the international community, by distracting the Serbs from the coming Croatian attack, by reducing the vulnerability of UNPROFOR personnel to hostage-taking, and by making certain territorial questions easier for the parties to resolve—is not evidence of a conspiracy. It is a tragic irony. No evidence reviewed in the process of assembling this report suggests that any party, Bosnian or international, engineered or acquiesced in the fall of Srebrenica, other than those who ordered and carried out the attack on it. My personal belief is that human and institutional failings, at many levels, rather than wilful conspiracy, account for why the Serbs were not prevented from overrunning the safe area of Srebrenica.

486. A second question concerns the possibility that the United Nations, or one or more of its Member States, had intelligence indicating that a Serb attack on Srebrenica was being prepared. I can confirm that the United Nations, which relied on Member States for such intelligence, had no advance knowledge of the Serb offensive. Indeed, the absence of an intelligence-gathering capacity, coupled with the reluctance of Member States to share sensitive information with an organization as open, and from their perspective, as "insecure" as the United Nations, is one of the major operational constraints under which we labour in all our missions. As to whether any intelligence was available to Member States, I have no means of ascertaining this; in any case none was passed on to the United Nations by those Member States that might have been in a position to assist.

487. Had the United Nations been provided with intelligence that revealed the enormity of the Bosnian Serbs' goals, it is possible, though by no means certain, that the tragedy of Srebrenica might have been averted. But no such excuse can explain our failure in Zepa: before they began their advance into Zepa, the Serbs made a public announcement regarding their plans. Zepa was not overrun because of a lack of intelligence, but because the international community lacked the capacity to do anything other than to accept its fall as a fait accompli.

E. Role of the Security Council and Member States

488. With the benefit of hindsight, one can see that many of the errors the United Nations made flowed from a single and no doubt well-intentioned effort: we tried to keep the peace and apply the rules of peacekeeping when there was no peace to keep. Knowing that any other course of action would jeopardize the lives of the troops, we tried to create—or imagine—an environment in which the tenets of peacekeeping—agreement between the parties, deployment by consent, and impartiality—could be upheld. We tried to stabilize the situation on the ground through ceasefire agreements, which brought us close to the Serbs, who controlled the larger proportion of the land. We tried to eschew the use of force except in self-defence, which brought us into conflict with the defenders of the safe areas, whose safety depended on our use of force.

489. In spite of the untenability of its position, UNPROFOR was able to assist in the humanitarian process, and to mitigate some—but, as Srebrenica tragically underscored, by no means all—the suffering inflicted by the war. There are people alive in Bosnia today who would not be alive had UNPROFOR not been deployed. To this extent, it can be said that the 117 young men who lost their lives in the service of UNPROFOR's mission in Bosnia and Herzegovina did not die in vain. Their sacrifice and the good work of many others, however, cannot fully redeem a policy that was, at best, a half-measure.

490. The community of nations decided to respond to the war in Bosnia and Herzegovina with an arms embargo, with humanitarian aid and with the deployment of a peacekeeping force. It must be clearly stated that these mea-

sures were poor substitutes for more decisive and forceful action to prevent the unfolding horror. The arms embargo did little more than freeze in place the military balance within the former Yugoslavia. It left the Serbs in a position of overwhelming military dominance and effectively deprived the Republic of Bosnia and Herzegovina of its right, under the Charter of the United Nations, to self-defence. It was not necessarily a mistake to impose an arms embargo, which after all had been done when Bosnia and Herzegovina was not yet a State Member of the United Nations. Once that was done, however, there must surely have been some attendant duty to protect Bosnia and Herzegovina, after it became a Member State, from the tragedy that then befell it. Even as the Serb attacks on and strangulation of the "safe areas" continued in 1993 and 1994, all widely covered by the media and, presumably, by diplomatic and intelligence reports to their respective Governments, the approach of the members of the Security Council remained largely constant. The international community still could not find the political will to confront the menace defying it.

491. Nor was the provision of humanitarian aid a sufficient response to "ethnic cleansing" and to an attempted genocide. The provision of food and shelter to people who have neither is wholly admirable, and we must all recognize the extraordinary work done by UNHCR [United Nations High Commissioner for Refugees] and its partners in circumstances of extreme adversity, but the provision of humanitarian assistance could never have been a solution to the problem in that country. The problem, which cried out for a political/military solution, was that a State Member of the United Nations, left largely defenceless as a result of an arms embargo imposed upon it by the United Nations, was being dismembered by forces committed to its destruction. This was not a problem with a humanitarian solution.

492. Nor was the deployment of a peacekeeping force a coherent response to this problem. My predecessor openly told the Security Council that a United Nations peacekeeping force could not bring peace to Bosnia and Herzegovina. He said it often and he said it loudly, fearing that peacekeeping techniques would inevitably fail in a situation of war. None of the conditions for the deployment of peacekeepers had been met: there was no peace agreement—not even a functioning ceasefire—there was no clear will to peace and there was no clear consent by the belligerents. Nevertheless, *faute de mieux*, the Security Council decided that a United Nations peacekeeping force would be deployed. Lightly armed, highly visible in their white vehicles, scattered across the country in numerous indefensible observation posts, they were able to confirm the obvious: there was no peace to keep.

493. In so doing, the Security Council obviously expected that the "warring parties" on the ground would respect the authority of the United Nations and would not obstruct or attack its humanitarian operations. It soon became apparent that, with the end of the cold war and the ascendancy of irregular forces—controlled or uncontrolled—the old rules of the game no longer held. Nor was it sufficiently appreciated that a systematic and ruthless campaign such as the one conducted by the Serbs would view a United

Nations humanitarian operation, not as an obstacle, but as an instrument of its aims. In such an event, it is clear that the ability to adapt mandates to the reality on the ground is of critical importance to ensuring that the appropriate force under the appropriate structure is deployed. None of that flexibility was present in the management of UNPROFOR.

F. Failure to fully comprehend the Serb war aims

494. Even before the attack on Srebrenica began, it was clear to the Secretariat and Member States alike that the safe areas were not truly "safe". There was neither the will to use decisive air power against Serb attacks on the safe areas, nor the means on the ground to repulse them. In report after report the Secretariat accordingly and rightly pointed out these conceptual flaws in the safe area policy. We proposed changes: delineating the safe areas either by agreement between the parties or with a mandate from the Security Council; demilitarizing the safe areas; negotiating full freedom of movement. We also stressed the need to protect people rather than territory. In fact, however, these proposals were themselves inadequate. Two of the safe areas—Srebrenica and Zepa—were delineated from the beginning, and they were cited in our reports as relatively more successful examples of how the safe area concept could work. The same two safe areas were also demilitarized to a far greater extent than any of the others, though their demilitarization was by no means complete. In the end, however, the partial demilitarization of the enclaves did not enhance their security. On the contrary, it only made them easier targets for the Serbs.

495. Nonetheless, the key issue—politically, strategically and morally—underlying the security of the "safe areas" was the essential nature of "ethnic cleansing". As part of the larger ambition for a "Greater Serbia", the Bosnian Serbs set out to occupy the territory of the enclaves; they wanted the territory for themselves. The civilian inhabitants of the enclaves were not the incidental victims of the attackers; their death or removal was the very purpose of the attacks upon them. The tactic of employing savage terror, primarily mass killings, rapes and brutalization of civilians, to expel populations was used to the greatest extent in Bosnia and Herzegovina, where it acquired the now infamous euphemism of "ethnic cleansing". The Bosnian Muslim civilian population thus became the principal victim of brutally aggressive military and paramilitary Serb operations to depopulate coveted territories in order to allow them to be repopulated by Serbs.

496. The failure to fully comprehend the extent of the Serb war aims may explain in part why the Secretariat and the peacekeeping mission did not react more quickly and decisively when the Serbs initiated their attack on Srebrenica. In fact, rather than attempting to mobilize the international community to support the enclave's defence we gave the Security Council the impression that the situation was under control, and many of us believed that to be the case. The day before Srebrenica fell we reported that the Serbs were not attacking when they were. We reported that the Bosniacs had fired on an UNPROFOR blocking position when it was the Serbs. We failed to men-

tion urgent requests for air power. In some instances in which incomplete and inaccurate information was given to the Council, this can be attributed to problems with reporting from the field. In other instances, however, the reporting may have been illustrative of a more general tendency to assume that the parties were equally responsible for the transgressions that occurred. It is not clear, in any event, that the provision of more fully accurate information to the Council—many of whose members had independent sources of information on the ongoing events—would have led to appreciably different results.

497. In the end, these Bosnian Serb war aims were ultimately repulsed on the battlefield, and not at the negotiating table. Yet the Secretariat had convinced itself early on that the broader use of force by the international community was beyond our mandate and anyway undesirable. In a report to the Security Council the Secretary-General spoke against a "culture of death", arguing that peace should be pursued only through non-military methods. When, in June 1995, the international community provided UNPROFOR with a heavily armed rapid reaction force, we argued against using it robustly to implement our mandate. When decisive action was finally taken by UNPROFOR in August and September 1995, it helped to bring the war to a conclusion.

G. Lessons for the Future

498. The fall of Srebrenica is replete with lessons for this Organization and its Member States—lessons that must be learned if we are to expect the peoples of the world to place their faith in the United Nations. There are occasions when Member States cannot achieve consensus on a particular response to active military conflicts, or do not have the will to pursue what many might consider to be an appropriate course of action. The first of the general lessons is that when peacekeeping operations are used as a substitute for such political consensus they are likely to fail. There is a role for peacekeeping—a proud role in a world still riven by conflict—and there is even a role for protected zones and safe havens in certain situations; but peacekeeping and war fighting are distinct activities which should not be mixed. Peacekeepers must never again be deployed into an environment in which there is no ceasefire or peace agreement. Peacekeepers must never again be told that they must use their peacekeeping tools—lightly armed soldiers in scattered positions—to impose the ill-defined wishes of the international community on one or another of the belligerents by military means. If the necessary resources are not provided—and the necessary political, military and moral judgements are not made—the job simply cannot be done.

499. Protected zones and safe areas can have a role in protecting civilians in armed conflict, but it is clear that either they must be demilitarized and established by the agreement of the belligerents, as in the case of the "protected zones" and "safe havens" recognized by international humanitarian law, or they must be truly safe areas, fully defended by a credible military deterrent. The two concepts are absolutely distinct and must not be con-

fused. It is tempting for critics to blame the UNPROFOR units in Srebrenica for its fall, or to blame the United Nations hierarchy above those units. Certainly, errors of judgement were made—errors rooted in a philosophy of impartiality and non-violence wholly unsuited to the conflict in Bosnia—but this must not divert us from the more fundamental mistakes. The safe areas were established by the Security Council without the consent of the parties and without the provision of any credible military deterrent. They were neither protected areas nor safe havens in the sense of international humanitarian law, nor safe areas in any militarily meaningful sense. Several representatives on the Council, as well as the Secretariat, noted this problem at the time, warning that, in failing to provide a credible military deterrent, the safe area policy would be gravely damaging to the Council's reputation and, indeed, to the United Nations as a whole.

500. The approach by the United Nations Secretariat, the Security Council, the Contact Group and other involved Governments to the war in Bosnia and Herzegovina had certain consequences at both the political and the military level. At the political level, it entailed continuing negotiations with the architects of the Serb policies, principally, Mr. Milosevic and Mr. Karadzic. At the military level, it resulted in a process of negotiation with and reliance upon General Mladic, whose implacable commitment to clear eastern Bosnia—and Sarajevo if possible—of Bosniacs was plainly obvious and led inexorably to Srebrenica. At various points during the war, those negotiations amounted to appeasement.

501. The international community as a whole must accept its share of responsibility for allowing this tragic course of events by its prolonged refusal to use force in the early stages of the war. This responsibility is shared by the Security Council, the Contact Group and other Governments which contributed to the delay in the use of force, as well as by the United Nations Secretariat and the mission in the field. Clearly the primary and most direct responsibility lies however with the architects and implementers of the attempted genocide in Bosnia. Radovan Karadzic and Ratko Mladic, together with their major collaborators, have been indicted by the International Tribunal for the Former Yugoslavia. To this day, they remain free men. They must be made to answer for the barbaric crimes with which they have been charged.

502. The cardinal lesson of Srebrenica is that a deliberate and systematic attempt to terrorize, expel or murder an entire people must be met decisively with all necessary means, and with the political will to carry the policy through to its logical conclusion. In the Balkans, in this decade, this lesson has had to be learned not once, but twice. In both instances, in Bosnia and in Kosovo, the international community tried to reach a negotiated settlement with an unscrupulous and murderous regime. In both instances it required the use of force to bring a halt to the planned and systematic killing and expulsion of civilians.

503. The United Nations experience in Bosnia was one of the most difficult and painful in our history. It is with the deepest regret and remorse that

we have reviewed our own actions and decisions in the face of the assault on Srebrenica. Through error, misjudgement and an inability to recognize the scope of the evil confronting us, we failed to do our part to help save the people of Srebrenica from the Serb campaign of mass murder. No one regrets more than we the opportunities for achieving peace and justice that were missed. No one laments more than we the failure of the international community to take decisive action to halt the suffering and end a war that had produced so many victims. Srebrenica crystallized a truth understood only too late by the United Nations and the world at large: that Bosnia was as much a moral cause as a military conflict. The tragedy of Srebrenica will haunt our history forever.

504. In the end, the only meaningful and lasting amends we can make to the citizens of Bosnia and Herzegovina who put their faith in the international community is to do our utmost not to allow such horrors to recur. When the international community makes a solemn promise to safeguard and protect innocent civilians from massacre, then it must be willing to back its promise with the necessary means. Otherwise, it is surely better not to raise hopes and expectations in the first place, and not to impede whatever capability they may be able to muster in their own defence.

505. To ensure that we have fully learned the lessons of the tragic history detailed in this report, I wish to encourage Member States to engage in a process of reflection and analysis, focused on the key challenges the narrative uncovers. The aim of this process would be to clarify and to improve the capacity of the United Nations to respond to various forms of conflict. I have in mind addressing such issues as the gulf between mandate and means; the inadequacy of symbolic deterrence in the face of a systematic campaign of violence; the pervasive ambivalence within the United Nations regarding the role of force in the pursuit of peace; an institutional ideology of impartiality even when confronted with attempted genocide; and a range of doctrinal and institutional issues that go to the heart of the United Nations ability to keep the peace and help protect civilian populations from armed conflict. The Secretariat is ready to join in such a process.

506. The body of this report sets out in meticulous, systematic, exhaustive and ultimately harrowing detail the descent of Srebrenica into a horror without parallel in the history of Europe since the Second World War. I urge all concerned to study this report carefully, and to let the facts speak for themselves. The men who have been charged with this crime against humanity reminded the world and, in particular, the United Nations, that evil exists in the world. They taught us also that the United Nations global commitment to ending conflict does not preclude moral judgements, but makes them necessary. It is in this spirit that I submit my report on the fall of Srebrenica to the General Assembly, and to the world.

NORTHERN IRELAND LEADERS ON STATUS OF THE PEACE PROCESS
November 16 and 17, 1999

The peace process in Northern Ireland, which got off to a promising start in the spring of 1998, staggered intermittently through the following year and a half before getting back on track toward the end of 1999. But the Herculean efforts that were necessary just to keep the province's leaders talking to each other demonstrated anew the difficulties of bringing lasting peace to a people who had known sectarian conflict and hatred for centuries.

Most Protestants wanted Northern Ireland to remain a province of the United Kingdom, while most Catholics favored joining the Republic of Ireland, with its majority Catholic population. Guerrilla warfare between extremists on both sides broke out in 1969 and raged until 1997, when the Irish Republican Army (IRA), the most important Catholic guerrilla group, declared a ceasefire. More than 3,200 people had died and thousands had been injured during the nearly three decades of violence.

Under the persuasive prodding of former U.S. senator George Mitchell, D-Maine, representatives of Northern Ireland's majority Protestants and minority Catholics agreed April 10, 1998, to a process of resolving their differences peacefully, at the ballot box, rather than with guns and bombs. In a later referendum, Northern Ireland's voters overwhelmingly supported the agreement—called the "Good Friday agreement" after the day on which it was reached. (Agreement signed, Historic Documents of 1998, p. 203)

Repeated Hurdles

Despite the yearning for peace among most of Northern Ireland's 1.6 million residents, every one of the steps needed to put the Good Friday accord into action was dogged with controversy, indicating that leaders of the two sides still deeply distrusted each other. On numerous occasions, British prime minister Tony Blair and his Republic of Ireland counterpart, Bertie Ahern, found it necessary to intervene to keep the process rolling. Despite the frequency of the crises, optimists argued that at each point Northern Ireland's leaders ended up deepening their commitment to peace and mov-

ing farther away from the hatreds of the past. Pessimists noted that extremists on both sides still had the ability to undermine the majority's desire for peace.

Most often the prime issue involved a demand by Protestant leaders that the IRA begin handing over its presumably large arsenal of weapons—a process known as "decommissioning." The IRA had rejected decommissioning as the equivalent of surrender and pointed instead to its adherence to a cease-fire declared in July 1997. As a practical matter, the IRA decommissioning issue served mainly to poison relations between the leading Protestant political party, the Ulster Unionists, and Sinn Fein, the political arm of the IRA.

Decommissioning was at the heart of a crisis that developed in mid-July 1999 and ran through most of the rest of the year. On July 15 the Ulster Unionists boycotted what was to have been the opening session of the new Northern Ireland Assembly. The party's leader, David Trimble, who had been designated "first minister" (or prime minister) of a new Northern Ireland government, said he and his party would refuse to sit in the government with Sinn Fein unless the IRA began disarming. Protestants had summarized this position as "no guns, no government." Trimble's announcement produced an angry reaction from his designated deputy on the Catholic side, Seamus Mallon, a leader of the moderate Democratic and Labor Party. Mallon accused the Unionists of "dishonoring" the peace agreement, announced his resignation as deputy first minister, and stormed out of the parliament building in Belfast, appropriately named Stormont.

The impasse left the British government with no alternative but to delay its plans, under the Good Friday accord, to hand over political power to the new Northern Ireland government. In effect, the peace process was put on hold while the various parties rethought their positions and the British and Irish governments looked for new ways of getting things back on track. Blair, who had made peace in Northern Ireland one of his signature themes, expressed deep disappointment but said: "I won't give up."

Mitchell's Negotiations

Blair's first step following the mid-July collapse of the peace process was to call in former senator Mitchell, who was widely respected for his ability to bridge the wide gulf separating the two sides in Northern Ireland. With evident reluctance, Mitchell agreed to chair another round of talks among the region's political leaders in hopes of finding a way to revive the peace process. One of the major problems Mitchell faced was that some of the leaders with whom he was dealing were under pressure from extremists within their own ranks not to make any more concessions. Trimble, in particular, faced intense opposition from many Protestants who believed that he had abandoned his own principles by accepting compromise.

Mitchell began meeting with Northern Ireland leaders in August, exploring various ways of moving beyond the issue of IRA decommissioning. It took eleven weeks of on-and-off meetings, but in mid-November Mitchell was able to put together a deal breaking the impasse.

In a series of carefully scripted statements November 16, Adams and Trimble reaffirmed their parties' commitment to the peace process and made subtle, but important, concessions to each other. The two men long had expressed contempt for one another, but under Mitchell's guidance had seemed to develop a grudging mutual respect.

Adams, who had been an active IRA militia member before turning to politics, said Sinn Fein "is totally committed to the implementation of the Good Friday agreement in all its aspect" and expressed confidence that the IRA "remains committed to the objective of a permanent peace." In a direct statement intended to ease Protestant fears, Adams pledged that decommissioning "is an essential part of the peace process."

Trimble, for years one of the most hard-line Protestant leaders, read a remarkably conciliatory statement: "For too long much of the unrest in our community has been caused by a failure to accept the differing expressions of cultural identity," he said. The people of Northern Ireland needed to develop "mutual respect and tolerance rather than division and alienation."

Trimble's most important concession was to agree to sit in the same government with Sinn Fein if the IRA would send a representative to an independent commission, chaired by retired Canadian general John de Chastelain, that was supervising the disarmament of Northern Ireland's paramilitary groups. The next day, November 17, the IRA released a brief statement saying it would name a representative to meet with the disarmament commission. "In our view, the Good Friday agreement is a significant development, and we believe its full implementation will contribute the achievement of lasting peace," the IRA said. Observers said it was significant that the statement did not include the IRA's traditional pledge never to hand over its weapons.

Putting the Deal in Place

Mitchell's agreement called for a series of steps leading to the appointment of a unified cabinet that would govern Northern Ireland. The first move came November 27, when Trimble persuaded his colleagues in the Ulster Unionist Party to accept the assurances that resulted from Mitchell's negotiations. But Trimble added a significant condition that was not part of the original agreement: if the IRA had not begun disarming by January 31, 2000, the Ulster Unionists would pull out of the new Northern Ireland government.

Following his party's meeting, Trimble addressed himself, rhetorically, to Adams: "We've done our bit. Now, Mr. Adams, it's over to you. We jumped. You follow."

Two days later, on November 29, the parties represented in the Northern Ireland Assembly nominated candidates for the new twelve-member cabinet. As had been planned previously, Trimble was named first minister and

Mallon, reversing his angry resignation four months earlier, was his deputy. By far the most controversial appointment was that of Martin McGuinnes, a high school dropout who reportedly had been a former IRA commander, as education minister. Adams, despite his stature as Sinn Fein's political leader, did not take a seat in the cabinet.

A rush of events on December 2 put key elements of the Good Friday peace agreement in place for the first time. The new cabinet took office in Belfast, formally assuming the responsibility of government that Britain had exercised since disbanding the previous Northern Ireland government after the outbreak of violence in 1969. The British Parliament had earlier approved legislation turning authority over to the new government. Two representatives of the hard-line Protestant Democratic Unionist Party boycotted the cabinet session, denouncing the presence of Sinn Fein members.

Also on December 2, the IRA announced that it had appointed a representative to meet with the disarmament commission, as it had promised to do in conjunction with Mitchell's negotiations. The name of the representative was not made public, but the IRA's willingness to meet with the commission was considered an important first step toward decommissioning.

In Dublin, Irish prime minister Ahern signed legislation, previously approved by voters and the parliament, renouncing clauses in the Irish constitution that claimed Northern Ireland to be part of the Republic of Ireland. The elimination of the constitutional claim had been a significant element in the Good Friday agreement, providing a degree of comfort to Protestants in the north.

Another symbolically important step took place at Buckingham Palace in London, where Irish president Mary McAleese had lunch with Queen Elizabeth II. Speaking afterward of the events that seemed to confirm the reality of peace, McAleese, a native of Belfast, said: "This is a day many people thought would never see dawn."

Another such day came December 13, when the two governments of Northern Ireland and the Irish Republic held their first joint meeting in the historic Northern Ireland city of Armagh, the ecclesiastical capital of both the Anglican and Catholic churches in Ireland. The two cabinets met as the North-South Ministerial Council, a summit session intended by the Good Friday agreement to satisfy the desire of many Catholics for closer ties with the south. Items on the council's agenda included issues of concern to both parts of Ireland, such as promoting tourism and protecting fishing grounds. It was the first official meeting of representatives from the two parts of Ireland since the Republic of Ireland became independent in 1922 and Ireland was divided.

In his opening remarks, Ahern said the joint meeting was part of the process of the "consolidation of peace and the promotion of reconciliation. Too many lives have been shattered or stunted, too many opportunities wasted, by the collective failures of the days gone past." he said. "This meeting is symbolic of a different and better way."

Following are three statements on the status of the peace process in Northern Ireland: first, a statement November 16, 1999, by David Trimble, leader of the Ulster Unionist Party; then a statement the same day by Gerry Adams, leader of Sinn Fein (the political arm of the Irish Republican Army); and finally a statement issued November 17, 1999, by the Irish Republican Army:

STATEMENT BY DAVID TRIMBLE

The Ulster Unionist Party [UUP] remains totally committed to the full implementation of the Belfast Agreement in all its aspects.

It is our belief that the establishment of the new political institutions and the disarmament of all paramilitary organisations will herald a new beginning for all sections of our people—a new, peaceful, and democratic society, free from the use or threat of force.

The UUP recognises and accepts that it is legitimate for nationalists to pursue their political objective of a united Ireland by consent through exclusively peaceful and democratic methods.

The UUP is committed to the principles of inclusivity, equality, and mutual respect on which the institutions are to be based. It is our intention that these principles will extend in practice to all areas of public life, and be endorsed by society as a whole.

The UUP sees a new opportunity for all our traditions in Northern Ireland to enter a new era of respect and tolerance of cultural differences and expression.

For too long, much of the unrest in our community has been caused by a failure to accept the differing expressions of cultural identity.

Disagreements over language issues, parades and other events must be resolved if the stability and tolerance we all want to see are to be realised.

These issues, in future, will be the means to promote mutual respect and tolerance rather than division and alienation. The UUP is committed to securing equality and mutual respect for all elements of our diverse culture.

The Agreement will help bring this about by providing a framework for a new political dispensation which recognises the full and equal legitimacy of our different identities and aspirations.

We now have a chance to create a genuine partnership between unionists and nationalists in a novel form of government. It offers us the opportunity to put past failures behind us.

This new government has the task of rebuilding our damaged economy and the social fabric of our community. It must also strive to eliminate the causes of disadvantage and promote greater prosperity for all.

Only when violence has no part to play and where only democratic politics will be used to further community goals will we have a fully matured as a society. We look forward with confidence to meeting this challenge.

Both of our traditions have suffered as a result of our conflict and division. This is a matter of deep regret and makes it all the more important that we now put the past behind us. The establishment of inclusive political institutions and the commencement of the process of decommissioning are the first steps in this process.

If, in our view, a genuine and meaningful response is forthcoming to Monday's statement from the Independent International Commission on Decommissioning, the way will then be clear

for the establishment of the political institutions envisaged in the Belfast Agreement.

Unionist, loyalist, nationalist, and republican must take these steps together to secure a new era of co-operation, reconciliation and mutual respect.

STATEMENT BY GERRY ADAMS

Sinn Fein is totally committed to the implementation of the Good Friday Agreement in all its aspects. We believe that the wholehearted implementation of the Agreement has the capacity to transform the existing situation through constructive and dynamic political development.

It is an unprecedented opportunity to start afresh. An opportunity to put behind us the failures, the tragedy and the suffering of the past.

There is no doubt that we are entering into the final stages of the resolution of the conflict.

The IRA cessation [cease-fire] which has now been in place for a total of almost four years represents an important and positive contribution by the IRA to the resolution of the conflict. IRA guns are silent and the Sinn Fein leadership is confident that the IRA remains committed to the objective of a permanent peace.

By providing an effective political alternative we can remove the potential for conflict. That conflict must be for all of us now a thing of the past, over, done with and gone.

There has been a particular focus on arms. This issue is addressed directly in the Good Friday Agreement. Sinn Fein accepts that decommissioning is an essential part of the peace process. We believe that the issue of arms will be finally and satisfactorily settled under the aegis of the de Chastelain Commission [the Independent Commission on Decommissioning] as set out in the Agreement. All parties to the Agreement have an obligation to help bring decommissioning about. Sinn Fein is committed to discharging our responsibilities in this regard.

Decommissioning can only come about on a voluntary basis. The Good Friday Agreement makes clear that the context required for its resolution is the

implementation of the overall settlement, including the operation of its institutions and using the mechanism of the de Chastelain Commission. This is a
collective responsibility.

Sinn Fein has total and absolute commitment to pursue our objectives by
exclusively peaceful and democratic means in accordance with the Good Friday Agreement. For this reason we are totally opposed to any use of force or
threat of force by others for any political purpose.

We are totally opposed to punishment attacks.

In the Executive [the new Northern Ireland cabinet] the two Sinn Fein Ministers will make and honour the pledge of office which includes a commitment to non-violence and exclusively peaceful and democratic means.

Under the terms of the Agreement any member of the Executive can be
removed from office for failure to meet his or her responsibilities, including
those set out in the Pledge of Office.

All sections of our people have suffered profoundly in this conflict. That
suffering is a matter of deep regret but makes the difficult process of removing conflict all the more imperative. Sinn Fein wishes to work with, not
against, the unionists and recognises this as yet another imperative. For Sinn
Fein co-operation and accommodation is the objective of this process.

We reiterate our total commitment to doing everything in our power to
maintain the peace process and to removing the gun forever from the politics
of our country.

STATEMENT BY THE IRISH REPUBLICAN ARMY

The IRA is committed unequivocally to the search for freedom, justice and
peace in Ireland. In our view, the Good Friday agreement is a significant
development, and we believe its full implementation will contribute to the
achievement of lasting peace.

We acknowledge the leadership given by Sinn Fein throughout this
process.

The IRA is willing to further enhance the peace process and consequently,
following the establishment of the institutions agreed on Good Friday last
year, the IRA leadership will appoint a representative to enter into discussions with Gen. John de Chastelain and the Independent International Commission on Decommissioning.

COMMERCE DEPARTMENT ON Y2K PREPARATIONS
November 17, 1999

Years of effort costing billions of dollars helped prevent major disruptions of computer systems as 1999 rolled over to year 2000. There were no massive computer failures anywhere in the world; airplanes did not fall out of the sky; power generating plants did not stop working on a cold winter's night; and the 6 billion people on Earth safely celebrated the beginning of 2000 in whatever manner they chose.

For years before the event, it was unclear just what would happen at the stroke of midnight December 31, 1999. Starting in the late 1980s, experts began worrying about outdated computer systems—or even new ones still being produced—that used only two digits to designate the year. When 99 became 00, would computers freeze up or spew out enormous quantities of invalid data?

Rather than wait for answers to those questions, government agencies and millions of private businesses and organizations bought new computer equipment, rewrote old computer programs or purchased new ones, and repeatedly tested their systems. In the United States, these efforts peaked in 1998, when governments and business spent more than $30 billion to make their systems "Y2K —Year 2000—compliant." From 1995 to 2001, total U.S. spending to protect against Y2K problems was expected to reach about $100 billion, according to a study released November 17, 1999, by the Commerce Department. That figure was far below many previous estimates, including a projection of $300 billion made in 1997 by the Gartner Group, a consulting agency that tried to track spending on Y2K issues. (Y2K preparedness, Historic Documents of 1997, p. 534; Historic Documents of 1998, p. 543)

Getting Ready for Y2K

In hindsight, some people thought it was much ado about nothing, that a matter of two simple digits could have cost so much money and caused so many people so much worry. But in the years leading up to 2000 there was growing anxiety about Y2K, especially in the heavily industrialized countries that depended on computers or computerized systems for everything from balancing bank accounts to keeping airplanes from crashing into each other.

The basic problem was that millions of computer programs written from the 1950s and even into the 1990s used just the last two digits of the year as a space-saving measure. During the early years of widespread computer use, even large-scale systems operated with levels of memory that would later be considered tiny. By 1999 most home personal computers were much more powerful than the giant room-size systems NASA used to design major space programs, such as the mission that put men on the Moon in 1969. If they thought about the Y2K problem at the time, authors of the early computer programs assumed they would be replaced by the end of the century. But many of those programs kept on running well past their expected life spans. To save money, businesses, individuals, government agencies, and others replaced their computer hardware but kept using the old programs with just two digits for the date.

Warnings by computer experts about the "Y2K bug" began to take hold in the public consciousness by the middle of the 1990s. At that point the federal government took the threat of computer malfunctions very seriously. Regulatory agencies demanded that banks and public utilities meet specific criteria within tight deadlines for fixing and testing their computer systems. President Bill Clinton appointed a high level Council on Year 2000 Conversion, chaired by John A. Koskinen. The council was given extraordinary power to demand changes at government agencies. Congress held numerous hearings and traded charges (often tinged by partisanship) with the administration about who was taking the matter more seriously.

Spurred in part by the government and in part by their own desires to avoid problems, major corporations started investing in Y2K readiness in 1995. Retired programmers who could write in now-obsolete computer languages such as COBOL found themselves in a seller's market, courted by businesses now frantic to update their old systems. As the years passed, the preparation became more intense. According to estimates by the International Data Corporation, total U.S. spending on Y2K preparation was about $5 million in 1995, $15 billion in 1996, $27 billion in 1997, $32 billion in 1998, and $29 billion in 1999.

Many companies and organizations used their Y2K preparations as an opportunity to update entire computer systems. The result was a boom in the computer industry, which during the late 1990s also benefited from the phenomenal growth of interest in the Internet, the most important new communications medium since television. Over the long term, the Commerce Department study said, the updated computer systems should improve productivity.

Economists said increased spending on computer systems probably added marginally to economic growth in 1999, which was the eighth straight year of economic expansion. By late 1999 most economists had dismissed earlier projections that widespread computer failures related to Y2K could plunge the economy into recession. In the November 17 Commerce Department study, Robert J. Shapiro, the undersecretary of commerce for economic affairs, predicted that any computer failures would have at most a "transient effect" on U.S. economic growth.

Another side benefit was that many large organizations discovered for the first time just how many computer systems they had. The Defense Department, for example, put together a list of 2,101 "crucial" computer systems—such as those used to manage nuclear weapons and plot the flights of military planes—and 5,500 other programs that were not quite as vital. Making all those programs and systems ready for 2000 cost the Pentagon, and taxpayers, about $3.6 billion, by far the biggest chunk of the $8.38 billion spent by all federal agencies on Y2K readiness. "It's very frustrating to say that we had to spend $3.6 billion," Deputy Defense Secretary John Hamre told the New York Times. *"But we could not stand the consequence if we had not spent the $3.6 billion."*

Smaller organizations—corner grocery stores, auto repair shops, small town governments—were slower to catch on to the significance of the Y2K problem. In many cases, the managers of small businesses and organizations failed to realize that their computers, or even pieces of technical equipment using embedded computer chips, might have a problem recognizing January 1, 2000. That situation changed as publicity about the Y2K bug became more difficult to avoid, especially during 1998 and the early months of 1999. But many small businesses deliberately chose to take a wait-and-see attitude: if something went wrong after the first of the year in 2000, that would be the time to fix it. Koskinen estimated that 400,000 to 500,000 small organizations adopted what he called a "fix on failure" strategy.

In the last half of 1999 government agencies and businesses began issuing public statements assuring the public and their customers that they had done all they could to prepare for the year 2000. President Clinton said November 10 that he expected "no major national breakdowns" because of Y2K computer failures. Banks mailed statements to depositors telling them not to worry about disappearing accounts; utilities claimed that power plants would keep running; and the Federal Aviation Administration (FAA) offered repeated assurances (greeted skeptically by many) that its aging computer systems would in fact be able to keep track of planes in the air on New Year's Day. To further bolster public confidence, organizations that offered essential public services promised to have plenty of employees on hand for any emergencies that might arise at the stroke of midnight.

Even so, an unknown number of Americans decided to take matters into their own hands, just in case. Gas-fired power generators suddenly became popular items in 1999, and by late in the year many manufacturers and retailers had trouble meeting the demand. Bottled water, canned goods, and flashlights also sold well. A few people hoarded large quantities of staple items, and some even cleaned out old bomb shelters dating from the 1950s.

762

Experts advised people to have plenty of cash on hand, just in case banks had trouble with automated teller machines and other systems. To meet the expected demand, the Federal Reserve Board distributed $80 billion in cash to banks and other financial institutions late in the year.

Another issue that arose late in December was concern about terrorism. Authorities on December 14 arrested an Algerian man who attempted to smuggle bomb-making equipment from Canada into Washington state. That man and a Canadian woman arrested five days later in Vermont were said to be linked to a terrorist organization in Algeria. The arrests caused widespread concerns that terrorists might target western nations during year 2000 celebrations. The FBI released a study concluding that some U.S.- based antigovernment extremist groups might consider the year 2000 as the beginning of the Apocalypse predicted in the New Testament. The FBI suggested that law enforcement agencies be on guard for possible violence associated with such groups. (Security threats, p. 499)

With all the assurances about U.S. readiness for Y2K gradually winning public acceptance, attention turned to other countries. Officials in other highly industrialized countries, especially in Europe, said their computer systems were just as up-to-date as those in the United States. Germany, which got a late start in dealing with Y2K, put its overall spending on the problem at $84 billion—nearly matching the U.S. total.

But many people wondered about Russia, with its nuclear arsenal, its troubled economy, and its computer systems that could not possibly have been updated to the same extent as those in the West. With just a few days to go before December 31, experts said widespread failures were likely in Russia's already trouble-prone natural gas, electrical, telephone, and air traffic control systems. The State Department ordered its "nonessential" employees in Russia, Ukraine, and other former Soviet republics home over New Year's. Most experts were less concerned about developing countries, especially in Africa, which were not highly dependent on computer systems.

An Anticlimax

To the surprise of just about everyone—especially the experts who had predicted problems overseas—few computer-related problems occurred anywhere in the world on January 1, 2000 (a Saturday), or during the first business days of the new year. A small number of computer systems did have trouble both in the United States and overseas, but some experts said the number of problems was less than normal.

The FAA experienced temporary problems with some of its computers, and the Federal Reserve Bank in Chicago momentarily misplaced about $700,000 in tax payments on January 4. Private firms reported few computer failures or interruptions. Some experts said there may have been more problems than were reported, but executives did not want to acknowledge them. Despite earlier predictions of shortages of consumer goods due to hoarding, grocery stores across the country had full shelves in the early days of 2000.

The greatest surprise was what happened—or did not happen—overseas. With only minor exceptions, there were no major power outages or other serious computer-related problems anywhere in the world. Russia's electrical power system kept working and, most important, its missiles with nuclear warheads stayed in storage.

Perhaps inevitably, there was a backlash. Some people, especially overseas, voiced suspicion that the Y2K fuss was a hoax, possibly a plot by computer companies to generate business. "We're a country that can't afford to waste money, and that's just what we did with this hoax," Mariana Gonzalez, a street merchant in Buenos Aires, Argentina, told the Washington Post. *"We can't feed our families and we spent millions on a sham to make foreign companies rich."*

Pressed to explain why everything went so smoothly, computer experts, government officials, and economists offered several theories. First, they said, all the effort put into Y2K readiness paid off. Koskinen said that thousands, and possibly millions, of computer systems would have failed if government and business had not spent time and money to make sure they did not. Some of the money spent on Y2K fixes probably was wasted, these experts said, but it was impossible to know that ahead of time.

Officials involved in Y2K programs also said they might have underestimated the amount of work that was done in the final months of 1999 to fix computer systems. Some of the predictions made during the year were based on outdated information, Koskinen said.

Worries about collapsing computer systems in the rest of the world—notably Russia—might have stemmed from overestimating how much other countries depend on computers. "If we had a failing, it may be that we extrapolated to the rest of the world the kind of business practices that we have developed here," the Pentagon's Hamre said.

> *Following is the executive summary of the report, "The Economics of Y2K and the Impact on the United States," released November 17, 1999, by the Economics and Statistics Administration of the U.S. Department of Commerce:*

As a result of programming decisions made during their creation, computer software and hardware may not recognize the Year 2000 accurately, causing operational errors. This report assesses the economic implications of this Y2K problem for the U.S. economy. The Department of Commerce's Economics and Statistics Administration reviewed how firms and governments should be expected to react in the face of the known Y2K problems and compared these results with available progress reports on Y2K readiness and other published Y2K economic assessments.

Overall Assessment & Key Judgements: Y2K is having an impact on U.S. business activity well in advance of the actual 1999 to 2000 changeover.

Expenditures by firms and public agencies to hunt down and correct error-prone technologies have been running on the order of $30 billion a year since 1997 and will total in the neighborhood of $100 billion. Since the economy is essentially fully employed, the Y2K expenditures are coming at the expense of productivity-enhancing investments and consumption. Once Y2K is resolved, more resources will be available for both.

It appears that Y2K problems will not be of sufficient size or scope to have more than a transient effect on overall U.S. economic growth. With no shortage of information about the problem, firms are correcting what is clearly a messy but not intractable situation. Y2K readiness and assessment reports by government agencies, the private sector, and private consultants are, for the most part, optimistic. While international organizations have reported a lower level of Y2K preparedness in many foreign countries, the countries that are highly dependent on information technology, and thus exposed to substantial risks, are reported to be well along with their fixes. There appears to be little chance that Y2K disruptions abroad will be transmitted to the United States to a degree that could substantially damage the economy. There are still important unknowns, and no one knows with certainty the precise economic consequences. However, the U.S. economy has faced many such pressures and has proven to be highly resilient in recent years.

How Firms Can Be Expected to React to Y2K: At the firm level, the Y2K problem is not that different from other risks businesses face every day. Firms can be expected to balance, from their own points of view, the perceived costs and benefits of identifying, fixing, and testing for Y2K problems and developing contingency plans.

- In competitive markets, where it is difficult to pass on new costs to customers, firms can be expected to spend enough to avoid significant losses while accepting a risk of some failures. The level of precautionary Y2K spending among firms may vary, depending on the degree of a firm's risk aversion and its financial means.
- In more concentrated markets, where there is a greater ability to pass on costs, firms can be expected to make efforts to figure out what their competitors are doing, and defensively to copy that behavior. The variation in spending between firms will probably be less in these more concentrated markets.
- For well regulated markets and government agencies, where there is a greater ability to pass on costs and where a sustained Y2K failure could be severely disruptive for others, there will be a strong incentive to find and fix all Y2K problems. But in countries that are poorly governed, or where monopoly firms or public services are poorly managed, these are the areas of greatest risk.

Clearly, some firms will make rational choices that include risks of failures. Some of these decisions will end up being wrong, and some profits and jobs will be affected as a result. It is unlikely these errors will be large enough to cascade into an economy-wide disruption, but this is not knowable with certainty.

Economic Basis for the Governmental and Public Role in Y2K: Even with the best of intent and the most rational decisions possible, the effects of these firm-level Y2K remediation decisions on the general economy could be influenced by special factors. Clearly, any sustained failure in critical infrastructure system, such as telephone or electricity, would be very disruptive, could have cascading effects, and is outside the control of most firms. Misinformation about the Y2K problem or the state of its resolution—whether or not the misinformation is deliberate—could lead to incorrect actions or levels of investment in Y2K fixes. Also, private decisions on Y2K spending can have good or bad effects on the broader society. Left to their own devices, firms might choose Y2K strategies that, while rational from their view, could still have negative implications for other people.

The potential for these factors to influence private Y2K decisions provides a strong public policy justification for the executive and legislative branches of government, industry regulators, industry associations and consultants, and the media to pay close attention to Y2K vulnerabilities. Public scrutiny has increased the level of private investment in fixing Y2K, thus reducing the potential external effects on society as a whole. In principle, governmental activities intended to mitigate the impact of the problem could also encourage behavior that makes the problem more likely. Government Y2K policies and programs have tried to avoid the danger of such "moral hazard" by insisting that responsibility to fix Y2K problems lies with the individuals, firms and agencies involved.

Domestic Y2K Readiness: The Y2K-problem is, at its core, a technological error that can be tested and corrected. By most accounts, the domestic U.S. economy is generally well-prepared.

The President's Council on the Year 2000 Conversion believes that "important national systems will make a successful transition to the Year 2000," and that it has a "high degree of confidence" in financial institutions, electric power, telecommunications, and the federal government. The Senate Special Committee on the Year 2000 Technology Problem concludes that sectors "critical to the safety and well-being of Americans, as well as to the economy, have made significant progress in the last eight months. . . ." Both reports indicate continuing concern for certain domestic sectors, including health care, local government, small business, and education, without however, finding general economy-wide risks. Private sector Y2K consultants and polls on corporate Y2K readiness, with a few exceptions, have the same general views.

An additional consideration supports these optimistic assessments: Surveys suggest that the majority of firms have already experienced some Y2K failures, and reports indicate that these have produced temporary, fixable disruptions. There will be a spike in failures at the turn of the year, but it may not be as large or as significant as commonly expected.

International Y2K Readiness and Implications for the U.S. Economy: Some concern remains about the level of international preparations and how foreign Y2K problems might effect the U.S. economy. However, for the most part, economically-sound behavior appears to be occurring overseas as well. U.S. firms that depend on suppliers overseas have a strong incentive to make sure that they are Y2K ready and that there are contingency plans in place—e.g., inventories, alternative suppliers—in case there are Y2K related disruptions. No information indicates that U.S. firms are doing less overseas than they are doing domestically.

Overseas problems are most likely to occur in countries with highly centralized, poorly supervised organizations and where there is current, severe economic distress. However, these nations do not play a major economic role in the U.S. economy. The major U.S. trading partners of Canada, Mexico, Europe, and Japan—where information technology plays a large role in the economy—report a strong degree of preparation and Y2K readiness.

For a foreign nation's Y2K failures to present a sustained threat to our economy, the foreign nation and its firms would have to be IT-intensive, very poorly Y2K prepared, important economically to the U. S., and have significant Y2K-related links that could generate sustained economic disruption. Available country-level assessments do not indicate any nations where all four of these risk factors to the U.S. are present.

The structure of economic incentives to U.S. firms, the reports of U.S. firm-level preparations involving the overseas supply chain, and country-level assessments of the major U.S. trading partners are consistent with the expectation of transient effects in trade-dependent sectors of the U.S. economy. Additional inventories, contingency preparations, and the time lags between foreign production and domestic use suggest that disruptions abroad should not immediately affect U.S. producers and ultimately, may not affect them very much. Trade takes place between tens of thousands of individuals and firms, and that is where Y2K readiness, contingency planning, and response to any glitches when they occur will rest. The incentive to get fixes or work-arounds in place quickly will be very high.

Estimates of U.S. Y2K Spending: Cumulative U.S. spending to address the Y2K problem is difficult to estimate. However, based upon several methodologically conservative estimates, cumulative Y2K readiness spending appears to be in the neighborhood of $100 billion, or about $365 per U.S. resident. Y2K spending, which started as early as 1995, appears to have peaked in 1998 and 1999 at about $30 billion per year.

Effects on Productivity: Spending to fix the Y2K technological errors increases costs and creates a diversion of spending from other productive investments. Some of the Y2K spending may involve 'shifting forward' new, productive, software and hardware investments which would have occurred eventually, offsetting to some extent the drag on productivity. Because Y2K spending has occurred over a number of years and is small relative to the economy, it is difficult to estimate the extent of productivity effects with assurance. For the future, the lifting of the Y2K repair burden should free resources that can be used in ways that will raise productivity.

Inventory and GDP Effects: Y2K contingency planning by firms and Y2K-related consumer behavior may have implications for inventory shifts and the composition of GDP at the turn of the year. Because of these issues,

767

consensus economic forecasts anticipate some inventory build-up now, offset by a reduction in the early part of next year. Also, Y2K contingency planning may involve, at least for some firms, a 'lock-down' that could reduce installations, if not orders, of software and hardware from what they otherwise would have been in the fourth quarter of 1999. As with the productivity effects, it will be very difficult to estimate after the fact these inventory and capital spending effects with either precision or assurance.

Consumer Behavior Concerns: A sudden rise in risk aversion associated with Y2K concerns—translated into unusual demand for cash or household goods—could prove disruptive to finance and commerce even with advance preparation. Current polls, however, suggest that the public is becoming less worried about Y2K as the date approaches. And financial institutions appear to be among the best prepared for Y2K. Most importantly, even if risk aversion rises, two-way markets ensure that the choice of holding more cash or hoarding goods will come at higher prices that reward those who accept modest risks.

Need to Avoid Complacency: While the general assessments of Y2K readiness and the implications for the U.S. economy as a whole are optimistic, Y2K glitches will surely happen and disrupt the firms and individuals involved. All firms and individuals should be sure that they have taken steps to identify, fix and test for Y2K problems, and put in place appropriate contingency plans.

OSHA ON PROPOSED ERGONOMICS STANDARDS
NOVEMBER 22, 1999

The Occupational Safety and Health Administration (OSHA) issued proposed regulations November 22, 1999, that the federal agency said would help protect millions of workers from common workplace injuries such as carpal tunnel syndrome and back injury. The so-called ergonomics standards would require about 1.6 million employers to identify and fix workplace hazards that contributed to musculoskeletal disorders, or MSDs. "Work-related musculoskeletal disorders . . . are the most prevalent, most expensive and most preventable workplace injuries in the country," Secretary of Labor Alexis M. Herman said at a news conference. Herman said the regulations would spare an average of 300,000 workers a year from painful, frequently debilitating injuries and save employers $9 billion a year in workers' compensation claims and other costs. About 27 million workers would be protected under the regulations.

The regulations were widely hailed by unions and several medical and professional associations that had long urged OSHA to act. But business leaders and several Republican legislators, who had managed to prevent OSHA from issuing the rules for several years, denounced them for being too vague, too broad, and too costly. Several groups threatened to challenge the new regulations in court. OSHA was not expected to issue final regulations until 2000.

A Common Workplace Problem

Each year about 1.8 million workers suffered MSDs, caused most often by overexertion or repetitive motion. About one-third of those injuries were serious enough to require the worker to take time off, and such injuries accounted for about one-third of all workers' compensation costs. MSD injuries were common in manual handling jobs, such as lifting and turning patients, sorting and delivering packages, handling baggage, and stocking grocery store or warehouse shelves. They were also common in manufacturing jobs, such as working on an assembly line, inspecting products, meat cutting and packing, and sewing clothing.

769

Women suffered disproportionately from MSDs because a large number of them worked in jobs that required heavy lifting, awkward postures, or repetitive motion. According to OSHA, women suffered 70 percent of the carpal tunnel syndrome cases and 62 percent of the tendinitis cases that required time off from work; more than 100,000 women each year sustained back injuries that forced them to take time off from work. MSDs currently cost $15–$20 billion a year in workers' compensation costs; total costs were put at as much as $60 billion a year.

Ergonomics was the study of ways to fit the job to the worker to minimize the occurrence of injuries to muscles, tendons, ligaments, joints, and spinal discs. Although many scientific questions about the causes and diagnoses of specific MSDs had not yet been answered, a large body of scientific evidence directly linked MSDs to on-the-job physical stress, and many employers had found that intervention to reduce physical stresses decreased the incidence of injury. Many interventions were simple and often relatively inexpensive. Such fixes included changing the height of a computer keyboard to minimize wrist strain, adjusting the height of the work surface to minimize leaning, stooping, and reaching; providing mechanical lifting equipment to relieve back strain; and repositioning tools or equipment, again to minimize damaging body motion. Encouraging workers to take short breaks from their repetitive tasks could help reduce injuries, as could rotating jobs on an assembly line.

In response to workers' complaints, hundreds of companies had already instituted ergonomics programs to reduce injuries. Companies said the changes cut their costs and boosted productivity as well as their employee's morale. According to OSHA more than ninety case studies showed that ergonomics programs cut MSD injury rates by an average of 70 percent. Despite these high rates of success, OSHA said it acted on the proposed rules because about 50 percent of employees and more than 70 percent of general industry workplaces were not covered by a company ergonomics program.

The Proposed Regulations

The proposed regulations were focused on jobs rather than workplaces. All general industry employers with workers involved in manual handling or manufacturing jobs would be required to implement a basic ergonomics program for those workers. Under the basic program, the company would have to provide information to employees and set up a system for employees to report signs and symptoms of MSDs. The company would be required to make someone responsible for administering the problem, including responding promptly to employee's reports of MSDs. OSHA said about 1.6 million general industry employers would have to set up this basic program initially. (Companies engaged in agricultural, construction, and maritime activities were exempt.)

Other employers with jobs that resulted in MSDs would also be covered, but only after a documented MSD occurred. OSHA said it expected about

300,000 employers to fall into this category. Companies that already had ergonomics programs were grandfathered, so long as they met the reporting requirements set out by the standards and their programs continued to hold down or eliminate MSDs.

Once the basic program was in place, employers would not be required to do anything unless and until a work-related MSD was reported. The injury had to be serious enough to require medical treatment, days away from work, or assignment to light-duty work, and it had to be directly connected to activities that formed the core of the work. For example, OSHA said, tendinitis in a poultry processor would be covered but a back injury sustained by that same worker while she changed a water bottle would not be covered.

When a covered MSD was reported, a company had two options. It could do a "quick fix" or institute a full program. The quick fix option was intended for problems that could be resolved within ninety days. In workplaces where many employees reported MSDs, employers would have to set up more extensive programs that involved analyzing jobs to assess risk factors, instituting controls to abate those risks, training employees, and providing prompt health care at no cost to the employee. In what was easily the most controversial provision of the package, the standards required employers to pay full wages and benefits for up to six months to recovering employees who were reassigned to light duty because of their injuries. Employees who could not work at all during the six-month period were to be paid 90 percent of their wages and 100 percent of their benefits. Workers' compensation allowed employers to pay only 60 percent of wages.

OSHA officials said the various options were intended to avoid a "one-size-fits-all" approach to regulation and to encourage employers to tailor ergonomics programs to their individual circumstances. The standards were "designed to limit what employers need to do while effectively protecting workers," said Charles N. Jeffress, assistant secretary of labor for occupational health and safety. He estimated that three-fourths of all general industry employers would not need to do anything until a documented MSD occurred. Even then, the agency said, costs for most employers would be minimal—an average of $150 a year for each work station fixed. Total costs were put at $4.2 billion a year, compared with estimated average annual savings of $9 billion.

Opposition from Business Groups, Republican Lawmakers

Opposition to the proposed standards was immediate, passionate, and predictable. Business groups and their allies in Congress had been lobbying against the regulations since OSHA began work on them in the early 1990s. In 1995 Congress passed legislation prohibiting the agency from using funds to issue ergonomics standards. The legislation was one of the first by the new Republican majority designed explicitly to address its business constituency's demand for less regulation. Congress continued the funding prohibition in 1996 and 1997. In 1998 Congress did not block funding for the rules but instead directed the National Academy of Sciences to study the connection between repetitive tasks and repetitive stress injuries. In August 1999 the House voted along party lines to bar OSHA from issuing its regulations until after the academy's report came out, which was not expected until 2001. When the Senate failed to act on the measure, OSHA decided to go ahead and issue the regulation.

Critics castigated OSHA for issuing its rules before the academy study was complete. "We simply do not have the scientific and medical proof to back up OSHA's proposed rule," five Republican House members said in a joint statement. Others said the Clinton administration was trying to rush the standards through before the 2000 presidential election to boost Vice President Al Gore's presidential chances. "Vice President Gore owes a lot to labor unions," one business official said. OSHA officials denied the allegation, noting that they had been studying ergonomics problems for more than a decade and that Elizabeth Dole, briefly a Republican presidential candidate in 1999, had initiated the formal process for developing the ergonomic standards when she was secretary of labor in the Bush administration. They also pointed to an existing academy study, which concluded that MSDs were directly related to work and that measures to alleviate physical stresses on the job reduced MSD injuries.

Other opponents complained that OSHA had seriously underestimated the costs of complying with the regulations. Kevin Burke, vice president of Food Distributors International (FDI), which represented food wholesalers and distributors, said that in the first year the rules would cost FDI members alone as much as $26 billion to retrofit their operations to comply with the rules and $6 billion a year after that. Those costs "would result in closed plants and warehouses and lost jobs, and would . . . be reflected in the cost of goods," he warned.

The Small Business Administration, an independent government agency, also disputed OSHA's cost estimates, saying that the pay and benefits guarantees for injured workers could substantially increase claims filed for injuries. "If this potential is realized," the agency said, "employees will benefit from reduced injuries and illnesses, but employers will experience a net increase in workers' compensation premiums and related costs." Some employer groups said that the regulations were so broadly written that employers would be required to cover health care costs for all MSDs, including those that were caused from sports and other activities not associated with the workers' jobs. "The standard is so badly written, so broadly written, that an employer is not going to know what to do," said Randel Johnson of the U.S. Chamber of Commerce. He said the chamber would challenge the rules in court and lobby Congress to block them from taking effect.

Following are texts of two background documents that accompanied the proposed ergonomics regulations issued November 22, 1999, by the Occupational Safety and Health Administration,

*describing the agency's proposed ergonomics regulations and
explaining why they were necessary:*

OSHA'S PROPOSED ERGONOMICS STANDARD

Ergonomics is the science of fitting the job to the worker. Ergonomics programs can prevent work-related musculoskeletal disorders (MSDs) that occur when there is a mismatch between the worker and the task. Each year 1.8 million workers experience injuries related to overexertion or repetitive motion, and 600,000 are injured severely enough to require time off work. OSHA's proposed standard is designed to help prevent these injuries.

Who's Covered?
- General industry employers with workers involved in manual handling or manufacturing production jobs (about 1.6 million worksites).
- Other general industry employers with one or more workers who experience work-related MSDs after the final standard takes effect (about 300,000 employers each year).
- 75% of general industry employers will not need to take any action!

What Are the Benefits?
- 3 million MSDs will be prevented over 10 years, an average of 300,000 per year.
- 27.3 million workers at 1.9 million worksites will be protected.
- $22,500 savings in direct costs for each MSD prevented.
- $9 billion average savings each year. (Currently MSDs cost $15 to $20 billion in workers' compensation costs with total costs as high as $45 to $60 billion each year.)

What Are the Costs?
- Fixing a work station averages $150 per year.
- Employers will pay $4.2 billion (including $875 million now lost by workers whose income and benefits are not fully covered by workers' compensation).

What Is a Work-Related Musculoskeletal Disorder?
A musculoskeletal disorder is an injury or disorder of the muscles, tendons, ligaments, joints cartilage and spinal discs. To be considered covered, an MSD injury must be:
- Diagnosed by a health care professional, result in a positive physical finding or serious enough to require medical treatment, days away from work or assignment to light duty work—i.e., an "OSHA-recordable" injury.

773

- Directly related to the employee's job. (For example, a warehouse worker's back injury would be covered, but that worker's carpal tunnel syndrome may not.)
- Specifically connected to activities that form the core or a significant part of the worker's job. (For example, a poultry processor might report tendinitis, but a back injury incurred while changing the water bottle occasionally would not be covered.)

What Would the Proposal Require?

- **Basic Program**—for employers with manual handling or manufacturing production jobs:
  - *Management leadership and employee participation*
    - Name someone to be responsible for ergonomics and supply resources and training for the program.
    - Be sure company policies do not discourage employees from reporting problems and let employees know how they can be involved in the ergonomics program.
  - *Hazard information and reporting*
    - Provide information to employees periodically on:
      - Ergonomic risk factors (force, repetition, awkward postures, static postures, contract stress, vibration, cold temperatures).
      - Signs and symptoms of musculoskeletal disorders.
      - Importance of reporting signs and symptoms early to prevent damage and how to make reports.
      - Requirements of this standard.
    - Set up a system for employees to report signs and symptoms of MSDs and respond promptly to reports.
- **Quick Fix**—for problem jobs that can be fixed right away:
  - Promptly care for an injured employee.
  - Work with employees to eliminate the MSD hazard within 90 days.
  - Verify that the fix worked within another 30 days.
  - Keep a record of Quick Fix controls.
  - Establish a full ergonomics program if the fix fails or another MSD of the same type occurs in that job within 36 months.
- **Full Program**—for employers with a covered MSD. Includes the basic program plus:
  - *Job hazard analysis and control*
    - Analyze problem jobs for ergonomic risk factors.
    - Work with employees to eliminate or materially reduce MSD hazards using engineering, administrative and/or work practice controls.
    - Use personal protective equipment to supplement other controls.
    - Track progress, and when jobs change, identify and evaluate MSD hazards.
  - *Training*
    - Train employees in jobs with covered MSDs, their supervisors and

staff responsible for the ergonomics program.
- Teach recognition of MSD hazards, the ergonomics program at the site and control measures used to reduce hazards.
- Conduct training initially, periodically and at least every 3 years at no cost to employees and in language they understand (e.g., Spanish).
- *MSD Management—for workers who have covered MSDs.*
  - Provide prompt response to an injured employee and access to a health care professional, if needed, for evaluation, management and follow-up at no cost to the employee.
    - Provide information to the health care professional about the job, the MSD hazards and the ergonomics standard.
    - Obtain a written opinion from the health care professional on how to manage the employee's recovery and ensure that the health care professional shares it with the worker.
  - Provide necessary work restrictions and work restriction protection (WRP) during the recovery period (100% pay and benefits for employees put on light duty; 90% pay and 100% benefits for employees who must be removed from work). WRP benefits last until the employee can return to work OR the MSD hazards are fixed OR 6 months have passed—which-ever comes first. WRP can be offset by workers' compensation or similar benefits.
- *Program Evaluation*
  - Evaluate the program periodically-at least every 3 years.
  - Consult with employees on program effectiveness and deficiencies.
  - Correct any deficiencies.
- *Recordkeeping*—for employers with 10 or more employees. Retain most records for only 3 years.
- **Grandfather Clause**—Employers who have already developed ergonomics programs won't need to begin again, provided that their ergonomics programs:
  - Meet the basic obligations and recordkeeping requirements of the standard.
  - Were implemented and evaluated before the standard became effective.
  - Are eliminating or materially reducing MSD hazards.

When Is an Employer in Compliance?

An employer has met the requirements of the standard when the controls eliminate or materially reduce MSD hazards. Employers can opt for an incremental process, trying one control and adding others if an injured employee does not improve or another MSD occurs in that job.

When Can an Employer Discontinue an Ergonomics Program?

IF MSD hazards are eliminated or materially reduced **AND** no covered MSD is reported for 3 years, employers may stop all but the following aspects of their ergonomics programs:

- For manufacturing or manual handling jobs:
  - Management leadership and employee participation
  - Hazard information and reporting
  - Maintenance of implemented controls and training related to those controls
- For other general industry jobs where a covered MSD had been reported:
  - maintenance of controls and training related to those controls. . . .

ERGONOMICS STATEMENTS FROM OSHA

I. Introduction

A. Overview

The preamble to this proposed ergonomics program standard discusses the data and events leading OSHA to propose the standard, the Agency's legal authority for proposing this rule, requests for information on a number of issues, and a section describing the significance of the ergonomic-related risks confronting workers in manufacturing, manual handling, and other general industry jobs. The preamble also contains a summary of the Preliminary Economic and Initial Regulatory Flexibility Analysis, a summary of the responses OSHA has made to the findings and recommendations of the Small Business Regulatory Fairness Enforcement Act Panel convened for this rule, a description of the information collections associated with the standard, and a detailed explanation of the Agency's rationale for proposing each provision of the proposed standard.

B. The Need for an Ergonomics Standard

Work-related musculoskeletal disorders (MSDs) currently account for one-third of all occupational injuries and illnesses reported to the Bureau of Labor Statistics (BLS) by employers every year. These disorders thus constitute the largest job-related injury and illness problem in the United States today. In 1997, employers reported a total of 626,000 lost workday MSDs to the BLS, and these disorders accounted for $1 of every $3 spent for workers' compensation in that year. Employers pay more than $15–$20 billion in workers' compensation costs for these disorders every year, and other expenses associated with MSDs may increase this total to $45–$54 billion a year. Workers with severe MSDs can face permanent disability that prevents them from returning to their jobs or handling simple, everyday tasks like combing their hair, picking up a baby, or pushing a shopping cart.

Thousands of companies have taken action to address and prevent these problems. OSHA estimates that 50 percent of all employees but only 28 percent of all workplaces in general industry are already protected by an ergonomics program, because their employers have voluntarily elected to implement an ergonomics program. (The disparity in these estimates shows that most large companies, who employ the majority of the workforce, already have these programs, and that smaller employers have not yet implemented them.) OSHA believes that the proposed standard is needed to bring this protection to the remaining employees in general industry workplaces who are at significant risk of incurring a work-related musculoskeletal disorder but are currently without ergonomics programs.

C. The Science Supporting the Standard

A substantial body of scientific evidence supports OSHA's effort to provide workers with ergonomic protection. . . . This evidence strongly supports two basic conclusions: (1) there is a positive relationship between work-related musculoskeletal disorders and workplace risk factors, and (2) ergonomics programs and specific ergonomic interventions can reduce these injuries.

For example, the National Research Council/National Academy of Sciences found a clear relationship between musculoskeletal disorders and work and between ergonomic interventions and a decrease in such disorders. According to the Academy, "Research clearly demonstrates that specific interventions can reduce the reported rate of musculoskeletal disorders for workers who perform high-risk tasks." . . . A scientific review of hundreds of peer-reviewed studies involving workers with MSDs by the National Institute for Occupational Safety and Health (NIOSH) also supports this conclusion.

The evidence, which is comprised of peer-reviewed epidemiological, biomechanical and pathophysiological studies as well as other published evidence, includes:

- More than 2,000 articles on work-related MSDs and workplace risk factors;
- A 1998 study by the National Research Council/National Academy of Sciences on work-related MSDs;
- A critical review by NIOSH of more than 600 epidemiological studies (1997);
- A 1997 General Accounting Office report of companies with ergonomics programs; and
- Hundreds of published "success stories" from companies with ergonomics programs;

Taken together, this evidence indicates that:

- High levels of exposure to ergonomic risk factors on the job lead to an increased incidence of work-related MSDs;
- Reducing these exposures reduces the incidence and severity of work-related MSDs;
- Work-related MSDs are preventable; and

- Ergonomics programs have demonstrated effectiveness in reducing risk, decreasing exposure and protecting workers against work-related MSDs.

As with any scientific field, research in ergonomics is ongoing. The National Academy of Sciences is undertaking another review of the science in order to expand on its 1998 study. OSHA will examine this and all research results that become available during the rulemaking process, to ensure that the Agency's ergonomics program standard is based on the best available and most current evidence. However, more than enough evidence already exists to proceed with a proposed standard. In the words of the American College of Occupational and Environmental Medicine, the world's largest occupational medical society, "there is an adequate scientific foundation for OSHA to proceed with a proposal and, therefore, no reason for OSHA to delay the rulemaking process. . . ."

D. Employer Experience Supporting the Standard

Employers with companies of all sizes have had great success in using ergonomics programs as a cost-effective way to prevent or reduce work-related MSDs, keeping workers on the job, and boosting productivity and workplace morale. A recent General Accounting Office (GAO) study of several companies with ergonomics programs found that their programs reduced work-related MSDs and associated costs (GAO/HEHS–97–163). The GAO also found that the programs and controls selected by employers to address ergonomic hazards in the workplace were not necessarily costly or complex. As a result, the GAO recommended that OSHA use a flexible regulatory approach in its ergonomics standard that would enable employers to develop their own effective programs. The standard being proposed today reflects this recommendation and builds on the successful programs that thousands of proactive employers have found successful in dealing with their ergonomic problems. . . .

INSTITUTE OF MEDICINE ON MEDICAL MISTAKES
November 29, 1999

Medical mistakes may kill between 44,000 and 98,000 hospital patients a year, according to a report released November 29, 1999, by the Institute of Medicine. The institute, an arm of the National Academy of Sciences, estimated that more than half of the mistakes were preventable and set a goal of cutting the number of mistakes in half within five years. "To err is human," the report said, "but errors can be prevented."

The report offered several recommendations for improving patient safety, including establishing a national center to study and devise strategies for reducing error, and a system of mandatory and voluntary reporting of errors so that the health care profession could learn how to prevent the same mistakes from happening again. President Bill Clinton, Washington legislators, and professional health organizations responded quickly, promising to take immediate steps to implement the report's recommendations.

The Scope of the Problem

Mistakes were not a matter of "recklessness" by individual doctors and nurses, but grew out of the manner in which hospitals, clinics, and pharmacies were operated, the report said. Most common mistakes involved medicines given at the wrong time, in the wrong dose, in dangerous combinations, or to the wrong person. The report said that 7,000 people died each year as a result of medication errors. Doctors' notoriously indecipherable handwriting caused some mistakes, as did drug names that sounded similar. Misunderstanding and lack of communication accounted for many errors. Medical knowledge and technology sometimes outpaced the ability of health providers to keep up, and most health professionals were not required to have their competency retested once they had their licences. Most serious errors occurred in busy settings such as emergency rooms and intensive care units, but mistakes occurred throughout the health care system—in physician's offices, nursing homes, community clinics, and home health care settings.

"These stunningly high rates of medical errors . . . are simply unacceptable in a medical system that promises to 'first do no harm,' " wrote William Richardson, president of the W. K. Kellogg Foundation and chairman of the panel of medical safety experts who wrote the report. Medical "errors can be prevented by designing systems that make it hard for people to do the wrong thing and easy for people to do the right thing," Richardson said.

Preventable medical errors were costly not only in terms of human deaths and injuries, the report said. Total national costs—from lost income and productivity, disability, and health care costs—were estimated to range from $17 billion to $29 billion a year; health care costs accounted for more than half of that total. Preventable errors involving drugs administered in hospitals could cost the nation as much as $2 billion a year, the panel said. Less tangible were the costs of lost public confidence in the health care system.

Some hospitals were already taking steps to cut down the number of medical mistakes. Computerized prescriptions reduced the problem of illegible handwriting. Software was available that sent a warning if a patient should not use the prescribed drug. Hospitals were marking limbs while the patient was still awake to ensure against operation on or removal of the wrong arm or leg. The Food and Drug Administration was taking steps to keep names of new drugs from sounding too much like names of those already on the market.

Despite those efforts, the panel said, there "was no cohesive effort" to improve patient safety. The current system for dealing with medical mistakes relied on a combination of peer review, state and federal regulations, malpractice lawsuits, and evaluations by private accrediting agencies. These venues considered individual or institutionwide mistakes, but no single agency was charged with coordinating a national effort to "design safety" into the overall health care system. To achieve that objective the panel made several recommendations:

- *The federal government should establish a Center for Patient Safety within the Department of Health and Human Services to conduct medical safety research and devise best practices, including prototypes of safety systems. The report said it would cost $30 million to $35 million to set up the center and as much as $100 million a year to run it.*
- *Hospitals and other health care delivery institutions should be required to report all serious mistakes to a state agency that would look for patterns of problems that could then be solved. According to the report, about twenty states required such reports, but the information required varied widely. Information about mistakes that had resulted in death or serious injury would be available to the public. Nonserious mistakes would be collected in a confidential database that would not be available for public review but that might suggest ways to improve medical safety.* (Hospital accreditation, p. 412)

- *All health practitioners should be examined periodically for competence and knowledge of safety practices.*

The reporting recommendations were expected to be controversial because of the confidentiality and liability issues involved. Doctors and other health care professionals were often reluctant to admit to mistakes for fear of inviting internal discipline or malpractice charges. "Safety is a cultural matter, and unless you create a cultural environment in which it becomes safe to talk about errors and near misses, you can't get to work on the root causes of error," said Donald M. Berwick, a professor of health care policy at Harvard and a member of the panel that wrote the report. "You can't use fear or blaming of individuals as a foundation for safety improvement. We want to set up an environment where more errors will be revealed."

Nancy Dickey, past president of the American Medical Association, expressed some skepticism about the recommendation, however. Everyone may "talk about a culture of safety," she said, "but we still live in an environment of blame." Richard H. Wade, senior vice president of the American Hospital Association, said "we agree that the nation needs a better system of reporting and tracking these errors, but a new federal agency many not be the answer. Mandatory reporting can be useful, but it must not become punitive. People will be reluctant to report mistakes if they're afraid of being punished."

Lucian Leape, a professor of health policy at Harvard Medical School and a panel member, said that the risk of discipline or liability was not the only thing preventing doctors from admitting to errors. "Physicians are taught that it's [their] job not to make a mistake. It's like a sin. The whole concept of error as sin, as a moral failing, is deeply ingrained in medicine, and it is very destructive."

The panel's recommendations on reporting errors could also pose a dilemma for federal lawmakers who were supporting legislation to give patients the right to sue their health care plans for treatment denials that resulted in further injury or illness. Such a right would likely intensify the culture of blame that the expert panel said was currently blocking the path to improved medical safety.

Swift Reaction

Reaction to the report's call for action was swift and supportive. In a statement from the White House Rose Garden on December 7, President Clinton announced that he was directing government agencies that provide or finance health care to "lead by example" and apply the latest and best techniques for reducing medical errors in the programs they administer. These programs included Medicare, Medicaid, and veterans and military health programs. The president also said the three hundred or so private health plans that insured federal employees would be required to institute quality improvement and patient safety practices by 2001 if they wanted to continue to do business with the federal government. Altogether some 85 million people would be covered under the president's directives.

Clinton also said he had asked the interagency health care quality task force to report to him within sixty days on ways to implement the report's recommendations. He further announced that he was convening a national conference with state health officials in March 2000 to promote best practices to prevent medical error, and he promised to ask for additional funding to develop quality improvement and patient safety techniques.

On Capitol Hill, Sen. Edward M. Kennedy, D-Mass., was putting together legislation to be introduced in 2000 to implement many of the panel's recommendations, including setting up a national center on patient safety. Kennedy, the senior Democrat on the Senate Health, Education, Labor and Pension Committee, said the committee's Republican chairman, James Jeffords, and Republican member Bill Frist, a doctor from Tennessee, had signaled their interest in holding hearings on patient safety.

The American Hospital Association announced that it was forming a partnership with the Institute for Safe Medication Practices, which would provide hospitals with the latest information on best practices for reducing errors in prescribing and dispensing medicines. The nonprofit institute reviewed medication errors reported by health care professionals across the country and worked with drug companies on labeling and packaging issues to prevent such errors.

Following is the executive summary of a report on medical mistakes, "To Err Is Human: Building a Safer Health System," issued November 29, 1999, by the Institute of Medicine:

The knowledgeable health reporter for the *Boston Globe*, Betsy Lehman, died from an overdose during chemotherapy. Willie King had the wrong leg amputated. Ben Kolb was eight years old when he died during "minor" surgery due to a drug mix-up.

These horrific cases that make the headlines are just the tip of the iceberg. Two large studies, one conducted in Colorado and Utah and the other in New York, found that adverse events occurred in 2.9 and 3.7 percent of hospitalizations, respectively. In Colorado and Utah hospitals, 8.8 percent of adverse events led to death, as compared with 13.6 percent in New York hospitals. In both of these studies, over half of these adverse events resulted from medical errors and could have been prevented.

When extrapolated to the over 33.6 million admissions to U.S. hospitals in 1997, the results of the study in Colorado and Utah imply that at least 44,000 Americans die each year as a result of medical errors. The results of the New York Study suggest the number may be as high as 98,000. Even when using the lower estimate, deaths due to medical errors exceed the number attributable to the 8th leading cause of death. More people die in a given year as a result of medical errors than from motor vehicle accidents (43,458), breast cancer (42,297), or AIDS (16,516).

Total national costs (lost income, lost household production, disability and health care costs) of preventable adverse events (medical errors resulting in injury) are estimated to be between $17 billion and $29 billion, of which health care costs represent over one-half.

In terms of lives lost, patient safety is as important an issue as worker safety. Every year, over 6,000 Americans die from workplace injuries. Medication errors alone, occurring either in or out of the hospital, are estimated to account for over 7,000 deaths annually.

Medication-related errors occur frequently in hospitals and although not all result in actual harm, those that do, are costly. One recent study conducted at two prestigious teaching hospitals, found that about two out of every 100 admissions experienced a preventable adverse drug event, resulting in average increased hospital costs of $4,700 per admission or about $2.8 million annually for a 700-bed teaching hospital. If these findings are generalizable, the increased hospital costs alone of preventable adverse drug events affecting inpatients are about $2 billion for the nation as a whole.

These figures offer only a very modest estimate of the magnitude of the problem since hospital patients represent only a small proportion of the total population at risk, and direct hospital costs are only a fraction of total costs. More care and increasingly complex care is provided in ambulatory settings. Outpatient surgical centers, physician offices and clinics serve thousands of patients daily. Home care requires patients and their families to use complicated equipment and perform follow-up care. Retail pharmacies play a major role in filling prescriptions for patients and educating them about their use. Other institutional settings, such as nursing homes, provide a broad array of services to vulnerable populations. Although many of the available studies have focused on the hospital setting, medical errors present a problem in any setting, not just hospitals.

Errors are also costly in terms of opportunity costs. Dollars spent on having to repeat diagnostic tests or counteract adverse drug events are dollars unavailable for other purposes. Purchasers and patients pay for errors when insurance costs and copayments are inflated by services that would not have been necessary had proper care been provided. It is impossible for the nation to achieve the greatest value possible from the hundreds of millions of dollars spent on medical care if the care contains errors.

But not all the costs can be directly measured. Errors are also costly in terms of loss of trust in the system by patients and diminished satisfaction by both patients and health professionals. Patients who experience a longer hospital stay or disability as a result of errors pay with physical and psychological discomfort. Health care professionals pay with loss of morale and frustration at not being able to provide the best care possible. Employers and society, in general, pay in terms of lost worker productivity, reduced school attendance by children, and lower levels of population health status.

Yet silence surrounds this issue. For the most part, consumers believe they are protected. Media coverage has been limited to reporting of anecdotal cases. Licensure and accreditation confer, in the eyes of the public, a "Good Housekeeping Seal of Approval." Yet, licensing and accreditation processes have focused only limited attention on the issue, and even these minimal efforts have confronted some resistance from health care organizations and providers. Providers also perceive the medical liability system as a serious impediment to systematic efforts to uncover and learn from errors.

The decentralized and fragmented nature of the health care delivery system (some would say "nonsystem") also contributes to unsafe conditions for patients, and serves as an impediment to efforts to improve safety. Even within hospitals and large medical groups, there are rigidly-defined areas of specialization and influence. For example, when patients see multiple providers in different settings, none of whom have access to complete information, it is easier for something to go wrong than when care is better coordinated. At the same time, the provision of care to patients by a collection of loosely affiliated organizations and providers makes it difficult to implement improved clinical information systems capable of providing timely access to complete patient information. Unsafe care is one of the prices we pay for not having organized systems of care with clear lines of accountability.

Lastly, the context in which health care is purchased further exacerbates these problems. Group purchasers have made few demands for improvements in safety. Most third party payment systems provide little incentive for a health care organization to improve safety, nor do they recognize and reward safety or quality.

The goal of this report is to break this cycle of inaction. The status quo is not acceptable and cannot be tolerated any longer. Despite the cost pressures, liability constraints, resistance to change and other seemingly insurmountable barriers, it is simply not acceptable for patients to be harmed by the same health care system that is supposed to offer healing and comfort. "First do no harm" is an often quoted term from Hippocrates. Everyone working in health care is familiar with the term. At a very minimum, the health system needs to offer that assurance and security to the public.

A comprehensive approach to improving patient safety is needed. This approach cannot focus on a single solution since there is no "magic bullet" that will solve this problem, and indeed, no single recommendation in this report should be considered as *the* answer. Rather, large, complex problems require thoughtful, multifaceted responses. The combined goal of the recommendations is for the external environment to create sufficient pressure to make errors costly to health care organizations and providers, so they are compelled to take action to improve safety. At the same time, there is a need to enhance knowledge and tools to improve safety and break down legal and cultural barriers that impede safety improvement. Given current knowledge about the magnitude of the problem, the committee believes it would be irresponsible to expect anything less than a 50 percent reduction in errors over five years.

In this report, safety is defined as freedom from accidental injury. This definition recognizes that this is the primary safety goal from the patient's perspective. Error is defined as the failure of a planned action to be completed as intended or the use of a wrong plan to achieve an aim. According to noted expert James Reason, errors depend on two kinds of failures: either the correct action does not proceed as intended (an error of execution) or the original intended action is not correct, (an error of planning). Errors can happen in all stages in the process of care, from diagnosis, to treatment, to preventive care.

Not all errors result in harm. Errors that do result in injury are sometimes called preventable adverse events. An adverse event is an injury resulting from a medical intervention, or in other words, it is not due to the underlying condition of the patient. While all adverse events result from medical management, not all are preventable (i.e., not all are attributable to errors). For example, if a patient has surgery and dies from pneumonia he or she got postoperatively, it is an adverse event. If analysis of the case reveals that the patient got pneumonia because of poor hand washing or instrument cleaning techniques by staff, the adverse event was preventable (attributable to an error of execution). But the analysis may conclude that no error occurred and the patient would be presumed to have had a difficult surgery and recovery (not a preventable adverse event).

Much can be learned from the analysis of errors. All adverse events resulting in serious injury or death should be evaluated to assess whether improvements in the delivery system can be made to reduce the likelihood of similar events occurring in the future. Errors that do not result in harm also represent an important opportunity to identify system improvements having the potential to prevent adverse events.

Preventing errors means designing the health care system at all levels to make it safer. Building safety into processes of care is a more effective way to reduce errors than blaming individuals (some experts . . . believe improving processes is the *only* way to improve quality). The focus must shift from blaming individuals for past errors to a focus on preventing future errors by designing safety into the system. This does not mean that individuals can be careless. People must still be vigilant and held responsible for their actions. But when an error occurs, blaming an individual does little to make the system safer and prevent someone else from committing the same error.

Health care is a decade or more behind other high-risk industries in its attention to ensuring basic safety. Aviation has focused extensively on building safe systems and has been doing so since World War II. Between 1990 and 1994, the U.S. airline fatality rate was less than one-third the rate experienced in mid century. In 1998, there were no deaths in the United States in commercial aviation. In health care, preventable injuries from care have been estimated to affect between three to four percent of hospital patients. Although health care may never achieve aviation's impressive record, there is clearly room for improvement.

To err is human, but errors can be prevented. Safety is a critical first step in improving quality of care. The Harvard Medical Practice Study, a seminal

research study on this issue, was published almost ten years ago; other studies have corroborated its findings. Yet few tangible actions to improve
patient safety can be found. Must we wait another decade to be safe in our
health system?

Recommendations

The IOM Quality of Health Care in America Committee was formed in June
1998 to develop a strategy that will result in a threshold improvement in quality over the next ten years. This report addresses issues related to patient
safety, a subset of overall quality-related concerns, and lays out a national
agenda for reducing errors in health care and improving patient safety.
Although it is a national agenda, many activities are aimed at prompting
responses at the state and local levels and within health care organizations
and professional groups.

The committee believes that although there is still much to learn about the
types of errors committed in health care and why they occur, enough is
known today to recognize that a serious concern exists for patients. Whether
a person is sick or just trying to stay healthy, they should not have to worry
about being harmed by the health system itself. This report is a call to action
to make health care safer for patients.

The committee believes that a major force for improving patient safety is
the intrinsic motivation of health care providers, shaped by professional
ethics, norms and expectations. But the interaction between factors in the
external environment and factors inside health care organizations can also
prompt the changes needed to improve patient safety. Factors in the external
environment include availability of knowledge and tools to improve safety,
strong and visible professional leadership, legislative and regulatory initiatives, and actions of purchasers and consumers to demand safety improvements. Factors inside health care organizations include strong leadership for
safety, an organizational culture that encourages recognition and learning
from errors, and an effective patient safety program.

In developing its recommendations, the committee seeks to strike a balance between regulatory and market-based initiatives, and between the roles
of professionals and organizations. No single action represents a complete
answer, nor can any single group or sector offer a complete fix to the problem. However, different groups can, and should, make significant contributions to the solution. The committee recognizes that a number of groups are
already working on improving patient safety, such as the National Patient
Safety Foundation and the Anesthesia Patient Safety Foundation.

The recommendations contained in this report lay out a four-tiered
approach:

- establishing a national focus to create leadership, research, tools and
  protocols to enhance the knowledge base about safety;
- identifying and learning from errors through the immediate and strong
  mandatory reporting efforts, as well as the encouragement of voluntary

efforts, both with the aim of making sure the system continues to be made safer for patients;

- raising standards and expectations for improvements in safety through the actions of oversight organizations, group purchasers, and professional groups; and
- creating safety systems inside health care organizations through the implementation of safe practices at the delivery level. This level is the ultimate target of all the recommendations.

Leadership and Knowledge

Other industries that have been successful in improving safety, such as aviation and occupational health, have had the support of a designated agency that sets and communicates priorities, monitors progress in achieving goals, directs resources toward areas of need, and brings visibility to important issues. Although various agencies and organizations in health care may contribute to certain of these activities, there is no focal point for raising and sustaining attention to patient safety. Without it, health care is unlikely to match the safety improvements achieved in other industries.

The growing awareness of the frequency and significance of errors in health care creates an imperative to improve our understanding of the problem and devise workable solutions. For some types of errors, the knowledge of how to prevent them exists today. In these areas, the need is for widespread dissemination of this information. For other areas, however, additional work is needed to develop and apply the knowledge that will make care safer for patients. Resources invested in building the knowledge base and diffusing the expertise throughout the industry can pay large dividends to both patients and the health professionals caring for them and produce savings for the health system.

> **RECOMMENDATION 4.1** Congress should create a Center for Patient Safety within the Agency for Health Care Policy and Research. This center should
> - set the national goals for patient safety, track progress in meeting these goals, and issue an annual report to the President and Congress on patient safety; and
> - develop knowledge and understanding of errors in health care by developing a research agenda, funding Centers of Excellence, evaluating methods for identifying and preventing errors, and funding dissemination and communication activities to improve patient safety.

To make significant improvements in patient safety, a highly visible center is needed, with secure and adequate funding. The Center should establish goals for safety; develop a research agenda; define prototype safety systems; develop and disseminate tools for identifying and analyzing errors and evaluate approaches taken; develop tools and methods for educating consumers about patient safety; issue an annual report on the state of patient safety, and recommend additional improvements as needed.

The committee recommends initial annual funding for the Center of $30 to $35 million. This initial funding would permit a center to conduct activities in goal setting, tracking, research and dissemination. Funding should grow over time to at least $100 million, or approximately 1% of the $8.8 billion in health care costs attributable to preventable adverse events. This initial level of funding is modest relative to the resources devoted to other public health issues. The Center for Patient Safety should be created within the Agency for Health Care Policy and Research because the agency is already involved in a broad range of quality and safety issues, and has established the infrastructure and experience to fund research, educational and coordinating activities.

Identifying and Learning from Errors

Another critical component of a comprehensive strategy to improve patient safety is to create an environment that encourages organizations to identify errors, evaluate causes and take appropriate actions to improve performance in the future. External reporting systems represent one mechanism to enhance our understanding of errors and the underlying factors that contribute to them.

Reporting systems can be designed to meet two purposes. They can be designed as part of a public system for holding health care organizations accountable for performance. In this instance, reporting is often mandatory, usually focuses on specific cases that involve serious harm or death, may result in fines or penalties relative to the specific case, and information about the event may become known to the public. Such systems ensure a response to specific reports of serious injury, hold organizations and providers accountable for maintaining safety, respond to the public's right to know, and provide incentives to health care organizations to implement internal safety systems that reduce the likelihood of such events occurring. Currently, at least twenty states have mandatory adverse event reporting systems.

Voluntary, confidential reporting systems can also be part of an overall program for improving patient safety and can be designed to complement the mandatory reporting systems previously described. Voluntary reporting systems, which generally focus on a much broader set of errors and strive to detect system weaknesses before the occurrence of serious harm, can provide rich information to health care organizations in support of their quality improvement efforts

For either purpose, the goal of reporting systems is to analyze the information they gather and identify ways to prevent future errors from occurring. The goal is not data collection. Collecting reports and not doing anything with the information serves no useful purpose. Adequate resources and other support must be provided for analysis and response to critical issues.

RECOMMENDATION 5.1   A nationwide mandatory reporting system should be established that provides for the collection of standardized information by state governments about adverse events that result in death or serious harm. Reporting should initially be required of hospitals and eventually be required of other institutional and ambulatory care delivery settings. Congress should

- designate the Forum for Health Care Quality Measurement and Reporting as the entity responsible for promulgating and maintaining a core set of reporting standards to be used by states, including a nomenclature and taxonomy for reporting;
- require all health care organizations to report standardized information on a defined list of adverse events;
- provide funds and technical expertise for state governments to establish or adapt their current error reporting systems to collect the standardized information, analyze it and conduct follow-up action as needed with health care organizations. Should a state choose not to implement the mandatory reporting system, the Department of Health and Human Services should be designated as the responsible entity; and
- designate the Center for Patient Safety to:
  (1) convene states to share information and expertise, and to evaluate alternative approaches taken for implementing reporting programs, identify best practices for implementation, and assess the impact of state programs; and
  (2) receive and analyze aggregate reports from States to identify persistent safety issues that require more intensive analysis and/ or a broader-based response (e.g., designing prototype systems or requesting a response by agencies, manufacturers or others).

RECOMMENDATION 5.2 The development of voluntary reporting efforts should be encouraged. The Center for Patient Safety should

- describe and disseminate information on external voluntary reporting programs to encourage greater participation in them and track the development of new reporting systems as they form;
- convene sponsors and users of external reporting systems to evaluate what works and what does not work well in the programs, and ways to make them more effective;
- periodically assess whether additional efforts are needed to address gaps in information to improve patient safety and to encourage health care organizations to participate in voluntary reporting programs; and
- fund and evaluate pilot projects for reporting systems, both within individual health care organizations and collaborative efforts among health care organizations.

The committee believes there is a role both for mandatory, public reporting systems and voluntary, confidential reporting systems. However, because of their distinct purposes, such systems should be operated and maintained separately. A nationwide mandatory reporting system should be established by building upon the current patchwork of state systems and by standardizing the types of adverse events and information to be reported. The newly established Forum for Health Care Quality Measurement and Reporting, a public/ private partnership, should be charged with the establishment of such standards. Voluntary reporting systems should also be promoted and the participation of health care organizations in them should be encouraged by accrediting bodies.

RECOMMENDATION 6.1 Congress should pass legislation to extend peer review protections to data related to patient safety and quality improvement that are collected and analyzed by health care organiza-

tions for internal use or shared with others solely for purposes of improving safety and quality.

The committee believes that information about the most serious adverse events which result in harm to patients and which are subsequently found to result from errors should not be protected from public disclosure. However, the committee also recognizes that for events not falling under this category, fears about the legal discoverability of information may undercut motivations to detect and analyze errors to improve safety. Unless such data are assured protection, information about errors will continue to be hidden and errors will be repeated. A more conducive environment is needed to encourage health care professionals and organizations to identify, analyze, and report errors without threat of litigation and without compromising patients' legal rights.

Setting Performance Standards and Expectations for Safety

Setting and enforcing explicit standards for safety through regulatory and related mechanisms, such as licensing, certification, and accreditation, can define minimum performance levels for health care organizations and professionals. Additionally, the process of developing and adopting standards helps to form expectations for safety among providers and consumers. However, standards and expectations are not only set through regulations. The actions of purchasers and consumers affect the behaviors of health care organizations, and the values and norms set by health professions influence standards of practice, training and education for providers. Standards for patient safety can be applied to health care professionals, the organizations in which they work, and the tools (drugs and devices) they use to care for patients.

> **RECOMMENDATION 7.1 Performance standards and expectations for health care organizations should focus greater attention on patient safety.**
>
> - **Regulators and accreditors should require health care organizations to implement meaningful patient safety programs with defined executive responsibility.**
> - **Public and private purchasers should provide incentives to health care organizations to demonstrate continuous improvement in patient safety.**

Health care organizations are currently subject to compliance with licensing and accreditation standards. Although both devote some attention to issues related to patient safety, there is opportunity to strengthen such efforts. Regulators and accreditors have a role in encouraging and supporting actions in health care organizations by holding them accountable for ensuring a safe environment for patients. After a reasonable period of time for health care organizations to develop patient safety programs, regulators and accreditors should require them as a minimum standard.

Purchaser and consumer demands also exert influence on health care organizations. Public and private purchasers should consider safety issues in their contracting decisions and reinforce the importance of patient safety by providing relevant information to their employees or beneficiaries. Purchasers should also communicate concerns about patient safety to accrediting bodies to support stronger oversight for patient safety.

RECOMMENDATION 7.2   Performance standards and expectations for health professionals should focus greater attention on patient safety.

- **Health professional licensing bodies should**
  (1) **implement periodic re-examinations and re-licensing of doctors, nurses, and other key providers, based on both competence and knowledge of safety practices; and**
  (2) **work with certifying and credentialing organizations to develop more effective methods to identify unsafe providers and take action.**
- **Professional societies should make a visible commitment to patient safety by establishing a permanent committee dedicated to safety improvement. This committee should**
  (1) **develop a curriculum on patient safety and encourage its adoption into training and certification requirements;**
  (2) **disseminate information on patient safety to members through special sessions at annual conferences, journal articles and editorials, newsletters, publications and websites on a regular basis;**
  (3) **recognize patient safety considerations in practice guidelines and in standards related to the introduction and diffusion of new technologies, therapies and drugs;**
  (4) **work with the Center for Patient Safety to develop community-based, collaborative initiatives for error reporting and analysis and implementation of patient safety improvements; and**
  (5) **collaborate with other professional societies and disciplines in a national summit on the professional's role in patient safety.**

Although unsafe practitioners are believed to be few in number, the rapid identification of such practitioners and corrective action are important to a comprehensive safety program. Responsibilities for documenting continuing skills are dispersed among licensing boards, specialty boards and professional groups, and health care organizations with little communication or coordination. In their ongoing assessments, existing licensing, certification and accreditation processes for health professionals should place greater attention on safety and performance skills.

Additionally, professional societies and groups should become active leaders in encouraging and demanding improvements in patient safety. Setting standards, convening and communicating with members about safety, incorporating attention to patient safety into training programs and collaborating across disciplines are all mechanisms that will contribute to creating a culture of safety.

RECOMMENDATION 7.3   The Food and Drug Administration (FDA) should increase attention to the safe use of drugs in both pre-and post-marketing processes through the following actions:

- **develop and enforce standards for the design of drug packaging and labeling that will maximize safety in use;**
- **require pharmaceutical companies to test (using FDA-approved methods) proposed drug names to identify and remedy potential sound-alike and look-alike confusion with existing drug names; and**
- **work with physicians, pharmacists, consumers, and others to establish appropriate responses to problems identified through post-marketing surveillance, especially for concerns that are perceived to require immediate response to protect the safety of patients.**

The FDA's role is to regulate manufacturers for the safety and effectiveness of their drugs and devices. However, even approved products can present safety problems in practice. For example, different drugs with similar sounding names can create confusion for both patients and providers. Attention to the safety of products in actual use should be increased during approval processes and in post-marketing monitoring systems. The FDA should also work with drug manufacturers, distributors, pharmacy benefit managers, health plans and other organizations to assist clinicians in identifying and preventing problems in the use of drugs.

Implementing Safety Systems in Health Care Organizations

Experience in other high-risk industries has provided well-understood illustrations that can be used to improve health care safety. However, health care management and professionals have rarely provided specific, clear, high-level, organization-wide incentives to apply what has been learned in other industries about ways to prevent error and reduce harm within their own organizations. Chief Executive Officers and Boards of Trustees should be held accountable for making a serious, visible and on-going commitment to creating safe systems of care.

> **RECOMMENDATION 8.1 Health care organizations and the professionals affiliated with them should make continually improved patient safety a declared and serious aim by establishing patient safety programs with defined executive responsibility. Patient safety programs should**
>
> - **provide strong, clear and visible attention to safety;**
> - **implement non-punitive systems for reporting and analyzing errors within their organizations;**
> - **incorporate well-understood safety principles, such as, standardizing and simplifying equipment, supplies and processes; and**
> - **establish interdisciplinary team training programs for providers that incorporate proven methods of team training, such as simulation.**

Health care organizations must develop a culture of safety such that an organization's care processes and workforce are focused on improving the reliability and safety of care for patients. Safety should be an explicit organizational goal that is demonstrated by the strong direction and involvement of governance, management and clinical leadership. In addition, a meaningful patient safety program should include defined program objectives, personnel, and budget and should be monitored by regular progress reports to governance.

RECOMMENDATION 8.2 Health care organizations should implement proven medication safety practices.

A number of practices have been shown to reduce errors in the medication process. Several professional and collaborative organizations interested in patient safety have developed and published recommendations for safe medication practices, especially for hospitals. Although some of these recommendations have been implemented, none have been universally adopted and some are not yet implemented in a majority of hospitals. Safe medication practices should be implemented in all hospitals and health care organizations in which they are appropriate.

Summary

This report lays out a comprehensive strategy for addressing a serious problem in health care to which we are all vulnerable. By laying out a concise list of recommendations, the committee does not underestimate the many barriers that must be overcome to accomplish this agenda. Significant changes are required to improve awareness of the problem by the public and health professionals, to align payment systems and the liability system so they encourage safety improvements, to develop training and education programs that emphasize the importance of safety and for chief executive officers and trustees of health care organizations to create a culture of safety and demonstrate it in their daily decisions.

Although no single activity can offer the solution, the combination of activities proposed offers a roadmap toward a safer health system. The proposed program should be evaluated after five years to assess progress in making the health system safer. With adequate leadership, attention and resources, improvements can be made. It may be part of human nature to err, but it is also part of human nature to create solutions, find better alternatives and meet the challenges ahead.

December

U.S. Trade Representative on
  World Trade Organization Talks . . . 797

Reports on Human Rights
  Violations in Kosovo 802

European Council on a New
  European Defense Force 817

Department of Justice Report
  on Capital Punishment 828

Surgeon General's Report
  on Mental Health 836

Former President Carter on
  the Panama Canal Transfer 850

Cartoonist Charles M. Schulz
  on His Retirement 856

United Nations Report on the
  1994 Genocide in Rwanda 860

Remarks at Peace Talks
  Between Israel and Syria 890

Vermont Supreme Court on
  the Rights of Homosexuals 898

UN Human Rights Official
  on the War in Chechnya 909

Boris Yeltsin on His Resignation
  as Russian President 917

U.S. TRADE REPRESENTATIVE ON WORLD TRADE ORGANIZATION TALKS
December 3, 1999

Deep conflicts in the economic and political interests of industrialized and developing countries led to the collapse in 1999 of an attempt to begin a new round of negotiations on global trade issues. The United States and some European countries had hoped to launch a "Millennium round" of negotiations on a complex series of trade issues, under the auspices of the World Trade Organization (WTO), beginning in 2000. But during a stormy four-day session in Seattle—punctuated by massive street demonstrations that erupted into a day of unexpected violence—representatives of the WTO's 135 member countries found little to agree on, and so plans for the negotiations were put on hold.

U.S. and European officials reached agreement later in December on several limited issues relating to global trade talks. But as of the end of 1999 it appeared likely that wide-ranging negotiations, of the type contemplated at the Seattle meeting, would not get underway at least until after a new U.S. president took office in 2001. "Things are going to just limp along until there can be a wholesale rethinking of the trade strategy," Julius Katz, a trade consultant who had been deputy trade negotiator during the Bush administration, said.

The failure of the WTO talks did not auger well for the Clinton administration's hopes of getting Congress to approve a bilateral trade agreement with China in 2000. U.S. and Chinese officials in November had agreed on a sweeping trade agreement intended, in part, to help pave the way for China's entry into the WTO. (China trade agreement, p. 724)

The Trade Negotiations System

The United States and its key trading partners had been negotiating regularly since the 1930s about the underlying principles of global trade. For most of those years, until the 1990s, most of the talks centered around tariffs—the taxes that each country imposed on goods imported from other countries. Following World War II the global trade talks were conducted under a system known as the General Agreement on Tariffs and Trade (GATT). The last round of negotiations under GATT (known as the Uruguay Round because the negotiations began there in 1986) was concluded in 1994. (Uruguay Round, Historic Documents of 1994, p. 555)

A principle outcome of the Uruguay Round was the formation of the WTO, a global agency based in Geneva with significant power to enforce trading standards and to mediate disputes between countries. Key European countries began pressing in 1998 for another round of trade talks to deal with the many complex issues that were arising because of the increasing importance of worldwide trade. The Clinton administration agreed to join the call for more negotiations, and plans were laid for the meeting in Seattle to establish an agenda for the negotiations, which were expected to last for at least three years. Following the announcement of the Seattle meeting, environmental groups, labor unions, and other special interest groups said they would be on hand to draw attention to issues they said trade negotiations routinely ignored.

Key Issues in Dispute

Even before the Seattle meeting got underway, some experts said the time was not right for the opening of a new round of multilateral trade talks. Most important, these experts said, there was no consensus about how to approach the many issues facing trade negotiators, much less a consensus on how to resolve those issues. The first sign that the skeptics might be right came a week before the scheduled November 30 opening of the Seattle meeting. Representatives of about twenty key trading countries met in Geneva to try to develop an agenda for the Seattle meeting but were unable to do so.

The thousands of delegates and observers had just arrived in Seattle for the WTO meeting when another sign of trouble arose. As an estimated 30,000 demonstrators from environmental groups, labor unions, and other organizations marched peacefully in downtown Seattle to protest various aspects of the WTO agenda, a small number of protesters turned violent November 30—smashing windows, looting storefronts, and throwing rocks at police. The Seattle police, who for months had prepared for dealing with peaceful demonstrators, were surprised by the violence. At first the police stood by, then they sprayed tear gas and fired rubber bullets at many of the peaceful protesters. The police and National Guard troops, who were called in December 1 to restore order, arrested nearly 600 protesters; nearly all of those arrested were later let go. In the meantime, Seattle's image as a progressive, easy-going city suffered untold damage from the media coverage of the violence. The city's merchants also suffered an estimated $3 million loss in property damage and about three times that much in lost business.

Inside the convention center where WTO delegates were meeting, the atmosphere was only marginally more peaceful. Negotiators attempted to confront dozens of trade matters but made little progress on any. In the end, three major underlying issues blocked an agreement to schedule a formal round of negotiations: a rash of disputes over agricultural trade policy, demands by developing nations for a greater say in how the WTO made decisions, and the Clinton administration's effort to make labor and environmental standards a central part of future trade deals.

As was always the case with multilateral trade negotiations, agriculture issues were among the most contentious. As had been the case for years, some of the most heated disputes were between the United States and its allies in the European Union. The United States had long demanded that European countries halt farm subsidies, and European nations in turn insisted on their right to bar imports from the United States of such products as genetically altered food items and beef from hormone-treated cattle. The Seattle meeting produced no serious progress on these issues.

There was general agreement in Seattle about the need for more "openness" and "transparency" in WTO deliberations, but no formal agreement on how to go about it. The most important negotiations on multilateral trade deals were almost always conducted in secret, and in most cases only a handful of powerful countries made the key decisions. Moreover, WTO deliberations on trade disputes between countries were conducted entirely in secret, with members of the public and special interest groups having no opportunity to influence decisions.

President Bill Clinton started campaigning before the Seattle meeting for more openness within the WTO, and he repeated that message in a speech to the assembled delegates. "I think it's imperative that the WTO become more open and accessible," he said. "If the WTO expects to have public support grow for our endeavors, the public must see and hear and, in a very real sense, actually join in the deliberations."

The Seattle meeting produced no concrete action on the secrecy issue. But two weeks later, during a December 17 meeting at the White House, Clinton and Romano Prodi, the recently elected president of the European Commission, agreed to push within the WTO for interim steps such as making trade organization documents and decisions available more widely and more quickly than in the past.

Clinton's Push on Labor Standards

Aside from the street demonstrations, the aspect of the Seattle meeting that received the most public attention was the Clinton administration's proposal to incorporate labor and environmental issues into trade negotiations. At the least, labor and environmental groups wanted to ensure that U.S. laws would not be undermined by trade deals or decisions rendered by the WTO. In one case frequently cited by environmentalists, the WTO ruled that the United States could not bar imports of shrimp from Asian countries that did not use fishing nets intended to protect endangered sea turtles.

In the months leading up to the Seattle meeting, the Clinton administration had reached general agreement with U.S. labor leaders on an approach for putting labor issues on the WTO agenda; that approach called for the creation of a WTO "working group" to come up with recommenda-

*tions for fair labor standards, such as prohibitions on the use of child labor
or forced labor.*

*U.S. officials viewed the study group proposal as a reasonable compro-
mise, but representatives of many developing countries viewed it as a
threat by the world's wealthiest, most powerful country to impose its standards on them. Delegates from Brazil, Egypt, India, and other countries
said the United States was planning to use labor standards as a back-door
means of keeping out their nations' products. These delegates also said they
worried about allowing the WTO to become a powerful international agency
with authority to police workshops all over the world. The representatives
of developing countries voiced yet another suspicion: Clinton, they said,
was merely playing to domestic U.S. politics, hoping to shore up support
among labor unions for the presidential candidacy in 2000 of his vice president, Al Gore.*

*Clinton inadvertently heightened the suspicions of developing countries
when he suggested in an interview with the* Seattle Post-Intelligencer, *published as the WTO meeting began, that the WTO eventually might apply
sanctions to countries that violated fair labor standards. Clinton's aides
then had to spend days trying to assure delegates that the president had
misspoken and was not advocating sanctions.*

*As an alternative to Clinton's proposed WTO working group, delegates
from some countries suggested turning the issue of labor standards over to
the International Labor Organization, an affiliate of the United Nations. The
administration and U.S. labor leaders resisted that proposal, saying that the
labor organization was a toothless agency with little power or influence.*

*The deadlock in Seattle meant that the issue of labor standards was dead,
at least for the time being. Even so, U.S. labor leaders portrayed the events
in Seattle as helping their cause, saying that the public protests and the
intense debate within the WTO meant that issues such as international
labor and environmental standards would at some point have to be taken
into account. "The breakdown [in the talks] reflects the first step in a serious coming to terms with pivotal issues: accountability, democratic procedures, workers' and human rights, and the environment," AFL-CIO President John J. Sweeney said after the meeting.*

> *Following is the text of a statement by Charlene Barshefsky, the
> U.S. trade representative and the chair of the ministerial meet-
> ing of the World Trade Organization held in Seattle from Novem-
> ber 30, 1999, to December 3, 1999, in which she announced that
> the meeting had failed to reach agreement on a new round of
> multilateral trade negotiations:*

Let me begin by offering my sincere thanks to Director-General [Mike]
Moore, to our Working Group Chairs and Co-Chairs, the WTO Secretariat, and

to each of the delegations representing their governments here at this Ministerial, for their very hard and productive work over the past week. I would also like to thank our hosts in the Seattle community for their hospitality and patience during a sometimes very difficult week.

Over the past four days, we engaged in intense discussion and negotiations on one of the core questions facing the world today: the creation of a global trading economy for the next century. The delegates have taken up some of the most profound and important issues and policy decisions imaginable, including issues that previous Rounds could not resolve, and matters that have not come before the trading system in the past. They took up these issues with good will and mutual respect, and made progress on many of them.

However, the issues before us are diverse, complex and often novel. And together with this, we found that the WTO has outgrown the processes appropriate to an earlier time. An increasing and necessary view, generally shared among the members, was that we needed a process which had a greater degree of internal transparency and inclusion to accommodate a larger and more diverse membership.

This is a very difficult combination to manage. It stretched both the substantive and procedural capacity of the Ministerial, and we found as time passed that divergences of opinion remained that would not be overcome rapidly. Our collective judgment, shared by the Director-General, the Working Group Chairs and Co-Chairs, and the membership generally, was that it would be best to take a time out, consult with one another, and find creative means to finish the job.

Therefore, Ministers have agreed to suspend the work of the Ministerial. During this time, the Director-General can consult with delegations and discuss creative ways in which we might bridge the remaining areas in which consensus does not yet exist, develop an improved process which is both efficient and fully inclusive, and prepare the way for successful conclusion. The Ministerial will then resume its work.

Again, I wish to thank Director-General Moore, the Seattle community, and all our delegations for their hard work and their participation in these talks. Our work together has been a honor and a privilege for me, and I look forward to its continuation in the weeks and months ahead.

REPORTS ON HUMAN RIGHTS VIOLATIONS IN KOSOVO
December 6 and 9, 1999

Televised images and other news reporting made it clear during 1999 that the tiny Yugoslav province of Kosovo suffered one of the most devastating upheavals of the last half of the twentieth century. Two reports issued in early December laid out in grisly detail the full extent of Kosovo's misfortune. An estimated 10,000 people had been killed and about 1.5 million people—90 percent of the ethnic Albanian population—had been forced out of their homes before and during NATO's eleven-week war to end the Yugoslav government's anti-Albanian terror campaign there. After the war was over, nearly all the Albanians returned, but most of the local Serbian population fled and some of the Serbs who remained were targeted for revenge. (Kosovo war, pp. 134, 285, 304)

The most comprehensive document on human rights abuses in Kosovo was issued December 6 by the Organization for Security and Cooperation in Europe (OSCE), a multinational agency that during late 1998 and early 1999 had tried to monitor a cease-fire in Kosovo. The OSCE issued two reports: one covering the situation in Kosovo from 1998 to the end of NATO's air war against Yugoslavia on June 10, 1999, and one covering mid-June through the end of October. On December 9 the U.S. State Department released another detailed report on human rights violations in Kosovo, focusing on events since the March 24 start of the NATO war.

Both reports pointed to the Yugoslav government, headed by President Slobodan Milosevic, and Serbian security forces acting under Belgrade's direction, as the principal violators of human rights in Kosovo. Kosovo was a province of Serbia, one of the two constituent republics remaining in the Federal Republic of Yugoslavia after its breakup in 1991–1992. An Albanian independence movement in Kosovo launched attacks against the Serbian-dominated government early in 1998, leading to a gradual escalation of conflict that resulted in the NATO air campaign from March 24 to June 10.

The International War Crimes Tribunal for the former Yugoslavia, a UN affiliate, on May 27 charged Milosevic and four senior aides with ordering murders, forced deportations, and other crimes against humanity against Albanians in Kosovo. Louise Arbour, the tribunal's chief prosecutor, said arrest warrants for the four men had been delivered to all UN member states. Indicted along with Milosevic were Milan Milutinovic, the president of Serbia; Dragoljub Ojdanic, chief of staff of the Yugoslav armed forces; Nikola Sainovic, deputy prime minister of Yugoslavia; and Vlajko Stojilkovic, the Yugoslav minister of internal affairs.

The two senior Serbian leaders in Bosnia—Radovan Karadzic and General Ratko Mladic—were indicted by the same tribunal in 1995 for war crimes during the 1992–1995 Bosnian war. Both men remained at large in Bosnia four years after their indictment. (Bosnia war, p. 735)

Serbian Campaign Against Kosovar Albanians

The OSCE and State Department reports detailed how local police, Serbian security forces, and the Yugoslav army used violence and repression to terrorize Albanians, who made up the majority of the population in Kosovo. Murder, imprisonment, torture, forced expulsion, rape, destruction of homes, and theft of personal possessions—all were common tactics used with brutal efficiency.

The OSCE report said that the "arbitrary killing" of Kosovo civilians was "both a tactic in the campaign to expel Kosovo Albanians, and an objective in itself"; in other words, the Serbs sought to remove all or most of the Albanian people from Kosovo either by killing them or forcing them to leave. In most cases, attacks on the Albanians were systematic and carefully planned, indicating that the security forces were working from a strategy developed by the central government in Belgrade. Only rarely did the attacks appear to be the result of a breakdown in authority, the reports said.

All ethnic Albanian Muslims in Kosovo were potential victims of Serbian attacks, but the OSCE report said that the Serbians specifically targeted certain elements of the population. Military-age ethnic Albanian men were the most vulnerable because they were considered to be potential "terrorists," the government's word for members of a separatist guerrilla force, the Kosovo Liberation Army. Serbian authorities also specifically sought out and persecuted the intellectual, social, and political elite of the Kosovar Albanians—in essence, anyone in a leadership position. In addition, the OSCE report cited evidence of the "murderous targeting" of children, apparently with the aim of terrorizing and punishing adults.

Robbing Albanians of their money and possessions was another "prime motivator" for the security forces, the OSCE report said. Virtually every Albanian refugee reported having his or her money, jewelry, and other personal possessions confiscated. In addition, the security forces routinely forced Albanian refugees to hand over passports, personal identification cards, and any other papers or possessions showing their names and places of residence; the object appeared to be to strip the Albanians of any identify as Kosovars. In its report, the State Department said that about half of all Kosovar refugees were forced to give up their identity papers. An unknown number of refugees also were forced to sign papers saying they were leaving Kosovo voluntarily.

After the NATO air strikes began March 24, Serbs frequently used groups of Kosovar Albanians as "human shields," the State Department said. Albanians were forced to travel with Serbian military convoys and were positioned at sites that were likely targets for NATO bombers, the report said.

The Serbian campaign to force ethnic Albanians from Kosovo was a success, at least temporarily. According to estimates compiled by the OSCE and the United Nations High Commissioner for Refugees, some 90 percent of the region's 1.6 million ethnic Albanians were uprooted from their homes between 1998 and the end of the war in June 1999. The majority—an estimated 863,000—were expelled, either by physical force or terror, into neighboring countries. More than half of those refugees (440,200) ended up in Albania, and nearly one-third (247,400) sought refuge in the former Yugoslav republic of Macedonia. Another 590,000 were internally displaced within Kosovo; they were forced out of their homes and took up temporary residence elsewhere in the province, often having to move repeatedly during the course of the war.

During the NATO air campaign, the Yugoslav government insisted that Kosovar Albanians were leaving their homes voluntarily to avoid NATO bombs. Both the U.S. and the OSCE reports categorically rejected that contention, noting that the refugees were forced from their homes by armed Serbian security forces.

In seeking to eliminate Albanians as a factor in Kosovar society, the Serbs wiped out entire neighborhoods and villages by burning the houses of residents after they had been expelled. The State Department report said that more than 1,200 residential areas were at least partially burned by Serbian security forces after the NATO bombardment began; that figure included some 500 villages. Serbian forces had destroyed an unknown number of villages during fighting in 1998.

Determining how many Albanians were killed was more difficult, and various estimates were subject to dispute. The State Department estimated that 10,000 Albanians were killed before and during the NATO war; that figure was based on the number of bodies recovered by late 1999, missing-person reports, and U.S. intelligence information (such as satellite images of mass grave sites).

Carla del Ponte, the chief UN war crimes investigator for Kosovo, said on November 10 that 11,334 people had been reported missing. As of that date investigators had exhumed 2,108 bodies from 195 sites, she said, and another 334 sites were thought to contain at least 2,100 bodies. Investigators suspended their excavation of graves in November and were expected to resume the grisly work in the spring of 2000. The whereabouts of the remaining 7,000 or so persons reported to be missing was unclear; some could have been found but not reported to authorities, some could be buried in unidentified graves, and some bodies could have been burned or hidden.

Seeking Revenge After the War

As could have been expected, some ethnic Albanians returning to their homes in Kosovo after the NATO war sought revenge against Serbs or other minorities whom the Albanians accused of taking part in the Serbian ethnic cleansing. The ethnic Albanians used many of the same tactics against the Serbs that had been used against them: murder, torture, burning of homes and villages, and other forms of intimidation.

Before NATO launched its attacks on Serb forces in late March, some 200,000 Serbs lived in Kosovo. Immediately after the war tens of thousands of Serbs fled, most into neighboring Serbia. The State Department report said approximately 97,000 Serbs remained in Kosovo as of December.

In its report, the OSCE said many Kosovar Albanians appeared to apply the concept of "collective guilt" to Serbs, regardless of whether the individuals involved had participated in or even supported the government's campaign against the Albanians.

The State Department report estimated that 200 to 400 Serbian residents were killed and thousands of homes and apartments belonging to Serbs had been destroyed in the months after the war. In one widely reported incident on July 23, fourteen Serb farmers were killed in their fields near the village of Gradsko, in south central Kosovo. The Serbian Orthodox Church said that more than forty churches and monasteries had been damaged in attacks following the NATO war. Among them was a new cathedral that had been under construction in Pristina, the capital of Kosovo, before the war; it was heavily damaged by a bomb in July.

Another group of postwar victims were the Roma (Gypsies), who remained in Kosovo during the war and were accused by the Albanians of doing "dirty work" for the Serbs, such as disposing of bodies. The OSCE said some Kosovar Albanians also were victims of retribution after the war simply because they "had not been seen to suffer" during the conflict. Among them were a small minority of Catholic Albanians who remained in the province during the war and were not harassed by the Serbs to the same extent as Muslim Albanians. Kosovo's small community of Muslim Slavs also suffered postwar revenge attacks, the OSCE said, simply because they spoke Serbo-Croatian.

The OSCE report said the lack of a "strong law enforcement system" in Kosovo following the war had "contributed to the lawlessness" in the region. European nations had promised to provide several thousand trained police offices for Kosovo following the war, but only a fraction of the number promised had arrived. UN officials responsible for governing Kosovo and commanders of NATO's peacekeeping force repeatedly appealed during the last half of the year for more police officers.

In the months after the war, the Yugoslav government denounced violence against remaining Serbs in Kosovo, saying their suffering exceeded that of the Albanians. Harold Koh, the assistant secretary of state for *human rights, rejected such contentions and said that acts of retribution—while inexcusable—were at a "substantially lower level" than the original Serb atrocities.*

> *Following are excerpts from two reports, "Ethnic Cleansing in Kosovo: An Accounting," issued December 9, 1999, by the U.S. State Department, describing human rights violations in Kosovo during 1999; and from the executive summary of the "Report on Human Rights Findings of the OSCE Mission in Kosovo: As Seen, As Told, Part II," issued December 6, 1999, by the Organization for Security and Cooperation in Europe describing human rights violations in Kosovo from mid-June to late October 1999:*

STATE DEPARTMENT REPORT

Overview

The following is a general account of atrocities committed by Serbian forces against ethnic Albanians in Kosovo primarily between March 1999 and late June 1999. Most of the information is compiled from victims and witness accounts provided to KFOR [the NATO peacekeeping force in Kosovo], the International Criminal Tribunal for the former Yugoslavia (ICTY), and other international organizations, supplemented by diplomatic and other reporting available as of early November 1999.

Since the signing of the military withdrawal agreement and departure of Serbian forces from Kosovo, earlier reports of Serbian war crimes in Kosovo, including the detention and summary execution of military-aged men and the destruction of civilian housing, have been confirmed by journalists and international organizations. According to press reports, Serbian troops and militias continued to rape women, loot property, burn homes and mosques, and murder Kosovar Albanians while withdrawing from Kosovo. Since the Serbian withdrawal, virtually all Kosovar Albanian survivors have returned to their villages and towns. However, there has also been a mass exodus of Serbian civilians who—despite KFOR efforts to protect them—are fearful of retribution from returning Kosovar Albanians and the influence of former members of the UCK [Albanian initials for the Kosovo Liberation Army]. KFOR troops have intervened on numerous occasions to prevent further violence in Kosovo.

War crime investigators and forensic teams from a number of countries and staff of the ICTY have begun investigating the numerous sites of mass graves and mass executions in Kosovo. KFOR has established security at many of the locations of alleged atrocities and requested returning family members not to disturb the potential evidence at any of the sites. Many family members choose to rebury their relatives without waiting for forensic investigations, however.

Kosovar Albanians have reported mass executions and mass graves at about 500 sites in the province. As of early November 1999, the ICTY has conducted site investigations at about 200 of these and has confirmed finding bodies at over 160 of the sites. Numerous accounts indicate that Serbian forces took steps to destroy forensic evidence of their crimes. This included execution methods that would allow the Serbs to claim their victims were collateral casualties of military operations, and burning or otherwise disposing of bodies. Over 2,100 bodies have been found by the ICTY among the some 200 atrocity sites that have been field investigated so far. However, the total number of bodies reported to the ICTY at over 500 gravesites is more than 11,000. If the pattern established among these 200 sites holds for all of the remaining sites—claimed by all sources—that have yet to be field investigated, we would expect the total number of bodies to be found at the known gravesites to be over 6,000. To this total must be added three important categories of victims: (1) those buried in mass graves whose locations are unknown, (2) what the ICTY reports is a significant number of sites where the precise number of bodies cannot be counted, and (3) victims whose bodies were burned or destroyed by Serbian forces. Press reporting and eyewitness accounts provide credible details of a program of destruction of evidence by Serbian forces throughout Kosovo and even in Serbia proper. The number of victims whose bodies have been burned or destroyed may never be known, but enough evidence has emerged to conclude that probably around 10,000 Kosovar Albanians were killed by Serbian forces.

As a result of Serbian efforts to expel the ethnic Albanian majority from Kosovo, almost one million Kosovar Albanians left the province after Serbian forces launched their first security crackdown in March 1998, with most having fled after March 1999. Based on the scope and intensity of Serbian activities throughout the province, as many as 500,000 additional Kosovars appear to have been internally displaced. In sum, about 1.5 million Kosovar Albanians (at least 90 percent of the estimated 1998 Kosovar Albanian population of the province) were forcibly expelled from their homes. Virtually all Kosovar Albanians who desired to return to Kosovo have done so at this time.

Thousands of homes in at least 1,200 cities, towns, and villages were damaged or destroyed. Victims report that Serbian forces harassed them with forced extortion and beatings, and that some were strafed by Serbian aircraft. Reports of organized rape of ethnic Albanian women by Serbian security forces during the conflict continue to be received. According to the victims, Serbian forces conducted systematic rapes in Djakovica, and at the Karagac and Metohia hotels in Pec.

With the return of international organizations to Kosovo in late June 1999, an unambiguous picture has unfolded, showing the scope and intensity of the ethnic cleansing campaign waged in the province.

Refugees have reported that Serbian forces systematically separated military-aged ethnic Albanian men—ranging from as young as age 14 years to 59 years old—from the population as they expelled the Kosovar Albanians from their homes. An exact accounting of the number of men killed is impossible because of Serbian efforts to destroy bodies of their victims, but clearly it includes civilians, combatants who were killed while prisoners of war as defined under the laws of armed conflict, and combatants killed while participating in hostilities. Forensic investigations will provide some, but not all, of the answers as to the relative proportions of each category.

Documenting the Abuses

The following is a partial list of war crimes, violations of international humanitarian law, or other human rights violations reported throughout Kosovo:

Forcible Displacement of Ethnic Albanian Civilians

Serbian authorities conducted a campaign of forced population movement on a scale seldom seen in Europe since the 1940s. They drove the vast majority of the ethnic Albanian population from their homes. The Serbian regime's claim that this population outflow was the result of voluntary flight in fear of NATO airstrikes is not supported by the accounts of victims. Victims consistently reported being expelled from their homes by Serbian forces at gunpoint, in contrast to the fighting of 1998, when the bulk of the internally displaced persons (IDPs) and refugees fled to escape the crossfire or to avoid reprisals by Serbian security forces. Many victims were herded onto trains and other organized transport and expelled from the province. In addition, Serbian forces expelled the majority of Kosovar Albanians from urban areas such as Djakovica. Refugees say that those forced to remain behind were used as human shields.

Serbian forces also disguised themselves as refugees to prevent targeting from NATO aircraft. Refugees claimed that on May 6, Serbian forces dressed in white hats and jackets with Red Cross and Red Crescent logos moved with convoys of IDPs between Djakovica and Brekovac. In order to conceal their military cargo, Serbian forces covered their wagons with plastic tarpaulins taken from NGOs [nongovernmental organizations].

In contrast to 1998, when Serbian security forces attacked small villages, Yugoslav Army units and armed civilians this year joined the police in systematically expelling ethnic Albanians at gunpoint from both villages and the larger towns of Kosovo. Serbian authorities forced many refugees to sign disclaimers saying they were leaving Kosovo of their own free will. Victims also reported that the Serbian forces confiscated their personal belongings and documentation, including national identity papers, and told them to take a last look around because they would never return to Kosovo. Many of the places targeted had not been the scenes of previous fighting or UCK activity. This indicates that the Serbian expulsions were an exercise in ethnic cleansing and not a part of a legitimate security or counter-insurgency operation, but instead a plan to cleanse the province of a significant proportion of its ethnic Albanian population.

Looting of Homes and Businesses

There are numerous reports from victims and the press of Serbian forces going house to house robbing residents before burning their homes. In addition, Kosovar Albanian victims claimed that Serbian forces robbed them of all their personal belongings before they crossed the borders.

Widespread Burning of Homes

Over 1,200 residential areas, including over 500 villages, were burned after late March, 1999. Most Serbian homes and stores remained intact during the conflict, and Serbian civilians in many towns painted a Cyrillic "S" on their doors so that Serbian forces would not attack their homes by mistake. The destruction is much more extensive and thorough than that which occurred in the summer of 1998. Many settlements were totally destroyed in an apparent attempt to ensure that the Kosovar Albanian population could not return. Serbian forces reportedly burned all houses previously rented to the OSCE in Vucitrn, Stimlje, and Kosovska Mitrovica. Mass burnings of villages waned towards the end of the campaign, by time many Kosovar Albanian homes had been abandoned. Those homes that were still intact were sometimes taken over by Serbian security forces.

Kosovar Albanians have reported that over 500 villages burned from late March 1999. . . .

Use of Human Shields

Serbian forces compelled Kosovar Albanians to accompany Serbian military convoys and shield facilities throughout the province. The extent to which civilians were used to shield military assets is difficult to measure, because Serbian units also escorted or herded Kosovar Albanians in the course of military operations.

Beginning in mid-April, Serbian forces used Kosovar Albanian men to shield military convoys from NATO airstrikes. Serbian forces reportedly removed young Kosovar Albanian men from refugee columns and forced them to form a buffer zone around Serbian convoys. Numerous Kosovar Albanians claimed to have witnessed and participated in this activity on the roads between Pec, Djakovica, and Kosovska Mitrovica.

In at least one instance—Korisa—Serbian forces intentionally positioned ethnic Albanians at sites that they believed were targets for NATO airstrikes. In other instances, unconfirmed reports say Kosovar Albanians were kept concealed within NATO target areas apparently to generate civilian casualties that could be blamed on NATO. In addition, Kosovar Albanian reports claimed that Serbian forces compelled Kosovar Albanian men to don Serbian military uniforms, probably so they could not be distinguished by NATO and UCK surveillance.

Detentions

Kosovar Albanians have claimed that Serbian forces systematically separated military-aged ethnic Albanian men—ranging from as young as 14 to 59 years old—from the population as they expelled Kosovar Albanians from their homes.

Refugees reported early in April that Serbian forces used the Ferro-Nickel factory in Glogovac as a detention center for a large number of Kosovar Albanians.

According to refugees, a cement factory in Deneral Jankovic had also been temporarily used as a detention center for Kosovar Albanians. The prisoners reportedly were released in late April.

From May 21 to early June, some 2,000 Kosovar Albanian men entered Albania after being detained by Serbian forces for three weeks in a prison in Smrekovnica near Srbica. Serbian authorities were apparently looking for UCK members and sympathizers among the prisoners. While detaining the men, the Serbian authorities forced them to dig trenches and physically abused many of them. After interrogations, the detainees were loaded on buses and driven to Zhure, from where they walked to the border.

Summary Executions

Kosovar Albanians have provided accounts of summary executions and mass graves at about 500 sites throughout Kosovo. In just one example, Serbian security forces reportedly locked an entire family into a house in the Drenica area and burned them alive. In addition to random executions, Serbian forces apparently targeted members of the Kosovar Albanian intelligentsia including lawyers, doctors, and political leaders. Survivors reported that Serbian forces burned bodies exhumed from mass graves in an apparent attempt to destroy forensic evidence of war crimes. . . .

Exhumation of Mass Graves

Kosovar Albanian refugees claim that Serbian forces exhumed bodies from mass grave sites from the outset of the conflict, apparently in an attempt to minimize evidence of atrocities. Reports indicate that in some instances Serbian forces re-interred bodies of executed ethnic Albanians in individual graves, while in others corpses were burned. Moving bodies from mass graves to individual graves has impeded the location of execution sites and hampered the ability of forensic investigators to discriminate between "regular" graves and graves containing massacre victims.

One of the most egregious examples is also one of the best-documented. In April, Serbian forces massacred Kosovar Albanian civilians in a field near Izbica, in north-central Kosovo. After the massacre, local Kosovar Albanians buried the victims in individual graves, an event videotaped by a local dentist from a nearby village. The videotape was smuggled out of Kosovo by the UCK. In May, the Department of State showed how the location of the videotape could be corroborated from overhead imagery. Serbian forces, during their retreat from Kosovo in early June, destroyed the graves at Izbica along with other graves of their victims—a fact that the Department of Defense confirmed through imagery at a press briefing in June.

According to Kosovar Albanian reports, Serbian forces in Lipljan, probably in early May, exhumed the bodies of ethnic Albanians who had been executed on April 18. After moving the bodies to a building in the village, Serbian forces reportedly ordered the surviving family members to rebury them in individual graves.

Similarly, Serbian forces exhumed the bodies of at least 50 ethnic Albanians in Glogovac and transported the bodies to the nearby village of Cikatovo on May 15, according to refugee reports. The bodies were then buried in individual graves.

Kosovar Albanians reported in mid-June that Serbian police excavated bodies from a mass grave in Kacanik and moved them to a local cemetery. Residents indicated that the bodies might be those killed by Serbian police in early April.

Rape

Numerous reports by Kosovar Albanian refugees reveal that the organized and individual rape of Kosovar Albanian women by Serbian forces was widespread. According to Kosovar Albanians, Serbian forces systematically raped women in Djakovica and Pec. Kosovar Albanian women reportedly were separated from their families and sent to an army camp near Djakovica, where they were raped repeatedly by Serbian soldiers. In Pec, Kosovar Albanians said that Serbian forces rounded up young Kosovar Albanian women and took them to the Hotel Karagac, where they were raped repeatedly. The commander of the local base was said to have used a roster of soldiers' names to allow all of his troops an evening in the hotel. A victim who escaped her captors reported that Serbian forces used a second hotel in Pec, the Metohia, for raping Kosovar Albanian women. In addition to these three specific accounts, numerous Kosovar Albanians claim that during Serbian raids on their villages, young women were gang raped in homes and on the sides of roads. There are probably many more incidents that have not been reported because of the stigma attached to the survivors in traditional Kosovar Albanian society. Medical facilities have reported abortions among refugee women who reported being raped by Serbian forces.

Violations of Medical Neutrality

Serbian forces systematically attacked Kosovar Albanian physicians, patients, and medical facilities. Violations of medical neutrality by Serbian forces include killings, torture, detention, imprisonment, and forced disappearances of Kosovar physicians. In March and April, Serbian health care providers, police and military expelled Kosovar Albanian patients and health care providers from health facilities as protective cover for military activities. The NGO Physicians for Human Rights has received reports of the destruction of at least 100 medical clinics, pharmacies, and hospitals.

811

Identity Cleansing

There are multiple reports of Serbian forces confiscating identity and property documents including passports, land titles, automobile license plates, identity cards, and other forms of documentation from Kosovar Albanians as they were forced out of villages or as they crossed international borders into Albania or Macedonia. Physicians for Human Rights reports that nearly 60 percent of respondents to its survey observed Serbian forces removing or destroying personal identification documents. Physicians for Human Rights also reported that the intent to destroy the social identity of Kosovar Albanians is also reflected in the number of places of worship, schools, and medical facilities that were destroyed by Serbian forces. . . .

Postscript: Albanian Retribution and Missing Persons

Ethnic violence in Kosovo did not halt with the end of the international conflict, the withdrawal of Serb forces, the deployment of NATO troops and the UN Mission, or the return of Kosovar refugees. This continued violence has affected both sides, but proportionally the Serbs and other minorities have suffered most heavily. Serbs have been subjected to kidnapping, murder, arson, grenade attacks, shootings, and a variety of other intimidation tactics, including bombing places of worship. NGOs have also recently documented abuses against Serb patients in hospitals in Kosovo and intimidation of Serb physicians.

Since June 10, between 200 and 400 Serb residents of Kosovo have been killed, thousands of Serb homes and apartments have been torched, destroyed, or looted, and according to Serbian Orthodox Church officials, more than 40 Serbian Orthodox churches and monasteries have been damaged or destroyed. In one of the worst incidents, on July 23, 1999, 14 Serb farmers were killed while working their fields near the village of Gradsko. On August 11, an international forensic team completed a site investigation at Llapushnica and confirmed finding a mass grave containing seven bodies. While none of the bodies had been positively identified at that time, preliminary indications suggest that the victims were Serbs.

The Roma population has also been the focus of retribution, being accused of collaborating in the expulsion of Kosovar Albanians. Historical animosity against the Roma community has also played a role. A July 20 statement condemning attacks on Serbs and Roma was released by the former UCK leadership, and former UCK leader Hashim Thaqi publicly denounced the July 23 Gradsko attack. There is no evidence that the former UCK leadership is orchestrating the violence. On the other hand, Kosovar Albanians have neither identified the perpetrators of these crimes, nor has the condemnation of these abuses by leaders of the Kosovar Albanian population been as broad, sustained, or effective as the circumstances warrant.

Prior to 1999, there were an estimated 200,000 Serbs in Kosovo. Today, some 97,000 remain, according to KFOR. This report documents all that we can now confirm about war crimes that occurred in Kosovo before the end of the conflict. Although this volume is far more detailed than the first edition, which was published before international investigators had physical access to alleged mass grave sites in Kosovo, this second volume still does not and cannot fully document the horrors that took place during the Spring of 1999 and before. Meanwhile, the question of violence and persecution against ethnic Serbs, Roma and other, as well as the question of Kosovar Albanian detainees and missing persons deserves a documentary approach and detailed reporting that the United States continues to support both financially and politically.

The United States is also committed to supporting NATO and UNMIK [United Nations Mission in Kosovo] efforts to break the cycle of violence. In the long term, the solution will lie in developing robust and pluralistic Kosovar institutions dedicated to respecting the rule of law. With logistical and financial assistance from the U.S., the police academy in Kosovo recently graduated its first class, a group of Kosovars, selected and trained to enforce the laws and guarantee due process without regard to ethnic background. In addition, the U.S. and the international community are focusing resources and training on integrating former UCK members into the Kosovo Protection Force (KPC).

OSCE and the United Nations High Commissioner for Refugees (UNHCR) released a joint report on November 3, 1999 on the situation of ethnic minorities in Kosovo, which observed that the overall situation remains tense. Movement out of Kosovo of persons from minority groups, particularly Serbs and Roma, continues. The report notes that fear is usually the major factor, but increasingly concerns about lack of access to humanitarian assistance, medical facilities, education, pensions, and employment are causing displacement. It states that this exclusion from such facilities and opportunities are either the direct result of a lack of freedom of movement brought on by the security situation or a consequence of real or perceived discrimination in the delivery of public services which are now predominantly, if not exclusively, Kosovar Albanian-run.

Finally, there is a further set of human rights issues emanating from Serbian authorities' actions in Kosovo. According to Amnesty International, as many as 23,000 conscientious objectors, draft evaders, and deserters from the Yugoslav Army during the Kosovo conflict may face trial before former Republic of Yugoslavia (FRY) military courts. At least several hundred conscientious objectors reportedly are imprisoned in the FRY, along with draft evaders and deserters. Meanwhile, at least 2,000 ethnic Albanians, and perhaps a significantly higher number, are reportedly held in Serbian detention facilities—some without formal charges against them. While Belgrade has released the names of approximately 2,000 of these detainees and released a few hundred in the past few weeks, ethnic Albanians claim that thousands more could be held in Serbian prisons. NGOs have documented that these detainees include women and children. The United States government calls upon Serbian authorities to release all imprisoned conscientious objectors, account for and unconditionally return detained Kosovar Albanians to their families in Kosovo, and suspend legal proceedings against both groups immediately.

OSCE REPORT

Findings of the Report

In the period covered by *Kosovo/Kosova: As Seen, As Told Part II* [mid-June to late October 1999], no community has escaped breaches of human rights, including the Kosovo Albanians. Particularly in the Kosovska Mitrovica/Mitrovice area, their freedom of movement and rights of access to education and healthcare have been violated. The report testifies to this and does not minimise the effect on the individuals concerned. However, the overwhelming weight of evidence points to violations against non-Albanians.

One discernible leitmotif emerges from this report. Revenge. Throughout the regions the desire for revenge has created a climate in which the vast majority of human rights violations have taken place. Through the assailant's eyes, the victims had either participated, or were believed to have participated, in the large-scale human rights abuses described in *Kosovo/Kosova: As Seen, As Told*; or they were believed to have actively or tacitly collaborated with the Yugoslav and Serbian security forces. Within this climate of vindictiveness a third category of victims emerged: those individuals or groups who were persecuted simply because they had not been seen to suffer before.

While the desire for revenge is only human, the act of revenge itself is not acceptable and must be recorded and addressed. The effects on the Kosovo Albanian population of accumulated discrimination and humiliation over the past decade is documented and cannot be doubted. Neither can it be doubted that the ethnic cleansing during the war had a deeply traumatic impact on the Kosovo Albanian community, leaving virtually no family untouched. Given this stark backdrop to the post-war setting, only a strong law enforcement system can prevent the climate of vindictiveness that perpetuates violence. The absence of such a robust response has contributed to the lawlessness that has pervaded post-war Kosovo/Kosova, leaving violence unchecked.

The first, obvious, group that suffered revenge attacks are the Kosovo Serbs. Despite the generally accepted premise that many of those who had actively participated in criminal acts left along with the withdrawing Yugoslav and Serbian security forces, the assumption of collective guilt prevailed. The entire remaining Kosovo Serb population was seen as a target for Kosovo Albanians. The report repeatedly catalogues incidents throughout the area where vulnerable, elderly Kosovo Serbs have been the victims of violence. The result of this has been a continuous exodus of Kosovo Serbs to Serbia and Montenegro and an inevitable internal displacement towards mono-ethnic enclaves, adding fuel to Serb calls for cantonisation.

Other particular victims of violence documented in the report are the Roma and Muslim Slavs. Many Kosovo Albanians labeled the Roma as col-

laborators: accused of carrying out the dirty work, such as disposing of bodies, they were tainted by association with the regime in Belgrade. The report
documents the decimation of the Roma community in many parts of
Kosovo/Kosova, driven from their homes in fear of their lives. The Muslim
Slav community, largely concentrated in the west of Kosovo/Kosova, may
share the same faith as the Kosovo Albanians, but they are separated by language. To be a Serbo-Croat speaker in Kosovo/Kosova is to be a suspect and
can be enough in itself to incite violence. Other non-Albanians that feature in
the report as victims of human rights violations include the Turks and Croats.

A disturbing theme that the report uncovers is the intolerance, unknown
before, that has emerged within the Kosovo Albanian community. Rights of
Kosovo Albanians to freedom of association, expression, thought and religion have all been challenged by other Kosovo Albanians. The report reveals
that opposition to the new order, particularly the (former) UCK's [Albanian
initials for the Kosovo Liberation Army] dominance of the self-styled munic-
ipal administrations, or simply a perceived lack of commitment to the UCK
cause has led to intimidation and harassment. A further aspect of inter-
Kosovo Albanian intolerance has been the challenges made in the Pec/Peje
area to the rights of Catholic Albanians to express their religion.

Violence has taken many forms: killings, rape, beatings, torture, house-
burning and abductions. Not all violence has been physical, however, fear
and terror tactics have been used as weapons of revenge. Sustained aggression, even without physical injury, exerts extreme pressure, leaving people
not only unable to move outside their home, but unable to live peacefully
within their home. In many instances, fear has generated silence, in turn
allowing the climate of impunity to go unchecked. The report shows that not
only have communities been driven from their homes, but also that the current climate is not conducive to returns. As a result, the spiral of violence has
driven a wedge between Kosovo/Kosova's communities, making ever more
elusive the international community's envisioned goal of ethnic co-existence.

The report highlights that although many incidents were disparate, individual acts of revenge, others have assumed a more systematic pattern and
appear to have been organised. The evidence in part points to a careful targeting of victims and an underlying intention to expel. This leads to one of the
more sensitive areas of the report, namely the extent of UCK involvement in
the period from June to October 1999. A consistent reporting feature has been
assumed UCK presence and control. The report is littered with witness statements testifying to UCK involvement, both before and after the demilitarisa-
tion deadline of 19th September ranging from reports of UCK 'police' to more
recent accusations of intimidation by self-proclaimed members of the provisional Kosovo Protection Corps (TMK) [a successor to the Kosovo Liberation
Army]. It is clear that the UCK stepped in to fill a law and order void, but this
'policing' role is unrestrained by law and without legitimacy. The highest levels of the former UCK leadership and current provisional TMK hierarchy have
openly distanced themselves from any connection of their members to the
violence that has taken place. They highlight the ease with which criminal ele-

ments who were never part of the UCK are now exploiting the UCK umbrella for their own nefarious purposes. Close scrutiny by the international community is needed to prove, or disprove, the veracity of these claims.

The report also highlights many instances of other human rights violations, such as denied access to public services, healthcare, education and employment which have also been used as a tool by both the Kosovo Albanians and the Kosovo Serbs to prevent the integration of traditionally mixed institutions. Restricted access to education, with its long-term implications for the life-chances of those affected; poor healthcare; limited employment opportunities—these are the emerging elements that lock segments of the population into a cycle of poverty and divide communities both on ethnic and on economic grounds. They constitute violations of civil, political, economic, social and cultural rights.

Conclusions

It is clear that the deficiency in the law enforcement capability provided by the international community and the lack of sufficient assistance in the administration of justice has fostered the climate within which the human rights violations documented in this report have taken place: impunity for the acts committed has resulted from failures to conduct serious investigations and this impunity, in turn, has perpetuated the violence. Establishing the rule of law is an essential element of OMIK's [the OSCE Mission in Kosovo] institution building mandate. Whoever the victims are, and even if they were themselves responsible for human rights or humanitarian law violations, their rights are inalienable and cannot be negated: life, liberty, security of person, freedom from harassment and a fair trial are rights, not privileges. For those who perpetrated, encouraged and organised the violations listed in this report, those rights also pertain. Additional investigative resources must therefore be put in place urgently, including investigators and forensic teams and the facilities to enable them to function. The legal and judicial framework must be strengthened so that periods of pre-trial detention can be reduced and trials conducted in a timely manner. The infusion of more international police and international judicial experts would greatly assist in ending the cycle of impunity.

The international community, through UNMIK [United Nations Mission in Kosovo], has the opportunity to positively influence the development of civil society in Kosovo/Kosova. Support for UNMIK's efforts to establish the rule of law is central, and critical, to this. With the rule of law comes the redress of grievance and freedom from arbitrary and discriminatory action. The OSCE Mission in Kosovo is committed, together with its UNMIK and Kosovo/Kosova partners, to work for the improvement of human rights conditions in the area. By identifying and denouncing the violations that have been committed to date, we are all better positioned to construct a Kosovo/Kosova that is founded on the principles of respect for human rights and fundamental freedoms.

EUROPEAN COUNCIL ON A NEW EUROPEAN DEFENSE FORCE
December 10, 1999

After years of talk about the need for a European defense force to react to emergencies outside the purview of the North Atlantic Treaty Organization (NATO), European leaders decided during 1999 to take action. The leaders of the European Union (EU) agreed December 10, 1999, to develop a crisis reaction force of up to 60,000 troops. The force, to be in place by 2003, would respond to security threats—such as the 1999 crisis in Kosovo—in the absence of action by the broader NATO alliance.

The United States, which for more than fifty years had provided a security blanket for Europe, was ambivalent about the prospect of a European-led security force. Washington for years had been urging European nations to step up their defense spending, which had fallen dramatically after the collapse of communism and the Soviet Union in the early 1990s. But U.S. officials—and some leaders in Europe, as well—expressed concern about any move that had the potential to weaken the political and security ties between the United States and Europe.

An Evolving Consensus in Europe

Perhaps as much as any single event since World War II, NATO's eleven-week war in Kosovo during the spring of 1999 illustrated for European leaders just how dependent they were on the United States for their security. Washington supplied the vast bulk of the military resources—airplanes, satellite reconnaissance, precision-guided bombs and missiles—needed to attack Serbian military and infrastructure targets. Without these U.S. resources, European nations would have taken much longer to mount such a massive strike against Serbia and might not have been able to bring the campaign to a successful conclusion. Just as important, the Clinton administration provided much of the political resolve behind NATO's determination to act in Kosovo. Without a push from Washington, Europe might not have taken such an aggressive posture to counter Serbia's terror tactics against the ethnic Albanian majority in Kosovo. (Kosovo war, p. 134)

The Kosovo war was a "watershed" event for Europeans, Karl Kaiser, a German foreign policy analyst told the New York Times. *"For Europe, it has brought a crushing realization of the asymmetry of military power between it and the United States, and the need to do something about that." One reason for doing something, some Europeans said, was a concern that a situation similar to the Kosovo crisis might arise in which Washington might not want to get involved. In such a case, NATO's massive military power— based primarily on U.S. forces—might not be available.*

Europe's first step toward developing a united military posture, separate from NATO, came at a European summit meeting in Cologne on June 3— just two weeks after NATO's fiftieth anniversary summit and one week before the Kosovo conflict ended. At that meeting, the EU officially took over the Western European Union, a long dormant counterpart to NATO, and announced that it would develop plans for a "rapid reaction" force. At the same time, the EU named Javier Solano, a Spaniard who had been the NATO secretary general, as its first "high representative" for foreign and defense policy.

In the following months, Britain, France, Germany, and Italy developed a proposal for a European crisis intervention force of 50,000 to 60,000 troops. The proposal called for the EU to establish political and security committees, along with a military staff, to put the force in place by 2003. The committees and the military staff would be based in Brussels, which already served as the headquarters of both the EU and NATO. To avoid unnecessary duplication, European leaders said the troops assigned to the force would be the same units that Europe would contribute to any NATO deployment in a crisis.

European leaders adopted the proposal at a EU summit meeting December 9–10 in Helsinki. When the summit meeting was called, approval of the defense force was to have been the central item on the agenda. But by the time of the meeting, all key issues relating to the new force had been decided, and the leaders devoted their time to expressing concern about Russia's attacks on separatist guerrillas in Chechnya and debating conditions for admitting new members to the EU, particularly Turkey. (War in Chechnya, p. 910; Turkish membership in the EU, p. 119)

Keeping the United States in Europe

Most European officials insisted that their plans did not mean that Europe no longer wanted the United States involved in defense matters. Nor did European members of NATO plan to abandon the North Atlantic alliance, they said. Rather, they said they were simply acting to correct Europe's inability to police its own neighborhood without having to rely so heavily on Washington. "In the trans-Atlantic alliance, we don't have too much America, we have too little Europe," German defense minister Rudolf Scharping said.

The proposal adopted December 10 by European leaders specifically referred to NATO as "the foundation of the collective defense of its mem-

bers," and said the European force would be deployed only in cases "where NATO as a whole is not engaged." To reinforce the point, German chancellor Gerhard Schroeder said: "There must and will be no thought of competition" between NATO and the EU on defense matters.

As with any development involving a group of fifteen countries, some European leaders put a somewhat different emphasis on Europe's move to create an independent security force. French president Jacques Chirac, the latest in a succession of French leaders eager to shift Europe's political center of gravity from Washington to Paris, praised the move as giving reality to "our vision of a multipolar world." With that comment, Chirac was reflecting long-standing European concern that the "bipolar" world of the cold war—in which the United States and the Soviet Union were the two superpowers—was being replaced by a "unipolar" world dominated just by the United States. The French foreign minister, Hubert Vedrine, went so far as to describe the United States as a "hyperpower" that had not demonstrated much interest in an equal partnership with its European allies.

In their public comments, U.S. officials said they fully supported Europe's move, and they played down speculation that the United States would feel that its role in Europe was being diminished. "There should be no confusion about American's position on the need for a stronger Europe," Deputy Secretary of State Strobe Talbott said at a December 15 meeting of NATO foreign ministers. "We are not against it; we are not ambivalent; we are not anxious; we are for it. We want to see a Europe that can act effectively through the alliance or, if NATO is not engaged, on its own."

Even so, Clinton administration officials privately expressed worry about the possible "duplication" of NATO's efforts and said it was difficult to imagine a serious crisis situation in Europe that the United States—and therefore NATO—would not want to address. European officials countered that they were concerned about Washington's demonstrated reluctance to commit ground troops to actual combat. They noted, for example, that President Bill Clinton all but ruled out the use of ground troops in Kosovo. Chirac and other Europeans also warned about what they viewed as an upsurge in isolationist sentiment in the United States, pointing in particular to the Senate's rejection in October of the comprehensive test ban treaty. (Test ban treaty, p. 600)

The gap between U.S. and European military capabilities was mirrored by—and in part the consequence of—a disparity in defense spending. The Clinton administration for years had been calling on NATO allies in Europe to increase their military budgets so they could shoulder a greater share of the alliance burden. U.S. defense secretary William S. Cohen noted that the United States was spending about 3.2 percent of its gross domestic product on defense—more than double the percentage in Germany and substantially higher than any other European country. Cohen and other U.S. officials said they wondered how Europe would meet its existing commitments to NATO, let alone the added costs of creating a European crisis-reaction force.

A related issue between the United States and its European allies concerned NATO's role in confronting security threats that might originate outside of the North Atlantic region. As an example, U.S. officials noted that North Korea was developing a long-range ballistic missile capable of hitting targets in parts of Europe. Cohen told his NATO counterparts at a meeting in Brussels in December that the threat from North Korea "is real." But few European officials seemed deeply concerned about the prospect of a military attack by North Korea or another "rogue" nation, such as Iraq or Iran. (North Korean missile issue, p. 568)

> *Following are excerpts from a communiqué issued December 10, 1999, by leaders of the European Union (acting in their capacity as the European Council), in which they announced the formation of a defense force to respond to crises; the communiqué is followed by excerpts from three annexes, prepared by the presidency of the European Council, providing details for the operation of the new defense force:*

DEFENSE FORCE COMMUNIQUÉ EXCERPTS

Common European Policy on Security and Defence

25. The European Council adopts the two Presidency progress reports (see Annex IV) on developing the Union's military and non-military crisis management capability as part of a strengthened common European policy on security and defence.

26. The Union will contribute to international peace and security in accordance with the principles of the United Nations Charter. The Union recognises the primary responsibility of the United Nations Security Council for the maintenance of international peace and security.

27. The European Council underlines its determination to develop an autonomous capacity to take decisions and, where NATO as a whole is not engaged, to launch and conduct EU-led military operations in response to international crises. This process will avoid unnecessary duplication and does not imply the creation of a European army.

28. Building on the guidelines established at the Cologne European Council and on the basis of the Presidency's reports, the European Council has agreed in particular the following:

- cooperating voluntarily in EU-led operations, Member States must be able, by 2003, to deploy within 60 days and sustain for at least 1 year military forces of up to 50,000-60,000 persons capable of the full range of Petersberg tasks [crisis intervention tasks defined by a previous EU [European Union] summit];

- new political and military bodies and structures will be established within the Council to enable the Union to ensure the necessary political guidance and strategic direction to such operations, while respecting the single institutional framework;
- modalities will be developed for full consultation, cooperation and transparency between the EU and NATO, taking into account the needs of all EU Member States;
- appropriate arrangements will be defined that would allow, while respecting the Union's decision-making autonomy, non-EU European NATO members and other interested States to contribute to EU military crisis management;
- a non-military crisis management mechanism will be established to coordinate and make more effective the various civilian means and resources, in parallel with the military ones, at the disposal of the Union and the Member States. . . .

DETAILS OF OPERATION

Annex IV: Presidency Reports to the Helsinki European Council on "Strengthening the Common European Policy on Security an Defense" and on "Non-military Crisis Management of the European Union"

The Presidency has responded as a matter of priority to the mandate given by the Cologne European Council to strengthen the common European policy on security and defence by taking the work forward in military and non-military aspects of crisis management. The work has been based on the provisions of the Treaty on European Union [EU] and the guiding principles agreed at Cologne, which have been reaffirmed by the Member States.

Work has yielded *two separate progress reports* to the European Council, which are intended to be complementary. The reports propose concrete measures and provide guidance for further work to take the necessary decisions by the end of the year 2000 towards the objectives set at Cologne. During the Portuguese Presidency, consideration will be given as to whether or not Treaty amendment is judged necessary.

To assume their responsibilities across the full range of conflict prevention and crisis management tasks defined in the EU Treaty, the Petersberg tasks, the Member States have decided to develop more effective military capabilities and establish new political and military structures for these tasks. In this connection, the objective is for the Union to have an autonomous capacity to take decisions and, where NATO as a whole is not engaged, to launch and then to conduct EU-led military operations in response to international crises.

Also in order to assume these responsibilities, the Union will improve and make more effective use of resources in civilian crisis management in which the Union and the Members States already have considerable experience. Special attention will be given to a rapid reaction capability.

All these measures will be taken in support of the Common Foreign and Security Policy and they will reinforce and extend the Union's comprehensive external role. With the enhancement and concertation of military and civilian crisis response tools, the Union will be able to resort to the whole range of instruments from diplomatic activity, humanitarian assistance and economic measures to civilian policing and military crisis management operations.

NATO remains the foundation of the collective defence of its members, and will continue to have an important role in crisis management.

The development of the common European policy on security and defence will take place without prejudice to the commitments under Article 5 of the Washington Treaty and Article V of the Brussels Treaty, which will be preserved for the Member States party to these Treaties. Nor shall the development of the common European policy on security and defence prejudice the specific character of the security and defence policy of certain Member States. Further steps will be taken to ensure full mutual consultation, cooperation and transparency between the EU and NATO.

The Union will contribute to international peace and security in accordance with the principles of the United Nations Charter. The Union recognises the primary responsibility of the United Nations Security Council for the maintenance of international peace and security. Following up the principles and objectives of the OSCE [Organization for Security and Cooperation in Europe] Charter for European Security, the Union will cooperate with the UN, the OSCE, the Council of Europe and other international organisations in a mutually reinforcing manner in stability promotion, early warning, conflict prevention, crisis management and post-conflict reconstruction.

Annex 1 to Annex IV: Presidency progress report to the Helsinki European Council on strengthening the Common European Policy on Security and Defence

Introduction

Recalling the guiding principles agreed at Cologne, the European Union should be able to assume its responsibilities for the full range of conflict prevention and crisis management tasks defined in the EU Treaty, the Petersberg tasks.

The European Union should have the autonomous capacity to take decisions and, where NATO as a whole is not engaged, to launch and then to conduct EU-led military operations in response to international crises in support of the Common Foreign and Security Policy (CFSP). The action by the Union will be conducted in accordance with the principles of the UN Charter and the principles and objectives of the OSCE Charter for European Security. The Union recognises the primary responsibility of the United Nations Security Council for the maintenance of international peace and security.

For this purpose, the following has been agreed:

A common European headline goal will be adopted for readily deployable military capabilities and collective capability goals in the fields of command and control, intelligence and strategic transport will be developed rapidly, to be achieved through voluntary co-ordinated national and multinational efforts, for carrying out the full range of Petersberg tasks.

New political and military bodies will be established within the Council to enable the Union to take decisions on EU-led Petersberg operations and to ensure, under the authority of the Council, the necessary political control and strategic direction of such operations. Principles for cooperation with non-EU European NATO members and other European partners in EU-led military crisis management will be agreed, without prejudice to the Union's decision-making autonomy.

Determination to carry out Petersberg tasks will require Member States to improve national and multinational military capabilities, which will at the same time, as appropriate, strengthen the capabilities of NATO and enhance the effectiveness of the Partnership for Peace (PfP) in promoting European security.

In presenting this report, the Presidency has taken note of the fact that Denmark has recalled Protocol no 5 to the Amsterdam Treaty on the position of Denmark.

Military Capabilities for Petersburg Tasks

Member States recall their commitment made at Cologne and their determination to give the EU appropriate capabilities, without unnecessary duplication, to be able to undertake the full range of Petersberg tasks in support of the CFSP. Such capabilities will enable them to conduct effective EU-led operations as well as playing, for those involved, their full role in NATO and NATO-led operations. More effective European military capabilities will be developed on the basis of the existing national, bi-national and multinational capabilities, which will be assembled for EU-led crisis management operations carried out with or without recourse to NATO assets and capabilities. Particular attention will be devoted to the capabilities necessary to ensure effective performance in crisis management: deployability, sustainability, interoperability, flexibility, mobility, survivability and command and control, taking account of the results of the WEU [Western European Union] audit of assets and capabilities and their implications for EU-led operations.

To develop European capabilities, Member States have set themselves the headline goal: by the year 2003, cooperating together voluntarily, they will be able to deploy rapidly and then sustain forces capable of the full range of Petersberg tasks as set out in the Amsterdam Treaty, including the most demanding, in operations up to corps level (up to 15 brigades or 50,000–60,000 persons). These forces should be militarily self-sustaining with the necessary command, control and intelligence capabilities, logistics, other combat support services and additionally, as appropriate, air and naval elements. Member States should be able to deploy in full at this level within 60 days, and within this to provide smaller rapid response elements available and deployable at very high readiness. They must be able to sustain such a deployment for at least one year. This will require an additional pool of deployable units (and supporting elements) at lower readiness to provide replacements for the initial forces.

Member States have also decided to develop rapidly collective capability goals in the fields of command and control, intelligence and strategic transport, areas also identified by the WEU audit. They welcome in this respect decisions already announced by certain Member States which go in that direction:

- to develop and coordinate monitoring and early warning military means;
- to open existing joint national headquarters to officers coming from other Member States;
- to reinforce the rapid reaction capabilities of existing European multinational forces;
- to prepare the establishment of a European air transport command;
- to increase the number of readily deployable troops;
- to enhance strategic sea lift capacity.

The General Affairs Council, with the participation of Defence Ministers, will elaborate the headline and capability goals. It will develop a method of consultation through which these goals can be met and maintained, and through which national contributions reflecting Member States' political will and commitment towards these goals can be defined by each Member State, with a regular review of progress made. In addition, Member States would use existing defence planning procedures, including, as appropriate, those available in NATO and the Planning and Review Process (PARP) of the PfP. These objectives and those arising, for those countries concerned, from NATO's Defence Capabilities Initiative (DCI) will be mutually reinforcing. The European NATO members who are not EU Member States, and other countries who are candidates for accession to the European Union will be invited to contribute to this improvement of European military capabilities. This will enhance the effectiveness of EU-led military operations and will, for those countries concerned, contribute directly to the effectiveness and vitality of the European pillar of the NATO.

Member States welcome the recent progress made towards the restructuring of European defence industries, which constitutes an important step forward. This contributes to strengthening the European industrial and technological defence base. Such developments call for increased efforts to seek further progress in the harmonisation of military requirements and the planning and procurement of arms, as Member States consider appropriate.

Decision-making

The Council decides upon policy relevant to Union involvement in all phases and aspects of crisis management, including decisions to carry out Petersberg tasks in accordance with Article 23 of the EU Treaty. Taken within the single institutional framework, decisions will respect European Community competences and ensure inter-pillar coherence in conformity with Article 3 of the EU Treaty.

All Member States are entitled to participate fully and on an equal footing in all decisions and deliberations of the Council and Council bodies on EU-led operations. The commitment of national assets by Member States to such operations will be based on their sovereign decision. Member States will participate in the ad hoc committee of contributors in accordance with the conditions provided for by paragraph 24.

Defence Ministers will be involved in the common European security and defence policy (CESDP); when the General Affairs Council discusses matters related to the CESDP, Defence Ministers as appropriate will participate to provide guidance on defence matters. The following new *permanent* political and military bodies will be established within the Council:

a) *A standing Political and Security Committee (PSC)* in Brussels will be composed of national representatives of senior/ambassadorial level. The PSC will deal with all aspects of the CFSP, including the CESDP, in accordance with the provisions of the EU Treaty and without prejudice to Community competence. In the case of a military crisis management operation, the PSC will exercise, under the authority of the Council, the political control and strategic direction of the operation. For that purpose, appropriate procedures will be adopted in order to allow effective and urgent decision taking. The PSC will also forward guidelines to the Military Committee.

b) *The Military Committee (MC)* will be composed of the Chiefs of Defence, represented by their military delegates. The MC will meet at the level of the Chiefs of Defence as and when necessary. This committee will give military advice and make recommendations to the PSC, as well as provide military direction to the Military Staff. The Chairman of the MC will attend meetings of the Council when decisions with defence implications are to be taken.

c) *The Military Staff (MS)* within the Council structures will provide military expertise and support to the CESDP, including the conduct of EU-led military crisis management operations. The Military Staff will perform early warning, situation assessment and strategic planning for Petersberg tasks including identification of European national and multinational forces.

As an *interim* measure, the following bodies will be set up within the Council as of March 2000:

a) Fully respecting the Treaty provisions, the Council will establish a standing interim political and security committee at senior/ambassadorial level tasked to take forward under the guidance of the Political Committee the follow up of the Helsinki European Council by preparing recommendations on the future functioning of the CESDP and to deal with CFSP affairs on a day-to-day basis in close contacts with the SG/HR [Secretary General/High Representative].

b) An interim body of military representatives of Member States' Chiefs of Defence is established to give military advice as required to the interim political and security committee.

c) The Council Secretariat will be strengthened by military experts seconded from Member States in order to assist in the work on the CESDP and to form the nucleus of the future Military Staff.

The Secretary General/High Representative (SG/HR), in assisting the Council, has a key contribution to make to the efficiency and consistency of the CFSP and the development of the common security and defence policy. In conformity with the EU Treaty, the SG/HR will contribute to the formulation, preparation and implementation of policy decisions. In the interim period, the SH/HR, Secretary General of the WEU, should make full use of WEU assets for the purpose of advising the Council under Article 17 of the EU Treaty.

Consultation and Cooperation with Non-EU Countries and with NATO

The Union will ensure the necessary dialogue, consultation and cooperation with NATO and its non-EU members, other countries who are candidates for accession to the EU as well as other prospective partners in EU-led crisis management, with full respect for the decision-making autonomy of the EU and the single institutional framework of the Union.

With European NATO members who are not members of the EU and other countries who are candidates for accession to the EU, appropriate structures will be established for dialogue and information on issues related to security and defence policy and crisis management. In the event of a crisis, these structures will serve for consultation in the period leading up to a decision of the Council.

Upon a decision by the Council to launch an operation, the non-EU European NATO members will participate if they so wish, in the event of an operation requiring recourse to NATO assets and capabilities. They will, on a decision by the Council, be invited to take part in operations where the EU does not use NATO assets.

Other countries who are candidates for accession to the EU may also be invited by the Council to take part in EU-led operations once the Council has decided to launch such an operation.

Russia, Ukraine and other European States engaged in political dialogue with the Union and other interested States may be invited to take part in the EU-led operations. All the States that have confirmed their participation in an EU-led operation by deploying significant military forces will have the same rights and obligations as the EU participating Member States in the day-to-day conduct of such an operation.

In the case of an EU-led operation, an ad-hoc committee of contributors will be set up for the day-to-day conduct of the operation. All EU Member States are entitled to attend the ad-hoc committee, whether or not they are participating in the operation, while only contributing States will take part in the day-to-day conduct of the operation.

The decision to end an operation will be taken by the Council after consultation between the participating states within the committee of contributors.

Modalities for full consultation, cooperation and transparency between the EU and NATO will be developed. Initially, relations will be developed on an informal basis, through contacts between the SG/HR for CFSP and the Secretary General of NATO. . . .

DEPARTMENT OF JUSTICE REPORT ON CAPITAL PUNISHMENT
December 12, 1999

Long-standing controversies over the death penalty heated up in 1999, as the states executed 98 prisoners, 30 more than in 1998 and the most since 1951, when 105 prisoners were put to death. Two states accounted for half of the executions: Texas with 35 and Virginia with 14. At year's end 3,625 prisoners were on death row.

Defenders of capital punishment said that the increased number of executions would enhance the death penalty's deterrent effect on crime. But the quickened pace of executions, together with the exoneration of eight men wrongly sentenced to death, a botched electrocution in Florida, and a commuted sentence in honor of a visit from the pope, may have done more to strengthen arguments of death penalty opponents. They focused on these and other events to underscore their contention that the death penalty was arbitrary, unconstitutionally cruel, and ran the risk of being imposed in error. By year's end several states were considering adopting moratoriums on capital punishment, and public support for the practice appeared to be declining slightly.

Weakening Support for the Death Penalty?

The U.S. Supreme Court outlawed the death penalty in 1972 but then reversed itself in 1976, ruling that capital punishment did not violate the Constitution if procedures were in place to guard against arbitrary and discriminatory application of it. Since that ruling thirty-eight states and the federal government had instituted the death penalty for specific offenses, impelled in part by soaring crimes rates, including record numbers of murders. Proponents of the death penalty argued that it was a deterrent to crime. Opponents argued that capital punishment had not been shown to have a deterrent effect. They also pointed to a number of disparities and vagaries in the way the death sentence was imposed, including the fact that some state judicial systems and political systems were more prone than others to impose the death penalty and carry it out. Opponents' appeals for an end to capital punishment fell on seemingly deaf ears, however. Since the death penalty was reinstated, public opinion polls showed that the public was unwavering in its support. Most polls consistently showed that 70 to 80 percent of the public backed capital punishment. (Reinstatement of the death penalty, Historic Documents of 1976, p. 489)

By the late 1990s there were signs that support was beginning to soften. Violent crime rates had declined significantly, easing public fears somewhat. In addition, most of the states that permitted death sentences also offered juries the option of life imprisonment without parole in some instances, an alternative that appealed to those members of the public who had reservations about the death penalty but thought that convicted criminals should pay for their crimes. In 1999 a series of unrelated events appeared to further weaken support for the death penalty. (Crime statistics, p. 614)

According to the Death Penalty Information Center, which opposed capital punishment, eight men were exonerated and released from death row in 1999. One of these was Anthony Porter, who had been convicted of murder in Illinois and had been on death row for sixteen years. He was exonerated after a journalism class at Northwestern University showed that the murder had been committed by another man, who confessed to the crime. Death penalty opponents said the releases illustrated the high risks of executing innocent people, but others argued that the exonerations showed that the system worked. One supporter told the Washington Post *that "the anti-death penalty people can't point to any case of an innocent person being put to death."*

Questionable evidence in the death sentence of a Virginia man led to a questionable Supreme Court decision, in the opinion of many death penalty foes. Tommy David Strickler, who was convicted and sentenced to death in 1990 for kidnapping and killing a young woman, appealed his conviction in 1996 after learning that the key eyewitness had initially told police that she could not identify the kidnappers and did not even remember being at the scene of the kidnapping. In a 7–2 ruling handed down June 17 the Supreme Court acknowledged that admission of the suppressed evidence "might have changed the outcome of the trial" and that there was a "reasonable possibility" that the jury might have spared Strickler from the death penalty. But the majority said Strickler had failed to meet the standard of showing a "reasonable probability" that the outcome would have been different. Strickler was executed later in the year.

In Florida an outcry over the third botched electrocution since 1990 forced Gov. Jeb Bush to call for a special legislative session to consider switching the method of execution to lethal injection. Allen Lee Davis died in the electric chair in July for murdering a pregnant woman and her two daughters, but not before bleeding profusely from the nose. Photographs of the execution, posted on the Internet by a Florida Supreme Court justice opposed to the electric chair, also showed that Davis was still breathing for a few seconds after the power was turned off. In two earlier cases, parts of inmates' bodies caught fire as they were being electrocuted. Earlier in the year, the U.S. Supreme Court agreed to hear arguments in another case from Florida challenging the use of the electric chair as cruel and unusual punishment. Florida was one of four states where the sole means of execution was electrocution; the other three were Alabama, Georgia, and Nebraska.

In Missouri a request from the pope saved one convict from execution. In January Gov. Mel Carnahan, a Democrat who supported the death penalty, commuted Darrell Mease's death sentence to life imprisonment at the request of Pope John Paul II, who was visiting St. Louis at the time Mease was scheduled to be executed. The Roman Catholic Church opposed the death penalty. Republicans in the state were outraged by Carnahan's decision. Two months later, after announcing that he would run for the U.S. Senate in 2000, Carnahan refused clemency in a controversial case where the evidence for conviction was questionable. Death penalty opponents accused Carnahan of using the death penalty to win political support among the state's conservatives, an allegation he denied. (Pope on the death penalty, Historic Documents of 1995, p. 145)

Domestic and international civil rights groups continued to pressure the federal government as well as the states to abandon the death penalty. In the United States, the National Council of Synagogues and the ecumenical committee of the National Conference of Catholic Bishops agreed in December to work together to abolish the death penalty. On April 18 the United Nations Human Rights Commission voted, 30–11, for a moratorium on the death penalty. Sponsored by the European Union, the resolution urged countries to reduce progressively the offenses for which the death penalty could be imposed and asked countries not to use it at all for people under age eighteen, pregnant women, and anyone who had "any form of mental disorder." Twelve countries abstained, including the United States. In 1998 only China and Congo executed more people than the United States. An investigator for the UN Human Rights Committee wrote a blistering report in 1998 denouncing the United States for its arbitrary and discriminatory use of the death penalty. (UN report, Historic Documents of 1998, p. 183)

Profile of Death Row

On December 12 the Bureau of Justice Statistics issued a report on capital punishment in the United States during 1998. It was the latest in a series of annual reports on the death penalty. According to the bureau, sixty-six men and two women were executed in 1998, primarily by lethal injection. Forty of those executed were white, eighteen were black, eight were Hispanic, one was American Indian, and one was Asian. Nearly half of the executions took place in Texas (twenty) and Virginia (thirteen). California held the largest number of prisoners on death row, followed by Texas, Florida, and Pennsylvania. Nineteen people were awaiting execution in federal prisons.

Despite efforts by Congress, the Supreme Court, and state legislatures to speed up the appeals process, the time between conviction and execution did not change much in 1998. The average stay on death row for the sixty-eight inmates executed in 1998 was ten years and ten months, just three months shorter than the average stay for the seventy-four inmates executed in 1997. Experts said that one reason the number of executions increased in 1999 was that many people who had been on death row since the late 1980s and early 1990s were reaching the end of their appeals, and for that reason they also expected the number of executions to increase in the next few years.

Following are excerpts from the report, "Capital Punishment 1998," released December 12, 1999, by the Department of Justice's Bureau of Justice Statistics:

Eighteen States executed 68 prisoners during 1998. The number executed was 6 fewer than in 1997. The prisoners executed during 1998 had been under sentence of death an average of 10 years and 10 months, 3 months less than that for inmates executed in 1997.

At yearend 1998, 3,452 prisoners were under sentence of death. California held the largest number on death row (512), followed by Texas (451), Florida (372), and Pennsylvania (224). Nineteen prisoners were under a Federal sentence of death.

During 1998, 30 States and the Federal prison system received 285 prisoners under sentence of death. Texas (39 admissions), California (31), Alabama and Florida (25 each) accounted for 42% of those sentenced to death.

During 1998, 66 men and 2 women were executed. Of those executed, 35 were non-Hispanic whites; 18 were non-Hispanic blacks; 8, white Hispanics; 5, whites with unknown Hispanic origin; 1, American Indian; and 1, Asian. Sixty of the executions were carried out by lethal injection, 7 by electrocution, and 1 by lethal gas.

From January 1, 1977, to December 31, 1998, 500 executions took place in 18 States. Nearly two-thirds of the executions occurred in 5 States: Texas (164), Virginia (59), Florida (43), Missouri (32), and Louisiana (24).

Capital Punishment Laws

At yearend 1998 the death penalty was authorized by 38 States and the Federal Government. During 1998 no State enacted new legislation authorizing capital punishment.

The New York Court of Appeals struck portions of the New York death penalty provision in December 1998 (*Hynes v. Tomei*). The affected portions of the statute barred imposition of a death sentence in cases where a guilty plea was entered by a defendant while a defendant pleading not guilty would have to stand trial and face the possibility of a death sentence. . . . These provisions were ruled to violate defendants' fifth amendment right against self-incrimination and sixth amendment right to a jury trial.

Statutory Changes

During 1998, 13 States revised statutory provisions relating to the death penalty. Most of the changes involved additional aggravating or mitigating circumstances, procedural amendments, and revisions to capital offenses. . . .

Method of Execution

As of December 31, 1998, lethal injection was the predominant method of execution (34 States).

Eleven States authorized electrocution; 5 States, lethal gas; 3 States, hanging; and 3 States, a firing squad.

Seventeen States authorized more than 1 method—lethal injection and an alternative method—generally at the election of the condemned prisoner; however, 5 of these 17 stipulated which method must be used, depending on the date of sentencing; 1 authorized hanging only if lethal injection could not be given; and if lethal injection is ever ruled unconstitutional, 1 authorized lethal gas, and 1 authorized electrocution. . . .

Minimum Age

In 1998 eight jurisdictions did not specify a minimum age for which the death penalty could be imposed.

In some States the minimum age was set forth in the statutory provisions that determine the age at which a juvenile may be transferred to criminal court for trial as an adult. Fourteen States and the Federal system required a minimum age of 18. Sixteen States indicated an age of eligibility between 14 and 17.

Characteristics of Prisoners Under Sentence of Death at Yearend 1998

Thirty-seven States and the Federal prison system held a total of 3,452 prisoners under sentence of death on December 31, 1998, a gain of 124, or 3.7% more than at the end of 1997.

The Federal prison system count rose from 14 at yearend 1997 to 19 at yearend 1998. Three States reported 39% of the Nation's death row population: California (512), Texas (451), and Florida (372). Of the 39 jurisdictions with statutes authorizing the death penalty during 1998, New Hampshire had no one under a capital sentence, and New York, Kansas, South Dakota, Colorado, New Mexico, and Wyoming had 4 or fewer.

Among the 38 jurisdictions with prisoners under sentence of death at yearend 1997, 23 had more inmates than a year earlier, 6 had fewer inmates, and 9 had the same number. California had an increase of 25, followed by Alabama (19) and Ohio (16). Illinois and Virginia had the largest decrease (4 each).

During 1998 the number of black inmates under sentence of death rose by 78; the number of whites increased by 42; and the number of persons of other races rose from 56 to 60.

The number of Hispanics sentenced to death rose from 291 to 314 during 1998. Thirty-eight Hispanics were received under sentence of death, 7 were removed from death row, and 8 were executed. Four-fifths of the Hispanics were held in 4 States: California (97), Texas (93), Florida (43), and Arizona (20).

During 1998 the number of women sentenced to be executed increased from 44 to 48. Eight women were received under sentence of death, two were removed from death row, and two were executed.

Women were under sentence of death in 17 States. Half of all women on death row at yearend were in California, Texas, Florida, and Pennsylvania. . . .

Men were 99% (3,404) of all prisoners under sentence of death. Whites predominated (55%); blacks comprised 43%; and other races (1.7%) included 29 American Indians, 18 Asians, and 13 persons of unknown race. Among those for whom ethnicity was known, 10% were Hispanic. . . .

Among inmates under sentence of death on December 31, 1998, for whom information on education was available, three-fourths had either completed high school (38%) or finished 9th, 10th, or 11th grade (38%). The percentage who had not gone beyond eighth grade (14%) was larger than that of inmates who had attended some college (10%). The median level of education was the 11th grade.

Of inmates under a capital sentence and with reported marital status, more than half had never married; about a fourth were married at the time of sentencing; and nearly a fourth were divorced, separated, or widowed.

Among all inmates under sentence of death for whom date of arrest information was available, half were age 20 to 29 at the time of arrest for their capital offense; 13% were age 19 or younger; and less than 1% were age 55 or older. The average age at time of arrest was 28 years. On December 31, 1998, 37% of all inmates were age 30 to 39, and 69% were age 25 to 44. The youngest offender under sentence of death was age 18; the oldest was 83.

Entries and Removals of Persons Under Sentence of Death

Between January 1 and December 31, 1998, 30 State prison systems reported receiving 285 prisoners under sentence of death; the Federal Bureau of Prisons received 5 inmates. Forty-two percent of the inmates were received in 4 States: Texas (39), California (31), and Arkansas and Florida (25 each).

All 256 prisoners who had been received under sentence of death had been convicted of murder. By gender and race, 142 were white men, 129 were black men, 3 were American Indian men, 3 were Asian men, 1 was a self-identified Hispanic male, 3 were white women, 3 were black women, and 2 were self-identified Hispanic women. Of the 285 new admissions, 36 were Hispanic men and 2 were Hispanic women.

Twenty-two States reported a total of 80 persons whose sentence of death was overturned or removed. Appeals courts vacated 43 sentences while upholding the convictions and vacated 35 sentences while overturning the convictions. Florida (16 exits) had the largest number of vacated capital sentences. Texas reported one commutation of a death sentence.

As of December 31, 1998, 48 of the 80 persons who were formerly under sentence of death were serving a reduced sentence, 15 were awaiting a new trial, 10 were awaiting resentencing, 1 was resentenced to time served, and 4 had no action taken after being removed from under sentence of death. No information was available on the current status of two inmates.

In addition, 13 persons died while under sentence of death in 1998. Ten of these deaths were from natural causes—3 in California, 2 each in Illinois and Alabama, and 1 each in Missouri, Texas, and Nevada. Two suicides occurred in North Carolina. One inmate in Texas was shot during an escape and subsequently died.

From 1977, the year after the Supreme Court upheld the constitutionality of revised State capital punishment laws, to 1998, a total of 5,709 persons entered prison under sentence of death. During these 22 years, 500 persons were executed, and 2,137 were removed from under a death sentence by appellate court decisions and reviews, commutations, or death.

Among individuals who received a death sentence between 1977 and 1998, 2,830 (50%) were white, 2,347 (41%) were black, 449 (8%) were Hispanic, and 83 (1%) were of other races. The distribution by race and Hispanic origin of the 2,137 inmates who were removed from death row between 1977 and 1998 was as follows: 1,113 whites (52%), 877 blacks (41%), 116 Hispanics (5%), and 31 persons of other races (2%). Of the 500 who were executed, 281 (56%) were white, 178 (36%) were black, 34 (7%) were Hispanic, and 7 (1%) were of other races.

Criminal History of Inmates
Under Sentence of Death in 1998

Among inmates under a death sentence on December 31, 1998, for whom criminal history information was available, 65% had past felony convictions, including 9% with at least one previous homicide conviction.

Among those for whom legal status at the time of the capital offense was reported, 40% had an active criminal justice status. Less than half of these were on parole, and about a fourth were on probation. The others had charges pending, were incarcerated, had escaped from incarceration, or had some other criminal justice status.

Criminal history patterns differed by race and Hispanic origin. More blacks (69%) than whites (63%) or Hispanics (61%) had a prior felony conviction.

About the same percentage of blacks (9%), whites (8%), and Hispanics (8%) had a prior homicide conviction. A slightly higher percentage of Hispanics (24%) or blacks (20%) than whites (15%) were on parole when arrested for their capital offense.

Since 1988, data have been collected on the number of death sentences imposed on entering inmates. Among the 3,169 individuals received under sentence of death during that time, about 1 in every 7 entered with 2 or more death sentences. . . .

Executions

According to data collected by the Federal Government, from 1930 to 1998, 4,359 persons were executed under civil authority. [Military authorities carried out an additional 160 executions, 1930–1998.]

After the Supreme Court reinstated the death penalty in 1976, 29 States executed 500 prisoners. . . .

During this 22-year period, 6 States executed 345 prisoners: Texas (164), Virginia (59), Florida (43), Missouri (32), Louisiana (24), and Georgia (23). These States accounted for more than two-thirds of all executions. Between 1977 and 1998, 278 white non-Hispanic men, 178 black non-Hispanic men, 34 Hispanic men, 4 American Indian men, 3 Asian men, and 3 white non-Hispanic women were executed.

During 1998 Texas carried out 20 executions; Virginia executed 13 persons; South Carolina, 7; Arizona, Florida, and Oklahoma, 4 each; Missouri and North Carolina, 3 each; and Alabama, Arkansas, California, Georgia, Illinois, Indiana, Maryland, Montana, Nevada, and Washington, 1 each. Sixty-six persons executed in 1998 were male and two were female. Forty were white; 18 were black; 8 were Hispanic; 1 was American Indian; and 1 was Asian. . . .

The 500 executions accounted for 8% of those at risk. A total of 2,137 prisoners (35% of those at risk) received other dispositions. About the same percentage of whites (9%), blacks (7%), and Hispanics (7%) were executed. Somewhat larger percentages of whites (37%) and blacks (35%) than Hispanics (25%) were removed from under a death sentence by means other than execution.

Among prisoners executed from 1977 to 1998, the average time spent between the imposition of the most recent sentence received and execution was more than 9 years. White prisoners had spent an average of 9 years, and black prisoners, 10 years and 3 months. The 68 prisoners executed in 1998 were under sentence of death an average of 10 years and 10 months.

For the 500 prisoners executed between 1977 and 1998, the most common method of execution was lethal injection (344). Other methods were electrocution (141), lethal gas (10), hanging (3), and firing squad (2). . . .

Among prisoners under sentence of death at yearend 1998, the average time spent in prison was 7 years and 4 months, up 3 months from that of 1997. . . .

The median time between the imposition of a death sentence and yearend 1998 was 75 months. Overall, the average time for women was 6.2 years, slightly less than that for men (7.4 years). On average, whites, blacks, and Hispanics had spent from 80 to 92 months under a sentence of death.

SURGEON GENERAL'S REPORT ON MENTAL HEALTH
December 13, 1999

Approximately one in five Americans experiences a mental disorder in any given year, but nearly two-thirds of them never seek treatment, according to a landmark report on mental health released December 13, 1999, by Surgeon General David Satcher. The stigma attached to mental illness and inadequate insurance were the main factors preventing treatment, but the report also said many people were not aware that effective treatments for many mental disorders, including the most severe, were available. The report emphasized that mental illnesses were "not the result of moral failings or limited will power" but legitimate, physical illnesses that were responsive to specific treatments. As a result, the report's principal advice was to "seek help if you have a mental health problem or think you have symptoms of a mental disorder."

According to the report, mental illnesses, including major depression and suicide, were the second leading cause, after heart conditions, of lost health and productivity in developed economies such as the United States. In 1996 direct treatment of mental disorders, substance abuse, and Alzheimer's cost $99 billion (mental disorders alone cost $69 billion); indirect costs for mental disorders alone cost $79 billion. An estimated 33–50 percent of the homeless population and an estimated 15–20 percent of the prison population were thought to be suffering from some mental disorder. Moreover, about 15 percent of all adults with mental disorders also suffered from alcohol or drug abuse, making effective treatment more difficult. Suicide, which was typically associated with mental disorders and substance abuse, was a leading cause of death in the United States. About 30,000 people killed themselves each year, a statistic that led Satcher to call suicide a serious public health problem earlier in the year. (Surgeon general's report on suicide prevention, p. 439)

The 500-page report on mental health was based on a review of more than 3,000 research papers, journal articles, and books, as well as on information gathered at a White House Conference on Mental Health in

June. That conference was chaired by Tipper Gore, the wife of the vice president and a long-time advocate on behalf of the mentally ill. "For all the progress that we have made on mental health, mental illness is still very much feared, and it's very much misunderstood," Gore said at White House news conference, where the report was formally released. "It's our responsibility to change those attitudes. No law or government program is going to do that for us," she said.

Gore and Satcher clearly hoped that focusing attention on the problem would help erase the stigma of mental disorders, encourage more people to seek treatment, and expand the supply of services available. Advocates for the mentally ill saw the report as an opportunity to press for greater public funding of mental health services and for health insurance "parity"—equal treatment under health insurance plans for mental and physical illness. During the White House Conference on Mental Health in June, President Bill Clinton announced that insurance companies offering health plans to federal employees would be required to offer the same coverage for mental disorders as they did for physical ones, but few private plans offered health insurance "parity." Satcher said he supported full parity, which he said was an "affordable and effective objective."

Erasing the Stigma of Mental Disorders

The report stressed three key findings: that "mental health is fundamental to overall health and the public health of the nation"; that mental illnesses were indistinguishable from other forms of illness; and that effective treatments now existed for most diagnosable mental disorders. The report suggested that readers consider mental health and mental illness as points on a continuum. Mental health was defined as "a state of successful performance of mental functions, resulting in productive activities, fulfilling relationships with other people, and the ability to adapt to change and to cope with adversity." Mental illness referred to all mental disorders that could be diagnosed. Mental disorders were conditions "characterized by alterations in thinking, mood, or behavior (or some combination thereof) associated with distress and/or impaired functioning," the report stated. Examples were Alzheimer's disease (thinking), depression (mood), and attention-deficit/hyperactivity disorder (behavior and thinking). Alterations in any of these functions contribute to "patient distress, impaired functioning, or heightened risk of death, pain, disability, or loss of freedom."

The report used the term mental health problems *to mean "signs and symptoms of insufficient intensity or duration to meet the criteria for any mental disorder" and warned that such symptoms and signs could be disabling if not dealt with. For example, the report said, among older people bereavement symptoms, if left unattended, could lead to depression, which in turn could lead to suicide, heart attack, or other disorders. (The highest rate of suicide was among white men over the age of sixty-five, who accounted for 20 percent of all suicides in the United States.)*

The report said that a great deal was still unknown about the causes of mental disorders. Although no one gene had been found to be responsible for any specific disorder, variations in multiple genes contributed to disruption of healthy brain function "that, under certain environmental conditions, results in mental illness." Scientists also recognized that socioeconomic factors affected vulnerability, making some demographic and economic groups more prone than others to experience mental health problems, and some disorders.

If science had not nailed down the causes of mental disorders, it nonetheless had produced what Satcher described as "a vast array of safe and effective" treatment options ranging from drug therapies, to counseling, to psychotherapy. Yet "critical gaps" existed between those who needed service and those who received service, and between the most effective treatment and what the patient actually received. Only about 10 percent of adults used mental health services in the health sector in any given year, while another 5 percent sought informal care from social services, agencies, schools, religious organizations, or self-help groups.

The primary reason for the gap in treatment was social stigma, which had been exacerbated in recent years by a spreading public perception that people with mental illnesses tended to be violent. The report acknowledged that some people with mental disorders were in fact violent and that violence was likely to be more of a problem for people diagnosed with both a mental disorder and substance abuse. The fact was, however, that the overall risk of violence was low, the report said, and there was "very little risk of violence or harm to a stranger from casual contact with an individual who has a mental disorder."

Another major reason that people with medical disorders did not seek treatment was the cost. Some 44 million people lacked any health insurance coverage at all, while plans covering millions of others did not offer the same coverages for mental disorders as for physical problems, making mental health care unaffordable for many. In 1996 Congress enacted a law that required health insurance plans that offered mental health benefits to set the same annual and lifetime limits on benefits for both mental illnesses and physical ailments. (1996 health care law, Historic Documents of 1996, p. 388; health care coverage, p. 561)

Health insurers could and did set different benefit levels for copayments, deductibles, inpatient hospital stays, and outpatient treatment. As a result, patients typically paid a higher share of the costs of their treatment for mental illness than for physical illness, a situation that many advocates for the mentally ill said was unfair and discriminatory. As of the end of 1999, twenty-eight states had enacted parity laws, and parity legislation had been introduced in both the House and Senate. Although the report did not take a stand on the issue, it said that where care had been managed, parity had resulted in "negligible cost increases."

"I think [the report is] going to highlight the great disparities regarding mental health treatment, the blatant discrimination that's been taking place,"

said Rep. Marge Roukema, R-N.J., who was sponsoring legislation to require mental health parity. Moreover, she said, the report "documents the cost-effectiveness of early treatment to help people. This is no longer opinion—this is established fact." Insurers, however, warned that parity would cause premiums to rise by as much as 5 percent. Carmella Bocchino of the American Association of Health Plans said there would have to be "trade-offs. Do we give up other parts of the benefits package, or are we looking to rising health care costs?" She said the nation would benefit from "an honest debate" about how to implement and pay for improved mental health care coverage.

The mental health report contained specific chapters on mental disorders in children, working-age adults, and older adults, including descriptions of the disorders affecting these populations and the kinds of treatments available for them. The report also discussed the organization of mental health care financing and services and ways to remove the barriers to quality health care for all those who need it. The report was prepared, under Satcher's guidance, by the Substance Abuse and Mental Health Services Administration and the National Institute of Mental Health, both within the Department of Health and Human Services.

Mental Illness and the Prison Population

In the first comprehensive survey of its kind, the Bureau of Justice Statistics reported July 11 that in 1998 an estimated 283,800 inmates in the nation's prisons and jails were mentally ill and that another 547,800 inmates with mental illness had been released on probation. Women were more likely to be mentally ill than men, with the highest rate of illness (40 percent) among white female state prisoners under age twenty-five. Paula Ditton, the author of the report, said she found the figures "startlingly high" and speculated that some mental patients released from hospitals into communities as part of the mainstreaming movement that began in the early 1970s may have ended up in prison. The bureau classified inmates as mentally ill if they said they were currently experiencing a mental or emotional condition or if they reported an overnight stay in a mental hospital or other treatment facility.

The report also found that the mentally ill were somewhat more likely than other prisoners to have committed a violent crime and that they were more than twice as likely to have been physically or sexually abused at some time before their incarceration. "This does not mean that mentally ill offenders are more violent than others offenders," Ditton said. The disproportion could occur, she said, because it might be easier for the police to catch mentally ill offenders and because juries and judges might be more inclined to convict and sentence mentally ill violent offenders.

Among state prisoners, 37 percent of the mentally ill were abused before their imprisonment, compared with 15 percent of other prisoners. Seventy-eight percent of the mentally ill female inmates had been abused, compared with 50 percent of the other female inmates. Mentally ill inmates were also twice as likely to be homeless. "What really comes through here is that the mentally ill are far more likely to come from homes that are troubled, either with parents who have been incarcerated or abused alcohol or drugs," said Allen Beck, chief of correction statistics for the bureau. "What is cause and what is effect is hard to sort out, but there is a consistent set of negative indicators—alcohol dependence, drug use, life experiences. It's a package of really co-occurring problems."

Following are excerpts from the preface and chapter 1 of "Mental Health: A Report of the Surgeon General," released December 13, 1999, by Surgeon General David Satcher at a White House news conference:

Preface

The past century has witnessed extraordinary progress in our improvement of the public health through medical science and ambitious, often innovative, approaches to health care services. Previous Surgeons General reports have saluted our gains while continuing to set ever higher benchmarks for the public health. Through much of this era of great challenge and greater achievement, however, concerns regarding mental illness and mental health too often were relegated to the rear of our national consciousness. Tragic and devastating disorders such as schizophrenia, depression and bipolar disorder, Alzheimer's disease, the mental and behavioral disorders suffered by children, and a range of other mental disorders affect nearly one in five Americans in any year, yet continue too frequently to be spoken of in whispers and shame. Fortunately, leaders in the mental health field—fiercely dedicated advocates, scientists, government officials, and consumers—have been insistent that mental health flow in the mainstream of health. I agree and issue this report in that spirit.

This report makes evident that the neuroscience of mental health—a term that encompasses studies extending from molecular events to psychological, behavioral, and societal phenomena—has emerged as one of the most exciting arenas of scientific activity and human inquiry. We recognize that the brain is the integrator of thought, emotion, behavior, and health. Indeed, one of the foremost contributions of contemporary mental health research is the extent to which it has mended the destructive split between "mental" and "physical" health.

We know more today about how to treat mental illness effectively and appropriately than we know with certainty about how to prevent mental illness and promote mental health. Common sense and respect for our fellow humans tells us that a focus on the positive aspects of mental health demands our immediate attention.

Even more than other areas of health and medicine, the mental health field is plagued by disparities in the availability of and access to its services. These disparities are viewed readily through the lenses of racial and cultural diversity, age, and gender. A key disparity often hinges on a person's financial status; formidable financial barriers block off needed mental health care from too many people regardless of whether one has health insurance with inadequate mental health benefits, or is one of the 44 million Americans who lack any insurance. We have allowed stigma and a now unwarranted sense of hopelessness about the opportunities for recovery from mental illness to erect these barriers. It is time to take them down.

Promoting mental health for all Americans will require scientific know-how but, even more importantly, a societal resolve that we will make the needed investment. The investment does not call for massive budgets; rather, it calls for the willingness of each of us to educate ourselves and others about mental health and mental illness, and thus to confront the attitudes, fear, and misunderstanding that remain as barriers before us. It is my intent that this report will usher in a healthy era of mind and body for the Nation.

David Satcher, M.D., Ph.D.
Surgeon General

Introduction and Themes

This first Surgeon General's Report on Mental Health is issued at the culmination of a half-century that has witnessed remarkable advances in the understanding of mental disorders and the brain and in our appreciation of the centrality of mental health to overall health and well-being. The report was prepared against a backdrop of growing awareness in the United States and throughout the world of the immense burden of disability associated with mental illnesses. In the United States, mental disorders collectively account for more than 15 percent of the overall burden of disease from all causes and slightly more than the burden associated with all forms of cancer. These data underscore the importance and urgency of treating and preventing mental disorders and of promoting mental health in our society.

The report in its entirety provides an up-to-date review of scientific advances in the study of mental health and of mental illnesses that affect at least one in five Americans. Several important conclusions may be drawn from the extensive scientific literature summarized in the report. One is that a variety of treatments of well-documented efficacy exist for the array of clearly defined mental and behavioral disorders that occur across the life span. Every person should be encouraged to seek help when questions arise about mental health, just as each person is encouraged to seek help when questions arise about health. Research highlighted in the report demonstrates that mental health is a facet of health that evolves throughout the lifetime. Just as each person can do much to promote and maintain overall health regardless of age, each also can do much to promote and strengthen mental health at every stage of life.

Much remains to be learned about the causes, treatment, and prevention of mental and behavioral disorders. Obstacles that may limit the availability or accessibility of mental health services for some Americans are being dismantled, but disparities persist. Still, thanks to research and the experiences of millions of individuals who have a mental disorder, their family members, and other advocates, the Nation has the power today to tear down the most formidable obstacle to future progress in the arena of mental illness and health. That obstacle is stigma. Stigmatization of mental illness is an excuse for inaction and discrimination that is inexcusably outmoded in 1999. As evident in the chapters that follow, we have acquired an immense amount of knowledge that permits us, as a Nation, to respond to the needs of persons with mental illness in a manner that is both effective and respectful.

Overarching Themes

Mental Health and Mental Illness: A Public Health Approach

The Nation's contemporary mental health enterprise, like the broader field of health, is rooted in a population-based public health model. The public health model is characterized by concern for the health of a population in its entirety and by awareness of the linkage between health and the physical and psycho- social environment. Public health focuses not only on traditional areas of diagnosis, treatment, and etiology, but also on epidemiologic surveillance of the health of the population at large, health promotion, disease prevention, and access to and evaluation of services.

Just as the mainstream of public health takes a broad view of health and illness, this Surgeon General's Report on Mental Health takes a wide-angle lens to *both* mental health and mental illness. In years past, the mental health field often focused principally on mental illness in order to serve individuals who were most severely affected. Only as the field has matured has it begun to respond to intensifying interest and concerns about disease prevention and health promotion. Because of the more recent consideration of these topic areas, the body of accumulated knowledge regarding them is not as expansive as that for mental illness.

Mental Disorders Are Disabling

The burden of mental illness on health and productivity in the United States and throughout the world has long been profoundly underestimated. Data developed by the massive Global Burden of Disease study, conducted by the World Health Organization, the World Bank, and Harvard University, reveal that mental illness, including suicide, ranks second in the burden of disease in established market economies, such as the United States.

Mental illness emerged from the Global Burden of Disease study as a surprisingly significant contributor to the burden of disease. The measure of calculating disease burden in this study, called Disability Adjusted Life Years (DALYs), allows comparison of the burden of disease across many different disease conditions. DALYs account for lost years of healthy life regardless of whether the years were lost to premature death or disability. The disability component of this measure is weighted for severity of the disability. For example, major depression is equivalent in burden to blindness or paraplegia, whereas active psychosis seen in schizophrenia is equal in disability burden to quadriplegia.

By this measure, major depression alone ranked second only to ischemic heart disease in magnitude of disease burden. Schizophrenia, bipolar disorder, obsessive-compulsive disorder, panic disorder, and post-traumatic stress disorder also contributed significantly to the burden represented by mental illness.

Mental Health and Mental Illness: Points on a Continuum

As will be evident in the pages that follow, "mental health" and "mental illness" are not polar opposites but may be thought of as points on a continuum. *Mental health* is a state of successful performance of mental function, resulting in productive activities, fulfilling relationships with other people, and the ability to adapt to change and to cope with adversity. Mental health is indispensable to personal well-being, family and interpersonal relationships, and contribution to community or society. It is easy to overlook the value of mental health until problems surface. Yet from early childhood until death, mental health is the springboard of thinking and communication skills, learning, emotional growth, resilience, and self-esteem. These are the ingredients of each individual's successful contribution to community and society. Americans are inundated with messages about *success*—in school, in a profession, in parenting, in relationships—without appreciating that successful performance rests on a foundation of mental health.

Many ingredients of mental health may be identifiable, but mental health is not easy to define. In the words of a distinguished leader in the field of mental health prevention, ". . . built into any definition of wellness . . . are overt and covert expressions of values. Because values differ across cultures as well as among subgroups (and indeed individuals) within a culture, the ideal of a uniformly acceptable definition of the constructs is illusory." In other words, what it means to be mentally healthy is subject to many different interpretations that are rooted in value judgments that may vary across cultures. The challenge of defining mental health has stalled the development of programs to foster mental health, although strides have been made with wellness programs for older people.

Mental illness is the term that refers collectively to all diagnosable mental disorders. Mental disorders are health conditions that are characterized by alterations in thinking, mood, or behavior (or some combination thereof) associated with distress and/or impaired functioning. Alzheimer's disease exemplifies a mental disorder largely marked by alterations in thinking (especially forgetting). Depression exemplifies a mental disorder largely marked by alterations in mood. Attention-deficit/hyperactivity disorder exemplifies a mental disorder largely marked by alterations in behavior (overactivity) and/or thinking (inability to concentrate). Alterations in thinking, mood, or behavior contribute to a host of problems—patient distress, impaired functioning, or heightened risk of death, pain, disability, or loss of freedom.

This report uses the term "mental health problems" for signs and symptoms of insufficient intensity or duration to meet the criteria for any mental disorder. Almost everyone has experienced mental health problems in which the distress one feels matches some of the signs and symptoms of mental disorders. Mental health problems may warrant active efforts in health promotion, prevention, and treatment. Bereavement symptoms in older adults offer a case in point. Bereavement symptoms of less than 2 months' duration do not qualify as a mental disorder, according to professional manuals for diagnosis. Nevertheless, bereavement symptoms can be debilitating if they are left unattended. They place older people at risk for depression, which, in turn, is linked to death from suicide, heart attack, or other causes. Much can be done—through formal treatment or through support group participation—to ameliorate the symptoms and to avert the consequences of bereavement. In this case, early intervention is needed to address a mental health problem before it becomes a potentially life-threatening disorder.

Mind and Body Are Inseparable

Considering health and illness as points along a continuum helps one appreciate that neither state exists in pure isolation from the other. In another but related context, everyday language tends to encourage a misperception that "mental health" or "mental illness" is unrelated to "physical health" or "physical illness." In fact, the two are inseparable.

Seventeenth-century philosopher Rene Descartes conceptualized the distinction between the mind and the body. He viewed the "mind" as completely separable from the "body" (or "matter" in general). The mind (and spirit) was seen as the concern of organized religion, whereas the body was seen as the concern of physicians. This partitioning ushered in a separation between so-called "mental" and "physical" health, despite advances in the 20th century that proved the interrelationships between mental and physical health.

Although "mind" is a broad term that has had many different meanings over the centuries, today it refers to the totality of mental functions related to thinking, mood, and purposive behavior. The mind is generally seen as deriving from activities within the brain but displaying emergent properties, such as consciousness.

One reason the public continues to this day to emphasize the difference between mental and physical health is embedded in language. Common parlance continues to use the term "physical" to distinguish some forms of health and illness from "mental" health and illness. People continue to see mental and physical as separate functions when, in fact, mental functions (e.g., memory) are physical as well. Mental functions are carried out by the brain. Likewise, mental disorders are reflected in physical changes in the brain. Physical changes in the brain often trigger physical changes in other parts of the body too. The racing heart, dry mouth, and sweaty palms that accompany a terrifying nightmare are orchestrated by the brain. A nightmare is a mental state associated with alterations of brain chemistry that, in turn, provoke unmistakable changes elsewhere in the body.

Instead of dividing physical from mental health, the more appropriate and neutral distinction is between "mental" and "somatic" health. Somatic is a medical term that derives from the Greek word soma for the body. Mental health refers to the successful performance of mental functions in terms of thought, mood, and behavior. Mental disorders are those health conditions in which alterations in mental functions are paramount. Somatic conditions are those in which alterations in nonmental functions predominate. While the brain carries out all mental functions, it also carries out some somatic functions, such as movement, touch, and balance. That is why not all brain diseases are mental disorders. For example, a stroke causes a lesion in the brain that may produce disturbances of movement, such as paralysis of limbs. When such symptoms predominate in a patient, the stroke is considered a somatic condition. But when a stroke mainly produces alterations of thought, mood, or behavior, it is considered a mental condition (e.g., dementia). The point is that a brain disease can be seen as a mental disorder or a somatic disorder depending on the functions it perturbs.

The Roots of Stigma

Stigmatization of people with mental disorders has persisted throughout history. It is manifested by bias, distrust, stereotyping, fear, embarrassment, anger, and/or avoidance. Stigma leads others to avoid living, socializing or working with, renting to, or employing people with mental disorders, especially severe disorders such as schizophrenia. It reduces patients' access to resources and opportunities (e.g., housing, jobs) and leads to low self-esteem, isolation, and hopelessness. It deters the public from seeking, and wanting to pay for, care. In its most overt and egregious form, stigma results in outright discrimination and abuse. More tragically, it deprives people of their dignity and interferes with their full participation in society.

Explanations for stigma stem, in part, from the misguided split between mind and body first proposed by Descartes. Another source of stigma lies in the 19th-century separation of the mental health treatment system in the United States from the mainstream of health. These historical influences exert an often immediate influence on perceptions and behaviors in the modern world.

Separation of Treatment Systems

In colonial times in the United States, people with mental illness were described as "lunaticks" and were largely cared for by families. There was no concerted effort to treat mental illness until urbanization in the early 19th century created a societal problem that previously had been relegated to families scattered among small rural communities. Social policy assumed the form of isolated asylums where persons with mental illness were administered the reigning treatments of the era. By the late 19th century, mental illness was thought to grow "out of a violation of those physical, mental and moral laws which, properly understood and obeyed, result not only in the highest development of the race, but the highest type of civilization." Throughout the history of institutionalization in asylums (later renamed mental hospitals), reformers strove to improve treatment and curtail abuse. Several waves of reform culminated in the deinstitutionalization movement that began in the 1950s with the goal of shifting patients and care to the community.

Public Attitudes About Mental Illness: 1950s to 1990s

Nationally representative surveys have tracked public attitudes about mental illness since the 1950s. To permit comparisons over time, several surveys of the 1970s and the 1990s phrased questions exactly as they had been asked in the 1950s.

In the 1950s, the public viewed mental illness as a stigmatized condition and displayed an unscientific understanding of mental illness. Survey respondents typically were not able to identify individuals as "mentally ill" when presented with vignettes of individuals who would have been said to be mentally ill according to the professional standards of the day. The public was not particularly skilled at distinguishing mental illness from ordinary unhappiness and worry and tended to see only extreme forms of behavior—namely psychosis—as mental illness. Mental illness carried great social stigma, especially linked with fear of unpredictable and violent behavior.

By 1996, a modern survey revealed that Americans had achieved greater scientific understanding of mental illness. But the increases in knowledge did not defuse social stigma. The public learned to define mental illness and to distinguish it from ordinary worry and unhappiness. It expanded its definition of mental illness to encompass anxiety, depression, and other mental disorders. The public attributed mental illness to a mix of biological abnormalities and vulnerabilities to social and psychological stress. Yet, in comparison with the 1950s, the public's perception of mental illness more frequently incorporated violent behavior. This was primarily true among those who defined mental illness to include psychosis (a view held by about one-third of the entire sample). Thirty-one percent of this group mentioned violence in its descriptions of mental illness, in comparison with 13 percent in the 1950s. In other words, the perception of people with psychosis as being dangerous is stronger today than in the past.

The 1996 survey also probed how perceptions of those with mental illness varied by diagnosis. The public was more likely to consider an individual with schizophrenia as having mental illness than an individual with depression. All of them were distinguished reasonably well from a worried and unhappy individual who did not meet professional criteria for a mental disorder. The desire for social distance was consistent with this hierarchy.

Why is stigma so strong despite better public understanding of mental illness? The answer appears to be fear of violence: people with mental illness, especially those with psychosis, are perceived to be more violent than in the past.

This finding begs yet another question: Are people with mental disorders truly more violent? Research supports some public concerns, but the overall likelihood of violence is low. The greatest risk of violence is from those who have dual diagnoses, i.e., individuals who have a mental disorder as well as a substance abuse disorder. There is a small elevation in risk of violence from individuals with severe mental disorders (e.g., psychosis), especially if they are noncompliant with their medication. Yet the risk of violence is much less for a stranger than for a family member or person who is known to the person with mental illness. *In fact, there is very little risk of violence or harm to a stranger from casual contact with an individual who has a mental disorder.* Because the average person is ill-equipped to judge whether someone who is behaving erratically has any of these disorders, alone or in combination, the natural tendency is to be wary. Yet, to put this all in perspective, the overall contribution of mental disorders to the total level of violence in society is exceptionally small.

Because most people should have little reason to fear violence from those with mental illness, even in its most severe forms, why is fear of violence so entrenched? Most speculations focus on media coverage and deinstitutionalization. One series of surveys found that selective media reporting reinforced the public's stereotypes linking violence and mental illness and encouraged people to distance themselves from those with mental disorders. And yet, deinstitutionalization made this distancing impossible over the 40 years as the population of state and county mental hospitals was reduced from a high of about 560,000 in 1955 to well below 100,000 by the 1990s. Some advocates of deinstitutionalization expected stigma to be reduced with community care and commonplace exposure. Stigma might have been greater today had not public education resulted in a more scientific understanding of mental illness.

Stigma and Seeking Help for Mental Disorders

Nearly two-thirds of all people with diagnosable mental disorders do not seek treatment. Stigma surrounding the receipt of mental health treatment is among the many barriers that discourage people from seeking treatment. Concern about stigma appears to be heightened in rural areas in relation to larger towns or cities. Stigma also disproportionately affects certain age groups, as explained in the chapters on children and older people.

The surveys cited above concerning evolving public attitudes about mental illness also monitored how people would cope with, and seek treatment for, mental illness if they became symptomatic. (The term "nervous breakdown" was used in lieu of the term "mental illness" in the 1996 survey to allow for comparisons with the surveys in the 1950s and 1970s.) The 1996 survey found that people were likelier than in the past to approach mental illness by coping with, rather than by avoiding, the problem. They also were more likely now to want *informal* social supports (e.g., self-help groups). Those who now sought *formal* support increasingly preferred counselors, psychologists, and social workers.

Stigma and Paying for Mental Disorder Treatment

Another manifestation of stigma is reflected in the public's reluctance to pay for mental health services. Public willingness to pay for mental health treatment, particularly through insurance premiums or taxes, has been assessed largely through public opinion polls. Members of the public report a greater willingness to pay for insurance coverage for individuals with severe mental disorders, such as schizophrenia and depression, rather than for less severe conditions such as worry and unhappiness. While the public generally appears to support paying for treatment, its support diminishes upon the realization that higher taxes or premiums would be necessary. In the lexicon of survey research, the willingness to pay for mental illness treatment services is considered to be "soft." The public generally ranks insurance coverage for mental disorders below that for somatic disorders.

Reducing Stigma

There is likely no simple or single panacea to eliminate the stigma associated with mental illness. Stigma was expected to abate with increased knowledge of mental illness, but just the opposite occurred: stigma in some ways intensified over the past 40 years even though understanding improved. Knowledge of mental illness appears by itself insufficient to dispel stigma. Broader knowledge may be warranted, especially to redress public fears. Research is beginning to demonstrate that negative perceptions about severe mental illness can be lowered by furnishing empirically based information on the association between violence and severe mental illness. Overall approaches to stigma reduction involve programs of advocacy, public education, and contact with persons with mental illness through schools and other societal institutions.

Another way to eliminate stigma is to find causes and effective treatments for mental disorders. History suggests this to be true. Neurosyphilis and pellagra are illustrative of mental disorders for which stigma has receded. In the early part of this century, about 20 percent of those admitted to mental hospitals had "general paresis," later identified as tertiary syphilis. This advanced stage of syphilis occurs when the bacterium invades the brain and causes neurological deterioration (including psychosis), paralysis, and death. The discoveries of an infectious etiology and of penicillin led to the virtual elimination of neurosyphilis. Similarly, when pellagra was traced to a nutrient deficiency, and nutritional supplementation with niacin was introduced, the condition was eventually eradicated in the developed world. Pellagra's victims with delirium had been placed in mental hospitals early in the 20th century before its etiology was clarified. Although no one has documented directly the reduction of public stigma toward these conditions over the early and later parts of this century, disease eradication through widespread acceptance of treatment (and its cost) offers indirect proof.

Ironically, these examples also illustrate a more unsettling consequence: that the mental health field was adversely affected when causes and treatments were identified. As advances were achieved, each condition was transferred from the mental health field to another medical specialty. For instance, dominion over syphilis was moved to dermatology, internal medicine, and neurology upon advances in etiology and treatment. Dominion over hormone-related mental disorders was moved to endocrinology under similar circumstances. The consequence of this transformation, according to historian Gerald Grob, is that the mental health field became over the years the repository for mental disorders whose etiology was unknown. This left the mental health field "vulnerable to accusations by their medical brethren that psychiatry was not part of medicine, and that psychiatric practice rested on superstition and myth."

These historical examples signify that stigma dissipates for individual disorders once advances render them less disabling, infectious, or disfiguring. Yet the stigma surrounding *other* mental disorders not only persists but may be inadvertently reinforced by leaving to mental health care only those behavioral conditions without known causes or cures. To point this out is not intended to imply that advances in mental health should be halted; rather, advances should be nurtured and heralded. The purpose here is to explain some of the historical origins of the chasm between the health and mental health fields.

Stigma must be overcome. Research that will continue to yield increasingly effective treatments for mental disorders promises to be an effective antidote. When people understand that mental disorders are not the result of moral failings or limited will power, but are legitimate illnesses that are responsive to specific treatments, much of the negative stereotyping may dissipate. Still, fresh approaches to disseminate research information and, thus, to counter stigma need to be developed and evaluated. Social science research has much to contribute to the development and evaluation of anti-stigma programs. As stigma abates, a transformation in public attitudes should occur. People should become eager to seek care. They should become more willing to absorb its cost. And, most importantly, they should become far more receptive to the messages that are the subtext of this report: mental health and mental illness are part of the mainstream of health, and they are a concern for all people. . . .

FORMER PRESIDENT CARTER ON THE PANAMA CANAL TRANSFER
December 14, 1999

Just two words—"It's yours"—ended nearly a century of U.S. ownership of one of the most important waterways in the world: the Panama Canal. With those words, former president Jimmy Carter, who in 1978 had convinced a skeptical Senate to approve treaties transferring the canal to Panama in 1999, formally handed over the canal in a ceremony closing a long-running chapter of U.S. imperialism.

But reminders of the emotions that the canal treaty had triggered two decades earlier remained in both the United States and Panama. American conservatives who had bitterly opposed the treaty were still warning in 1999 that Washington was giving a vital asset to an unstable country that was unprepared to manage it. In Panama there were conflicting sentiments: pride in finally achieving full national sovereignty after a century of U.S. domination, residual anger at the United States for all the wrongs both real and imagined done to Panama during that century, and nervousness about the country's ability to handle its new responsibility. There was even some resentment in Panama that the sitting U.S. president, Bill Clinton, skipped the historic occasion. (Panama Canal treaty, Historic Documents of 1977, p. 591; Historic Documents of 1978, p. 177)

Panama had been part of Colombia until 1903, when the United States inspired a rebellion that led to the creation of an independent country. The new country's leaders signed an agreement with the United States providing for construction of the canal, along with U.S. ownership of nearly 400,000 acres of land and lakes surrounding it. After a decade of work that cost the lives of 5,600 workers, the canal was inaugurated in August 1914. It quickly became an important shipping corridor, cutting weeks off the time needed for ships to travel between the Atlantic and Pacific oceans. The United States, with its military bases and ownership of the canal, was the dominant partner in a relationship that had many tense moments. Among them was an incident in 1964 when students tried to raise the Panamanian flag in the Canal Zone; twenty-two Panamanians and four U.S.

Marines died in subsequent clashes, leading to a brief suspension of diplomatic relations between the two countries.

Changes Since the Treaty

In 1977 Carter, then in his first year as president, completed negotiations on the canal treaties with General Omar Torrijos, one of the most powerful and popular of Panama's numerous military dictators. The treaties were wildly popular in Panama, where they were seen as restoring the country's lost independence. But conservatives in the United States bitterly denounced Carter's act as a betrayal, and they tried unsuccessfully to block approval of the treaties in the Senate.

By 1999, when the final stage of the treaties was to take effect, the world had changed dramatically. The cold war, which had been a powerful factor animating U.S. opponents to the treaty, had ended. The Soviet Union—once said by many in the United States to be positioning itself to control the canal after Panama owned it—had collapsed. Panama was no longer under the control of military strongmen. Despite continuing poverty, corruption, and economic woes, Panama had become a functioning democracy with the regular transfer of power from one elected government to another. On September 1 Panama inaugurated its first woman president, Mireya Moscoso, the widow of one of the country's most important nationalist leaders in modern times, Arnulfo Arias.

The United States also had undergone profound changes in the years since the Panama Canal treaty was headline news, not the least of which was its becoming the sole superpower in the world. The United States of 1977–1978 was still haunted by the Watergate scandal, confronting the economic uncertainty of high inflation, and profoundly worried by the military might of the Soviet Union. All those concerns were distant memories for most Americans by 1999.

Much of the once-dominant U.S. presence in Panama already had disappeared by 1999. The Canal Zone—a U.S.-run, five-mile-wide strip bordering the canal all the way from the Caribbean Sea (at the northwest) to the Gulf of Panama (at the southeast)—was dissolved in 1979 and taken under Panamanian control. The U.S. military had pulled out of three major facilities—Howard Air Force Base, Fort Clayton, and Albrook Field—and Panama was planning to convert them to commercial facilities. Panamanian officials for years had carried most of the responsibility for running the canal, through its management office, the Panama Canal Commission. Once Panama took control, the commission was to be replaced by the new Panama Canal Authority under Panamanian leadership.

Changes also were underway at the canal itself. The commission was in the midst of a modernization project to replace aging equipment, including the locomotives (called "mules") that pulled large ships through the canal. The canal also was being widened and deepened so it could accommodate much larger container ships than those for which the canal was built at the beginning of the twentieth century. About 14,000 ships passed through the canal annually; officials said they expected traffic to increase by about 20 percent once the canal was modernized.

Renewed Concerns in the United States

One thing that had not changed in the two decades since Jimmy Carter signed the 1977 treaties was the anxiety among some conservatives in the United States about the loss of U.S. control over the canal. The generalized fears of treaty opponents became more specific in 1997 when Panama decided to award contracts for the management of two of the numerous ports at either end of the canal to a multinational company based in Hong Kong, Hutchison Whampoa Ltd.

Some U.S. conservatives expressed concern about the contracts at the time they were awarded, and the level of criticism rose as the date for handing over the canal approached. Senate Majority Leader Trent Lott, R-Miss., wrote to Defense Secretary William Cohen in August warning that the Hong Kong company was linked to the communist government in Beijing. "U.S. naval ships will be at the mercy of Chinese-controlled pilots, and could even be denied passage through the Panama Canal," he said. Retired admiral Thomas Moorer, a former chairman of the Joint Chiefs of Staff, wrote in New American, *the magazine of the right-wing John Birch Society, that with the turnover of the canal "communist China will become the de facto new owners and rulers of the Panama Canal."*

U.S. and Panamanian officials, along with executives of Hutchison Whampoa, dismissed those criticisms, noting that the company had no control over shipping in the canal and that the 1977 treaty gave the U.S. naval priority in use of the canal during an emergency. Moreover, they noted that Hutchison Whampoa was a publicly traded company with operations worldwide; its top managers in Panama were British and American, and none of its employees there were Chinese.

Carter, who had battled many of the same critics in pushing the treaty through the Senate twenty-one years earlier, denounced them as "demagogues" who had "exaggerated problems and spoke about catastrophic events. There are still some in my country spreading false stories about the security of the canal."

Handing over the Canal

Under the treaty, Panama was to assume ownership of the canal at noon on December 31, 1999, but U.S. and Panamanian officials agreed to hold a ceremonial transfer two weeks earlier, on December 14. President Clinton decided not to attend, citing pressing business, including the opening of negotiations in Washington between Israel and Syria. U.S. officials said Clinton wanted the focus of attention to be on Panama, not on the United States, but some observers said the White House was more concerned about reviving old tensions about the canal treaties within the United States. Clinton asked Carter to represent him, along with Secretary of State Madeleine K. Albright. But Albright also decided at the last minute not to attend, leaving Commerce Secretary William Daley as the highest ranking current official on the U.S. delegation.

The ceremony took place at the Miraflores Locks, just outside Panama City. Carter, President Moscoso, several Latin American heads of state, and King Juan Carlos of Spain arrived on board one of the new "mules" that symbolized the determination of both countries to modernize the canal.

In his speech celebrating the occasion, Carter recalled the controversy that had plagued the canal throughout its history and the bitter opposition in the United States to the treaty turning it over to Panama. During the intervening years, he said, there had been "a harmonious step-by-step transfer" of Canal operations to Panama. "Today there is mutual respect between our two nations, a canal that is secure and superbly managed by an independent authority, real and firmly established democracy in Panama, and principals of competition and free enterprise now prevailing in the management of adjacent facilities in the former Canal Zone," he said.

Moscoso praised Carter for his vision in signing the canal treaties but pointedly made no mention of Clinton. She said Panama's assumption of control over the canal marked "the consolidation of our sovereignty and the recovery of our national territory." She offered assurances that Panama would meet its responsibilities to maintain the canal for international shipping.

Carter and Moscoso exchanged diplomatic notes confirming the transfer of control of the canal. Moscoso later said Carter told her, "It's yours" after he signed the U.S. note.

At sunset on December 30, a small detachment of U.S. military personnel hauled down the last U.S. flag that had flown over the Panama Canal Commission headquarters, folded it, and presented it to U.S. ambassador Simon Ferro. Officials had planned to take down the flag on December 31—when Panama planned a large formal ceremony—but apparently decided to play down the significance of the event by acting a day ahead of time. It was one last example of how ambivalent the relationship between Panama and the United States had been for nearly a century. "Somehow I think it would have been nobler to lower the flag at today's ceremony," Panama's foreign minister, Jorge Ritter, said on December 31.

> *Following is the text of a speech delivered December 14, 1999, by former president Jimmy Carter during a ceremony in Panama marking the transfer of control of the Panama Canal from the United States to Panama:*

I am honored to represent the United States of America as leader of a distinguished delegation on this historic occasion. It is important to understand the past, to acknowledge the present, and to plan for the future.

I would like first to thank the heroes of the past: our own President Theodore Roosevelt for his vision and political courage; George Goethals for his brilliant engineering feat (with special thanks for a design that avoids the threat of the Y2K bug); and William Gorgas, whose research saved the lives of tens of thousands of workers from deadly disease. At the same time, we cannot forget the tens of thousands of workers who came here from 97 nations, many of whom gave their lives in this challenging work.

From the first, the 1903 Panama Canal Treaty created controversy. It was never seen by any Panamanian when it was drafted and signed, and became both a source of pride in the United States and a symbol of colonialism and subjugation to many citizens of Panama. The key phrase was "control in perpetuity as though it were sovereign," which created an inevitable argument about actual title to the Canal Zone. This issue became increasingly contentious, and President Eisenhower agreed to restraints concerning flying the American flag in certain areas of the Zone. When this agreement was violated in 1964, a total of 24 American and Panamanian soldiers were killed in the resulting confrontation. Panama broke diplomatic relations with the United States, and some other Latin American nations threatened to take the same action. President Lyndon Johnson promised to negotiate a new treaty, but political opposition in the United States prevented the fulfillment of this promise.

This situation continued to fester under Presidents Richard Nixon and Gerald Ford, with negotiations on a text but no effort being made to have a new treaty ratified by an obdurate U.S. Senate. Despite the need for a close partnership, our two nations lost the delicate balance of trust and cooperation necessary for the safe operation of the canal.

When I became president in 1977, we resumed negotiations and were successful in forging a good document under the leadership of Ellsworth Bunker and Sol Linowitz, who worked with Panama's ambassadors Royo and Escobar. In both nations, there were citizens who made deliberately false statements, exaggerated real differences and predicted future catastrophes—all designed to mislead citizens and inflame latent passions. (There are still a few demagogues in the United States who are continuing these same practices.)

Despite formidable political difficulties, we forged a strong bipartisan coalition to combat these negative forces. The specific challenge was to convince at least two-thirds of the U.S. Senators to approve the negotiated treaties (one for this century and the other for the future). I had full support from key Republicans, including Presidents Nixon and Ford, Minority Leader Howard Baker, former Secretary of State Henry Kissinger, David Rockefeller and, perhaps most important of all, John Wayne!

After extremely heated debates, the final result was that 84 percent of Democrats and 42 percent of Republicans voted to ratify the treaties. Some of them paid a terrible political price for this courageous action. For instance, of the 20 Senators who supported the treaties and faced re-election in 1978, only seven of them returned to serve another term.

I came to Panama to exchange the ratified treaty documents, and discussed with President Omar Torrijos some concerns about the future of his country. He promised that human rights would be honored, that those living in exile would be invited to return (including Arnulfo Arias), to insure freedom of the press, and to permit the establishment of political parties and a process of democratic elections. My judgment is that he did his best to fulfill these commitments.

Under the terms of the treaties, the Zone was erased in 1979, and Panama was no longer a geographically divided nation. Since then, there has been a harmonious step-by-step transfer to Panama of the operation and control of the canal. Today there is mutual respect between our two nations, a canal that is secure and superbly managed by an independent authority, real and firmly established democracy in Panama, and principles of competition and free enterprise now prevailing in the management of adjacent facilities in the former Canal Zone.

We have made good plans for the future. At the beginning of the new year, the second treaty gives the United States the right and duty to defend the canal against external threats and for our ships to go to the head of the line in a state of emergency. We expect this to be done in close cooperation with the government of Panama.

It is crucial that the United States continue to provide cooperation and support as Panama faces the challenges that are now being inherited. There is always some threat to the operation of an exposed facility like the canal. Serious problems of drug trafficking will continue within this area of our world. We will have to protect from further environmental damage the watershed that provides 52 million gallons of fresh water for each passing ship. With increasing global commerce, there will be a need for constant modernization and expansion of these crucial facilities. There is still unexploded ordnance, even exposed on the surface, in the former firing range. I understand that President Clinton has promised President Moscoso to address this unresolved issue during the coming year.

Having just exchanged documents to transfer control of the canal to Panama, we must now pledge ourselves to continue the present state of cooperation and mutual respect during the next millennium. I am confident of a bright future for this vital waterway, and for the people of our two nations.

CARTOONIST CHARLES M. SCHULZ ON HIS RETIREMENT
December 14, 1999

Good Grief! That was response of millions of fans when they heard that cartoonist Charles M. Schulz was retiring and ending his daily comic strip, "Peanuts." Arguably the world's most popular cartoon, "Peanuts" had run for almost fifty years. Schulz, seventy-seven, who was recuperating from surgery for colon cancer, made his announcement December 14, 1999. "I feel very blessed to have been able to do what I love for almost 50 years," the cartoonist said in a statement, explaining that he had decided he needed to "focus on my health and my family without the worry of a daily deadline."

(Schulz died in his sleep at his home in Santa Rosa, California, on February 13, 2000, the day the last original Sunday "Peanuts" strip ran. The cause of death was the colon cancer, a spokesman said. In the strip Schulz had signed a farewell: "Charlie Brown, Snoopy, Linus, Lucy . . . how can I ever forget them. . . ." His friend, cartoonist Lynn Johnston, told the Associated Press that Schulz's death was "as if he had written it that way.")

When Schulz announced his retirement, his strip ran in 2,600 papers, in seventy-five countries, and in twenty-one languages, reaching an estimated 355 million readers daily. Together with books, television specials, and licensing the use of the familiar cartoon characters for thousands of consumer products, Schulz earned an estimated $30 million to $40 million a year. Schulz seemed unfazed by his success, insisting on drawing every frame of every strip. "Peanuts" began October 2, 1950, and continued with only one interruption—a five-week hiatus when he turned seventy-five—until his retirement. The last daily strip ran January 3, 2000. United Features Syndicate planned to fill the void with old strips, starting with those that appeared in 1974 and continuing indefinitely.

Schulz was renowned in the cartoon business for drawing all his own strips without assistance from other artists or humorists. "It was always his effort to do the best he could possibly do, no matter what," said Johnston, the creator of "For Better or for Worse." "There are very few people who could sustain the work that [Schulz has] done, alone, for fifty years."

The World's Longest Running Story

From the outset, the characters in "Peanuts" embodied the doubts, anxieties, and longings of childhood, along with perseverance and the hope that somehow things would improve. They rarely did. Charlie Brown, the round-headed kid with the zigzag on his shirt, always had the football pulled away from his kick at the last second, lost innumerable kites in the trees, and managed a baseball team that in fifty years never won a single game. (Charlie hit one home run, on March 30, 1993.) Snoopy, Charlie Brown's dog, never spoke nor strayed far from the roof of his doghouse but lived a rich and varied fantasy life, revealed in thought balloons. Two of his best-loved persona were the World War I Flying Ace, always caught in an dogfight with the cursed Red Baron, and the novelist, whose master work began: "It was a dark and stormy night." Lucy, the bossy fussbudget, who was called "crab grass on the lawn of life" by her little brother Linus, dispensed psychiatric counseling from a curbside stand for five cents a visit. "Happiness is a warm puppy," she told Snoopy on April 25, 1960. When Lucy wasn't giving advice, she was pulling the football away from Charlie Brown, dropping the umpteenth fly ball in the outfield, or mooning after Schroeder, who played Beethoven on a toy piano with the black keys painted on.

Other characters included Linus, his security blanket (a term Schulz coined) clutched in his hand, who waited many an autumn night for the Great Pumpkin to appear; Peppermint Patty, the tomboy who often slept through class and got D-minuses for her efforts; Marcie, who called Peppermint Patty "sir" and shared test answers with her; and Franklin, an African American boy who played on the softball team and had no anxieties or obsessions. Adults were never seen in the cartoon. Nor was the Little Red-Haired Girl, who was the love of Charlie Brown's life. She was modeled after Schulz's real-life love when he was a young man in St. Paul. Schulz said "she chose someone else as I was about to propose to her and that broke my heart." One commentator said the strip was "arguably the longest story ever told by one human being."

Loss was a major theme in the strip. As Schulz put it, "All the loves are unrequited; all the baseball games are lost; all the test scores are D-minuses, and the football is always pulled away." When asked once why he did not have any happy endings, Schulz replied that there was "nothing funny about the person who gets to kick the football." Schulz's second wife, Jeannie, once commented, perhaps not surprisingly, that all the characters in "Peanuts" reflected facets of Schulz's personality. "He's crabby like Lucy, diffident like Charlie Brown. There's a lot of Linus—he's philosophical and wondering about life."

The Building of an Empire

Schulz was born November 26, 1922, in Minneapolis. Although his full name was Charles Monroe, he quickly acquired the nickname "Sparky," after the horse in the comic strip "Barney Google." Schulz wanted to be a cartoonist from childhood and practiced by drawing pictures of "Popeye." In high school he sold a drawing to "Ripley's Believe It or Not!" but the cartoons he submitted for his school yearbook were rejected. After high school Schulz took a correspondence course from Art Instruction, Inc., but was soon drafted into the army, serving in France and Germany from 1943 to 1945. After the war, Schulz went back to cartooning, lettering the comics at a Catholic magazine, drawing a weekly cartoon called "Li'l Folks" for the St. Paul Pioneer Press, *and occasionally selling a cartoon to the* Saturday Evening Post. *In 1949 he submitted some of his "Li'l Folks" strips to United Features Syndicate, which liked the strip but insisted on changing the name to "Peanuts" because "Li'l Folks" was too similar to the name of another strip. Schulz later said he never liked the new name.*

Schulz's first strip appeared October 2, 1950. It showed two children sitting on a curb watching Charlie Brown approach. "Well! Here comes ol' Charlie Brown! Good ol' Charlie Brown. . . . Yes, Sir! Good ol' Charlie Brown!" they say as Charlie walks past them. "How I hate him!" But the public loved him. By 1953 the strip was a proven success, and Schulz was earning $30,000 a year. In 1952 he also began to turn out "Peanuts" books, and in 1958 he began to license use of the "Peanuts" characters on merchandise. Eventually they appearing on thousands of products from greeting cards, to clothing, to dolls and toys, to school lunch boxes. Schulz reviewed all applications for use of his images and rejected a few, including ashtrays and sugar-laden breakfast cereals.

The first animated cartoon, "A Charlie Brown Christmas," was aired in 1965. It had run for thirty-four consecutive years as of the 1999 holiday season and was still garnering top ratings. Other television specials and feature films followed, as well as commercials for Metropolitan Life Insurance Company. The characters found themselves memorialized in a rock song ("Snoopy and the Red Baron" by the Royal Guardsmen), an off-Broadway play ("You're a Good Man, Charlie Brown"), and a concerto by Ellen Taaffe Zwilich, which premiered at Carnegie Hall. Snoopy was the official mascot of the National Aeronautics and Space Administration, and in the first moon landing in 1969 the lunar module was named Snoopy and the command module was called Charlie Brown.

Despite his great success, Schulz maintained a quiet routine, going from his home to his office each work day, where he used a yellow legal pad to sketch out ideas for his strip. By all accounts, he was a melancholy man, afflicted with many of the anxieties and doubts that his characters expressed so well. Schulz said that he once woke up in the night, thinking, "Good grief, who are all these little people? Must I live with them for the rest of my life?" Millions of devoted fans were delighted that the answer was yes.

Following are a statement released December 14, 1999, by the cartoonist Charles M. Schulz, announcing that he was retiring and ending his comic strip, "Peanuts"; and a comment by President Bill Clinton December 15 on Schulz's retirement:

SCHULZ'S ANNOUNCEMENT

Dear Readers, Colleagues, Fellow Cartoonists and Friends near and far:

I have always wanted to be a cartoonist, and I feel very blessed to have been able to do what I love for almost 50 years. That all of you have embraced Snoopy, Charlie Brown, Lucy and Linus and all the other PEANUTS characters has been a constant motivation for me.

It is important for me to tell you personally that I have decided to retire from drawing the PEANUTS comic strip, effective with the daily release of Tuesday, January 4th, 2000 (and Sunday release of February 13th), in order to concentrate on my treatment for and recuperation from colon cancer. Although I feel better following my recent surgery, I want to focus on my health and my family without the worry of a daily deadline.

Thank you for your kindness and support over the years and for the outpouring of good wishes since my surgery.

Sincerely,
Charles M. Schulz

STATEMENT BY BILL CLINTON

Like all readers of "Peanuts," I was saddened by the news that Charles M. Schulz will retire his beloved comic strip on January 4. But every one of his fans understands that this difficult decision is the right one for Mr. Schulz's health and for his family.

The characters Charles Schulz created are more than enduring icons. Charlie Brown, Linus, Snoopy, Pig Pen, and Lucy taught us all a little more about what makes us human. Virtually every day for a half-century, Charles Schulz has shown us that a comic strip can transcend its small space on the page. It can uplift, it can challenge, it can educate its readers even as it entertains us. "Peanuts" has done all of these things. I wish Charles Schulz a speedy recovery and a fulfilling retirement.

UNITED NATIONS REPORT ON THE 1994 GENOCIDE IN RWANDA
December 16, 1999

Faster and more decisive action by the United Nations might have prevented or at least reduced the scale of the 1994 genocide in Rwanda that killed an estimated 800,000 people, an independent study commissioned by the UN reported December 16, 1999. UN member states—most importantly the United States—lacked the "political will" to act in Rwanda, the study said, leaving an ill-equipped UN peacekeeping force there able to do little more than watch in horror as Hutu extremists slaughtered thousands of members of a rival ethnic group, the Tutsi.

Coupled with a November 5 report acknowledging the UN's failure to prevent the massacre of several thousand Bosnian Muslim men and boys in the town of Srebrenica in July 1995, the report provided evidence for those who argued that the world body had hidden behind its neutrality when confronted with enormous problems. "There can be no neutrality in the face of genocide, no impartiality in the face of a campaign to exterminate part of a population," the Rwanda inquiry panel said. (Bosnia report, p. 735)

UN Secretary General Kofi Annan, who wrote the report on Bosnia and was himself criticized for failures during the Rwanda genocide, apologized to the people of Rwanda for the UN's failures. "All of us must bitterly regret that we did not do more to prevent" the genocide in Rwanda, Annan said in a statement. "On behalf of the United Nations I acknowledge this failure and express my deep remorse." Reflecting on such tragedies, Annan had told the UN General Assembly in September that "massive, systematic violations of human rights—wherever they might take place—should not be allowed to stand."

During a trip to Africa in March 1998, President Bill Clinton apologized for U.S. inaction during the genocide. "We in the United States and the world community did not do as much as we could have and should have done to try to limit what occurred in Rwanda in 1994," Clinton told a group of massacre survivors. U.S. officials had said that the administration's reaction to the crisis in Rwanda was colored by fear of repeating a

1993 experience in Somalia, where eighteen U.S. Army Rangers were killed while participating in a failed mission to restore order. (Clinton apology, Historic Documents of 1998, p. 160)

Conducting the Study

Annan commissioned the study in March 1999. It was conducted by a three-member panel that was chaired by former Swedish prime minister Ingvar Carlsson and included former South Korean foreign minister Han Sung-Joo and retired lieutenant general Rufus M. Kupolati of Nigeria. In its report, the panel echoed many of the conclusions presented in a highly critical report, "Leave None to Tell the Story: Genocide in Rwanda," issued in March 1999 by Human Rights Watch.

Carlsson faulted the U.S. government for failing to cooperate with the inquiry, saying the Clinton administration had refused to make available vital documents or senior officials who were in office at the time. Secretary of State Madeleine K. Albright, who was the U.S. ambassador to the UN at the time of the massacres, declined to meet with the panel. The State Department rejected Carlsson's assertion, saying two senior officials familiar with U.S. documents from the period had met with panel and answered questions.

In a briefing for reporters, Carlsson recalled finding a pair of shoes still lying in a Rwandan churchyard where civilians had gone, in vain, for protection. "It was a pair of small shoes from, evidently, a three-year-old girl, her crime being that she was a Tutsi or belonged to a moderate Hutu family," he said. "She probably didn't know about the world yet. I can assure you I will never forget those two shoes."

Background to the Genocide

Conflict between the Hutu and Tutsi broke out in October 1990, when a Tutsi-led rebel force attacked forces aligned with the Rwandan government headed by long-time president Juvenal Habyarimana, a Hutu. The government responded with an intense anti-Tutsi campaign, and the war raged inconclusively for nearly three years until a rebel advance in 1993 set the stage for a peace agreement negotiated by the Organization of African Unity, with help from the UN. Signed August 4, 1993, the agreement called for a power-sharing arrangement between Habyarimana's government and the rebels, with a cease-fire to be monitored by a UN peacekeeping force.

Just a week after the peace accord was signed, the UN Security Council received an assessment from a human rights monitor warning that attacks on Tutsis raised the question of whether genocide was being committed. That report recommended steps to prevent further human rights abuses. Carlsson's team said that report "seems to have been largely ignored by the key actors within the United Nations system."

In September 1993 a joint delegation of the Rwandan government and rebels appealed to then UN secretary general Boutros-Ghali to send a peacekeeping force to the country immediately, arguing that the cease-fire was in danger of collapse. The Rwandans asked for a force of 4,260 peacekeep-

861

ers. Boutros-Ghali told the delegation that the Security Council was unlikely to approve a force of that size, and that any deployment of peace-keepers would take at least two or three months.

Boutros-Ghali ultimately recommended a force of 2,548 with a broad mandate to monitor the cease-fire, including helping to disarm the combatants. The Security Council on October 5 approved a peacekeeping force but with a more limited mandate of investigating cease-fire violations, helping with the delivery of humanitarian supplies, and assisting in providing security for Kigali, the Rwandan capital. Called the United Nations Assistance Mission in Rwanda (UNAMIR), the force was not given a mandate to use military force or to confiscate weapons.

During the final two months of 1993—as the UN peacekeeping mission was gearing up—the security situation in Rwanda deteriorated, with an estimated sixty people killed in violent incidents. The inquiry said one of the most worrisome developments was the organizing of armed militia groups. At the end of 1993 the peacekeeping force reached a strength of 1,300 troops; it reached a maximum strength of 2,539 in late March 1994.

Warnings, Then the Killing Begins

On January 11, 1994 UNAMIR's commander, Canadian Brigadier General Romeo A. Dallaire, sent a cable to UN headquarters passing on warnings from a highly placed Rwandan government official of a plot by a powerful Hutu militia group, known as the Interahamwe, to provoke an attack on Belgian units of the peacekeeping force in hopes of forcing them to leave. Dallaire's cable said the informant also had said the militia was heavily armed and appeared to be planning to kill all Tutsis in Kigali, the capital.

Dallaire said he planned to take military action to thwart the attacks mentioned by his informant, including confiscating the weapons. In response, Annan—then undersecretary general in charge of peacekeeping— said Dallaire had no mandate to take direct action. Instead, Annan ordered Dallaire to take his information to Rwandan president Habyarimana and demand that the government stop any violence by the militias. Confronted with information about the plot, Habyarimana denied any knowledge and promised to look into the situation.

This was the first of several episodes during the early months of 1994 in which Dallaire and his political counterpart, UN Special Representative Jacques-Roger Booh Booh, sought permission to intervene to stop attacks on civilians, only to be told by UN headquarters that UNAMIR had no legal mandate to do so. Officials in New York said Dallaire could confiscate weapons held by militia groups, but only if he acted in conjunction with the Rwandan security forces. Dallaire's appeals were supported on a least two occasions by the foreign minister of Belgium, which had contributed the best-armed contingent of troops to the UN peacekeeping force.

The security situation in Rwanda deteriorated rapidly during the first three months of 1994 as the Interahamwe militia launched sporadic attacks on Tutsis and other government opponents. In late February the leaders of two opposition parties were assassinated; one of the parties was an extremist Hutu faction that believed the government was too lenient in its treatment of the Tutsi. In the meantime, the peace agreement between the government and the Tutsi rebels was falling apart; numerous attempts by UN officials and other international leaders to win agreement on a coalition government mandated by the peace accord failed.

The trigger for the genocide was the April 6, 1994, shooting down by unknown assailants of an airplane carrying President Habyarimana and President Cyprien Ntaryamira of Burundi. The two leaders, who were returning from a regional summit, were killed. Military officers immediately took control of the Rwandan government, and the next day Hutu extremists killed key officials, including the country's prime minister, who had taken refuge in a UN office. The military, acting with the Interahawame militia, took over the government and set in motion a violent campaign to eliminate moderate Hutu political leaders and as much of the Tutsi population as possible.

Operating from plans that clearly had been laid months earlier, the extremists at first targeted individual political opponents and then launched a campaign of indiscriminate slaughter of Tutsis and moderate Hutus, killing them by the thousands. Within weeks all levels of Rwandan Hutu society were participating in the killings: soldiers, policemen, farmers, businessmen, school teachers, even religious leaders were wielding guns and machetes against Tutsis and any Hutus who refused to cooperate with the killings. Because intermarriage among Hutu and Tutsi had been common, the killings split many families. The government and militia leaders offered rewards to many of those doing the killing. An estimated 200,000 people were killed in just two weeks.

Shortly after the killings began, the Tutsi guerrillas—with support from some neighboring countries—launched counterattacks and gradually began to overwhelm the Hutu forces. The guerrillas captured Kigali, the capital, on July 4, and ten days later drove the main remnants of the Hutu government from northern Rwanda. By that point, the UN inquiry said, some 800,000 people had been killed. In its report, Human Rights Watch estimated that the Tutsi forces killed 25,000 to 30,000 people, mostly Hutus, during the counterattack that brought them to power.

More than a million Hutus—including extremist Hutu leaders and thousands of armed members of the Interahamwe militia—fled the country, most into neighboring Zaire, where the UN and other agencies established refugee camps. Three years later thousands of those refugees were slaughtered by Tutsi guerrillas, backed by the new Tutsi-led Rwandan government, as they rampaged through eastern Zaire on a campaign that led to the ouster of Zaire's long-time dictator, Mobutu Sese Seko. (Mobutu overthrow, Historic Documents of 1997, p. 877)

The Failure to Respond

In its report, the inquiry panel detailed step-by-step how the United Nations at all levels—from peacekeepers on the scene to the member nations represented on the Security Council—failed to take steps that might have prevented or at least reduced the scale of the genocide in Rwanda. The fail-ure, the panel said, "was a failure by the United Nations system as a whole."

With an armed force of 2,500, UNAMIR should have been able to stop the killings at an early stage, the panel said. But UNAMIR was hampered by orders from New York that limited its ability to take credible action. The panel also cited several specific failings of UNAMIR, most of which resulted from the typical unwillingness of UN member nations to provide adequate resources for peacekeeping missions. UNAMIR, the panel said, was under-manned, ill-equipped, suffered from command-and-control problems, and lacked any useful intelligence-gathering capabilities.

During the early stage of the genocide UNAMIR was unable to save sev-eral political leaders who had asked for protection, as well as Rwandan civilians who worked for UNAMIR and other UN agencies. The report described a notorious incident in which an estimated 2,000 civilians, including government officials targeted by Hutu extremists, had fled to the grounds of a technical school near Kigali, hoping for UN protection from rampaging Hutu forces. Fearing for their own lives, Belgian peacekeepers on April 11 left the school even though, as the report said, "there could not have been any doubts as to the risk of massacre which awaited the civil-ians." The manner in which the peacekeepers left the civilians at the school, "including attempts to pretend to the refugees that they were not in fact leaving, was disgraceful," the report said.

Even so, other peacekeepers displayed "acts of courage" in protecting civilians, sometimes at the risk of their own lives, the panel said. Fourteen peacekeepers died during the genocide; among them were ten Belgian peace-keepers who were tortured and murdered on April 7, leading the Belgian government to withdraw the rest of its troops from UNAMIR a week later.

UN officials, including Boutros-Ghali and Annan, also came under seri-ous criticism in the report. In particular, the inquiry faulted senior UN staff for their planning of the peacekeeping mission, noting for example that it was based on overly optimistic assumptions and faulty intelligence about the political and security situation in Rwanda. One of the most egre-gious errors, the panel said, was the failure by UN officials to take into account warnings about the possibility of continued ethnic conflict in Rwanda; one such warning came in August 1993 from the UN's own human rights observer in Rwanda who specifically said a genocide was possible. In a similar vein, the panel said it was "incomprehensible" that UN headquarters did not act more decisively in response to Dallaire's cable indicating that the Hutu militia was planning to massacre Tutsis.

The Rwandan genocide vividly demonstrated numerous institutional weaknesses at the UN Security Council, the panel said. The council often took weeks to respond to even the most urgent crises, member nations failed to share information that might have improved decisionmaking, council representatives sometimes failed to question the information presented to them or even to examine documents placed at their disposal (such as Dal-

laire's cable), and council decisions usually reflected political concerns by member nations rather than the realities of the situation under discussion.

The Security Council failed to take decisive action throughout the most serious phases of the killing in Rwanda, the inquiry panel said. On April 21, as the genocide was reaching its height, the council voted to pare UNAMIR back to a token force of 270 troops, an action the inquiry panel said demonstrated the council's "lack of political will to do more to stop the killing." The council later reversed that decision, first voting to keep UNAMIR in place and then voting on May 17 to establish a much larger force (called UNAMIR II), which was unable to take the field for weeks because of the reluctance of member nations to provide troops. The Security Council also voted to impose an arms embargo against Rwanda—a step that came much too late to have any impact on the killing.

One little-noticed reason for the Security Council's failure in the Rwanda crisis was the fact that the Rwandan government was at the time a member of the council, the panel said. The presence of "a party to the conflict" severely hindered the council's ability to deal with the situation, the panel said.

The inquiry panel saved its most damning criticism for the member nations of the UN, including the United States, for the failure of "political will" that virtually paralyzed the world body. The panel offered numerous examples of how the major powers represented on the Security Council balked at measures that might have made a difference in Rwanda. At the outset of deliberations over sending peacekeepers to Rwanda, for example, the U.S. delegation argued for a "symbolic" presence of just 100 troops. The U.S. stance, as echoed in varying degrees by Britain, France, and other Security Council powers, continued to haunt UN deliberations throughout the crisis period.

Because the United States traditionally paid 30 percent of the UN peacekeeping budget, Washington's reluctance on the matter was a major factor in persuading Boutros-Ghali that the Security Council would not support the more substantial peacekeeping force in Rwanda that experts on the scene had recommended. The same concern prevented Boutros-Ghali and his aides from allowing UNAMIR to take a more active stance in trying to prevent the violence.

On May 3, less than a month after the Rwandan genocide began, President Clinton signed an executive order (Presidential Decision Directive 25) establishing strict limits on U.S. support for and participation in UN peacekeeping activities. Although the directive was a response to the failed UN mission in Somalia the year before and was not specifically related to the ongoing events in Rwanda, it had the effect of hardening U.S. resistance to any serious international response to the genocide.

Recommendations for the Future

The inquiry panel offered fourteen recommendations to improve the UN's capacity to manage future peacekeeping missions and to deal with conflicts such as the one in Rwanda. Several recommendations dealt with technical and institutional issues, such as the flow of information within the UN system and the development of an "early warning system" to improve the UN's ability to anticipate crises.

The inquiry panel also tackled the more difficult question of how the UN responds to cases of massive human rights violations. The world body could no longer afford to take a "neutral" position in the internal disputes of member nations, the panel said. "The United Nations—and in particular the Security Council and troop contributing countries—must be prepared to act to prevent acts of genocide or gross violations of human rights wherever they take place. The political will to act should not be subject to double standards."

Secretary General Annan said he accepted and agreed with the inquiry panel's report, noting that his earlier report on the Srebrenica massacre in Bosnia had reached many of the same conclusions. "Of all my aims as secretary general, there is none to which I feel more deeply committed than that of enabling the United Nations never again to fail in protecting a civilian population from genocide or mass slaughter."

Rwanda War Crimes Tribunal

The December 16 release of the UN report came in the midst of a serious crisis in a long-running effort by the UN's International War Crimes Tribunal to bring to justice those responsible for the 1994 genocide in Rwanda. The tribunal, based in Arusha, Tanzania, in 1998 convicted three former Rwandan officials on genocide charges; they were the first persons ever convicted under the Genocide Convention of 1948. (Convictions, Historic Documents of 1998, p. 614)

In November 1999 a UN appeals court at The Hague, Netherlands, ordered the war crimes tribunal to release Jean-Bosco Barayagwica, a former Rwandan official who had been held on genocide charges and was alleged to have established a radio station that incited Hutu attacks on the Tutsis in 1994. The appeals court said prosecutors in Arusha had violated Barayagwica's rights by holding him for more than a year before he was indicted, in October 1997. The case illustrated chronic problems the war crimes tribunal experienced in investigating the genocide and bringing to justice those deemed to have been most responsible for it.

The appellate court decision infuriated the Tutsi-led government of Rwanda, which immediately announced that it was suspending all cooperation with the war crimes tribunal. Tribunal officials said they were helpless to proceed unless they had active cooperation from Rwanda, which controlled access to witnesses and information necessary for trials on genocide charges. The standoff was unresolved at the end of 1999.

Deteriorating Situation in Burundi

As the year ended UN officials were struggling to deal with a renewed crisis of relations between the Hutu and the Tutsi in neighboring Burundi, where an estimated 200,000 people had died in ethnic clashes since 1993. In September 1999 the Tutsi-led government in Burundi forced an estimated 300,000 to 350,000 Hutus into fifty-four "regroupment" camps. The government said the forced removal of the Hutus was necessary to protect them from ongoing conflict between the government and Hutu guerrillas. But human rights groups, the U.S. State Department, and other observers denounced the action as a counterinsurgency tactic aimed at depriving the Hutu rebels of supporters. Observers said the camps were crowded and disease-ridden and that hundreds of people were dying in them each week.

Former South African president Nelson Mandela in December accepted appointment as an international mediator in the Burundi conflict, succeeding former Tanzanian president Julius Nyerere, who died in October. Mandela was considered one of the few world leaders with enough stature to have a chance of convincing the warring parties to end what had appeared to be an eternal conflict in the region.

Following are excerpts from the "Report of the Independent Inquiry into the Actions of the United Nations During the 1994 Genocide in Rwanda," released December 16, 1999:

I. Introduction

Approximately 800,000 people were killed during the 1994 genocide in Rwanda. The systematic slaughter of men, women and children which took place over the course of about 100 days between April and July of 1994 will forever be remembered as one of the most abhorrent events of the twentieth century. Rwandans killed Rwandans, brutally decimating the Tutsi population of the country, but also targetting moderate Hutus. Appalling atrocities were committed, by militia and the armed forces, but also by civilians against other civilians.

The international community did not prevent the genocide, nor did it stop the killing once the genocide had begun. This failure has left deep wounds within Rwandan society, and in the relationship between Rwanda and the international community, in particular the United Nations. These are wounds which need to be healed, for the sake of the people of Rwanda and for the sake of the United Nations. Establishing the truth is necessary for Rwanda, for the United Nations and also for all those, wherever they may live, who are at risk of becoming victims of genocide in the future.

In seeking to establish the truth about the role of the United Nations during the genocide, the Independent Inquiry hopes to contribute to building renewed trust between Rwanda and the United Nations, to help efforts of reconciliation among the people of Rwanda, and to contribute to preventing similar tragedies from occurring ever again. The Inquiry has analysed the role of the various actors and organs of the United Nations system. Each part of that system, in particular the Secretary-General, the Secretariat, the Security Council and the Member States of the organisation, must assume and acknowledge their respective parts of the responsibility for the failure of the international community in Rwanda. Acknowledgement of responsibility must also be accompanied by a will for change: a commitment to ensure that catastrophes such as the genocide in Rwanda never occur anywhere in the future.

The failure by the United Nations to prevent, and subsequently, to stop the genocide in Rwanda was a failure by the United Nations system as a whole. The fundamental failure was the lack of resources and political commitment devoted to developments in Rwanda and to the United Nations presence there. There was a persistent lack of political will by Member States to act, or to act with enough assertiveness. This lack of political will affected the response by the Secretariat and decision-making by the Security Council, but was also evident in the recurrent difficulties to get the necessary troops for the United Nations Assistance Mission for Rwanda (UNAMIR). Finally, although UNAMIR suffered from a chronic lack of resources and political priority, it must also be said that serious mistakes were made with those resources which were at the disposal of the United Nations. . . .

The 1948 Convention on the Prevention and Punishment of the Crime of Genocide lays down the criteria for what acts are to be considered a genocide, one of the most heinous crimes which can be committed against a human population. Essentially, the Convention requires both that certain acts have been committed, and that they be done with a particular intent: that of destroying, in whole or in part, a national, ethnic, racial or religious group, as such. The Security Council used the same criteria in outlining the mandate of the International Criminal Tribunal for Rwanda (ICTR), contained in resolution 955 . The ICTR has determined that the mass killings of Tutsi in Rwanda in 1994 constituted genocide. It was a genocide planned and incited by Hutu extremists against the Tutsi.

[Section II provides a detailed summary of the events leading up to the genocide in 1994, the acts of genocide, and the United Nation's response to those events].

III. Conclusions

The Independent Inquiry finds that the response of the United Nations before and during the 1994 genocide in Rwanda failed in a number of fundamental respects. The responsibility for the failings of the United Nations to prevent and stop the genocide in Rwanda lies with a number of different actors, in particular the Secretary-General, the Secretariat, the Security Council, UNAMIR and the broader membership of the United Nations. This international responsibility is one which warrants a clear apology by the Organization and by Member States concerned to the Rwandese people. As to the responsibility of those Rwandans who planned, incited and carried out the genocide against their countrymen, continued efforts must be made to bring them to justice—at the International Criminal Tribunal for Rwanda and nationally in Rwanda.

In the following chapter, the Inquiry wishes firstly to identify the overriding failure in the response of the United Nations: the lack of capacity of the United Nations peacekeeping mission in place to deal with the realities of the challenge it was faced with. Subsequently, the Inquiry will point to a number of other mistakes and failings in the response of the United Nations during the period under review.

1. The overriding failure

The overriding failure in the response of the United Nations before and during the genocide in Rwanda can be summarized as a lack of resources and a lack of will to take on the commitment which would have been necessary to prevent or to stop the genocide. UNAMIR, the main component of the United Nations presence in Rwanda, was not planned, dimensioned, deployed or instructed in a way which provided for a proactive and assertive role in dealing with a peace process in serious trouble. The mission was smaller than the original recommendations from the field suggested. It was slow in being set up, and was beset by debilitating administrative difficulties. It lacked well-trained troops and functioning materiel. The mission's mandate was based on an analysis of the peace process which proved erroneous, and which was never corrected despite the significant warning signs that the original mandate had become inadequate. By the time the genocide started, the mission was not functioning as a cohesive whole: in the real hours and days of deepest crisis, consistent testimony points to a lack of political leadership, lack of military capacity, severe problems of command and control and lack of coordination and discipline.

A force numbering 2,500 should have been able to stop or at least limit massacres of the kind which began in Rwanda after the plane crash which killed the Presidents of Rwanda and Burundi. However, the Inquiry has found that the fundamental capacity problems of UNAMIR led to the terrible and humiliating situation of a UN peacekeeping force almost paralysed in the face of a wave of some of the worst brutality humankind has seen in this century.

Despite the failures of UNAMIR, it should be said that United Nations personnel within UNAMIR and in the programmes and agencies also performed acts of courage in the face of the chaos that developed in Rwanda, and did save the lives of many civilians, political leaders and United Nations staff, sometimes at the risk of their own lives. In particular the peacekeepers who remained throughout the genocide, including the Force Commander and the contingents of Ghana and Tunisia, deserve recognition for their efforts to counteract some of the worst brutality humanity has seen under extremely difficult circumstances. The archives of the United Nations bear testimony to the multitude of requests, from within Rwanda, from Member States and from NGO's [nongovernmental organizations] asking for help to save persons at risk during the genocide. Statistics are difficult to find, but it may be worth quoting an internal list from UNAMIR's own archives which states that 3,904 displaced people had been moved by UNAMIR during the fighting in Kigali between 27 May and 20 June 1994.

2. The inadequacy of UNAMIR's mandate

The decisions taken with respect to the scope of the initial mandate of UNAMIR were an underlying factor in the failure of the mission to prevent or stop the genocide in Rwanda. The planning process failed to take into account remaining serious tensions which had not been solved in the agreements between the parties. The United Nations mission was predicated on the success of the peace process. There was no fall-back, no contingency planning for the eventuality that the peace process did not succeed.

The overriding failure to create a force with the capacity, resources and mandate to deal with the growing violence and eventual genocide in Rwanda had roots in the early planning of the mission. The signing of the Arusha Accords in August 1993 was generally hailed with optimism and relief following the years of difficult negotiations between the Rwandan parties. Although tensions clearly persisted below the surface, not least within the Government delegation, the international community received the Accords as the starting point towards peace and power-sharing in Rwanda.

The over-optimistic assumption by the parties to the Arusha Agreement [the 1996 Rwandan peace accord] that an international force could be deployed in about a month meant that the United Nations was fighting the clock from the first days of preparing for UNAMIR. The initial planning process suffered from insufficient political analysis. [UNAMIR commander Brigadier General Romeo A.] Dallaire has acknowledged that the reconnaissance mission, which he headed, lacked the necessary political competence to make a correct in-depth analysis of the political situation and the underlying realities between the ex-belligerents of the Arusha Peace Agreement. The mission was apparently not even aware of the disturbing report published only a couple of weeks before by the Special Rapporteur of the Commission on Human Rights on Summary and Extrajudicial Executions about the situation in Rwanda. In the report, the Rapporteur supported the findings of a number of human rights NGOs earlier that year. He pointed to an extremely serious human rights situation, and discussed at some length the possibility that a genocide was being committed in Rwanda. That a report of this nature was not taken into account in the midst of planning a large United Nations peacekeeping presence in Rwanda shows a serious lack of coordination on the part of the United Nations organs concerned. Indeed, Dallaire informed the Inquiry that, had there been more depth in the political assessment and had he been aware of the report, he would have reconsidered the force level recommendations by the reconnaissance mission. *The responsibility for this oversight in the planning of UNAMIR lies with the parts of the UN Secretariat concerned, in particular the Center for Human Rights and DPKO* [the UN Department of Peacekeeping Operations].

The reconnaissance mission had estimated that a force of 4,500 troops was required to fulfil the mandate in Rwanda. However, the Secretariat believed that it would not be possible to get Council support for that number of troops. This picture of the political commitment at the time was probably correct: the United States delegation had suggested to the United Nations that a symbolic presence of 100 be sent to Rwanda. Even France, which had been pushing for a United Nations presence in Rwanda, felt that 1,000 would suffice. Dallaire's figures were pared down even before they were presented to the Council. On 24 September, by then two weeks after the end of the original transitional period, the Secretary-General recommended a peacekeeping force numbering 2,548 military personnel.

If the mandate which the Security Council gave UNAMIR in its resolution 872 (1993) was more limited than the Secretary-General's proposal to the Council, then it was even more distant from the original broad concept agreed on by the parties in the Arusha Accords. The difference was not without importance. The interpretation of the real scope of the mandate given by the Council became a debated issue months before the genocide broke out, as will be shown below. The limitation of the mandate . . . was an early and public sign of the limits to the engagements which the Security Council was prepared to assume in Rwanda. The United States presented a number of amendments to the draft resolution which weakened the mandate, including in relation to the disarmament of civilians. . . .

The responsibility for the limitations of the original mandate given to UNAMIR lies firstly with the United Nations Secretariat, the Secretary-General and responsible officials within the DPKO for the mistaken analysis which underpinned the recommendations to the Council, and for recommending that the mission be composed of fewer troops than the field mission had considered necessary. The Member States which exercised pressure upon the Secretariat to limit the proposed number of troops also bear part of the responsibility. Not least, the Security Council itself bears the responsibility for the hesitance to support new peacekeeping operations in the aftermath of Somalia, and specifically in this instance for having decided to limit the mandate of the mission in respect to the weapons secure area.

3. The implementation of the mandate

Further serious difficulties arose with respect to the implementation of UNAMIR's mandate. UNAMIR's mandate was cautious in its conception; it was to become equally so in its application on the ground. Headquarters consistently decided to apply the mandate in a manner which would preserve a neutral role of UNAMIR under a traditional peacekeeping mandate. This was the scope of action that was perceived to have support in the Security Council. Despite facing a deteriorating security situation which would have motivated a more assertive and preventive role for the United Nations, no steps were taken to adjust the mandate to the reality of the needs in Rwanda.

The cable sent by Dallaire . . . on 11 January regarding contacts with an informant brought into focus key aspects of how UNAMIR implemented its mandate. The Inquiry believes that serious mistakes were made in dealing with the cable.

Firstly, the information contained in the cable, and in particular the information indicating the existence of a plan to exterminate Tutsi, was so important that it should have been given the highest priority and attention and shared at the highest level. Mistakes were made both in UNAMIR and in the Secretariat in this regard. . . .

Secondly, it is incomprehensible to the Inquiry that not more was done to follow-up on the information provided by the informant. Having decided to share the information with President Habyarimana with the aim of getting him to act on it, constant pressure should have been put on the President to see to it that he took the action he had promised. . . .

Lastly, the *threat against the Belgian contingent [of UNAMIR] should have been followed up* more clearly, not only in relation to the security of that particular contingent, but equally as part of the strategic discussions within the Secretariat and with the Security Council on the role of UNAMIR in Rwanda. The United Nations knew that extremists on one side hoped to achieve the withdrawal of the mission. Therefore, the strategy of the United Nations to use the threat of withdrawing UNAMIR as leverage in relation to the President to achieve progress in the peace process could actually have been one which motivated extremist obstructions rather than prevented them.

Questions have been raised as to the wisdom of inviting Belgium, a former colonial power, to participate in UNAMIR. The threats against the Belgian contingent described in the Dallaire cable as well as on the radio and through other forms of propaganda, show the difficulties inherent in that participation. In the case of UNAMIR it must be said, however, that Belgium was providing well-equipped troops which were not being offered by others, and that both parties had accepted that they participate in the mission.

4. Confusion over the rules of engagement

[Section 4 details uncertainties among various officials, including the leaders of the peacekeeping force, about the "rules of engagement" that determined how they were to respond to violent situations]. . . .

5. Failure to respond to the genocide

a. After the Presidential plane [carrying Rwandan President Habyarimana] was shot down [on April 6, 1994], the situation in Kigali quickly descended into chaos. Roadblocks were set up, massacres of Tutsi and opposition and moderate politicians began. Soon, the RPF [the Tutsi-led rebel group] broke out of its complex, and were strengthened by forces from outside the capital. In addition to the killings of civilians, fighting broke out between the Presidential Guards and the RPF. UNAMIR was faced with hundreds of calls for help, from politicians, staff members and others. Thousands of people sought refuge at sites where UNAMIR was present, including about 5,000 people who had gathered at the field hospital already by 8 April.

When the genocide began, the weaknesses of UNAMIR's mandate became devastatingly clear. The natural question is why a force numbering 2,500 could not stop the actions of the militia and RGF soldiers who began setting up roadblocks and killing politicians and Tutsi in the early hours after the crash. Could UNAMIR not have deterred, by its presence and a show of determination, the terrible sequence of violence that followed?

The correspondence between UNAMIR and Headquarters during the hours and days after the plane crash shows a force in disarray, with little intelligence about the true nature of what is happening and what political and military forces are at play, with no clear direction and with problems even communicating among its own contingents. The mission was under rules of engagement not to use force except in self defence. It had taken upon itself to protect politicians, but then in certain cases did not do so in the face of threats by the militia. Civilians were drawn to UNAMIR posts but the mission proved incapable of sustaining protection of them. The Force Commander found quite early on that he did not have the practical command of all his troops: for all practical purposes the Belgian peacekeepers came under the command of their national evacuation troops, and within days, the Bangladeshi contingent was no longer responding to orders from UNAMIR Headquarters. In short, the correspondence between Kigali and Headquarters, and the information provided to the Security Council in the early days of the genocide, show an operation prevented from performing its political mandate related to the Arusha agreement, incapable of protecting the civilian population or civilian United Nations staff and at risk itself. Furthermore, UNAMIR was sidelined in relation to the national evacuation operations conducted by France, Belgium, the United States and Italy. The responsibility for this situation must be shared between the leadership of UNAMIR, the Secretariat and troop contributing countries.

United Nations archives show that the DPKO very quickly began to discuss the possibility of a withdrawal of UNAMIR as one option which might become necessary. . . . The instinctive reaction within the Secretariat seems to have been to question the feasibility of an effective United Nations response, rather than actively investigating the possibility of strengthening the operation to deal with the new challenges on the ground.

Soon, however, the unilateral decision by Belgium to withdraw its troops in the wake of the tragic killing of the ten Belgian peacekeepers brought the United Nations mission near the brink of disintegration. The decision by the Belgian Government to withdraw was followed by rapid indications from Bangladesh that it might do the same. In a letter to the President of the Security Council dated 21 April, the Bangladeshi Permanent Representative raised a number of security concerns for which United Nations guarantees were sought. There was therefore a significant risk that the peacekeeping force would disintegrate.

The problems UNAMIR was faced with regarding command and control in the early days of the genocide included the unauthorized evacuation by members of the civilian police component, which were under UNAMIR command, and the embarrassing instance where Bangladeshi peacekeeping troops refused to allow colleagues from the Belgian contingent inside the Amahoro stadium complex where they were seeking refuge.

The Inquiry believes that it is essential to preserve the unity of United Nations command and control, and that troop contributing countries, despite the domestic political pressures which may argue the reverse, should refrain from unilateral withdrawal to the detriment and even risk of ongoing peacekeeping operations

The loss of ten peacekeepers is a terrible blow to any troop contributing country. However, even if the Belgian Government felt that the brutal murder of its para-commandos and the anti-Belgian rhetoric in Rwanda at the time made a continued presence of its own contingent impossible, *the Inquiry finds the campaign to secure the complete withdrawal of UNAMIR difficult to understand.* The analysis of the situation in Rwanda, which was presented as an underlying argument for withdrawal, painted a picture of ongoing massacres, in addition to the fighting between the parties. However, the focus seems to have been solely on withdrawal rather than on the possibilities for the United Nations to act, with or without Belgium.

Discussions within the Security Council during these first weeks of the genocide show a body divided between those, such as the United States, who were sympathetic to the Belgian campaign to withdraw the mission, and others, with the NAM [nonaligned movement] Caucus in the forefront, advocating a strengthening of UNAMIR. In presenting his three options to the Security Council in a report dated 20 April, the Secretary-General did state that he did not favour the option of withdrawal. Although the Secretary-General has argued that he made his preference for strengthening UNAMIR clear through a statement by his spokesman to the press, *the Inquiry believes that the Secretary-General could have done more to argue the case for reinforcement in the Council.*

The decision by the Security Council on 21 April to reduce UNAMIR to a minimal force in the face of the killings which were by then known to all, rather than to make every effort to muster the political will to try and stop the killing has led to widespread bitterness in Rwanda. *It is a decision which the Inquiry finds difficult to justify. The Security Council bears a responsibility for its lack of political will to do more to stop the killing.*

The Secretary-General's letter of 29 April, asking the Security Council to reconsider its decision to reduce the mandate and strength of the mission, was a welcome shift in focus towards the need for the United Nations to act to stop the killing. The need to do so was no longer presented as subordinate to the two-party cease-fire negotiations. However, the response of the Security Council took weeks to agree on, a costly delay in the middle of the genocide. . . .

. . . The delay in decision-making by the Security Council was a distressing show of lack of unity in a situation where rapid action was necessary. Almost three weeks after the Secretary-General's letter, the Council finally authorized UNAMIR II [an expanded peacekeeping force] on 17 May.

b. The lack of will to act in response to the crisis in Rwanda becomes all the more deplorable in the light of the reluctance by key members of the International Community to acknowledge that the mass murder being pursued in front of global media was a genocide. The fact that what was occurring in Rwanda was a genocide brought with it a key international obligation to act in order to stop the killing. The parties to the 1948 Convention took upon themselves a responsibility to prevent and punish the crime of genocide. This is not a responsibility to be taken lightly. Although the main action required of the parties to the Convention is to enact national legislation to provide for jurisdiction against genocide, the Convention also explicitly opens the opportunity of bringing a situation to the Security Council. Arguably, in this context, the members of the Security Council have a particular responsibility, morally if not explicitly under the Convention, to react against a situation of genocide.

However, as the mass killings were being conducted in Rwanda in April and May 1994, and although television was broadcasting pictures of bloated corpses floating down the river from Rwanda, there was a reluctance among key States to use the term genocide to describe what was happening. The Secretary-General did so in an interview for US television on 4 May 1994, one of the earliest in the international community to do so. The Secretary-General's report to the Security Council . . . on 30 May 1994 formally included the word genocide. However, when certain members of the Council proposed that the resolution on UNAMIR II include such a determination, others refused.

The delay in identifying the events in Rwanda as a genocide was a failure by the Security Council. The reluctance by some States to use the term genocide was motivated by a lack of will to act, which is deplorable. If there is ever to be effective international action against genocide, States must be prepared to identify situations as such, and to assume the responsibility to act that accompanies that definition. The Inquiry hopes that the stronger recognition given today to the need to ensure human security and to guarantee the safety of individual human beings from human rights violations, will also mean that States will not shy away from identifying events as genocide, and responding to them with action.

It is important to add the following: the imperative for international action is not limited to cases of genocide. The United Nations and its member states must also be prepared to mobilise political will to act in the face of gross violations of human rights which have not reached the ultimate level of a genocide. Particular emphasis must be placed on the need for preventive action: the will to act needs to be mobilised before a situation escalates to a genocide. . . .

Members of the [Rwandan] Interim Government have since been indicted at the ICTR [International Criminal Tribunal for Rwanda] for their roles in the Rwandan genocide. One question that arises from the Inquiry's study of the archives of the UN is whether the accountability of these persons for the ongoing massacres was made sufficiently clear to them at the time. To an extent, this brings into focus a recurrent dilemma in crisis management: whether to negotiate with those in control irrespective of the acts they may have committed. *In the view of the Inquiry, the United Nations had an obligation to make absolutely clear to the members of the so-called Interim Government the individual responsibility which accompanies the commission of genocide and war crimes.*

6. Peacekeeping overburdened: inadequate resources and logistics

Rwanda was to prove a turning point in United Nations peacekeeping, and came to symbolize a lack of will to commit to peacekeeping, and above all, to take risks in the field. UNAMIR came about following a dramatic expansion of the number of peacekeeping troops in the field after the end of the Cold War. However, by the second half of 1993, the enthusiasm for United Nations peacekeeping of previous years was on the wane among key member states, the capacity of the Secretariat, in particular the DPKO, to administer the approximately 70,000 peacekeepers wearing blue berets was overstretched, and several existing operations were facing severe difficulties.

In a report to the Security Council dated 14 March 1994 entitled "Improving the capacity of the United Nations for peacekeeping", the Secretary-General outlined the unprecedented growth of United Nations peacekeeping during the preceding five years. At the same time, however, he also mentioned that international enthusiasm for peacekeeping was diminishing. He pointed out the difficult financial situation the United Nations was facing, with over $1 billion in outstanding assessments to peacekeeping operations.

UNAMIR's poor quality and lack of capacity had a key effect on the way the mission dealt with the unfolding crisis after 6 April. However, the lack of resources and logistics had been a serious problem for UNAMIR from its inception, and continued to be so during the mission's later stages. It is significant that even the resolution establishing UNAMIR already included an invitation to the Secretary-General to consider ways of reducing the total maximum strength of UNAMIR. The Secretary-General was asked to seek economies in planning and executing the phased deployment, and to report regularly on what had been achieved in this regard. Even the Belgian contingent, which was the strongest in UNAMIR, faced problems with recycled materiel and lack of arms. The Bangladeshi contingent arrived without even the most basic supplies. Troops lacked necessary training in a number of respects. . . .

The responsibility for the logistical problems faced by UNAMIR lies both with the Department of Peacekeeping Operations, in particular its Field Administration and Logistics Division (FALD), and with individual troop contributors. FALD should not have allowed UNAMIR to have the dire lack of resources described above. By April, six months after the establishment of the mission, these fundamental logistics problems should have been dealt with. However, the Inquiry also finds that troop contributors to UNAMIR did not provide their contingents with basic weaponry and other materiel for which they were responsible. The constant pressure by the Security Council on UNAMIR to save money and cut resources also created problems in a situation where the mission was too weak to start with.

7. The shadow of Somalia

It has often been said that UNAMIR was an operation which was created in the shadow of Somalia. In particular the deaths of the Pakistani and US peacekeepers in Somalia in 1993 had a deep effect on the attitude towards the conduct of peacekeeping operations. For instance, the UN commission of inquiry set up to study these tragic deaths in Somalia, whose report came out just as preparations were being made to strengthen UNAMIR in the wake of the genocide, concluded that "the UN should refrain from undertaking further peace enforcement actions within the internal conflicts of States"

For the Government of the United States the events in Mogadishu were a watershed in its policy towards UN peacekeeping. By May 1994, when the genocide in Rwanda began, President Clinton had enacted PDD25, a directive which placed strict conditions on US support for United Nations peacekeeping. The killings of the peacekeepers in Somalia also had a restrictive effect on the UN Secretariat, in particular with regard to the risks that could be assumed during peacekeeping operations and in respect to the interpretation of mandates. This legacy of Somalia was of particular importance to the conduct of UNAMIR.

8. Focus on achieving a cease-fire

[This section details the preoccupation by UN officials with preserving the August 1993 cease-fire between the Rwandan government and the Tutsi-led guerrilla group, the RPF].

... The Inquiry finds it disturbing that records of meetings between members of the Secretariat, including the Secretary-General, with officials of the so-called Interim Government show a continued emphasis on a cease-fire, more than the moral outrage against the massacres, which was growing in the international community.

The persistent attempts to view the situation in Kigali after the death of the President as one where the cease-fire had broken down and therefore needed to be restored through negotiations, rather than one of genocide in addition to the fighting between the RGF [the government's security forces] and RPF, was a costly error of judgment. *It was an error committed by the Secretariat, the leadership of UNAMIR and the Members of the Security Council. Several Council members have criticized the quality of the analysis provided to them by the Secretariat in this instance.* For a number of the non-permanent members at the time, a key to realizing the genocidal perspective to the killings in Rwanda was information provided to them by the NGO community.

9. Lack of analytical capacity

A problem in the United Nations response to the situation in Rwanda was the weaknesses apparent in the capacity for political analysis, in particular within UNAMIR, but also at Headquarters. With respect to UNAMIR, a key problem identified by the Force Commander in an interview with the Inquiry was the weak political representation in the reconnaissance mission to Rwanda in August 1993 and the lack of real understanding the team had about the underlying political realities of the Rwandan peace process. Once UNAMIR was set up, there was a lack of capacity for intelligence analysis. *At Headquarters there was not sufficient focus or institutional resources for early warning and risk analysis. Much could have been gained by a more active preventive policy aimed at identifying the risks for conflict or tension, including through an institutionalized cooperation with academics, NGOs and better coordination within different parts of the United Nations system dealing with Rwanda.*

A key issue in the analysis of the flow of information is whether it should have been possible to predict a genocide in Rwanda. The Inquiry has received very different replies to this question, both from Rwandese and international actors whom it interviewed. As indicated above, early indications of the risk of genocide were contained in NGO and United Nations human rights reports of 1993. The Inquiry is of the view that these reports were not sufficiently taken into account in the planning for UNAMIR. UNAMIR was viewed as a traditional peacekeeping operation under Chapter VI, established at the request of the parties to a two-sided conflict to assist them in the implementation of a peace agreement. Despite warning signs during the Arusha process, in particular related to the lack of commitment by extremists within the President's party to the peace process and to power-sharing, very little if anything seems to have been done in terms of contingency planning for the eventuality that the peace agreement was threatened or challenged. UNAMIR was established without a fall-back position or a worst-case scenario. There were warning signs of the possibility of a genocide in Rwanda, and furthermore clear indications that mass killings were being planned and could take place in Rwanda in early 1994. That failure to formulate a determined response to these warnings is due in part to the lack of correct analysis, both in UNAMIR and within the Secretariat, but also by key Member States.

One of the main tasks of UNAMIR was to monitor the observance of the Arusha Agreement. The delays in this process which were evident already during the first weeks of UNAMIR's presence in Rwanda took place against a backdrop of a steadily worsening security situation. Reports from the field did refer to the rising number of killings, serious ethnic tension, militia activities and the import and distribution of arms. Although the description of these threats in cables to Headquarters seemed at times divorced from the usually separate analysis of the difficulties incurred in the political process, these worrying factors were reported to Headquarters, in increasingly alarming tones. . . .

These [reports from the field and UN headquarters responses to them] are examples which, together with others cited in this report, such as the handling of the Dallaire cable, and the analysis of developments after the genocide began, show an institutional weakness in the analytical capacity of the United Nations. The responsibility for this lack of analytical capacity falls primarily on the Secretariat under the leadership of the Secretary-General.

10. The lack of political will of Member States

Another reason for the main failure of the international community in Rwanda was the lack of political will to give UNAMIR the personnel and materiel resources the mission needed. Even after the Security Council decided to act to try and stop the killing, and reversed its decision to reduce UNAMIR, the problems that the Secretariat had faced since UNAMIR's inception in getting contributions of troops from Member States persisted. . . . *In sum, while criticisms can be levelled at the mistakes and limitations of the capacity of UNAMIR's troops, one should not forget the responsibility of the great majority of United Nations Member States, which were not prepared to send any troops or materiel at all to Rwanda. . . .*

A general point about the need for political will is that such will must be mobilised equally in response to conflicts across the globe. *It has been stated repeatedly during the course of the interviews conducted by the Inquiry that the fact that Rwanda was not of strategic interest to third countries and that the international community exercised double standards when faced with the risk of a catastrophe there compared to action taken elsewhere.*

11. Failure to protect political leaders

UNAMIR was tasked with the protection of a number of politicians who were of key importance to the implementation of the Arusha Agreement. Moderate and opposition politicians quickly became targets as violence started after the crash of the Presidential plane. Some of them were saved, among them the Prime Minister Designate, Mr Twagiramungu. A number of others, however, were killed by members of the Presidential Guards and elements of the Rwandese army. . . .

[The following section provides details on the killings of numerous political leaders who had sought protection by UN forces].

There is a pattern to these events which shows a failure by UNAMIR troops to guarantee the protection to these political personalities that they had been assured and expected. It is regrettable that not more could be done to resist the attacks by the Presidential Guards and other extremist elements against these politicians. As mentioned above, the Rules of Engagement which governed the mission permitted the use of force in self-defence, as well as action to prevent crimes against humanity. On the other hand, it must be recognized that the extremist forces had had time to observe the strength of the UNAMIR guard posts and overwhelm them with larger force. . . .

The failure in these instances seems to be attributable in some instances to a lack of direction from UNAMIR Headquarters, but also to the peacekeepers themselves, who by not resisting the threat to the persons they were protecting in some of the cases outlined above, as would have been covered by their Rules of Engagement, showed a lack of resolve to fulfil their mission.

12. Failure to protect civilians

The role of UNAMIR in the protection of civilians during the genocide is one of the most debated and painful issues of this period. Considerable efforts were made by members of UNAMIR, sometimes at risk to themselves, to provide protection to civilians at risk during the massacres. However, there do not seem to have been conscious and consistent orders down the chain of command on this issue. During the early days of the genocide, thousands of civilians congregated in places where UN troops were stationed, i.a., the Amahoro Stadium and the Ecole Technique at Kicukiro. And when UNAMIR later came to withdraw from areas under its protection, civilians were placed at risk. Tragically, there is evidence that in certain instances, the trust placed in UNAMIR by civilians left them in a situation of greater risk when the UN troops withdrew than they would have been otherwise.

According to the Force Commander and the Deputy Force Commander, the order to evacuate was not given by UNAMIR Headquarters. The order would seem to have been taken by the Belgian command within UNAMIR. There is no doubt that the decision to evacuate the school, leaving thousands of refugees behind at the mercy of the waiting forces of the Interahamwe, is one which has caused enormous pain to the Rwandan people, in particular the survivors of the genocide. The perception that the UN knowingly abandoned a group of civilians has damaged trust in the United Nations severely.

When the UNAMIR contingent at ETO [the Ecole Technique mentioned above] left, there could not have been any doubt as to the risk of massacre which awaited the civilians who had taken refuge with them. Indeed, the Interahamwe and the RGF had for days been stationed outside the school. The manner in which the troops left, including attempts to pretend to the refugees that they were not in fact leaving, was disgraceful. *If such a momentous decision as that to evacuate the ETO school was taken without orders from the Force Commander, that shows grave problems of command and control within UNAMIR.*

The Inquiry notes that the International Criminal Tribunal for Rwanda recently convicted Mr Georges Rutaganda of genocide and sentenced him to life imprisonment, i.a. for his role in the assault on ETO.

13. Failure to protect national staff

It is a tragic aspect of modern conflict that United Nations and associated as well as other humanitarian personnel are increasingly the targets of violence during armed conflict. The genocide in Rwanda took its toll among the personnel of the United Nations: fourteen peacekeepers and a number of local civilian staff were brutally killed. The efforts to strengthen the protection of United Nations and associated personnel since 1994 have been most encouraging, but more could still be done, not least in order to broaden the scope of the protection afforded by the United Nations convention on this subject.

The Inquiry met with several persons who were members of the national staff of the United Nations in Rwanda at the time of the genocide. When the international civilian staff of the United Nations were evacuated, national staff were left behind. There is considerable bitterness among the national staff at what is perceived as a double standard within the United Nations as to the safety of different groups of staff members. It was even alleged that United Nations staff members may have been at greater risk than others as a result of their employment with the organisation. The United Nations regulations at the time precluded the evacuation of national staff. While the decisions taken at the time may have been in conformity with United Nations regulations, there can be no doubt of the damage caused by these rules to the trust between members of staff. The Inquiry feels that the subsequent change in staff regulations permitting the relocation within the country of national staff is a positive step, but also feels that it is necessary to look actively at the possibility of providing for evacuation in cases where relocation may be a less preferable option. It goes without saying that each staff member, international or national, must know precisely what protection can be expected in times of crisis. *The mistaken perception among national staff members in Rwanda that the United Nations would and could protect them shows that a serious failure on the part of those in charge of security—in particular the Special Representative and the designated security official—to provide correct information to staff members.*

14. Flow of information

[This section provides details on lapses in the flow of information among UN representatives in the field, officials at UN headquarters in New York, members of the Security Council, and member nations represented on the Security Council].

15. Organizational problems

Organizational problems existed both within UNAMIR and within Headquarters which affected the capacity of the United Nations to respond to the events in Rwanda. . . .

The relationship between the Secretary-General and the Security Council is a unique feature of the Charter of the United Nations. The Secretary-General has the opportunity, but also the responsibility, to bring to the attention of the Council issues which require action. The Secretary-General can have a decisive influence on decision-making in the Council, and has the capacity to mobilize political will among the membership on key issues on the agenda. Boutros-Ghali was absent from New York during much of the key period of the genocide. The Inquiry understands that Secretaries-General cannot be present at every meeting of the Security Council. The archives show almost daily cables informing the Secretary-General of the unfolding events in Kigali and Headquarters related to Rwanda, and sometimes replies to Headquarters with comments by the Secretary-General. The Inquiry concludes that the Secretary-General was kept informed of key developments in Rwanda. However, the role of the Secretary-General in relation to the Council in true crisis situations such as that of the Rwandan genocide, is one which can only to a limited extent be performed by proxy. *Without the opportunity of direct personal contacts between the Secretary-General and the Security Council as a whole, and with its members, the role of the Secretary-General in influencing Council decision-making cannot be as effective or powerful as if he were present.*

16. National evacuations: international troops in different roles

The rapid deployment of the national contingents to evacuate expatriates from Kigali saved lives among the expatriate community. Nonetheless, the lack of coordination on the ground with the United Nations before the operations is a matter of concern. The leadership of UNAMIR, or of the Secretariat, should have been better informed about the evacuations being planned.

The rapidity of the response, whereby the French operation was dispatched within hours of the shooting down of the aircraft, also shows a disconnect in the analysis of the situation between these key Member States of the United Nations and UNAMIR. Immediately upon receipt of the information about the crash, France, Belgium, US and Italy evidently believed the situation to be so volatile as to warrant immediate evacuation of their nationals. During these first hours after the crash, UNAMIR was still struggling to identify the nature of what had happened, and to establish basic communication among its own units.

One particular element of concern to the Inquiry is the different roles played by Belgian troops during these crucial hours. The Belgian contingent was still the best equipped and strongest of UNAMIR. The arrival of Belgian national troops blurred the perception of the Kibat contingent. Dallaire also stated to the Inquiry that the Belgian troops within UNAMIR also began taking orders from, and sharing materiel, with the evacuation force. This undermined the capacity of UNAMIR to act in the early days of the genocide.

17. Operation Turquoise

[This section discusses the role of a French-led force, Operation Turquoise, which was sent to Rwanda in late June, after most of the killing in the Rwandan genocide had taken place. The inquiry panel said it was "unfortunate" that the resources committed by France and the other countries involved in Operation Turquoise were not made available to the UN at an earlier date].

18. Rwanda as a member of the Security Council

The fact that Rwanda, represented by the Habyarimana government, was a member of the Security Council from January 1994 was a problem in the Security Council's handling of the Rwanda issue. In effect, one of the parties to the Arusha Peace Agreement had full access to the discussions of the Council and had the opportunity to try to influence decision-making in the Council on its own behalf. That a party to a conflict on the agenda of the Council, which was the host country of a peacekeeping operation, later subject to an arms embargo imposed by the body of which it was a member, shows the damaging effect of Rwanda's membership on the Council.

The damage was evident in the actions of the Rwandan representatives on the Security Council during this period. Both Secretariat officials and representatives of Members of the Council at the time have told the Inquiry that the Rwandan presence hampered the quality of the information that the Secretariat felt it possible to provide to the Council and the nature of the discussion in that body.

19. Final observations

On 15 November, 1999, a few weeks before the presentation of this report, the Secretary-General published a report on the fall of Srebrenica. Clearly, some of the criticisms directed at the actions of the United Nations in that report and the lessons learned drawn from them are also relevant to the present analysis of the role of the United Nations in Rwanda.

One such point is that "a deliberate and systematic attempt to terrorize, expel or murder an entire people must be met decisively with all necessary means, and with the political will to carry the policy through to its logical conclusion" (§502). Faced in Rwanda with the risk of genocide, and later the systematic implementation of a genocide, the United Nations had an obligation to act which transcended traditional principles of peacekeeping. In effect, there can be no neutrality in the face of genocide, no impartiality in the face of a campaign to exterminate part of a population. *While the presence of United Nations peacekeepers in Rwanda may have begun as a traditional peacekeeping operation to monitor the implementation of an existing peace agreement, the onslaught of the genocide should have led decision-makers in the United Nations—from the Secretary-General and the Security Council to Secretariat officials and the leadership of UNAMIR—to realize that the original mandate, and indeed the neutral mediating role of the United Nations, was no longer adequate and required a different, more assertive response, combined with the means necessary to take such action.*

The Inquiry agrees with the Secretary-General that "[W]hen the international community makes a solemn promise to safeguard and protect innocent civilians from massacre, then it must be willing to back its promise with the necessary means."

[Referring to paragraph 504 of the Srebrenica report] The experience of the Rwandan genocide makes it necessary to add that the United Nations must be aware that its presence in conflict areas also raises among those same civilians an expectation of protection which must be borne in mind when analysing the means necessary to conduct an operation. Whether or not an obligation to protect civilians is explicit in the mandate of a peacekeeping operation, the Rwandan genocide shows that the United Nations must be prepared to respond to the perception and the expectation of protection created by its very presence.

In his report, the Secretary-General encouraged Member States to engage in a process of reflection to clarify and to improve the capacity of the United Nations to respond to various forms of conflict. Among the issues highlighted, he mentioned the gulf between mandate and means and an institutional ideology of impartiality even when confronted with attempted genocide. As is clear from the above, both of those issues formed part of the key failings of the UN in Rwanda. The Inquiry believes that the process of analysis and discussion suggested in the Srebrenica report should be undertaken promptly in order to address the mistakes of peacekeeping at the end of this century and to meet the challenges of the next one. The Inquiry hopes that the present report will add impetus to such a process.

There are institutional lessons to be learned from the Rwandan crisis with regard to the capacity and willingness of the United Nations to conduct peacekeeping operations. However, there are also lessons which need to be learned which relate specifically to the relationship between the United Nations and Rwanda.

The United Nations failed the people of Rwanda during the genocide in 1994. It is a failure for which the United Nations as an organization, but also its Member States, should have apologized more clearly, more frankly, and much earlier. The present report seeks to identify the scope and reasons of that failure. Based on the conclusions drawn about the problems in the response by the United Nations, the Inquiry has also formulated recommendations for the future. In so doing, the Inquiry hopes to provide a basis on which to build a better relationship between the Government and people of Rwanda on the one hand, and the United Nations on the other. This will require a true will for healing on both sides. The meetings which the Inquiry has held with both Rwandese and United Nations officials during the course of its work have shown that this will exists.

A renewed partnership will be necessary to deal with the challenges ahead. The aftermath of the genocide is still a reality—in the pain of those who lost loved ones, in the efforts to build reconciliation between Rwandans, in the challenges of bringing those responsible to justice, and in the continued problems of displacement as well as in the efforts to find ways to balance the needs and interests of those who survived the genocide within Rwanda and those returning from lives as refugees abroad. It is also still a reality in the continued existence of the Interahamwe as an armed force in the Great Lakes region, and in the continued instability in that area. The challenges of the future are ones where the United Nations can help Rwanda to rebuild and reconcile.

IV. Recommendations

. . . The Inquiry is aware that a number of steps have been taken over the past few years to improve the capacity of the United Nations to respond to conflicts, and specifically to respond to some of the mistakes made in Rwanda. For instance, welcome changes have been made with regard to how the Secretariat briefs the Security Council. Internal structures have also been set up with the aim of improving the Secretariat's capacity for early warning and early action. However, there is still need for determined action if the United Nations is to be better prepared to prevent future catastrophes than it was to prevent and respond to the tragedy in Rwanda. The Inquiry makes the following recommendations for action.

1. An action plan to prevent genocide. The Inquiry recommends that the Secretary-General initiate a United Nations action plan to prevent genocide. More than five years after the genocide in Rwanda, the time has come to make the obligation under the Genocide Convention to "prevent and to punish" genocide a concrete reality in the daily work of the United Nations. The plan should aim to increase awareness and capacity system-wide to prevent and counteract genocide and other massive human rights violations, and should result in the implementation in practice of the lessons learned from the tragedies of Rwanda and the former Yugoslavia. Each part of the United Nations system, including Member States, should examine what active steps they should take to counteract such horrific crimes. The plan should include a follow-up mechanism to ensure that such steps are taken. An action plan to prevent genocide could provide concrete input to the World Conference Against Racism, Racial Discrimination, Xenophobia and Related Intolerance scheduled for the year 2001.

As part of the plan, efforts at improving early warning and preventive capacity should include the prevention of genocide as a particular component. Specific training should be given to staff both at Headquarters, in agencies and programmes, and not least, personnel in field missions, to identify warning signs, analyse them, and translate warnings into appropriate action. Use should be made of the competence developed over the past years within the International Tribunals for the former Yugoslavia and Rwanda. In the technical field, enhanced cooperation between Member States and the United Nations should aim to improve capacity to block hate media. The plan should establish networks of cooperation with humanitarian organisations, academic institutions and other non-governmental organisations with the aim of enhancing early warning and early response capacity. An intensified dialogue should be established between the Secretariat and the Security Council on the need for preventive action, and when necessary, on the need for enforcement measures to counteract genocide and other massive human rights violations in the future.

Planning for peacekeeping operations should whenever relevant include the prevention of genocide as a specific component. In situations where a peacekeeping operation might be confronted with the risk of massive killings or genocide it must be made clear in the mandate and Rules of Engagement of that operation that traditional neutrality cannot be applied in such situations, and the necessary resources be put at the disposal of the mission from the start.

Identify situations as genocide when warranted and assume the concomitant responsibility to act. States must be prepared to identify situations as genocide when the criteria for that crime are met, and to assume the responsibility to act that accompanies that definition. More attention needs to be given to preventing crises from escalating or erupting into genocide.

2. The Inquiry recommends that action be taken to improve the capacity of the United Nations to conduct peacekeeping operations, and in particular to ensure the sufficiently rapid deployment of missions into the field. The issue is not a new one, and similar recommendations have been made by other bodies, but while the need has been repeated many times, the problem remains. The United Nations remains the only organization which can bring global legitimacy to peacekeeping efforts. Important initiatives can be taken at the regional level, but the United Nations must be prepared and willing to exercise the responsibility for international peace and security enshrined in its Charter, no matter where the conflict. The Inquiry hopes that the Secretary-General and the Member States of the Organization will use the opportunity provided by the Millennium Summit and Assembly next year to mobilise the political will necessary to solve the current problems facing United Nations peacekeeping, to look clearly at the challenges ahead, at what needs to be learnt from past failures, including in Rwanda, and what can be done to meet the challenges of tomorrow. This entails in particular:

- **Ensuring the necessary resources for peacekeeping.** Member States must be prepared to provide the necessary troops at short notice to the United Nations. Participation in initiatives such as the United Nations standby-arrangements needs to be increased, but equally importantly, matched by the political will to allow those resources committed to be deployed in specific conflict situations.

  The credibility of United Nations peacekeeping depends on operations being given the resources necessary to fulfil their mandates.

  It also requires that troop contributors refrain from withdrawing unilaterally from a peacekeeping operation when that withdrawal may be expected to jeopardize or put in danger the operation in question. Close coordination is necessary with the Secretariat about any decision to withdraw or reduce a contingent.
- **Increasing preparedness to conduct contingency planning,** both for expected new peacekeeping operations and to meet possible needs to adjust mandates of existing operations.
- **Taking action to make logistical resources rapidly available** to contingents lacking in material, either by enhancing the use of the logistic base at Brindisi or by means of donor contributions. The Secretariat should be provided with the resources to enable it to function as a clearing-house for needs and available materiel and training resources. Concrete discussions should be held between the United Nations and relevant regional and subregional organisations on how to improve the availability of materiel for peacekeeping. The Inquiry urges that new momentum be given to solving the recurrent need for logistical support for troop contingents from developing countries.
- **Ensuring that mandates fully meet the needs on the ground.** The overriding concern in formulating mandates must be what presence is needed on the ground, not short-term financial constraints. The Security Council should be presented with proposals reflecting the real needs of a mission, not ones tailored to a previously perceived consensus. Mandates must be made robust enough already from the beginning of a mis-

sion. They should also be flexible enough to allow the Force Commander the lee-way to adapt to changing circumstances on the ground.

- **Ensuring that the leadership of an operation arrives in a well-planned manner.** The Special Representative of the Secretary-General should be appointed early, should preferrably have experience from peace negotiations which may have preceded a peacekeeping mission, and should be among the first to take up his post in the mission area. Good cooperation between the civilian and military leadership of a mission is essential.
- **Ensuring full coordination between the Secretariat and other affected agencies in the planning and deployment of peacekeeping operations.** It is also important to further improve coordination and cooperation between peacekeeping operations and NGOs active in the mission area.
- **Ensuring that Lessons Learned from previous missions are integrated into the planning of new peacekeeping operations.**
- **Improve cooperation between the United Nations on the one hand, and regional and subregional organizations on the other.** Existing contacts could be intensified, not least in order to enhance concrete cooperation with respect to peacekeeping activities. Regular and direct contacts between the Security Council and representatives of regional and subregional organizations active in the field of peace and security should be increased.
- **There should never be any doubt as to which Rules of Engagement apply during the conduct of a peacekeeping mission.** Rules of Engagement must be given formal approval by Headquarters.

3. **The United Nations—and in particular the Security Council and troop contributing countries—must be prepared to act to prevent acts of genocide or gross violations of human rights wherever they may take place. The political will to act should not be subject to double standards.**

4. **Improve the early warning capacity of the United Nations, in particular its capacity to analyse and react to information.** Steps have been taken to improve the awareness of the need for early warning and early action within different parts of the Secretariat. Nonetheless, the Inquiry feels it essential both to continue to improve the capacity of the organization to analyse and respond to information about possible conflicts, and its operational capability for preventive action. Further enhancement of the cooperation between different Secretariat departments, UNSECOORD, programmes and agencies and outside actors, including regional and subregional organizations, NGOs and the academic world, is essential. As outlined under paragraph 1 above, the Inquiry believes that the prevention of genocide merits particular attention within the scope of early warning activities.

5. **Improve efforts to protect civilians in conflict and potential conflict situations.** Specific provisions related to the protection of civilian pop-

ulations should be included in the mandates of peacekeeping operations wherever appropriate and ensure the necessary resources for such protection. In this context, the Inquiry supports intensified efforts by the Secretary-General and the Security Council to follow-up on the recommendations contained in the Secretary-General's recent report on the protection of civilians in armed conflict.

A strong and independent role for the Secretary-General is an essential component in efforts by the United Nations to prevent conflict. The Secretary-General deserves the constant support of the membership of the organization in his attempts to promote an early resolution to conflict.

6. Seek further improvements in the security of United Nations and associated personnel, including local staff. The Secretary-General should actively consider expanding the possibility of evacuation to national staff of the United Nations. Members of the national staff must be kept clearly informed of the rules which apply to them. There should be no scope for misunderstanding about their status in the event of an evacuation.

7. Ensure full cooperation between officials responsible for the security of different categories of UN personnel in the field. Ensure functioning means of communication between such officials.

8. Improve the flow of information within the United Nations system. The trend towards a more coordinated approach to the prevention and resolution of conflicts means that information must be shared with all parts of the United Nations system involved in such efforts. In particular, an effective flow of information must be ensured between the Executive Office of the Secretary-General and the substantive departments of the Secretariat as well as between Headquarters and the field.

9. Further improve the flow of information to the Security Council. When the Secretary-General does not personally brief the Security Council, that task should fall on the officer most qualified from the substantive point of view to do so, which is often the case today. The Inquiry supports the continuation of the practice of briefings by representatives of substantive departments, but also encourages direct participation in the consultations of the whole by the High Commissioners for Refugees and Human Rights, Special Representatives of the Secretary-General and when relevant, UN funds and programmes. The more direct the flow of information, the better.

10. Improve the flow of information on human rights issues. Information about human rights must be a natural part of the basis for decision-making on peacekeeping operations, within the Secretariat and by the Security Council. Reports by the Secretary-General to the Security Council should include an analysis of the human rights situation in the conflict concerned. Human rights information must be a brought to bear in the internal deliberations of the Secretariat on early warning, preventive action and peacekeeping. And increased efforts need to be made to ensure that the necessary human rights competence exists as part of the staff of UN missions in the field.

11. National evacuation operations must be coordinated with UN missions on the ground.

12. Membership of the Security Council. The fact that Rwanda was a member of the Security Council before and during the genocide was a problem. While recognizing the complexity of this issue, the Inquiry believes that consideration should be given in the course of ongoing discussions on the reform of the Council, to strengthening the possibility of other members of the Security Council or the General Assembly suspending the participation of a representative of a member state on the Council in exceptional circumstances such as that related to Rwanda. Article 27 (3) of the Charter of the United Nations, which provides that in decisions under Chapter VI, a party to a dispute shall abstain from voting in the Security Council, should be applied consistently. The difficulties inherent in the participation in Council action by the party to a conflict should also be borne in mind when electing new non-permanent members to the Council.

13. The international community should support efforts to rebuild Rwandan society after the genocide, paying particular attention to the need for reconstruction, reconciliation and respect for human rights. Donors should bear in mind the importance of balancing and meeting the needs of survivors, returning refugees and other groups affected by the genocide.

14. The United Nations should acknowledge its part of the responsibility for not having done more to prevent or stop the genocide in Rwanda. The Secretary-General should seek actively ways to launch a new beginning in the relationship between the United Nations and Rwanda, recognising the failures of the past but also establishing a commitment to cooperation in the future.

REMARKS AT PEACE TALKS BETWEEN ISRAEL AND SYRIA
December 15, 1999

The election of a new Israeli prime minister who was committed to reaching agreements with his Arab neighbors revitalized the Middle East peace process in 1999. Retired general Ehud Barak, elected in May 1999, lost no time in reaching out to former foes he had fought on the battlefield. By year's end, Barak was conducting simultaneous negotiations with both the Palestinians and Syria in hopes of reaching comprehensive peace accords during 2000.

Barak injected new energy and meaning into a peace process that had been stalled during much of the tenure of the man he handily defeated at the polls, Benjamin Netanyahu. A hard-line critic of peace negotiations, Netanyahu had made concessions at the bargaining table only under extreme pressure, usually from the United States. Barak made it clear that he, too, would be a tough negotiator, but one much more dedicated to putting Israel at peace with its neighbors. Barak said he would model his approach after his mentor, former Israeli prime minister Yitzhak Rabin, another former general who became convinced of the need to end the seemingly eternal warfare in the Middle East. Rabin was assassinated in 1995 after signing an important peace agreement with his long-time foe, Palestinian leader Yasir Arafat. (Rabin assassination, Historic Documents of 1995, p. 689; Barak election, p. 359)

The year also saw the death of the man who, perhaps more than any other individual, had come to symbolize the drive for peace in the Middle East: Jordan's King Hussein. The king, sixty-three, had suffered for several years from non-Hodgkins lymphoma, a form of cancer, and had undergone treatment at the Mayo Clinic in Minnesota. Near death, Hussein returned to Jordan on February 5, and the following day the government transferred his powers to his thirty-seven-year-old son, Crown Prince Abdullah. Hussein died February 7, leaving behind an unparalleled legacy for such a troubled region as the Middle East. He was the longest-serving ruler in the region, having taken over the throne of the Hashemite kingdom of Jordan at age sixteen in 1952, just a year after his grandfather, King Abdullah, was assassinated.

Hussein led his country into the disastrous war against Israel in 1967—losing control over the West Bank of the Jordan River. But in later years he turned to the peace table as the best way of settling differences and became the region's most consistent and persuasive advocate of conciliation. Hussein signed a formal peace treaty with Rabin in 1994, and in 1998 he intervened at a crucial moment to help salvage U.S.-sponsored peace talks between Israel and the Palestinians. Abdullah promised to continue his father's policies. (Jordan-Israel peace agreement, Historic Documents of 1994, p. 329)

Israel-Palestinian Talks

Peace talks between Israel and the Palestinians had been stalled since December 1998, when Netanyahu froze implementation of the Wye River peace agreement. That agreement, reached at a Maryland retreat as the result of insistent prodding by President Bill Clinton, called for Israel to turn over to the Palestinians 13 percent of the land it occupied on the West Bank in exchange for antiterrorism guarantees by the Palestinians. Since 1967 Israel had erected hundreds of Jewish settlements on the West Bank, in many cases crowding out Palestinians who had lived in the region for generations.

In the Wye agreement Arafat also promised that the Palestine Liberation Organization, which he headed, would revoke sections in its charter calling for the destruction of Israel. With Clinton in attendance, the Palestine National Council followed through on that promise on December 14, 1998. Israel also turned over about two hundred square miles of West Bank land to the Palestinians, but Netanyahu—under intense pressure from right-wing political factions in his government—refused late in 1998 to carry out further steps under the Wye accord. (Wye accord, Historic Documents of 1998, p. 742)

Immediately after taking office, Barak unnerved the Palestinians by saying he did not plan to make the next round of West Bank land transfers to the Palestinians that were required under the Wye River agreement. Instead, he said, the two sides should move immediately to broader "final status" negotiations covering all issues—including the most contentious one of all, the future of Jerusalem. Barak backed down from that position during his first meeting with Arafat, on July 11, just five days after taking office. Arafat reportedly demanded that Barak begin to fulfill Israel's responsibilities under the Wye accord, and Barak agreed.

Two months later, on September 4, Barak and Arafat met again at Sharm el Sheik, on the Red Sea in Egypt, and signed an agreement that reformulated the Wye River accord. Negotiated by the leaders in separate meetings with Secretary of State Madeleine K. Albright, the new agreement called for Israel to turn over additional West Bank land to the Palestinians in three stages, bringing the total portion of the West Bank under Palestin-

ian control to 40 percent. Barak also agreed to release 350 Palestinian pris-
oners held in Israeli jails, 200 of whom would be released immediately. In
return, Arafat agreed to turn over to Israel a list of all members of the
Palestinian security forces. The agreement also allowed Palestinians to
travel freely, for the first time, between the West Bank and the Gaza Strip
(the two areas where most Palestinians lived), and allowed the Palestini-
ans to build a seaport in Gaza—a project intended to help stimulate the
weak local economy.

More important, the accord established an ambitious schedule for fur-
ther talks toward a final settlement resolving the most difficult issues
between Israel and the Palestinians, including the status of Jerusalem, the
exact borders between Israel and the Palestinian territory, and the fate of
Jewish settlements in the occupied territories and of Palestinian refugees.
That schedule called for agreement by February 13, 2000, on a "framework"
for resolving those issues, and then for a final agreement on all of them by
September 2000.

In a speech at the signing ceremony, Albright noted that future negotia-
tions between the Israelis and Palestinians would be even more difficult
than those in the past. "The issues are tough, laden with emotion, and
deeply rooted in the region's troubled past," she said. "They involve life and
death issues for both sides."

The two sides moved quickly to carry out the first elements of the Sharm
el Sheik agreement. Israel released 199 prisoners on September 9 (one pris-
oner, who had been scheduled for release later in September declined an
early release), and turned over 7 percent of West Bank land (about 200
square miles) on September 10. The Palestinians also handed over the
promised list of security force members. Israel opened the promised "safe
passage" route between the West Bank and the Gaza Strip on October 25; its
main immediate effect was to allow thousands of unemployed Palestinians
from Gaza to seek work in the West Bank, where jobs were more plentiful.

President Clinton met with Barak and Arafat in Oslo, Norway, on
November 2 during a service honoring the memory of Rabin. Barak and
Arafat agreed in Oslo on the pace of talks leading toward the February
2000 deadline for a framework agreement and promised to avoid inflam-
matory statements that might undermine the negotiations. Talks between
senior Israeli and Palestinian negotiators on the framework got underway
November 9, with both sides acknowledging that meeting the deadline
would be difficult.

The next key step that Barak and Arafat had agreed on—the transfer of
an additional 5 percent of West Bank land to the Palestinians by November
15—was held up for weeks because of a dispute over territory to be
included. Israel insisted that it had the sole right to decide what land to
turn over, while the Palestinians said that was a shared responsibility.
After nearly five weeks of disagreement on the matter, Barak and Arafat
met December 21 in the West Bank town of Ramallah and reached agree-
ment on exactly what land was to be transferred. The actual transfer was

expected to take place early in 2000. The two sides also sparred early in December over Israel's continued construction of Jewish settlements on the West Bank. After Palestinian representatives walked out of negotiations, Barak pledged on December 7 to halt further construction, at least for the time being.

Israel-Syria Talks

Difficult as they might have been at most points, negotiations between Israel and the Palestinians had become fairly routine by the late 1990s. The same could not be said for links between Israel and its implacable enemy: Syria The two countries had conducted numerous negotiations over the years since the 1967 war, but the United States was almost always the intermediary. No Israeli prime minister had ever sat at the same nego-tiating table with Syrian president Hafez al Assad or even with one of Assad's senior aides. Former secretary of state Warren M. Christopher shuttled back and forth between Israel and Syria more than twenty times during the early years of the Clinton administration but failed to reach any firm agreements; those talks were halted in early 1996.

Seeking to take advantage of the new leadership in Israel, the Clinton administration during the summer put out feelers to Assad, attempting to judge his interest in reviving talks with Israel. During her Middle East trip that culminated in the Sharm el-Sheik Israel-Palestinian agreement, Albright met with Assad in Damascus on September 4, but failed to get his commitment on new talks. Over the next several weeks Clinton made nearly three dozen telephone calls to Barak and Assad, and Albright returned to the region and met again with Assad on December 7. U.S. offi-cials said the essence of their appeal was that Barak's election offered a unique opportunity for Israel and Syria to settle their differences. Clinton also asked Assad to think of his legacy; at age sixty-eight the Syrian leader was known to be in failing health.

The appeals by Clinton and Albright worked: on December 8 Clinton announced that Assad and Barak had agreed to resume negotiations between the two countries, with an initial round of meetings to take place in the United States. Barak would represent Israel, and Foreign Minister Farouk al-Shara would represent Syria. Clinton's national security advi-sor, Samuel R. Berger, said the all issues between Israel and Syria "will be on the table," including the most divisive issue: the future of the Golan Heights, a strategic piece of land that Israel had captured during the 1967 war.

Barak and Shara met at the White House a week later, on December 15, and in public statements said both countries were committed to finding points of agreement. Barak's statement was brief and to the point: "We came here to put behind us the horrors of war and to step toward peace," he said, adding that it would take "seriousness, determination, and devo-tion" to reach that goal. Shara—apparently with an eye toward the Arab audience listening to his words—took a less conciliatory approach, refus-

*ing to shake hands in public with Barak and even avoiding direct eye con-
tact with him. In his remarks he reviewed Syria's grievances with Israel,
complained about the international media's coverage of the 1967 war, and
insisted that there could be no peace agreement unless Israel gave Syria
back "all its occupied land."*

*Both sides said that phrase would be at the heart of the negotiations.
Syria demanded that Israel return all the Golan Heights, back to the borders in effect on June 4, 1967, before the outbreak of the Six Days War.
Rabin reportedly had agreed, before he was murdered, to return most of the
Golan Heights, but there were varying interpretations about how much of
a withdrawal he had proposed. At the heart of the matter was the question
of whether Israel meet Syria's demand for control over portions of the eastern shoreline of the Sea of Galilee.*

*After two days of meetings, mediated at times by Clinton and at times
by Albright, Barak and Shara agreed to begin formal negotiations on January 3, 2000, at a location near Washington. Announcing the talks, Clinton said "the journey will be tough," but he said the leaders had agreed that
"there should be no looking back, for the sake of our generation and generations yet to come."*

*Barak on December 13 won support from the Israeli parliament (the
Knesset) for his talks with Syria. Israel would have to pay "a heavy territorial price," he said, referring to the certainty that the Golan Heights
would be returned to Syria. But refusing to negotiate peace with Syria
"could cost us in blood" over the longer term, he said. Parliament's endorsement was made possible only because two dozen members abstained on the
issue, indicating that Barak likely would have difficulty winning approval
of any peace deal he negotiated.*

*Following are the complete remarks by President Bill Clinton,
Israeli prime minister Ehud Barak, and Syrian foreign minister Farouk al-Shara at a ceremony December15, 1999, at the
White House marking the first high-level peace negotiations
between Israel and Syria:*

President Bill Clinton: Good morning. It is an honor to welcome Prime
Minister [Ehud] Barak, Foreign Minister [Farouk] al-Shara, and the members
of the Israeli and Syrian delegations here to the White House.

When the history of this century is written, some of its most illustrious
chapters will be the stories of men and women who put old rivalries and conflicts behind them, and looked ahead to peace and reconciliation for their children. What we are witnessing today is not yet peace, and getting there will
require bold thinking and hard choices. But today is a big step along that path.

Prime Minister Barak and Foreign Minister al-Shara are about to begin
the highest-level meeting ever between their two countries. They are pre-

pared to get down to business. For the first time in history, there is a chance of a comprehensive peace between Israel and Syrian, and indeed, all its neighbors.

That Prime Minister Barak and Foreign Minister al-Shara chose to come here to Washington reminds us of one other fact, of course, which is the United States' own responsibility in this endeavor. Secretary Albright and I, and our entire team, will do everything we possibly can to help the parties succeed. For a comprehensive peace in the Middle East is vital not only to the region, it is also vital to the world, and to the security of the American people. For we have learned from experience that tensions in the region can escalate, and the escalations can lead into diplomatic, financial, and, ultimately, military involvement, far more costly than even the costliest peace.

We should be clear, of course, the success of the enterprise we embark upon today is not guaranteed. The road to peace is no easier, and in many ways it is harder than the road to war. There will be challenges along the way, but we have never had such an extraordinary opportunity to reach a comprehensive settlement.

Prime Minister Barak, an exceptional hero in war, is now a determined soldier for peace. He knows a negotiated peace, one that serves the interests of all sides, is the only way to bring genuine security to the people of Israel, to see that they are bound by a circle of peace.

President [Hafez al] Assad, too, has known the cost of war. From my discussion with him in recent months, I am convinced he knows what a true peace could do to lift the lives of his people and give them a better future. And Foreign Minister al-Shara is an able representative of the President and the people of Syria.

Let me also say a brief word about the continuing progress of the Palestinian track. Chairman Arafat also has embarked on a courageous quest for peace, and the Israelis and the Palestinians continue to work on that.

We see now leaders with an unquestioned determination to defend and advance the interest of their own people, but also determined to marshal the courage and creativity, the vision and resolve, to secure a bright future based on peace, rather than a dark future under the storm clouds of continuing, endless conflict.

At the close of this millennium, and in this season of religious celebration for Jews, for Muslims, for Christians, Israelis, Palestinians, Syrians, Lebanese, all have it within their power to end decades of bitter conflict. Together, they can choose to write a new chapter in the history of our time. Again, let me say that today's meeting is a big step in the right direction. And I am profoundly grateful for the leaders of both nations for being here.

We have just talked and agreed that it would be appropriate for each leader to say a few brief words on behalf of the delegation. We will take no questions, in keeping with our commitment to do serious business and not cause more problems than we can solve out here with you and all your helpful questions.

But I will begin with Prime Minister Barak.

Prime Minister Ehud Barak: We came here to put behind us the horrors of war and to step forward toward peace. We are fully aware of the opportunity, of the burden of responsibility, and of the seriousness, determination and devotion that will be needed in order to begin this march, together with our Syrian partners, to make a different Middle East where nations are living side by side in peaceful relationship and in mutual respect and good-neighborliness.

We are determined to do whatever we can to put an end and to bring about the dreams of children and mothers all around the region to see a better future of the Middle East at the entrance to the new millennium. Thank you very much.

Foreign Minister Farouk al-Shara: Although it's very cold, I prepared a statement, and I would like to thank, first of all, President Clinton for all the efforts that he exerted with his Secretary of State and the peace team here in Washington. And also, I what like to convey the best greetings and wishes from President Assad, and his high appreciation for the efforts which you and Secretary Albright have exerted for the resumption of the peace talks between Syria and Israel from the point at which they stopped in 1996.

Your announcement, Mr. President, was warmly welcomed, both in Syria and in the Arab world, and its positive echoes resonated in the world at large. That is because it promises, for the first time, the dawn of a real hope to achieve an honorable and just peace in the Middle East.

And as you have mentioned in your letter of October 12, 1999 to President Assad, the issues have crystallized and difficulties defined. That is why if these talks are to succeed as rapidly as we all desire, no one should ignore what has been achieved until now, or what still needs to be achieved.

It goes without saying that peace for Syria means the return of all its occupied land; why, for Israel, peace will mean the end of the psychological fear which the Israelis have been living in as a result of the existence of occupation, which is undoubtedly the source of all adversities and wars. Hence, ending occupation will be balanced for the first time by eliminating the barrier of fear and anxieties, and exchanging it with a true and mutual feeling of peace and security. Thus, the peace which the parties are going to reach will be established on justice and international legitimacy. And thus, peace will be the only triumphant, after 50 years of struggle.

Those who reject to return the occupied territories to their original owners in the framework of international legitimacy send a message to the Arabs that the conflict between Israel and Arabs is a conflict of existence in which bloodshed can never stop, and not a conflict about borders which can be ended as soon as parties get their rights, as President Assad has stressed at these meetings more than once before, and after Madrid peace conference.

We are approaching the moment of truth, as you have said, and there is no doubt that everyone realizes that a peace agreement between Syria and Israel, and between Lebanon and Israel, would indeed mean for our region the end of a history of wars and conflicts, and may well usher in a dialogue of civilization and an honorable competition in various domains—the political, cultural, scientific, and economic.

Peace will certainly pose new questions to all sides, especially for the Arab side, who will wonder after reviewing the past 50 years, whether the Arab-Israeli conflict was the one who solely defied the Arab unity, or the one which frustrated it.

During the last half-century, in particular, the vision of the Arabs and their sufferings were totally ignored, due to the lack of a media opportunity for them which conveys their points of view to international opinion. And the last example of this is what we have witnessing during the last four days of attempts to muster international sympathy with the few thousand of settlers in the Golan, ignoring totally more than half a million Syrian people who were uprooted from tens of villages on the Golan, where their forefathers lived for thousands of years and their villages were totally wiped out from existence.

The image formulated in the minds of Western people and which formulated in public opinion was that Syria was the aggressor, and Syria was the one who shelled settlements from the Golan prior to the 1967 war. These claims carry no grain of truth in them—as Moshe Dayan, himself, has explained in his memoirs, that it was the other side who insisted on provoking the Syrians until they clashed together and then claimed that the Syrians are the aggressors.

Mr. President, the peace talks between Israel and Syria have been ongoing for the last eight years, with off and on, of course. We hope that this is going to be the last resumption of negotiations which will be concluded with a peace agreement, a peace based on justice and comprehensivity; an honorable peace for both sides that preserves rights, dignity and sovereignty. Because only honorable and just peace will be embraced by future generations, and it is the only peace that shall open new horizons for totally new relations between peoples of the region.

President Assad has announced many years ago that peace is the strategic option of Syria. And we hope that peace has become the strategic option for others today, in order to have or to leave future generations a region that is not torn with wars, a region whose sky is not polluted by the smell of blood and destruction.

We all here agree that we are at a threshold of an historic opportunity, an opportunity for the Arabs and Israelis alike, and for the United States and the world at large. Therefore, we all have to be objective and show a high sense of responsibility in order to achieve a just and comprehensive peace, a peace that has been so long awaited by all the peoples of our region and the world at large.

Thank you, Mr. President.

President Clinton: Thank you very much, ladies and gentlemen. We're going to work.

VERMONT SUPREME COURT ON THE RIGHTS OF HOMOSEXUALS
December 20, 1999

Gay rights advocates won some major victories in 1999 in their push for equal treatment for homosexuals. The most significant breakthrough came in Vermont, where the state supreme court ruled December 20, 1999, that the state had to give homosexual couples all the same rights and protections that it extended to heterosexual couples. But efforts to strengthen the military's "don't ask, don't tell" policy fell short. In December, after a young army private was court-martialed and sentenced to life imprisonment for the brutal beating death of a gay soldier, President Bill Clinton said the policy was "out of whack" and that military leaders were not carrying it out as he had intended.

Equal Treatment for Same-Sex Couples

Throughout the 1990s the gay political community successfully sought equal treatment on several fronts for gay couples. Several state legislatures adopted legislation prohibiting discrimination against gays in jobs and other areas of daily life and giving them benefits traditionally enjoyed only by married couples, such as property rights and spousal rights regarding medical care. Several major private companies also agreed to extend health insurance coverage to the partners of their gay employees. But no state had yet sanctioned same-sex marriages, something that many in the gay community wanted, not only because a legally recognized marriage entailed a host of benefits and rights (as well as obligations), but also because many gay couples wanted their private commitments to each other publicly acknowledged. Conservatives as well as moderates and liberals who supported gays on other rights issues balked at governmental recognition of same-sex marriages.

Gay activists had thought their best opportunity for winning state approval of same-sex marriages was in Hawaii. In 1993 the state supreme court had ruled that Hawaii's failure to recognize such marriages was tantamount to gender discrimination; the court sent the case back to the lower courts for further consideration. In the ensuing uproar, Congress enacted legislation barring federal recognition of homosexual marriages and stipulating that states did not have to recognize the validity of gay marriages licensed in other states. At least thirty states passed legislation prohibiting same-sex marriages. One of these was Hawaii, where voters in 1998 approved a constitutional amendment barring gay marriages by a 2-to-1 margin. The gay community held out hope that the state supreme court might overturn that amendment when the original case returned to it, but on December 10 the high court ruled that the amendment had made the case moot. (Same-sex marriages, Historic Documents of 1996, p. 687)

With the legal battle in Hawaii concluded, the only state with a viable challenge was Vermont, where three homosexual couples had sued for the right to marry in 1997. Their challenge had been rejected by a Vermont superior court, and they appealed to the state supreme court. In its ruling on December 20 the supreme court sidestepped moral and religious arguments and based its decision on the equal protection portions of the state constitution. "The laudable governmental goal of promoting a commitment between married couples . . . provides no reasonable basis for denying the legal benefits and protections of marriage to same-sex couples, who are no differently situated with respect to this goal than their opposite-sex counterparts," the court wrote. To extend equal rights to gay couples "who seek nothing more, nor less, than legal protection and security for their avowed commitment to an intimate and lasting relationship is simply, when all is said and done, a recognition of our common humanity."

The court left it to the state legislature to decide whether the benefits would come through formal marriage or a legal system of domestic partnerships. Whatever the legislature chose, the court said, it "must conform with the constitutional imperative to afford all Vermonters the common benefit, protection, and security of the law." Because the ruling was based on Vermont law, rather than federal law, it could not be appealed to the U.S. Supreme Court.

Although many questions still remained as a result of the decision, the gay community was jubilant. "We've never gotten this kind of official recognition," said Bernatrice Dohrn, legal counsel for the Lambda Legal Defense Fund. "They're saying it's a social good that we be who we are, that we be in strong and loving families. It's so simple and yet it's never happened before. This is a huge thing for gay people." Many conservatives did not agree. Gary Bauer, the former president of the Family Research Council and a candidate for the Republican presidential nomination, said the decision was "deeply disturbing. . . . It begins in a fundamental way to redefine marriage as between a man and a woman, and once you abandon that, all things are possible."

Gays in the Military

The military's controversial "don't ask, don't tell" policy came under heavy attack in 1999 from gay activists and others who said that instead of diminishing prejudice against gays in the military, the policy was actually contributing to increased harassment. The policy was put into place in 1994, after political outrage forced Clinton to recant his 1992 campaign promise to allow openly gay men and women to join the armed forces. The policy allowed gays to serve in the military but barred them from declaring their homosexuality or engaging in homosexual acts. At the same time, the armed forces were ordered to stop actively searching for gays and investigate only when "credible information" surfaced about a person's sexual orientation. (Clinton plan to remove military homosexual ban, Historical Documents of 1993, p. 153)

The idea was that homosexuals who were willing to keep their sexual orientation private would be able to serve in the military without fear of being hunted out and discharged. But the number of gays and lesbians discharged from the services began to increase almost immediately. In 1998 more than 1,100 service members were discharged for being homosexual, nearly double the number in 1993, the year before the policy went into effect. The Pentagon said most of those discharged had volunteered the information that they were gay simply to get out of the military. Gay rights advocates argued that the policy itself had failed. Too often, they said, people were investigated because they were rumored or perceived to be gay or because they had reported harassment or threats that had triggered investigation of their conduct rather than of the alleged harassers.

In August the Pentagon sought to strengthen the policy by requiring mandatory training on antiharassment guidelines for all military personnel, including law enforcement personnel, commanders, and supervisors. "I've made it clear there is no room for harassment or threats in the military," Defense Secretary William Cohen said issuing the new guidelines. The guidelines were issued just weeks after Pfc. Barry L. Winchell, who was gay, was beaten to death with a baseball bat in his barracks at Fort Campbell, Ky. In December Pvt. Calvin Glover was court-martialed and sentenced to life in prison for the death. At Glover's trial it was revealed that for several months Winchell had been the butt of taunts and threats that had gone unreprimanded by superiors; one superior even joined in the harassment. Winchell finally fought back, knocking down Glover, who came back a day later and beat Winchell to death in his sleep. Following the trial Defense Secretary Cohen ordered spot checks of military bases around the country to determine what problems were preventing effective implementation of the don't ask, don't tell policy.

In his remarks December 11, President Clinton acknowledged that the policy had been a failure, but he stopped short of recommending that homosexuals be allowed to serve openly in the military, pointing out that he had already done that in 1993 and been frustrated in his efforts. Clinton's comments came after his wife, Hillary Rodham Clinton, called for an open policy on gays in the military during her campaign for a New York Senate seat. Vice President Al Gore, widely expected to be the Democratic presidential nominee in 2000, also called for an end to the policy. "Gays and les-

*bians should be allowed to serve their country without discrimination,"
Gore said on December 14.* (Clinton on gay rights, Historic Documents of
1997, p. 760)

Other Developments

*Several other major decisions affecting gay rights occurred in 1999,
many of them in Europe.*

*On August 4 the New Jersey supreme court ruled that the Boy Scouts was
not a private organization and that its expulsion of a gay Eagle Scout in
1990 was not protected by the First Amendment guarantee of the right of
free association. The court said the Boy Scouts was equivalent to a public
accommodation, like a restaurant or a school, because it was not selective
in its membership. Its decision to expel the scout was therefore a violation
of New Jersey's antidiscrimination laws. The court, which decided the case
unanimously, also rejected the Boy Scouts' claim that homosexuality was
immoral. The ruling was squarely at odds with a decision handed down by
the California supreme court in March 1998. There the court held that Boy
Scouts was a private organization not covered by the state's civil rights
laws and therefore had the right under the constitutional protections of
freedom of association and freedom of expression to expel homosexuals,
agnostics, and atheists.*

*The European Court of Human Rights unanimously ruled September 27
that Britain's ban on homosexuals in the military was a violation of the
basic human right to privacy. The Court served as the court of last resort
for members of the European Union. The British government announced in
December that it would lift the ban.*

*The French Parliament on October 13 voted to give legal status to unmar-
ried couples, including same-sex couples. Virtually any two people, no matter what their relationship, would be allowed to enter into a "civil solidarity pact," which would then entitle them to the same rights as married
couples in such matters as income taxes, housing, inheritance, and social
welfare. The legislation made France the first traditionally Catholic country to sanction same-sex unions. The law was subsequently declared constitutional and was expected to take effect sometime in 2000.*

*The newly merged Exxon Mobil Corporation announced in early Decem-
ber that it was abandoning Mobil's policy of providing health care coverage
to the partners of its homosexual employees. Those already receiving benefits would continue to get them, but new employees and employees who
formed a same-sex partnership in the future would not. Another newly
merged petroleum giant, BP-Amoco, was planning to extend domestic partnership benefits beginning April 1, 2000. Amoco had offered the benefits
before the merger, BP had not.*

Following are excerpts from the majority opinion in the case of
Baker v. State of Vermont, *in which the Vermont Supreme Court
ruled December 20, 1999, that the state had to give homosexual*

901

couples all the rights and protections that it extended to hetero-
sexual couples:

AMESTOY, C. J. [Chief Justice Jeffrey L. Amestoy] May the State of Vermont exclude same-sex couples from the benefits and protections that its
laws provide to opposite-sex married couples? That is the fundamental question we address in this appeal, a question that the Court well knows arouses
deeply-felt religious, moral, and political beliefs. Our constitutional responsibility to consider the legal merits of issues properly before us provides no
exception for the controversial case. The issue before the Court, moreover,
does not turn on the religious or moral debate over intimate same-sex relationships, but rather on the statutory and constitutional basis for the exclusion of same-sex couples from the secular benefits and protections offered
married couples.

We conclude that under the Common Benefits Clause of the Vermont Constitution, which, in pertinent part, reads,

> That government is, or ought to be, instituted for the common benefit, protection,
> and security of the people, nation, or community, and not for the particular emol-
> ument or advantage of any single person, family, or set of persons, who are a part
> only of that community. . . .

. . . plaintiffs may not be deprived of the statutory benefits and protections
afforded persons of the opposite sex who choose to marry. We hold that the
State is constitutionally required to extend to same-sex couples the common
benefits and protections that flow from marriage under Vermont law.
Whether this ultimately takes the form of inclusion within the marriage laws
themselves or a parallel "domestic partnership" system or some equivalent
statutory alternative, rests with the Legislature. Whatever system is chosen,
however, must conform with the constitutional imperative to afford all Vermonters the common benefit, protection, and security of the law.

Plaintiffs are three same-sex couples who have lived together in committed relationships for periods ranging from four to twenty-five years. Two of
the couples have raised children together. Each couple applied for a marriage
license from their respective town clerk, and each was refused a license as
ineligible under the applicable state marriage laws. Plaintiffs thereupon filed
this lawsuit against defendants—the State of Vermont, the Towns of Milton
and Shelburne, and the City of South Burlington—seeking a declaratory judgment that the refusal to issue them a license violated the marriage statutes
and the Vermont Constitution.

The State, joined by Shelburne and South Burlington, moved to dismiss the
action on the ground that plaintiffs had failed to state a claim for which relief
could be granted. The Town of Milton answered the complaint and subsequently moved for judgment on the pleadings. Plaintiffs opposed the motions
and cross-moved for judgment on the pleadings. The trial court granted the

State's and the Town of Milton's motions, denied plaintiffs' motion, and dismissed the complaint. The court ruled that the marriage statutes could not be construed to permit the issuance of a license to same-sex couples. The court further ruled that the marriage statutes were constitutional because they rationally furthered the State's interest in promoting "the link between procreation and child rearing." This appeal followed.

I. The Statutory Claim [omitted]

II. The Constitutional Claim

Assuming that the marriage statutes preclude their eligibility for a marriage license, plaintiffs contend that the exclusion violates their right to the common benefit and protection of the law guaranteed by Chapter I, Article 7 of the Vermont Constitution. They note that in denying them access to a civil marriage license, the law effectively excludes them from a broad array of legal benefits and protections incident to the marital relation, including access to a spouse's medical, life, and disability insurance, hospital visitation and other medical decisionmaking privileges, spousal support, intestate succession, homestead protections, and many other statutory protections. They claim the trial court erred in upholding the law on the basis that it reasonably served the State's interest in promoting the "link between procreation and child rearing." They argue that the large number of married couples without children, and the increasing incidence of same-sex couples with children, undermines the State's rationale. They note that Vermont law affirmatively guarantees the right to adopt and raise children regardless of the sex of the parents, and challenge the logic of a legislative scheme that recognizes the rights of same-sex partners as parents, yet denies them—and their children—the same security as spouses.

In considering this issue, it is important to emphasize at the outset that it is the Common Benefits Clause of the Vermont Constitution we are construing, rather than its counterpart, the Equal Protection Clause of the Fourteenth Amendment to the United States Constitution. . . .

As we explain in the discussion that follows, the Common Benefits Clause of the Vermont Constitution differs markedly from the federal Equal Protection Clause in its language, historical origins, purpose, and development. While the federal amendment may thus supplement the protections afforded by the Common Benefits Clause, it does not supplant it as the first and primary safeguard of the rights and liberties of all Vermonters.

[Sections A–D omitted.]

E. The Standard Applied

With these general precepts in mind, we turn to the question of whether the exclusion of same-sex couples from the benefits and protections incident to marriage under Vermont law contravenes Article 7 [the Common Benefits Clause]. The first step in our analysis is to identify the nature of the statutory classification. As noted, the marriage statutes apply expressly to opposite-sex couples. Thus, the statutes exclude anyone who wishes to marry someone of the same sex.

Next, we must identify the governmental purpose or purposes to be served by the statutory classification. The principal purpose the State advances in support of the excluding same-sex couples from the legal benefits of marriage is the government's interest in "furthering the link between procreation and child rearing." The State has a strong interest, it argues, in promoting a permanent commitment between couples who have children to ensure that their offspring are considered legitimate and receive ongoing parental support. The State contends, further, that the Legislature could reasonably believe that sanctioning same-sex unions "would diminish society's perception of the link between procreation and child rearing . . . [and] advance the notion that fathers or mothers . . . are mere surplusage to the functions of procreation and child rearing." The State argues that since same-sex couples cannot conceive a child on their own, state-sanctioned same-sex unions "could be seen by the Legislature to separate further the connection between procreation and parental responsibilities for raising children." Hence, the Legislature is justified, the State concludes, "in using the marriage statutes to send a public message that procreation and child rearing are intertwined."

Do these concerns represent valid public interests that are reasonably furthered by the exclusion of same-sex couples from the benefits and protections that flow from the marital relation? It is beyond dispute that the State has a legitimate and long-standing interest in promoting a permanent commitment between couples for the security of their children. It is equally undeniable that the State's interest has been advanced by extending formal public sanction and protection to the union, or marriage, of those couples considered capable of having children, i.e., men and women. And there is no doubt that the overwhelming majority of births today continue to result from natural conception between one man and one woman. . . .

It is equally undisputed that many opposite-sex couples marry for reasons unrelated to procreation, that some of these couples never intend to have children, and that others are incapable of having children. Therefore, if the purpose of the statutory exclusion of same-sex couples is to "further the link between procreation and child rearing," it is significantly under-inclusive. The law extends the benefits and protections of marriage to many persons with no logical connection to the stated governmental goal.

Furthermore, while accurate statistics are difficult to obtain, there is no dispute that a significant number of children today are actually being raised by same-sex parents, and that increasing numbers of children are being conceived by such parents through a variety of assisted-reproductive techniques. . . .

Thus, with or without the marriage sanction, the reality today is that increasing numbers of same-sex couples are employing increasingly efficient assisted-reproductive techniques to conceive and raise children. . . . The Vermont Legislature has not only recognized this reality, but has acted affirmatively to remove legal barriers so that same-sex couples may legally adopt and rear the children conceived through such efforts. . . .

Therefore, to the extent that the State's purpose in licensing civil marriage was, and is, to legitimize children and provide for their security, the statutes plainly exclude many same-sex couples who are no different from opposite-sex couples with respect to these objectives. If anything, the exclusion of same-sex couples from the legal protections incident to marriage exposes their children to the precise risks that the State argues the marriage laws are designed to secure against. In short, the marital exclusion treats persons who are similarly situated for purposes of the law, differently. . . .

The question thus becomes whether the exclusion of a relatively small but significant number of otherwise qualified same-sex couples from the same legal benefits and protections afforded their opposite-sex counterparts contravenes the mandates of Article 7. It is, of course, well settled that statutes are not necessarily unconstitutional because they fail to extend legal protection to all who are similarly situated. . . .

While the laws relating to marriage have undergone many changes during the last century, largely toward the goal of equalizing the status of husbands and wives, the benefits of marriage have not diminished in value. On the contrary, the benefits and protections incident to a marriage license under Vermont law have never been greater. They include, for example, the right to receive a portion of the estate of a spouse who dies intestate and protection against disinheritance through elective share provisions . . ; preference in being appointed as the personal representative of a spouse who dies intestate . . ; the right to bring a lawsuit for the wrongful death of a spouse . . ; the right to bring an action for loss of consortium . . ; the right to workers' compensation survivor benefits . . ; the right to spousal benefits statutorily guaranteed to public employees, including health, life, disability, and accident insurance . . ; the opportunity to be covered as a spouse under group life insurance policies issued to an employee . . ; the opportunity to be covered as the insured's spouse under an individual health insurance policy . . ; the right to claim an evidentiary privilege for marital communications . . ; homestead rights and protections . . ; the presumption of joint ownership of property and the concomitant right of survivorship . . ; hospital visitation and other rights incident to the medical treatment of a family member . . ; and the right to receive, and the obligation to provide, spousal support, maintenance, and property division in the event of separation or divorce. . . .

While other statutes could be added to this list, the point is clear. The legal benefits and protections flowing from a marriage license are of such significance that any statutory exclusion must necessarily be grounded on public concerns of sufficient weight, cogency, and authority that the justice of the deprivation cannot seriously be questioned. Considered in light of the extreme logical disjunction between the classification and the stated purposes of the law—protecting children and "furthering the link between procreation and child rearing"—the exclusion falls substantially short of this standard. The laudable governmental goal of promoting a commitment between married couples to promote the security of their children and the community as a whole provides no reasonable basis for denying the legal ben-

efits and protections of marriage to same-sex couples, who are no differently
situated with respect to this goal than their opposite-sex counterparts. Promoting a link between procreation and childrearing similarly fails to support
the exclusion. We turn, accordingly, to the remaining interests identified by
the State in support of the statutory exclusion.

The State asserts that a number of additional rationales could support a legislative decision to exclude same-sex partners from the statutory benefits and
protections of marriage. Among these are the State's purported interests in
"promoting child rearing in a setting that provides both male and female role
models," minimizing the legal complications of surrogacy contracts and sperm
donors, "bridging differences" between the sexes, discouraging marriages of
convenience for tax, housing or other benefits, maintaining uniformity with
marriage laws in other states, and generally protecting marriage from "destabilizing changes." The most substantive of the State's remaining claims relates
to the issue of childrearing. It is conceivable that the Legislature could conclude that opposite-sex partners offer advantages in this area, although we
note that child-development experts disagree and the answer is decidedly
uncertain. The argument, however, contains a more fundamental flaw, and
that is the Legislature's endorsement of a policy diametrically at odds with the
State's claim. In 1996, the Vermont General Assembly enacted, and the Governor signed, a law removing all prior legal barriers to the adoption of children
by same-sex couples. At the same time, the Legislature provided additional
legal protections in the form of court-ordered child support and parent-child
contact in the event that same-sex parents dissolved their "domestic relationship." In light of these express policy choices, the State's arguments that Vermont public policy favors opposite-sex over same-sex parents or disfavors the
use of artificial reproductive technologies, are patently without substance.

Similarly, the State's argument that Vermont's marriage laws serve a substantial governmental interest in maintaining uniformity with other jurisdictions cannot be reconciled with Vermont's recognition of unions, such as first-
cousin marriages, not uniformly sanctioned in other states. . . . In an
analogous context, Vermont has sanctioned adoptions by same-sex partners,
notwithstanding the fact that many states have not. . . . Thus, the State's claim
that Vermont's marriage laws were adopted because the Legislature sought to
conform to those of the other forty-nine states is not only speculative, but
refuted by two relevant legislative choices which demonstrate that uniformity
with other jurisdictions has not been a governmental purpose.

The State's remaining claims (e.g., recognition of same-sex unions might
foster marriages of convenience or otherwise affect the institution in "unpredictable" ways) may be plausible forecasts as to what the future may hold,
but cannot reasonably be construed to provide a reasonable and just basis for
the statutory exclusion. The State's conjectures are not, in any event, susceptible to empirical proof before they occur.

Finally, it is suggested that the long history of official intolerance of intimate same-sex relationships cannot be reconciled with an interpretation of
Article 7 that would give state-sanctioned benefits and protection to individ-

uals of the same sex who commit to a permanent domestic relationship. We find the argument to be unpersuasive for several reasons. First, to the extent that state action historically has been motivated by an animus against a class, that history cannot provide a legitimate basis for continued unequal application of the law. . . . As we observed recently . . . "equal protection of the laws cannot be limited by eighteenth-century standards." Second, whatever claim may be made in light of the undeniable fact that federal and state statutes—including those in Vermont—have historically disfavored same-sex relationships, more recent legislation plainly undermines the contention. . . . In 1991, Vermont was one of the first states to enact statewide legislation prohibiting discrimination in employment, housing, and other services based on sexual orientation. . . . Sexual orientation is among the categories specifically protected against hate-motivated crimes in Vermont. . . .

Thus, viewed in the light of history, logic, and experience, we conclude that none of the interests asserted by the State provides a reasonable and just basis for the continued exclusion of same-sex couples from the benefits incident to a civil marriage license under Vermont law. Accordingly, in the faith that a case beyond the imagining of the framers of our Constitution may, nevertheless, be safely anchored in the values that infused it, we find a constitutional obligation to extend to plaintiffs the common benefit, protection, and security that Vermont law provides opposite-sex married couples. It remains only to determine the appropriate means and scope of relief compelled by this constitutional mandate.

F. Remedy

It is important to state clearly the parameters of today's ruling. Although plaintiffs sought injunctive and declaratory relief designed to secure a marriage license, their claims and arguments here have focused primarily upon the consequences of official exclusion from the statutory benefits, protections, and security incident to marriage under Vermont law. While some future case may attempt to establish that—notwithstanding equal benefits and protections under Vermont law—the denial of a marriage license operates per se to deny constitutionally-protected rights, that is not the claim we address today.

We hold only that plaintiffs are entitled under Chapter I, Article 7, of the Vermont Constitution to obtain the same benefits and protections afforded by Vermont law to married opposite-sex couples. We do not purport to infringe upon the prerogatives of the Legislature to craft an appropriate means of addressing this constitutional mandate, other than to note that the record here refers to a number of potentially constitutional statutory schemes from other jurisdictions. These include what are typically referred to as "domestic partnership" or "registered partnership" acts, which generally establish an alternative legal status to marriage for same-sex couples, impose similar formal requirements and limitations, create a parallel licensing or registration scheme, and extend all or most of the same rights and obligations provided by the law to married partners. . . .

Further, while the State's prediction of "destabilization" cannot be a ground for denying relief, it is not altogether irrelevant. A sudden change in the marriage laws or the statutory benefits traditionally incidental to marriage may have disruptive and unforeseen consequences. Absent legislative guidelines defining the status and rights of same-sex couples, consistent with constitutional requirements, uncertainty and confusion could result. Therefore, we hold that the current statutory scheme shall remain in effect for a reasonable period of time to enable the Legislature to consider and enact implementing legislation in an orderly and expeditious fashion. . . . In the event that the benefits and protections in question are not statutorily granted, plaintiffs may petition this Court to order the remedy they originally sought. . . .

III. Conclusion

While many have noted the symbolic or spiritual significance of the marital relation, it is plaintiffs' claim to the secular benefits and protections of a singularly human relationship that, in our view, characterizes this case. The State's interest in extending official recognition and legal protection to the professed commitment of two individuals to a lasting relationship of mutual affection is predicated on the belief that legal support of a couple's commitment provides stability for the individuals, their family, and the broader community. Although plaintiffs' interest in seeking state recognition and protection of their mutual commitment may—in view of divorce statistics— represent "the triumph of hope over experience," the essential aspect of their claim is simply and fundamentally for inclusion in the family of State-sanctioned human relations.

The past provides many instances where the law refused to see a human being when it should have. . . . The challenge for future generations will be to define what is most essentially human. The extension of the Common Benefits Clause to acknowledge plaintiffs as Vermonters who seek nothing more, nor less, than legal protection and security for their avowed commitment to an intimate and lasting human relationship is simply, when all is said and done, a recognition of our common humanity.

The judgment of the superior court upholding the constitutionality of the Vermont marriage statutes under Chapter I, Article 7 of the Vermont Constitution is reversed. The effect of the Court's decision is suspended, and jurisdiction is retained in this Court, to permit the Legislature to consider and enact legislation consistent with the constitutional mandate described herein.

UN HUMAN RIGHTS OFFICIAL
ON THE WAR IN CHECHNYA
December 20, 1999

Three years after failing to quash an independence movement in the tiny republic of Chechnya, the Russian military moved back into the province in September 1999, launching brutal assaults that killed thousands of civilians and drove more than 200,000 people from their homes. Russian president Boris Yeltsin and his prime minister, Vladimir Putin, said the attacks were necessary to drive out terrorists who had planted bombs that killed more than 300 Russians in August and September. But it appeared that Moscow's real aim was to reverse the results of its disastrous 1994–1996 war to drive out an Islamic government in Chechnya that had declared independence from Russia.

At least in its beginning months, the new war in Chechnya drew broad support from the Russian public—in contrast to the previous war, when mounting casualties among Russian soldiers rapidly swelled public opposition to the intervention. The early success of the war drove up the popularity of Putin, who was widely considered to be Yeltsin's hand-picked successor. Yeltsin on December 31 resigned and named Putin as acting president, making him the clear front-runner in elections scheduled for 2000. At the same time, Moscow was facing increasingly vocal criticism from Western leaders and international organizations who said the Russian army's apparently indiscriminate bombing was killing thousands of civilians. (Yeltsin resignation, p. 918)

Background to the Conflict

Chechnya was one of Russia's smallest republics, with a land area of just more than 6,000 square miles, located in the northern Caucasus Mountains just north of Georgia and about 80 miles west of the Caspian sea. The area was conquered by Russia in 1859 and incorporated into communist Russia in 1921, four years after the revolution. In November 1991, just before the collapse of the Soviet Union, Chechnya declared its independence. About three-fourths of the 1 million people in the province were native Chechens, an Islamic people who had been in the area for centuries. Most of the remaining 250,000 were Russians who had settled there under Soviet role.

Yeltsin, who had campaigned for the presidency of Russia in 1991 on a platform of allowing considerable autonomy to local regions, at first took no action in response to the Chechen declaration of independence. But in late 1994 Yeltsin ordered the army into Chechnya, declaring that the province was an integral part of Russia. Army generals believed that capturing the Chechen capital, Grozny, and driving the independent government there from power would take just a few weeks. But Chechens proved to be superb guerrilla fighters able to withstand massive assaults by the Russian army. The war lasted nearly two years and was a disaster for Moscow, which pulled out of Chechnya in 1996. The army killed tens of thousands of Chechens, but thousands of Russian soldiers also died, and for the first time in Russian history public outrage at the failure of a military campaign played a major role in the Kremlin's decision to retreat. The elected Chechen separatist government, headed by president Aslan Maskhadov, remained in power, serving as a reminder to Moscow of the limits to its military power. (War in Chechnya, Historic Documents of 1995, p. 93)

In August 1999 a force of several thousand Islamic guerrillas, headed by a Chechen warlord, moved into neighboring Dagestan and declared an Islamic republic. The Russian army launched massive attacks—most of them from the air—that drove most of the guerrillas out. Even so, at least 230 Russian soldiers died in the fighting, which continued at a low level well into September.

Apartment Bombings in Moscow

A series of unexplained bombings in August and September—which Russian authorities attributed to Chechen "terrorists"—threw millions of Russians into a panic and gave Moscow political justification to move into Chechnya.

The first bombing came August 31, when an explosion ripped through Moscow's upscale shopping area called Manezh, near the Kremlin. One person was killed and about forty others were wounded. On September 4 an apartment complex in Dagestan housing Russian army officers and their families was bombed, killing sixty-four people.

Then two massive bombs destroyed apartment buildings in Moscow. The first, on September 8, killed 94 people and wounded 200 others at an apartment complex in the southeastern section of Moscow. Four days later, 119 people were killed and 200 others injured when a bomb totally destroyed an eight-story brick apartment building on a major road leading south out of Moscow. The latter bombing occurred on a day that had been set aside for mourning the victims of those killed in the September 9 blast. Finally, on September 16, a bomb went off in an apartment complex in Volgodonsk, in southern Russia about 700 miles from Moscow, killing more than 20 people and wounding dozens more.

Authorities said there were similarities in the apartment bombings: they occurred in the early morning, when occupants were sleeping, and in two cases swarthy men using false identification papers had rented space on the ground floors of the buildings and left behind sacks that were labeled as containing "sugar" but in fact were filled with a powerful explosive.

Following the September 13 bombing, Yeltsin went on national television and angrily said that "terrorism has declared war on the Russian people," and he blamed the Chechen independence movement. He said Russian forces would seal off Chechnya, and he ordered a sweeping security search of all 33,000 apartment buildings in Moscow.

Russian Troops Move into Chechnya

Russian warplanes launched a bombing campaign against Chechnya on September 23, attacking a reported arms depot and radar installation at the Grozny airport and an oil refinery on the outskirts of the city. A week of increasingly intensive bombing drove tens of thousands of Chechens from their homes, most into the neighboring province of Ingushetia, and set the stage for a land invasion by Russian troops on September 30.

Prime Minister Putin at first said the ground action was intended merely to establish a buffer zone to prevent Chechen guerrillas from infiltrating into other parts of Russia. But news reports suggested that Moscow had finally decided to sever Chechnya in two pieces: an area of relatively level terrain in the north under Russian control, with the mountainous southern part left in the hands of the separatists. On October 1 Putin said the Russian government was withdrawing its recognition of Maskhadov as the elected leader of Chechnya and would instead deal with a Chechen "parliament" based in Moscow that Russian authorities had attempted to install in Grozny near the close of the 1994–1996 war.

Within a month of the invasion, Russian forces had captured the northern third of Chechnya and had approached within a few miles of Grozny, in the center of the province, and had begun heavy bombing of the city. The Russian army on November 13 captured Gudermes, Chechnya's second largest city, and then concentrated forces around Grozny. By the middle of November Moscow had committed more than 100,000 ground troops to the battle.

At least in the early months of the conflict, the Russian public appeared to rally behind the government and troops in the field—in sharp contrast to the public's alarmed reaction to the slaughter of civilians and Russian soldiers in the 1994–1996 war. Analysts said the principal difference was that Russians accepted the government's explanation that the latest war was a necessary attack on terrorists. It also appeared that army generals were much more cautious in 1999 than they had been in the earlier war, with the result that fewer Russian soldiers were dying in combat.

On November 26 Russian forces stepped up their attacks on Grozny, launching thousands of bombs and artillery shells on the capital. Russian generals said the military was planning a lengthy siege of the capital and would construct bases for a permanent presence in Chechnya. The statements seemed to indicate that the military was accepting the fact that earlier predictions of a rapid victory in Chechnya were overly optimistic. Chechen fighters were avoiding direct confrontations with the Russian military, instead relying on the guerrilla hit-and-run attacks that had served them well during the 1994–1996 war.

The army on December 6 dropped leaflets on the city telling residents they had just five days to leave or face death. "Use any means possible" to get out, the leaflet said, and the army announced that a "safe corridor" would be established so civilians could leave the city. The government later said it had not set any ultimatum for Grozny residents, but the warning caused panic in Grozny and set off alarm bells in capitals around the world. Bombings of the supposed "safe corridor" also convinced many Grozny residents that they it might be better to stay than to try to leave.

Russian troops made their first attempt to enter Grozny on December 15 but were immediately surrounded by thousands of Chechen troops and forced to beat a hasty retreat. The army kept up its assault through the rest of December, bombing the city at night and sending armed convoys into outlying areas during the day in an attempt to root out Chechen guerrillas. At year's end Russian forces were still on the city's outskirts, but what remained of the city from the 1994–1996 war was rapidly being destroyed.

Western Leaders Step up Criticism

The war put international leaders—especially in Europe and the United States—in a difficult position. On the one hand, most were appalled by the brutality of the Russian offensive, which bore some similarities to the campaigns of ethnic terror that had raged through the former Yugoslavia during the 1990s. But on the other hand Western leaders gave a high priority to maintaining stability in Russia, which in their view meant bolstering the Kremlin's moderate leaders who supported the country's transition to a free-market economy and democracy. Officials in Washington, London, Berlin, and other Western capitals feared that too strong a reaction against the war in Chechnya might needlessly stir up nationalist sentiment within Russia against the West, with repercussions that could not be foreseen. Western leaders also sympathized with Moscow's instinctive desire to react against terrorists who had killed hundreds of Russian civilians. In addition, the Clinton administration was conducting sensitive diplomatic negotiations with Moscow on arms control and other issues, most notably Washington's plan to seek amendment of the 1972 U.S.-Soviet antiballistic missile treaty to allow possible construction of an antimissile "shield."

During a summit meeting on the Middle East held in Oslo early in November, President Bill Clinton made a personal appeal to Putin to scale back the attacks, but Putin rebuffed the plea, saying Russia was trying to eliminate terrorism. Administration officials gradually escalated their criticism of the Russian offensive, with Stephen Sestanovich, a senior advisor to Secretary of State Madeleine K. Albright, telling the Senate Foreign

Relations Committee on November 4 that Russia's use of "indiscriminate force against innocent civilians is indefensible, and we condemn it."

The first highly critical international condemnation of Russian action came November 16 when Mary Robinson, the United Nations High Commissioner for Human Rights, issued a statement saying she was disturbed that "serious violations of human rights and of humanitarian law" were taking place in Chechnya. Among the specifics Robinson cited were that the "indiscriminate and disproportionate use of force" was causing a high level of casualties among civilians, that "vulnerable populations" such as children and the elderly were not given an opportunity to escape the bombing, and that Russia had failed to provide adequate humanitarian supplies for nearly 200,000 refugees, most of them in Ingushetia.

Robinson appealed to Moscow to stop the "devastating impact of military operations on the civilian population," to establish "humanitarian corridors" for civilians to escape the fighting, and to allow international agencies to provide humanitarian supplies to refugees. Sadako Ogata, the United Nations High Commissioner for Refugees, toured refugee camps on the Chechen border November 19 and said thousands of refugees were in need of food, shelter, and other supplies.

The first open break between Moscow and the West on Chechnya came November 18, during a summit meeting in Istanbul of the fifty government leaders represented in the Organization for Security and Cooperation in Europe. Responding to criticism from fellow leaders, Yeltsin launched into an impassioned defense of Russia's military action in Chechnya, saying it was a response to "the bloody wave of terrorist acts that have swept over Moscow and other cities and towns of our country." Other countries "have no right to criticize Russia over Chechnya," Yeltsin said, reminding his fellow leaders of "the aggression of NATO headed by the United States that was mounted against Yugoslavia" during the war over Kosovo earlier in 1999. Yeltsin said the United States had killed civilians in Yugoslavia.

Clinton directly challenged Yeltsin, pointing his finger at the Russian leader and calling for an end to the bomb and artillery attacks that had killed thousands of civilians. "If the attacks on civilians continue, the extremism Russia is trying to combat will only intensify," he said. "In order to isolate and undermine the terrorists, there must be a political dialogue and a political settlement." Although it garnered headlines, the confrontation between Yeltsin and Clinton appeared to have no effect on the war.

The Russian army's December 6 demand that residents leave Grozny shocked European nations that had been reluctant to criticize Moscow. German chancellor Gerhard Schroeder sent Yeltsin and Putin a message demanding that they revoke the ultimatum. French president Jacques Chirac described Russia's actions in Chechnya as "unacceptable" and Italian prime minister Massimo D'Alema said European nations might have to consider "economic pressure" if Russia failed to heed the criticism.

Western nations exerted some economic pressure early in December when the International Monetary Fund (IMF) suspended distribution of a

*$640 million loan that was part of a broader $4.5 billion "stabilization"
package to bolster Russia's economy. Officially, the IMF said it acted
because Moscow had failed to meet several economic requirements, and
officials in Washington and European capitals said the loan suspension
was not directly linked to the events in Chechnya. But several of those same
officials said the IMF's action might help call Moscow's attention to the serious concerns in the rest of the world about what was happening in Chechnya. Clinton said during a December 8 press conference that the United
States should not suspend its direct aid to Russia, most of which went to
help the Russians safeguard their nuclear weapons and related supplies
and to promote democratic institutions. But Clinton said over the long
term he expected leaders in Moscow would find the war in Chechnya to be
"very costly" because it had undermined international support for Russia.*

*As the war continued into December, international organizations
stepped up their campaigns on behalf of Chechen civilians. On December
20, Francis M. Deng, the UN's special representative for "internally displaced persons" (refugees who remained in their own country), issued a
strongly worded appeal to Moscow to "protect civilians from indiscriminate attacks and other acts of violence." Also on December 20 Human
Rights Watch, a U.S.-based organization that advocated universal standards for human rights, sent a letter to the UN Security Council asking it
to convene an independent inquiry of events in Chechnya. "Russian forces
have bombed and shelled dozens of towns and villages still inhabited by
civilians, actions that have killed and maimed untold numbers of people
and shown contempt for international humanitarian law." Human Rights
Watch cited in particular reports that Russian forces had conducted "summary executions" of civilians and looted property in the town of Alklan-
Yurt at the beginning of December. A videotape showing Russian troops
carting off private possessions from the town was shown on Russian television later in December.*

*As of the end of the year, the UN Security Council had taken no action on
the matter. Russia was one of five permanent Security Council members
able to exercise a veto over council actions.*

*Following is the text of a statement issued December 20, 1999,
by Francis M. Deng, the representative of the United Nations secretary general on internally displaced persons, in which he
called on the Russian government to protect civilians in Chechnya from attacks by the Russian military:*

Over the past few months, more than 250,000 persons have been forcibly
displaced as a result of the conflict in Chechnya, and their numbers continue
to grow, following the warning issued by Russian forces on 6 December to the
people of Grozny to leave their homes or face intensified attack.

The overwhelming majority of the internally displaced remain within the borders of the Russian Federation, principally in Chechnya and Ingushetia. As such they are internally displaced persons and responsibility for meeting their assistance and protection needs rests first and foremost with the Russian Government. As Representative of the Secretary-General on Internally Displaced Persons, it is incumbent upon me to call on the Government of the Russian Federation to assume this responsibility and, in particular, to address the following concerns.

Protection and Safety of Civilians: Russian military operations are endangering the physical security of civilians and preventing them from gaining access to safety. Reports indicate that many civilians remain trapped by military action while others, including many elderly and infirm, are unable or are too frightened to leave in search of protection and safety. Many of those who have left have been subject to military attack or harassment, or have been obliged to pay bribes at checkpoints set up by Russian forces. It is incumbent upon the Russian Government to protect civilians from indiscriminate attacks and other acts of violence.

Arbitrary Detention: There are reports that Russian forces have established 'filtration camps at the border to detain internally displaced Chechens suspected of sympathising with the Chechen cause, as well as members of their families. Arbitrary detention of non-combatants contravenes international standards.

Looting and Pillaging: Property left behind by the displaced reportedly is being looted and pillaged by Russian forces.

Subsistence Needs: Many of the internally displaced persons in camps in Ingushetia are not receiving adequate supplies of basic essentials such as heating supplies, clothing, bedding and cooking facilities, and lack access to medical care and social services.

Shelter: With winter fast approaching, the availability of appropriate shelter for internally displaced persons who have fled to Ingushetia is of particular concern. There are reports of severe overcrowding in both private accommodation and in camps for the displaced. Some internally displaced persons, including children, are having to sleep outdoors in the cold.

Access to Humanitarian Assistance: The Russian Government should do everything possible to facilitate the delivery of humanitarian aid to the displaced by international humanitarian organisations, and increase its own assistance to those in need. It must take effective steps to guarantee the security of displaced persons and of international humanitarian workers in areas under its control. The security situation and bureaucratic obstacles have been preventing international relief organisations from gaining access to the internally displaced, supplying them with assistance and monitoring the delivery of the assistance.

Voluntary Return: The Russian authorities must ensure that the return of internally displaced persons to their homes takes place voluntarily and under conditions of safety. There are reports that camp authorities in Ingushetia are pressuring some displaced persons to return to their homes in Chechnya even though conditions are far from safe and they lack the materials to repair their homes.

As Representative of the Secretary-General, I call upon the Russian authorities to observe the relevant principles of international law as restated in the Guiding Principles on Internal Displacement.

I also join the voices of many around the world in urging the Security Council to discuss the conflict in Chechnya and to give special focus to the internally displaced and the humanitarian dimension of the conflict.

BORIS YELTSIN ON HIS RESIGNATION
AS RUSSIAN PRESIDENT
December 31, 1999

Boris Yeltsin, whose courage and determination helped bring down communism and the Soviet state but whose personal failings undermined the transformation of Russia into a capitalist democracy, sudden resigned on New Year's Eve and handed power to a relatively unknown aide, Prime Minister Vladimir Putin. A former colonel in the Soviet secret service, Putin was expected to be a formidable candidate in Russia's third free presidential election, scheduled for March 2000.

Yeltsin's surprise resignation was just the last in a series of erratic moves during his fifteen years on the world stage. Ever since then Soviet leader Mikhail Gorbachev put him in charge of the Communist Party in Moscow in 1985, Yeltsin had confounded both supporters and opponents with his flair for dramatic gestures and swift tactical changes. The most enduring image of him in history books was likely to be his unexpected appearance atop a tank in Moscow in August 1991, when he confronted the Soviet generals who had attempted a coup against Gorbachev.

As Yeltsin walked out of the Kremlin on the afternoon of December 31, Russia was a vastly different place from the country he took over following the collapse of the Soviet Union at the end of 1991. In terms of government, Russia had adopted the ballot box as the tool for choosing its leaders. Russia clearly had not yet developed all the elements of a smoothly functioning civil democracy, but most Russians seemed to agree by 1999 that there would be no turning back to the rigid, unelected authoritarianism of the czars and commissars. Yeltsin and his aides had dismantled the other central feature of communism: state control of the economy. A "Wild West" capitalism had emerged in its place, one in which a handful of scheming businessmen—known as the "oligarches"—became fabulously wealthy while millions of Russians lived in poverty. Despite the hardships and economic dislocations, capitalism appeared to have taken hold in Russia.

In his nationally televised address announcing his resignation, Yeltsin asked Russians to forgive him for failing to transform Russia "in one fell swoop, in one leap, jump from the dreary, stagnant totalitarian past into a bright, affluent and civilized future." He had thought it could be done, he said, "but it didn't work out."

Yeltsin's Rise to Power

Yeltsin was a Communist Party boss in the Ural Mountain region of Sverdlovsk in 1985 when Gorbachev, who had himself just assumed power in the Kremlin, installed him as party chief in Moscow. Yeltsin quickly developed a popular following and a willingness to criticize the slow pace of reforms, alarming Gorbachev, who dumped him from his leadership posts. Yeltsin then took advantage of Gorbachev's electoral reforms and in 1990 won election as parliamentary chairman in the Russian republic (the most important of the Soviet republics at the time). In June 1991 he became the first freely elected president of the Russian republic, establishing himself as Gorbachev's main rival. In August 1991 Soviet generals staged a coup against Gorbachev and placed him under house arrest. Yeltsin courageously faced down the generals when he climbed atop a tank outside the Kremlin and the coup collapsed, establishing Yeltsin as the country's preeminent political leader. Gorbachev returned to office but resigned in December 1991 after Yeltsin and the leaders of Belarus and Ukraine declared the Soviet Union to be disbanded.

Yeltsin moved quickly to consolidate reforms. In January 1992 he decreed an end to communist control of the economy and hired young reformers—advised by Western economists—to dismantle elements of the Soviet state. Key decisions made at that point later came back to haunt Yeltsin and Russia, most importantly the rapid privatization of huge industrial enterprises, which were bought at a fraction of their value by former Communist Party officials and opportunistic businessmen. Fundamental weaknesses of the old Soviet economy quickly became evident, and millions of Russians lost their jobs and pensions as outdated and inefficient factories were closed. The harsh realities of Russia's sudden jerk into raw capitalism threw millions of people into poverty, but Yeltsin held the course.

Public dissatisfaction with rising unemployment and skyrocketing inflation emboldened the communist majority in the Russian parliament and their supporters, who seized government buildings and attacked riot police in September 1993. Facing what appeared to be an attempted coup, Yeltsin declared martial law and ordered the shelling of parliament—an undemocratic move that ended in the deaths of more than 150 people but saved his government, and possibly democracy itself. Two months later voters approved a new constitution that gave the president sweeping emergency powers but also formally established free enterprise as the country's economic system and guaranteed individual rights, including the right to own private property.

In December 1994 Yeltsin made what he later said was his biggest mistake, allowing Russian army generals to invade the southern republic of

Chechnya in an attempt to oust Islamic leaders who had declared indepen-
dence. A brutal war lasting nearly two years killed tens of thousands of peo-
ple, including many Russian soldiers, and ended in a failure for Moscow.
Ironically, a repeat of that war was under way as Yeltsin resigned. (Chechnya war, p. 909)

Despite serious health problems and growing public disenchantment
with the rough edges of capitalism, Yeltsin staged a come-from-behind cam-
paign to win a second term as president in July 1996. He defeated the
leader of a resurgent Communist Party, which had used its influence in
parliament to undermine many of Yeltsin's reforms. Yeltsin spent much of
the rest of 1996 and the early part of 1997 in the hospital, recovering first
from heart surgery and then from pneumonia. Long absences for health
reasons were to become common during his last years in office. Yeltsin also
was plagued with numerous charges of corruption involving his family,
particularly his daughter, Tatyana Dyachekno, who was generally consid-
ered his closest political advisor. (Yeltsin reelection, Historic Documents of
1996, p. 430)

The multiple shortcomings of the Russian economy culminated in a vir-
tual collapse in August 1998, when the country was forced to default on
much of its internal debt and devalue the ruble. Western leaders, who had
invested billions of dollars to finance Russia's transformation to capital-
ism, were shaken but said they were committed to the reform process. (Economic collapse, Historic Documents of 1998, p. 601)

Opponents in parliament in late 1998 revived what had been a lagging
effort to impeach Yeltsin because of his handling of the war in Chechnya.
The impeachment move died in May 1999, just three months after U.S.
president Bill Clinton survived an impeachment drive in the U.S. Congress.
But Yeltsin continued his erratic attempts to find a prime minister who
could take responsibility for public policy without posing too much of a
challenge to the president's authority. In May he fired Prime Minister
Yevgeny Primakov, who had been in office just eight months, and elevated
Sergei Stepashin, his interior minister, to the post. Yeltsin abruptly fired
Stepashin on August 9, after he served just three months, and installed
Putin as acting prime minister. Perhaps more important, Yeltsin declared
Putin, who was little known outside the Kremlin, to be his preferred suc-
cessor as president.

A series of bombings in Moscow and two other cities starting at the end
of August killed more than 300 people and caused widespread panic in
Russia. Yeltsin and Putin declared that "terrorists" from Chechnya were
responsible, and in September the military launched air attacks on the
Chechen capital, Grozny, leading to a land invasion at the end of the
month.

Because it was portrayed as an antiterrorism campaign, the war in
Chechnya proved to be enormously popular in Russia, and it made Putin—
widely perceived as the architect of the war—the country's most popular
politician. Parties aligned with the Kremlin did surprisingly well in par-

liamentary elections held December 19, giving Putin the opportunity to achieve a working majority, which no Russian leader had enjoyed since the collapse of communism.

The endorsement of Putin at the polls clearly played a major role in Yeltsin's decision to resign less than two weeks later and hand the government over to his designated successor. Yeltsin said as much in his resignation speech: "To hold onto power for another half year, when the country has a strong man who is worthy of being president and with whom practically every Russian today ties his hope for the future? Why should I get in his way? Why wait another six months?"

Assessing Yeltsin's Tenure

In the wake of Yeltsin's resignation, most analysts described him as the figure who was most capable of leading Russia out of communism and of expressing a vision for his country as a free society. Even Gorbachev, who introduced what seemed at the time to be revolutionary reforms in the Soviet system, lacked Yeltsin's drive for a clean break with the past. Many others saw in the late 1980s that Soviet communism had become a hollow shell; only Yeltsin had the courage and the stature to give it the push that made it collapse.

Yeltsin, according to most assessments, was not a detail man. Having lived all his life in the Soviet system, and having spent many years working his way through the party bureaucracy, he was incapable of putting in place the myriad elements necessary for a civil society with a functioning democracy and a free economy. Yeltsin turned that job over to eager reformers, none of whom had any more working experience than he did with the day-to-day realities of free markets and democratic political institutions. As one experiment after another failed, Yeltsin's typical response was to fire one set of aides and replace them with another. He brought in legions of experts from Western countries but often rejected their advice as being impractical or ill-suited to Russian society.

Yeltsin also looked the other way as opportunists stole much of the nation's wealth, making corruption one of the dominant factors in the economy. "What do you expect," a reformist politician quoted Yeltsin as saying when he was warned of corruption at high levels. "Russia has always been corrupt."

Frequent and lengthy illnesses, perhaps worsened by legendary bouts of drinking, severely weakened Yeltsin's ability to govern. In his final years Yeltsin exercised leadership by surprise. He installed and then fired prime ministers and other key aides without warning and, it often seemed, without any reason other than to keep his government and his opponents off balance. "He returned to the old Russian czarist tradition," Lilia Stevenson, a Yeltsin biographer, told the Washington Post.

Despite his failings, critics and supporters alike agreed that Yeltsin made it unlikely that Russia itself would return to its old traditions, whether czarist or communist. One of his fiercest political enemies, the ultranationalist leader Vladimir Zhirinovsky, put Yeltsin's legacy in the simplest and most basic terms: "He gave us freedom."

Putin in Charge

A native of St. Petersburg (called Leningrad when he was born), Putin graduated from Leningrad State University in 1975 and immediately went to work for the Soviet Union's intelligence service, the KGB. He spent most of the 1980s in East Germany, then returned to Leningrad in 1989 and in 1991 went to work for the city's reformist mayor, Anatoly Sobchak. Five years later he was recruited for work in the Kremlin and rose rapidly through a succession of jobs, becoming head of the KGB's successor agency (the Federal Security Service) in 1998, and then Yeltsin's national security advisor in March 1999.

On August 9 Yeltsin plucked Putin from relative obscurity, named him acting prime minister, and declared him to be his favored successor as president in elections scheduled for June 2000. At the time, Putin had no personal base of support other than Yeltsin and colleagues from his past jobs, and he had not demonstrated any of the personal charisma necessary for a high-level political leader. One of Putin's five predecessors as prime minister, Yevgeny Primakov, was mounting a presidential bid and seemed to be gaining support.

After Putin had been in office less than a month, the bombings of apartment buildings in Moscow and other cities handed Putin his first big challenge, and he rose to it with a firm hand that reassured many Russians. The attack on Chechnya proved to be unexpectedly popular, as well. By the time of the December elections, opinion polls showed Putin to be the most trusted politician in Russia, and two brand new parties aligned with him captured more than 30 percent of the vote—enough to give Putin leverage with the parliament. After Yeltsin resignation announced his resignation, most analysts agreed that Putin seemed to be the strongest candidate for the 2000 elections, which by law were moved up to late March, from the original schedule of June.

One of Putin's first official actions was to sign a decree giving Yeltsin immunity from prosecution. The decree offered Yeltsin legal protection for his home, personal possessions, and private papers. Yeltsin had been beset on almost a daily basis by numerous allegations about corruption among family members and friends, but no serious evidence of corrupt behavior involving him personally had emerged.

In a speech televised at midnight, Putin assured Russians that "there will be no power vacuum" during the transition. "Freedom of speech, freedom of conscience, freedom of the press, the right to private property—all these basic principles of a civilized society will be reliably protected by the state," he said.

Following is the text of a speech delivered December 31, 1999, by Russian president Boris Yeltsin, in which he announced that he was resigning and turning the government over to Vladimir Putin as acting president:

My fellow Russians,

Only a little time remains until the "magic" date in our history. The year 2000 is arriving, a new century and a new millennium. We have all been contemplating this date with regard to ourselves, figuring out, first in childhood, and then when we were grown up how old we would be in the year 2000, how old our mother and our children would be. And it once seemed to be so remote, that unusual New Year. And now this day has come.

Dear friends, today I am addressing you for the last time with a New Year message. But that is not all. Today I am addressing you for the last time as the President of Russia. I have made a decision. I have brooded over it long and painfully. Today, on the last day of the outgoing century, I am resigning.

I have heard it said many times that Yeltsin would be holding on to power by all means, that he would never relinquish it to anyone. This is a lie. This is beside the point. I have always said that I would not diverge one step from the Constitution, that the elections to the Duma should take place at the time fixed by the Constitution. And that is the way it happened.

And likewise I wanted the presidential election to take place on time, in June 2000. It would have been very important for Russia. We are creating a vital precedent of civilized and voluntary transfer of power from one president of Russia to another, a newly-elected one.

And yet, I have decided otherwise. I am leaving. I am leaving ahead of time. I have realized that it is necessary for me to do so. Russia must enter the new millennium with new political leaders, with new faces, with new intelligent, strong, energetic people. And we, those who have been in power for many years—we must leave.

Having seen with what hope and confidence people voted in the Duma election for a new generation of politicians, I have realized that I have accomplished the main work of my life. Russia will never again revert to its past. Russia will now move only forward. And I should not get in the way of the natural course of history.

To hold on to power for another six months when the country has a strong man who is worthy of becoming a president and on whom practically every Russian now pins his hopes for the future? Why should I get in his way? Why wait another six months? No. This is not me. This is not in my nature.

Today, on this exceedingly important day for me I would like to speak a little more personally than usual.

I want to ask your forgiveness. I want to ask your forgiveness because many of our dreams have not come true, because some things that seemed simple to us have turned out to be tormentingly difficult. I ask your forgiveness for not living up to some of the hopes of the people who believed that we would be able in one fell swoop, in one leap, jump from the dreary, stagnant totalitarian past into a bright, affluent and civilized future. I myself believed in this. It seemed that we would overcome everything in one leap.

But it didn't work out—in one leap. I have proved to be too naive in some things, in some cases problems have proved to be too complex. We were pushing our way forward through mistakes and setbacks. Many people in these complex times have experienced upheavals. But I want you to know— I never said it, but today it is important for me to say it to you. The pain of each of you has echoed in me, in my heart, in my sleepless nights, in my agonizing over what should be done to make people's lives if only a little easier and better. I have never had a more important task.

I am leaving. I have done all I could. And not for reasons of health, but in view of the totality of the problems. Coming to replace me is a new generation, a generation of those who can do more and better. In accordance with the Constitution, before retiring I signed a decree transferring the duties of the President of Russia to the Chairman of the Government, Vladimir Vladimirovich Putin. For three months, in accordance with the Constitution, he will be the head of state. And in three months' time, also under the Constitution, the election of the President will take place.

I have always been confident of the extraordinary wisdom of the Russian people. So, I have no doubt about the choice you will make at the end of March 2000. As I bid you farewell I would like to say to each and every one of you, be happy. You deserve happiness. You deserve happiness and tranquillity.

A Happy New Year! I congratulate you on the new century, my dear fellow Russians!

CUMULATIVE INDEX, 1995–1999

A

Abacha, Sani
  coup in Nigeria, **1999** 274
  death of, **1998** 220; **1999** 274
  executions of dissidents in Nigeria, **1995** 696–697
Abington Township School District v. Schempp, **1995** 547
Abiola, Moshood K.O., Yoruba leader imprisonment and death, **1999** 273–274
Abortion
  antiabortion violence, attorney general on, **1998** 809–814
  Catholic church, opposition to, **1998** 811–812
  Catholic teaching on, **1995** 145–146, 149–151, 153–155, 157–158, 161
  Democratic Party platform on, **1996** 623–624, 639
  Dole position on, **1996** 496
  Foster nomination and, **1995** 61–62
  Republican Party platform on, **1996** 496–497, 518–519
  UN population conference, **1995** 583
Abraham Lincoln Opportunity Foundation (ALOF), **1997** 6–7
Abrecht, Gary I., on shooting of fellow Capitol police officers, **1998** 516–517
Abubakar, Abdulsalami, Nigerian president, **1999** 274
Acheson, Dean, role in NATO, **1999** 121
Acquired immunodeficiency syndrome. *See* AIDS (acquired immunodeficiency syndrome)
Acupuncture, NIH panel on, **1997** 749–759
ADA. *See* Americans with Disabilities Act (ADA, 1990)
Adams, Gerry
  Northern Ireland peace process, **1999** 755, 758–759
  on Omagh bombing, **1998** 206
  Sinn Fein leader's Great Britain visit, **1998** 204
  visa for U.S. visit, **1995** 728; **1998** 204
Adams v. Richardson, **1995** 245
Adarand Constructors v. Peña, **1995** 307–326, 371, 485–486; **1997** 190, 191, 193, 194; **1998** 855–856

Advertising
  of distilled spirits, on television, **1996** 770–775
  of tobacco products, **1996** 590–591, 596–598; **1997** 38, 332, 334, 336–337
Advertising Council, adult attitudes toward children, **1997** 424, 426; **1999** 386
Advisory Commission on Intergovernmental Relations (ACIR), unfunded mandates legislation, **1995** 142–143
Advisory Committee on Religious Freedom Abroad, report, **1998** 19–29
Affirmative action
  ban, federal appeals court panel on, **1997** 183–194
  California legislation, **1996** 759–763
  Clinton endorsement of, **1995** 483–496, 574–575; **1997** 315
  Clinton presidential debate on, **1996** 728
  Dole opposition to, **1995** 483–484, 574–575
  federal government plans, **1995** 307–326
  in public schools, **1998** 855–868
  student success stories, **1997** 321
Afghanistan
  human rights, **1999** 531–534
  humanitarian aid, **1999** 526–527
  land mine casualties, **1995** 47, 48
  political situation, UN secretary general on, **1999** 524–535
  UN economic sanctions, **1999** 524
  U.S. airstrikes against terrorists, **1998** 555, 586–591
  U.S. economic sanctions, **1999** 525–526
Africa
  AIDS, spread of, **1999** 489–498, 587–588
  Central African refugee crisis, **1996** 809–815
  Clinton state visit, **1998** 159–168, 221; **1999** 54, 428
  conflict in, UN Secretary General on, **1998** 220–232
  Democratic Party platform, **1996** 645
  economic development, **1997** 352–355
  land mine problem, **1995** 47–49, 50–51
  peacekeeping mission of UN High Commissioner for Refugees, **1999** 428–438
  population growth, **1999** 587–588
  Republican Party platform, **1996** 543–544

925

CUMULATIVE INDEX, 1995–1999

Sub-Saharan HIV/AIDS epidemic, **1998**
882–884; **1999** 489
U.S. policy, **1998** 159–168; **1999** 54
African National Congress (ANC), **1996** 250;
1998 164
human rights abuses, **1998** 755–758
Mbeki presidential inauguration, **1999**
297–303
South African Truth and Reconciliation Com-
mission report findings, **1998** 755–758,
769–771
African Nuclear Weapon Free Zone Treaty, **1995**
236, 237
African Trade and Development Act, **1998** 45;
1999 54
African Americans
and cocaine penalties sentencing, **1997**
245–247, 252
teenage birth rates, **1998** 261–262
A.G. Edwards, welfare-to-work program, **1997**
622
Agency for Health Care Policy and Research
(AHCPR), end-of-life care, **1997** 328, 329
Agency for International Development (AID)
Atwood resignation, **1999** 700
Turkey earthquake relief, **1999** 467, 469–471
Agostini v. Felton, **1997** 361–381
Agricultural policy
commodity price supports, **1995** 70–71; **1996**
199–200
Democratic platform on, **1996** 648
farm bill, **1996** 199–203, 696
Republican platform on, **1996** 537–538
Agriculture Department (USDA)
biotechnology in agriculture, secretary Glick-
man on, **1999** 401–411
dietary guidelines, **1996** 3–16
farm bill, secretary Glickman on, **1996**
199–203
food safety initiative, **1997** 690–698
meat inspection rules, **1996** 414–417
Aguilar v. Felton, **1997** 361–381
Ahern, Bertie, Northern Ireland peace agreement, **1998** 203–219; **1999** 753
Aid to Families with Dependent Children
(AFDC), elimination of, **1996** 452; **1997** 618;
1998 357; **1999** 261
AIDS (acquired immunodeficiency syndrome)
in African nations, **1999** 428, 489–498
children with, **1999** 386–387
global epidemic, UN report on, **1998** 878–889
minorities and, **1996** 447–448
prevention and control of, **1995** 65; **1997**
81–93
research
Clinton comments on, **1995** 428, 433,
434–435; **1997** 38, 761
federal programs, **1996** 156–166
Helms opposition to, **1995** 428, 433, 459
programs needed, **1997** 91–92
on "triple therapy," **1997** 81–82
testing, for pregnant women, **1995** 441–452
Air Force (U.S.), Roswell incident, **1997** 395–405
Airplane crashes. *See* Aviation safety
Akayesu, Jean-Paul, genocide trials, **1998** 616
A.L.A. Schechter Poultry Corp. v. U.S., **1995**
187, 192
Alaska, Tongass National Forest, protection of
roadless lands, **1999** 593–594

Albania, political situation, **1997** 360
Albemarle Paper Co. v. Moody, **1998** 450
Albert, Speer, on Turkey's supply of chromite to
Nazi Germany, **1998** 292
Albright, Madeleine K.
Africa, economic assistance, **1999** 430
Armenia-Azerbaijan relations, **1999** 640
chemical weapons treaty, **1997** 195–201
Congo visit, **1997** 880–885
diplomatic posts evaluation, **1999** 690–692
Israel-Palestinian talks, **1999** 891–892, 894
Kosovo peace negotiations, **1999** 135
land mines, **1997** 847
NATO
future of, **1998** 912–919
membership ceremony, **1999** 121, 127–133
North Korea, U.S. relations, **1999** 571–572
nuclear weapons test moratorium, **1999** 603
Panama Canal transfer ceremony, absence
from, **1999** 852–853
religious freedom, **1997** 563; **1998** 19, 21, 23
Rwanda genocidal war, **1999** 861
terrorism, **1998** 587
UN secretary candidates, **1996** 825
UN weapons inspection in Iraq, **1998** 936
U.S. consulate in Vietnam, **1997** 489–492;
1999 475–479
U.S. embassy bombings, **1998** 558, 560–561;
1999 307
U.S. sanctions
against Cuba, **1998** 32
against Iraq, **1997** 770
U.S.-Iran relations, **1998** 689–690
on Zaire leader Kabila, **1998** 161
Alcohol, Tobacco, and Firearms (ATF) Bureau
guns, estimates of number of, **1995** 466–467
National Tracing Center, **1995** 469
Waco incident, **1999** 480
Alcohol use
federal survey results, **1996** 577–578; **1999**
460, 462
health benefits of drinking, **1996** 3–4, 16
liquor advertising on television, **1996** 770–775
Alden v. Maine, **1999** 334, 335, 336–349
Alexander, Duane, child health care, **1997** 425
Alexander, Jane, future of the arts, **1997** 700
Alexander, Kent B., **1996** 447
Algeria, terrorist organizations, **1999** 499
Aliyev, Heydar, **1999** 640
Allchin, James, **1999** 656
Allegheny County v. Greater Pittsburgh ACLU,
1995 399, 401, 402
Allen, Ernie, on sex offenders, **1997** 384
Allen, George, and balanced budgets, **1995** 11
Allen, Paul, **1999** 655
Allen v. Illinois, **1997** 393
Alley, Wayne, **1997** 624
Altman, Drew E., managed cared, **1997** 788
Alvarez, Aida, welfare system, **1997** 620
America Online, indecent materials restrictions,
1997 444
America Reads Challenge, **1997** 35, 64–65; **1998**
77, 88
American Association of Retired Persons
(AARP), health care, **1997** 790
American Automobile Association (AAA),
aggressive driving, **1997** 551
American Bar Association (ABA), independent
counsel legislation, **1999** 168

926

American Campaign Academy, **1997** 10, 15
American Cancer Society (ACS)
  dietary guidelines, **1996** 3, 5
  thyroid cancer and radiation, **1997** 591
  value of mammograms, **1997** 144, 145
American Citizens' Television (ACTV), **1997** 7
American Civil Liberties Union (ACLU)
  affirmative action, **1996** 761–762
  drug testing, of students, **1995** 341
  gay rights, **1996** 286
  on gay rights to march in parade, **1995** 327–335
  Internet and free speech, **1997** 444–458
  Internet pornography ban, **1996** 354–355
  juvenile curfew laws, **1996** 327
  on race-based redistricting ruling, **1995** 372
  school vouchers, **1997** 364
American Constitutional Law Foundation
  (ACLF). *See Meyer v. American Constitutional Law Foundation (ACLF)*
American Council on Education (ACE), teacher
  quality, **1999** 64, 66
American Enterprise Institute, independent
  counsel report, **1999** 168
American Federation of Labor-Congress of
  Industrial Organizations (AFL-CIO)
  Kirkland retirement, **1995** 680–681
  labor movement advances, **1999** 630–638
  Sweeney's election remarks, **1995** 680–685
American Forest and Paper Association, **1999** 595
American Heart Association (AHA), dietary
  guidelines, **1996** 3, 5
American Hospital Association, patient safety, **1999** 782
American Legion, Dole speech on social issues, **1995** 573–580
American Library Association (ALA), Internet
  pornography ban, **1996** 354–355
American Medical Association (AMA)
  end-of-life care education and practice reform, **1996** 329
  labor unions for medical profession, **1999** 633
  medical records privacy, **1997** 583
  physician-assisted suicide
    doctor and patient privilege, **1999** 442
    opposition to, **1996** 124; **1997** 460
American Opportunities Workshop (AOW), **1997** 6–7
American Pain Society, **1997** 328
Americans for Tax Reform, **1998** 894
Americans with Disabilities Act (ADA, 1990)
  and AIDS discrimination, **1998** 378–392
  definition of disability, Supreme Court on, **1999** 317–332
  and EEOC guidelines on mental disabilities, **1997** 127–141
AmeriCorps, **1995** 34, 82, 438; **1997** 35, 40; **1999** 56
  and church volunteers, **1997** 244
  program expansion, **1997** 239
  program objectives, **1997** 243
  rebuilding burnt churches, **1997** 311–312
  training for private sector jobs, **1997** 621
  volunteers helping flood victims, **1997** 243
Ames, Aldrich H., espionage case, **1995** 532–533; **1996** 794
Amir, Yigal, assassin of Yitzhak Rabin, **1995** 689
Amish, religious freedom issues, **1997** 407

Amtrak
  train accident in Arizona desert, **1995** 178
  train accident in Silver Spring, Maryland, **1996** 189–190
ANC. *See* African National Congress (ANC)
Anderson, Gerald, Roswell incident, **1997** 401
Andrews, David, U.S. bombing of Chinese
  embassy, **1999** 307
Angelou, Maya, at Million Man March, **1995** 656
Angola
  conflict in, **1999** 431
  landmine problem, **1995** 48–49
  UN role in, **1995** 355
Annan, Kofi
  Afghanistan
    humanitarian aid, **1999** 526–527
    UN peace negotiations, **1999** 525
  Africa
    conflict in, **1998** 220–232
    UN assistance, **1999** 429
  Congo, war in, **1999** 645–653
  on global economy, **1999** 393
  India, nuclear testing, **1998** 327
  Indonesia, human rights, **1999** 513
  Iraq, UN weapons inspections, **1998** 935, 936
  Kosovo conflict, **1998** 830, 831; **1999** 288
  Rwanda genocidal war, **1998** 222; **1999** 860
  Srebenica massacre, UN response, **1999** 735, 737, 741
  UN secretary general, **1997** 152–153
  UN secretary general appointment, **1996** 824–827
  on worldwide population growth, **1999** 585
Anti-Defamation League, church arson preven-
  tion, **1997** 311
Anti-Drug Abuse Act, **1997** 248, 249, 250
Anti-Personnel Landmine Ban Treaty, **1998** 541
Antitrust, Microsoft Corp. case, **1999** 654–689
Apartheid, South African Truth and Reconcilia-
  tion Commission report, **1998** 755–758
Apfel, Kenneth S., social security reform, **1998** 98
Apparel industry, code of conduct to end sweat-
  shops, **1997** 206–211
Apple, R. W., on issue of morality, **1997** 21
Applewhite, Marshall Herff, Heaven's Gate cult
  leader, **1997** 122–124
Arafat, Yasir
  Israeli-Palestinian peace accord, **1996** 337
  West Bank agreement, **1995** 622–624, 626–628
  Wye River peace agreement, **1998** 742–745, 751–753; **1999** 891–892
Arbour, Louise, Kosovo human rights investiga-
  tions, **1999** 290, 803
Archer, Bill (R-Texas)
  House Speaker elections, **1998** 802
  IRS reform, **1997** 663
  on social security and budget surplus, **1999** 43
Argentina
  aid to Nazi Germany, **1997** 259, 262, 263; **1998** 291, 292
  allied relations and negotiations with, **1998** 295–298
  German assets, **1997** 267
Arias, Arnulfo, president of Panama, **1999** 851
Arizona
  drug use survey, **1999** 464
  medical use of marijuana, **1996** 755–756

Arizonans for Official English v. Arizona, **1997** 189

Arkin, William M., on "smart" weapons, **1997** 494–495

Arlington National Cemetery, Tomb of the Unknowns, disinternment remarks, **1998** 281–283

Armenia
relations with Azerbaijan, **1999** 640–641
shootings in parliament, **1999** 639–642

Armey, Richard (R-Texas)
Chinese nuclear-espionage matter, **1999** 237–238
gift limits to members of Congress, **1995** 701
and Gingrich ethics violations, **1997** 5
health care reform, **1997** 791
legal immigration, **1995** 565
Republican senior leader, **1998** 952

Army (U.S.)
extremist activity in, task force on, **1996** 178–185
sexual harassment in the military, **1997** 654–660

Arnold, Jim, on moon ice findings, **1998** 116, 119

Arson, **1999** 622

Arts and humanities
decency in the arts, Supreme Court on, **1998** 405–418
NEA report on future of, **1997** 699–710

Asia
Democratic Party platform, **1996** 644–645
financial crisis, **1997** 832–843; **1998** 532, 602, 722–734, 923; **1999** 87
Northeast Asia weapons development, **1996** 216–217
Republican Party platform, **1996** 544

Asia-Pacific Economic Cooperation (APEC) group, **1995** 74

al-Assad, Hafez, Syrian president, **1999** 362, 364

Assassinations
al-Sadr, Ayatollah Mohammed Sadeq, **1999** 145
Evers, Medgar, **1995** 456
Habyarimana, Juvenal, **1998** 614; **1999** 863
Kennedy, John F., **1997** 104; **1999** 422
Kennedy, Robert F., **1999** 422
Malcolm X, **1995** 657
Ntaryamira, Cyprien, **1999** 863
Rabin, Yitzhak, **1995** 622, 689–695; **1996** 337; **1998** 742; **1999** 890
Sarkisian, Vazgen, **1999** 639
Uwilingiyimana, Agathe, **1998** 614

Association of Southeast Asian Nations (ASEAN)
Cambodian censure, **1997** 640
future of, **1997** 643–644

Astronomy
age of the universe, **1996** 265–269
birth of stars, **1995** 288–293
Hubble space telescope, **1995** 288–293; **1996** 265–269; **1998** 115
multiplanet solar system, discovery of, **1999** 173–178

Asylum, political
U.S. policy, **1998** 26–28
women, new U.S. rules on, **1995** 276–280

Atef, Mohammad, **1998** 555

Atlantis (space shuttle), **1995** 419–421

Atomic bombs, *Enola Gay* exhibit (Smithsonian Institution), **1995** 55–58

Atomic Energy Act, **1997** 107; **1999** 241

Attorneys general, tobacco settlement, **1998** 842–854

Atwood, J. Brian, resignation from AID, **1999** 700

Austria, euro currency, **1998** 271

Automobile industry, electric automobiles, **1996** 17–20

Automobile safety
aggressive driving, **1997** 550–561
air bag regulations, **1996** 801–806; **1997** 774–779

Aviation safety
air traffic control system, **1997** 114–115, 119–120
airline safety enforcement, GAO report on, **1998** 169–179
Boeing 737 mechanical problems, **1999** 115–116
Brown, Ron, mission crash, **1996** 204–209
Egyptair flight 990 crash, **1999** 113
FAA and airline safety inspections, **1996** 237–246; **1997** 115; **1999** 113–114
GAO report and recommendations, **1997** 113–121
Kennedy, John F., Jr. crash, **1999** 422–427
Swiss Air Flight 111 fire, **1998** 171
TWA flight 800 crash, **1996** 231, 233, 237, 662–663; **1997** 116, 780–786; **1998** 171–172
United Airlines crash, **1999** 116
USAir crash, **1999** 116
ValuJet flight 592 crash, **1996** 237–240; **1997** 113, 116; **1998** 172
White House Commission recommendations, **1997** 116–119
Y2K conversion, **1998** 548, 549

Aviation security
requirements, GAO report on, **1996** 662–671
Transportation Department investigations of, **1999** 114–115
White House Commission recommendations, **1997** 115, 120–121

Aviation Security Advisory Committee, **1996** 664–665

Azerbaijan, relations with Armenia, **1999** 640

Aziz, Tariq, UN weapons inspections, **1997** 768–769

AZT (azidothymidine), therapeutic use with pregnant women, **1995** 441–452

B

Babbitt, Bruce, on endangered species, **1995** 360

Babbitt v. Sweet Home Chapter of Communities for a Greater Oregon, **1995** 359–368

Bacon, Kenneth H., on "smart" weapons, **1997** 494

Bailweg, Lawrence F., **1997** 661–662

Baker, Howard H., Jr.
on independent counsel legislation, **1999** 167–168
National Commission on the Separation of Powers, **1998** 908
tobacco industry lobbyist, **1997** 335

Baker, James, chemical weapons treaty, **1997** 201

Balanced budget
bipartisan agreement, **1997** 602–610; **1998** 801

Clinton plan for, **1996** 53; **1997** 29, 33; **1998** 40
Democratic Party platform, **1996** 627–628
during Clinton administration, **1998** 42–43
and government shutdowns, **1995** 737–745; **1996** 53; **1997** 33, 231, 603; **1998** 501, 800
Republican Party platform, **1996** 505–506
Balanced Budget Act (1997), **1998** 88–89
Balanced budget amendment
bipartisan issue, **1995** 10–11; **1998** 801
Clinton and Republican impasse, **1995** 737–745; **1997** 3
Clinton response, **1995** 32–33; **1996** 24; **1997** 30
Clinton's line-item veto, **1997** 611
Dole support for, **1995** 575
Republican leaders and, **1996** 696
Senate response to, **1995** 165, 169
signing ceremony, **1997** 602–610
Ball, Robert M., social security investments, **1998** 101
Ballot initiatives, Supreme Court on, **1999** 3–14
Baltimore (Maryland), school uniform policy, **1996** 91
Bandelier National Monument (New Mexico), **1995** 124
Banks and banking
Japanese economic crisis, **1998** 534–535
Y2K conversion compliance, **1998** 546, 548
Barak, Ehud
Israel prime minister on new government programs, **1999** 359–367
Israel-Syria peace negotiations, **1999** 890, 891, 896
Baran, Jan, lawyer for Gingrich ethics case, **1997** 4
Barayagwica, Jean-Bosco, **1999** 866
Barbour, Haley, tobacco industry lobbyist, **1997** 335
Barkdale, James, on Microsoft Corp. antitrust case, **1999** 656, 659
Barr, Bob (R-Ga.), House Judiciary Committee impeachment inquiry, **1998** 709–710
Barr, Michael L., on aviation accidents, **1999** 424
Barre, Raymond, euro currency proposal, **1998** 272
Barrett, Thomas M. (D-Wis.), House Judiciary Committee impeachment inquiry, **1998** 711
Barry, Marion S.
at Million Man March, **1995** 656
as figurehead, **1996** 784
as mayor of Washington, **1995** 498
as "race-hustling poverty pimp," **1997** 31
Barshefsky, Charlene, U.S.-China bilateral trade agreement, **1999** 724, 726, 728–734
Barzani, Massoud, Iraq situation report, **1996** 680–686
Baseball, major league
McGwire home run record, **1998** 626–631
Ripken on breaking Gehrig's consecutive game record, **1995** 588–590; **1998** 628–629
Sosa home run record, **1998** 626–627, 626–628
al-Bashir, Omar Hassan, U.S. airstrike in Sudan, **1998** 587
Bates, Tom, California term limits, **1997** 887
Bauer, Gary, same-sex marriages, **1999** 899
Baxter Healthcare, manufacturer of breast implants, **1995** 516
Bazell, W.W., Roswell incident, **1997** 395

Beasley, Michele, on political asylum for women, **1995** 277
Beck, Allen, mental illness of prisoners, **1999** 840
Beckman, John C., space mission failures, **1999** 715
Becton, Julius W., Jr., new superintendent of D.C. schools, **1996** 785
Begin, Menachem, **1998** 744
Belarus, nuclear weapons nonproliferation, **1996** 220, 221
Belgium, euro currency, **1998** 271
Bell, Griffin B., National Commission on the Separation of Powers, **1998** 908, 910
Bell, Robert G., defense policy, **1997** 814
Bellamy, Carol
HIV/AIDS pandemic in Africa, **1999** 489–498
vaccination of children, **1999** 387
on worldwide poverty, **1999** 585
Belo, Carlos Ximenes (bishop), East Timor independence, **1999** 513, 515
Benjamin, Joel, chess champion, **1997** 274
Bennett, Robert F. (R-Utah)
Clinton censure resolution, **1999** 21
Clinton impeachment trial, **1999** 21, 29
medical records security, **1997** 583
Bennett, Robert S., presidential immunity case, **1997** 290
Benton Foundation, public access to communications media, **1999** 371
Benz, Jeffrey G., **1999** 109
Berger, Samuel R. "Sandy"
Chinese nuclear-espionage matter, **1999** 237–238
on Russian nuclear weapons, **1997** 515
Bergier, Jean-François, **1998** 293
Berlin, Fred, on sex offenders, **1997** 384–385
Berliner, Don, Roswell incident, **1997** 400
Berman, Howard L. (D-Calif.), House Judiciary Committee impeachment inquiry, **1998** 703–704
Berthelot, Rene, and European Commission scandal, **1999** 156
Berwick, Donald M., **1999** 781
Bessette, Lauren, death of, **1999** 422
Bhutto, Benazir, **1999** 624
Biafra, independence movement, **1995** 697
Biden, Joseph R., Jr. (D-Del.)
chemical weapons treaty, **1997** 196
on Foster, surgeon general nomination, **1995** 62
nuclear test ban treaty, **1999** 604, 609
Bijur, Peter I., statement on racial slurs of Texaco executives, **1996** 764–769
Bilingual education, California initiative, **1998** 313–319
bin Laden, Osama
embassy bombings, **1998** 555–558; **1999** 53, 525, 691
survives U.S. airstrikes, **1998** 586
Binder, Alan B., on moon ice findings, **1998** 114, 116, 119
Bioethics
cloning research, **1997** 212–220
euthanasia, Catholic teaching on, **1995** 146, 155–158
genetic testing in the workplace, **1998** 63–72
sex selection technique, **1998** 65–66
Biological diversity, genetically altered foods, **1999** 401–411

Biological weapons
  Clinton administration policy, **1998** 49–50
  Gulf War syndrome, **1997** 740–745
  UN weapons inspection in Iraq, **1997** 768;
    1998 934–944
  worldwide proliferation of, **1996** 210–230
Biological Weapons Convention, **1998** 50
Biotechnology, in agriculture, **1999** 401–411
Birch, Elizabeth
  Clinton and gay rights, **1997** 760, 762
  same-sex marriages, **1996** 689
Birth rates. *See under* Teenage pregnancy
Bittman, Robert, Lewinsky scandal investigations, **1998** 567, 569–576
Blackmun, Harry A., gay rights to march, **1995** 327–335
Blacks
  apology for racism to, **1995** 336–338
  college enrollment, **1997** 186
  labor market, **1999** 101–102
  race-based redistricting, **1995** 369–384
Blair, Steven N., on exercise, **1996** 419
Blair, Tony
  at economic summit (Denver), **1997** 342
  on death of Diana (princess of Wales), **1997** 647, 649
  euro currency in Britain, **1999** 76
  on European Commission reforms, **1999** 157
  on greenhouse gas emissions, **1997** 481
  Hong Kong transfer ceremony, **1997** 502
  inaugural election as prime minister, **1997** 277–283
  Northern Ireland peace agreement, **1998** 203–219; **1999** 753–754
Blassie, Michael J., disinterment from Tomb of the Unknowns, **1998** 281–282
Blendon, Robert J., child heath care survey, **1997** 425
Bliley, Thomas J., Jr. (R-Va.), on tobacco regulations, **1995** 672
Blocher, Christoph, **1997** 259
Blumenthal, Sidney, and Clinton impeachment trial, **1999** 17
Blumstein, Alfred
  on carjackings, **1999** 616
  crime reports, **1996** 732–734; **1999** 615
  on homicide rate, **1995** 710
  on juvenile curfew laws, **1996** 327
BMW of North America, Inc. v. Ira Gore, Jr., **1996** 274–283
Board of Education of Central School District No. 1 v. Ball, **1995** 395
Board of Education of Kiryas Joel School v. Grumet, **1997** 362, 366
Board of Education of Westside Community Schools (Dist. 66) v. Mergens, **1995** 392–393, 398
Boaz, David, on computer access, **1999** 370
Boehlert, Sherwood (R-N.Y.), Gingrich resignation, **1998** 802
Bokat, Stephen
  disability, definition of, **1999** 319
  on sexual harassment liability, **1998** 440
Bolling v. Sharpe, **1995** 313
Bonior, David (D-Mich.), and Gingrich ethics violation complaint, **1995** 748, 751; **1996** 839
Bono, Mary (R-Calif.), House Judiciary Committee impeachment inquiry, **1998** 713
Bono, Sonny (R-Calif.), death of, **1998** 41

Booh, Jacques-Roger Booh, **1999** 862
Boren, David, chemical weapons treaty, **1997** 201
Borges, Francisco, NAACP treasurer, **1995** 454
Bork, Robert H.
  Cox fired by, **1998** 906
  Supreme Court nomination rejected, **1998** 696
Bosnia
  civil war, **1995** 717–718; **1998** 827
  Dayton peace agreement, **1999** 735–736
  elections, **1996** 817–818
  NATO peacekeeping mission, **1997** 342; **1998** 49; **1999** 120–121, 286, 735–737
  political situation report, **1996** 816–823
  Republican Party platform, **1996** 540
  UN peacekeeping mission, **1995** 717–726; **1996** 818–819; **1997** 151, 154, 155
  UN role in, **1995** 351
Botha, Pietr W., repressive government in South Africa, **1998** 756–757, 762–763
Botswana, Clinton state visit, **1998** 159
Bouchard, Lucien, Quebec independence, **1998** 592–595
Boucher, Rick (D-Va.), House Judiciary Committee impeachment inquiry, **1998** 704–705
Boutros-Ghali, Boutros
  Bosnian conflict, **1999** 738
  chemical weapons treaty, **1996** 740–743
  International Olympics Committee investigations, **1999** 109
  Rwanda genocidal war, **1999** 861–862
  UN fiftieth anniversary remarks, **1995** 350, 352–353
  UN secretary general
    final statements as, **1996** 824–825, 827–830
    relations with Congress, **1997** 152–153
  UN summit on poverty, **1995** 136
Bowers v. Hardwick, **1996** 285
Bowles, Camilla Parker, **1997** 648
Bowles, Erskine, balanced budget agreement, **1997** 604
Boxer, Barbara (D-Calif.), **1995** 409
Boy Scouts of America, policy on gay members, **1999** 901
Brademus, John, status of the arts, **1997** 700
Bradley, Bill (D-N.J.), retirement from Senate, **1995** 558–562
Brady gun control bill
  proposal to repeal, **1995** 463
  Republican opposition to, **1996** 601
Brady, James S.
  at Democratic Party convention, **1996** 601
  wounded in Reagan assassination attempt, **1995** 463–464
Brady, Sarah, Brady gun control bill, **1995** 463
Bragdon v. Abbott, **1998** 378–392
Brandeis, Louis D., on government, **1997** 626, 627
Branham, Lynn S., sex offenders legislation, **1997** 382
Branzburg v. Hayes, **1998** 401
Brassard, Jacques, Quebec independence, **1998** 594
Brazil, economic conditions, **1998** 76, 722; **1999** 87
Breaux, John B. (D-La.), on Clinton state of the union address, **1995** 26
Breitenstein, A. G., medical records privacy, **1997** 582

Breyer, Stephen G.
  affirmative action, federal government plans,
    1995 309, 323–326
  congressional term limits, **1995** 260
  disability, definition of, **1999** 319, 320, 325–332
  drug testing of students, **1995** 339–346
  endangered species on private lands, **1995**
    359–368
  free speech
    ballot initiatives, **1999** 6
    Internet and, **1997** 445
  gay rights discrimination, **1996** 286
  gun-free school zone, **1995** 184, 190–191,
    196–200
  HIV as a disability, **1998** 379, 388–389
  line-item veto, **1997** 612; **1998** 421, 431–433,
    433–437
  parochial school aid, **1997** 363, 375–380,
    380–381
  physician-assisted suicide, **1997** 461, 472–473,
    478–479
  presidential immunity, **1997** 292
  race-based redistricting, **1995** 371, 380–384;
    1996 370, 381–383, 383–387
  religious freedom, **1997** 408, 417–420
  religious publications, **1995** 386, 393–395
  religious symbols, **1995** 387, 396–404
  sex offenders, right to confine, **1997** 383–384,
    392–394
  sexual harassment, **1999** 215
  states rights, **1999** 333, 345–349
Bribery, of public officials, combating, **1997**
  800–807
Brickman, Lester, **1995** 517
Bridgewater, Bill, **1995** 464
Brimmer, Andrew F., **1996** 784
Bristol-Myers, manufacturer of breast implants,
  1995 516
Broder, David S., on Clinton state of the union
  address, **1995** 24
Bromwich, Michael R., FBI crime laboratory
  report, **1997** 221–228
Bronfman, Edgar, **1997** 262
Brookings Institution, independent counsel
  report, **1999** 168
Brothers to the Rescue, **1996** 93–97
Brown, Curtis, *Discovery* space shuttle mission,
  1998 778–786
Brown, Judie, on embryonic research, **1998** 66
Brown, Lee P., drug-free schools, **1995** 341
Brown, Ronald H.
  Corporate Citizenship Award, **1996** 42
  death of, **1996** 204–209
  on labor-management relations report, **1995**
    15, 17
Brown, Sarah, on teenage pregnancy, **1999** 386
Brown, Willie L., California term limits, **1997**
  887
Brown & Williamson Tobacco Corp., tobacco
  claims settlement, **1997** 331; **1998** 842
Brown v. Board of Education, **1995** 456, 458
Bryant, Ed (R-Tenn.), House Judiciary Commit-
  tee impeachment inquiry, **1998** 708
Bryant, Robert, antiabortion violence, **1998**
  813–814
Buchanan, Patrick J.
  on English as official language, **1995** 573
  as presidential candidate, **1996** 496, 563–564
  at Republican Party convention, **1996** 478

*Buckley v. American Constitutional Law Foun-
  dation (ACLF)*, **1999** 5–14
Buckley v. Valeo, **1998** 435; **1999** 11
Budget deficit
  during Republican administrations, **1997** 605
  reduction
    CEA report on, **1997** 53, 60–61; **1998** 86
    Clinton plan for, **1995** 72–73; **1996** 21, 24,
      51, 52, 65–67; **1997** 50–51; **1998** 74, 77,
      81–82
    and current economic expansion, **1999**
      95–97
    GAO report, **1996** 147–155
    and investment, **1995** 80–81
    zero deficit, **1998** 42
  worldwide, and admission to European Union,
    1998 273
Budget surplus
  Clinton plan for, **1998** 74–75, 98; **1999** 90
  Clinton remarks on, **1999** 350–356
  Congressional Budget Office on, **1998** 500–
    509
  projections, **1999** 42
Buitenen, Paul van, European Commission cor-
  ruption, **1999** 156
Bumpers, Dale (D-Ark.), Clinton impeachment
  trial defense summation, **1999** 20, 29–40
Burg, Avraham, **1999** 362
Burger King, jobs for welfare recipients, **1997**
  34, 622
Burlington Industries, Inc. v. Ellerth, **1998**
  439–442, 453–465
Burma, religious persecution, **1997** 567–568
Burton, Dan (R-Ind.)
  on financial disclosure for members of Con-
    gress, **1995** 701
  Waco incident, **1999** 482
Burundi
  assassination of president Cyprien
    Ntaryamira, **1999** 863
  political situation, **1999** 866–867
  refugees in Tanzania, **1999** 435
Bush, George
  domestic policy, underground nuclear test
    ban, **1999** 601
  economic policy
    budget compromise, **1997** 602
    fighting recession, **1995** 55, 56–57, 61–65
    research and development, **1995** 65
  foreign policy, Vietnam relations, **1995** 473
  National Rifle Association resignation, **1995**
    208–211
  Persian Gulf War, **1995** 55, 59–60
  volunteerism summit, **1997** 40, 238–239,
    240–241
Bush v. Vera, **1996** 368–387
Bushnell, Prudence, U.S. embassy security con-
  cerns, **1998** 556, 557
Buthelezi, Mangosuthu Gatsha, and Zulu-based
  Inkatha Freedom Party, **1995** 102; **1998** 758
Butler, R. Paul, planet explorations and discov-
  ery, **1999** 174, 176–177
Butler, Richard, UN weapons inspections in Iraq,
  1997 768–769; **1998** 936, 937; **1999** 147–148
Butler v. Michigan, **1997** 454
Butts, Calvin O., III, **1995** 337
Buyer, Steve (R-Ind.), House Judiciary Commit-
  tee impeachment inquiry, **1998** 707–708
Byock, Ira, end-of-life care, **1997** 325

Byrd, Robert C. (D-W.Va.)
  Clinton impeachment trial, **1999** 17
  line-item veto, **1997** 612; **1998** 420–421
  nuclear test ban treaty, **1999** 602
  Senate historian, **1998** 153
  on unfunded mandates, **1995** 143
Byrd v. Raines, **1997** 612
Byrnes, James, "speech of hope," **1996** 655, 658

C

Cabana, Robert, **1998** 932
Cady, John R., food safety agency, opposition to,
  1998 523
Caldera, Louis, Korean War massacre, army secretary on, **1999** 552–558
California
  affirmative action, Proposition 209, **1996**
    759–763; **1997** 183–194
  ballot initiatives, **1999** 4
  bilingual education initiative, Proposition 227,
    1998 313–319
  drug use survey, **1999** 464
  immigration, Proposition 187, **1995** 563
  medical use of marijuana, Proposition 215,
    1996 755–758
  taxation and spending limits, Proposition 13,
    1999 4
  term limits, Proposition 140, **1997** 886–891
  welfare reform, **1999** 260–261
Cambodia
  Khmer Rouge demise, State Department on,
    1998 971–975
  land mine casualties, **1995** 47, 48
  political situation after coup, State Depart-
    ment on, **1997** 639–646
  UN role in, **1995** 355
  U.S. aid policy, **1997** 640, 645
Camdessus, Michel
  Asian financial crisis, **1997** 832–843; **1998** 722
  Russian economic crisis, **1998** 604
Campaign finance
  attorney general investigations, **1997** 822–831;
    1998 890–902
  Chinese government and, **1998** 976
  congressional hearings, **1997** 825–826
  during presidential elections, **1997** 21
  reform, **1996** 551, 553–554; **1997** 31, 33,
    826–827; **1998** 50
  reform legislation, **1999** 42, 56
Campbell, Keith, cloning research, **1997** 213,
  214–215
Campolo, Tony, churches and volunteers, **1997**
  243
Canada, Quebec independence, **1998** 592–598
Canady, Charles T. (R-Fla.)
  affirmative action programs, **1995** 485; **1998**
    856–857
  gay rights legislation, **1996** 286
  House Judiciary Committee impeachment
    inquiry, **1998** 706
  same-sex marriages, **1996** 688
  school prayer amendment, **1995** 548
Cancer
  carcinogens in the diet, **1996** 71–79
  deaths declining, NCI report on, **1996** 790–793
Cancer, breast
  mammograms for diagnosis of, **1997** 142–149
  mortality rates, **1996** 791–793; **1997** 142

rescue of South Pole doctor, **1999** 611–613
  treatment with drug tamoxifen, **1998** 194–202
Cancer, lung, mortality rates, **1996** 791–793
Cancer, thyroid, from nuclear testing fallout,
  1997 591–601
Cannon, Christopher B. (R-Utah), House Judiciary Committee impeachment inquiry, **1998**
  712
Capital punishment
  Catholic teaching on, **1995** 146–147, 152–153;
    1999 830
  Justice Department report on, **1999** 828–835
  in Nigeria, hanging of dissidents, **1995**
    696–699
  in South Africa, constitutional ban, **1996** 251
  in South Africa, court ruling on, **1995** 283–287
  for Timothy McVeigh, for Oklahoma City
    bombing, **1997** 626
  in U.S., UN report on, **1998** 183–193
Capitol Square Review v. Pinette, **1995** 385,
  387, 396–404
Capitol (U.S.), service for slain Capitol police-
  men, **1998** 510–517
Capps, Walter (D-Calif.), death of, **1998** 41
Card, David, minimum wage, **1996** 564
Cardin, Benjamin (D-Md.), and Gingrich ethics
  violations case, **1997** 17–19
Carey, Ron
  statement on UPS strike, **1997** 631–634
  Teamsters union president ousted, **1997** 628,
    630–631
Carjackings, **1999** 616
Carlsson, Ingvar, **1999** 861
Carneal, Michael, **1998** 736–737
Carr, Michael, *Galileo* imaging team, **1997** 204
Carrie, Elliott, on crime rates, **1999** 615
Carter, Jimmy
  economic policy, inflation and, **1998** 501
  foreign policy
    Bosnia cease-fire negotiations, **1995** 719
    China relations, **1997** 95
    Panama Canal transfer ceremony, **1999**
      850–855
  volunteerism summit, **1997** 238, 239, 240–241
Cartolini, Nestor Cerpa, Peruvian hostage leader,
  1997 235
Carville, James, on Paula Corbin, **1997** 290
Casper, Gerhard, separation of powers, **1998** 911
Cassell, Christine, end-of-life care, **1997** 325
Cassidy, Edward Idris (cardinal), Holocaust
  repentance report, **1998** 121–130
Castle, Michael N. (R-Del.), **1998** 953
Castro, Fidel, state visit of Pope John Paul II,
  1998 30–31
Catholic church, Holocaust, or "Shoah," repentance, **1998** 121–130
Censorship, decency standards in the arts, **1998**
  405–418
Census Bureau (U.S.)
  aging of U.S. population, **1996** 296–301
  foreign-born population, **1995** 563–569
  health insurance coverage, **1999** 561–567
  immigration report, **1997** 175–182
  income inequality, **1996** 396–400
  measures of well-being report, **1999** 390–400
Centennial Olympic Park (Atlanta), bombing
  incident, **1996** 233, 445–449
Center for Democracy and Technology, medical
  records privacy, **1997** 582

Center for International Security and Cooperation (Stanford University), Chinese technology transfer, **1999** 239–240

Center for Patient Safety, proposed, **1999** 780, 782

Center on Budget and Policy Priorities, income inequality, **1999** 391

Center to Improve Care of the Dying, **1997** 329

Centers for Disease Control and Prevention (CDC)
  AIDS
    cases and deaths, **1997** 81
    HIV infection cases and, **1998** 380
    HIV transmission risk during dental treatment, **1998** 380
    testing of pregnant women, **1995** 441–452
  cigarette smoking, **1999** 539–540
  drug-resistant bacteria and overuse of antibiotics, **1999** 185, 186–187, 190, 192–193, 195
  FoodNet program (foodborne illnesses), **1998** 529–530
  obesity and overeating, **1997** 159–160
  smoking among teenagers, **1998** 845

Central Intelligence Agency (CIA)
  chemical weapons warnings during Gulf War, **1997** 742
  Chinese nuclear-espionage matter, **1999** 238
  creation of, **1997** 811
  Iraq political situation, **1996** 680–686
  Nicholson espionage case, **1996** 794–800
  Roswell incident, **1997** 397
  Russian nuclear testing, **1999** 604
  TWA flight 800 crash, **1997** 780
  U.S. bombing of Chinese embassy, **1999** 306, 309

Chabad-Lubavitch v. Burlington, **1995** 397

Chabad-Lubavitch v. Miller, **1995** 397

Chabot, Steve (R-Ohio), House Judiciary Committee impeachment inquiry, **1998** 709

Chafee, John H. (R-R.I.)
  Clinton impeachment trial, **1999** 20
  war hero, **1999** 39

Chambers, Ray, volunteerism summit, **1997** 243

Chaote, Pat, Reform Party vice-presidential nomination, **1996** 552

Chapman, Clark, *Galileo* imaging team, **1997** 204

Charest, Jean, **1998** 594

Charles (prince of Great Britain)
  at Hong Kong transfer ceremony statement, **1997** 502, 504–505
  on death of Diana, **1997** 647
  royal family affairs, **1997** 648

Chaskalson, Arthur, South African court ruling on death penalty, **1995** 284, 285–287

Chavez-Thompson, Linda
  AFL-CIO union leader, **1995** 681, 683
  race relations panel, **1997** 316, 322

Chavis, Benjamin, Jr., resignation from NAACP, **1995** 453

Chechnya, war in, **1995** 93–94, 99–100; **1996** 432; **1999** 909–916

Chemical weapons
  Clinton administration policy on, **1998** 49–50
  Gulf War syndrome, **1997** 740–745
  UN weapons inspection in Iraq, **1997** 768; **1998** 934–944
  verification issue, **1999** 603
  worldwide proliferation of, **1996** 210–230

Chemical Weapons Convention (CWC)
  Clinton support for, **1995** 358; **1997** 42
  secretary of state on, **1997** 195–201
  Senate ratification, **1998** 50
  Senate ratification fails, **1996** 210–211
  UN secretary general on, **1996** 740–743

Cheney, Daniel, TWA flight 800 crash, **1997** 782

Cheney, Richard B. "Dick"
  chemical weapons treaty, **1996** 741
  nuclear test ban treaty, **1999** 601, 608

Chernomyrdin, Viktor S., Russian economic reform, **1995** 94–95; **1998** 602–605

Chestnut, Jacob J., Capitol policeman slain, **1998** 510–517

Chestnut, Wei Ling (Mrs. Jacob J.), **1999** 44

Chicago Housing Authority (CHA), **1995** 294–301

Child abuse
  HHS report, **1996** 778
  ILO report, **1996** 776–783
  violent crimes against, **1999** 617

Child care, White House Conference on, **1998** 47

Child development, Perot Reform Party nomination speech on, **1996** 560–561

Child health
  AIDS epidemic impact on, **1998** 886–887; **1999** 386–387
  federal funding, **1998** 88
  indicators of, **1999** 388–389
  insurance coverage, **1999** 566–567
  smoking prevention programs, **1999** 49
  surveys on well-being of children, **1997** 424–425
  vaccinations for children, **1999** 387

Child labor
  report, **1996** 776–783
  workplace protections, **1997** 207

Child nutrition, diets of children, **1999** 385

Child support
  case enforcement, **1997** 38, 618
  Democratic Party platform, **1996** 638

Child welfare
  reform, **1996** 457–458
  well-being of children report, **1997** 425; **1999** 384–400

Children
  adult attitudes toward, **1997** 422–443; **1999** 386
  behavior and social indicators, **1999** 389
  dangers and threats to, **1999** 385
  economic security indicators, **1999** 388
  nuclear testing fallout, effect on, **1997** 592–593
  population and family characteristics, **1999** 387–388
  in poverty, **1999** 384–385

Chiles, Lawton (D-Fla.) (1971-1989), on Cuban immigrants, **1995** 204

China, People's Republic of (PRC)
  Clinton-Jiang news conference, **1998** 466–478
  Cultural Revolution, **1997** 95, 97–98
  Gang of Four, **1997** 97–98
  Hong Kong transfer ceremony, **1997** 501–506
  human rights in, **1996** 133–138; **1997** 735–738
  Japan relations, **1998** 540–541
  missile threat to U.S., **1998** 487–488
  North Korean relations, **1999** 577
  nuclear secrets theft, U.S. accusations of, **1999** 235–256, 304
  nuclear weapons development, **1996** 217

population control, **1999** 586–587
religious persecution, **1997** 562, 563, 568–570
technology transfer, **1998** 976–982
Tiananmen Square protest, **1997** 94, 95,
  728–729, 736–737; **1998** 467–468
U.S. bombing of embassy in Yugoslavia, **1999**
  236, 304–316, 726
U.S. relations, **1999** 304–316
  most-favored nations status, **1997** 731
U.S. summit meeting, **1997** 728–739
U.S-China bilateral trade agreement, **1999**
  724–734, 797
Chirac, Jacques
  apology for French complicity with Nazis,
    1995 478–482
  European defense force, **1999** 819
  inaugural address of French president, **1995**
    228–232
  NATO charter with Russia, **1997** 515
  NATO participation of France, **1997** 516
  nuclear nest ban treaty, **1999** 603
  social welfare system, **1997** 341
Chisholm v. Georgia, **1999** 338, 345
Choice in Dying (New York City), **1997** 330
Chopko, Mark, school voucher plans, **1997** 364
Chrétien, Jean
  at economic summit (Denver), **1997** 342
  land mines ban treaty, **1997** 844
  Quebec independence, **1998** 594–595
Christopher, Warren M.
  chemical weapons treaty, **1996** 742
  on land mines, **1995** 46
  NATO expansion plans, **1996** 655–661; **1997**
    515
  Vietnam relations, **1995** 472
Chun Doo Hwan, **1997** 893, 894
Chung, Johnny, **1997** 825, 829
Church Arson Prevention Act (1966), **1997** 301,
  306, 307, 308
Church of Lukumi Babalu Aye, Inc. v. Hialeah,
  1997 421
Church and state separation, parochial school
  aid, **1997** 361–381
CIA. *See* Central Intelligence Agency (CIA)
Cin-Made Co., **1996** 43
Cisneros, Henry G.
  on housing shortages for low-income people,
    1996 167
  and President's Service Summit, **1997** 40
  public housing takeover in Washington (D.C.),
    1995 499
Cities, state of, HUD report on, **1998** 364–377
*City of Boerne v. Flores, Archbishop of San
  Antonio*, **1997** 406–421
City of Cleburne v. Cleburne Living Ctr., **1997**
  191
City of Richmond v. J.A. Croson Co., **1995** 308,
  315–316, 322, 323; **1997** 191, 193; **1998** 862, 867
Civil rights
  Clinton political discourse and citizenship
    speech, **1995** 426–660
  Democratic Party platform on, **1996** 650–652
Clark, Marcia, Simpson prosecutor's rebuttal,
  1995 613, 619–621
Clark, Wesley K., Kosovo crisis, NATO campaign,
  1999 137–138
Clarke, Richard, computer infrastructure secu-
  rity, **1998** 677
Clay, Henry, as Speaker of the House, **1995** 6–7

Clayton, Paul, medical records security, **1997**
  581
Clean Air Act, **1998** 92–93
Clean Water Initiative, **1998** 51
Clinger, William F. (R-Pa.), on unfunded mandates legislation, **1995** 141–142
Clinton, Bill
  on advertising of distilled spirits, **1996**
    770–771, 774–775
  affirmative action endorsement, **1998** 856
  campaigns and elections
    acceptance speech, **1996** 602–603, 609–
      622
    Chinese government contributions, **1999**
      237
    finance practices, **1997** 822–825, 827–831
    finance reform, **1997** 30–31, 33
    postelection statements, **1996** 747–749,
      749–753
    presidential campaign, **1997** 21
    presidential debates, **1996** 707–709,
      709–718, 724–731
  commerce secretary
    Mickey Kantor appointment, **1996** 204
    Ronald Brown, statement on death of, **1996**
      204–209
  on Contract with America, **1995** 427–428, 430
  defense policy
    building defense budget, **1999** 53–54
    chemical and biological weapons, **1998**
      49–50
    computer security, **1996** 312; **1998** 677
    land mines ban treaty, **1997** 844, 846
    military homosexual ban, **1997** 761
    national security issues, **1997** 40–43
    national security needs, **1997** 811, 814
    nuclear nonproliferation treaty, **1995**
      233–238
    nuclear test ban treaty, **1999** 600–607
    security abroad, **1995** 38–40
    U.S. role, **1996** 31–32
    weapons development and nonproliferation
      policy, **1996** 227–228
  domestic policy
    affirmative action endorsement, **1995**
      483–496, 574–575
    antiterrorism bill, **1996** 231–236
    apparel workplace investigations, **1997**
      206–211
    aviation security, **1996** 662–664
    child care programs, **1998** 47–48
    church arson prevention, **1997** 303, 306,
      310, 311
    consumer product liability, **1996** 275–276
    crime bill, **1995** 33–34; **1996** 29; **1997** 39
    drug control policy, Dole challenge to, **1996**
      572
    farm bill, **1996** 199
    health care reform, **1995** 74–75; **1998** 46–
      47
    juvenile curfews, **1996** 325
    patients' bill of rights, **1999** 562–563
    proposals, **1998** 39–40
    same-sex marriages, **1996** 687–690; **1997**
      761
    tobacco claims settlement, **1997** 331–332,
      335
    unfunded mandates legislation, **1995**
      141–145

volunteerism summit, **1997** 40, 238–244
welfare reform, **1995** 25, 74–75; **1996**
  450–461; **1997** 33–34, 617–622; **1998** 46,
  356–357
economic policy
  balanced budget, **1995** 24–25, 32–33; **1996**
    53; **1997** 30, 33, 602–605; **1998** 40, 77
  balanced budget amendment, signing cere-
    mony, **1997** 605–608
  budget deficit reduction, **1998** 77
  budget impasse, **1995** 737–745
  budget surplus, **1998** 502; **1999** 350–356
  corporate responsibility, **1996** 41–42
  Democratic convention speech, **1996**
    610–612
  expanding the middle class, **1995** 34–38
  minimum wage advocate, **1996** 563–569
economic reports, **1995** 69–76; **1996** 50–54;
  1997 52–54; **1998** 73–79; **1999** 85–92
economic summits, Denver, **1997** 341–342
education policy
  Democratic convention speech on, **1996**
    612–613
  education and training programs, **1999** 53
  inaugural address on, **1997** 24–25
  national education standards, **1997** 29, 30,
    34–35
  state of the union address on, **1997** 34–37;
    1998 43–44; **1999** 46–48
  uniforms in public schools, **1996** 84
environmental policy, **1996** 30–31; **1997** 39;
  1998 51–52
  Everglades restoration project, **1996** 80–83;
    1997 39
  pesticide regulation reform, **1996** 467–
    470
  Utah's Red Rocks region preservation, **1997**
    39
executive orders
  security clearances, **1995** 532–545
  striking workers, **1995** 129–133
foreign policy
  activist policy, **1999** 699–710
  African state visit, **1998** 159–168, 221; **1999**
    54, 428
  Bosnia, NATO peacekeeping mission, **1995**
    717–726; **1996** 818–819; **1998** 49
  Chechnya war, **1999** 913
  chemical weapons treaty, **1997** 195,
    196–197
  China
    apology for U.S. bombing of Chinese
      embassy, **1999** 304
    news conference, **1998** 466–478
    summit meeting, **1997** 728–739
  Cuba, boat people agreement, **1995** 203–
    207
  Cuban airline attack response, **1996** 95–97
  Democratic convention acceptance speech,
    1996 621–622
  East Timor, UN peacekeeping forces, **1999**
    513
  Indonesia, political situation, **1999** 718–723
  Iraq, air strikes against, **1998** 934–944
  Israel, eulogy for Yitzhak Rabin, **1995** 692
  Israel-Syria peace negotiations, **1999**
    894–895, 897
  Kosovo, air war against Serbian forces,
    1999 134–143

Middle East
  West bank agreement, **1995** 622, 625–626
  Wye River peace agreement, **1998**
    747–749, 750; **1999** 52–53, 700
Northern Ireland, peace efforts, **1995**
  727–733; **1998** 204
peacekeeping missions, **1999** 52–53
on religious freedom, **1998** 19, 22–23
Russia, economic crisis, **1998** 601–613
Rwanda genocidal war, U.S. apology for
  inaction, **1999** 860–861
Turkey, visit after earthquake, **1999** 467
UN secretary general, statement on, **1996**
  824–825, 826–827
U.S. embassy bombings, **1998** 558, 561–563
Vietnam, diplomatic relations, **1995**
  472–477
Foster nomination, **1995** 67–68
gay rights, speech to Human Rights Campaign,
  1997 760–766
government reform, reinventing government,
  1995 30–31
health care policy
  AIDS research, **1995** 428, 433, 434–435
  consumers bill of rights, **1997** 787
human radiation experiments, apology for,
  1995 633–638
impeachment trial, **1999** 15–40, 351
inaugural addresses, **1997** 20–26
Korean War veterans memorial dedication,
  1995 506, 509–511
medical research, **1997** 37–38
Nazi Germany, investigations into neutral aid
  to, **1997** 257–272
on Oklahoma City bombing, **1995** 176–177
political discourse and citizenship speech,
  1995 426–440
presidency
  approval ratings, **1999** 42
  censuring the president, **1998** 633, 699
  line-item veto, **1997** 611–616
on race-based redistricting, **1995** 371
racism
  commencement speech on, **1997** 314–324
  and inaugural address, **1997** 22
  pleas to end in America, **1995** 646–654;
    1997 22, 29, 315
  race initiative, State of the Union address
    on, **1999** 56–57
Schulz, Charles (cartoonist), retirement, statement on, **1999** 859
security
  clearances for government employees,
    1995 532–545
  Pennsylvania Avenue closing, **1995** 254–258
  shooting of Capitol policemen, **1998**
    515–516
sexual harassment suit, **1997** 21, 290–298;
  1998 39, 565, 633–634, 638–639, 962; **1999**
  16, 21–22
space program
  support for, **1996** 471
  talk with woman astronaut Shannon Lucid,
    1996 691–694
state of the union addresses, **1995** 24–42;
  1996 21–35; **1997** 29–44; **1998** 38–54; **1999**
  41–57
terrorism, U.S. airstrikes against terrorists,
  1998 586–591

trade policy
"fast-track" negotiations, **1997** 612; **1998** 75
and labor practices, **1998** 45
market expansion, **1997** 53–54
NAFTA, remarks on, **1997** 541–549
WTO meeting in Seattle, **1999** 799
UN fiftieth anniversary remarks, **1995** 350–358
Waco compound incident, **1995** 293–301
White House Travel Office probe, **1997** 21
Whitewater investigation, **1997** 21; **1998** 633
World War II fiftieth anniversary commemoration, **1995** 216–221
Clinton, Hillary Rodham
Democratic convention (1996), **1996** 602
gays in the military, **1999** 900
remarks at UN Conference on Women, **1995** 581–587
Starr investigation, **1998** 566
Whitewater investigation, **1996** 22, 839; **1997** 21; **1998** 393–394; **1999** 22
Clinton v. City of New York, **1998** 419–437
Clinton v. Jones, **1997** 290–298
Cloning
of humans, **1997** 213–214, 341, 351
research, **1997** 212–220
Coats, Dan (R-Ind.), timing of U.S. airstrikes, **1998** 587–588
Coble, Howard (R-N.C.), House Judiciary Committee impeachment inquiry, **1998** 704
Coburn, Tom (R-Okla.), physician-assisted suicide, **1999** 442
Cocaine
sentencing for sales of, **1997** 245–254
use in U.S., **1996** 575–576, 579; **1999** 460, 463
See also Crack cocaine
Cochran, Johnnie L., Simpson defense attorney's closing arguments, **1995** 613, 615–618
Cohen, Eliot, "smart" weapons performance, **1996** 403
Cohen, William S. (defense secretary)
antiharassment training for military personnel, **1999** 900
appointment, **1996** 673
burial at sea of John F. Kennedy Jr., **1999** 424
cost-cutting measures, **1997** 812
defense spending, **1999** 819
Gulf War syndrome investigations, **1997** 741
Iraq, air strikes against, **1998** 936–937
Kosovo, NATO air strikes, **1999** 127
NATO expansion, **1997** 516
North Korean missile threat, **1999** 820
Panama Canal, U.S. Policy, **1999** 852
sexual harassment and discrimination in the military, **1997** 656
Tomb of the Unknowns, disinterment remarks, **1998** 281–283
U.S. embassy bombings, **1998** 558, 559–560
women in the military, **1998** 335–336
Cohen, William S. (R-Maine)
limits on gifts to members of Congress, **1995** 701
retirement from Congress, **1995** 558–559
Cohen v. Jenkintown Cab Co., **1998** 398, 402, 404
Cole, James M.
special counsel appointment, **1995** 749
special counsel report on Gingrich ethics violations, **1997** 3–19
Cole, Philip, cancer death rates, **1996** 790

Coleman, Russell, death penalty case, **1998** 185–186
Coles, Matthew, and Americans with Disabilities Act, **1998** 380
College Savings Bank v. Florida Prepaid Postsecondary Ed. Expense Bd., **1999** 334, 340
Colleges and universities
accreditation reform, **1998** 5, 17
affirmative action in California, **1996** 759–763; **1997** 186
computer-related field graduates, **1997** 670
costs of higher education, **1998** 3–18, 43–44
HOPE scholarship program, **1998** 43, 78, 87; **1999** 46
minority enrollment, **1997** 186
Pell Grant scholarships, **1998** 43, 87
police corps opportunities, **1997** 244
segregation, Southern Education Foundation report on, **1995** 239–253
student aid programs, **1996** 115–117; **1998** 18
tuition tax credit proposal, **1997** 30, 36; **1998** 87
Colorado
ballot initiatives legislation, **1999** 3–14
gay rights legislation, **1996** 284–295, 689
Colorado for Family Values, gay rights legislation, **1996** 285
Columbine High School (Littleton, Colo.), shooting incident, **1999** 179–184, 615
Colwell, Rita, on South Pole emergency rescue operation, **1999** 611–613
Combest, Larry (R-Texas)
government secrecy, **1997** 103
intelligence community, **1996** 796
Commerce Department
secretary Mickey Kantor appointment, **1996** 204–209
secretary Ronald Brown, death of, **1996** 204–209
technology worker shortage, **1997** 669–678
Y2K preparations, **1999** 760–768
Commission on the Future of Worker-Management Relations, report of, **1995** 15–23
Commission on Protecting and Reducing Government Secrecy, report, **1997** 103–112
Commission to Assess the Ballistic Missile Threat to the United States (Rumsfeld Commission), **1998** 481–499
Communications Decency Act (CDA; 1996), **1996** 353; **1997** 444–458
Community Empowerment Act, **1997** 71
Compassion in Dying, **1997** 462
Comprehensive Environmental Response, Compensation, and Liability Act (1980), **1995** 113
Comprehensive Nuclear Test Ban Treaty (CNTBT), **1995** 234–237, 553–557; **1998** 49
postponed by India and Pakistan nuclear testing, **1998** 326, 329
ratification defeated by Congress, **1999** 43, 53, 600–610, 699, 819
Republican Party platform opposition to, **1996** 542
Computers
chess victory of IBM computer, **1997** 273–276
digital divide in access to, **1999** 368–383
E-rate program, **1999** 371
medical records security, **1997** 580–587
Microsoft Corp. monopoly case, **1999** 654–689
security, GAO report on, **1998** 676–686

security issues, **1997** 711–720
technology workers, shortage of, **1997** 669–678
threats to Pentagon systems, **1996** 312–324
year 2000 (Y2K) conversion, **1997** 534–540; **1998** 543–554; **1999** 51, 760–768
See also Internet
Conboy, Kenneth, **1997** 631
Conference on Urgent Actions for Nuclear Non-Proliferation and Disarmament, **1998** 541
Congo, Republic of
conflict in, **1999** 428, 430, 431, 435–436, 645–653
humanitarian situation, **1999** 649–650
Kabila leadership, **1998** 161
Lusaka cease-fire agreement, **1999** 434, 436, 646–647, 647–649
political situation, **1997** 877–885; **1998** 220
UN peacekeeping mission, **1997** 151, 154, 155, 156
See also under its earlier name Zaire
Congress
close of 104th Congress, congressional leaders on, **1996** 695–703
religion and congressional powers, **1997** 406–421
Republican control of
first one hundred days, House Leaders on, **1995** 165–175
opening remarks, **1995** 3–14
resignations, Packwood speech, **1995** 592–599
retirements, **1995** 558–559
term limits, **1995** 259–275
unfunded mandates legislation, **1995** 141–145
U.S. Vietnam policy, **1995** 474–475
See also House of Representatives; Senate
Congress of National Black Churches, **1997** 304, 306
Congressional Black Caucus, cocaine penalties, sentencing for, **1997** 247
Congressional Budget Office (CBO)
budget surplus, **1998** 500–509
cost of unfunded federal mandates, **1995** 141, 142, 144
Congressional ethics
Gingrich House ethics violations, **1995** 746–751; **1996** 838–849; **1997** 3–19, 603
limits on gifts to members, **1995** 700–709
Connerly, Ward, affirmative action, **1996** 761; **1997** 186, 317
Consolidated Edison Co. v. NLRB, **1995** 198
Constantine, Thomas A., warning letter to doctors on prescribing drugs for suicide, **1997** 462
Constitution (South Africa), text of new constitution, **1996** 249–264
Constitution (U.S.)
Article I, commerce clause, gun-free school zone, **1995** 183–200; **1999** 335
First Amendment
establishment clause
parochial school aid, **1997** 361–381
religion in schools, **1995** 546–547
religious publications, **1995** 386, 388–395
religious symbols, **1995** 387, 396–404
free speech
ballot initiative petitions, **1999** 5
decency in the arts, **1998** 405–418
gay rights to march, **1995** 327–335
on the Internet, **1997** 444–458

Internet pornography ban, **1996** 353–361
religious publication, **1995** 385–395
religious symbols, **1995** 385, 387, 396–404
religious freedom, **1997** 406–421
Fourth Amendment, drug searches, **1995** 339–349
Tenth Amendment, reserved powers, congressional term limits, **1995** 259–275
Eleventh Amendment, states' rights, immunity from suits, **1999** 333–356
Fourteenth Amendment
due process
damages for consumer product liability, **1996** 274–283
physician-assisted suicide, **1996** 125–126; **1997** 459–479
religious freedom, **1997** 406–421
sex offenders, right to confine, **1997** 382–394
equal protection
affirmative action, **1995** 307–326; **1997** 183–194; **1998** 855–868
gay rights, **1996** 284–295
physician-assisted suicide, **1996** 123–124; **1997** 329
redistricting, race-based, **1995** 369–384; **1996** 368–387
religious freedom, **1997** 406–421
double jeopardy clause, sex offenders, right to confine, **1997** 382–394
ex post facto clause, sex offenders, right to confine, **1997** 382–394
free exercise clause, religious freedom, **1997** 406–421
Consumer price index, **1997** 59; **1998** 73, 74, 79
for 1998, **1999** 86
projections for 1996 to 1998, **1996** 69
Consumers
health care bill of rights, **1997** 787–799
product liability, Supreme Court on, **1996** 274–283
Contraception, Catholic teaching on, **1995** 145–146, 149–151
Contract with America
CEA challenges to, **1995** 70
Clinton comments on, **1995** 427–428, 430
during first one hundred days of Congress, **1995** 165–167
Gingrich comments on, **1995** 4, 8–9, 168, 170
Gingrich strategic plan, **1998** 696, 800
and line-item veto, **1998** 419
unfunded mandates legislation, **1995** 141–142
Contracts, government, striking workers and, **1995** 129–133
Controlled Substances Act, **1997** 459, 462; **1999** 442
Convention on Biological Diversity, **1999** 403
Convention on Conventional Weapons (CCW), **1995** 52–53, 54; **1997** 845
Convention on the Safety of United Nations and Associated Personnel, **1998** 541
Conyers, John, Jr. (D-Mich.)
church arson prevention, **1997** 306
on Clinton impeachment, **1998** 697
House Judiciary Committee impeachment inquiry, **1998** 701–702
Starr report public release, **1998** 636
Cook, Richard, space mission failures, **1999** 714

Cook, Robin, Rushdie death threat lifted, **1998** 690–691

Cook, Suzan Johnson, race relations panel, **1997** 317, 322; **1998** 668

Coomaraswamy, Radhika, Afghanistan, human rights, **1999** 527

Cooper Institute for Aerobics Research, physical activity report, **1996** 419–420

Cooperative Threat Reduction (CTR) program, **1996** 143, 228–230

Copyright, agreement with Vietnam, **1997** 490

Corder, Frank Eugene, **1995** 255

Corporate mergers, FTC Chairman on, **1998** 338–353

Corporate Responsibility, Conference on, **1996** 41–49

Corporations
  responsibility, **1996** 633
  sponsorship of national parks, **1996** 582

Costantino, Joseph, tamoxifen trials, **1998** 198–200

Coulson, Danny O., Waco incident, **1999** 481

Council of Economic Advisers (CEA), annual reports (Clinton), **1995** 69–71, 76–91; **1996** 50–51, 55–70; **1997** 50–52, 54–73; **1998** 73–76, 79–97; **1999** 85–88, 92–102

Council of State Governments, position on ballot initiatives, **1999** 5

Council on Food Safety, establishment of, **1998** 523

Courts, federal
  impeachment of judges, **1999** 18
  judicial vacancies, **1998** 48
  Republican Party platform reforms, **1996** 515–516

Courts, federal appeals
  affirmative action ban panel, **1997** 183–194
  California term limits, **1997** 886–891
  Internet pornography ban, **1996** 353–361
  Microsoft Corp. antitrust case, **1999** 654–689
  physician-assisted suicide, **1996** 121–132

Cox, Archibald, special prosecutor fired, **1998** 906

Cox, Christopher (R-Calif.)
  Chinese technology transfer, **1998** 977, 979–982
  House committee on national security and theft of nuclear secrets chair, **1999** 236

Cox committee. *See* House Select Committee on U.S. National Security and Military/Commercial Concerns with the People's Republic of China

Cox, Patrick, on European Commission, **1999** 157

Crack cocaine
  epidemic ebbing, **1997** 682
  users, **1999** 460

Craig, Gregory B., Clinton impeachment trial, **1999** 19

Craig, Larry (R-Idaho), nuclear testing fallout, **1997** 591

Crash at Corona (Berliner and Friedman), **1997** 400

Cresson, Edith, European Commission corruption, **1999** 156–157

Crime
  bribery of public officials, combating, **1997** 800–807
  Clinton proposals, **1995** 33–34; **1996** 29–30; **1997** 39

counterfeiting of U.S. currency, **1996** 98–105
  Democratic Party platform, **1996** 634–636
  Dole convention speech on, **1996** 492–493
  Republican Party platform, **1996** 521–524

Crime in the United States (FBI report), **1995** 710–716; **1996** 732–739; **1997** 681–689; **1998** 869–877; **1999** 614–622

Crime statistics
  FBI report on, **1995** 710–716; **1996** 732–739; **1997** 681–689; **1998** 869–877; **1999** 614–622
  trends for children, **1999** 384

Criminal justice system
  sentencing for cocaine penalties, **1997** 245–254
  Simpson trial, **1995** 611–621

Critical Infrastructure Protection, President's Commission on, **1997** 711–720

Croatia
  civil war, **1998** 827
  Ustasha regime wartime treasury, **1998** 293, 310–312

Crowe, William J.
  embassy security, **1999** 690, 691
  on nuclear test ban treaty, **1998** 49

Cruzan v. Director, Missouri Dept. of Health, **1996** 122, 127, 130; **1997** 465, 471

Cuba
  boat people agreement, **1995** 203–207
  civilian airplanes attack, **1996** 93–97; **1998** 33
  Hurricane Georges damage, **1998** 790
  religious freedom, **1997** 564, 571–572
  religious freedom, papal address on, **1998** 30–37
  travel restrictions, **1995** 205
  U.S. economic sanctions, **1995** 204; **1996** 95–97; **1998** 30, 32–33

Cults
  Branch Davidian sect, **1995** 177, 209; **1996** 362; **1997** 123; **1999** 480–488
  Heaven's Gate mass suicide, **1997** 122–126
  Jonestown (Guyana) suicide, **1997** 123

Cummins, Anthony, **1997** 407

Cuomo, Andrew M., affordable housing, **1999** 392

Cuomo, Mario M., at Democratic Party convention, **1996** 601–602

Curran, James W., voluntary AIDS testing for pregnant women, **1995** 442

Currency
  counterfeiting of U.S., **1996** 98–105
  "Euro" coins and bills, **1998** 271–280

Currie, Betty, Lewinsky scandal, **1998** 574–576, 583, 635, 644–645, 650–651

Currie, Nancy J., **1998** 931

Cyprus
  political situation, **1997** 360
  Republican Party platform on, **1996** 541

Czech Republic, NATO membership, **1997** 514, 516; **1999** 119, 120, 122–124

D

Daily, Edward, Korean War massacre incident, **1999** 552–553

D'Alema, Massimo, **1999** 913

D'Alessandro, David, olympics bribery scandal, **1999** 107

Daley, William
  computer access initiative, **1999** 371
  Panama Canal transfer ceremony, **1999** 853

Dallaire, Romeo A., **1999** 862
D'Amato, Alfonse M. (R-N.Y.)
    neutral aid to Nazi Germany, **1997** 262
    Whitewater investigations, **1996** 839
Dan, Wang, **1996** 134
Danforth, John C., Waco investigation, **1999** 165,
    480, 482–488
Darden, Christopher, Simpson prosecutor's
    rebuttal, **1995** 612, 618–619
Daschle, Tom (D-S.D.)
    104th Congress
        first one hundred days, Democratic
            response, **1995** 165, 174–175
        remarks on closing of, **1996** 698–699
    nuclear test ban treaty, **1999** 602
    Starr report, **1998** 633
Dash, Samuel
    Democratic counsel resignation, **1998** 699
    on independent counsel legislation, **1999** 168
Davis, LaShonda, **1999** 216
Davis v. Monroe County Board of Education,
    1999 216–234
De Klerk, Frederick W.
    bombing cover-up charges, **1998** 757
    death penalty and, **1995** 283–284
    National Party withdrawal from South African
        coalition government, **1996** 251
    South African government leader, **1999**
        297–298
    South African human rights issues, **1998** 756
de Mello, Vieira, East Timor independence, **1999**
    511
de Tocqueville, Alexis, on the Congress, **1995**
    6–7
Dean, Richard, **1996** 33–34
Death and dying, end-of-life care report, **1997**
    325–330
Death penalty. *See* Capital punishment
Death rates. *See* Mortality rates
Defenders of Wildlife, **1995** 360
Defense Base Closure and Realignment Act
    (1990), **1995** 410
Defense Base Closure and Realignment Commis-
    sion, military base closings, **1995** 407–418
Defense contractors, corporate mergers, **1998**
    341
Defense Department
    base closings, **1995** 407–418
    computer security, **1996** 312–324
    computer system inventory, **1999** 762
    Cooperative Threat Reduction (CTR) program,
        1996 143, 228–230
    cost-cutting measures, **1997** 811–812
    military construction bills, **1997** 613
    nuclear weapons proliferation report, **1996**
        210–230
    terrorist bombing in Saudi Arabia, **1996**
        672–679
    Tomb of the Unknowns disinternment
        remarks, **1998** 281–283
    Y2K conversion, **1999** 762
Defense Information Systems Agency (DISA),
    computer security, **1996** 313, 315–316, 322, 323
Defense policy
    European defense force, **1999** 817–827
    Republican Party platform on, **1996** 541–543
Defense spending
    Clinton proposal to increase, **1999** 53–54
    cost-cutting measures, **1997** 811–812
    Dole support for, **1995** 576

DeGeneres, Ellen, **1997** 761
Dehr, Donald, **1999** 109
Delahunt, Bill (D-Mass.), House Judiciary Com-
    mittee impeachment inquiry, **1998** 709
Delaney, James J. (D.-N.Y.), and carcinogens in
    food, **1996** 73, 467
DeLay, Tom (R-Texas)
    Clinton campaign contributions, **1999** 237
    Clinton resignation campaign, **1998** 954
    and Gingrich ethics violations, **1997** 4, 5
    Republican senior leader, **1998** 952
Dellinger, Walter E. III
    on affirmative action, **1997** 185
    on physician-assisted suicide, **1996** 124
Dellums, Ronald V. (D-Calif.), praise from Gin-
    grich, **1995** 4, 8
Demining Assistance Program, **1995** 47–48
Demirchian, Karen, shooting of, **1999** 639
Democratic Party
    campaign finances
        attorney general investigations, **1998**
            890–902
        Chinese contributions to, **1997** 825
    Gephardt comments on role of, **1995** 6
    platform, **1996** 623–652
Democratic Party convention (Chicago, 1996),
    1996 600–622
Deng, Francis M., Chechnya war, **1999** 914–
    916
Deng Xiaoping
    and GATT, **1999** 725
    president Jiang Zemin on death of, **1997**
        94–100, 728
Dennis, W. Glenn, Roswell incident, **1997** 396
"The Deputy" (Hochhuth), **1998** 123
Deri, Aryeh, Israeli Shas Party leader, **1999** 360,
    361
DeSeve, G. Edward, computer security issues,
    1998 678
Detroit Bank v. U.S., **1995** 313
Deutch, John
    computer security, **1996** 312; **1997** 711–712
    government secrecy, **1997** 103
    Iraq situation report, **1996** 680–686
    national security, **1999** 502–503
    Nicholson espionage case, **1996** 794–800
Developing countries
    economic aid, **1997** 481–482
    economic situation, **1999** 392–394
DeWaal, Caroline Smith, food safety agency,
    1998 523
Diabetes
    and job accommodations, **1998** 380–381
    research and treatment, **1997** 217–218
Diana (princess of Wales)
    death of, **1997** 647–653; **1999** 422
    land mines ban, **1997** 845
Dickey, Jay (R-Ark.), embryonic research fund-
    ing, **1998** 66
Dickey, Nancy, medical safety, **1999** 781
Dicks, Norman (D-Wash.), Chinese technology
    transfer, **1998** 977, 979–982; **1999** 236
Diet
    and carcinogens, **1996** 71–79
    federal dietary guidelines, **1996** 3–16
    and health, **1997** 160–161
    obesity, Surgeon general's report on, **1997** 167
    obesity and overeating, **1997** 159–160
Dillingham, Gerald L., FAA and airline safety
    inspections, **1996** 239, 240–246

Dillingham, Steven D., on FAA procedures, **1997** 114

DiMaggio, Joe, baseball record, **1995** 588–589

Dingell, John D. (D-Mich.), patients' bill of rights, **1999** 562

Disabled persons
definition of, Supreme Court on, **1999** 317–332
EEOC employer guidelines on mental disabilities, **1997** 127–141
HIV-positive people, Supreme Court on, **1998** 378–392

Disaster relief
floods of Red River (North Dakota and Minnesota), **1997** 229–233
Hurricane Mitch relief effort, UN report on, **1998** 789–798

Discrimination, job
definition of disabled, Supreme Court on, **1999** 317–332
EEOC employer guidelines on mental disabilities, **1997** 127–141
and sexual harassment, **1998** 438

Diseases
drug-resistant infections and, **1999** 185–199
Gulf War syndrome, **1997** 740–745
infectious diseases, **1996** 302–311; **1997** 348–349
See also Infectious diseases

Distilled Spirits Council of the United States (DISCUS), on liquor advertising on television, **1996** 770–775

District of Columbia
federal support for, **1998** 51
financial crisis, **1995** 497–505
financial crisis in schools, **1996** 784–789
home rule, **1995** 497, 500
home rule charter, **1995** 497
Korean War veterans memorial, **1995** 506–511

District of Columbia Financial Responsibility and Management Assistance Authority, school crisis report, **1996** 784–789

Ditton, Paula, mental illness of prisoners, **1999** 839

Dixon, Alan J. (D-Ill.), military base closings, **1995** 408

Dixon, Julian C. (D-Calif.), **1995** 499

Doctors Without Borders (Medicins sans Frontieres), **1999** 288, 491

Dodd, Thomas J. (D-Conn.) (1953-1957; 1959-1971), Clinton presidential nomination speech, **1996** 602

Dohrn, Beatrice, same-sex marriages, **1999** 899

Dolan, Michael P.
apology to taxpayers, **1998** 131
IRS disputes with taxpayers, **1997** 662

Dole, Elizabeth, Republican Party convention speech, **1996** 479

Dole, Robert (R-Kan.)
affirmative action, **1995** 483–484, 574–575; **1996** 759
Clinton state of the union, Republican response to, **1996** 21–23, 35–38
Congress
limits on gifts to members of, **1995** 701, 702
resignation from Senate, **1996** 270–273
term limits, **1995** 259
defense policy, chemical weapons treaty, **1996** 211, 742

domestic policy
abortion issue, **1996** 496
consumer product liability, **1996** 275–276
drug prevention programs, **1996** 570, 572
social issues speech, **1995** 573–580
on striking workers, **1995** 130
tobacco sales to children, **1996** 592
welfare reform, **1996** 451
economic policy, minimum wage, **1996** 565
on Farrakhan and Million Man March, **1995** 647, 657
foreign policy
Bosnia peacekeeping mission, **1998** 49
chemical weapons treaty, **1997** 196, 197
U.S.-Vietnam relations, **1995** 472
Foster nomination, **1995** 63
Gingrich supporter, **1997** 5
independent counsel legislation, **1999** 168
presidential campaign, **1997** 21
debates, **1996** 707–709, 709–718, 724–731
postelection statement, **1996** 747–749, 753–754
Republican convention acceptance speech, **1996** 478–480, 486–495
war hero, **1999** 39
World War II service record, **1996** 31

Dombeck, Mike, national forest road construction moratorium, **1999** 592, 594–595

Domenici, Pete V. (R-N.M.)
immigration policy, **1996** 636–637
mental health treatment, **1996** 389–390
war hero, **1999** 39

Dominican Republic, hurricane damage and relief efforts, **1998** 789, 790

Donahue, Thomas R., **1995** 681, 683

Dorgan, Byron (D-N.D.), nuclear test ban treaty, **1999** 601–602

Dow Chemical, breast implants lawsuits, **1995** 517

Dow Corning, manufacturer of breast implants, bankruptcy of, **1995** 515, 516, 517

Dowd, Edward, Waco incident, **1999** 483

Downing, Wayne, Saudi Arabia bombing investigation, **1996** 673–674, 675–679

DPRK (Democratic People's Republic of Korea). *See* North Korea

Drug enforcement
Clinton administration proposals, **1997** 39
Democratic Party platform, **1996** 635–636
Republican Party platform, **1996** 524–525

Drug Enforcement Administration (DEA), warnings to doctors on prescription drugs for suicide, **1997** 459, 462–463; **1999** 441, 442

Drug testing, random, **1995** 339–349

Drug trafficking
prevention programs, **1997** 350
sentencing for cocaine penalties, **1997** 245–254

Drug use
in Arizona, **1999** 464
in California, **1999** 464
declining, **1998** 48
federal surveys, **1996** 570–579; **1999** 459–464
illicit drug use, **1999** 461–462
needle-exchange programs for addicts, **1997** 81, 82, 87–88
prevention programs, **1996** 30
trends in new use, **1999** 463–464

Drugs
    antibiotics and drug-resistant bacteria, **1999**
    185–199
    generic AIDS drugs, **1999** 491–492
Duberstein, Kenneth, International Olympics
    Committee investigations, **1999** 108, 109
Duffus, James III, testimony on National Park
    Service, **1995** 120–128
Duisenberg, Willem F.
    European Central Bank president appoint-
    ment, **1998** 273
    European Central Bank president on euro cur-
    rency, **1999** 75–84
Dunlap, Albert J., **1996** 44
Dunlop, John T., Commission on the Future of
    Worker-Management Relations chairman, **1995**
    15
Dunn, Jennifer (R-Wash.), Clinton state of the
    union address, Republican response, **1999** 43,
    58–60
Duran, Francisco Martin, **1995** 256
Durbin, Richard (D-Ill.), on independent counsel,
    1999 167
Durmus, Osman, on earthquake in Turkey, **1999**
    466

E

Eagleburger, Lawrence S.
    chemical weapons treaty, **1997** 195–196
    Cuban foreign policy, **1998** 33
Earned Income Tax Credit (EITC), **1995** 78;
    1996 28, 54, 59
Earth Summit (Rio de Janeiro), **1999** 403
Earthquakes
    Colombia, Red Cross relief, **1999** 468
    in Turkey, U.S. aid, **1999** 465–471
East Timor
    independence, UN human rights commis-
    sioner on, **1999** 511–523
    UN peacekeeping forces, **1999** 513–514,
    718–719
    UN Transitional Administration, **1999** 514
Easterling, Barbara, **1995** 681, 683
Eastern Slavonia, UN peacekeeping mission,
    1997 151, 154, 156
Eastman Kodak Company, nuclear testing warn-
    ings, **1997** 593
Echaveste, Maria, apparel industry sweatshops,
    1997 209
Economic development
    aid to developing countries, **1997** 481–482
    community empowerment zones, **1997** 39, 71
    empowerment zones and enterprise communi-
    ties, **1998** 90–991; **1999** 91
    set-aside programs abolished, **1998** 856
    small and medium-sized enterprises, **1997**
    344–345
    in the U.S., **1999** 50
Economic performance
    CBO projections, **1998** 502, 505–509
    CEA projections, **1995** 71, 76–77, 79–80; **1996**
    68–70; **1997** 51–52, 63–69; **1998** 79–81, 84–85;
    1999 88
    Clinton economic report, **1996** 52–53; **1998**
    73–79
    Democratic Party platform, **1996** 626–629
    and human development, UN report on, **1996**
    438–444

"misery index," **1996** 52; **1997** 59; **1999** 95
    peacetime expansion, **1999** 42
    stock market volatility, **1997** 721–727
Economic recession
    Asian financial crisis, **1998** 722
    during Bush administration, **1995** 55, 56–57,
    61–65
    Japanese economic crisis, **1998** 532–542, 722
    in the United States, **1998** 532
Economic reports, Clinton and CEA, **1995**
    69–91; **1996** 50–70; **1997** 50–73; **1998** 73–97;
    1999 85–102
Economic sanctions
    against Afghanistan, **1999** 524, 525–526
    against countries denying religious freedom,
    1998 19, 21
    against Cuba, **1998** 30, 32–33
    against India, for nuclear testing, **1998** 327,
    328–329
    against Pakistan, for nuclear testing, **1998**
    327, 328–329
Economic summits, Denver, **1997** 340–360
Ecstasy (drug), use among teenagers, **1999**
    460–461
Education
    accountability, **1999** 47–48, 90–91
    California bilingual education initiative, **1998**
    313–319
    CEA on human capital investment, **1997** 53,
    64–66
    character counts program, **1997** 36
    Clinton administration and, **1995** 82; **1996** 27,
    53, 62; **1997** 24–25, 29, 34–37, 64–65; **1999**
    46–48, 90–91
    Clinton Democratic nomination speech, **1996**
    612–613
    Democratic Party platform on, **1996** 629–631
    federal funding for more teachers and train-
    ing, **1999** 66–67
    G.I. Bill for America's Workers, **1997** 37
    Head Start program, **1998** 88
    job skills training, **1998** 82
    literacy, America Reads Challenge, **1997** 35,
    64–65; **1998** 77, 88
    literacy for adults, **1999** 50
    national education standards, **1997** 30, 34–35;
    1998 44, 88
    Perot Reform Party nomination speech on,
    1996 559–561
    Republican Party platform, **1996** 527–529
    teacher testing, **1998** 57
    worldwide, UNICEF report on, **1998** 920–928
    See also Colleges and universities; Schools;
    Teachers
Education Accountability Act, **1999** 47–48
Education Amendments (1972), gender discrimi-
    nation ban, **1999** 216
Education Department
    State of American Education address, **1996**
    106–117
    uniforms in public schools, **1996** 84–92
Educational attainment, of foreign-born, **1997**
    180
Edwards v. South Carolina, **1995** 331
Eigen, Peter, on bribery of public officials, **1997**
    801
Eisen, Phyllis, on immigrant legislation, **1995**
    565

Eisenach, Jeffrey, and GOPAC activities, **1997** 8, 13
Eisenhower, Dwight, nuclear test ban, **1999** 601
Eizenstat, Stuart E., neutral nations aid to Nazi Germany, **1997** 257–258; **1998** 291–312
El Niño/La Niña, impact from, **1998** 726, 947–948
El Salvador, hurricane and flood damage, **1998** 791
Elderly
  opportunities and challenges of, **1997** 343–344
  population in U.S., **1996** 296–301
  Republican Party platform on, **1996** 532–533
  suicide prevention, **1999** 454
Elders, Jocelyn, surgeon general resignation, **1995** 61
Elizabeth (queen of England)
  death of Diana, statements on, **1997** 647–648, 650–651
  speech for new prime minister, **1997** 277–283
Ellis Island (New York City), deteriorating condition of, **1995** 124, 125
Ellwood, Robert, on cults, **1997** 124
Embassies
  bombings in Africa, **1998** 555–563; **1999** 524
  consolidation proposal, **1999** 691
  diplomatic posts evaluation, State Department on, **1999** 690–698
  human rights and religious freedom issues, **1998** 25–26
  security lapses, **1998** 557; **1999** 690–692
  U.S. bombing of Chinese embassy in Yugoslavia, **1999** 304–316, 726
Employee benefits
  Clinton administration policy, **1996** 27–39
  corporate responsibility for, **1996** 41–49
  for partners of homosexual employees, **1996** 689
Employment Division v. Smith, **1997** 406–407, 410, 411, 416, 418–420, 421
Employment Nondiscrimination Act, **1997** 762, 764; **1999** 56
Endangered Species Act (1973), Supreme Court on, **1995** 359–368
Energy Department (DOE)
  GAO report on nuclear cleanup priorities, **1995** 113–119
  human radiation experiments, **1995** 633–634
  [nuclear] material protection, control, and accounting (MPC&A) systems, **1996** 142–146
Energy policy, Republican Party platform on, **1996** 536–537
England-Joseph, Judy A., testimony on Chicago Housing Authority, HUD takeover of, **1995** 294–301
Engle v. Vitale, **1995** 547
Engler, John, and balanced budgets, **1995** 11
English, as U.S. official language, **1995** 573–574, 577–578; **1996** 521
Enola Gay (B-29 bomber), Smithsonian Institution exhibit, **1995** 55–58
Enterprise zones, community empowerment zones, **1997** 39, 71
Entrapment, Barry on drug charges, **1995** 498
Environmental Defense Fund, genetically altered crops, **1999** 403
Environmental protection
  biotechnology in agriculture, **1999** 401–411
  CEA report on, **1998** 92–93

Clinton administration, **1996** 30–31, 64–65; **1997** 39
Clinton clean air fund proposal, **1999** 55–56
Clinton Democratic acceptance speech, **1996** 619–621
Democratic Party platform on, **1996** 648–650
electric automobile production, **1996** 17–20
Everglades restoration project, **1996** 80–83
farm legislation and, **1996** 200–201
forest lands, Clinton "roadless initiative," **1999** 592–599
global issues, **1997** 345–348
Lands Legacy Initiative, **1999** 56
Livability Agenda, **1999** 56
pesticide regulation reform, **1996** 467–470
Republican Party platform on, **1996** 533–535
UN earth summit conference
  New York City, **1997** 480–488
  Rio de Janeiro, **1997** 480, 860; **1999** 403
UN global warming treaty, **1997** 859–876
Environmental Protection Agency (EPA), pesticides in food, **1996** 467–469
Equal Employment Opportunity Commission (EEOC)
  discrimination claims, **1997** 322
  employer guidelines on mental disabilities, **1997** 127–141
Equal opportunity
  CEA report on, **1998** 97
  Republican Party platform, **1996** 517–518
Ercan, Ahmet, on earthquakes in Turkey, **1999** 467
Ergonomics, OSHA standards, **1999** 769–778
Ericksen, Michael, on addictive power of cigarette smoking, **1999** 539
Eritrea, border dispute with Ethiopia, **1999** 431
Espionage
  Ames case, Senate report on, **1996** 794
  Chinese theft of U.S. nuclear secrets, **1999** 235–256
  Nicholson case, CIA-FBI statement on, **1996** 794–800
  Pitts case, **1996** 794, 795–796
Esposito, Bill, FBI crime laboratory report, **1997** 224
Espy, Mike
  agriculture secretary resignation, **1998** 906
  corruption charges, **1998** 906, 907–908
Estabrook, Ronald, **1996** 72–73
Ethiopia, border dispute with Eritrea, **1999** 431
Euro-Atlantic Partnership Council (EAPC), **1997** 518, 520–521
European Central Bank (ECB), monetary policy, **1999** 75–84
European Coal and Steel Community, **1998** 272
European Commission
  establishment of, **1999** 155–156
  reform report, **1999** 155–164
European Community (EC), **1998** 271
European Council, European defense force proposal, **1999** 817–827
European Security and Defence Identity (ESDI), **1997** 522
European Space Agency, and International Space Station, **1998** 930
European Union (EU)
  euro currency, and monetary policy, **1999** 75–84

euro currency adopted, **1998** 271–280; **1999** 155
European defense force, **1999** 817–827
expansion
  membership for Turkey, **1999** 466–467
  potential members, **1999** 158
genetically altered seeds moratorium, **1999** 403
See also European Commission
Euthanasia, Catholic teaching on, **1995** 146, 155–158
Evans, Lane (D-Ill.), apparel industry sweatshops, **1997** 209
Everglades (Florida), restoration of, **1996** 80–83
Evers, Medgar
  assassination, **1995** 456
  NAACP activities, **1995** 455
Evers-Williams, Myrlie, address as new NAACP chairman, **1995** 453–462
Executive orders
  race initiative, **1998** 668
  security clearances, **1995** 532–545
  striking workers, **1995** 129–133
Exon, Jim (D-Neb.), ban on Internet pornography, **1996** 353–354
Extraterrestrial life
  Galileo's inspection of Jupiter's moon, **1997** 202–205
  life on Mars, **1996** 471–477; **1997** 510
Extremists, in U.S. Army, task force on, **1996** 178–185
Exxon Mobil Corporation, homosexual employees policy, **1999** 901

F

FAA. *See* Federal Aviation Administration (FAA)
Faden, Ruth, **1995** 633–634, 635–636
Fagan, Jeffrey, crime rate declining, **1997** 681
Fagnoni, Cynthia M., welfare reform, congressional testimony on, **1999** 258–259, 261–271
Fair Labor Standards Act (FLSA), **1999** 336–337, 341, 344, 345, 347, 349
Faircloth, Lauch (R-N.C.), church arson prevention, **1997** 306
Families
  adult attitudes toward children, **1997** 422–443
  Democratic Party platform on, **1996** 646–647
  Republican Party platform on, **1996** 526–527
  strengthening American families, **1996** 25–26
Families USA, **1997** 790
Family and Medical Leave Act, **1997** 38; **1998** 47, 78; **1999** 48
Faragher v. City of Boca Raton, **1998** 439–442, 443–452
Farrakhan, Louis, and Million Man March, **1995** 453, 455, 646, 647–648, 655–669
Fayed, Emad "Dodi," **1997** 647, 649
FBI. *See* Federal Bureau of Investigation (FBI)
FCC. *See* Federal Communications Commission (FCC)
FCC v. Pacifica Foundation, **1997** 447–448, 451
FDA. *See* Food and Drug Administration (FDA)
Federal Aviation Administration (FAA)
  airline safety enforcement, **1998** 169–179
  aviation security requirements, **1996** 663–671
  fuel tank requirements, **1997** 782
  inspection program, **1997** 115, 116; **1999** 113–114

performance of, **1997** 113
TWA flight 800 crash, **1997** 780
and White House Commission report, **1997** 113–121
Y2K conversion, impact of, **1999** 762
Federal Aviation Reauthorization Act, **1998** 170
Federal Bureau of Investigation (FBI)
  crime laboratory credibility, **1997** 785–786
  crime laboratory report, **1997** 221–228
  espionage, Nicholson case, **1996** 794–800
  "Freemen" surrender, **1996** 362–367
  TWA flight 800 crash, **1997** 780–786
  uniform crime report, **1995** 710–716; **1996** 732–739; **1997** 681–689; **1998** 869–877; **1999** 614–622
  Waco incident, **1999** 480–488
Federal Communications Commission (FCC)
  campaign advertising, **1998** 50
  liquor advertising, **1996** 772
  telecommunications company mergers, **1998** 339, 340–341
  television rating system, **1997** 527
  v-chip requirement ruling, **1997** 527
Federal Emergency Management Agency (FEMA)
  arson prevention and training grants, **1997** 304, 309–310
  Red River floods, **1997** 232
Federal, Food, Drug and Cosmetic Act, Delaney Clause, **1996** 73, 467–468
Federal Interagency Forum on Child and Family Statistics
  well-being of children indicators, **1997** 425
  well-being of children report, **1999** 384, 387–400
Federal judges, impeachment of, **1999** 18
Federal Mediation and Conciliation Service, **1997** 629
Federal Railroad Administration (FRA), railroad safety regulations, **1996** 189–198
Federal Trade Commission (FTC)
  corporate mergers, **1998** 338–353
  liquor advertising, **1996** 772–773
Feingold, Russell D. (D-Wis.)
  campaign finance reform, **1997** 31, 33, 827; **1998** 50, 893; **1999** 56
  Clinton impeachment trial, **1999** 17
Feinstein, Dianne (D-Calif.), **1995** 409
  Clinton censure resolution, **1999** 21
Fel-Pro, Inc., **1996** 42
Feldblum, Chai, disability, definition of, **1999** 319
Feldman, William, on moon ice findings, **1998** 116, 119
FEMA. *See* Federal Emergency Management Agency (FEMA)
Ferro, Simon, Panama Canal transfer ceremony, **1999** 853
Fetal research, Catholic teaching on, **1995** 155
Field v. Clark, **1998** 428
Fields, Cleo (D-La.), **1995** 370
Financial institutions, mergers, **1998** 339–340
Finland, euro currency, **1998** 271
First, Neal, cloning research, **1997** 212, 215
Fischer, Joschka, nuclear weapons proliferation, **1999** 603
Fischer, Stanley, Thailand economy, **1998** 725
Fisher v. U.S., **1998** 402

Fisheries, conservation of, UN treaty on, **1995** 524–531

Flag, respect for, Dole view on, **1995** 579

Flinn, Kelly, **1997** 656

Floods
  in Red River area, Clinton remarks, **1997** 229–233
  in Venezuela, **1999** 469

Florida, death row executions, **1999** 829–830

Florida v. College Savings Bank, **1999** 334

Flowers, Robert B., **1997** 742

Foley, James B., on international bribery, **1997** 801

Foley, Kathleen M., end-of-life care, **1997** 326

Food and Drug Administration (FDA)
  acupuncture treatments, **1997** 750
  cigarette regulations, authority for, **1999** 538–539
  cigarette regulations, proposed, **1995** 670–679; **1997** 331
  drug names, **1999** 780
  food inspections, **1997** 692; **1998** 523–524
  food safety system, **1997** 690
  nicotine as a drug, **1997** 331, 333
  nicotine levels in cigarettes, **1997** 333, 334
  silicone breast implants, **1995** 515–523
  smoking as "pediatric disease," **1997** 336
  tobacco sales to children, regulations against, **1996** 589–599

Food and Drug Administration Modernization Act (1997), **1998** 89

Food Quality Protection Act, **1996** 467–470

Food safety
  agency, GAO proposal, **1997** 693
  agency established, **1998** 523
  agriculture department initiative, **1997** 690–698
  foodborne illness, GAO report on, **1998** 521–531
  genetically altered foods, **1999** 401–411
  Hazard Analysis and Critical Control Points (HACCP), **1996** 415, 416–417; **1997** 690, 694–697; **1998** 521–522, 525, 527, 528
  meat inspection rules, **1996** 414–417
  pesticide regulation reform, **1996** 46–470

Food Safety and Inspection Service (FSIS), **1998** 523–524, 523–528

Food stamp program
  cutbacks, **1996** 453
  use declining, **1999** 391
  Y2K computer conversion, **1998** 553

Ford, Gerald R.
  oil price shocks, **1998** 501
  volunteerism summit, **1997** 238, 239–240

Ford, Leslie, tamoxifen trials, **1998** 200–201

Ford Motor Co. v. EEOC, **1998** 450

Foreign aid, congressional opposition to, **1999** 700–702

Foreign Corrupt Practices Act, **1997** 800–807

Foreign Espionage Act, **1999** 241

Foreign policy
  activist policy, Clinton on, **1999** 699–710
  Clinton Democratic Party convention, **1996** 621–622
  diplomatic posts evaluation, State Department on, **1999** 690–698
  religious persecution, U.S. position on, **1998** 19–29
  Republican Party platform, **1996** 538–546

U.S. role as world leader, **1995** 580

U.S.-Japan relations, **1998** 540–542

Forests, protection of, Clinton administration proposal, **1999** 592–599

Forgione, Pascal D., Jr., teacher quality survey, **1999** 65

Fortier, Lori, testimony in Oklahoma City bombing case, **1997** 624–625

Fortier, Michael J., and Oklahoma City bombing, **1995** 177; **1997** 624–625

Foster, Henry W., Jr.
  surgeon general nomination, **1995** 61–68
  surgeon general nomination, NAACP support for, **1995** 454
  and White House travel office firings, **1998** 394

Foster, Vincent W., Jr.
  meeting with attorney James Hamilton, **1998** 393
  suicide, **1998** 633

Fowler, Donald
  abortion issue, **1996** 624
  Democratic Party fund-raising violations, **1996** 839–840

Fox, James Alan, juvenile crime, **1995** 711; **1998** 871; **1999** 615

France
  Chirac apology for complicity with Nazis, **1995** 478–482
  Chirac inaugural address, **1995** 228–232
  euro currency, **1998** 271

Frank, Barney (D-Mass.)
  House Judiciary Committee impeachment inquiry, **1998** 702
  same-sex marriages, **1996** 688

Frankel, Jeffrey, U.S. economic growth, **1999** 88

Franklin, Benjamin, on power of God, **1995** 14

Franklin, John Hope, presidential advisory panel on race relations, **1997** 314, 316, 322, 323; **1998** 665, 668

Franks, Gary A. (R-Conn.), **1995** 372

Free Access to Clinic Entrances, **1998** 810

Freedman, Wendy L., age of universe controversy, **1996** 265–268

Freedom of Access to Clinic Entrances (FACE) Act, **1998** 810, 814

Freeh, Louis J.
  "Freemen" surrender, **1996** 362–367
  investigations into campaign finance practices, **1997** 824, 830–831
  Nicholson espionage case, **1996** 794–800
  on Russian intelligence efforts, **1996** 794
  Waco incident investigation, **1999** 481

Freemen (militia group), surrender of, FBI statement on, **1996** 362–367

Frey, Robert, on corporate management and responsibility, **1996** 43

Friedman, Michael
  food recalls, **1997** 691
  on tamoxifen trials, **1998** 197

Friedman, Stanton T., Roswell incident, **1997** 400

Frist, Bill (R-Tenn.)
  during shooting of Capitol policemen, **1998** 511
  patient safety hearings, **1999** 782

Frohnmayer, David, on ballot initiatives, **1999** 5

Frontiero v. Richardson, **1995** 313

Frost, Gary L., **1995** 337

FTC. *See* Federal Trade Commission (FTC)
Fuhrman, Mark, racist police detective in Simpson trial, **1995** 612–613, 617, 646; **1997** 74
Fujimori, Alberto K., Peruvian hostage crisis, **1997** 234–236
Fullilove v. Klutznick, **1995** 312, 314, 321, 323–324
Fulz, Keith O., aviation security, testimony on, **1996** 665–671
Fund for Rural America, **1996** 201
Funk v. U.S., **1998** 398, 402

G

Gaffney, Frank J., Jr., **1996** 741
Gallegly, Elton (R-Calif.), House Judiciary Committee impeachment inquiry, **1998** 705–706
Gangs, legislation controlling, **1997** 39
Garcia v. San Antonio Metropolitan Transit Authority, **1999** 334, 347
Garofalo, Lucia, **1999** 499
Garrow, David, **1995** 657
Gartner Group, on year 2000 computer conversion, **1997** 534, 536
Garvey, Jane E., aviation fuel tank requirements, **1997** 782
Garvey, Steve, baseball record, **1995** 588
Gates, William, **1999** 655
Gay, Hobart R., Korean War massacre incident, **1999** 556
Gay rights
  Clinton speech to Human Rights Campaign, **1997** 760–766
  discrimination against gays, Supreme Court on, **1996** 284–295
  parade marchers, **1995** 327–335
  same-sex marriages, **1996** 687–690; **1997** 761; **1999** 4
  and security clearances, **1995** 532, 533; **1997** 761
Gearhart, John, on embryonic research, **1998** 66
Gebser v. Lago Vista Independent School District, **1998** 442; **1999** 222, 228, 229
Gehrig, Lou, baseball record, **1995** 588–591
Gekas, George (R-Pa.), House Judiciary Committee impeachment inquiry, **1998** 703
General Accounting Office (GAO)
  aviation safety enforcement, **1998** 169–179
  aviation safety report, **1997** 112–121
  aviation security requirements, **1996** 662–671
  computers, Y2K (year 2000) conversion, **1997** 534–540; **1998** 543–554
  counterfeiting of U.S. currency, **1996** 98–105
  deficit reduction, **1996** 147–155
  District of Columbia financial crisis, **1995** 497–505
  drug-resistant bacteria, **1999** 185–199
  FAA and airline safety inspections, **1996** 237–246
  food safety, foodborne illness, **1998** 521–531
  Food Safety Agency proposal, **1997** 693
  Gulf War
    "smart" weapons effectiveness, **1997** 493–500
    "smart" weapons performance, **1996** 403–413
  Gulf War syndrome, **1997** 741
  health insurance coverage, **1998** 139–150
  HUD programs, **1996** 169

National Park Service
  conditions, **1996** 580–588
  testimony, **1995** 120–128
  nuclear material in the former Soviet Union, **1996** 139–146
  nuclear wastes cleanup, **1995** 113–119
  Pentagon computer systems, threats to, **1996** 312–324
  railroad safety, **1996** 189–198
  Roswell incident, **1997** 397
  social security system solvency, **1998** 98–109
  terrorism, **1997** 711
  UN peacekeeping operations report, **1997** 150–157
  welfare reform, **1998** 354–363; **1999** 257–271
General Accounting Office (GAO) computers, security of systems, **1998** 676–686
General Agreement on Tariffs and Trade (GATT)
  CEA report on, **1998** 83
  Uruguay Round, **1995** 74, 85; **1997** 53; **1999** 798
  See also under its later name World Trade Organization (WTO)
General Motors
  selling electric automobiles, **1996** 17–20
  UAW strike, **1998** 320–325
Genetics
  biotechnology in agriculture, **1999** 401–411
  cloning research, **1997** 212–220
  genetic testing in the workplace, **1998** 63–72
  human genome project, **1997** 37–38
Genocide. *See under* Rwanda
Gephardt, Richard A. (D-Mo.)
  104th Congress
    closing remarks, **1996** 699–701
    first one hundred days, democratic response, **1995** 165, 172–174
    opening remarks, **1995** 3–6
  free trade agreements, **1997** 543; **1998** 75
  House impeachment vote, **1998** 961–962, 967
  House Speaker elections, **1997** 3; **1998** 803
  Starr report, **1998** 633, 636
Geremek, Bronislav, at NATO membership ceremony for Poland, **1999** 121, 126–127
German unification, **1998** 816
Germany
  euro currency, **1998** 271
  Gerhard Schroeder's legislative plans, **1998** 815–826
Ghana, Clinton state visit, **1998** 159
Gianni, Matthew, on conservation of world fisheries, **1995** 524
Gibbons v. Ogden, **1995** 186–187
Gibson, Everett K., **1996** 471, 474–476
Gibson, John M., Capitol policeman slain, **1998** 510–517
Gibson, Lynn (Mrs. John M.), **1999** 44
Gibson, Robert "Hoot," **1995** 420–424
Gibson, William F., and NAACP scandal, **1995** 453–454
Gidzenko, Yuri, **1998** 932
Gifford, Kathie Lee, apparel industry sweatshop investigations, **1997** 206–207, 209
Gildenberg, Bernard D., Roswell incident, **1997** 400
Gilmore, James S. III, on terrorism, **1999** 502
Gingrich, Newt (former House Speaker, R-Ga.)
  affirmative action, **1997** 316
  antimissile defense policy, **1998** 483

balanced budget amendment, **1995** 738–740, 744–745
  signing ceremony, **1997** 604, 608–610
budget controversy, **1996** 148; **1997** 3; **1998** 800
Clinton debate, **1995** 427; **1996** 21
Clinton visit to China, **1998** 469
Congress
  first one hundred days, **1995** 165, 167–172
  House ethics rules violations, **1995** 746–751; **1996** 838–849; **1997** 3–19, 603; **1998** 800–801
  House Speaker reelection, **1997** 3–4
  House Speaker resignation, **1998** 698, 799–808, 951
  limit on gifts to members of, **1995** 701
  lobbyist registration bill, **1995** 702
  opening remarks, **1995** 3–5, 6–14
  shooting of Capitol policemen, **1998** 514–515
Jiang Zemin state visit, **1997** 730
minimum wage, **1996** 565
national security commission member, **1999** 500
on NEA funding, **1998** 407
at Republican Party convention, **1996** 478
Renewing American Civilization course, **1997** 7–11, 14–15
welfare reform bill, **1996** 461
Ginsberg v. New York, **1997** 447, 451, 454–457
Ginsburg, Ruth Bader
  affirmative action, federal government plans, **1995** 309, 320–326
  congressional term limits, **1995** 260
  disability, definition of, **1999** 319–320, 325–332
  drug testing of students, **1995** 339–346
  endangered species on private lands, **1995** 359–368
  free speech
    ballot initiatives, **1999** 5–12
    decency and the arts, **1998** 408
    and the Internet, **1997** 445
  gay rights discrimination, **1996** 286
  gun-free school zone, **1995** 184
  HIV as a disability, **1998** 379, 389
  line-item veto, **1998** 421
  parochial school aid, **1997** 363, 374–375, 375–380, 380–381
  physician-assisted suicide, **1997** 461, 472–473, 478
  punitive damages, for consumer product liability, **1996** 275, 282–283
  race-based redistricting, **1995** 371, 380–384; **1996** 370, 381–383, 383–387
  religious freedom, **1997** 408
  religious publications, **1995** 386, 393–395
  sex offenders, right to confine, **1997** 384, 392–394
  sexual harassment, **1998** 461; **1999** 215
  states rights, **1999** 333, 345–349
Giuliani, Rudolph W., parochial school aid, **1997** 363
Glacier National Park, **1995** 126
Glantz, Stanton A., on secondhand smoke, **1995** 673
Glenn, John
  campaign finances, **1998** 894

Discovery space shuttle mission, **1998** 53–54, 776–786, 930
  election campaigns, **1998** 777
Glickman, Dan (agriculture secretary)
  biotechnology in agriculture, **1999** 401–411
  on farm bill, **1996** 199–203
  food recalls, **1997** 691–692
  food safety system, **1997** 693–698; **1998** 523
  meat inspection rules, **1996** 414–417
Global Climate Coalition, **1997** 862
Global warming
  and record high temperatures, **1998** 945–950
  UN treaty conference (Kyoto), **1997** 481, 859–876; **1998** 945, 947
Glover, Calvin, beating death of Barry L. Winchell, **1999** 900
Glover v. Patten, **1998** 399
Golan Heights, Israeli-Syria negotiations, **1995** 623
Goldin, Daniel S.
  Glenn space shuttle mission, **1998** 777
  life on Mars, **1996** 471–477; **1997** 510
  Mars mission failures, **1999** 712, 714
Goldman, Ronald L., murder of, **1995** 611–621; **1997** 74
Gonorrhea, **1999** 193
Goodlatte, Robert W. (R-Va.), House Judiciary Committee impeachment inquiry, **1998** 707
GOPAC (political action committee), and Gingrich ethics violations, **1995** 748–751; **1996** 840–848; **1997** 6–14
Gorbachev, Mikhail S.
  economic summit (London), **1997** 340
  Russian leader, **1999** 917
Gore, Al, Jr. (Vice president)
  aviation safety report, GAO on, **1997** 113–121; **1998** 171–172; **1999** 114
  campaigns and elections
    acceptance speech, **1996** 602, 603–608
    attorney general investigations of campaign finance, **1998** 898–902
    finance practices, **1997** 823–824, 825, 827–831
    presidential, **1999** 800
    vice-presidential debates, **1996** 707–709, 718–724
  church arson prevention, **1997** 310
  defense policy, gays in the military, **1999** 900–901
  environmental issues
    Everglades restoration project, **1996** 80–83
    global warming, **1997** 861
  foreign policy, South Africa, U.S. trade sanctions, **1999** 491
  gay rights, Ellen DeGeneres "coming out," **1997** 761
  House impeachment vote, **1998** 968–969
  IRS and customer service, **1998** 131–138
  job discrimination, and genetic testing, **1998** 64–65
  nuclear nonproliferation treaty, **1995** 234, 238
  school violence, Columbine High School commemoration speech, **1999** 179–184
  shooting of Capitol policemen, **1998** 515
  television rating system, **1997** 529–531
  and UN summit on poverty, **1995** 135
  volunteerism summit, **1997** 238

Gore, Tipper
  and education, **1997** 36
  mental health initiative, **1999** 49, 837
Gorton, Slade (R-Wash.), **1995** 359
Goss v. Lopez, **1995** 348
Government ethics, Republican Party platform,
  1996 512–513
Government reorganization
  Clinton reinventing government plan, **1995** 75,
    83–85; **1996** 32–34, 54, 63–64
  Democratic Party platform, **1996** 639–640
  reduction in size of, **1997** 54
  Republican Party platform, **1996** 511–513
Grachev, Pavel S., Chechnya War, **1995** 94
Gradison, Bill, on health insurance premiums,
  1998 141–142
Graham, Lindsey (R-S.C.)
  Clinton impeachment inquiry, **1998** 699
  House Judiciary Committee impeachment
    inquiry, **1998** 712–713
Graham, Thomas, Jr., nuclear nonproliferation
  treaty, extension of, **1995** 233–238
Gramm, Phil (R-Texas)
  abortion opponent, **1995** 62
  as presidential candidate, **1995** 573
Grams, Rod (R-Minn.), Cuban foreign policy,
  1998 33
Grand Rapids School District v. Ball, **1997** 361,
  368–371, 373, 375–379
Great Britain
  death of princess Diana, **1997** 647–653
  election of prime minister Blair, **1997** 237–283
  Eurocurrency, rejection of, **1997** 278
  Northern Ireland peace agreement, **1998**
    203–219
Greece, earthquake relief for Turkey, **1999** 466
Greeley, Ronald, and *Galileo* imaging, **1997**
  204
Green v. County School Bd., **1998** 865
Greenhouse gas emissions
  earth summit (Rio de Janeiro), **1997** 860
  and global warming, **1998** 945
  Great Britain policy, **1997** 481
  reduction of, **1997** 861–862
  U.S. policy, **1997** 861–862
Greenhouse, Linda, on congressional term limits,
  1995 259
Greenpeace International, world fisheries con-
  servation, **1995** 524–525
Greenspan, Alan
  and economic expansion, **1997** 51; **1998**
    75–76, 502
  monetary policy, **1999** 86
  stock market volatility, **1997** 721–727
Gregory v. Ashcroft, **1995** 186
Gregory v. Chicago, **1995** 331
Griffey, Ken, Jr., and home run championship,
  1998 627
Griffin, Arlee, Jr., **1995** 337
Griffin v. Wisconsin, **1995** 342
Gross domestic product (GDP), **1996** 69; **1998**
  73, 79; **1999** 95–96
Group of Eight (*formerly* G-7)
  final statement, **1997** 340–360
  food safety, **1999** 405
  Kosovo conflict, **1999** 286
  NATO expansion, **1997** 340, 516
  sanctions against India and Pakistan for
    nuclear testing, **1998** 328

Group of Seven (G-7), world debt relief, **1999**
  701–702
Group of Twenty, **1999** 393–394
Guatemala
  hurricane and flood damage, **1998** 791
  peace agreement, **1996** 850–856
Guinier, Lani, on minority rights, **1995** 611
Guisti, Carlos, death of Peruvian hostage, **1997**
  235
Gun control
  assault weapons in crime, **1995** 470–471
  automatic weapons, **1995** 468
  Clinton administration proposals, **1999** 42, 43,
    54–55
  Democratic Party platform on, **1996** 634–635
  firearm use, **1996** 733
  gun use in crimes, **1995** 463–471
  gun-free school zones, Supreme court report
    on, **1995** 183–200; **1998** 735–736
  Republican Party platform, **1996** 519
Gun-Free School Zones Act (1990), **1995**
  185–186
Gun-Free Schools Act (1994), **1998** 735–736
Gunderson, Steve (R-Wis.), **1996** 688
Gusmao, Jose Alexandre, **1999** 515

H

Habibie, B.J.
  East Timor, UN peacekeeping forces, **1999**
    513
  East Timor independence, **1999** 512
  elections in Indonesia, **1999** 514, 718, 719
  president of Indonesia, **1998** 284–288; **1999**
    719–720
Habiger, Eugene E., nuclear weapons security,
  1999 240
Habitat for Humanity
  low-income housing, **1999** 56
  and rebuilding of burnt churches, **1997** 304,
    306, 311
Habyarimana, Juvenal
  assassination of, **1998** 614; **1999** 863
  Rwanda genocidal war, **1999** 861, 862
Hackworth, Donald E., General Motors UAW
  strike statement, **1998** 323, 324–325
Hagel, Chuck (R-Neb.), food safety system, **1997**
  692
Hagelin, John, **1996** 707
*Hague v. Committee for Industrial Organiza-
  tion*, **1995** 334
Haines, Gerald K., Roswell incident, **1997** 397
Haiti
  elections in, and UN, **1995** 355
  hurricane damage, **1998** 789, 790
  UN peacekeeping mission, **1997** 150, 151, 154,
    155, 156
Hall, James E.
  air bag safety, **1997** 775
  air safety standards for foreign airlines, **1999**
    113
  aviation safety, congressional testimony on,
    1999 116–118
  and de-icing procedures, **1998** 171
  on National Transportation Safety Board fund-
    ing, **1999** 115
  on railroad safety, **1996** 189
  TWA flight 800 crash, **1997** 781, 783–786
Hall, Tony P. (D-Ohio), abortion issue, **1996** 624

947

Hamilton, James, meeting with Foster, posthumous confidentiality, **1998** 393
Hamilton, Lee H. (D-Ind.),
    government secrecy, **1997** 103
    national security commission member, **1999** 500
Hamre, John, Y2K computer conversion, **1998** 545; **1999** 762
Han Sung-Joo, **1999** 861
Handgun control. *See* Gun control
Hanford Nuclear Reservation (Washington), cleanup efforts, **1995** 114–115, 117–118
Hans v. Louisiana, **1999** 339
Hansen, Charles M., Jr., on labor unions, **1999** 632
Harkin, Tom (D-Iowa)
    apparel industry sweatshops, **1997** 209
    disability legislation, **1999** 319
    farm bill opponent, **1996** 200
    nuclear testing fallout, **1997** 593
Harris, Eric, Columbine High School shooter, **1999** 179
Harris, Fred R., poverty and race, **1998** 667–668
Harris v. Forklift Systems, Inc., **1998** 462
Hart, Gary (*formerly* D-Colo.), national security commission member, **1999** 500
Hartzler, Joseph H., **1997** 623
Harvard School of Public Health, survey on children, **1997** 424–425
Hashimoto, Ryutaro
    at economic summit (Denver), **1997** 342
    on hostage crisis in Peru, **1997** 234–237
    Japanese economic stimulus package, **1998** 532, 535
Hasson, Kevin J., **1995** 386
Hastert, Dennis (R-Mich.), candidate for House Speaker, **1998** 954
Hatch, Orrin G. (R-Utah)
    affirmative action opponent, **1997** 185–186
    physician-assisted suicide, **1997** 462
    religious freedom, **1997** 408–409
Hate crimes
    church arson cases, **1997** 301–313
    extremists in U.S. Army, task force on, **1996** 178–185
    FBI report, **1997** 686; **1998** 874; **1999** 616–617, 619
Hate Crimes Prevention Act, **1999** 56
Havel, Vaclav, NATO membership for Czech Republic, **1997** 516
Hawaii, same-sex marriages, **1996** 689; **1999** 4, 898–899
Hawkins, Vernon, **1996** 784
Head Start program, federal support for program, **1997** 36, 73
Health
    benefits of drinking, **1995** 3–4, 16
    benefits for girls in sports, **1997** 158–171
    CEA report, **1998** 88–90
    connective tissue disease and breast implants, **1995** 520–521
    marijuana for medical uses, **1996** 755–758
    physical exercise, benefits of, **1996** 418–429
    See also Child health
Health and Human Services (HHS) Department
    child abuse and neglect, **1996** 778
    federal dietary guidelines, **1996** 3–16
    hospital oversight, inspector general on, **1999** 412–421

    medical records privacy, **1997** 580–587
    welfare reform studies, **1999** 269–270
Health care
    acupuncture treatments, NIH panel on, **1997** 747–759
    and deficit reduction, **1996** 67
    Democratic Party platform, **1996** 631–632
    end-of-life care, **1997** 325–330
    hospital care quality, **1999** 412–421
    long-term care proposals, **1999** 46
    mammograms and mastectomy, **1997** 38
    mammograms controversy, **1997** 142–149
    medical mistakes, Institute of Medicine on, **1999** 779–793
    medical records security, **1997** 580–587
    patients' bill of rights, **1997** 787–799; **1998** 46–47, 89, 140; **1999** 48–49, 562–563
    Republican Party platform, **1996** 529–530
    spending, **1998** 142
    for women, **1997** 38
Health Care Finance Administration (HCFA), hospital quality oversight, **1999** 412–421
Health care reform, Clinton proposals, **1995** 74–75, 88–90; **1997** 38
Health insurance
    Clinton administration proposals, **1999** 49
    coverage
        Census Bureau on, **1999** 561–567
        GAO report, **1998** 139–150
    coverage for children, **1999** 566–567
    for mental health treatment, **1996** 388–390
    portability, **1999** 564
    uninsured, increasing numbers of, **1998** 142–143; **1999** 563–564
    universal coverage, **1999** 564
Health Insurance Portability and Accountability Act (HIPAA, 1996), **1997** 72; **1998** 78, 140–142, 143–150
Health maintenance organizations (HMOs). *See* Managed care
Health, public
    drug-resistant bacteria as threat to, **1999** 185–199
    Gulf War syndrome, **1997** 740–745
    infectious diseases, **1996** 302–311; **1997** 348–349
    nuclear testing fallout, **1997** 591–601
    silicone breast implants, **1995** 515–523
    suicide prevention, **1999** 439–455
    See also Child health
Hearn, Ruby P., child health care, **1997** 425
Heath, Clark, nuclear testing fallout, **1997** 591
Hecker, JayEtta Z., impact of NAFTA, **1997** 543
Heffron v. International Soc. for Krishna Consciousness, Inc., **1995** 398
Hefley, Joel (R-Colo.), park service opponent, **1995** 121
Helms, Jesse (R-N.C.)
    AIDS research, opposition to, **1995** 428, 433, 459
    chemical weapons treaty opponent, **1996** 741; **1997** 196
    death penalty in U.S., **1998** 185
    government secrecy, **1997** 103
    nuclear test ban treaty, **1999** 601, 608, 699
    on tobacco industry, **1996** 592
    U.S. role in UN, **1995** 350–351; **1997** 153; **1999** 701

Henderson, Wade, affirmative action programs, **1998** 856

Hendricks, Leroy, sex offender confinement case, **1997** 382–394

Henry, Greg, planet detection, **1999** 175

Herbert, Victor, acupuncture, **1997** 750

Herbert v. Lando, **1998** 402

Heritage Forests Campaign, **1999** 594

Herman, Alexis
apparel industry sweatshops, **1997** 209
consumer health care, **1997** 787, 791
UPS strike, **1997** 630
welfare system, **1997** 620

Herman, Alexis M., ergonomics standards, **1999** 769

Hester, Jeff, on Hubble space telescope pictures, **1995** 291–293

Heyman, I. Michael, *Enola Gay* exhibit announcement, **1995** 55–58

Hicks, John J., FBI crime laboratory report, **1997** 223

Hicks, Katherine, **1997** 661

Hill, Christopher, Kosovo political situation, **1998** 830

Hinson, David R., FAA and airline safety, **1996** 237–238

Hirabayashi v. U.S., **1995** 313; **1997** 190

Hispanics
college enrollment, **1997** 186
labor market, **1999** 101–102
teenage birth rates, **1998** 261–262

Historically black colleges and universities (HBCUs), **1995** 241, 247, 249

HIV. *See* Human immunodeficiency virus (HIV) infection

Hochhuth, Rolf, **1998** 123

Hoffa, James P., **1997** 628

Hohamad, Mahathir, **1997** 833

Holbrooke, Richard C.
Bosnia
Dayton peace agreement, **1999** 737, 740
Declaration of New York, **1999** 737
Congo, Lusaka agreement, **1999** 647
East Timor refugees, **1999** 515
Kosovo peace negotiations, **1998** 830; **1999** 136

Holmes Norton, Eleanor (D-D.C.), **1995** 499

Holocaust
French complicity with Nazis, apology for, **1995** 478–482
Nazi-confiscated art, return of, **1998** 294–295
neutral nations aid to Nazi Germany, **1998** 299–312
Roman Catholic church repentance for, **1998** 121–130
Swiss banks and, **1998** 293–294
victims of, restitution investigations, **1997** 257–272

Homeless persons, national survey of, **1999** 392

Homicide, rate of, **1995** 710, 714; **1999** 620

Homosexual rights
gays in the military, **1999** 899–901
military ban, **1997** 761; **1999** 901
same-sex marriages, **1996** 687–690; **1999** 898–899
same-sex marriages in France, **1999** 901
Vermont Supreme Court on, **1999** 898–908

Honberg, Ronald S., on EEOC guidelines on mental disabilities, **1997** 129

Honduras, hurricane damage, UN situation report, **1998** 789–791, 792–798

Hong Kong
political situation, **1997** 358–359, 501, 503–504; **1998** 468
stock market plunge, **1997** 722, 834
transfer to China ceremony, **1997** 501–506

Hong Soon Young, Korean War massacre incident, **1999** 553

Hoover, J. Edgar, and "Verona" project, **1997** 104

Hopewell Furnace National Historic Site (Pennsylvania), **1995** 124, 125

Hopwood v. State of Texas, **1998** 862–863

Horn, Steve (R-Calif.), Y2K computer conversion crisis, **1998** 545

Horowitz, Michael, religious persecution, **1997** 562–563

Hospitals
medical mistakes, Institute of Medicine report on, **1999** 779–793
quality of, **1999** 412–421

Hostages
Japanese in Peru, **1997** 234–237
U.S. in Iran, **1995** 351

House Judiciary Committee
impeachment inquiry, **1998** 695–721
impeachment trial, **1999** 15–40

House of Representatives
Chinese technology transfer, **1998** 976–982
impeachment vote, **1998** 958–970
physician-assisted suicide legislation, **1999** 441–442
Speaker of the House
election, **1997** 3–4
Gingrich resignation, **1998** 698, 799–808, 951
Livingston resignation, **1998** 799, 951–957, 959, 962
Wright resignation, **1997** 5; **1998** 800
transfer of power from Democratic to Republican Party, **1995** 3–14

House Resources Committee, on endangered species, **1995** 360–361

House Select Committee on U.S. National Security and Military/Commercial Concerns with the People's Republic of China, report, **1999** 235–256

House Standards of Official Conduct Committee (Ethics committee), Gingrich violations, **1995** 746–751; **1996** 838–849; **1997** 3–19

Housing
affordable, lack of, **1998** 253–259, 355, 364; **1999** 391–392
public, Chicago Housing Authority, HUD takeover of, **1995** 294–301
rental housing market crisis, **1996** 167–177
Republican Party platform, **1996** 509–510

Housing and Urban Development Department (HUD)
Chicago Housing Authority takeover, **1995** 294–301
church arson rebuilding program, **1997** 302–303, 304, 308–309
cities, state of the, **1998** 364–377
housing the poor, **1998** 253–259, 355, 364
rental housing market, **1996** 167–177

Hu Jintao, on U.S. bombing of Chinese embassy, **1999** 305

949

Huang, John, campaign finance contributions, **1997** 825; **1998** 894
Hubbard, Scott, on *Lunar Prospector* mission, **1998** 118
Hubbell, Webster L., indictment, **1998** 633
Hubble space telescope
  age of the universe, **1996** 265–269
  birth of stars, **1995** 288–293
  mission repairs, **1999** 712
  planet outside the solar system, **1998** 115
Huerta, Michael P., on year 2000 computer conversion, **1997** 534–535
Hughes Space and Communications Co., **1999** 237, 250
Human experimentation
  radiation experiments, **1995** 633–638
  in testing biological weapons, **1997** 768
Human genome project, **1997** 37–38
Human immunodeficiency virus (HIV) infection
  in African nations, **1999** 489–498
  children infected with, **1999** 387
  as a disability, Supreme Court on, **1998** 378–392; **1999** 317
  transmission risks during dental treatment, **1998** 379–380
  in U.S., **1997** 84
  worldwide epidemic, **1998** 878–889
  worldwide estimates, **1997** 83–84
  worldwide impact of, **1996** 306–307; **1997** 348–349
  young people and, **1998** 888–889
Human rights
  in Afghanistan, **1999** 531–534
  Chechnya war, **1999** 909–916
  in China, **1996** 133–138; **1997** 729, 735–738; **1998** 467–468, 469–470
  and democracy, G-8 statement on, **1997** 355–356
  East Timor independence and, **1999** 511–523
  in Iraq, **1999** 144–152
  in Kosovo, **1999** 802–816
  Kosovo conflict, **1998** 837–839
  in Nigeria, **1995** 696–699
  Pope John Paul II UN speech on, **1995** 639–645
  South African Truth and Reconciliation Commission report, **1998** 755–775
  State Department reports on, **1996** 133–138
  UN and, **1995** 358
  UN Conference on Women, **1995** 581–587
Human Rights Campaign, **1997** 760–766; **1999** 4
Human Rights Watch
  Kosovo conflict, **1999** 290
  religious vs. political rights, **1997** 563
Hume, John, Northern Ireland peace negotiations, **1998** 203
Hun Sen, Cambodian coup, **1997** 639–641; **1998** 971, 972
Hundler, Donald W., on electric vehicles, **1996** 19, 20
Hungary, NATO membership, **1997** 514, 516; **1999** 119, 120
Hunt, James B. "Jim" (North Carolina governor), teaching standards, **1997** 35; **1999** 47
Hunt v. Blackburn, **1998** 398
Hunter v. Erickson, **1997** 188, 192
Huntress, Wesley, on moon ice findings, **1998** 114, 117

Hurley v. Irish-American Gay, Lesbian and Bisexual Group of Boston, **1995** 327–335
Hurricanes, UN report on damage, **1998** 789–798
Hussein ibn Talal (king of Jordan)
  death of, **1999** 890–891
  eulogy for Yitzhak Rabin, **1995** 691, 693–694
  Middle East peace negotiations, **1999** 890–891
  West Bank peace agreement, **1995** 622
  Wye River peace agreement, **1998** 744, 753–754
Hussein, Saddam
  attempts to oust, **1998** 938
  chemical weapons policy, **1997** 198; **1998** 49–50
  human rights in Iraq, **1999** 144–145
  political situation report, **1996** 680–686
  UN air strikes against Iraq, **1998** 934–944; **1999** 53
  UN weapons inspections, **1997** 767
Hutchinson, Asa (R-Ark.)
  House Judiciary Committee impeachment inquiry, **1998** 711
  House Judiciary Committee impeachment trial, **828** 18
Hutchison Whampoa Ltd., **1999** 852
Hyde, Henry J. (R-Ill.)
  and antiterrorism bill, **1995** 179
  church arson prevention, **1997** 306
  extra-marital affair, **1998** 697
  House impeachment inquiry, **1998** 696, 697, 700–701
  House Judiciary Committee and impeachment trial, **1999** 16, 17–19, 22–29
  House vote on impeachment, **1998** 959
  physician-assisted suicide legislation, **1997** 462; **1999** 441–442
  on Reno conflict of interest, **1997** 824
  Starr report public release, **1998** 636

I

IBM
  benefits for partners of homosexual employees, **1996** 689
  chess victory of "Deep Blue" computer, **1997** 273–276
Idaho National Engineering Laboratory, nuclear waste cleanup, **1995** 118
Idaho v. Coeur d'Alene Tribe of Idaho, **1999** 348
Illinois v. Krull, **1995** 346
ILO. *See* International Labor Organization (ILO)
IMF. *See* International Monetary Fund (IMF)
Immigration
  aid to immigrants, **1996** 452–453, 455–456; **1997** 34
  California, Proposition 187, **1995** 563
  Census Bureau report, **1997** 175–182
  Cuban and Haitian refugee boatlifts, U.S. policy on, **1995** 203–207
  Democratic Party platform, **1996** 636–637
  foreign-born population, in U.S., **1995** 563–569; **1997** 175–182
  legal immigrants, number of, **1995** 564–656
  Republican Party platform, **1996** 520–521
  U.S. strength in diversity, **1997** 43
Immigration and Naturalization Service (INS)
  abolition proposal, **1997** 175
  political asylum
    from religious persecution, **1998** 26–28
    for women, new rules on, **1995** 276–280

Impeachment, presidential
  Clinton impeachment
    articles of impeachment, **1998** 964–967;
      1999 20
    censure resolution, **1999** 21
    grounds for, in Starr report, **1998** 637–638
    House Judiciary Committee inquiry, **1998**
      695–721
    House votes, **1998** 958–970
    Starr independent counsel investigations,
      1998 38–39, 393, 395, 565–566, 905, 907,
      960
    Starr investigation report, **1998** 632–664
    and timing of air strikes against Iraq, **1998**
      937
    trial, statements from, **1999** 15–40
  Johnson impeachment, **1998** 697, 959; **1999**
    15
  Nixon impeachment, House vote, **1998** 959
Inaugural addresses, Clinton, **1997** 20–26
Income distribution
  basic needs report, **1999** 391, 394–400
  human development, UN report on, **1996**
    438–444
  inequality
    CEA on, **1997** 52
    Census Bureau on, **1996** 396–400; **1999**
      390–391
    in developing countries, **1999** 392–393
  median income of foreign-born, **1997** 181
Independent counsel
  dissatisfaction with, **1998** 634
  future of, Starr congressional testimony on,
    1999 165–172
  in Lewinsky affair, **1998** 565
  role of the, **1998** 905–911
Inderfuth, Karl F., India and Pakistan economic
  sanctions, **1998** 329
India
  cyclone in Bay of Bengal, **1999** 468–469
  Lahore Declaration, **1999** 623–624
  missile threat to U.S., **1998** 491–492
  nuclear weapons testing, **1998** 483, 541; **1999**
    623–624
  relations with Pakistan, **1999** 623–629
  weapons of mass destruction proliferation,
    1996 213, 222–223
Indiana, welfare reform, **1999** 258
Individuals with Disabilities Education Act, **1999**
  318
Indonesia
  economic crisis, **1998** 722, 724; **1999**
    720–721
  elections, **1999** 719–720
  IMF aid package, **1997** 836; **1999** 721
  independence movements, **1999** 721–722
  political situation, **1998** 604; **1999** 718–
    723
  Suharto resignation, **1998** 284–288, 722
  unemployment, **1998** 726
  See also East Timor
Indyk, Martin S., U.S.-Iran relations, **1998** 689
Infant mortality, worldwide, **1996** 306
Infectious diseases
  World Health Organization report on, **1996**
    302–311
  worldwide prevention, **1997** 348–349
Inflation rate, **1996** 51, 69; **1997** 50, 53; **1998** 74,
  75

Information Technology Agreement (ITA), **1998**
  92
Information Technology Association of America
  (ITAA), technology worker shortage, **1997** 669,
  670
Infrastructure, protecting, **1997** 711–720
Inglis, Bob (R-S.C.), House Judiciary Committee
  impeachment inquiry, **1998** 706–707
Inglis, Oliver Michael, **1998** 616
Ingraham v. Wright, **1995** 348
Inman, Bobby Ray, embassy security, **1999** 691
Inouye, Daniel K. (D-Hawaii), war hero, **1999** 39
INS. *See* Immigration and Naturalization Service
  (INS)
INS v. Chadha, **1998** 427
Institute of Medicine (IOM)
  end-of-life care report, **1997** 325, 327–328
  medical mistakes, **1999** 779–793
  thyroid cancer from radiation study, **1997** 592,
    594, 598
Insurgent groups, and weapons development,
  1996 224–225
Intelligence community
  expanding powers of, **1996** 796–797
  Republican Party platform on, **1996** 547–548
Interest rates, **1997** 721; **1998** 76
Interior Department (U.S.), on endangered
  species, **1995** 359
Internal Revenue Service (IRS)
  citizen advocacy, **1998** 50–51
  Customer Service Task Force report, **1998**
    131–138
  impact of year 2000 computer conversion on,
    1997 535
  mistakes and abuses, **1997** 661–668
  reform bill, **1997** 663; **1998** 51, 56
  reforms and customer service, **1998** 131–138
  and tax exempt organizations, **1997** 9–13, 15
International Campaign to Ban Landmines, **1997**
  845
International Convention on Civil and Political
  Rights (ICCPR), and death penalty, **1998** 183,
  184, 189, 190, 192, 466, 469
International Criminal Tribunal for Rwanda,
  1998 614–625; **1999** 866
International Labor Organization (ILO)
  child labor report, **1996** 776–783
  labor standards, **1999** 52, 800
International Monetary Fund (IMF)
  Asian financial crisis, **1997** 832–843; **1998**
    723–724
  debt reduction, **1999** 702
  India and Pakistan loans suspended, **1998** 328
  Indonesia economy, **1999** 721
  Japanese economy, **1998** 534
  Russian economic crisis, **1998** 601, 604
  Russian loan suspension, **1999** 913–914
  U.S. support for, **1998** 46
International Olympics Committee (IOC),
  bribery scandal investigations, **1999** 105–112
Internet
  digital divide in access to, **1999** 368–383
  free speech, Supreme Court on, **1996** 353–361;
    1997 444–458
  future generation, **1998** 53
  Internet Explorer vs. Netscape Navigator,
    1999 654–689
  into the classrooms, **1997** 37
  into the hospitals, **1997** 37

Microsoft Corp. antitrust case, **1999** 654–689
online investing, **1999** 20
pornography ban, **1996** 353–361
public release of Starr report on, **1998**
  636–637
Iran
  chemical weapons stockpile, **1997** 198
  counterfeiting of U.S. currency, **1996** 100
  Great Britain diplomatic relations, **1998**
    687–689
  Khatami presidential election, **1997** 284–289
  missile tests, **1998** 482
  missile threat, **1998** 489–490
  nuclear weapons proliferation, **1996** 212
  religious persecution of Baha'i sect, **1997** 564,
    572–573
  Rushdie death threat lifted, **1998** 687–691
  U.S. diplomatic relations, **1998** 689–690
  U.S. hostages in, UN efforts fail, **1995** 351
  weapons development, **1996** 212, 218, 219
Iraq
  chemical weapons use, **1996** 212; **1997**
    740–745; **1998** 49–50
  human rights report, **1999** 144–152
  missile threat to U.S., **1998** 482, 490–491
  nuclear weapons, **1996** 212
  oil-for-food program, **1999** 146–147
  Operation Desert Fox, **1999** 53
  political situation, CIA report on, **1996**
    680–686
  religious persecution, **1997** 564, 573–574
  UN sanctions against, **1995** 355–356; **1997**
    767, 769–770
  weapons development, **1996** 212, 218, 219
  weapons inspections, UN Special Commis-
    sion, **1997** 767–773; **1999** 147–148
Ireland
  euro currency, **1998** 271
  Republican Party platform, **1996** 541
Ireland, Northern
  Clinton on peace efforts in, **1995** 727–733
  Good Friday agreement, **1999** 753–754, 756
  peace agreement, **1998** 203–219
  peace process, **1999** 753–759
Ireland, Patricia, same-sex marriages, **1996** 687
Irish Republican Army (IRA)
  cease-fire agreement, **1995** 727
  peace process and decommissioning of, **1999**
    753–759
  Sinn Fein, **1995** 728–729
Irish-American Gay, Lesbian and Bisexual Group
  of Boston (GLIB), **1995** 327–335
IRS. *See* Internal Revenue Service (IRS)
Ismail, Razali, UN earth summit, **1997** 482
Isolationism, Clinton challenges, **1995** 350, 357
Israel
  Barak on new government programs, **1999**
    359–367
  Hebron withdrawal, **1996** 339–340
  land mine warfare, **1995** 51
  Netanyahu election as prime minister, **1996**
    337–342
  political situation, **1999** 359–367
  religious persecution, **1997** 574–575
  Syria peace negotiations, **1999** 890–897,
    893–894
  Syria relations, **1999** 362
  Turkey, earthquake rescue teams, **1999**
    466–467

Wye River agreement with Palestinians, **1998**
  742–754; **1999** 52–53, 700, 891–893
Israel, occupied territories, West Bank agree-
  ment, **1995** 622–630
Istook, Ernest J., Jr. (R-Okla.), lobbyist legisla-
  tion, **1995** 702–703
Italy, euro currency, **1998** 271
Ivey, William J., decency in the arts, **1998** 406,
  407
Izetbegovic, Alija, **1995** 719

J

Jackson, Jesse L.
  Clinton's affirmative action speech, **1995** 485
  Democratic national conventions, **1996**
    601–602
  individual retirement accounts, opposition to,
    1998 100
  Million Man March, **1995** 656
  as "race-hustling poverty pimp," **1997** 31
  on Texaco executives racial slurs, **1996** 765,
    766
Jackson, Michael, NATO Kosovo commander,
  1999 288
Jackson, Thomas P., line-item veto, **1997** 612
Jackson, Thomas Penfield, Microsoft antitrust
  case, **1997** 654–689
Jackson-Lee, Sheila (D-Texas), House Judiciary
  Committee impeachment inquiry, **1998** 707
Jacobson, Michael, **1996** 5
Jacoby v. Arkansas Dept. of Ed., **1999** 336
Jaffee v. Redmond, **1996** 388–395
Japan
  China relations, **1998** 540–541
  economic crisis, **1998** 532–542
  economic situation, **1997** 835
  hostage crisis in Peru, **1997** 234–237
  North Korean relations, **1999** 576–577
  Russia relations, **1998** 540
  Tokyo subway terrorist nerve gas incident
    (Arum Shinrikyo), **1999** 502, 503
  UN treaty conference (Kyoto), **1997** 481,
    859–876; **1998** 945, 947
  U.S. foreign policy, **1998** 540–542
  World War II, apology for suffering, **1995**
    302–306
Jarrell, Jerry, hurricane damage, **1998** 790
Jeffords, James M. (R-Vt.)
  health insurance for disabled persons, **1999**
    49
  health insurance premiums, **1998** 141
  patient safety hearings, **1999** 782
Jehovah's Witness, religious freedom issues,
  1997 407, 564, 572
Jenkins, Bill (R-Tenn.), House Judiciary Commit-
  tee impeachment inquiry, **1998** 710
Jeremiah, David, Chinese nuclear-espionage mat-
  ter, **1999** 238
Jerusalem, status of, U.S. policy on, **1995** 623
Jet Propulsion Laboratory, *Galileo's* inspection
  of Jupiter's moon, **1997** 202–205
Jewell, Richard, Olympic Park bombing suspect
  case, **1996** 445, 446–447
Jews
  French apology for complicity with Nazis,
    1995 478–482
  Roman Catholic church Holocaust repentance
    statement, **1998** 121–130

Jiang Zemin
  China-U.S. summit meeting, **1997** 728–739;
    1999 726
  and Clinton news conference in China, **1998**
    466–478
  on death of Deng Xiaping, **1997** 94–100
  on earthquake in Taiwan, **1999** 468
  Hong Kong transfer ceremony statement,
    1997 502, 505–506
  Japan state visit, **1998** 541
Job creation
  Democratic Party platform, **1996** 629, 632–633
  Republican Party platform, **1996** 506–507
  technology worker shortage, **1997** 669–678
Job discrimination. *See* Discrimination, job
Jobless rate. *See* Unemployment rate
Joe Dimaggio Children's Hospital, **1999** 385
John Paul II
  Catholic-Jewish relations during the Holo-
    caust, **1998** 121–122, 124
  on Gospel of Life ("culture of death"), **1995**
    145–161
  on human rights, UN speech, **1995** 639–645
  land mines ban, **1997** 845
  religious freedom in Cuba, **1998** 30–37
Johns Hopkins Sexual Disorders Clinic (Balti-
  more), **1997** 385
Johnson, Andrew, impeachment, **1998** 697, 959;
  1999 15
Johnson, David R., Salt Lake Olympics Commit-
  tee, **1999** 106, 107
Johnson, Lyndon Baines, economic policy, **1998**
  500–501
Johnson, Magic, AIDS victim, **1998** 880–881
Johnson, Mitchell, **1998** 736
Johnson, Nancy L. (R-Conn.), **1995** 748
Johnston, J. Bennett (D-La.), **1995** 114–115
Johnston, Lloyd D., drug use among adolescents,
  1996 571
Joint Commission on the Accreditation of Health
  Care Organizations, **1999** 413
Jones, Ben, **1995** 748, 750; **1996** 840
Jones, David, on nuclear test ban treaty, **1998** 49
Jones, Paula Corbin, sexual harassment suit,
  1997 21, 290–298; **1998** 39, 565, 633–634,
  638–639, 962; **1999** 16, 21–22, 166
Jordan, Anthony, Baptist view on women and the
  family, **1998** 334
Jordan, Barbara (D-Texas), immigration reform,
  1995 565
Jordan, Larry R., on extremists in the military,
  1996 179
Jordan, Vernon, Jr., Lewinsky scandal, role in,
  1998 577–580, 635, 649–650; **1999** 17
Joste, Bruce, tobacco industry fraud suit, **1999**
  538
Journal of the American Medical Association
  (JAMA)
  end-of-life care report, **1997** 325–330
  physical activity report, **1996** 420
Juan Carlos (king of Spain), Panama Canal transfer ceremony, **1999** 853
Judicial system, federal court appointments,
  1998 48
Jupiter, NASA explorations, **1999** 175–176
Jupiter Communications, online stock trading
  study, **1999** 203
Juppé, Alain, French government programs,
  1995 229–230

Justice Department
  Bureau of Justice Statistics, use of guns in
    crime report, **1995** 463–471
  capital punishment report, **1999** 828–835
  curfews for juveniles, **1996** 325–333
  FBI crime laboratory, Office of the Inspector
    General (OIG) investigations, **1997** 221–228
  protective function privilege for Secret Ser-
    vice officers, **1998** 396, 566
  race-based redistricting, **1995** 369–372,
    378–379
  tobacco industry health risks fraud allega-
    tions, **1999** 536–551
Juvenile justice system
  curfew ordinances, **1996** 325–333
  death penalty, **1998** 187
  Democratic Party platform, **1996** 635
  juvenile crime bill, **1998** 48
  Republican Party platform, **1996** 522–523
  rise in juvenile crime, **1995** 711
  violent crime, **1996** 733
J.W. Hampton, Jr. & Co. v. U.S., **1998** 436

K

Kabbah, Ahmad, Sierra Leone peace negotia-
  tions, **1999** 430
Kabila, Laurent
  Congo leadership, **1998** 161; **1999** 430,
    645–646
  Zaire coup and new Congo leader, **1997** 877,
    879–885
Kaczynski, David, role in conviction of brother
  as Unabomber, **1998** 233–234
Kaczynski, Theodore J.
  Unabomber manifesto, **1995** 600–610
  Unabomber sentencing, **1998** 233–252
Kaden, Lewis B., **1999** 692
Kaiser, Karl, European defense force, **1999** 818
Kallstrom, James, TWA flight 800 crash, **1997**
  781, 783–786
Kambanda, Jean, genocide trials, **1998** 614–625
Kanka, Megan, sex offender victim, **1997** 384
Kansas, Sexually Violent Predator Act, **1997**
  382–394
Kansas City (Missouri), school uniform policy,
  1996 90
Kansas v. Hendricks, **1997** 382–394
Kantor, Mickey, commerce secretary appoint-
  ment, **1996** 204
Kaplan v. Burlington, **1995** 397
Karadzic, Radovan, war criminal, **1995** 718;
  1999 738, 803
Karlan, Pamela, **1995** 372
Karon, John M., AIDS statistics, **1996** 158–159
Karrazi, Kamal, Rushdie death threat lifted, **1998**
  691
Kartman, Charles, U.S.-North Korea diplomatic
  relations, **1999** 570
Kashmir, India-Pakistan disputes, **1999** 624–625
Kasich, John (R-Ohio), welfare reform, **1996**
  461–462
Kasparov, Garry, chess victory of IBM computer,
  1997 273–276
Kassebaum-Baker, Nancy Landon (R-Kan.)
  chemical weapons treaty, **1997** 201
  integration of women for military training,
    1997 657
  striking workers, **1995** 130
  women in the military, **1998** 336

Katz, Harvey, on UAW General Motors strike, **1998** 321–322

Katz, Julius, trade negotiations, **1999** 797

Katzenbach v. Morgan, **1997** 415

Kaufman, Frank J., Roswell incident, **1997** 401

Kavan, Jan, at NATO membership ceremony for Czech Republic, **1999** 121, 122–124

Kazakstan, nuclear weapons, **1996** 219–221

Kean, Thomas H.
  race relations panel, **1997** 316, 322; **1998** 668
  racial stereotyping, **1998** 666

Keating, Frank, on Oklahoma City bombing, **1995** 176, 179–180

Keeler, William (cardinal), antiabortion issue, **1998** 812

Kelling, George, violent crime, **1997** 682

Kelly, James, UPS strike statement, **1997** 634–635

Kemp, Jack F.
  vice-presidential campaign, Republican Party acceptance speech, **1996** 478, 480, 481–486
  vice-presidential debates, **1996** 707–709, 718–724

Kendall, David E., grand jury investigations, **1998** 567

Kennard, William E.
  ballot initiatives, **1999** 6
  telecommunications industry mergers, **1998** 341

Kennedy, Anthony M.
  affirmative action, federal government plans, **1995** 308, 310–319
  congressional term limits, **1995** 260–261, 270
  disability, definition of, **1999** 319, 320
  drug testing of students, **1995** 339–346
  endangered species on private lands, **1995** 359–368
  free speech, and the Internet, **1997** 445
  gay rights discrimination, **1996** 284–286, 287–291
  gay rights to march, **1995** 327–335
  gun-free school zone, **1995** 184, 192–194, 260
  HIV as a disability, **1998** 379, 381–388
  line-item veto, **1998** 421, 430–431
  parochial school aid, **1997** 363
  physician-assisted suicide, **1997** 461
  race-based redistricting, **1995** 369, 371, 373–380; **1996** 369, 371–379, 381
  religious freedom, **1997** 407–417
  religious publications, **1995** 385–395
  religious symbols, **1995** 387, 396–400
  sex offenders, right to confine, **1997** 383
  sexual harassment, **1998** 439–441, 453–461; **1999** 215, 217, 227–234
  states rights, immunity from suits, **1999** 333, 335, 336–344

Kennedy, Carolyn Bessette, death of, **1999** 422

Kennedy, David, death of, **1999** 423

Kennedy, Edward M. (D-Mass.)
  Chappaquiddick incident, **1999** 422–423
  church arson prevention, **1997** 306
  eulogy for John F. Kennedy Jr., **1999** 422–427
  health insurance costs, **1998** 141
  health insurance for disabled persons, **1999** 49
  on minimum wage, **1996** 564
  patient safety legislation, **1999** 782
  religious freedom, **1997** 409
  same-sex marriages, **1996** 688

Kennedy, John F.
  assassination of, **1999** 422
    CIA involvement, **1997** 104
  on leadership, **1997** 49
  tax cut proposal, **1999** 93

Kennedy, John F., Jr., eulogy for, **1999** 422–427

Kennedy, Joseph P., II (D-Mass.), liquor advertising, **1996** 772

Kennedy, Michael, death of, **1999** 423

Kennedy, Patrick F., embassy security, **1998** 557

Kennedy, Robert F., assassination of, **1999** 422

Kennesaw State College (KSC), Gingrich Renewing American Civilization course, **1997** 8, 14

Kenya, embassy bombings, **1998** 555–563; **1999** 53, 524, 690

Kerner Commission report, update on, **1998** 667–668

Kerr, Donald M., Jr., FBI crime laboratory director, **1997** 221

Kerrey, Bob (D-Neb.)
  IRS reform, **1997** 663
  social security reform, **1998** 100
  on U.S.-Vietnam relations, **1995** 472
  war hero, **1999** 39

Kerry, John (D-Mass.)
  global warming, **1997** 862
  U.S.-Vietnam relations, **1995** 472

Kessler, David A.
  cigarette regulations, **1995** 670–679
  FDA regulations, testimony on, **1996** 598–599
  silicone breast implants, **1995** 515–523
  smoking and health panel, **1997** 334

Kessler, Gladys, **1995** 131

Kevorkian, Jack ("Dr. Death"), physician-assisted suicide cases, **1996** 122; **1997** 329; **1999** 442

Keynes, John Maynard, **1999** 93

Khamenei, Ayatollah Ali, **1998** 688, 689

Khatami, Mohammed
  Iran presidential election, **1997** 284–289; **1998** 687, 688
  U.S.-Iran relations, **1998** 687

Khieu Samphan, **1998** 972–975

Khmer Rouge, collapse of the, **1998** 971–975

Khomeini, Ayatollah Ruholla
  death of, **1998** 688
  Rushdie death threat, **1998** 687

Kilberg, William, on sexual harassment policy, **1998** 441

Kim Dae-jung
  Japan relations, **1998** 541
  relations with North Korea, **1999** 576
  South Korean elections, **1997** 835, 892–897

Kim Il Sung, and Korean War, **1995** 507

Kim Jong Il, **1997** 894, 895

Kim Un Yong, International Olympics Committee investigations, **1999** 106, 108

Kim Young Sam
  Korean War veterans memorial dedication, **1995** 506, 508–509
  South Korean president, **1997** 892, 893

King, Jeffrey C., on maternal mortality, **1996** 344–345

King, Martin Luther, Jr., celebration of on Inauguration Day, **1997** 22, 25

King, Willie, victim of medical mistake, **1999** 782

Kinkel, Kipland P. "Kip," **1998** 736

Kinkel, Klaus, NATO expansion, **1996** 657

Kinnock, Neil, European Commission commissioner, **1999** 156, 158

Kiriyenko, Sergei, Russian economy, **1998** 603, 604
Kirkingburg v. Albertson's, **1999** 319
Kirkland, Lane, retirement from AFL-CIO, **1995** 680–681
Kirkpatrick, Jeane J., nuclear test ban treaty, **1999** 608
Kissinger, Henry A.
  Cuban foreign policy, **1998** 33
  International Olympics Committee investigations, **1999** 109
  nuclear test ban treaty, **1999** 601
Kittinger, Joseph W., Jr., Roswell incident, **1997** 396, 401
Kitzhaber, John, physician-assisted suicide, **1997** 463
Klausner, Richard
  cancer death rates, **1996** 790
  mammogram advocate, **1997** 144, 145–149
  on tamoxifen trials, **1998** 194, 197–198, 202
Klebold, Dylan, Columbine High School shooter, **1999** 179
Klein, Joel, Microsoft Corp. antitrust ruling, **1999** 658–659
Kleinfield, Andrew J., **1997** 184
Kocharian, Robert, shootings in Armenian parliament, **1999** 639–642
Koh, Harold, on violence in Kosovo, **1999** 805–806
Kohl, Helmut
  at economic summit (Denver), **1997** 342
  euro currency plans, **1998** 272–273
  German economic reforms, **1998** 816–817
  German unification, **1998** 816
  reelection defeat, **1998** 273, 815; **1999** 77
Kolb, Ben, death of, **1999** 782
Kolbe, Jim (R-Ariz.), social security reform, **1998** 101
Koller, Arnold, **1997** 259
Konopliv, Alex, gravity map of the moon, **1998** 117
Koop, C. Everett, smoking and health, **1997** 332, 334
Koop, James Charles, antiabortion protester, **1998** 811
Kopechne, Mary Jo, death of, **1999** 423
Korea, Democratic Republic of (North Korea). *See* North Korea
Korea, Republic of (South Korea). *See* South Korea
Korean war (1950-1953)
  background, **1995** 507–508
  land mine warfare, **1995** 50
  No Gun Ri massacre, **1999** 552–558
  veterans memorial dedication, **1995** 506–511
Korematsu v. U.S., **1995** 313
Koresh, David, Branch Davidian cult leader, **1997** 123; **1999** 480
Koskinen, John A., Y2K conversion, **1998** 543–544; **1999** 761, 764
Kosovo war
  human rights violations, **1999** 802–816
  NATO air war against Serbian forces
    Clinton announcement, **1999** 134–143
    UNSC resolution on, **1999** 285–296
  NATO bombing campaign, **1999** 119, 122
  Racak massacre, **1999** 135
  UN economic assistance, **1999** 429

UN situation report, **1998** 827–841
U.S. involvement, **1999** 601
Kouchner, Bernard, NATO peacekeeping mission in Kosovo, **1999** 287–288
KPMG Peat Marwick, volunteer program, **1997** 240
Kreps, Juanita M., Commission on the Future of Worker-Management Relations member, **1995** 15
Krikalev, Sergei, **1998** 932
Krueger, Alan B., minimum wage, **1996** 564
Ku Klux Klan
  church arson cases, **1997** 302
  religious symbols, **1995** 387, 396–404
Kunkel, Dale, television rating system, **1997** 528
Kupolati, Rufus M., **1999** 861
Kurdish peoples
  Iraq situation report, **1996** 680–686
  and Iraqi chemical weapons, **1996** 740
Kyl, John (R-Ariz.)
  chemical weapons treaty, **1996** 741, 742
  computer security issues, **1998** 678

L

La Bella, Charles, campaign finance investigations, **1998** 891
Labor-management relations, future of, **1995** 15–23
Labor market, developments in, **1999** 97–102
Labor unions
  labor movement advances, **1999** 630–638
  for medical profession, **1999** 632–633
  World Trade Organization and, **1999** 799–800
LaHood, Ray (R-Ill.), House impeachment vote, **1998** 961
Lake Mead National Recreation Area (Nevada), **1995** 124, 126, 127
Lamb's Chapel v. Center Moriches Union Free School District, **1995** 390–391, 393, 398, 399
Lamm, Richard D., Reform Party candidate, **1996** 551
Land mines
  global ban on antipersonnel land mines, **1997** 358, 844–858
  Kosovo conflict, **1998** 837
  military history of, **1995** 49–51
  State Department report on, **1995** 46–54
  treaty banning, **1997** 844–858; **1998** 541
Languages, official, English in states of U.S., **1995** 573–574, 577–578
Lao Tsu, on leadership, **1998** 154
LaPierre, Wayne, and the National Rifle Association, **1995** 208–215
Largent, Steve (R-Okla.), Clinton state of the union address, Republican response, **1999** 58, 60–63
Latin America
  Democratic Party platform, **1996** 645
  Republican Party platform, **1996** 545–546
Lau v. Nichols, **1998** 313
Law, Bernard (cardinal), antiabortion issue, **1998** 812
Law enforcement
  aggressive driving and, **1997** 554, 556–558
  "broken windows" theory, **1997** 682–683
  community policing, **1997** 39

employees in U.S., **1996** 739; **1997** 689; **1998** 877; **1999** 622
police corps, **1997** 244
Lawrence, David M., health care, **1997** 791
Lawyers, attorney-client privilege, Supreme Court on, **1998** 393–404
Le Van Bang, Vietnam ambassador, **1997** 489
Leach, Jim (R-Iowa), on Gingrich as House Speaker, **1997** 3–4
Leahy, Patrick (D-Vt.)
  farm legislation, **1996** 200–201
  land mines ban, **1997** 845, 846
  medical records security, **1997** 582–583
Leape, Lucian, medical mistakes, 28, 781
Leavitt, Mike (Utah governor), Salt Lake olympics corruption scandal, **1999** 106
Leavy, Edward, **1997** 184
Lebanon, UN peacekeeping mission, **1997** 151, 154, 155, 156
Lebow, Cynthia, on National Transportation Safety Board, **1999** 115
Lee, Barbara Combis, death with dignity, **1997** 462
Lee, Bill, nomination for Office of Civil Rights, **1997** 765
Lee, Martin, Hong Kong dissident, **1997** 502
Lee v. Weisman, **1995** 547
Lee, Wen Ho, espionage accusations, **1999** 235, 241
Legislative reform, Clinton on unfunded mandates legislation, **1995** 141–145
Lehman, Betsy, death of, **1999** 782
Lehrer, Jim, in presidential and vice-presidential debates, **1996** 709–731
Lemon v. Kurtzman, **1997** 372
Leshner, Alan, research on marijuana for medical purposes, **1996** 757
Levin, Carl M. (D-Mich.), limits on gifts to members of Congress, **1995** 701, 702
Levine, Arnold J., AIDS research, **1996** 157
Levitt, Arthur, online investing, SEC chairman on, **1999** 203–214
Levy, David, Israel foreign minister appointment, **1999** 362
Levy, Mark, union for interns and medical residents, **1999** 633
Lewinsky, Monica
  job search, **1998** 582–584, 635, 647–649, 659–660
  Jordan (Vernon) involvement, **1998** 577–580, 584, 635, 649–650, 660; **1999** 17
  scandal
    alleged Clinton affair, **1998** 38–39; **1999** 601
    Clinton apology to the nation, **1998** 568–569
    Clinton denial to staff, **1998** 581–582
    Clinton grand jury testimony, **1998** 564–585, 651–652, 655–656
    Clinton public denials, **1998** 566; **1999** 15
    Clinton refusal to testify, **1998** 661–662
    Clinton-Lewinsky denial of affair, **1998** 38–39, 565
    Clinton-Lewinsky meetings, **1998** 572–574, 656–657
    dress stains and DNA sample, **1998** 639
    Flynt of *Hustler* magazine muckraking campaign, **1998** 953
    gifts, concealment of evidence, **1998** 583–584, 635, 643–645, 656–657, 658–659
    secretary Betty Currie's role, **1998** 574–576, 583, 650–651
    sexual relationship, **1998** 570–572, 584–585, 640–641
    Starr report, **1998** 632–664
    Tripp (Linda) tapes, **1998** 565–566
  testimony, **1998** 576–577
Lewis, John (D-Ga.)
  affirmative action programs, **1998** 859
  civil rights, **1995** 372
Lewis, Pamela A., affirmative action, **1996** 761
Lewis, Stephen, AIDS epidemic in Africa, **1999** 490
Liability, Supreme Court on punitive damages, **1996** 274–283
Libya
  U.S. airstrikes against, **1998** 586
  weapons proliferation, **1996** 212–213, 218; **1997** 198
Lieberman, Joseph I. (D-Conn.)
  affirmative action programs, **1995** 485
  Clinton censure resolution, **1999** 21
Life expectancy
  in African countries declining, **1998** 879, 886
  worldwide, **1996** 305; **1999** 588
Liggett Group Inc., smoking and addiction, **1997** 333
Lin Biao, coup attempt, **1997** 97
Lindsey, Bruce R., presidential attorney-client privilege, **1998** 393
Little, Greg, tobacco industry fraud suit, **1999** 538
Livingston, Robert L. (R-La.)
  air strikes against Iraq, **1998** 937
  on Clinton education agenda, **1997** 29
  extra-marital affair, **1998** 953
  House Speaker challenge, **1998** 802
  House Speaker resignation, **1998** 799, 951–957, 959, 962
Lobbyists, registration and financial disclosure, **1995** 700, 702–703
Locke, Gary (Washington State governor), **1997** 43
Lofgren, Zoe (D-Calif.), House Judiciary Committee impeachment inquiry, **1998** 707
Logdson, John M., space exploration cost reduction, **1999** 712
Long Beach (Calif.), school uniform policy, **1996** 89
Lopez, Alfonso, Jr., **1995** 183
Loprest, Pamela, welfare reform report, **1999** 259
Loral Space and Communications Systems Ltd., **1999** 237, 250
Lorillard Tobacco Co., claims settlement, **1997** 331; **1998** 842
Los Alamos National Laboratory (LANL), nuclear secrets theft, **1999** 235, 241
Lott, Trent (R-Miss.)
  air strikes against Iraq, **1998** 937, 961
  balanced budget agreement, **1997** 604
  campaign finance reform, **1997** 31, 827; **1998** 893
  chemical weapons treaty, **1996** 742; **1997** 196–197
  Clinton state of the union address, Republican response, **1998** 40–41, 54–59

Congress
  closing remarks at 104th Congress, **1996**
    701–703
  limits on gifts to members of, **1995** 701
  Senate "Leaders Lecture Series," **1998** 151
  Senate majority leader election, **1996** 271
  shooting of Capitol policemen, **1998**
    513–514
  health care reform, **1997** 791
  Jiang Zemin state visit, **1997** 730
  liquor advertising, **1996** 772
  nuclear test ban treaty, **1999** 600–603, 607–610
  Panama Canal, U.S. policy, **1999** 852
  television rating system, **1997** 529
Loving v. U.S., **1997** 296
Loving v. Virginia, **1995** 313
Lucid, Shannon W., space flight, **1996** 691–694;
  1999 611
Lugar, Richard G. (R-Ind.)
  chemical weapons treaty, **1996** 741
  NATO expansion, **1997** 517
  nuclear materials in former Soviet states,
    1996 141
  nuclear test ban treaty, **1999** 602, 608
Lundgren v. Superior Court (Ct. App. 1996),
  1997 189
Luxembourg, euro currency, **1998** 271
Lynch v. Donnelly, **1995** 399
Lynn, Joanne, end-of-life care, **1997** 327, 328–330

M

McAleese, May, **1999** 756
McAndrew, James, Roswell incident, **1997**
  396–405
McCaffrey, Barry R.
  cocaine penalties, sentencing for, **1997** 246
  drug control programs, **1996** 617
  drug czar appointment, **1996** 30
  drug use among teenagers, **1996** 571–572
  drug use survey, **1999** 459, 461
  marijuana law enforcement, **1996** 756; **1997**
    462
McCain, John (R-Ariz.)
  campaign finance investigations, **1996** 840
  campaign finance reform, **1997** 31, 33,
    826–827; **1998** 50, 893; **1999** 56
  International Olympics Committee investiga-
    tions, **1999** 108
  line-item veto, **1997** 611; **1998** 422
  on presidential credibility abroad, **1995** 720
  Republican Party convention nomination
    speech, **1996** 479
  television rating system, **1997** 529
  tobacco claims settlement, **1998** 841
  on U.S.-Vietnam relations, **1995** 472–473
  war hero, **1999** 39
McCollum, Bill (R-Fla.), House Judiciary Committee impeachment inquiry, **1998** 702–703
McConnell, Mitch (R-Ky.), limits on gifts to members of Congress, **1995** 701
McCulloch v. Maryland, **1999** 347
McCurry, Michael D.
  on outreach events, **1997** 761
  security clearance reform, **1995** 532
McDowell, Barbara, gun control laws, **1995** 185
McEntee, George, W., **1995** 681
McGowan, Daniel, health care, **1997** 791
McGuinnes, Martin, **1999** 756

McGuinness, Jeffrey C., **1995** 130
McGwire, Mark
  home run record, **1998** 626–631
  use of steroids, **1999** 461
McHugh, James T., **1995** 145–146
McKay, David S., **1996** 472, 474–476
McKay, James C., Meese investigation, **1998** 906
McKinney, Cynthia A. (D-Ga.), **1995** 370
McKinney, Gene C., military sexual harassment
  case, **1997** 656–657; **1998** 336
McLaughlin v. Florida, **1995** 313
McLaury, Bruce K., **1996** 785
McMillan, John L., and DC home rule charter,
  1995 497
Macroeconomic policy, **1999** 93–94
McVeigh, Timothy, and Oklahoma City bombing,
  1995 177; **1996** 178; **1997** 623–627; **1999**
  480
Madison, James, on the constitution, **1997**
  416
Madrid Declaration on Euro-Atlantic Security
  and Cooperation, **1997** 514–526
Major, John
  ousted by Tony Blair, **1998** 204
  as prime minister, **1997** 277–278, 279
Malaysia
  economic crisis, **1998** 722
  financial crisis, **1997** 833
Mallon, Seamus, Northern Ireland peace agreement, **1998** 205; **1999** 754, 756
Maltais, Vern, Roswell incident, **1997** 401
Mammograms, **1997** 38, 142–149
Managed care
  health insurance coverage, Census Bureau on,
    1999 561–567
  and patients rights, **1998** 46–47
Mandela, Nelson
  Burundi conflict mediator, **1999** 867
  Clinton state visit, **1998** 161–167
  on death penalty, **1995** 283
  on executions in Nigeria, **1995** 697, 698
  land mines ban, **1997** 845
  remarks opening Parliament, **1995** 101–109
  South African constitution, **1996** 249
  South African leadership and legacy, **1999**
    297–299
  South African Truth and Reconciliation Com-
    mission report, **1998** 756
Mandela, Winnie, human rights abuses, **1998**
  758, 771–772
Manley, Audrey F., physical activity report, **1996**
  418
Mansfield, Mike (D-Mont.), on civility in the Sen-
  ate, **1998** 151–158
Mao Zedong, **1997** 94, 95, 97, 98
Mapplethorpe, Robert, **1998** 406
Marbury v. Madison, **1997** 417; **1998** 909
Marcy, Geoffrey, planet explorations and discov-
  ery, **1999** 174–177
Marijuana
  decriminalization of, **1996** 571
  legalization for medical use, **1996** 755–758;
    1997 462
  use in U.S., **1996** 575, 579; **1999** 460, 463
Maris, Roger, home run record, **1998** 626
Markey, Edward (D-Mass.), television rating sys-
  tem, **1996** 833; **1997** 529
Marriage, same-sex marriages, **1996** 687–690;
  1997 761

Mars
life on, NASA statements on, **1996** 471–477
NASA explorations, **1999** 175–176
Marsh, Robert T., infrastructure commission
chairman, **1997** 712
Marshall, F. Ray, Commission on the Future of
Worker-Management Relations member, **1995**
15
Martin, Graham, former ambassador to Vietnam,
1997 489
Martinez, Marty (D-Calif.), apparel industry
sweatshops, **1997** 209
Martinez, Ricardo
aggressive driving, **1997** 550
air bag regulations, **1996** 801–806; **1997**
774–775
Martonyi, Janos, at NATO membership ceremony
for Hungary, **1999** 121, 124–125
*Marya S. Norman-Bloodsaw et al. v. Lawrence
Berkeley Laboratory et al.*, **1998** 66–72
Maryland, welfare reform, **1999** 258
Maskhadov, Aslan, Chechnya war, **1999** 910
Maternal mortality, UNICEF report on, **1996**
343–352
Matloff, Norm, **1997** 669
Matsch, Richard P., **1997** 624
Mayer, Thomas, on European economy, **1999** 78
Mayhew, Patrick, meeting with Gerry Adams of
Sinn Fein, **1995** 728
Mayor, Michael, planet detection, **1999** 173–174
Mazur, Jay, apparel industry workplace monitor-
ing, **1997** 208
Mbeki, Thabo
amnesty, **1998** 759
ANC human rights violations, **1998** 756
South Africa presidential inauguration speech,
1999 297–303
U.S. trade sanctions, **1999** 491
Mead, Kenneth, and airport security, **1999** 114
Mease, Darrell, death sentence commuted, **1999**
830
Medicaid
eligibility, **1998** 88; **1999** 564
for persons with disabilities, **1999** 320
reform, **1996** 451, 557
spending growth, **1997** 52, 63–64
Medical records, privacy issue, **1997** 580–587,
795
Medicare
budget surplus and, **1999** 42, 43, 45–46, 90,
354–356
coverage for mammograms, **1997** 38
reform, **1996** 557, 712–713; **1998** 89, 93–94
spending growth, **1997** 52, 63–64
Meehan, Martin T. (D-Mass.)
campaign finance reform, **1997** 33; **1998** 893;
1999 56
House Judiciary Committee impeachment
inquiry, **1998** 708–709
Meek v. Pittenger, **1997** 366, 377
Meese, Edwin, III, investigation of, **1998** 906
Megawati Sukarnoputri, **1999** 718–720
Meisinger, Susan R.
on EEOC guidelines on mental disabilities,
1997 129
on sexual harassment policy and practice,
1998 441
Memphis (Tenn.), school uniform policy, **1996**
91

Mental health
EEOC mental disabilities guidelines, **1997**
127–141
surgeon general's report on, **1999** 836–849
therapist-patient privilege, Supreme Court on,
1996 388–395
White House Conference on, **1999** 49
Mental retardation, death penalty, **1998** 187–188
MERCOSUR (customs union), **1998** 95
Meritor Savings Bank v. Vinson, **1998** 438,
445–446, 449, 455–457, 460, 463
Metro Broadcasting, Inc. v. FCC, **1995** 308, 312,
315–316, 322–323
Metzler, Cynthia, apparel industry sweatshops,
1997 209
Mexico
immigration to U.S., **1997** 176–177
religious persecution, **1997** 564
Meyer v. Grant, **1999** 5
Meyerhoff, Al, **1996** 72
Mfume, Kweisi (D-Md.)
at Million Man March, **1995** 656
new president and CEO of NAACP, **1995** 453,
454–455
on Texaco executives racial slurs, **1996** 765,
766
Michel, Robert H. (R-Ill.), **1998** 800
Michigan Dept. of State Police States v. Stitz,
1995 342
Microsoft Corporation, antitrust case, **1999**
654–689
Middle-Class Bill of Rights, **1995** 73–74, 86–87
Middle East
Democratic Party platform, **1996** 645
Republican Party platform on, **1996** 544–545
weapons development, **1996** 217–218
Middle East peace
Barak comments on, **1999** 364–366
Declaration of Principles, **1995** 622; **1998**
742
statement of G-8, **1997** 359
terrorist opposition to, **1995** 39
U.S. role in, **1995** 623–624
West Bank agreement, **1995** 622–630
Wye River peace agreement, **1998** 742–754;
1999 52–53, 700
Milbank Memorial Fund, end-of-life care guidelines, **1997** 329
Military bases, closing of, commission report,
1995 407–418
Military personnel
bombing in Saudi Arabia, **1996** 672–679
gays in the military, **1999** 899–901
homosexual ban, **1997** 761
homosexual ban lifted in Britain, **1999** 901
sexual harassment, Army report on, **1997**
654–660; **1998** 335–336
Military strength
Democratic Party platform, **1996** 642–644
readiness for future wars, **1997** 813
Miller, George (D-Calif.)
apparel industry sweatshops, **1997** 209
and Gingrich ethics violation complaint, **1995**
748, 751
Miller v. California, **1997** 449–450
Miller v. Johnson, **1995** 369–384; **1996** 369
Million Man March
Clinton remarks on, **1995** 646, 655
Farrakhan's remarks at, **1995** 655–669

Mills, Cheryl D., Clinton impeachment trial, **1999** 19
Milosevic, Slobodan
 Bosnia conflict, **1995** 717, 719
 Kosovo conflict, **1998** 828–831; **1999** 134–136, 139, 285–286
 war crimes, **1999** 738, 802–803
Milutinovic, Milan, war criminal, **1999** 803
Miner, Roger J., **1996** 123–124
Minimum wage
 Clinton proposals for raising, **1995** 70; **1996** 59; **1999** 42, 43, 88
 Clinton's remarks on, **1996** 563–569
 Democrat vs. Republican position on, **1996** 697
 increase in, effect on welfare rolls, **1999** 257
Minorities
 presidential advisory board on race relations report, **1998** 665–675
 race-based redistricting, **1995** 369–384; **1996** 368–387
Mir (space station)
 Lucid flight experience, **1996** 691–694; **1999** 611
 news conference from space, **1995** 419–425
 service and decommissioning of, **1998** 929–930
Missile systems
 antimissile defense system, **1998** 483–484
 scud-based missile infrastructures, **1998** 488–492
 threats to U.S., Rumsfeld Commission on, **1998** 481–499
Missing in action (MIAs), accounting for in Southeast Asia, **1995** 472–473, 475; **1999** 476
 Vietnam, negotiations with, **1997** 491
Missouri, death row executions, **1999** 830
Mitchell, George J. (D-Maine)
 independent counsel legislation, **1999** 168
 olympic bribery scandal investigations, **1999** 107–108, 109
 tobacco industry lobbyist, **1997** 335
Mitchell, George J. (*former* D-Maine)
 Bosnia, Dayton peace agreement, **1999** 736
 Northern Ireland peace negotiations, **1998** 204–205; **1999** 753, 754–755
Mitterrand, François
 antipoverty proposal, **1995** 135
 and deportation of Jews, **1995** 479
Miyazawa, Kichi, Japanese monetary policy, **1998** 533
Mladic, Ratko, war criminal, **1995** 718; **1999** 738, 739, 803
Mobutu Sese Seko, ousted from Zaire, **1997** 877–879; **1998** 161, 220, 615; **1999** 428, 645, 863
Modjeski, Leland William, **1995** 256
Molinari, Susan (R-N.Y.)
 Republican Party convention keynote speech, **1996** 479
 welfare reform, **1996** 462
Molitoris, Jolene, on railroad safety regulations, **1996** 190
Monaghan, Henry P., on commerce clause, **1995** 185
Monetary policy
 euro currency, **1998** 271–280; **1999** 75–84
 European corporate bond market, **1999** 77–78
Monsanto, jobs for welfare recipients, **1997** 34, 622

Montt, Efrain Rios, **1996** 851
Moore, Charles B., Roswell incident, **1997** 400
Moore, Henson, forest preservation, **1999** 595
Moorer, Thomas, Panama Canal transfer, **1999** 852
Moose, George E., UN death penalty report, **1998** 185
Morgan v. Nucci, **1998** 864
Morris, Dick, Clinton campaign strategist resignation, **1996** 601
Mortality rates
 cancer deaths, **1996** 790–793
 for children, **1999** 384
 worldwide, **1996** 305–306
Morton, David, North Korean, UN humanitarian aid, **1999** 572
Moscoso, Mireya
 first woman president of Panama, **1999** 851
 Panama Canal transfer ceremony, **1999** 853
Mosser, Thomas, victim of Unabomber, **1998** 234, 235, 237–238
Movesian, Musheg, **1999** 639
Moynihan, Daniel Patrick (D-N.Y.)
 government secrecy, **1997** 103–104
 health insurance for disabled persons, **1999** 49
 social security reform, **1998** 100
 welfare reform, **1996** 452
Mozambique, UN role in, **1995** 355
Mubarak, Hosni
 eulogy for Yitzhak Rabin, **1995** 691, 694–695
 West Bank peace agreement, **1995** 622
Mukai, Chiaki, Japanese astronaut, **1998** 776
Mulligan, Deirdre K., medical records privacy, **1997** 582
Mulroney, Brian, Canadian cabinet members, **1998** 594
Mumcu, Erkan, on earthquake in Turkey, **1999** 466
Mundy, Carl E., Jr., chemical weapons, **1997** 201
Murayama, Tomichi, apology for World War II suffering, **1995** 302–306
Murder rate. *See* Homicide, rate of
Murdoch, Rupert, **1995** 749–759
Murkowski, Frank H. (R-Alaska)
 global warming, **1997** 862
 Hanford cleanup, **1995** 114–115
Murphy v. United Parcel Service, **1999** 319
Murray, Gilbert P., victim of Unabomber, **1998** 234, 237
Museveni, Yoweri K., Ugandan leadership, **1998** 161; **1999** 646
Musharraf, Pervez, military coup, **1999** 623–629
Mussa, Michael, Asian monetary policy, **1998** 725

N

NAACP. *See* National Association for the Advancement of Colored People (NAACP)
Nader, Ralph, on corporate mergers, **1998** 341–342
Nadler, Jerrold (D-N.Y.)
 House impeachment vote, **1998** 961, 963
 House Judiciary Committee impeachment inquiry, **1998** 705
Nagorno-Karabakh conflict, **1999** 640–641
Nakajima, Hiroshi, on infectious diseases, **1996** 302

Namibia, UN role in, **1995** 355
Nandan, Satya, **1995** 524, 526–527
Nathan, Irv, independent counsel statute, **1998** 908
Nation of Islam, **1995** 453, 455, 646, 657
National Aeronautics and Space Administration (NASA)
  age of the universe estimates, **1996** 265–269
  Climate Orbiter mission to Mars investigation, **1999** 711–717
  Discovery space shuttle mission, **1998** 776–786
  Galileo mission to Jupiter's moons, **1997** 202–205
  Hubble space telescope, birth of stars, **1995** 288–293
  International Space Station, **1998** 929–933
  life on Mars, **1996** 471–477
  Lunar Prospector findings of moon ice, **1998** 113–120
  multiplanet solar system discovery, **1999** 173–178
  Pathfinder mission to Mars, **1997** 509–513
National Air and Space Museum, *Enola Gay* exhibit, **1995** 55–58
National Association for the Advancement of Colored People (NAACP)
  church arson prevention, **1997** 311
  Evers-Williams address, **1995** 453–462
  on race-based redistricting, **1995** 372
National Association of Evangelicals, **1997** 311
National Association of Secondary School Principals, sexual harassment in schools, **1999** 218
National Association of Securities Dealers (NASD)
  regulation of, **1999** 204–205
  suitability rule, **1999** 205
National Bioethics Advisory Commission, cloning of humans moratorium, **1997** 213–214
National Board for Professional Teaching Standards, **1997** 35
National Campaign to Prevent Teen Pregnancy, **1998** 263; **1999** 386
National Cancer Institute (NCI)
  breast cancer drug tamoxifen, **1998** 194–202
  cancer deaths declining, **1996** 790–793
  funding, **1998** 53
  mammogram controversy, **1997** 142–149
  nuclear testing fallout, **1997** 591–601
National Center for Education Statistics (NCES), teacher quality survey, **1999** 64–71
National Center for Health Statistics (NCHS), teenage pregnancy report, **1998** 260–267; **1999** 385
National Center for Missing and Exploited Children, sex offenders, **1997** 384
National Center for Tobacco-Free Kids, **1997** 335
National Church Arson Task Force (NCATF), report, **1997** 301–313
National Commission on the Causes and Prevention of Violence, **1999** 615
National Commission on the Cost of Higher Education, report on college costs, **1998** 3–18
National Commission on Separation of Powers report, **1998** 905–911
National Conference of Roman Catholic Bishops
  antiabortion crusade, **1998** 811–812
  physician-assisted suicide, opposition to, **1996** 124

National Coordinator for Security, Infrastructure Protection, and Counter-Terrorism, **1998** 677
National Council on the Arts, decency standards, **1998** 406
National Council of Churches
  church arson prevention, **1997** 304, 306, 311
  religious freedom, **1997** 408
National Crime Victimization Survey (NCVS), **1998** 869–870
  use of guns in crime, **1995** 463–471
National Declassification Center, **1997** 105, 108–109
National Defense Panel, national security needs, **1997** 811–821
National Earthquake Information Center (U.S.), **1999** 465
National Economic Council (NEC), **1997** 62
National Education Goals Panel, **1996** 106
National Endowment for the Arts (NEA)
  decency in the arts, **1998** 405–418
  funding, **1998** 406, 407–408
  future of nonprofit arts, **1997** 699–710
National Endowment for the Arts v. Finley, **1998** 405–418
National Foreign Affairs Training Center (NFATC), religious persecution training, **1998** 27
National Highway Traffic Safety Administration (NHTSA)
  aggressive driving, **1997** 550–561
  automobile air bag regulations, **1996** 801–806; **1997** 774–779
National Household Survey on Drug Abuse (NHSDA), **1996** 570–579; **1999** 459–464
National Institute of Child Health and Human Development, **1997** 425
National Institutes of Health (NIH)
  acupuncture, panel on, **1997** 749–759
  AIDS research, **1996** 156–166; **1997** 38, 83
  end-of-life care research, **1997** 327, 330
  funding for, **1998** 53
National Labor Relations Board, on labor unions for hospital interns and medical residents, **1999** 633
National Labor Relations Board v. Jones & Laughlin Steel Corp., **1995** 188, 191–192
National Labor Relations Board v. Mackay Radio and Telegraph, **1995** 129
National League of Cities (NLC), child welfare, **1999** 385
National Longitudinal Study of Adolescent Health, **1997** 424
National Nuclear Security Administration, **1999** 240–241
National Oceanic and Atmospheric Administration (NOAA), global warming and record high temperatures, **1998** 946
National Park Service (NPS)
  GAO report on deteriorating conditions, **1996** 580–588
  GAO testimony on management of, **1995** 120–128
  new parks, **1996** 581
National Performance Review (NPR), report, **1995** 75, 83–85
National Research Council (NRC)
  carcinogens in the diet, **1996** 71–79
  medical records security, **1997** 581

National Rifle Association (NRA)
  assault weapon ban repeal efforts, **1995**
    464–465
  Bush resignation from, **1995** 208–215
National School Boards Association
  child welfare, **1999** 385
  drug-testing for athletes, **1995** 341
  sexual harassment of students, **1999** 215
National Science Foundation
  emergency rescue of South Pole doctor, **1999**
    611–613
  funding, **1998** 53
National security
  clearances of government employees, **1995**
    532–545
  computer security, GAO report on, **1998**
    676–686
  computer security threats, **1996** 312–324;
    1997 111–112
  declassifying government secrets, **1997** 105,
    108–109
  Democratic Party platform, **1996** 641–644
  Dole Republican convention speech on, **1996**
    493
  in federal buildings, **1995** 178–179
  government secrecy report, **1997** 103–112
  infrastructure protection, **1997** 711–720
  "leaking" of information, **1997** 106
  missile threat, Rumsfeld Commission on,
    1998 481–499
  National Defense Panel needs report, **1997**
    811–821
  nuclear weapons secrets theft by China, U.S.
    accusations of, **1999** 235–256, 304
  Pennsylvania Avenue closing, **1995** 254–258
  Pentagon Papers case, **1997** 104, 105–106
  threats in the next century, **1999** 499–510
  U.S. nuclear strategy, **1997** 811, 814
  "Verona" project, **1997** 104
National Security Act, **1997** 811
National Security Council (NSC), creation of,
  1997 811
National Socialism, in Germany, **1998** 127
National Socialist Party of America v. Skokie,
  1995 331
National Survey of America's Families, **1999**
  259
National Telecommunications and Information
  Administration, report, **1999** 368–383
National Transportation Safety Board (NTSB)
  aviation safety, **1999** 115
  railroad safety recommendations, **1996** 189,
    191
  TWA flight 800 crash, **1997** 780–786
  ValuJet crash, **1996** 238
National Union for the Total Independence of
  Angola, **1999** 431
Native Americans
  religious freedom, **1997** 406–407, 410
  teenage birth rates, **1998** 261
NATO. *See* North Atlantic Treaty Organization
  (NATO)
Natural disasters, **1999** 468–469
  See also Earthquakes
Natural resources
  national forests, Clinton "roadless initiative,"
    1999 592–599
  National Park Service, GAO testimony on,
    1995 120–128

Natural Resources Defense Council (NRDC),
  world fisheries conservation, **1995** 524
Navarro Valls, Joaquin, on UN Conference on
  Women, Vatican views, **1995** 583–584
Nazi concentration camps
  French apology for complicity with Nazis,
    1995 478482
  French complicity with Nazis, **1995** 478
  gold from victims of, **1997** 269
  refugees from to Switzerland, **1997** 265
Nazi Germany
  anti-Semitism and the Shoah, **1998** 127–129
  confiscated art, return of, **1998** 294–295
  neutral nations aid to, **1997** 257–272; **1998**
    291–312
Ndiaye, Bacre Waly, death penalty in U.S., **1998**
  183–193
Needle exchange programs, for drug users, **1997**
  81, 82, 87–88
Netanyahu, Benjamin
  Israeli prime minister election, **1996** 337–342
  Israeli prime minister election defeat, **1999**
    359–360, 890
  Wye River peace agreement, **1998** 742–747,
    749–750; **1999** 891
Netherlands, euro currency, **1998** 271
Nettles, Bonnie Lu Trousdale, Heaven's Gate cult
  leader, **1997** 122–124
Nettleton, Joyce A., **1996** 72
Neuborne, Bert, **1995** 327
New Jersey, Megan's Law, for sex offenders,
  1997 382, 384
New Jersey v. T.L.O., **1995** 342, 347, 348
Newman, Jim, **1998** 932
Nicaragua, hurricane damage, **1998** 789, 791
Nichols, Terry L., and Oklahoma City bombing,
  1995 177; **1996** 178; **1997** 223, 623–627
Nicholson, Harold James, espionage case, **1996**
  794–800
Nickles, Don (R-Okla.), on Clinton legislative
  program, **1999** 42
Nicotine addiction, tobacco companies and,
  1995 670–679; **1997** 333; **1999** 546–548
Nielsen, Jerri, South Pole doctor, **1999** 611–613
Nigeria
  elections, **1999** 428
  human rights in, **1995** 696–699
  inauguration of president Obasanjo, **1999**
    272–282
  political conditions, **1998** 220
  religious persecution, **1997** 575–576
  U.S. policy, **1999** 275–276
  U.S. response to hanging of dissidents, **1995**
    696–699
Nixon, Richard M.
  oil pricing, **1998** 501
  presidential immunity, **1997** 291
Nixon v. Fitzgerald, **1997** 294, 295
Nobel Peace Prize
  Rabin, Peres, and Arafat acceptance speeches,
    1995 691
  Rotblat and nuclear disarmament, **1995** 553
  Williams, Jody, land mines ban campaign,
    1997 846
Norfolk (Virginia), school uniform policy, **1996**
  91–92
North American Free Trade Agreement (NAFTA)
  CEA report on, **1995** 85; **1997** 53, 61–62, 68;
    1998 83, 95

Clinton economic report, **1995** 74
Clinton on impact of, **1997** 541–549
Republican Party support for, **1996** 510
North Atlantic Treaty Organization (NATO)
  Bosnia peacekeeping mission, **1995** 717–726;
    1997 342; **1998** 49; **1999** 286
  charter with Russia, **1997** 514, 515
  and European defense force, **1999** 817–827
  and European nations, **1995** 93, 100
  expansion
    Clinton support for, **1997** 40, 341; **1998**
      48–49, 613; **1999** 54
    cost issues, **1997** 517
    G-8 discussions, **1997** 340, 516
    Russian opposition to, **1998** 612–613
    secretary of State report on, **1996** 655–661
    statements marking, **1999** 119–133
    summit meeting and, **1997** 514–526
  fiftieth anniversary, Washington summit, **1998**
    912; **1999** 119, 121–122
  French participation, **1997** 516
  future of
    Clinton administration of, **1999** 120
    secretary of state on, **1998** 912–919
  historical background, **1999** 119–120
  Kosovo crisis
    air war, **1999** 119, 122
      Clinton announcement, **1999** 134–143
      UN resolution on, **1999** 285–296
    airstrikes threatened, **1998** 829–831
  Republican Party platform, **1996** 539
  summit meeting (Madrid), **1997** 514–526
North Korea
  famine, **1999** 572
  missile threat to Europe, **1999** 820
  missile threat to U.S., **1998** 481–482, 489
  nuclear weapons proliferation, **1996** 211–212,
    215–217
  relations with South Korea, **1997** 895–896
  religious persecution, **1997** 564
  U.S. policy, **1999** 568–583
  See also Korean War
North, Oliver L., conviction and appeal, **1998**
  906
Northern Ireland. *See* Ireland, Northern
Norwood, Charlie (R-Ga.), patients' bill of rights,
  1999 562
Novelli, Bill, smoking and health, **1997** 335
Ntaryamira, Cyprien, assassination of, **1999** 863
Nuclear, chemical, and biological (NBC)
  weapons, proliferation of, **1996** 210–230
Nuclear energy, in former Soviet Union, **1996**
  139–146, 228–229
Nuclear freeze, African Nuclear Weapon Free
  Zone Treaty, **1995** 236, 237
Nuclear nonproliferation
  statement of G-8, **1997** 356–358
  treaty, extension of, **1995** 233–238, 554
Nuclear Non-Proliferation Treaty (NPT, 1968)
  extension of, **1995** 233–238, 554; **1996**
    228–229; **1997** 199
  UN role with, **1995** 358
Nuclear safety, **1997** 349
Nuclear technology
  sales to China, **1997** 729
  theft of, by China, **1999** 235–256, 304
Nuclear testing
  comprehensive ban on, **1995** 234–237,
    553–557; **1998** 49; **1999** 600–610, 699, 819

fallout, NCI report on, **1997** 591–601
  in India and Pakistan, **1999** 623–624
  UN on, **1998** 326–332
Nuclear waste management, cleanup priorities,
  GAO report on, **1995** 113–119
Nuclear weapons
  in former Soviet Union, **1996** 139–146
  missile threats, Rumsfeld Commission on,
    1998 481–499
  non-proliferation environment, **1998** 492–495
  North Korean nuclear agreement, **1997** 41
  proliferation of worldwide, Defense Depart-
    ment report on, **1996** 210–230
  Russian missiles, **1997** 515
  verification issue, **1999** 603–604
  See also Comprehensive Nuclear Test Ban
    Treaty (CNTBT)
Nunn, Sam (D-Ga.)
  chemical weapons treaty, **1996** 741; **1997** 201
  military base closings, **1995** 409
  nuclear materials in former Soviet states,
    1996 141
  retirement from Congress, **1995** 558–559
Nuon Chea, **1998** 972–975
Nutrition
  food guide pyramid, **1996** 4–5
  and vegetarian diets, **1996** 5, 8
Nyerere, Julius, death of, **1999** 867

O

Oakley, Phyllis E., refugee camps in Central
  Africa, **1996** 811–815
OAU. *See* Organization of African Unity (OAU)
Obasanjo, Olusegun, Nigerian president inaugu-
  ration speech, **1999** 272–282
Obuchi, Keizo, on Japanese economic crisis,
  1998 532–542
Occupational health
  EEOC employer guidelines on mental disabili-
    ties, **1997** 127–141
  ergonomics standards, **1999** 769–778
Occupational Safety and Health Administration
  (OSHA), ergonomics standards, **1999** 769–778
O'Connor, Sandra Day
  affirmative action, federal government plans,
    1995 307–308, 309–319
  attorney-client privilege, **1998** 395, 401–404
  congressional term limits, **1995** 260, 271–275
  disability, definition of, **1999** 318, 320,
    321–325, 325–332
  drug testing of students, **1995** 339, 340,
    346–349
  endangered species on private lands, **1995**
    359–368
  free speech
    ballot initiatives, **1999** 6
    decency in the arts, **1998** 405, 407, 408–415
    and the Internet, **1997** 445–446, 454–458
  gay rights discrimination, **1996** 286
  gay rights to march, **1995** 327–335
  gun-free school zone, **1995** 184, 192–194
  HIV as a disability, **1998** 380, 389–392
  line-item veto, **1998** 421, 431–433, 433–437
  parochial school aid, **1997** 362–363, 364–375
  physician-assisted suicide, **1997** 461, 472–473,
    478–479
  race-based redistricting, **1995** 369, 371,
    373–380; **1996** 369–370, 371–379, 379–380

religious freedom, **1997** 408, 410, 417–420
religious publications, **1995** 385–395
sex offenders, right to confine, **1997** 383
sexual harassment, **1998** 442; **1999** 215–217, 218–227
states rights, **1999** 333
Odeen, Philip A., **1997** 812
Odeh, Mohammad Sadeek, **1998** 558
Office of AIDS Research (OAR), report on, **1996** 156–166
Office of Civil Rights, Bill Lee nomination, **1997** 765
Office of Management and Budget (OMB), year 2000 computer conversion cost estimates, **1997** 535–540
Office of Technology Assessment (OTA) studies, U.S.-Russian space cooperation, **1995** 222–227
Ogata, Sadako
    Africa, UN economic assistance, **1999** 428–438
    Congo, economic conditions, **1999** 646
Oh, Angela E., race relations panel, **1997** 317, 322; **1998** 668
Oil industry, corporate mergers, **1998** 338–339
Ojdanic, Dragoljub, war criminal, **1999** 803
O'Keefe, William K., **1997** 862
Oklahoma, welfare reform, **1999** 258
Oklahoma City bombing incident, **1999** 502
    and antiterrorism bill, **1996** 231–232
    FBI crime laboratory reports, **1997** 221, 223
    and gun control laws, **1995** 183, 465
    McVeigh and Nichols trial and sentencing, **1997** 623–627; **1999** 480
    militia group involvement, **1996** 178
    prayer service for victims, **1995** 176–182
O'Leary, Dennis O., hospital care oversight, **1999** 414
O'Leary, Hazel R.
    campaign finance practices, **1997** 824, 825, 828, 829
    human radiation experiments, **1995** 633–634
Olmstead v. L.C., **1999** 319, 320, 325–332
Olson, Pamela F., IRS disputes with taxpayers, **1997** 661
Olympics Committee. *See* International Olympics Committee (IOC)
Omnibus Budget Reconciliation Act (1993)
    deficit reduction plan, **1996** 55–56
    earned income tax credit expansion, **1995** 78
Oncale v. Sundowner Offshore Services, Inc., **1998** 441–442
Open Society Institute, **1997** 329
Operation Desert Storm
    "smart" weapons effectiveness, GAO report, **1997** 493–500
    "smart" weapons performance report, **1996** 403–413
Oregon, physician-assisted suicide legislation, **1997** 461–463; **1999** 441–442
Oregon v. Mitchell, **1997** 413–414, 415
Organization for Economic Cooperation and Development (OECD)
    combating bribery of public officials, **1997** 26.800–807
    Kosovo conflict, **1998** 830–831
Organization for Security and Cooperation in Europe (OSCE), Kosovo human rights violations, **1999** 802–806, 814–816

Organization of African Unity (OAU)
    Congo, Lusaka cease-fire agreement, **1999** 650
    Ethiopia-Eritrea border dispute, **1999** 431
    Summit (Algiers), **1999** 438
Organized crime
    efforts to combat, **1997** 349–350
    and NBC weapons, **1996** 225
O'Scannlain, Diarmuid F., affirmative action court opinion, **1997** 184, 186–194
Osgood, James, **1997** 626
Overseas Facilities Authority (OFA), **1999** 693, 695–696
Overseas Presence Advisory Panel, diplomatic posts evaluation report, **1999** 690–698
Overseas Private Investment Corporation (OPIC), **1998** 165; **1999** 50
Al-'Owahili, Mohammed Rashed Daoud, **1998** 558

P

Pacific Gas & Electric Co. v. Public Utilities Commission of California, **1995** 333
Packwood, Bob (R-Ore.), resignation from Senate, **1995** 592–599
Padget, Ellie, computer security issues, **1998** 676
Padre Island National Seashore (Texas), **1995** 123
Pakistan
    Lahore Declaration, **1999** 623–624
    military coup, **1999** 623–629
    missile threat to U.S., **1998** 492
    nuclear weapons testing, **1998** 326–332, 467, 541; **1999** 623–624
    relations with India, **1999** 623–629
    religious persecution, **1997** 564, 576–577
    weapons of mass destruction proliferation, **1996** 213, 222–223
Palestine Liberation Organization (PLO)
    West Bank agreement, **1995** 622–630
    Wye River peace agreement, **1998** 742–754; **1999** 53–54, 700, 891–893
Palila v. Hawaii Dept. of Land and Natural Resources, **1995** 366
Pan Am (Lockerbie) bombing, **1996** 662
Panama Canal treaties, transfer ceremony, Carter speech, **1999** 850–855
Panama Refining Co. v. Ryan, **1998** 436
Paramilitary organizations
    "Freemen" surrender to FBI, **1996** 362–367
    Waco and Ruby Ridge incidents, **1995** 178
Parden v. Terminal R. Co. of Ala. Docks Dept., **1999** 340
Paris Club
    Honduran and Nicaraguan disaster relief efforts, **1998** 792
    Russian participation, **1997** 341, 342–343
Paris Reparations Conference (1946), **1997** 269–270
Park Chung Hee, **1997** 894
Parker, Mike (D-Miss.), on vote for Speaker of the House, **1995** 3
Parker, Paul Michael "Mike" (D-Miss.), Gingrich resignation, **1998** 803
Parks, Rosa, at Million Man March, **1995** 6565
Partnership for Peace, **1997** 521
Pastrana, Andres, peace negotiations, **1999** 468
Patagonia, **1996** 43
Pataki, George E., **1997** 613

Patients' Bill of Rights, **1997** 787–799; **1998** 46–47, 89, 140; **1999** 48–49, 562–563
Patten, Chris
at Hong transfer ceremony, **1997** 502
on Hong Kong political situation, **1997** 501
Paul, Henri, **1997** 647
Paul, William, AIDS research, **1996** 157
Pavelic, Ante, **1998** 293
Paxon, Bill (R-N.Y.), and Gingrich ethics violations, **1997** 5
Payne, Billy, on Centennial Olympic Park bombing, **1996** 448
Pease, Ed (R-Ind.), House Judiciary Committee impeachment inquiry, **1998** 711
Pell, Claiborne (D-R.I.), UN charter, **1995** 354
Pelosi, Nancy (D-Calif.), and Gingrich ethics violations case, **1997** 4
Peña, Federico
FAA and airline safety, **1996** 238
and railroad safety regulations, **1996** 191
Pennsylvania Avenue (Washington, D.C.), closing of, **1995** 178, 254–258
Pension plans. *See* Retirement plans; Social security
Pentagon
bombing in Saudi Arabia, **1996** 672
computer systems, security matters, **1998** 676–677
computer systems, threats to, **1996** 312–324
Pentagon Papers case, **1997** 104, 105–106
Peres, Shimon
defeat by Netanyahu, **1996** 337
eulogy for Yitzhak Rabin, **1995** 692–693
West Bank peace agreement, **1995** 622, 624, 689–690
Perez v. U.S., **1995** 198
Perot, H. Ross
presidential debates, **1996** 550
presidential election (1996), nomination, **1996** 550–562
Perry, William J.
air safety after Brown mission crash, **1996** 205–206
extremists in U.S. Army, task force on, **1996** 178
military base closings, **1995** 407, 408
North Korea, U.S. policy, **1999** 568–583
nuclear weapons proliferation, **1996** 210
terrorist bombing in Saudi Arabia, **1996** 672, 674
Persian Gulf War
Gulf War syndrome, **1997** 740–745
"smart" weapons effectiveness, GAO report, **1997** 493–500
"smart" weapons performance report, **1996** 403–413
UN backing for, **1995** 351
Personal Responsibility and Work Opportunity Reconciliation Act (PRWORA, 1996), **1998** 357; **1999** 261
Peru, hostage crisis, **1997** 234–237
Pesticides, regulation reform, **1996** 467–470
Pétain, Henri Philippe, complicity with Nazis, **1995** 478
Peterson, Douglas "Pete," U.S. ambassador to united Vietnam, **1997** 489; **1999** 476
Philip Morris
claims settlement, **1997** 331; **1998** 842

FDA regulations on tobacco sales, **1996** 598–599
Phoenix (Arizona), school uniform policy, **1996** 92
Physical Fitness and Sports, President's Council on, **1997** 158–171
Physician-assisted suicide
and end-of-life care, **1997** 326
federal appeals court on, **1996** 121–132
legalization of, **1997** 329
Oregon ballot measure approved, **1997** 461–463
Supreme Court on, **1997** 459–479
Physicians for Responsible Negotiations, **1999** 633, 812
Pickering, Thomas R.
U.S. airstrikes against terrorists, **1998** 587
U.S. bombing of Chinese embassy, **1999** 306–316
Pike, John, space mission failures, **1999** 715
Pilcher, Carl, on *Lunar Prospector* mission, **1998** 118
Pinchot, Gifford, **1999** 593, 596
Pinchot, Peter, **1999** 593
Piot, Peter
AIDS epidemic in Africa, **1999** 489
HIV/AIDS epidemic, **1998** 878
Pitofsky, Robert
FTC chairman on corporate mergers, **1998** 338–353
on unionization of doctors, **1999** 633
Pitts, Earl Edwin, espionage case, **1996** 794, 795–796
Pius XII (pope), and Jews during the Holocaust, **1998** 122, 123
Planned Parenthood of Southeastern Pa. v. Casey, **1996** 125–127; **1997** 373, 465–466
Plessy v. Ferguson, **1995** 456
Plowden, Warren, on sexual harassment in schools, **1999** 218
Poe v. Ullman, **1997** 189, 476
Poindexter, John M., indictment and appeal, **1998** 906
Pol Pot, death of, **1998** 972
Poland, NATO membership, **1997** 514, 516; **1999** 119, 120, 126–127
Police conduct, for access to medical records, **1997** 583
Political action committees (PACs), GOPAC and Gingrich ethics violations, **1995** 748–751
Pollard, Jonathan J., **1998** 743–744
Ponte, Carla del, Kosovo war crimes investigations, **1999** 804
Pontifical Commission for Religious Relations with the Jews, **1998** 121, 124
Population
aging in U.S., **1996** 296–301
control in China, **1999** 586–587
worldwide, **1996** 305; **1999** 584–591
Pornography
decency in the arts, Supreme Court on, **1998** 405–418
and the Internet, **1997** 444–458
Internet ban, **1996** 353–361
Porter, Anthony, **1999** 829
Portman, Rob (R-Ohio), IRS reform, **1997** 663
Portugal
aid to Nazi Germany, **1997** 259, 262, 263; **1998** 291, 292

allied relations and negotiations with, **1998** 298–301
euro currency, **1998** 271
German assets, **1997** 267
Posner, Paul L., on deficit reduction, **1996** 147–148
Posner, Richard, Microsoft Corp. antitrust case, **1999** 654–689
Pound, Richard W., International Olympics Committee investigations, **1999** 106
Poverty
  Capability Poverty Measure, **1996** 439
  children in, **1999** 384–385
  rates in America, **1997** 53, 60, 69; **1998** 74, 85, 365
    for African Americans, **1999** 390
    for the elderly, **1998** 99, 104
    for foreign-born, **1997** 181
    for Hispanics, **1999** 390
  and sports opportunities for girls, **1997** 158–159, 168–169
  UN summit on, **1995** 134–140
Powell, Colin L.
  chemical weapons, **1997** 201, 742
  on Farrakhan and Million Man March, **1995** 657
  on nuclear test ban treaty, **1998** 49
  President's Volunteerism Summit, **1997** 40, 238–244
  Republican Party convention speech, **1996** 478–479
Powell v. McCormack, **1995** 262, 264, 267
Pratt Kelly, Sharon, mayor of Washington, **1995** 498
Precourt, Charles, **1995** 423
Pregnancy
  AIDS testing for pregnant women, **1995** 441–452
  maternal deaths, **1996** 343–352
  See also Teenage pregnancy
President, censuring president Clinton, **1998** 633, 699
Presidential Advisory Commission on Consumer Protection and Quality in the Health Care Industry, **1997** 787–799; **1998** 89, 140
Presidential commissions
  on Consumer Protection and Quality in the Health Care Industry, **1997** 787–799; **1998** 89, 140
  on Critical Infrastructure Protection, **1997** 711–720
  worker-management relations, future of, **1995** 15–23
Presidential debates
  Clinton-Dole debates, **1996** 707–709, 709–718, 724–731
  Perot Reform Party exclusion from, **1996** 50, 552, 707
Presidential immunity, Supreme Court on, **1997** 290–298
Presidential impeachment. *See* Impeachment, presidential
President's Advisory Committee on Human Radiation Experiments, **1995** 633–638
President's Commission on Critical Infrastructure Protection, **1998** 677
President's Council for One America, **1998** 667, 673

President's Council on Physical Fitness and Sports, benefits for girls report, **1997** 158–171
President's Summit for America's Future (Philadelphia), **1997** 40, 238–244, 323
Presidio (San Francisco), national park status, **1996** 581
Primakov, Yevgeny
  confirmation as prime minister, **1998** 605–606
  NATO expansion, **1996** 656
  Russian economic plan, **1998** 606
  UN weapons inspections in Iraq, **1997** 769
Princeton Survey Research Associates, on children, **1997** 425
Prisoners of war (POWs), Vietnam, ambassador Peterson, **1997** 489–490
Prisons
  incarceration rates rising, **1998** 871–872; **1999** 616
  mental illness of prison population, **1999** 839–840
Privacy
  attorney-client privilege, and posthumous confidentiality, **1998** 393–404
  genetic testing in the workplace, **1998** 63–72
  of medical records, **1997** 580–587
Prodi, Romano
  at economic summit (Denver), **1997** 342
  European Commission
    address to, **1999** 158–164
    presidential appointment, **1999** 157–158
  trade policy, **1999** 799
Progress and Freedom Foundation (PFF), **1997** 8–9, 14
Project on Death in America, **1997** 326, 329
Property rights, activists and endangered species, **1995** 360–361
Public Agenda, adult attitudes toward children survey, **1997** 422–443
Public health. *See* Health, public
Public officials, combating bribery of, OECD treaty, **1997** 800–807
Pueher, Joseph W., **1998** 978
Putin, Vladimir
  as acting prime minister of Russia, **1999** 917, 921
  Chechnya war, **1999** 909, 911

Q

Quebec, independence, Canadian Supreme Court on, **1998** 592–598
Quindel, Barbara Zack, **1997** 630
Quinlan, Karen Ann, right-to-die case, **1996** 122

R

Rabe, David, **1998** 407
Rabin, Yitzhak
  assassination of, **1995** 622, 689–695; **1996** 337; **1998** 742; **1999** 890
  political life of, **1995** 690–691
  West Bank agreement, **1995** 622, 623, 628–630
Race relations
  Clinton administration race initiative, **1998** 74, 665; **1999** 56–57
  Clinton commencement speech on, **1997** 313–324
  and Clinton inauguration, **1997** 22
  presidential advisory board report, **1998** 665–675

presidential advisory panel, **1997** 316–317
racial reconciliation, things you can do, **1998** 674–675
Racial segregation, race-based redistricting, **1995** 369–384
Racial stereotyping, **1998** 672
Racism
  apology to African-Americans for, **1995** 336–338
  church arson cases, **1997** 301–313
  Clinton plea to end in America, **1995** 646–654; **1997** 22, 29, 315
  and diversity in America, **1997** 43
  Texaco executives racial slurs, **1996** 764–769
Radiation, human radiation experiments, **1995** 633–638
Ragsdale, James, Roswell incident, **1997** 401
Railroads
  Amtrak, train accidents, **1995** 178; **1996** 189–190
  safety, GAO report on, **1996** 189–198
Raines, Franklin D., balanced budget agreement, **1997** 604
Raines v. Byrd, **1998** 423
Rait, Ken, forest preservation, **1999** 594
Ralston, Joseph W., Joint Chiefs of Staff nomination, **1997** 656
Ramo, Roberta Cooper, **1999** 109
Ramsey, David J., acupuncture, **1997** 749
Ranariddh, Norodom (prince of Cambodia), **1997** 639; **1998** 971
Rangel, Charles B. (D-N.Y.), on Clinton state of the union address, **1995** 26
Rape
  during Kosovo conflict, **1999** 811
  FBI report, **1996** 737; **1997** 687–688; **1998** 875; **1999** 620
Ray, Charles, consul general in Vietnam, **1999** 476
Reagan, Nancy, volunteerism summit, **1997** 238, 240–241
Reagan, Ronald
  defense policy, **1997** 814
    chemical weapons disposal, **1997** 198
    nuclear weapons ban, **1999** 604
  economic policy
    deficit spending, **1998** 501
    supply-side economics, **1999** 94
  foreign policy, Kim Dae-jung arrest intervention, **1997** 893
Record, James F., Saudi Arabia bombing investigation, **1996** 673–674
Reed, Bruce
  on welfare rolls decline, **1999** 257
  welfare system, **1997** 619
Reed v. Reed, **1995** 313
Rees-Jones, Trevor, **1997** 647, 649
Reeve, Christopher, at Democratic Party convention, **1996** 601
Reform Party convention, Perot presidential nomination, **1996** 550–562
Refugees
  Africa, UNCHR Ogata's address on, **1999** 432–438
  Central African refugee crisis, **1996** 809–815
  Central American escaping hurricane and flood damage, **1998** 791
  Cuban boat people, U.S. Policy on, **1995** 203–207

Jews to Switzerland, **1997** 264–265
of religious persecution, U.S. policy, **1998** 26–28
Regents of the University of California v. Bakke, **1995** 313–314
Regulatory reform
  CEA economic report on, **1997** 61
  Republican Party platform, **1996** 514
Rehnquist, William H.
  affirmative action, federal government plans, **1995** 308
  attorney-client privilege, **1998** 395, 397–401
  Clinton impeachment trial, **1999** 10, 16, 21
  congressional term limits, **1995** 260, 271–275
  disability, definition of, **1999** 318, 320
  drug testing of students, **1995** 339–346
  endangered species on private lands, **1995** 360, 366–368
  free speech
    ballot initiatives, **1999** 6, 12–14
    and the Internet, **1997** 445, 454–458
  gay rights discrimination, **1996** 286, 291–295
  gay rights to march, **1995** 327–335
  gun-free school zones, **1995** 184, 185–192
  HIV as a disability, **1998** 379–380, 389–392
  line-item veto, **1998** 421
  on Packwood investigation, **1995** 593
  parochial school aid, **1997** 363
  physician-assisted suicide, **1997** 460–461, 463–472
  punitive damages, for consumer product liability, **1996** 275, 282–283
  race-based redistricting, **1995** 369, 371, 373–380; **1996** 368–369, 371–379
  religious freedom, **1997** 408
  religious publications, **1995** 385–395
  religious symbols, **1995** 387, 396–400
  sex offenders, right of confine, **1997** 383
  sexual harassment in schools, **1999** 215, 227–234
  states rights, **1999** 333
Reich, Robert B.
  apparel industry investigations, **1997** 209
  on corporate responsibility, **1996** 41–49
  on illegal immigrants and the labor force, **1995** 565
  on income inequality, **1996** 396
  on labor-management relations report, **1995** 15, 17
Reinhardt College, Gingrich's Renewing American Civilization course, **1997** 8–9
Reinhardt, Stephen, **1996** 123
Reischauer, Robert D., balanced budget agreement, **1997** 602
Reiss, David, on AIDS policy, **1997** 82
Religion, in public schools, **1995** 546–552
Religious freedom
  in Cuba, **1997** 564, 571
  in Cuba, papal address on, **1998** 30–37
  Supreme court case, **1997** 406–421
  U.S. foreign policy, **1998** 19–29
Religious Freedom Day, **1998** 23
Religious Freedom Restoration Act (RFRA), Supreme Court on, **1997** 406–421; **1999** 335
Religious persecution
  church arson cases, **1997** 301–313
  State Department report, **1997** 562–579
  U.S. policy, **1998** 26–28

Reno, Janet
   antiabortion violence, **1998** 809–813
   campaign finance investigations, **1997**
      822–831; **1998** 890–902
   church arson cases, **1997** 301–303, 310
   FBI crime laboratory investigations, **1997**
      221–222
   Lewinsky affair investigations, **1998** 565–566
   marijuana law enforcement, **1996** 756
   Microsoft Corp. antitrust ruling, **1999** 658
   Nicholson espionage case, **1996** 797–798
   physician-assisted suicide, **1997** 463; **1999**
      441–442
   school safety, **1998** 738–739
   sentencing for cocaine penalties, **1997** 246
   special counsel regulations, **1999** 165, 168–169
   tobacco industry fraud, **1999** 537
   and violent crime, **1995** 710; **1998** 869
   Waco investigations, **1999** 480–488
Reno v. American Civil Liberties Union, **1997**
   444–458
Renton v. Playtime Theatres, Inc., **1997**
   447–448
Republican Party
   election losses, **1998** 801–802
   fundraising efforts, **1998** 894
   and opening remarks of 104th Congress, **1995**
      3–14
   platform, **1996** 496–549
   state of the union address
      Dole's response, **1996** 21–23, 35–38
      Dunn and Largent's response, **1999** 58–63
      Lott's response, **1998** 40–41, 54–59
      Watts' response, **1997** 31, 44–49
      Whitman's response, **1995** 25, 43–45
   welfare reform bill, **1996** 450–463
Republican Party convention (San Diego, 1996),
   1996 478–496
Research and development, CEA report on,
   1997 66–67; **1998** 82–83
Resolution on Racial Reconciliation, **1995**
   336–338
Resource Conservation and Recovery Act
   (RCRA, 1976), **1995** 113
Ressem, Ahmed, **1999** 499
Reston, James, acupuncture, **1997** 749–750
Retirement plans
   Democratic Party platform, **1996** 632
   Universal Savings Accounts (USAs), **1999** 46,
      90
Richardson, Bill (D-N.M.)
   GAO report on national parks, **1996** 581
   on political compromise, **1996** 468
Richardson, Bill (Energy Dept. secy.), nuclear
   weapons security, **1999** 240–241
Richardson, Elliott, attorney general resignation,
   1998 906
Richardson, James T., on Star of Bethlehem,
   1997 125
Richardson, William, on medical mistakes, **1999**
   780
Richmond (Virginia), school uniform policy,
   1996 90
Richness, Michael, nicotine addiction, **1998** 845
Rifkind, Robert S., on Catholic/Jewish relations,
   1998 123
Riggs, Frank (R-Calif.)
   affirmative action programs, **1998** 858
   bilingual education funding, **1998** 315

Riley, Richard W.
   national education standards, **1997** 35
   parochial school aid, **1997** 363
   school safety, **1998** 738
   State of American Education address, **1996**
      106–117
   teacher shortage, **1999** 65
Rimer, Barbara, mammogram advocate, **1997**
   144, 145–149
Ripken, Cal, Jr., on breaking consecutive baseball game record, **1995** 588–591; **1998** 628–629
Ritter, Jorge, Panama Canal transfer ceremony,
   1999 853
Ritter, William Scott, Jr., UN weapons inspection
   in Iraq, **1998** 935–936
R.J. Reynolds Tobacco Co.
   Joe Camel advertising campaign, **1997** 332,
      334
   tobacco settlement, **1998** 842
RJR Nabisco Holdings Corporation, tobacco
   claims settlement, **1997** 331
Robert Wood Johnson Foundation
   child health care survey, **1997** 425
   end-of-life care research, **1997** 326, 329, 330
Roberts, Pat (R-Kan.), farm bill, **1996** 200
Robertson, Pat, on Clinton impeachment, **1999**
   42
Robinson, Mary
   Chechnya war human rights violations, **1999**
      913
   East Timor independence, **1999** 511–523
Robinson, Robert A., **1997** 693
Robles, Joseu, Jr., military base closings, **1995**
   409
Rocky Flats (Colorado), nuclear weapons facil-
   ity, **1995** 114, 117
Rodgers, Kathy, sexual harassment rulings, **1998**
   439–440
Rodionov, Igor, NATO expansion, **1996** 657
*Rodriguez de Quijas v. Shearson/American
   Express, Inc.*, **1997** 374
Rodu, Brad, cancer death rates, **1996** 790
Rogan, James E. (R-Calif.), House Judiciary
   Committee impeachment inquiry, **1998** 712
Rogers, Melissa, religious freedom, **1997** 408
Rogers, Richard M., Waco incident, **1999** 481
Rogers v. EEOC, **1998** 462
Rogers, William D., Cuban foreign policy, **1998**
   33
Roh Tae Woo, **1997** 894
Romania, NATO membership candidacy, **1997**
   516; **1999** 122
Romer v. Evans, **1996** 284–295
Romney, George, volunteerism summit, **1997**
   238
Ronald McDonald House Charities, **1997** 424,
   426; **1999** 386
Roosevelt, Franklin Delano
   Gingrich comments on presidency of, **1995** 4
   national forest preservation efforts, **1999** 596
   New Deal measures and commerce clause,
      1995 184
Rosenbaum, Mark, and affirmative action, **1997**
   284–285
*Rosenberger v. Rector and Visitors of the Uni-
   versity of Virginia*, **1995** 385–395; **1997** 368,
   376
Roslin Institute (Scotland), cloning research,
   1997 212–220

Ross, Carl, forest preservation, **1999** 594

Ross, Jane L., social security shortfall, **1998** 99–100

Ross, Jerry, **1998** 932

Roswell (New Mexico), UFO citings, Air Force report, **1997** 395–405

Rotblat, Joseph, Nobel Peace prize winner, **1995** 553

Roth, Stanley O., Cambodian political situation, **1997** 641–646

Roth, William V., Jr. (R-Del.)
  health insurance for disabled persons, **1999** 49
  IRS hearings, **1997** 661
  Senate Finance Committee chairman, **1995** 592

Rothman, Steven R. (D-N.J.), House Judiciary Committee impeachment inquiry, **1998** 711

Rothstein, Barbara J., **1996** 123

Rowland, Diane, on Medicaid, **1998** 143

Roy, Joe, on extremists in the military, **1996** 178–179

Rubin, Howard A., on year 2000 computer conversion, **1997** 534

Rubin, James P.
  Afghanistan, U.S. humanitarian aid, **1999** 527
  Kosovo, NATO airstrikes in, **1998** 829
  Pakistan military coup, **1999** 625
  on sub-Saharan African conflict, **1998** 220

Rubin, Robert E.
  Asian financial crisis, **1997** 832; **1998** 725
  on closing Pennsylvania Avenue, **1995** 255
  IRS and customer service, **1998** 132–138
  IRS reform, **1997** 663
  and National Church Arson Task Force, **1997** 302, 310
  Vietnam economic relations, **1997** 490

Ruby Ridge incident, **1995** 178

Ruckleshaus, William D., resignation, **1998** 906

Rudman, Warren B. (*formerly* R-N.H.)
  Chinese technology transfer study, **1999** 239
  Gulf War syndrome investigations, **1997** 740
  national security commission member, **1999** 500, 501–502

Rudolph, Eric Robert, antiabortion bombing case, **1998** 810

Ruff, Charles F.C., Clinton impeachment trial, **1999** 19

Rufo v. Inmates of Suffolks County Jail, **1997** 366

Rugova, Ibrahim, Kosovo conflict, **1999** 288

Rumsfeld, Donald H., missile threat to U.S., **1998** 481–499

Rushdie, Salman, death threat lifted, **1998** 687–691

Russia
  economic conditions, **1998** 75–76, 601–603, 722; **1999** 87
  elections, **1995** 94; **1996** 139, 430–437; **1997** 515
  foreign policy, **1995** 100
  Japan relations, **1998** 540
  media, **1995** 98
  missile threat, **1998** 487
  NATO charter and cooperation, **1996** 656; **1997** 514, 515, 518, 521–522
  nuclear proliferation, **1996** 219–221
  nuclear testing, **1999** 604
  Paris Club membership, **1997** 341, 342–343
  privatization of, **1995** 96–97
  religious freedom, **1997** 564, 577–578
  Republican Party platform, **1996** 540
  and U.S. space station, **1995** 222–227, 419–425; **1998** 929–930
  Yeltsin
    address to parliament, **1996** 430–437
    at economic summit (Denver), **1997** 340–342
    economic crisis, **1998** 601–613
    election victory, **1996** 139, 430–437; **1997** 515
    state of the nation address, **1995** 92–101

Ruth, Henry, and independent counsel legislation, **1999** 168

Rwanda
  Clinton state visit, **1998** 159
  genocidal war
    Clinton apology for U.S. inaction, **1998** 160; **1999** 861
    UN report, **1999** 860–889
    UN response, **1998** 222; **1999** 735
    UN Tribunal on, **1998** 614–625
  refugee camps, State Department report, **1996** 809–815
  refugee relief, **1999** 434–435
  UN Assistance Mission in Rwanda (UNAMIR), **1999** 862, 863–865, 869–884
  UN humanitarian aid programs, **1999** 429
  UN peacekeeping mission, failure of, **1997** 151, 154, 155, 156; **1999** 860–889

S

Sable Communications of Cal., Inc. v. FCC, 1997 450

al-Sadr, Ayatollah Mohammed Sadeq, assassination of, **1999** 145

Saenz v. Roe, **1999** 261

Safe and Drug-Free School Act, **1999** 55

Sagan, Carl, **1997** 509

Sainovic, Nikola, war criminal, **1999** 803

St. Patrick's Day Parade, **1995** 327–335

Samaranch, Juan Antonio, International Olympics Committee investigations, **1999** 106, 108, 109

Sandage, Allan R., age of universe controversy, **1996** 265–266, 268

Sanders, Bernard (I-Vt.), apparel industry sweatshops, **1997** 209

Sanderson, Robert "Sandy," antiabortion protester victim, **1998** 810

Sankoh, Foday, Sierra Leone peace negotiations, **1999** 430–431

Santer, Jacques
  on euro currency, **1998** 274, 275–280
  European Commission commissioner, **1999** 156–157

Santorum, Rick (R-Pa.), Cuban foreign policy, **1998** 33

Sarkisian, Aram, Armenian prime minister appointment, **1999** 639–640

Sarkisian, Vazgen
  Armenian prime minister, **1999** 641
  assassination of, **1999** 639

Saro-Wiwa, Ken, execution of, **1995** 696–699

Sasser, James, U.S. bombing of Chinese embassy, **1999** 305–306

Satcher, David (surgeon general)
on drug AZT therapy for pregnant women, **1995** 441
mental health, **1999** 836–849
on physical activity, **1996** 419
school violence study, **1999** 181
suicide prevention, **1999** 439–455, 836
teenage smoking, **1998** 845
Saudi Arabia
religious persecution, **1997** 564, 578–579
terrorist bombing, **1996** 672–679
Savage, Gus (D-Ill.), on white racism, **1995** 656–657
Save America's Forests, **1999** 594
Sawhill, Isabel, on teenage pregnancy, **1998** 263
Scalia, Antonin
affirmative action, federal government plans, **1995** 308, 319–320
attorney-client privilege, **1998** 395, 401–404
ballot initiatives, **1999** 6
congressional term limits, **1995** 260, 271–275
disability, definition of, **1999** 318
drug testing of students, **1995** 339–346
endangered species on private lands, **1995** 360, 366–368
free speech
decency in the arts, **1998** 405, 407, 415–417
and the Internet, **1997** 445
gay rights discrimination, **1996** 284, 286, 291–295
gay rights to march, **1995** 327–335
gun-free school zone, **1995** 184
HIV as a disability, **1998** 380, 389–392
line-item veto, **1998** 421, 431–433, 433–437
parochial school aid, **1997** 363
physician-assisted suicide, **1997** 461
punitive damages, for consumer product liability, **1996** 275
race-based redistricting, **1995** 369, 371, 373–380; **1996** 369, 381
religious freedom, **1997** 406–408, 409–417
religious publications, **1995** 385–395
religious symbols, **1995** 387, 396–400
sex offenders, right to confine, **1997** 383
sexual harassment, **1998** 441, 442, 452, 461–465; **1999** 215, 227–234
state rights, **1999** 333
Scanlon, William J.
health insurance coverage report, **1998** 143–150
on insurance premium rates, **1998** 141
Scharping, Rudolf, European defense force, **1999** 818
Schechter Poultry Corp. v. U.S., **1998** 436
Scheinberg, Phyllis F., GAO testimony on railroad safety, **1996** 189–198
Schiff, Steven, Roswell incident, **1997** 397
Schlesinger, James
national security commission member, **1999** 500
nuclear test ban treaty, **1999** 601, 608
Schlickeisen, Rodger, **1995** 360
School integration
colleges and universities, **1995** 239–253
Little Rock Central High School 40th anniversary, **1997** 317
School violence
Columbine High School shootings, **1999** 179–184

federal response, **1999** 181–182
legislative efforts to control, **1999** 55
school safety report, **1998** 735–741
school shooting incidents, **1999** 180–181
School-to-Work Opportunities Act, **1995** 73
Schools
affirmative action ban, **1998** 855–868
charter schools, **1998** 88; **1999** 48
D.C. schools, financial crisis, **1996** 784–789
enrollment of children, **1999** 389
Perot Reform Party nomination speech on, **1996** 559–561
religion in public schools, **1995** 546–552
school safety, federal report on, **1998** 735–741
uniforms policy in public schools, **1996** 84–92
voucher plans, **1997** 363–364
See also Education; Teachers
Schools, private, parochial school aid, **1997** 361–381
Schopf, William, **1996** 472
Schroeder, Gerhard
bail-out of bankrupt company, **1999** 77
and European Commission reforms, **1999** 157
European defense force, **1999** 819
German chancellor inaugural speech, **1998** 815–826
and interest rates, **1998** 274
political profile, **1998** 817–819
Schroeder, Patricia (D-Colo.), maternal mortality rate, **1996** 344
Schuller, Robert, **1997** 43
Schultz, Marjorie, affirmative action proponent, **1997** 186
Schulz, Charles M., retirement and death of, **1999** 856–859
Schumer, Charles (D-N.Y.)
House Judiciary Committee impeachment inquiry, **1998** 703
religious freedom, **1997** 409
Schwailer, Terryl, **1996** 672–674
Schwartz, Bernard L., **1998** 978
Schwarzkopf, H. Norman, chemical weapons, **1997** 201
Schweitzer, LeRoy, Freeman leader, **1996** 363, 365
Science and technology
federal support for, **1995** 82–83
Republican Party platform, **1996** 508–509
Scott, Robert C. (D-Va.), House Judiciary Committee impeachment inquiry, **1998** 706
Scowcroft, Brent, chemical weapons, **1997** 201
Scrutton, Hugh Campbell, victim of Unabomber, **1998** 234, 238–239
Seattle (Wash.), school uniform policy, **1996** 89–90
Secret Service, protective function privilege, **1998** 395–396, 566
Securities and Exchange Commission (SEC), online investing, **1999** 203–214
Seeber, Ronald, on unions, **1995** 682
Segal, Eli J., welfare reform, **1997** 622; **1998** 357
Seiple, Robert, religious freedom, **1998** 21
Seminole Tribe of Fla. v. Florida, **1999** 334, 336, 340, 345–346
Senate
campaign finance hearings, **1998** 893–894
Mansfield on civility in the, **1998** 151–158

Senate Select Committees, Ethics, Packwood
expulsion recommended by, **1995** 592–597
Senegal, Clinton state visit, **1998** 159
Sensenbrenner, F. James, Jr. (R-Wis.), on Clinton
impeachment, **1999** 18
Sentencing Reform Act (1984), **1997** 250–251,
253
Separation of powers
and line-item veto, **1998** 419–437
National Commission on Separation of Pow-
ers report, **1998** 905–911
Serbia, war in Kosovo, **1998** 827–841; **1999**
134–143, 285–296
Serrano, Andres, **1998** 406
Serushago, Omar, genocide trials, **1998** 616
Service Employees International Union (SEIU)
home care workers union, **1999** 630, 631–632
hospital quality oversight, **1999** 414
Sex education
abstinence-only programs, **1997** 83, 89
safe sex for teenagers, **1997** 81, 82–83
Sex offenders
confining, Supreme Court on, **1997** 382–394
Megan's Law in New Jersey, **1997** 382, 384
Sex selection, ethics of embryonic research,
1998 66
Sexual assault and harassment
Clinton-Jones law suit, **1997** 21, 290–298;
1998 39, 565, 633–634, 638–639, 962; **1999**
16, 21–22
of girls in athletic settings, **1997** 170
in the military, Army report on, **1997** 654–660
of the same sex, **1998** 441–442
of a student
by a classmate, **1999** 215–234
by a teacher, **1998** 442
in the workplace, Supreme Court opinion on,
1998 438–465
Shabazz, Betty, at Million Man March, **1995** 656
Shadley, Robert D., sexual abuses on base, **1997**
655
Shaiken, Harley, on labor movement, **1999**
632
Shalala, Donna
consumer health care, **1997** 787, 791
dietary guidelines, **1996** 3
drug use among children, **1996** 570–572
drug use survey, **1999** 459, 461
girls in sports, **1997** 158–159
marijuana use, **1996** 756–757
medical records privacy, **1997** 580–587
physical activity, **1996** 4, 418
teenage pregnancy, **1998** 260
welfare system, **1997** 620
Shalikashvili, John M.
antipersonnel land mines, **1997** 847
on test ban treaty, **1998** 49
Shapiro, Robert J., impact of Y2K computer failures, **1999** 762
Shapiro, Stephen
school voucher plans, **1997** 364
student rights, **1995** 341
al-Shara, Farouk, Israel-Syria peace negotiations,
1999 896–897
Sharif, Nawaz
India-Pakistan Lahore Declaration, **1999**
623–624
ousted from Pakistan, **1999** 623, 625–626
Pakistani nuclear testing, **1998** 327

Shattuck, John, religious freedom and human
rights, **1998** 20
Shaw, Eugene (R-Fla.), welfare reform, **1996** 463
Shaw v. Hunt, **1996** 368; **1998** 866–867
Shaw v. Reno, **1995** 370, 373–376, 378, 380–382,
384; **1996** 368, 370; **1997** 190, 193
Shays, Christopher (R-Conn.), campaign finance
reform, **1997** 33; **1998** 893; **1999** 56
Shea, Jamie, on U.S. bombing of Chinese
embassy, **1999** 305
Shelby, Richard C. (R-Ala.), on Clinton's perfor-
mance, **1999** 42
Shelton, Henry, Joint Chiefs of Staff nomination,
1997 656
Shenandoah National Park (Virginia), **1995**
123–124
Shepherd, Bill, **1998** 932
Sherbert v. Verne, **1997** 410, 411
Sherrill, Kenneth, Clinton and gay rights, **1997**
760
Shoemaker, Eugene, **1998** 114
Shook, Karen H., **1996** 785
Shultz, George P., Cuban foreign policy, **1998** 33
Siegfried, Richard S., sexual harassment in the
military, **1997** 654
Sierra Leone
Lomé agreement, **1999** 433–434, 436
peace negotiations, **1999** 428, 430, 433–434,
436
UN peacekeeping forces (ECOWAS), **1999**
431
war atrocities, **1999** 430
Simpson, Alan K. (R-Wyo.), immigration laws,
1995 563
Simpson, Nicole Brown, **1995** 611–621; **1997** 74
Simpson, O.J. (Orenthal James)
closing arguments in trial, **1995** 611–621
final verdict, **1997** 29–30
jurors' remarks, **1997** 74–80
and racism, **1995** 646
Singer, Israel, **1997** 262
*Skinner v. Railway Labor Executives' Associa-
tion*, **1995** 342, 343, 344, 345
Slany, William Z., **1997** 257, 261
Sleeper, Jim, on racism, **1998** 667
Slepian, Barnett, murder of, **1998** 809–811
Slovakia, NATO membership candidacy, **1999**
122
Slovenia, NATO membership candidacy, **1997**
516
Small Business Job Protection Act (1996), **1996**
563–569
Smaltz, Donald C., Espy investigation, **1998** 906,
907–908
Smith, Franklin L., removed from D.C. schools,
1996 784–785
Smith, John F., Jr., GM electric vehicle develop-
ment, **1996** 19–20
Smith, Lamar (R-Texas)
and Gingrich ethics case, **1997** 4
House Judiciary Committee impeachment
inquiry, **1998** 705
illegal immigrants, **1995** 565
Smith, Sidney C., Jr., on cigarette regulations,
1995 670
Smith v. County of Albemarle, **1995** 397
Smith v. Reeves, **1999** 339
Smithsonian Institution, *Enola Gay* exhibit,
1995 55–58

Smoking
  children and tobacco sales, FDA regulations, **1996** 589–599
  cigarette advertising bans, **1997** 38, 332
  cigarette regulations
    FDA authority, **1999** 538–539
    FDA proposals, **1995** 670–679
  declining levels, **1999** 460
  fraud of tobacco industry, allegations of, **1999** 536–661
  Gore's vice-presidential acceptance speech, **1996** 607–608
  reduction, **1999** 539–540
  secondhand smoke, effects of, **1995** 673
  tobacco company accountability, **1999** 49–50
  trends, and declining death rates from, **1996** 791
  young adults and, **1997** 332, 335, 336; **1998** 47, 89; **1999** 49, 384
    increasing levels, **1999** 460
Snowe, Olympia (R-Maine)
  integration of women for military training, **1997** 657
  sexual harassment in the Army, **1997** 656
Social security
  benefits for those who work, **1999** 320
  budget surplus and, **1998** 40, 98; **1999** 42, 43, 45–46, 90, 354–356
  reform, CEA report on, **1998** 93–94
  solvency, GAO report, **1998** 98–109
  spending growth, **1997** 52, 63–64
  strengthening the system, **1998** 43, 75
  Y2K conversion compliance, **1998** 545, 550
Social Security Disability Insurance, **1999** 320
Solano, Javier
  European defense force, **1999** 818
  Kosovo air attacks, **1999** 136, 139
Solar system, exploration of, multiplanet solar system discovery, **1999** 173–178
Solomon, Gerald B. H. (R-N.Y.), air strikes against Iraq, **1998** 937, 961
Solow, Robert M., on minimum wage, **1996** 564
Somalia, UN peacekeeping mission, **1997** 151, 154, 155, 156; **1998** 222
Sons of the Gestapo, **1995** 178
Soros, George
  end-of-life care, **1997** 326
  physician-assisted suicide, **1997** 462
  Russian economy, **1998** 603
Sosa, Sammy
  baseball home run record, **1998** 626–628
  relief efforts in Dominican Republic, **1999** 54
Souter, David H.
  affirmative action, federal government plans, **1995** 309, 323–324
  congressional term limits, **1995** 260
  disability, definition of, **1999** 319, 323, 325–332
  drug testing of students, **1995** 339, 340, 346–349
  endangered species on private lands, **1995** 359–368
  free speech
    ballot initiatives, **1999** 6
    decency in the arts, **1998** 407, 417–418
    and the Internet, **1997** 445
  gay rights discrimination, **1996** 286
  gay rights to march, **1995** 327–335
  gun-free school zone, **1995** 184, 195–196, 196–200

HIV as a disability, **1998** 379
line-item veto, **1998** 421
parochial school aid, **1997** 363, 375–380, 380–381
physician-assisted suicide, **1997** 461, 476–478
race-based redistricting, **1995** 371, 380–384; **1996** 370, 383–387
religious freedom, **1997** 408, 421
religious publications, **1995** 386, 393–395
religious symbols, **1995** 387, 396–404
sex offenders, right to confine, **1997** 384, 392–394
sexual harassment, **1998** 439–441, 443–452; **1999** 215
states rights, **1999** 333, 335–336, 345–349
South Africa
  Clinton state visit, **1998** 159
  death penalty, Supreme Court ruling, **1995** 283–287
  elections, **1999** 428
  Inkatha Freedom Party (IPC), **1995** 102; **1998** 758, 766–767, 773–774
  Mbeki presidential inauguration, **1999** 297–303
  Pan Africanist Congress (PAC), **1998** 772–773
  Truth and Reconciliation Commission
    establishment of, **1995** 103, 107
    report, **1998** 755–775
  UN role in, **1995** 355
  U.S. trade sanctions, **1999** 491
  See also African National Congress (ANC)
South Asian Association for Regional Cooperation, **1998** 329
South Carolina, welfare reform, **1999** 258
South Carolina v. Katzenbach, **1997** 412, 413
South Dakota, ballot initiatives, **1999** 3–4
South Korea
  economic situation, **1997** 896–897; **1998** 722, 723
  elections, **1997** 835, 892–897
  financial crisis, **1997** 834–835, 892, 894
  IMF aid package, **1997** 836, 892
  political situation, **1997** 896
  relations with North Korea, **1997** 896–897; **1999** 576
  security, **1997** 897
  unemployment, **1998** 726
  See also Korean war
Southern Baptist Convention, **1995** 336–338
  on women and the family, **1998** 333–336
Southern Christian Leadership Conference, **1997** 311
Southern Education Foundation, segregation report, **1995** 239–253
Soviet Union (former)
  Afghanistan invasion, **1999** 524
  collapse of, **1999** 120
  Democratic Party platform, **1996** 644
  Mir space station, **1998** 929–930
  nuclear material in, **1996** 139–146
  weapons development, **1996** 219–221
Space exploration
  Climate Orbiter mission to Mars investigation, **1999** 711–717
  Clinton support for, **1997** 37
  Discovery flight of John Glenn, **1998** 776–786
  Endeavor shuttle mission, **1998** 929–933
  Galileo's inspection of Jupiter's moons, **1997** 202–205

International Space Station, **1998** 929–933
life on Mars, **1996** 471–477; **1997** 510
Lunar Prospector findings of moon ice, **1998** 113–120
Mir space station, **1995** 419–425; **1996** 691–694; **1998** 929–930; **1999** 611
Pathfinder mission to Mars, **1997** 509–513; **1999** 712
Polar Lander mission investigation, **1999** 711–717
Republican Party platform, **1996** 548
Salyut Soviet space stations, **1998** 929
Sojourner mission to Mars, **1999** 712
Unity space station, **1998** 931–933
woman astronaut Shannon Lucid, **1996** 691–694; **1999** 611
Zarya Russian control module, **1998** 931–933
Space station
    Clinton support for, **1997** 37
    international agreement, **1997** 351
    Sagan Memorial Station, **1997** 509
    U.S.-Russian
        cooperative effort, **1995** 222–227, 419–425
        news conference from space, **1995** 419–425
Space Telescope Science Institute, **1996** 269
Spain
    aid to Nazi Germany, **1997** 259, 262, 263; **1998** 291
    allied relations and negotiations with, **1998** 301–304
    euro currency, **1998** 271
    German assets, **1997** 267
Special counsel, Waco investigations, **1999** 165, 480–488
Specter, Arlen (R-Pa.)
    Clinton impeachment trial, **1999** 20–21
    intelligence community, **1996** 796
    national security, **1999** 503
    Saudi Arabia terrorist bombing, **1996** 674–675
Speer, Lisa, on world fisheries conservation, **1995** 524
Spence, Floyd D. (R-S.C.), terrorist bombing in Saudi Arabia, **1996** 675
Spencer, Earl, eulogy for Diana (princess of Wales), **1997** 648, 651–653
Sperling, Gene
    apparel industry code of conduct, **1997** 207, 209
    U.S.-China trade agreements, **1999** 726, 730
Speth, James Gustave, human economic development report, **1996** 438–444
Sports
    chess victory of IBM computer, **1997** 273–276
    health benefits for girls, **1997** 158–171
Spotted owl, northern, Endangered Species Act and, **1995** 359–368
Spratt, John M., Jr. (D-S.C.), Chinese technology transfer, **1996** 98; **1999** 236, 237
Sprint, jobs for welfare recipients, **1997** 34, 622
Spudis, Paul, **1996** 473
Squibb, manufacturer of breast implants, **1995** 516
Srebenica massacre, UN report, **1999** 735–752, 860
Staniecki, Ted, parochial school aid, **1997** 363
Starbucks Coffee, **1996** 43
Starovoitova, Galina, murder of, **1998** 606
Starr, Kenneth W.
    attorney-client privilege, **1998** 393, 395

Clinton investigations as independent counsel, **1999** 166–167
Clinton rebuttal to Starr report, **1998** 654–664
grand jury investigations, **1998** 567
independent counsel
    future of, **1999** 165–172
    investigations, **1998** 38–39, 565–566, 907, 960; **1999** 15–16, 22
    report to Congress, **1998** 632–653
START. *See* Strategic Arms Reduction Treaty
State Department
    Cambodia, Khmer Rouge demise, **1998** 971–975
    Cambodian coup, **1997** 639–646
    Central African refugee crisis, **1996** 809–815
    diplomatic posts evaluation, **1999** 690–698
    human rights in China reports, **1996** 133–138
    Kosovo human rights violations, **1999** 803, 806–814
    land mine crisis, **1995** 46–54
    NATO expansion, **1996** 655–661
    religious freedom abroad, **1998** 19–29
    religious persecution report, **1997** 562–579
    U.S. bombing of Chinese embassy, **1999** 304–316
    Vietnam, U.S. consulate in, **1997** 489–492
    See also under names of secretary of state
State of the Union addresses
    Clinton, **1995** 24–45; **1996** 21–35; **1997** 29–49; **1998** 38–54; **1999** 41–63
    Republican responses to, **1996** 21–23, 35–38; **1997** 31, 44–49; **1998** 40–41, 54–59; **1999** 43, 58–60
States' rights, Supreme Court on, **1999** 333–356
Statue of Liberty, reduced visitor hours, **1995** 124
Steinberg, Elan, **1997** 262
Steinhoff, Jeffrey C., District of Columbia financial crisis, **1995** 500–505
Stephens, Gene, **1995** 464
Stern, Andrew L., on hospital oversight, **1999** 414
Stevens, John Paul
    affirmative action, federal government plans, **1995** 308–309, 317–318, 320–323
    ballot initiatives, **1999** 6
    congressional term limits, **1995** 260, 262, 263–270
    disability, definition of, **1999** 319, 320
    drug testing of students, **1995** 339, 340, 346–349
    endangered species on private lands, **1995** 359–368
    free speech, Internet and, **1997** 444–446, 446–454
    gay rights discrimination, **1996** 286
    gay rights to march, **1995** 327–335
    gun-free school zone, **1995** 184, 195, 196–200
    HIV as a disability, **1998** 379, 388–389
    line-item veto, **1997** 612; **1998** 421, 422–430
    parochial school aid, **1997** 363
    physician-assisted suicide, **1997** 461, 473–476
    presidential immunity, **1997** 291–298
    punitive damages, for consumer product liability, **1996** 274, 276–282
    race-based redistricting, **1995** 371, 380–384; **1996** 370, 381–383
    religious freedom, **1997** 408, 417
    religious publications, **1995** 386, 393–395

sex offenders, right to confine, **1997** 384, 392–394
sexual harassment, **1998** 442; **1999** 215
states rights, **1999** 333, 345–349
therapist-patient privilege, **1996** 388–389, 390–395
welfare reform, **1999** 260
Stewart, Payne, death of, **1999** 424
Stiglitz, Joseph E.
  on AIDS epidemic, **1997** 83
  economic crisis and the poor, **1998** 725
  on economic growth, **1996** 51
  on income inequality, **1997** 52
  Indonesian economic crisis, **1998** 724
Stock market
  buying on margin, **1999** 210
  crash of 1987, **1997** 724
  day-trading, **1999** 206–207, 208–209
  Jiang Zemin visit to, **1997** 730
  limit orders, **1999** 209–210
  online investing, **1999** 203–214
  ownership of stocks, **1999** 86
  suitability rule, **1999** 205
  volatility, **1997** 721–727, 834
Stojilkovic, Vlajko, war criminal, **1999** 803
Storer v. Brown, **1999** 7
Strategic Arms Reduction Treaty (START II)
  congressional actions on, **1995** 234, 236
  Russian support for, **1995** 234, 236
Strategic Arms Reduction Treaty (START III), **1999** 53
Strategic Defense Initiative (SDI)
  defense spending for, **1998** 484
  Republican Party platform on, **1996** 541
Strickler, Tommy David, death sentence, **1999** 829
Striking workers
  on federal contracts, **1995** 129–133
  steelworkers strike, **1997** 291
  United Auto Workers General Motors strike, **1998** 320–325
  UPS strike, **1997** 628–635; **1998** 320
Stromberg v. California, **1995** 331
Studds, Gerry E. (D-Mass.), **1995** 360
Student achievement, sports participation and, **1997** 168
Student aid
  Clinton program, **1995** 82
  Hope scholarship program, **1998** 43, 78, 87; **1999** 46
  tuition tax credit proposal, **1997** 30, 36
Students
  random drug testing of, **1995** 339–349
  religious publications, **1995** 385–395
Study to Understand Prognoses and Preferences for Outcomes and Risks of Treatment (SUPPORT), **1997** 329, 330
Sturckow, Rick, **1998** 932
Substance Abuse and Mental Health Services Administration (SAMHSA), **1999** 461
Sudan
  conflict in, **1999** 431
  religious persecution, **1997** 564
  U.S. airstrikes against terrorists, **1998** 555, 586–591
Sudarsono, Juwono, **1999** 720
Suharto
  Indonesian president resignation, **1998** 284–288, 722

ousted as president, **1999** 512, 718
pardon for corruption, **1999** 721
Suicide
  physician-assisted, House bar on, **1999** 441–442
  prevention, surgeon general on, **1999** 439–455, 836
  protective factors, **1999** 450–451
  risk factors, **1999** 449–450
Sulmasy, Daniel P., end-of-life care, **1997** 327, 328–330
Sun Microsystems, **1999** 659
Superfund, enactment of, **1995** 113
Supplemental Security Income (SSI), **1999** 320
Supply-side economics, **1999** 94–95
Supreme Court
  affirmative action, federal government plans, **1995** 307–326, 484–485
  attorney-client privilege, **1998** 393–404
  ballot initiatives, **1999** 3–14
  congressional term limits, **1995** 259–275
  disability, definition of, **1999** 317–332
  drug testing of students, **1995** 339–349
  endangered species on private lands, **1995** 359–368
  free speech, on the Internet, **1997** 444–458
  gay rights, **1995** 327–335; **1996** 284–295
  gun-free school zones, **1995** 183–200; **1999** 335
  HIV infection, as a disability, **1998** 378–392
  liability, punitive damages, **1996** 274–283
  liquor advertising, **1996** 771–772
  patient-therapist privilege, **1996** 388–395
  physician-assisted suicide, **1997** 459–479
  presidential immunity, **1997** 290–298
  race-based redistricting, **1995** 369–384
  racial gerrymandering, **1996** 368–387
  religious symbols and publications, **1995** 385–404
  residential signs, **1995** 289–297
  sex offenders, confining, **1997** 382–394
  sexual harassment, **1998** 438–465; **1999** 215–234
  states rights, **1999** 333–356
  welfare reform, double-tier benefits, **1999** 260–261
Supreme Court opinions
  Abington Township School District v. Schempp, **1995** 547
  Adams v. Richardson, **1995** 245
  Adarand Constructors, Inc. v. Peña, **1995** 307–326, 485–486; **1997** 190, 191, 193, 194; **1998** 855–856
  Agostini v. Felton, **1997** 361–381
  Aguilar v. Felton, **1997** 361–381
  A.L.A. Schechter Poultry Corp. v. U.S., **1995** 187, 192
  Albemarle Paper Co. v. Moody, **1998** 450
  Alden v. Maine, **1999** 334–349
  Allegheny County v. Greater Pittsburgh ACLU, **1995** 399, 401, 402
  Allen v. Illinois, **1997** 393
  Babbitt v. Sweet Home Chapter of Communities for a Greater Oregon, **1995** 359–368
  BMW of North America, Inc. v. Ira Gore, Jr., **1996** 274–283
  Board of Ed. of Central School District No. 1 v. Ball, **1995** 395

Board of Ed. of Kiryas Joel School v. Grumet, **1997** 362, 366

Board of Ed. of Westside Community Schools (Dist. 66) v. Mergens, **1995** 392–393, 398

Bolling v. Sharpe, **1995** 313

Bowers v. Hardwick, **1996** 285

Bragdon v. Abbott, **1998** 378–392

Branzburg v. Hayes, **1998** 401

Brown v. Bd. of Education, **1995** 456, 458

Buckley v. American Constitutional Law Foundation (ACLF), **1999** 5–14

Buckley v. Valeo, **1998** 435; **1999** 11

Burlington Industries, Inc. v. Ellerth, **1998** 439–442, 453–465

Bush v. Vera, **1996** 368–387

Butler v. Michigan, **1997** 454

Byrd v. Raines, **1997** 612

Capitol Square Review v. Pinette, **1995** 385, 387, 396–404

Chabad-Lubavitch v. Burlington, **1995** 397

Chabad-Lubavitch v. Miller, **1995** 397

Chisholm v. Georgia, **1999** 338, 345

Church of Lukumi Babalu Aye, Inc. v. Hialeah, **1997** 421

City of Boerne v. Flores, Archbishop of San Antonio, **1997** 406–421

City of Cleburne v. Cleburne Living Ctr., **1997** 191

City of Richmond v. J.A. Croson Co., **1995** 308, 315–316, 322, 323; **1997** 193; **1998** 862, 867

Clinton v. City of New York, **1998** 419–437

Clinton v. Jones, **1997** 290–298

Cohen v. Jenkintown Cab Co., **1998** 398, 402, 404

College Savings Bank v. Florida Prepaid Postsecondary Ed. Expense Bd., **1999** 334, 340

Consolidated Edison Co. v. NLRB, **1995** 198

Cruzan v. Director, Missouri Dept. of Health, **1996** 122, 127, 130; **1997** 465, 471

Davis v. Monroe County Board of Education, **1999** 216–234

Detroit Bank v. U.S., **1995** 313

Edwards v. South Carolina, **1995** 331

Employment Division v. Smith, **1997** 406–407, 410, 411, 416, 418–420, 421

Engle v. Vitale, **1995** 547

Faragher v. City of Boca Raton, **1998** 439–442, 443–452

FCC v. Pacifica Foundation, **1997** 447–448, 451

Field v. Clark, **1998** 428–429

Fisher v. U.S., **1998** 402

Florida v. College Savings Bank, **1999** 334

Ford Motor Co. v. EEOC, **1998** 450

Frontiero v. Richardson, **1995** 313

Fullilove v. Klutznick, **1995** 312, 314, 321, 323–324

Funk v. U.S., **1998** 398, 402

Garcia v. San Antonio Metropolitan Transit Authority, **1999** 334, 347

Gebser v. Lago Vista Independent School District, **1998** 442; **1999** 222, 228, 229

Gibbons v. Ogden, **1995** 186–187

Ginsberg v. New York, **1997** 447–448, 451, 454–457

Glover v. Patten, **1998** 399

Goss v. Lopez, **1995** 348

Grand Rapids School District v. Ball, **1997** 361, 368–371, 375–379

Gregory v. Ashcroft, **1995** 186

Gregory v. Chicago, **1995** 331

Griffin v. Wisconsin, **1995** 342

Hague v. Committee for Industrial Organization, **1995** 334

Hans v. Louisiana, **1999** 339

Harris v. Forklift Systems, Inc., **1998** 462

Heffron v. International Soc. for Krishna Consciousness, Inc., **1995** 398

Herbert v. Lando, **1998** 402

Hirabyashi v. U.S., **1995** 313; **1997** 190

Hunt v. Blackburn, **1998** 398

Hunter v. Erickson, **1997** 188, 192

Hurley v. Irish-American Gay, Lesbian and Bisexual Group of Boston, **1995** 327–335

Idaho v. Coeur d'Alene Tribe of Idaho, **1999** 348

Illinois v. Krull, **1995** 346

Ingraham v. Wright, **1995** 348

INS v. Chadha, **1998** 427

Jacoby v. Arkansas Dept. of Ed., **1999** 336

Jaffee v. Redmond, **1996** 388–395

J.W. Hampton, Jr. & Co. v. U.S., **1998** 436

Kansas v. Hendricks, **1997** 382–394

Kaplan v. Burlington, **1995** 397

Katzenbach v. Morgan, **1997** 415

Kirkingburg v. Albertson's, **1999** 319

Korematus v. U.S., **1995** 313

Lamb's Chapel v. Center Moriches Union Free School District, **1995** 390–391, 393, 398, 399

Lau v. Nichols, **1998** 313

Lee v. Weisman, **1995** 547

Lemon v. Kurtzman, **1997** 372

Loving v. U.S., **1997** 296

Loving v. Virginia, **1995** 313

Lynch v. Donnelly, **1995** 399

McCulloch v. Maryland, **1999** 347

McLaughlin v. Florida, **1995** 313

Marbury v. Madison, **1997** 417

Meek v. Pittenger, **1997** 366, 377

Meritor Savings Bank v. Vinson, **1998** 438, 445–446, 449, 455–457, 460, 463

Metro Broadcasting, Inc. v. Federal Communications Commission, **1995** 308, 312, 315–316, 322–323

Meyer v. Grant, **1999** 5

Michigan Dept. of State Police States v. Stitz, **1995** 342

Miller v. California, **1997** 449–450

Miller v. Johnson, **1995** 369–384; **1996** 369

Murphy v. United Parcel Service, **1999** 319

National Endowment for the Arts v. Finley, **1998** 405–418

New Jersey v. T.L.O., **1995** 342, 347, 348

Nixon v. Fitzgerald, **1997** 294, 295

NLRB v. Jones & Laughlin Steel Corp., **1995** 188, 191–192

NLRB v. Mackay Radio and Telegraph, **1995** 129

Olmstead v. L.C., **1999** 319, 320, 325–332

Oncale v. Sundowner Offshore Services, Inc., **1998** 441–442

Oregon v. Mitchell, **1997** 413–414, 415

Pacific Gas & Electric Co. v. Public Utilities Commission of Calif., **1995** 333

Palila v. Hawaii Dept. of Land and Natural Resources, **1995** 366
Panama Refining Co. v. Ryan, **1998** 436
Parden v. Terminal R. Co. of Ala. Docks Dept., **1999** 340
Perez v. U.S., **1995** 198
Planned Parenthood of Southeastern Pa. v. Casey, **1996** 125–127; **1997** 373, 465–466
Plessy v. Ferguson, **1995** 456
Poe v. Ullman, **1997** 189, 476
Powell v. McCormack, **1995** 262, 264, 267
Raines v. Byrd, **1998** 423
Reed v. Reed, **1995** 313
Regents of the University of California v. Bakke, **1995** 313–314
Reno v. American Civil Liberties Union, **1997** 444–458
Renton v. Playtime Theatres, Inc., **1997** 447–448
Rodriquez de quijas v. Shearson/American Express, Inc., **1997** 374
Rogers v. EEOC, **1998** 462
Romer v. Evans, **1996** 284–295
Rosenberger v. Rector and Visitors of the University of Virginia, **1995** 385–395; **1997** 368, 376
Rufo v. Inmates of Suffolks County Jail, **1997** 366
Sable Communications of Cal., Inc. v. FCC, **1997** 450
Saenz v. Roe, **1999** 261
Schechter Poultry Corp. v. U.S., **1998** 436
Seminole Tribe of Fla. v. Florida, **1999** 334, 336, 340, 345–346
Shaw v. Hunt, **1996** 368; **1998** 866–867
Shaw v. Reno, **1995** 370, 373–376, 380–382, 384; **1996** 368; **1997** 190, 193
Sherbert v. Verne, **1997** 410, 411
Skinner v. Railway Labor Executives' Assn., **1995** 342, 343, 344, 345
Smith v. County of Albemarle, **1995** 397
Smith v. Reeves, **1999** 339
South Carolina v. Katzenbach, **1997** 412, 413
Storer v. Brown, **1999** 7
Stromberg v. California, **1995** 331
Sutton v. United Air Lines, **1999** 318, 320–325
Swidler & Berlin v. U.S., **1998** 393–404
Thornburg v. Gingles, **1995** 370
Tinker v. Des Moines Independent Community School Dist., **1995** 331; **1999** 223
Train v. City of New York, **1998** 433
Trammel v. U.S., **1998** 402
Treasury Employees v. Von Raab, **1995** 342, 344, 345
TVA v. Hill, **1995** 363–364
United Jewish Organizations of Williamsburgh, Inc. v. Carey, **1995** 376
United States Term Limits, Inc. v. Hill, **1995** 263
United States Term Limits, Inc. v. Thornton, **1995** 259–275
United States v. Bass, **1995** 189
United States v. Curtiss-Wright Export Corp., **1998** 429
United States v. Darby, **1995** 188
United States v. Fordice, **1995** 239, 242, 245–247
United States v. Hays, **1995** 370
United States v. Lopez, **1995** 183–200, 260
United States v. Martinez-Fuerte, **1995** 342
United States v. Nixon, **1997** 297; **1998** 401, 402
United States v. Osborn, **1998** 399
United States v. Zolin, **1998** 403
Upjohn Co. v. U.S., **1998** 398, 402
Vacco, Attorney General of N.Y. v. Quill, **1997** 459–479
Vernonia School District 47J v. Acton, **1995** 339–349; **1999** 223
Walz v. Tax Commission of City of New York, **1997** 372
Washington v. Davis, **1997** 190
Washington v. Glucksberg, **1997** 459–479
Washington v. Seattle School District No. 1, **1997** 188
Wesberry v. Sanders, **1995** 265
West Virginia Bd. of Education v. Barnette, **1995** 331
Wickard v. Filburn, **1995** 188
Widmar v. Vincent, **1995** 391, 392, 393, 398, 399
Wisconsin v. Yoder, **1997** 411
Witte v. U.S., **1997** 391
Witters v. Washington Dept. of Services for the Blind, **1997** 362, 368–371, 378–379
Wolman v. Walter, **1997** 366
Wygant v. Jackson Bd. of Education, **1995** 314–315; **1997** 191
Zauderer v. Office of Disciplinary Counsel of Supreme Court of Ohio, **1995** 333
Zobrest v. Catalina Foothills School District, **1997** 362, 368–371, 377–378
Surgeon general
  Elders resignation, **1995** 61
  mental health, **1999** 836–849
  nomination of Dr. Henry W. Foster, Jr., **1995** 61–68
  nutrition and health report, **1997** 167
  physical exercise, benefits of, **1996** 418–429
  suicide prevention, **1999** 439–455
Sutton v. United Air Lines, **1999** 318, 320–325
Sweatshop Watch, **1997** 208
Sweden
  aid to Nazi Germany, **1997** 259, 262, 263; **1998** 291, 292
  allied relations and negotiations with, **1998** 304–307
  liquidation of German assets, **1997** 267
Sweeney, John J.
  labor movement advances, **1999** 630–638
  new AFL-CIO president, election remarks, **1995** 680–685
  U.S.-China trade agreement opponent, **1999** 728
  WTO talks in Seattle, **1999** 800
Swidler & Berlin v. U.S., **1998** 393–404
Swiss Foundation for Solidarity, **1997** 259
Switzerland
  aid to Nazi Germany, **1997** 257–272; **1998** 293–294
  refugee policy, **1997** 264–265
Symington, Fife, and tax cuts, **1995** 43
Syria
  Israel relations, **1999** 362
  peace negotiations, U.S. role, **1995** 622–624
  peace negotiations with Israel, **1999** 890–897

T

Taiwan (Republic of China)
  earthquake relief, **1999** 465, 467–468
  one China policy, Clinton and Jiang on, **1997** 735, 738
  Republican Party platform, **1996** 544
Talabani, Jalal, **1996** 680
Talbott, Strobe
  Armenian negotiations, **1999** 640
  European defense force, **1999** 819
  Russian elections speech, **1996** 431, 432–437
Taliaferro, Capt. Jeff, **1999** 53
Tambo, Oliver, ANC leader in exile, **1999** 299
Tan, C. J., chess victory for IBM computer, **1997** 275
Tang Jiaxuan, U.S. bombing of Chinese embassy, **1999** 305–306, 307
Tanzania
  Burundi refugees in, **1999** 435
  embassy bombings, **1998** 555–563; **1999** 53, 524, 690
Tatum, Wilbert A., on criminal justice system, **1995** 611–612
Tax reform
  child tax credit, **1998** 90
  and deficit reduction, **1996** 67
  Democratic Party platform, **1996** 628–629
  Earned Income Tax Credit (EITC), **1995** 78; **1996** 28
  Perot Reform Party nomination speech on, **1996** 558–559
  Republican Party platform on, **1996** 503–505
  tax cut legislation, **1999** 352
  tax cuts as economic stimulus, **1999** 93–94
Taxman, Sharon, affirmative action case, **1997** 185
Taxpayer Relief Act (1997), **1998** 90
Taylor, Gene (D-Miss.), on vote for Speaker of the House, **1995** 3
Taylor, Michael R., meat safety inspections, **1996** 415
Teachers
  quality, federal report on, **1999** 64–71
  shortages of, **1999** 64–65
Teamsters union, UPS strike, **1997** 628–635
Technology and Literacy Challenge initiative, **1997** 65
Technology transfer, China's role in, **1998** 467, 976–982
Technology workers, shortage of, **1997** 669–678
Teenage pregnancy
  declining levels, **1999** 384, 385–386
  Democratic Party platform, **1996** 638–639
  National Center for Health Statistics report on, **1998** 260–267
  prevention programs, **1995** 61, 65–67
  sports participation and prevention of, **1997** 170
Teenage smoking, **1997** 332, 335, 336; **1998** 47, 89, 845–846; **1999** 49, 384
Teenagers
  adult attitudes toward, **1997** 422–443
  murder rate, **1999** 615
See also Youth
Tejeda, Frank (D-Texas), death of, **1997** 43, 44
Telecommunications
  access to electronic services, **1999** 368–383
  industry mergers, **1998** 339, 340–341
  telephone penetration, **1999** 373–374

Telecommunications Act (1996), **1999** 371
Telecommunications industry, E-rate program, **1999** 371
Television
  rating system, **1996** 831–837; **1997** 527–533
  v-chips for blocking programs, **1997** 527, 529
Temporary Assistance to Needy Families (TANF), **1996** 452; **1997** 618; **1998** 354, 357, 358, 362, 363; **1999** 258, 261–271
Tenet, George J.
  Chinese nuclear-espionage matter, **1999** 238
  missile threat to U.S., **1998** 483
Tennessee, welfare reform, **1999** 258
Ter-Petrosian, Levon, **1999** 641
Tereby, Susan, **1998** 115
Term limits
  California state legislature, federal appeals court on, **1997** 886–891
  congressional, **1995** 259–275; **1996** 696–697
Terrorism
  antiterrorism bill, **1995** 178–179; **1996** 231–236
  aviation security requirements, **1996** 666–667
  bombings, **1997** 714
    in African embassies, **1998** 555–563; **1999** 53
    in Lebanon, **1998** 555–556
    in Northern Ireland, **1998** 206
    Olympic Park bombing, **1996** 445–449
    in Saudi Arabia, **1996** 672–679
  border arrests of potential terrorists, **1999** 499, 763
  combating, **1997** 351
  countering, **1999** 502–503
  GAO report, **1997** 711
  Pan America Flight 103 (Lockerbie, Scotland), **1995** 176
  Republican Party platform, **1996** 543
  threats in the next century, **1999** 499–510
  Unabomber manifesto on society's ills, **1995** 600–610
  Unabomber sentencing memorandum, **1998** 233–252
  U.S. airstrikes against terrorists, **1998** 586–591
  and weapons of mass destruction, **1996** 223–224
  World Trade Center Building (New York City), **1995** 176
  See also Oklahoma City bombing incident; World Trade Center bombing
Texaco, Inc., racial slurs by executives, **1996** 764–769
Thaci, Hashim, Kosovo conflict, **1999** 288
Thagard, Norman, **1995** 419–425
Thailand
  financial crisis, **1997** 833–834, 838; **1998** 722, 723
  IMF aid package, **1997** 836
  unemployment, **1998** 726
Thatcher, Margaret
  at Hong Kong transfer ceremony, **1997** 502
  as prime minister, **1997** 277–278
Thernstrom, Abigail, **1995** 372; **1997** 316
Thiessen, March, UN death penalty, **1998** 185
Thomas, Bob, race relations panel, **1998** 668
Thomas, Clarence
  affirmative action, federal government plans, **1995** 308, 320
  attorney-client privilege, **1998** 395, 401–404

confirmation hearings, **1998** 439
congressional term limits, **1995** 260, 271–275
disability, definition of, **1999** 319
drug testing of students, **1995** 339–346
endangered species on private lands, **1995** 360, 366–368
free speech
  ballot initiatives, **1999** 6
  decency in the arts, **1998** 405, 415–417
  and the Internet, **1997** 445
gay rights discrimination, **1996** 286, 291–295
gay rights to march, **1995** 327–335
gun-free school zone, **1995** 184, 194–195
HIV as a disability, **1998** 380, 389–392
parochial school aid, **1997** 363
physician-assisted suicide, **1997** 461
punitive damages, for consumer product liability, **1996** 275
race-based redistricting, **1995** 369, 371, 373–380; **1996** 369, 381
religious freedom, **1997** 408
religious publications, **1995** 385–395
religious symbols, **1995** 387, 396–400
sex offenders, right to confine, **1997** 383, 385–392
sexual harassment, **1998** 441, 452, 461–465; **1999** 215, 227–234
sexual harassment accusations against, **1998** 439
states rights, **1999** 333
Thomas, Dorothy, on women's rights, **1995** 581
Thomas, Oliver, religious freedom, **1997** 408
Thomas, Robert, race relations panel, **1997** 316–317
Thomas-Keprta, Kathie, **1996** 474, 476
Thompson, David R., California term limits, **1997** 887, 889–891
Thompson, Fred (R-Tenn.), campaign finance investigations, **1998** 891
Thompson, Linda Chavez, race relations, **1998** 668
Thompson, Robert, race relations panel, **1997** 322
Thompson, Tommy, and balanced budgets, **1995** 11, 43
Thomson, James A., on embryonic research, **1998** 66
Thornburg v. Gingles, **1995** 370
Threshold Test Ban Treaty (1974), **1995** 553–554
Tibet, Chinese policies, **1997** 570, 739
Timber industry, endangered species and, **1995** 359–368
Tinker v. Des Moines Independent Community School Dist., **1995** 331; **1999** 223
Tobacco
  consumption in the Americas, **1996** 578
  sales to children, **1996** 589–599
  state attorneys general settlement, **1998** 842–854
  use survey, **1999** 462–463
Tobacco industry
  accountability for smoking-related illnesses, **1999** 49–50
  cigarette regulations, resistance of, **1995** 670–679
  claims settlement, **1997** 331–339; **1998** 842–854; **1999** 536–537
  health risks fraud accusations, **1999** 536–661

nicotine addiction controversy, **1995** 670–679; **1999** 546–548
Tobin, James, **1995** 135
Torricelli, Robert G. (D-N.J.)
  and balanced budget amendment, **1997** 30–31
  on independent counsel, **1999** 167
Torrijos, Omar, Panama Canal treaties, **1999** 851
Tower, John G. (R-Texas) (1961-1985), defense secretary nomination defeated, **1998** 696
Trade
  open markets
    CEA report on, **1997** 61–62, 68; **1998** 83–84, 91–92; **1999** 91
    Clinton administration and, **1995** 85; **1997** 51; **1998** 45, 78; **1999** 51–52
    Republican Party platform, **1996** 510–511
    U.S. market expansion, **1996** 61; **1997** 53–54, 58
Trade deficit
  Perot Reform Party nomination speech, **1996** 556–557
  U.S. with Japan, **1996** 729–730
Trade negotiations
  labor standards as part of, Clinton administration, **1999** 799–800
  presidential "fast-track" negotiations, **1997** 612; **1998** 75, 95; **1999** 43
  Uruguay Round, **1995** 74, 85; **1997** 53, 61–62; **1998** 83
  U.S. China bilateral agreement, **1999** 724–734, 797
  U.S.-Vietnam agreements, **1999** 477–478
  WTO meeting in Seattle, **1999** 797–801
Trade Representative (U.S.), World Trade Organization talks, **1999** 797–801
Train v. City of New York, **1998** 433
Trammel v. U.S., **1998** 402
Transparency International, **1997** 801
Treasury Employees v. Von Raab, **1995** 342, 344, 345
Treaty of Peace and Friendship (Japan-China), **1998** 540–541
Tribe, Laurence H.
  on congressional authority and commerce clause, **1995** 185
  on Constitutional law, **1995** 259–260
Trichet, Jean-Claude, **1998** 273
Trimble, David, Northern Ireland peace negotiations, **1998** 203–206; **1999** 754, 755–756, 757–758
Tripp, Linda R., Lewinsky confidante, **1998** 565, 634; **1999** 22
Troutt, William E., National Commission on the Cost of Higher Education, **1998** 3
Truman, Harry S
  atomic bomb controversy, **1995** 56
  equality for all Americans, **1997** 762
  and steelworkers strike, **1997** 291
  and Swiss relations with Nazi Germany, **1997** 259
  and "Verona" project, **1997** 104
  on world peace, **1997** 42
Trumka, Richard L., **1995** 681, 683
Tuberculosis, and drug-resistant bacteria, **1999** 192–193
Tucker, C. DeLores, **1995** 455
Tucker, Jim Guy, indictment, **1998** 633; **1999** 22
Tudjman, Franjo, Bosnia accord, **1995** 719
Tung Chee-hwa, **1997** 501; **1998** 468

Tunney, John V. (D-Calif.) (1965-1977), and endangered species act, **1995** 365
Turkey
  aid to Nazi Germany, **1997** 259, 262, 263; **1998** 291
  earthquakes, U.S. aid, **1999** 465–471
  European Union candidacy, **1999** 158
  European Union membership issue, **1999** 466–467
  German assets, **1997** 267
  NATO ally, **1997** 269
  return of Nazi valuables, **1998** 292–293
Turkey, allied relations and negotiations with, **1998** 307–310
Tuskegee Syphilis Study, **1995** 62
Tutu, Desmond
  on death penalty, **1995** 283
  Truth and Reconciliation Commission, **1998** 755–756
TVA v. Hill, **1995** 363–364

U

Uganda, Clinton state visit, **1998** 159
Ukraine
  NATO cooperation, **1997** 518, 522
  nuclear weapons, **1996** 219–221
Unabomber, manifesto on society's ills, **1995** 600–610
Unanian, Nairi, **1999** 639
Underwood, Julie, on sexual harassment of students, **1999** 215
Unemployment rate, **1997** 50, 53, 59, 70; **1998** 73–74, 75, 79, 85, 364
  of foreign-born, **1997** 180
  in Indonesia, **1998** 726
  in South Korea, **1998** 726
  in Thailand, **1998** 726
  in U.S.
    for 1995, **1996** 51, 55, 69
    for 1998, **1999** 86
    for minorities, **1999** 87
Unger, Laura, on online investing, **1999** 206
UNICEF (United Nations Children's Fund)
  AIDS in Africa, **1999** 489–498
  child welfare reports, **1996** 776, 777–778; **1999** 386–387
  Clinton praises, **1995** 351, 356
  education worldwide, **1998** 920–928
  history of, **1996** 777
  maternal deaths, report on, **1996** 343–352
Unidentified flying objects (UFOs), Roswell incident, Air Force report, **1997** 395–405
Uniforms, in public schools, **1996** 84–92
Union of Needletrades, Industrial and Textile Employees (UNITE), **1999** 632
UNITA. *See* National Union for the Total Independence of Angola
United Airlines
  Boeing 737 crash, **1999** 116
  jobs for welfare recipients, **1997** 34, 622
United Auto Workers (UAW), General Motors strike, **1998** 320–325
United Jewish Organizations of Williamsburgh, Inc. v. Carey, **1995** 376
United Nations
  African conflict, UN secretary general on, **1998** 220–232

Bosnia, peacekeeping operation, **1995** 351–352
chemical weapons convention, **1996** 740–743; **1997** 195–201
fiftieth anniversary commemoration, **1995** 350–358
global warming treaty, **1997** 859–876
HIV infection worldwide estimates, **1997** 83–84
HIV/AIDS epidemic, **1998** 878–889
Hurricane Mitch damage report, **1998** 789–798
India, nuclear testing, **1998** 326–332
Iraq
  air strikes against, **1998** 934–944
  sanctions against, **1995** 355–356; **1997** 767, 769–770
North Korea, humanitarian aid, **1999** 572
Pakistan, nuclear testing, **1998** 326–332
peacekeeping operations, GAO report on, **1997** 150–157
reform efforts, **1997** 351–352
Rwanda genocidal war, report on, **1999** 860–889
secretary general appointment, **1996** 824–830
Srebenica massacre, UN role, **1999** 735–752
U.S. death penalty, **1998** 183–193
U.S. dues payment, **1997** 152–153; **1998** 50; **1999** 54, 700–701
worldwide population, **1999** 584–591
United Nations conferences
  Environment and Development (New York City), **1997** 488
  Nuclear Non-Proliferation Treaty Review and Extension Conference, **1995** 233–238
  Population and Development, International Conference on (Cairo, 1994), **1995** 136, 583
  Straddling Fish Stocks and Highly Migratory Fish Stocks, International Conference on, **1995** 524–531
  World Conference on Women (4th, Beijing), **1995** 136, 581–587; **1996** 138
  World Summit for Social Development, **1995** 134–140
United Nations Development Programme (UNDP), **1996** 438–444; **1999** 393
United Nations Educational, Scientific, and Cultural Organization (UNESCO), U.S. withdrawal from, **1995** 351
United Nations High Commissioner for Refugees (UNHCR)
  asylum for victims of religious persecution, **1998** 28
  Kosovo conflict refugees, **1999** 289, 804
  promoting peace in Africa, **1999** 428–438
United Nations Human Rights Commission
  death penalty in U.S., **1998** 183–193
  East Timor independence, **1999** 511–523
  human rights in Iraq, **1999** 144–152
  religious freedom in multilateral institutions, **1998** 29
United Nations Children's Fund. *See* UNICEF
United Nations Military Observer Group, **1997** 152
United Nations Programme on HIV/AIDS (UNAIDS), **1998** 878–889; **1999** 489
United Nations Security Council
  Cuban attack on civilian aircraft, **1996** 93–94
  Iraq, weapons inspection in, **1997** 767–773

peacekeeping mission mandate, **1997** 153–154
Resolution 1199, Kosovo conflict, **1998** 829, 830
Resolution 1203, Kosovo war crimes tribunal, **1998** 831
Resolution 1244, Kosovo conflict, NATO-led peacekeeping forces, **1999** 138–139, 285–296
Resolution 1258, Congo, UN peacekeeping forces, **1999** 647
Resolution 1272, East Timor, UN administration of, **1999** 514
United Nations Special Commission (UNSCOM), air strikes against Iraq, **1998** 934–944
United Nations Truce Supervisory Organization, **1997** 152
United Parcel Service (UPS)
jobs for welfare recipients, **1997** 34, 622
Teamsters union strike, **1997** 628–635; **1998** 320
United States Agency for International Development (USAID). *See* Agency for International Development (AID)
United States Commission on Immigration Reform, **1995** 564–565
United States Commission on National Security/21st Century, **1999** 499–510
United States v. Bass, **1995** 189
United States v. Curtiss-Wright Export Corp., **1998** 429
United States v. Darby, **1995** 188
United States v. Fordice, **1995** 239, 242, 245–247
United States v. Hays, **1995** 370
United States v. Lopez, **1995** 183–200, 260
United States v. Martinez-Fuerte, **1995** 342
United States v. Nixon, **1997** 297; **1998** 401, 402
United States v. Osborn, **1998** 399
United States v. Zolin, **1998** 403
United States Term Limits, Inc. v. Hill, **1995** 263
United States Term Limits, Inc. v. Thornton, **1995** 259–275
University of Texas, affirmative action program, **1996** 762–763
University of Virginia, religious publications, **1995** 388–395
Upjohn Co. v. U.S., **1998** 398, 402
Uranium, highly-enriched uranium supplies in former Soviet Union, **1996** 140, 142–143
The Urban Institute, welfare reform report, **1999** 258, 259–260, 269
Urban League, computer access programs, **1999** 371
Uruguay Round, **1995** 74, 85; **1997** 53, 61–62; **1998** 83, 92
U.S. Bancorp, online stock trading study, **1999** 203
U.S. Conference of Mayors, job shortages in cities, **1998** 365
Usery, William J., Jr., Commission on the Future of Worker-Management Relations member, **1995** 15
Uwilingiyimana, Agathe, assassination of, **1998** 614

V

Vacco, Attorney General of N.Y. v. Quill, 1997 459–479
Vacco, Dennis, apparel industry sweatshops, **1997** 206

Vajpayee, Atai Bihari
India nuclear testing, **1998** 326, 329–330
state visit to Pakistan, **1999** 624
Valenti, Jack, television rating system, **1996** 831, 834, 836–837
Values
and adult attitudes toward children survey, **1997** 422–443
Dole social issues speech, **1995** 573–580
ValuJet crash, **1996** 237–240; **1997** 113
van der Stoel, Max, human rights in Iraq, **1999** 144–152
Varmus, Harold, on embryonic research funding ban, **1998** 66
Vatican
Evangelium Vitae (Gospel of Life), **1995** 145–161
UN Conference on Women, objections to plan of action, **1995** 583
Vedrine, Hubert, European defense force, **1999** 819
Venezuela, floods in, **1999** 469
Ventura, Stephanie, on teenage pregnancy, **1999** 385
Vernonia School District 47J v. Acton, **1995** 339–349; **1999** 223
Vessey, Gen. John W., Jr., Vietnam POW/MIAs investigations, **1995** 473, 475
Veterans
Gulf War syndrome report, **1997** 740–745
Tomb of the Unknowns (Arlington National Cemetery), disinterment remarks, **1998** 281–283
Veterans Affairs Department (DVA), Gulf War syndrome report, **1995** 275; **1997** 742
Veto, line-item
Clinton's use of, **1997** 611–616
congressional passage of, **1995** 169–170; **1996** 149, 696
unconstitutional, Supreme Court on, **1998** 419–437, 909
Vice president, Gore nomination acceptance speech, **1996** 602, 603–608
Vice presidential debates, Gore-Kemp debates, **1996** 707–709, 718–724
Vichy government, complicity with Nazis, **1995** 478–479
Victims Rights Amendment, **1997** 39
Vietnam
U.S. consulate, secretary of state on, **1997** 489–492; **1999** 475–479
U.S. diplomatic relations, **1995** 472–477; **1997** 489–492; **1999** 475–479
U.S. economic sanctions against, **1995** 474; **1997** 489; **1999** 476
Vietnam war, landmine warfare, **1995** 50
Violence
against children, **1999** 617
aggressive driving, **1997** 550–561
FBI crime report, **1995** 710–716; **1997** 681–689; **1998** 869–877; **1999** 614–622, 618–619
school safety report, **1998** 735–741
shooting of Capitol policemen, **1998** 510–517
shootings in schools, **1998** 735–737
Violence Against Women Act, **1995** 277
Violence shootings in Armenian parliament, **1999** 639–642

Violent Crime Control and Law Enforcement Act (1994), **1997** 247
Volker, Paul A., commission on neutral aid to Nazi Germany, **1997** 260
Voter referendums. *See* Ballot initiatives
Voter registration
  Farrakhan on minority drive, **1995** 656, 666–667
  NAACP campaign, **1995** 454, 462
Voting districts, minority-dominated, **1995** 369–384
Voting Rights Act (1965), race-based redistricting, **1995** 369–384
Voucher systems, in public schools, **1997** 363–364
Vrooman, Robert S., Chinese nuclear-espionage matter, **1999** 241

W

Waco (Texas) incident
  Branch Davidian mass suicide, **1997** 123
  cult compound attack, **1995** 177; **1996** 362
  NRA criticism of ATF role, **1995** 209
  and Oklahoma City bombing incident, **1997** 623–624
  special counsel investigations, **1999** 165, 480–488
Wade, Richard H., medical mistakes, **1999** 781
Wadsworth, Deborah, adult attitudes toward children, **1997** 423–424
Wages and salaries, **1999** 87–88, 98–99
  See also Minimum wage
Wahid, Abdurrahman, president of Indonesia, **1999** 514, 718–723
Walchholz, Bruce, **1997** 592
Walker, William, **1999** 135
Walpole, Robert, Chinese nuclear-espionage matter, **1999** 238–239
Walsh, Jim (R-N.Y.), on legal immigrants rights, **1995** 565
Walsh, Lawrence E.
  on independent counsel legislation, **1999** 168
  Iran-contra affair, **1998** 905–906; **1999** 165
Walsum, Peter Van, on Kosovo conflict, **1999** 287
Walz v. Tax Commission of City of New York, **1997** 372
War crimes
  Kosovo conflict, **1995** 718; **1998** 381; **1999** 738, 739, 802–804
  Rwanda tribunal, **1998** 614–625; **1999** 866
Warner, John W. (R-Va.)
  Cuban foreign policy, **1998** 33
  House vote on impeachment, **1998** 958
  nuclear test ban treaty, **1999** 602, 604, 608
  on test ban treaty, **1995** 56
Washington, welfare reform, **1999** 258
Washington Policy Group, Inc. (WPG), **1997** 8
Washington, Thomas L., on NRA fundraising letter, **1995** 209
Washington v. Davis, **1997** 190
Washington v. Glucksberg, **1997** 459–479
Washington v. Seattle School District No. 1, **1997** 188
Washington, Walter E., mayor of Washington, **1995** 498
Waters, Maxine (D-Calif.)
  cocaine possession sentencing, **1997** 247

House Judiciary Committee impeachment inquiry, **1998** 708
  minority business competition, **1998** 856
Watt, Melvin (D-N.C.)
  on affirmative action, **1995** 309
  House Judiciary Committee impeachment inquiry, **1998** 706
Watts, J. C. (R-Okla.)
  affirmative action programs, **1998** 859
  Clinton state of the union address, Republican response, **1997** 31, 44–49
  Republican senior leader, **1998** 952
Waxman, Henry A. (D-Calif.), Waco incident, **1999** 482
Waxman, Seth P., FDA cigarette regulation, **1999** 539
Weapons
  land mine crisis, **1995** 46–54
  of mass destruction, **1996** 210–230; **1998** 935
  "smart" weapons effectiveness, GAO report, **1997** 493–500
  "smart" weapons performance report, **1996** 403–413
Weaver, Rander, and Ruby Ridge incident, **1995** 178
Wei Jingsheng, Chinese dissident released, **1997** 730–731
Weiler, Edward, space mission failures, **1999** 713, 715
Weinberg, Daniel, income inequality report, **1996** 397, 398–400
Welch, Tom, Salt Lake Olympics Committee, **1999** 106, 107
Weld, William F.
  abortion issue, **1996** 497
  and balanced budgets, **1995** 11
Welfare policy
  Democratic Party platform on, **1996** 637–639
  Dole Republican convention speech on, **1996** 490–492
  immigrant benefits, **1997** 177–178
Welfare reform
  CEA report on, **1995** 87–88; **1997** 70–72; **1998** 85, 89–90
  Clinton plan, **1995** 74–75; **1996** 65; **1997** 33–34, 617–622; **1998** 46
  double-tier benefits, Supreme Court on, **1999** 260–261
  GAO report on, **1998** 354–363; **1999** 257–271
  Gingrich comments on, **1995** 4–5, 11–13
  Republican bill, **1996** 450–463
Welfare-to-work programs, **1997** 619, 622; **1998** 90, 356, 357, 362; **1999** 50
Wells, John Calhoun, **1997** 629
Wennberg, John E., end-of-life care, **1997** 326
Wesberry v. Sanders, **1995** 265
Wessinger, Catherine, on cults, **1997** 124
Wessmann v. Gittens, **1998** 855–868
West, Togo D., Jr.
  extremists groups in the military, **1996** 178, 179
  sexual harassment in the military, **1997** 654
West Virginia Bd. of Education v. Barnette, **1995** 331
Weston, Russell Eugene, Jr., slaying of Capitol policemen, **1998** 510–517
Wexler, Robert (D-Fla.), House Judiciary Committee impeachment inquiry, **1998** 710

White, Byron R., gay rights to march, **1995**
327–335
White House
Pennsylvania Avenue closing, **1995** 254–258
plane crash on White House lawn, **1995** 255
shooting incidents, **1995** 256
Travel Office probe, **1997** 21; **1998** 394, 565,
633
White House Commission on Aviation Safety and
Security (Gore Commission), report, GAO on,
1997 113–121; **1998** 170–171
White House Conference
on Child Care, **1998** 47
on Early Learning and the Brain, **1997** 36
on Mental Health, **1999** 49, 836–837
on Social Security, **1998** 40, 43, 98–99
White House Millennium Program, **1998** 52–53;
1999 57
White supremacy, Farrakhan's remarks on evils
of, **1995** 663–665
Whitehurst, Frederick
FBI crime laboratory complaints, **1997**
222–224, 225–227
FBI crime laboratory evidence in Oklahoma
City bombing case, **1997** 625
Whitewater investigation, **1996** 22; **1997** 21;
1998 393–394, 565, 633; **1999** 22
Whitman, Christine Todd
and balanced budgets, **1995** 11
response to Clinton state of the union address,
1995 25, 43–45
Wickard v. Filburn, **1995** 188
Widmar v. Vincent, **1995** 391, 392, 393, 398,
399
Widnall, Sheila, **1997** 656
Wigand, Jeffrey, nicotine addiction, **1997** 333
Wilken, Claudia, California term limits, **1997** 887
Wilkins, Roger, **1995** 658
Wilkins, Roy, **1995** 455, 459
Will, George F., on sexual harassment in schools,
1999 217–218
Willadsen, Steen M., cloning research, **1997** 212,
215
Willemssen, Joel C., Y2K computer crisis, **1998**
545, 547–554
Willey, Kathleen, Clinton sexual misconduct
charges, **1998** 698
Williams, Anthony A., **1996** 784
Williams, David, FBI crime laboratory reports,
1997 222–223
Williams, Debra, affirmative action case, **1997**
185
Williams, Harrison A., Jr. (D-N.J.) (1953-1957;
1959-1982), Abscam scandal, **1995** 594
Williams, Jody, land mines ban, **1997** 845–846
Williemssen, Joel C., on year 2000 computer con-
version, **1997** 535
Willis, Daniel K., violent aggressive driving study,
1997 551
Willis, Kent, **1996** 85
Wilmut, Ian, cloning research, **1997** 212–220
Wilson, James Q., violent crime, **1997** 682
Wilson, Pete (governor), on affirmative action,
1996 759–760, 762
Wilson, Pete (R-Calif.)
abortion issue, **1996** 497
and balanced budgets, **1995** 11
and health care reform, **1995** 43
Winchell, Barry L., death of, **1999** 900

Winter, William F., **1998** 668
race relations panel, **1997** 316, 322
Wirth, Timothy, **1995** 126
Wisconsin, welfare reform, **1999** 258
Wisconsin v. Yoder, **1997** 411
Wisenberg, Solomon L., Lewinsky scandal inves-
tigations, **1998** 567, 576–585
Witt, James Lee, Red River floods, **1997** 232
Witte v. U.S., **1997** 391
*Witters v. Washington Dept. of Services for the
Blind*, **1997** 362, 368–371, 378–379
Wolf, Frank (R-Va.), comments at bipartisan
prayer service, **1995** 8
Wolfensohn, James, Asian economic crisis, **1998**
725, 726–734
Wolfowitz, Paul D., missile threat, **1998** 481
Wolman v. Walter, **1997** 366
Women
and the family, Southern Baptist Convention
statement on, **1998** 333–337
mammogram controversy, **1997** 142–149
in the military, **1997** 654–660; **1998** 335–336
in space exploration, **1996** 691–694
UN World Conference on, **1995** 136, 581–587;
1996 138
violence against, **1999** 527
Wood, Tom, on racial preferences, **1997** 184
Woodham, Luke, **1998** 736
Woodpecker, red cockaded, **1995** 359–368
Woolsey, James R., missile threat, **1998** 481
Work teams, role in future of labor-management
relations, **1995** 16–17
Workplace
apparel industry sweatshops, **1997** 206–211
future of, **1995** 15–23
genetic testing in the, **1998** 63–72
World Bank
and AIDS prevention programs, **1997** 83
Asian financial crisis, **1998** 722–734
debt reduction, **1999** 702
U.S. debt, **1997** 42
World Health Organization (WHO)
acupuncture treatment, **1997** 750
Clinton praises, **1995** 351, 356
infectious diseases, **1996** 302–311
pain management guidelines, **1997** 328
pharmaceutical quality control, **1997** 348
suicide prevention, **1999** 440, 443
World Jewish Congress
German confiscations of gold, **1997** 258
neutral aid to Nazi Germany, **1997** 257, 260,
262
World Jewish Restitution Organization, **1997** 260
World Meteorological Organization (WMO),
global warming report, **1998** 945–950
World Summit for Social Development, **1995**
134–140
World Trade Center bombing, **1999** 502
FBI crime laboratory report, **1997** 221, 223,
225–226
World Trade Organization (WTO)
antimonopoly powers, **1999** 393
Clinton administration negotiations, **1997** 543
GATT creation of, **1997** 53; **1999** 798
generic drug trade, **1999** 492
labor standards and, **1999** 800–801
membership request
for China, **1997** 730; **1999** 724
for Russia, **1997** 341

organized labor, **1999** 630
role of, **1997** 58, 61, 68
Seattle meeting (Millennium round), **1999** 797–801
World War II
declassification of documents, **1997** 271
fiftieth anniversary commemoration, **1995** 216–221
Holocaust, Catholic church repentance for, **1998** 121–130
Holocaust victims restitution, **1997** 270–271
Japanese apology for suffering, **1995** 302–306
landmine warfare, **1995** 50
Nazi confiscated art, return of, **1998** 294–295
neutral nations aid to Nazi Germany, **1997** 257–272; **1998** 291–312
Tripartite Gold Commission (TGC), **1997** 266, 271
U.S. postwar policy, **1997** 268–270
Wright, Jim (D-Texas) (1955-1989)
ethics charges, **1995** 746; **1996** 839; **1997** 5
House Speaker resignation, **1997** 5; **1998** 800
Wright, Susan Webber
Clinton contempt ruling, **1999** 21–22
Clinton sexual harassment suit, **1998** 566; **1999** 21–22
Wu, David (R-Ore.), physician-assisted suicide, **1999** 442
Wurst, Andrew, **1998** 736
Wyden, Ron (D-Ore.)
elected to Senate, **1995** 592
physician-assisted suicide, **1997** 462–463
tobacco claims settlement, **1998** 845
Wygant v. Jackson Bd. of Education, **1995** 314–315; **1997** 191

Y

Y2K (Year 2000) conversion, **1997** 534–540; **1998** 543–554; **1999** 51, 760–768
Year 2000 Conversion Council, **1998** 543–544
Yeltsin, Boris N.
Chechnya war, **1999** 909–910, 913
economic summits
Denver, **1997** 340–342
Tokyo, **1995** 93
election victory, **1996** 139, 430–437; **1997** 515
NATO expansion, **1999** 120
NATO summit meeting, **1997** 515
priorities for 1995, **1995** 100–101

religious freedom legislation, **1997** 564
resignation as Russian president, **1999** 917–923
Russian economic crisis, **1998** 601–613
Soviet economic reforms, **1995** 93, 96–98
state of the nation speech, **1995** 92–101
Yokich, Stephen P., **1995** 682
Yosemite National Park, **1995** 126
Young, Andrew, on Centennial Olympic Park bombing, **1996** 448–449
Youth
adult attitudes toward, **1997** 422–433
HIV epidemic and, **1998** 888–889
juvenile curfew laws, **1996** 325–333
smoking by, FDA regulations of tobacco sales, **1996** 589–599
suicide prevention, **1999** 453–454
See also Teenagers
Youth Crime Watch of America, **1999** 385
Yugoslavia
U.S. bombing of Chinese embassy, **1999** 304–316
war in Kosovo, **1998** 827–841; **1999** 119, 134–143
Yurek, Stephen R., on sexual harassment in schools, **1999** 218

Z

Zaire
Mobutu ousted from, **1997** 877–879; **1998** 161, 220, 615; **1999** 428
Rwandan refugee camps, **1996** 809–815
See also under its later name Congo, Republic of
Zare, Richard, **1996** 474
Zauderer v. Office of Disciplinary Counsel of Supreme Court of Ohio, **1995** 333
Zeman, Milos, **1999** 702
Zhironovsky, Vladimir, **1995** 94
Zhou Enlai, **1997** 95
Zhu Bangzao, U.S.-China relations, **1999** 236
Zhu Rongji, U.S.-China trade negotiations, **1998** 468; **1999** 726
Zimring, Franklin, prison populations, **1998** 871
Zobrest v. Catalina Foothills School District, **1997** 362, 368–371, 377–378
Zyuganov, Gennady, opposes Yeltsin, **1995** 92; **1996** 139, 431